DIGITAL SYSTEM DESIGN
AND MICROPROCESSORS

McGraw-Hill Series in Computer Organization and Architecture

Bell and Newell: *Computer Structures: Readings and Examples*
Cavanagh: *Digital Computer Arithmetic: Design and Implementation*
Gear: *Computer Organization and Programming*
Hamacher, Vranesic, and Zaky: *Computer Organization*
Hayes: *Computer Architecture and Organization*
Hayes: *Digital System Design and Microprocessors*
Hwang and Briggs: *Computer Architecture and Parallel Processing*
Kogge: *The Architecture of Pipelined Computers*
Siewiorek, Bell, and Newell: *Computer Structures: Principles and Examples*
Stone: *Introduction to Computer Organization and Data Structures*
Stone and Siewiorek: *Introduction to Computer Organization and Data Structures: PDP-11 Edition*

McGraw-Hill Computer Science Series

Ahuja: *Design and Analysis of Computer Communication Networks*
Barbacci and Siewiorek: *The Design and Analysis of Instruction Set Processors*
Ceri and Pelagatti: *Distributed Databases: Principles and Systems*
Donovan: *Systems Programming*
Filman and Friedman: *Coordinated Computing: Tools and Techniques for Distributed Software*
Givone: *Introduction to Switching Circuit Theory*
Goodman and Hedetniemi: *Introduction to the Design and Analysis of Algorithms*
Katzan: *Microprogramming Primer*
Keller: *A First Course in Computer Programming Using Pascal*
Kohavi: *Switching and Finite Automata Theory*
Liu: *Elements of Discrete Mathematics*
Liu: *Introduction to Combinatorial Mathematics*
MacEwen: *Introduction to Computer Systems: Using the PDP-11 and Pascal*
Madnick and Donovan: *Operating Systems*
Manna: *Mathematical Theory of Computation*
Newman and Sproull: *Principles of Interactive Computer Graphics*
Payne: *Introduction to Simulation: Programming Techniques and Methods of Analysis*
Révész: *Introduction to Formal Languages*
Rice: *Matrix Computations and Mathematical Software*
Salton and McGill: *Introduction to Modern Information Retrieval*
Shooman: *Software Engineering: Design, Reliability, and Management*
Tremblay and Bunt: *An Introduction to Computer Science: An Algorithmic Approach*
Tremblay and Bunt: *An Introduction to Computer Science: An Algorithmic Approach, Short Edition*
Tremblay and Manohar: *Discrete Mathematical Structures with Applications to Computer Science*
Tremblay and Sorenson: *An Introduction to Data Structures with Applications*
Tucker: *Programming Languages*
Wiederhold: *Database Design*
Wulf, Levin, and Harbison: *Hydra/C.mmp: An Experimental Computer System*

DIGITAL SYSTEM DESIGN AND MICROPROCESSORS

John P. Hayes

University of Michigan

McGraw-Hill Book Company

New York St. Louis San Francisco Auckland Bogotá Hamburg
Johnannesburg London Madrid Mexico Montreal New Delhi
Panama Paris São Paulo Singapore Sydney Tokyo Toronto

For Terrie

This book was set in Times Roman by Photo Data, Inc.
The editor was Eric M. Munson;
the production supervisor was Leroy A. Young.
Project supervision was done by Cobb/Dunlop Publisher Services Incorporated.
Halliday Lithograph Corporation was printer and binder.

DIGITAL SYSTEM DESIGN AND MICROPROCESSORS

1234567890 HALHAL 8987654

ISBN 0-07-027367-7

Library of Congress Cataloging in Publication Data

Hayes, John P. (John Patrick), date
   Digital system design and microprocessors.

   (McGraw-Hill series in computer organization and
   architecture)
   Bibliography: p.
   1. Digital integrated circuits.   2. Logic design.
3. Microprocessors.   4. Microcomputers—Programming.
I. Title. II. Series.
TK7874.H393 1984   001.64   83-25160
ISBN 0-07-027367-7

CONTENTS

PREFACE

Since the introduction of integrated circuits (ICs) in the early 1960s, immense changes have taken place in the way in which digital systems are designed and manufactured. Continued improvements in IC technology have greatly increased the range and complexity of the functions that can be incorporated into the tiny, inexpensive chip of semiconductor material that forms a typical IC. The building blocks now available to the system designer range from chips containing a few transistors to those that contain 100,000 or more. An important milestone was reached around 1970, when it became possible to include all the functions of the central processing unit (CPU) of a general-purpose programmable digital computer in a single IC; this CPU-on-a-chip is called a microprocessor. Microprocessors and other products of large-scale integration have drastically altered the economics of digital system design. They have also profoundly changed the design process itself, by adding software design or programming to traditional hardware (logic) design. The low cost, small size, and programmability of microprocessors make them suitable for an enormous number of applications, ranging from hand-held electronic games to the control of industrial robots. For this reason, the study of microprocessors and their applications in system design has assumed an important place in engineering and applied science curricula.

OBJECTIVES AND PHILOSOPHY

The primary purpose of this book is to serve as the text for a one- or two-term course on digital system design aimed at undergraduate students specializing in electrical engineering, computer engineering, or computer science. It should also be useful as a text for microprocessor-oriented courses in other disciplines, as a main or supplementary text for computer organization courses, and as a text for self-study. Because of the rather diverse backgrounds of the intended readership, as well as the breadth of topics that must be covered, a special effort has been made to provide a self-contained book. Thus the reader with no previous exposure to digital hardware design will find here an introduction to the relevant concepts in electronics and IC technology, along with a thorough treatment of standard logic design techniques. The reader with little or no software experience, on the other hand, will find programming techniques developed from basic principles using both assembly-level and high-level programming languages. The more experienced reader will find, in addition to the core material on logic design and microprocessor-based systems, coverage of such advanced topics as microprogramming and multi-processor design. Note too that the presentation allows individual chapters to be skipped without significant loss of continuity.

The book attempts to cover all major aspects of digital system design, from the gate and register-transfer levels that employ small- and medium-scale (SSI/MSI) ICs, to the microprocessor level using large- and very-large-scale (LSI/VLSI) ICs. Logic gates, register-level devices, and microprocessors are treated as members of a hierarchy of design components for digital systems, all of whose characteristics must be familiar to the system designer. While the book is directly concerned with practical design issues, the material is presented in terms of general principles wherever possible. In particular, an effort is made to treat hardware and software design in a consistent and balanced fashion as complementary aspects of the design of microprocessor-based systems. There is also an emphasis throughout the book on good notation and good design practice such as structured programming.

Unlike some other books in the field, this one is not tied to any commercial IC series or microprocessor family. This reflects its concern with general design principles, and the need to accommodate the rapid rate of change of digital system technology. It nevertheless is also desirable to expose the reader to real-world products in some detail; consequently extensive use is made of examples drawn from commercially available products. These examples have been carefully chosen in the basis of their ability to illustrate fundamental concepts, and the extent to which they are used, and will continue to be used, in industry. For example, the enormously popular and well-established 7400 series of SSI/MSI ICs is used to illustrate gate- and register-level design methods. The Intel 8080/8085 and the Motorola 6800 are the major 8-bit microprocessor examples used, while 16-bit microprocessors are represented by the Intel 8086 (iAPX 86) and the Motorola 68000. Bit-sliced microprocessors are illustrated by the Advanced Micro Devices 2900 series. Microprocessors are treated as families of components rather than as isolated devices. This makes it easy to bring such popular microprocessors as the Zilog Z80, a member of the 8080/8085 family, into the discussion. It also allows the extremely useful and powerful support circuits, such as programmable input-output (IO) controllers and arithmetic coprocessors, found in most microprocessor families to be placed in their proper context. Assembly language programming is mainly illustrated by the assembly languages of the 8080/8085 and 6800 microprocessors, and Pascal serves as the sample high-level programming language. A simple register-transfer language (RTL) that is completely consistent with Pascal is used throughout the book for descriptive purposes, along with conventional flowcharts and block diagrams.

OVERVIEW OF THE BOOK

The text is presented in two main parts. The first half (Chaps. 1–4) deals primarily with digital hardware and its role in the design of nonprogrammable systems. The remainder of the book (Chaps. 5–8) is concerned with programmable systems, in which microprocessors and software design play central roles.

Chapter 1 (Introduction to Digital Systems) presents an overview of system design concepts, and provides a broad introduction to the technological basis of microprocessor-based systems. The historical developments in switching circuit technology and digital computer design leading to one-chip microprocessors and microcomputers are traced. At the same time, the fundamental concepts of IC technology, computer organization, and programming are introduced. The applications of microprocessors in digital systems are surveyed, and illustrated with several detailed examples. The nature of the design process for microprocessor-based systems is also examined.

Chapter 2 (Integrated Circuit Technology) provides the basic information on ICs needed to understand their use in system design. A self-contained treatment of the key relevant concepts from electric circuit theory is presented. The methods used to fabricate ICs, and their significance to the system designer, are discussed. The characteristics of TTL and MOS logic families are examined. Various practical issues such as loading constraints and noise elimination are also covered here.

The next two chapters deal with logic design using standard ICs. Chapter 3 (Design Using Small-Scale Integration) begins with the basic concepts of logic design and binary numbers. The design of combinational and sequential logic circuits at the gate level is studied, with examples drawn from the popular 7400 series of ICs. The aspects of switching theory and Boolean algebra that are relevant to current design practice are treated in detail. In Chap. 4 (Design Using Medium- and Large-Scale Integration), we turn to the use of more complex MSI/LSI design components. The principal MSI design components (multiplexers, arithmetic circuits, registers, etc.) and their design characteristics are considered, again drawing examples from the 7400 series. The register-transfer approach to digital system design is presented in this chapter. Also introduced formally here is a register-transfer language derived from the programming language Pascal. The major component types at the LSI level are surveyed, and memory design using ROMs and RAMs is considered in depth. Finally, the use of ROMs as general-purpose design components is discussed.

The structure and application of some representative microprocessor families are investigated in Chap. 5 (Basic Microprocessor Organization). A simple 1-bit microprocessor intended for industrial control applications, the Motorola 14500, serves as the introductory example. The general principles of CPU organization, including instruction sets, data types, and external communication methods, are then presented. Two influential 8-bit microprocessor series, the Motorola 6800 and Intel 8080/8085, are thoroughly described and compared. Some important derivatives of these microprocessors, including the Motorola 6801 one-chip microcomputer and the Zilog Z80 microprocessor, are briefly discussed.

The principles of computer programming as they apply to microprocessor-based systems are examined in Chap. 6 (Microcomputer Programming). The program development process and programming language selection are analyzed, emphasizing the need for systematic and well-structured design approaches. Assembly language programming is discussed using the 6800 and 8080/8085 assembly languages as examples. Programming microprocessor-based systems via high-level languages is also discussed, with Pascal serving as the main example. Numerous sample programs appear throughout this chapter.

Chapter 7 (Interfacing Techniques) is devoted to the important issue of connecting microprocessors to the outside world. The interfacing needs of common digital input-output (IO) devices, including keyboards and LED displays, are examined. Analog IO devices such as transducers and stepping motors are treated next, along with the methods for converting signals between analog and digital forms. Microprocessor bus structures are studied, with emphasis on standard buses represented by the Multibus (IEEE 796 standard bus). Input-output programming methods, interrupt-driven IO, and direct memory access (DMA) are covered in this chapter using programmable IO interface circuits from the major microprocessor families.

The last chapter (Chap. 8: Advanced Microprocessor Organization) addresses the design of more powerful microprocessor-based digital systems. The characteristics of 16-bit microprocessors are reviewed, and are illustrated by the Intel 8086 and Motorola 68000. Bit slicing and microprogramming are considered, with the Advanced Micro Devices 2900 bit-sliced microprocessor family acting as the example. Finally, microcomputer systems with more than one programmable processor are studied, including systems containing arithmetic coprocessors, IO processors, and multiple CPUs (multiprocessors).

Each chapter concludes with a summary, suggestions for further reading, and a comprehensive set of problems. The problems, most of which have been class-tested, have been designed so that they can be solved using only the information available in this book. Many of the problems are also intended to augment concepts encountered in the text.

COURSE PLANS

Digital System Design and Microprocessors was designed as the text for a one- or two-term undergraduate course at approximately the sophomore–junior level. It has been used by the author primarily for a one-semester (15-week) course called Introduction to Digital System Design Using Microprocessors, in which the audience has ranged from juniors to graduate students. The bulk of the material for this course is drawn from Chaps. 4 through 8. It is recommended that students using the book for a one-term course have some prior familiarity with switching theory, and with basic computer organization and programming. If the book is used for a two-term course sequence, then no specific prerequisites are necessary. Typically the first course of such a sequence is called

Introduction to Digital Logic Design, and covers Chaps. 1 through 4; the second course, which may be called Microprocessor/Microcomputer Design and Applications, covers Chaps. 5 through 8. The material of this book has also been used successfully for an intensive two-week short course taken by practicing engineers and technical managers. If laboratory work is included in any of these courses, then this book will need to be supplemented with appropriate laboratory manuals and IC manufacturers' data manuals; otherwise no supplementary materials should be necessary.

Table P.1 shows a possible outline for a single 15-week course based on this book, while Table P.2 gives a plan for a two-course sequence covering two 10-week quarter terms. Since each chapter and major section is reasonably self-contained, a course instructor should have considerable flexibility to modify the choice of topics covered or the sequence of topic presentation in order, say, to coordinate the course lectures with a specific sequence of laboratory experiments.

Table P.1 Sample outline for a 15-week, one-semester course based on this book.

Week	Topics	Text reference
1	Introduction. Historical review. Significance and applications of microprocessors.	Chap. 1
2	IC technology overview. System design using ICs.	Secs. 2.2–2.3
3	Gate-level logic design review. 7400-series SSI/MSI components.	Chap. 3. Sec. 4.1
4	MSI components (continued). Register-transfer design.	Secs. 4.1–4.2
5	LSI components. ROMs and RAMs. Memory system design.	Sec. 4.3
6	Simple microprocessor (14500). Basic computer organization.	Secs. 5.1–5.2
7	CPU organization and instruction sets. 8-bit microprocessor families (6800 and/or 8080/8085).	Sec. 5.2. Sec. 5.3 and/or 5.4
8	8-bit microprocessor families (continued). Midterm examination.	Sec. 5.3 and/or 5.4
9	Program development and language selection. Microprocessor programming in assembly and/or high-level programming languages.	Secs. 6.1–6.2
10	Microprocessor programming (continued).	Secs. 6.3–6.4
11	Microprocessor programming (continued). IO interfacing.	Sec. 7.1
12	Digital and analog IO devices. Analog–digital conversion methods.	Sec. 7.2
13	Bus structures. IO programming. Interrupts.	Sec. 7.3
14	DMA. 16-bit microprocessor families (8086 and/or 68000)	Secs. 7.3–8.1
15	Selected topic from: bit-sliced microprocessors; special-purpose processors; multimicroprocessors.	Sec. 8.2–8.3

Table P.2 Sample outline for a sequence of two 10-week (quarter-term) courses based on this book.

Week	Topics	Text reference
	Course 1: *Introduction to Digital Logic Design*	
1	Introduction. Digital system concepts. Historical review.	Secs. 1.1–1.2
2	Basic electronics concepts. IC technology overview.	Secs. 2.1–2.2
3	TTL and MOS logic families. Design using ICs.	Sec. 2.3
4	Logic design concepts. Binary number representation.	Sec. 3.1
5	Combinational and sequential components and circuits. 7400-series SSI components.	Sec. 3.2
6	Boolean algebra. Combinational circuit design.	Sec. 3.3
7	Combinational and sequential circuit design.	Secs. 3.3–4.1
8	MSI components. Register-transfer design.	Secs. 4.1–4.2
9	LSI components. Memory circuits (ROMs and RAMs).	Sec. 4.3
10	Programmable digital systems. Microprocessors and their applications.	Sec. 5.1. Sec. 1.3
	Course 2: *Microprocessor/Microcomputer Design and Applications*	
1	Review of digital design concepts. Microprocessors and their applications.	Chap. 1
2	Basic computer organization. CPUs and instruction sets.	Secs. 5.1–5.2
3	8-bit microprocessor family (6800 or 8080/8085).	Sec. 5.3 or 5.4
4	8-bit microprocessor family (continued)	
5	Program design. Language selection. Assembly language programming.	Secs. 6.1–6.3
6	Assembly language programming (continued)	Sec. 6.3
7	IO interfacing. Basic IO devices and buses.	Secs. 7.1–7.2
8	IO programming. Interrupts and DMA.	Sec. 7.3
9	16-bit microprocessors (8086 and/or 68000)	Sec. 8.1
10	Bit-sliced microprocessors (2900) and microprogramming.	Sec. 8.2

ACKNOWLEDGMENTS

I would like to thank my many students at the University of Michigan, the University of Southern California, and various industrial organizations who contributed to the shaping of this book. Thanks are also due my microprocessor-laboratory teaching assistants, especially John P. Shen and Thirumalai Sridhar. The support and love of my wife Terrie, as well as her assistance in proofreading, are very much appreciated.

John P. Hayes

ONE

INTRODUCTION TO DIGITAL SYSTEMS

"Much interest was expressed by several of the party to learn on what subject the Chinese were most anxious to have information. Count Strzelecki told them that the subject of most frequent inquiry was Babbage's Calculating Machine. On being further asked as to the nature of the inquiries, he said they were most anxious to know whether it would go into the pocket."

[Charles Babbage: *Passages from the Life of a Philosopher,* 1864]

This chapter examines the elements of digital system design, and provides a broad overview of the technological basis of the revolution in system design brought about by microprocessors. The terminology and descriptive methods common to all types of systems are introduced. The important distinction between structure and behavior is discussed, as is the hierarchical nature of complex systems. The microprocessor can be regarded as a result of the confluence of two evolutionary streams—one in electronic circuit technology, and the other in the design of digital computers. These evolutionary processes are traced in detail, not only for their historical interest, but also for the insight they give into the continuing rapid changes occurring in microprocessor design. Finally, the role of the microprocessor as a component in complex systems is examined. The range of applications for microprocessors is surveyed, and the procedures used in microprocessed-based design are discussed.

1.1 SYSTEM CONCEPTS

Two fundamental aspects of every system—structure and behavior—are examined in this section. Complexity levels and their implications are discussed, and some physical factors governing system design are introduced.

1.1.1 Structure and Behavior

In ordinary discourse the word "system" is encountered in many different contexts, for example:

The solar system
The digestive system
The metric system
The postal system
A hi-fi audio system
A computer system

In each instance system suggests a set of related things or parts that are linked together to form a unified whole. Thus a hi-fi system consists of various components such as a turntable, an amplifier, and loudspeakers, all linked together by electrical cables. A system also has a well-defined function or behavior, which can be distinguished from the functions of its component parts. The function of the hi-fi system is to transform information stored on phonograph records into audible sound, something that no one of the system components can perform by itself.

A system often consists of many parts that are linked by subtle or poorly understood relationships. Systems of this kind are said to be *complex*. One natural system that is highly complex is the human brain. Its complexity can be measured roughly by the fact that it contains about 10^{10} brain cells or neurons, each of which is itself a (sub)system of considerable complexity. Even in systems of very high complexity such as the brain, it is assumed that there are understandable order and regularity within the system; this assumption is reflected in the word *systematic*.

In this book we are concerned with a class of man-made systems called digital systems. A *digital system* may be defined here as a set of interconnected components that process information in digital or discrete form. (The significance of the term "digital" is explored later in this section.) In most digital systems of interest, the fundamental components from which the systems are constructed are tiny electronic devices called integrated circuits (ICs). The links between these electronic components are signal paths such as wires over which (digital) information can be transmitted. Modern digital systems cover an enormous range of complexity. The components available for constructing these systems range from single on–off switches to entire computers. The number of components in a digital system can range from one or two to many thousands. Our understanding of a digital system is usually inversely proportional to its complexity. Systems composed of small numbers of fairly simple switches are well understood, whereas those with thousands of such switches are often poorly understood.

Because we must deal with many different types of digital systems, from the very simple to the highly complex, it is useful at the outset to consider the basic properties common to all such systems. This not only will provide a unifying theme to our discussion, but will also give us a uniform language for describing the systems of interest.

As noted above, a system contains objects called components that are related or connected by links. Frequently a system component is treated as a primitive entity or "black box" whose internal structure is not of interest. In other situations the same component C may itself be regarded as a system with internal components of its own. In this case C may be referred to as a *subsystem* of the original system.

Figure 1.1 lists the components and links that can be associated with some well-known systems. The identification of a system's components and links is a subjective process that often can be carried out in several different ways. Thus the metric system for everyday use treats the units meter (m), gram (g), and second (s) as primitive components or building blocks of the system; this system is therefore called the MGS (meter-gram-second) system. Electrical engineers, on the other hand, prefer to treat the kilogram (kg)—that is, 1000 g—rather than the gram as the basic unit of mass. They also add the unit of electric current, the ampere (A), as a primitive unit, thereby obtaining the MKSA (meter-kilogram-second-ampere) system. Note that the links in the metric system are the abstract rules for constructing composite units of measurement from the basic units and a set of standard prefixes denoting multiplicative factors. Thus the composite quantity microsecond (μs) is formed by linking the prefix micro (denoting one millionth) to the basic unit second.

The components and links of a system are examples of mathematical entities called sets. A *set* is simply a collection of objects called the members of the set. The set is usually represented by a list of its members, in which the members are separated by commas, and the entire set is enclosed by braces. Thus we could describe the components of the hi-fi system of Fig. 1.1 by the four-member set:

$$\{\text{Turntable, Amplifier, Left loudspeaker, Right loudspeaker}\} \qquad (1.1)$$

System	Components	Links
Solar	Sun Planets Asteroids	Gravitation Distance
Hi-fi	Turntable Amplifier Loudspeakers	Electrical cables
Metric	Measurement units 　meter 　gram 　second Multiplicative prefixes 　kilo- 　hecto- 　deka- 　deci- 　etc.	Rules for constructing composite units of measurement

Figure 1.1 Components and links of some familiar systems.

More generally, we use symbolic names to represent a set and its members. Thus we can define the component set C of an abstract system S containing n components in the following way.

$$C = \{C_0, C_1, \ldots, C_{n-1}\} \tag{1.2}$$

Set notation may also be used for the links of a system. The links in our hi-fi example might be represented by the following two-member set.

$$\{\text{Turntable-to-amplifier cable, Amplifier-to-loudspeakers cable}\} \tag{1.3}$$

In general a set of m links may be written as

$$L = \{L_0, L_1, \ldots, L_{m-1}\} \tag{1.4}$$

Note that each link defines a connection or relationship between the members of some subset of the set of components. Another way of specifying a link is to list the set of components that it links together. We therefore could rewrite (1.3) as follows:

$$\{ \{\text{Turntable, Amplifier}\},$$
$$\{\text{Turntable, Left loudspeaker, Right loudspeaker}\} \}$$

With these preliminaries we may now define the *structure G* of a system S as the combination of its component set C and its link set L. More formally, we may write

$$G = (C, L) \tag{1.5}$$

or in words,

$$\text{Structure} = (\text{Components, Links}) \tag{1.6}$$

In Eqs. (1.5) and (1.6) we use parentheses rather than braces to mark off the members of a set. Parentheses indicate that the order in which the set members are listed is significant. Thus the system structure G defined by Eq. (1.5) is a two-member ordered set (also called a pair) whose left member is a set of components C and whose right member is a set of links L. If we state that $H = (A, B)$ denotes a system structure, then we know that A denotes components and B denotes links, and not the reverse.

A convenient and natural way to represent the structure of a system is by means of a *block diagram,* in which components are represented by rectangular boxes called blocks, and links are denoted by lines connecting the blocks. Specifically, a link L_i corresponds to one or more connected lines that touch all the blocks representing the components connected by L_i. The name or function of a component is usually written in the corresponding block, while the name or function of a link may be written beside the corresponding lines in the block diagram. Figure 1.2 is a block diagram of the hi-fi system defined by Eqs. (1.1) and (1.3).

In most fields of science and engineering, specialized forms of block diagrams have been developed for representing the systems of interest. When the number of component types is small, economy and clarity of representation are increased by using distinct symbols instead of blocks for the various component types. Figure 1.3a is a generalized block diagram for a small electronic circuit. (This circuit forms a device called a NAND gate, which will be encountered frequently in later chapters.) In practice standard

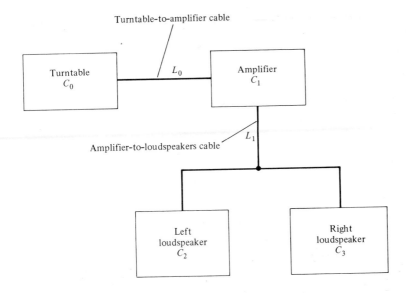

Turntable-to-amplifier cable

Amplifier-to-loudspeakers cable

Figure 1.2 Block diagram representing the structure of a hi–fi system.

symbols are used for electronic components, and the block diagram of Fig. 1.3a is normally replaced by the schematic diagram of Fig. 1.3b. Note that the external devices D_A, D_B, D_C, and the power supply, which are shown explicitly in Fig. 1.3a, are shown only by implication in Fig. 1.3b. Finally, Fig. 1.3c shows a single special symbol that is used to represent the entire NAND gate. This standard symbol is used in logic circuit design, where a NAND gate is treated as a primitive component or building block.

So far we have only considered the question: How is the system constructed? We now turn to the equally important question: What does the system do? In many of the systems of interest here, the components transmit *signals* to one another via the system's links. These signals are typically electrical in nature, and contain information in some suitably encoded form. The two links L_0 and L_1 in the hi-fi system shown in Fig. 1.3, for example, transmit information in the form of time-varying electric signals whose variations mirror those of the sound signals to be reproduced by the system.

In systems whose links are signal transmission paths, the components usually are devices that process or transform information. The entire system then can be viewed as an information-processing device. A component (which may be the entire system) receives a set of signals $X = (X_0, X_1, X_2, \ldots)$, called *input signals,* from other components, which it uses to generate a set of *output signals* $Z = (Z_0, Z_1, Z_2, \ldots)$ that it can transmit to other components. The relationship between X and Z is taken to define the behavior of the component or system in question. Thus we can say that a device's *behavior* is known if, for every input signal X_i to the device, we know the corresponding output signal Z_i produced by the device. The behavior F of a system or a system component can be defined, at least in principle, by the pair (X, Z) where the sets X and Z

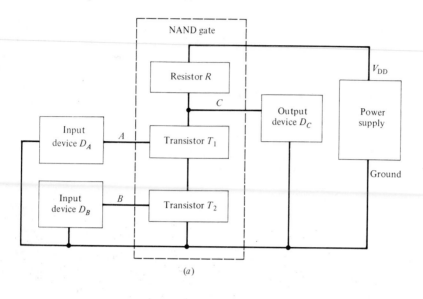

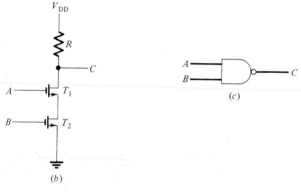

Figure 1.3 Three structural descriptions of a NAND gate: (*a*) general block diagram; (*b*) electric circuit diagram; (*c*) logic circuit symbol.

contain all corresponding pairs of input-output (IO) signals of interest. We therefore can write

$$F = (X, Z) \qquad (1.7)$$

or, less formally,

$$\text{Behavior} = (\text{Input signals, Output signals}) \qquad (1.8)$$

[Compare Eqs. (1.5) and (1.6), which define system structure.] In complex systems the number of IO signal pairs is often too large to permit their explicit listing as in (1.7), and we must resort to other, more concise, representations of system behavior. For example, it may be useful to treat F as a mathematical function or mapping from X, the input signals or independent variables, to Z, the output signals or dependent variables. The IO relationship implied by (1.7) then can be rewritten in the following form:

$$Z = F(X)$$

To illustrate the foregoing concepts, consider again the NAND circuit of Fig. 1.3. It has two main input signals denoted A and B, and an output signal denoted C. The signal values or signal states of interest here are electric voltage levels. In many applications we can restrict our attention to just two voltage levels: a high voltage V_H, which corresponds roughly to the power supply voltage V_{DD}, and a low voltage V_L corresponding to the zero or ground voltage level. This restriction makes A, B, and C into two-state or binary signals. (Later we will see that it is useful to represent binary values somewhat more abstractly by the digits 0 and 1.) We can completely define the behavior of this NAND circuit according to (1.7) by specifying all possible combinations of the input signal values and the corresponding output values. This is done in a tabular form called a *truth table* in Fig. 1.4a. Figure 1.4 also shows two other useful ways of describing the same behavior. In Fig. 1.4b the behavior of the NAND gate is given by a statement in a formalized version of English, with the symbol $:=$ (sometimes written $\leftarrow$ or $=$) denoting "becomes" or "is assigned the value." Behavioral descriptions in a formal language of this kind are encountered frequently throughout this book. Figure 1.4c shows another type of behavioral description called a *flowchart*. The behavior specified by the flowchart is determined by tracing all possible paths from the box labeled "Start" to the box labeled "Stop." Each rectangular box defines certain IO actions that should take place when the box in question is reached. The outgoing arrow from each box points

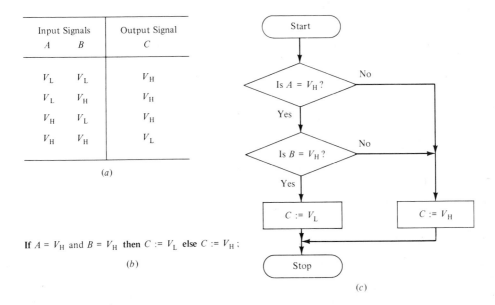

Input Signals A	B	Output Signal C
V_L	V_L	V_H
V_L	V_H	V_H
V_H	V_L	V_H
V_H	V_H	V_L

(a)

If $A = V_H$ and $B = V_H$ then $C := V_L$ else $C := V_H$;

(b)

(c)

Figure 1.4 Three behavioral descriptions of a NAND gate: (a) truth table; (b) formal language statement; (c) flowchart.

to the next set of actions in the current path. A fork in a path is indicated by a diamond-shaped box. If the condition specified in the diamond is true, the outgoing arrow labeled "Yes" is followed; if the condition is false, the "No" exit is used. The reader should verify that the three descriptions of NAND-gate behavior given in Fig. 1.4 do indeed contain the same information.

It is important to recognize that the concepts of system structure and system behavior are independent. Knowledge of a system's structure does not imply knowledge of its behavior, and vice versa. One can construct a complex electronic system from a wiring diagram (a complete structural description) without knowing how the resulting system behaves. Conversely, it is possible to know the behavior of a complex system— how to operate a computer, for example—without knowing anything about the underlying structure of the system in question. In general, a given system behavior can be obtained in many different ways. For example, the electromechanical system depicted in Fig. 1.5 has the NAND-gate behavior specified by Fig. 1.4, even though this system has little structural resemblance to the electronic NAND gate appearing in Fig. 1.3. This second NAND gate is composed of two electromechanical switches called *relays,* which are controlled by the electric input signals A and B; the relays replace the electronic switches (transistors) of Fig. 1.3. When a high voltage V_H is applied to a relay's input line, the relay becomes magnetized and pulls its armature switch from its normal closed position to the open position. The positions of the two armature switches in Fig. 1.5 determine the value of the output signal C. C is connected directly to V_H whenever at least one armature switch is closed, that is, at least one relay has V_L applied to its input line. Otherwise C assumes the ground voltage level V_L via a circuit to ground through the output device.

The behavior of a system with many components can be determined from the behavior of the components and the system structure. Thus by knowing the behavior of the resistor R and the transistors T_1 and T_2 used to construct the NAND gate of Fig. 1.3, one can deduce the system behavior described in Fig. 1.4. Often a block diagram of a system implicitly or explicitly defines the functions of the components used; such a diagram can serve as both a structural and a behavioral description of the system in question. The fact that many system descriptions provide information on both system structure and behavior tends to blur the distinction between these concepts.

The study of systems has two fundamental aspects, analysis and synthesis. As suggested by Fig. 1.6, *analysis* is concerned with the determination of a system's behavior, given its structure and the behavior of its components. Conversely, *synthesis* or *design* is the determination of a system structure that exhibits a given behavior. Normally the system must be synthesized using specified component and link types, and certain design objectives must be met. A common design objective is to minimize the total cost of the components and links used to construct the system. Another important design goal is to maximize the system's efficiency of operation or performance. Performance is often measured by the system's speed of operation, or its utilization of energy or other costly resources. Typically many design alternatives exist that exhibit various trade-offs between cost and performance. It is the designer's task to choose between the possible trade-offs, which are often vague and difficult to quantify, to obtain the system that best fits a given situation.

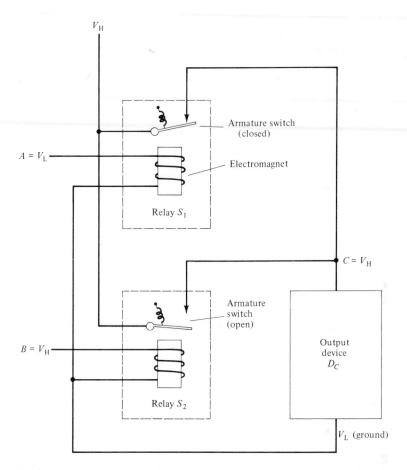

Figure 1.5 NAND gate constructed from electromechanical relays.

1.1.2 Complexity Levels

Many systems of interest here are extremely complex, that is, they contain very large numbers of basic components and links. A big computer system, for instance, may be constructed from thousands of individual electronic components that are interconnected by millions of wires. Computer programs (which may be termed software systems) are routinely written that contain thousands of individual instructions. To cite an extreme example, some versions of the main control program, or operating system, written for the IBM System/360 computer series in the 1960s contained over 2 million instructions.

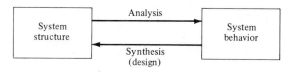

Figure 1.6 Relationship of structure and behavior.

Human beings have difficulty comprehending the structure or behavior of systems that contain more than a few dozen components. This raises a fundamental question: How do we deal with systems of extremely high complexity such as are frequently encountered in digital system hardware and software design? One important answer, which is rooted in the principle of the division of labor, is to break up the system under consideration into subsystems of manageable complexity.

Consider the task of analyzing or synthesizing a highly complex system S. We can begin by viewing S as being composed of a small set of components $\{S_1, S_2, \ldots, S_n\}$, where each S_i represents a (sub)system that is intrinsically less complex than S itself. S_i in turn may be decomposed into a small set of simpler components $\{S_{i_1}, S_{i_2}, \ldots, S_{i_m}\}$. The S_{i_j}'s then can be broken down into even simpler components, and so on. Thus it is possible to view S at a series of different levels, which we may call *complexity levels,* each of which is characterized by specific types of primitive components and links. To examine the internal structure of a primitive component from some complexity level, we must move down to the next lowest complexity level.

Figure 1.7 shows several well-defined complexity levels at which a particular complex system, a digital computer, may be treated. In Fig. 1.7a the entire computer is viewed as a one-component system represented by a block diagram composed of a single block; this is the highest complexity level. Figure 1.7b shows the computer as a five-component system. The components recognized at this level are the central processing

(a)

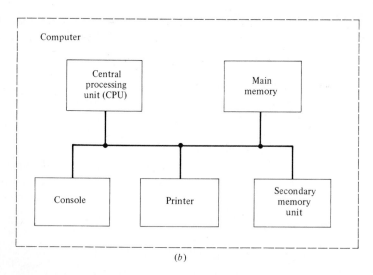

(b)

Figure 1.7 Views of a computer at various complexity levels.

Figure 1.7 continued.

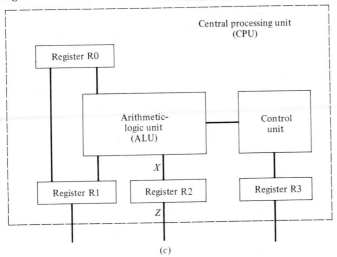

(c)

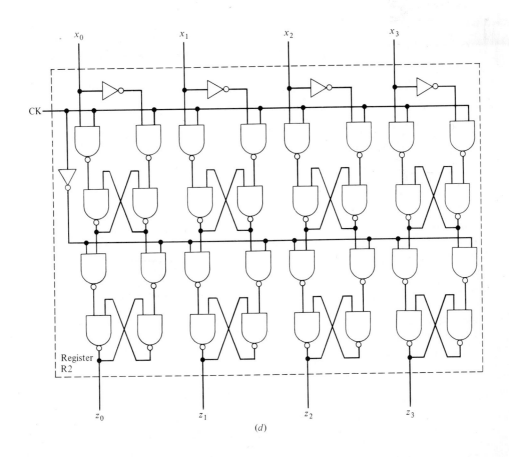

(d)

unit (CPU), which is the component responsible for instruction execution, the main memory used to store instructions that are awaiting execution, and three IO devices: a user's console with a keyboard and video display, a hardcopy printer, and a secondary memory device such as a magnetic disk storage unit. In Fig. 1.7c one of the foregoing units, the CPU, is further decomposed into a system comprising temporary storage devices called registers, a control unit, and a data-processing circuit called an arithmetic-logic unit or ALU, which performs most of the operations specified by instructions to the computer. Finally, Fig. 1.7d illustrates an even lower complexity level at which we can view the internal design of a CPU register. Here the system components are devices called logic gates. The gates process binary data and are represented by special symbols instead of blocks. The larger semicircular symbol denotes a NAND gate (see Figs. 1.3 and 1.4), while the smaller triangular symbol denotes another type of gate called an inverter or NOT gate. (An inverter is actually a one-input version of a NAND.) The three complexity levels illustrated by Figs. 1.7b, 1.7c, and 1.7d are called the *processor, register,* and *gate levels,* respectively, where the level name indicates an important component type that is treated as primitive in that particular level. Note that Fig. 1.7 by no means exhausts the number of complexity levels. Gates, for example, can be decomposed further into transistors, resistors, and so on, yielding the *electronic circuit level* depicted in Fig. 1.3.

The higher the complexity level at which a system is viewed, the fewer components are needed to describe the system, but the components themselves are more complex. Increasing the complexity level, therefore, implies coalescing subsystems composed of low-level components into a single higher-level component. This is basically a simplification process. At any level, the internal structure of the components recognized at that level constitutes irrelevant detail. Increasing the complexity level also simplifies the behavioral description of a system. For example, the input and output signals (x_0, x_1, x_2, x_3) and (z_0, z_1, z_2, z_3) of the gate-level circuit appearing in Fig. 1.7d are coalesced into the simpler higher-level signals X and Z in the register-level circuit of Fig. 1.7c.

The processor, register, and gate levels illustrated in Fig. 1.7 are the main complexity levels used in this book. Other levels are also of interest, especially the electronic circuit level depicted in Fig. 1.3. People concerned with different aspects of the design or application of a digital system such as a computer tend to view the system at different levels. Thus the manager of a data-processing center tends to view computers at the processor level. A programmer, on the other hand, is also interested in the register level, particularly as it pertains to the CPU. In the design of a computer system, the design process is often divided up by complexity level, and different people may be responsible for the design tasks at the various levels. Processor-level structure and behavior are specified by designers called (*computer*) *architects*. At the register and gate levels, the design process is carried out by *logic designers*.

Figure 1.8 shows a more abstract picture of the various complexity levels in the computer of Fig. 1.7. The components belonging to a particular level are represented by dots that are placed in a row. Each component is connected by a line to all the components that contribute to its internal structure at the next lowest complexity level. The resulting diagram clearly shows that there is a hierarchical order or ranking among the components defined by the complexity levels. Similar hierarchies are found in many complex

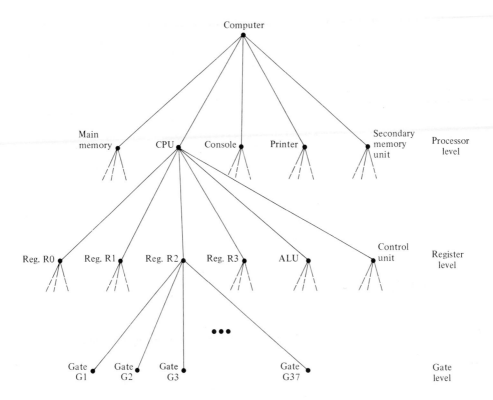

Figure 1.8 Hierarchical organization of the computer in Fig. 1.7.

organizations, as in an army, where complexity level corresponds to military rank. Systems with the organization depicted in Fig. 1.8 are referred to as *hierarchical systems*.

The design and analysis of a complex hierarchical system can often be greatly simplified by exploiting its hierarchical organization. As an illustration, consider a hypothetical system S with a hierarchy of three complexity levels: L_1 (the highest level), L_2, and L_3 (the lowest level). Suppose that 25 components are recognized at level L_1, which includes five different component types. In other words, five copies of each of five different level-L_1 component types are needed to construct S. Furthermore, assume that every component on level L_i can be decomposed into 25 level-L_{i+1} components of five different types. Let the components on level L_3 be those from which S ultimately must be fabricated. Clearly S comprises a total of $25^3 = 15,625$ level-L_3 components. If we attempted to design S directly as a one-level system of 15,625 components, the complexity of the design process would probably be overwhelming. A much more efficient approach is to carry out the design level by level along the following lines.

1. Design S using level-L_1 components.
2. Design each of the five level-L_1 component types using level-L_2 components.
3. Design each of the five level-L_2 component types using level-L_3 components.

The foregoing design approach, often called *top-down* design, reduces the design of S to the design of eleven 25-component systems, each of which uses five component types. Thus we deal directly with $11 \times 25 = 275$ components, instead of the 15,275 that would have been encountered if the design process had not been decomposed by complexity levels.

The fundamental electronic building blocks of modern digital systems are *integrated circuits* (ICs). A typical IC is an electronic circuit that is manufactured from a single, tiny piece of silicon called a *chip*. The complexity of an IC may be measured by the number of logic gates it contains. Current manufacturing methods allow IC complexity to range from one gate per chip to 10^5 or more gates per chip. The ICs are often classified into three groups on the basis of the number of gates they contain. Those with small-scale integration (SSI) contain roughly 1 to 100 gates. Medium-scale integration (MSI) covers the range 100 to 1000 gates per chip, whereas large-scale integration (LSI) and very-large-scale integration (VLSI) refer to thousands of gates per chip. Typically, LSI/VLSI, MSI, and SSI ICs correspond to design components at the processor, register, and gate complexity levels respectively. A CPU that is built into a single LSI/VLSI chip is called a *microprocessor*, and is a key component of many systems.

1.1.3 Physical Considerations

Physical variables such as temperature, pressure, length, velocity, current, and voltage are called *analog* or continuous variables. They are characterized by the fact that they can change value by arbitrarily small amounts. This means that within any range of variation, no matter how small, an analog quantity can assume an infinite number of different values. Hence if we plot a graph of an analog function $f(x)$ against x, we obtain a continuous curve. Figure 1.9 shows graphs for some diverse analog quantities as functions of time.

A continuous variable f is often represented or measured by another continuous variable g whose changes in value are similar or analogous to those of f. (This analogy between the measured and the measuring variables is the reason for the term "analog signal.") For example, the speed or velocity of an automobile is usually measured by an interval marked by a needle on the dial of a speedometer; see Fig. 1.10a. The speedometer is designed so that an increase or decrease in the car's velocity causes a proportional increase or decrease in the length of the interval marked off by the speedometer needle. The speedometer therefore may be called an analog measuring instrument. Another analog instrument is a mercury thermometer that measures temperature by the length of a column of mercury in a capillary tube. As temperature rises and falls, the length of the mercury column increases and decreases in proportion to the temperature changes. Many analog devices use electrical quantities such as current, voltage, or resistance as the analog signal for representing the physical variables of interest.

A system whose signals all are analog is called an *analog system*. A variety of analog systems have been designed for computation purposes. One of the simplest and best-known analog computers is a *slide rule*. Numbers on a slide rule are represented over continuous ranges by intervals marked on scales that can be moved relative to one

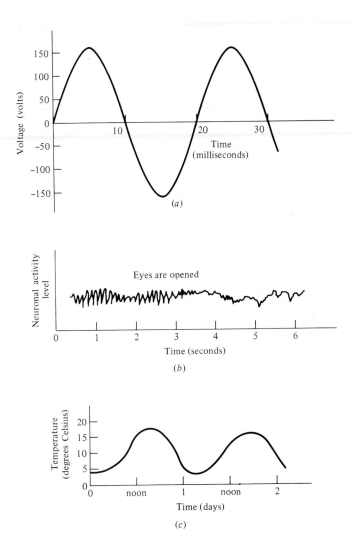

Figure 1.9 Examples of analog signals: (*a*) mains voltage waveform; (*b*) human encephalogram; (*c*) ambient temperature chart.

another. By adding and subtracting intervals on various scales, many useful mathematical operations can be performed. For example, multiplication and division are done using two logarithmic scales on which the number *n* marks an interval whose length is proportional to log *n*. If the intervals marked *n* and *m* on two identical logarithmic scales are added by placing them end to end as shown in Fig. 10b, then the number *p* marking the sum of the two interval lengths represents the product *mn*. This is a consequence of the following basic property of logarithms:

$$\log m + \log n = \log mn \qquad (1.9)$$

Note that $p = mn$ can be read directly from one of the two logarithmic scales. Division is implemented in a similar manner by the subtraction of intervals on the same scales. Mechanical analog computers such as the slide rule are many centuries old. Electromechanical and electronic analog computers were developed and used extensively during the first half of the twentieth century.

When used for measurement or computation, analog devices have a serious deficiency: The accuracy with which an analog value can be read is limited. If two values are very close together, they cannot be readily distinguished. In the analog devices of Fig. 1.10, for example, a value can be read with a precision of at most three decimal digits. While this may be adequate for everyday needs, many scientific and engineering tasks require a precision of eight digits or more. To obtain greater precision in analog devices such as those of Fig. 1.10, the effective length of the number scales must be greatly increased, which usually is not feasible. Furthermore, the interpolation process required when a pointer falls between two marks on an analog scale is inherently error-prone.

We can avoid these limitations in accuracy by using digital or discrete signals in place of analog. A *digital* variable is one that can assume only a finite set of n values; the n allowed values are often represented by the numerical digits $0, 1, 2, \ldots$. Of particular

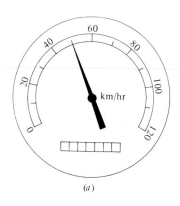

(a)

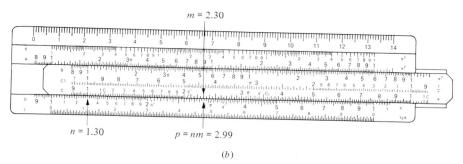

(b)

Figure 1.10 Two analog devices: (a) automobile speedometer; (b) slide rule.

interest are *binary* variables that have the two values 0 and 1, and *decimal* variables that have the 10 values 0, 1, 2, 3, 4, 5, 6, 7, 8, and 9. The internal representation of information in most digital systems uses binary digital signals. A number can be represented by a sequence of m digital signals. By increasing *m*, a relatively simple process that takes up little space, essentially any desired degree of accuracy can be obtained. Figure 1.11 shows a digital light-emitting diode (LED) display unit of the type used in many electronic pocket calculators. Six decimal digits are displayed in this example. A slide rule that allowed comparable precision would be enormously long and unwieldy. Thus when LSI circuit technology greatly lowered the cost of digital pocket calculators in the early 1970s, analog slide rules became obsolete. More recently, digital techniques have been introduced to improve the fidelity or accuracy of home audio systems, another traditional bastion of analog techniques. Analog computers have been superseded in most applications by digital computers.

Figure 1.12a shows the graph of an ideal binary signal as it varies with time. There are exactly two signal values denoted by 0 and 1, and at the points of time marked 1, 2, and 3, instantaneous changes of value occur. In practical systems these digital signals are

Figure 1.11 Digital display unit employing light–emitting diodes (LEDs).

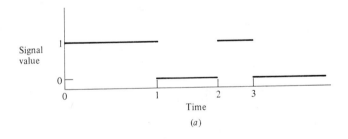

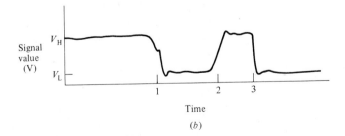

Figure 1.12 Binary digital waveform: (*a*) ideal; (*b*) actual.

represented by inherently analog quantities such as voltage. Thus in Fig. 1.12b the two digital signals 0 and 1 are represented by the two voltage levels V_L and V_H respectively. Since voltage is a continuous quantity, a voltage change from V_L to V_H, or vice versa, requires the signal to pass through all voltage values between V_L and V_H. Consequently, as Fig. 1.12b indicates, changes between V_L and V_H cannot take place instantaneously. These deviations from the ideal behavior can be taken care of by proper system design to ensure that digital signals are used only after value transitions have been completed. Furthermore, signals that should remain constant tend to fluctuate about their nominal values V_L or V_H as a result of minor imperfections in the behavior of physical components and signals. This means that 0 and 1 should correspond to a small range of voltage values around V_L and V_H respectively. Thus, while signal waveforms such as that of Fig. 1.12b can be treated as digital for many purposes, the designer must be aware of their analog aspects. It should also be noted that, while most manufactured electronic systems process digital signals, nature remains mostly analog. Consequently a digital system must often deal with analog signals at its point of contact or *interface* with the outside world.

The most basic digital component, called a *switch*, transforms a binary input signal x into a binary output signal z. The transistors of Fig. 1.3 and the relays of Fig. 1.5 are examples of switches. Figure 1.13 shows the abstract structure and behavior of a switch. Switches can be built using many different technologies, for both the signal medium and the signal switching mechanism. A relay is classed as an electromechanical device because its input and output signals are electric, while its switching action involves mechanical movement of the armature. Electronic switches such as transistors also employ electric signals, but involve no mechanical movement. Their operation is based solely on the flow of electrons and other carriers of electric charge. Since electric currents have speeds approaching the speed of light (300,000 km/s or 30 cm/ns), electronic switches are among the fastest known. Furthermore, they can be manufactured in extremely small and inexpensive packages. For these reasons—high speed, small size, and low cost—electronic switching circuits form the basic building blocks of most digital systems. Other switch technologies are used, however, particularly at the interfaces between an electronic system and the outside world. Switches can be based on various electrical, optical, mechanical, pneumatic, and hydraulic principles.

One of the most common types of switches is illustrated by Fig. 1.14. This is a manually operated on–off switch S that controls an electric circuit containing a battery and a light bulb. The values of the input signal x can be identified with the positions of the switch contacts (open or closed), or with the corresponding positions of the operator's hand (raised or lowered). The switch's output signal z can be associated with any one of

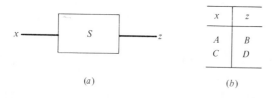

x	z
A	B
C	D

(a)

(b)

Figure 1.13 Abstract switch: (a) structure; (b) behavior.

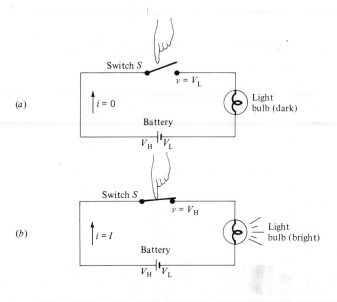

Figure 1.14 Electric circuit with manual on–off switch: (*a*) switched off; (*b*) switched on; (*c*) truth table.

several circuit parameters: the voltage v at one of the switch's terminals, the current i flowing around the circuit, or the illumination level of the light bulb. The relations between the various choices of x and z are described in the truth table of Fig. 1.14c. A system composed of interconnected switches is called a *switching circuit*. The NAND gates of Figs. 1.3 and 1.5 are examples of simple switching circuits, while a digital computer is a very complex switching circuit.

To be able to connect two signal-carrying links or *lines* v and w within a switching circuit to each other, the signal values carried by the lines must be physically compatible. Thus if the signal values used by v are the voltage levels V_L and V_H, these voltages must also be the signal values of line w. If signals are transmitted in the form of voltage pulses of a certain duration, then both v and w, and the devices connected to them, must be able to accommodate pulses of the same duration. If v and w carry physically different types of signals, for example, the voltage levels V_L and V_H in one case and the illumination levels dark and bright in the other case, then v and w are incompatible. Physically incompatible signal lines can be connected by means of a *transducer,* a device that transforms signals from one physical type to another. The on–off switch S of Fig. 1.14 can be regarded as a mechanical-to-electrical transducer, because it converts a mechanical signal (hand or contact position) into an electric signal (current or voltage). If the

an output "line," then the entire circuit of Fig. 1.14 becomes a mechanical-to-optical transducer.

Energy is required to transmit signals through a system. Every physical component absorbs some energy from its input signals in order to change the values of its output signals. Thus a signal that is propagated through a series of components tends to change from its original value, unless it is suitably restored or regenerated. Electric currents and voltages, for example, decay in magnitude and must be restored by a process called signal *amplification*. This process can be implemented by circuits called *amplifiers* or *drivers*. Alternatively, signal amplification circuits can be included in the system components themselves.

An input line x of a component absorbs a certain amount of energy from incoming signals; this energy may be termed the *load $L(x)$* imposed by x. An output line z can only supply signals at a certain maximum energy level $D(z)$ called the *drive capability* of z. Clearly if z is connected to or drives n lines $x_1, x_2, \ldots, x_n$, we require

$$D(z) \geq L(x_1) + L(x_2) + \cdots + L(x_n)$$

or, in other words,

$$\text{Output drive} \geq \text{Total input load} \tag{1.10}$$

If the total load exceeds the drive capability on some line, then the signals appearing on the line deteriorate in quality, and the system may function erratically, or even fail completely. Drive and load mismatches are usually corrected by the use of amplifiers and other "signal conditioning" devices.

1.2 EVOLUTION OF MICROPROCESSORS

This section surveys the historical developments in digital circuit technology and computer design that led to one-chip microprocessors and microcomputers.

1.2.1 Switch Technology

A fundamental component of all digital systems is a high-speed switch capable of controlling the flow of a rapidly changing electric current. The earliest requirement for such a switch was as a detector in a radio receiver, which is a device used to convert a high-frequency alternating current obtained from the receiving antenna into a direct current that can be used to produce sound. The conversion of alternating to direct current is called *rectification*; hence a detector is a special type of rectifier. A detector behaves as a mechanical switch that closes to permit current flow in one direction, and opens to block current flow in the reverse direction. Of the many ingenious devices used as detectors, two are of particular importance in the history of electronics: the crystal diode and the diode vacuum tube.

Early crystal detectors consisted of a small piece of crystalline material such as galena (lead sulfide PbS), to which was attached a thin metallic wire called a cat's whisker; see Fig. 1.15. The rectifying properties of this device were known as far back as

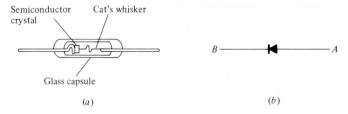

Figure 1.15 Point–contact semiconductor diode: (*a*) cross section; (*b*) symbol.

1874 (Braun & MacDonald, 1978), but the theory behind its operation was not under-stood until the 1930s. We now recognize that the crystals used are semiconductors, so that crystal detectors, now usually called semiconductor *diodes*, can be regarded as forerunners of modern semiconducter devices such as transistors and integrated circuits. The most important semiconductor, silicon (Si), was used in crystal diodes as far back as 1906. Figure 1.16 illustrates the use of a semiconductor diode as a switch. The relative voltages applied to the diode terminals *A* and *B* are denoted by + (positive) and − (negative) signs. When these voltages are as shown in Fig. 1.16a, in which case the diode is said to be forward biased, electric current flows from *A* to *B*, and the diode behaves as a closed mechanical switch, as in Fig. 1.16b. When the voltages applied to the diode terminals are reversed as in Fig. 1.16c, the diode behaves as the open switch of Fig. 1.16d, and is said to be reverse biased. Note that the arrow part of the diode symbol indicates the direction in which current flow is allowed.

The U.S. inventor Thomas A. Edison (1847–1931) observed in 1883 that a light bulb to which a small metallic plate is added can act as a rectifier. An electric current can flow between the heated filament and the plate in one direction only. This phenomenon, called the Edison effect, was employed by the Englishman John A. Fleming (1849–1945) to build a detector for use in radio receivers. Fleming's device, which is called a diode *vacuum tube* or diode *valve*, consists of a heated element (the cathode) surrounded by a metal plate (the anode) as depicted in Fig. 1.17. Its rectifying property derives from the fact that the cathode emits electrons that are attracted to a positively charged anode, but are repelled, thus blocking current flow, when the anode is negatively charged. Although much bulkier than the crystal diode, and requiring an auxiliary power supply to heat the cathode, the diode vacuum tube displaced the crystal diode in many

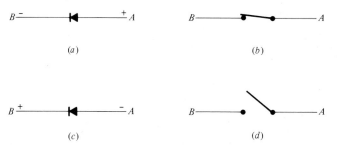

Figure 1.16 Use of a semiconductor diode as an on-off switch.

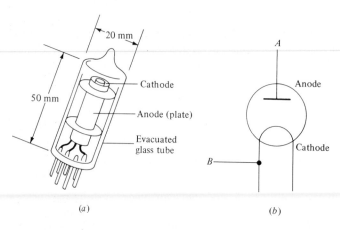

Figure 1.17 Vacuum-tube diode: (*a*) physical structure; (*b*) symbol.

applications because of its higher reliability. (Early crystal diodes had a movable cat's whisker that required delicate manual adjustment.) Interest in the semiconductor diode revived during World War II, however, when its small size and resulting ability to rectify ultrahigh-frequency signals made it more suitable than a vacuum tube as a detector in radar circuits.

Diodes can be interconnected to form various types of switching circuits. However, diodes alone do not suffice for the construction of large switching circuits because they cannot amplify signals. As signals propagate through diode circuits, the corresponding current and voltage levels deteriorate and become unusable. Some form of signal amplification is needed to restore the signals to usable levels. The two most important forms of electronic amplifiers evolved from diode rectifiers. The diode vacuum tube gave rise to the triode and other forms of amplifying vacuum tubes, while the crystal diode, after a much longer delay, led to a semiconductor amplifier, the transistor.

In 1906, not long after Fleming introduced the diode tube, an American, Lee de Forest (1873–1961), announced his invention of the Audion, a three-element vacuum tube or triode, which was capable of amplifying the feeble currents encountered in radio receivers. To make the triode, De Forest inserted a piece of wire shaped like a gridiron between the cathode and anode of a Fleming-type diode. This third electrode, called the grid, controls the flow of electrons between the cathode and the anode. In particular, a small change in the signal applied to the grid can produce a similar but much larger change in the signal appearing at the anode, thus effecting the desired amplification.

Vacuum-tube technology developed very rapidly, probably because the underlying physical principles are relatively simple and were quickly understood. An incandescent cathode emits electrons that are attracted to a positively charged anode. The intermediate grid either attracts or repels electrons, depending on its voltage relative to the cathode, and thereby influences the cathode–anode current flow. The voltage appearing at the anode is an amplified copy of the grid voltage. With the addition of feedback circuits, the triode can be made to oscillate and become a source of high-frequency signals. Triode circuits also can be built that act as digital storage devices or memories.

The triode soon spawned vacuum tubes with additional electrodes and improved operating characteristics. Until the establishment of the transistor in the mid-1950s, the tube remained the principal component of electronic circuits. In one application, domestic television sets, it was not displaced by the transistor until the 1970s. During the period 1946–1954 approximately, vacuum tubes were the main components used in the high-speed switching and storage circuits of digital computers. Computers of that era are called *first-generation* machines, a term that is largely synonymous with the use of vacuum tubes.

The vacuum tube has obvious disadvantages: It is bulky, it is fragile, and it consumes a large amount of power. Beginning in the 1920s, attempts were made in several countries to construct small crystal or "solid-state" amplifiers to replace vacuum tubes (Braun & MacDonald, 1978). Two major obstacles faced the early experimenters: The electrical properties of semiconductors were not fully understood, and small quantities of impurities in the materials being used significantly affected their behavior. Julius E. Lilienfeld (1882–1963), a professor of physics at the University of Leipzig, filed patent applications in the 1920s and 1930s on various transistor-like devices, but nothing came of this work. Experiments were conducted with many semiconductor materials, such as copper oxide and selenium, and rectifiers for power supplies were manufactured from these materials in large quantities in the 1930s.

After World War II, during which crystal diodes of the kind shown in Fig. 1.15 were used extensively, considerable research was carried out in the United States on the properties of the semiconductors, germanium and silicon. In 1947 John Bardeen and Walter H. Brattain of Bell Laboratories demonstrated a semiconductor device capable of amplification. This device, called a *point-contact transistor,* consisted of a germanium crystal (the base) with two closely spaced wires (the emitter and collector) touching its surface. It thus resembled a crystal diode with two cat's whiskers. An electric current flowing between the emitter and base is capable of controlling a much larger current flowing between the collector and the base. Thus a signal injected into the emitter appears in amplified form at the collector, so that the transistor acts as a semiconductor triode. Unlike the vacuum-tube triode, the transistor requires no heated filament or vacuum, and it is much smaller than an equivalent tube.

In 1950 William B. Shockley, also of Bell Laboratories, published a theoretical analysis of a different type of transistor, the *junction transistor.* It is so called because its electrical behavior depends on phenomena occurring at a junction formed by two types of semiconductors called n type and p type. In an n-type semiconductor, electrical conduction is primarily by means of negatively (n) charged electrons, whereas in p-type material conduction is primarily by means of positively (p) charged holes. (A hole corresponds roughly to the absence of an electron.) A semiconductor can be made p-type or n-type by introducing appropriate impurities called dopants into its crystal structure. A junction transistor consists of a piece of n-type (p-type) semiconductor sandwiched between two pieces of p-type (n-type) material to form a pnp or npn configuration. Figure 1.18 shows a representative early junction transistor. The two outer layers form the emitter and collector, and replace the cat's whiskers used in point-contact transistors; the central layer forms the base. Junction transistors were first constructed in 1951. They soon superseded point-contact transistors, which had proved to be unreliable and

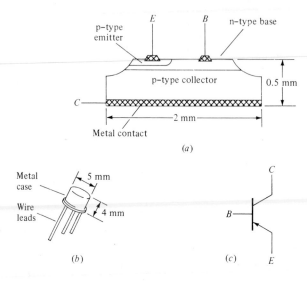

Figure 1.18 Bipolar junction transistor ca. 1958: (*a*) cross section (unencapsulated); (*b*) physical structure; (*c*) symbol.

difficult to manufacture. Bardeen, Brattain, and Shockley received the Nobel prize for physics in 1956 for their contributions to the invention of the transistor.

Transistors of the kinds discussed so far are collectively referred to as *bipolar transistors*, because their electrical behavior directly involves charge carriers of two polarities, negative electrons and positive holes. Another type of transistor, called the unipolar or, more commonly, the *field-effect transistor* (FET), employs only one type of charge carrier. In an FET an electric field is used to control current flow in a semiconductor, in much the same way as the field created by the grid controls the anode–cathode current in a triode vacuum tube. Field-effect transistors were the subject of investigation by Lilienfeld, Shockley, and others for many years; however, largely because of the difficulty of obtaining semiconductor materials of sufficient purity, FETs did not become commercially viable until the 1960s.

Like a bipolar transistor, a FET consists of a tiny piece of semiconductor material with three terminals called, in this case, the source, the gate, and the drain. When appropriate voltages are applied to the FET terminals, a current flows between the source and the drain through a narrow conducting channel in the semiconductor substrate. A voltage applied to the gate, which is superimposed over the conducting channel, can alter the channel's width, and thereby alter the magnitude of the source-drain current.

There are two main types of FETs: junction FETs and insulated-gate FETs. In the junction type, the gate portion of the transistor takes the form of a p-type (n-type) layer surrounding an n-type (p-type) conducting channel. In the more common *insulated-gate FET,* the gate is an electrode that is separated from the semiconductor substrate by a thin layer of insulating material such as silicon dioxide. Early insulated-gate FETs used a metal such as aluminum for the gate material, so that all insulated-gate FETs are usually referred to as *MOS (metal-oxide-semiconductor)* transistors or MOSFETs. The structure of a MOSFET is depicted in Fig. 1.19. Modern MOSFETs often use the semiconductor

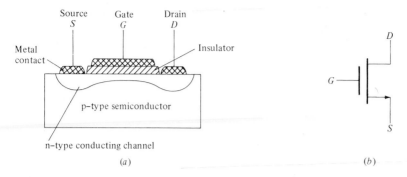

Figure 1.19 Metal–oxide–semiconductor (MOS) field–effect transistor ca. 1970: (*a*) cross section; (*b*) symbol.

silicon as the gate material instead of metal. Note that the two transistors in the NAND circuit of Fig. 1.3 are MOSFETs.

1.2.2 Printed and Integrated Circuits

Until World War II almost all electronic circuits were assembled manually. The various components—vacuum tubes, resistors, capacitors, etc.—were mounted on a supporting base, such as a metal box, called a chassis. Links between the components were established by means of insulated wires that were usually soldered to the terminals of the components. Borrowing concepts from the long-established printing and engraving industries, the Englishman Paul Eisler introduced the modern printed circuit around 1940. In a printed circuit connections are formed by strips of conducting foil bonded to an insulating board on which the system components are mounted. The foil connection patterns are created by printing and etching, thus allowing automation to be introduced into electronic circuit manufacture.

Figure 1.20 illustrates the most basic print-and-etch process for making a printed circuit. The process starts with a stiff board of some insulating material that has a thin (35 μm or so) sheet of copper foil bonded to one surface as shown in Fig. 1.20a. The foil is then coated with a layer of acid-resistant photographic emulsion called a *photoresist*. A photographic template or *mask* containing an image of the desired connector pattern is then superimposed on the photoresist as shown in Fig. 1.20b. The assembly is exposed to a suitable radiation source, such as ordinary or ultraviolet light, causing the image on the mask to be transferred to the photoresist. The board is then immersed in a developing solution, which removes the exposed photoresist. Next the board is immersed in a copper etchant such as ferric chloride ($FeCl_4$) solution, which removes the copper that is not protected by the photoresist. The remaining photoresist then is removed, resulting in an exact image in copper foil of the pattern on the photomask. Mounting holes for the components are drilled, and the components can be mounted on the board, now called a *printed-circuit board* (PCB) as shown in Fig. 1.20c. Finally, the components must be soldered to the PCB; this can be done in a single step by dipping the foil side of the PCB into a bath of molten solder.

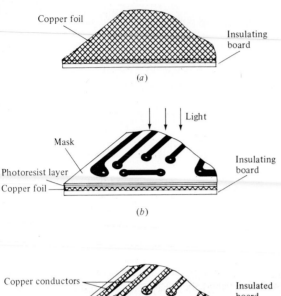

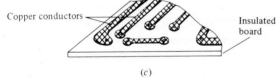

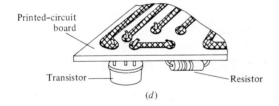

Figure 1.20 Printed-circuit manufacture: (*a*) copper-clad board; (*b*) printing step; (*c*) printed-circuit board (PCB) after etching and drilling; (*d*) PCB with components mounted.

The use of PCBs grew rapidly in the 1950s, particularly in the United States, and many refinements were introduced. For example, multilayer PCBs were developed that contained a dozen or more conducting layers, and efficient methods were devised for automatically interconnecting conductors on different layers.

Beginning in the 1950s, other aspects of printing technology were adapted for the production of entire circuits, including the printing of various types of electronic components. The motivations for these developments were to reduce circuit size, to improve circuit uniformity and reliability, and to reduce production costs by allowing further automation of the manufacturing process. Two important processes developed in the 1950s and still often used, allow electronic circuits to be fabricated in the form of thick or thin films of various materials on an insulating substrate.

Thick-film circuits depend on the use of special pastelike inks that have various degrees of electrical conductivity. The inks are applied to masks containing screened openings to create ink patterns on an inert insulating substrate; this process is essentially the same as silk-screen printing. Heating is then employed to harden the ink. By using various inks and several printing steps, conductors, resistors, and capacitors can be printed on a common substrate to form a complete electric circuit. Semiconductor devices such as transistors and (crystal) diodes that require a regular crystalline structure cannot be produced by screen printing, thus limiting thick-film technology to the manufacture of fairly simple circuits.

Thin-film circuits are also formed by depositing thin layers (films) of materials with various electrical properties onto a common substrate. In this case, however, the processing is done in vacuo, and various methods are employed to transfer the film material to the substrate. Figure 1.21 depicts a widely used deposition technique called vacuum evaporation. The substrate on which the thin-film circuit is to be formed is placed in a vacuum chamber. A mask with openings where film deposition is desired is placed over the substrate. A small amount of the film material is then introduced into the chamber and heated electrically, causing it to vaporize. Because of the high vacuum in the apparatus, atoms of the evaporated material travel in straight lines to the substrate and condense on the parts of the substrate that are unprotected by the mask. By repeated evaporations of this kind, films of different materials can be superimposed to produce relatively complex circuits. For example, a thin-film MOSFET of the type shown in Fig. 1.19a can be formed by the following four steps.

1. Deposit a film of semiconductor material on the substrate.
2. Deposit metallic conductors to form the source and drain contacts.
3. Deposit a film of insulating material in the gate position.
4. Deposit a metallic film on the gate insulator to form the gate contact.

The manufacture of transistors using thin-film techniques remains relatively difficult and costly (Kabaservice, 1978).

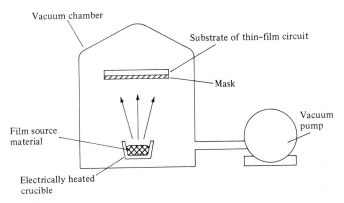

Figure 1.21 Thin-film circuit manufacture by vacuum deposition.

Several important improvements were made in transistor manufacturing methods in the 1950s. The zone refining technique devised by William G. Pfann at Bell Laboratories in 1954 allowed the production of large semiconductor crystals of extremely high purity (less than one part of impurities per billion). The controlled introduction of impurities to create the p- and n-type regions of bipolar transistors (see Fig. 1.19a) was greatly improved by the diffusion process developed at Bell Laboratories and elsewhere. By using photographic masking techniques of the kind discussed earlier, a semiconductor substrate is exposed to a vapor containing the desired impurity types to create p- or n-type "islands" within the substrate. The depth of the impurity diffusion can be regulated accurately by varying the temperature and duration of the diffusion process. Thus by a sequence of diffusions using different masks and impurity types, the three-layer transistor structure of Fig. 1.19a could be produced within a single piece of semiconductor material.

The earliest transistors were fabricated from germanium. However, silicon has several properties that make it more attractive for transistor manufacture. It is one of the most abundant elements on earth, whereas germanium is relatively rare. Silicon transistors can operate at higher temperatures than their germanium equivalents. When a piece of silicon is heated in the presence of oxygen, a layer of silicon dioxide (SiO_2), which is an excellent insulator, forms on the surface of the silicon. The thickness of this oxide layer also can be precisely controlled. By using vacuum evaporation techniques of the kind illustrated in Fig. 1.21, metal conductors, particularly aluminum conductors, can be deposited on SiO_2 (and also on bare silicon), to which they adhere firmly. Finally, openings can be created in an SiO_2 layer using a print-and-etch process analogous to that used in PCB manufacture. This allows the oxide layer to be used as a mask for the selective diffusion of impurities into the underlying silicon substrate.

The first commercial silicon transistors were produced by Texas Instruments in 1954. In 1958 Jean A. Hoerni of Fairchild devised the very important *planar process* for making bipolar transistors from silicon. As its name implies, this process allows a transistor to be created from a single flat piece of silicon, now referred to as a chip. Three techniques characterize the planar process: the use of SiO_2 layers as masks, the use of photolithographic print-and-etch methods to create patterns of openings in the oxide layer, and the use of multiple diffusions to create p- and n-type regions. A later addition was a technique called epitaxy. This involves the vapor deposition of high-purity silicon on a silicon substrate of lower purity, while preserving the substrate's crystal structure in the deposited epitaxial layer. Like the PCB and film manufacturing techniques considered above, the planar transistor manufacturing process has many of the characteristics of a printing operation. Besides permitting transistor dimensions to be controlled more precisely, it also allows many transistors to be manufactured simultaneously from a single wafer of silicon.

The planar process set the stage for the next major innovation: the fabrication of a multicomponent circuit in a single silicon chip. Such circuits, now called integrated circuits (ICs), were first designed in 1958–1959 by Jack S. Kilby at Texas Instruments and Robert S. Noyce at Fairchild (Wolff, 1976; Braun & McDonald, 1979). Independently, they devised methods for making a complete set of electronic components, including resistors, capacitors, diodes, and transistors, in silicon using the planar process. Two additional problems also had to be solved to produce practical ICs: the electrical isolation of individual components from the common and electrical conducting semiconductor substrate, and the provision of conducting paths between the terminals of selected components. The component isolation problem was solved by Noyce (and, independently, by Kurt Lehovec at Sprague Electric Company) by noting that a junction between p-type and n-type semiconductors acts as a diode, which, when reverse biased as in Fig. 1.16c, acts as an open circuit. Thus, by surrounding each component with an appropriate reverse-biased pn junction, it can be electrically isolated from the substrate and the other components of the IC. Kilby and Noyce observed that the component interconnection problem could be solved by the use of vacuum evaporation techniques (see Fig. 1.21) to deposit metal (aluminum is most suitable) on the chip surface, using an oxide layer to separate it from underlying components or substrate. The provision of conducting paths in this manner is called metalization. Thus, by a sequence of processing steps involving the use of photographic masks, diffusion, oxidation, epitaxy, and metalization, a complete circuit can be manufactured from a single chip of silicon crystal. Figure 1.22 shows the cross section of a simple IC consisting of a bipolar transistor and a resistor. The transistor structure is essentially the same as that of the *discrete* (i.e., nonintegrated) transistor appearing in Fig. 1.18. The resistor consists of the p-type region lying between contacts 1 and 2; the n-type region surrounding the resistor proper forms with the p-type substrate a pn junction that serves to isolate the resistor from the substrate.

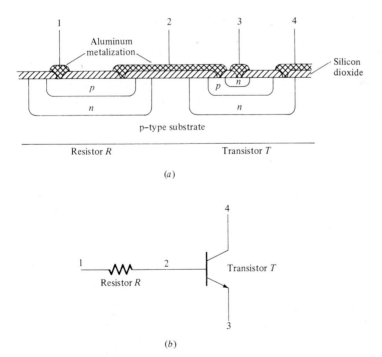

Figure 1.22 Simple integrated circuit (IC): (*a*) cross section; (*b*) equivalent electric circuit.

The first commercial IC was produced by Fairchild in 1961. Shown in surface view in Fig. 1.23, this IC was a 1-bit register, also called a *flip-flop*, and comprised four bipolar transistors and two resistors. Since 1961 IC manufacturing technology has developed at an extraordinarily rapid pace. A major objective of this development has been to reduce the physical size of transistors and other IC components, thereby increasing the number of components, or *component density*, of the IC. A measure of the progress made can be seen in Fig. 1.24, which shows a one-chip microprocessor, the Motorola 68000. It was introduced in 1980 and contains about 70,000 MOS transistors within a 6.25-mm by 7.15-mm silicon chip. This microprocessor is packaged in a 64-pin *dual-in-line package* (DIP), which is a standard way of encapsulating IC chips and providing them with rigid external contacts (pins). Standard DIPs contain two rows of pins, with pins spaced 0.1 inch (2.54 mm) apart in each row. Thus, as in Fig. 1.24, the IC package may be much bigger than the IC chip it contains.

At the present time, most ICs fall into two main groups, bipolar and MOS, depending on the types of transistors they contain. Integrated MOS transistors generally can be made smaller than equivalent bipolar transistors; hence MOS technology is most often used to make ICs such as microprocessors and microcomputers that have very high component densities. Bipolar ICs generally exhibit higher operating speeds than their MOS counterparts. Within the two main IC technologies there are many sub-technologies, which differ in the manufacturing processes used, or in the manner in which the transistors are interconnected to form larger devices such as logic gates. For

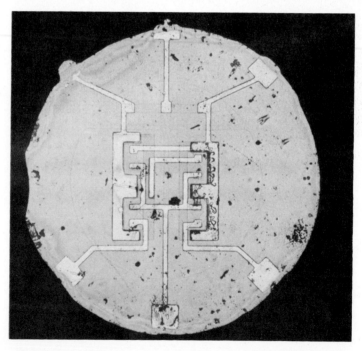

Figure 1.23 The first commercial IC, introduced in 1961. *(Courtesy Fairchild Camera and Instrument Corp.)*

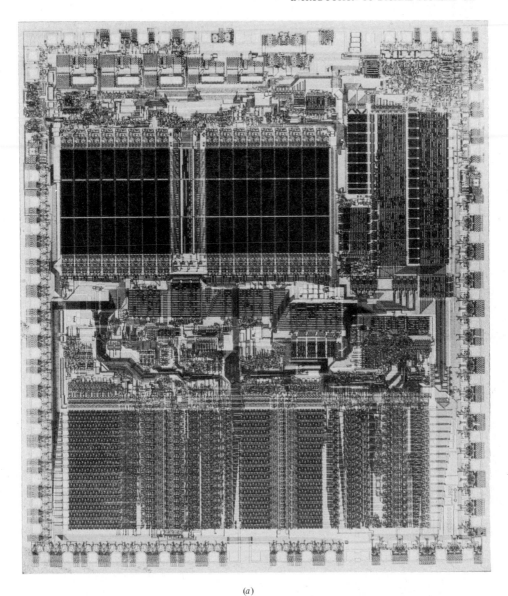

(a)

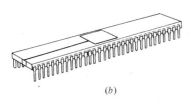

(b)

Figure 1.24 (a) Photomicrograph of the Motorola 68000 microprocessor chip introduced in 1980. *(Courtesy Motorola Inc.)*; (b) 64-pin dual in-line package (DIP) containing the 68000 chip.

example, TTL (transistor-transistor logic), ECL (emitter-coupled logic), and I²L (integrated injection logic) are three important bipolar subtechnologies that differ in various physical characteristics. The MOS IC subtechnologies include nMOS (n-channel MOS), which is illustrated by the MOSFET of Fig. 1.19, pMOS (p-channel MOS), and CMOS (complementary MOS). Another widely used IC classification parameter is component density. Figure 1.25 illustrates a typical classification into small-, medium-, large-, and very-large-scale integration. The component density ranges given in this illustration are somewhat subjective since the maximum achievable IC component density varies considerably with the (sub)technology used. Furthermore, as manufacturing methods have been refined, IC component densities have tended to increase rapidly.

Modern IC manufacturing processes are highly automated and allow large batches of ICs to be produced simultaneously. As a result they can be manufactured at a very low cost per unit. Thus a relatively simple microprocessor chip containing, say, 5000 transistors can be sold for a few dollars—the price of a single transistor in the 1950s. A remarkable aspect of IC technology is the fact that IC prices vary rather little with component density. This can be explained by the analogy that the price of a book varies little with the number of words it contains. Thus the cost of a digital system is often proportional to the number of ICs used to construct it. A fundamental trend in system design, therefore, is to use fewer ICs, but to increase their component density or complexity. The one-chip microcomputer embodying a complete digital system in a single IC is the culmination of this trend.

The search for electronic amplifiers and switches was originally motivated by the needs of the communication industries, principally the radio, television, and telephone industries. Up to the 1950s most electronic systems were analog rather than digital. With the appearance of electronic digital computers in the 1940s, the use of digital design techniques began to increase. As computers proliferated in the 1960s and 1970s, they began to employ huge numbers of ICs, and the development of high-density ICs for the computer market increased rapidly. In 1970 the first LSI chips appeared in the form of computer memory units. In 1971 Intel Corporation introduced what is generally regarded as the first commercial microprocessor, the 4004. The first commercial one-chip microcomputer containing all the features of a digital computer that can be miniaturized was the 8048 microcomputer from Intel, which was introduced in 1976. (A patent application on a one-chip microcomputer was filed by Texas Instruments in 1971 and subsequently granted.) The 4004 was rapidly followed by many other microprocessors

IC Type	Approximate Number of Components (usually transistors) per Chip
SSI	One to 100
MSI	100 to 1000
LSI	1000 to 10,000
VLSI	More than 10,000

Figure 1.25 Classification of ICs based on component density. (Millman, 1979.)

and microcomputers produced by the major semiconductor firms. The low cost of the microprocessor made it economically feasible and desirable to use digital computer technology in an enormous number of new applications, including many traditionally analog fields of engineering such as communications and instrumentation.

Although the microprocessor is a product of LSI technology, it is also a product of digital computer technology. Many of the most important innovations in digital computer design, some of which have yet to appear in microprocessors, were first introduced before 1960 (Myers, 1982). Thus, to appreciate fully the origins and capabilities of microprocessors and microcomputers, we must turn to the evolution of digital computers.

1.2.3 Digital Computers

Throughout recorded history, human beings have invented mechanical devices to aid in calculations. One of the oldest such aids is the *abacus,* which consists of a frame on which beads or counters can be positioned to represent numbers. By manipulating the beads according to certain rules, the four fundamental operations of arithmetic—addition, subtraction, multiplication, and division—can be performed. The abacus is essentially a digital storage device incapable of carrying out calculations by itself; it is merely a memory aid to a human computer.

The first successful attempts to devise automatic calculating machines appear to have been made in Europe in the seventeenth century. In 1642 the French philosopher and scientist Blaise Pascal (1623–1662) built a mechanical adding machine. The basis of Pascal's adder was a mechanism for the automatic transfer of carry digits when forming the sum of two numbers, the numbers themselves being represented by the positions of counter wheels. Around 1671 Gottfried Leibniz (1646–1716) extended Pascal's machine to perform multiplication and division automatically. The mechanical calculator underwent further development in the second half of the nineteenth century, when the commercial production of practical four-function desk calculators was started. The important innovations of that period include the use of depressible keys for data and command entry, and the use of electric motors to increase operating speed.

The foregoing mechanical calculators (and their modern electronic equivalents) can be characterized as single-step devices, because they are able to perform only one arithmetic operation at a time. Numerical calculations often require many steps, using different operations and operands (data) at each step. A single-step calculator requires a human operator to enter manually the operations and data needed for every step. The first attempt to build a computing machine capable of automatic multistep calculations was made by Charles Babbage (1792–1871) in England in 1823. This machine, called a *difference engine,* was designed to compute tables of functions such as logarithms and trigonometric functions. The function is represented by a polynomial, which is evaluated by a technique (the method of finite differences) based on repeated addition. Only a few difference engines were ever built, including Babbage's small demonstration machine.

In the 1830s Babbage conceived of a much more powerful mechanical computer, which he called the Analytical Engine. This machine was to be a general-purpose computer capable of carrying out any mathematical calculation automatically. It embodied all the essential components of a modern digital computer system, namely:

1. A processor called the "mill" able to add, subtract, multiply, and divide
2. A memory unit (the store) constructed from decimal counting wheels and having a capacity of 1000 50-digit numbers
3. Various IO mechanisms, including a punched-card reader, a card punch, and a printer

The actions of the Analytical Engine were to be specified by a program composed of a chain of punched cards, where a card could define either a number or an operation to be performed. While Babbage's difference engine was constrained to perform the same sequence of operations on different data, the Analytical Engine could change the sequence of its operations automatically in response to conditions encountered during a computation. (This important innovation is now called conditional branching.) The Analytical Engine was never completed, in large part because of the inadequacies of the mechanical technology available to Babbage.

The first successful general-purpose digital computers were built in the 1930s, a full century after Babbage began working on the Analytical Engine. In Germany Konrad Zuse constructed several small mechanical computers. One of these, called the Z3, used electromechanical relays (cf. Fig. 1.5) and binary instead of decimal number representation. The Z3 was completed in 1941 and seems to have been the first operational general-purpose computer. Independently in the United States, a mainly mechanical general-purpose digital computer was designed by Howard H. Aiken (1900–1973), a professor of physics at Harvard University. Aiken's machine, first known as the Automatic Sequence Controlled Calculator, and later as the Harvard Mark I, was constructed in cooperation with the International Business Machines Corporation (IBM), then a leading manufacturer of office equipment. In many ways the Harvard Mark I, which started operation in 1944, was a successful realization of Babbage's goals for the Analytical Engine. The Mark I, like the Analytical Engine, used decimal counter wheels for its main memory. A later computer, the Harvard Mark II, built by Aiken and his colleagues, used electromechanical relays. Many relay computers were built in the 1940s, but they were quickly superseded by computers based on faster and more reliable electronic technologies.

Vacuum-tube technology underwent considerable development after the introduction of the triode in 1906, but it was not applied to computer design until the 1930s. The first electronic digital computer employing vacuum tubes appears to have been a machine designed by John V. Atanasoff at Iowa State University in the late 1930s. This was a relatively small computer intended to solve up to 30 simultaneous linear equations. Its main computing mechanism was an add–subtract unit for binary numbers that contained about 300 vacuum tubes. A supporting memory unit was constructed from a rotating drum on which capacitors, each capable of storing one binary digit or *bit,* were mounted. Various IO devices were provided, including a card reader and a card punch. Although its construction was essentially complete by 1942, Atanasoff's computer was abandoned before it was ever actually used. Several other vacuum-tube computers were also successfully completed in the early 1940s, notably by Zuse in Germany, and a series of machines named Colossus, which were built in England and used for wartime cryptanalysis.

The first widely known electronic digital computer was the ENIAC (Electronic Numerical Integrator and Calculator) built at the University of Pennsylvania under the direction of John W. Mauchly (1907–1980) and J. Prespert Eckert. (Although Eckert and Mauchly obtained a patent on the electronic digital computer, a 1973 court decision credited Atanasoff with this invention, and declared the Eckert–Mauchly patent invalid.) The ENIAC was completed in 1946 and was used for a wide variety of computations until 1955. Physically it was very large, containing about 18,000 vacuum tubes and weighing about 30 tons (27,000 kg). The ENIAC contained vacuum-tube switching circuits capable of addition, subtraction, multiplication, division, and the extraction of square roots. These circuits processed 10-digit decimal numbers, where each digit was represented by a pattern of 10 binary digits or bits. The main memory of the ENIAC consisted of twenty 10-digit storage registers, also built from vacuum tubes. The IO devices included a card reader, a card punch, and a printer. The ENIAC was programmed by manually setting several thousand switches, and by plugging and unplugging a large number of cables.

A serious shortcoming of early computers such as the Harvard Mark I and the ENIAC was the use of separate storage media for programs and data. For example, in the ENIAC active data were stored in high-speed vacuum-tube registers, whereas programs were stored in the form of manual switch and cable settings. As a result, the task of modifying a program, or introducing a new program, was both slow and cumbersome. A new electronic computer called the EDVAC (Electronic Discrete Variable Automatic Computer) proposed by the ENIAC's designers, including Eckert, Mauchly, and John von Neumann (1903–1957), embodied what is now called the *stored program concept,* in which a single relatively large memory is used for storing both instructions and data during program execution. The plans for the EDVAC, first published in a draft report by von Neumann in 1945, were widely circulated and had considerable influence. Even more influential was the design of a computer, now known as the IAS (Institute of Advanced Studies) computer, which was built by von Neumann and his colleagues at the Institute for Advanced Studies in Princeton in the period 1946–1952. The IAS computer served as the prototype for most subsequent computers, and the term "von Neumann computer" has become synonymous with standard computer architecture.

Figure 1.26 shows the structure of a typical "first-generation" computer of the IAS type. At its heart is a *central processing unit,* or *CPU,* which is responsible for program execution and acts as the main controller of the computer. A program, that is, a sequence of instructions, and its associated data that are awaiting execution are stored in a common *main memory M*. The CPU continually fetches instructions and data from M and processes the data as specified by the instructions. The CPU typically has two main parts: an instruction unit or *I-unit* responsible for fetching instructions and data from M, and an execution unit or *E-unit,* which performs the actions specified by the instructions. The *E*-unit typically contains switching circuits that implement addition, subtraction, and other operations: collectively these circuits form the *arithmetic-logic unit* (ALU) of the computer. The ALU also contains high-speed temporary storage devices (registers),

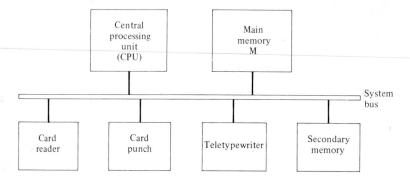

Figure 1.26 Organization of a typical first-generation computer.

which store the information needed by the CPU to process an instruction. One of these registers, called the accumulator (AC), acts as the main data register of the CPU. For example, a typical addition instruction, which might be written symbolically as ADD X, causes the contents of a memory location designated X to be brought into the CPU, where it is added to the contents of the accumulator AC. Using a notation to be introduced later in this chapter, we will describe the behavior of this instruction in the following self-explanatory form: $AC := AC + M[X]$. In general, instructions of IAS-like machines fall into three main groups:

1. Data-transfer instructions that copy or move information without changing it from one part of the computer to another
2. Data-processing instructions such as add, subtract, and compare, which transform data in a well-defined way
3. Program-control instructions, such as conditional branch instructions, which determine the sequence in which instructions are executed

Besides the CPU and M, a typical computer contains some IO or peripheral devices. The IO devices include secondary memories that serve as a backup memory for M. A secondary memory unit usually has a large storage capacity, and is slower but less expensive than M. As indicated in Fig. 1.26, the various components of the computer communicate via a set of shared electrical cables referred to as the *system bus*. It is worth noting that the representative first-generation computer organization depicted in Fig. 1.26 is the same as that found in most current microcomputer systems.

Two other important characteristics of modern digital computers were firmly established by the EDVAC and IAS designs: the use of binary or base-2 number representation, and the grouping of information into n-bit units called *words*, where all n bits are manipulated simultaneously or in parallel. Most CPU circuits, memory locations, and communication paths (buses) are designed to accommodate words of length n. Furthermore, the basic instructions and data items are assigned lengths that are integral multiples or submultiples of the standard word size. For example, the IAS computer itself has a word size $n = 40$ bits. Numbers in this machine are 40 bits, or one word, in length, with the leftmost bit denoting the sign of the number (0 for positive and 1 for negative). All IAS instructions are 20 bits or a halfword long. Most computers now employ a word size that is a power of 2; 4-bit, 8-bit, and 16-bit word lengths are typical of microcomputers.

The rate of construction of vacuum-tube digital computers increased rapidly in the late 1940s. This period also saw the beginnings of the digital computer manufacturing industry. In 1947 Eckert and Mauchly, the designers of the ENIAC, formed a company (which was later to become the Univac Division of Sperry Corporation) to manufacture electronic computers. This company produced the Univac (Universal Automatic Computer) I, one of the first commercially successful digital computers, in 1951. In the same year Ferranti Ltd. in England delivered the Ferranti Mark 1, a commercial electronic computer derived from a pioneering computer project at Manchester University. International Business Machines Corporation, which was responsible for the fabrication of the Harvard Mark I electromechanical computer, also entered the electronic computer market with the very successful 700 series introduced in 1953. The company quickly achieved worldwide dominance in the manufacture and sale of large-scale digital computers, a position it has since maintained.

The use of vacuum tubes in digital computers was mainly confined to the switching and storage circuits within the CPU. Cost considerations precluded the use of vacuum tubes for constructing the main memory M. A variety of less costly but slower devices such as acoustic delay lines, which stored information in the form of continuously propagating sound waves, were used for M. By 1954 main memory technology was dominated by ferrite core memories composed of tiny rings (cores) of a magnetic material called ferrite. Each ferrite core could store a single bit of information. Secondary memories also relied on magnetic storage technologies, particularly magnetic disk and tape devices.

While the early 1950s saw rapid improvements in digital computer hardware technology, there were also important developments in the methods used for producing computer programs, that is, computer software. The earliest computers were programmed exclusively in *machine language,* which is the binary code that can be executed directly by the CPU. A significant reduction in programming difficulty resulted from the introduction of *assembly languages,* which are programming languages that allow instructions to be written in symbolic form using easily remembered names for the operations and operands of each instruction. A special program called an *assembler* is required to translate the assembly-language (source) program into a machine-language (object) program before it is executed. Figure 1.27 shows assembly-language and machine-language versions of a simple program written for an early microprocessor, the Motorola 6800. These programs are designed to implement the addition operation described by the following algebraic equation:

$$\alpha = \beta + 150 \tag{1.11}$$

The variables α and β have been assigned to the main memory locations specified by the numerical addresses 9 and 10 respectively. The current values of these variables are stored in the designated memory locations; these values must be transferred to the CPU

Instruction	Comment
ALPHA EQU 9	Equate the symbol ALPHA to the main memory location M[9] whose address is nine.
BETA EQU 10	Equate the symbol BETA to the main memory location M[10] whose address is 10.
LDA A BETA	Copy (load) the contents of main memory location M[BETA] into accumulator A in the CPU.
ADD A #150	Add the number 150 to the contents of A, and store the result in A.
STA A ALPHA	Copy (store) the contents of A into the main memory location M[ALPHA].

(a)

Instruction	Comment
10010110	LDA A. (Load the accumulator A from the main memory location whose address follows.)
00001010	Binary form of memory address 10.
10001011	ADD A immediate. (Add to the accumulator A the number whose value follows immediately.)
10010110	Binary form of the number 150.
10010111	STA A. (Store the accumulator A in the memory location whose address follows.)
00001001	Binary form of memory address 9.

(b)

Figure 1.27 (a) Assembly-language and (b) machine-language versions of a simple addition program for the Motorola 6800 microprocessor.

before they can be used by a programmer. In the assembly-language program of Fig. 1.27a, α and β are represented by the mnemonic names ALPHA and BETA, which were created by the programmer. In the machine-language program, on the other hand, α and β must be expressed as 8-bit binary numbers. Similarly, the operation part of an instruction can be represented by Motorola-defined symbolic acronyms in the assembly-language case, whereas machine-language operations use a much less readable binary code. For example, the "load accumulator A" instruction of Fig. 1.27 is written as LDA A in assembly language and as 10010110 in machine language.

In the 1950s transistors slowly began to replace vacuum tubes as the main electronic components in CPU design. One of the earliest *second-generation* or transistor computers was the TX-O, an experimental machine built at the Massachusetts Institute of Technology's Lincoln Laboratories, which began operating in 1953. Commercial transistor computers were introduced by many companies in the late 1950s and early 1960s. For instance, in 1959 IBM began delivering the 7090, a large computer intended for scientific applications, which was a transistorized version of the IBM 709, a vacuum-tube computer.

As computer usage increased, the difficulty of writing computer programs became a major cause for concern. While assembly languages are much easier to use than machine languages, they have characteristics that make them unsuitable for many software design tasks. Assembly languages, like machine languages, are computer-specific, so that assembly-language programs written for one type of computer cannot be used (without considerable difficulty) on a different type of computer. Assembly language usually has little resemblance to the language (e.g., English) in which a computer user can most easily describe a problem to the computer. In general, only a single, relatively simple action can be defined by a statement in assembly language; the statements of Fig. 1.27a are typical. This means that very long and possibly complex assembly-language programs are needed to specify many computational tasks.

In the mid-1950s another class of programming languages, called *high-level languages,* was introduced. These languages are intended to allow computer programs to be specified in a form that is close to the users' problem specification language, and relatively independent of the particular computer being used. An early and very successful high-level programming language is FORTRAN (Formula Translation), which was developed by IBM and intended mainly for scientific and engineering applications. It allows complex numerical operations to be written in a form resembling conventional mathematical equations. For example, Eq. (1.11) can be written in FORTRAN thus:

$$ALPHA = BETA + 150$$

The five-statement assembly-language program of Fig. 1.27a can be replaced by the two-statement FORTRAN program of Fig. 1.28. Like an assembly-language program, a FORTRAN program must be translated into the machine language of the computer that is to execute it. This translation is carried out by a program called a (FORTRAN) *compiler,* which converts the high-level language statements into equivalent statements in machine language. FORTRAN compilers have been written for every widely used computer, and hence FORTRAN programs, unlike assembly-language programs, can be run on almost every computer. For this reason, FORTRAN and other high-level programming languages are said to be *machine-independent.* Another important high-level language of the 1950s is COBOL (Common Business Oriented Language), which has an English-like syntax and was intended for business-oriented rather than scientific applications. Since the 1950s, dozens of high-level programming languages have been introduced for various applications, although FORTRAN and COBOL continue to be among the most popular.

In 1964 IBM introduced a very influential computer series called the System/360 (Amdahl et al., 1964). This series includes many computer models that vary widely in cost and performance but share a common system organization and assembly language.

Instruction	Comment
INTEGER ALPHA, BETA	Treat the variables ALPHA and BETA as (fixed-point) integers.
ALPHA = BETA + 150	Add 150 to BETA and assign the resulting value to ALPHA.

Figure 1.28 FORTRAN program that is equivalent to the assembly language program in Fig. 1.27a.

Although often considered to be the earliest *third-generation* or IC-based computer family, the System/360 does not use ICs; instead it employs thick-film circuits on which tiny discrete transistors are mounted. Ferrite-core technology is used for main memory.

Figure 1.29 shows the organization of a typical System/360 computer; implementation details vary considerably from model to model. Figure 1.30 shows a computer system employing the System/360 Model 30. Several different word sizes are used that are multiples of 8 bits or 1 byte; 32 bits is the nominal CPU word length. The CPU contains sixteen 32-bit general-purpose registers that replace the accumulator of earlier machines. An ALU processes numerical data in fixed-point or integer formats, using both binary and decimal number codes. A separate ALU may be used to process numbers in a format called floating point, which allows nonintegral or "real" numbers to be represented in an efficient manner. An I-unit is responsible for fetching and interpreting instructions from the external memory M. In many System/360 models the I-unit is *microprogrammed,* which means that its actions are specified by a set of low-level programs called microprograms stored in a special memory, the control memory, within the I-unit itself. Microprogramming greatly enhances the flexibility of a CPU, making it relatively easy for the manufacturer to make additions and changes to the CPU's instruction set.

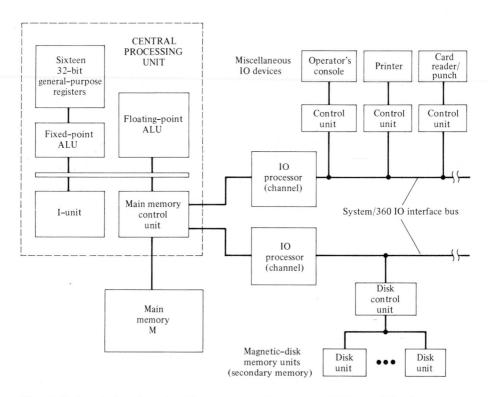

Figure 1.29 Organization of a typical third-generation computer in the IBM System/360 series.

Figure 1.30 IBM System/360 Model 30 computer installation ca. 1968. *(Courtesy International Business Machines Corp.)*

Another important aspect of the System/360 is the use of special processors called *input–output processors* or IOPs (IBM uses the term *channel* for IOP) to supervise operations involving IO devices. A typical IO operation consists of the transfer of a block of words between main memory M and some IO device such as a disk memory unit or a card reader. In simple computers with an organization like that of Fig. 1.26, IO operations are often controlled directly by the CPU. An IOP frees the CPU from the simple but time-consuming tasks associated with IO operation control, and allows IO operations to proceed in parallel with CPU operations. As shown in Fig. 1.29, a System/360 computer may have one or more IOPs, each with direct access to M. An IOP communicates with IO devices via device-specific control units. Each IOP is connected to its IO control units by means of a shared bus, which constitutes the System/360 IO interface bus. The IOPs are designed to execute a small and specialized instruction set intended mainly for data-transfer operations. Ultimate control over the IO system of a System/360 computer is retained by the CPU, since it can execute instructions that start, stop, or check the status of any IOP.

Most computers manufactured around 1960 were large and costly *mainframe* machines. Despite the reductions in physical size and power consumption resulting from the replacement of vacuum tubes by transistors, a typical computer system still occupied a large room (see Fig. 1.30) and cost hundreds of thousands of dollars. Much of this cost was for computer hardware, with the CPU and M among the more costly items. Considerable effort was devoted to developing ways of using the available computer resources as efficiently as possible. An important step in this direction was the development of the *operating system*, a supervisory program usually supplied by the computer manufacturer that allows many users to use the various resources of a computer concurrently. For example, an operating system can allow one user's program to be executed by the CPU while other programs are engaged in IO operations supervised by IOPs. Many programs can be active in the computer at the same time, with the operating system responsible for scheduling the various activities of each program. Operating systems also can carry out automatic transfers of programs and data between main and secondary memory, thus enabling the computer to execute programs that are larger than the available main memory space. Operating systems began to be designed for most large computers around 1960; one of the most complex operating systems was written by IBM for the System/360 series.

Although the System/360 introduced no great changes in computer design (it did not even use the then available IC technology), it nevertheless had a profound influence on the digital computer industry. During the six-year production life (1964–1970) of the series, IBM delivered about 33,000 System/360 computers. This created a huge market for computer hardware and software that are compatible with the System/360. Many of the features of this series, including its assembly language, its IO interface, and its operating system conventions, became de facto industry standards that continued to influence commercial computer design into the 1980s. In 1970 IBM introduced the System/370, which uses semiconductor ICs for both the CPU and M but retains the System/360 organization and instruction set largely intact. Later IBM series, designated 303X, 4300, and so on, also retain a high degree of compatibility with the System/360–370 series. Significantly, other computer manufacturers have produced, and continue to produce, computer series based on the System/360–370 design. Notable examples include the Amdahl Corporation's 470 series introduced in 1976, and the Ryad series produced in the U.S.S.R. and other eastern European countries.

In 1965 Digital Equipment Corporation (DEC) introduced the PDP-8 (Programmed Data Processor Eight), one of the first of a class of small computers now referred to as *minicomputers*. Minicomputers are characterized by a short CPU word size (12 bits in the case of the PDP-8) and relatively low cost (about $15,000 per system). Their low cost and small physical size allowed minicomputers to be used in many new computer applications, such as industrial process control. The first PDP-8s employed discrete transistor technology, but an IC version was introduced in 1967. By 1970 small-scale and medium-scale ICs were found in almost all new computers. At that time, MOS LSI chips were also being mass produced, mainly for use in computer main memories and pocket calculators. The stage was set for the next major development, the one-chip CPU, or microprocessor.

1.2.4 Microprocessors and Microcomputers

In the late 1960s many semiconductor manufacturers were experimenting with ways to exploit the relatively new MOS LSI/VLSI technology in the design of complex digital systems such as programmable calculators, computer terminals, and general-purpose minicomputers. One such effort was begun by Intel Corporation under the direction of

Marcian E. Hoff, Jr., in 1969 to develop a small set of LSI chips for use in a calculator series to be produced by the now defunct Japanese firm, Busicom Corporation. Unlike previous calculator chips, the Intel chip set was organized as a general-purpose computer that could be programmed during manufacture to act as a calculator. In 1971 Intel began marketing this chip set, which was designated the MCS-4 (Microcomputer Set Four) series, as a "programmable controller for logic replacement" (Intel, 1974). The MCS-4 series originally contained four pMOS ICs: the 4001 read-only memory (ROM) chip; the 4002 random-access memory (RAM) chip, which forms a read–write memory; the 4003 IO interface chip, which is a special type of register; and the 4004 CPU chip. The 4004 is now generally recognized as the first commercially produced microprocessor.

The 4004 is a general-purpose CPU designed to process 4-bit data words; it therefore is called a 4-bit microprocessor. It contains 16 general-purpose temporary registers, an ALU consisting mainly of a 4-bit adder circuit, and all the logic needed to process a repertoire of 45 instruction types. The 4001 ROM chip is intended for program storage; its contents are defined during chip manufacture by a process called mask programming. Each 4001 chip has a storage capacity of 2K bits organized as 256 8-bit words (bytes). This 8-bit memory word size reflects the fact that 4004 instructions are either 8 or 16 bits in length. The 4001 ROM chip also contains several IO ports, that is, connection points for simple IO devices that can be accessed via CPU instructions. Thus, in principle, a small microcomputer can be built using just two members of the MCS-4 family, a 4004 chip acting as the CPU, and a 4001 acting as the program memory and IO interface circuit. In practice a typical system based on the MCS-4 chip set might contain a dozen or more ICs. This, however, represents a significant reduction in complexity over equivalent systems constructed from SSI or MSI circuits.

The MCS-4 was rapidly followed by other microprocessor series from various manufacturers. As production volume increased, microprocessor prices dropped substantially. This greatly stimulated the demand for these new design components, which were much more powerful and flexible than any previously available at comparable prices. It was soon perceived that a huge market existed for microprocessor chip sets, so that by the end of 1975, almost 40 different microprocessor types were in production. In 1972 Intel introduced the first 8-bit microprocessor, the 8008, which used the same pMOS technology as the 4004. The 8008 was superseded by a faster and more powerful microprocessor, the 8080, which employed nMOS technology and was introduced in 1973. The 8080 was extremely successful, and came to be one of the most widely used and imitated 8-bit microprocessors. Another popular early microprocessor was the Motorola 6800 introduced in 1974, which is also an 8-bit nMOS device that is broadly similar to the 8080.

The first-generation computer organization illustrated by Fig. 1.26 is typical of early microcomputers. Figure 1.31 shows an eight-chip microcomputer constructed from the Intel MCS-80 series of ICs, which is centered around the 8080 microprocessor. The CPU consists of the 8080 chip itself and two "support" chips, the 8024 clock generator that supplies the main timing signals for the microcomputer, and the 8028 "system controller" that serves to increase the system bus drive capability. The 8080 contains an 8-bit ALU capable of binary addition and subtraction, seven general-purpose 8-bit registers including an accumulator, and the logic circuits needed to process over 70 different

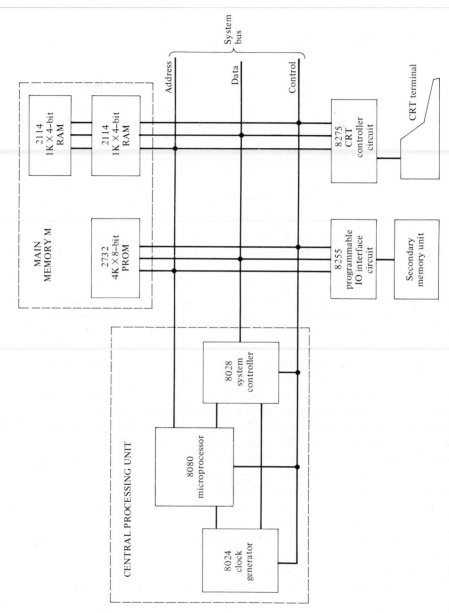

Figure 1.31 Organization of a microcomputer based on the Intel 8080 microprocessor.

instruction types. Eight bits is also the main memory word size. In the particular system of Fig. 1.31 main memory M is composed of a user-programmable ROM or PROM (programmable ROM) chip, and a two-chip RAM with a combined capacity of 5K bytes. (Note that in measuring memory capacity, 1K denotes 1024, which is the power of 2 that is closest to 1000.) The 8080 uses 16 bits to address a location in M, allowing main memory capacity to be increased to a maximum of $2^{16} = 64K$ bytes. The microcomputer system bus that links the CPU and M is composed of three subbuses: an 8-bit bidirectional bus used for data transmission to or from a storage location in M, a 16-bit address bus whose contents specify the memory location to be used, and various control lines whose exact number is application-dependent. The two IO interface chips appearing in Fig. 1.31 present much the same appearance to the CPU as the memory chips; each contains various addressable locations to which or from which the CPU can transfer data. The 8255 is a general-purpose interface chip whose characteristics can be modified under program control to match those of a wide variety of IO devices. The 8275 is a special-purpose chip for interfacing a standard CRT-type terminal to an 8080-based microcomputer. All the ICs in Fig. 1.31 except the 8024 and 8028 may be classified as LSI devices; see Fig. 1.25.

Calculator chips containing all the functions of a simple nonprogrammable pocket calculator in a single IC first appeared in 1971. The organization of these chips resembled that of a one-chip microcomputer, but they were not readily adaptable for performing other functions. In 1974 Texas Instruments introduced the TMS 1000 series of one-chip microcomputers; these were designed to be mask-programmable for use in a wide range of relatively simple applications such as calculators, domestic appliance control, and electronic games. The TMS 1000 is a pMOS chip containing a 4-bit CPU, a 1K- by 8-bit mask-programmable ROM for program storage, a 64K- by 4-bit RAM for temporary data storage, and several IO ports for communicating with IO devices. The TMS 1000 executes a small instruction set that is microprogrammed, and hence can be redefined by mask-programming the CPU's control memory during the IC manufacturing process. This flexibility combined with very low cost—in large quantities, less than $5 per IC—has made the TMS 1000 the most widely used microcomputer. About 20 million units were produced in 1979 alone, far more than any other microprocessor or microcomputer.

In 1976 Intel introduced the first 8-bit one-chip microcomputer series, the MCS-48. A representative microcomputer chip in this family is the 8048, which includes an 8-bit CPU, a 1K- by 8-bit mask-programmable ROM, a 64K- by 8-bit RAM for data storage, and three 8-bit IO ports. A measure of the progress in computer technology in the 30-year period from 1946 to 1976 can be seen from the comparison between the ENIAC and the 8048 in Fig. 1.32. The functional capabilities of these machines as measured by main memory capacity and bits processed per second are broadly similar. However, the physical size and power consumption of the 8048 are less by a factor of around 10^5 than those of the ENIAC. In addition, the cost of the 8048 is less by a factor of 10^5 or so than that of the ENIAC, assuming that they were mass produced under comparable conditions.

The functional capabilities of microprocessors and microcomputers have continued to increase rapidly with improvements in LSI/VLSI technology. Microprocessors with

Parameter	ENIAC	8048
Volume	8.5×10^5 cm³ (a large room)	6.9 cm³ (a 40-pin DIP)
Weight	2.7×10^6 g	30 g
Power consumption	1.4×10^5 W	1.5 W
Program storage (ROM) capacity	16K bits (relays and manual switches)	8K bits (transistors)
Data storage (RAM) capacity	1K bits (vacuum tubes)	0.5K bit (transistors)
Time to compute sum of two 10-digit numbers	200 μs	200 μs

Figure 1.32 Comparison of a 1946 vacuum-tube computer, the ENIAC, and a 1976 one-chip microcomputer, the Intel 8048.

CPU word sizes of 16 and 32 bits have appeared; for example, the Motorola 68000 shown in Fig. 1.24. The FOCUS CPU, introduced in Hewlett-Packard's 9000 series of desktop computers in 1982, is a 32-bit microprocessor containing 450,000 transistors in a silicon chip whose area is only 32.5 mm² (Canepa et al., 1983). It is now possible to construct a microcomputer containing most of the features of second- and third-generation mainframe computers such as the System/360 Model 30 (Fig. 1.30) using just a handful of ICs.

Microprocessors and microcomputers have been responsible for a huge increase in the production of general-purpose computers, most of which have been used in new applications such as word processing and personal computing. The influence of microprocessors goes far beyond their use in general-purpose computers, however; they have had a profound impact on all aspects of digital system design. They are extremely flexible design components that can be tailored to specific applications by means of software placed in their program memories, and by attaching them to appropriate IO devices. The low cost and small size of microcomputers allow them to be used in applications such as domestic appliance and automobile engine control, where digital computers, or indeed any form of digital system, were never used before.

1.3 MICROPROCESSOR-BASED SYSTEMS

Starting with two typical applications, the point-of-sale terminal and an industrial process control system, this section considers the role of microprocessors in digital system design. The process of designing a microprocessor-based system is also examined.

1.3.1 Point-of-Sale Terminal

The electromechanical cash register has been a fixture in retail stores since the nineteenth century; it is estimated that in 1970 over 3 million of these devices were being used in the United States alone (Purchase, 1974). A cash register is basically a nonprogrammable mechanical calculator that is a direct descendant of the machines of Pascal and others mentioned in the preceding section. It has the following capabilities.

1. It can accept numbers (representing prices and related quantities) and commands that are entered via levers or keys.
2. It can perform addition to compute the total cost of a sales transaction with a customer.
3. It can display its input data and results on an indicator device.
4. It can print the same data on a strip of paper, thus providing the customer and the store with a permanent record of the sales transaction.

Despite its long-established position in the relatively conservative retail industry, the cash register has been largely superseded by a much more powerful and cost-effective microprocessor-based system called a *point-of-sale (POS) terminal.*

Figure 1.33 shows the structure of a typical POS terminal. It has much the same basic organization as the general-purpose computers depicted in Figs. 1.26 and 1.31. At its heart is a microprocessor that acts as the system controller. The behavior of the system is defined by a set of special-purpose programs stored in the ROM portion of main memory. A common shared bus is used for internal communication. Connected to this bus are various IO devices, including an electronic keyboard, a digital display unit (see Fig. 1.11), and a printer. Clearly these devices can implement electronically all the functions of an electromechanical cash register. Programs must be written and placed in the terminal's ROM program memory that can fetch and decode data from the keyboard, compute sales totals, and transfer data to the display and printer. These tasks are relatively simple, and use only a small fraction of the microprocessor's computational ability. In a POS terminal the microprocessor is also used to perform a new set of tasks that could not possibly be done by the old-fashioned cash register.

As Fig. 1.33 shows, the POS terminal may be connected to a variety of additional IO devices. In a large retail store or chain of stores with many POS terminals, they may all be linked to a central computer that maintains a large data base concerning the store's operation. A description of each sales transaction is automatically transmitted from the POS terminals to this central computer where it can be used to update sales records, initiate automatic reordering of needed merchandise, monitor the store's cash flow, and so on. The link between the POS terminal and the central computer can be a special cable; alternatively public or private telephone lines may be used. A similar link can be established between a POS terminal and a computer at a credit-card service bureau. A special IO device can be attached to the POS terminals that reads a customer's credit card number, for example, from a magnetically encoded strip attached to the credit card. This number is then transmitted to the computer at the credit bureau, which checks the customer's credit-worthiness and transmits a credit authorization or denial message back

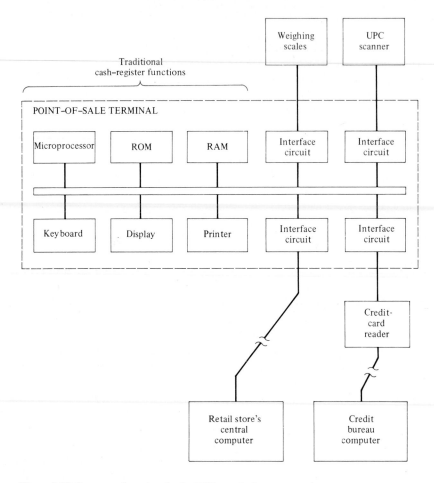

Figure 1.33 Structure of a point-of-sale (POS) terminal.

to the POS terminal. The entire process normally takes a fraction of a second. Details of the sales transaction also can be sent to the credit bureau where it can be used to update the credit-card accounts of both the customer and the store. Thus the use of a micro-processor in the POS terminal allows much of the costly paperwork associated with inventory control and billing to be automated or eliminated.

The POS terminal can also be used to reduce another major cost of operating a retail sales business—the task of associating prices with individual items of merchandise. For example, scales that produce an electrically coded output can be attached to the POS terminal. The terminal is programmed to read automatically the weight W of any item I placed on the scales. If the terminal operator enters the price P per unit weight of I via the keyboard, then the terminal can compute the cost of I by performing the multiplication $P \times W$. A much more sophisticated method of price determination becomes possible if a universal product code (UPC) scanner is attached to the POS terminal. The scanner uses electrooptical techniques to read the standard UPC symbol that is now printed on many products by their manufacturers. The UPC symbol is a decimal number represented by a sequence of light and dark bars of various widths. It serves as a unique identification number for the type of item to which it is attached. Figure 1.34 shows the UPC symbol assigned to *Scientific American* magazine. To determine the price of an item identified by a UPC symbol, the symbol is passed in front of the UPC scanner, which reads and decodes the symbol, and generates an electronic version of it. The POS terminal then sends the UPC symbol information to the store's central computer, which looks in its data base to obtain the current price of the item in question. The price is instantly returned to the POS terminal, where it is displayed and printed. This method of establishing the price of items eliminates the expensive chore of manually stamping a price on each item in the store. It also makes it easy for the store to change the price of an item; all that is required is to change the corresponding entry in the price table maintained by the central computer.

Figure 1.35 is a flowchart that outlines the behavior of the POS terminal of Fig. 1.33. The rectangular boxes represent major actions by the terminal; they also typically correspond to programs or subroutines in the system software. The POS terminal's control programs continually scan or poll the various input devices to determine when a key is depressed, when a UPC symbol passes in front of the UPC scanner, and so forth. Once input data have been recognized, the various programs that process the data are activated. The complexity of these programs varies considerably. The program to decode keyboard signals is usually fairly simple, since each key can be designed to produce a well-defined binary electric signal. A relatively complex program is needed to decode the UPC symbol, since the POS terminal must take into account variations in UPC symbol size, print quality, symbol orientation, and scanning speed. If telephone lines are used to link the POS terminal to external computers, the POS terminal must be able to generate all the signals needed to dial up the external computers, interact with them, and finally terminate the telephone call by "hanging up."

1.3.2 Cable Manufacturing Control

Microprocessors are used extensively to improve productivity and quality control in manufacturing operations. To illustrate this important application area, which is referred to as industrial process control, we examine the use of a microprocessor-based controller in a plant that manufactures telephone cable (Smyth, 1975).

A basic step in cable manufacture is coating the metal wires used as conductors with an insulating layer or jacket. In this example the insulating material is a thermoplastic

Figure 1.34 Example of a universal product code (UPC) symbol.

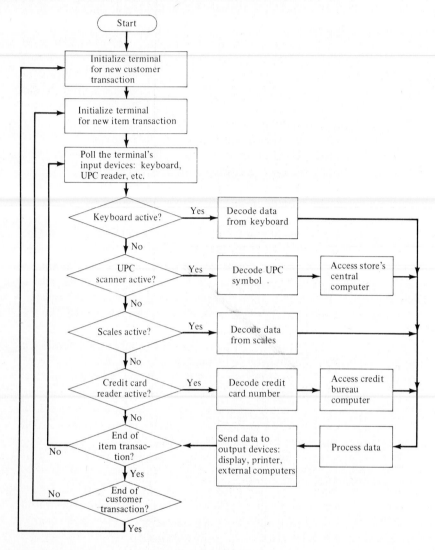

Figure 1.35 Flowchart of POS terminal behavior.

resin called polyethylene, which is applied to the cable by means of the equipment depicted in Fig. 1.36. Uninsulated cable is drawn through an extrusion machine that uses heat and pressure to apply a continuous coating of polyethylene to the cable. The cable is then cooled by passing it through a water trough. To meet the desired quality goals, the evenness and thickness of the insulating jacket must be held within precise limits. The system therefore includes various measurement and error-correcting mechanisms linked to a microprocessor whose purpose is to maintain the required quality control in the manufacturing process. Special instruments mounted on the water trough monitor the thickness of the insulating jacket. When the jacket fails to meet its thickness specifica-

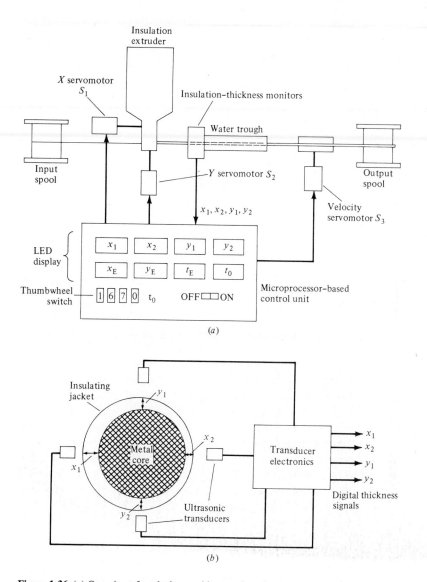

Figure 1.36 (a) Overview of a telephone cable manufacturing process; (b) insulation thickness monitoring.

tions, corrections are made by moving the position of the extruder head relative to the cable, and by altering the speed at which the cable is drawn through the extruder. These corrections are carried out by three electric motors called *servomotors*; two of these control the position of the extruder, and the third controls the cable speed.

The thickness of the insulation jacket is measured at four points that are equally spaced around the cable's circumference as shown in Fig. 1.36b. The measuring instruments are ultrasonic transducers that operate on essentially the same principles as sonar. Each transducer can transmit a sequence of sound pulses at the moving cable.

These pulses pass through the layer of insulation and are reflected by the metal core of the cable. A reflected signal or echo returns to the transducer, which converts it into an electric signal. Since sound travels at different velocities in air and in the solid insulation, the arrival time of an echo at the transducer varies with the thickness of the insulation at the point of measurement. The electronic circuits associated with the transducer generate a digital number representing the insulation thickness in a form that can be used directly by the main control unit. The four thickness parameters x_1, x_2, y_1, and y_2 are recomputed at regular intervals and made available to the control unit. The desired or nominal thickness t_0 of the insulation jacket is entered manually by means of thumbwheel switches. The average thickness t of the insulation layer actually being applied to the cable at any time can be computed by the controlling microprocessor using the formula

$$t = \frac{x_1 + x_2 + y_1 + y_2}{4}$$

Thus the error t_E in the insulation thickness is given by

$$t_E = \frac{x_1 + x_2 + y_1 + y_2}{4} - t_0 \tag{1.12}$$

Clearly t_E is zero when the measured and desired thicknesses coincide. It is positive when the jacket being applied is too thick, and negative when the jacket is too thin. Now t can be increased (decreased) by decreasing (increasing) the velocity of the cable through the extruder; the cable velocity in turn is determined by the speed of the velocity servomotor S_3. Thus, to correct the average thickness of the insulating jacket, the microprocessor computes t_E according to Eq. (1.12) and transmits to S_3 a signal that is proportional to t_E. This causes S_3 either to speed up or to slow down until subsequent values of t_E become zero.

It is obviously possible for t_E to be zero while, at the same time, the insulation thickness varies significantly around the cable's circumference. This situation arises when the center of the portion of the cable that is in the extruder and the center of the ring of insulating material being applied by the extruder do not coincide; Fig. 1.36b illustrates this. To guard against this possibility, the microprocessor computes two additional error parameters: the horizontal *eccentricity* x_E defined by the equation

$$x_E = \frac{x_1 - x_2}{t_0}$$

and the vertical eccentricity y_E defined by

$$y_E = \frac{y_1 - y_2}{t_0}$$

The eccentricities x_E and y_E are both zero when the insulation thickness at the four points of measurement is constant, which probably means that the insulation is being applied satisfactorily. If, however, $y_E > 0$, that is, $y_1 > y_2$, then the insulation is too thick at the top of the cable or too thin at the bottom. The microprocessor therefore transmits a signal that is proportional to y_E to the servomotor S_2, causing it to move the extruder head upward to equalize y_1 and y_2, thereby reducing y_E to zero. If $y_E < 0$, then S_2 moves the extruder head downward until again y_E becomes zero.

In a similar fashion, the horizontal eccentricity x_E is used as an error signal to drive the X servomotor S_1. S_1 moves the extruder head left or right to reduce x_E to zero, thereby centering the cable core in the horizontal direction.

Figure 1.37 summarizes, by means of a flowchart, the actions of the software required for the microprocessor-based controller in this example. The microprocessor periodically scans the thumbwheel switches and the signals generated by the insulation-

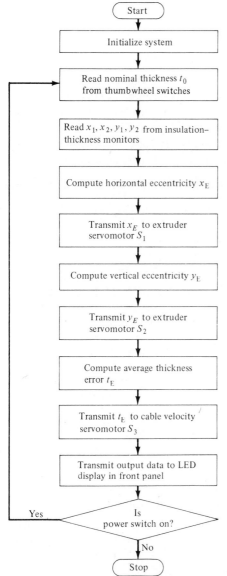

Figure 1.37 Flowchart of insulation thickness control process.

thickness monitors. It computes the error estimates t_E, x_E, and y_E, which it then transmits to the appropriate servomotors and LED displays. Note that many details of the system's behavior are omitted from Fig. 1.37. For example, the microprocessor must convert the numbers t_0, x_1, y_1, etc., into several forms for use by different parts of the system. Binary number formats are used for internal computations, whereas ordinary decimal formats are used by the LED displays and the thumbwheel switches on the front panel of the control unit. The numbers must also be reformatted for transmission as control signals to the servomotors. Since the servomotors and other IO devices in the system are much slower than the microprocessor, the latter must compute the times at which these IO devices are ready to respond to new commands.

1.3.3 Microprocessor Applications

Systems employing microprocessors may be divided into two broad categories—those whose primary function is computation, and those whose primary function is control. In a *computing system* the role of the microprocessor is to produce data $f(X)$ that are some specified function f of specified input data X. In the case of an instrumentation or communication system, $f(X)$ may simply be a modified form of X. In a *control system*, on the other hand, the purpose of the microprocessor is to maintain within specified operating limits some other system S that is subject to disturbance variables D that tend to move S outside its acceptable operating range. S provides the control system C with input data D' indicating the nature of the disturbance D. This information is used by C to compute correction signals E, which are then fed back to S and used to counteract the disturbance. Figure 1.38 illustrates these general concepts. The POS terminal and the cable manufacture controller discussed earlier are typical examples of microprocessor-based systems whose main functions are computation and control respectively.

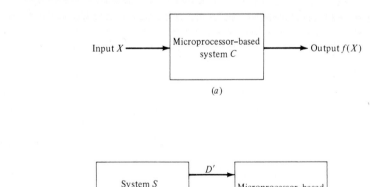

Figure 1.38 Role of microprocessors in (*a*) computation and (*b*) control.

The notions of computation and control are intimately related, and are often difficult to separate. For instance, the microprocessor in the POS terminal of Fig. 1.33 may be said to control the scales, the credit-card reader, and its other IO devices. Conversely the microprocessor-based control system C of Fig. 1.38b may be regarded as a computer with input $X = D'$ and output $f(X) = E$. A hierarchical system (see Sec. 1.1.2) often has subsystems that are viewed as control units, while other subsystems may be most conveniently regarded as computing units.

Figure 1.39 lists some representative uses of microprocessors and microcomputers. Toys form one of the largest markets for these devices, taking advantage of the power of a computer to create a huge variety of imaginative and interesting games. Microprocessors are also being incorporated into relatively simple domestic devices such as ovens, washing machines, air conditioners, television sets, and burglar alarms. A microprocessor-controlled room air conditioner, for example, can be programmed to adjust automatically to complex changes in outside temperature and room occupancy, thereby achieving substantial reductions in energy consumption. Microprocessors can be used in automobiles to control ignition timing, fuel injection, pollutant emission, braking, and dashboard instrumentation. They can control an automobile engine over a much wider range of operating conditions than the electromechanical controllers they replace, which can result in substantial improvements in engine performance, fuel economy, and exhaust emissions.

Microprocessors are also being used extensively in commercial and industrial applications. In the form of low-cost general-purpose computers, they allow small businesses to automate inventory control, billing, recordkeeping, and similar accounting operations. As word processors, microcomputers are being introduced into offices, where they can increase the efficiency of processing letters, reports, and other textual material. They can be used, for example, to check spelling or hyphenation, thus acting as a kind of mechanized dictionary. The influence of the microprocessor-based POS terminal on the retail sales industry has been discussed in detail. In manufacturing industries, microprocessors have been incorporated into many machine tools and process control systems, and have speeded the development of industrial robots that can replace human assembly-line workers. In these applications the objectives are to increase productivity (computers can be made to work 24 hours a day) and to improve the quality of the finished product. Microprocessors are now used routinely in many types of

Automobiles	Biomedical equipment
Electronic toys and games	Industrial process controllers
Household appliances	Measuring instruments
Personal computers	Navigation equipment
Pocket calculators	POS terminals
	Small business computers
	Telecommunications equipment
(a)	*(b)*

Figure 1.39 Important application areas for microprocessors: (*a*) domestic and (*b*) industrial and commercial.

measuring instruments to increase reliability and accuracy. Navigation systems have been greatly improved by microprocessors. An exotic example is the cruise missile, which guides itself to a target by detecting and identifying features of the terrain over which it is passing. The terrain is scanned by radar and other means, and the resulting data are processed by on-board microcomputers to carry out the difficult tasks of feature recognition. Significant advances in medicine, particularly in the areas of patient monitoring and the design of artificial limbs and other prostheses, can also be attributed to the introduction of microprocessors and microcomputers.

The technology of microprocessor-based systems is relatively new, and it can be expected that the advances outlined above will be eclipsed by future developments. For example, the ability of current computer systems to process visual images or speech is very limited. Since these are the most convenient communication media for human beings, it would be very useful to be able to use them to communicate with machines. Traffic accidents could be decreased if a car's braking and steering mechanisms could be connected to a control system capable of scanning the car's surroundings and identifying hazards. A typewriter that could "take dictation" by generating typescript directly from spoken input would be an asset to most businesses. More sophisticated industrial robots than now exist could eliminate many jobs that are tedious, dangerous, or cannot be performed efficiently by people.

The digital systems of interest in this book typically contain the following major subsystems:

1. A system controller C organized as a computer and composed of digital electronic components
2. Input-output devices that enable C to communicate with its environment
3. Ancilliary devices such as power supplies and cooling equipment

Input-output devices make use of a variety of physical technologies based on electrical, mechanical, magnetic, optical, and acoustic phenomena, and may process signals in either digital or analog form. The system controller C often takes the form of a network of ICs mounted on PCBs (cf. Fig. 1.20). Our concern here is mainly with the design of C and its interfaces with IO devices.

In some cases, C is reduced to one or two ICs that are specially designed for a particular application; custom circuits of this sort may be very costly. In most cases it is much more economical in terms of design effort and component cost to construct C from standard off-the-shelf components, including ICs of various complexity levels and discrete (nonintegrated) devices. The mixed nature of the component complexity levels typically encountered is illustrated by Fig. 1.40, which shows the circuit of an experimental digital speedometer for a bicycle. This system is based on the Intel 8085, a widely used 8-bit microprocessor. The bicycle's speed is sensed by means of a light beam that passes through the spokes of a wheel and impinges on a photoelectric transducer. When the light beam is interrupted by the passage of a spoke, a signal is transmitted to the microprocessor, which, directed by a program stored in the 8708 PROM chip, computes the bicycle's current velocity and displays it on the three-digit LED display. The 8156 chip contains a RAM or read–write memory that the system control program uses for

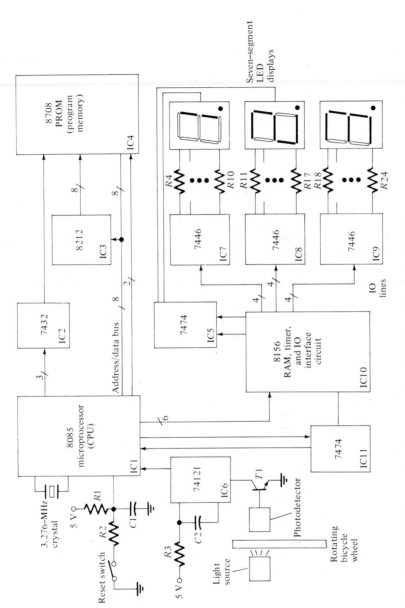

Figure 1.40 Circuit diagram of a microprocessor-based digital speedometer for a bicycle.

temporary data storage, as well as several IO ports or connection points for IO devices (the LED displays in this case). The 8156 also contains a programmable timer, which is used for various time computations in this application. Note that while most of the system's functions are incorporated into only three ICs, the 8085, the 8708, and the 8156, a large number of "support" circuits are present; indeed they are essential for the proper operation of the system. For example, the three 7446s are required to decode the 4-bit binary-coded decimal (BCD) digits produced from output ports on the 8156 into 7-bit words that can be applied to the seven-segment LED displays. The 7446s also amplify the relatively weak signals generated by the 8156 to meet the high current requirements of the LEDs. Two of the six NOT gates in the 7404 chip are used as drivers for decimal points on the LED display. Each seven-segment display also uses seven current-limiting resistors. Discrete components are also found in the reset circuitry and elsewhere in the system. A parts list for the circuit of Fig. 1.40 appears in Fig. 1.41.

From the foregoing example it can be concluded that a microprocessor-based system can contain ICs ranging in complexity from VLSI to SSI (see Fig. 1.25), not to mention discrete circuits. The types of components needed are determined by many application-dependent factors. These factors, which are usually difficult to specify, include the functions to be performed, system operating speed, component driving and loading limits, and component availability. A digital system designer can expect to use components from all complexity levels, and so must be reasonably familiar with the components and design rules associated with each level.

Figure 1.42 defines four commonly recognized complexity levels in electronic system design. As discussed in Sec 1.1.2, each level is determined by the components and signal types treated as primitive at that level. The more complex the functions

Component	Generic Part Number	Description	Function Performed
IC1	8085	8-bit microprocessor	Central processing unit (CPU)
IC2	7432	Four 2-input OR gates	PROM control signal generation
IC3	8212	8-bit register	Address register for PROM
IC4	8708	1024- by 8-bit PROM	Storage of system software (main memory)
IC5	7404	Six NOT gates	Drivers for LED decimal points
IC6	74121	One-shot pulse generator	Sends interrupt pulse to CPU
IC7:IC9	7446	LED display decoder/drivers	Drivers for LED digit segments
IC10	8156	256- by 8-bit RAM, programmable timer, IO interface circuit	Temporary data storage (main memory), LED interfacing, and miscellaneous functions
IC11	7474	Two D-type flip-flops	⎫
R1		51-kΩ resistor	⎪
R2		1.5-kΩ resistor	⎬ Miscellaneous signal timing
R3		5-kΩ resistor	⎪
R4:R24		220-Ω resistors	⎭ Used to limit current in LEDs
C1:C2		1-µF capacitors	Miscellanous timing
T1	2N659	Bipolar npn transistor	Amplifier for photodetector

Figure 1.41 Parts list for the circuit in Fig. 1.40.

Complexity Level	Primitive Signals	Representative Primitive Components	Component Functions	Corresponding Circuit Types
Electronic	Analog	Transistor	Switching and amplification	Discrete
		Resistor	Voltage and current control	
		Capacitor		
Gate	Bit	Gate	Logical operations such as AND or OR	SSI
		Flip-flop	1-bit memory	
Register	Word	Register	One-word memory	MSI
		Multiplexer	Word routing	
		Decoder	Word-pattern interpretation	
		Adder	Addition and subtraction of numbers	
Processor	Block	(Micro)processor	Instruction processing	LSI and VLSI
		Read-only memory	Program storage	
		Random-access memory	Data storage	
		IO interface circuit	Communication with IO devices	

Figure 1.42 Four important complexity levels and their characteristics.

performed by the primitive components, the higher the complexity level. A component at any level is functionally equivalent to a system constructed from components taken from the next lowest complexity level. Figure 1.7 illustrates this hierarchical aspect of system structure. The technological evolution described in Sec. 1.2 can be viewed as a fairly steady progression toward higher complexity levels in the primitive building blocks available for system design. Typically the newer, more complex, components are used for many, but by no means all, of the tasks performed by multicomponent systems built from older, less complex, components. The complexity level of a system comprising components from various levels is usually considered to be that of its most complex components, and the designer's primary concern is with design at that level. In this book we deal mainly with digital system design at the processor level where, as Fig. 1.42 shows, the primitive components are microprocessors, memories, IO interface circuits, and the like, and the primitive "signals" are blocks of words such as programs and data sets. The design techniques associated with lower complexity levels are examined in the early chapters.

1.3.4 Design Methodology

As discussed earlier, the goal of the system designer is to define a structure that has a specified behavior and meets certain cost and performance constraints. When the number of primitive components needed to build the system is large, then, for the reasons outlined earlier, the design process is generally broken down into several independent and specialized design tasks. These tasks are distinguished by the types of components with which they deal and their complexity levels.

Consider, for example, the design of a large computer system that is to be constructed from SSI and MSI ICs, and is to be programmed in various high-level programming languages. The design is carried out in several major stages, each of which may be assigned to a different group of designers. The first step is to specify the overall structure and behavior of the computer at a high level, typically the processor level of Fig. 1.42. The resulting design is referred to as the *architecture* or "system design" of the computer. The term architecture covers the main hardware subsystems (CPU, memory, buses, etc.), the software subsystems (instruction set, operating system, compilers, etc.), and their interrelationships. Once the architecture has been determined, the detailed design of the computer can begin. The task of implementing the hardware subsystems using MSI and SSI devices is termed *logic design,* and corresponds to the register and gate levels of Fig. 1.42. The detailed design of the software subsystems, a task called *system programming,* corresponds roughly to the register level. Systems programs are often written in an assembly language defined by the system architects.

As the example of Figs. 1.41 and 1.42 indicates, a microprocessor-based system can incorporate aspects of all the main complexity levels. Since the system is relatively small, the entire design can be assigned to a single engineer who must, to some extent, carry out the functions of system architect, logic designer, and system programmer.

Figure 1.43 gives a more detailed view of the steps in the system design problems of interest here. The first step is to determine the specifications of the system, that is, its desired behavior, and the main constraints on the design process, such as the project deadlines and budget. This planning stage usually requires close interaction between the system architects and the ultimate users of the system. The design proper then begins; for the reasons described in Sec. 1.1.2, a system is often designed in several hierarchical steps. In the scheme of Fig. 1.43 two design steps are distinguished. In the preliminary or architectural design stage, the major hardware and software elements of the system are

Design Step	Actions Required
Planning	Obtain specifications of the desired system behavior. Estimate overall project costs and work schedule.
Preliminary design (architecture)	Define and document the overall design or architecture of the system. Specify the main component technologies to be used.
Detailed design	Define and document the detailed hardware and software structure of the system.
Prototype construction	Build a working model of the system.
Debugging	Test the prototype and compare its actual behavior with the system specifications. Modify the prototype design until satisfactory operation is achieved.
Final documentation	Complete the system documentation, including the manuals needed to use and maintain the system.

Figure 1.43 Main steps in designing a complex system."

specified. The component technologies to be employed, such as IC types and programming languages, are also identified at this stage. The result is a set of block diagrams, flowcharts, and other documents describing the system design at the processor level. In the second or detailed design step, the complete structure of all the subsystems defined in the preceding step is worked out in terms of the primitive hardware and software components. This results in a set of design documents, including logic circuits, flowcharts, and program listings. While the design is now complete, it is probably not correct unless the system in question is very simple. There are likely to be numerous design errors or "bugs" resulting from the failure of the designers to meet all the original specifications for the system. Moreover, the specifications themselves are often found to be incorrect or incomplete.

The debugging process begins with the construction of a working model or prototype according to the design that has just been completed. The prototype system is then operated, and its behavior is analyzed and compared with the desired behavior. More often than not, design errors are uncovered that necessitate changes in the system design. These changes are then incorporated into the prototype, which is retested for proper operation. The process of testing for errors and correcting them is continued until no more errors are detected, and the prototype performs satisfactorily. This type of debugging is often very costly to implement, and hence it is usually desirable to organize the preliminary and detailed design steps so that the probability of design errors is minimized. Finally, the important step of documenting the system design is completed. Documentation is required in the form of operating manuals for the system's users and service manuals for maintenance of the system and future modifications.

The percentage of the total design cost of the system expended in the preceding design steps is application dependent, and thus is difficult to determine in general. Figure 1.44 shows some statistical data for the cost in person-months of design effort associated with some major steps in the design of (large) computer systems. Two types of design projects are represented, hardware-only projects and software-only projects. In each case only about half the total design effort is devoted to the design process per se (steps 1 through 3 in Fig. 1.44). Note that a very large amount of time is devoted to testing and debugging the design, particularly in the case of software systems. This indicates that the duration of the design process can be significantly reduced by shortening the debugging

Design Step	Percentage of System Design Cost in Person-Months	
	Hardware Design Project	Software Design Project
1. Planning	1	1
2. Preliminary design	7	19
3. Detailed design	43	25
4. Debugging	29	40
5. Documentation	20	15
	100%	100%

Figure 1.44 Breakdown of design costs for two kinds of computer design projects. (Phister, 1978.)

step. The common phenomenon of "cost overrun" in complex system design projects is often a consequence of underestimating the difficulties of debugging the initial designs.

Various tools can be employed to simplify the tasks involved in a design project of the kind just discussed. Analytic or mathematical design algorithms are particularly useful design aids whenever appropriate ones are available. For example, a branch of mathematics called Boolean algebra has found considerable application in digital system design. It is one of the basic tools for hardware system analysis at the gate and register levels. Boolean algebra is the basis of various design algorithms that are useful for implementing relatively small subsystems, such as the control logic of a CPU. However, like most exact mathematical approaches, Boolean algebra can rarely be used to capture all the features of a complex system that are of concern to a designer. For instance, the gate-level behavior of a microprocessor, in principle, can be defined precisely by means of a set of Boolean equations. The number of equations and variables needed is so enormous, however, that it is hardly feasible to specify these equations, let alone use them to obtain solutions to realistic logic design problems.

In practice analytic methods can be used only to a limited extent in digital system design. Most system designs are developed in an *ad hoc* or heuristic fashion from similar systems built in the past. The evolution of digital computer design discussed in Sec. 1.2 provides a good illustration of this. The preliminary planning and architectural design steps (see Fig. 1.43) are carried out by human designers who are guided primarily by their knowledge and experience. For the remaining design steps, there exist various practical design tools that can assist the human designers. These tools usually include a computer, so that the design process may be referred to as *computer-aided design* (CAD). The CAD computer is often used to carry out the following tasks:

1. Simulation: Computer programs that mimic (i.e., simulate) the relevant structure and behavior of the target system are executed via the CAD computer. This allows trial designs to be analyzed without actually constructing the system in question.
2. Program preparation: The CAD computer is used for text editing, program translation (assembly or compilation), and similar tasks associated with software design.
3. Hardware design: Hardware design algorithms can be programmed for and be executed by the CAD computer.
4. Hardware–software integration: This includes the task of transferring programs and data to PROM chips, thus converting them to "hardware."
5. Design debugging: The CAD computer can be used as a test instrument in debugging preliminary or prototype designs.
6. Documentation: It can store the system documentation in an easily manipulated form.

A special CAD tool for designing microprocessor-based systems that has evolved since the introduction of the microprocessor is called a *microprocessor* (or *microcomputer*) *development system* (MDS), and it can perform all the tasks listed above. A typical MDS is a general-purpose computer system with the structure depicted in Fig. 1.45. At its heart is a *development computer C*, which contains a CPU (occasionally several CPUs), a main memory, and some general-purpose IO interface circuits. The CPU often

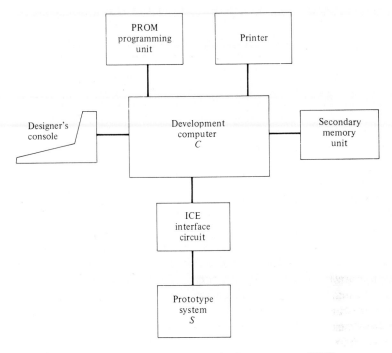

Figure 1.45 Organization of a microprocessor development system (MDS).

contains the same microprocessor that is to be used in the target system S that is being designed. Therefore, C can directly execute machine-language programs intended for S, and do so in precisely the same manner as S. A video terminal or teletypewriter may be used as the designer's console for communication with the development computer. A high-capacity secondary memory unit, such as a magnetic disk memory, is also included in the MDS for storing both design data and the systems programs needed to operate the MDS. The latter usually include text editors, program translators, simulators, debugging programs, and an operating system or executive program that manages the various resources of the MDS. A major task of the operating system is to maintain program and data files in an orderly fashion in the secondary memory unit. Other common IO devices in an MDS are a PROM programming unit to "burn" information into PROM chips, and a hard-copy printer. As Fig. 1.45 indicates, the MDS can also be directly connected to a hardware-implemented prototype of S, allowing the MDS to control and monitor the activities of the prototype; this process is called *in-circuit emulation* (ICE). It is particularly useful during final system debugging since it allows the MDS to be used as a powerful test instrument that is both hardware- and software-compatible with the system being tested.

Figure 1.46 shows a microprocessor design laboratory based on a commercial MDS, the Tektronix Model 8560 (Tektronix, 1982). The basic 8560 unit (appearing in the front center of Fig. 1.46) houses a development computer and a secondary memory that employs magnetic-disk storage devices with a capacity of over 300 million bits.

Figure 1.46 Microprocessor design laboratory employing the Tektronix 8560 MDS. *(Courtesy Tektronix Inc.)*

Several CRT terminals, which serve as designers' consoles or work stations, can be attached to a single 8560, thus allowing a group of designers to cooperate on the development of software for the target microprocessor system. Additional components, such as printers, PROM programming units, and ICE interface circuits, can also be attached directly to the 8560. The 8560 is an an example of a *universal MDS*, so called because it can support the development of many different types of microprocessors. This is accomplished by the use of microprocessor-specific ICE interface circuits, and by software executed by the 8560's development computer (actually a DEC Model PDP-11/23 microcomputer) that allows the 8560 to mimic the behavior of the target microprocessor.

The design of a microprocessor-based system using an MDS as the main design aid proceeds as follows: In the planning step (see Fig. 1.43) the overall system specifications and project plans are established. In the next step the architecture of the target system S is defined. The microprocessor family to be used to build S is selected, as well as the programming language(s) and MDS to be used. Design-aid availability is often a significant factor in the choice of microprocessor. The detailed design of S can now proceed. All the software design can be implemented using the MDS. Programs are entered via the console keyboard. They then can be translated into executable machine language form by the development computer C. C is also used to execute these programs for test purposes. The designer may go further and program C to create an environment that simulates the hardware of the target system S. Thus the complete design for S can be simulated and tested before a hardware prototype is built. The design and construction of a hardware prototype usually are carried out in parallel with the software design. Once the programs for S have been tested and debugged as far as is possible on the MDS, they can be burned into PROM chips via the MDS's PROM programming unit. The resulting programmed PROMs can then be plugged into the prototype hardware, thereby integrating the hardware and software designs. More often than not, the combined system fails, even though no design errors were discovered in the hardware and software when tested separately. A common reason for system failure at this stage is a mismatch, often a subtle one, in the timing of operations involving hardware–software interaction. The MDS may be used to detect problems of this sort via its ICE facility. A special ICE interface circuit is used to link the prototype system to the MDS, which allows the CPU of the MDS to control or monitor the actions of the prototype as it carries out its functions. Accurate timing measurements can be made by the MDS and displayed on its console. Using the ICE facility, the designer may instruct the prototype to execute a program one instruction at a time, halting after each instruction cycle and displaying its status on the designer's console; this useful debugging procedure is called *single-stepping* or program tracing. Design changes are made to the prototype until it is found to operate correctly. At this point the final (production) versions of the system S can be manufactured.

Although it is very useful in developing a microprocessor-based system, an MDS is by no means essential. Almost any general-purpose computer can be provided with the software needed for program preparation and simulation of the target system. Many of the functions of the ICE feature of an MDS can be carried out by a stand-alone test instrument called a *logic analyzer* (Kneen, 1980).

Finally, it should be emphasized that a careful and systematic approach to each step in the entire design process is very important to its successful completion. In many cases most of the cost and complexity of the design reside in the development of the control software for the system being designed. This software may contain hundreds or thousands of lines of instructions. The system hardware, in contrast, may be relatively simple, consisting of only a handful of ICs. The systematic top-down approach discussed in Sec. 1.1.2 is especially useful for the design of complex software. This means that a large control program should be decomposed in a hierarchical manner into small program modules whose individual structure and behavior can be easily understood and verified.

1.4 SUMMARY

The term "system" is one of great generality, and so is not easily defined. It typically denotes a collection of objects that interact in a complex but orderly fashion. Every system has two important aspects: its structure, defined by its components and links, and its behavior, defined by the relations among its IO variables or signals. System structure can be described by means of block diagrams, where the blocks denote components and the lines between them denote links. For specific types of systems, such as electronic or logic circuits, the blocks are often replaced by special symbols, where a symbol's shape represents a component type. System behavior can be represented by various means, including flowcharts, truth tables, and textual descriptions written in informal languages, such as English, or in formal languages, such as computer programming languages or mathematical notation. System analysis is concerned with determining the behavior of a system, given the structure of the system and the behavior of its components. System design or synthesis, on the other hand, is concerned with building a structure that displays a given behavior. The art of the system designer is to construct a system that achieves the desired behavior at the lowest possible cost.

Most complex systems, both natural and artificial, exhibit a hierarchical organization that allows the system to be studied at several different complexity levels. For example, digital systems may be viewed at the electronic, gate, register, and processor levels. Each level is distinguished by the components and signals that are treated as primitive. A primitive component at one level appears as a multicomponent (sub)system when viewed at the next lowest complexity level. The design of a complex system such as a computer or a large computer program is usually implemented most efficiently by giving it a hierarchical organization, which is then implemented level by level, beginning at the highest complexity level and ending at the lowest. This is termed top-down design.

Systems that process information can be characterized by the types of signals they process. Such signals fall into two principal classes: analog signals, which can vary over a continuous range, and digital signals, which can only assume a finite set of values. Most digital systems, when viewed at their lowest complexity level, employ only two signal values, conventionally denoted by 0 and 1. In a physical system the binary values 0 and 1 actually represent two values of some analog physical quantity such as voltage. Moreover, the physical components from which digital systems are built exhibit various analog properties, such as causing continuous signal fluctuations or having continuous drive requirements. These analog aspects of physical systems often add significant complications to the digital system design process.

Most modern digital systems are composed of high-speed switching devices capable of rapidly changing the value of an electric signal. Crystal diodes and diode vacuum tubes were the earliest such switches. The triode vacuum tube, introduced in 1906, was the first electronic switch capable of signal amplification, and formed the basis of all electronic systems, both digital and analog, for about 50 years. The transistor, a much smaller and more reliable electronic switch fabricated from semiconducting materials, began to replace vacuum tubes in the 1950s. Also around this time, automated methods for electronic circuit assembly, including the use of printed-circuit boards and thick- or thin-film circuits, began to supersede manual assembly methods. Based on various printing technologies, these techniques allowed complex electronic circuits to be mass produced in a precise and compact form.

A manufacturing technique called the planar process was devised in 1958 that allowed many transistors to be constructed simultaneously on the surface of a small wafer of semiconductor. Shortly thereafter methods were introduced for fabricating other types of electronic components and interconnections between components on a common semiconductor substrate. The result was the integrated circuit (IC), which was first produced commercially in 1961. Rapid advances in IC manufacturing technology were made in the 1960s, with silicon assuming the role of the semiconductor of choice for most ICs. These advances were characterized by a continual increase in the maximum number of components (transistors or logic gates) that could be included in a single mass-produced IC. A measure of the rate of increase in IC component density is given by

Moore's law (Moore, 1965), which states that the number of components per IC chip could be expected to double every year, at least for the period 1965–1975. The accuracy of this prediction is borne out by Fig. 1.47. In high-volume production, the cost per IC chip tends to be very low and relatively independent of component density. Consequently, as component density increases, the cost per component decreases, making the newer, denser ICs more attractive to the system designer. By 1970 the point had been reached where the central processing unit (CPU) of a computer could be squeezed onto a single IC. This resulted in the appearance of the one-chip CPU or microprocessor. A few years later the one-chip microcomputer appeared.

The foregoing developments in electronic circuit manufacturing technology were paralleled by developments in the design and implementation of digital computers. The origins of computers go back much further, however. Mechanical four-function calculators were constructed in the seventeenth century, while the central principles of the general-purpose programmable digital computer were formulated by Babbage in the nineteenth century. Electronic digital computers based on vacuum-tube technology were first successfully built in the 1940s. The organization of the modern computer was established in these first-generation machines. This organization comprises a CPU used for program execution, a main memory used for program and data storage, and IO devices such as punched card readers, printers, and secondary memory units. Early computers were programmed mainly in low-level machine and assembly languages, and provided very limited hardware and software facilities to the computer user.

The introduction of transistors gave rise to the second generation of electronic computers in the mid-1950s. Transistor computers were much more compact and reliable than their vacuum-tube counterparts, allowing significant increases in hardware complexity. High-level programming languages such as FORTRAN and COBOL came into general use in the 1950s, and made computers accessible to many new users. Computers

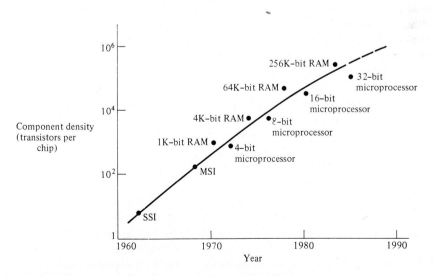

Figure 1.47 Growth of maximum achievable IC component density.

were also supplied with operating systems and other systems software that allowed them to be used more easily and more efficiently. In 1964 IBM announced the very influential System/360 computer series, many of whose hardware and software conventions became de facto industry standards. Usually regarded as the first third-generation computer, the System/360 marked the tentative introduction of IC technology into the manufacture of large computers. More extensive use of SSI and MSI circuits resulted in the appearance of minicomputers, whose relatively small size and low cost engendered a significant increase in the use of computers in specialized industrial and scientific applications. The development of LSI technology around 1970 saw a further reduction in computer size and cost with the advent of microprocessors and microcomputers. The first microprocessors were characterized by small word size, 4 or 8 bits, and rather limited instruction repertoires. As IC component densities increased (see Fig. 1.47), microprocessors began to acquire the hardware and software features of second and third-generation machines, a process that still continues.

Because of their low cost, small size, and flexibility, microprocessors have had an enormous impact on all aspects of digital system design. They are universal design components in that they can be customized for particular applications by supplying them with appropriate control programs and IO devices. A microprocessor-based system, therefore, has the structure of a general-purpose digital computer. The inclusion of microprocessors has resulted in great improvements in such traditional digital systems as cash registers and traffic-light controllers. Many formerly analog systems, such as electronic measuring instruments and automobile engine control systems, have been replaced by microprocessor-controlled digital systems that provide greater accuracy and flexibility, and, in many cases, do so at lower cost. Microprocessors have also stimulated creation of an ever-increasing number of entirely new types of systems such as "intelligent" household appliances and industrial robots.

Although a microprocessor-based system can consist of just a single IC, it often contains numerous ICs and discrete components representing several different complexity levels, all of which must be familiar to the system's designer. System development typically involves the following design steps: project planning, architectural design, detailed design, debugging, and documentation. Careful structuring of the design process is required to prevent the need for an excessive amount of effort in the debugging phase. Often the most complex portion of the system being designed is the control software, which is best designed in a top-down manner. A useful aid in the design of a microprocessor-based system is a microprocessor development system (MDS).

1.5 FURTHER READING

An introduction to digital systems from a modern engineering viewpoint can be found in Motil's text (Motil, 1972). Simon provides a penetrating analysis of the nature of complex systems (Simon, 1981). Gall's book *Systemantics,* as its name implies, is an amusing but insightful account of systems and their limitations (Gall, 1975). A comprehensive and well-illustrated history of the development of electronic technology and systems, including computers, is given in *Electronics* (1980). An authoritative account of the historical development of digital computers can be found in Randell (1982). Braun and McDonald's *Revolution in Miniature* is a very satisfying treatment of the history and impact of semiconductor technology (Braun & McDonald, 1978), while the early development of microprocessors has been described by Noyce and Hoff (1981). The design process for microprocessor-based systems is surveyed by Tseng (1982), and a wide-ranging and provocative essay on the present and future impact of microprocessors appears in Evans (1980).

1.6 PROBLEMS

1.1 For each of the following well-known systems, list a possible set of components and links that define the system structure in the manner of Fig. 1.1.

(*a*) The human circulatory system
(*b*) The decimal system
(*c*) The Goren system of bidding in bridge
(*d*) The Scandinavian Airlines System
(*e*) The international monetary system

1.2 The various diagrams listed below can be regarded as specialized block diagrams representing systems. In each case identify the symbols that represent blocks and lines interconnecting blocks.

(*a*) A road atlas of the United States
(*b*) A flowchart for a computer program
(*c*) A crossword puzzle
(*d*) A genealogical chart or family tree

1.3 A flowchart F, such as that of Fig. 1.4c, is a useful method for representing the behavior of a system S. F is clearly a particular type of block diagram. Block diagrams, however, are used to define a system's structure. Does this mean that F must also define the structure of S? Justify your answer.

1.4 Hypergraphs are a class of mathematical objects of interest to topologists. A *hypergraph H* is a pair (V, E) where V is a set of objects called vertices and E is a set of objects called edges, each of which consists of a subset of V. When each edge in E contains just two vertices from V, H is called simply a *graph*. Discuss the relevance of graphs and hypergraphs to the task of describing system structure and behavior.

1.5 People who deal with complex systems are often divided into those who analyze and those who design or synthesize. This dichotomy is apparent in such job titles as psychoanalyst and fashion designer. Identify the type of work, either analysis or synthesis, associated with each of the following jobs.

(*a*) Accountant
(*b*) Bomb disposal expert
(*c*) Chef
(*d*) Computer programmer
(*e*) TV repairperson

1.6 "How complex or simple a structure is depends critically on the way we describe it" (Simon, 1981). Write a brief essay on the applicability of this statement to microprocessor-based systems.

1.7 Select any system S from the list in Fig. 1.1. Define two distinct complexity levels at which S can be described. Identify the structure and behavior recognized at each of the two complexity levels. Show how each component at the higher complexity level can be defined in terms of components and links taken from the lower complexity level.

1.8 What are the advantages of designing a large computer program as a hierarchy of small program modules? Suggest some general qualitative criteria for determining what constitutes a suitable program module within a system of this kind.

1.9 The systematic design approach for hierarchical systems discussed in Sec. 1.1.2 is top-down in the sense that detailed design begins at the highest complexity level and ends at the lowest. There is a complementary design approach called *bottom-up* design that begins at the lowest complexity level and terminates at the highest. Give an example of a bottom-up design process unrelated to computer systems. Write a brief note on the relative merits of top-down and bottom-up methods, indicating situations in which each is more suitable than the other.

1.10 What are the advantages and disadvantages of representing system variables in digital rather than analog form? Explain why digital methods for recording music on records and tapes were introduced around 1980 to replace older analog methods.

1.11 The use of logarithm tables to perform multiplication and division is based on the same principle as the slide rule. In each case multiplication and division are reduced to addition and subtraction respectively. Is the use of logarithm tables for these operations an analog or a digital process? Explain your answer.

1.12 Suppose that a certain slide rule has scales that are 10 cm long, permitting multiplication and division to be performed with up to three digits of precision. Estimate how long the slide rule would have to be to equal the eight digits of precision provided by many electronic pocket calculators.

1.13 Semiconductor materials in the form of crystal diodes were used to construct high-speed electronic switches (rectifiers) before 1900.

(*a*) Explain why crystal diodes are, by themselves, inadequate for the design of complex digital systems.

(*b*) Why did more than 50 years elapse before the development of semiconductor switches (transistors) that were suitable for constructing complex digital systems?

1.14 List the advantages of transistors over vacuum tubes as the basic switching elements in general-purpose digital computers.

1.15 Explain why, among the hundreds of available semiconducting materials, silicon has achieved the preeminent position in the manufacture of integrated circuits.

1.16 Why do most current LSI and VLSI circuits use MOS rather than bipolar transistor circuits?

1.17 The progress of IC manufacturing technology can be gauged by the cost c to the system designer of a basic component such as a simple logic gate, e.g., a two-input NAND. If an IC containing 1000 gates costs \$1, then c is \$0.001 per gate. Give some arguments supporting the contention that c has tended to be approximately halved annually by progress in IC manufacturing methods.

1.18 Mechanical computing systems ranging from Pascal's calculating machine to modern cash registers operate much more slowly than their electronic counterparts. What other disadvantages have mechanical digital systems compared with electronic systems?

1.19 Write an essay on the evolution of the physical components used to construct CPUs from Babbage's Analytical Engine to the Intel 8080.

1.20 Comment on the significance of the fact that in many general-purpose computing machines, including slide rules, difference engines, and microprocessors, the only arithmetic operations that can be performed directly are addition and subtraction.

1.21 Describe the functions performed by each of the following components of a microcomputer system: the CPU, main memory, the system bus, an IO port.

1.22 What is the stored program concept in computer design, and why was it introduced? Explain why many microprocessor-based systems do not use this design concept. (As a result they are occasionally referred to as *Harvard-class* machines after the Harvard Mark 1 computer.)

1.23 In the machine-language program of Fig. 1.27b, lines 1 and 4 each contain the same bit pattern 10010110. Line 1 represents the instruction operation or opcode load accumulator A, whereas line 4 represents the numerical operand 150. Suppose that during the execution of this program, the CPU fetches the word 10010110 from main memory. How does it determine whether to treat this word as an opcode or an operand?

1.24 What are the advantages of using high-level languages such as FORTRAN to program digital computers? Under what circumstances, if any, is it more desirable to use assembly or machine languages?

1.25 Describe how microprocessors can be used to improve the performance and ease of use of the following domestic appliances:

(*a*) Hi-fi systems

(*b*) Television sets

(c) Microwave ovens

(d) Burglar alarm systems

(e) Washing machines

1.26 The introduction of POS terminals with UPC scanners allowed supermarkets to discontinue the costly process of stamping prices on individual items. This action was opposed by some consumer groups on the grounds that it prevented customers from determining the prices they had paid for individual items after leaving the store, thereby making "comparison shopping" more difficult. Explain how POS terminals can be used to solve this problem while retaining the UPC system.

1.27 Consider the microprocessor-based insulation control system shown in Fig. 1.36. Assume that the jacket thickness always lies in the range 0 to 0.5 mm. Each ultrasonic transducer generates a 10-bit binary number that represents jacket thickness. What is the smallest possible error in jacket thickness that can be detected by the transducers? State any assumptions that you make.

1.28 Consider the parts list for a microprocessor-based speedometer appearing in Fig. 1.41.

(a) Identify all the MSI parts used.

(b) Identify all the gate-level parts used.

1.29 Construct a flowchart that describes the operation of the digital speedometer of Fig. 1.40. The flowchart should fit on one page and have roughly the same level of detail as the flowcharts appearing in Figs. 1.35 and 1.37.

1.30 Consider the data in Fig. 1.44 on the distribution of design effort in computer development projects. Suggest why a significantly higher percentage of total development is devoted to testing and debugging in software projects, compared with hardware projects.

1.31 The following statement appears in a textbook on the design of microprocessor-based systems: "It is not necessary to allow time for debugging, since systems implemented using the steps described in this book *always work*." Explain why the author's claim is highly suspect.

1.32 Write an essay analyzing the relative merits of the top-down and bottom-up design approaches (see Prob. 1.9) in the case of microprocessor-based systems. In your analysis consider overall design time, debugging requirements, and the implementation of changes after the design has been completed.

1.33 List the ways in which a microprocessor development system (MDS) can be used as a tool in the design of a new microprocessor-based system.

CHAPTER

TWO

INTEGRATED CIRCUIT TECHNOLOGY

"With the advent of the transistor and the work in semiconductors, generally, it now seems possible to envisage electronic equipment in a solid block with no connecting wires. The block may consist of layers of insulating, conducting, rectifying and amplifying materials, the electrical functions being connected directly by cutting out areas of the various layers."

[G.W.A. Dummer: *Proc. of Symp. of the IRE-AIEE-RTMA*, Washington, D.C., May 1952]

Integrated circuits (ICs), which are electronic circuits manufactured on a single, tiny piece of semiconductor material, are the fundamental components of modern digital systems. In this chapter those aspects of electric circuit theory and electronics needed in the design of microprocessor-based systems are presented in a self-contained manner. The processes used to manufacture ICs, as well as their significance, are discussed. The electrical characteristics of the principal families of ICs used in logic design are examined. The logic families considered in detail here include TTL (transistor-transistor logic) and the most widely used MOS (metal-oxide-semiconductor) families. Various practical issues in the construction of systems from ICs are also discussed, including loading requirements, interconnection methods, and noise suppression.

2.1 ELECTRONICS CONCEPTS

Microcomputers, like most digital systems, are constructed from physical devices whose underlying behavior is electronic in nature. A full understanding of these systems requires some familiarity with basic electric circuit theory and electronics. A concise summary of the relevant concepts from these fields is presented in this section.

2.1.1 Introduction

The international system of units called *SI* (from the French name *Système International d'Unités*) is used throughout this book for measuring physical quantities. This standard system, which is an extension of the familiar metric system, employs the basic units listed in Fig. 2.1a. From these few primitive units, a large number of more complex units of measurement are derived. For example, the unit of force, which is called a newton (N), is defined as the force required to accelerate a mass of 1 kilogram at a rate of 1 meter per second per second. Using the standard SI abbreviation we can write

$$N = kg \cdot m \cdot s^{-2}$$

The unit of energy or work is called the joule (J) and is the work done or energy required when a force of 1 newton moves its point of application through a distance of one meter, that is,

$$J = N \cdot m = kg \cdot m^2 \cdot s^{-2}$$

Figure 2.1b lists some representative derived units; note that all are named for famous scientists.

Quantity	Unit	Symbol	Equivalent Quantities in Other Systems of Units
length	meter	m	39.3701 inches (in.)
mass	kilogram	kg	2.2046 pounds (lb.)
time	second	s	1/60 minute (min.)
electric current	ampere	A	
temperature	kelvin	K	1 degree Celsius (°C) or 9/5 degree Fahrenheit (°F)

(*a*)

Quantity	Unit	Symbol	Definition in Terms of Other SI Units
force	newton	N	1 kilogram-meter per second^2
work (energy)	joule	J	1 newton-meter = 1 watt-second
power	watt	W	1 joule per second = 1 volt-ampere
charge	coulomb	C	1 ampere-second
electric potential (voltage)	volt	V	1 joule per coulomb
resistance	ohm	Ω	1 volt per ampere
capacitance	farad	F	1 coulomb per volt
magnetic flux	weber	Wb	1 volt-second
inductance	henry	H	1 weber per ampere

(*b*)

Figure 2.1 (*a*) Some basic and (*b*) some derived units of the SI metric system.

All SI units may be multiplied by positive or negative powers of 10 by attaching certain standard prefixes to their names; in the case of mass units, the prefixes are attached to the stem "-gram." Some commonly used power-of-10 prefixes are listed in Fig. 2.2. For example, the unit microsecond is formed by attaching the prefix micro, denoting 10^{-6}, to the basic unit second, thereby forming a unit denoting one millionth of a second. The symbol for a microsecond is μs, which is formed by combining the symbol μ (the Greek letter mu), which represents micro, with the symbol s for second. The SI system has two major advantages over other systems of units. It is a decimal system since all units for measuring a given physical quantity such as length are related by powers of 10 only, for example, meters, centimeters, kilometers. Second, the SI system employs identical units for both mechanical and electrical quantities. Thus the joule is both the mechanical unit of work (1 newton-meter) and the electrical unit of work (1 watt-second).

Matter is composed of atoms, each consisting of a relatively large center or nucleus surrounded by tiny orbiting particles called *electrons*. Both the electrons and the nucleus have a property called electric *charge*, which creates an attractive force that holds the atom together. The electron can be considered the smallest carrier of electric charge. By convention, the charge on the electron is taken to be negative; it has a fixed magnitude of 1.602×10^{-19} C. Thus if $-e$ denotes the electron charge, we have

$$ e = 1.602 \times 10^{-19} \text{ C} \tag{2.1} $$

The electric charge associated with the atomic nucleus is due to particles called protons, each of which has a charge $+e$ that is equal in magnitude but opposite in sign to that of an electron. In a normal atom the positive charges of the protons are exactly balanced by the negative charges of the electrons, so that the electric charge of the atom as a whole is zero. A piece of matter that has no overall electric charge is said to be electrically *neutral*. If electrons are added to a neutral substance, it becomes negatively charged; if electrons are removed, it becomes positively charged.

Certain substances such as amber (whose Greek name is *elektron*) and many modern plastic materials can be charged by rubbing. For example, running a plastic comb through one's hair can result in a transfer of electric charge that leaves the hair positively

Prefix	Symbol	Meaning	Representative Example
tera	T	10^{12}	1 terabit $= 10^{12}$ bits
giga	G	10^{9}	1 gigahertz $= 1$ GHz $= 10^{9}$ hertz
mega	M	10^{6}	1 megawatt $= 1$ MW $= 10^{6}$ watts
kilo	k	10^{3}	1 kilohm $= 1$ kΩ $= 1000$ ohms
centi	c	10^{-2}	1 centimeter $= 1$ cm $= 0.01$ meter
milli	m	10^{-3}	1 milliampere $= 1$ mA $= 0.001$ ampere
micro	μ	10^{-6}	1 microvolt $= 1$ μV $= 10^{-6}$ volts
nano	n	10^{-9}	1 nanosecond $= 1$ ns $= 10^{-9}$ seconds
pico	p	10^{-12}	1 picofarad $= 1$ pF $= 10^{-12}$ farads

Figure 2.2 Some power-of-10 prefixes used with the SI units.

charged and the comb negatively charged. Roughly speaking, electrons are rubbed off the hair onto the comb. It is sometimes observed that electrically charged hair tends to stand on end. This is a consequence of the fundamental fact that bodies whose charges are of the same kind, either both positive or both negative, tend to repel each other. Thus the individual hairs charged by rubbing with a comb acquire the same kind of charge and repel one another, thereby making the hair stand on end. Conversely a positively charged body and a negatively charged body tend to attract each other. The attraction between the electrons and protons of an atom is of this type. These phenomena are succinctly summarized in the following law:

Unlike charges attract; like charges repel.

Electrons may be thought of as moving in several fixed orbits around the atomic nucleus, rather like planets orbiting the sun. The attractive force between two bodies with unlike charges decreases as the distance between them increases. Hence the electrons in the orbit that is furthest from the nucleus are the ones that are most easily dislodged from the atom, as by friction or by heating. Thermal agitation of the atoms of solid materials, even at room temperature, results in the ejection of electrons from the outer orbits of the atoms. These free electrons tend to diffuse slowly through the solid, repelling one another, and occasionally being captured by an atom that lacks one or more electrons and therefore is positively charged. Substances with a plentiful supply of free electrons at room temperature are called *conductors*; those that have very few free electrons, and thus are poor conductors of electricity, are called *insulators*. Certain materials with conducting properties intermediate between conductors and insulators are called *semiconductors*. Modern electronic devices, ranging from transistors to single-chip microcomputers, are fabricated by the judicious combination of conductors, insulators, and semiconductors.

The attractive or repulsive force between charged bodies can be measured by the usual units of mechanical force, which are newtons in the SI system; see Fig. 2.1b. Suppose that a force of F newtons is exerted on a charged particle of q coulombs at a point p. There is an *electric field E* at p, which is defined by the force equation

$$F = qE \qquad \text{N} \tag{2.2}$$

Note the analogy between (2.2) and the mechanical force equation (Newton's second law):

$$F = mA \qquad \text{N}$$

where m denotes mass and A denotes acceleration. Thus E, whose units are newtons per coulomb, measures the accelerating force exerted by charged particles.

To move an electrically charged body through a region of space containing an electric field, work (either positive or negative) must be done. The work done in moving a positive charge of 1 coulomb from point a to point b is called the *potential difference* or, more often, the *voltage* from a to b, and is denoted by v_{ab}. Clearly,

$$v_{ab} = -v_{ba}$$

The unit of voltage is the volt, which is the work required to push a charge of 1 coulomb a distance of 1 meter through an electric field of magnitude 1 newton per coulomb. Thus a volt is equal to 1 newton-meter per coulomb or 1 joule per coulomb. If point a is taken as a reference point for voltage measurement, then we can refer to v_{ab} as the voltage of point b, and denote it by v_b. Since $v_{aa} = v_a = 0$, point a is said to be at zero volts or *ground* potential. The purpose of a battery, electric generator, or other power supply unit is to generate electric charge carriers that have specific voltage levels. Many electronic circuits require a power supply unit that provides two voltage levels: a reference or ground voltage, and a voltage that has a level of $+5$ volts relative to the ground voltage.

Suppose that the voltage terminals of a battery are connected to the ends of an electrical conductor such as a metal wire. This creates an electric field in the conductor, which causes the negatively charged free electrons to move toward the positive terminal of the battery. The flow of electrons or other electrically charged particles in this manner is called an *electric current*. The unit of current in the SI system is the ampere (A), which is also one of the basic units listed in Fig. 2.1. One ampere corresponds to 1 coulomb of charge flowing past a measurement point per second. Thus from (2.1), it is equivalent to a flow of 1.602×10^{19} electrons per second, which is about four times the current drawn by a flashlight bulb. The currents flowing in electronic systems are often much smaller, and are typically measured in milliamperes.

Most of the systems of interest in this book are electric circuits. Figure 2.3a shows the essential elements of an electric circuit—a *power supply* and a *load device*. Figure 2.3b shows, in standard schematic form, the circuit of a flashlight, in which the power supply is a battery and the load device is a light bulb. The power supply maintains a potential difference of V volts between the terminals of the load, and supplies the energy

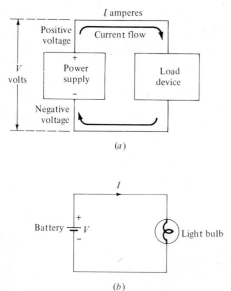

(a)

(b)

Figure 2.3 (a) Essentials of an electric circuit; (b) circuit of a flashlight.

needed to drive the electric charge carriers through it. As a charge of q coulombs flows around the circuit, it loses energy in the amount of qV joules in passing through the load. In the circuit of Fig. 2.3b the energy taken by the load from the electric current is converted into light and heat. As the q-coulomb charge flows through the power supply, it regains the energy qV joules. In the battery case this energy is obtained from a chemical reaction occurring in the battery. Suppose that a steady current of I amperes flows through the circuits of Fig. 2.3. It follows from the definitions of current and voltage that the energy consumed by the load or generated by the power supply in 1 second is VI joules. Hence the *power P* consumed by the load or supplied by the power source is given by the equation

$$P = VI \qquad W \tag{2.3}$$

A useful analogy can be drawn between the electric circuit of Fig. 2.3a and the hydraulic system of Fig. 2.4. The flow of electric current through wires in the first case corresponds to the flow of water through pipes in the second case. The pressure difference between two points in the hydraulic system corresponds to the potential difference or voltage between the corresponding points in the electric circuit. If there is no pressure or potential difference between the points, then no current flows; the larger the difference, the larger is the current flow. Thus voltage can be viewed as the electrical pressure that causes an electric current to flow. In Fig. 2.4 the mill wheel removes energy from the falling water. This energy is restored by the water pump, which transfers the water from a position of low (potential) energy to one of high energy. In a similar way, an electric power supply pumps charge carriers from a low to a high potential energy level.

Electrons play a central role in the combination of atoms to form compound structures such as molecules. Of interest here is the formation of regular solid structures called crystals. A *crystal* is a body in which all the atoms are aligned in a uniform three-dimensional pattern. This pattern is a result of interaction between the electrons called the *valence* electrons, which are in the outermost orbits of adjacent atoms. Consider, for instance, the element silicon, which is the primary raw material for modern electronic circuits. A silicon atom has 32 electrons and 32 protons, and there are four valence electrons in the outside orbit. In a silicon crystal every atom a is equidistant from four other atoms that are positioned at the vertices of a tetrahedron centered on a. Each of the valence electrons of a is shared with one of its four neighboring atoms, as suggested in Fig. 2.5. Every atom of the crystal, therefore, appears to have eight valence electrons instead of four. This linking of electrons creates a bond, called a covalent bond, between

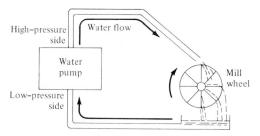

Figure 2.4 Hydraulic system analogous to the electric circuit of Fig. 2.3a.

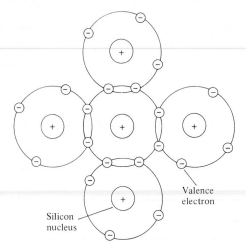

Figure 2.5 Covalent bonds between atoms in a silicon crystal.

the atoms that serves to hold the crystal together. Note that the crystal as a whole is electrically neutral because the same numbers of electrons and protons are present.

At very low temperatures such as 0 K (absolute zero), the valence electrons of a silicon crystal are not free to move, so the crystal behaves as an insulator. As temperature increases, a valence electron can acquire enough thermal energy to allow it to break free from its parent atom and wander through the crystal. Free electrons of this kind permit a silicon crystal to be a fair conductor of electric current—that is, a semiconductor—at room temperature. When an electron leaves its original position in the crystal structure of Fig. 2.5, a vacancy is left that is termed a *hole*. A hole can be thought of as a current carrier with a charge of $+e$. Suppose that a hole exists in some atom a_1 due to an escaped electron. An adjacent atom a_2 can release a valence electron that jumps to a_1 and "fills" the hole. Of course, this creates a new hole in a_2. The foregoing process can be interpreted as a positively charged hole moving from a_1 to a_2. Thus an electric current flowing in a semiconductor such as silicon has two components, as depicted in Fig. 2.6: free electrons flowing in one direction, and holes flowing in the opposite direction. Holes move by a sequence of jumps between adjacent atoms; they thus have lower mobility (are slower) than free electrons, which can move relatively long distances

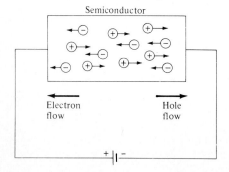

Figure 2.6 Electric current flow in a semiconductor.

before interacting with atoms. The electrical properties of a semiconductor can be profoundly altered by the addition of minute amounts of impurities, a topic discussed later in this section.

2.1.2 Direct-Current Circuits

In the simple electric circuit of Fig. 2.3a there is a power supply that acts as the source of electric energy, and a load device that receives electric energy and converts it to other forms of energy such as heat, light, or mechanical work. In general, an *electric circuit* consists of a set of *sources* (power supplies) and *elements* (load devices) linked together by *connectors*. The connection points in the circuit are called *nodes* or *terminals*. The electrical elements of interest here include resistors, capacitors, diodes, and transistors. The connectors of interest are conductors of electricity such as wires and the various conductors built into integrated circuits. The term *electronic circuit* or system is applied rather loosely to electric circuits of the kind found in television sets, computers, and the like, which are characterized by the fact that the voltages and currents they contain represent either digital or analog information; electronic circuits therefore may be equated with information-processing electric circuits. Circuits containing semiconductor devices such as transistors are generally referred to as electronic, whether or not they process information.

We first examine a class of electric/electronic circuits called *direct-current* or *dc* circuits, in which the voltages and currents associated with each element and source are fixed in direction. In many cases the electrical parameters are fixed in magnitude as well as direction, that is, they do not vary with time. A power supply such as a battery can be viewed as either a current or a voltage source in a dc circuit. It is useful to define an ideal *voltage source,* represented by the symbol of Fig. 2.7a, which produces a constant voltage V whose value is therefore independent of the amount of current drawn from the source. A voltage source is only an approximate model for a real battery, since the output voltage from a battery tends to decrease as the current drawn from it increases. Similarly, a *current source* is an ideal device that produces a constant current I under all conditions; it is represented by the circuit symbol of Fig. 2.7b. The two terminals of a voltage-current source are designated positive ($+$) and negative ($-$), where by convention a positive current composed of positively charged current carriers emerges from the positive terminal and returns to the negative terminal. Since electrons carry negative charges, they flow into the positive terminal of a power source. Note that the current $+I$

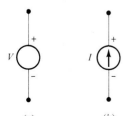

(a)   (b)   **Figure 2.7** Standard symbols for (a) voltage source and (b) current source.

flowing through a connector in one direction is equivalent to the current $-I$ flowing through the same connector in the opposite direction.

Suppose that an ideal voltage source whose output voltage is V is connected to a two-terminal load device D as in Fig. 2.3a. If the resulting steady current I flowing through D is directly proportional to V, then we can write

$$V = RI \tag{2.4}$$

where the constant of proportionality R is called the *resistance* of D. The unit of resistance is the ohm (Ω), where 1 ohm is the resistance of a device that allows 1 ampere to flow through it when a voltage of 1 volt is applied across it. Equation (2.4) is called *Ohm's law*—which, like the unit of resistance, is named for the German physicist Georg Ohm (1787–1854). Ohm's law is applicable to most materials that are held at a constant temperature. Conductors have low resistance (fractions of an ohm), whereas insulators have very high resistance (megohms). Electrical elements designed to have a specific fixed resistance are called *resistors,* and are represented by the symbol shown in Fig. 2.8. Many devices, such as a light bulb or the heating element of an electric oven or toaster, can be accurately modeled by an ideal resistor. Suppose, for instance, that the light bulb of the flashlight circuit in Fig. 2.3b has resistance $R = 10\ \Omega$. If the battery voltage is 3 V, then the current flowing in the circuit is given by Ohm's law [Eq. (2.4)]:

$$I = V/R = 3/10 = 0.3\ \text{A}$$

By Eq. (2.3), the power generated by the battery, which is also the power consumed by the light bulb, is

$$P = VI = 0.9\ \text{W}$$

The analysis of electric circuits often involves the calculation of the voltages and currents at various places in the circuit. This analysis is usually based on two fundamental principles known as Kirchoff's laws, after the German scientist Gustav Kirchoff (1824–1887). The first of these is *Kirchoff's current law,* which may be stated as follows:

The algebraic sum of all the currents entering a node of the circuit is zero.

Here "algebraic" means that the direction or sign (positive or negative) of each current must be taken into account. This law is an immediate consequence of the fact that the same number of charge carriers enter a node as leave it; in other words, electric charge is conserved. It also suggests that an electric current flows somewhat like a liquid; compare Fig. 2.4, where the current entering any pipe is equal, but opposite in sign, to the current leaving the pipe. The second analysis principle, which is called *Kirchoff's voltage law,* states that

The algebraic sum of all the potential differences around any closed path (loop) of the circuit is zero.

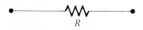

R

Figure 2.8 Symbol for a resistor of R ohms.

This law expresses the fact that the energy produced by the power sources is equal to that consumed by the load elements; in other words, electric energy is conserved.

Consider the circuits of Figs. 2.9 and 2.10, which illustrate the use of Kirchoff's laws. Figure 2.9 represents a battery B that is connected to or drives a load L. The battery is modeled by an ideal voltage source of V volts that is connected to an r-ohm resistor, where r represents the internal resistance of the battery. The load L is modeled by a resistor of R ohms. When the circuit is switched on, a constant (direct) current I flows through it, as indicated in the figure. I may be calculated by applying Ohm's law and Kirchoff's voltage law in the following manner. By Ohm's law the potential differences or voltage drops across r and R are rI and RI respectively. The circuit forms a single closed path or loop; hence by Kirchoff's voltage law the sum of the voltage drops around this loop is zero, that is,

$$rI + RI - V = 0$$

This equation immediately yields the desired current I thus:

$$I = \frac{V}{r + R}$$

The voltage V_B appearing across the battery terminals in Fig. 2.9 is $V - rI = RI$, so that V_B decreases as R decreases. If R is reduced to zero, in which case B is said to be

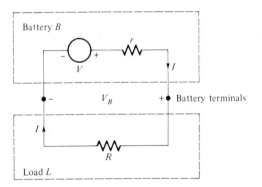

Figure 2.9 Electric circuit model for a battery driving a load.

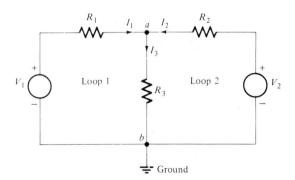

Figure 2.10 Circuit containing several resistors and voltage sources.

short-circuited, V_B becomes zero and I assumes its maximum value V/r. If r is also reduced to zero, then I tends to infinity. Thus the internal resistance serves to limit the amount of current that can be drawn from the battery. If I is reduced to zero by disconnecting the load from the battery B, then B is said to be *open-circuited*, and V_B becomes V, its maximum value.

Figure 2.10 shows a somewhat more complex circuit containing several resistors and voltage sources. Node b is *grounded*, as indicated by the special ground symbol, so that $V_b = 0$ serves as the reference voltage. Suppose that we need to compute the currents I_1, I_2, and I_3 flowing through the resistors R_1, R_2, and R_3 respectively. The circuit contains two loops, as indicated in the figure. Applying Kirchoff's voltage law to these loops yields the two equations

$$V_1 - R_1 I_1 - R_3 I_3 = 0 \tag{2.5}$$

$$V_2 - R_2 I_2 - R_3 I_3 = 0 \tag{2.6}$$

The application of Kirchoff's current law to node a yields another equation:

$$I_1 + I_2 - I_3 = 0 \tag{2.7}$$

The three equations (2.5)–(2.7) can be solved for the three unknowns, I_1, I_2, and I_3 using standard algebraic methods. It can easily be shown, for example, that

$$I_3 = \frac{R_2 V_1 + R_1 V_2}{R_1 R_2 + R_1 R_3 + R_2 R_3} \tag{2.8}$$

Once the currents flowing in the circuit are known, the voltage at any node can easily be calculated. For instance, the voltage V_a of node a is the potential difference across the terminals of resistor R_3, since $V_b = 0$. By Ohm's law, $V_a = R_3 I_3$, and hence by Eq. (2.8),

$$V_a = \frac{R_3(R_2 V_1 + R_1 V_2)}{R_1 R_2 + R_1 R_3 + R_2 R_3}$$

The concept of an equivalent circuit is an important one in electric circuit theory. Suppose that N_1 is a complex subcircuit of some circuit N. It is often possible to find a simple circuit N_1^*, called an *equivalent circuit* of N_1, which can be substituted for N_1 in N so that the currents and voltages at the nodes on the boundary or interface between N_1 and the rest of N are unchanged by the substitution. In other words N_1 and N_1^* appear to have identical electrical characteristics when viewed from their IO terminals.

To illustrate this equivalence concept, consider the resistive networks of Fig. 2.11. The circuit of Fig. 2.11a, in which n elements are connected end to end, is called a *series* or *cascade* connection, while the circuit of Fig. 2.11b is called a *parallel* connection. It is of interest to find simple equivalent circuits that can replace series or parallel circuits of this kind. Suppose that a voltage V_{ab} is applied across the terminals of the series circuit of Fig. 2.11a. This forms a closed loop through which a current I flows. Clearly by Kirchoff's voltage law and Ohm's law we have

$$V_{ab} = R_1 I + R_2 I + \cdots + R_n I$$

$$= (R_1 + R_2 + \cdots + R_n)I \tag{2.9}$$

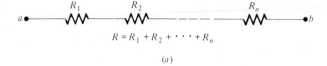

$$R = R_1 + R_2 + \cdots + R_n$$

(a)

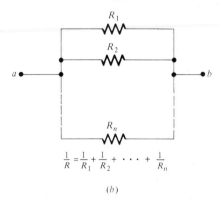

$$\frac{1}{R} = \frac{1}{R_1} + \frac{1}{R_2} + \cdots + \frac{1}{R_n}$$

(b)

Figure 2.11 Set of resistors connected (a) in series and (b) in parallel.

In comparing Eqs. (2.4) and (2.9) we see that the n resistors in series are equivalent to a single R-ohm resistor that satisfies the equation

$$R = R_1 + R_2 \cdots + R_n \qquad (2.10)$$

If R is substituted for the series circuit of Fig. 2.11a, the interface parameters V_{ab} and I remain unchanged. Similarly we can find a single resistor R that is equivalent to the parallel connection of Fig. 11b. Again let a voltage V_{ab} be applied to the terminals of the circuit, and let I_j denote the resulting current flowing through resistor R_j for $j = 1, 2, \ldots$, n. Let I be the current entering node a. Kirchoff's current law implies that

$$I = I_1 + I_2 + \cdots + I_n$$

Hence by Ohm's law,

$$\frac{V_{ab}}{R} = \frac{V_{ab}}{R_1} + \frac{V_{ab}}{R_2} + \cdots + \frac{V_{ab}}{R_n}$$

Therefore,

$$\frac{1}{R} = \frac{1}{R_1} + \frac{1}{R_2} + \cdots + \frac{1}{R_n} \qquad (2.11)$$

Equations (2.10) and (2.11) are very useful for simplifying resistive circuits.

   Many electric circuits have just two external terminals; those of Fig. 2.11 are examples. A general *two-terminal circuit* can be viewed as a black box of the sort shown in Fig. 2.12a, where the voltage V and the current I appearing at the external terminals

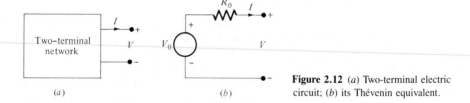

Figure 2.12 (*a*) Two-terminal electric circuit; (*b*) its Thévenin equivalent.

are of main interest. It can be shown that any two-terminal circuit consisting of resistors and voltage or current sources has the simple equivalent circuit shown in Fig. 2.12b, which consists of a voltage source V_0 in series with a resistor R_0. This circuit is called a *Thévenin equivalent circuit* after the nineteenth century French telegraph engineer M. L. Thévenin, who invented it.

Figure 2.13 illustrates two typical applications of resistors in the design of digital systems. In Fig. 2.13a a resistor R is being used to limit the current drawn by a *light-emitting diode* (LED), which forms an output device of the circuit N. When the output voltage V_{out} of N is zero, the output current I_{out} is also zero, and the LED is dark. When $V_{out} = 5$ V, then a current I_{out} flows through the LED, causing it to emit light whose intensity is proportional to the magnitude of I_{out}. Now the voltage drop across a

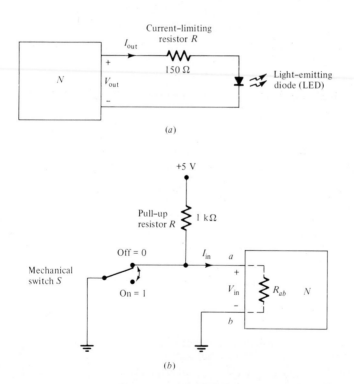

Figure 2.13 Two applications of resistors: (*a*) current-limiting resistor; (*b*) pull-up resistor.

conducting LED is approximately constant (at about 2 V) independent of I_{out}, and hence a large and dangerous current could flow through the LED unless a *current-limiting resistor* such as R were placed in series with it. The value of R is chosen to reduce I_{out} to a safe value that also causes the LED to produce light of reasonable intensity; a typical value of I_{out} is 20 mA.

Another important use of resistors is depicted in Fig. 2.13b. Here a mechanical on–off switch S is being used to generate the logic values 0 and 1 on an input line of the circuit N. Assume that a high voltage V_H in the range 2.4 to 5 V represents logical 1, while a low voltage V_L in the range 0.4 to 0 V (ground) represents logical 0. (These are the standard voltage levels used in many logic circuits.) N imposes a load that can be represented by the equivalent resistance R_{ab}, called the input resistance of N, which exists between the terminals a and b. Typically R_{ab} is a very large resistance—for example, 100 kΩ—so that N draws little current from its input circuits. Now consider the action of the switch S. If S is in the upper (off) position as shown in Fig. 2.13b, then the terminal a of N is connected directly to ground, so that the desired logical 0 value is applied to it. A current $I = 5$ mA flows through the external resistor R to ground via S. If S is in the lower (on) position, then a current I_{in} flows into terminal a, which is defined by the equation

$$I_{in} = \frac{5}{R + R_{ab}}$$

With $R = 1$ kΩ and $R_{ab} = 100$ kΩ, I_{in} is approximately 50 μA. Hence the voltage drop RI_{in} across R is about 0.05 V, which means that 4.95 V is applied to terminal a, a voltage that is well within the logical 1 range. If R were reduced to zero, then the voltage on a would be 5 V; however, the circuit would no longer work with the switch in the off position, since a would be connected to 5 V and ground simultaneously, resulting in indeterminate operation. Since R can be regarded as pulling terminal a up to the logical 1 value when the switch is on, R is termed a *pull-up resistor*.

2.1.3 Dynamic Circuits

In the previous subsection we discussed only circuits in which the various electrical parameters of interest (voltage, current, power, etc.) remain constant for long periods. If such parameters are plotted on a graph as a function of time, a simple *timing diagram* of the kind shown in Fig. 2.14a is obtained. Electrical parameters that vary with time are encountered in many situations. Figure 2.14b, for instance, shows another timing diagram, in which the magnitude of the parameter being plotted falls off with time. This might represent the voltage appearing at the terminals of an automobile battery over the battery's lifetime. Time-varying or *dynamic* electrical quantities will be denoted by small letters, and frequently will be described by timing diagrams. For example, v or $v(t)$ will be used to denote the (instantaneous) value of a voltage at the time instant t, while i or $i(t)$ will denote an instantaneous current.

Figure 2.15 depicts timing diagrams of a type called *periodic*, because they are formed from a fixed pattern that is repeated periodically at intervals of T seconds. T is called the *period* or cycle time of the periodic variable. From their wavelike appearance, the graphs of Fig. 2.15 are also referred to as *waveforms*. The number of cycles per

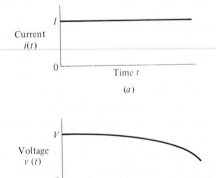

(a)

(b)

Figure 2.14 Timing diagrams for: (a) constant direct current and (b) decaying direct voltage.

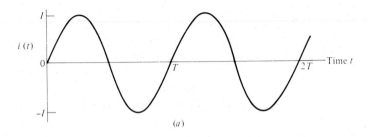

(a)

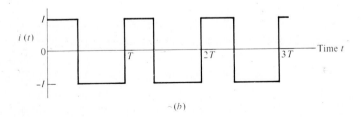

(b)

Figure 2.15 Periodic current waveforms: (a) sine wave; (b) square wave.

second f is called the *frequency* of the waveform. Frequency is measured in units called hertz (Hz), where 1 Hz is 1 cycle per second. Clearly,

$$f = \frac{1}{T} \quad \text{Hz}$$

The waveform of Fig. 2.15a is called a *sine wave* because it is the graph of the following sine equation:

$$i(t) = I \sin 2\pi f t$$

The instantaneous current $i(t)$ is said to be *sinusoidal*. Household electric current in the United States has a sinusoidal waveform with a frequency $f = 60$ Hz. The waveform of Fig. 15b is called a *square wave,* and $i(t)$ in this case is digital rather than analog since $i(t)$ can only assume the two values $\pm I$. Because the electric currents represented by Fig. 2.15 change direction continuously, they are referred to as *alternating (ac) currents*.

Figure 2.16 shows the sorts of electrical timing diagrams encountered in digital systems. The waveforms, voltage waveforms in this case, are confined to two values V_H and V_L, which typically represent the logic values 1 and 0 respectively. Figure 2.16a shows a periodic waveform of the type used as a synchronizing or clock signal in digital circuits. The waveform of Fig. 16b, which represents a stream of logical data, has no discernible pattern and is therefore *aperiodic*. This waveform consists of alternating intervals of value V_H and V_L. One such interval of value V_H (V_L) is called a V_H (V_L) *pulse,* so that waveforms such as those of Fig. 2.16 can be called *pulse sequences*. The frequency of an aperiodic pulse sequence may be defined as the average number of V_H pulses generated per second.

In addition to the sources and resistors considered so far, there are several electrical elements that play an important role in dynamic circuits. An element called a capacitor is illustrated in Fig. 2.17. In its simplest form a *capacitor* consists of two conducting plates that are separated by a thin insulator as indicated in Fig. 2.17a. Suppose that a charge of q coulombs is removed from one plate and transferred to the other. This results in a stable situation in which the opposite charges on the two plates attract each other via an electric field through the insulator; the insulator prevents a current from flowing between the plates that would neutralize their charges. In this state the capacitor is said to be storing a charge q. If the capacitors terminals a and b are connected via an external conductor K, then a current flows through K that discharges the capacitor, that is, neutralizes both of its plates. Since work can be done by this current, a capacitor is clearly an energy-storage element.

Suppose that a capacitor stores a charge of q coulombs. A potential difference of, say, v volts must exist between the plates of the capacitor. The ratio of the stored charge q

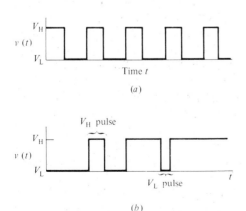

Figure 2.16 Digital waveforms: (*a*) periodic; (*b*) aperiodic.

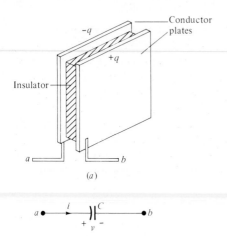

Figure 2.17 (*a*) Structure (simplified) of a capacitor; (*b*) symbol for a capacitor of C farads.

to the potential difference v across the capacitor is a constant C called the *capacitance* of the device. Capacitance is measured in units called farads (F); hence

$$C = \frac{q}{v} \quad \text{F} \tag{2.12}$$

The standard symbol for a capacitor of C farads is shown in Fig. 2.17b.

Suppose that a capacitor C is connected to an external circuit so that it is either charging or discharging. Let v denote the instantaneous voltage applied to C at any time, and let i be the corresponding current in C. Since i represents charge flowing per unit time, i is related to the instantaneous charge q stored in C by the integral equation

$$q = \int i \, dt$$

We therefore can rewrite Eq. (2.12) in the form

$$C = \frac{1}{v} \int i \, dt$$

from which it follows that

$$i = C \frac{dv}{dt} \tag{2.13}$$

Hence the current flowing in a capacitor is proportional to the rate of change of the voltage applied to the capacitor.

When a fixed external voltage v is applied to a capacitor C, the capacitor begins to charge rapidly until it stores a charge of $q = Cv$ coulombs. At that point, C is fully charged and no further current flows. Thus a fully charged capacitor to which a steady voltage is applied acts as an open circuit. If v is constant, then $dv/dt = 0$; therefore, by (2.13), $i = 0$. Suppose, on the other hand, that the voltage v applied to C is time varying;

that is, $dv/dt \neq 0$. Then C acts as a load device, transmitting a time-varying current $i \neq 0$, and consuming energy. If v changes value very rapidly, that is, if dv/dt is very large, then i can also assume very large values. Clearly large values of dv/dt are found in (periodic or aperiodic) voltage waveforms of very high frequency, such as the megahertz frequencies occurring in computer circuits. Consequently, when a voltage of very high frequency is applied to C, the capacitor approximates a short circuit offering little resistance to current flow. In summary, a capacitor allows little or no current to flow through it when it is subjected to a low frequency or steady voltage, while a high-frequency signal can flow through it largely unimpeded. Many of the uses of capacitors in digital system design are direct consequences of this general property.

The power consumption of a capacitor is easily calculated as follows: By definition $p = vi$; therefore, by (2.13),

$$p = Cv \frac{dv}{dt} \quad W \tag{2.14}$$

Since power is work or energy generated per unit time, the energy w stored in C is given by the relation

$$w = \int p \, dt \quad J$$

Hence from (2.14) we obtain

$$w = \int Cv \, dt = \frac{1}{2}Cv^2 \quad J \tag{2.15}$$

So far we have only considered phenomena arising from the electric field that surrounds every charged particle. This is the only force field associated with stationary charges. A moving electric charge also creates a magnetic field around itself. Thus a wire carrying an electric current is surrounded by a magnetic field with properties similar to those of the magnetic field of a permanent magnet. Conversely, if a conductor is held in a time-varying magnetic field (e.g., the field of a moving magnet), a voltage is induced between the ends of the conductor. The interaction of an electric current and its associated magnetic field determines the properties of another important electrical element called an inductor.

As Eq. (2.13) indicates, a capacitor has the property that the current i flowing through it directly proportional to the rate of change of the voltage v applied to it. An *inductor* may be defined as an element with the property that the voltage v across it is directly proportional to the rate of change of the current i flowing through it; that is,

$$v = L \frac{di}{dt} \tag{2.16}$$

The proportionality constant L in (2.16) is called the *inductance* of the device in question, and is measured in henries (H). v is the voltage induced in the inductor by the time-varying magnetic field created by i. Practical inductors are formed from coils of insulated wire as illustrated in Fig. 2.18a; the coiling serves to concentrate the magnetic field surrounding the wire. The standard circuit symbol for an inductor appears in Fig. 2.18b.

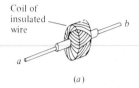

Coil of
insulated
wire

(a)

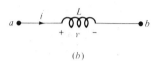

(b)

Figure 2.18 (a) Structure of an inductor; (b) symbol for an inductor of L henries.

The behavior of an inductor L closely parallels that of a capacitor C with voltages and currents interchanged, and magnetic fields replacing electric fields. For example, the energy stored in the magnetic field of an inductor L is given by the equation

$$w = \tfrac{1}{2}Li^2 \quad \text{J}$$

which is analogous to Eq. (2.15). While a capacitor presents an open circuit ($i = 0$) to a steady voltage or current source, an inductor presents a short circuit ($v = 0$). An inductor presents an open circuit ($i = 0$) to a time-varying source of very high frequency. In general, inductors are used much less often than capacitors in the electronic circuits of interest in this book.

It is important to realize that all real electric devices possess the properties of resistance, capacitance, and inductance to some degree. A short wire used as a connector in a circuit has a nonzero resistance R; however, R is usually so small that it can be ignored under most circumstances. Since a current flowing through a wire also creates electric and magnetic fields around it, causing different parts of the wire to interact with one another, the wire also has nonzero capacitance and inductance. Again these quantities are usually negligible; they may become significant at extremely high frequencies, however. Stray capacitance and inductance can also exist between different conductors in a circuit, producing unwanted interactions between the signals on the conductors. Thus a current flowing in one conductor can induce a small voltage of irregular waveform called *noise* in some other conductor that is adjacent to it (see Fig. 1.12).

Figure 2.19 shows an example of a resistance-capacitance (RC) circuit that is sometimes used to model the behavior of a physical connector. R represents the inherent resistance of the material, such as copper or aluminum, from which the connector is made, while C represents stray capacitance between the conductor and ground. Figure 2.19 also shows the effect of R and C on an ideal voltage pulse applied to the connector. Although V_{in} changes instantaneously from 0 to V volts at time t_1, V_{out} changes gradually. At t_1, C begins to charge at a rate whose magnitude depends on the values of R and C. Thus V_{out} rises gradually from 0 toward V as indicated in Fig. 2.19c. Similarly V_{out} falls gradually at t_2 since C discharges at a finite rate through R. Thus the capacitance C has the effect of rounding off the corners of square pulses; inductance has a similar effect.

The stray resistance, capacitance, and inductance of a connector or circuit element also affect some other aspects of the signals being transferred. For example, the gradual

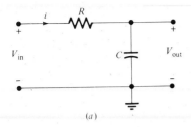

(a)

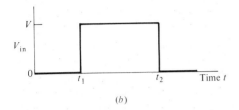

(b)

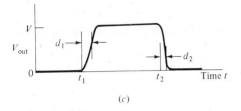

(c)

Figure 2.19 (a) Resistance-capacitance (RC) circuit representing a physical connector; (b) input pulse to the connector; (c) resulting output pulse.

signal changes depicted in Fig. 2.19c imply that changes in V_{in} are delayed before reaching V_{out}. Thus there is a rise-time delay d_1 before a change from 0 to V propagates through the circuit of Fig. 2.19a, and a fall-time delay d_2 before a change from V to 0 is propagated. Furthermore, if a current i flows through R, then $V_{out} = V_{in} - Ri$, so that V_{in} is degraded by the amount Ri before it reaches V_{out}. In addition, there is a power loss of Ri^2 watts in the resistance R. There is a further power loss due to C that depends on the frequency of the waveform being transmitted. The combined loading effect of all the resistance, capacitance, and inductance of a circuit is called the *impedance* of the circuit and is denoted by Z.

2.1.4 Semiconductor Devices

Semiconductors are solid materials whose electrical resistance is intermediate between that of conductors and insulators. Many semiconducting materials are known, including the elements silicon (Si) and germanium (Ge), and chemical compounds such as gallium arsenide (GaAs). We are concerned here only with silicon, which, in crystalline form, is by far the most important semiconductor currently used in the manufacture of electronic circuits.

As noted earlier, two kinds of electric charge carriers, electrons and holes, are present in semiconductors. In a pure semiconductor crystal the number of free electrons equals the number of holes, so that the crystal as a whole is electrically neutral. This balance between the charge carriers can be changed drastically by the addition of very small amounts of other substances to the crystal, a process called *doping*. The added substances, which are referred to as *impurities,* are typically used in concentrations of one impurity atom per 10^8 atoms of silicon. Each impurity atom replaces a silicon atom in the crystal structure so the crystal's physical structure is basically unchanged by the doping. However, the impurity atoms greatly increase the available supply of free electrons or holes, thereby altering the electrical characteristics of the crystal. Suppose that a substance such as arsenic (As) that has five valence electrons per atom is used to dope a silicon crystal. This increases the available supply of free electrons in the crystal since only four of an arsenic atom's valence electrons are needed to bind it to the surrounding silicon atoms (cf. Fig. 2.5). Semiconductor material doped in this fashion is called *n-type,* because negatively charged electrons become the predominant or *majority carriers* of electric current. Of course, holes are also available for electrical conduction, but they constitute the *minority carriers* in n-type semiconductor. If an impurity such as boron (B) that has only three valence electrons per atom is added to a pure silicon crystal, a surplus of holes results. Semiconductors doped in this way are called *p-type,* since positively charged holes are the majority carriers, while electrons are the minority carriers.

Two key components in electronic circuit design, diodes and transistors, are formed from single crystals of silicon that contain both p-type and n-type regions. The simpler of these is represented by the *junction diode* in Fig. 2.20. It is a two-terminal device composed of a single silicon crystal containing a p-type region in direct contact with an n-type region. The boundary between the two regions is called a *pn junction,* and gives the junction diode its name. A junction diode is the modern replacement for the point-contact crystal diode (Fig. 1.15) used in early radio receivers, and has numerous uses in electronic circuit design.

The essential features of diode behavior are illustrated in Fig. 2.21. The small squares denote stationary charged atoms, and the circles denote mobile charge carriers. Consider first the situation in Fig. 2.21a, where no external voltage is applied, in which case the diode is said to be *unbiased.* The p and n regions initially contain high

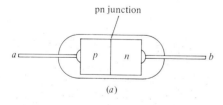

(a)

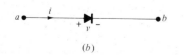

(b)

Figure 2.20 Junction semiconductor diode: (*a*) cross section; (*b*) symbol.

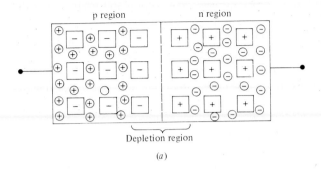

(a)

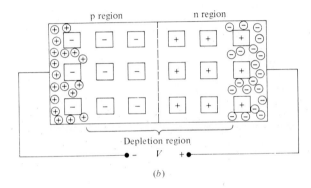

(b)

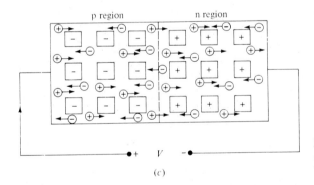

(c)

Figure 2.21 Behavior of a junction diode: (*a*) unbiased; (*b*) reverse biased; (*c*) forward biased.

concentrations of holes and free electrons respectively. It might be expected that the holes and electrons would diffuse across the pn junction until they became evenly distributed throughout the semiconductor material. In fact, this does not happen. Some initial diffusion of charge carriers does occur, but it causes a buildup of charge near the pn junction, which prevents further diffusion. For example, holes from the p region that cross the junction into the n region leave behind negatively charged atoms in the p region near the junction, as depicted in Fig. 2.21a. The negative atoms form a barrier that tends to repel any electrons that stray into the p region from the n region. A similar barrier of positively charged atoms forms in the n region near the pn junction, which tends to repel holes from the p region. Thus the p and n regions of the junction diode retain their original majority carrier concentrations, except for a small region around the pn junction. The latter region is largely devoid of mobile charge carriers and is therefore called the *depletion region*.

Now suppose that a voltage source S—a battery, for example—is connected to the terminals of a junction diode. If the negative terminal of S is connected to the p region of the diode as in Fig. 2.21b, the diode is said to be *reverse biased*. The positive terminal of S attracts the negatively charged electrons in the n region of the diode, and the negative terminal of S attracts the holes in the p region. Consequently majority carriers of both types are pulled away from the pn junction, so that little or no current can flow through the diode. A reverse-biased pn junction therefore acts as an open switch. If the connections to the source S are reversed, so that the positive terminal of S is connected to the diode's p region, then the diode is said to be *forward biased*. In this case majority carriers are propelled away from the battery terminals and can cross the pn junction. This permits a large current to flow through the diode, so that a forward-biased diode behaves as a closed switch. Note that when majority carriers have been propelled across the pn junction, at which point they become minority carriers, excess majority and minority carriers tend to neutralize each other, a process called *recombination*. This recombination releases a certain amount of energy, which, in the case of a light-emitting diode (LED), appears in the form of visible light (cf. Fig. 2.13).

On the basis of the foregoing somewhat simplified analysis, we can conclude that a junction diode has the voltage–current characteristics shown in Fig. 2.22a. No current flows while the diode is reverse biased, and an arbitrarily large current can flow while the diode is forward biased. A real junction diode has the voltage–current relationship depicted in Fig. 2.22b, which takes some secondary effects into account. The depletion region of the unbiased diode shown in Fig. 2.21a creates a small voltage drop v_{DR} across the pn junction, which opposes a forward-biasing external voltage v. Very little current flows through the diode until v exceeds v_{DR}, after which a relatively large current can flow. When the diode is reverse biased, a small current can flow through the diode because of the presence of minority carriers, some of which can be propelled across the pn junction by a reverse-biasing external voltage. If this reverse voltage is sufficiently large, then the minority carriers can collide with atoms of the crystal with sufficient energy to break the covalent electron bond, thereby releasing new charge carriers that can collide with other atoms, and so on. This condition is called *avalanche breakdown*, and it allows a large reverse current to flow through the diode. The normal operating range of a junction diode is indicated in Fig. 2.22b.

Figure 2.23 shows a representative application of a semiconductor diode in a circuit called a *rectifier*, whose function is to convert an alternating voltage into a direct voltage. Assume that the input to the rectifier is a sine wave v_{in} of the kind appearing in Fig. 2.23b. During the first half of each cycle of v_{in}, the diode D is forward biased, so that a current flows through the diode that drives the load device, and also charges the capacitor C. During the second half of a v_{in} cycle, D is reverse biased so no current flows through it. C, however, can now discharge through the load, supplying current to it until the start of the

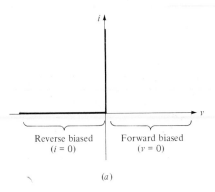

Reverse biased
$(i = 0)$

Forward biased
$(v = 0)$

(a)

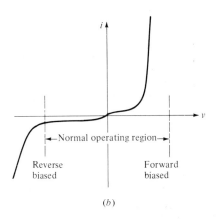

←Normal operating region→

Reverse
biased

Forward
biased

(b)

Figure 2.22 Voltage–current relationship of a junction diode: (a) ideal and (b) actual.

next v_{in} cycle. Thus the load device sees the voltage v_{out} whose waveform is in Fig. 2.23c; v_{out} approximates a steady direct voltage. If C were not present, v_{out} would consist of the top half of the sine wave, as indicated by the broken line in Fig. 2.23c. Thus C smooths out most of the fluctuations in v_{out}; such smoothing or filtering tasks form a major class of applications of capacitors in electronic design.

Many electronic circuits involve the transmission of electric signals through a series of subcircuits or stages, with some signal processing taking place in each stage. Each stage has some impedance, which would eventually degrade the current and voltage levels of the signals being processed to the point where they are no longer usable. Degraded signals of this sort must be restored periodically by an electronic circuit called an *amplifier*. Figure 2.24 shows, in simplified form, the general structure of an amplifier. The key component of this circuit is an amplifying element containing three or more interacting electrodes. The main amplifying devices are vacuum tubes, which are now largely obsolete, and bipolar and MOS transistors. Transistors are three-terminal devices fabricated from a single silicon crystal containing both p- and n-type regions. In general an amplifier produces an output current or voltage that is approximately linearly

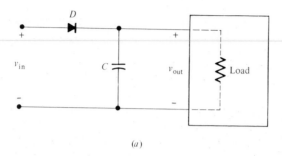

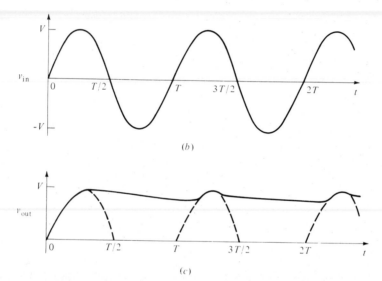

Figure 2.23 (*a*) Rectifier circuit; (*b*) alternating input voltage waveform; (*c*) dc output voltage waveform.

proportional to its input current or voltage. If s_{in} is the input voltage or current signal and s_{out} is the corresponding output signal, then

$$s_{out} = A\ s_{in}$$

where A is called the *gain* of the amplifier.

Voltages and currents are analog quantities that can vary continuously over an infinite range of values. We will be primarily concerned with binary digital circuits where there are only two signal values of interest, which are denoted abstractly by the symbols 0 and 1. If the IO signals of the amplifier circuit of Fig. 2.24a are binary, then the circuit is referred to as an *(amplifying) switch*. A typical switch has two states of operation:

1. An *off* state in which the output current i_{out} is zero; since no current flows through the load resistance R, $v_{out} = V$.

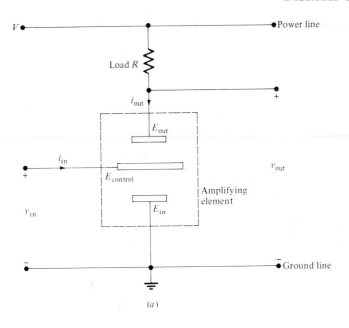

(a)

Amplifying Element	Electrode Names		
	$E_{control}$	E_{in}	E_{out}
Vacuum tube (valve)	Grid	Cathode	Anode (plate)
Bipolar (junction) transistor	Base	Emitter	Collector
MOS (field-effect) transistor	Gate	Source	Drain

(b)

Figure 2.24 (a) General structure amplifier; (b) representative amplifying elements.

2. An *on* state in which i_{out} has its maximum value; if the resistance between the input and output electrodes is then approximately zero, we obtain $i_{out} = V/R$ and $v_{out} = 0$.

Thus an amplifying switch allows a (small) voltage v_{in} to move the output voltage v_{out} through the full voltage range of the circuit's power supply. Complex circuits such as microcomputers make extensive use of transistor-based switches of this general type.

The *bipolar* or *junction transistor* is illustrated schematically in Fig. 2.25; Fig. 1.18 indicates the physical structure of a typical discrete transistor of this kind. It consists of three doped regions sandwiched together in either the pnp sequence of Fig. 2.25a or the

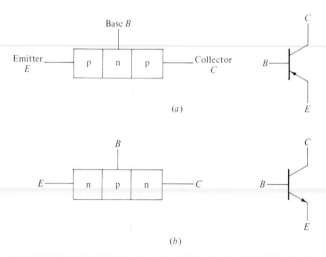

Figure 2.25 Structure and symbol for (a) pnp bipolar transistor and (b) npn bipolar transistor.

npn sequence of Fig. 2.25b. In each case the transistor contains two pn junctions, whose interaction determines the bahavior of the transistor. The central doped region, which is called the *base*, acts as the control electrode $E_{control}$; the two outer regions, called the *emitter* and *collector*, serve as E_{in} and E_{out}.

The action of the npn transistor of Fig. 2.25b may be summarized as follows: Suppose that the n-type emitter is grounded (i.e., held at 0 V), the p-type base is connected to a small positive voltage v, and the n-type collector is connected to a large positive voltage V. The base-emitter pn junction is then forward biased as in Fig. 2.21c, so that electrons are injected into the base and holes are injected into the emitter, causing a current i_{in} the flow from the emitter to the base. The base region is made extremely narrow, so that almost all the electrons injected into the base by i_{in} are transferred into the collector via diffusion. These injected electrons allow a large current i_{out} to flow between the collector and the emitter. If v, and therefore i_{in}, are reduced to zero, then the base no longer supplies electrons to the collector, and i_{out} also becomes zero. Thus i_{out} varies in a manner that is roughly proportional to i_{in}; that is,

$$i_{out} = A\ i_{in}$$

The current gain A of a bipolar transistor is typically 100 or more. A pnp transistor operates in essentially the same way as an npn transistor with the polarities (positive and negative signs) of the external voltages reversed. Bipolar transistors are so called because charge carriers of both polarities, positive holes and negative electrons, contribute directly to their operation.

Figure 2.26 illustrates the second type of transistor, the *MOS (metal-oxide semicon-ductor)* transistor or *field-effect transistor (FET)*. Like the bipolar transistor, it exists in two complementary forms, *pMOS* and *nMOS*, where the p or n prefix indicates the polarity of the (majority) charge carrier used to conduct current through the transistor. A pMOS (nMOS) transistor consists of two islands of p-type (n-type) material embedded in

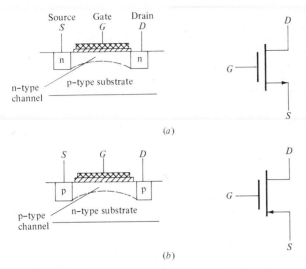

Figure 2.26 Structure and symbol for (*a*) nMOS transistor and (*b*) pMOS transistor.

a semiconductor substrate of the opposite polarity. These islands, called the *source* and the *drain*, form two of the transistor's electrodes. The output current i_{out} flows between the source and the drain through a region of the substrate called the channel. Superimposed above the channel, and separated from the substrate by a thin layer of silicon dioxide insulator, is a (metal) electrode called the *gate*. This is the control electrode, and corresponds to the base in a bipolar transistor. A voltage applied between the gate electrode and the substrate creates an electric field in the channel region (the field effect), which controls the magnitude of i_{out}. To illustrate this action, consider an nMOS transistor in which both the source terminal and the substrate material are grounded. Suppose that a small positive voltage v_{in} is applied to the gate, while a large positive voltage V is applied to the drain. The pn junction between the source and the substrate is unbiased, and the pn junction between the drain and the substrate is reverse biased, so that no current flows between the source or drain and the substrate. The positive voltage v_{in} on the gate tends to attract electrons to the channel region under the gate, converting that part of the p-type substrate into n-type material temporarily. This n-type channel region constitutes a conducting path between the n-type source and drain regions, and allows a relatively large source-drain current to flow; the magnitude of this current i_{out} is roughly proportional to v_{in}. When v_{in} is reduced to zero, the temporary n-type channel disappears and i_{out} also becomes zero. Note that the gate electrode and the underlying substrate act very much like the plates of a capacitor, storing a charge in the layer of insulator that separates them. Because of the delay associated with charging and discharging this capacitance (cf. Fig. 2.19c), MOS transistors tend to have larger propagation delays (slower operating speeds), than their bipolar counterparts.

If a bipolar or MOS transistor is used as the amplifying element in Fig. 2.24a, a simple amplifier circuit results. Many practical amplifiers contain additional circuit elements to increase gain, reduce delay, adjust the shape of the output signal waveform, and so on. Logic devices such as NAND gates (see Fig. 1.3) are typically designed around transistor amplifiers, with additional components to perform logical operations. Many different circuit configurations are used for logic gates; these circuit types are divided into *logic families* with such names as TTL (transistor-transistor logic) and CMOS (complementary MOS). Logic families will be considered in more detail later.

2.2 INTEGRATED CIRCUITS

Modern electronic systems make extensive use of integrated circuits, that is, circuits manufactured from a single monolithic piece (chip) of semiconductor material. In this section we examine the methods employed to make ICs, and the basic transistor circuits used to perform logical operations.

2.2.1 Manufacturing Processes

Electronic circuits are composed of conductors, insulators, and various types of semi-conductors. To fabricate an IC, it is necessary to be able to combine these materials to form a solid circuit containing all the required electric devices and their interconnec-tions. The element silicon by itself can, with suitable physical or chemical modification, act as a conductor, an insulator, or a p-type or n-type semiconductor. Integrated-circuit fabrication typically begins with a set of thin disks or *wafers* of crystalline silicon, each of which serves as the foundation or *substrate* on which a large number of identical IC chips can be fabricated simultaneously. Figure 2.27 indicates in general terms how a silicon substrate can be altered to form regions with the various desired electrical properties. In its pure state crystalline silicon is a poor conductor of electricity. Polycrystalline silicon—or *polysilicon*—is composed of many minute silicon crystals or grains that are packed together in irregular fashion. The grain boundaries have the effect of increasing the density of available charge carriers, thereby increasing the electrical conductivity of the silicon so that it approaches that of a metal. Polysilicon finds various uses in IC fabrication; for instance, it is often used instead of metal to form the electrodes of MOS transistors. In most cases, however, a metal such as aluminum, which is a better

Conducting Property	Materials Used	Fabrication Methods
Conductor	Aluminum, polysilicon	Vacuum deposition
Semiconductor		
Pure	Pure silicon	Crystal growth from liquid
p- or n-type	Doped silicon	Diffusion, ion implantation, epitaxy
Insulator	Silicon dioxide pn junctions	Oxidation
		Doping (see above)

Figure 2.27 Fabrication of conductors, semiconductors, and insulators in a silicon IC.

conductor of electricity than polysilicon, is used to create conducting pathways within an IC. Metal and polysilicon regions are typically created by vacuum deposition on the silicon substrate using apparatus similar to that of Fig. 1.21. Very good adhesion is obtained between the different materials, so that metal, silicon, and polysilicon layers form a single continuous solid.

Various techniques are known for adding impurities to pure silicon to create p-type and n-type semiconducting regions. A popular method is *diffusion*, in which the silicon substrate is heated to a high temperature in a furnace while being exposed to gases containing the desired impurity materials or dopants. Impurity atoms diffuse into the exposed silicon surface to create a doped layer. Note that this technique may be used to convert p-type silicon to n-type, and conversely. Impurity atoms may also be injected into the silicon via a high-velocity beam of ions—that is, electrically charged atoms of the desired impurity, a method called *ion implantation*. A third approach, called *epitaxy*, is to deposit a layer of doped crystalline silicon on the silicon substrate. This is done in such a way that the added epitaxial layer and the underlying substrate form a single crystal; in other words, the atoms of the epitaxial layer and the substrate are aligned with one another in crystalline fashion.

An especially valuable property of silicon is the fact that silicon dioxide—*oxide* for short—is an excellent insulator. It is also very hard and durable, and is unaffected by many chemicals used in the etching steps of IC fabrication. A layer of oxide can easily be formed on a silicon substrate by heating it in the presence of certain substances containing oxygen; this process is called *oxidation*. Oxide layers are typically used to separate metal conductors from semiconductors in an IC. A second insulation mechanism used in ICs is the reverse-biased pn junction. As illustrated in Fig. 2.21b, such a junction approximates an open switch, and so can be used to insulate p-type and n-type semiconductor regions from one another.

The manufacturing processes outlined above are characterized by the fact that each creates a layer of new material on the surface of a silicon wafer. As a result an IC is composed of a few thin layers of conductors, insulators, and semiconductors on a thick silicon substrate that provides mechanical support for the circuit. The depth of the various surface layers is measured in micrometers (microns), while the surface area of the IC is generally measured in square millimeters. An IC is therefore essentially a two-dimensional or planar device. All the electrical elements of the IC are laid out on its surface in a nonoverlapping manner; the interconnections between the elements can overlap to a limited extent.

An IC is constructed in a sequence of steps each of which creates a layer of some specific material on the surface of the circuit. For example, a diffusion step is used to create p-type or n-type regions in some subset of the circuit's components, while a metalization step creates connections among components. Each step requires that certain regions on the surface of a wafer be exposed to a fabrication process such as diffusion of impurities or deposition of metal, while the remaining parts of the wafer are shielded from this process. Thus in each step a layer of some material must be placed on selected areas of the wafer according to a precise geometrical configuration or pattern; this operation is called *patterning*. The required pattern for each layer is first formed on a photographic template called a *mask*. Then, by using methods analogous to photoengraving, an exact image of the mask is transferred to the surface of the IC wafer so that the new surface layer is formed only in the regions of the wafer that correspond to either the opaque or the transparent regions of the mask. The complexity and cost of manufacturing an IC may be measured by the number of masks (i.e., the number of patterning operations) it requires; six masks is a typical number.

Figure 2.28 illustrates a representative IC patterning step. The starting point is a silicon wafer that already may have several circuit layers on its working surface. A uniform layer of new material is first placed on the wafer surface as shown in Fig. 2.28b; the nature of this layer, which we will refer to as L, depends on the particular patterning operation to be performed. In diffusion and insulating steps L is usually silicon dioxide and is formed by oxidizing the silicon surface of the wafer in a special furnace. In other processes, such as metalization and epitaxy, L is formed by depositing new material on the wafer surface.

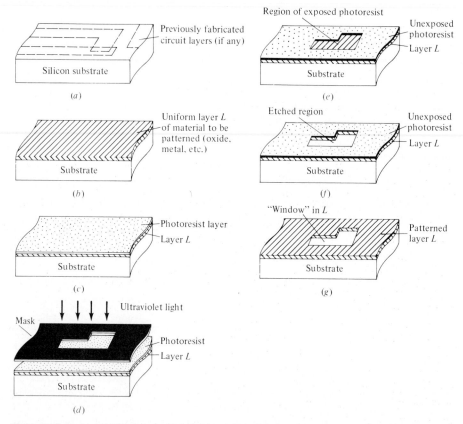

Figure 2.28 Integrated–circuit patterning process: (*a*) bare silicon wafer; (*b*) wafer coated with layer L of material to be patterned; (*c*) photoresist coating; (*d*) masking and exposure; (*e*) photoresist development; (*f*) etching of layer L; (*g*) photoresist removal.

The remaining task is to move selected areas of L, which generally take the form of polygon-shaped "windows," so that the desired geometrical pattern is formed in L. To this end L is coated with a thin layer of material called photoresist (or simply resist), as shown in Fig. 2.28c. Photoresist is light-sensitive like the coating on ordinary photographic film. It also has the property of resisting attack by the chemicals used to etch L, and hence the term "resist." The photoresist layer is then exposed to ultraviolet light, or other suitable forms of radiation, via a photographic mask placed on or near the surface of the wafer; this step is illustrated in Fig. 2.28d. Each desired window in L is represented by a transparent region of the mask, so that the areas of the photoresist layer that are exposed to the external radiation mark the windows of L. Next the photoresist is developed by means of an appropriate developing agent that dissolves the exposed photoresist, but leaves the unexposed photoresist intact as shown in Fig. 2.28e. At this point an etchant is applied to the wafer surface that attacks the material of L but does not affect the photoresist material. This removes the material of the L layer in the window regions that are unprotected by photoresist, resulting in the situation depicted in Fig. 2.28f. Finally, the remaining photoresist is dissolved by a suitable solvent, yielding the patterned layer L of Fig. 2.28g, which contains an exact image of the mask. If L is intended solely to act as a conducting, semiconducting, or insultating layer, then one fabrication step has been completed and a new one can be initiated. In the case of a diffusion process, an additional step is required. The material of the patterned layer L is silicon dioxide, and the windows of Fig. 2.28g are placed over silicon areas whose impurity content is to be altered. The wafer is then placed in a diffusion furnace that allows impurity atoms to diffuse into the parts of the wafer surface that are not protected by the oxide layer.

The design of a complex IC is a long and costly process. It has two closely related aspects:

1. System or functional design that involves selection of appropriate circuit components, and determination of their interconnections to meet the given behavioral specifications
2. Circuit layout that involves specification of the mask patterns for the various components, and the placement of these patterns and their interconnections on a plane corresponding to the surface of the IC chip

The system design problem here is similar to other hardware design problems such as the design of a system on a printed-circuit board using ICs as components. In this case the components must be chosen so that the corresponding IC layouts can be readily constructed. Often a library of standard IC designs is maintained for such common components as registers and amplifiers. The IC designer can draw on predefined designs of this sort, which are sometimes called *macrocells*, in designing new circuits. A major goal in IC layout is the minimization of the total wafer area occupied by the circuit. This, of course, maximizes the number of copies of the IC that can be fabricated simultaneously on a single silicon wafer, thereby reducing the cost per chip.

Once the system design and layout of a new circuit have been completed, the layout description is converted into a set of masks for the various patterning steps needed to manufacture the IC. Each mask shows the geometrical pattern of a particular layer of each IC on the wafer. The mask used in a metalization step, for example, shows a pattern of aluminum connectors, and is quite similar to the masks used to make printed circuit boards (see Fig. 1.20), but is on a much smaller scale. Mask design generally begins with a large-scale drawing of the desired pattern. Mask patterns may be drawn manually, or they may be generated semiautomatically using *computer-aided design* (CAD). In the latter case, the layout information must be specified in digital form, as a computer program, for example, which can be used to control a pattern-generating machine. CAD methods are essential to the production of LSI/VLSI devices such as microprocessors and microcomputers. Once completed, the large-scale mask is reduced photographically by a factor of a thousand or so until it is the size of the IC itself. The final mask used in the IC production process is typically a glass plate about the size of the silicon wafer. Enough copies of the IC mask pattern are packed onto this disk to cover the entire wafer.

The starting point in the manufacture of an IC is a large crystal of silicon that has the form of a cylinder and is about 10 cm in diameter. Such crystals are obtained by pulling a small seed crystal slowly from a bath of molten silicon. Some of the molten silicon solidifies and adheres to the seed crystal, thereby enlarging it. Elaborate precautions are taken to ensure the purity and uniformity of the silicon. Controlled amounts of p-type or n-type impurities can be added to the molten silicon to produce a crystal that is uniformly doped. The crystal cylinder is sawn into thin wafers, which are then highly polished to provide a smooth surface on which ICs can be fabricated.

Figure 2.29 outlines the process by which ICs are manufactured from the silicon wafer. A series of patterning operations involving oxidation, diffusion, metalization, and similar processes are performed to produce multiple copies of the desired IC on the wafer. Each IC chip (or *die,* as it is often called at this stage) is then tested by a testing machine that uses needle-like probes to make contact with various contact points on the chip. Test signals are injected into the circuit, and the circuit's responses are recorded and checked. If the chip fails to meet its predetermined electrical and functional specifications, then it is marked with ink and subsequently is discarded. After all circuits have been probed and tested, they are removed from the wafer. This is most frequently done by scribing horizontal and vertical lines along the chip boundaries with a diamond-tipped tool. Pressure is then applied to the wafer, causing the individual chips to break off. The chips marked defective are eliminated at this stage.

The next step is to encapsulate the IC chip in a package that provides mechanical protection for the chip, and large electrical terminals called *leads* or *pins* for connecting the chip to other circuits. First the chip is firmly attached to a protective case of plastic or ceramic material that contains the necessary number of pins. Then connections are made between the pins and relatively large metal areas on the chip called the *pads*. This may be done by means of fine wires that are bonded to the chip pads and the package pins. The entire package is then hermetically sealed. The packaged IC is subjected to a final battery of tests. The circuits that pass these tests are now ready for shipment.

Figure 2.30 shows three of the most commonly used IC package types. The leads or pins of these packages are all designed for easy mounting on printed circuit boards. The metal-case *TO-5 package* (TO stands for transistor outline) of Fig. 2.30a is used mainly for single transistors and fairly simple ICs. The most widely used package is the *dual in-*

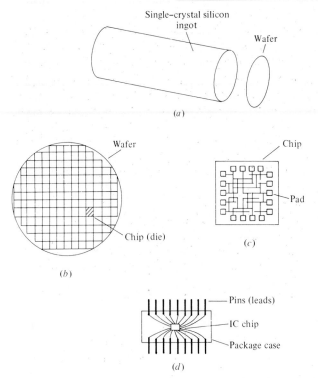

Figure 2.29 Major steps in IC manufacture: (*a*) wafer preparation; (*b*) patterned wafer; (*c*) separated IC chip; (*d*) packaged chip.

Figure 2.30 Three common IC packages: (*a*) TO–5 package; (*b*) dual in–line package (DIP); (*c*) flatpack.

line package (DIP) of Fig. 2.30b. It is characterized by two parallel rows of pins attached at right angles to the package case. Adjacent pins in each row are 0.1 inch (2.54 mm) apart. The total number of pins used in DIPS varies from 2 to 64 or more; a typical LSI circuit requires about 40 pins. The *flatpack* package of Fig. 2.30c is similar to a DIP, but is thinner and has its pins in the same plane as the case.

Generally speaking, several hundred chips are fabricated simultaneously on a single silicon wafer. A significant number of these chips fail the wafer probe tests and must be rejected. Integrated-circuit manufacturing defects have many sources. Since the features on an IC mask are often only a few micrometers wide, ICs are easily destroyed by tiny defects on the wafer surface, or slight misalignments of the masks used in patterning. A speck of dust on a mask can cause a region of a circuit containing perhaps several connectors or transistors to be improperly processed, rendering the entire IC inoperable. The percentage of correctly working chips obtained from a wafer is called the *yield* for that particular IC. Since the cost of processing a wafer is fixed, the higher the yield, the lower is the cost per chip. When production of an IC begins, particularly in the case of an IC involving new circuit layout methods or processing methods, the yield obtained is often quite small, perhaps 15 percent. As the manufacturer gains experience with the production of the IC, yields tend to improve, often dramatically, allowing the price of the IC to be reduced. The chip packaging process is one of the most difficult steps to automate; it therefore tends to be one of the more costly manufacturing steps. The production cost of an IC is also influenced by the cost of testing it at various stages in the production process. Testing complex ICs such as microprocessors and large memory chips can be very time consuming, and contributes significantly to the overall production costs.

2.2.2. Passive Components

Next we examine the techniques used to manufacture specific electrical elements into a silicon IC, beginning with *passive* devices that are incapable of signal amplification. The pn junction discussed earlier has a key role in the structure of many IC elements, including resistors, transistors, and diodes. These elements are frequently built from a sequence of p-type and n-type layers that are separated by pn junctions. A major use of these pn junctions is to isolate components from one another. We therefore first examine the fabrication of a single pn junction on the surface of a silicon wafer. This is generally done using some version of the planar process, which, as discussed in Sec. 1.2, was originally developed by Fairchild in 1958, and was a key step in the establishment of IC technology.

Figure 2.31 illustrates the planar process for making a pn junction. The starting point is a silicon wafer that has been uniformly doped with p-type impurity during the crystal growth phase. This forms a p-type substrate on which an "island" of n-type silicon is created to form the desired pn junction. A layer of silicon dioxide about 1 μm thick is grown on the wafer surface. Then the patterning process of Fig. 2.28 is used to pattern the oxide layer so that an opening or window is formed that defines the desired n-type region; this is illustrated in Fig. 2.31b. An n-type region is created under the window by a diffusion step in which the wafer is heated to a very high temperature while exposed to a gas containing appropriate n-type impurity material such as phosphorous. The impurity atoms diffuse into the parts of the wafer surface that are unprotected by the oxide layer. This forms a layer of n-type semiconductor directly under the oxide window, as depicted in Fig. 2.31c. The depth of this layer, which is generally a few micrometers, can be precisely controlled by setting the temperature and duration of the diffusion step. Once the wafer is returned to room temperature, diffusion of the impurity atoms halts, and the new n-type region becomes a permanent part of the wafer. The boundary between the diffused n-type region and the p-type substrate constitutes the required pn junction. The procedure of Fig. 2.31 can also be used to form a p-type island in an n-type

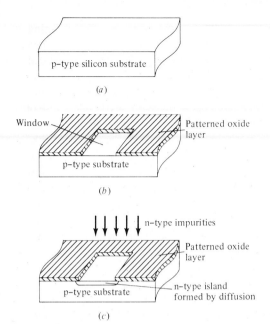

(a)

(b)

(c)

Figure 2.31 Fabrication of a pn junction by the planar process.

substrate. By repeating the planar process several times, alternating layers of p-type and n-type material can be produced.

If the pn junction of Fig. 2.31c is reverse biased, the island is effectively isolated electrically from the substrate; an electrical element can be built into the island by additional fabrication steps. Figure 2.32 shows an alternative way of producing islands of n-type material in a p-type substrate. This process is used to fabricate bipolar ICs, because it yields a more suitable pn junction for isolating bipolar transistors than the diffused junction of Fig. 2.31. First an n-type epitaxial layer is grown on the surface of a p-type substrate. Then a diffusion step is carried out using p-type impurities; this produces a p-type "moat" that surrounds the desired n-type island. The p-type diffusion layer is made to penetrate the expitaxial layer completely, so that it effectively becomes part of the substrate. A component such as a transistor can then be built into the n-type island by additional patterning steps. This is the standard method used for component isolation in bipolar ICs. Special pn junctions of this type are not needed in MOS ICs because, as Fig. 2.26 shows, an MOS transistor is automatically isolated from the substrate by a pn junction. As a result MOS transistors can be packed more closely together than bipolar transistors.

Perhaps the simplest IC element to manufacture is a junction diode. Figure 2.33 shows the structure of such a diode as it might appear in a bipolar IC. It is fabricated in the following steps, which are intended to accommodate transistor fabrication also.

1. An n-type island is formed over a p-type substrate by means of the epitaxy and diffusion technique of Fig. 2.32; this step provides an isolating pn junction for all devices on the same wafer.

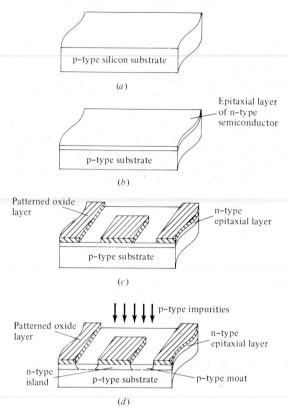

Figure 2.32 Standard junction isolation process for bipolar ICs.

2. A second diffusion is carried out, this time using p-type impurities to create a p-type island within the n-type island.
3. A patterned oxide layer is formed that insulates the wafer surface, except where it is desired to make contact with the underlying p- and n-type regions. Windows are positioned in the oxide layer at all desired contact points.
4. A patterned metal (aluminum) layer is formed that makes contact with the diode via the oxide windows, and provides interconnections between devices on the chip.

The resulting device contains two pn junctions that act as junction diodes; see Fig. 2.33c. The inner pn junction defines the main circuit diode D_1. The outer pn junction D_2 serves to isolate D_1 from the substrate and other devices on the same IC. The substrate is normally maintained at the maximum negative voltage used in the circuit, so that D_2 is always reverse biased, thereby isolating the n-type epitaxial island from the substrate. Arbitrary signal voltages can then be applied to the terminals a and b of the circuit diode D_1 without affecting the rest of the IC, except as provided by the metal interconnections.

Another fairly simple IC component is a resistor, which is an essential element in biopolar ICs. (As will be seen later, transistors are often used in place of resistors in MOS circuits.) Figure 2.34 outlines one possible way of forming a resistor in a bipolar IC. It

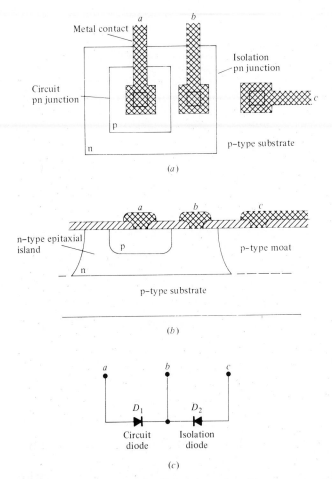

Figure 2.33 Integrated junction diode: (*a*) top view; (*b*) cross section; (*c*) equivalent circuit.

uses exactly the same sequence of fabrication steps as the junction diode of Fig. 2.33. As in the diode case, the outer pn junction serves to isolate the circuit element. The inner p-type region forms the resistor proper. The value of the resistance produced, R ohms, is determined by the length and cross-sectional area of this region, as well as by the resistance offered by the p-type material. Since (doped) silicon is a semiconductor, it has relatively low electrical resistance, and consequently it may be necessary to make the p region very long and narrow in order to produce high values of R. This tends to consume an excessive amount of the available wafer area. A further problem is that it is difficult to control the value of R during manufacture; R may vary by as much as 20 percent from the desired value.

A number of special effects occur at the junction between a metal and a semiconductor. In most cases a simple low-resistance contact between the metal and the semiconductor is required at such a junction; this is the case for the devices of Figs. 2.33 and 2.34.

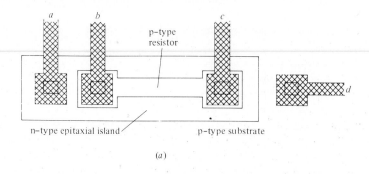

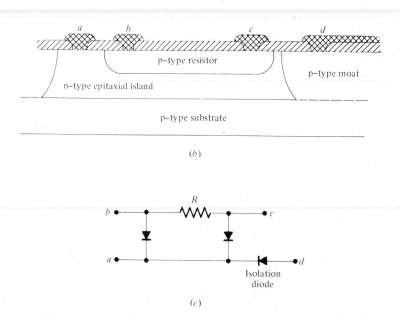

Figure 2.34 Integrated resistor: (*a*) top view; (*b*) cross section; (*c*) equivalent circuit.

Since aluminum can act as a p-type impurity, there is some tendency for a small p-type region to form under an aluminum contact to an n-type region, for example, contact *b* of Fig. 2.33. This spurious effect can be counteracted by doping the n-type region under the contact more heavily than usual. This heavily doped region is denoted n^+, where the plus superscript indicates the heavy doping; it is formed by a separate diffusion step. An n^+ region is normally placed under contact *a* of Fig. 2.34.

The contact between a metal and a semiconductor can also act as a rectifier called a *Schottky diode*. This phenomenon is the basis of the crystal detector of Fig. 1.15. The metal–semiconductor interface must be extremely clean and free of defects for it to act as a rectifier; careful processing thus is needed to produce a Schottky diode by the deposition of metal on a silicon wafer. The presence of impurities or n^+ doping at the contact swamps the rectifying property to produce a nonrectifying contact termed an *ohmic contact*. As will be discussed later, Schottky diodes are useful for improving the performance of bipolar ICs. An integrated Schottky diode is illustrated in Fig. 2.35.

Capacitors can be formed in ICs in a number of ways. Most IC devices contain considerable stray capacitance, which is often exploited in lieu of explicit capacitors. For example, a reverse-biased pn junction can serve as a capacitor with the depletion layer (see Fig. 2.21) acting as the insulator. However, its behavior is far from that of an ideal capacitor, because the width of the depletion layer, and therefore the effective capacitance, varies with the applied voltage. A better integrated capacitor can be made as illustrated in Fig. 2.36, which uses silicon dioxide as the insulator. A layer of semiconductor serves as one plate, while a metal layer serves as the other. A heavily doped n^+ region is employed to reduce contact resistance of the connection to the lower semiconductor plate. This device, although commonly used in bipolar ICs, is called an *MOS capacitor*—a name reflecting its composition from superimposed metal, oxide, and semiconductor layers. A typical MOS transistor has a capacitance of 40 pF or so; larger capacitors are avoided because of the large area they need.

Integrated-circuit resistors and capacitors of the types discussed usually can be manufactured economically only with a small range of values, thus limiting their usefulness. Transistors, on the other hand, despite their appearance of greater complexity, can be manufactured more easily using most IC technologies, and they occupy less chip area. There is thus a tendency to substitute transistors for resistors and capacitors

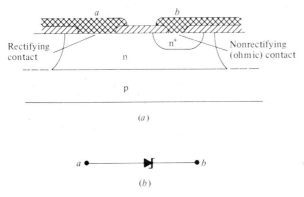

Figure 2.35 Integrated Schottky diode: (*a*) cross section; (*b*) symbol.

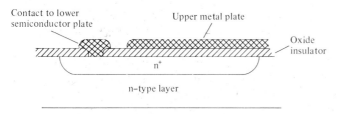

Figure 2.36 Cross section of an MOS capacitor.

wherever possible. As a result, most LSI/VLSI circuits, particularly MOS ICs, consist almost entirely of transistors. We turn next to the design of transistors for integrated circuits.

2.2.3 Transistors

As observed earlier, there are two distinct classes of transistors, bipolar junction transistors and MOS field-effect transistors. Bipolar transistors contain three alternating layers of p-type and n-type material, and thus come in two varieties, npn and pnp, as indicated in Fig. 2.25. Additional semiconductor layers are often used to provide pn junction isolation from the wafer substrate, or to improve the transistor's electrical behavior. The npn transistor is used somewhat more frequently than the pnp type in IC designs, because it has slightly superior electrical characteristics. Figure 2.37a shows in cross section the essential structure of an integrated npn transistor. It is quite similar to the junction diode of Fig. 2.33, but contains an extra n-type island. This type of transistor is manufactured in the following steps.

1. An n-type island is formed on a p-type wafer by the epitaxy and moat diffusion process described in Fig. 2.32. The pn junction thus created will isolate the transistor from the substrate, while the n-type island will act as the collector of the transistor.

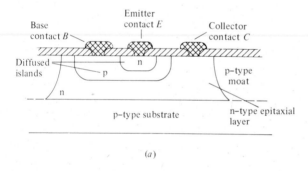

(a)

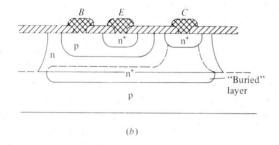

(b)

Figure 2.37 Cross section of an npn transistor: (a) basic structure; (b) structure with buried n^+ layer.

2. A p-type diffusion is carried out, yielding a p-type island that constitutes the base region.
3. An n-type diffusion is performed to produce the emitter region within the base region.
4. A patterned oxide layer is formed with windows that define contact points to the transistor's base, emitter, and collector regions.
5. A patterned metal layer is produced that makes the necessary connections to the transistor.

Figure 2.37b shows another npn transistor with better electrical properties. The metal contact to the n-type collector region is improved by doping the contact area more heavily. This n^+ contact layer is produced in the same diffusion step used to form the emitter region, and so does not require a special mask. The performance of the transistor can be further improved by creating an n^+-type "buried" layer under the connector as shown in Fig. 2.37b. This requires a new n^+ diffusion step, which is performed before the n-type epitaxial layer is grown on the wafer surface. The buried layer serves to lower the resistance between the collector contact and the collector region of the transistor. During the second n^+ (emitter) diffusion step, the buried layer tends to diffuse upward, as suggested by the broken lines in Fig. 2.37b, to join the n^+ island at the collector contact. Note the same use of an n^+ layer in the MOS capacitor of Fig. 2.36. The pnp transistors have essentially the same structure as npn transistors, with the p- and n-type regions interchanged. Figure 2.38 shows how a pnp transistor might be manufactured on a wafer that also contains npn transistors of the kind appearing in Fig. 2.37b. The n-type epitaxial region is now used for isolation purposes only, while the outer p-type island serves as the collector. An extra p^+-type island is added to the structure of Fig. 2.37b to act as the emitter of the pnp transistor; a p^+ layer is also used to improve the contact to the p-type collector region. Many variations of these processes for producing bipolar transistors exist, which attempt to reduce the chip area used or to improve such operating characteristics as power consumption or switching speed.

As the simplified cross-sectional diagrams of Fig. 2.26 suggest, MOS transistors are somewhat easier to fabricate than their bipolar counterparts. The source and drain regions can be produced in a single diffusion step, so that they form two islands in a substrate of opposite polarity. An oxidation step is used to provide the insulating layer under the gate, while a subsequent metalization step creates the metal gate, and the necessary contacts to the source and drain. Figure 2.39 shows the structure of a pMOS transistor of this type. The pn junction between the p-type regions forming the source, drain, and channel and the n-type substrate is reverse biased during normal operation, thereby isolating the transistor proper from the substrate. Thus no special pn junction is needed for isolation purposes, which is an important advantage of MOS circuits. The metal gate of Fig. 2.39 must be aligned precisely between the source and drain regions, and hence special care must be taken during the metalization step.

As in the case of bipolar transistors, there are many different ways of fabricating MOS transistors in integrated circuits. Figure 2.40 illustrates the widely used *silicon-*

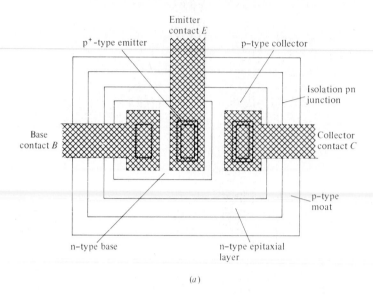

(a)

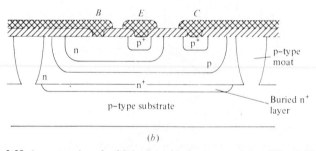

(b)

Figure 2.38 A pnp transistor for fabrication with the npn transistor of Fig. 2.37a: (a) top view; (b) cross section.

gate method for the nMOS case. Distinguished by the use of a polysilicon layer for the gate electrode instead of metal, the process is as follows:

1. First a p-type silicon wafer is subjected to oxidation and patterning to define the gate, source, and drain regions, whose relative positions are as in the metal-gate transistor of Fig. 2.39. The n-type diffusion to form the source and drain is not performed at this point, however.
2. A very thin layer of oxide is now grown over the entire surface of the wafer, as shown in Fig. 2.40b.
3. A layer of polysilicon is grown on the wafer surface and patterned to create the gate electrode as indicated in Fig. 2.40c; the thin oxide layer constitutes the gate insulator.

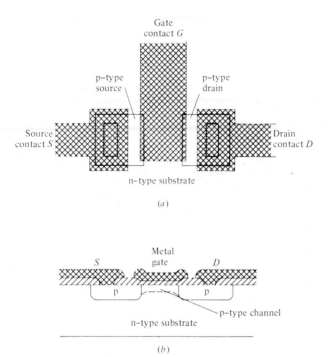

Figure 2.39 Metal-gate pMOS transistor: (*a*) top view; (*b*) cross section.

4. The wafer is etched to remove the thin oxide layer from all areas except those protected by polysilicon. This exposes the thick oxide windows created in step 1, which define the source and drain areas.

5. An n-type diffusion is performed that produces the source and drain electrodes as indicated in Fig. 2.40d. Note that the (poly)silicon gate is "self-aligning," because its edges are also edges of the source and drain diffusion windows. Thus the problem of accurately aligning separate diffusion and metal masks to define the gate electrode has been eliminated.

6. A third (thick) oxidation layer is grown, which is patterned to define contact windows to the gate, source, and drain regions.

7. A final metalization step creates the necessary metal contacts to the transistor.

It can be seen from Fig. 2.40 that an nMOS transistor fabricated by the silicon-gate process consists of diffusion, polysilicon, and metal layers that are insulated from one another by silicon dioxide. This allows the polysilicon and diffusion layers to be used as connectors by themselves, although their higher electrical resistance makes them inferior to metal connectors. This higher resistance is tolerable in VLSI circuits where connectors are very short and carry small electric currents. Thus if the metal connectors are eliminated, the nMOS transistor of Fig. 2.40f reduces to the very simple structure of Fig. 2.41, consisting of a polysilicon "connector" that crosses over a diffusion

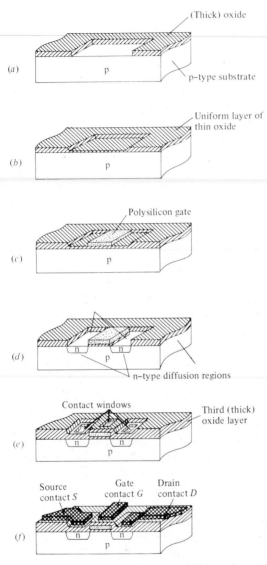

Figure 2.40 Fabrication of a silicon-gate nMOS transistor: (*a*) first oxidation; (*b*) second (thin) oxidation; (*c*) polysilicon gate patterning; (*d*) etching and source-drain diffusion; (*e*) third oxidation; (*f*) addition of metal contacts.

"connector." The two connectors are separated from each other by a thin oxide layer and, as in Fig. 2.40d, there is no diffusion region under the crossover region. The crossover region therefore acts as the transistor's gate, while the two ends of the diffusion connector act as the source and drain. This simplified MOS transistor is the basis of an important VLSI design methodology that allows system designers who are not specialists in IC

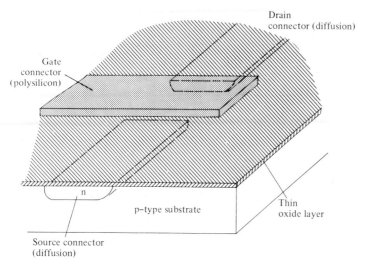

Figure 2.41 Simplified nMOS transistor with polysilicon and diffusion connectors.

design to design complex chips, including microprocessors and microcomputers; the interested reader is referred to Mead and Conway (1980) for details.

2.2.4 Transistor Circuits

The actions of bipolar and MOS transistors were described informally in Sec. 2.1. Figure 2.42 shows some voltage–current graphs that provide a more detailed picture of bipolar transistor action. The circuit of Fig. 2.42a, consisting of an npn transistor T and a (load) resistor R, is a specific instance of the general amplifier circuit of Fig. 2.24a. A bipolar transistor is considered to be a current-controlled amplifier, where the base current I_B controls the larger collector current I_C.* The relationship between I_B, I_C, and the collector voltage $V_C = V_{out}$ is illustrated by Fig. 2.42b. For simplicity we assume that the input voltage $V_B = V_{in}$ is proportional to the input current I_B. This assumption and the data of Fig. 2.42b lead to the IO voltage relationship depicted in Fig. 2.42c. Two states of operation of the circuit are of particular interest. When $V_{in} = 0$, both I_B and I_C are also approximately zero, in which case the transistor is said to be operating in the *cutoff* region or the switched-off state. Since the current I_C through the load resistor R is zero, $V_{out} = V_C$, its maximum possible value. As V_{in} and I_B are increased, I_C also increases. The point

---

* The following standard naming conventions for the currents and voltages associated with a transistor are employed throughout this book. Let X be the first letter appearing in the name of a transistor electrode (base, collector, emitter, gate, source, or drain). Then we have:

V_X = (average) voltage appearing at X

I_X = (average) current flowing into X

V_{XX} = power supply voltage connected to X

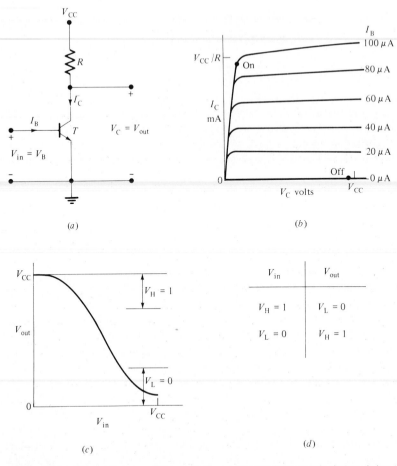

Figure 2.42 (a) Basic bipolar amplifier circuit (inverter); (b) voltage-current characteristics; (c) input-output voltage characteristics; (d) logical behavior (truth table).

is eventually reached where further increase in I_B causes little or no increase in I_C, in which case the transistor is said to be in *saturation* or the fully switched-on state. In this condition I_C is approximately V_{CC}/R, its maximum possible value, while V_{out} is close to zero. Thus the saturation and cutoff regions represent the operating conditions where the circuit's output voltage V_{out} assumes its minimum value zero and its maximum value V_{CC} respectively. Note that these voltage values, zero (ground) and V_{CC}, correspond to the two voltages provided by the circuit's power supply.

It is usual to associate the output voltages of a transistor operating in or near the cutoff and saturation regions with the logic values 0 and 1, where the higher voltage V_H

corresponds to 1 and the lower voltage V_L corresponds to 0. In most cases V_H and V_L also correspond to the power supply voltages. In the circuit of Fig. 2.42a, for instance,

$$V_H = V_{CC} = \text{logical } 1$$

$$V_L = 0 = \text{logical } 0$$

Because actual voltage signals fluctuate, it is necessary to make the logical 0 and 1 values correspond to voltage ranges rather than single voltage values, as indicated in Fig. 2.42c. The allowable 0 and 1 voltage ranges are precisely defined for commercial digital ICs. The voltage values falling between the 0 and 1 ranges represent indeterminate or unknown conditions from a logical point of view; this indeterminate region is only encountered while signals are switching from one logic value to the other. Figure 2.42d summarizes the logical behavior of the circuit of Fig. 2.42a under static or steady-state conditions. Note that a 0 input signal yields a 1 output signal, and vice versa. For this reason, the circuit in question is variously called an *inverter* (0 and 1 are each other's inverses) or a NOT gate (not-0 is 1 and not-1 is 0) when used in a digital system.

Figure 2.43 illustrates the dynamic or time-varying behavior of the bipolar amplifier circuit. In the off state the two pn junctions of T are effectively reverse biased and so present significant capacitance to the input signal I_B or V_B. In the on or saturated state the pn junctions of T are forward biased, and more closely resemble perfect conductors. It follows that switching the transistor between the on and off states involves changing the distribution of charge carriers, a change that cannot take place instantaneously. Thus, like the RC circuit of Fig. 2.19, output signal changes are delayed with respect to input signal changes, leading to the IO waveforms of Fig. 2.43. The average delay between input and output signal changes is called the *switching time* or *propagation delay* of the

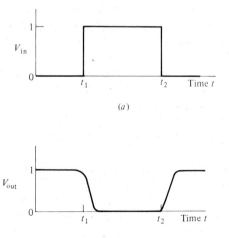

(a)

(b)

Figure 2.43 Dynamic behavior of a transistor inverter.

circuit. It is generally desirable to make this switching time as small as possible. Practical bipolar inverters or amplifiers therefore contain additional circuitry to decrease switching time, and otherwise improve the circuit's performance.

Figure 2.44a shows the structure of a basic MOS amplifier circuit that is essentially the same as the bipolar circuit of Fig. 2.42a, with an nMOS transistor replacing the npn bipolar transistor. An MOS transistor is a voltage-driven device, so that the input gate voltage V_G replaces the input base current I_B as the controlling parameter. The IO voltage relationship of the MOS amplifier is plotted in Fig. 2.44b; it is quite similar to that of Fig. 2.42c. The output voltage $V_{out} = V_D$ varies inversely as the input voltage $V_{in} = V_G$. The logic values 0 and 1 can again be associated with the saturation condition ($V_D \approx 0$ and $I_D \approx V_{DD}/R$) and the cutoff condition ($V_D \approx V_{DD}$ and $I_D \approx 0$) respectively. The waveforms of Fig. 2.43 also describe the dynamic behavior of this MOS inverter. The construction of an MOS transistor implies that the gate electrode and the underlying silicon substrate act as the plates of a relatively large capacitor. In most MOS circuits the substrate is held at ground potential, so that the gate capacitance must charge and discharge through the maximum voltage range of zero to V_{DD} volts. This gate capacitance is larger than the corresponding input capacitance in a bipolar inverter, resulting in longer charge–discharge times, and hence longer switching times. Therefore, MOS circuits tend to be slower than the corresponding bipolar circuits. The large input capacitance of an MOS transistor also allows it to be used as a memory element, since a packet of charge carriers, representing logical 0 or 1, can be stored for relatively long periods in the gate-substrate capacitor.

Digital systems are often constructed from transistor circuits called *logic gates*. A typical gate takes the form of an (inverting) amplifier like those of Figs. 2.42 and 2.44, preceded by an input circuit or stage that combines the input logic signals according to certain rules that define the function of the gate. (Logic gates and their behavior are examined in depth in Chap. 3.) Additional circuit stages may be included in a gate to increase its switching speed, improve the shape of its output waveforms, and so on.

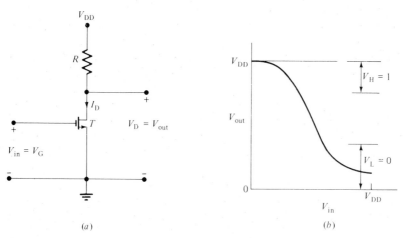

(a)   (b)

Figure 2.44 (a) Basic MOS amplifier circuit (inverter); (b) input-output voltage characteristics.

Several generic circuit configurations are known for constructing logic gates; these constitute the IC *logic families*. For example, the important *TTL* (*transistor-transistor logic*, also abbreviated T²L) family is characterized by the use of transistors for both the input stage and the subsequent amplifier stage(s). Circuits of the older, and now obsolete, *DTL* (*diode-transistor logic*) family use diodes instead of transistors in the input stage. Besides sharing a common electronic circuit structure, family members are *compatible* with one another. Compatibility in this context means using the same current or voltage signal ranges to represent logic values, and generating output signals that can be directly connected to the input lines of other family members. Different families may be incompatible in one or more ways, necessitating the use of special interface circuits to link members of the different families in a common circuit.

An ideal logic family of ICs would combine high-speed operation, low power consumption, low production cost, and ease of use in system design. The existence of numerous incompatible logic families stems from the fact that all practical logic families deviate from the ideal in some respect. For example, bipolar logic families are relatively fast, but also have relatively high power consumption. Some MOS families, on the other hand, have very low power consumption, but they tend to be slower than bipolar circuits performing the same functions. The digital system designer is therefore faced with several distinct IC families, whose use involves various trade-offs with respect to speed, power consumption, and other design factors.

Figure 2.45 lists some major IC families of interest to digital system designers. Early bipolar ICs employed either resistors as in *RTL* (*resistor-transistor logic*) or diodes as in DTL for forming logic combinations of their input signals. These logic families have been superseded by TTL, where transistors, including those with two or more emitters, are used for both logical operations and signal amplification. Most SSI and MSI ICs currently used in digital system design are manufactured using TTL technology. Another bipolar logic family *ECL* (*emitter-coupled logic*) uses a transistor circuit structure that results in shorter switching times than TTL, but at the expense of higher power consumption. This family is used to build large fast computers, but the high power

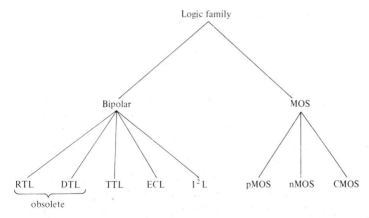

Figure 2.45 Some important IC logic families.

consumption of ECL circuits, which require special cooling facilities, greatly limits its use in microcomputers. The last bipolar family I^2L (*integrated injection logic*) is perhaps closest to being the ideal logic family. However, the technology for manufacturing I^2L circuits is complex and relatively immature; consequently they are not widely used at the present time. There are three major families in the MOS category. The *pMOS circuits* use pMOS field-effect transistors almost exclusively, while *nMOS circuits* use nMOS transistors. The pMOS ICs are somewhat easier to manufacture than equivalent nMOS circuits. However, pMOS circuits are inherently slower than nMOS, because the holes used as charge carriers in pMOS transistors have lower mobility than the electrons used in the nMOS case. The *CMOS* (*complementary MOS*) circuits combine both pMOS and nMOS transistors in approximately equal numbers in a manner that results in extremely low power consumption. All the MOS logic families are used in the manufacture of microprocessors. New variants of the foregoing families are constantly appearing in the marketplace. For instance, *Schottky TTL* is a version of TTL that adds Schottky diodes to standard TTL circuits to reduce their switching time.

2.3 DESIGN USING ICs

The characteristics of three important IC families—TTL, nMOS, and CMOS—are discussed next. Various practical issues in the design of digital systems from ICs are considered, including loading constraints and interconnection techniques.

2.3.1 Transistor-Transistor Logic

Transistor-transistor logic has long been one of the most popular logic families. Many low-cost TTL ICs in the SSI/MSI range are commercially available. The TTL gates are characterized by the use of two or more stages of transistor circuits for performing logical operations and signal amplification. They are relatively fast devices; a TTL gate has a switching time (propagation delay) of 10 ns or less. The power consumption of TTL gates, on the other hand, can be relatively high, with the figure of 10 mW per gate being typical. As we will see later, there are several TTL subfamilies that trade off speed and power consumption in various ways. These gates tend to use more IC chip area than equivalent MOS gates. This fact, coupled with the generally higher power requirements of TTL, tends to limit the use of TTL and other bipolar technologies in the production of LSI/VLSI circuits.

To illustrate the design of TTL circuits, we consider the logic gates defined in Fig. 2.46. The *AND gate* of Fig. 2.46a is characterized by the fact that the output signal z (usually represented by a high voltage V_H) is 1 if the input signals x_1 *and* x_2 are also 1; $z = 0$ otherwise. The behavior of the AND gate, that is, the AND logical function, is fully defined by the truth table in Fig. 2.46a. Figure 2.46b specifies another important logic gate, the NAND gate. The name NAND is an abbreviation of NOT AND, and stems from the fact that the NAND truth table can be obtained by inverting, or forming the NOT function of, the output column of the corresponding AND gate truth table. Thus the output of a NAND gate is 0 if and only if all input signals are 1. NAND is one of the most

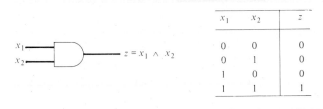

x_1	x_2	z
0	0	0
0	1	0
1	0	0
1	1	1

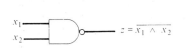

$z = x_1 \wedge x_2$

(*a*)

x_1	x_2	z
0	0	1
0	1	1
1	0	1
1	1	0

$z = \overline{x_1 \wedge x_2}$

(*b*)

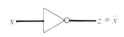

$z = \overline{x}$

x	z
0	1
1	0

(*c*)

Figure 2.46 Symbols and truth tables for three basic logic gates: (*a*) AND gate; (*b*) NAND gate; (*c*) inverter or NOT gate.

useful logic functions, and can readily be implemented using many different technologies (cf. Figs. 1.3–1.5). As will be seen in Chap. 3, NAND is a universal logic operation, which means that any digital system can be constructed using only NAND gates as building blocks. The inverter or NOT gate, which is also defined in Fig. 2.46, can be regarded as a one-input version of a NAND gate. The AND operation is denoted by the special symbol $\wedge$ in this book, and the inversion operation is denoted by an overbar. Thus, as shown in Fig. 2.46b, the output function implemented by the NAND gate can be represented by the logic equation

$$z = \overline{x_1 \wedge x_2}$$

An *n*-input NAND gate, where $n = 1, 2, 3, \ldots$, generates the function

$$z = \overline{x_1 \wedge x_2 \wedge \cdots \wedge x_n}$$

An electronic circuit that constitutes a simple TTL NAND gate appears in Fig. 2.47a. Like most TTL gates, its input signals x_1 and x_2 are applied to the emitters of a multiemitter transistor. Such transistors are easily constructed in bipolar ICs by adding extra emitter islands to the basic transistor structure of Fig. 2.37. The behavior of this TTL gate can best be understood by considering the roughly equivalent DTL circuit of Fig. 2.47b. Here the multiemitter transistor T_1 is replaced by a set of diodes, one for each pn junction in T_1. The subcircuit composed of the diodes D_1 and D_2 and the resistor R_1 behaves like an AND gate for the following reasons. If an input signal, say x_1, is set to 0 (ground voltage), the corresponding input diode D_1 becomes forward biased, so that $y = x_1 = 0$. If x_1 and x_2 are both set to 1, then D_1 and D_2 are reverse biased. Essentially no current flows through R_1 under these conditions, so the potential of line y becomes

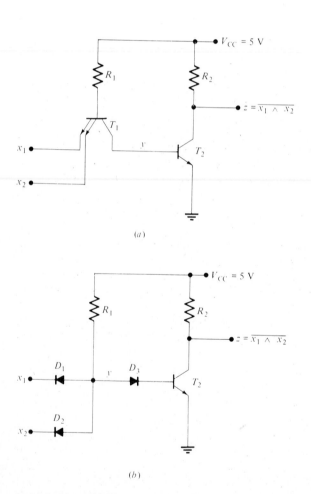

(a)

(b)

Figure 2.47 (a) Essentials of a TTL NAND circuit; (b) roughly equivalent DTL circuit.

approximately $V_{CC} = 1$. The logic signal appearing on line y is, therefore, the AND function of the gate's imputs, that is,

$$y = x_1 \wedge x_2$$

Now y is also the input to an inverter composed of T_2 and R_2 (cf. Fig. 2.42), so that the output signal z is $\bar{y}$. It follows that z realizes the desired NAND function, namely,

$$z = \overline{x_1 \wedge x_2}$$

The multiemitter transistor T_1 of Fig. 2.47a takes up less chip area and has better electrical characteristics than the corresponding diode circuit of Fig. 2.47b. For instance, T_1 speeds up the operation of the circuit by rapidly withdrawing the stored charge from the base of T_2 when the latter is changing from the saturated to the cutoff state. Figure 2.48 shows a possible IC design for this TTL NAND gate. A p-type substrate is used. It contains three n-type epitaxial islands: one for the two resistors R_1 and R_2, one for the normal npn transistor T_2, and one for the slightly larger multiemitter transistor T_1. The p-type diffusion step needed for the base regions of T_1 and T_2 is also used to form the resistors. Note that the resistors and transistors in this IC have the structures shown in more detail in Figs. 2.34 and 2.37 respectively.

The performance of the TTL gate of Fig. 2.47a has several deficiencies. Suppose, for example, that it is required to drive an output load device that possesses a fairly large input capacitance C. Thus a load capacitance of C farads is effectively connected between the output line z and ground. When the output transistor T_2 is switched off, implying the z should be logical 1, or about V_{CC} volts, a current I must flow through R_2 to

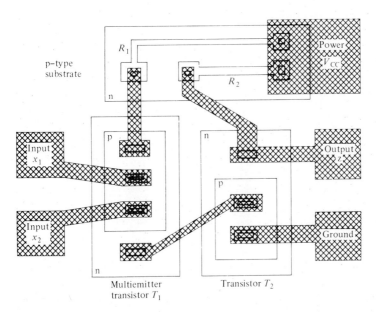

Figure 2.48 Possible IC implementation of the TTL NAND gate of Fig. 2.47a.

charge C to the V_{CC} level. As Fig. 2.19 indicates, charging and discharging a capacitor takes time, and introduces a signal propagation delay that increases with the values of R_2 and C. Since R_2 also must have a fairly large value (1.6 kilohms is typical), the maximum current that can be drawn through R_2 is fairly small. This limits the number of other gates that can be connected to the output of the TTL gate under consideration, since the input circuits of every gate draw some current from the circuit that feeds or drives them. The maximum number of other gates from the same family that can be connected to the output of a gate G is called the *fan-out* of G. (The *fan-in* of G is the maximum number of gates that can be connected to the input lines of G, which is simply the number of input lines present in G.) Thus we can say that the simple TTL gate of Fig. 2.47a has low fan-out or, equivalently, low output drive capability.

The performance of the foregoing TTL gate can be greatly improved by adding another amplifier stage to increase its output drive capability. Figure 2.49 shows such a design, which is found in many commercial TTL ICs. The output signal y generated by transistor T_2 is further amplified by the output stage containing two transistors T_3 and T_4 connected in a "totem-pole" configuration. The stages containing T_1 and T_2 operate in essentially the same way as the circuit of Fig. 2.47a: When either primary input signal x_1 or x_2 is 0, T_1 switches on, causing T_2 to switch off; when $x_1 = x_2 = 1$, T_1 is off while T_2 is on. When T_2 is off, there is no voltage drop across R_4, so T_4 switches off. At the same time, the collector y of T_2 goes to a high voltage level, causing T_3 to switch on. Hence the gate output signal z assumes the 1 value required for the NAND function. Note that in this state, an output device can draw a relatively large current through the small resistor R_3. Thus the output drive of this circuit is higher than that of the circuit in Fig. 2.47a. Now consider the case when T_2 is switched on and z should be 0. The resistors R_2 and R_4 are chosen so that the base w of T_4 assumes a low voltage level (about 0.7 volt), which,

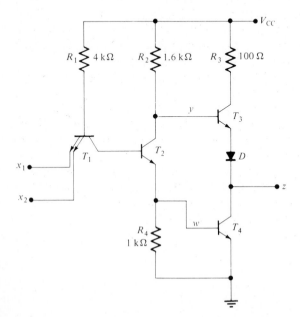

Figure 2.49 TTL NAND circuit of the type used in commercial ICs.

however, is sufficient to switch T_4 into the on (saturated) state. The voltage applied to the base y of T_3, which is at approximately the same potential as w when T_2 is on, might be expected to turn T_3 on also. This is prevented by the diode D, which reduces the base-to-emitter voltage drop across T_3 to a level that forces it into the cutoff region. Thus only T_4 is switched on, causing z to be pulled down to the desired 0 level. In this state the gate presents a relatively low resistance to any other gates that are connected to z. It thus can draw current from a relatively large number of other gates while maintaining z in the logical 0 voltage range. Hence the fan-out of this TTL gate is high both when $z = 1$ and when $z = 0$. Note that when $z = 1$, the gate acts as a *current source* that supplies current to its output line, while if $z = 0$, it acts as a *current sink*, drawing current from its output line. The low internal resistance of the output stage of Fig. 2.49 compared with that of Fig. 2.47a means that the capacitance presented by load devices can be charged and discharged faster, resulting in shorter switching times. We conclude, therefore, that the addition of the totem-pole output stage to the basic gate of Fig. 2.47a increases both the circuit's operating speed and its output drive capability.

Because of their popularity, many common TTL logic circuits have been standard-ized, and are available from numerous IC manufacturers. There is an important group of TTL circuits known as the *7400 series*, which includes hundreds of different ICs with standard numerical part numbers that all begin with the digits 74, a convention originally introduced by Texas Instruments. The 7400 designation refers to "commercial-grade" ICs with an operating temperature range of 0 to 70°C. There is also a *5400 series* containing ICs that are identical to the corresponding 7400-series members, but have the "military" temperature range of -55 to 125°C. All 7400-series devices require a single 5-V power supply. High voltages in the range 2 to 5 V represent logical 1, and low voltages in the range 0 (ground) to 0.8 V represent logical 0. Most members of this series are available packaged in DIPs or flatpacks of the kind depicted in Fig. 2.30. All 7400- or 5400-series ICs with the same part number, say 74xyz or 54xyz, can be expected to have similar pin assignments, perform the same logical functions, and have the same electri-cal characteristics. Different ICs in the series have similar IO drive requirements, and therefore are electrically compatible with one another.

Figure 2.50 describes two SSI members of the 7400 series. The circuit of Fig. 2.50a, whose part number is 7404, contains six separate inverters, and is referred to informally

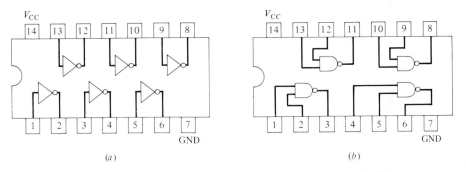

Figure 2.50 Two 7400-series ICs: (*a*) 7404 hex inverter; (*b*) 7400 quad two–input NAND.

as a "hex" inverter IC. It is housed in a 14-pin package (DIP or flatpack) with the pin assignments indicated in the figure. Twelve pins are assigned to the IO lines of the six inverters; the remaining two pins are assigned to power (V_{CC} or 5 V) and ground (GND or 0 V). The IC with the part number 7400 (not to be confused with the series name) contains four 2-input NAND gates, and so is called a quad NAND-gate IC. It is also housed in a 14-pin package with the indicated pin assignment. Relatively simple ICs of the foregoing types are available for less than $1 from many suppliers. There are also 7400-series ICs in the MSI and LSI ranges. Complete listings of the currently available 7400 circuits can be found in the catalogs, often called TTL or logic data books, provided by the major IC manufacturers (Texas Instruments, 1973; National Semiconductor, 1981b).

Besides the *standard* TTL family considered thus far, several other TTL subfamilies are available, which differ in their switching speed, power consumption, and other considerations. *Schottky TTL* is a family in which Schottky diodes (see Fig. 2.35) are connected between the base and collector terminals of most transistors in the corresponding standard TTL circuits. The Schottky diodes prevent the transistors from entering the fully saturated region, thereby eliminating the charge-storage delays associated with saturation. This allows the transistors to switch state more rapidly, but at the expense of higher power consumption. Figure 2.51 shows a Schottky-clamped transistor of the type found in Schottky TTL ICs. A variant of Schottky TTL, called *low-power Schottky TTL*, uses different resistance values to reduce power consumption; unfortunately operating speed is also reduced to the standard TTL level. Figure 2.52 lists some typical perfor-

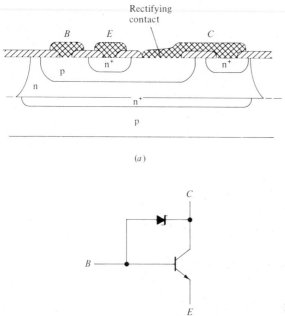

(a)

(b)

Figure 2.51 Schottky-clamped integrated npn transistor: (*a*) cross section; (*b*) equivalent circuit.

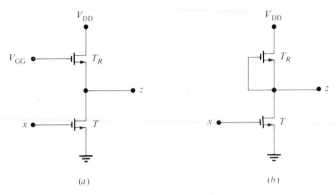

Figure 2.54 Two all-transistor nMOS inverter circuits.

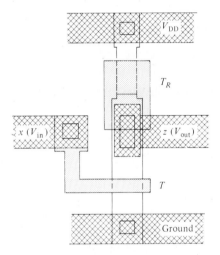

Figure 2.55 Integrated-circuit implementation of the nMOS inverter of Fig. 2.54*b* using silicon–gate technology.

subjected to a special processing step (ion implantation) to modify its electrical characteristics, so that it behaves like a resistor rather than a switch.

MOS logic gates are easily constructed by connecting additional switching transistors in series or in parallel with the switch T of an inverter. Figure 2.56 shows a two-input nMOS NAND gate formed by placing a second transistor in series with the transistor T of the inverter design in Fig. 2.54a. The input signals x_1 and x_2 are applied to the gate terminals of transistors T_1 and T_2 respectively. If both x_1 and x_2 are 1, then transistors T_1 and T_2 assume the on (switch closed) state, setting z to 0, as in Fig. 2.53a. If either x_1 or x_2 is 0, then one of the transistors T_1 or T_2 is off (switch open), allowing T_R to pull the output signal z up to 1 as illustrated in Fig. 2.53b. Thus z realizes the NAND function $\overline{x_1 \wedge x_2}$ as required.

The structure of an MOS transistor is such that the gate electrode and the underlying substrate region act as the plates of a capacitor. Thus MOS logic circuits present a relatively large capacitance C to signals applied to their input lines. In the inverters of

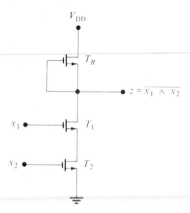

Figure 2.56 An nMOS NAND circuit.

Fig. 2.54, for instance, V_{in}, the input voltage corresponding to the logical signal x, is connected across, or "sees," the gate-substrate capacitance C of transistor T. The speed at which C can be charged and discharged limits the circuit's overall operating speed. This incidental capacitance C has another important property, namely, it can store the current value of the input signal V_{in} if the source of V_{in} is temporarily disconnected. In other words, the input capacitance C remembers V_{in} for short periods, say a few hundred milliseconds, until stray discharge paths in the IC cause any stored charge in C to leak away. This charge storage property is exploited in a class of MOS logic circuits called *dynamic* circuits, in which individual subcircuits are periodically disconnected from the power supply by means of periodic control signals called *clock* signals. During periods when a subcircuit is disconnected from its power source, information on its state is stored in the capacitance C of the various transistors present. Before a charge stored in C can leak away, the power is reconnected to restore C to its fully charged level, a process termed *refreshing*. This continuous switching on and off of the power supply connections reduces a circuit's average power consumption, and can also lead to simpler circuits for certain operations. Logic circuits that do not control the power connections in the foregoing fashion are termed *static* circuits.

Figure 2.57 contains an example of a dynamic MOS logic circuit *SR* that is called a *shift register*. It is basically formed by connecting in series identical copies of the MOS inverter circuit considered previously. The output z_j of inverter stage I_j is connected to the input x_{j+1} of the next inverter stage I_{j+1} via a transistor switch S_j. The gate terminals of the S_j's are connected to a pair of clock signals ϕ_1 and ϕ_2, which control the dynamic operation of the circuit. These signals, which together form a *two-phase clock* signal, have the waveforms depicted in Fig. 2.57b. The waveforms are identical, but out of phase (out of step) with each other. An important aspect of the ϕ_1 and ϕ_2 waveforms is that they are nonoverlapping in the sense that ϕ_1 and ϕ_2 never assume the logic value 1 simultaneously. ϕ_1 is connected to the odd-numbered transistors $S_1, S_3, \ldots$, while ϕ_2 is connected to even-numbered transistors $S_0, S_2, \ldots$. Hence when transistors $S_1, S_3, \ldots$ are switched on, transistors $S_0, S_2, \ldots$ are switched off, and vice versa. When S_j is off, little or no current can be drawn by I_{j+1} from the power supply via the preceding stage I_j.

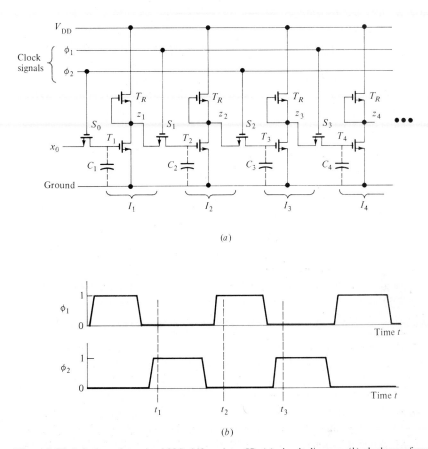

(a)

(b)

Figure 2.57 A 2-phase dynamic nMOS shift register SR: (a) circuit diagram; (b) clock waveforms.

The signal z_j applied by I_j to I_{j+1} is, however, stored in the input capacitance C_{j+1} associated with I_{j+1} and represented by a capacitor in the circuit diagram of Fig. 2.57a.

The dynamic shift register SR of Fig. 2.57 behaves as follows. Suppose that the input signal $x_0(t_1) = 1$ is applied to input line x_0 at time t_1. Since ϕ_2 is then 1, as indicated in Fig. 2.57b, S_0 switches on, allowing a 1 to be applied to the input x_1 of inverter stage I_1. This causes the input capacitance C_1 of I_1 to be charged to the 1 voltage level. Now $\phi_1 = 0$ at t_1 so S_1 is switched off, preventing the changes occurring in I_1 from affecting the next stage I_2. At time t_2, ϕ_1 is 1, while ϕ_2 is 0. The change in ϕ_2 causes S_0 to switch off, but the stored charge in C_1 causes transistor T_1 to remain on; that is, the state of I_1 does not change. Since S_1 is now on, the output signal $z_1(t_2) = 0$ of I_1 is connected to the input x_2 of I_2. This allows C_2 to discharge via S_1 and T_1, so that the output of I_2 assumes the value $z_2 = \bar{z}_1(t_2) = x_0(t_1) = 1$. In other words, during the period t_1 to t_3 representing one complete clock cycle, the external input signal $x_0(t_1)$ is transferred unchanged from line x_0 to line z_2. At the same time $x_2(t_1)$ is transferred to line z_4, $x_4(t_1)$ is transferred to z_6, and so on. Thus as long as the clock signals ϕ_1 and ϕ_2 are active, information is shifted continuously from left to right in *SR*, and hence its name shift register. Each pair of adjacent inverters can be viewed as storing 1 bit of information for one clock period; hence if *SR* contains $2n$ inverter stages, it can store up to n bits of information simultaneously. If the rightmost output line z_{2n} of *SR* is connected to the leftmost input x_0, a closed circuit is obtained around which data can be circulated, and therefore stored, indefinitely. This type of shift register is a basic memory device in dynamic MOS logic circuits. A variety of other circuit structures and clocking techniques are used to design dynamic circuits.

An important MOS logic family with extremely low power consumption is CMOS (complementary metal-oxide-semiconductor). In CMOS circuits pMOS and nMOS transistors are paired in a way that eliminates the need for load resistors or transistors, thereby also eliminating the power loss associated with any electrical resistance. The transistors used in CMOS circuits all act as switches, and their power consumption is primarily due to stray capacitance. Because of this a CMOS circuit's power consumption, although very small, tends to increase with the circuit's operating frequency. In addition to having low power requirements, CMOS devices are relatively insensitive to fluctuations in logic signal levels or the power supply voltage, and are readily made compatible with TTL circuits. The main disadvantage of CMOS is the use of a larger number of transistors per gate than other logic families, which tends to increase circuit complexity and chip area.

Figure 2.58 shows a fundamental CMOS inverter circuit comprising two transistors, a pMOS transistor T_1 and an nMOS transistor T_2. When the input signal x becomes 1, T_1 switches off while T_2 switches on, causing the output line z to be connected to ground (logical 0) via T_2; this is illustrated in Fig. 2.58b. Conversely, when x becomes 0, T_1 switches on and T_2 switches off, so that z is connected to V_{DD} (logical 1) via T_1 as shown in Fig. 2.58c. The complementary roles played by the pMOS and nMOS transistors in the operation of this circuit are at the root of the name CMOS. The same approach can be used to implement other logic functions. For example, it is easily verified that the CMOS circuit of Fig. 2.59 acts as a two-input NAND gate. Note again how the pMOS and nMOS transistors complement one another. Also note that more transistors are needed than in the nMOS NAND gate of Fig. 2.56.

The layout of an IC that implements the CMOS inverter of Fig. 2.58 is shown in Fig. 2.60. Circuit fabrication is complicated by the fact that the pMOS and nMOS transistors must be electrically isolated from each other. This isolation is achieved by forming a p-type island in the n-type substrate around each nMOS transistor. The pn junction between this island and the substrate provides the necessary isolation. Note that a connection must be made to the p-type island surrounding T_2 since the input (gate) voltage of T_2 must be connected between the gate electrode of T_2 and the p-type island of T_2, which constitutes a "local" substrate. All such p-type regions in a CMOS circuit must be connected together, but this is a minor design complication.

The CMOS technology is being used successfully to manufacture logic circuits whose complexity ranges from SSI to VLSI. Common SSI and MSI logic functions are provided by the *4000 series* of CMOS ICs, which was originated by RCA, but is now supplied by many semiconductor manufacturers. This series is analogous to the 7400 series of TTL ICs, although the part numbers used for corresponding logic functions are

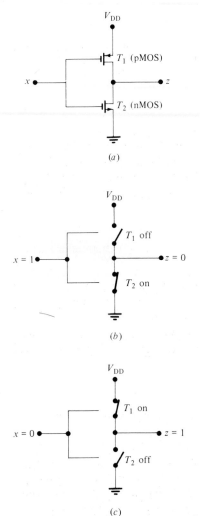

(a)

(b)

(c)

Figure 2.58 CMOS inverter: (a) circuit diagram; (b) switching behavior with $x = 1$; (c) switching behavior with $x = 0$.

unrelated. For example, the 4011 CMOS IC is a quad two-input NAND circuit, which thus is logically equivalent to the 7400 IC of Fig. 2.50b. Note, however, that 4000- and 7400-series ICs differ significantly in such electrical properties as power consumption, operating speed, and drive capability. Recently a CMOS version of the 7400 series, designated the 74C00 series, has become available (National Semiconductor, 1981a).

2.3.3. Loading Considerations

The binary logic values used in digital systems are represented by two voltage ranges: a high-voltage range, which we have denoted by V_H, represents logical 1, while a low-voltage range V_L represents logical 0. Figure 2.61 shows the actual voltage ranges

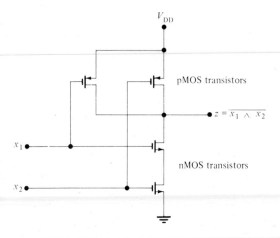

Figure 2.59 CMOS NAND circuit.

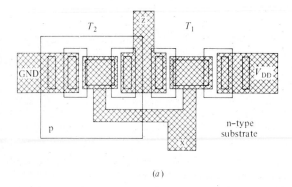

(a)

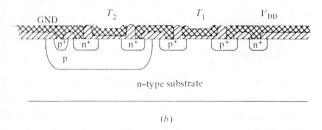

(b)

Figure 2.60 IC implementation of the CMOS inverter of Fig. 2.58a: (a) top view; (b) cross section.

employed in standard TTL circuits; other logic families also use these, or similar, voltage ranges. Any voltage in the range 0.0 to 0.8 V denotes logical 0, while any voltage level in the range 2.0 to 5.0 V denotes logical 1. The intermediate range 0.8 to 2.0 V should occur only when a signal is changing from one logical value to the other. Steady voltages lying in this transition region are forbidden in logic design, because they do not correspond to logical 0 or 1, and their effect on circuit behavior is uncertain.

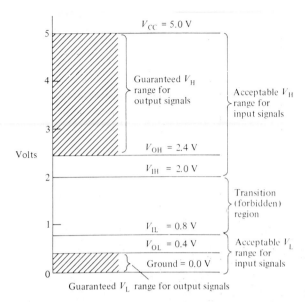

Figure 2.61 Standard voltage specifications for logic signals in 7400-series TTL ICs.

The output signals produced by standard TTL circuits are usually guaranteed to lie in the narrower or more conservative voltage ranges that are represented by the shaded areas in Fig. 2.61. A standard TTL output line whose output current does not exceed a specified maximum value is guaranteed to produce a V_H signal in the range 2.4 to 5.0 V, and a V_L signal in the range, 0.0 to 0.4 V. In practice voltage signals tend to fluctuate around any desired value due to variations in component characteristics and unpredictable interactions of a minor nature between different signals; these unwanted effects are collectively called *noise*. The 0.4-V differences between the worst-case values of the guaranteed and acceptable voltage ranges in Fig. 2.61 allow for signal fluctuations, and therefore are sometimes called *noise margins*. Thus an output signal of 0.4 V representing logical 0, which is applied to a line *L*, can fluctuate between 0.0 and 0.8 V without causing incorrect operation of any TTL circuits having input lines connected to *L*.

Suppose that some output signal of a circuit N_0 is connected as an input signal to another circuit N_1 as illustrated in Fig. 2.62a. N_0 is then said to *drive* N_1, while N_1 *loads* N_0. N_0 transmits logical information to N_1 by causing the voltage applied to the interconnection line *L* to assume values in the V_H and V_L ranges. Corresponding to these voltage levels, electric currents denoted I_H and I_L flow through line *L*. The exact values assumed by these voltage and current parameters are determined by the electrical characteristics of N_0 and N_1, particularly the resistance they offer to input or output signals. The electrical behavior of the interconnection may be analyzed by means of the equivalent circuits appearing in Fig. 2.62, which show simplified versions of the input and output stages found in the various logic families introduced earlier.

Figure 2.62b shows the situation when N_0 is transmitting a logical 1 signal to N_1 by setting the voltage V on *L* to V_H. A current I_H, called a *source current* I_H, flows out from N_0 and into N_1. Similarly, when a logical 0 is being transmitted from N_0 to N_1, a current

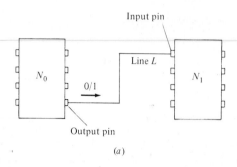

(a)

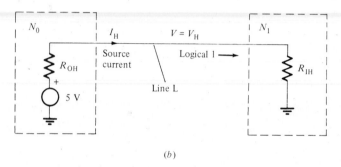

(b)

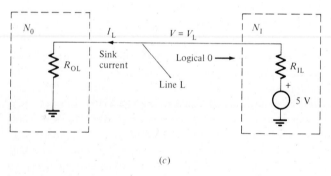

(c)

Figure 2.62 (a) Logic signal connection between two ICs; (b) equivalent circuit with output voltage V_H (logical 1); (c) equivalent circuit with output voltage V_L (logical 0).

I_L, called a *sink current*, flows into N_0. Note that the direction of logic signal flow and current flow are independent, and should not be confused. The value of the voltage V appearing on the line L is determined by the following equations, which are obtained directly from the equivalent circuits of Fig. 2.62:

$$V_H = I_H R_{IH} = 5 - \frac{5 R_{OH}}{R_{IH} + R_{OH}}$$

$$(2.17)$$

$$V_L = 5 - I_L R_{IL} = \frac{5 R_{OL}}{R_{IL} + R_{OL}}$$

From these equations we see that as the input load resistance R_{IH}/R_{IL} imposed by N_1 decreases, V_H decreases and V_L increases, while the currents I_H and I_L both increase. If the input resistance of N_1 is too small, implying that N_0 and N_1 are incompatible or mismatched, the nontransition values of the voltage V on L may move into the forbidden region, resulting in indeterminate logical behavior. Mismatching may also result in excessively high values of the currents I_H and I_L, which could damage N_0 or N_1.

To prevent such mismatching, IC manufacturers specify minimum and maximum allowable values for the currents and voltages appearing on all IO lines of each IC type; these limiting values are the same for all members of a logic family. Figure 2.63 defines the parameters generally found in IC specifications (data sheets), and gives the standard values used for various TTL subfamilies. The voltage parameters correspond to the limits of the acceptable input values and guaranteed output values discussed earlier and illustrated in Fig. 2.61. The currents I_{IL} and I_{IH} associated with an input line represent the worst-case loads imposed by the line on any line driving it to the V_L and V_H levels respectively. The currents I_{OL} and I_{OH} are the worst-case currents provided by an output line, and represent that line's drive capability. The values of these voltage and current parameters for any particular IC, as well as other useful design information, can be found in the manufacturer's data sheet for the IC in question. Figure 2.64 shows the data sheet for Fairchild's version of the 74LS00 IC, a quad two-input NAND circuit employing low-power Schottky technology (Fairchild, 1975). As the data sheet indicates, the Fairchild part number 9LS00XC (subsequently abbreviated to XC) is equivalent to the 74LS00 part number. It can be seen that the figures given for input and output voltage and current limits are identical to the generic figures for the 74LS00 series listed in Fig. 2.63. Note that the values of I_{OL} and I_{OH} are given implicitly in Fig. 2.64 under the heading "Test Conditions."

Much additional information that is useful to the system designer can be found in manufacturers' data sheets. Figure 2.64, for example, states that the power supply voltage V_{CC} of the 74LS00, which is nominally 5 V, can range from 4.75 to 5.25 V without affecting circuit operation. This implies that fluctuations in the power supply voltage must not exceed ±5 percent of the nominal 5-V value. The military grade 54LS00 part (denoted 9LS00XM or XM), which is also described in Fig. 2.64, can tolerate power supply fluctuations of ±10 percent. The data sheet specifies the current drawn from the power supply under various conditions. I_{CCL} and I_{CCH} denote the current drawn from the power supply when all gate output signals are held at V_L and V_H, respectively; the figures given under the heading TYP (typical) are average values. Let I_{CC} denote the average current drawn by the 74LS00, which may be approximated by $(I_{CCL} + I_{CCH})/2$. Thus the average power consumption of the 74LS00 is given by

$$P = \frac{V_{CC}(I_{CCL} + I_{CCH})}{2}$$

Taking the "typical" figures from the data sheet, we obtain

$$P = \frac{5.0(2.4 + 0.8)}{2} = 8.0 \text{ mW}$$

Parameter	General Specifications	TTL Logic Family Specifications		
		7400	74S00	74LS00
Input voltages	V_{IL}: The maximum acceptable input voltage representing V_L (logic 0)	0.8 V	0.8 V	0.7 V
	V_{IH}: The minimum acceptable input voltage representing V_H (logic 1)	2.0 V	2.0 V	2.0 V
Output voltages	V_{OL}: The maximum guaranteed output voltage representing V_L	0.4 V	0.5 V	0.3 V
	V_{OH}: The minimum guaranteed output voltage representing V_H	2.4 V	2.5 V	2.4 V
Input currents (load currents)	I_{IL}: The maximum input current required when $V = V_{OL}$	1.6 mA	2.0 mA	0.36 mA
	I_{IH}: The maximum input current required when $V = V_{OH}$	20 µA	50 µA	40 µA
Output currents (drive currents)	I_{OL}: The minimum guaranteed output current when $V = V_{OL}$	16 mA	20 mA	8 mA
	I_{OH}: The minimum guaranteed output current when $V = V_{OH}$	400 µA	1000 µA	400 µA

Figure 2.63 Standard voltage and current specifications for three TTL logic subfamilies.

QUAD 2-INPUT NAND GATE

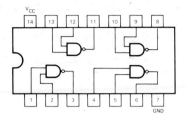

GUARANTEED OPERATING RANGES

PART NUMBERS	SUPPLY VOLTAGE			TEMPERATURE
	MIN	TYP	MAX	
9LS00XM / 54LS00XM	4.5 V	5.0 V	5.5 V	−55°C to 125°C
9LS00XC / 74LS00XC	4.75 V	5.0 V	5.25 V	0°C to 75°C

X = package type; F for Flatpak, D for Ceramic Dip, P for Plastic Dip. See Packaging Information Section for packages available on this product.

DC CHARACTERISTICS OVER OPERATING TEMPERATURE RANGE (unless otherwise specified)

SYMBOL	PARAMETER		LIMITS			UNITS	TEST CONDITIONS (Note 1)
			MIN	TYP	MAX		
V_{IH}	Input HIGH Voltage		2.0			V	Guaranteed Input HIGH Voltage
V_{IL}	Input LOW Voltage	XM			0.7	V	Guaranteed Input LOW Voltage
		XC			0.8		
V_{CD}	Input Clamp Diode Voltage			−0.65	−1.5	V	V_{CC} = MIN, I_{IN} = −18 mA
V_{OH}	Output HIGH Voltage	XM	2.5	3.4		V	V_{CC} = MIN, I_{OH} = −400 µA, V_{IN} = V_{IL}
		XC	2.7	3.4			
V_{OL}	Output LOW Voltage	XM,XC		0.25	0.4	V	V_{CC} = MIN, I_{OL} = 4.0 mA, V_{IN} = 2.0 V
		XC		0.35	0.5	V	V_{CC} = MIN, I_{OL} = 8.0 mA, V_{IN} = 2.0 V
I_{IH}	Input HIGH Current			1.0	20	µA	V_{CC} = MAX, V_{IN} = 2.7 V
					0.1	mA	V_{CC} = MAX, V_{IN} = 10 V
I_{IL}	Input LOW Current				−0.36	mA	V_{CC} = MAX, V_{IN} = 0.4 V
I_{OS}	Output Short Circuit Current (Note 3)		−15		−100	mA	V_{CC} = MAX, V_{OUT} = 0 V
I_{CCH}	Supply Current HIGH			0.8	1.6	mA	V_{CC} = MAX, V_{IN} = 0 V
I_{CCL}	Supply Current LOW			2.4	4.4	mA	V_{CC} = MAX, Inputs Open

AC CHARACTERISTICS: T_A = 25°C (See Page 4-50 for Waveforms)

SYMBOL	PARAMETER	LIMITS			UNITS	TEST CONDITIONS
		MIN	TYP	MAX		
t_{PLH}	Turn Off Delay, Input to Output	3.0	5.0	10	ns	V_{CC} = 5.0 V
t_{PHL}	Turn On Delay, Input to Output	3.0	5.0	10	ns	C_L = 15 pF

NOTES:
1. For conditions shown as MIN or MAX, use the appropriate value specified under recommended operating conditions for the applicable device type.
2. Typical limits are at V_{CC} = 5.0 V, T_A = 25°C.
3. Not more than one output should be shorted at a time.

Figure 2.64 Data sheet for the 74LS00 quad two-input NAND IC. *(Courtesy Fairchild Camera and Instrument Corp.)*

Hence this version of the 74LS00 IC can be expected to consume 8.0 mW of power, or about 2.0 mW per gate. As the higher MAX (maximum) values given for I_{CCL} and I_{CCH} indicate, the maximum power consumption of this circuit can be two or three times greater than P.

The number of input lines connected to, and therefore driven by, an output line L of some circuit N_0, is termed the fan-out of L. The fan-out of L in Fig. 2.62a is one, while its fan-out in Fig. 2.65a is k. Each line to which L fans out imposes a load on L by acting as a current source or sink, and therefore affects the voltage V applied to L by the driving circuit N_0. If the fan-out of L is too great, N_0 may be overloaded, causing V to assume forbidden values. The designer therefore must be aware of the maximum permissible fan-out of every output line in the circuit under consideration.

Fan-out constraints may be analyzed by means of the equivalent electric circuits appearing in Figs. 2.65b and 2.65c. For simplicity, assume that the devices $N_0, N_1, \ldots ,$ N_k all belong to the same logic family, and so have the same values of the parameters listed in Fig. 2.63. Consider the circuit of Fig. 2.65b, where the voltage V on L is V_H. Each of the load devices $N_1, N_2, \ldots , N_k$ may draw a maximum current of I_{IH} from L; thus the worst-case load current drawn from L is kI_{IH}. N is guaranteed to supply a current I_{OH} when V is in the V_H region. Hence proper circuit operation is guaranteed if the inequality

$$I_{OH} \geq kI_{IH} \qquad (2.18)$$

is satisfied. A similar analysis applied to the circuit in Fig. 2.65c for the case where V is V_L yields a second inequality

$$I_{OL} \geq kI_{IL} \qquad (2.19)$$

The fan-out k of L is considered to be acceptable if both of the inequalities (2.18) and (2.19) are satisfied. These inequalities are easily generalized to cover fan-out where several different logic families are involved.

Suppose, for instance, that the circuits $N_0, N_1, \ldots , N_k$ appearing in Fig. 2.65a are all 7400-series standard TTL ICs. Substitution of the appropriate current values from Fig. 2.63 into (2.18) and (2.19) yields

$$400 \geq 40k$$

$$16 \geq 1.6k$$

The largest value of k satisfying these inequalities is 10. Hence we conclude that a standard TTL output line is limited to a fan-out of 10 or less when driving standard TTL inputs. Now consider the case where N_0 is a low-power Schottky IC in the 74LS00 series, while $N_1, N_2, \ldots , N_k$ are 7400-series ICs. Again inserting the appropriate data from Fig. 2.63 into inequalities (2.18) and (2.19), we obtain

$$400 \geq 40k \qquad (2.20)$$

$$8 \geq 1.6k \qquad (2.21)$$

Although (2.20) allows k to be as high as 10, (2.21) limits k to 5. Hence a 74LS00-series IC can drive at most five 7400-series inputs.

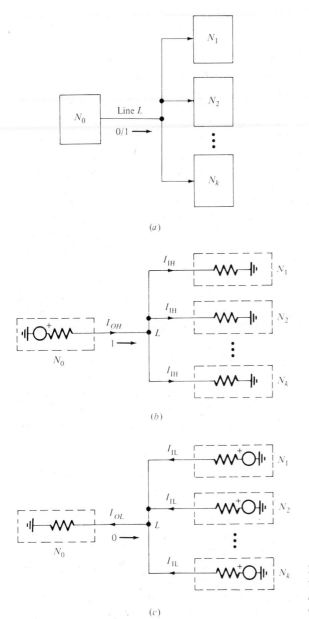

Figure 2.65 (*a*) Circuit with line *L* of fan-out *k*; (*b*) equivalent circuit with *L* at V_H (logical 1); (*c*) equivalent circuit with *L* at V_L (logical 0).

The electrical characteristics of the IO lines in pMOS and nMOS circuits are usually designed to be very similar to those of 7400-series standard TTL circuits, which are listed in Fig. 2.63. For example, the Intel 8085 microprocessor chip, which uses dynamic nMOS circuitry, requires a 5-volt power supply, and has V_H and V_L ranges that are very close to the 7400-series ranges. The drive capability of the output lines of the 8085 is specified as follows (Intel, 1979):

$$I_{OL} = 2 \text{ mA} \quad \text{with} \quad V_{OL} = 0.45 \text{ V}$$
$$I_{OH} = -400 \text{ } \mu\text{A} \quad \text{with} \quad V_{OH} = 2.4 \text{ V} \tag{2.22}$$

From Eqs. (2.18) and (2.19) and the data of Fig. 2.63, we see that an 8085 output signal can drive one 7400- or 74S00-series input; however, it can drive five 74LS00-series inputs. An output line, like those of the 8085 microprocessor, is called *TTL compatible* if it can drive at least one *standard TTL load*, that is, an input line having the input current requirements of a 7400-series device. The input currents required by MOS circuits are generally much lower than those of TTL circuits. Thus for input lines of the 8085 microprocessor we have

$$I_{IL} = I_{OL} = 10 \text{ } \mu\text{A} \tag{2.23}$$

Consequently a TTL circuit can drive a large number of MOS loads. The current values given in (2.22) and (2.23) are typical of nMOS logic circuits.

Frequently in digital system design it is found that some line L has a maximum output current that is insufficient to drive all the input lines that must be connected to it. A current amplifier called a *buffer* may be used to rectify this problem, as illustrated in Fig. 2.66a. The buffer B, which is represented by a triangle symbol in logic diagrams, is

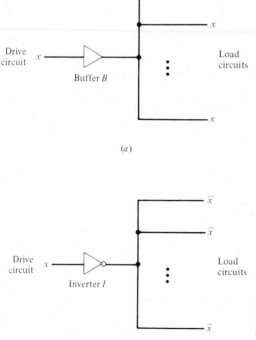

(a)

(b)

Figure 2.66 Increasing output drive (fan-out) capability via: (a) a noninverting buffer; (b) an inverting buffer.

inserted in L to increase the output drive current available. The term buffer may be applied to any logic gate that provides relatively large output currents. The TTL gates, particularly inverters, are often used as buffers in MOS circuits. For example, if an inverter from the 7404 IC of Fig. 2.50a is inserted in an output line of the 8085 microprocessor, the line's drive capability or maximum fan-out is increased from one to ten standard TTL loads. Unlike an inverter, the buffer B of Fig. 2.66a does not alter the logic values being transmitted through it; it does, however, increase their propagation delay.

From the viewpoint of circuit loading, CMOS presents a special case. The output drive currents of CMOS ICs are comparable to those of other MOS families; however, the input currents required are about a thousand times less. A typical value of the input current (I_{IL} or I_{IH}) required by a CMOS line is 10 pA (picoamperes), a consequence of the extremely high input resistance of CMOS logic circuits. Hence a very large number of CMOS loads can be driven by a circuit from any standard logic family, including TTL, nMOS, and CMOS itself. A maximum fan-out of 50 or so is recommended in CMOS circuit design, since the total capacitance of the load circuits increases with fan-out, which may increase the signal propagation delay to an unacceptable level. The CMOS circuits have some other unusual electrical characteristics. They can operate satisfactorily with power supply voltages ranging from 3 to 15 V; as a result they are quite insensitive to fluctuations in the power supply voltage. The current drawn by a CMOS circuit, and therefore its power consumption, tends to increase with the power supply voltage and, unlike other logic families, with the frequency of the signals being processed.

2.3.4 Interconnection Methods

A digital system is composed of ICs and other electronic components mounted on a suitable base and interconnected or wired together. The base material, which is typically a fiberglass or plastic board, provides mechanical support for the system. Various schemes are used to make the electrical interconnections between the components. Figure 2.67 illustrates two widely used interconnection methods: printed circuits and wire-wrapped circuits. In the case of Fig. 2.67a the components are mounted on a printed-circuit board (PCB) consisting of a rigid insulation board or card on which metal connections are created by a print-and-etch technique. (See Fig. 1.20 for an outline of the PCB manufacturing process.) Holes are drilled in the PCB to accommodate the pins of the ICs and other components; these holes also pass through the appropriate printed connections for each pin. Solder is then applied to the underside of the board to form a strong mechanical and electrical connection between the pins and the printed conductors. Printed-circuit boards of this type are used extensively in mass-produced systems. They may have two or more layers of printed connections. Two-layer boards are frequently employed, since they allow horizontal connections to be placed on one side of the board, and vertical connections on the other, thus alleviating the wire crossover problem that is a consequence of having all connectors in the same plane. Soldering provides good low-cost electrical connections; its main drawback is that soldered components are difficult to remove and replace.

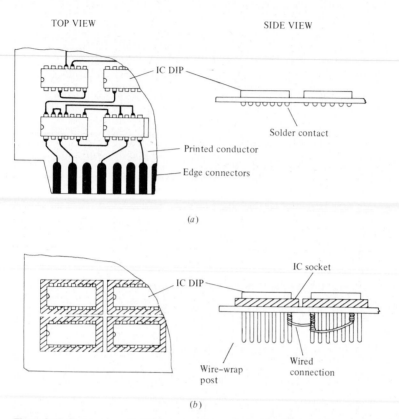

TOP VIEW   SIDE VIEW

(a)

(b)

Figure 2.67 Two common circuit interconnection methods: *(a)* printed-circuit board (PCB); *(b)* wire-wrapped board.

Figure 2.67b depicts another interconnection method called *wire wrapping*. Each IC is inserted into a special wire-wrap socket, which is firmly attached to a supporting board. A wire-wrap socket has square metal posts or pins that protrude from the underside of the board as indicated; the pins of an IC inserted into the socket are connected to these posts. Insulated silver-plated copper wire is used to connect different posts, and thus interconnect different ICs. The insulation is stripped from the end of a piece of wire and the exposed wire is wrapped in a single tight layer around a post by means of a special tool. Two or three different wires can be attached to each post, depending on its length. Contrary to what one might expect, wire wrapping is a permanent and very reliable interconnection method, because the contact areas between the wire and the corners of the post are airtight and under extremely great pressure. Wire wrapping also has the advantage of allowing ICs to be packed very close together, since no board area is taken up by printed connections. However, this is balanced by the fact that the overall depth of the circuit is much greater than that of an equivalent PCB, due to the presence of the IC sockets and the wire-wrap posts. Integrated-circuit replacement is very easy, but care must be taken not to bend or break any pins when inserting ICs into sockets. Wire wrapping is expensive for mass production, but is very attractive for systems that are to be produced in small quantities.

A very-low-cost and flexible interconnection method, which is intended for experimental circuit construction or *breadboarding*, is shown in Fig. 2.68. The circuit is constructed on a so-called breadboard consisting of a metal or plastic base on which are mounted breadboard socket strips, each consisting of an array of socket holes embedded in an insulating medium. Each hole contains a spring-loaded electrical contact, and is able to accommodate a single DIP pin or a solid copper wire (approximately 22-gauge wire). The holes are spaced 0.1 inch apart, so that a standard DIP can be plugged directly into a socket strip. The contacts embedded in the strip are electrically connected in vertical groups of five as indicated in Fig. 2.68; additional groups of 25 contacts are present along the outer (horizontal) edges of the strip. The DIPs are inserted horizontally so that they straddle the center line of a strip. In the case of smaller DIPs such as the 14-pin DIPs used in Fig. 2.68, four contact holes in a group of five are available for making connections to any DIP pin. The connections are formed by pieces of insulated wire whose ends are stripped and simply plugged into socket holes. Clearly this is a very flexible interconnection technique, since wires and ICs can be changed very easily.

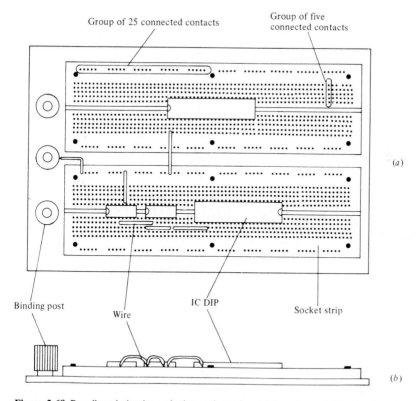

Figure 2.68 Breadboard circuit employing socket strips; (*a*) top view and (*b*) side view.

While eminently suitable for design development and experimentation purposes, bread-board socket strips are not used in production, because the wires are easily shaken loose.

In small digital systems all electronic components can be placed on a single PCB or wire-wrapped board, resulting in a *single-board system*. Larger systems requiring several circuit boards are usually housed in metal enclosures or *cabinets*. A cabinet of the kind often used for large microcomputers, such as the development computer in the MDS system of Fig. 1.46, appears in Fig. 2.69. It accommodates a power supply unit that converts mains alternating voltage to the direct-voltage levels needed by the system's electronic circuit boards. The latter are mounted vertically in a *card cage* containing vertical slots that support the PCBs. The bottom of each circuit board is fitted with a set of edge connectors that plug into a socket mounted in the card cage. The edge-connector sockets are wired together to provide interboard electrical connections; they are also connected to sockets in the rear of the cabinet that provide links to external IO devices. Major control switches and display devices such as LEDs are usually mounted on the front panel of the cabinet. Access to the system for maintenance purposes is achieved by removing the top cover, as shown in the figure. Since appreciable heat is generated by the circuit boards and the power supply, provision must be made for ventilation of the cabinet; sometimes electric cooling fans are also built into the cabinet.

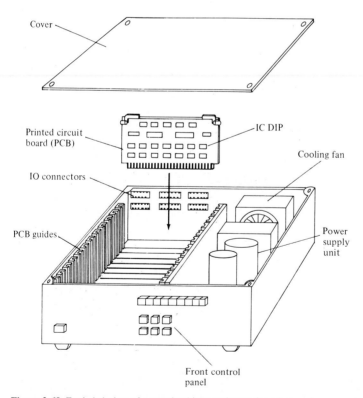

Figure 2.69 Exploded view of a metal cabinet enclosure for a large microcomputer system.

Often many components in a system must be able to transfer data words of the same general type to one another. To reduce the number of physical interconnections needed for such communication, a small set of shared lines called a *bus* may be used. More generally, any group of *n* related lines or wires may be termed an *n*-bit bus. Various buses appear in the microprocessor-based system of Fig. 1.40, for example, the 8-bit address-data bus linking the microprocessor and the PROM. The edge connectors of the boards used in the system of Fig. 2.69 are usually designed for connection to a standard bus that links the boards to one other. Besides reducing the number of wires needed, a bus also reduces the number of terminals (DIP pins or edge connectors) required by the communicating devices. Buses, therefore, play an important role in reducing interconnection costs in complex systems.

For proper operation, only one of the devices connected to a shared bus can place information on the bus at any time; in other words, there can only be one data source during bus communication. More than one device can act as a data destination; however, there is usually only one source and one destination device using the bus at any time. There is no inherent difficulty in connecting a bus line L to the inputs of many gates in the possible destination devices; this is the normal fan-out situation depicted in Figs. 2.65 and 2.66. A problem arises when the output lines of two or more gates in the possible source devices are connected to L. The output signal of a standard logic gate is always either 0 or 1. If one gate attempts to place a 0 on L while another gate attempts to place a 1 on L, an indeterminate condition results since L cannot assume the values 0 and 1 simultaneously. The direct connection of the output lines of standard gates in this fashion is therefore forbidden in logic circuit design. The question then arises: How can two or more logic circuits drive a common bus line?

The foregoing problem is neatly solved by a special class of TTL logic elements called *three-state* or *Tri-State** gates. A three-state gate differs from a conventional logic gate in having an extra input line E called the *enable* (or sometimes the *disable*) input. When $E = 1$, in which case the gate G in question is said to be *enabled*, G produces 0 and 1 output signals in the usual fashion. When $E = 0$, however, causing G to become *disabled*, the output line of G assumes a new logic value, which is denoted by Z and is called the *high-impedance state*. Disabling a three-state gate has the effect of creating an extremely high impedance or resistance in the gate's output line, which effectively disconnects the gate from the output L. For many purposes it can be assumed that a disabled gate has an open circuit, that is, an infinite resistance, in its output line. Thus the Z logic value may be equated to the voltage level of a conductor that has no voltage sources connected to it, or is *"floating."* Negligible current is drawn by the output line of a three-state gate that is disabled. Thus the outputs of many three-state gates can be connected to a common bus line L provided the following rule of operation is obeyed: No more than one three-state gate G driving L should be enabled at any time. When enabled, G is the only signal source that is logically connected to L, and hence it can place 0's and 1's on L without interference from any other three-state gates whose outputs are wired to L.

---

* The term "Tri-State" is a registered trademark of National Semiconductor Corporation, which introduced this design concept in 1970. We will use the generic term "three-state gate" here.

Figure 2.70 describes two representative three-state gates: a noninverting buffer, sometimes called a three-state (bus) driver, and a two-input NAND gate. The usual logic symbols introduced already are used for three-state gates, with the extra enable input attached to the body of the symbol as indicated. A variety of three-state gate types can be found in the 7400 series of TTL ICs. Figure 2.71 shows a 4-bit bus that is attached to two signal sources A and B. Two copies of a 7400-series IC, the 74126 three-state quad buffer, are used to interface the devices to the bus. An alternative to three-state gates for driving bus lines is provided by another class of TTL devices called *open-collector gates* (see Prob. 2.38). Open-collector bus circuits use fewer gates than three-state circuits, but they are more difficult to design, and operate more slowly.

The interconnection design issues addressed so far are applicable to circuits containing wires that are no more than about 50 cm in length. When longer connections are used, various electrical phenomena come into play that can interfere with logic signal transmission. We consider these phenomena next in conjunction with other electrical effects that cause logic circuits to misbehave.

2.3.5 Noise Suppression

Noise in an electric circuit may be defined as unwanted signals that are caused by various internal and external electrical conditions. Noise signals interact with the normal logic

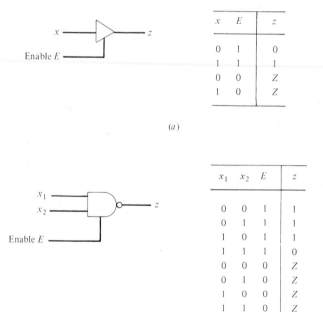

(a)

(b)

Figure 2.70 Symbols and truth tables for two three-state logic gates: (a) noninverting buffer or (bus) driver; (b) two-input NAND gate.

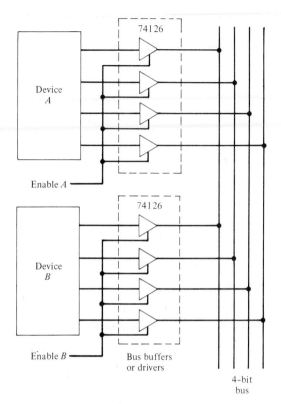

Figure 2.71 Connecting to a bus via three–state buffers.

signals in digital circuits, distorting their waveforms as illustrated in Fig. 2.72. A small amount of noise is normal in all circuits, and does not interfere with circuit operation. For example, if a circuit is designed to meet the TTL voltage specifications appearing in Fig. 2.61, signal voltages can fluctuate in the 0.4-V noise margin regions between the guaranteed output and acceptable input values without altering circuit behavior. If large noise signals such as the noise-induced voltage *spike* of Fig. 2.72b are present, the circuit may misbehave. Therefore, steps should be taken during the design process to ensure that the effects of noise are kept within acceptable limits.

The external sources of noise affecting digital systems are electromagnetic radiation from "noisy" electric equipment, and fluctuations in the ac power supply. The former may be reduced by attaching noise-suppression circuitry to the noise source; alternatively the affected circuit can be placed in a metal enclosure to shield it from the offending radiation. A regulated power supply unit can filter noise from the ac power lines, supplying a steady direct voltage despite moderate fluctuations in its input voltage. Internal noise in a circuit is due to unwanted interactions between different parts of the circuit itself. It is usually minor, and so can be ignored in systems that operate at low frequencies, carry small electric currents, and contain short interconnection lines. In

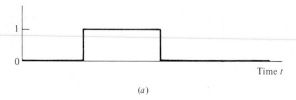

(a)

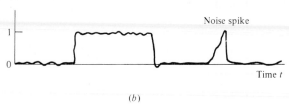

(b)

Figure 2.72 Digital signal waveforms: (a) ideal; (b) actual with noise spike.

general, noise problems tend to increase with a circuit's physical size and operating speed. Here we consider three major sources of internal circuit noise:

1. Power and ground distribution problems
2. Signal crosstalk
3. Transmission-line effects

We next examine each of these problems in turn, and discuss briefly some design methods to circumvent them.

Every IC has at least two pins that must be connected to the power and ground terminals of a power supply, so that it obtains the electric energy it needs to function. Thus power and ground lines must be distributed to all ICs in a system, as indicated in Fig. 2.73a. The power supply unit must typically maintain the voltage (usually 5 V) supplied to each IC within 5 percent of the nominal voltage level. In a system with many ICs, relatively large electric currents are drawn from the power supply unit, and hence the conductors used to distribute the power and ground signals must be large enough to carry the necessary currents. Even large power and ground connectors have some electrical resistance, which, under certain conditions, can cause excessive voltage fluctuations or noise affecting circuit operation. This resistance can be minimized by keeping the power and ground lines as short and as direct as possible. Better yet, the individual conductors can be replaced by a conducting sheet or plane. In many cases it is more practical to use a grid of conductors that approximates a plane, and provides low-resistance connections to large numbers of components. Single-board systems such as those of Fig. 2.67 frequently employ a *ground plane* or grid to which all ground connections are made.

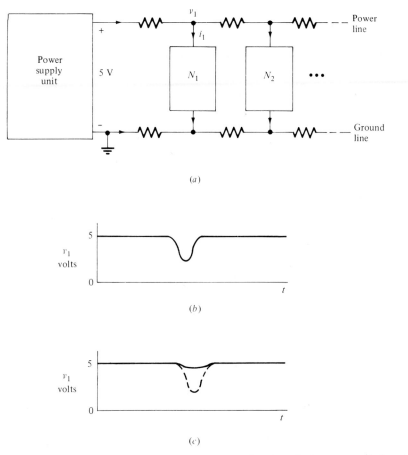

Figure 2.73 (a) Distribution of power and ground lines; (b) noise spike in power supply line; (c) effect of decoupling capacitor.

As observed earlier in our discussion of circuit loading, the current drawn by a logic element depends on the signals applied to its input lines, which in turn determine the signals appearing at its output lines. As these signals vary, the current drawn by the logic element fluctuates, often quite rapidly and over a wide range. Consider the power distribution circuit of Fig. 2.73a, which supplies a 5-V signal to the ICs $N_1, N_2, \ldots$. The actual (instantaneous) voltage applied to some IC, say N_1, at any time is given by the equation

$$v_1 = 5 - ri_1$$

where i_1 is the instantaneous current drawn from the power supply by N_1, and r represents the small resistance of the various lines linking N_1 to the power supply unit. Changes in the logic signals associated with N_1 can cause sudden large increases or decreases in the magnitude of i_1, and therefore in the magnitude of v_1. Such voltage fluctuations appear as noise spikes in the power supply lines feeding N_1 as shown in Fig. 2.73b. These spikes are often of such short duration that there is insufficient time for them to propagate to the (regulated) power supply unit where they could be filtered out. Their duration may be sufficiently long, however, to cause improper operation of N_1 or other ICs in its immediate vicinity.

The foregoing noise problem is solved by the use of capacitors called *decoupling* or *bypass capacitors*, which are connected between the power and ground lines, and are distributed throughout the circuit at regular intervals. These capacitors filter out localized noise spikes in the manner suggested by Fig. 2.73c. They store sufficient energy to supply a few ICs with power for the duration of the noise spike, while maintaining the power-line voltage close to its nominal value. The number and size of the decoupling capacitors depend on the logic family being used; the relevant data can usually be found in manufacturers' data manuals. In a high-speed TTL circuit it is good practice to include one decoupling capacitor with a value of about $0.1\ \mu F$ for every four or five ICs. Few, if any, decoupling capacitors are needed in CMOS circuits because of their inherent insensitivity to the power supply voltage level. Figure 2.74 shows a well-designed power distribution method for a single-board memory system employing nMOS ICs. The power and ground lines are laid out as uniform grids so that each IC is effectively surrounded by a power line and a ground line. Decoupling capacitors are distributed evenly over the surface of the board; in this case, following the manufacturer's recommendations, one decoupling capacitor is used for every two ICs.

Another possible noise source in digital systems is *crosstalk*, which is the coupling of signals from one circuit to another via stray inductance and capacitance. These effects appear only when signals are in transition, that is, changing value. For example, a rapidly changing electric current in a wire can induce a small noise voltage in a physically adjacent wire. The magnitude of the noise voltage increases with the length of the adjacent portions of the two wires, and decreases with their separation; it also

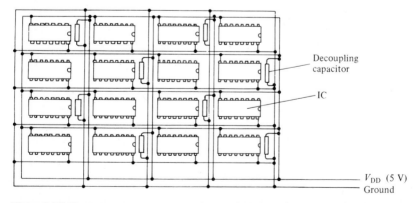

Figure 2.74 Single-board memory system with power and ground distribution grids and decoupling capacitors.

increases with the magnitude of the noise-inducing current. Thus crosstalk is mainly a problem in closely spaced conductors that carry fairly large fluctuating currents, and run parallel to each other over relatively long distances. Crosstalk therefore can be reduced by physically separating crosstalk-prone conductors. It also can be reduced by the use of a good ground plane or grid such as that of Fig. 2.74. Crosstalk between two conductors is greatly diminished by running a grounded conductor between them. Thus the ground grid in the system of Fig. 2.74 assists in isolating each IC from potential noise sources existing in the remainder of the circuit.

For many purposes it is sufficient to consider a wire or other connector as a perfect electrical conductor, or else as a conductor with a small lumped impedance (resistance, capacitance, or inductance); see Fig. 2.19. In reality impedance is distributed over the wire's entire length. This fact can alter considerably the wire's behavior when the signal propagation times through the wire are long relative to the rise (from 0 to 1) and fall (from 1 to 0) times of the signals being transmitted. The behavior of the wire under these conditions approximates that of a transmission line. A *transmission line* may be defined as two electrical conductors, such as a signal wire and ground, that are separated by a uniform insulating medium. At each point along an ideal transmission line, an applied electric signal "sees" a constant impedance Z_0, called the line's *characteristic impedance*. In other words, the instantaneous voltage v and current i at any point are related by the following generalized Ohm's law:

$$v = Z_0 i \qquad (2.24)$$

Figure 2.75 shows a transmission line L that links two devices A and B. Suppose that A generates a voltage pulse as indicated. The distributed capacitance and inductance of L cause the pulse to travel along L at a finite rate (about 0.2 m/ns). At the end of the line the pulse encounters the load resistance of B, namely R_B, at which the relation

$$v = R_B i \qquad (2.25)$$

must hold. If $R_B = Z_0$, then (2.24) and (2.25) are satisfied simultaneously, in which case the line is said to be *matched*. If, on the other hand, $R_B \neq Z_0$, a conflict or mismatch occurs at the end of the line when the traveling pulse suddenly sees a higher or lower impedance than Z_0. To resolve this conflict, a quantum change in v occurs at device B, which has the effect of transmitting a reverse or reflected pulse back along the transmission line to A. This pulse is positive-going, that is, in the same direction as the original pulse from A, if $R_B > Z_0$; the reflected pulse is negative-going if $R_B < Z_0$. Thus, on reaching A, the reflected pulse either increases or decreases the net voltage at A. Depending on the terminating resistance R_A at A, the pulse from B, in turn, may be reflected back to B. Thus several such pulses of diminishing magnitude may be reflected back and forth through the transmission line until all the pulse energy has been dissipated. Figure 2.75 shows in simplified form two possible situations occurring when R_B and R_A are both less than the characteristic impedance Z_0. In Fig. 2.75b the pulse length T is assumed to be much greater than the round-trip signal propagation time from A to B and back to A again. The various pulses meeting at A combine to yield the distorted effective waveform shown in the figure. Notice that the transmission-line reflections have several effects on the pulse waveform: it rises more slowly, its maximum value is

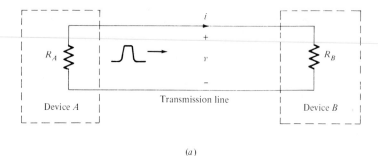

(a)

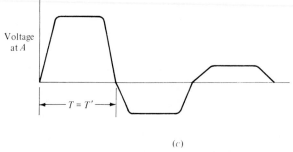

(b)

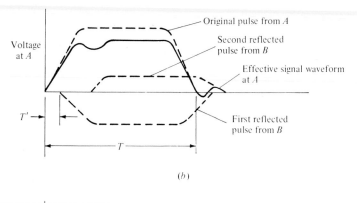

(c)

Figure 2.75 *(a)* Transmission line connecting two devices; *(b–c)* effect at source of reflections from destination.

diminished, and several spurious oscillations occur, which is an effect called *ringing*. When T and T' are roughly equal, the situation illustrated in Fig. 2.75c arises. In this case the reflected signals produce several well-formed noise pulses, which can induce errors in logic devices that are attached to the transmission line.

A wire in a digital system and nearby ground conductors can behave very like a transmission line, especially when the wire is fairly long and is transmitting rapidly changing signals. Variations in the capacitance between the wire and ground resemble mismatched load impedances attached to a transmission line, and therefore can produce reflections of the kind depicted in Fig. 2.75. Long wires that are carelessly routed with respect to ground are thus noise-prone. It is desirable to run long wires at an approximately fixed distance from a ground conductor so that the resulting connection resembles a uniform transmission line. Single wires, whose characteristic impedance is about 150 Ω, can be used without difficulty with most TTL and MOS circuit families for distances up to about 0.5 m. Over longer distances a *twisted pair* connection may be used that is a transmission line created by twisting together two insulated wires, with the twists spaced uniformly along the entire line. One wire connects the logic signal source and destination, and the other is grounded at both ends. A twisted pair interconnection has a characteristic impedance of about 100 Ω. This is much less than the input impedance of most gates, and hence reflections will occur unless impedance-matching circuitry is attached to the end of the twisted pair (see Prob. 2.44). A twisted pair may be used to connect logic circuits separated by distances up to about 3 m. Over still longer distances buffer circuits called *line drivers* and *receivers* should be used that are designed to match the characteristic impedance of the transmission line linking them.

2.4 SUMMARY

Integrated circuits (ICs) are the basic building blocks of digital systems. Digital information is represented by electric voltage or current levels. Voltage represents the electrical pressure or potential difference that causes an electric current to flow. Electric current, which is the amount of electric charge flowing per unit time, is measured in amperes. Electrons are the usual carriers of electric charge in most materials; in semiconductors holes also serve as charge carriers.

Three fundamental laws govern the behavior of electric circuits: Ohm's law ($V = RI$), Kirchoff's current law (the algebraic sum of the currents entering a node is zero), and Kirchoff's voltage law (the algebraic sum of the voltages around a closed loop is zero). The parameter R relating voltage to current is called resistance, and is measured in ohms. Circuit elements designed to have a constant resistance are called resistors. Direct-current (dc) circuits carry signals that do not change in magnitude or direction over the period of interest. They can be modeled by electric networks containing idealized voltage or current sources, and resistors that act as power-dissipating load elements. Time-varying electric signals are necessary for information processing. Digital information is normally represented by a sequence of pulses containing voltages that fall into two ranges V_H and V_L, which correspond to logical 1 and 0 respectively. Capacitors and inductors are electrical elements that can store and transmit time-varying signals. All practical electric devices contain some resistance, capacitance, and inductance; the net loading effect of these parameters is termed impedance.

Semiconductor components play an essential role in electronic circuits. By selectively doping a piece of semiconductor material—silicon is the usual choice—it can be converted into n-type semiconductor in which electrons are the majority carrier of electric charges, or p-type semiconductor in which holes are the majority carriers. The boundary between contiguous n-type and p-type semiconductor regions forms a pn junction, which functions as a simple switch called a diode. When forward biased, a pn junction or other diode approximates a closed switch, whereas a reverse-biased pn junction acts as an open switch blocking the flow of electric current. The addition of a third p-type or n-type region to a pn junction diode produces a three-terminal element called a bipolar transistor, which is capable of signal amplification. Another type of transistor, the MOS (metal-oxide-semiconductor) transistor, is also composed of several types of semiconductor material, but operates on different (field effect) principles. Transistors, either bipolar or MOS, are the key components of all ICs.

The manufacture of ICs begins with a large cylindrical crystal of pure silicon that is sliced into thin disks or wafers. The wafer constitutes the base on which a large number of identical copies of an IC can be made simultaneously. Various doping techniques such as diffusion and ion implantation are used to create p- and n-type regions on the surface of the wafer. Electrical conductors are formed by depositing a metal (usually aluminum) on the wafer. Insulators are formed by oxidizing the wafer surface to produce silicon dioxide, an excellent insulating material. Circuit components also may be isolated from one another by means of reverse-biased pn junctions placed around the components. A complete IC is produced by a series of patterning steps, each of which transfers a specific pattern from a photographic mask to a layer of conductor, insulator, or semiconductor material on the surface of the wafer. Integrated-circuit fabrication therefore resembles photoengraving, and is a process that can be highly automated. After all patterning steps have been completed, the individual ICs are separated in the form of chips or dice, and are inserted in appropriate packages, such as DIPs.

All standard electronic elements can be included, in principle, in an IC. Capacitors and inductors require very large amounts of chip area, and so are rarely included explicitly in digital ICs. Bipolar ICs are constructed mainly from bipolar transistors and resistors, while MOS circuits are fabricated almost entirely from MOS transistors. The MOS circuits generally require less chip area and consume less power than do functionally equivalent bipolar circuits. Hence MOS technology is used most often for circuits that require large- or very-large-scale integration (LSI or VLSI). Bipolar circuits are used primarily when small- or medium-scale integration (SSI or MSI) is needed.

Digital circuits can be designed in several different ways, using either bipolar or MOS techniques, to perform logical operations. The possible circuit structures are grouped into classes called logic families, whose members are electrically compatible with one another. The most widely used bipolar family is TTL (transistor-transistor logic), which employs multiemitter input transistors and several high-speed amplifier stages. Schottky diodes can be included in TTL circuits to increase speed (Schottky TTL) or, with other circuit changes, to reduce power consumption (low-power Schottky TTL). Many common logic functions are available in a standard series of TTL ICs called the 7400 series. There are three main MOS logic families—pMOS, nMOS, and CMOS. The pMOS and nMOS circuits are quite similar, but use p-type and n-type MOS transistors respectively. The nMOS circuits are the faster of the two, but are somewhat more difficult to manufacture. The complexity and power consumption of MOS circuits may be reduced by using dynamic logic, which employs capacitors to store information and is controlled by special clock signals. The CMOS logic circuits contain both pMOS and nMOS transistors, which operate in complementary fashion. CMOS circuits are distinguished by extremely small power consumption and insensitivity to fluctuations in the power supply voltage.

When interconnecting ICs to form a digital system, certain precautions must be taken to ensure that electrical parameters are kept within acceptable limits. For example, precise voltage ranges that must be used to represent logical 0 and 1 are specified for such IC families as the 7400 TTL series. To maintain all signal voltages within these ranges, certain loading or fan-out constraints must be met. Generally speaking the worst-case total current drawn by the set of load devices connected to an IC N must not exceed the maximum output current that can be supplied by N, under all operating conditions. The necessary data for loading calculations can be found in standardized form in the manufacturer's data sheets for the ICs being used. The signal voltage ranges and the limiting input-output (IO) currents used for standard TTL ICs are also frequently used to specify the loading requirements of other logic families, including pMOS and nMOS. Buffer gates are used to increase a circuit's drive capability.

The interconnection methods used for electronic systems include printed-circuit and wire-wrapped boards; printed-circuit boards (PCBs) are normally used for mass-produced systems. When many devices must process the same data, a set of shared lines called a bus may be used to interconnect them. Connection of output circuits to a high-speed bus is accomplished via three-state (buffer) gates. A three-state gate has an extra output value, the high-impedance state Z, which serves logically to disconnect the gate's output line from the bus line to which it is physically connected.

Spurious electric signals called noise occur to some extent in all electronic circuits. Excessive noise can result in improper circuit operation, and therefore must be prevented. Noise problems are most severe in very fast circuits, circuits carrying high currents, and those containing long interconnection lines. Among the major internal noise sources found in digital systems are power and ground lines, signal crosstalk between adjacent conductors, and transmission-line effects. All can be reduced by providing low-resistance conducting planes or grids for the distribution of power and ground signals to all parts of the system. Sudden changes in the current requirements of an IC can produce large noise signals in the power lines connected to the IC and adjacent circuits. This type of noise can be suppressed by decoupling capacitors. Crosstalk, which is caused by the electrical coupling of neighboring circuits, can be prevented by careful system layout. Under certain conditions, any signal line in conjunction with nearby ground conductors, can behave as a transmission line. Uneven load conditions along such a line produce reflections that can distort and delay signal waveforms. These undesirable noise effects can be minimized by making all connections as short and as uniform as possible.

2.5 FURTHER READING

A readable nontechnical overview of IC technology and its impact appears in *Scientific American* (1977). There are many good textbooks on basic electrical circuit theory (Fitzgerald et al., 1981) and electronics (Kabaservice, 1978; Millman, 1979). The fabrication of ICs is also covered in detail in several books (Roddy, 1978; Colclaser, 1980). The major logic circuit families and their characteristics are discussed by Kabaservice (1978), Millman (1979), and Roddy (1978). The design of large-scale MOS circuits is covered in Carr and Mize (1972) and Mead and Conway (1980). Manufacturers' design manuals and data books also provide much useful information on design using various IC families, for example, the Fairchild *TTL Applications Handbook* (Fairchild, 1973); these books emphasize such practical design considerations as loading requirements and noise suppression. Good treatments of practical design issues in the microprocessor system context can be found in Blakeslee (1979) and Stone (1982).

2.6 PROBLEMS

2.1 Express each of the following units of measurement in terms of the basic SI units listed in Fig. 2.1a. For example, 1 kilovolt is expressed as 10^3 kg · m² · s⁻³ · A⁻¹.

    (*a*) A "unit" of electric energy consumpton, which is defined as equal to 1 kilowatt-hour (kWh).

    (*b*) A calorie, which is the amount of heat energy required to raise the temperature of 1 gram of water by 1 degree Celsius.

    (*c*) The SI unit of pressure (force per unit area), which is called a pascal, and is denoted by the symbol Pa.

2.2 Explain why the kilogram rather than the gram was chosen as the basic or primitive unit of mass in the SI system. (This is one of the SI system's few irregularities.)

2.3 The ratio of the voltage to the current at a pair of terminals is called the *impedance* between the terminals. Under certain conditions the impedance of a capacitor of C farads can be represented by the expression $(\omega C)^{-1}$. Calculate the units in which the parameter ω is measured.

2.4 Explain why on cold dry days an electric shock can sometimes be felt on touching a metal door knob or radiator after walking across a deep carpet.

2.5 Consider the battery-load circuit of Fig. 2.9. Prove that the maximum power is transferred from the battery to the load when the resistance R of the load is equal to the internal resistance r of the battery.

2.6 A car battery has an open-circuit voltage of 12 V. To start the car, the battery must supply a current of 80 A to the starter motor, which can be viewed as a resistive load of 0.1 Ω. On a certain winter's day, the internal resistance of the car battery climbs from its normal value of 0.02 Ω to 0.2 Ω. Will the car start on that day?

2.7 Figure 2.76 shows a circuit that can model the IO behavior of any two-terminal electrical network composed of voltage or current sources and resistors. It is called a *Norton equivalent circuit,* and is closely related to the Thévenin equivalent circuit defined in Fig. 2.12. Determine the relationships between the circuit parameters V_0, R_0, I_0' , and R_0' in the two equivalent circuits.

2.8 Consider the LED circuit of Fig. 2.13a. The LED emits light when $V_{out} = 5$ V, in which case there is a potential difference of 2 V across the terminals of the LED.

    (*a*) Under these conditions, what is the current I_{out} flowing through the LED?

    (*b*) What is I_{out} if V_{out} is changed to 10 V?

2.9 Let the single LED in the circuit of Fig. 2.13a be replaced by two identical LEDs in series. Assume that at least 15 mA must flow through an LED of the type used here for it to light up.

    (*a*) What is the smallest value of the applied voltage V_{out} that will make both LEDs light up?

    (*b*) Suppose that $V_{out} = 5$ V. What must the resistance of the current-limiting resistor R be to allow 20 mA to flow through the LEDs?

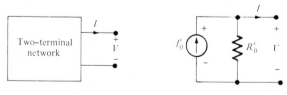

      (*a*)   (*b*)

Figure 2.76 (*a*) Two-terminal electric circuit; (*b*) its Norton equivalent.

2.10 In Fig. 2.11 formulas are given for computing the equivalent resistance of n resistors that are connected in series or in parallel. Find an analogous set of formulas for computing the equivalent capacitance of n capacitors $C_1, C_2, \ldots, C_n$ that are connected (a) in series and (b) in parallel. Explain your reasoning.

2.11 Explain why connecting a capacitor between the power and ground lines can smooth out fluctuations in the power supply voltage.

2.12 Explain why the voltage–current relationship of an actual junction diode depicted in Fig. 2.22b deviates from the ideal relationship of Fig. 2.22a.

2.13 What are the properties of silicon that make it especially suited to the manufacture of integrated circuits?

2.14 Draw a clearly labeled diagram showing in cross section the structure of an integrated pnp transistor that is constructed on an n-type silicon wafer. Junction isolation from the substrate should be provided.

2.15 What is the minimum number of IC masks needed in the manufacture of the bipolar transistor of Fig. 2.38? List the mask steps in their correct sequence, and describe briefly the patterning operation carried out with each mask.

2.16 How many IC masks are needed to manufacture the pMOS transistor of Fig. 2.39? List the masks in sequence and outline the patterning step for which each mask is used.

2.17 Explain why an nMOS field-effect transistor occupies a smaller area on a p-type silicon wafer than an equivalent npn bipolar transistor.

2.18 Why is a VLSI circuit containing, say, 15,000 transistors likely to cost less to design, manufacture, and sell if MOS rather than bipolar IC technology is used?

2.19 What is the minimum number of IO pins that must be included in DIPs containing the following TTL circuits?

  (a) Quad three-input AND gates
  (b) Dual four-input NAND gates
  (c) A single eight-input NAND gate

2.20 Suppose that the (idealized) input waveforms of Fig. 2.77b are applied to the NAND gate of Fig. 2.77a.

  (a) Construct the corresponding waveform for the output signal z assuming that the gate has zero propagation delay.
  (b) Repeat part (a) assuming that the gate has a propagation delay of 5 ns, so that changes in z lag the corresponding input changes by 5 ns.

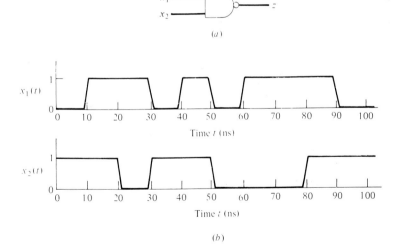

Figure 2.77 (a) NAND gate; (b) input waveforms applied to the NAND gate.

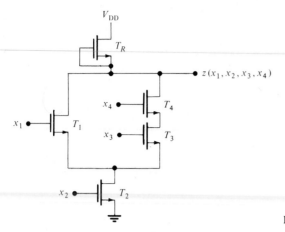

Figure 2.78 Complex nMOS circuit.

2.21 Figure 2.78 shows an nMOS circuit that realizes the four-input logic function $z(x_1, x_2, x_3, x_4)$. Construct a truth table for this circuit.

2.22 Design pMOS inverter and NAND circuits that are the pMOS counterparts of the nMOS circuits given in Figs. 2.54a and 2.56.

2.23 Figure 2.79 defines two important logic gates called *OR* and *NOR gates* (cf. the AND and NAND gates defined in Fig. 2.46). The output of the OR gate of Fig. 2.79a is 1 when either x_1 *or* x_2 or both are 1. The NOR function corresponds to NOT OR, and is obtained by inverting the output of an OR gate. Repeat Prob. 2.20 replacing the NAND gate (*a*) by an OR gate and (*b*) by a NOR gate.

2.24 Design an nMOS circuit analogous to the NAND circuit of Fig. 2.56 that implements the two-input NOR function defined in Fig. 2.79b.

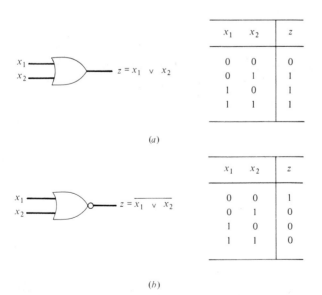

Figure 2.79 Symbols and truth tables for two more basic logic gates: (*a*) OR gate; (*b*) NOR gate.

2.25 Suppose that the following changes are made to the nMOS NAND gate of Fig. 2.56.
(*a*) The nMOS transistors T_R, T_1, and T_2 are replaced by equivalent pMOS transistors.
(*b*) V_{DD} is changed from $+5$ to -5 V.
Construct a truth table for the logic function realized by the resulting pMOS circuit.

2.26 So far we have assumed that logical 1 always corresponds to the higher or more positive voltage range denoted by V_H, while logical 0 corresponds to the lower voltage range V_L. This is the usual assumption made in logic design, and is termed the *positive logic* convention. Although much less common than positive logic, *negative logic* in which 1 corresponds to V_L and 0 corresponds to V_H is sometimes encountered. Let G be a two-input gate that realizes the logic function z when the positive logic convention is used. Determine the logic function z' realized by G when negative logic is assumed, and z is each of the following functions: AND, NAND, NOT, OR, NOR. (The last two functions are defined in Fig. 2.79.)

2.27 Construct a truth table for the nMOS gate of Fig. 2.78 assuming that the negative logic convention defined in Prob. 2.26 is used instead of the usual positive logic convention.

2.28 Suppose that each inverter stage I_j of the two-phase dynamic MOS shift register of Fig. 2.57 is redesigned as shown in Fig. 2.80. T_R is replaced by a load transistor T'_R that can be switched on and off by the appropriate clock signal ϕ_i. When $\phi_i = 1$, I'_R behaves like the original load transistor T_R; however, when $\emptyset_i = 0$, T'_R behaves like an open circuit between V_{DD} and T_j.
(*a*) Assuming that the modified shift register SR' is driven by the clock signals defined in Fig. 2.57b, describe in detail the behavior of SR' during the single clock period t_1 to t_3.
(*b*) Explain why SR' consumes less power on the average than the original shift register SR.

2.29 Figure 2.81 shows a CMOS logic circuit realizing the three-input logic function $z(x_1, x_2, x_3)$. Construct a truth table for this circuit.

2.30 Design a CMOS circuit analogous to the NAND circuit of Fig. 2.59 that realizes the two-input NOR function defined in Fig. 2.79b.

2.31 Write a brief essay comparing and contrasting the TTL, nMOS, and CMOS logic families from the viewpoints of propagation delay, power consumption, and reliability in a noisy environment.

2.32 Explain why in the standard TTL voltage specifications appearing in Fig. 2.61, the acceptable V_H range, which spans 3.0 V, is much wider than the acceptable V_L range, which spans only 0.8 V.

2.33 Let L be an output line of a 74S00-series Schottky TTL IC. Calculate the maximum number of input lines that can be driven by L for each of the following possible load device types:
(*a*) Standard TTL
(*b*) Schottky TTL
(*c*) Low-power Schottky TTL

2.34 Suppose that an output line L from a standard 7400-series TTL IC is driving two standard TTL loads. Calculate how many additional 74LS00-series low-power Schottky TTL loads can be connected to L.

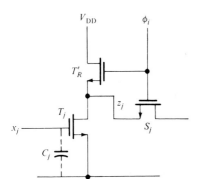

Figure 2.80 Modified inverter stage for two-phase dynamic nMOS shift register.

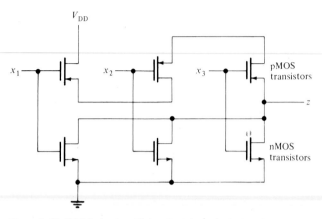

Figure 2.81 CMOS circuit realizing the 3-input logic function $z(x_1,x_2,x_3)$.

2.35 Figure 2.82 shows a partial data sheet (Fairchild, 1975) for a certain IC that is a member of a TTL logic subfamily. Calculate the maximum number of standard TTL loads that can be driven by an output line of the part designated XC in this data sheet.

2.36 Write a short essay comparing and contrasting printed circuits and wire-wrapped circuits from the viewpoints of manufacturing cost, reliability, and maintainability.

2.37 Most interconnection lines in logic circuits are unidirectional, that is, they can transmit signals in one direction only; a bidirectional line can transmit data in either direction (but in only one direction at a time). Explain how three-state gates can be used to create a 1-bit bidirectional bus linking two devices A and B, so that each device can send data to and receive data from the other device by means of a single line.

2.38 A simplified open-collector NAND gate can be formed by removing the resistor R_2 from the TTL NAND circuit of Fig. 2.47a. Figure 2.83 shows how two such open-collector (OC) gates can be used to drive a bus line L. The external resistor has approximately the same value as the resistor R_2 that was removed from the collector branch in the output amplifier stage of each gate. Construct a truth table for the logic function $z(x_1, x_2, x_3, x_4)$ appearing on L. Note that under certain conditions, an OC gate may be considered to put its output line in the high-impedance state Z.

DC CHARACTERISTICS OVER OPERATING TEMPERATURE RANGE (unless otherwise specified)

SYMBOL	PARAMETER		LIMITS			UNITS	TEST CONDITIONS (Note 1)
			MIN	TYP	MAX		
V_{IH}	Input HIGH Voltage		2.0			V	Guaranteed Input HIGH Voltage
V_{IL}	Input LOW Voltage	XM			0.7	V	Guaranteed Input LOW Voltage
		XC			0.8		
V_{CD}	Input Clamp Diode Voltage			−0.65	−1.5	V	V_{CC} = MIN, I_{IN} = −18 mA
V_{OH}	Output HIGH Voltage	XM	2.5	3.4		V	V_{CC} = MIN, I_{OH} = −1.2 mA, V_{IN} = V_{IL}
		XC	2.7	3.4			
V_{OL}	Output LOW Voltage	XM,XC		0.25	0.4	V	V_{CC} = MIN, I_{OL} = 12 mA, V_{IN} = 2.0 V
		XC		0.35	0.5	V	V_{CC} = MIN, I_{OL} = 24 mA, V_{IN} = 2.0 V
I_{IH}	Input HIGH Current			1.0	20	μA	V_{CC} = MAX, V_{IN} = 2.7 V
					0.1	mA	V_{CC} = MAX, V_{IN} = 10 V
I_{IL}	Input LOW Current				−0.36	mA	V_{CC} = MAX, V_{IN} = 0.4 V
I_{OS}	Output Short Circuit Current (Note 3)		−30		−100	mA	V_{CC} = MAX, V_{OUT} = 0 V
I_{CCH}	Supply Current HIGH			0.45	1.0	mA	V_{CC} = MAX, V_{IN} = 0 V
I_{CCL}	Supply Current LOW			3.0	6.0	mA	V_{CC} = MAX, Inputs Open

Figure 2.82 Partial data sheet for a TTL IC. (*Courtesy Fairchild Camera and Instrument Corp.*)

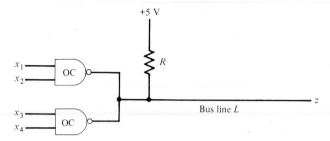

Figure 2.83 Use of open-collector NAND gates to drive a bus line.

2.39 What is meant by a ground plane or grid? List the ways in which it helps to reduce noise in digital circuits.

2.40 Explain the role of decoupling capacitors in the design of high-speed digital systems.

2.41 A ribbon cable consisting of many, perhaps 25, parallel insulated wires forming a flat strip or ribbon is sometimes used for interconnection purposes in digital systems. It is generally recommended that when making long connections with ribbon cable, only every second wire in the cable be used for logic signal transmission; the remaining wires should be grounded. Explain the purpose of this apparently wasteful interconnection rule.

2.42 Explain in general qualitative terms how transmission-line effects in the interconnections of a digital system can cause the following problems: spurious signal pulses and longer than normal signal propagation times.

2.43 Consider the ideal transmission line of Fig. 2.75a. The voltage v at any point can be broken into two components: v^+, which represents the net voltage propagating from left to right, that is, from the signal source; and v^-, which is the net voltage propagating from right to left. Hence we have

$$v = v^+ + v^-$$

In a similar way we can decompose the current i at any point along the transmission line as follows:

$$i = i^+ + i^-$$

By considering these representations of v and i, prove that device B produces an inverted reflected voltage when $R_B < Z_0$, and a noninverted reflected voltage when $R_B > Z_0$.

2.44 Figure 2.84 shows the use of a twisted-pair connected to link two widely separated TTL circuits. The resistors R_1 and R_2 form an impedance-matching termination circuit for the twisted pair, which is treated as an ideal transmission line. The values of R_1 and R_2 are chosen to allow minimal but adequate drive currents to be drawn by the load circuit B. If $R_2 = 330 \ \Omega$, and the characteristic impedance of the twisted pair is 132 Ω, calculate an appropriate resistance value for R_1.

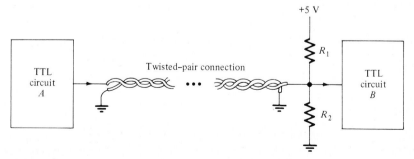

Figure 2.84 Twisted-pair transmission line with termination circuit.

THREE

DESIGN USING SMALL-SCALE INTEGRATION

"The time must come when the inevitable results of the admirable investigations of the late Dr. Boole must be recognized for their true value, and the plain and palpable form in which the [Jevons logic] machine presents those results will, I hope, hasten the time."

[W. S. Jevons: *Principles of Science,* 1874]

An IC containing up to about 100 electronic devices is considered to employ small-scale integration (SSI). Such circuits are used to fabricate simple logic elements such as switches, gates, and flip-flops, which process or store binary information. This chapter examines SSI components and their uses in the design of digital systems. The elements of logic design are reviewed, including the properties of the basic logic elements, the different types of logic circuits, and the representation of information in binary form. Combinational and sequential SSI ICs are considered, with examples drawn from the popular 7400 series of commercially produced ICs. Systematic design procedures, which are based on Boolean algebra and are suitable for designing small logic circuits, are discussed.

3.1 LOGIC DESIGN CONCEPTS

We first consider how information is represented in binary or logical form. The basic types of logic components are then introduced, and the two main types of logic circuits, combinational and sequential, are characterized.

3.1.1 Logic Values

Digital circuits are characterized by the use of a small number of signal levels or values to represent information. For example, n voltage levels $V_1, V_2, \cdots, V_n$ could represent the possible values of an n-valued digital variable. The most useful figure for n in electronic digital circuits is two, resulting in two-valued or binary variables. Two voltage levels, a high voltage V_H and a low voltage V_L, are generally used for binary variables in electronic circuits. In standard TTL circuits, for instance, V_H corresponds to voltages in the range 2.0 to 5.0 V, while V_L corresponds to voltages in the range 0.0 to 0.8 V; see Fig. 2.61.

There are several advantages to restricting digital signals to two rather than, say, 10 values.

1. Switches, which are fundamental components of digital systems, are inherently binary in nature because they have two stable states, on and off.
2. The fewer values used, the wider is the separation between them, and the less the likelihood of minor noise fluctuations changing a signal value (voltage) V_i to an adjacent value $V_{i\pm1}$.
3. Since voltage is inherently an analog or continuous quantity, a signal change from V_i to a nonadjacent value V_{i+2} must pass through the intermediate value V_{i+1}. Thus a spurious V_{i+1} signal is produced which, if present for a sufficiently long time, can cause a malfunction. With binary signals there are no intermediate signal values of this kind.

Thus binary digital circuits are inherently easier to construct and tend to be more reliable than circuits that process signals that can assume three or more values; the latter are referred to as *multivalued logic circuits*.

Although binary signal values are associated with specific voltage levels, it is usual to represent them by the abstract symbols 0 (logical zero) and 1 (logical one), which are termed *logic values*. While there are strong analogies between these logic values and the numbers 0 and 1, the concepts of logic value and number are quite distinct. In logic design the values 0 and 1 are usually made to correspond to the voltage levels V_L (the lower voltage) and V_H (the higher voltage), respectively, a convention called positive logic. Occasionally the opposite convention is used that associates 1 with V_L and 0 with V_H; this is known as negative logic. Only the positive logic convention is used in this book.

The terms logic design and logic value suggest a connection with the discipline of logic, which may be defined as the science of proper reasoning. Classical logic is a branch of philosophy and, under the name mathematical or symbolic logic, a branch of mathematics. It is concerned with the correctness of sentences or propositions such as: If man is an animal and all animals are mortal, then man is mortal. A sentence of this kind has two possible values, namely, **true** and **false**, and therefore can be regarded as a binary variable. Thus classical logic and logic design are both concerned with binary variables; they also share a common mathematical basis. Figure 3.1 gives the correspondence between the variables and values of various binary systems.

A *logic element* is a circuit component whose input and output signals are confined to the values 0 and 1. It is represented in circuit diagrams by means of a box as illustrated in Fig. 3.2a, or in the case of very common logic elements, by a special symbol. Systems or networks formed by interconnecting logic elements are termed *logic circuits*. A logic circuit whose output values at any time are completely determined by the combination of

Discipline	Variables	Values Assigned to Variables	
Electronic circuit design	Voltage signals	V_H (high voltage)	V_L (low voltage)
Logic design	Logic signals	1 (logical one)	0 (logical zero)
Classical logic	Sentences or propositions	**true**	**false**

Figure 3.1 Some disciplines concerned with binary quantities.

values applied to its input lines is called a *combinational circuit*. Let N be a combinational circuit with n input signals $x_1, x_2, \cdots, x_n$ and m output signals $z_1, z_2, \cdots, z_m$. Each output signal z_i can be viewed as a *logic function* from the 2^n values specified by $x_1, x_2, \cdots, x_n$ into the values 0 and 1 appearing on line z_i; this is indicated explicitly by writing the output signal in the form $z_i(x_1, x_2, \cdots, x_n)$. N is said to *realize* or *implement* the logic function $z_i(x_1, x_2, \cdots, x_n)$. Clearly the behavior of N is defined by the logic functions z_1, $z_2, \cdots, z_m$. A common way of specifying these functions is to list all 2^n possible input combinations along with the corresponding output values in a table called a truth table, a name that again reflects the link with classical logic. Figure 3.2b shows a truth table for the three-input two-output combinational circuit of Fig. 3.2a. In general, the truth table for an n-input m-output combinational circuit contains 2^n rows, n input columns, and m output columns.

There are various situations in which it is useful to have other signal values besides 0 and 1 in logic circuits; these additional values also may be termed logic values. The basic values 0 and 1 represent the signals appearing on a perfect conductor C to which a voltage source supplying the voltage signals V_L and V_H, respectively, is connected. One might raise the question: What is the logic value appearing on C when it is not connected to any

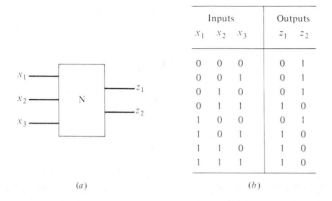

(a) *(b)*

Figure 3.2 (*a*) Combinational circuit or component and (*b*) its truth table.

voltage source whatsoever, that is, if C is isolated or floating? A third value, denoted by Z and called the high-impedance state, may be assigned to C under these circumstances. This terminology derives from the fact that an isolated conductor presents an extremely high electrical impedance to any signal source subsequently connected to it; Z is also the usual symbol for electrical impedance. As discussed in Sec. 2.3.4, 0, 1, and Z are the possible values of the output signals generated by a class of logic elements called three-state gates.

It might also be asked: What happens if V_L and V_H, or equivalently 0 and 1, are applied simultaneously to the conductor C? This is a conflict situation in which C is likely to assume a voltage level that represents neither 0 nor 1. A fourth logic value denoted U *(unknown)* is then needed to specify the state of C. Logic circuits are invariably designed so that the U value is never produced under normal operating conditions; it may appear, however, when a fault is present in that circuit. Additional logic values may be needed for certain types of logic circuits. For most purposes, it suffices to use the two fundamental values 0 and 1, with occasional use of other values, especially Z.

3.1.2 CSA Circuits

The key components of integrated logic circuits are transistors, which function as electronic switches that can block or transmit logic signals. The LSI/VLSI circuits of the type used to manufacture microprocessors and microcomputers are composed almost entirely of MOS transistor switches. We now briefly consider the logical behavior of such circuits based on the CSA (connector-switch-attenuator) theory described in Hayes (1982). These circuit models occupy a complexity level, which may be called the *switch level*, that is intermediate between the electronic circuit level discussed in Chap. 2 and the conventional gate-level logic circuits studied in the remainder of this chapter.

Consider an ideal electrical conductor C to which various voltage signals $x_1, x_2, \cdots,$ x_k are applied. C assumes an (output) voltage level z_C, which is a function of the applied (input) voltages. Hence we may write

$$z_C = \#(x_1, x_2, \cdots, x_k)$$

where $\#$ denotes a *connection function* computed by the conductor C. If the input signals $x_1, x_2, \cdots, x_k$ and the output signal z_C are confined to voltages corresponding to logic values in the set $V_4 = \{0, 1, U, Z\}$, then $\#$ may be interpreted as a logic function or logic operator on V_4. The question then arises: Given the values of $x_1, x_2, \cdots, x_k$, what is the value of $\#(x_1, x_2, \cdots, x_k)$?

It is reasonable to assume that if all the input logic signals applied to C have the same value $x \in V_4$, than z_C also has the value x. Hence we obtain

$$\#(x, x, \cdots, x) = x \qquad \text{for all } x \in V_4$$

If at some point $z_C = Z$, that is, C is in the high-impedance or floating state, and $x \in \{0, 1, U\}$ is applied to C, then we would expect x to override Z and force z_C to the new value x. Thus the values 0, 1, U are seen as *logically stronger* than Z, a relation denoted by the symbol $>$ which is read as "is logically stronger than" or "overrides." Note that in this context $>$ is not the same as the numerical relation "is greater than." Hence we can write

$$0 > Z; \quad 1 > Z; \quad U > Z$$

It is also convenient to use the symbol $\geq$ to denote the relation "is of equal or greater logical strength than" among logic values. Thus we can write $x \geq x$ for any $x \in V_4$. If the input signals to C include both 0 and 1, then from the voltage interpretations of the logic values, z_C can be expected to assume the unknown value U. Therefore,

$$\#(0, 1, \cdots, x) = U$$

This implies that $0 \not\geq 1$ and $1 \not\geq 0$, so that 0 and 1 are incomparable with respect to the relation $\geq$. Moreover, U is logically stronger than any other member of V_4, that is,

$$U > 0; \quad U > 1; \quad U > Z$$

The foregoing analysis of the logical behavior of a connector can be summarized by the following *Connection Rule*:

Let C be a connector to which the input signals $x_1, x_2, \cdots, x_k \in V_4$ are applied. C then produces the output value $z_C = \#(x_1, x_2, \cdots, x_k)$ where z_C is the logically weakest member of V_4 such that $z_C \geq x_i$ for $i = 1, 2, \cdots, k$. (3.1)

For example, $\#(0, 1, 1, Z) = U$ and $\#(Z, 0, Z, 0) = 0$. Figure 3.3 gives a complete truth table for $\#(x_1, x_2, \cdots, x_k)$ in the case where $k = 2$.

An *abstract switch* S is a logic element with two states, on and off, and three input-output (IO) terminals: a control terminal K whose value determines the state of S, and two symmetric input-output "data" terminals D_1 and D_2. The symbol appearing in Fig. 3.4a is

x_1	x_2	z_C
0	0	0
0	1	U
0	U	U
0	Z	0
1	0	U
1	1	1
1	U	U
1	Z	1
U	0	U
U	1	U
U	U	U
U	Z	U
Z	0	0
Z	1	1
Z	U	U
Z	Z	Z

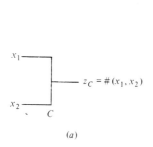

(a)

(b)

Figure 3.3 (a) Connector C with two input signals; (b) its truth table with respect to V_4.

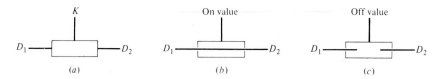

Figure 3.4 Positive switch: (*a*) symbol; (*b*) behavior when switched on; (*c*) behavior when switched off.

used to represent a switch in circuit diagrams. When S is in the on state, D_1 and D_2 are effectively linked via a connector through S as illustrated in Fig. 3.4b. When S is switched off, D_1 and D_2 are disconnected as shown in Fig. 3.4c. A switch therefore may be viewed as a controlled connector. Two basic types of switches are described in Fig. 3.5: a *positive switch,* which is turned on by $K = 1$ and turned off by $K = 0$; and a *negative switch,* which is turned on by $K = 0$ and turned off by $K = 1$. As indicated in Fig. 3.5, an abstract switch models various kinds of physical switches. For example, an nMOS transistor switch can be modeled by a positive switch S with the transistor's gate input corresponding to the control input K of S; the transistor's source and drain terminals correspond to the data terminals of S. In a similar way, a negative gate can model a pMOS transistor.

A circuit composed of connectors and switches only is called a *CS (connector-switch) circuit.* (The term *switching circuit* may also be used; however, this term is usually employed as a synonym for logic circuits in general.) Figure 3.6a shows an example of a CS circuit N_1 composed of two negative switches S_1 and S_2, two positive switches S_3 and S_4, and six connectors $C_0{:}C_5$. Two external input signals x_1 and x_2 are applied to N_1 and a single output signal z_1 is produced by N_1. The logical constants 0 and 1, representing ground and power respectively, are also applied to N_1. Connector-switch circuits are normally designed to process binary variables; thus the inputs x_1 and x_2 and the output z_1 of N_1 can be expected to be confined to the values 0 and 1.

Type	Symbol	Behavior	Examples
Positive	K	$K = 1$: on $K = 0$: off	(1) nMOS transistor (2) npn bipolar transistor (3) Normally off (electro) mechanical switch
Negative	K	$K = 0$: on $K = 1$: off	(1) pMOS transistor (2) pnp bipolar transistor (3) Normally on (electro) mechanical switch

Figure 3.5 Two basic switch types.

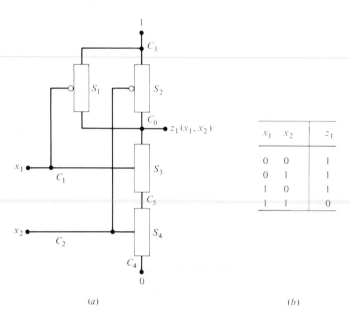

Figure 3.6 CS NAND circuit N_1: (a) circuit diagram; (b) truth table.

The truth table for N_1, which appears in Fig. 3.6b, may be constructed as follows: Suppose that $x_1 = x_2 = 0$. This input combination switches S_1 and S_2 on, while switching S_3 and S_4 off. S_1 and S_2 then create a connecting path from C_3 to the output connector C_0, thereby applying 1 to C_0. Since S_3 and S_4 are off, C_0 is disconnected from the 0 source C_4. Thus S_3 only applies the signal Z, which is equivalent to applying no signal, to C_0. Hence $z_{C_0} = \#(1, Z) = 1$, implying that $z_1(0, 0) = 1$. Next suppose that $x_1 = 0$ and $x_2 = 1$. This input combination switches S_1 and S_4 on, while switching S_2 and S_3 off. Again a connection exists from C_3 to C_0 but not from C_4 to C_0; consequently $z_{C_0} = \#(1, Z) = 1 = z_1(0, 1)$. It can be shown similarly that $z_1(1, 0) = 1$. Finally, consider the case where $x_1 = x_2 = 1$. This combination causes S_3 and S_4 to switch on, thus connecting C_4 to C_0. S_1 and S_2, on the other hand, are switched off, which disconnects C_3 from C_0. It follows that $z_{C_0} = \#(Z, 0) = 0 = z_1(1, 1)$, yielding the last row of the truth table for N_1. Note that N_1 exactly models the structure and behavior of the CMOS transistor circuit appearing in Fig. 2.59. N_1 therefore is a CS implementation of the NAND logic function.

As discussed above, a switch models certain aspects of the digital behavior of a transistor. It can also be useful to introduce digital or logical models of other electrical elements such as resistors and capacitors. For example, resistors acting as pull-up load elements play a central role in the logical operation of the pMOS and nMOS circuits examined in Sec. 2.4. To model the digital behavior of a resistor, some more logic values are necessary. As noted already, the logic values 0, 1, U, Z forming V_4 have a property called logical strength. Additional logic values can be created by splitting 0, 1, and U into n subvalues having different logical strength levels thus:

$$0 = 0_1, 0_2, \cdots, 0_n = \tilde{0}$$

$$1 = 1_1, 1_2, \cdots, 1_n = \tilde{1}$$

$$U = U_1, U_2, \cdots, U_n = \tilde{U}$$

where a tilde denotes the weakest value in each group. Particularly useful in the analysis of MOS logic circuits is the case where $n = 2$ and there are seven logic values, $V_7 = \{0, 1, U, \tilde{0}, \tilde{1}, \tilde{U}, Z\}$. Figure 3.7 shows graphically the strength relationships among the members of V_4 and V_7. If a value x appears above another value x', then x is logically stronger than x'. Different values lying on the same horizontal line are incomparable. For example, the weak unknown value $\tilde{U}$ in V_7 is logically stronger than $\tilde{0}$ or $\tilde{1}$, but it is weaker than 0 or 1. U and Z are the strongest and weakest values, respectively, in each set.

The behavior of a connector C when signals defined on V_7 are applied to it is a direct extension of its behavior with respect to V_4. It suffices to replace V_4 by V_7 in the Connection Rule (3.1) to obtain a rule for computing $\#(x_1, x_2, \cdots, x_k)$ when the x_i's are members of V_7. For example, $\#(\tilde{0}, \tilde{1}, \tilde{0}, Z) = \tilde{U}$, $\#(0, \tilde{0}, \tilde{1}, \tilde{U}) = 0$, and $\#(0, \tilde{0}, \tilde{1}, 1) = U$.

Figure 3.8 defines a logic element called an *attenuator*, which serves to generate the weak values $\tilde{0}, \tilde{1}, \tilde{U}$ from the strong values $0, 1, U$ respectively. As suggested by Fig. 3.9,

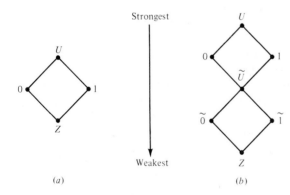

Figure 3.7 Strength relationships among logic value sets: (a) V_4; (b) V_7.

x	z
0, $\tilde{0}$	$\tilde{0}$
1 $\tilde{1}$	$\tilde{1}$
U $\tilde{U}$	$\tilde{U}$
Z	Z

(a) (b)

Figure 3.8 Symbol and truth table for an attenuator.

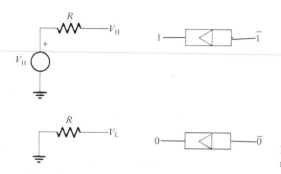

Figure 3.9 Correspondence between a resistor and an attenuator.

an attenuator is the digital equivalent of an analog resistor. The strong signals 0 and 1 correspond to V_L and V_H voltage signals that are obtained from ideal voltage sources that have infinite current drive capability or, equivalently, zero internal resistance. Such voltage sources are closely approximated by power and ground lines, or by the output signals of an amplifier circuit. The weak signals 0 and 1, on the other hand, correspond to V_L and V_H signals obtained from voltage sources with low-current drive capability. Such sources have a nonzero internal resistance that may be represented by an attenuator. Logical strength therefore can be interpreted as representing the (current) drive capability or override capability of a logic signal. Thus an attenuator has the effect of reducing current drive, and so may be regarded as the inverse of an amplifier; this analogy is suggested by the use of a reversed amplifier (triangle) symbol within the symbol for an attenuator. Figure 3.10 gives the definition of an amplifier with respect to V_7. Circuits composed of connectors, switches, attenuators, and other logic elements are called *CSA (connector-switch-attenuator) circuits*.

A CSA circuit N_2 containing two switches and an attenuator appears in Fig. 3.11a. N_2 realizes the two-input function $z_2(x_1, x_2)$. If the input signals x_1 and x_2 are confined to the set $\{0, 1\}$, then it is easily shown that N_2 has the behavior specified by the truth table of Fig. 3.11b. When $x_1 = x_2 = 1$, the two switches S_1 and S_2 are turned on, creating a path from C_5 to C_0 that applies 0 to C_0. The attenuator A continuously applies $\tilde{1}$ to C_0, but because $0 > \tilde{1}$, the output signal of N_2 is $z_2(1, 1) = \#(0, \tilde{1}) = 0$. If either x_1 or x_2 is 0, then the connection from C_5 to C_0 is broken, and C_0 receives only the signal Z from S_1. The attenuator then pulls C_0 up to the 1 level, implying that $z_2 = \#(Z, \tilde{1}) = \tilde{1}$. Ignoring strength levels, N_2 implements the same NAND function as the CS circuit N_1 of Fig. 3.6a. In fact, N_2 models the structure and behavior of the nMOS NAND circuit shown in

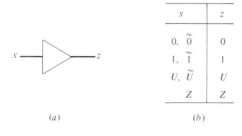

x	z
$0, \tilde{0}$	0
$1, \tilde{1}$	1
$U, \tilde{U}$	U
Z	Z

(*a*)   (*b*)

Figure 3.10 Definition of an amplifier with respect to V_7.

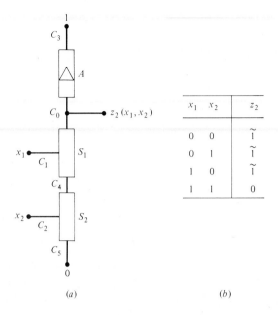

(a)   (b)

Figure 3.11 CSA NAND circuit N_2:
(a) circuit diagram; (b) truth table.

Fig. 2.56. The differences in the strength levels of the output logic signals of N_2 mirror the differences in output drive capability between the output high and output low states of the underlying electronic circuit of Fig. 2.56. Note that in both cases an extra amplifier stage can be added to convert the weak output signals to strong ones.

Connector-switch-attenuator theory is especially useful for analyzing circuits such as three-state and open-collector gates (see Sec. 2.3.4), which can drive their output lines to the high-impedance state Z. Consider, for instance, the bus-driving circuit of Fig. 2.83. Figure 3.12 shows an equivalent CSA circuit. The elements N, which represent the open-collector NAND gates in the original circuit, have the behavior defined in Fig. 3.12b. This truth table is the same as that of an ordinary NAND gate with Z replacing 1 or

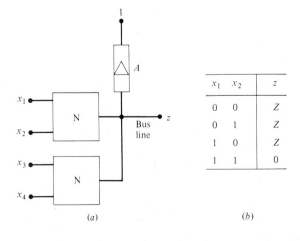

(a)   (b)

Figure 3.12 CSA model for the bus circuit of Fig. 2.83: (a) circuit diagram; (b) truth table of the element N.

$\bar{1}$. The output of the circuit of Fig. 3.12a is 0 whenever one of the N's produces a 0 on its output line. When all the N's produce the output Z, then the attenuator A, which represents the pull-up resistor R of the original circuit, forces z to 1. Hence z always assumes values from the set $\{0, \bar{1}\}$. In recognition of the explicit role of the connector C in determining the output function z, the circuit of Fig. 3.12a is said to contain *wired logic,* with the connector C acting as a *wired gate.* In fact, connectors play a central role in determining the logical operation of all types of switching circuits.

3.1.3 Combinational Circuits

Digital circuits are designed to process binary information. To concentrate on the functional aspects of such circuits, we move to a higher level of abstraction than the CSA level. This level is called the gate or logic level, and is characterized by the use of a logic element called a gate as the basic component. The internal structure of a gate may be seen as either a CSA circuit or an analog electronic circuit. Figures 3.6 and 3.11, for example, show two possible CSA implementations of a two-input NAND gate, while the corresponding electronic circuits appear in Figs. 2.59 and 2.56 respectively. At the gate level, gates become primitive components whose internal structure is not of interest. In moving from switches to gates, several other simplifications are made:

1. The concept of logical strength is dropped, so that only the two fundamental logic values 0 and 1 are retained.
2. While CSA circuits are inherently bidirectional—that is, logic signals can flow in either direction through any two-terminal connector—gate circuits are inherently unidirectional. This implies that each terminal of a gate is either an input or an output terminal of the gate, but not both.
3. Power and ground connections are not shown in gate-level circuits, since they represent constant logic signals that are not directly involved in information processing. Thus the interconnection structure of a gate-level circuit is significantly simpler than that of the underlying CSA or electronic circuit.

Throughout the remainder of this book we will be mainly concerned with "pure" logic circuits in which only the values 0 and 1 appear as signals. Occasionally it will be useful to introduce additional values such as Z, which again will require the use of CSA concepts. Note that gates and similar components can be combined with CSA switches in the same circuit, provided all signals are confined to the set $\{0, 1\}$ during normal operation. It is also sometimes useful to redefine gate behavior in terms of an expanded logic value set such as V_4 or V_7.

A *gate* G may be defined formally as a combinational logic element with n input lines or signals $x_1, x_2, \cdots, x_n$ and one output line or signal z. G realizes some logic function $z(x_1, x_2, \cdots, x_n)$, where $x_1, x_2, \cdots, x_n, z$ assume values from the set $\{0, 1\}$. Like any system component, G can be represented in structural (block) diagrams, which in this context are called *logic diagrams,* by means of the general block symbol shown in Fig. 3.13a. The function z realized by G then may be written into the block. The most common gate types use the distinctively shaped circuit symbols appearing in Figs.

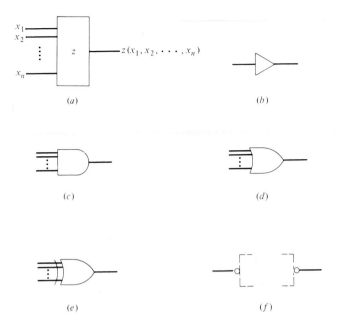

(a) (b)

(c) (d)

(e) (f)

Figure 3.13 Basic logic symbols: (a) general block symbol; (b) buffer; (c) AND; (d) OR; (e) EXCLUSIVE-OR; (f) inversion (NOT).

3.13b–3.13f. The triangle symbol of Fig. 3.13b denotes a buffer or driver element that is used for electronic signal amplification. Viewed as a logic element, a buffer performs the trivial identity operation that maps 0 onto 0 and 1 onto 1. The distinctive shapes of Figs. 3.13c–3.13e denote nontrivial logic functions called AND, OR, and EXCLUSIVE-OR respectively. Finally, the logic function called inversion or NOT, which maps 0 onto 1 and 1 onto 0, may be denoted by a small circle or bubble. This inversion symbol is not used by itself, but instead may be attached to the IO terminals of any of the other symbols in Fig. 3.13, giving rise to a variety of different gate symbols and types.

The input-output behavior of any gate can be completely described by means of a truth table. Figure 3.14a shows the truth table for a simple (noninverting) buffer. It also shows an alternative but rarely used symbol for a buffer obtained by attaching inversion circles to both terminals of the basic buffer symbol. Here the two inversions cancel each other, so that the resulting gate acts as a noninverting buffer. Figure 3.14b shows two possible symbols and the truth table for another one-input gate, the inverter or NOT gate.

Figure 3.15 defines the six most important multi-input gate types used in logic design, and shows the most common circuit symbols used to represent them. The design of electronic circuits to implement some of these gates was examined in Chap. 2. Here we are concerned only with the gates' logical behavior, which is defined by the truth table of Fig. 3.15b. The AND gate is so named because its output signal z_{AND} is 1 if and only if $x_1 = 1$ *and* $x_2 = 1$ *and* $\cdots$ *and* $x_n = 1$. Similarly, the output z_{OR} of the OR gate is 1 if and only if $x_1 = 1$ *or* $x_2 = 1$ *or* $\cdots$ *or* $x_n = 1$. Thus there is only one input combination, namely, $(x_1, x_2, \cdots, x_n) = (1, 1, \cdots, 1)$, which causes an AND gate to generate a 1, while only the

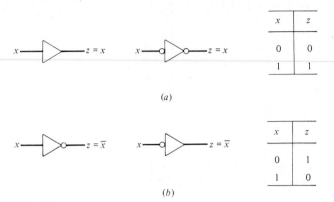

Figure 3.14 Symbols and truth tables for: (*a*) noninverting buffer; (*b*) inverter or NOT gate.

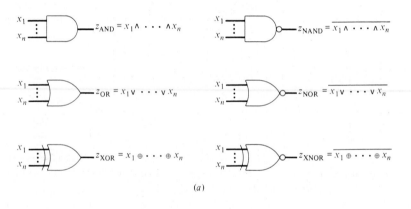

x_1	x_2	$\cdots$	x_{n-1}	x_n	z_{AND}	z_{NAND}	z_{OR}	z_{NOR}	z_{XOR} (n odd)	z_{XNOR} (n odd)	z_{XOR} (n even)	z_{XNOR} (n even)
0	0		0	0	0	1	0	1	0	1	0	1
0	0		0	1	0	1	1	0	1	0	1	0
0	0		1	0	0	1	1	0	1	0	1	0
0	0		1	1	0	1	1	0	0	1	0	1
		$\cdots$										
1	1		1	0	0	1	1	0	0	1	1	0
1	1		1	1	1	0	1	0	1	0	0	1

(*b*)

Figure 3.15 Six basic gate types: (*a*) symbols; (*b*) truth tables.

combination $(0, 0, \cdots, 0)$ causes an OR gate to produce a 0. The EXCLUSIVE-OR gate is somewhat more difficult to define. When $n = 2$, a two-input EXCLUSIVE-OR gate produces a 1 if and only if $x_1 = 1$ or $x_2 = 1$, but not both at once. It is thus similar to an OR gate except that the input combination $(x_1, x_2) = (1, 1)$ is excluded from the set of 1-producing input combinations. A general n-input EXCLUSIVE-OR gate can be defined as a gate that produces a 1 if and only if an odd number of its input signals are 1. For this reason, an EXCLUSIVE-OR gate is sometimes called a *parity check gate* since its output signal indicates the parity (evenness or oddness) of the number of 1s applied to its input lines.

The three gates called NAND, NOR, and EXCLUSIVE-NOR in Fig. 3.15 may be formed by inverting the output signal of the corresponding AND, OR, and EX-CLUSIVE-OR gates. Thus the output signal z_{NAND} of a NAND gate is 0 if and only if all inputs to the gate are 1, while z_{NOR} is 1 if and only if all inputs are 0. An EXCLUSIVE-NOR gate produces a 1 if and only if an even number of input signals are 1. Note that when $n = 1$, NAND, NOR, and EXCLUSIVE-NOR all reduce to NOT gates or inverters. Multi-input NAND and NOR gates are especially useful as logic design components for several reasons:

1. Each type is functionally complete in the sense that any logical function, that is, any truth table, can be realized by a logic circuit composed of NAND gates only, or one composed of NOR gates only. The other gates listed in Fig. 3.15 do not have this property.
2. NAND and NOR gates can be constructed from simple transistor circuits, examples of which appear in Chap. 2. AND and OR gates, on the other hand, usually require more complex transistor implementations. For instance, a NAND circuit followed by an extra inverting stage is needed to implement the AND function using most MOS logic families. EXCLUSIVE-OR and EXCLUSIVE-NOR have even more complex transistor implementations.

To be able to represent the behavior of logic circuits in mathematical form, as functional equations, for example, it is useful to introduce special operator symbols to denote the operations performed by gates. In this book we employ the widely used symbols $\wedge$, $\vee$, $\oplus$, and $^-$ (overbar) to represent the AND, OR, EXCLUSIVE-OR, and NOT operations respectively. Hence, as indicated in Fig. 3.15, we can write

$$z_{AND}(x_1, x_2, \ldots, x_n) = x_1 \wedge x_2 \wedge \ldots \wedge x_n$$

$$z_{OR}(x_1, x_2, \ldots, x_n) = x_1 \vee x_2 \vee \ldots \vee x_n$$

$$z_{XOR}(x_1, x_2, \ldots, x_n) = x_1 \oplus x_2 \oplus \ldots \oplus x_n$$

$$z_{NOT}(x_1) = \overline{x}_1$$

Special operator symbols are rarely used for the NAND, NOR, or EXCLUSIVE-NOR functions; we therefore combine the preceding symbols as follows:

$$z_{NAND}(x_1, x_2, \ldots, x_n) = \overline{x_1 \wedge x_2 \wedge \ldots \wedge x_n}$$

$$z_{NOR}(x_1, x_2, \ldots, x_n) = \overline{x_1 \vee x_2 \vee \ldots \vee x_n}$$

$$z_{XNOR}(x_1, x_2, \ldots, x_n) = \overline{x_1 \oplus x_2 \oplus \ldots \oplus x_n}$$

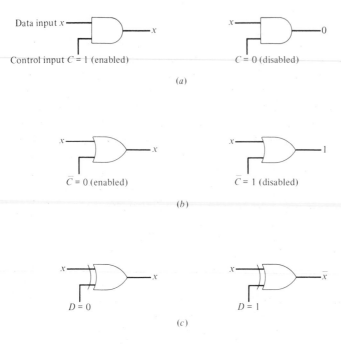

Figure 3.16 Use of gates to control logic signal flow: (a) AND; (b) OR; (c) EXCLUSIVE-OR.

The AND and OR operations are frequently indicated by the symbols for numerical multiplication and addition, namely, juxtaposition (or ·) and +; hence the reader can expect to encounter the following notation:

$$z_{AND}(x_1, x_2, \ldots, x_n) = x_1 x_2 \ldots x_n$$

$$z_{OR}(x_1, x_2, \ldots, x_n) = x_1 + x_2 + \ldots + x_n$$

The use of $\wedge$ (which resembles a capital A for AND) and $\vee$ (from the Latin *vel* meaning or) as symbols for AND and OR, respectively, avoids any confusion between logical and numerical operations, both of which are encountered in digital system design.

It can be helpful to view gates as devices for controlling the flow of logic signals through a circuit. A gate may be "opened" to allow a particular signal applied to one of its input lines to pass through it; it may be "closed" to block signal transmission through the gate. This idea, which is the origin of the term "gate," suggests that a logic gate can act as a unidirectional switch. This viewpoint is illustrated in Fig. 3.16 for various two-input gates. One input line C to each gate is used to control the transmission of the other input signal x through the gate; C may be termed a *control input* and x a *data input*. In the case of the AND gate of Fig. 3.16a, when $C = 1$, the output signal $z = x$, so that x passes unchanged through the gate. Under this condition, the AND gate is said to be *enabled*, and C is said *to gate* x through the gate. When, however, $C = 0$, z is forced to 0 independently of the value of x, and the gate is said to be *disabled*. In the case of the OR gate of Fig. 3.16b, the gate is enabled when the control signal $\bar{C} = 0$; it is disabled when

$\bar{C} = 1$. In the case of the EXCLUSIVE-OR gate of Fig. 3.16c, there are no enabled or disabled conditions; x is transmitted unchanged through the gate when $D = 0$, and x is inverted during transmission through the gate when $D = 1$.

Combinational circuits can be constructed by connecting two or more gates together in such a way that the resulting circuit realizes a well-defined set of logic functions. Combinational circuits have two main uses in digital systems:

1. As *data transfer circuits* that control the flow of logic signals (data) from one part of the system to another
2. As *data processing circuits* that process or transform data, thereby performing useful computation

Figure 3.17 shows an example of a data transfer circuit called a *multiplexer*, which is designed to control the transfer of data from a set of input buses, in this case the two buses $X = (x_0, x_1, x_2, x_3)$ and $Y = (y_0, y_1, y_2, y_3)$, to the output data bus $Z = (z_0, z_1, z_2, z_3)$. Clearly only one of X and Y can transmit data to Z at any one time. Two control input lines are connected to this circuit: a select or address line S and an enable line $\bar{E}$. This multiplexer M therefore constitutes a 10-input four-output combinational circuit com-

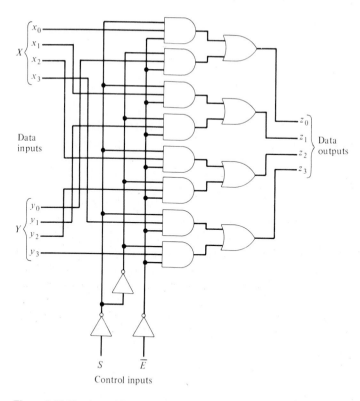

Figure 3.17 Two-input 4-bit multiplexer circuit M.

posed of AND, OR, and NOT gates. From the behavior of its constituent gates, it is easily verified that M behaves as follows:

1. When $\bar{E} = 1$, in which case the multiplexer is disabled, all output signals z_0, z_1, z_2, z_3 of M are forced to 0. This is so because $\bar{E}$ is connected to an inverter that applies 0 to an input of every AND gate of M. This forces the outputs of all the ANDs to 0, which in turn forces the OR gates to produce 0 on each of the primary output lines of M.

2. When $\bar{E} = 0$, in which case the multiplexer is enabled, the value of z_i for $i = 0, 1, 2, 3$ is determined by the other control signal S as follows:

$$z_i = x_i \quad \text{when} \quad S = 0$$

$$z_i = y_i \quad \text{when} \quad S = 1$$

The control signal S thus selects one of the input buses X or Y whose data are then transmitted to the output bus Z when the multiplexer is enabled.

It is possible to describe the behavior of the multiplexer M more formally by means of a truth table; however, since M has 10 primary input variables, such a table would have $2^{10} = 1024$ rows, making it rather impractical. An equally rigorous but much more concise description of M's behavior can be conveyed by means of a set of equations called *logic* or *Boolean equations*, which make use of the logic operations introduced above. Four logic equations of the following form suffice to specify the input-output behavior of M:

$$z_i = \bar{E} \wedge [(x_i \wedge \bar{S}) \vee (y_i \wedge S)] \qquad i = 0, 1, 2, 3,$$

The properties of such equations will be considered later.

In the logic circuits of Figs. 3.16 and 3.17, input and output lines are divided into data and control lines, a distinction that is based on the intended functions of the circuits in question. Data lines can assume the values 0 and 1 in arbitrary fashion, and no particular significance is attached to either value. A control line usually specifies an action or function F to be carried out by the circuit. When the control line C assumes one of its values, the action F is carried out, in which case C is said to be *activated* or *asserted*. When C assumes the opposite value, F is not performed, and C is said to be *deactivated* or *deasserted*. Certain naming conventions are used in logic design to indicate the value, 0 or 1, needed to activate a control line; unfortunately these conventions are not always used consistently in the literature. A control signal that is activated by 1, or is *active high*, is given a name with no overbar, for example, ENABLE, and is applied to lines that do not terminate in inversion circles. A control signal that is activated by 0, or is *active low*, may be indicated in one of the following ways:

1. By giving the signal a name with an overbar, for example, $\overline{\text{ENABLE}}$, and by not inserting inversion circles in the corresponding line.
2. By giving the signal a name without an overbar, and inserting a single inversion circle in the corresponding line.

Figure 3.18 illustrates the use of these naming rules. Note that they are only of value for lines that are associated with a single well-defined control function.

An example of a combinational logic circuit intended for data processing is given in Fig. 3.19. This is the logic diagram of a commerical medium-scale IC in the 7400-series of TTL circuits, the 74283 4-bit binary *adder* (Texas Instruments, 1981). It computes the arithmetic sum

$$Z = X + Y + C_{in}$$

where X, Y, and Z are 4-bit binary numbers, and C_{in} denotes a 1-bit input carry signal. It also generates an output carry signal C_{out}. The C_{in} and C_{out} signals allow n copies of the 74283 to be connected together to form a $4n$-bit adder circuit. As Fig. 3.19 indicates, the 74283 is a nine-input five-output combinational circuit containing 36 gates of six different types. To understand this and other data-processing circuits, it is necessary to consider how numerical data are represented using just the two symbols 0 and 1.

3.1.4 Binary Numbers

The smallest unit of information in a logic circuit is a single variable x that can assume the two values 0 and 1. Such a two-valued or binary variable can represent a control signal such as the multiplexer enable signal $\bar{E}$ in Fig. 3.17, or a data signal such as the carry-in signal C_{in} in the adder of Fig. 3.19. Often two or more binary variables are grouped to form an ordered set X called a word and denoted by $(x_1, x_2, \ldots, x_n)$ or $x_1 x_2 \ldots x_n$. Each component variable x_i of X may be called a binary digit or bit, and hence $X = x_1 x_2 \ldots x_n$ is an n-bit word. In the logic circuits of Figs. 3.17 and 3.19 the signals $X = x_0 x_1 x_2 x_3$, $Y = y_0 y_1 y_2 y_3$, and $Z = z_0 z_1 z_2 z_3$ constitute 4-bit data words. The words processed by the multiplexer may denote arbitrary numerical or nonnumerical information. The adder, on the other hand, is designed to process number words that use a specific binary code.

Binary numbers are encountered in almost all digital systems. For example, the memory and IO devices of a microcomputer are selected for read or write operations by

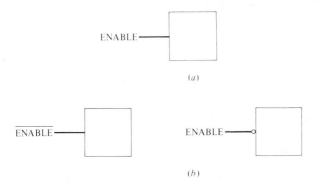

Figure 3.18 Common signal naming conventions: (*a*) active state is high (ENABLE = 1); (*b*) active state is low (ENABLE = 0).

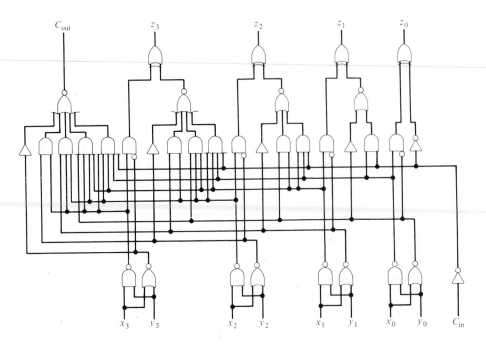

Figure 3.19 Logic circuit for the 74283 4-bit binary adder IC.

means of address words, where each address is treated as a binary number. All micro-processors contain arithmetic-logic circuits intended to process arithmetic or numerical data, as well as nonnumerical or "logical" data. We now consider how numbers are represented in such systems. For the present we will assume that the only number words of interest are whole numbers or integers.

The usual decimal number system used by human beings has two key characteristics: it employs 10 distinct symbols or digits $0, 1, 2, \ldots, 9$, and each digit position within a number is associated with a specific power of 10 called the *weight* of the digit. In an ordinary decimal integer, the rightmost or least significant digit is the units digit whose weight is 1, that is, 10^0. The next digit to the left denotes 10s and has weight 10 or 10^1. The next digit after that has weight 10^2, and so on, as illustrated in Fig. 3.20a. Using this positional notation, whose origins are several thousand years old, a number symbol has a value equal to the weighted sum of its digits; for example,

$$1109 = 1 \times 10^3 + 1 \times 10^2 + 0 \times 10^1 + 9 \times 10^0$$

The same positional notation is used for binary numbers in digital systems, except that the number of available digits is reduced from 10 to two, namely, 0 and 1, and the weight of each digit is a power of two instead of a power of 10. Figure 3.20b shows the binary number 10001010101, which also represents the integer 1109 because

$$1109 = 1 \times 2^{10} + 0 \times 2^9 + 0 \times 2^8 + 0 \times 2^7 + 1 \times 2^6 + 0 \times 2^5 + 1 \times 2^4$$
$$+ 0 \times 2^3 + 1 \times 2^2 + 0 \times 2^1 + 1 \times 2^0$$

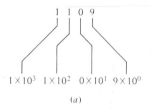

(a)

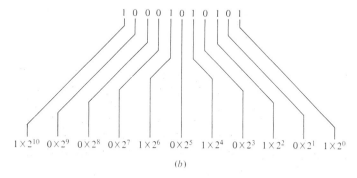

(b)

Figure 3.20 Two representations of the integer 1109: (a) decimal; (b) binary.

In general, if r distinct digits are available, and each digit has a weight r^i, then r is called the *radix* or *base* of the number system. The radix r associated with a particular number word is sometimes indicated by using r as a subscript thus:

$$1109_{10} = 10001010101_2$$

Usually the radix is clear from the context, and the subscript r is omitted. It is convenient to write the binary representation of an n-bit integer N in the form $x_{n-1}x_{n-2} \ldots x_1x_0$; this allows N to be expressed in the form

$$N = \sum_{i=0}^{n-1} x_i 2^i \qquad (3.2)$$

where 2^i is the weight of bit x_i. The second column of Fig. 3.21 gives the 4-bit binary representations of the numbers zero through 15; these are the number codes used by the adder circuit in Fig. 3.19. Note also that in constructing truth tables, we have followed the usual convention of listing the rows in the ascending binary number sequence determined by the input signal combinations (cf. Fig. 3.15).

As the examples of Figs. 3.20 and 3.21 demonstrate, binary numbers are longer and less readable for human beings than the equivalent decimal numbers. A convenient shorthand notation for binary numbers is obtained by using radix 16, that is, the *hexadecimal* number system. As defined in Fig. 3.21, 16 digits are used in hexadecimal

Decimal	Binary	Hexadecimal	Binary-coded Decimal (BCD)
00	0000	0	00000000
01	0001	1	00000001
02	0010	2	00000010
03	0011	3	00000011
04	0100	4	00000100
05	0101	5	00000101
06	0110	6	00000110
07	0111	7	00000111
08	1000	8	00001000
09	1001	9	00001001
10	1010	A	00010000
11	1011	B	00010001
12	1100	C	00010010
13	1101	D	00010011
14	1110	E	00010100
15	1111	F	00010101

Figure 3.21 Various representations of the unsigned integers 0 through 15.

numbers, the 10 decimal digits $0, 1, \ldots, 9$ and six additional digits denoted by the letters A, B, C, D, E, F. For example,

$$455_{16} = 1109_{10} = 10001010101_2 \tag{3.3}$$

because

$$455_{16} = 4 \times 16^2 + 5 \times 16^1 + 5 \times 16^0 = 1109$$

A binary integer can be converted to hexadecimal by replacing groups of 4 bits by the corresponding hexadecimal digit. Conversely, a given hexadecimal number can be converted to binary by replacing each digit by the equivalent 4-bit binary code. This conversion process is illustrated by the following example.

$$\underbrace{1111}_{F}\underbrace{0000}_{0}\underbrace{1001}_{9}\underbrace{0101}_{5}{}_2 = F095_{16} \tag{3.4}$$

Conversion between decimal and binary numbers is not so simple. Equation (3.2) can be used to convert a given binary number to its decimal equivalent. The summation on the right hand side of (3.2) is evaluated using ordinary decimal arithmetic, a process involving addition of a series of powers of two; the latter can be obtained by repeated multiplication by two. To convert a given decimal number to binary form, it is necessary to factor it into powers of two. This may be done by repeated division by two, as illustrated in Fig. 3.22 for the numbers given in Fig. 3.20. The remainder, either 0 or 1, produced by each division by two corresponds to 1 bit of the desired binary number.

Divisor $)$ Dividend
$\qquad$ Quotient Remainder $=$ bit x_i of weight 2^i

2	) 1109	
2	) 554	$1 = x_0$
2	) 277	$0 = x_1$
2	) 138	$1 = x_2$
2	) 69	$0 = x_3$
2	) 34	$1 = x_4$
2	) 17	$0 = x_5$
2	) 8	$1 = x_6$
2	) 4	$0 = x_7$
2	) 2	$0 = x_8$
2	) 1	$0 = x_9$
	0	$1 = x_{10}$

Figure 3.22 Conversion of the decimal number 1109 to its binary equivalent $x_{10}\, x_9 \cdots x_0$.

To simplify conversion to and from binary representation, it is often useful to encode a decimal number $d_{n-1}d_{n-2} \ldots d_1 d_0$ where $d_i \in \{0, 1, \ldots, 9\}$ in the following way: Replace each decimal digit d_i by its 4-bit binary equivalent as defined by Fig. 3.21. The resulting $4n$-bit word is called a *BCD* (*binary-coded decimal*) number, and will be indicated here by the subscript BCD. Thus we have.

$$\underbrace{010001010101}_{4 \quad 5 \quad 5}{}_{\text{BCD}} = 455_{10} \tag{3.5}$$

Note that the binary and BCD codes for the same number are generally quite different [cf. Eqs. (3.3) and (3.5)]. The BCD representation of the number 1109_{10} defined by Eq. (3.3) is

$$\underbrace{0001000100001001}_{1 \quad 1 \quad 0 \quad 9}{}_{\text{BCD}}$$

Each 4-bit segment of a BCD number represents a single digit whose weight is a power of 10; therefore the underlying radix is 10. Only 10 of the 16 possible 4-bit patterns are needed to represent BCD digits; the six patterns 1010 to 1111 are not used. Hence the binary word appearing on the left-hand side of Eq. (3.4) is not a valid BCD number pattern. While the BCD number format clearly simplifies decimal number conversion, it has the drawback of requiring more bits to represent a given number than the ordinary binary number (radix 2) code. Figure 3.21 lists the 8-bit BCD numbers from 0 to 15. The largest 8-bit BCD number is

$$10011001_{\text{BCD}} = 99_{10}$$

whereas the largest 8-bit binary number is

$$11111111_2 = 255_{10}$$

So far we have only considered *unsigned* integers that include no symbols for the plus and minus signs needed to distinguish positive and negative numbers. Unsigned numbers are simply regarded as positive numbers with the plus sign omitted. Thus the

n-bit addresses of a computer system are treated as unsigned binary integers denoting address numbers from zero to $2^n - 1$. In many applications both positive and negative numbers must be processed. An obvious way to indicate a number's sign is to append an extra sign bit s to the left end of the unsigned number thus:

$$sx_{n-2}\ x_{n-3}\ \dots\ x_0$$

$$\underset{\text{sign}}{|}\quad \underset{\text{magnitude}}{\underbrace{\qquad\qquad}}$$

This way of constructing signed binary numbers is called *sign-magnitude* (SM) code. By convention, $s = 0$ denotes plus or a positive number, and $s = 1$ denotes minus or a negative number. The $n - 1$ rightmost bits of an SM number indicate its size or magnitude. To change the sign of a given SM number, all that is needed is to invert or complement the sign bit s. For example,

$$01101000_{SM} = +104_{10}$$

$$11101000_{SM} = -104_{10}$$

The basic arithmetic operations add, substract, multiply, and divide can be performed using unsigned or SM binary numbers in essentially the same ways as these operations are performed manually with decimal numbers. Since the available digits are restricted to 0 and 1, the addition of 1 to 1 results in a sum bit 0 and a carry bit 1; in other words,

$$1 + 1 = 10_2 = 2_{10}$$

Subtraction of 1 from 0 results in a difference bit 1 and a borrow bit 1. Figure 3.23 shows examples of various arithmetic calculations using both decimal and binary numbers. Note that the unsigned binary addition of Fig. 3.23a is performed automatically by the adder circuit of Fig. 3.19.

The result of a binary arithmetic operation on n-bit words is typically required to be an n-bit word. If the full result is an $(n + 1)$-bit word, as in the case of the binary addition of Fig. 3.23a, *overflow* is said to occur. Overflow is indicated by the generation of a carry (or borrow) signal from the leftmost or most significant bit in the magnitude part of the n-bit result; this is the second bit from the left in the case of SM numbers. Sometimes overflow can be ignored, and the proper result taken to be the n rightmost bits of the result. For example, in address computations that involve unsigned binary numbers, the result of adding 1 to the largest address number thus

$$
\begin{array}{r}
111 \dots 11 \\
000 \dots 01 \\
\hline
1\quad 000 \dots 00
\end{array}
$$

is taken to be zero by simply ignoring the final carry bit, thereby truncating the result to n bits. This truncation effectively converts the address numbers into a circular list in which the address $00 \dots 0$ immediately follows the address $11 \dots 1$. In other cases overflow may signal an improper result, and the overflow condition must be detected so that appropriate corrective action can be taken.

1110_2	Augend	14
1011_2	Addend	11
$1\ \overline{1001}_2$	Sum	25
	(a)	
1001_{SM}	Augend	-1
1101_{SM}	Addend	-5
$\overline{1110}_{SM}$	Sum	-6
	(b)	
1110_2	Minuend	14
1011_2	Subtrahend	11
$\overline{0011}_2$	Difference	3
	(c)	
0001_{SM}	Minuend	$+1$
1101_{SM}	Subtrahend	-5
$\overline{0110}_{SM}$	Difference	$+6$
	(d)	
1010_2	Multiplicand	10
1100_2	Multiplier	12
$\overline{0000}$		20
0000	Partial	
1010	products	10
1010		
$\overline{1111000}_2$	Product	120
	(e)	

Figure 3.23 Examples of arithmetic operations on binary and decimal numbers: (a) unsigned addition; (b)signed addition; (c)unsigned subtraction; (d) signed subtraction; (e) unsigned multiplication.

Although SM code is the direct binary counterpart of the decimal number code used by human beings, another binary number representation called *twos complement* (TC) is most often used in digital computers, mainly because it simplifies the implementation of certain arithmetic operations. Positive TC numbers are exactly the same as the equivalent SM numbers, for example,

$$01101000_{TC} = 01101000_{SM} = +104_{10} \qquad (3.6)$$

The sign bit of a positive TC number is 0, and the remaining bits represent the number's magnitude in the standard fashion. Negative TC numbers are quite different from their SM counterparts. To negate a TC number (either positive or negative), the two-step negation algorithm given in Fig. 3.24 may be used. Suppose that this algorithm is applied to the TC number appearing in (3.6). Step 1 changes 01101000 to 10010111. Then in step 2, one is added to 10010111 to yield 10011000; consequently,

$$10011000_{TC} = 11101000_{SM} = -104_{10}$$

It is easily shown (see Prob. 3.12) that the leftmost bit s of a TC number N is always 1 when N is negative; thus s represents the sign of a TC number as it does in the SM case. Figure 3.25 compares the SM and TC codes when 4-bit words are used. Note that there are two SM representations of zero, but only one TC zero.

The key advantage of twos complement in digital system design is that during addition and subtraction, all bits of the TC numbers, including the sign bits, can be treated uniformly, assuming there is no overflow (see Prob. 3.13). Figure 3.26 illustrates TC addition using negative numbers. On comparing this with the unsigned addition in

Step 1: Complement each bit of the given TC number $N = x_{n-1} x_{n-2} \ldots x_0$ to obtain N' $= \bar{x}_{n-1} \bar{x}_{n-2} \ldots \bar{x}_0$.

Step 2: Add one to N' using unsigned binary addition and ignoring any carry generated from the leftmost bit position. The resulting n-bit sum is the TC representation of $-N$.

Figure 3.24 Algorithm for negating a twos-complement number.

Sign Magnitude	Twos Complement	Decimal
1111	1001	−7
1110	1010	−6
1101	1011	−5
1100	1100	−4
1011	1101	−3
1010	1110	−2
1001	1111	−1
1000	0000	−0
0000	0000	+0
0001	0001	+1
0010	0010	+2
0011	0011	+3
0100	0100	+4
0101	0101	+5
0110	0110	+6
0111	0111	+7

Figure 3.25 Various representations of the signed integers −7 through +7.

1110_{TC}	Augend	−2
1011_{TC}	Addend	−5
1 1001_{TC}	Sum	−7

Figure 3.26 Example of addition using twos-complement numbers.

Fig. 3.23a, we see that the proper TC sum is obtained by adding the TC addend to the TC augend bit by bit, treating the signs like the other (magnitude) bits. In contrast, the sign bits must be given special treatment to obtain the correct result in the SM addition example of Fig. 3.23b. Hence a single addition process, which in a microprocessor is specified by a binary addition instruction, can be applied uniformly to all bits of TC numbers. This facilitates the addition of long numbers, which, because of the short word size (k bits) characteristic of microprocessors, must be broken down into k-bit segments and added separately. Even though only the leftmost segment of a TC number contains the sign bit, all segments can be added via the same instruction. A further advantage of the TC code is that both addition and subtraction can be implemented together by a single circuit of the type shown in Fig. 3.27. The 4-bit adder subcircuit used here is the 74283 logic circuit for (unsigned) binary addition of Fig. 3.19, which computes the sum

$$Z = X + Y' + C_{in} \tag{3.7}$$

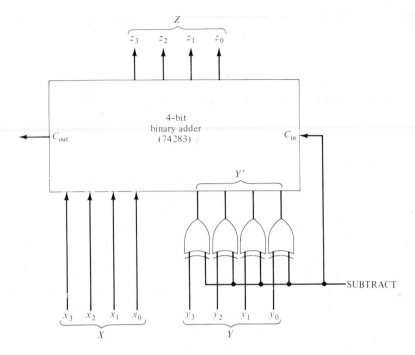

Figure 3.27 Logic circuit that performs addition and subtraction on 4-bit twos-complement numbers.

The carry input C_{in} of this adder is connected to an external control signal called SUBTRACT, which when set to 1 (activated) causes subtraction to be performed; addition is performed when SUBTRACT = 0. Suppose that SUBTRACT = 0. Then C_{in} = 0, and the four EXCLUSIVE-OR gates make $Y' = Y$ (cf. Fig. 3.16c). Hence (3.7) reduces to the addition

$$Z = X + Y$$

as required. On the other hand, if SUBTRACT = 1, then C_{in} = 1 and $Y' = \bar{Y}$. Hence (3.7) implies that the operation

$$Z = X + \bar{Y} + 1$$

is performed. But since $\bar{Y} + 1$ is $-Y$ in TC code, the desired subtraction

$$Z = X - Y$$

is obtained.

Binary integers are a special case of a class of numbers called *fixed-point* binary numbers, in which a binary point (corresponding to a decimal point in decimal numbers) is implicitly or explicitly located in a fixed position in the number format. Thus in the integer $x_{n-1}x_{n-2} \ldots x_0$, an implicit binary point lies immediately to the right of the least significant (units) bit x_0. No significant conceptual change results from assuming that the binary point is in some other fixed position. Relocating the binary point in the number format has the effect of multiplying every number by a constant factor that is a positive or negative power of two. An entirely different class of numbers, called *floating-point* numbers, will be introduced in Chap. 5. Floating-point number codes are more suitable than fixed-point codes for representing very large and very small numbers.

3.1.5 Sequential Circuits

The output signals $Z(t)$ of an ideal combinational logic circuit N of the type considered so far are completely determined by the combination of input signals $X(t)$ applied to N at time t. In other words, N has no memory, and therefore imposes no delay on the logic signals that pass through it. Physical signals are propagated at a finite speed that is limited by the speed of light (approximately 300 000 km/s or 0.3 m/ns). Electric signals are also delayed by inductive and capacitive effects as illustrated by Fig. 2.19. In logic design it is usual to combine all delay sources into a form that can be represented by a logical *delay element* D of the type defined in Fig. 3.28. The behavior of D is given by the equation

$$z(t) = x(t - t_p)$$

This means that the output from D at time t has the value possessed by its input line t_p time units earlier; D therefore imposes a t_p-second delay on all logic signals that pass through

$x(t) \longrightarrow \boxed{D \atop t_p} \longrightarrow z(t) = x(t - t_p)$

(a)

$\begin{matrix} x_1(t) \\ x_2(t) \end{matrix} \longrightarrow$ ⟫∘$\longrightarrow \boxed{t_p} \longrightarrow z(t) = \overline{x_1(t - t_p) \wedge x_2(t - t_p)}$

(b)

$\begin{matrix} x_1(t) \\ x_2(t) \end{matrix} \longrightarrow$ ⟫∘$\longrightarrow z(t) = \overline{x_1(t - t_p) \wedge x_2(t - t_p)}$

(c)

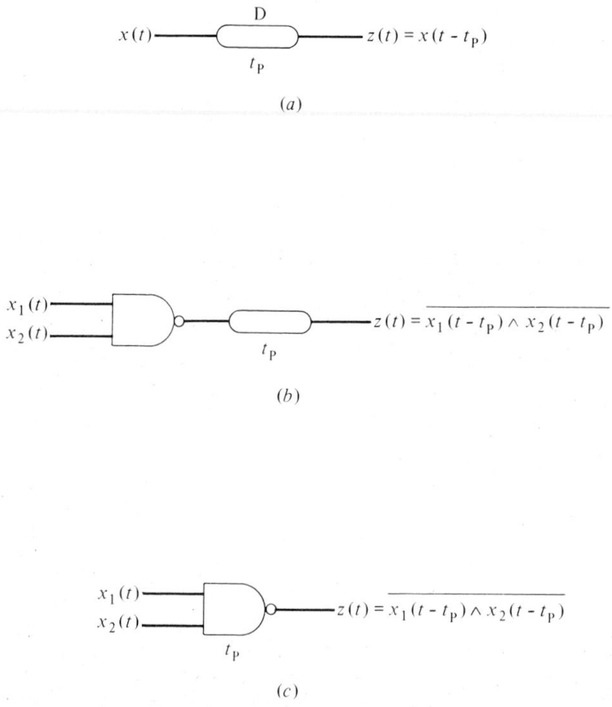

Figure 3.28 (a) Symbol for a delay element. Model of a NAND gate with (b) explicit propagation delay t_p and (c) implicit propagation delay t_p.

it. Since D must "remember" its input values for t_P seconds, it constitutes a simple memory device. By inserting a delay element of size t_P into a line carrying the signal x, a fixed delay of duration t_P is assigned to x. Figure 3.28b shows how a practical NAND gate with a propagation or switching delay of t_P seconds may be modeled by means of an ideal (zero-delay) NAND gate and a delay element. Usually gate delays are not shown explicitly in logic diagrams; instead the desired delay t_P is implicitly assigned to the gate symbol as indicated in Fig. 3.28c. t_P is then referred to as the *typical* or *nominal propagation delay* of the gate; its value can be found in IC manufacturers' data sheets as, for example, in Fig. 2.64.

The delay element D has a finite memory span of t_P seconds; input signals occurring before time $t - t_P$ cannot influence the output of D at time t or later. To obtain a memory device whose memory span is of unlimited duration, that is, a memory that does not "forget," a circuit containing feedback is required. *Feedback* is a closed signal path that allows a circuit's output signals also to be used as input signals to the circuit. All the (combinational) logic circuits considered so far in this chapter are *feedforward* or *acyclic* circuits in which there is no feedback.

A very simple logic circuit N containing feedback appears in Fig. 3.29a, which provides two different perspectives on the feedback paths. N consists of two inverters I_1 and I_2, each having propagation delay t_P, and two logic signals z_1 and z_2. The circuit has two stable configurations or *states* of its logic signals z_1 and z_2, namely,

$$z_1z_2 = 01$$

$$z_1z_2 = 10$$

as shown in Fig. 3.29b. When $z_1z_2 = 01$, for example, inverter I_1 has input signal $z_2 = 1$ and output signal $z_1 = 0$, and therefore does not change state. Similarly, inverter I_2 has complementary input and output signals and is also stable. Thus N can maintain or *store* either of the states 01 or 10 indefinitely. The other two possible states 00 and 11 are unstable, as indicated in Fig. 3.29c. Suppose that $z_1z_2 = 00$ at time t. After t_P seconds, the inverter outputs change to 1, making $z_1z_2 = 11$. This is again an unstable condition, causing the inverter outputs to change back to 00 after another t_P seconds. Under these conditions N oscillates continually between states 00 and 11. In its two stable states 01 and 10, N can store 1 bit of information. Either z_1 or z_2 can be regarded as the stored variable; if one is specified, the other follows from the relation $z_1 = \bar{z}_2$.

To make the circuit of Fig. 3.29 into a practical memory device, a means of changing its state is needed. Figure 3.30a shows one way of doing this, which adds two input lines called S (set) and R (reset) to the inverters of Fig. 3.29, thereby changing them to NOR gates. (For another approach using bidirectional IO lines, see Prob. 3.7.) The resulting circuit is called an *SR (set–reset) latch*. (It is also called an SR or RS flip-flop; however, we prefer to use the term flip-flop in a somewhat more restricted sense defined below.) Figure 3.30b describes the behavior of an SR latch L in a format similar to a truth table. Like the two-inverter memory circuit of Fig. 3.29, L has two stable states: a *set* state corresponding to $z_1z_2 = 10$, and a *reset* state $z_1z_2 = 01$. When S = R = 0, the latch remains indefinitely in its current stable state; the input combination SR = 00 therefore may be termed the *quiescent* input. On changing SR to 10, that is, on enabling the set line, L changes to the set state $z_1z_2 = 10$, where it remains as long as SR = 10 or 00.

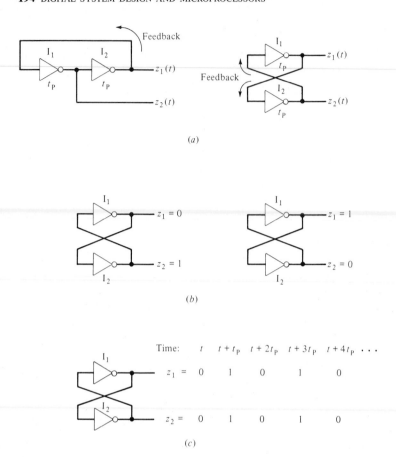

Figure 3.29 (a) Memory circuit N composed of two inverters; (b) stable states of N; (c) unstable states of N.

Similarly, making SR = 01, that is, enabling the reset line, sends L to the reset state z_1z_2 = 01, where it remains as long as SR = 01 or 00. Note that at least $2t_P$ seconds, where t_P is the delay of each NOR gate, are required for a complete transition between the set and reset states. Finally, suppose that the input combination 11 is applied to L in either of its stable states. Then, as Fig. 3.30b indicates, z_1z_2 becomes 00. If SR subsequently reverts to the quiescent condition, then oscillation may result, effectively destroying the information stored in the latch. Thus the input combination SR = 11 is forbidden when designing circuits with SR latches.

Figure 3.31a gives the standard circuit symbol used for an SR latch. The latch is considered to store a variable denoted Q, which is called a *state variable*. The output lines are therefore labeled Q and $\overline{Q}$, while the input lines are labled S and R as indicated. Q = 1 denotes the set state (latch storing 1), while Q = 0, or, equivalently, $\overline{Q}$ = 1, denotes the reset state (latch storing 0). The behavioral data of Fig. 3.30b are usually condensed into the format of Fig. 3.31b, which is called a *state table*. Each row of the state table corresponds to a stable state S_i of the latch, and each column I_j represents a

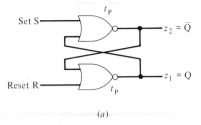

(a)

Time = t				$t + t_P$		$t + 2t_P$		$t + 3t_P$		Comment
S	R	z_1	z_2	z_1	z_2	z_1	z_2	z_1	z_2	
0	0	0	1	0	1	0	1	0	1	State of L is unchanged
0	0	1	0	1	0	1	0	1	0	
0	1	0	1	0	1	0	1	0	1	
1	0	1	0	1	0	1	0	1	0	
0	1	1	0	0	0	0	1	0	1	L is reset
1	0	0	1	0	0	1	0	1	0	L is set
1	1	0	1	0	0	0	0	0	0	Forbidden input combination
1	1	1	0	0	0	0	0	0	0	
0	0	0	0	1	1	0	0	1	1	Unstable condition

(b)

Figure 3.30 SR latch L: (a) logic circuit; (b) IO behavior.

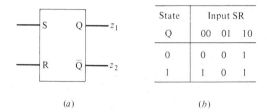

State	Input SR		
Q	00	01	10
0	0	0	1
1	1	0	1

Figure 3.31 SR latch: (a) symbol; (b) state table.

(a)   (b)

valid input combination SR. The entry S_{ij} in row S_i and column I_j is the next state assumed by the latch when its present state is S_i and the input combination I_j is applied to it. Only stable states and valid input combinations are shown in the state table. A state table thus conveys IO behavioral data in much the same way as a truth table does in the case of combinational circuits. The behavior of the latch can also be described by a time-dependent logic equation thus:

$$Q(t + T) = \bar{R}(t) \wedge [S(t) \vee Q(t)] \qquad (3.8)$$

where $T \geq 2t_P$ is a time interval that is sufficiently long to allow a new stable state to be reached. Equation (3.8) states that Q becomes 1 at time $t + T$ if and only if R = 0 at time t, and either S = 1 or Q = 1, or both.

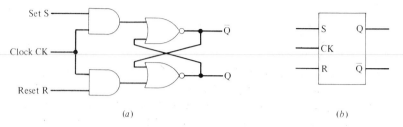

Figure 3.32 Clocked SR latch: (a) logic circuit; (b) symbol.

It is very useful to add an extra input line CK (for clock) to an SR latch to control precisely the times at which the latch changes state. The clock input CK is so called because it is typically connected to a periodic clock signal that is employed to synchronize the activities of a set of associated memory devices in a logic circuit. Figure 3.32 gives the circuit diagram and symbol for the modified latch, which is called here a *clocked SR latch*. (Again the term flip-flop is often used for this device in the literature.) When CK = 0, the quiescent input combination 00 is applied via the AND gates to the SR latch, which therefore cannot change state. Thus setting CK to 0 disables the latch by blocking the main S and R input signals. When CK = 1, in which case the latch is said to be enabled or clocked, the latch responds to the signals on S and R as described above. Some other useful latch types that can be derived from the basic SR latch will be considered later.

The only function of the clock input signal CK in a clocked latch is to fix the time at which the latch begins to respond to signals on its main input lines. When CK is enabled, the latch's state and output variables Q and $\overline{Q}$ begin to change immediately, and changes may continue as long as CK = 1. Hence the process of storing new information $Q(t + T)$ in a latch immediately begins to destroy the old stored information $Q(t)$. There are many situations in digital system design where it is necessary to retain the value of $Q(t)$ while $Q(t + T)$ is being computed; this is the case whenever $Q(t + T)$ is a function of $Q(t)$. Under these circumstances a memory device is required whose old state can be read unchanged while a new state is being written into the memory. The name flip-flop is used for a class of 1-bit clocked memory devices with this property. In a flip-flop a clock signal determines the time at which the circuit begins to change state as it does in a clocked latch; however, a clock signal also determines a later time at which the output signals of the flip-flop are allowed to change value. Only input changes are timed in a clocked latch; in a flip-flop both input and output changes are timed.

Figure 3.33 shows a type of flip-flop called an *SR (set–reset) master–slave flip-flop* derived from the SR latch. It contains two clocked SR latches L_1 and L_2 called the master and slave latches respectively. The clock circuitry of the flip-flop is designed so that L_1 is disabled when L_2 is enabled, and vice versa. The main S and R inputs set and reset the master latch L_1 in the normal fashion when CLOCK = 1. However, enabling L_1, disables the slave latch L_2; since the flip-flop's output signals Q and $\overline{Q}$ are obtained from L_2, these signals remain unchanged while L_1 is enabled. When the flip-flop's clock signal CLOCK returns to 0, L_2 becomes enabled while L_1 is disabled. Consequently the state of L_1 is transferred directly to L_2, during which time the flip-flop's output signals may change. In

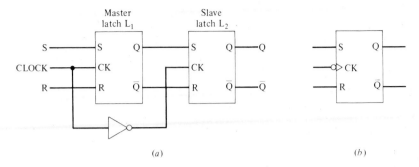

Figure 3.33 SR master–slave flip–flop: (*a*) logic circuit; (*b*) symbol.

summary, the SR flip-flop responds to its S and R input signals like an SR latch when CLOCK becomes 1; its outputs do not change until CLOCK returns to 0. Similar symbols are used for SR latches and flip-flops as indicated in Fig. 3.33b. The arrowhead symbol placed after the clock terminal CK, in combination with the inversion circle, means that the flip-flop's outputs change only on the falling edge of the clock signal, that is, when CK falls from 1 to 0. An arrowhead symbol (which is termed a dynamic signal indicator) without an inversion circle marks a line that is enabled by a rising signal; the transition between levels enables the desired function rather than the final level reached.

A logic circuit whose output signals at any time are determined by (a sequence of) previous input signal combinations, as well as the input combination at time t, is called a *sequential circuit*. The influence of the previous input signals is recorded in the sequential circuit's memory, which is usually a set of latches or flip-flops. The information in the memory elements constitutes the *internal state Y(t)* of the circuit. The output signals of the circuit are logic functions of $Y(t)$ and the current input combination $X(t)$, and can hence be expressed as $Z[X(t), Y(t)]$. Z is computed by combinational circuits; combinational circuits are also used to control the inputs to the memory elements, and therefore determine the sequential circuit's next state. The behavior of a sequential circuit can be described by a state table such as that of Fig. 3.31b, or by a set of (sequential) logic equations such as (3.8).

Most sequential circuits encountered in digital system design are *synchronous* sequential circuits, which means that all memory elements are clocked latches or flip-flops whose clock inputs are connected to a common clock signal CLOCK. This permits CLOCK to synchronize all state transitions, and allows the time between successive state changes to equal one period of the clock signal. The use of clock signals in this manner greatly simplifies the design and operation of sequential circuits, since minor differences in signal propagation delays in different parts of the circuit can be ignored. Unclocked or *asynchronous* sequential circuits are therefore relatively uncommon.

Sequential circuits have two major uses in digital systems:

1. As *memories* to store information while it is being processed
2. As *control circuits* to generate the control signals necessary to select and enable a sequence of data-transfer or data-processing steps in the execution of complex multistep tasks

As noted earlier, a simple data-transfer or data-processing step is usually performed by combinational circuits. It is sometimes more efficient to use a sequential circuit for a data-processing step; hence sequential circuits whose main function is data processing also exist. Combinational and sequential circuits operating in conjunction provide all the storage, transfer, processing, and control functions needed in digital systems like microcomputers.

Memories are perhaps the most common sequential subcircuits found in digital systems. An n-bit word may be stored in a set of n latches or a set of n flip-flops; the latter is called an n-bit register. A random-access memory (RAM) is constructed from a two-dimensional array of simple latches. Figure 3.34a shows an example of a sequential circuit called a *shift register*, which has many uses in digital design, including storage, control, and data processing. This particular circuit is found in the 7491 IC, a member of the 7400 series of TTL logic circuits. It contains eight SR master–slave flip-flops such as that of Fig. 3.33, and some associated control circuitry. The 7491 has eight state variables designed $y_0, y_1, \ldots, y_7$ in Fig. 3.34, and hence has $2^8 = 256$ distinct internal states. It has three input lines A, B, C and two output lines z_1, z_2. The input line C, which is also referred to as the clock input, controls the operation of the shift register. When C is enabled (which requires a dynamic transition of C from 0 to 1 and back to 0), the information y_i stored in each flip-flop is transferred to the flip-flop on its right, that is, the information stored in the flip-flops is shifted one bit position to the right during one clock period; hence the name shift register. The leftmost flip-flop acquires a new state y_0, which is determined by the externally applied A and B signals, while the contents y_7 of the rightmost flip-flop are lost, or shifted out to be used by external circuits. Note how the clock signal C is connected to the CK inputs of all the flip-flops, thus ensuring that they act in unison during a shifting operation. In other words, C synchronizes the state change step in all the flip-flops.

The behavior of the 7491 can be described by a state table of the sort shown in Fig. 3.34b. The complete table contains 64 rows and eight columns. The column headed $--0$ represents all the input combinations for which the clock signal C is disabled. Since the circuit does not change state under that condition, it is customary to omit clock signals completely from state tables. Thus the variable C and the $--0$ column can be deleted from Fig. 3.34b, reducing it to a 64×4 state table. The transitions described by the table are then assumed to take place when the implicit clock signal is properly enabled. The entries in Fig. 3.34b are pairs of the form $Y(t + T), Z(t)$, where $Y(t + T)$ is the next state of the circuit and $Z(t)$ is the current output; this is the general form of an entry in the state table of a sequential machine. The large number of states possible in this circuit makes a state table a cumbersome descriptive tool. The circuit's behavior can be described much more concisely by means of a set of logic equations; again for simplicity the clock variable C is omitted from these equations. The following set of *next-state equations* define the method used to compute the next values of the eight state variables:

$$y_0(t + T) = A(t) \wedge B(t)$$
$$y_{i+1}(t + T) = y_i(t) \qquad \text{for } i = 0, 1, \ldots, 6$$

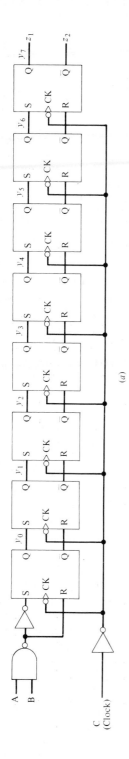

(a)

State	Input ABC				
$y_0y_1y_2y_3y_4y_5y_6y_7$	- - 0	001	011	101	111
00000000	00000000,01	00000000,01	00000000,01	00000000,01	00000000,01
00000001	00000001,10	00000000,10	00000000,10	00000000,10	10000000,10
00000010	00000010,01	00000001,01	00000001,01	00000001,01	10000001,01
00000011	00000011,10	00000001,10	00000001,10	00000001,10	10000001,10
00000100	00000100,01	00000010,01	00000010,01	00000010,01	10000010,01
...			...		
11111110	11111110,01	01111111,01	01111111,01	01111111,01	11111111,01
11111111	11111111,10	01111111,10	01111111,10	01111111,10	11111111,10

(b)

Figure 3.34 7491 8-bit shift register IC: (a) logic circuit; (b) state table.

199

The output signals of the 7491 are specified by the following set of *output equations*:

$$z_1(t) = y_7(t)$$
$$z_2(t) = \bar{y}_7(t)$$

3.2 SSI COMPONENTS

We turn next to the simplest class of ICs used in digital system design. These ICs employ small-scale integration (SSI), which is characterized by a maximum component density of about 100 transistors or 30 logic gates per chip. Representative combinational and sequential SSI circuit elements are described in this section, and some design issues involved in using them are discussed.

3.2.1 Combinational ICs

The basic building blocks of combinational circuits, namely, logic gates, have already been introduced. There are two kinds of single-input gates—noninverting buffers that realize the logic function $z = x$, and inverters or NOT gates that realize the function $z = \bar{x}$. There are six multi-input gates, AND, NAND, OR, NOR, EXCLUSIVE-OR, and EXCLUSIVE-NOR, whose general definitions can be found in Fig. 3.15. Figure 3.35 lists the two-input versions of all these gates. Note that the gates form complementary pairs thus:

$$z_{NOT}(x) = \bar{z}_{BUFFER}(x) = \bar{x}$$

$$z_{NAND}(x_1, x_2) = \bar{z}_{AND}(x_1, x_2) = \overline{x_1 \wedge x_2}$$

$$z_{NOR}(x_1, x_2) = \bar{z}_{OR}(x_1, x_2) = \overline{x_1 \vee x_2}$$

$$z_{XNOR}(x_1, x_2) = \bar{z}_{XOR}(x_1, x_2) = \overline{x_1 \oplus x_2}$$

Several variants of the basic gate types, which were mentioned in Sec. 2.3.4, are also listed in Fig. 3.35. Three-state gates have an extra control input line E (enable). When $E = 1$, a three-state gate behaves like an ordinary gate of the same type, generating 0 and 1 output signals. When $E = 0$, however, the gate's output line assumes the high-impedance state Z. Under the latter condition, the gate is logically disconnected from all circuits attached to its output line. Three-state gates are particularly useful for connecting circuits to bus lines, as illustrated in Fig. 2.71.

Another logic gate variant is the open-collector (OC) gate type in the TTL logic families. (The significance of the name "open collector," which refers to the output transistor stage of the gate, is discussed in Prob. 2.38.) Like a three-state gate, the output line of an OC gate assumes the high-impedance state Z for certain input combinations; this Z value replaces the normal 1 value produced by the basic gate. A group of OC gates can be connected to a common output (bus) line L in such a way that only the logic values 0 and 1 appear on L. Figure 3.36a shows such a circuit N formed from OC NAND gates. The common output line L is connected to the power supply V_{CC}, which represents

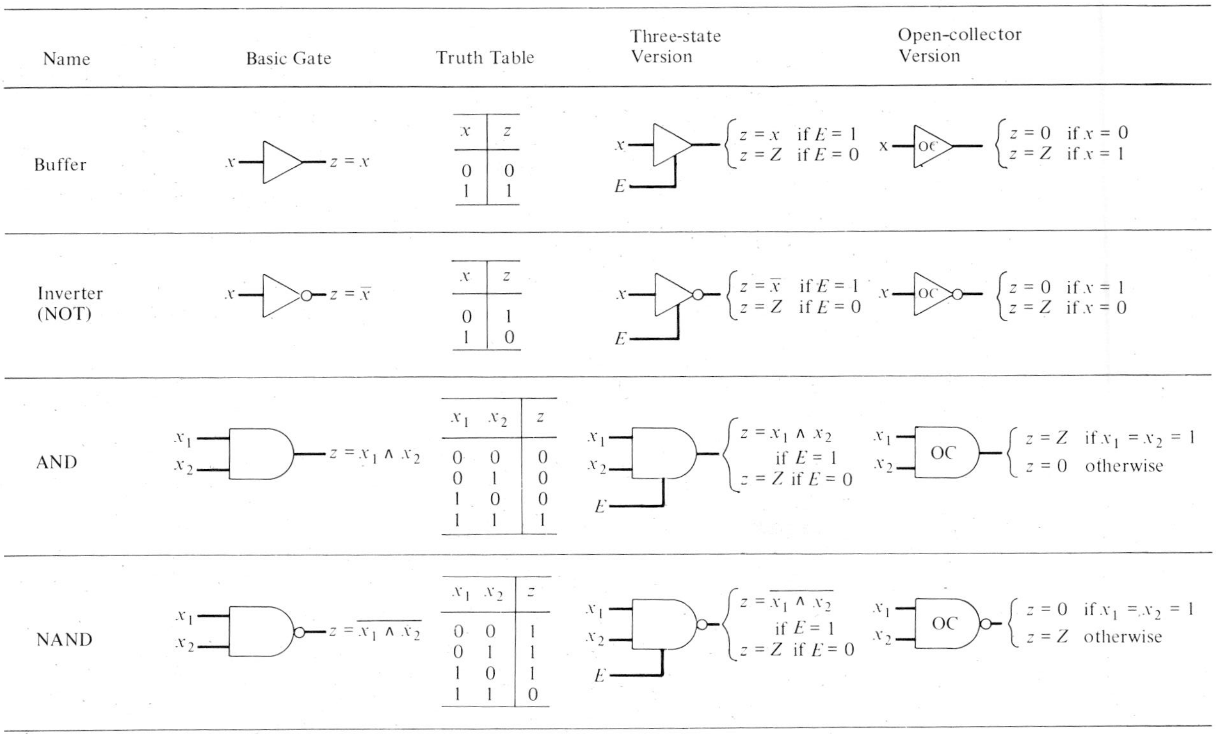

Name	Basic Gate	Truth Table	Three-state Version	Open-collector Version
Buffer	$z = x$	$\begin{array}{c\|c} x & z \\ \hline 0 & 0 \\ 1 & 1 \end{array}$	$\begin{cases} z = x & \text{if } E = 1 \\ z = Z & \text{if } E = 0 \end{cases}$	$\begin{cases} z = 0 & \text{if } x = 0 \\ z = Z & \text{if } x = 1 \end{cases}$
Inverter (NOT)	$z = \bar{x}$	$\begin{array}{c\|c} x & z \\ \hline 0 & 1 \\ 1 & 0 \end{array}$	$\begin{cases} z = \bar{x} & \text{if } E = 1 \\ z = Z & \text{if } E = 0 \end{cases}$	$\begin{cases} z = 0 & \text{if } x = 1 \\ z = Z & \text{if } x = 0 \end{cases}$
AND	$z = x_1 \wedge x_2$	$\begin{array}{cc\|c} x_1 & x_2 & z \\ \hline 0 & 0 & 0 \\ 0 & 1 & 0 \\ 1 & 0 & 0 \\ 1 & 1 & 1 \end{array}$	$\begin{cases} z = x_1 \wedge x_2 & \text{if } E = 1 \\ z = Z & \text{if } E = 0 \end{cases}$	$\begin{cases} z = Z & \text{if } x_1 = x_2 = 1 \\ z = 0 & \text{otherwise} \end{cases}$
NAND	$z = \overline{x_1 \wedge x_2}$	$\begin{array}{cc\|c} x_1 & x_2 & z \\ \hline 0 & 0 & 1 \\ 0 & 1 & 1 \\ 1 & 0 & 1 \\ 1 & 1 & 0 \end{array}$	$\begin{cases} z = \overline{x_1 \wedge x_2} & \text{if } E = 1 \\ z = Z & \text{if } E = 0 \end{cases}$	$\begin{cases} z = 0 & \text{if } x_1 = x_2 = 1 \\ z = Z & \text{otherwise} \end{cases}$

Figure 3.35 The basic logic gates and commonly used variants.

(*Figure 3.35 continued*)

Name	Basic Gate	Truth Table			Three-state Version	Open-collector Version
		x_1	x_2	z		
OR	$z = x_1 \vee x_2$	0	0	0		
		0	1	1		
		1	0	1		
		1	1	1		
NOR	$z = \overline{x_1 \vee x_2}$	0	0	1		
		0	1	0		
		1	0	0		
		1	1	0		
EXCLUSIVE-OR	$z = x_1 \oplus x_2$	0	0	0		
		0	1	1		
		1	0	1		
		1	1	0		
EXCLUSIVE-NOR	$z = \overline{x_1 \oplus x_2}$	0	0	1		
		0	1	0		
		1	0	0		
		1	1	1		

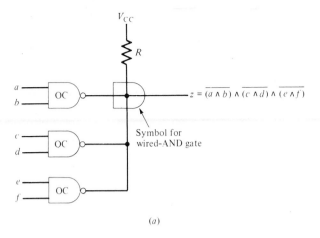

(a)

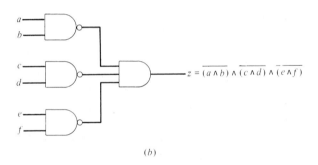

(b)

Figure 3.36 (a) Logic circuit containing open-collector NAND gates; (b) equivalent circuit containing ordinary NAND gates.

logical 1, by a pull-up resistor R. As defined in Fig. 3.35, an OC NAND gate produces 0 at its output terminal if all its input signals are 1; it produces the Z value if at least one of the input signals is 0. If any OC NAND gate in the circuit N produces a 0, the output z of N also becomes 0. If, on the other hand, all the OC NANDs produce the output Z, the resistor R pulls up z to the 1 level. Hence N is equivalent to the circuit of Fig. 3.36b in which the OC NAND gates are replaced by ordinary NANDs, and the output line L with its pull-up resistor R is replaced by an AND gate. (A more rigorous analysis of N's behavior can be made using the CSA theory of Sec. 3.1.2; see Prob. 3.6.)

Since the output connection of the circuit in Fig. 3.36a performs the AND function, it is referred to as a wired-AND gate. The standard way to indicate the presence of a wired-AND gate in a logic diagram is to superimpose an AND symbol over the connector in question, as is done in Fig. 3.36a. Wired-OR gates also occur, and are similarly indicated by the OR symbol in logic diagrams. Note that if ordinary gates have their output lines wired together in the manner of Fig. 3.36a, an invalid logic circuit results because the output signal will be undefined if one of the connected gates outputs a 0 while another outputs a 1. The main advantage of OC gates is the fact that by allowing wired gates, circuits with fewer gates can be constructed; this is illustrated by Fig. 3.36. Open-collector gates tend to be slower and more subject to noise than ordinary gates or three-state gates, and consequently they are little used in microprocessor-based systems.

The majority of commercially available ICs in the SSI range contain from one to six gates, all of the same type. The number of gates in the IC is limited by the number of pins on the IC package, as well as the number of input lines, or the fan-in, of each gate. A few SSI circuits contain gates of several types that are interconnected to form simple general-purpose logic circuits. The SSI ICs are housed in relatively small packages, 14-pin DIPs or flatpacks being typical. The 7400 series of ICs, which was introduced in Chap. 2, includes a large and widely used set of SSI circuits, all with standard names (part numbers beginning with 74) and internal configurations. Although primarily used for TTL logic families, including "standard" TTL (the 7400 series proper), Schottky TTL (the 74S00 series), and low-power Schottky TTL (the 74LS00 series), 7400-series devices are also being produced in other logic families such as CMOS. For these reasons, we will restrict our discussion of commercial ICs to circuits that are found in the various versions of the 7400 series.

Figure 3.37 shows the logic circuits and pin assignments of a representative selection of combinational SSI circuits in the 7400 series; for a complete listing of the hundreds of available types, manufacturers' data books should be consulted, (e.g., National Semiconductor, 1981a, 1981b; Texas Instruments, 1981). Most of these ICs have 14 pins including power (V_{CC}) and ground (GND) pins; a few have 16 pins. All the basic gate types are available, with various numbers of inputs per gate. A 14-pin package allows a maximum of six independent one-input gates to be included in one IC, since each gate requires one input pin and one output pin for a total of 12 pins, in addition to power and ground. Thus we find buffers and inverters appearing in "hex" or six-gate groups in Fig. 3.37. A 14-pin package also can accommodate four independent two-input gates, each of which requires three pins. Thus the 7400 series has many ICs containing "quad" (quadruple) sets of two-input gates, where the gate types can be AND, OR, NAND, NOR, EXCLUSIVE-OR, or EXCLUSIVE-NOR. Other gate sizes are also provided, especially in the case of the NAND function, where gate fan-in can range from two to 13 as demonstrated by Figs. 3.37h–3.37l.

Many of the ICs appearing in Fig. 3.37 are also available in open-collector versions. Some are also supplied in buffer versions that have higher than usual fan-out or output-current drive capability. For example, the logic diagram for the quad two-input NAND gates appearing in Fig. 3.37h is applicable to each of the following 7400-series ICs:

1. The 7400 quad two-input NAND gates
2. The 7403 quad two-input NAND gates with open collectors
3. The 7437 quad two-input NAND buffers
4. The 7438 quad two-input NAND buffers with open collectors

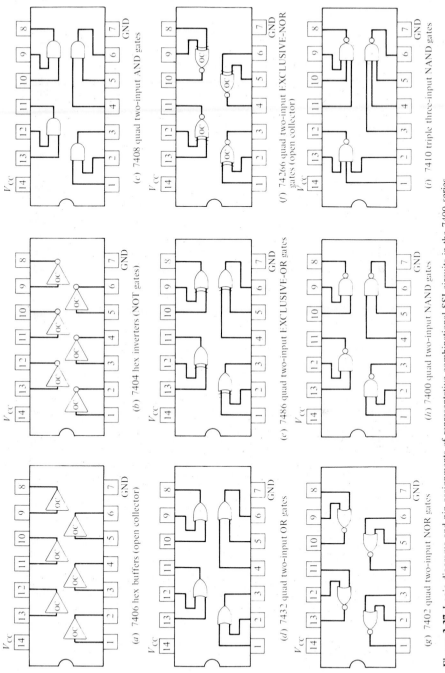

Figure 3.37 Logic diagrams and pin assignments of representative combinational SSI circuits in the 7400 series.

(a) 7406 hex buffers (open collector)

(b) 7404 hex inverters (NOT gates)

(c) 7408 quad two-input AND gates

(d) 7432 quad two-input OR gates

(e) 7486 quad two-input EXCLUSIVE-OR gates

(f) 74266 quad two-input EXCLUSIVE-NOR gates (open collector)

(g) 7402 quad two-input NOR gates

(h) 7400 quad two-input NAND gates

(i) 7410 triple three-input NAND gates

205

(*Figure 3.37 continued*)

(*j*) 7420 dual four-input NAND gates

(*k*) 7430 eight-input NAND gate

(*l*) 74133 13-input NAND gate

(*m*) 74126 quad three-state buffers

(*n*) 74366 hex three-state inverters with common two-input NOR enable

(*o*) 74134 three-state 12-input NAND gate

(*p*) 7455 4-4-input AND-OR-INVERT gate

(*q*) 7451 2-2-input and 3-3-input AND-OR-INVERT gate

(*r*) 7454 3-2-2-3-input AND-OR-INVERT gate

206

As discussed in Sec. 2.3.1, there are also faster (the 74S00 Schottky TTL series) and lower-power (the 74LS00 low power Schottky series) versions of many 7400-series ICs. Also commercially available are CMOS ICs that are compatible with the foregoing TTL series (the 74C00 series). There are relatively few three-state devices in the 7400 series, since three-state gates are mainly employed for driving the bus lines that interconnect major subcircuits. Three representative three-state ICs appear in Figs. 3.37m–3.37o. Numerous additional three-state circuits are supplied by National Semiconductor in a series of TTL ICs with part numbers in the range DM8000–DM8999 (National Semiconductor, 1981b). The three 7400-series ICs appearing in Figs. 3.37p–3.37r are examples of composite combinational circuits called *AND-OR-INVERT "gates."* This name stems from the fact that these ICs contain circuits composed of several AND gates whose outputs are connected to a NOR gate, that is, an OR-INVERT gate. These circuits thus contain two levels of logic gates, and they allow more complex logic functions to be realized by a single IC than is possible with the other SSI ICs.

To illustrate the use of the foregoing SSI ICs, consider the design of an adder circuit for 1-bit binary numbers, a so-called *full adder*. This circuit has the external connections shown in Fig. 3.38a. There are two input data bits x and y, and a carry-in line C_{in}. The output signals of the full adder consist of a sum bit z and a carry-out bit C_{out} (cf. the 4-bit binary adder in Fig. 3.19). The full adder must compute the sum

$$C_{out}, z = x + y + C_{in} \qquad (3.9)$$

where C_{out}, z denotes a 2-bit result. Equation (3.9) implies that the full adder has the truth table of Fig. 3.38b. C_{out} is set to 1 if and only if the addition produces the result two (10 in binary) or three (11). From this truth table the following logic equations defining z and C_{out} are readily derived.

$$z = x \oplus y \oplus C_{in} \qquad (3.10)$$

$$C_{out} = (x \wedge y) \vee (x \wedge C_{in}) \vee (y \wedge C_{in}) \qquad (3.11)$$

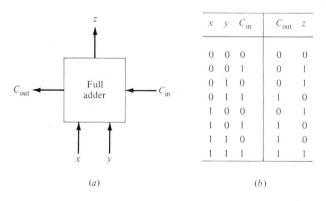

x	y	C_{in}	C_{out}	z
0	0	0	0	0
0	0	1	0	1
0	1	0	0	1
0	1	1	1	0
1	0	0	0	1
1	0	1	1	0
1	1	0	1	0
1	1	1	1	1

(a)   (b)

Figure 3.38 One-bit binary adder (full adder): (a) input-output signals and (b) truth table.

These equations imply that the full adder can be realized by the logic circuit of Fig. 3.39 in which the three-input EXCLUSIVE-OR gate implements Eq. (3.10), and the two-level AND-OR subcircuit implements Eq. (3.11).

Now suppose that the full adder is to be constructed using only ICs that appear in Fig. 3.37. This means that the gates in the logic design of the full adder must be assigned to a set of ICs that can be interconnected to yield the desired logic functions z and C_{out}. This assignment of logic elements to ICs is sometimes called the *IC partitioning problem*, because the gates in the logic circuit must be divided or partitioned into groups, each of which can be assigned to a particular IC (Breuer, 1972). The main objective in solving this problem is to use as few ICs as possible, since the cost of a multicomponent system is usually proportional to the number of components used. In comparing the logic circuit of Fig. 3.39 with the available ICs, we see that no three-input EXCLUSIVE-OR gate is available for realizing z. However, by using a pair of two-input EXCLUSIVE-OR gates from the 7486 quad two-input EXCLUSIVE-OR IC (Fig. 3.37e), we can construct a two-gate EXCLUSIVE-OR circuit that implements (3.10) thus:

$$z = (x \oplus y) \oplus C_{in} \qquad (3.12)$$

The AND-OR circuit realizing C_{out} in Fig. 3.39 could be assigned to two ICs such as the 7408 quad two-input AND and the 7432 quad two-input OR ICs, which appear in Figs. 3.37c and 3.37d respectively. This would result in a three-IC implementation of the full adder. The AND-OR format of (3.11) and the corresponding circuit in Fig. 3.39 suggest that z can be realized by a single AND-OR-INVERT gate such as the 7454 appearing in Fig. 3.37r. This will require that the output of the AND-OR-INVERT gate be inverted (complemented) to convert it to an AND-OR circuit. One of the two unused EXCLU-SIVE-OR gates in the 7486 can be used as an inverter as shown in Fig. 3.16c. We thus arrive at the two-IC implementation of the full adder that appears in Fig. 3.40. Two of the four EXCLUSIVE-OR gates in the 7486 realize z according to Eq. (3.12). Three of the AND gates and the NOR gate of the 7454 realize $\overline{C}_{out}$ thus:

$$C = \overline{C}_{out} = \overline{(x \wedge y) \vee (x \wedge C_{in}) \vee (y \wedge C_{in})}$$

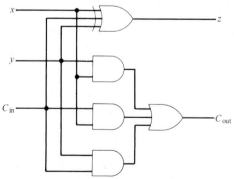

Figure 3.39 Possible logic circuit for a full adder.

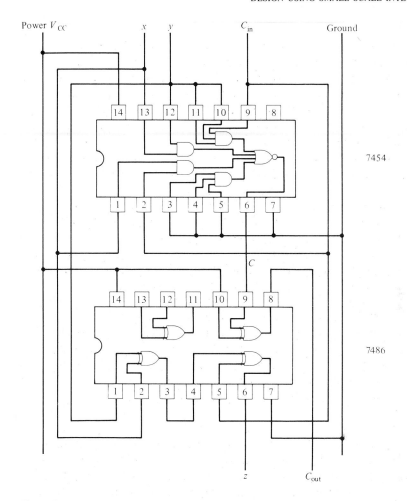

Figure 3.40 Two-IC implementation of a full adder.

The output of the 7454 is then applied to an input of an EXCLUSIVE-OR gate in the 7486 whose other input is held at the constant 1 value; this gate produces the desired carry-out signal as follows:

$$C_{out} = \overline{C}_{out} \oplus 1$$

It can be seen that certain gates are unused in Fig. 3.40, while some gates have both used and unused inputs. As will be discussed later in this section, the unused input lines can always be connected either to constant values (supplied by V_{CC} and ground), or to other used signal lines. Thus, all inputs of the unused AND gate in the 7454 IC, for instance, are connected to ground (logical 0), thereby forcing its output to 0 so that it has no effect on the output signal produced by the NOR gate.

3.2.2 Sequential ICs

It was observed earlier in this chapter that the fundamental memory element in digital systems is a device with two stable states, one representing the set or store-1 condition, and the other representing the reset or store-0 condition. The SR latch of Figs. 3.30 and 3.31 is an asynchronous memory device whose outputs can change immediately in response to signal changes on the set (S) and reset (R) input lines. More useful are clocked latches such as that of Fig. 3.32 in which a clock signal CK enables the latch, and allows state transitions in several latches to be synchronized. The clocked SR latch cannot respond to signal changes on the S or R lines until CK = 1. Once stabilized, the latch's output signals Q and $\overline{Q}$ remain constant as long as CK = 0. Clocked latches (and also flip-flops) are often supplied with a pair of auxiliary asynchronous set and reset lines called *preset* (PR) and *clear* (CLR) respectively. Figure 3.41 shows the clocked SR latch of Fig. 3.32 with the addition of preset and clear inputs. PR = 1 sets the latch independent of the values of S, R, and CK, while CLR = 1 resets it. The input combination PR = CLR = 1 is forbidden because it results in the same kind of indeterminate behavior that occurs when S = R = 1; see Fig. 3.30b. The preset and clear inputs are generally used to initialize a circuit to a fixed starting state before normal (clocked) operation of the circuit begins.

While latches have many uses in digital systems, they are unsuitable for applications where the current state Q(t) is needed while the next state Q(t + T) is being established. This is the case in the shift register of Fig. 3.34, for example, where the output $y_i(t)$ of each flip-flop must be held constant while the next states $y_i(t + T)$ and $y_{i+1}(t + T)$ are being computed. Latches are also unsuitable for circuits requiring external feedback from the outputs to the inputs of a memory element so that the next state is a function of the present state. In such cases a flip-flop, such as the SR flip-flop of Fig. 3.33, must be used. Flip-flops are characterized by the fact that the outputs Q and $\overline{Q}$ do not change until after the flip-flop has responded to the input signals that define its next state. Thus in the SR flip-flop, the master latch can only assume a new state while the clock CK is at the 1 level. The flip-flop's primary outputs Q and $\overline{Q}$, which are also the outputs of the slave latch, can change only when CK returns to 0. The behavior of these output signals is

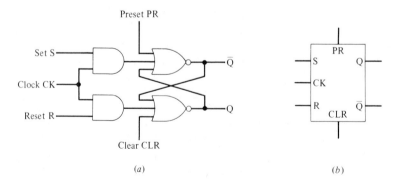

(a)

(b)

Figure 3.41 Clocked SR latch with preset and clear: (a) logic circuit; (b) symbol.

indicated by the circle and arrowhead symbols attached to the CK terminal in the standard flip-flop symbol of Fig. 3.33b.

A slightly modified version of the SR flip-flop called the *JK master–slave flip-flop*, or simply the *JK flip-flop*, is much more useful; it is defined in Fig. 3.42. The behavior of the JK flip-flop closely resembles that of the SR flip-flop, with the J and K inputs acting as the set and reset lines respectively. As in the SR case, JK = 00 is the quiescent input combination, JK = 10 sets the flip-flop, and JK = 01 resets it. Unlike the SR case, however, JK = 11 is a valid input combination that always causes the JK flip-flop to change state. This is attributed to the presence of the two extra AND gates in the circuit of Fig. 3.42a that cause JK = 11 to the transmitted as either 10 or 01 to the inputs of the master SR-type latch, depending on the current values of the flip-flop's outputs Q and $\overline{Q}$. The foregoing behavior is summarized in the state table of Fig. 3.42c. As always, the indicated state changes only take place when an appropriate clock signal is applied. The behavior of the JK flip-flop can also be described by the following logic (next-state) equation:

$$Q(t + T) = [J(t) \wedge \overline{Q}(t)] \vee [\overline{K}(t) \wedge Q(t)] \qquad (3.13)$$

State tables and equations usually describe the behavior of a sequential machine in terms of its initial and final stable states only. To display the precise times at which signals, including state variables, change value, a timing diagram is useful. Figure 3.43

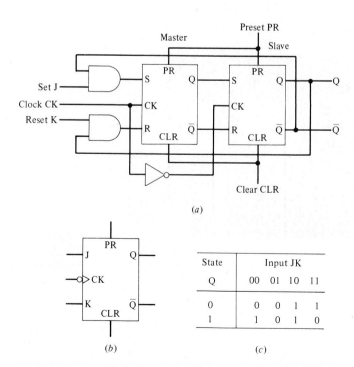

(a)

(b)

(c)

State	Input JK			
Q	00	01	10	11
0	0	0	1	1
1	1	0	1	0

Figure 3.42 JK master-slave flip-flop: (a) logic circuit; (b) symbol; (c) state table.

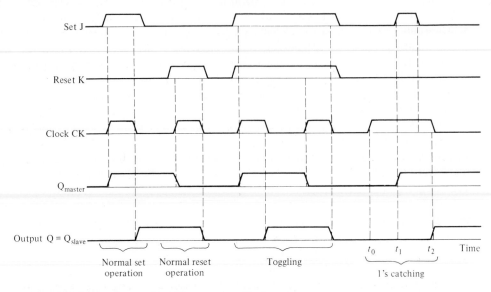

Figure 3.43 Timing diagram for a JK master-slave flip-flop.

is a timing diagram that illustrates the behavior of the JK flip-flop of Fig. 3.42. The flip-flop is normally set by applying 10 to JK and then raising the clock signal CK from 0 to 1 and holding it at the 1 level long enough for the master latch's output Q_{master} to become 1. The master latch responds continuously to the JK signals while CK = 1, hence J and K should remain constant for the duration of the clock pulse with CK = 1. Similarly Q_{master} is normally reset to 0 by applying JK = 01 to the flip-flop for the duration of one clock pulse. The flip-flop's output signal Q, which is also the output Q_{slave} of the slave latch, does not change until CK falls from 1 to 0. If J and K are held continuously at the 1 level, then the JK flip-flop changes state repeatedly, or *toggles*, with every clock pulse as indicated in the timing diagram.

Certain undesirable behavior can occur in a JK flip-flop of the master–slave type if the J and K signals are not held constant while CK = 1. This is illustrated on the right-hand side of Fig. 3.43 where a short 1 pulse (e.g., a noise pulse) is applied to J while the clock is at the 1 level. This pulse causes Q_{master} to change from 0 to 1 at time t_1. When the clock subsequently returns to 0 (at time t_2), Q = Q_{slave} also changes from 0 to 1. At this point, however, J = K = 0, which is the quiescent input condition. Thus the final state of the flip-flop does not reflect the JK input conditions present at either the start t_0 or the end t_2 of the clock pulse in question. This property of JK master–slave flip-flops is called *1s catching*, because the master latch "catches" a 1 pulse while Q = 0 and the clock is enabled; a similar *0s catching* phenomenon can occur when Q = 1. Thus if the J and K signals cannot be held constant while CK = 1, improper state changes may take place.

The 1s and 0s catching property of the JK master–slave flip-flop can be avoided by using another type of JK flip-flop called *edge-triggered*. A *positive edge-triggered JK flip-flop* is one whose next state is determined by the JK signals present when the clock signal changes from 1 to 0. In other words, the positive (0-to-1) edge of the clock pulse triggers the next state change, and hence the flip-flop's name. As long as the clock remains at the 1 level, changes in the J and K signals do not affect the next state. When the clock returns to 0, the flip-flop's outputs Q and $\overline{Q}$ assume their new values, as in the master–slave case. Figure 3.44 shows the timing behavior of the positive edge-triggered JK flip-flop for the same J, K, and clock waveforms used in Fig. 3.43. Note that the rightmost 1 pulse on J has no effect. A *negative edge-triggered JK flip-flop* is similar to the positive type, but has the polarity of its clock reversed. Hence its next state is determined by the JK signals present when the clock changes from 1 to 0, and the flip-flop's outputs change when the clock returns from 0 to 1. To contrast the JK flip-flop of Fig. 3.42 with the edge-triggered types, the former is sometimes called *level-triggered*, since a new next state can be established as long as the clock signal is held at the level that enables the master latch. There are no standard circuit symbols to distinguish edge triggering from level triggering in flip-flops. The JK flip-flop symbol of Fig. 3.42b is therefore also the symbol for a positive-edge JK flip-flop; by eliminating the inversion circle on CK, the symbol for a negative edge-triggered JK flip-flop is obtained.

There is another useful class of 1-bit memory devices called D latches and D flip-flops, where D denotes delay. A clocked *D latch* is defined in Fig. 3.45. It is formed by adding an inverter to a clocked SR latch, so that the main input line D of the D latch is connected to S, and $\overline{D}$ is connected to R. Thus D = 1 makes SR = 10 and sets the latch, while D = 0 makes SR = 01 and resets it. As in the JK design, the forbidden input combination SR = 11 is never applied to the SR latch. The behavior of the D latch can be expressed by the equation

$$Q(t + T) = D(t)$$

Thus when the latch is enabled (CK = 1), the Q output signal is the same as the D input signal, but is delayed by T seconds. The D latch can be viewed as a clocked delay element, which explains its name.

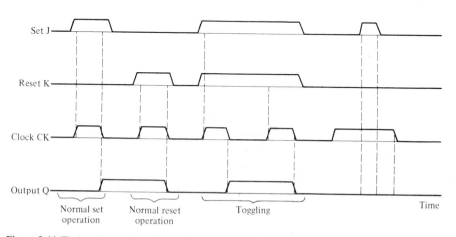

Figure 3.44 Timing diagram for a JK positive edge-triggererd flip-flop.

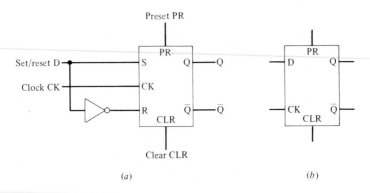

Figure 3.45 Clocked D latch: (*a*) logic circuit; (*b*) symbol.

Figure 3.46 indicates how a clocked D latch can be combined with a clocked SR latch in a master–slave configuration to produce a *D flip-flop*. In this version of a D flip-flop, the master D latch is enabled by CK = 0. As long as the clock CK remains at 0, the state of the master latch varies continuously in response to changes on the D input line. When CK returns to 1, the state of the master latch is fixed and is transferred to the slave latch, causing the primary outputs of the D flip-flop to change. Hence the positive (0-to-1) edge of the clock CK times the next state change and the output signal change; consequently this D flip-flop is also termed positive edge triggered. A negative edge-

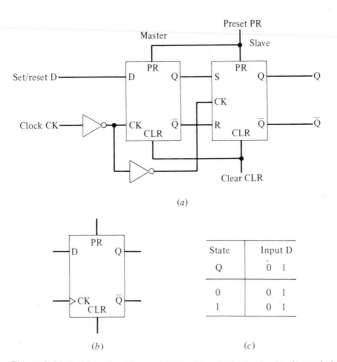

Figure 3.46 Positive edge-triggered D flip-flop: (*a*) logic circuit; (*b*) symbol; (*c*) truth table.

triggered D flip-flop is obtained by inverting the clock signals applied to the two internal latches.

Figure 3.47 describes some basic latch and flip-flop ICs found in the 7400 series. The 74279 shown in Fig. 3.47a contains four independent unclocked latches, each consisting of a pair of cross-coupled NAND gates (cf. Fig. 3.31a). The use of NAND instead of NOR gates requires the set and reset functions to be activated by 0 rather than 1 signals; therefore, these latches are named $\overline{SR}$ latches. The 7475 in Fig. 3.47b contains four clocked D-type latches that are grouped into two pairs, each with its own clock line. The majority of sequential SSI circuits in the 7400 series contain JK flip-flops; three representative examples appear in Fig. 3.47c–3.47e. The 74107 contains two indepen-dent level-triggered JK flip-flops of the master–slave type defined in Fig. 3.43. The 74106 and 7470 contain JK edge-triggered flip-flops with negative and positive edge triggering respectively. The 74106 contains two independent flip-flops, while the 7470 contains a single flip-flop with additional gates attached to its JK input lines. The 7474 IC shown in Fig. 3.47f contains two independent D-type positive edge-triggered flip-flops. Many additional flip-flop variants can be found in manufacturers' TTL data books.

Figure 3.48 shows an example of a sequential logic circuit that is easily implemented using the foregoing ICs. It is a *Johnson counter*, also called a *walking-ring* or *shift counter*, which is useful in control applications. It consists of a set of flip-flops whose inputs and outputs are linked together as in a shift register (cf. Fig. 3.34a), except that the inverted output $\overline{Q}$ of the last flip-flop is connected to the input of the first flip-flop, forming a closed loop. D flip-flops are used in Fig. 3.48, but they could be replaced by JK flip-flops. The purpose of the counter is to generate a specific sequence of 4-bit words $z_3z_2z_1z_0$ in response to a sequence of 1-pulses applied to the main input line x. The counter can be placed in the initial state $z_3z_2z_1z_0 = 0000$ by activating the CLEAR input line. A 1 pulse applied to x causes the following state transitions:

$$z_0(t + T) = z_1(t)$$

$$z_1(t + T) = z_2(t)$$

$$z_2(t + T) = z_3(t)$$

$$z_3(t + T) = \bar{z}_0(t)$$

resulting in the next state 1000. It is easily seen that a train of 1-pulses applied to x causes $z_3z_2z_1z_0$ to assume the following sequence of values

$$0000$$
$$1000$$
$$1100$$
$$1110$$
$$1111$$
$$0111$$
$$0011$$
$$0001$$

at which point the initial state 0000 reappears. Thus the counter generates a sequence of eight distinct 4-bit patterns or numbers, and so constitutes a modulo-8 counter. These

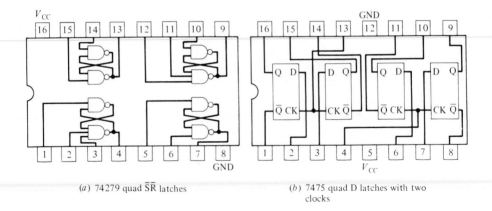

(a) 74279 quad $\overline{S}\overline{R}$ latches

(b) 7475 quad D latches with two clocks

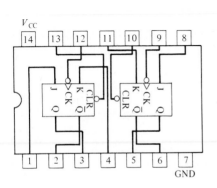

(c) 74107 dual JK (master-slave) flip-flops with clear

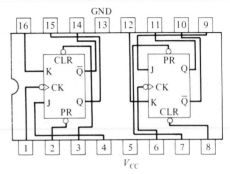

(d) 74106 dual negative edge-triggered JK flip-flops with preset and clear

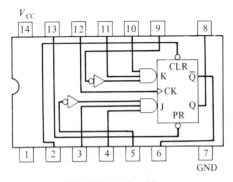

(e) 7470 AND-gated positive edge-triggered JK flip-flop with preset and clear

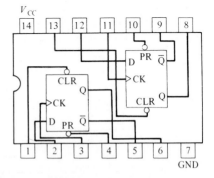

(f) 7474 dual positive edge-triggered D flip-flops with preset and clear

Figure 3.47 Logic diagrams and pin assignments of representative sequential SSI ICs in the 7400 series.

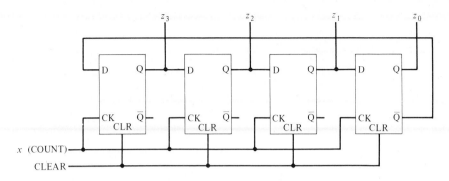

Figure 3.48 Four-bit Johnson counter.

patterns have the advantage that they are easily decoded to obtain eight distinct signals that can be used to activate eight sequential operations (see Prob. 3.25). Figure 3.49 shows a straightforward implementation of the Johnson counter by means of two 7474 dual D flip-flop ICs. These flip-flops are positive edge triggered; therefore, the counter's output $z_3z_2z_1z_0$ changes value immediately after x changes from 0 to 1.

3.2.3 Timing Considerations

The speed of operation of a combinational or sequential logic circuit is ultimately determined by the propagation delays of its constituent ICs. Values of these delay parameters, and other useful timing information, can be found in the appropriate IC data sheets. For example, Fig. 3.50 shows the timing data typically supplied with combinational ICs, in this case the two ICs composing the full adder circuit of Fig. 3.40. The

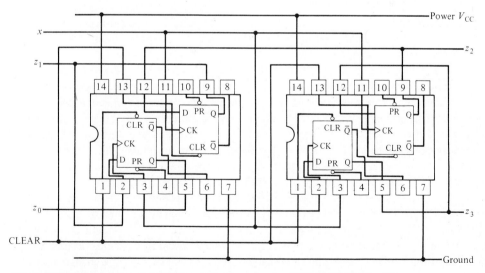

Figure 3.49 Implementation of 4-bit Johnson Counter using two 7474 dual D flip-flop ICs.

		Propagation Delay (ns)					
		t_{PLH}			t_{PHL}		
IC Type	MIN	TYP	MAX	MIN	TYP	MAX	Test Conditions
7454	–	13	22	–	8	15	Load capacitance C_L = 15 pF Load resistance R_L = 400 Ω,
7486	–	15	23	–	11	17	C_L = 15 pF, R_L = 400 Ω, 0 applied to other input
	–	18	30	–	13	22	C_L = 15 pF, R_L = 400 Ω, 1 applied to other input

Figure 3.50 Timing data for two combinational 7400 series ICs.

circuit propagation delay is presented in two parts, t_{PLH} and t_{PHL}, called the *low-to-high-output* and the *high-to-low-output propagation delays* respectively. t_{PLH} is the delay after an input signal change occurs that causes the output of the circuit to change from low (0) to high (1), until the output signal actually changes from 0 to 1. Similarly, t_{PHL} is the delay between input and output signal changes when the output goes from 1 to 0. In each case typical (TYP) and maximum (MAX) or worst-case values are given in Fig. 3.50. The figures given for the 7486 apply to any of the four independent EXCLUSIVE-OR gates contained in this IC. Suppose, for instance, that both inputs x_1 and x_2 of an EXCLUSIVE-OR gate in the 7486 are 1, causing the gate's output signal z to be 0. Let x_1 be changed from 1 to 0 at time t. Then z changes from 0 to 1 at time $t + t_{PLH}$ where, according to the data of Fig. 3.50, t_{PLH} is typically 18 ns, but is guaranteed not to exceed 30 ns. Note that the propagation delays of the 7486 vary with the input signal combinations applied to the gates. Other combinational ICs have more easily described propagation delays. Thus in the case of the 74LS00 quad NAND IC whose data sheet appears in Fig. 2.64, we find that $t_{PLH} = t_{PHL} = t_P$.

The propagation delays, both typical and worst-case, of a large circuit may be determined by summing the appropriate propagation delays of its component ICs. All possible signal transmission paths through the circuit must be considered, especially the longest paths that determine the maximum delays. Care must be taken that for each signal change affecting an output line of some IC, the correct delay value t_{PLH} or t_{PHL} is chosen to account for that IC's contribution to the overall circuit propagation delay. Consider again the adder of Fig. 3.40. By using the timing data for its component ICs given in Fig. 3.50, we can compute the maximum propagation delay of signals transmitted to the carry-out line C_{out} as follows. There are two cases to consider, depending on the way in which the output signal C of the 7454 AND-OR-INVERT gate changes. If C changes from 0 to 1, then the 7454 contributes a propagation delay of at most 22 ns. C is applied to an input line of an EXCLUSIVE-OR gate in the 7486 whose other input is held constantly at 1. Thus from Fig. 3.50 we see that if C changes from 0 to 1, causing C_{out} to change from 1 to

0, the EXCLUSIVE-OR gate's propagation delay is at most 22 ns. Hence the total delay imposed on the signal transmitted to C_{out} is at most $22 + 22 = 44$ ns. Now suppose that C changes from 1 to 0, causing C_{out} to change from 0 to 1. Under these conditions the maximum delay due to the 7454 is 15 ns, while that due to the 7486 is 30 ns, so that the total maximum delay is 45 ns. Hence the worst-case delay associated with C_{out} is 45 ns. By a similar analysis it can be shown that the maximum propagation delay of signals transmitted to the sum output line z of the adder is 53 ns. We conclude that the maximum time for the adder in question to compute the result C_{out}, z is 53 ns.

Additional timing data are necessary to define the behavior of clocked sequential circuits. In general, input signals to a sequential circuit—in particular, the clock signal itself—must be held at the 0 or 1 levels long enough for the circuit to respond to the current input conditions, for example, to complete a transition to a new internal stable state. In some cases constraints must be placed on the times at which input signals change relative to the clock signal. Figure 3.51 gives some representative timing data for 7400-series flip-flops (Texas Instruments, 1981). The clock signal CK is defined by two *pulse-width* parameters denoted t_W, which specify the minimum periods for which CK must be high (1) and low (0). In the case of the 7474 dual D flip-flop, for instance, the clock must be 1 for at least 30 ns and 0 for at least 37 ns to ensure proper operation. Thus the minimum clock period T_{min} for the 7474 is $30 + 37 = 67$ ns. Hence the *maximum clock frequency* f_{max} at which the 7474 is guaranteed to operate is given by the equation

$$f_{max} = 1/T_{min} \approx 15 \text{ MHz} \tag{3.14}$$

f_{max} is often included as a parameter in the data sheets of sequential ICs. For the 7474 the minimum (MIN) value of f_{max} is 15 MHz, as given by Eq. (3.14); a typical (TYP) value of f_{max} is 25 MHz. The foregoing values of t_W and f_{max} are directly applicable to the counter circuit of Fig. 3.49, which is composed solely of 7474s. We conclude, therefore, that the 1-pulses to be counted that are applied to the x (clock) line of this circuit must be at least 30 ns in duration, and must be spaced at least 37 ns apart.

Edge-triggered flip-flops, such as those of the 7474, are enabled by either the positive (0-to-1) or negative (1-to-0) edge of a clock signal that is present at some instant of time t. The flip-flop's main input signals (D or J and K) must be constant or stable for some minimum length of time preceding t, which is called the *setup time* t_{setup}. This is necessary to ensure that the flip-flop's internal state is stable when the enabling edge of

recommended operating conditions

		SERIES 54/74			'70			'72, '73, '76, '107			'74			'109			'110			'111			UNIT
					MIN	NOM	MAX	MIN	NOM	MAX	MIN	NOM	MAX	MIN	NOM	MAX	MIN	NOM	MAX	MIN	NOM	MAX	
Supply voltage, V_{CC}	Series 54	4.5	5	5.5	4.5	5	5.5	4.5	5	5.5	4.5	5	5.5	4.5	5	5.5	4.5	5	5.5				V
	Series 74	4.75	5	5.25	4.75	5	5.25	4.75	5	5.25	4.75	5	5.25	4.75	5	5.25	4.75	5	5.25				
High-level output current, I_{OH}				−400			−400			−400			−800			−800			−800				μA
Low-level output current, I_{OL}				16			16			16			16			16			16				mA
Pulse width, t_W	Clock high	20			20			30			20			25			25						ns
	Clock low	30			47			37			20			25			25						
	Preset or clear low	25			25			30			20			25			25						
Input setup time, t_{setup}		20↑			0↑			20↑			10↑			20↑			0↑						ns
Input hold time, t_{hold}		5↑			0↓			5↑			6↑			5↑			30↑						ns
Operating free-air temperature, T_A	Series 54	−55		125	−55		125	−55		125	−55		125	−55		125	−55		125				°C
	Series 74	0		70	0		70	0		70	0		70	0		70	0		70				

↑↓ The arrow indicates the edge of the clock pulse used for reference: ↑ for the rising edge, ↓ for the falling edge.

Figure 3.51 Timing data for some sequential ICs in the 7400 series. (*Courtesy Texas Instruments, Inc.*)

the clock signal appears. At time t the flip-flop begins to respond to the main input signals; since it takes some time for the flip-flop to reach a new stable state, the main input signals must remain unchanged for a minimum period after t, which is called the *hold time* t_{hold}. Figure 3.52 illustrates the concepts of setup and hold time for a positive edge-triggered device. The data in Fig. 3.51 imply that for a 7474 D flip-flop, $t_{setup} = 20$ ns and $t_{hold} = 5$ ns. Consequently a pulse applied to the D input line must be at least 25 ns in duration.

3.2.4 Fan-in/Fan-out Constraints

We consider next two key issues encountered when SSI ICs are used to implement an abstract logic design. Frequently the number of input lines or fan-in of a gate G in the original logic circuit is not the same as the fan-in of the gates available in the ICs used to implement G; we may term this the *fan-in problem*. A related issue, which was addressed in electrical terms in Sec. 2.3.3, is the *fan-out problem*—namely, ensuring that the number of input lines to which the output z of G is connected (i.e., the fan-out of G) does not exceed a specified maximum value.

The fan-in problem is illustrated by the full adder circuit examined earlier; see Figs. 3.38–3.40. The original logic design of Fig. 3.39 contains a three-input EXCLUSIVE-OR gate whose fan-in exceeds that of the gates in the 7486 quad two-input EXCLUSIVE-OR circuit used in Fig. 3.40. This problem is solved by using two EXCLUSIVE-OR gates from the 7486 that are connected in series to form a two-gate circuit that is logically equivalent to a three-input EXCLUSIVE-OR. Conversely the 7454 AND-OR-INVERT gate contains more inputs than needed to implement the relevant part of Fig. 3.39, resulting in gates that have various combinations of used and unused inputs. For instance, only two of the three inputs of one of the 7454's three-input AND gates are used, while no inputs of the remaining three-input AND gate are used.

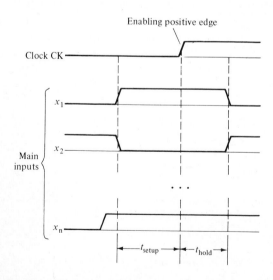

Figure 3.52 Setup and hold times in a positive edge-triggered device.

To increase fan-in, a multigate circuit that realizes the desired gate function with the specified number of inputs must be designed. This can be done in many ways. The AND, OR, and EXCLUSIVE-OR functions are quite easy to expand in this fashion, since a treelike interconnection of gates of any one type is logically equivalent to a single gate of the same type that has greater fan-in. Figure 3.53a illustrates this kind of fan-in expansion for the AND function. Another AND circuit composed of a set of NAND gates feeding a NOR gate appears in Fig. 3.53b. By inserting inverters into the output lines of the circuits of Figs. 3.53a and 3.53b, NAND circuits of high fan-in are obtained. Another two ways of increasing NAND fan-in are demonstrated in Fig. 3.53c and 3.53d. Note that at least three levels of gates are required if only NAND gates are available. Each gate introduces a propagation delay, and hence the circuits of Fig. 3.53 can be expected to be slower than a single equivalent multi-input gate. The other gate types can be expanded in a similar manner.

To decrease fan-in, a means of disabling unused input lines is necessary. As depicted in Fig. 3.54, this can always be done for the basic gates by connecting the unused inputs to constant logic signals, 0 in the case of OR, NOR, EXCLUSIVE-OR, and EXCLU-SIVE-NOR, and 1 in the case of AND and NAND. An alternative approach that usually results in shorter interconnections is to tie unused inputs to some used input line x of the gate. This simply causes several copies of the same signal x to be applied to the gate in question. Such duplicated input signals do not affect the output function realized by AND, OR, NAND, or NOR gates. However, in the case of EXCLUSIVE-OR and

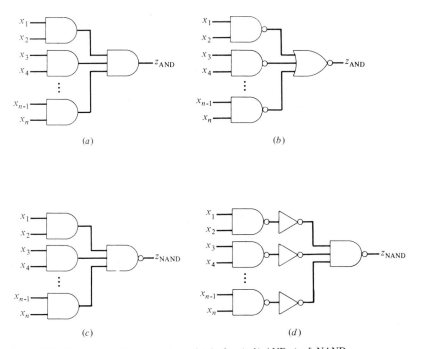

Figure 3.53 Some ways of increasing gate fan-in for: (a,b) AND; (c,d) NAND.

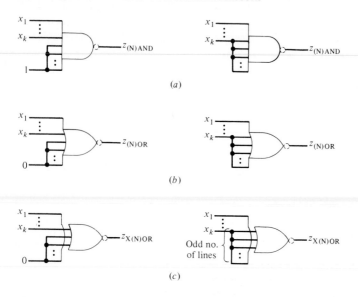

Figure 3.54 Some ways of decreasing gate fan-in for: (*a*) AND and NAND; (*b*) OR and NOR; (*c*) EX-CLUSIVE-OR and EXCLUSIVE-NOR.

EXCLUSIVE-NOR gates, it must be ensured that the number of gate input lines carrying the signal x is always odd. An even number of replicated signals will cancel one another, causing the gate's output function to become independent of the variable x. For example,

$$x \oplus x = 0$$

whereas

$$x \oplus x \oplus x = x$$

It might also be asked: What happens if an unused input line is left disconnected or floating? The answer depends on the logic family being used. Floating inputs are not permitted in CMOS circuits; unused inputs must always be connected to logic signals, as in Fig. 3.54. The electrical design of most TTL circuits is such that floating inputs normally assume the logical 1 level. Thus it is permissible to leave the unused preset (PR) inputs to the D flip-flops in the counter circuit of Fig. 3.49 disconnected, since they float to the 1 level, which, as indicated by the inversion circle, is the inactive condition. Note that the three inputs of the unused AND gate in this circuit cannot be left disconnected, because the AND gate's output line is an unused input to a NOR gate, which therefore must be forced to 0. Sometimes a floating input line can act as a receiving antenna for noise signals, allowing it to become either 0 or 1 randomly. Thus it is generally advisable to connect all unused lines to well-defined logic signals in accordance with the IC manufacturer's guidelines.

The fan-out limitations of an IC are normally specified in electrical terms in its data sheets; the interpretation of these electrical data is examined in Sec. 2.2.3. Figure 3.55 summarizes the fan-out characteristics of three important TTL logic families. Standard

IC Type of Source (Output) Line	Maximum Number of Destination (input) Lines		
	Standard TTL (7400 Series)	Schottky TTL (74S00 Series)	Low-Power Schottky TTL (74LS00 Series)
Standard TTL	10	6	20
Schottky TTL	12	10	40
Low-power Schottky TTL	5	4	10

Figure 3.55 Fan-out constraints for ICs in the 7400, 74S00, and 74LS00 series.

TTL ICs are made so that each output line can drive up to 10 input lines on ICs of the same logic family. The same output line can be connected to at most six inputs of Schottky TTL ICs, but can be connected to as many as 40 inputs of low-power Schottky ICs. When normal fan-out limits must be exceeded, extra buffer elements may be used, as illustrated in Fig. 2.66. Logic gates designated as buffer gates can also be used as they have higher than normal fan-out limits. For example, the 7437 standard TTL IC, which is a quad two-input NAND buffer IC with the structure depicted in Fig. 3.37h, has three times the normal output drive capability. Thus an output of the 7437 can fan out to a maximum of 30 standard TTL inputs instead of the usual 10.

3.3 SYSTEMATIC DESIGN METHODS

By themselves, SSI components are most often used to design relatively simple logic circuits; they also play a significant role as interconnecting elements in more complex systems. A formal theory of logic design (switching theory) has existed since the 1930s, and is applicable to modern logic design using SSI ICs. This section examines classical switching theory and its uses in the design of small combinational and sequential logic circuits.

3.3.1 Design Process

Figure 3.56 lists the steps in designing a small system using SSI-level ICs. This is a particular instance of the general system design process discussed in Sec.1.3.4. As in any design task, the primary goal here is to obtain a system that has the correct behavior, in terms of both the logic functions generated and the speed at which the circuit operates. A secondary goal is to minimize the total cost of the system. The cost of a small logic circuit is most conveniently measured by the number of hardware components used to implement it. Within any particular IC complexity range such as SSI, there is little variation in cost among the different types of ICs available. Thus hardware cost minimization essentially reduces to the problem of minimizing the total number of ICs used.

Design Step	Actions Required
Planning	Obtain specifications of the desired system behavior. Determine the IC technology and logic families to be used.
Preliminary design	Specify the overall design or architecture of the system. Identify the major combinational and sequential subcircuits.
Logic design	Implement the logic circuits identified in the preceding step using appropriate gate and flip-flop types. Partition the logic circuit into ICs of the chosen logic families.
Physical design	Build, debug, and document a prototype version of the system.

Figure 3.56 Main steps in designing a digital system using SSI ICs.

Classical switching theory is concerned with the design of logic circuits from individual gates and flip-flops. It provides various systematic design procedures whose goal is to realize specified logic functions by means of the minimum number of gates and flip-flops. These procedures are computationally complex, which limits their use in practice to small circuits containing few input variables and states, typically less than 10. Furthermore, they make certain simplifying assumptions about the logic circuits being designed, for example, by limiting the number of circuit levels to two or three, or by ignoring fan-in/fan-out constraints. Consider again the full adder circuit of Fig. 3.39, which realizes z and C_{out} using the minimum number of standard logic gates. The physical implementation of this circuit by means of 7400-series ICs, which appears in Fig. 3.40, uses the minimum number of ICs, but not the minimum number of gates. In fact this circuit contains a number of unused gates. Such minor inefficiency in gate usage is relatively unimportant because it does not affect the number of ICs needed. The multiplexer circuit of Fig. 3.17, which is basically a two-level circuit composed of AND, OR, and NOT gates, is representative of the kind of circuit obtainable by standard gate-minimization techniques. More complex logic circuits such as the 4-bit adder of Fig. 3.19 are generally designed by *heuristic* methods, which rely on unsystematic, intuitive, or ad hoc design decisions. Heuristic designs can be expected to contain more than the minimum number of components, although good designs of this type are often quite close to minimal. The use of excessive numbers of gates or flip-flops to implement a circuit is undesirable from the viewpoints of circuit cost, operating speed, power consumption, and maintenance. Consequently gate and flip-flop minimization is still useful as an abstract design objective, even if true minimality is rarely achieved in practice.

A complex digital system can be broken down into a set of combinational subcircuits $C_1, C_2, \ldots$, and a set of simple sequential subcircuits $S_1, S_2, \ldots$, as suggested by Fig. 3.57. Each of these subcircuits may be associated with a specific set of functions performed by the system. The sequential subcircuits are typically plain memory circuits (sets of latches or flip-flops), or else memory circuits with limited data-processing capability such as shift registers or counters. The main data-transfer and data-processing operations are carried out in the combinational subcircuits. In the synchronous systems

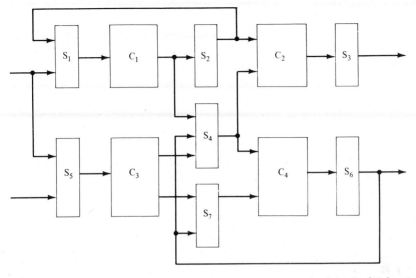

Figure 3.57 High-level view of a system composed of combinational subcircuits $\{C_i\}$ and sequential subcircuits $\{S_i\}$.

of interest here, all the memory elements are connected to a common clock signal CLOCK, so that all can change state simultaneously.

Every synchronous sequential logic circuit can be reduced, in principle, to the structure shown in Fig. 3.58 consisting of a memory M and a combinational circuit C. M includes all the memory elements found in the sequential circuits $S_1, S_2, \ldots$ of Fig. 3.57, while C includes $C_1, C_2, \ldots$ and the combinational portions of $S_1, S_2, \ldots$. C is responsible for generating the primary output signals Z of the circuit, as well as the signals Y' that determine the next state of M. The inputs to C are the primary input signals X and the current state Y provided by M. The memory M is easy to design, since it is typically just a set of flip-flops with certain common control signals such as clock and clear. The major problem is therefore to design the combinational part C. The systematic design of combinational circuits is heavily based on Boolean algebra, to which we turn next.

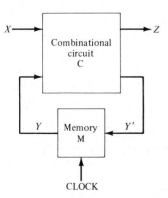

Figure 3.58 General structure of a synchronous sequential circuit.

3.3.2 Boolean Algebra

Boolean algebra, which is named for the English mathematician George Boole (1815–1864), was originally introduced to provide a symbolic method for analyzing human logic (Boole, 1854). Almost a century later it was found to provide a means as well for analyzing logical machines. In general an *algebra* consists of a set of elements K, a set of functions or operators P that operate on the members of K, and a set of axioms or basic laws that define the properties of K and P. In ordinary numerical algebra, K is the set of real numbers and P is the set of numerical operations addition, subtraction, multiplication, division, exponentiation, and so on. The axioms of ordinary algebra are the rules that we use, often instinctively, to manipulate and evaluate algebraic expressions. A sampling (by no means complete) of such axioms follows:

$$x + (y + z) = (x + y) + z$$

$$x(yz) = (xy)z$$

$$x + y = y + x$$

$$xy = yx$$

$$x(y + z) = xy + xz \qquad (3.15)$$

$$x + 0 = x$$

$$x1 = x$$

$$x + (-x) = 0$$

$$x(x^{-1}) = 1$$

A *Boolean algebra* may be defined as a set K of Boolean values or constants, along with a set P of three operators AND, OR, and NOT. For reasons that will become clear shortly, we denote the AND, OR, and NOT operators by the symbols $\wedge$, $\vee$, and $^-$ (overbar), respectively, which we have been using to denote the logic operations performed by AND, OR, and NOT gates. K contains 2^n elements, where n is a nonzero integer, and includes two special elements denoted 0 and 1. Thus in the simplest two-valued Boolean algebra, $K = \{0, 1\}$. Figure 3.59 lists a useful and complete set of axioms for any Boolean algebra.

On comparing the axioms of Fig. 3.59 with those of ordinary algebra included in Eq. (3.15), it can be seen that many are essentially the same, with AND ($\wedge$) and OR ($\vee$) replacing multiplication (denoted by juxtaposition rather than an explicit operator symbol) and addition ($+$) respectively. For instance, each algebra contains a pair of associative laws that state that the order in which a particular operator from P is applied to three members of K is of no consequence. The special identity elements 0 and 1 of Boolean algebra play roles analogous to those of the numbers 0 and 1 in ordinary algebra. The logical inverse $\bar{x}$ roughly corresponds to both the additive inverse $-x$ obtained by subtraction and the multiplicative inverse x^{-1} obtained by division. There are, however, significant differences between the two algebras. For example, only one of the two distributive laws appearing in Fig. 3.59 has a counterpart in ordinary algebra, because

$$x(y + y) = xy + xz$$

but

$$x + (yz) \neq (x + y)(x + z)$$

The idempotent laws and De Morgan's laws are also peculiar to Boolean algebra.

Other properties of Boolean algebra can be derived as theorems from the given axioms. Consider, for example, the following Boolean equation:

$$x \vee (\bar{x} \wedge y) = x \vee y \qquad (3.16)$$

The left-hand side of Eq. (3.16) can be reduced systematically to the right-hand side in the following manner.

$$x \vee (\bar{x} \wedge y) = (x \vee \bar{x}) \wedge (x \vee y) \text{ by axiom 4b (distributivity of } \vee \text{ over } \wedge)$$

$$= 1 \wedge (x \vee y) \qquad \text{by axiom 7b (properties of the inverse)}$$

$$= (x \vee y) \wedge 1 \qquad \text{by axiom 3a (commutativity of } \wedge)$$

$$= x \vee y \qquad \text{by axiom 5b (properties of the identity element 1)}$$

It will be observed that the axioms of Fig. 3.59 are listed in dual pairs, where the *dual* E^d of any Boolean expression or equation E is obtained by replacing every occurrence of $\wedge$,

No.	Statement of Axioms	Name
1	For any $x, y, z \in K$, $x \wedge y \in K$, $x \vee y \in K$ and $\bar{z} \in K$	Closure property
2	(a) $x \wedge (y \wedge z) = (x \wedge y) \wedge z$ (b) $x \vee (y \vee z) = (x \vee y) \vee z$	Associative laws
3	(a) $x \wedge y = y \wedge x$ (b) $x \vee y = y \vee x$	Commutative laws
4	(a) $x \wedge (y \vee z) = (x \wedge y) \vee (x \wedge z)$ (b) $x \vee (y \wedge z) = (x \vee y) \wedge (x \vee z)$	Distributive laws
5	K contains two unique identity elements 0 and 1 with the following properties: (a) $x \vee 0 = x$ (b) $x \wedge 1 = x$ (c) $x \wedge 0 = 0$ (d) $x \vee 1 = 1$	Properties of identity elements
6	For every $x \in K$ there exists a unique inverse element $\bar{x} \in K$ with the following properties: (a) $x \wedge \bar{x} = 0$ (b) $x \vee \bar{x} = 1$	Properties of inverse elements
7	(a) $x \wedge x = x$ (b) $x \vee x = x$	Idempotent laws
8	(a) $\overline{x \wedge y} = \bar{x} \vee \bar{y}$ (b) $\overline{x \vee y} = \bar{x} \wedge \bar{y}$	De Morgan's laws
9	$\bar{\bar{x}} = x$	Involution law

Figure 3.59 Complete set of axioms for Boolean algebra.

$\vee$, 0 and 1 by $\vee$, $\wedge$, 1, and 0 respectively. If E is a valid equation or law of Boolean algebra, then E^d also must be a valid equation. This is a consequence of the fact that if every axiom used in a proof of E is replaced by its dual axiom, the result is a proof of E^d. Thus the dual of Eq. (3.16) is

$$x \wedge (\bar{x} \vee y) = x \wedge y$$

and is another valid law of Boolean algebra.

Consider a Boolean algebra defined with respect to the set of elements K, for example, $K = \{0, 1\}$. An n-variable *Boolean function* z is a mapping from the set $(x_1, x_2, \ldots, x_n)$, where $x_i \in K$ for $i = 1, 2, \ldots, n$ onto the element $z(x_1, x_2, \ldots, x_n) \in K$. Such functions may be defined by means of truth tables, or else by means of algebraic expressions, that is, *Boolean expressions*, that contain only variables defined on K, and the operators AND, OR, and NOT. For example, the n-variable Boolean AND and NAND functions are defined by the following Boolean expressions:

$$z_{\text{AND}}(x_1, x_2, \ldots, x_n) = x_1 \wedge x_2 \wedge \ldots \wedge x_n$$

$$z_{\text{NAND}}(x_1, x_2, \ldots, x_n) = \overline{x_1 \wedge x_2 \wedge \ldots \wedge x_n}$$

New Boolean operators can also be defined in terms of the basic AND, OR, and NOT operators. Sometimes a special symbol $|$ (the Scheffer stroke symbol) is used as a NAND operator; it may be defined as follows:

$$z_{\text{NAND}}(x_1, x_2) = x_1 \mid x_2 = \overline{x_1 \wedge x_2} \tag{3.17}$$

More useful is the EXCLUSIVE-OR operator symbol $\oplus$, which can be specified thus:

$$z_{\text{XOR}}(x_1, x_2) = x_1 \oplus x_2 = (\bar{x}_1 \wedge x_2) \vee (x_1 \wedge \bar{x}_2) \tag{3.18}$$

There is an intimate relationship between Boolean algebra and (combinational) logic functions or circuits. Consider the class of all combinational logic functions K_n of the form $z(x_1, x_2, \ldots, x_k)$ defined on the logic values $\{0, 1\}$, where k varies from 0 to n. Each distinct function z has a unique representation by means of a 2^n-row truth table with n input columns and one output column. Since each entry in the output column can be either 0 or 1, there are

$$\underbrace{2 \times 2 \times \cdots \times 2}_{2^n \text{ times}} = 2^{2^n}$$

distinct functions in K_n. Figure 3.60 lists K_2, the $2^{2^2} = 16$ functions of up to two variables. Earlier we defined the logical operators AND, OR, and NOT using the same notation that we have introduced for the operators of Boolean algebra. Given the logic functions z_1 and z_2 from K, we can use the logical operators to construct new members of K_n as follows:

$$z_1(x_1, \ldots, x_k) \wedge z_2(x_m, \ldots, x_p)$$

$$z_1(x_1, \ldots, x_k) \vee z_2(x_m, \ldots, x_p) \tag{3.19}$$

$$\bar{z}_1(x_1, x_2, \ldots, x_k)$$

It is easily seen that if we substitute the set of logic functions K_n for K, and the logic operators AND, OR, and NOT for the corresponding Boolean operators in the definition of a Boolean algebra given in Fig. 3.59, all the laws listed, which become logic equations, remain true. We therefore reach the following important conclusion:

The set K_n of all logic functions of up to n variables along with the logical (gate) operators AND, OR, and NOT form a Boolean algebra.

This particular type of Boolean algebra is sometimes called *switching algebra*.

Thus all the laws of Boolean algebra apply to logic functions, so there is no real confusion in using the same symbols for the operators of Boolean algebra and those used to describe logic functions. In fact it is customary in switching theory and logic design to treat the adjectives Boolean and logic(al) as interchangeable when applied to such terms as function, equation, expression, and circuit.

The correspondence between Boolean algebra and logic circuits follows from the fact that a Boolean/logic expression denoting a Boolean/logic function can be mapped directly into a logic circuit that realizes the function in question. This mapping is illustrated by Fig. 3.61, which shows circuits corresponding to the three Boolean/logic expressions in (3.19). Note that the operators $\wedge$, $\vee$, and $^-$ are mapped into AND, OR, and NOT gates respectively. The variables or subexpressions that are operated on by some operator f correspond to signals that are applied to the inputs of the gate G_f that represents f in the logic circuit. Parentheses can be used in a straightforward fashion to denote gates; for example, $(x_1 \wedge x_2 \wedge \ldots \wedge x_n)$ denotes an n-input AND gate, $(x_1 \vee x_2 \vee \ldots \vee x_n)$ denotes an n-input NOR gate, and so on. With this convention, the equations

$$z = (x \oplus y \oplus C_{in})$$
$$C_{out} = ((x \wedge y) \vee (x \wedge C_{in}) \vee (y \wedge C_{in})) \tag{3.20}$$

describe both the structure and behavior of the full adder logic circuit appearing in Fig. 3.39. Similarly the IC implementation of this circuit given in Fig. 3.40 is described by the equations:

$$z = ((x \oplus y) \oplus C_{in})$$
$$C_{out} = \overline{(1 \oplus \overline{((x \wedge y) \vee (x \wedge C_{in}) \vee (y \wedge y \wedge C_{in}) \vee (0 \wedge 0 \wedge 0))}} \tag{3.21}$$

No. of Variables	Logic/Boolean Functions
0	$z = 0;\quad z = 1$
1	$z = x_1;\quad z = x_2;\quad z = \bar{x}_1;\quad z = \bar{x}_2$
2	$z = x_1 \wedge x_2;\quad z = \bar{x}_1 \wedge x_2;\quad z = x_1 \wedge \bar{x}_2;\quad z = \bar{x}_1 \wedge \bar{x}_2;$ $z = x_1 \vee x_2;\quad z = \bar{x}_1 \vee x_2;\quad z = x_1 \vee \bar{x}_2;\quad z = \bar{x}_1 \vee \bar{x}_2;$ $z = x_1 \oplus x_2;\quad z = \bar{x}_1 \oplus x_2$

Figure 3.60 The set K_2 of the 16 Boolean/logic functions of up to two variables.

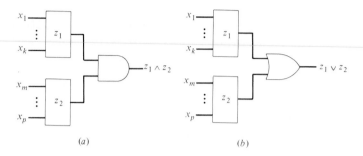

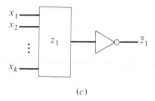

Figure 3.61 Logic circuits corresponding to the Boolean/logic expressions (3.19).

Boolean expressions are used principally to describe the functional behavior rather than the interconnection structure of logic circuits. If a particular combination of 0/1 values is substituted for the primitive variables appearing in a Boolean expression E representing a Boolean function z, and E is evaluated using the laws of Boolean algebra, then the corresponding value of z is obtained. If this is done for all 2^n possible combinations of values of the variables, then the complete truth table for z is derived from E. Thus a Boolean expression provides in a compact form, whose structure corresponds to a logic circuit, all the behavioral information contained in a truth table. Two Boolean expressions and the corresponding logic circuits can be said to be *(functionally) equivalent* if they yield the same truth table.

The important task of verifying the correctness of a logic circuit can be reduced to that of determining whether two sets of Boolean equations, one representing the circuit's specifications and the other representing its implementation, are functionally equivalent. Let us now prove that the IC network of Fig. 3.40 correctly implements the abstract logic circuit of Fig. 3.39 by verifying that the sets of equations (3.20) and (3.21) that describe the structures of these circuits are functionally equivalent. A direct but computationally tedious approach is to derive truth tables from each set of equations and compare these tables bit by bit. The desired equivalence can be proved more rapidly by showing that corresponding equations can be reduced to the same form by applying the laws of Boolean algebra. Consider, for instance, the two equations for C_{out}. From the definition of the EXCLUSIVE-OR operator $\oplus$ in Eq. (3.18) we obtain

$$1 \oplus E = (\bar{E} \wedge 1) \vee (E \wedge 0)$$

$$= \bar{E} \vee 0 \qquad \text{by axioms 5b and 5c}$$

$$= \bar{E} \qquad \text{by axiom 5a}$$

By using this result and axiom 9, the equation for C_{out} in (3.21) can be transformed to

$$C_{out} = (x \wedge y) \vee (x \wedge C_{in}) \vee (y \wedge y \wedge C_{in}) \vee (0 \wedge 0 \wedge 0)$$

which, using axioms 7a (idempotence) and 5a, reduces to the C_{out} equation in (3.20). The equivalence of the expressions for the function z in (3.20) and (3.21) follows from the easily proved fact that the $\oplus$ operator is associative, that is, it obeys an associative law such as those in axioms 2 of Fig. 3.59.

3.3.3 Two-level Forms

We have seen that an essentially unlimited number of Boolean expressions or logical expressions—henceforth we will use these terms interchangeably—can specify the same logic function. Corresponding to these expressions are an equally large number of different logic circuit configurations that realize the function. For example, all the following Boolean expressions denote the two-variable EXCLUSIVE-OR function:

$$x_1 \oplus x_2$$

$$(x_1 \vee x_2) \wedge (\bar{x}_1 \vee \bar{x}_2) \tag{3.22}$$

$$[(x_1 \mid (x_1 \mid x_2)) \mid (x_2 \mid (x_1 \mid x_2))]$$

Logic circuits corresponding to these expressions are given in Fig. 3.62.

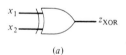

(a)

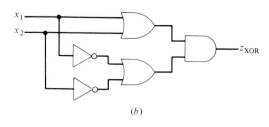

(b)

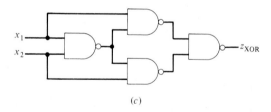

(c)

Figure 3.62 Logic circuits corresponding to the expressions (3.22) defining the EXCLUSIVE-OR function.

Systematic logic design procedures are known only for combinational circuits with very specific and fairly simple structures corresponding to certain simple types of Boolean expressions. An example of such an expression is

$$z_1 = (x_1 \wedge \bar{x}_2) \vee (\bar{x}_1 \wedge \bar{x}_3) \vee (\bar{x}_2 \wedge \bar{x}_4) \vee (\bar{x}_1 \wedge x_2 \wedge x_4) \vee (x_1 \wedge x_3 \wedge x_4) \qquad (3.23)$$

which is termed a *sum-of-products (SOP) expression* for z_1. This name is a consequence of the analogy alluded to earlier between the numerical operators multiply and plus, and the logical operators AND and OR. If (3.23) is rewritten with $+$ and juxtaposition replacing $\vee$ and $\wedge$, it assumes the form

$$z = x_1 \bar{x}_2 + \bar{x}_1 \bar{x}_3 + \bar{x}_2 \bar{x}_4 + \bar{x}_1 x_2 x_4 + x_1 x_3 x_4$$

which, apart from the presence of the inversion operator $(^-)$, resembles a sum-of-products expression in ordinary algebra. Quantities of the form x_i or $\bar{x}_i$ in Boolean expressions are called *literals*. A set of literals linked by the AND operator $\wedge$ constitutes a (logical) *product term*. A Boolean SOP expression is formed by linking a set of product terms by means of the $\vee$ (logical sum) operator. An SOP expression E defining the function z corresponds to a logic circuit composed of AND and OR gates. Each of the product terms in E is realized by an AND gate. The outputs of the AND gates are connected to the inputs of the OR gate, whose output is then the desired function. We call circuits of this type *AND-OR circuits*. Figure 3.63a shows the AND-OR circuit corresponding to Eq. (3.23).

The duality of the AND and OR operations means that a Boolean function also can be defined by *product-of-sums (POS) expressions* that take the form of a logical product of logical sum terms. For instance, the function z_1 defined by (3.23) can also be defined by the following POS expression:

$$z_1 = (\bar{x}_1 \vee \bar{x}_2 \vee x_3) \wedge (\bar{x}_2 \vee \bar{x}_3 \vee x_4) \wedge (x_1 \vee x_2 \vee \bar{x}_3 \vee \bar{x}_4) \qquad (3.24)$$

A POS expression E can be realized directly by an *OR-AND circuit* consisting of a set of OR gates, one for every sum term in E, connected to an output AND gate. The OR-AND circuit realization of (3.24) can be found in Fig. 3.63b.

AND-OR and OR-AND circuits are examples of *two-level* combinational circuits, since every signal propagating from the input lines to the output lines passes through two gates. It is assumed that the input signals (literals) are available in both the normal or true form x_i and the inverted form $\bar{x}_i$; if not, inverters must be added to generate the $\bar{x}_i$'s. As Fig. 3.57 demonstrates, the inputs of a combinational circuit are often obtained from memory elements such as flip-flops, which produce output signals in both the true form Q and the inverted form $\bar{Q}$.

Every logic function can be specified by means of SOP and POS expressions, and so can be realized by two-level AND-OR and OR-AND circuits. This is a consequence of the existence for every logic function of unique SOP and POS expressions called *canonical* or *normal forms*. Consider, for example, the truth table for the four-variable function z_1 appearing in Fig. 3.64. z_1 can be expressed as the logical sum of the 11 simple functions $m_0, m_1, \ldots, m_{15}$, which are also defined in Fig. 3.64.

$$z_1 = m_0 \vee m_1 \vee m_2 \vee m_4 \vee m_5 \vee m_7 \vee m_8 \vee m_9 \vee m_{10} \vee m_{11} \vee m_{15} \qquad (3.25)$$

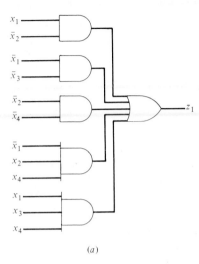

(a)

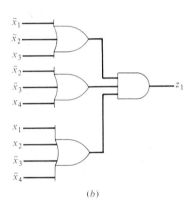

(b)

Figure 3.63 (a) AND-OR circuit implementing the SOP expression (3.23); (b) OR-AND circuit implementing the POS expression (3.24).

The output column of the truth table defining m_i has a 1 in some row i in which the output column of z_1 also has a 1; the m_i column has 0s everywhere else. Hence m_i, which is called a *minterm* of z_1, can be expressed by a product term containing four literals, one for each input variable of z_1. For instance,

$$m_2 = \bar{x}_1 \wedge \bar{x}_2 \wedge x_3 \wedge \bar{x}_4$$

because $m_2 = 1$ if $\bar{x}_1$ and $\bar{x}_2$ and x_3 and $\bar{x}_4$ are all 1, and $m_2 = 0$ otherwise. If product terms are substituted for the m_i's in (3.25), the following *canonical SOP expression* for z_1 is obtained.

$$\begin{aligned}
z_1 = \;& (\bar{x}_1 \wedge \bar{x}_2 \wedge \bar{x}_3 \wedge \bar{x}_4) \vee (\bar{x}_1 \wedge \bar{x}_2 \wedge \bar{x}_3 \wedge x_4) \vee (\bar{x}_1 \wedge \bar{x}_2 \wedge x_3 \wedge \bar{x}_4) \vee \\
& (\bar{x}_1 \wedge x_2 \wedge \bar{x}_3 \wedge \bar{x}_4) \vee (\bar{x}_1 \wedge x_2 \wedge \bar{x}_3 \wedge x_4) \vee (\bar{x}_1 \wedge x_2 \wedge x_3 \wedge x_4) \vee \\
& (x_1 \wedge \bar{x}_2 \wedge \bar{x}_3 \wedge \bar{x}_4) \vee (x_1 \wedge \bar{x}_2 \wedge \bar{x}_3 \wedge x_4) \vee (x_1 \wedge \bar{x}_2 \wedge x_3 \wedge \bar{x}_4) \vee \\
& (x_1 \wedge \bar{x}_2 \wedge x_3 \wedge x_4) \vee (x_1 \wedge x_2 \wedge x_3 \wedge x_4)
\end{aligned} \quad (3.26)$$

Row	Input Variables				Output Function	Minterms of z_1											Maxterms of z_1				
	x_1	x_2	x_3	x_4	z_1	m_0	m_1	m_2	m_4	m_5	m_7	m_8	m_9	m_{10}	m_{11}	m_{15}	M_3	M_6	M_{12}	M_{13}	M_{14}
0	0	0	0	0	1	1	0	0	0	0	0	0	0	0	0	0	1	1	1	1	1
1	0	0	0	1	1	0	1	0	0	0	0	0	0	0	0	0	1	1	1	1	1
2	0	0	1	0	1	0	0	1	0	0	0	0	0	0	0	0	1	1	1	1	1
3	0	0	1	1	0	0	0	0	0	0	0	0	0	0	0	0	0	1	1	1	1
4	0	1	0	0	1	0	0	0	1	0	0	0	0	0	0	0	1	1	1	1	1
5	0	1	0	1	1	0	0	0	0	1	0	0	0	0	0	0	1	1	1	1	1
6	0	1	1	0	0	0	0	0	0	0	0	0	0	0	0	0	1	0	1	1	1
7	0	1	1	1	1	0	0	0	0	0	1	0	0	0	0	0	1	1	1	1	1
8	1	0	0	0	1	0	0	0	0	0	0	1	0	0	0	0	1	1	1	1	1
9	1	0	0	1	1	0	0	0	0	0	0	0	1	0	0	0	1	1	1	1	1
10	1	0	1	0	1	0	0	0	0	0	0	0	0	1	0	0	1	1	1	1	1
11	1	0	1	1	1	0	0	0	0	0	0	0	0	0	1	0	1	1	1	1	1
12	1	1	0	0	0	0	0	0	0	0	0	0	0	0	0	0	1	1	0	1	1
13	1	1	0	1	0	0	0	0	0	0	0	0	0	0	0	0	1	1	1	0	1
14	1	1	1	0	0	0	0	0	0	0	0	0	0	0	0	0	1	1	1	1	0
15	1	1	1	1	1	0	0	0	0	0	0	0	0	0	0	1	1	1	1	1	1

Figure 3.64 Truth table for the function z_1, its minterms, and its maxterms.

Since z_1 and its minterms are uniquely defined by the positions of the output 0s and 1s in a standard truth table, a canonical SOP expression such as (3.26) serves as a function definition whose general structure is the same for all functions; hence the name canonical.

From duality considerations we can define a *canonical POS expression* that takes the form of a logical product of maxterms, where a *maxterm* is a logical sum term containing one literal for each input variable. A function z therefore has a maxterm M_i for every row i in its truth table for which $z = 0$. Thus the function z_1, which is defined along with its maxterms in Fig. 3.64, has the following canonical POS expression:

$$z_1 = M_3 \wedge M_6 \wedge M_{12} \wedge M_{13} \wedge M_{14}$$

$$= (x_1 \vee x_2 \vee \bar{x}_3 \vee \bar{x}_4) \wedge (x_1 \vee \bar{x}_2 \vee \bar{x}_3 \vee x_4) \wedge (\bar{x}_1 \vee \bar{x}_2 \vee x_3 \vee x_4) \wedge$$

$$(\bar{x}_1 \vee \bar{x}_2 \vee x_3 \vee \bar{x}_4) \wedge (\bar{x}_1 \vee \bar{x}_2 \vee \bar{x}_3 \vee x_4) \tag{3.27}$$

Again every logic function has a unique representation in this standard form.

The existence of (canonical) SOP and POS expressions for every logic function implies that every function can be realized by a two-level circuit containing only AND and OR gates, assuming that the input variables are available in both true and inverted form. If the input signals are available in one form only, an additional level of inverters can be added to the circuit. It follows that the gate types AND, OR, and NOT are *logically complete* in the sense that they suffice to implement any Boolean function. Other logically complete sets of gate types also exist. Among the basic gates AND, OR, EXCLUSIVE-OR, NAND, NOR, and EXCLUSIVE-NOR, only the NAND and NOR gate types are logically complete by themselves. This completeness can be proved simply by showing that all-NAND or all-NOR circuits can be used to implement the AND, OR, and NOT functions. Figure 3.65 does this for the NAND case. A NAND gate is changed to an inverter merely by reducing its fan-in to one as indicated in Fig. 3.65a. By using such a NAND inverter to invert the output of a k-input NAND gate as shown in Fig. 3.65b, the k-input AND function is realized. Finally, by inserting NAND inverters

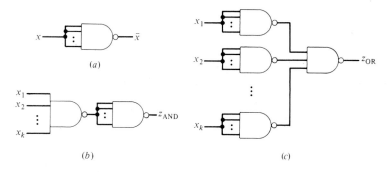

Figure 3.65 All-NAND implementations of: (*a*) NOT; (*b*) AND; (*c*) OR.

in the input lines of a k-input NAND gate as shown in Fig. 3.65c, the k-input OR function is obtained. The fact that this circuit yields the OR function is expressed by the equation

$$x_1 \vee x_2 \vee \ldots \vee x_k = \overline{\bar{x}_1 \wedge \bar{x}_2 \wedge \ldots \wedge \bar{x}_k}$$

which follows directly from one of the very useful De Morgan laws (axiom 8a in Fig. 3.59). Physical NAND and NOR gates are somewhat easier to fabricate using IC technology than AND or OR gates. As Fig. 3.37 implies, there are more NAND ICs in the 7400 TTL logic family than AND and OR ICs combined. These considerations, coupled with the logical completeness of NAND and NOR, make NAND and NOR gates particularly attractive in logic design. We turn next to the design of two-level all-NAND and all-NOR circuits.

Consider again the AND-OR realization of the four-variable function z_1, which appears in Fig. 3.63a. The output function is unchanged if two inversions are inserted in each of the circuit's internal lines as shown in Fig. 3.66a; the two inversions simply cancel out. The inversion circles attached to the output side of the AND gates convert them directly to NAND gates. The inversion circles attached to the input side of the OR gate also convert it to a NAND gate, because by De Morgan's laws

$$\overline{x_1 \wedge x_2 \wedge \ldots \wedge x_k} = \bar{x}_1 \vee \bar{x}_2 \vee \ldots \vee \bar{x}_k$$

Hence we can substitute a NAND gate for the output gate of Fig. 3.66a, yielding the two-level NAND-NAND circuit of Fig. 3.66b. We conclude, therefore, that a two-level all-NAND realization of a function z can be produced simply by replacing every gate in an AND-OR realization of z by a NAND gate. It can be proved in similar fashion that a NOR-NOR realization of z results from replacing all gates in an OR-AND realization of z by NOR gates. Consequently SOP and POS expressions directly describe NAND-NAND and NOR-NOR implementations respectively. Other gate combinations also can

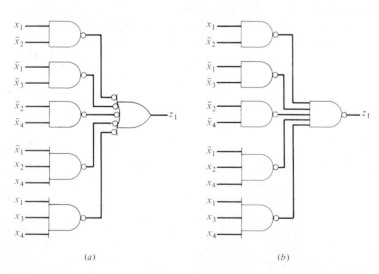

(a)   (b)

Figure 3.66 Conversion of the AND-OR circuit of Fig. 3.63a to a NAND-NAND circuit.

be used to obtain general two-level logic circuits, for instance, the AND-NOR structure found in the AND-OR-INVERT gates of the 7400 series; see Figs. 3.37p–3.37r.

In the discussion so far, fan-in/fan-out constraints have not been taken into account. It has implicitly been assumed that gates of the specified types with any desired fan-in are available. In an AND-OR realization of an n-variable logic function corresponding to a canonical SOP expression, AND gates having n inputs and an OR gate having up to $2^n - 1$ inputs may be required. If n is large, therefore, the fan-in of the IC gates available for implementing the function may be exceeded. Fan-in can be increased by using the approach depicted in Fig. 3.53, but this means increasing the number of levels in the circuit, thereby decreasing its operating speed. Since the input signals of a two-level circuit, which correspond to literals in the equivalent Boolean expression, typically fan out to many gates, additional input buffers may be needed. For example, inverters are included in the control input lines of the multiplexer circuit of Fig. 3.17, which is basically an AND-OR circuit, to help meet the fairly high fan-out requirements of these lines. Thus, while a two-level circuit easily can be modified to meet any given fan-in/fan-out constraints, this modification increases the number of levels, the number of gates, and the propagation delay of the circuit.

In practice two-level circuits are mainly used to implement functions involving small numbers of variables, or circuits having a simple structure, such as multiplexers. Circuits of this type occur throughout even the most complex digital systems. Some commercial MSI ICs implement two-level logic circuits. Logic functions that are unsuitable for two-level circuit realizations include multibit arithmetic functions. These functions are often implemented heuristically by multilevel circuits with many gate types, like the 4-bit addition circuit of Fig. 3.19. Even with the two-level restriction, there are many different ways to realize a given function. The two SOP expressions (3.24) and (3.26) both represent AND-OR realizations of the same function z_1. The circuit corresponding to (3.24) requires far fewer AND gates (five instead of 11), and its gates have smaller fan-in than the circuit corresponding to (3.26); clearly the former circuit is more desirable in every respect. An obvious question is how we obtain the simplest two-level circuit, which is usually considered to be one with the fewest gates, realizing a given logic function. This was a central problem of classical switching theory, and various solution methods are known; a representative and practical approach to this problem will be examined shortly.

To summarize, two-level combinational circuits have a number of advantages:

1. Any logic function can be realized by a two-level circuit; it is therefore a type of universal logic structure.
2. Except for the few logic functions realizable by one-level circuits, that is, the basic gate functions realizable by a single gate, two-level circuits have the minimum possible propagation delays, and therefore lead to the fastest logic circuits.
3. Two-level circuits can be constructed from many combinations of gate types; especially useful in this regard are NAND-NAND and NOR-NOR configurations.
4. Systematic procedures for designing two-level circuits containing the minimum number of gates are known, although their high computational complexity limits them to relatively small numbers of variables, say 10 or less.

The disadvantages of two-level circuits are their potentially high fan-in/fan-out require-ments, and the excessively large number of gates needed to implement some functions.

3.3.4 Gate Minimization

As discussed above, a logic function z can be represented by many different SOP and POS expressions, each corresponding to a different two-level logic circuit that realizes z. A product or sum term in any such expression corresponds to a gate in the two-level circuit. An SOP (POS) expression E will be called *minimal* if it has the following properties:

1. No SOP (POS) expression for z contains fewer product (sum) terms than E.
2. No literals can be deleted from any product (sum) term of E without altering the function being defined

Minimal SOP and POS expressions represent two-level circuits that contain the mini-mum number of gates, and have no unnecessary or *redundant* input lines to any gates. We now consider how such minimum-gate circuits can be constructed systematically. We will restrict our attention mainly to SOP expressions; dual results apply to the POS case.

Let t_1 be a product term containing the literal x_i. We can write

$$t_1 = t \wedge x_i$$

where t denotes the remaining literals, if any, of t_1, and is itself a product term. Let t_2 be the product term formed from t_1 by replacing the literal x_i by its complement $\bar{x}_i$.

$$t_2 = t \wedge \bar{x}_i$$

The terms t_1 and t_2 are said to be *(logically) adjacent* in the variable x_i. Suppose that an SOP expression E contains the two adjacent terms t_1 and t_2 thus:

$$E = (t \wedge x_i) \vee (t \wedge \bar{x}_i) \vee \ldots \tag{3.28}$$

By the distributivity property of $\wedge$ over $\vee$ (axiom 4a in Fig. 3.59), we can rewrite E as follows:

$$E = [t \wedge (x_i \vee \bar{x}_i)] \vee \ldots$$

Hence by axioms 6b and 5b,

$$E = t \vee \ldots \tag{3.29}$$

On comparing (3.28) and (3.29), we see that two product terms have been replaced by one simpler product term. Consequently two AND gates have been replaced by a single AND gate of lower fan-in in the corresponding AND-OR logic circuit. By repeated application of the equation

$$t = (t \wedge x_i) \vee (t \wedge \bar{x}_i) \tag{3.30}$$

a canonical SOP expression can be reduced to a minimal expression. This is the algebraic basis of minimization techniques for two-level circuits.

To formalize the process of merging terms in a Boolean expression, we need some additional terminology. A product term t is called an *implicant* of z if every input combination that makes $t = 1$ also makes $z = 1$; in other words, $t = 1$ implies that $z = 1$. An implicant t of z is called a *prime implicant* of z if the deletion of any literal from t creates a product term that is not an implicant of z. A prime implicant therefore cannot be merged with any other implicant of z using (3.30). Consider, for example, the following SOP expression for the three-variable function z_2.

$$z_2(x_1, x_2, x_3) = x_2 \vee (\bar{x}_1 \wedge \bar{x}_3) \vee (x_1 \wedge x_3) \tag{3.31}$$

The product term

$$t(x_1, x_2, x_3) = \bar{x}_1 \wedge \bar{x}_3$$

appearing in (3.31) is obviously an implicant of z_2. Suppose that the literal $\bar{x}_1$ is deleted from t yielding the simpler product term

$$t'(x_1, x_2, x_3) = \bar{x}_3$$

t' is not an implicant of z_2 because

$$t'(1, 0, 0) = 1$$

whereas

$$z_2(1, 0, 0) = 0$$

We therefore conclude that t is a prime implicant of z_2, as are the other two product terms in (3.31). Prime implicants are of interest because all product terms in a minimal SOP expression must be prime implicants of the function defined by the expression.

For logic functions of small numbers of variables, the minimization process can be performed manually using a modified truth table known as a *Karnaugh map,* for the IBM engineer Maurice Karnaugh who introduced it in 1953. Every 1 and 0 entry in the output column of a truth table for z represents a minterm or maxterm, respectively, of z, as indicated in Fig. 3.64. In a Karnaugh map the output column is redrawn as a two-dimensional array of cells or boxes, each containing a 0 or 1 entry. The 1-cells correspond to minterms, and the 0-cells to maxterms. The cells are so arranged that logically adjacent minterms or maxterms are approximately physically adjacent on the Karnaugh map. Prime implicants correspond to certain clusters of minterms on the map, and can be quickly identified by inspection.

Figure 3.67 shows the truth tables and Karnaugh maps for a pair of two-variable logic functions, $z_{OR} = x_1 \vee x_2$ and $z_{XOR} = x_1 \oplus x_2$. Karnaugh maps for two-variable functions are 2×2 arrays. Each cell is indexed by a binary number, which is the binary number in the input columns of the corresponding row of the truth table. For instance, the cell in the top left-hand corner has the index number $x_1 x_2 = 00$, and corresponds to the first row of the truth table. The indexes of two neighboring cells in the same row or column of the map differ in only one position, and hence denote logically adjacent cells. The two 1-cells in the right-hand column of the Karnaugh map of z_{OR} correspond to the

x_1	x_2	z_{OR}
0	0	0
0	1	1
1	0	1
1	1	1

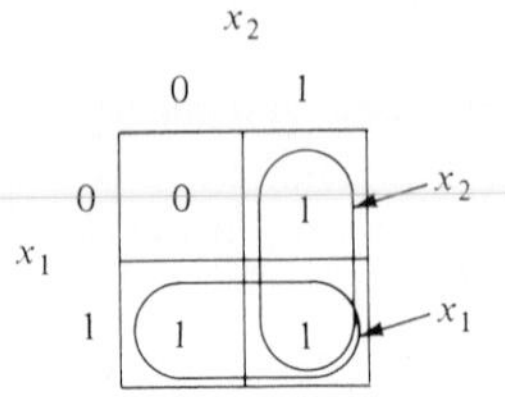

(a)

x_1	x_2	z_{XOR}
0	0	0
0	1	1
1	0	1
1	1	0

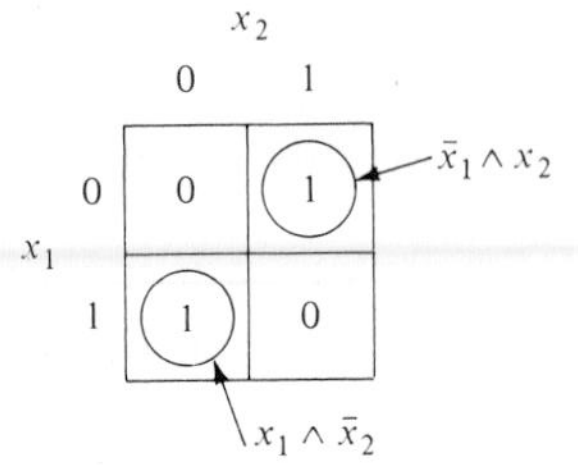

(b)

Figure 3.67 Truth tables and Karnaugh maps for: (a) $z_{OR} = x_1 \lor x_2$; (b) $z_{XOR} = x_1 \oplus x_2$.

minterms $m_1 = \bar{x}_1 \wedge x_2$ and $m_3 = x_1 \wedge x_2$ of z_{OR}. Since m_1 and m_3 are adjacent, we can merge them according to (3.30) thus:

$$m_1 \lor m_3 = (\bar{x}_1 \wedge x_2) \lor (x_1 \wedge x_2) = x_2$$

Hence x_2 is a prime implicant of z_{OR}, a fact that is indicated graphically in Fig. 3.67a by encircling the relevant 1-cells. Similarly, the 1-cells in the bottom row of the map for z_{OR} are encircled to show that x_1 is also a prime implicant of z_{OR}. Clearly z_{OR} has the minimal SOP expression

$$z_{OR} = x_1 \lor x_2$$

corresponding to a single two-input OR gate, which can be viewed as a degenerate two-level AND-OR circuit in which the AND gates have shrunk to single wires. The Karnaugh map of z_{XOR} in Fig. 3.67b shows that this function has two minterms, $m_1 = \bar{x}_1 \wedge x_2$ and $m_2 = x_1 \wedge \bar{x}_2$. These minterms are nonadjacent, and hence each is a prime implicant. It follows that z_{XOR} has the unique minimal SOP form

$$z_{XOR} = (\bar{x}_1 \wedge x_2) \lor (x_1 \wedge \bar{x}_2)$$

To handle three-variable functions, a Karnaugh map of the kind depicted in Fig. 3.68a is needed. The columns of the map are indexed so that physically adjacent cells differ in the value of only one input variable. Note, however, that the indexes of cells in corresponding rows from the first and last columns also differ in only one variable. Hence the first and last columns are regarded as (logically) adjacent by implicitly joining the left and right boundaries of the map. This implies that the minterms m_0 and m_2 corresponding to the cells at the ends of the top row are logically adjacent. Hence they can be merged as follows:

$$m_0 \wedge m_2 = (\bar{x}_1 \wedge \bar{x}_2 \wedge \bar{x}_3) \lor (\bar{x}_1 \wedge x_2 \wedge \bar{x}_3)$$

$$= \bar{x}_1 \wedge \bar{x}_3$$

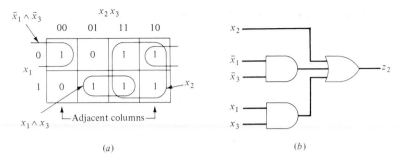

Figure 3.68 (a) Karnaugh map of the three-variable function z_2; (b) minimal-AND-OR realization of z_2.

to obtain a prime implicant of the function z_2; this prime implicant is indicated by the broken loop in Fig. 3.68a, which encloses the 1-cells with the indexes 000 and 010. z_2 has two other prime implicants corresponding to encircled 1-cells in Fig. 3.68a. The largest of these includes 1-cells representing the four minterms m_2, m_3, m_6, and m_7. The fact that these 1-cells can be denoted by a single product term can be seen by repeated application of the product-term merger rule (3.30).

$$m_2 \vee m_3 \vee m_6 \vee m_7 = ((\bar{x}_1 \wedge x_2 \wedge \bar{x}_3) \vee (\bar{x}_1 \wedge x_2 \wedge x_3)) \vee ((x_1 \wedge x_2 \wedge \bar{x}_3) \vee (x_1 \wedge x_2 \wedge x_3))$$

$$= (\bar{x}_1 \wedge x_2) \vee (x_1 \wedge x_2)$$

$$= x_2$$

Hence the four encircled 1s in Fig. 3.68a represent the prime implicant x_2 of z_2. It is easily seen that z_2 has a unique minimal SOP expression consisting of the logical sum of all three of its prime implicants thus:

$$z_2 = x_2 \vee (\bar{x}_1 \wedge \bar{x}_3) \vee (x_1 \wedge x_3) \tag{3.32}$$

A minimal AND-OR circuit implementing (3.32) appears in Fig. 3.68b.

Figure 3.69a shows a Karnaugh map for the four-variable function z_1 whose truth table was given in Fig. 3.64. As in the previous cases, the cells are indexed so that the indexes of neighboring cells in the same row or column differ in only one variable; hence they are both logically and physically adjacent. Boundary cells in the same row or column of the map must also be considered to be adjacent. Again certain clusters of 2^m 1-cells in the Karnaugh map can be identified with prime implicants. All two-cell clusters representing prime implicants of z_1 are marked in Fig. 3.69b, while all four-cell prime-implicant clusters are indicated in Fig. 3.69c. Note how the four corner cells of the Karnaugh map represent the prime implicant $\bar{x}_2 \wedge \bar{x}_4$. In general a group G of 2^m 1-cells on a Karnaugh map corresponds to a prime implicant if:

1. The cell indexes of G include all 2^m combinations of some m input variables, and a fixed combination of the remaining $n - m$ input variables.
2. Any group of 2^{m+1} that includes G and has property 1 contains at least one 0-cell.

With practice, all prime implicants of a function can be quickly identified from its Karnaugh map.

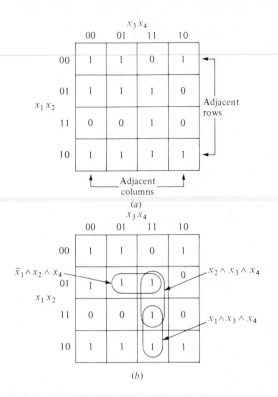

(a)

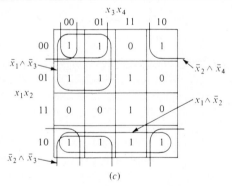

(b)

(c)

Figure 3.69 (a) Karnaugh map for the four-variable function z_1; (b) prime implicants covering two minterms; (c) prime implicants covering four minterms.

Having found all the prime implicants, it remains to select a minimal subset whose logical sum is the desired function z. This amounts to selecting a minimal set of prime-implicant clusters on the Karnaugh map that contain or *cover* all 1-cells of z. Such a set is called a *minimal prime-implicant cover* of z. If a prime implicant p is the only cover for some 1-cell or minterm m, then p is said to be *essential,* and must be included in every minimal cover of z. From Fig. 3.69 it can be seen that $\bar{x}_1 \wedge \bar{x}_3$ and $\bar{x}_2 \wedge \bar{x}_4$ are essential since they are the only prime implicants that cover the minterms $m_4 = \bar{x}_1 \wedge x_2 \wedge \bar{x}_3 \wedge \bar{x}_4$ and $m_2 = \bar{x}_1 \wedge \bar{x}_2 \wedge x_3 \wedge \bar{x}_4$ respectively. These essential terms cover all but four of the minterms of z_1.

It is easily seen from the Karnaugh map that two additional prime implicants are necessary to cover these minterms, yielding the minimal SOP expression

$$z_1 = (\bar{x}_1 \wedge \bar{x}_3) \vee (\bar{x}_2 \wedge \bar{x}_4) \vee (x_1 \wedge \bar{x}_2) \vee (x_2 \wedge x_3 \wedge x_4) \tag{3.33}$$

Note that the original SOP expression (3.23) used to define z_1 contains five prime implicants and is therefore nonminimal. Nevertheless no prime implicant can be deleted from (3.23) since each covers a minterm not covered by any other prime implicant forming (3.23). A minimal five-gate NAND-NAND circuit realizing (3.33) appears in Fig. 3.70 [cf. the six-gate circuit of Fig. 3.66b, which implements (3.23)].

A dual approach can be used to derive minimal POS expressions, and the corresponding minimum-gate two-level circuits, from the Karnaugh map. 0-cells that represent maxterms are merged using the equation

$$s = (s \vee x_i) \wedge (s \vee \bar{x}_i) \tag{3.34}$$

which is the dual of (3.30). The dual of a prime implicant is a *prime implicate,* which is a term composed of a sum of literals, none of which may be deleted. Every minimal POS expression is therefore a logical product of prime implicates. Prime implicates may be identified on the Karnaugh map by clustering 0-cells in the same way 1-cells are clustered to identify prime implicants. Figure 3.71a shows the Karnaugh map of Fig. 3.69 with all four of its prime implicates marked. Three of these are essential and suffice to cover all maxterms of the function. Hence z_1 has the unique minimal POS expression

$$z_1 = (\bar{x}_1 \vee \bar{x}_2 \vee x_3) \wedge (\bar{x}_2 \vee \bar{x}_3 \vee x_4) \wedge (x_1 \vee x_2 \vee \bar{x}_3 \vee \bar{x}_4) \tag{3.35}$$

Figure 3.71b shows the corresponding NOR-NOR realization of z_1; an AND-OR realization of (3.35) appears in Fig. 3.63b. Note that these circuits contain fewer gates than any circuit derived from a minimal SOP expression for z_1. In general, it is necessary to consider both SOP and POS forms to find the two-level realization with the fewest gates.

The Karnaugh map method is mainly useful for finding optimal two-level circuits of functions of up to four variables, although larger maps have been used. More complex functions can be treated by such well-known minimization techniques as the Quine-McCluskey algorithm (McCluskey, 1965), which generalize the map method, and make

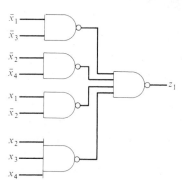

Figure 3.70 Minimal NAND-NAND realization of the four-variable function z_1.

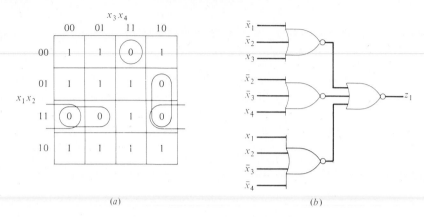

(a)   (b)

Figure 3.71 (a) Karnaugh map of z_1 showing its prime implicates; (b) minimal NOR-NOR realization of z_1.

it suitable for programming on a computer. The major steps in most such algorithms are as follows:

1. Find all prime implicants (implicates) of the function by systematically combining logically adjacent product (sum) terms.
2. Select a minimal set of prime implicants (implicates) that covers all minterms (maxterms) of the function.

The number of prime implicants and implicates of a function, and the amount of computation needed to find a minimal cover, tend to increase exponentially with the number of input variables. As noted earlier, large two-level circuits are also likely to violate the fan-in/fan-out constraints imposed by practical ICs.

    The foregoing issues are illustrated by the task of designing a 4-bit binary adder for unsigned or twos-complement numbers. Such an adder has nine input lines, including carry in C_{in}, and five output lines, including carry out C_{out}. Thus its truth table has 512 rows, nine input columns, and five output columns. As the multilevel realization given in Fig. 3.19 suggests, C_{out} is the most complex of the adder's output signals. It can be shown that C_{out} has 31 essential prime implicants, whose logical sum is C_{out}. This implies that a two-level SOP realization of C_{out} alone requires 32 gates, including a 31-input output gate. Moreover, a primary input variable can appear in up to 15 of the prime implicants of C_{out}, implying a minimum fan-out of 15 for certain lines.

    In cases such as this where two-level logic circuits are impractical, multilevel circuits derived by heuristic means are generally used. Consider once more the design of a binary adder. When adding multidigit numbers using pencil and paper, we usually add the numbers one digit at a time, starting with the least significant digits. As carries are produced, they are propagated to the left and included on the next addition step. This process is adapted to the addition of two binary numbers by adding 1 bit from each number in each addition step, with carry bits generated as needed. Clearly such an addition step can be performed by the full adder circuit defined in Fig. 3.38. By connecting four copies of this full adder in the cascade configuration of Fig. 3.72, a 4-bit

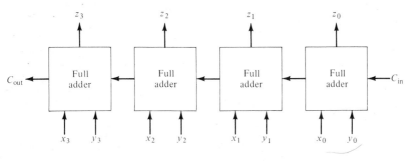

Figure 3.72 A 4-bit ripple-carry adder.

adder is obtained. Since carry signals are said to "ripple" from one full-adder stage to the next, this type of addition circuit is called a *ripple-carry adder*. If each full-adder stage is realized by the four-gate circuit of Fig. 3.39, then only 20 gates are needed for the complete circuit, and there are no fan-in or fan-out problems. The drawback of the ripple-carry adder is its large propagation delay. An input signal change on lines x_0, y_0, or C_{in} that alters C_{out} must propagate through all four full-adder stages, or a total of eight levels of gates. Thus we have a slower circuit than the ideal two-level implementation, but one that contains far fewer gates and meets practical fan-in/fan-out constraints. The 74283 design given in Fig. 3.19, which contains four gate levels and 36 gates, falls somewhere between ripple-carry adders and two-level adders in terms of speed and hardware cost.

3.3.5 Sequential Design

Any (synchronous) sequential machine with primary inputs X and primary outputs Z can be reduced, at least in principle, to the form of Fig. 3.58 consisting of a combinational part C and a (clocked) memory part M. M stores the current internal state Y of the machine, while C computes Z and the next state Y', both of which are logic functions of X and Y. We turn next to a systematic approach to the design of sequential logic circuits that have the general structure of Fig. 3.58, and implement C and M by means of gates and flip-flops respectively.

The starting point in the design process is to obtain specifications for the behavior of the circuit to be designed. From the initial informal specifications, a formal description of the desired behavior is constructed. A state table, which is the sequential equivalent of a combinational truth table, is very convenient for this purpose, although deriving an appropriate state table from informal system specifications may not be easy. In the initial state table, it suffices to represent internal states by symbolic such names as S_0, S_1, ... The states are then mapped onto a set of binary state variables y_0, y_1, ..., y_p where each y_i is the output Q of a flip-flop F_i in the memory circuit M. If there are q states, then we need p flip-flops, where

$$p = \lceil \log_2 q \rceil$$

and $\lceil k \rceil$ denotes the smallest integer greater than or equal to k. The mapping of symbolic states onto binary state variables is called *state assignment*. While the state assignment can be made in arbitrary fashion, a judicious assignment may reduce the number of gates in C.

To change y_i as required by a state transition specified in the state table, certain input signals must be applied to F_i; the values of these signals, of course, depend on the type of flip-flop used. Suppose, for instance, that F_i is a JK flip-flop whose main inputs are $J_i K_i$. To change y_i from 0 to 1 requires $J_i K_i = 10$ or 11, while to leave y_i unchanged at 0 requires $J_i K_i = 00$ or 01. Similarly, to change y_i from 1 to 0, we need $J_i K_i = 01$ or 11, and to leave y_i unchanged at 1 requires $J_i K_i = 00$ or 01. J_i and K_i are logic functions generated by C; their values therefore must be specified for all combinations of the primary input variables X and the state variables $Y = (y_1, y_2, \ldots, y_p)$. From the state table and the flip-flop specifications we can construct a truth table, called an *excitation* or *transition table*, for C. This table specifies the input signals (J_i and K_i in the above instance) to be applied to every flip-flop of M; it also defines the primary output signals Z. It remains to convert the excitation table to a combinational logic circuit, which can be done using any of the approaches examined earlier. Figure 3.73 summarizes the foregoing design process for sequential machines.

We next apply this design methodology to a simple but useful sequential circuit called a *serial adder*. As illustrated in Fig. 3.74 a serial adder has two main input lines x and y and an output line z. If two n-bit unsigned binary numbers $X = x_{n-1}x_{n-2} \ldots x_0$ and $Y = y_{n-1}y_{n-2} \ldots y_0$ are applied serially, that is, 1 bit at a time, to the input lines x and y, respectively, the sum

$$X + Y = Z = z_{n-1}z_{n-2} \ldots z_0$$

is generated bit by bit on the output line z. The least significant bits of Z are generated first, and the most significant bits last. Serial adders are contrasted with *parallel adders* such as the circuits of Figs. 3.19 and 3.72 in which all bits of the input numbers are processed simultaneously or in parallel.

During one step, corresponding to one clock period, a serial adder must add two incoming bits x_i and y_i and produce the sum bit z_i. Since this addition may result in the generation of a carry bit C_i, the carry bit must be stored internally for use in the next 1-bit addition step. Hence the operation of the adder can be described by the following arithmetic equation

$$C_i, z_i = x_i + y_i + C_{i-1} \tag{3.36}$$

Design Step	Actions Required
State-table specification	Obtain specifications of the desired system behavior. Convert to a symbolic state table.
State assignment	Select the flip-flop type to implement the memory subcircuit M. Assign a pattern of state variables (flip-flop outputs) to each state.
Combinational design	Construct a truth (excitation) table for the combinational subcircuit C. Carry out the logic design of C.

Figure 3.73 Systematic approach to sequential circuit design.

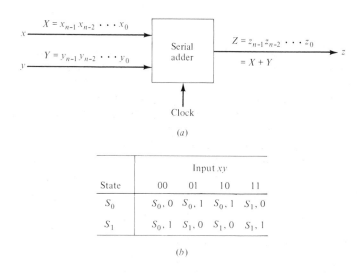

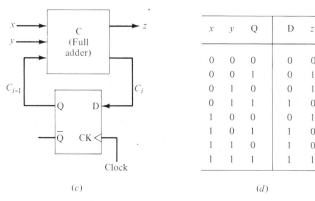

Figure 3.74 Serial binary adder: (*a*) input-output signals; (*b*) state table; (*c*) general structure using a D flip-flop; (*d*) excitation table.

To store the carry information, a serial adder must have two internal states S_0 and S_1 with the following interpretations:

S_0: Carry $C_{i-1} = 0$ produced during the preceding clock cycle
S_1: Carry $C_{i-1} = 1$ produced during the preceding clock cycle

Thus M must, in effect, record the value of C_{i-1}. From these states and the foregoing informal description of the behavior of a serial adder, we obtain the state table given in Fig. 3.74b. Each entry is of the form S_{i+1}, z_i, where S_{i+1} is the next internal state to be assumed and z_i is the current output signal from the adder. To determine an entry of the state table, say that of row S_0 and column 11, we consider the effect of applying the input combination $x_i y_i = 11$ to the adder when $C_{i-1} = 0$. Substituting into (3.36) yields

$$C_i, z_i = 1 + 1 + 0 = 1, 0$$

Hence, $z_i = 0$, and since $C_i = 1$, the next state must be S_1. We conclude that the entry in the truth table under these circumstances should be S_1, 0. The remaining entries may be similarly computed.

Since the serial adder has only two internal states, its memory M need only contain a single flip-flop. Let us assume that a D flip-flop of the kind defined in Fig. 3.46 is to be used. There are only two possible assignments of the the flip-flop's output Q to the states S_0 and S_1; we arbitrarily choose the following one:

$$S_0 \text{ corresponds to } Q = C_{i-1} = 0$$

$$S_1 \text{ corresponds to } Q = C_{i-1} = 1$$

To change a D flip-flop's state to $Q = d$ requires only setting $D = d$. Hence the carry signal C_i, which is to be recorded, can be applied directly to the D input of the flip-flop. This results in the circuit structure depicted in Fig. 3.74c. It should be clear from this that C acts as a full adder; therefore the excitation table for the serial adder, which appears in Fig. 3.74d, is identical to the full-adder truth table defined earlier in Fig. 3.38b.

Suppose that we wish to implement C for the serial adder by means of a two-level all-NAND circuit. Figure 3.75 shows Karnaugh maps for the functions D and z, which are derived directly from the excitation table of Fig. 3.74d. Clearly D and z have unique minimal sets of prime implicants corresponding to the SOP expressions

$$z = (\bar{x} \wedge \bar{y} \wedge Q) \vee (\bar{x} \wedge y \wedge \overline{Q}) \vee (x \wedge \bar{y} \wedge \overline{Q}) \vee (x \wedge y \wedge Q)$$

$$D = (x \wedge y) \vee (x \wedge Q) \vee (y \wedge Q) \tag{3.37}$$

A NAND-NAND realization of (3.37) appears in Fig. 3.76. Note that while extra NOT gates are necessary to produce $\bar{x}$ and $\bar{y}$, $\overline{Q}$ is automatically provided by the D flip-flop. An alternative realization of the combinational subcircuit C is given in Fig. 3.39.

There is a close correspondence between this serial adder and the parallel ripple-carry adder of Fig. 3.72. The serial adder completes an n-bit addition in n steps (clock cycles), whereas the ripple-carry adder carries out the same addition in just one step. However, the ripple-carry adder employs n serial adder subcircuits, while the serial adder requires only one. Roughly speaking, the parallel adder is n times faster than the serial adder, but uses n times more hardware. This type of trade-off between operating speed and hardware cost is encountered throughout digital system design.

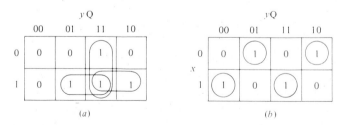

Figure 3.75 Karnaugh maps derived from the excitation table of the serial adder: (a) D; (b) z.

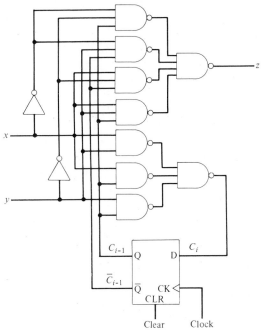

C_{i-1} Q   D C_i

$\overline{C}_{i-1}$ $\overline{Q}$ CK
      CLR

Clear   Clock

Figure 3.76 NAND implementation of the serial adder.

3.3.6 Design Example

As an illustration of the preceding design techniques, we now consider in detail the logic design of a widely used sequential circuit called an *up-down counter*. The main IO signals of an up-down counter appear in Fig. 3.77a. The output signals represent an unsigned binary number; for simplicity we limit this number to 2 bits $z_1 z_0$. There are two main input lines called COUNT and DOWN. A 1 signal applied to the COUNT line causes $z_1 z_0$ to be decremented by one if DOWN = 1, while $z_1 z_0$ is incremented by one if DOWN = 0. Thus the circuit counts either up or down in the normal binary counting sequence in response to 1-signals applied to COUNT; the direction of the counting is specified by the DOWN control line. The output of the up-down counter remains unchanged as long as COUNT = 0. A state table is easily constructed from the foregoing description; see Fig. 3.77b. The internal states S_i records the number of COUNT signals received so far; this number appears at the circuit's outputs as $z_1 z_0$. It is assumed that the arrival of a 1-signal on COUNT when $z_1 z_0 = 11$ changes $z_1 z_0$ to 00. This is called counting modulo-4, where the term *modulus* refers to the total number of different numerical values generated by the counter. The modulus is four in this case. The 4-bit Johnson counter of Fig. 3.48 is an example of a modulo-8 counter, which, however, can only count in one direction. (It also employs a nonstandard number code.)

The counter circuit of Fig. 3.77 has four states S_0, S_1, S_2, S_3, which can be specified by two state variables $y_1 y_0$. When the counter is in state S_i, a total of i 1s (modulo-4) have

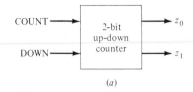

(a)

State	Input COUNT DOWN			
	00	01	10	11
S_0	$S_0, 00$	$S_0, 00$	$S_1, 01$	$S_3, 11$
S_1	$S_1, 01$	$S_1, 01$	$S_2, 10$	$S_0, 00$
S_2	$S_2, 10$	$S_2, 10$	$S_3, 11$	$S_1, 01$
S_3	$S_3, 11$	$S_3, 11$	$S_0, 00$	$S_2, 10$

(b)

Figure 3.77 Two-bit up-down counter: (a) input-output signals; (b) state table.

been received on the COUNT line. It is therefore natural to make a state assignment that uses the binary pattern $y_1 y_0$ denoting the number i to represent S_i thus:

State	$y_1 y_0$
S_0	00
S_1	01
S_2	10
S_3	11

(3.38)

This state assignment has the advantage that the circuit's output signals can be taken directly from the state variables, that is, $z_1 z_0 = y_1 y_0$. For demonstration purposes, we will use the randomly chosen, and less efficient, state assignment defined in Fig. 3.78a. We will also assume that edge-triggered JK flip-flops are to be used to implement the counter's memory part M. Two JK flip-flops F_0 and F_1 are required, whose Q outputs represent the state variables y_0 and y_1 respectively. As shown in Fig. 3.78b, the combinational part C of the counter must generate the input signals J_0, K_0, J_1, K_1 to the flip-flops that cause $y_1 y_0$ to change to $y_1' y_0'$ in accordance with the state transitions specified by the state table. C must also generate the primary output signals $z_1 z_0$. The JK input patterns needed to change the flip-flop states appear in Fig. 3.42c. This information allows us to convert the state table of the up-down counter (Fig. 3.77b) to the excitation table given in Fig. 3.78c.

Once the excitation table has been constructed, the design of the combinational circuit C is quite straightforward. We will use the Karnaugh-map method to derive a two-level SOP implementation. Six Karnaugh maps defining the six outputs of C as functions of COUNT, DOWN, y_1, y_0 appear in Fig. 3.79; each map corresponds to one output column of the excitation table. Minimal prime-applicant covers are easily determined by

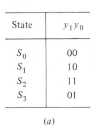

State	$y_1 y_0$
S_0	00
S_1	10
S_2	11
S_3	01

(a)

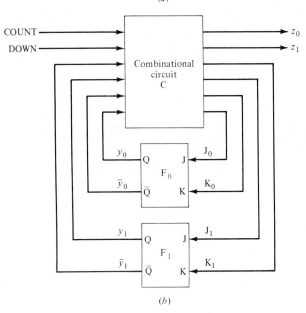

(b)

COUNT	DOWN	y_1	y_0	J_1	K_1	J_0	K_0	z_1	z_0
0	0	0	0	0	0	0	0	0	0
0	0	0	1	0	0	0	0	1	1
0	0	1	0	0	0	0	0	0	1
0	0	1	1	0	0	0	0	1	0
0	1	0	0	0	0	0	0	0	0
0	1	0	1	0	0	0	0	1	1
0	1	1	0	0	0	0	0	0	1
0	1	1	1	0	0	0	0	1	0
1	0	0	0	1	0	0	0	0	1
1	0	0	1	0	0	0	1	0	0
1	0	1	0	0	0	1	0	1	0
1	0	1	1	0	1	0	0	1	1
1	1	0	0	0	0	1	0	1	1
1	1	0	1	1	0	0	0	1	0
1	1	1	0	0	1	0	0	0	0
1	1	1	1	0	0	0	1	0	1

(c)

Figure 3.78 Two-bit up-down counter: (a) state assignment; (b) general structure using JK flip-flops; (c) excitation table.

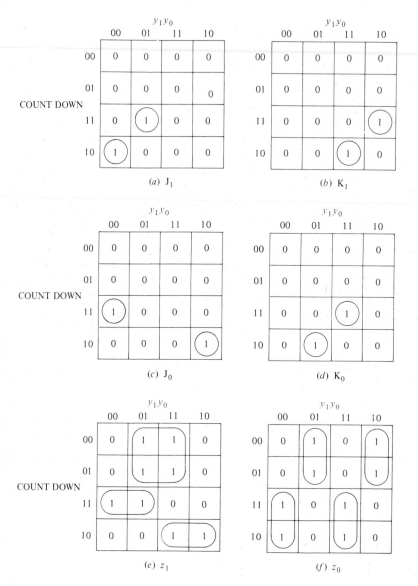

Figure 3.79 Karnaugh maps for the excitation table of Fig. 3.78c.

inspection, and are indicated by the encircled 1s in Fig. 3.79. The minimal covers give rise to the following SOP equations for C:

$$J_1 = (\text{COUNT} \wedge \text{DOWN} \wedge \bar{y}_1 \wedge y_0) \vee (\text{COUNT} \wedge \overline{\text{DOWN}} \wedge \bar{y}_1 \wedge \bar{y}_0)$$

$$K_1 = (\text{COUNT} \wedge \text{DOWN} \wedge y_1 \wedge \bar{y}_0) \vee (\text{COUNT} \wedge \overline{\text{DOWN}} \wedge y_1 \wedge y_0)$$

$$J_0 = (\text{COUNT} \wedge \text{DOWN} \wedge \bar{y}_1 \wedge \bar{y}_0) \vee (\text{COUNT} \wedge \overline{\text{DOWN}} \wedge y_1 \wedge \bar{y}_0) \qquad (3.39)$$

$$K_0 = (COUNT \wedge DOWN \wedge y_1 \wedge y_0) \vee (COUNT \wedge \overline{DOWN} \wedge \bar{y}_1 \wedge y_0)$$

$$z_1 = \overline{(COUNT \wedge y_0)} \vee (COUNT \wedge DOWN) \wedge \bar{y}_1) \vee (COUNT \wedge \overline{DOWN} \wedge y_1)$$

$$z_0 = (COUNT \wedge \bar{y}_1 \wedge y_0) \vee \overline{(COUNT} \wedge y_1 \wedge \bar{y}_0) \vee (COUNT \wedge \bar{y}_1 \wedge \bar{y}_0)$$
$$\vee (COUNT \wedge y_1 \wedge y_0)$$

These equations are easily converted to a two-level SOP realization of C.

In constructing the excitation table of Fig. 3.78c only the input combinations $J_iK_i = $ 10, 01, and 00 were used to set y_i, reset y_i, and leave y_i unchanged, respectively. In fact, any state transition of a JK flip-flop can be achieved with two input combinations; see Fig. 3.42c. For example, if y_i is to be left unchanged at the 0 value, we can apply either 00 or 01 to J_iK_i. In this case we "don't care" what value is applied to the reset input K_i. The symbol d, called the *don't care value*, is used to denote a logic signal that may be set either to 0 or to 1 without violating the constraints governing the circuit's behavior. Hence we can write $J_iK_i = 0d$ to denote the possible input signals to flip-flop F_i that leave y_i in the 0 state. Similarly, to keep y_i in the 1 state requires $J_iK_i = d0$. A transition from $y_i = 0$ to $y_i = 1$ is accomplished by $J_iK_i = 1d$, while $J_iK_i = d1$ changes y_i from 1 to 0. Thus a JK flip-flop allows various don't care input signals, which, as we show next, can be used to simplify the realization of C. Note that no corresponding flexibility in assigning inputs signals exists for D flip-flops.

Figure 3.80 shows a revised version of the excitation table for the up-down counter in which don't cares are used wherever possible. The corresponding Karnaugh maps for the flip-flop input signals appear in Fig. 3.81. Each d on these maps may be changed to 0 or 1 without affecting the counter's behavior. When constructing a minimal prime-implicant cover, d's are set to 1 to increase the size of the possible prime implicants, so that the specified 1-cells can be covered with fewer larger covers. As usual, prime implicants correspond to encircled cells in Fig. 3.81. The encircled d's are set to 1 and the

COUNT	DOWN	y_1	y_0	J_1	K_1	J_0	K_0	z_1	z_0
0	0	0	0	0	d	0	d	0	0
0	0	0	1	0	d	d	0	1	1
0	0	1	0	d	0	0	d	0	1
0	0	1	1	d	0	d	0	1	0
0	1	0	0	0	d	0	d	0	0
0	1	0	1	0	d	d	0	1	1
0	1	1	0	d	0	0	d	0	1
0	1	1	1	d	0	d	0	1	0
1	0	0	0	1	d	0	d	0	1
1	0	0	1	0	d	d	1	0	0
1	0	1	0	d	0	1	d	1	0
1	0	1	1	d	1	d	0	1	1
1	1	0	0	0	d	1	d	1	1
1	1	0	1	1	d	d	0	1	0
1	1	1	0	d	1	0	d	0	0
1	1	1	1	d	0	d	1	0	1

Figure 3.80 Excitation table with don't cares.

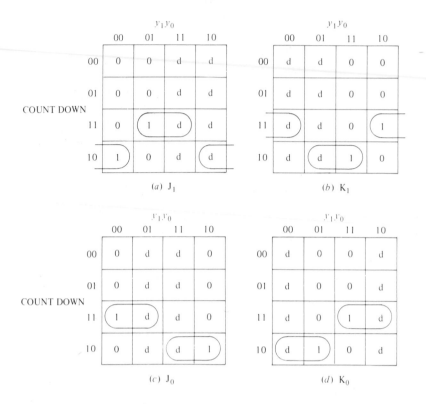

Figure 3.81 Karnaugh maps for the excitation table of Fig. 3.80.

remaining d's are set to 0. This results in the following set of SOP expressions for the JK input signals:

$$J_1 = (\text{COUNT} \wedge \text{DOWN} \wedge y_0) \vee (\text{COUNT} \wedge \overline{\text{DOWN}} \wedge \bar{y}_0)$$

$$K_1 = (\text{COUNT} \wedge \text{DOWN} \wedge \bar{y}_0) \vee (\text{COUNT} \wedge \overline{\text{DOWN}} \wedge y_0)$$

$$J_0 = (\text{COUNT} \wedge \text{DOWN} \wedge \bar{y}_1) \vee (\text{COUNT} \wedge \overline{\text{DOWN}} \wedge y_1)$$

$$K_0 = (\text{COUNT} \wedge \text{DOWN} \wedge y_1) \vee (\text{COUNT} \wedge \overline{\text{DOWN}} \wedge \bar{y}_1)$$

(3.40)

A NAND realization of the up-down counter is given in Fig. 3.82. The JK functions are defined by (3.40), while the output z_1z_0 is defined by (3.39). Figure 3.82 also shows a straightforward partitioning of the counter into nine 7400-series ICs from the small IC library of Figs. 3.37 and 3.47. NAND ICs with various fan-in values are used, as well as the 74106 dual edge-triggered JK flip-flop IC. Note the use of extra inverters in the COUNT and DOWN input lines that reduce the load imposed on circuits driving these lines to that of a single (inverter) gate. Since the COUNT signal must be supplied to 12 gates, which exceeds the maximum allowed fan-out (10 gates), COUNT is regenerated by two separate inverters, each with fan-out six. It should be noted that a different state assignment can yield a simpler counter circuit containing fewer gates and ICs (Prob. 3.49).

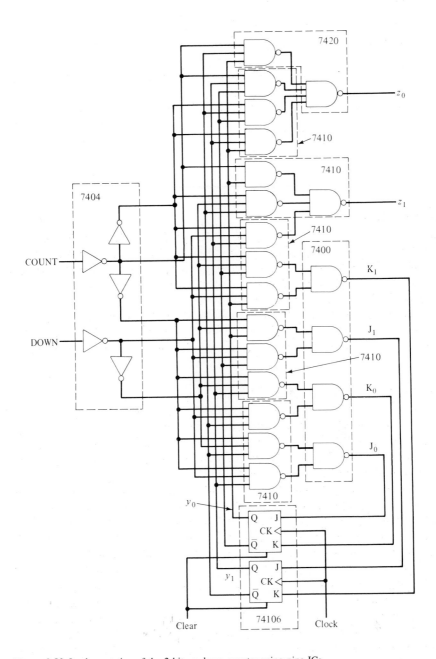

Figure 3.82 Implementation of the 2-bit up-down counter using nine ICs.

The SSI design methodology illustrated by the preceding example is suitable only for sequential machines with small state and excitation tables. To design, say, an 8-bit up-down counter using the same approach would require processing a state table with 256 states and a excitation table with 1024 rows, 10 input columns, and 24 output columns—a formidable task. Complex circuits of this sort are usually designed by heuristic approaches. For example, an 8-bit up-down counter can be decomposed into four identical 2-bit counter stages as depicted in Fig. 3.83. The counter stages are linked by carry/borrow signals in the same manner as the stages of the ripple-carry adder of Fig. 3.72. Each counter stage is essentially similar to the 2-bit up-down counter discussed above, with one extra output line CY (carry). An SSI implementation of the entire 8-bit counter in the style of Fig. 3.81 would contain around 40 ICs. Complex logic functions usually can be implemented more easily and with far fewer components by using ICs in the MSI range, as discussed in the next chapter.

3.4 SUMMARY

The integrated circuits used in digital system design process binary signals that assume only the two logic values 0 and 1. Additional signal values such as Z (the high-impedance state) and U (an unknown or indeterminate state) are sometimes useful. The structure and digital behavior of transistor switching circuits can be modeled very closely by means of CSA (connector-switch-attenuator) circuits. Usually, however, more abstract digital devices called logic gates are used to construct digital circuit models. The fundamental gate types include AND, OR, NOT, NAND, NOR, EXCLUSIVE-OR, and EXCLU-SIVE-NOR. Of these, NAND and NOR gates are the most important because they are functionally complete logic elements, and are easily fabricated using most IC technologies. Circuits composed of ideal zero-delay gates are called combinational logic circuits, because their output signals depend only on the current combination of input signals applied to the circuit. This implies that combinational circuits have no memory. Such circuits are used mainly as data-transfer circuits to control the flow of information in a system, and also as data-processing circuits to perform numerical or logical computation.

Various binary encoding schemes are employed to represent numbers in digital systems. The most basic scheme uses a positional notation in which each binary digit or bit of a number word is weighted by a power of two. Binary numbers formed in this way

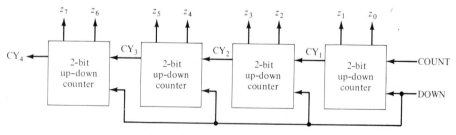

Figure 3.83 Eight-bit up-down counter.

are directly analogous to ordinary decimal numbers, but have a radix of 2 instead of 10. To simplify conversion between binary and decimal form, a number representation called BCD (binary coded decimal) may be used. Each 4-bit group within a BCD word denotes a decimal digit; the weight of the group is a power of 10. The BCD numbers are generally longer than equivalent binary (radix 2) numbers, and so occupy more storage space. A number may be either signed or unsigned. Signed numbers formed by appending a sign symbol (0 for positive and 1 for negative) to an unsigned number are said to be in sign-magnitude form. A more widely used code for signed binary numbers is twos complement, which is characterized by a special complement representation of negative numbers. Use of the twos-complement code simplifies the implementation of addition and subtraction.

All physical logic circuits have nonzero signal propagation delays. To enable a circuit to delay or remember an input signal for an indefinite period, feedback is necessary. A simple memory element called an SR (set–reset) latch can be formed from a pair of NOR gates whose outputs are fed back to their inputs. An SR latch has two stable states that can represent a stored 1 and a stored 0; certain input signals are forbidden to prevent unstable or indeterminate operation. By adding additional circuitry to a latch, a class of very useful memory elements called flip-flops can be formed. The time at which a flip-flop responds to changes in its input signals, as well as the time at which the flip-flop's output signals change, can be precisely controlled by means of a clock signal. The most widely used flip-flop types are D (delay) and JK-flip-flops. A circuit composed of gates and flip-flops is called a (synchronous) sequential circuit, since its behavior depends on the sequence in which input signals are applied to it. The major uses of sequential circuits are as memories and as control circuits.

Small-scale integration is used to manufacture gates and flip-flops. All the basic gate and flip-flop types are available in such commercial IC families as the very popular 7400 series of TTL devices. A typical SSI IC contains from one to six independent gates or flip-flops, all of the same type and having the same fan-in and fan-out specifications. A few SSI IC types contain several interconnected gates, for example, AND-OR-INVERT circuits. Many IC types are provided in three-state, open-collector, and buffer versions, in addition to the standard version. When using ICs, the designer must take into account signal propagation delays and fan-in/fan-out constraints. The relevant design information can be found in the manufacturer's data sheets for the particular IC or IC logic family being used.

A systematic approach to the design of small logic circuits has been known for many years. Its goals are to minimize the number of gates and flip-flops needed to realize a given function. The circuit to be designed is partitioned into a combinational subcircuit C and a memory subcircuit M. The memory M is composed of latches or flip-flops, and is used to store the internal state of the circuit. The major design problem is to implement the combinational circuit C, whose inputs are the external (primary) input signals X and the internal (secondary) state variables Y. The outputs of C are the primary output signals Z and the internal signals Y', which must be applied to M to determine the next state of the system.

The design of combinational circuits is greatly aided by a type of Boolean algebra called switching algebra. The elements of this algebra are logic variables and functions that are combined by means of Boolean or logical operators. A basic set of operators for Boolean algebra are denoted by the symbols $\wedge$ (AND), $\vee$ (OR), and $^{-}$ (NOT). The properties of a Boolean algebra are defined by a small set of basic laws or axioms. The importance of Boolean algebra in logic circuit design arises from the fact that the behavior (logic function) and, to a lesser extent, the structure of a logic circuit can be represented by one or more Boolean expressions involving $\wedge$, $\vee$, and $^{-}$, and possibly other operators. Thus combinational circuit design can be regarded as a problem of converting Boolean expressions into forms that correspond to practical logic circuits. The most useful of these forms are SOP (sum-of-products) and POS (product-of-sums) expressions, which correspond to two-level logic circuits. Any logic function can be realized by a two-level circuit, which therefore is a universal circuit structure. Two-level circuits also have the minimum propagation delay, and can be implemented by various types of gates, including NAND and NOR gates. Of special interest are minimal two-level circuits that have the fewest gates among all possible two-level realizations of a given function.

Given a truth table, Boolean expression, or similar specification of a logic function z, a minimal SOP realization of z can be constructed as follows: First determine all prime implicants of z. Then find a minimal set of prime implicants that cover all minterms of z. The logical sum (OR function) of the prime implicants in the minimal cover, with the prime implicants expressed as logical product terms (AND functions), is a minimal SOP expression for z. A minimum-gate two-level circuit of the AND-OR or NAND-NAND type can be obtained directly from the minimal SOP expression. For functions of up to four variables, the foregoing gate minimization problem is easily solved graphically by using a Karnaugh map to represent z. Computer programs can be used to solve this problem for functions of up to about 10 variables. Note that a two-level circuit designed in this fashion may have to be modified to meet practical fan-in/fan-out constraints.

The first step in the design of a sequential logic circuit is to construct a symbolic state table that formally defines the behavior of the desired circuit. If there are q distinct states in this state table, a set of $p = [\log_2 q]$ flip-flops is selected to implement the memory subcircuit M that stores the system's states. Each state is then assigned a unique pattern of values of the state variables $Y = y_{p-1}y_{p-2} \ldots y_1y_0$, where y_i is the signal appearing on the Q output line of the ith flip-flop. An excitation table, which constitutes a truth table for the combinational subcircuit C, is constructed from the state table and the flip-flop specifications. Finally the logic design of C is carried out using, for instance, the Karnaugh-map approach. Complex logic functions involving relatively large numbers of input-output and internal state variables are typically implemented by ad hoc or heuristic means.

3.5 FURTHER READING

There are many textbooks covering switching theory and logic design in the SSI context (Muroga, 1979; Fletcher, 1980). CSA theory is introduced in Hayes (1982), while gate minimization is covered in depth in McCluskey (1965), and Muroga (1979). Technical data on ICs in the various 7400-series logic families can be found in the TTL and CMOS catalogs (data books) published by such IC manufacturers as Fairchild, National Semiconductor, Signetics, and Texas Instruments. The two-volume set *Logic and Memory Experiments Using TTL IC's* (Larsen & Rony, 1978; Rony & Larsen, 1979) contains a great deal of useful information on logic design using 7400-series ICs.

3.6 PROBLEMS

3.1 Almost all electronic digital circuits are based on binary or two-valued signals that take their values from the set $\{0, 1\}$. What advantages and disadvantages would result from the use of multivalued signals employing, say, the 10 values $\{0, 1, 2, \ldots, 9\}$?

3.2 A common type of fault in integrated circuits is a *short circuit*, which causes two normally disconnected lines L_i and L_j to become connected. Suppose that the binary signals x_i and x_j are applied to L_i and L_j. Construct a truth table showing the effects of a short circuit between L_i and L_j on x_i and x_j, commenting on any difficulties encountered.

3.3 Construct realizations of the NOR function $\overline{x_1 \vee x_2}$ and the EXCLUSIVE-OR function $x_1 \oplus x_2$ using:
    (*a*) CS networks defined on V_4 (cf. Fig. 3.6)
    (*b*) CSA networks defined on V_7 (cf. Fig. 3.11)

3.4 Figure 3.84 defines a pair of amplifying switches that can be turned on and off by both weak and strong values from V_7. These switches can be used to model transistors with built-in amplification or gain.

    (*a*) Construct a CS circuit from these switches that acts as an amplifying circuit or buffer by transforming $\widetilde{0}$ and 0 into 0, and by transforming $\widetilde{1}$ and 1 into 1. Use as few switches as possible.

    (*b*) Construct a CS circuit that acts as an inverting buffer by transforming $\widetilde{0}$, 0 and $\widetilde{1}$, 1 into 1 and 0, respectively. Again use as few switches as possible.

3.5 Repeat Prob. 3.4 using CSA circuits containing connectors, attenuators, and positive, but not negative, amplifying switches.

3.6 The circuit of Fig. 3.36a mixes analog devices (the resistor R) and digital devices (the NAND gates) in a questionable way. Using CSA theory, construct a rigorous logical model for this circuit by defining all components with respect to V_7. Your answer should include a CSA circuit diagram and a truth table describing the circuit's behavior.

3.7 Figure 3.85a shows a latch of the type used as a 1-bit memory cell in large bipolar RAMs. It is simpler than the SR latch of Fig. 3.30 since the lines a and b are bidirectional, serving both as input (set and reset) and output (Q and $\overline{Q}$) lines. An appropriate CSA model for this memory cell apears in Fig. 3.85b. Construct a comprehensive tabular description of the behavior of this CSA circuit with respect to V_7 along the lines of Fig. 3.30b.

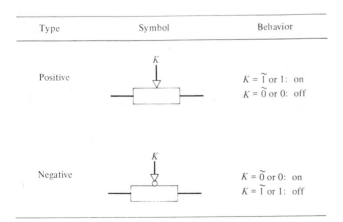

Type	Symbol	Behavior
Positive	K	$K = \widetilde{1}$ or 1: on $K = \widetilde{0}$ or 0: off
Negative	K	$K = \widetilde{0}$ or 0: on $K = \widetilde{1}$ or 1: off

Figure 3.84 Two types of amplifying switches.

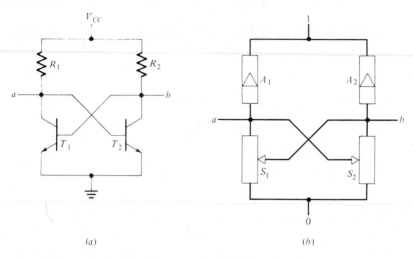

(a)   (b)

Figure 3.85 (a) Bipolar RAM cell; (b) its CSA equivalent.

3.8 Convert the following numbers into unsigned 8-bit binary form: 40_{10}, 40_{BCD}, 40_{16}, 123_{10}, $01F_{16}$.

3.9 Convert the following numbers into 8-bit twos-complement (TC) code: 40, -40, 40_{16}, -40_{16}, 01101001_{SM}, 10010010_{SM}.

3.10 Convert the following TC numbers into ordinary decimal form: 10010000, 0001000, 11111110, 01111111, 00000000, 11111111.

3.11 Compare and contrast the three binary number codes SM, TC, and BCD with respect to the following criteria:

(a) Storage space requirements
(b) Complexity of circuits for performing addition and subtraction
(c) Complexity of circuits for performing multiplication
(d) Ease of conversion to ordinary decimal form

3.12 Let n_{TC} be a nonzero twos-complement number with sign bit s. Prove that the sign bit of $-n_{TC}$ is always $\bar{s}$. (*Hint:* Consider the negation algorithm for TC numbers given in Fig. 3.24. Examine all cases in which the step of adding one to $\bar{n}_{TC}$ changes the sign bit.)

3.13 An n-bit TC number n_{TC} can also be negated by the following method. Let $z = 00 \ldots 0$ denote an n-bit word of 0s. Subtract n_{TC} from z using unsigned binary arithmetic and ignoring any borrow produced in the leftmost bit position; the result is $-n_{TC}$. For example,

$$
\begin{array}{lll}
z: & 00000000 = & 0_{10} \\
n_{TC}: & 01101000 = & +104_{10} \\
\hline
\text{Difference:} & 1\ 10011000 = & -104_{10}
\end{array}
$$

Thus we can write $-n_{TC} = 0 - n_{TC}$. Use this viewpoint on negation to prove that, provided there is no overflow, the correct sum of any two TC numbers is obtained by using unsigned binary addition.

3.14 Each of the gates listed in Fig. 3.86 is equivalent to a basic gate appearing in Fig. 3.15. Identify the equivalent gates.

Figure 3.86 Three gates containing input inversions.

3.15 Design equivalent circuits analogous to those of Fig. 3.53 that can be used to increase the fan-in of OR, NOR, EXCLUSIVE-OR, and EXCLUSIVE-NOR gates.

3.16 A logic circuit is said to be *well-behaved* if the logic values appearing on all lines of the circuit are always uniquely defined. Figure 3.87 shows a simple combinational circuit that is not well-behaved. Suppose that $x = 1$ in this circuit. If $z = 1$, then both inputs of the NAND gate are 1, which requires $z = 0$ on the output of the NAND. If $z = 0$, then 0 is applied to one input of the NAND requiring $z = 1$. Since z cannot be simultaneously 0 and 1, there is a logical inconsistency in this circuit. Note that if the propagation delay t_p is changed to a nonzero value, the circuit changes to a sequential circuit that is well-behaved.

(*a*) Explain what happens if a physical (nonideal) NAND gate is configured as shown in Fig. 3.87.

(*b*) Construct a combinational circuit containing feedback that is well-behaved. The existence of such circuits implies that feedback is not a property that is confined to sequential circuits.

3.17 Consider the open-collector (OC) logic circuit of Fig. 3.88 consisting of eight OC inverters and a pull-up resistor.

(*a*) What is the logic function realized by this circuit?

(*b*) Draw a wiring diagram for this circuit in the style of Fig. 3.40 using 7405 OC hex inverter ICs; assume that the 7405 has the same pin assignment as the 7404 normal inverter IC.

3.18 Open-collector logic is usually avoided in large digital systems for the following reasons:

(*a*) It is more subject to noise than standard TTL logic.

(*b*) Switching speeds are lower than standard logic.

(*c*) Faulty gates are more difficult to isolate in OC circuits.

Explain item (*c*).

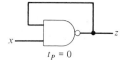

$t_p = 0$

Figure 3.87 Combinational circuit that is not well behaved.

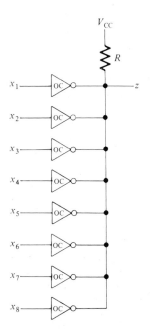

Figure 3.88 Logic circuit containing open-collector inverters.

3.19 A four-input 1-bit multiplexer M is to be designed. The data inputs of M are x_0, x_1, x_2, x_3 and the data output is z (cf. Fig. 3.17). Four control lines s_0, s_1, s_2, s_3 select the data input that is to be connected to the ouput z, where x_i is connected to z if and only if $s_i = 1$. M is enabled by another control input E.

(a) Draw a standard logic diagram for M using inverters and two-input AND and OR gates.

(b) Redesign M using three-state gates of any appropriate type to drive the output line z. Note that substantially fewer gates are needed using this approach.

3.20 The multiplexer M of Fig. 3.17 is to be implemented using only the 7400 quad two-input NAND IC.

(a) Redraw the logic diagram of Fig. 3.17 replacing all gates by two-input NANDs.

(b) Calculate the number of 7400s necessary to implement M.

3.21 Repeat Prob. 3.20 using 7402 quad two-input NOR ICs instead of the 7400 NANDs.

3.22 Implement the multiplexer circuit of Fig. 3.17 using any 7400-series ICs from the set given in Fig. 3.37. The design objective is to use as few ICs as possible.

(a) Give a parts listing showing the IC types used and the number of copies of each type needed.

(b) Draw a wiring diagram similar to Fig. 3.40 showing all connections to the ICs, including power and ground.

3.23 Show that the 4-bit ripple-carry adder of Fig. 3.72 can be implemented using six 7400-series ICs from Fig. 3.37.

3.24 Implement the 4-bit adder circuit of Fig. 3.19, which represents a single MSI IC from the 7400 series, using SSI ICs from Fig. 3.37. The primary design objective is to obtain a circuit that is as fast as possible, assuming that every gate has a fixed propagation delay $t_P = t_{PLH} = t_{PHL}$. A secondary goal is to use as few ICs as possible.

(a) Give a parts list showing the IC types used and the number used of each type.

(b) Draw a wiring diagram of the IC implementation similar to Fig. 3.40.

3.25 Consider the modulo-8 Johnson counter of Figs. 3.48 and 3.49. It is desired to decode the output sequence $Z_0 = 0000, Z_1 = 1000, Z_2 = 1100, \ldots$ so that when Z_i appears, the ith line c_i in the eight-line set c_0, $c_1, \ldots, c_7$ is activated. Show that a circuit composed of only two 7400 quad NAND ICs suffices to generate the c_i's.

3.26 Redesign the SR latch of Fig. 3.30 using NAND gates in place of NOR gates.

3.27 Show that the shift register of Fig. 3.34 will not work properly if clocked SR latches are substituted for the SR master–slave flip-flops.

3.28 Using NAND gates only, carry out the logic design of a clocked JK latch.

3.29 Redraw the timing diagram of Fig. 3.44 for a JK negative edge-triggered flip-flop, using the same input waveforms.

3.30 What is meant by 0s catching in a JK master–slave flip-flop? Illustrate your answer by an appropriate timing diagram. Explain why this problem does not occur in edge-triggered JK flip-flops.

3.31 Explain why the D flip-flop of Fig. 3.46 is considered to be edge triggered rather than level triggered. Complete the timing diagram of Fig. 3.89 for this flip-flop.

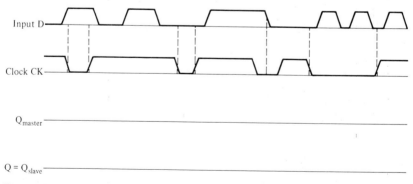

Figure 3.89 Partial timing diagram for a D flip-flop.

3.32 Using the data of Fig. 3.50, calculate typical values of the propagation delays t_{PLH} and t_{PHL} for each of the output lines of the adder circuit appearing in Fig. 3.40.

3.33 Prove that the maximum propagation delay of signals transmitted to the sum output z of the adder of Fig. 3.40 is 53 ns, and not 60 ns as might be expected from the fact that the 7486 EXCLUSIVE-OR IC can impose delays as high as 30 ns per gate; see Fig. 3.50.

3.34 Consider the timing data for the 7473 dual JK flip-flop IC given in Fig. 3.51.

(*a*) Determine the maximum frequency at which the 7473 is guaranteed to operate.

(*b*) What is the minimum width or duration of 1-pulses applied to the J or K inputs of the 7473 necessary to ensure proper operation?

3.35 Prove that the EXCLUSIVE-OR operator $\oplus$ obeys the following laws, which are useful when manipulating Boolean expressions:

$$x \oplus (y \oplus z) = (x \oplus y) \oplus z \qquad \text{(Associativity)}$$

$$x \oplus y = y \oplus x \qquad \text{(Commutativity)}$$

$$x \wedge (y \oplus z) = (x \wedge y) \oplus (x \wedge z) \qquad \text{(Distributivity of } \wedge \text{ over } \oplus)$$

Note, however, that $\oplus$ does not distribute over $\wedge$, that is,

$$x \oplus (y \wedge z) \neq (x \oplus y) \wedge (x \oplus z)$$

3.36 Consider the NAND operator $|$ defined in Eq. (3.17). Determine whether or not $|$ is associative or commutative.

3.37 The first six laws listed in Fig. 3.59 are sufficient to define a Boolean algebra. Prove this by deriving the remaining laws 7–9 as theorems, using only the first six laws in your proofs.

3.38 Using the axioms of Fig. 3.59 prove the following Boolean equations, which are known as the *absorption laws*.

$$x \wedge (x \vee y) = x$$

$$x \vee (x \wedge y) = x$$

3.39 Prove the following Boolean relations:

$$x_1 \vee x_3 \vee (\bar{x}_2 \wedge \bar{x}_4) = (x_1 \vee \bar{x}_2 \vee x_3) \wedge (x_1 \vee x_3 \vee \bar{x}_4)$$

$$((a \wedge b) \oplus (b \wedge c) \oplus (a \wedge c)) \vee (a \wedge b \wedge c \wedge d \wedge e \wedge f) = (a \vee b) \wedge (a \vee c) \wedge (b \vee c)$$

3.40 Consider the four-valued signal set $V_4 = \{0, 1, U, Z\}$, which is used in the analysis of CS networks in Sec. 3.1.2. Let the operators $\wedge$, $\vee$, and $^-$ be defined on V_4 as follows:

(*a*) For any $x, y \in V_4$, $x \wedge y = z$ where z is the logically strongest element in V_4 such that $z \leq x$ and $z \leq y$.

(*b*) For any $x, y \in V_4$, $x \vee y = z$ where z is the logically weakest element in V_4 such that $x \leq z$ and $y \leq z$.

(*c*) $\bar{0} = 1$, $\bar{1} = 0$, $\bar{U} = Z$, and $\bar{Z} = U$.

Prove that V_4 with the operators defined above constitutes a four-valued Boolean algebra. Show all your work.

3.41 (*a*) Prove that the NOR operator is logically complete by giving all-NOR implementations of the AND, OR, and NOT functions (cf. Fig. 3.65).

(*b*) Prove that the EXCLUSIVE-OR and EXCLUSIVE-NOR operators, by themselves or in combination, are logically incomplete.

3.42 Assuming that input variables are available in both true and inverted form, show that every logic function can be realized by a two-level AND-NOR or OR-NAND circuit. Explain why not all functions can be realized by two-level OR-NOR or AND-NAND circuits.

3.43 (*a*) Calculate the minterms and maxterms of the Boolean function

$$z = \overline{(x_1 \vee (\bar{x}_1 \wedge x_2 \wedge \bar{x}_3)) \vee (x_1 \oplus \bar{x}_2)}$$

(*b*) Express z in both canonical SOP form and canonical POS form.

	cd			
ab	00	01	11	10
00	1	d	d	d
01	d	d	0	0
11	0	d	0	0
10	d	d	0	1

Figure 3.90 Incompletely-specified 4-variable Karnaugh map.

3.44 Consider the incompletely specified Karnaugh map of Fig. 3.90. Assign the values 0 and 1 to the don't cares d to obtain the Karnaugh maps of four distinct and completely specified logic functions with the following properties:

(a) z_1 is a function of exactly two variables.
(b) z_2 has exactly five minterms.
(c) z_3 has exactly four prime implicants.
(d) z_4 has a prime implicant that cannot appear in any minimal SOP expression for z_4.

3.45 The function $z(x_1, x_2, x_3, x_4)$ has the following eight minterms: $m_0, m_4, m_5, m_8, m_{10}, m_{11} m_{13}, m_{15}$; where $m_0 = \bar{x}_1 \wedge \bar{x}_2 \wedge \bar{x}_3 \wedge \bar{x}_4$, and so on. Find minimal SOP and POS expressions for z. Construct a minimum-gate two-level circuit that realizes z.

3.46 Design a two-level combinational circuit to multiply two 3-bit signed numbers X and Y producing a 3-bit product Z, where $Z = X \times Y$ (modulo-4). Assume that SM numbers are used, and that an all-NOR implementation is required.

3.47 Repeat Prob. 3.46 using TC code instead of SM code.

3.48 A logic circuit N with the following specifications is to be realized using only type 7400 quad two-input NAND ICs.

(a) N has four primary inputs a, b, c, d and two primary outputs f, g.
(b) $f = 1$ whenever two or more of the input signals to N are 1; otherwise $f = 0$.
(c) $g = 1$ whenever an even number of 1 signals is applied to N; otherwise $g = \bar{f}$.

3.49 Redesign the 2-bit up-down counter of Fig. 3.77 using D flip-flops and the natural state assignment (3.38). Obtain both an excitation table and a logic diagram. Partition your logic circuit into 7400-series ICs from Figs. 3.37 and 3.47 using as few ICs as possible.

3.50 Carry out the logic design of the 2-bit counter stage used in Fig. 3.83. Use only JK flip-flops and NOR gates in your design.

3.51 Design a logic circuit N that serially multiplies an unsigned binary number of arbitrary length by 3. N has one input line x and one output line z. A number n is entered serially (bit by bit) on x with the least significant bit first; the product $3n$ emerges serially on z. Implement your design using any appropriate ICs from the set appearing in Figs. 3.37 and 3.47.

3.52 A sequential circuit N having two input lines $X = (x_1, x_2)$ and one output line z is to be designed. Sequences of 2-bit numbers are applied to X. N sets z to 1 if and only if the particular six-number sequence 2–1–3–2–2–0 is applied to X. N is therefore said to be an *acceptor* or *recognizer* of this sequence.

(a) Construct a state table for N.
(b) Carry out the logic design of N using JK flip-flops and NAND gates, and employing as few gates and flip-flops as possible.

FOUR

DESIGN USING MEDIUM- AND LARGE-SCALE INTEGRATION

"Reeling and Writhing, of course, to begin with," the Mock Turtle replied, "and then the different branches of arithmetic — Ambition, Distraction, Uglification and Derision."

[Lewis Carroll (Charles L. Dodgson): *Alice's Adventures in Wonderland*, 1865]

The term MSI is applied to ICs containing from about 100 to 1000 transistors, while LSI refers to ICs containing over 1000 transistors. MSI/LSI circuits can perform much more complex operations than the SSI circuits considered in Chap. 3. In this chapter the most important MSI devices and their applications are examined, again drawing many examples from the 7400 series. The register-transfer approach to complex system design at the MSI level is presented, and applied to the design of arithmetic circuits. The major types of LSI components and their characteristics are introduced, and IC memories of both the read-only (ROM) and read-write (RAM) varieties are discussed in detail. The use of ROMs as general-purpose design elements is also explored.

4.1 MSI COMPONENTS

We begin by examining the general characteristics of digital systems that employ MSI circuits. The principal MSI component types are introduced and their primary applications are discussed.

4.1.1 The MSI Level

Medium-scale ICs are an order of magnitude denser than the SSI circuits considered in the preceding chapter. They can contain up to about a thousand transistors or a few hundred logic gates per IC chip. They are thus capable of performing logical operations that are significantly more complex than the gate and flip-flop operations that are typical of the SSI design level. The 74283 4-bit adder of Fig. 3.19, which contains 36 gates, is an example of a commercially available MSI component. In addition to their higher densities, MSI devices are also distinguished by the fact that their IO signals can usually be grouped into multibit words or vectors. A word therefore can be regarded as the primitive unit of information at the MSI level. Words are typically used to represent numbers, characters, instructions, and so on.

The Boolean algebra used to describe the behavior of SSI components can be adapted to a limited extent to describe MSI and other word-oriented devices. Let $z(x_0, x_1, \cdots, x_{n-1})$ denote a Boolean (logic) function of n variables. This function maps the n binary variables $(x_0, x_1, \cdots, x_{n-1})$ onto the binary variable z. Suppose that each variable x_i is replaced by an m-bit word $X_i = (x_{i,0}, x_{i,1}, \cdots, x_{i,m-1})$. Then we can extend the function $z(x_0, x_1, \cdots, x_{n-1})$ to a function $Z(X_0, X_1, \cdots, X_{n-1})$ defined for m-bit words thus:

$$Z(X_0, X_1, \cdots, X_{n-1}) = (z(x_{0,0}, x_{0,1}, \cdots, x_{0,n-1}),$$
$$z(x_{1,0}, x_{1,1}, \cdots, x_{1,n-1})$$
$$\cdots \qquad\qquad\qquad (4.1)$$
$$z(x_{m,0}, x_{m,1}, \cdots, x_{m,n-1}))$$

It is not difficult to show that the set of functions of the type defined by (4.1) constitutes a $2^{2^{mn}}$-valued Boolean algebra. For example, a 4-bit NOR function may be defined as follows:

$$Z_{\text{NOR}}(X, Y) = (\overline{x_0 \vee y_0}, \overline{x_1 \vee y_1}, \overline{x_2 \vee y_2}, \overline{x_3 \vee y_3}) \qquad (4.2)$$

or, more concisely,

$$Z_{\text{NOR}}(X, Y) = \overline{X \vee Y} \qquad (4.3)$$

where $X = (x_0, x_1, x_2, x_3)$ and $Y = (y_0, y_1, y_2, y_3)$. Equations (4.2) and (4.3) define the operation of the 7402 quad two-input NOR gate IC (Fig. 3.37g). Hence the 7402 can be called a 4-bit *word gate* that performs the NOR operation on 4-bit words. The OR operator appearing in (4.3) is therefore an extension of the usual OR operator from binary variables to words, that is, ordered sets of binary variables. In an analogous way, the ordinary NOR gate symbol is used in Fig. 4.1a to represent a NOR word gate corresponding to the 7402 IC. Figures 4.1b and 4.1c show suitable symbols for two NAND ICs in the 7400 series that also can be viewed as implementing word gates. Note that the m lines used to transmit an m-bit word are coalesced into a single m-bit line or bus in Fig. 4.1. The number of 1-bit lines forming the bus is written alongside the corresponding line in a circuit diagram, and is marked by a slash. The symbolism of Fig. 4.1 provides a higher-level view of logic circuits that is appropriate to the MSI complexity level.

Unfortunately most MSI components cannot be described as simply as word gates. For example, the 4-bit adder IC of Fig. 3.19 is most easily described using arithmetic operations instead of Boolean operations thus:

$$C_{\text{out}}, Z = X + Y + C_{\text{in}} \qquad (4.4)$$

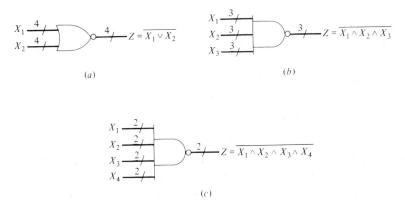

Figure 4.1 Symbols for word gates implemented by: (*a*) the 7402 quad two-input NOR; (*b*) the 7410 triple three-input NAND; (*c*) the 7420 dual four-input NAND.

where $X = x_3x_2x_1x_0$, $Y = y_3y_2y_1y_0$, and $Z = z_3z_2z_1z_0$ are 4-bit words representing binary numbers. The MSI circuits are further complicated by the fact that a particular component may process words of several different sizes simultaneously. For instance, in (4.4), X, Y, and Z are 4-bit words, while C_{out} and C_{in}, which denote carry signals, are 1-bit words. We conclude that it is not possible to base the analysis of general MSI networks on Boolean algebra alone.

Reflecting their functional complexity, there are no standard symbols for representing MSI elements in circuit diagrams. Except in a few cases such as word gates, a general block symbol or box is used as illustrated in Fig. 4.2. The function performed is written inside the block. The block's IO lines can represent buses of various sizes as specified by slash numbers. Thus the output bus Z of unit F in Fig. 4.2 contains m 1-bit lines, implying that the unit's output signal, which is also denoted by Z, is an m-bit word. If F is capable of performing several different operations on the "data" input signals X_1, X_2, $\cdots$, X_k, then "control" input signals $C = (c_1, c_2, \cdots, c_p)$ are used to select the specific operation to be performed at any time. A division of IO signals into data and control signals, as indicated in Fig. 4.2, is often found in components at the MSI and higher

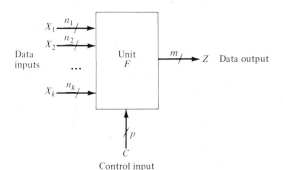

Data inputs

Control input

Figure 4.2 General symbol for an MSI component.

complexity levels. Figure 4.3 depicts possible symbols for two specific MSI ICs, the 74157 multiplexer and the 74283 adder; gate-level logic circuits for these ICs appear in Figs. 3.17 and 3.19 respectively. Note that when an MSI circuit is used as a system component, its internal structure in terms of gates and flip-flops is usually not of interest.

The MSI elements and the functions they perform are more difficult to classify than their SSI counterparts. The basic SSI components are gates, latches, and flip-flops. Figure 4.4 lists the most important types of MSI components, both combinational and sequential. Most are found in various versions in the 7400 IC series whose SSI members were discussed in Chap. 2. These versions are distinguished by different IC technologies (standard TTL, low-power Schottky TTL, CMOS, etc.), and different data word sizes (typically 2, 4, or 8 bits per word). As in the SSI case, the complexity of the functions included in a single IC chip is limited by the number of IO pins available. The MSI

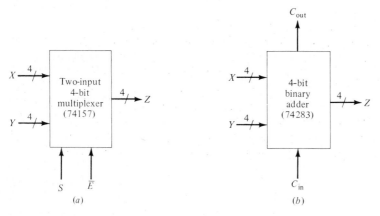

Figure 4.3 Examples of combinational MSI components in the 7400 IC series: (*a*) a multiplexer; (*b*) an adder.

Type	Element	Main Functions Performed
Combinational	Word gate	Logical (Boolean) operations
	Multiplexer	Data transfer; general function generation
	Decoder/encoder	Code or format conversion
	Adder	Addition and subtraction
	Shifter	Shifting and scaling
	Comparator	Data comparison
	Arithmetic-logic unit (ALU)	Numerical and logical operations
Sequential	(Multibit) latch	Data storage
	(Parallel) register	Data storage
	Shift register	Data storage; format conversion
	Counter	Control signal generation; timing

Figure 4.4 Representative MSI component types.

circuits are typically packaged in DIPs or flatpacks (see Fig. 2.30) with from 14 to 24 IO pins.

We now briefly outline the functions of the various MSI elements listed in Fig. 4.4; these functions are examined in detail later in this section. Although their complexity puts them in the SSI range, it is useful to view word gates as basic components at the MSI level. As noted, word gates perform the usual Boolean operations AND, OR, NAND, NOR, EXCLUSIVE-OR, EXCLUSIVE-NOR, and NOT on m-bit words, where $m \geq 1$; see Fig. 4.1. The primary function of a multiplexer (sometimes abbreviated MUX) is to allow words from several different sources to be transferred to a common destination. Select or address control signals determine which of several input (source) buses connected to the multiplexer is logically connected to its single output (destination) bus at any time. Figure 4.3a shows a multiplexer with two input buses X and Y, which are selected for connection to the output bus Z by the control line S; the word size in this case is 4 bits. Multiplexers also find limited use for generating arbitrary Boolean functions, implying that they constitute a type of universal logic element. There is a large class of combinational MSI elements that transform words from one format or code to another; these may be collectively termed decoder/encoder circuits. A (simple) *decoder* converts an n-bit word denoting an unsigned binary number i into a 2^n-bit word Z, in which the ith bit is 1 while the remaining $2^n - 1$ bits are 0. Z is sometimes said to be in 1-out-of-2^n code. Decoders of this type are useful in the design of addressing or selection circuitry where one of several possible actions must be selected. A (simple) *encoder* converts from 1-out-of-2^n code to n-bit binary code, and therefore is the inverse of a decoder. Other MSI decoder/encoder circuits handle number codes such as BCD, and also the special codes used by IO devices such as seven-segment LED displays.

A variety of arithmetic operations are implemented in MSI chips. Adder circuits such as that of Fig. 4.3b are used to perform binary addition. With suitable additional circuitry to perform negation, they can also be used for subtraction; see Fig. 3.27. A combinational *shifter* circuit is used to shift a word a specified number of bits to the left or right. Shifting has many uses. For example, shifting a binary number k-bit positions to the left (right) is equivalent to multiplication (division) by 2^k. Another useful MSI element is a *comparator*, which compares two input numbers X_1 and X_2 and issues output signals indicating their relative magnitudes, for example, $X_1 = X_2$, $X_1 > X_2$, or $X_1 < X_2$. The various logical and numerical operations discussed can be combined—at least for small word sizes—into a single multifunction circuit called an arithmetic-logic unit (ALU). More complex arithmetic operations such as general multiplication and division normally require ICs in the LSI/VLSI range.

The number of different types of sequential MSI components is fairly small. A set of n 1-bit latches, either clocked or unclocked, can be grouped into an n-bit latch chip. A similar group of n flip-flops forms an n-bit register. Such latches and registers are the basic storage devices for multibit words. In a simple n-bit latch or register all n bits of a word can be transferred to or from the latch or register simultaneously or in parallel. Shift registers, on the other hand, allow serial or 1-bit-at-a-time transfer of data to or from the register. An example of a typical 8-bit shift register in the 7400 series was discussed in Chap. 3; see Fig. 3.34. Figure 4.5 shows a suitable symbol for this shift register as a primitive MSI component. Shift registers are useful as data-storage elements, and for

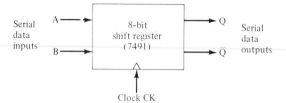

Figure 4.5 Example of a sequential MSI component in the 7400 IC series, an 8-bit shift register.

conversion of data streams from serial (bit-by-bit) to parallel (word-by-word) form. As Fig. 3.34 demonstrates, the individual storage cells of an MSI latch or register may use common control lines for the clock, clear, and similar signals. By adding a small amount of combinational logic to a parallel or shift register, a counter can be constructed. Counters are mainly employed in the design of control circuits. The logic design of various types of counters was considered in Chap. 3; see Figs. 3.48 and 3.82.

A digital system composed of MSI-level components typically contains registers, which are used for the temporary storage of data and control information, and combinational components, which are used to transfer and process the data. An example of such a system appears in Fig. 4.6a. Its purpose is to perform addition and subtraction on two 8-bit twos-complement numbers, and it is representative of the type of circuitry found inside a microprocessor. One input number is obtained from an 8-bit register A, while the other is obtained from an 8-bit bus B, which is normally connected to an external register or latch. When register A is clocked, the number appearing on bus B is added to the number stored in A if the control line SUBTRACT is set to 0; the number on B is subtracted from A if SUBTRACT $= 1$. In each case the result A $\pm$ B is stored in register A replacing the previously stored input operand. Note that the old contents of a register can be read out, and new data written in, during a single clock cycle. This property reflects the timing characteristics of the underlying flip-flops, and is not a property of

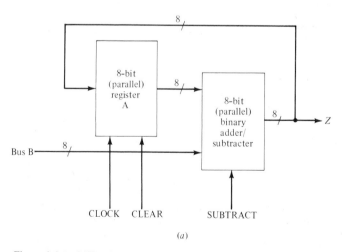

(a)

Figure 4.6 (a) MSI adder-subtracter for 8-bit twos-complement numbers; (b) its implementation using 7400-series ICs.

(Figure 4.6 continued)

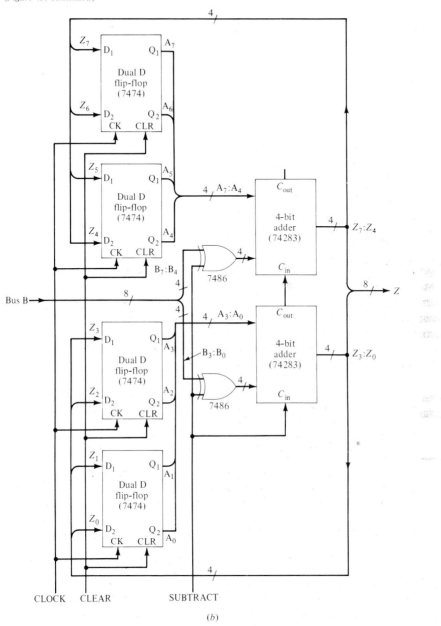

(b)

(Figure 4.6 continued)

latches; see Sec. 3.1.5. For example, if register A is composed of edge-triggered flip-flops, its output denoting the number A is applied to one of the adder/subtracter input as long as the clock signal CLOCK is stable. When CLOCK changes in the appropriate direction, for example, from 0 to 1 for positive edge triggering, the register assumes a new state determined by the output signals from the adder/subtracter.

An implementation of the foregoing arithmetic circuit using SSI and MSI ICs from the 7400 series appears in Fig. 4.6b. Two 4-bit adder ICs of type 74283 perform the required 8-bit TC addition. The carry-out signal C_{out} from the low-order adder stage constitutes the carry-in signal C_{in} of the high-order adder stage. The eight lines of bus B are connected to the adder via eight EXCLUSIVE-OR gates, which are used to complement B when subtraction is required. Thus when SUBTRACT $= 1$, $\overline{B} + 1$, denoting $-B$ in TC code, is applied to the adder (cf. Fig. 3.27). Finally, four 7474 dual D flip-flop ICs are used to implement the register in straightforward fashion. Some new symbolism, which it is hoped is self-explanatory, is introduced in Fig. 4.6b. The merging or diverging of lines to form larger or smaller buses is shown by lines in the circuit diagram that meet at a curved angle with no connection dot. For instance, the 4-bit output buses of the two adder ICs are merged to form the 8-bit bus $Z = Z_7:Z_0 = Z_7Z_6 \cdots Z_0$; these buses also diverge to 1-bit lines that are connected to the D inputs of the flip-flops. The eight EXCLUSIVE-OR gates are realized by two 7486s, which are represented by 4-bit word gates in Fig. 4.6b. These two word gates perform the following operation:

$$B \oplus SUBTRACT = (B_7 \oplus SUBTRACT, B_6 \oplus SUBTRACT, \ldots$$

$$B_0 \oplus SUBTRACT)$$

The entire circuit uses eight ICs, and contains about 80 gates and eight flip-flops.

Registers and latches are used extensively in MSI circuits for the temporary storage of data and control words. The behavior of such circuits often involves a sequence of *register-transfer operations,* during each of which information is read from registers (or latches), transformed, if required, by data-processing circuits, and then stored again. For this reason, the MSI level is also called the *register-transfer level* of design. A register-transfer operation can be completed during a single clock period, and thus corresponds to a single state transition of a sequential machine. One clock period, referred to as the (*machine*) *cycle time,* may be taken as the basic unit of time at the MSI complexity level.

The behavior of an MSI circuit can be described by any of the tools introduced in earlier chapters, including state tables, flowcharts, and narrative text. To keep the complexity of the behavioral descriptions at the same level as structural descriptions such as the block diagrams of Fig. 4.6, words are treated as single variables as much as possible. The contents of a register or latch may be denoted by a single state variable that can assume up to 2^n values, where n is the device's storage capacity in bits. A commonly used descriptive medium at the MSI or register-transfer level is a semiformal language, which resembles a computer programming language, and is referred to as a *register-transfer language* or RTL. The RTLs generally do not specify signal timing details, and consequently do not distinguish latches from registers. Although numerous RTLs have been defined, primarily for pedagogic purposes, no standard language presently exists. A typical RTL employs statements of the form

$$R_0 := F(R_1, R_2, \cdots, R_k);$$

which states that the operation F is performed on the contents of registers $R_1, R_2, \cdots, R_k$, and the result is transferred to register R_0. This statement may be qualified by a clause specifying when, or under what conditions, the register-transfer operation should take place, for example,

$$\textbf{if } C = 1 \textbf{ then } R_0 := F(R_1, R_2, \cdots, R_k); \tag{4.5}$$

The register transfer operation in (4.5) takes place during each clock cycle for which the control signal or condition denoted by C is 1; note that the clock signal is not explicitly mentioned. Circuit behavior is often described by a sequence of RTL statements that describe the operations that should take place in a corresponding sequence of machine cycles.

Figure 4.7 shows an RTL description of the actions necessary to perform the subtraction $\alpha - \beta$ using the circuit in Fig. 4.6. Three register-transfer operations are required, which can be carried out in three successive clock cycles. First the TC number $00 \cdots 0$ denoting zero is placed in register A. This can be done by simply activating the CLEAR control line. Then the minuend α is loaded into A via bus B and the adder/subtracter circuit. This data transfer is accomplished by a "dummy" addition step of the form

$$A := 0 + \alpha;$$

In the third clock period, the subtrahend β is placed on bus B. A subtraction operation is indicated by SUBTRACT $= 1$, which causes the result $\alpha - \beta$ to be computed and returned to A. The result is also made available to external circuits via the bus Z.

Logic design at the MSI level is normally done in heuristic or intuitive fashion; there are no general design algorithms analogous to the SSI design methods covered in Sec. 3.3. The following approach is typical. First the required behavior is specified as a sequence of register-transfer operations using flowcharts or RTL descriptions. Suitable MSI (and, if needed, SSI) components are selected to implement the register-transfer operations and associated control functions. Finally, the chosen components are interconnected so that all specified operations can be performed. Most register-transfer operations require linking registers to combinational data-transfer and data-processing circuits in a straightforward manner. An important aspect of MSI-level design is the selection of the components to be used. This requires a good understanding of the MSI circuit types listed in Fig. 4.4. Frequently a component having the required word size is not available off the shelf. It is then necessary to be able to use components of a given word size to implement components of the same type having a different, usually larger,

RTL Statement	Comment
$A := 0;$	Clear register A by setting CLEAR to 1
$A := A + \alpha;$	Place α on bus B and set SUBTRACT to 0 to perform an addition cycle that transfers α to A
$A := A - \beta;$	Place β on bus B and set SUBTRACT to 1 to perform a subtraction cycle that transfers $\alpha - \beta$ to A

Figure 4.7 RTL description of subtraction using the circuit of Fig. 4.6.

word size. For example, in the circuit of Fig. 4.6b, two 4-bit adder ICs are used to construct an 8-bit adder; there is currently no 8-bit adder IC in the 7400 series. Similarly, four dual flip-flop ICs must be used to form the 8-bit register A. The ability to expand the word size of components systematically is therefore a central issue in MSI design.

4.1.2 Multiplexers

A multiplexer is one of the most versatile combinational MSI circuits. The IO lines of a typical multiplexer are shown in Fig. 4.8. It has 2^m input data buses $X_0, X_1, \cdots, X_{2^m-1}$ and one output data bus Z, all of which are k bits wide. It also has a set of input control lines, including an m-bit select bus S and an enable line E. When $E = 0$ all lines in the output bus are forced to 0, that is, $Z = 0$, and the multiplexer is said to be disabled. When $E = 1$ the multiplexer is enabled and the signals on one of the input buses X_i are transferred to Z, that is $Z = X_i$, where i is the number represented in binary form by the bit pattern $s_{m-1}s_{m-2}$ $\cdots s_1s_0$ applied to the S bus. For example, if $m = 4$ and $s_3s_2s_1s_0 = 0111$, which is the binary form of the number seven, then the data on bus X_7 are transferred to Z through the multiplexer. Up to 2^m data sources can be attached to the input data buses of the multiplexer, and one data destination can be attached to Z. Hence, as its name implies, the select bus S selects one of several data sources to be connected to a single destination; for this reason, a multiplexer is also called a (data) selector. Only one k-bit word can be transferred via a multiplexer at any time, since the Z bus must be shared by all the data sources. Bus sharing of this sort is known as time-division multiplexing, and is the origin of the name multiplexer.

The main multiplexer types found in the 7400 IC series are specified in Fig. 4.9. The 74150 multiplexer of Fig. 4.9a has 16 data inputs $x_0, x_1, \cdots, x_{15}$, and so requires a 4-bit select bus S. The data x_i transmitted through the 74150 are inverted, that is, $z = \bar{x}_i$, as indicated by the inversion circle on the data output line. The enable signal E is also inverted, and hence the multiplexer is enabled by $E = 0$ and disabled by $E = 1$; when disabled, z is forced to 1. The 74151 multiplexer of Fig. 4.9b has eight input data lines, and so employs three select lines. It provides the output data in both true and complemented form. The 74153 depicted in Fig. 4.9c has four input data buses, each 2 bits wide. In our terminology it is a four-input 2-bit multiplexer; it is also referred to as a dual 4-to-1 multiplexer. It has two enable lines, one for each half of the 2-bit data buses. The final multiplexer of Fig. 4.9, the 74157, was encountered earlier. It is a two-input 4-bit

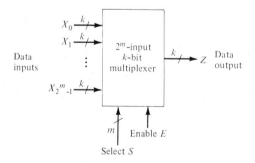

Figure 4.8 General 2^m-input k-bit multiplexer.

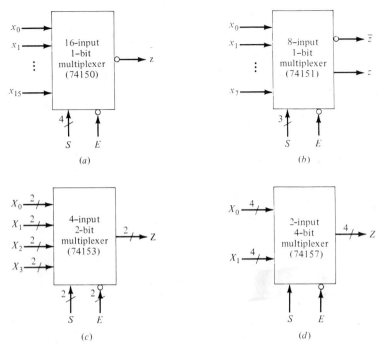

Figure 4.9 Some multiplexers from the 7400 series.

multiplexer, also known as a quad 2-to-1 multiplexer. The internal structure of the 74157 appears in Fig. 3.17; the logic design of the other multiplexer types is quite similar. Note that all the ICs of Fig. 4.9, except the 74150, require 16 pins; the 74150 requires 24.

A multiplexer is characterized by two major parameters: the number 2^m of input data buses available and the bus size k. 2^m may be termed the fan-in of the multiplexer. Both of these parameters may have to be modified to suit a particular application. The general 2^m-input k-bit multiplexer of Fig. 4.8 can be converted to an r-input s-bit multiplexer, where $r \leq 2^m$ or $s \leq k$, simply by not using unwanted input buses or unwanted lines within the data buses. Unused lines are tied to constant 0 or 1 values as recommended for the IC logic family being used. A large multiplexer can always be obtained by interconnecting several smaller multiplexers. For example, suppose that an r-input pk-bit multiplexer is to be designed from r-input k-bit multiplexers. This requires p copies of the r-input k-bit multiplexer. The corresponding k-bit data buses of all p component multiplexers are merged to form the desired pk-bit buses, and the corresponding S and E control lines are connected. Figure 4.10 demonstrates how three 74150 16-input 1-bit multiplexers are connected in this manner to yield a 16-input 3-bit multiplexer with inverted outputs.

Designing a multiplexer with a larger number of input data buses is slightly more difficult. Figure 4.11 shows a 32-input 1-bit multiplexer constructed from three smaller multiplexers. The 32 data sources are connected to the inputs of two 74150s, which select two of the data sources, namely, x_i and x_{i+16} where $s_3s_2s_1s_0$ denotes i, and connects them with inversion to lines y_0 and y_1 respectively. A third two-input multiplexer selects either

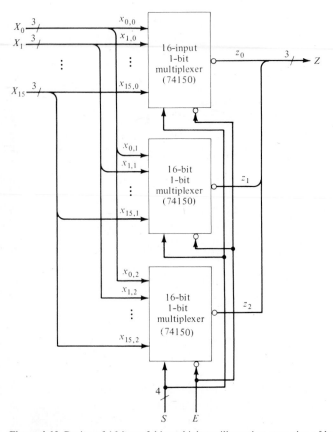

Figure 4.10 Design of 16-input 3-bit multiplexer illustrating expansion of bus size.

y_0 or y_1, as determined by the select signal s_4, and connects it to the primary output z. This multiplexer could consist of one quarter of a 74157 IC (Fig. 4.9d). Suppose, for instance, that it is desired to transfer data from x_{21} to z. Then the 5-bit select bus $S = s_4 s_3 s_2 s_1 s_0$ is set to $10101_2 = 21_{10}$. Since $s_3 s_2 s_1 s_0 = 0101_2 = 5_{10}$, the 74150s connect $\bar{x}_5$ and $\bar{x}_{5+16} = \bar{x}_{21}$ to y_0 and y_1 respectively. Now $s_4 = 1$ is applied to the select input of the output multiplexer, which selects y_1, and therefore transfers $\bar{x}_{21}$ from y_1 to z as required. The treelike structure of Fig. 4.11 can be generalized to handle any number of data inputs using any available multiplexer types as components. The data sources are connected to an input "column" of r_1 multiplexers, which select r_1 of the input data words. A subset of r_2 of these r_1 words is selected by a second column of multiplexers, and so on until a unique word is selected by the final multiplexer and transferred to the primary output bus. By combining the bus-width expansion technique of Fig. 4.10 with the bus-number expansion technique of Fig. 4.11, multiplexers of any size can readily be designed.

Besides their use for data selection or transfer, multiplexers can also serve as general-purpose Boolean function generators. Consider the 2^m-input 1-bit multiplexer in Fig. 4.12. For clarity, the data inputs have been renamed $c_0, c_1, \cdots, c_{2^m-1}$. Suppose that a

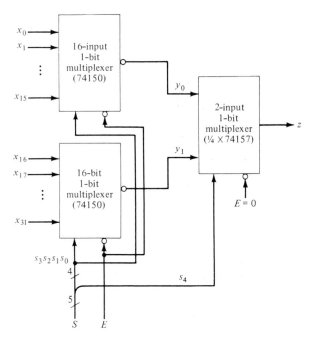

Figure 4.11 Design of a 32-input 1-bit multiplexer illustrating expansion of the number of input buses.

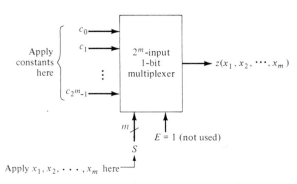

Figure 4.12 Use of a multiplexer as a Boolean function generator.

set of m Boolean variables $X = (x_1, x_2, \cdots, x_m)$ is applied to the m-line select bus $S = (s_{m-1}, s_{m-2}, \cdots, s_0)$, and the enable line E is set to 1. Then for each of the 2^m possible values of X, a different data value c_i is transferred to the multiplexer's output line z. The multiplexer is therefore producing a logic function $z(x_1, x_2, \cdots, x_m)$ whose values are specified as follows:

$$z(0, 0, \ldots, 0, 0) = c_0$$

$$z(0, 0, \ldots, 0, 1) = c_1$$

$$z(0, 0, \ldots, 1, 0) = c_2$$

$$\ldots$$

$$z(1, 1, \ldots, 1, 1) = c_{2^m-1}$$

Hence by connecting the c_i's to the appropriate constant values 0 and 1, the multiplexer can be made to realize any of the 2^{2^m} Boolean functions of m or fewer variables. A 1 is applied to c_i if m_i is a minterm of z; otherwise a 0 is applied to c_i. Consider, for example, the three-variable function

$$z_{XOR}(x_1, x_2, x_3) = x_1 \oplus x_2 \oplus x_3 \tag{4.6}$$

The values assumed by z_{XOR} are easily computed.

$$z_{XOR}(0, 0, 0) = 0 = c_0$$

$$z_{XOR}(0, 0, 1) = 1 = c_1$$

$$z_{XOR}(0, 1, 0) = 1 = c_2$$

$$z_{XOR}(0, 1, 1) = 0 = c_3$$

$$z_{XOR}(1, 0, 0) = 1 = c_4 \tag{4.7}$$

$$z_{XOR}(1, 0, 1) = 0 = c_5$$

$$z_{XOR}(1, 1, 0) = 0 = c_6$$

$$z_{XOR}(1, 1, 1) = 1 = c_7$$

Figure 4.13a shows a realization of this function using an eight-input 1-bit multiplexer.

An m-variable function can also be realized by a single 2^{m-1}-input 1-bit multiplexer if some input variable, say x_m, is available in both true and complemented form, and is applied to the data inputs of the multiplexer in addition to the constants 0 and 1. This

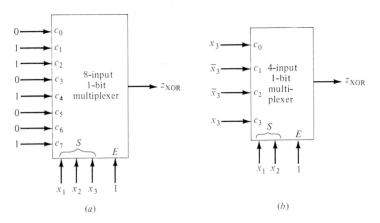

(a)

(b)

Figure 4.13 Realization of the three-variable function $z_{XOR}(x_1, x_2, x_3)$ using: (a) an eight-input multiplexer and (b) a four-input multiplexer.

scheme is illustrated in Fig. 4.13b, where the three-variable function $z_{XOR}(x_1, x_2, x_3)$ of (4.6) is implemented by a four-input multiplexer. Only the input variables x_1 and x_2 are applied to the multiplexer's select lines. Suppose that x_1 and x_2 are both set to 0. According to the first two rows of (4.7), if $x_3 = 0$, then $z_{XOR} = 0$, while if $x_3 = 1$, then $z_{XOR} = 1$. Hence when $(x_1, x_2) = (0, 0)$, $z_{XOR} = x_3$. Consequently, if x_3 is applied to the data input c_0 of the multiplexer, as shown in Fig. 4.13b, the behavior specified by the first two rows of (4.7) is obtained. Similarly, by applying $\bar{x}_3$ to data input c_1, the next two rows of (4.7) are realized, and so on. General rules for deciding which of the signals 0, 1 x_m or $\bar{x}_m$ to apply to each data input c_i can readily be deduced from this example (Prob. 4.6).

4.1.3 Decoders and Encoders

A general decoder circuit is depicted in Fig. 4.14. It has an m-bit input data bus $X = x_{m-1}x_{m-2} \cdots x_0$, and a 2^m-bit output data bus $Z = z_0z_1 \cdots z_{2^m-1}$. When the decoder is disabled $(E = 0)$, Z is forced to $00 \ldots 0$. When enabled $(E = 1)$, one specific output line z_i is set to 1, where i is the unsigned binary number represented by the bit pattern applied to X; all the remaining output lines are set to 0. Thus the decoder can be regarded as transforming data from ordinary m-bit binary number code to the format called 1-out-of-2^m code. For example, if $m = 3$ and $X = 101$, then the decoder produces the output word $Z = 00000100$, while if $X = 000$, the output becomes $Z = 10000000$. Decoders of this type are mainly used in the design of addressing circuits for memories and IO devices. In this application, the word X, which is termed an m-bit address, is intended to

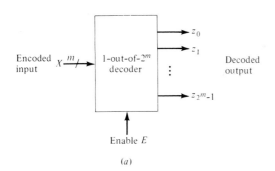

(a)

$x_{m-1}x_{m-2} \cdots x_1$ x_0				E	z_0 $z_1 \cdots z_{2^m-2}$ z_{2^m-1}			
d	d	d	d	0	0	0	0	0
0	0	0	0	1	1	0	0	0
0	0	0	1	1	0	1	0	0
		$\cdots$				$\cdots$		
1	1	1	0	1	0	0	1	0
1	1	1	1	1	0	0	0	1

(b)

Figure 4.14 General 1-out-of-2^m decoder: (*a*) symbol; (*b*) truth table.

select one out of up to 2^m memory or IO devices for a read or write operation. Each output z_i of the address decoder therefore must be attached to an appropriate input control line of the device to which the address number i has been assigned.

Figure 4.15 defines two representative decoder ICs found in the 7400 series. The 7445 of Fig. 4.15a is an example of a 1-out-of-10 decoder. It is frequently used to convert 4-bit BCD digits into 1-out-of-10 code for addressing IO devices like incandescent lamps, and so is also known as a *BCD-to-decimal decoder*. As indicated by the inversion bubbles, the 7445's output signals are active in the 0 (low) state. Hence when $X = 1000$ denoting the digit 8, the output $Z = 1111111101$ is produced, in which only z_8 is active. The 7445 has no enable input line; however, it is disabled ($Z = 1111111111$) by any of the six input combinations that does not represent a valid BCD digit. Note that if input line x_3 and output lines z_8 and z_9 are not used, the 7445 serves as a 1-out-of-8 decoder. A second commercial decoder circuit, the 74154 1-out-of-16 decoder, appears in Fig. 4.15b. Again the output signals are inverted, so that $Z = 11 \ldots 1$ denotes the disabled condition. The 74154 has two enable lines E_1 and E_2, which enable the decoder if and only if $E_1 = E_2 = 0$. The 7445 and 74154 require 16-pin and 24-pin packages, respectively.

Besides their applications in addressing circuits, decoders are also used for routing data from a common source to one of several destinations. Since this is the inverse of the data-routing operation performed by a multiplexer, it is called demultiplexing, and 1-out-of-n decoders are also termed n-output *demultiplexers*. Figure 4.16 shows the general 1-

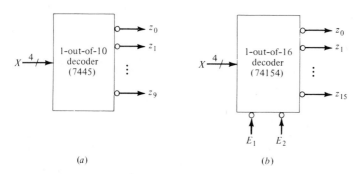

(a)   (b)

Figure 4.15 Two decoders from the 7400 series.

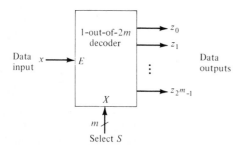

Figure 4.16 The 1-out-of-2^m decoder of Fig. 4.14 used as a 2^m-output demultiplexer.

out-of-2^m decoder from Fig. 4.14 in the role of a 2^m-output demultiplexer. The input data source x is now connected to the original enable input E, while the m original input address lines X are used as select control lines S as in a multiplexer. When S specifies the data destination address i, then $z_i = 1$ if $x = 1$, while $z_i = 0$ if $x = 0$, that is, $z_i = x$. In other words, the signal applied to input x is transferred to the output z_i, while all other output lines are held constant (at 0). A second enable line, such as is found in the 74154, can be used to enable the demultiplexing operation. Figure 4.17 shows a multiplexing–demultiplexing circuit that permits up to 16 different data signals to be transmitted over a common 1-bit data path. A 74150 16-input multiplexer selects one of 16 possible data sources, and a 74154 16-output demultiplexer (or 1-out-of-16 decoder) selects the corresponding data destination.

Decoders or demultiplexers can be expanded to handle larger numbers of IO lines in much the same way as multiplexers. Figure 4.18 demonstrates the treelike structure of large decoding circuits (cf. Fig. 4.11). Here the 32 output lines of a 1-out-of-32 decoder are obtained from two 74154s, each of which decodes the four low-order bits of the 5-bit input address word X. The high-order bit x_4 of X is supplied to a third 1-out-of-2 decoder whose output signals are used to enable the two 74154s. Suppose, for instance, that $X = 11101 = 29_{10}$, indicating that output z_{29} should be activated. Since $x_4 = 1$, the 1-out-of-2 decoder disables the upper 74154 ($y_0 = 1$) and enables the lower 74154 ($y_1 = 0$). The input combination $x_3x_2x_1x_0 = 1101 = 13_{10}$ applied to the lower 74154 causes its 13th output line, namely, $z_{13+16} = z_{29}$, to be activated; the remaining 31 outputs of the decoder are deactivated.

The name encoder is applied to a circuit having up to 2^m main inputs and m outputs, such that when one input x_i is active, the m-bit binary pattern representing the number i appears on the output bus. Hence an encoder generates the address i of an active input line x_i, in contrast with a decoder, which uses the address i to activate an output line z_i. Since there is nothing to prevent several input lines of an encoder from being activated simultaneously, encoding circuits are normally designed to respond to only one active input signal. This is done by assigning fixed priority values to the input lines, and designing the encoder, usually called a *priority encoder*, so that only the address of the active input with the highest priority is generated at any time. The overall structure and

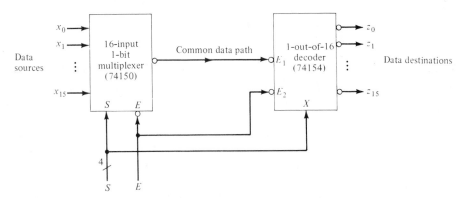

Figure 4.17 Circuit for data transmission between 16 source-destination pairs via time-division multiplexing.

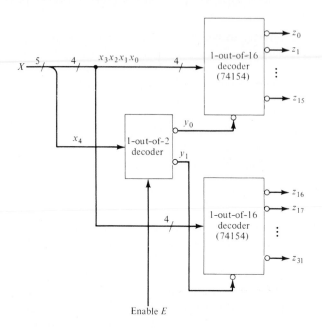

Figure 4.18 Design of a 1-out-of-32 decoding circuit illustrating decoder expansion.

behavior of a 2^m-input priority encoder is described in Fig. 4.19. Input x_i is assigned higher priority than x_j if $i > j$; consequently x_{2^m-1} has the highest priority, while x_0 has the lowest. The encoder's output Z is therefore set to the largest number i such that x_i is active. When all the input lines are inactive, the special output signal I (input inactive) is set to 1; otherwise I is held at 0.

Two priority encoders from the 7400 series are depicted in Fig. 4.20. The 74147 is a 10-input four-output priority encoder, which is the counterpart of the 7445 1-out-of-10 decoder of Fig. 4.15a. The 74147 actually has only nine input lines $x_1, x_2, \cdots, x_9$. If one or more of these lines is active, the address of the active line of highest priority is placed on the output bus Z. Note that all the IO lines of the 74147 are active in the 0 state. Suppose, for example, that $X = 111111100$, implying that x_8 and x_9 are active. Then the pattern 0110, which is the inverted form of $1001_2 = 9_{10}$, is produced on Z, since x_9 has a higher priority than x_8. When none of the 74147's input lines is active, which can be interpreted as the active condition for the missing x_0 line, the output is set to 1111. The 74158 of Fig. 4.20b is an eight-input priority encoder with a full complement of data and control lines. The input control line E enables the encoder in the normal fashion. The output control line I denotes inactive inputs; it is activated ($I = 0$) whenever all the input data lines are inactive, that is, $X = 11111111$ and $E = 0$. A second output control line G is useful for increasing the encoder size. It is activated ($G = 0$) only when there is at least one active input (implying that $I = 0$), and the encoder is enabled (implying that $E = 0$). Hence we can write $G = I \lor E$.

Encoders are more difficult to expand than most MSI components. Figure 4.21 shows one way of making a 16-input priority encoder from two copies of the 74148. Four

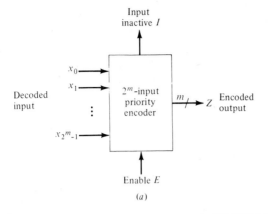

x_0	x_1	x_2	$\cdots$	x_{2^m-2}	x_{2^m-1}	E	z_{m-1}	z_{m-2}	$\cdots$	z_1	z_0	I
d	d	d		d	d	0	0	0		0	0	0
0	0	0		0	0	1	0	0		0	0	1
1	0	0		0	0	1	0	0		0	0	0
d	1	0		0	0	1	0	0		0	1	0
d	d	1		0	0	1	0	0		1	0	0
		$\cdots$						$\cdots$				
d	d	d		1	0	1	1	1		1	0	0
d	d	d		d	1	1	1	1		1	1	0

(b)

Figure 4.19 General 2^m-input priority decoder: (a) symbol; (b) truth table.

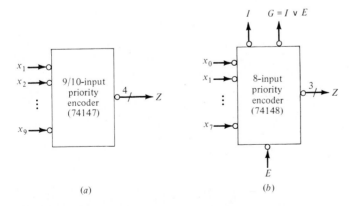

Figure 4.20 Two priority encoders from the 7400 series.

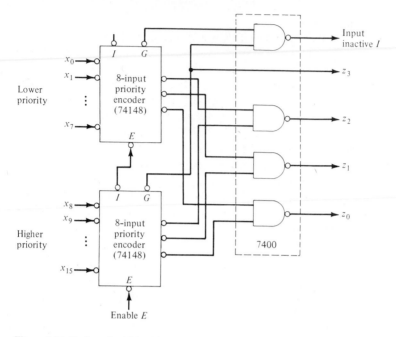

Figure 4.21 Design of a 16-input priority encoder.

additional gates are also needed, which can be obtained from a 7400 quad two-input NAND IC. Basically the two 74148s are connected in series via their I and E control lines. The higher-priority 74148 with the data inputs $x_8, x_9, \cdots, x_{15}$ disables the lower-priority 74148 when any one of the input lines to the former is active. The Z output signals of the two 74148s are merged via three NAND gates to yield the three low-order bits $z_2 z_1 z_0$ of the final output address; the fourth bit z_3 is obtained from the G output signal of the higher-priority 74148. A fourth NAND gate combines the G signals from the two 74148s to yield the input inactive indicator signal I for the 16-input encoder.

4.1.4 Arithmetic Circuits

Certain basic arithmetic functions can be implemented directly by combinational MSI circuits. Chip density and package pin restrictions limit the data types that can be processed by these circuits to short (1 to 4 bits) fixed-point numbers. The number codes most commonly used include unsigned binary and twos-complement; only these two cases will be considered here. Integrated-circuit complexity considerations also restrict the types of operations performed to addition, subtraction, and some associated functions. General multiplication and division can be implemented directly by combinational ICs in the LSI/VLSI range. Alternatively networks of MSI components can be designed to perform these operations according to various sequential algorithms.

Binary addition, which was introduced in Sec. 3.1, is perhaps the most fundamental arithmetic function. Adder circuits are generally designed to add two unsigned n-bit binary numbers producing an n-bit sum. Because of the manner in which the sign bit is defined for TC numbers, a standard adder can also add two TC numbers directly to obtain the proper TC sum. As discussed earlier (see Fig. 4.6), an adder can be used with only minor modification for TC subtraction also.

Figure 4.22a shows a simple adder IC from the 7400 series, the 7482 2-bit binary adder. It is composed of two 1-bit full adder stages of the standard kind defined in Fig. 3.38, which are connected in series or cascade as depicted in Fig. 4.22b. The carry-out signal from the low-order (rightmost) stage is applied to the carry-in line of the high-order stage, thus providing ripple-carry propagation between the stages. n copies of the 7482 can be cascaded in similar fashion via their carry-in/out lines to construct a $2n$-bit ripple-carry adder. While numbers of arbitrary length can be added by such circuits, the maximum addition time increases with n. This follows from the fact that a signal change affecting the high-order (leftmost) carry-out bit must propagate via the longest possible path through all stages of the adder.

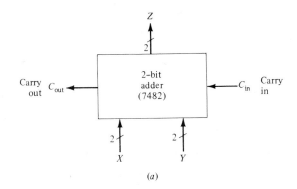

(a)

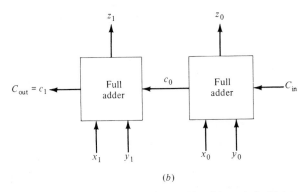

(b)

Figure 4.22 The 7482 2-input binary adder: (a) symbol; (b) internal structure illustrating ripple-carry propagation.

Faster addition can be achieved at the expense of more circuitry by replacing ripple-carry propagation by another technique called carry lookahead. Carry lookahead is employed in the internal design of the 74283, a 4-bit adder circuit that was encountered in Chap. 3. Figure 4.23a shows the IO connections of the 74283, and a somewhat simplified view of its internal structure appears in Fig. 4.23b. The 74283 contains four 1-bit adder stages $S_0:S_3$, each of which approximates a full adder without the carry-out line. S_i adds the data bits x_i, y_i and the carry-in bit c_i to produce a sum bit z_i. The distinguishing feature

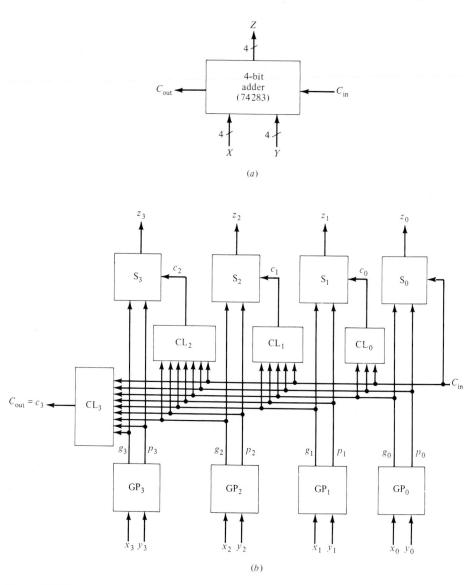

Figure 4.23 The 74283 4-bit binary adder: (a) symbol; (b) internal structure illustrating carry lookahead.

of the carry-lookahead approach is the method used to generate the c_i signals. For each S_i there is an associated subcircuit GP_i which produces two signals g_i and p_i called *generate* and *propagate*, respectively, and defined as follows.

$$g_i = x_i \wedge y_i$$
$$p_i = x_i \vee y_i$$

(4.8)

Now the ith carry-out signal c_i is defined by the usual carry equation:

$$c_i = (x_i \wedge y_i) \vee (x_i \wedge c_{i-1}) \vee (y_i \wedge c_{i-1})$$

Substituting from (4.8), we can rewrite this equation thus:

$$c_i = g_i \vee (p_i \wedge c_{i-1})$$

(4.9)

Applying Eq. (4.9) to the rightmost two stages of Fig. 4.23b yields

$$c_0 = g_0 \vee (p_0 \wedge C_{in})$$

(4.10)

and

$$c_1 = g_1 \vee (p_1 \wedge c_0)$$

(4.11)

Now if (4.10) is substituted into (4.11) we obtain

$$c_1 = g_1 \vee (p_1 \wedge g_0) \vee (p_1 \wedge p_0 \wedge C_{in})$$

Continuing, we can obtain sum-of-products expressions for all the c_i's in terms of the g_i's, the p_i's and C_{in}.

$$c_0 = g_0 \vee (p_0 \wedge C_{in})$$
$$c_1 = g_1 \vee (p_1 \wedge g_0) \vee (p_1 \wedge p_0 \wedge C_{in})$$
$$c_2 = g_2 \vee (p_2 \wedge g_1) \vee (p_2 \wedge p_1 \wedge g_0) \vee (p_2 \wedge p_1 \wedge p_0 \wedge C_{in})$$
$$C_{out} = c_3 = g_3 \vee (p_3 \wedge g_2) \vee (p_3 \wedge p_2 \wedge g_1) \vee (p_3 \wedge p_2 \wedge p_1 \wedge g_0)$$
$$\vee (p_3 \wedge p_2 \wedge p_1 \wedge p_0 \wedge C_{in})$$

(4.12)

The carry signals $c_0{:}c_3$ are generated by the carry-lookahead subcircuits $CL_0{:}CL_3$ in Fig. 4.23b. Carry-lookahead addition of this type therefore allows all c_i's to be computed simultaneously. In a ripple-carry adder, on the other hand, c_i must be generated before c_{i+1} can be determined. The interested reader can easily map Fig. 4.23b directly onto the gate-level logic design of the 74283 given earlier (Fig. 3.19).

In arithmetic processors it is often necessary to be able to compare the magnitudes of two numbers. For this purpose an IC such as the 7485 4-bit magnitude comparator of Fig. 4.24 is very useful. It is designed to compare two numbers A and B, which may be either 4-bit unsigned binary numbers or BCD digits, and activate one of three output signals $F = f_0 f_1 f_2$ indicating the conditions $A < B$, $A = B$, and $A > B$ respectively. The 7485 has three extra input lines $E = e_0 e_1 e_2$, which are used for expansion to deal with larger numbers. $4n$-bit numbers may be compared by n copies of the 7485 that are connected in series, with the F outputs of each 7485 connected to the corresponding E inputs of the 7485 handling the next 4 most significant bits. The 7485 comparing the most significant

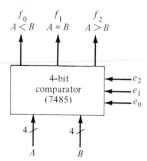

Figure 4.24 The 7485 4-bit magnitude comparator.

bits provides the final F outputs of the circuit. Figure 4.25 illustrates the design of a 12-bit comparator along these lines.

The more useful arithmetic and logic functions can be combined into a single multifunction IC called an arithmetic-logic unit (ALU). Two ALU circuits from the 7400 series are illustrated in Fig. 4.26; these ICs are designed to process 4-bit words representing either numbers or nonnumerical (logical) data. The 74181 can perform 16 arithmetic functions, including addition, subtraction, and magnitude comparison, and 16 digital operations including the AND, OR, NAND, NOR, and EXCLUSIVE-OR word-gate operations. A 5-bit control bus S selects the operation to be carried out by the 74181 at any time. The 74381 is a simplified version of the 74181. It has a repertoire of eight arithmetic-logic operations, which are defined in Fig. 4.26c. The operations include addition, two forms of subtraction, three standard logical operations, and two operations that set the 74381's main output data bus Z to 0000 or 1111.

Expansion of ALU circuits to accommodate larger data words is fairly straightforward. The 74181 is equipped with a pair of carry lines C_{in} and C_{out}. By cascading these lines as shown in Fig. 4.27a, the 74181's arithmetic operations can be extended to words of arbitrary size. The C_{in} and C_{out} lines propagate carry signals between adjacent copies of the 74181 during addition; they also propagate borrow signals during subtraction. Note

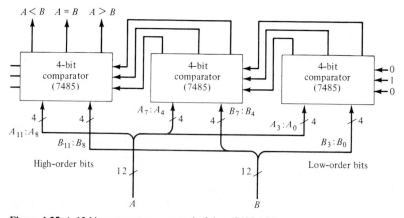

Figure 4.25 A 12-bit comparator composed of three 7485 4-bit comparators.

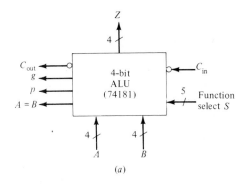

(a)

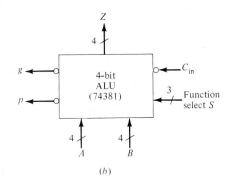

(b)

Function Select			
s_1	s_1	s_0	Function to be Performed
0	0	0	$Z := 0000$ (clear)
0	0	1	$Z := B - A$ (subtraction)
0	1	0	$Z := A - B$ (subtraction)
0	1	1	$Z := A + B$ (addition)
1	0	0	$Z := A \oplus B$ (exclusive-or)
1	0	1	$Z := A \vee B$ (or)
1	1	0	$Z := A \wedge B$ (and)
1	1	1	$Z := 1111$ (preset)

(c)

Figure 4.26 Two 4-bit ALU circuits from the 7400 series: (a) the 74181; (b) the 74381; (c) functions performed by the 74381.

that no connections between stages are needed for logical operations. The carry interconnection scheme of Fig. 4.27a is basically the ripple-carry propagation scheme used in the adder of Fig. 4.22b. It suffers from the same drawback, namely computation time for arithmetic operations increases with the data word size. To permit faster arithmetic operations, both the 74181 and the 74381 have provisions for implementing carry lookahead; indeed, this is the only type of carry generation allowed by the 74381. Each ALU produces the generate and propagate signals g and p needed to compute the interstage carry signals $c_3, c_7, \cdots$ according to Eqs. (4.12). An auxiliary circuit called a

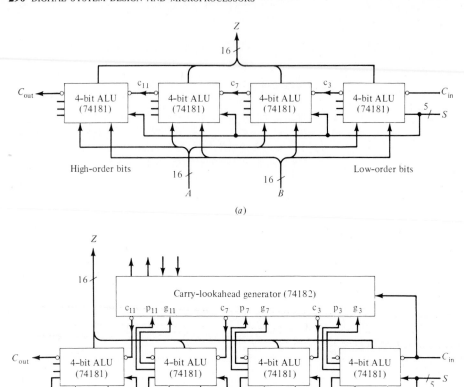

Figure 4.27 A 16-bit ALU circuit using (*a*) ripple carry; (*b*) carry lookahead.

carry-lookahead generator is required for the carry computations. The 7400 series contains the 74182 carry-lookahead generator IC, which generates three carry signals via a two-level combinational circuit implementing the first three equations of (4.12) with the subscripts 0, 1 and 2 replaced by 3, 7 and 11 respectively. Figure 4.27b shows a 16-bit ALU that uses carry lookahead. It is composed of four 74181 ALU ICs and a 74182 carry-lookahead generator. The g and p outputs of the 74181s are supplied to the 74182, which provides the carry-in signals for the three high-order stages of the ALU. A similar design can be used for word-size expansion with the 74381 ALU chip. The magnitude comparison output $A = B$ of the 74181 is designed so that the corresponding $A = B$ lines from all stages can be wired together to form wired-ANDs, as indicated in Fig. 4.27b.

4.1.5 Latches and Registers

The basic sequential circuits found at the MSI level are multibit latches and registers used for word storage. *Multibit latches* are composed of single 1-bit clocked or unclocked latches, whose timing characteristics they reflect. Latches are suitable for storage applications where there is no direct feedback from the outputs to the inputs of the latches. Where such feedback is present, registers, which are composed of flip-flops rather than latches, should be used. Unlike a latch, a register allows its present contents or state to be read while new data are being written into it. The behavioral differences between simple latches and flip-flops were examined in detail in Chap. 3; we will mainly be concerned with registers rather than multibit latches here.

Figure 4.28 shows the structure of a typical 8-bit latch, the 74100 D-type latch. It is composed of eight D latches, which are divided into two groups of four latches with a separate clock line for each group. By externally connecting these clock lines, a common

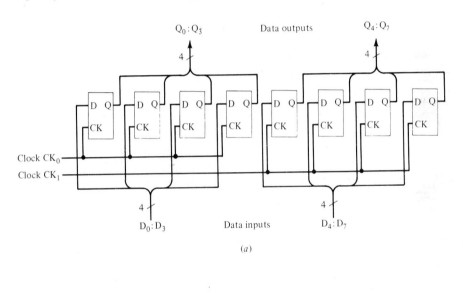

(a)

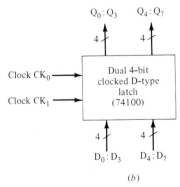

(b)

Figure 4.28 Typical MSI latch (74100) composed of eight clocked D latches: (a) logic circuit; (b) symbol.

clock signal can be applied to all eight latches. To minimize pin requirements, only the true or Q output of each D latch is externally accessible. Figure 4.29 shows a very similar 8-bit register from the 7400 series, the 74273 D-type register with clear. It contains eight positive edge-triggered D flip-flops with common clock and clear lines. Again only the Q and not the $\overline{Q}$ outputs of the flip-flops are available. Expansion of latches and registers to accommodate larger word sizes is a rather trivial process. It is illustrated by Fig. 4.6b where four 7474 2-bit registers are used to construct an 8-bit register. Only the control lines of the individual flip-flops, in this case the clock and clear lines, need to be connected to common signals in the obvious fashion.

In general an n-bit register is a set of n associated flip-flops. Registers are most often constructed from edge-triggered D flip-flops, as in Fig. 4.29, but other flip-flop types, such as level- or edge-triggered JK flip-flops, are also used. D flip-flops have the advantage of requiring only one input data line per stored bit, whereas JK flip-flops require two. Unless otherwise specified, the data input and output lines of an n-bit register R are assumed to be independent, allowing all bits of an n-bit word to be

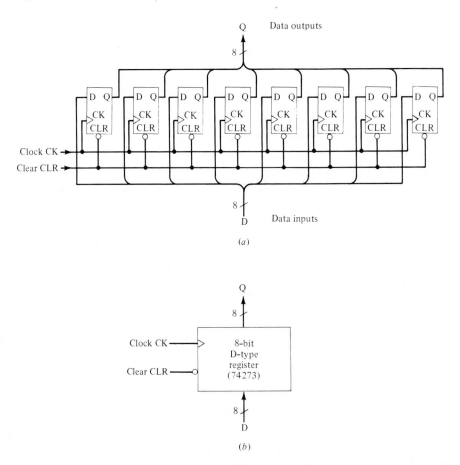

Figure 4.29 Typical parallel register (74273) composed of eight D flip-flops: (*a*) logic circuit; (*b*) symbol.

transferred to or from R simultaneously or in parallel, that is, in one clock cycle. This mode of data transfer is called *parallel IO*, in contrast with the *serial IO* mode of data transfer found in shift registers. Therefore R is sometimes called a parallel register, since it uses parallel IO exclusively. While the flip-flops of R have separate parallel data lines, they normally share the clock, clear, and preset control lines.

Like the parallel register R, a shift register SR is composed of a set of flip-flops. The flip-flops of SR are connected in series via their data lines to form a cascade of flip-flops F_0, F_1, $\cdots$, F_{n-1}. External access is provided to the leftmost and rightmost flip-flops F_0 and F_{n-1}. When appropriate control signals are activated, the stored data or state $Y = y_0$, $y_1, \cdots, y_{n-1}$ of SR is shifted one position either to the left or right. A left-shift operation transforms the contents of SR as follows:

$$y_1, y_2, \cdots, y_{n-1}, x := y_0, y_1, \cdots, y_{n-2}, y_{n-1} \qquad (4.13)$$

where x denotes a new data bit written into the rightmost flip-flop F_{n-1}. The old contents y_0 of the leftmost flip-flop F_0 are transferred out of SR to be stored in an external device or discarded. Similarly, a right-shift operation can be described by the following transformation:

$$x, y_0, \ldots, y_{n-3}, y_{n-2} := y_0, y_1, \ldots, y_{n-2}, y_{n-1} \qquad (4.14)$$

Shift registers are distinguished from parallel registers by their use of serial or bit-by-bit data transfer to or from external devices. A shift register may also allow parallel IO transfer, however. This gives rise to four possibilities: parallel-in, parallel-out, serial-in, and serial-out connections, which may be present in a shift register in various combinations. With parallel in/out connections a shift register can be used for data conversion from serial to parallel form, or vice versa; this is a major application of shift registers in digital systems.

The 7491 8-bit shift register studied earlier (Fig. 3.34), and shown again in symbolic form in Fig. 4.30a, is of the basic serial-in serial-out type. When the 7491 is clocked, a right shift takes place, causing the input data bit $A \wedge B$ to be loaded into the leftmost flip-flop, while the contents of the rightmost flip-flop are shifted out of the shift register in both true and complemented form. Figure 4.30 also lists some other representative shift registers from the 7400 series. The 74164 8-bit shift register of Fig. 4.30b is essentially the same as the 7491 with the addition of external connections to the Q signals of all flip-flops; a clear line has also been added. The internal state of the 74164 therefore is continuously available on its 8-bit output data bus Z, which constitutes a parallel output connection. The 74164 is consequently classified as a serial-in parallel-out shift register. Note that the output z_7 of the rightmost flip-flop also serves as an implicit serial data output line, if required. The 74165 IC depicted in Fig. 4.30c is an example of an 8-bit shift register with parallel-in and serial-out data transfer modes. When the load control line LD is inactive (LD = 1), the 74165 behaves like a basic serial-in serial-out shift register, with A, Q, and $\overline{Q}$ acting as the data IO lines. When the load line LD is set to 0, the data on the 8-bit input bus X are loaded in parallel into the shift register thereby completely redefining the state of the circuit. This parallel load operation is asynchronous, and is unaffected by the states of the clock CK or the serial data input line

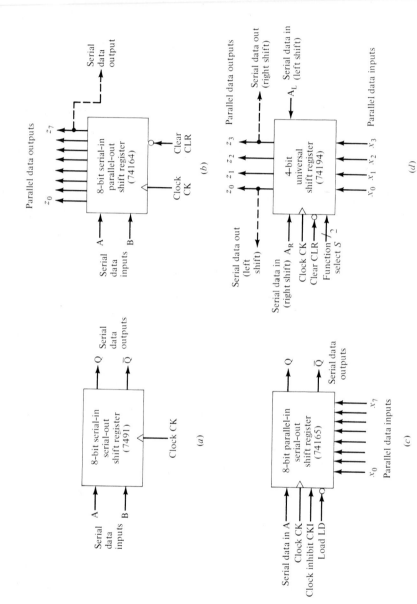

Figure 4.30 Some shift registers from the 7400 series.

294

A. The 74165 has a control line CKI called clock inhibit, which can be used to override the clock CK, thereby preventing shifting from taking place.

Figure 4.30d illustrates a very general type of shift register, which has all types of serial and parallel IO connections, and also allows shifting in both the left and right directions. This is the 74194 4-bit bidirectional parallel-in parallel-out shift register; it is called a *universal shift register* in IC manufacturers' data books. A 2-bit function select bus $S = s_1 s_0$ determines the IO data transfer mode to be used. When $S = 11$ data are loaded in parallel into the 74194 from the input data bus X; this load operation is synchronized with the next clock pulse. Parallel data output capability is provided continuously via the bus $Z = z_0 z_1 z_2 z_3$. When $S = 01$, the 74194 acts as a right-shift register with A_R as the serial input and z_3 as the serial output data lines. Changing S to 10 converts the 74194 into a left-shift register with A_L and z_0 serving as the serial data input and output lines respectively. The timing of the left and right shifts is controlled by the clock signal CK in the standard fashion. A clear line CLR allows the shift register to be asynchronously reset to the 0000 state. Figure 4.31 contains a 12-bit shift register constructed from three 74194s. The circuit is configured as a serial-in parallel-out shift register, making it suitable for converting a serial data stream into a parallel stream of 12-bit words.

4.1.6. Counters

Like shift registers, counters are composed primarily of flip-flops with a small amount of added combinational logic. The IO connections and state behavior of a general n-bit counter are given in Fig. 4.32. It contains n flip-flops that define the internal state of the counter; this state is made available externally via the n-bit data bus $Z = z_{n-1} z_{n-2} \cdots z_0$. Z is termed the count, and is normally treated as an unsigned binary number, although other number codes are sometimes used. The main control input of the counter is the count-in

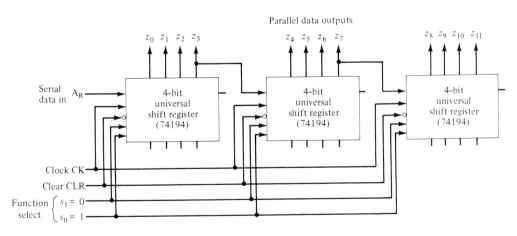

Figure 4.31 A 12-bit serial-in parallel-out right-shift register.

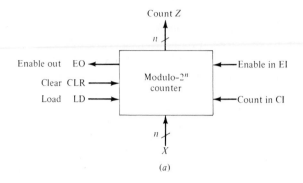

CLR	LD	EI	CI	z_{n-1}	z_{n-2}	$\cdots$	z_1	z_0	EO	z_{n-1}	z_{n-2}	$\cdots$	z_1	z_0
1	0	d	d	d	d		d	d	0	0	0		0	0
0	1	d	d	d	d		d	d	0	x_{n-1}	x_{n-2}		x_1	x_0
0	0	0	d	z_{n-1}	z_{n-2}		z_1	z_0	0	z_{n-1}	z_{n-2}		z_1	z_0
0	0	d	0	z_{n-1}	z_{n-2}		z_1	z_0	0	z_{n-1}	z_{n-2}		z_1	z_0
0	0	1	1	0	0		0	0	0	0	0		0	1
0	0	1	1	0	0		0	1	0	0	0		1	0
0	0	1	1	0	0		1	0	0	0	0		1	1
					$\cdots$						$\cdots$			
0	0	1	1	1	1		0	1	0	1	1		1	0
0	0	1	1	1	1		1	0	1	1	1		1	1
0	0	1	1	1	1		1	1	0	0	0		0	0

(b)

Figure 4.32 Modulo-2^n binary counter: (a) symbol; (b) state table.

line CI. When the counter is enabled (by setting the enable in line EI to 1), a pulse on CI causes the transformation

$$Z := Z + 1;$$

that is, it increments the count by one. Since CI triggers a single state change in the counter, it is also called the clock signal. A sequence of pulses on CI makes the counter pass through a sequence of states $Z = 0, 1, 2, \ldots$, and hence the counter effectively counts the number of pulses applied to its CI line. Eventually Z reaches a maximum value, after which it returns to zero. The number of different count values M assumed by Z is the modulus of the counter, and the counter itself is called a *modulo-M counter*.

In the counter of Fig. 4.32 the modulus M is 2^n, and the values of Z range from zero to $2^n - 1$ in the standard binary counting sequence. 2^n is clearly the maximum possible modulus for an n-bit counter. For example, a 4-bit counter can have a maximum modulus of 16, in which case it behaves as follows:

CI pulse no.:　　1 2 3 ... 14 15 16 17 18 ...
　Count Z:　0 1 2 3 ... 14 15　0　1　2 ...

Note that at any time the count Z is equal to the remainder obtained by dividing the number of CI pulses received since initialization by the modulus M; modulo-M counters are therefore sometimes known as *divide-by-M* counters. Four-bit counters are frequently designed with 10 as their modulus, in which case they are referred to as *decade counters*. Decade or modulo-10 counters are useful in the design of control circuits for decimal (BCD) data processing.

The counter of Fig. 4.32 can be initialized to the zero state $00 \ldots 0$ by activating its clear line CLR in the usual fashion. In addition, the data on the n-bit input bus $X = x_{n-1}x_{n-2} \ldots x_0$ can be loaded in parallel into the counter under control of the load line LD, thereby initializing the counter to any desired state X. The output enable line EO is activated only when the maximum count $M - 1$ is reached. The enable lines EI and EO are intended to simplify the design of larger counters, an issue to be addressed later.

Counter circuits fall into two main groups: *asynchronous* or *ripple counters*, in which the state variables $z_{n-1}z_{n-2} \cdots z_0$ may change at different times in response to pulses on CI, and *synchronous counters*, in which CI serves as a clock signal, causing all state variables to change simultaneously. Asynchronous counters use very little logic, but their untimed output signal changes make them less suitable for some digital systems than the synchronous type. Figure 4.33a shows a 4-bit asynchronous counter consisting of four JK flip-flops. Each flip-flop has its J and K inputs connected permanently to 1, so that when the flip-flop is clocked (by a 0-to-1 transition of its clock input CK), it always changes state or toggles. Thus a pulse applied to the counter's count in line CI causes the output z_0 of the rightmost flip-flop to change from 0 to 1; a second CI pulse changes z_0 from 1 back to 0, and so on. z_0 in turn is used to toggle the state of the second flip-flop, whose output z_1 therefore changes state in response to every second pulse applied to CI. Similarly the output z_2 and z_3 of the third and fourth flip-flop stages change state in response to every fourth and eighth CI pulse respectively. Hence the count $Z = z_3z_2z_1z_0$ passes through all 16 possible 4-bit states in the normal binary counting sequence thus:

$$
\begin{array}{cccc}
z_3 & z_2 & z_1 & z_0 \\
0 & 0 & 0 & 0 \\
0 & 0 & 0 & 1 \\
0 & 0 & 1 & 0 \\
0 & 0 & 1 & 1 \\
 & \cdot & \cdot & \cdot \\
1 & 1 & 1 & 0 \\
1 & 1 & 1 & 1
\end{array}
\tag{4.15}
$$

When $Z = 1111$ the next count pulse changes Z to 0000; this therefore is a modulo-16 asynchronous counter. Only the clock input of the rightmost flip-flop is connected directly to CI; the clock pulses controlling the remaining flip-flops must ripple asynchronously through the counter from right to left, thereby allowing the z_i's to change at different times.

Figure 4.33b shows a representative synchronous counter, which is also constructed from four JK flip-flops. CI is connected directly to the clock input CK of each flip-flop, allowing them all to change state simultaneously. The toggling of the flip-flop that produces output z_i is controlled by the signal $z_{i-1} \wedge z_{i-2} \wedge \cdots \wedge z_0$, which is generated by an i-input AND gate, so that z_i changes value only if $z_{i-1}z_{i-2} \cdots z_0 = 11 \cdots 1$. Consequently

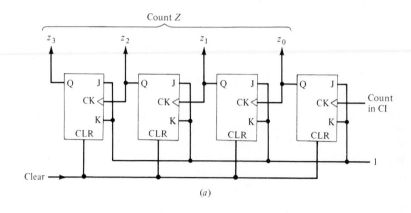

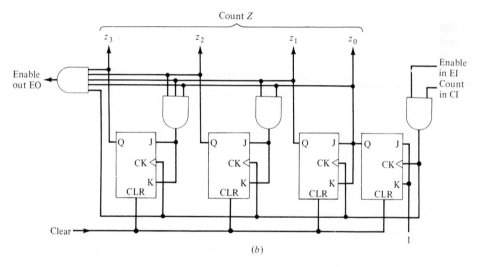

Figure 4.33 (a) Asynchronous and (b) synchronous modulo-16 counters.

the normal binary counting sequence (4.15) is again produced on Z, implying that the circuit of Fig. 4.33b is a synchronous modulo-16 counter. This circuit also illustrates the logic associated with the enable signals EI and EO.

The logic design of some other kinds of counters was examined in Chap. 3. The Johnson counter of Fig. 3.48, which is a slightly modified shift register, is a synchronous modulo-8 counter that produces a nonstandard 4-bit count sequence. Figures 3.78 and 3.82 define a modulo-4 up-down counter that is doubly synchronous because of the presence of a clock input in addition to the count-in line COUNT. In the up mode (DOWN = 0), this counter is a normal modulo-4 binary counter that behaves as follows:

$$\text{Count-in pulse no.:} \quad 1 \ 2 \ 3 \ 4 \ 5 \ 6 \ \ldots$$
$$\text{Count } Z: \quad 0 \ 1 \ 2 \ 3 \ 0 \ 1 \ 2 \ \ldots$$

In the down mode, however, it counts down modulo-4 thus:

$$\text{Count-in pulse no.:} \quad 1\ 2\ 3\ 4\ 5\ 6\ \ldots$$
$$\text{Count } Z:\quad 0\ 3\ 2\ 1\ 0\ 3\ 2\ \ldots$$

Figure 4.34 demonstrates how the enable lines EI and EO are used in counter expansion. Here three modulo-2^n counter stages S_2, S_1, and S_0 are interconnected to form a modulo-2^{3n} counter. The EI line of each stage S_i, except the rightmost stage, is connected to the EO line of the preceding stage S_{i-1}. As indicated in Fig. 4.32b, this EO signal remains at 0 until the maximum count $11 \ldots 1$ is reached by S_{i-1}. The next CI pulse changes EO to 1, thereby activating the EI line of S_i and allowing the count of S_i to be incremented by 1; at the same time S_{i-1} is reset to the $00 \ldots 0$ state. Note that EO is acting as a carry-out signal, so that the counter interconnection scheme of Fig. 4.34 closely resembles ripple-carry propagation (cf. Figs. 4.22b and 4.27a).

The modulus of a given counter can easily be changed by means of the scheme depicted in Fig. 4.35. The enable-out signal EO is used to initialize the counter by activating the load control LD when the maximum count $M - 1$ is reached. If the binary

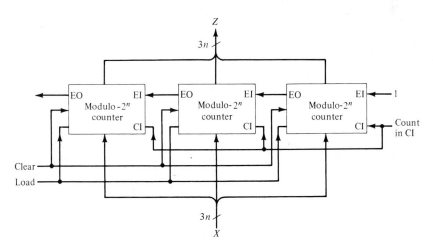

Figure 4.34 Modulo-2^{3n} counter illustrating counter expansion.

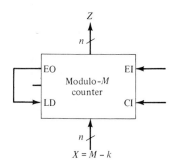

Figure 4.35 Conversion of a modulo-M counter to a modulo-k counter ($k \le M$).

number representing $M - k$ is applied to the input data bus X, then the counter is forced to behave as follows:

CI pulse no.:   1   2   ... $k-1$ k $k+1$

    Count Z: $M-k$ $M-k+1$ $M-k+2$ ... $M-1$ $M-k$ $M-k+1$ ...

Thus the counter generates a fixed sequence of k count values, effectively reducing its modulus from M to k.

A large number of different counter ICs, both synchronous and asynchronous, can be found in the 7400 series. Two examples of synchronous 4-bit counters from this series appear in Fig. 4.36. The 74163 is a modulo-16 counter providing all the functions of the general counter of Fig. 4.32. It has two enable-in lines EIP and EIT, which, with a slightly different definition of enable out EO, allow high-speed multistage counters to be built that employ a type of carry lookahead (see Prob. 4.26). Figure 4.36b shows the 74169, which is an up-down version of the 74163. When the control line UP is set to 1, the 74169 increments the count Z as in the 74163. When UP $= 0$, the 74169 decrements Z each time a count pulse is received, and therefore acts as a down counter. The symbols of Fig. 4.36a and 4.36b also apply to a pair of decade (modulo-10) counters, the 74160 (up) counter and the 74168 up-down counter respectively.

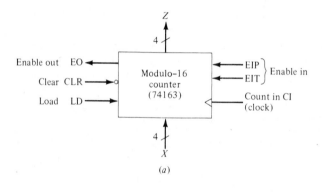

(a)

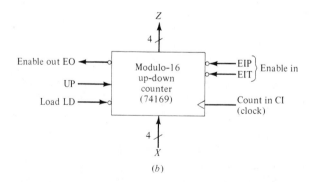

(b)

Figure 4.36 Two 4-bit synchronous counters from the 7400 series.

4.2 REGISTER-TRANSFER DESIGN

The organization and design of digital systems at the MSI or register-transfer level are considered next. The use of register-transfer languages or RTLs for describing such systems is examined. System design at this complexity level is discussed using a binary multiplier circuit as an example.

4.2.1 System Organization

The basic units of information in a register-transfer circuit are multibit words of various sizes. Registers play a central role in the operation of such circuits, because they are used to store words that are undergoing processing. A typical register-transfer operation involves the following steps.

1. Select and, if necessary, fetch or read the words stored in a set of registers R_1, R_2, $\cdots$, R_k. These words, which may also be denoted by R_1, R_2, $\cdots$, R_k are the input operands of the operation.
2. Transform the words R_1, R_2, $\cdots$, R_k via appropriate (combinational) circuits such as multiplexers, decoders, or ALUs, to produce one or more output operands or results. A result may be denoted by $F(R_1, R_2, \cdots, R_k)$, where F denotes the overall function or transformation carried out in this step.
3. Store or write the results into one or more registers, which may include original registers R_1, R_2, $\cdots$, R_k.

The foregoing operation is normally carried out during one (machine) cycle of the clock signal that controls all the registers of the system. When a single result word is generated, the register-transfer operation can be concisely described by a statement of the form

$$S := F(R_1, R_2, \cdots, R_k); \tag{4.16}$$

where S denotes the result and the register that stores it. When a set of m results is generated during one clock cycle, the operations performed can be described by a compound RTL statement as follows:

$$S_1 := F_1(R_1, R_2, \cdots, R_k),$$

$$S_2 := F_2(R_1, R_2, \cdots, R_k),$$

$$\cdots$$

$$S_m := F_m(R_1, R_2, \cdots, R_k); \tag{4.17}$$

Hence commas separate the various register-transfer operations occuring in parallel during a clock cycle, while a semicolon marks the end of the cycle. Complex multicycle operations are described by a sequence of RTL statements like (4.16) and (4.17).

To implement a set of register-transfer operations, MSI components of four types may be needed:

1. Word-storage devices such as registers and latches; note that the use of latches is restricted by their simple clocking mechanisms.
2. Processing circuits such as (word) gates, adders, comparators, ALUs, and multiplexers (configured as Boolean function generators).

3. Circuits such as buses, multiplexers (configured as data selectors), and decoders (configured as address decoders or demultiplexers) used to route data through the system.

4. Control circuits that generate the control signals (clear, enable, select, etc.) necessary to ensure that the desired register-transfer operations are carried out at the proper times and in the proper sequence; counters often play a central role in the design of control units.

Figure 4.6 shows a simple register-transfer circuit for binary addition and subtraction, and its implementation using 7400-series ICs. A more complicated circuit of the same general type appears in Fig. 4.37. This circuit performs arithmetic and logical operations on 4-bit words, and resembles the E-unit of a simple microprocessor. Three registers A, B, and C are provided for temporary data storage. Data words are transferred to and from this circuit via an input bus BUS_0 and two output buses BUS_1 and BUS_2. At the heart of the system is a 4-bit ALU, which is similar to the 74381 IC of Fig. 4.26. The two input operands applied to the ALU at any time may come from various sources as determined by a pair of multiplexers. The left (L) input operand can be obtained from either of the registers A or B, while the right (R) input operand is obtained from one of four possible sources: register A, register C, input bus BUS_0, or a constant source that provides the operand zero, that is, 0000. The result produced by the ALU is always stored in the A register. A demultiplexer allows the contents of A to be transferred to either one of the output buses BUS_1 or BUS_2.

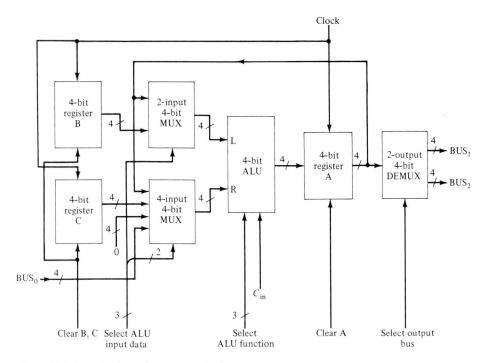

Figure 4.37 Example of a register-transfer circuit.

The circuit of Fig. 4.37 enables a variety of different register-transfer operations to be implemented, not all of which are useful. If the functions of the ALU are those listed in Fig. 4.26c, then the following useful operations (among many others) can be performed:

$$A := A + C;$$

$$A := A - B;$$

$$BUS_2 := B - C;$$

$$A := B - 0;$$

$$A := BUS_0 \oplus A;$$

Certain operations such as

$$A := B + B \qquad (4.18)$$

cannot be performed in a single clock cycle because B cannot be applied simultaneously to the L and R inputs of the ALU; the necessary direct data path from B to R does not exist. However, (4.18) can easily be obtained by two consecutive register-transfer operations thus:

$$A := B \oplus 0;$$

$$A := A + B; \qquad (4.19)$$

Longer sequences may be used to implement more complex functions. Suppose, for example, that B is to be multiplied by a positive integer n. The two-statement sequence (4.19) effectively multiplies B by two. We can obtain multiplication by n by repeating the second operation of (4.19) n times thus:

$$A := B \oplus 0;$$

$$A := A + B;$$

$$A := A + B;$$

$$\cdots$$

$$A := A + B;$$

This register-transfer "program" computes $n \times B$ by adding B to itself n times, and accumulating the partial sum in the A (accumulator) register.

The particular operation performed by a register-transfer circuit at any time is determined by a control unit, whose purpose is to apply appropriate signals to a set of external control lines of the circuit in question. In the example of Fig. 4.37, these control signals are listed at the bottom of the figure. Consider for instance, the control signals needed to specify the operation

$$A := B \wedge 0;$$

The select input lines of the two multiplexers must be set so that B is applied to the L input of the ALU, and 0 is applied to its R input. The 3-bit pattern that specifies the AND operation must be applied to the ALU function select lines. The remaining control lines must be set at suitable disabling or don't care values. For example, the various clear lines must be disabled, whereas any value may be assigned to the ALU's carry-in line C_{in}, because C_{in} is ignored during an AND operation.

The preceding example suggests that a register-transfer system has two main parts, a data-processing part and a control part, which are linked as indicated in Fig. 4.38 A *data-processing unit* such as the circuit of Fig. 4.37 performs the main computational tasks of the system, as well as any auxiliary data-transfer and storage functions. The *control unit* supplies the control signals necessary to select and sequence the operations of the data-processing subsystem. The overall action of the system of Fig. 4.38 is controlled by an external command, which can be supplied by, say, depressing a key on a keyboard. We can make a further distinction between special-purpose or nonprogrammable systems and general-purpose or programmable systems. A *nonprogrammable system* is designed to execute a small set of commands, perhaps as few as one. A pocket calculator and a point-of-sale terminal (see Sec. 1.4) are familiar examples of this type of system. A *programmable system* can perform an unlimited sequence of commands, which, if the data-processing unit is sufficiently general, allow essentially any desired operation to be performed. Computers of all types fall into this category. It should be noted that microprocessors and microcomputers are used extensively in both special-purpose and general-purpose systems. In this chapter we will limit our attention to nonprogrammable special-purpose digital systems.

Much of the complexity of a system such as that of Fig. 4.38 resides in the control unit. A suitable controller for a special-purpose system is depicted in Fig. 4.39. The data-processing unit to be controlled is assumed to carry out a fixed sequence of k register-transfer operations. These operations are initiated by a short pulse applied to the ON line. This sets the JK flip-flop, which in turn activates the enable input EI of a modulo-k counter. The counter then responds to pulses received from the system clock, and proceeds to increment through all its k states. When the counter's initial state is reached again, the counter automatically halts by disabling its EI input via the JK flip-flop, as indicated in Fig. 4.39. The modulo-k counter thus produces a sequence of k distinct count states during k consecutive clock cycles. These count states are translated into the k patterns of control signals used to select the desired sequence of register-transfer operations in the data-processing unit. The translation is implemented by the

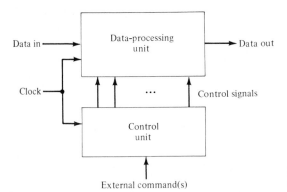

Figure 4.38 System partitioned into data-processing and control units.

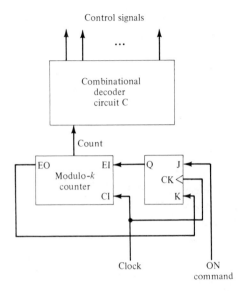

Control signals

Combinational
decoder
circuit C

Count

EO   EI   Q   J
Modulo-k CK
counter
CI   K

Clock   ON
command   **Figure 4.39** Simple control unit.

combinational circuit C, which can be viewed as a special-purpose decoder. C may be designed using the methods covered in Chap. 2. It is not difficult to generalize the control unit design of Fig. 4.39 to generate m different control-signal sequences in response to m different external commands. The controller of Fig. 4.39 is sometimes called *hardwired,* because its functions are permanently wired into the design, particularly that of the circuit C. Another, more flexible, control design technique called microprogramming is introduced later in this chapter.

4.2.2 Design Process

The MSI and SSI design methodologies differ in several important respects. The methods employed at the MSI and higher complexity levels are mainly heuristic and intuitive, a consequence of the complex behavior of the components used. Systematic cost minimization techniques such as the Karnaugh-map method for gate minimization (see Sec. 3.3.4) have no counterparts at the MSI or register-transfer level. Register-transfer designs are also usually decomposed into data-processing and control parts, which may be designed via quite different procedures. The formal tools used to describe circuit behavior at the SSI level are bit oriented, and include truth tables, state tables, and (sequential) Boolean equations. While these tools can be used in a more abstract word-oriented format at higher complexity levels, they are often replaced by flowcharts or RTLs.

Figure 4.40 enumerates the major steps in the design of a register-transfer system (cf. the general system design process of Fig. 1.43, and the SSI version of Fig. 3.56). As always, the main design objective is to produce a correctly working system, whose behavior and performance meet the system's specifications. A secondary goal is to minimize the cost of the system, which again may be measured by the total number of ICs

Design Step	Actions Required
Planning	Obtain specifications of the desired system behavior. Determine the IC technology and logic families to be used.
Preliminary design	Specify the overall design or architecture of the system. Identify the data-processing and control units, and specify their architectures.
Detailed design (logic design)	Implement the data-processing unit using the appropriate MSI component types. Identify the control signal sequences it requires, and implement the control unit.
Physical design	Build, debug, and document a prototype version of the system.

Figure 4.40 Main steps in designing a system at the register-transfer or MSI level.

it contains. While most of the ICs used in a typical register-transfer design fall into the MSI range, significant numbers of SSI ICs are also used for such mundane but essential tasks as signal inversion and buffering, simple logical operations, and the like.

The specifications of a register-transfer system often take the form of one or more algorithms that must be implemented in hardware. An *algorithm* defines in a step-by-step format the actions to be carried out to produce a desired result; typically each step can be equated directly to a register-transfer operation. For example, the behavior of a multiplier circuit can be defined as a sequence of steps involving the operations add and shift. The behavior of an industrial process controller may be specified in terms of the following operations: read data from sensors or other input devices, process the data, and finally issue commands to actuators and other output devices. Algorithms of this kind are often most conveniently described by means of flowcharts, or descriptions in (semi) formal languages like RTLs.

Consider the task of specifying the behavior of the adder/subtracter whose structure is given in Fig. 4.6. Viewed at the bit level of SSI design, this is a rather complex sequential circuit containing eight flip-flops and about 80 gates. It has 19 binary IO lines, and $2^8 = 256$ possible states. Thus a complete bit-level state table or a set of (sequential) Boolean equations describing this circuit would be excessively long and unmanageable. Figure 4.41 shows three behavioral descriptions of the adder/subtracter, which are at a level of abstraction that is appropriate to register-transfer design. For simplicity it is assumed that the CLEAR line is synchronized with the clock signal CLOCK. Figure 4.41a is a simplified state table in which the circuit's state and the data on the input bus are denoted by the word variables A and B respectively. This table gives the symbolic next state for each value of the main control lines CLEAR and SUBTRACT. The leftmost entry, for example, specifies the 2^{16} possible state transitions that can occur during one clock cycle when CLEAR = 0 and SUBTRACT = 0. A concise symbolic next-state entry is possible because all 2^{16} state transitions collectively define a single easily-specified arithmetic function, namely 8-bit binary addition. Figure 4.41b shows the circuit's behavior in flowchart form. A path through this flowchart that begins and ends at the top of the diagram specifies a register-transfer operation, that is, the action performed during one machine cycle. The states of the circuit's control signals determine the outcomes of the decisions indicated by the diamond-shaped boxes. Finally, Fig. 4.41c

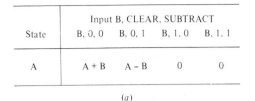

State	Input B, CLEAR, SUBTRACT			
	B, 0, 0	B, 0, 1	B, 1, 0	B, 1, 1
A	A + B	A – B	0	0

(a)

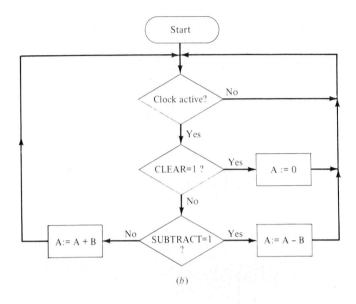

(b)

```
while  CLOCK = ACTIVE  do
    begin
    if  CLEAR = 1  then  A := 0
      else if  SUBTRACT = 1  then  A := A - B  else  A := A + B
    end;
```

(c)

Figure 4.41 Three formal behavioral descriptions of the adder/subtracter circuit of Fig. 4.6: (a) state table; (b) flowchart; (c) formal language (Pascal).

describes the circuit by means of a formal language, in this case the computer programming language Pascal. Most RTL descriptions of digital systems have a similar program-like appearance. Unlike programming languages, however, RTLs are capable of describing hardware features and timing details that are beyond the scope of languages, such as Pascal.

Once the system specifications have been constructed in a suitable algorithmic form, the preliminary architectural design is carried out. This is usually divided into two stages: First a data-processing unit is outlined, and then an appropriate control-unit architecture is specified. The major data operands and register-transfer operations required are derived from the system specifications. Thus from Fig. 4.41 we see that two 8-bit operands A and B are used, along with three operations: addition, subtraction, and clear. The registers needed for temporary data storage are identified; in the present example A is associated with a register, while B is associated with an input bus. Processing circuits must be specified that perform the desired register-transfer operations. In this case the A register itself provides the clear function, while the remaining operations are provided by a combinational adder/subtracter. The algorithmic specifications also determine the data paths that must be present in the system. For instance, the operations $A := A + B$ and $A := A - B$ imply the need for data paths from the A register and the B bus to the inputs of the adder/subtracter. They also imply the need for a (feedback) data path from the output of the adder/subtracter to the input of the A register. The foregoing analysis of the formal specifications results in the general structure depicted in Fig. 4.6a. The detailed logic design of the data-processing unit can now be done using the chosen logic family. The IC types available greatly influence the final design. Figure 4.6b shows one possible IC implementation of this data-processing circuit using a mixture of SSI and MSI ICs from the 7400 series.

The process of designing the data-processing portion of the system implicitly identifies the control signals to be used. For example, when multiplexers are chosen to route data through a circuit in the manner illustrated in Fig. 4.37, the multiplexers' select input lines automatically become control inputs of the overall circuit. Control signals are also introduced any time a component with more than one function is employed. The eight-function ALU of Fig. 4.37 requires a 3-bit control bus to select the function to be performed at any time. Each register-transfer operation of the data-processing unit is invoked by a specific bit pattern applied to its input control lines; this bit pattern is easily determined from the detailed design of the data-processing unit. Last, the logic design of the control unit that produces the required patterns of control signals must be carried out. The circuit of Fig. 4.39 is suitable for simple hardwired control units, and its main problem is the design of the combinational decoder circuit C. Provided the number of control signals is not large, and few long multicycle operations are required, the systematic design procedures discussed in Sec. 3.3 can be applied to the design of C. Very complex control units such as the I-unit of a microprocessor, where hundreds of different control signals are not uncommon, are designed heuristically, or by using other approaches such as microprogramming (to be discussed in Chap. 8).

4.2.3 Register-Transfer Languages

Formal languages for describing the structure and behavior of complex digital systems have existed for many years. One of the earliest was the Mechanical Notation devised by Babbage to describe his Analytical Engine (Babbage, 1864). With the advent of modern electronic computers, a class of formal descriptive languages, namely, computer programming languages, came into widespread use. High-level programming languages such as Pascal (see Fig. 4.41) are very suitable for specifying digital system behavior at the register-transfer level; they are less suited to describing hardware structure or implementation details. This is not surprising because high-level programming languages were explicitly designed to allow algorithms to be specified in a manner that is independent of the hardware configuration of the host computer. The RTLs, most of which are based on existing programming languages, attempt to remedy the foregoing deficiency by adding to the programming languages features that allow various aspects of circuit structure and timing to be specified.

Figure 4.42 lists some well-known RTLs, none of which, however, has achieved the status of a standard language. Interest in the use of RTLs for describing computers first arose in the 1950s (Reed, 1956). In 1964 the programming language APL was used in essentially unmodified form to prepare a massive description of the architecture of the IBM System/360 computer series (Falkoff et al., 1964). Several RTLs, notably AHPL and DDL, have extended APL to allow more explicit hardware descriptions. The programming language ALGOL, a forerunner of Pascal, influenced the RTLs CDL and ISP. The languages mentioned in Fig. 4.42 have found their major use as descriptive tools in textbooks on computer design. They have also been used to a limited extent in computer users' manuals, and as input-output languages for digital simulation programs and related design software.

Despite many differences in detail, all RTLs are broadly similar. In this book we make use of a simple RTL that has the essential features found in almost all RTLs. It is based on the programming language Pascal, which is illustrated in Fig. 4.41, and is studied in depth in Chap. 6. The fundamental element of this language and, indeed, of every RTL, is a *register-transfer statement* of the form

$$A := B; \qquad (4.20)$$

This states that the contents of a register B are to be copied to another register A. Note that at the register-transfer level of description, the nature of the flip-flops used in the registers, and the structure of the implied data path from the outputs of B to the inputs of A are often ignored. The names A and B can refer either to the registers themselves or to their contents. The size of a register and the names of the individual bits it stores are specified by *declaration statements*, which have the following format.

$$\textbf{register} \quad A[0:7], \ B[0:7]; \qquad (4.21)$$

Language	Related Programming Language	References
APL (A Programming Language)		Inverson, 1962; Blaauw, 1976
AHPL (A Hardware Programming Language)	APL	Hill and Peterson, 1978
CDL (Computer Design Language)	ALGOL	Chu, 1972
DDL (Digital Design Language)	APL	Duley and Dietmeyer, 1968; Dietmeyer and Duley, 1975
ISP (Instruction-Set Processor)	ALGOL	Bell and Newell, 1971; Siewiorek, Bell, and Newell, 1982

Figure 4.42 Some well-known register-transfer languages.

Statement (4.21) declares the existence of two 8-bit registers named A and B whose component bits are named A[0], A[1], ..., A[7] and B[0], B[1], ..., B[7] respectively. Registers can also be combined or concatenated to form new registers using the concatenation operator "." as follows.

$$\textbf{register} \quad REG = A.B;$$

This statement defines a 16-bit register named REG, which is formed by concatenating the A and B registers defined already in (4.21). The individual bits of REG are implicitly named REG[0], REG[1], ..., REG[15], which implies that REG[0] = A[0], REG[1] = A[1], ..., REG[7] = A[7], REG[8] = B[0], ..., REG[15] = B[7]. Combinational circuits are also implicitly declared by means of register-transfer statements of the form

$$A := F(B,C); \tag{4.22}$$

where F denotes the function performed by the circuit in question. The outputs of the B and C registers are connected to the inputs of the combinational circuit, causing it to compute the result F(B, C); this result is then transferred to the A register. The function F may also be defined by an arithmetic or logical expression using ordinary (Boolean) algebraic notation. For example, the statement

$$A := B \lor \overline{C};$$

specifies the existence of logic circuits that perform various Boolean operations on B and C, generating the result $F(B, C) = B \lor \overline{C}$, which is then transferred to A. Again the detailed structure of the logic circuits used is not of interest.

A statement such as (4.22) specifies a single register-transfer operation to be performed during a single clock cycle. Occasionally several register transfers are required to take place in the same clock period. In that case, the register-transfer operations are listed in the same statement separated by commas thus:

$$A := B, \quad B := 0, \quad C := F(A,B); \tag{4.23}$$

Statement (4.23) defines three register-transfer operations that are to occur simultaneously or in parallel. Note that ordinary programming languages cannot express parallelism of this sort. The list of register-transfer operations terminates with a semicolon. Semicolons are used to terminate all statements in this RTL. In the case of action (as opposed to declaration) statements, a semicolon serves to mark the end of a clock cycle. We shall refer to (4.23) as a *compound* register-transfer statement to distinguish it from *simple* register-transfer statements such as (4.20)–(4.22).

A multistep or multicycle operation is described by a set of (compound) register-transfer statements. It is clearly necessary to indicate the sequence in which the various register-transfer operations are to be performed. In the simplest case this can be done by listing the statements in the order in which the corresponding operations are required to take place. For instance, the three-statement sequence

$$A := B;$$

$$B := 0; \tag{4.24}$$

$$C := F(A,B);$$

has the following interpretation. First B is transferred to A. In the next clock cycle, zero is transferred to B, that is, the B register is cleared. Finally the transfer C := F(A,B) takes place in the third clock cycle. Hence (4.24) specifies three register-transfer operations that are required to occur in three consecutive clock cycles. In contrast (4.23) requires the same three operations to take place during a single clock cycle. Note that the results produced by (4.23) and (4.24), specifically the final contents of register C, may not be the same in the two cases.

A simple linear sequence of register-transfer operations can be controlled by a counter circuit such as that of Fig. 4.39, which generates a fixed sequence of control signals that select and enable each required operation in turn. Often the order in which a given set of operations is executed depends on the occurrence of certain internal conditions or states, or the arrival of external control signals. To account for this, various types of *conditional register-transfer statements* are possible. We will use the **if** statement format

$$\textbf{if } \text{COND } \textbf{then } A := F(B,C); \hspace{2cm} (4.25)$$

to indicate that the register transfer A := F(B, C) is to take place if and only if a condition denoted by COND is present in the circuit. Typical conditions are "control line C is active" and "register R contains zero." Often a condition has the form of a logical expression that must be true for the specified operation to take place. If the condition COND is not present when (4.25) is encountered, then no action takes place during the current clock cycle. Many different formats for expressing conditional register-transfer operations are found in RTLs. For example, the CDL statement

$$/\text{COND}/ \quad A \leftarrow F(B,C),$$

and the ISP statement

$$(\text{COND} \Rightarrow A \leftarrow F(B,C))$$

are both equivalent to (4.25). Figure 4.43 shows the essential hardware required to execute (4.25), assuming that COND corresponds to a control signal of the same name. This circuit constitutes the hardware structure described by statement (4.25).

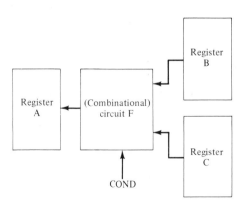

Figure 4.43 Circuit corresponding to the RTL statement: **if** COND **then** A := F(B,C).

It is sometimes useful to perform a register-transfer operation repeatedly, as long as some specified condition holds. This situation can be expressed concisely by means of a **while** conditional statement:

$$\textbf{while } \text{COND } \textbf{do } A := F(B,C);$$

In this example the register transfer $A := F(B,C)$ is executed cycle after cycle, as long as the condition COND holds. When this condition no longer holds, control shifts to the next consecutive register-transfer statement.

Figure 4.44 summarizes the main features of the RTL used in this book. In addition to **register** declarations, which were discussed above, a second type of item called a **terminal** can be declared using the same format. A **terminal** declaration statement identifies a terminal, wire, or bus that can carry, but not store, a signal or word. If T is declared to be a terminal, then the transfer statement

$$T := F(A,B);$$

means that T assumes the value $F(A, B)$ during the current clock cycle. This value is not stored by T, which would be the case if T were a register. As explained earlier, semicolons are used to separate or "delimit" consecutive clock cycles. The keywords **begin** and **end** act as delimiters that are used to group several consecutive RTL statements into a unit called a *block,* which can be used as the action part of an **if** or **while** statement. For example, the **while** statement

$$\textbf{while } \text{COND } \textbf{do begin } S1; S2; S3 \textbf{ end};$$

causes the three consecutive statements S1, S2, S3 to be executed repeatedly as long as the COND condition is present. The statements are executed in the sequence

$$S1; S2; S3; S1; S2; S3; S1; \ldots$$

As Fig. 4.44 indicates, an RTL statement may be preceded by a label terminating in a colon. A statement with label L can be referenced by a **goto** statement of the form

$$\textbf{goto } L;$$

which states that the next statement to be executed is the one labeled L. As discussed already, register-transfer operations and similar actions are specified by register-transfer statements, which may be conditional or unconditional, simple or compound. Commas are used to separate operations occurring in parallel within the same clock cycle. Conditions are defined by either **if** or **while** clauses. Figure 4.44 also shows the standard flowchart symbols corresponding to the various elements of the RTL.

An RTL description of a digital system typically has two parts: a declaration part that identifies major registers and other key components of the system, and an action part that defines the system's behavior in terms of sequences of conditional and unconditional register-transfer statements. The formal RTL statements may be augmented by informal explanatory comments in ordinary English; such comments are enclosed in braces { }. As in most RTLs and programming languages, no significance is attached to word spacing or indentation, although the manner in which an RTL description is laid out can influence its

RTL Element	Meaning	Equivalent Flowchart Symbol
register R1[1:k], R2 = A.B;	Declares R1 to be a *k*-bit register, and R2 to be a register formed by concatenating the (previously defined) registers A and B.	
terminal T1[0:k − 1], Z = X.Y;	Declares T1 to be a *k*-bit signal terminal, and Z to be a terminal formed by concatenating the (previously defined) terminals X and Y.	
begin ... end	Delimiters enclosing a sequence of RTL statements that are to be treated as a unit or block.	
L: R := F(R1, R2, ..., Rk);	A simple register-transfer statement with label L, which states: Compute the function F of registers R1, R2, ..., Rk, and transfer the result to register R. (The registers may also be replaced by terminals.)	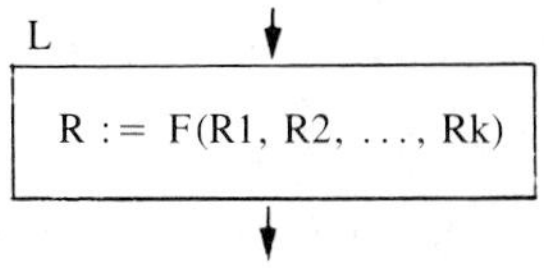
S1, S2, ..., Sm;	A compound register-transfer statement (unlabeled) containing m statements S1, S2, ..., Sm to be executed in parallel.	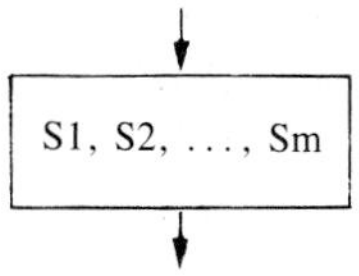
if C then S1 else S2;	If condition C holds, then execute statement or block S1, otherwise execute S2.	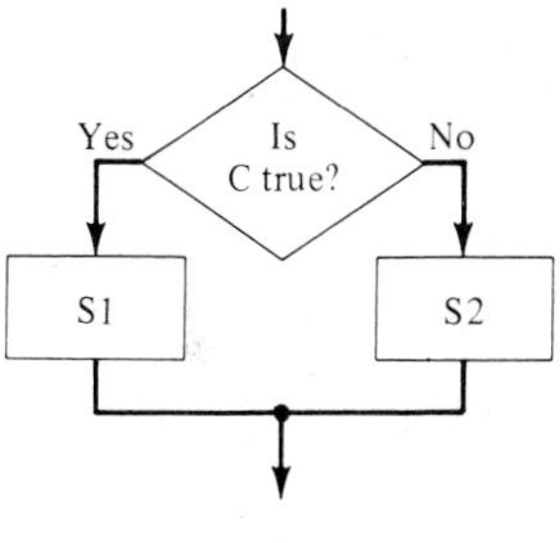
while C do S;	While condition C holds, repeatedly execute the statement or block S.	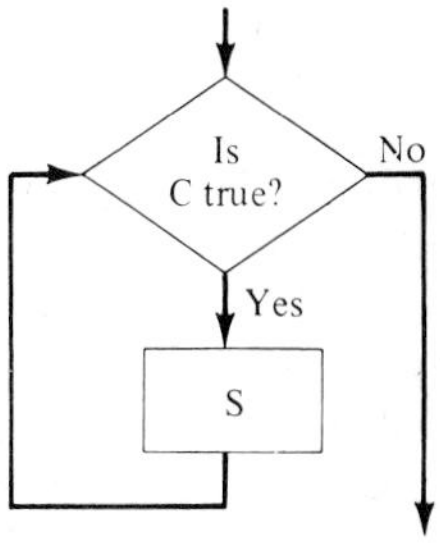
goto L;	The next RTL statement to be executed is the one labeled L.	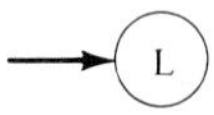

Figure 4.44 Simple Pascal-based RTL.

readability. It is common to use indentation to show the structure of complex RTL statements and **begin-end** blocks.

Figure 4.45 presents a detailed description of the adder/subtracter circuit of Fig. 4.6a, which illustrates most of the features of our RTL. The declaration part consists of two declaration statements. The 8-bit register A is defined by a **register** statement, and the two 8-bit buses B and Z are defined by a **terminal** declaration statement. The action part of the RTL description consists of a single compound **while** statement controlled by the clock signal CLOCK. When the clock is inactive, no operations are specified. When the clock is active, the compound **if** statement lying between **begin** and **end** is executed repeatedly. (The **begin** and **end** delimiters are actually superfluous here because they enclose only one, albeit complex, **if** statement.) This **if** statement specifies the major register-transfer operations to be performed—namely, clear, add, and subtract—and the conditions controlling their execution. The transfer operations $Z := A - B$ and $Z := A + B$ state that the functions to the right of the transfer symbol $:=$ are to be computed and applied to the bus Z during the current clock cycle. Since Z has no storage capability, its data may disappear during the next clock cycle; normally an external latch or register is provided to capture the data on Z. The register A, on the other hand, retains the data applied to it by the operations $A := 0$, $A := A - B$ or $A := A + B$ indefinitely, until it is changed by a subsequent register-transfer operation.

4.2.4 Multiplier Design

Logic circuits that perform binary multiplication and division tend to be significantly more complex than circuits for addition and subtraction. As a result, multiply and divide instructions are not found in the instruction repertoires of many microprocessors.

{Declaration part}

register A[0:7];

terminal B[0:7], Z[0:7];

{Action part}

while CLOCK = ACTIVE **do**

  begin

  if CLEAR = 1 **then** A := 0 **else**

    if SUBTRACT = 1 **then** Z := A − B, A := A −B

        else Z := A + B, A := A + B

  end;

Figure 4.45 RTL description of the adder/subtracter circuit of Fig. 4.6a.

Relatively complex operations of this sort may be implemented by sequential circuits or programs that compute the desired functions via a sequence of simple register-transfer operations. To illustrate the hardware design issues involved, we turn next to the realization of binary multiplication by means of register-transfer circuits.

The "long" multiplication technique used for pencil-and-paper calculations provides a convenient starting point in the development of an algorithm for hardware implementation. Suppose that an n-digit unsigned number Y, the multiplicand, is to be multiplied by another n-digit unsigned number X, the multiplier. The steps in long multiplication may be summarized as follows:

1. Multiply Y by each digit x_i of the multiplier X in turn, beginning with the least significant digit x_0. This yields a set of partial products of the form $x_i Y$.
2. Shift each partial product $x_i Y$ one digit position to the left with respect to the preceding partial product $x_{i-1} Y$.
3. Sum the n shifted partial products to form the final product XY.

Figure 4.46a shows an example of this pencil-and-paper technique applied to two 4-bit binary integers. Since the multiplier digits can only assume the values 0 and 1, each partial product $x_i Y$ is either Y or zero. The left-shift operation is tantamount to multiplication by two, hence the ith shifted partial product can be written as $2^i x_i Y$. The final result is obtained by adding the n shifted partial products thus:

$$XY = \sum_{i=0}^{n-1} 2^i x_i Y$$

Note that the product XY may contain up to $2n$ bits.

This pencil-and-paper algorithm for binary multiplication has several drawbacks that make it unsuitable for direct use in a hardware multiplier circuit. It requires n registers to store the partial products. Furthermore, these registers must all be linked to an adder—a $2n$-bit parallel adder would seem most suitable—to implement the final summation of the partial products. Figure 4.46b shows a modified multiplication method that replaces the n partial product registers by a single register A called the *accumulator* register. As each new partial product is determined, it is added to the contents of the accumulator, which therefore accumulates the sum of the (shifted) partial products. The multiplicand Y may be stored in a $2n$-bit shift register, which is left-shifted n times to provide the nonzero partial products. When the partial product is zero, the corresponding addition step is skipped. Thus the product XY is obtained in n steps, each involving a $2n$-bit addition operation followed by a left-shift operation performed by the register that stores the multiplicand.

Figure 4.46c illustrates a further modification to the multiplication algorithm, yielding a version that is suitable for hardware implementation. Instead of holding the contents of A stationary and left-shifting the multiplicand register, in this case the multiplicand register is fixed while the contents of A are right-shifted with respect to Y. Consequently Y may be stored in an ordinary n-bit register, and the addition operation can be implemented by an n-bit rather than a $2n$-bit adder. Since n-bit addition can

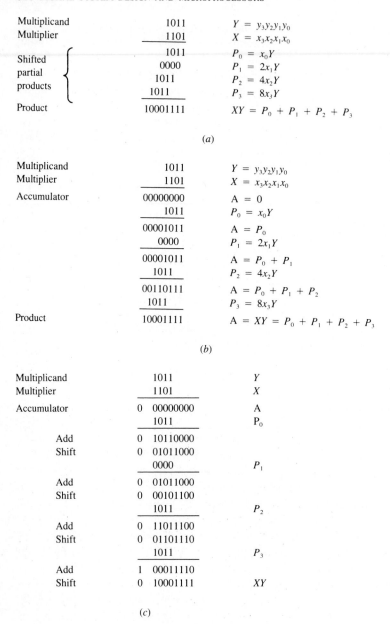

Multiplicand	1011	$Y = y_3y_2y_1y_0$
Multiplier	1101	$X = x_3x_2x_1x_0$
Shifted	1011	$P_0 = x_0Y$
partial	0000	$P_1 = 2x_1Y$
products	1011	$P_2 = 4x_2Y$
	1011	$P_3 = 8x_3Y$
Product	10001111	$XY = P_0 + P_1 + P_2 + P_3$

(a)

Multiplicand	1011	$Y = y_3y_2y_1y_0$
Multiplier	1101	$X = x_3x_2x_1x_0$
Accumulator	00000000	$A = 0$
	1011	$P_0 = x_0Y$
	00001011	$A = P_0$
	0000	$P_1 = 2x_1Y$
	00001011	$A = P_0 + P_1$
	1011	$P_2 = 4x_2Y$
	00110111	$A = P_0 + P_1 + P_2$
	1011	$P_3 = 8x_3Y$
Product	10001111	$A = XY = P_0 + P_1 + P_2 + P_3$

(b)

Multiplicand		1011	Y
Multiplier		1101	X
Accumulator	0	00000000	A
		1011	P_0
Add	0	10110000	
Shift	0	01011000	
		0000	P_1
Add	0	01011000	
Shift	0	00101100	
		1011	P_2
Add	0	11011100	
Shift	0	01101110	
		1011	P_3
Add	1	00011110	
Shift	0	10001111	XY

(c)

Figure 4.46 Unsigned binary multiplication: (a) using the normal pencil-and-paper approach; (b) modification using accumulated partial products; (c) further modification for machine implementation.

produce an $(n + 1)$-bit result, an extra storage location must be appended to the left end of the accumulator; consequently A is realized by a $(2n + 1)$-bit right-shift register. Thus we can implement the multiplication scheme of Fig. 4.46c using the following data registers:

1. A $(2n + 1)$-bit right-shift register forming the accumulator A. Following the conventions of our RTL, we can denote A and its contents by $A[2n:0]$.
2. An n-bit multiplier register denoted $Q[n-1:0]$, which stores X.
3. An n-bit multiplicand register denoted $M[n-1:0]$, which stores Y.

The product is computed in n steps or iterations, each of which involves an addition of the form

$$A[2n:n] := A[2n-1:n] + M; \qquad (4.26)$$

or

$$A[2n:n] := A[2n-1:n] + 0; \qquad (4.27)$$

The addition operation is followed by a 1-bit right-shift operation, which may be expressed as follows:

$$A[2n] := 0, A[2n-1:0] := A[2n:1];$$

To decide which of (4.26) or (4.27) is to be performed during the ith iteration, the corresponding multiplier bit x_i, which is originally stored in location $Q[i]$ of the multiplier register, must be inspected. A convenient way of inspecting x_i is to make Q a right-shift register like A. Q is then right-shifted during each add-shift iteration of the multiplication algorithm, so that the required bit x_i is always found in the rightmost cell of Q, namely, $Q[0]$. Thus the main add-shift step can be described by the following two RTL statements:

if $Q[0] = 1$ **then** $A[2n:n] := A[2n-1:n] + M;$

$A[2n] := 0, A[2n-1;0] := A[2n;1], Q[n-1] := 0, Q[n-2;0] := Q[n-1:1];$

Thus each add-shift step can be implemented in two clock cycles; a complete n-bit multiplication therefore requires at least $2n$ clock cycles.

Figure 4.47 shows the structure of the data-processing part of a multiplier unit that implements the foregoing multiplication scheme. Data storage is provided by the A, M, and Q registers; A and Q are right-shift registers. An n-bit parallel adder circuit is connected to M and the left half of A as indicated. A control unit, whose design will be discussed later, generates the control signals used to load the various registers, initiate shifts, and so on. Two n-bit buses designated DATA-IN and DATA-OUT are provided for entering the input operands X and Y, and removing the result XY. With this hardware organization established, we can now specify the detailed multiplication algorithm to be used. A concise formal description of this algorithm using our RTL appears in Fig. 4.48. The main registers A, M, and Q and the buses DATA-IN and DATA-OUT are declared by **register** and **terminal** statements respectively. It is also convenient to declare as a register a counter named COUNTER, which forms part of the control unit, as in Fig.

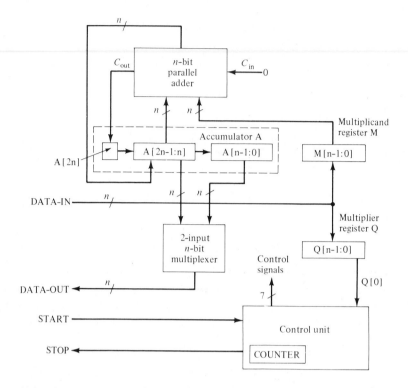

Figure 4.47 Structure of a multiplier circuit for unsigned binary numbers.

4.39. During multiplication COUNTER is incremented by 1 during every clock cycle. This could be indicated explicitly in Fig. 4.48 by including the register-transfer operation

$$\text{COUNTER} := \text{COUNTER} + 1$$

in each statement that corresponds to a clock cycle; for simplicity, this increment operation has been omitted from the RTL description.

A multiplication operation is initiated by the arrival of an external START signal. The multiplier responds by loading the multiplier operand X from the DATA-IN bus into the Q register, and clearing the accumulator A. These operations are performed in parallel during the first clock cycle. In the second clock cycle the multiplicand Y is transferred from the DATA-IN bus to the M register, which completes the loading of the input operands. The multiplication proper is now performed by a sequence of n add-and-shift operations requiring a total of $2n$ clock cycles. Bit Q[0] of the multiplier register determines whether or not addition should occur. After $2n$ clock cycles, the final result XY resides in the accumulator. As indicated in Fig. 4.48, two additional clock cycles are employed to transfer XY n bits at a time from the accumulator to the DATA-OUT bus. The control signal STOP is also activated to signal completion of the multiplication. The entire multiplication process, including the transfer of operands, requires $2n + 4$ clock cycles. Hence at a typical clock frequency of 2 MHz, a 16-bit multiplication can be completed in 18 μs.

{Declaration part}

register $A[2n:0]$, $M[n-1:0]$, $Q[n-1:0]$, $COUNTER[p-1:0]$;

{COUNTER is an iteration counter that is automatically incremented by 1 during every machine clock cycle.}

terminal $DATA\text{-}IN[n-1:0]$, $DATA\text{-}OUT[n-1:0]$;   {Input-output data buses}

{Action part}

{This algorithm multiplies two unsigned n-bit binary numbers X and Y. X must be placed on the DATA-IN bus during clock cycle 0, and Y must be placed on DATA-IN during clock cycle 1. The most significant half of XY is placed on the DATA-OUT bus during clock cycle $2n + 2$, and the least significant half of XY is placed on DATA-OUT during clock cycle $2n + 3$.}

while $CLOCK = ACTIVE$ **do**

  if $START = 1$ **then**

  begin

    $Q := DATA\text{-}IN$, $A := 0$, $COUNTER := 0$; {Load multiplier register; clear accumulator and counter.}

    $M := DATA\text{-}IN$;   {Load multiplicand register.}

    while $COUNTER < 2n + 2$ **do**

      begin   {Main add-shift step}

      if $Q[0] = 1$ **then** $A[2n:n] := A[2n-1:n] + M$;

      $A[2n] := 0$, $A[2n-1:0] := A[2n:1]$, $Q[n-1] := 0$, $Q[n-2:0] := Q[n-1:1]$;

      end;

    $DATA\text{-}OUT := A[2n-1:n]$, $STOP := 1$;   {Transfer the product XY from the accumulator to the DATA-OUT bus.}

    $DATA\text{-}OUT := A[n-1:0]$

  end;

Figure 4.48 RTL description of the behavior of the unsigned binary multiplier circuit of Fig. 4.47.

Figure 4.49 shows a control unit for the foregoing multiplier circuit, which is based on the sequence-counter design of Fig. 4.39. Seven major control signals have been identified. The CLEAR line is used to clear A at the start of a multiplication operation. The ADD signal is connected to the parallel load control line of the subregister A[2n:n]; when ADD is activated by the control unit, the output from the adder, that is, $A[2n-1:n] + M$, is loaded into A[2n:n]. ADD therefore directly controls the operation

$$A[2n:n] := A[2n-1:n] + M;$$

The SHIFT control line is used to right-shift both the A and the Q registers. The control signals LOAD-M and LOAD-Q are used to transfer data from DATA-IN to M and Q respectively; they therefore are connected to the parallel load control lines of the appropriate registers. The remaining two OUTPUT lines are used to transfer the $2n$-bit result from the A register to the DATA-OUT bus via a multiplexer, as indicated in Fig. 4.47. To complete the specification of the control unit, the behavior of the decoder circuit C must be defined. A truth table for C can easily be derived from the RTL description

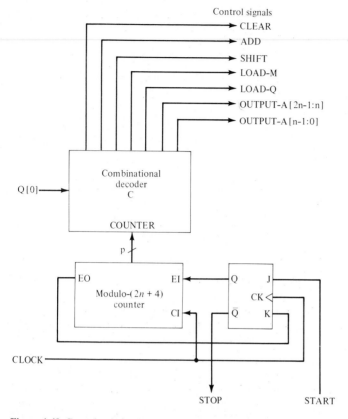

Figure 4.49 Control unit for the multiplier circuit of Fig. 4.47.

given in Fig. 4.48. Figure 4.50 shows such a table for $n = 8$. Note that the row sequence is determined by the value of COUNTER, and thus follows exactly the sequence of register-transfer operations specified by Fig. 4.48. The conversion of the data-processing unit of Fig. 4.47 and the control unit of Fig. 4.49 into IC circuits is straightforward.

Signed binary multiplication presents no difficulty if SM (sign-magnitude) number formats are used. The sign bits x_s and y_s are first separated from the magnitude parts X' and Y' of the input operands X and Y respectively. The multiplication process of Fig. 4.48 may then be applied directly to X' and Y' to produce the magnitude part $P' = X'Y'$ of the required result. The sign p_s of the product is obtained from the following simple calculation

$$\textbf{if } x_s = y_s \textbf{ then } p_s := 0 \textbf{ else } p_s := 1;$$

which is equivalent to

$$p_s := x_s \oplus y_s; \tag{4.28}$$

Thus the only extra hardware needed for SM multiplication is the logic circuitry to implement (4.28). The sign calculation can be performed in parallel with the magnitude multiplication, so no additional time penalty is incurred.

Multiplication of TC (twos-complement) numbers is more difficult, because negative numbers do not represent magnitude in the usual form. The foregoing SM multiplication method may be adapted to TC numbers using the following indirect approach, which first replaces any negative input operand by its positive counterpart. Recall that the SM and TC codes for positive numbers are identical. The positive operands are then multiplied to produce a positive result P. If the final product XY is positive, P is the result; otherwise P is negated. The required negation operations may be implemented using the method of Fig. 3.24, which is based on the relation

$$-N = \bar{N} + 1 \tag{4.29}$$

The logical inversion $\bar{N}$ required by (4.29) can be obtained by using the inverted outputs of the A, M, and Q registers, while the addition of one can be implemented by passing $\bar{N}$ through the original n-bit adder of Fig. 4.47 with the carry-in line C_{in} set to 1. New data paths are necessary to link the A, Q, and M registers to the adder; note that two passes through the adder are needed to negate the double-length product P.

Figure 4.51 gives a modified version of the multiplication algorithm of Fig. 4.48, which handles n-bit TC numbers. The sign bits of X and Y are stored in two flip-flops denoted XS and YS respectively. A flip-flop PS is also used to store the sign of the product XY. The registers Q and M store the (positive) magnitudes of X and Y, and are

Inputs	Outputs						
COUNTER	CLEAR	ADD	SHIFT	LOAD-M	LOAD-Q	OUTPUT-A[2n-1:n]	OUTPUT-A[n-1:0]
00000	1	0	0	0	1	0	0
00001	0	0	0	1	0	0	0
00010	0	Q[0]	0	0	0	0	0
00011	0	0	1	0	0	0	0
00100	0	Q[0]	0	0	0	0	0
00101	0	0	1	0	0	0	0
00110	0	Q[0]	0	0	0	0	0
00111	0	0	1	0	0	0	0
01000	0	Q[0]	0	0	0	0	0
01001	0	0	1	0	0	0	0
01010	0	Q[0]	0	0	0	0	0
01011	0	0	1	0	0	0	0
01100	0	Q[0]	0	0	0	0	0
01101	0	0	1	0	0	0	0
01110	0	Q[0]	0	0	0	0	0
01111	0	0	1	0	0	0	0
10000	0	Q[0]	0	0	0	0	0
10001	0	0	1	0	0	0	0
10010	0	0	0	0	0	1	0
10011	0	0	0	0	0	0	1

Figure 4.50 Truth table for the decoder circuit C of the multiplier control unit when $n = 8$.

{Declaration part}

register $A[2n-2:0]$, $M[n-2:0]$, $Q[n-2:0]$, COUNTER$[p-1:0]$, XS, YS, PS;

terminal DATA-IN$[n-1:0]$, DATA-OUT$[n-1:0]$;

{Action part}

{This is a modified version of the binary multiplication algorithm of Fig. 4.48, which handles n-bit TC numbers.}

while CLOCK $=$ ACTIVE **do**

  if START $= 1$ **then**

    begin   {Load input operands and convert to positive form, if necessary.}

    XS $:=$ DATA-IN$[n-1]$, Q $:=$ DATA-IN$[n-2:0]$, A $:= 0$, COUNTER $:= 0$;

    YS $:=$ DATA-IN$[n-1]$, M $:=$ DATA-IN$[n-2:0]$;

    PS $:=$ XS $\oplus$ YS, **if** XS $= 1$ **then** Q $:= \overline{Q} + 1$;
                  if YS $= 1$ **then** M $:= \overline{M} + 1$;

    while COUNTER $< 2n + 2$ **do**

      begin   {Main multiplication step}

      if Q$[0] = 1$ **then** A$[2n-2:n-1] :=$ A$[2n-3:n-1] +$ M;

      A$[2n-2] := 0$, A$[2n-3:0] :=$ A$[2n-2:1]$, Q$[n-2] := 0$, Q$[n-3:0] :=$ Q$[n-2:1]$

      end;

    if PS $= 1$ **then**

      begin   {Negate the $(2n-2)$-bit product in the accumulator.}

      A$[2n-2]$.A$[n-2:0] := \overline{A}[n-2:0] + 1$;   {Store carry-out bit in A$[2n-2]$.}

      A$[2n-2]$.A$[2n-3:n-1] := \overline{A}[2n-3:n-1] +$ A$[2n-2]$

      end;

    DATA-OUT $:=$ PS.PS.A$[2n-3:n-2]$, STOP $:= 1$;

    DATA-OUT $:=$ A$[n-1:0]$

  end;

Figure 4.51 RTL description of a multiplier circuit for twos-complement numbers.

thus $n-1$ bits long. The accumulator A is now a $(2n-1)$-bit register. Multiplication proceeds in the following manner. The input operands X and Y are entered via DATA-IN as before; the sign bits are placed in XS and YS, while the remaining parts of the operands go to Q and M. XS and YS are checked and, if necessary, the contents of Q or M, or both, are negated according to (4.29). An $(n-1)$-bit version of the unsigned binary multiplication technique of Fig. 4.48 is then executed, which produces a $(2n-2)$-bit result in A$[2n-3:0]$. If PS $= 1$, then A$[2n-3:0]$ is negated as indicated, in two steps. Note that the carry-out signal generated by adding one to the low-order half $\overline{A}[2n-3:0]$ must be added to the high-order half $\overline{A}[2n-3:n-1]$; this carry signal is stored in A$[2n-2]$. It remains to append the sign bit PS to rest of the result; it is convenient to append an additional leading 0 (if PS $=$ 0) or leading 1 (if PS $=$ 1) bit to make the final result exactly $2n$ bits long. Hence the product XY is expressed in the form PS.PS.A$[2n-3:0]$.

The foregoing technique for TC multiplication has two obvious drawbacks: Several extra clock cycles are added by the initial and final negation steps, and significant amounts of extra logic are required to perform the negations. More complex add-and-shift multiplication algorithms, such as Booth's algorithm (Cavanagh, 1984), are known that operate directly on both positive and negative operands, producing the proper TC product without the negation steps.

4.3 LSI AND MEMORIES

The use of LSI circuits in digital system design is examined in this section. The main types of LSI components are introduced. Memory circuits and some representative special-purpose data-processing circuits are examined in detail.

4.3.1. The LSI Level

The term large-scale integration, as defined earlier (Fig. 1.25), refers to ICs containing between 1,000 and 10,000 transistors. This component density is sufficient to allow a complete digital system, such as the electronic portion of a small microcomputer, to be built into a single IC chip. Consequently LSI devices can perform much more complex operations than the MSI devices of the preceding section. The preferred circuit technology for manufacturing LSI circuits is MOS, as a consequence of the higher component densities achievable. Like their MSI counterparts, LSI circuits are word oriented in that signals are typically grouped into words that are transmitted via buses and stored in registers. The words may also be grouped into blocks of words corresponding to programs or data sets; such blocks can be regarded as fundamental units of information at the LSI level. A summary of the most important LSI component types is given in Fig. 4.52.

Memory ICs, which are designed to store blocks of information, are used in huge numbers in the manufacture of computers and other large digital systems. A typical

Type	Element	Main Functions Performed
Memory	Read-only memory (ROM)	Permanent program or data storage
	Random-access memory (RAM)	Temporary program or data storage
General-purpose data processing	Microprocessor	Program execution
	Microcomputer	Program storage, execution, and interfacing with IO devices
Special-purpose data processing	Arithmetic circuits	Fixed-point and floating-point arithmetic operations
	IO device controllers	Control of specific IO devices

Figure 4.52 Representative LSI component types.

memory M is organized as an array of N m-bit latches, giving it a storage capacity of N m-bit words. Each word stored in M is assigned a unique address. By supplying the proper address to M, any desired word can be immediately retrieved or read from M, independent of its physical position within M. This property of integrated memory circuits is called *random access*. It is contrasted with the *serial access* mode of operation that characterizes shift registers and nonelectronic memories such as magnetic tape and disk units, where to retrieve certain stored data, other unwanted data must be scanned first. Two major kinds of semiconductor memories exist, ROMs and RAMs. A *read-only memory* (ROM) is designed to allow its stored data to be read, but not to be rewritten or changed, during normal system operation. The other type of memory, which is somewhat misleadingly called *random-access memory* (RAM), can be read from and written into during normal operation. Since ROMs and RAMs both use the same random-access retrieval mode, a more appropriate term for a RAM would be a read-and-write memory (RWM); however, the term RAM is well established with the foregoing meaning. ROMs are used to store programs and other permanent information; RAMs are typically employed as scratchpad memories to store intermediate results and similar temporary data. ROMs are also useful as general-purpose (Boolean) function generators.

A variety of general-purpose and special-purpose data-processing ICs are produced using LSI technology. In the general-purpose category we find microprocessors and one-chip microcomputers. A *microprocessor* is an integrated central processing unit (CPU) for a computer, and contains all the logic circuits necessary to fetch, decode, and execute instructions from an externally stored program. A (one-chip) *microcomputer* contains a microprocessor, memories (ROM and RAM) for program and data storage, and interface circuits for connecting with external IO devices. The instruction set of a typical microprocessor is such that any desired computation can be performed by executing an appropriate program. Hence microprocessors and microcomputers represent universal design components. Some computations may require extremely large amounts of computation time or memory space, thereby limiting the range of operations for which microprocessors and microcomputers can be usefully employed by themselves. LSI technology has also been successfully applied to the fabrication of special-purpose data-processing circuits that execute a small fixed set of operations very efficiently. For example, combinational LSI circuits that perform fixed-point binary multiplication are commercially available. Also available are more general (sequential) arithmetic processors that execute a full range of fixed-point and floating-point operations; they are used, for instance, in pocket calculators. Many special-purpose processors have been developed to control the operation of specific devices such as CRT terminals, printers, magnetic disk units, and communication lines, which constitute the IO devices of microprocessor-based systems. Often these special-purpose controllers are constructed from microcomputers that have been programmed during manufacture to carry out a specific set of IO control tasks.

Figure 4.53 shows a combinational multiplier circuit of a type that is appropriate for LSI. It multiplies two 4-bit unsigned binary numbers via a scheme similar to that of Fig. 4.46b, but dispensing with the accumulator and using multiple adders. Each row of AND gates in Fig. 4.53 computes a shifted partial product of the form $2^i x_i Y$. This partial product is then passed through an adder stage composed of three full adders, where it is

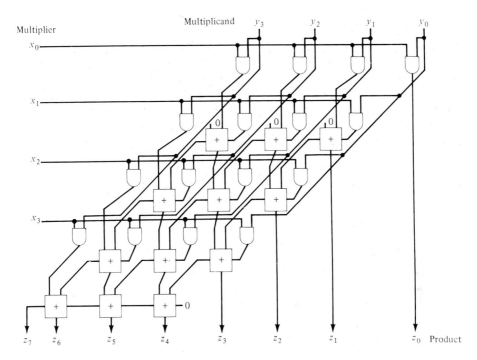

Figure 4.53 Combinational multiplier circuit suitable for LSI implementation.

added to the sum of the preceding partial products. The required shifting of the partial products is achieved via the spatial positioning of the AND gates and full adders. For a typical word size of $n = 8$ or 16, this approach requires far more hardware than an equivalent sequential multiplier circuit such as that of Fig. 4.47. This extra hardware is made feasible through LSI, and a significant reduction in multiplication time is achieved. The uniform array-like structure of the combinational multiplier also facilitates its implementation using a single IC.

Figure 4.54 shows the general structure of a microprocessor-based system composed of LSI ICs. At its heart is a microprocessor that serves as the main control unit of the system. It executes programs that are stored in the ROM part of the main memory M, while the RAM part of M serves as a working or scratchpad memory. An optional arithmetic circuit is shown here that serves as an extension to, or "coprocessor" of, the main microprocessor, and is used by the latter to execute the more complex arithmetic operations. Several IO control circuits link the microprocessor to the outside world, which is represented by a set of IO devices. A central shared bus forms the main communication path between the various system components. The organization and application of programmable microprocessor-based systems such as that of Fig. 4.54 are considered more fully in the remainder of this book. In this chapter we restrict our attention to the simpler LSI components, especially ROMs and RAMs, and their use in the design of nonprogrammable systems.

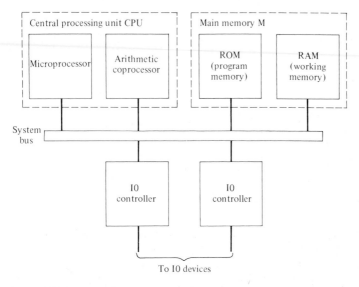

Figure 4.54 Structure of a microprocessor-based system.

Although LSI circuits contain an order of magnitude more internal components (transistors and gates) than MSI circuits, the number of IO pins available is only slightly greater. Forty is a typical number of pins attached to an LSI IC. It follows that communication among LSI circuits is word by word, as in register-level MSI design. This allows many of the design concepts for register-transfer circuits discussed in Sec. 4.2, including the use of word-oriented block diagrams and RTL descriptions, to be extended to LSI (and VLSI) design. Every microprocessor has its own built-in programming language, which in symbolic form (assembly language) can be used as an RTL to specify the behavior of a microprocessor-based system. The use of this language to define system behavior (assembly-language programming) constitutes a major part of the system design process, and is examined in Chap. 6.

4.3.2 Memory Technology

Many different technologies are available for storing binary information, and their physical characteristics vary over a wide range. Examples include semiconductor electronic circuits, magnetic ferrite cores, magnetic disks, punched cards, and printed paper. A computer system frequently contains memory units that employ several different technologies, a consequence of the fact that no one technology has all the desirable characteristics of an information store. In particular, inexpensive memories tend to be slow (memory speed may be measured by the time required to perform a read or write operation), while fast memories tend to be expensive. A general-purpose computer with the structure shown in Fig. 4.54 can be expected to have the following three types of memories:

1. A small but very fast memory composed of from eight to 16 registers and forming part of the CPU; this is sometimes called a *register file*.
2. A much larger but somewhat slower *main memory* M composed of ROM and RAM ICs; the capacity of M is usually measured in kilobytes, where a kilobyte, denoted by 1K bytes, is $2^{10} = 1024$ 8-bit words.
3. An even larger and slower *secondary memory* typically composed of magnetic disk and tape units, and having a capacity measured in millions of bytes (megabytes). Secondary memories are attached to a computer system as IO devices.

The foregoing memory subsystems are organized in a hierarchical fashion that allows the CPU to interact mainly with its register file and main memory. Blocks of information are transferred from time to time between main and secondary memory, giving the CPU indirect access to the latter via main memory M. Here we are concerned only with IC memories of the kind used to design M.

As mentioned already, memories of both the ROM and RAM types employ a storage and retrieval method called random access. Figure 4.55 outlines the structure of such a memory. Most of the area of the memory IC chip is occupied by an array of 1-bit storage cells. A group of *m* cells is used to store an *m*-bit word, and is assigned a unique *p*-bit

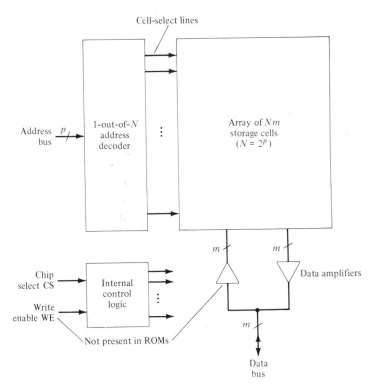

Figure 4.55 Structure of an integrated memory employing random access.

address, where $2^p = N$. Addresses are supplied to the memory via a p-bit memory address bus. The address is decoded by a 1-out-of-N decoder (the address decoder), which activates a select line S causing the corresponding cells to be selected for external access. In the ROM case, the contents of the selected m cells are transferred to the m-bit data bus, whence they are made available to external devices such as a CPU. A RAM requires an additional control line called the *write-enable* (WE) line, which indicates whether a read or a write operation is to be performed using the addressed cells. A read operation (WE = 0) proceeds in much the same way as a ROM read operation. In a write operation (WE = 1), data are transferred from the external data bus to the addressed cells, replacing their old contents. The data bus of a RAM often consists of m bidirectional lines; in a ROM a unidirectional (output) data bus suffices. Finally, ROM and RAM ICs have a general enable line termed the *chip-select* (CS) line, which must be active for the memory to respond to read or write requests. As we will see shortly, CS lines play an important role in the expansion of memory ICs to form larger memories.

The basic storage cell of most ROMs is a simple semiconductor switch that is permanently turned on or off, thereby generating a constant 1 or 0 data bit whenever it is accessed. A ROM must be "programmed" in advance to determine the data stored in its storage cells. This may be done in the IC fabrication process by selectively including contacts in cells where a closed switch is desired, and omitting the contacts where an open switch is desired. This process is termed *mask programming*, since the ROM contents are determined by the mask used in some patterning step, for example, metalization (see Sec. 2.2). The term ROM is sometimes restricted to memories manufactured in this manner. Another class of ROMs is manufactured with a fusible link included in every storage cell, which can be opened selectively or "blown" by passing an electric current through it. Such ROMs then can be programmed electrically after the ROM IC has been fabricated and packaged. Figure 4.56 shows the internal structure of a bipolar ROM IC of this type. Each storage cell consists of a transistor cell, which, when selected by the appropriate address, supplies a signal via a fusible link to some output data line D_i. This signal is V_{CC}, representing logical 1, if the fuse is intact, and 0 otherwise. The foregoing programming methods are irreversible, so that once a ROM has been programmed, its contents cannot subsequently be changed.

There is another important class of read-only memories called (*erasable*) *programmable read-only memories* (EPROMs, or simply PROMs), which can be reprogrammed many times. In a common type of PROM, a 1 or 0 is indicated by the presence or absence of a stored charge in a special type of MOS transistor whose gate electrode is encapsulated in silicon dioxide, an excellent insulator; see Fig. 4.57. As a result, a stored electronic charge can be retained on the gate for an extremely long period of time (many years), even with the frequent removal of small amounts of charge each time the stored charge is read. To program PROMs composed of transistor cells of this type, a high voltage (30 V or higher) is applied between the source and drain terminals of an uncharged cell for a fixed time, so that electrons are created with sufficient energy to penetrate the oxide insulation and collect on the buried gate electrode. Erasure or discharge of a cell is accomplished by the simple means of exposing the cell surface to ultraviolet light. This causes the insulation around the buried gate to break down temporarily, allowing the stored charge to leak away, thus returning the cell to the 0 state.

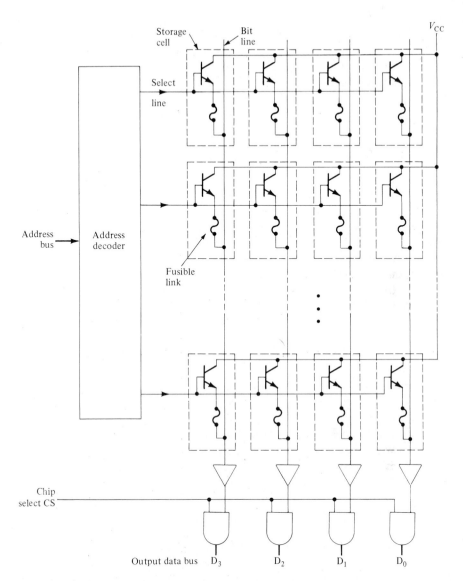

Figure 4.56 Structure of a bipolar ROM employing fusible links.

PROMs can readily be programmed by a system designer using a PROM programming unit, which is a standard component of microprocessor development systems; see Fig. 1.45. PROMs are particularly useful during the development phase of a new micro-processor-based system for the storage of the system's control software. This software can easily be changed or replaced to implement design changes or correct errors.

The circuits used to implement RAM cells are inherently more complex than those of ROMs, since a RAM cell must be capable of being written into (programmed) as well

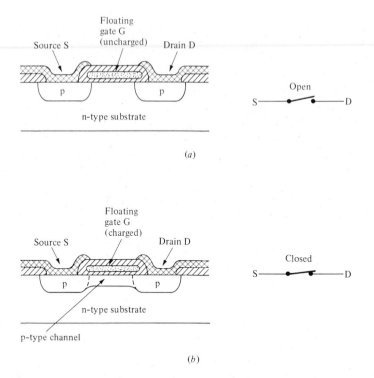

Floating gate G (uncharged)

Source S

Drain D

p

p

n-type substrate

Open

S———• •———D

(a)

Floating gate G (charged)

Source S

Drain D

p

p

n-type substrate

p-type channel

Closed

S———• •———D

(b)

Figure 4.57 Erasable PROM cell and an equivalent switch: (a) storing 0 (erased state); (b) storing 1.

as being read from during normal operation. The complexity of RAM cells varies from about one to six transistors. There is considerable economic incentive to keep the cells as simple as possible, consistent with reasonable production yields and reliability of operation. RAM ICs with a storage capacity of 64K bits (2^{16} bits) or more have been mass produced since the early 1980s.

Figure 4.58 shows a six-transistor RAM cell, which is basically an unclocked latch composed of two cross-coupled MOS inverters. The stored data are represented by the complementary pair of signals $Q, \overline{Q}$. The logical behavior of this type of memory cell is described in Fig. 3.29; it has two stable states corresponding to $Q = 0$ and $Q = 1$. To minimize the number of external interconnections to the cell, an important consideration in LSI design, a pair of bidirectional lines B_0 and B_1 called the *bit* (or *bit/sense*) lines are used for transferring data to and from the cell. A single *select* line S (also called a *word* line) is used to select the cell for both reading and writing. As explained in Sec. 2.3, each of the transistor pairs T_1, T_{R1} and T_2, T_{R2} forms an nMOS inverter, with T_{R1} and T_{R2} acting as resistors. The remaining two transistors T_3 and T_4 are used as IO switches to allow reading and writing via the bit lines.

When it is not being accessed, the RAM cell of Fig. 4.58 has its select line S held at 0. Consequently transistors T_3 and T_4 are switched off, effectively disconnecting the cell from the bit lines. The bit lines themselves are normally held at logical 1 via external pull-up resistors. First let us consider a read operation. The cell is selected by setting S to

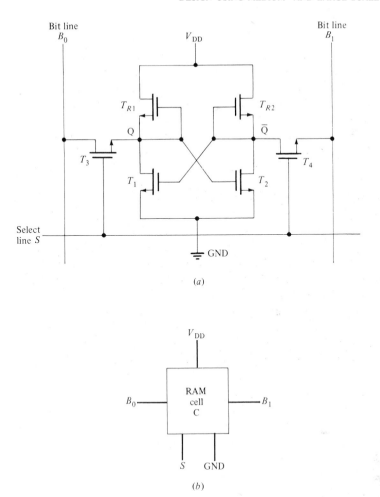

Figure 4.58 Six-transistor static nMOS RAM cell C: (*a*) electronic circuit; (*b*) symbol.

1, which switches T_3 and T_4 on thereby connecting the stored signals Q and $\overline{Q}$ to bit lines B_0 and B_1 respectively. If $Q = 1$, that is, the cell is storing 1, then $\overline{Q}$ pulls B_1 from its normal (weak) 1 state to 0. The resulting 0 pulse on B_1 is processed by an external amplifier, called a *sense* or *read amplifier,* which outputs a 1 signal to the appropriate external data line of the RAM. Since $Q = B_0 = 1$, there is no change on line B_0. In a similar manner, when the cell stores 0, indicated by $Q = 0$, Q produces a 0 signal on line B_0, while B_1 remains unchanged. Thus by monitoring the signals on either one of the bit lines, say B_0, the cell's state can be read out. Note that reading the cell has no effect on its state, and hence this type of cell is said to have *nondestructive readout.*

To write new data into the RAM cell, control circuits are required that can temporarily force the bit lines to the 0 value. Suppose, for instance, that we wish to write 1 into a cell that currently stores 0, implying that $Q = 0$ and $\overline{Q} = 1$. As in a read operation, S is set to 1, causing T_3 and T_4 to switch on. Then a (strong) 0 is applied to B_1, while a (strong) 1 is applied to B_0. This input combination causes the storage latch to change state (T_2 switches on and T_1 switches off), resulting in the new state $Q = B_0 = 1$ and $\overline{Q} = B_1 = 0$. This state remains in the cell when the select line returns to 0. If the cell already stores a 1, then writing 1 in the above manner does not affect the cell. To write 0 into the cell, S is set to 1, and the bit lines B_0 and B_1 are forced to 0 and 1 respectively. The behavior of this cell may also be analyzed using the CSA theory of Sec. 3.1.1. (Prob. 4.37).

Figure 4.59 shows, in simplified form, how storage cells of the foregoing type are connected to construct a complete RAM. Note the two-dimensional matrix or array

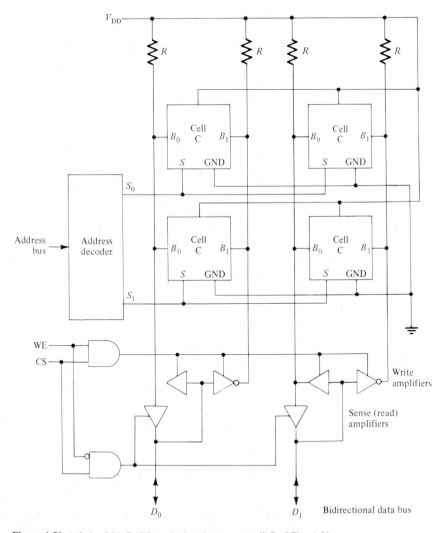

Figure 4.59 A 2- by 2-bit RAM employing the storage cell C of Fig. 4.58.

layout, also seen in Fig. 4.56, which is a basic characteristic of most ROMs and RAMs. Three-state logic is used to allow the same set of external data lines to serve as both input and output lines. During a write operation, which requires WE = 1, the sense amplifiers are disabled. This causes their output lines to assume the high-impedance state Z, thereby logically disconnecting them from the data bus. Similarly, during a read operation (WE = 0) the three-state write amplifiers are disabled, so that they have no effect on the bit lines.

The above type of RAM is called *static* because, except when new data are being written into the memory, the stored data can be retained unchanged for an indefinite period. There is another important class of RAMs called *dynamic RAMs* with the property that the stored data spontaneously decay or leak away, and must be restored at regular intervals. As discussed in Sec. 2.3, dynamic MOS circuits store information in the form of packets of electric charge in capacitors; the presence (absence) of a charge packet indicates a stored 1 (0). The major advantage of dynamic RAMs is the simplicity of their storage cells. As illustrated in Fig. 4.60, a dynamic storage cell can be constructed from a capacitor C and a single transistor T. C is the storage element, while T acts as a switch for charging and discharging C via the single bit line B. A select line S from the address decoder is used to turn T on and off, thereby allowing C to be selectively charged and discharged.

To write a data bit D into the dynamic RAM cell, D is applied to the bit line B. Then the select line S is set to 1, causing C to charge if $D = 1$, or discharge if $D = 0$. The value of D is thus stored in the form of a zero or full charge on C. For reading the contents of the cell, B is converted to an output line, and the cell is again selected by setting S to 1. If C is charged, that is, storing 1, it then discharges through the B line, producing a current pulse that is detected by a sense amplifier, and causing 1 to appear on the corresponding output data line of the RAM. If C is discharged before reading begins, no current pulse is produced on B, and a 0 data output is generated. Clearly this readout process is *destructive,* since reading a cell always leaves it in the 0 state. If the cell originally stored 1, the read operation must be immediately followed by a write 1 operation, which restores the original state. This extra write step is carried out automatically by the RAM's control circuits, and thus the destructive feature of the basic read process is shielded from the user.

The insulation of the capacitor C in the RAM cell of Fig. 4.60 is less than perfect; hence even if the cell is never read, a stored charge tends to leak away fairly rapidly, typically in a few milliseconds. To prevent the RAM's contents from being lost in this

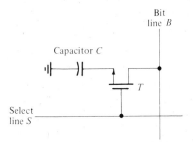

Figure 4.60 A one-transistor dynamic RAM cell.

way, they must be restored at regular intervals, a process called refreshing the memory. A cell can be refreshed simply by executing a read operation addressed to that cell; as discussed above, the read cycle includes an automatic rewrite that restores any stored charge to its maximum level. Accordingly, dynamic RAMs can be refreshed by an external control circuit that generates all addresses in sequence, and specifies a read operation for each address; the resulting data appearing on the RAM's data bus are ignored. In a microprocessor-based system refreshing can often be done while the RAM is otherwise idle, and hence its impact on the overall speed of operation of the system is usually quite small. Static RAMs require no refreshing, and therefore are simpler to use. However, their more complex storage cells—compare Figs. 4.58 and 4.60—means that fewer storage cells can be placed on a single IC chip of a given size and circuit technology. Thus the single-chip RAMs with the greatest storage capacity usually employ dynamic rather than static circuits.

Figure 4.61 summarizes the most important technology-dependent properties of integrated ROMs and RAMs. ROMs and dynamic RAMs generally achieve the highest storage capacity per IC. As discussed in Chap. 2, improvements in IC manufacturing technologies continue to increase the maximum economically achievable storage capacity of all types of memory ICs. The major disadvantages of dynamic RAMs are generally higher access times, and the need for circuits to control refreshing. Most types of RAMs are *volatile*, meaning that switching off the power to the RAM destroys the stored information. Semiconductor ROMs and most types of magnetic memories are nonvolatile.

4.3.3 Memory System Design

We now turn to the task of designing the main memory system of a computer using off-the-shelf memory ICs. Only RAMs will be considered explicitly; however, most of what is said also applies to ROMs—allowing, of course, for the fact that ROMs are read-only devices. RAMs are among the most common ICs found in microprocessor-based systems, and are commercially available in a variety of types and sizes from most semiconductor manufacturers. Some smaller RAM ICs can be found in the 7400 TTL series, for example, the 7489 64-bit RAM, which is organized as a 16- by 4-bit array. Large RAMs in the LSI/VLSI range usually employ either static or dynamic MOS circuits of the type discussed above. RAM ICs are organized as N- by m-bit arrays, where N is the number of addressable word-storage locations available and m is the word size, which generally ranges from one to eight.

Feature	ROM	Static RAM	Dynamic RAM
Contents alterable on-line?	No	Yes	Yes
Storage capacity per IC	Very high	High	Very high
Access time	Lowest	Lower	Low
Refreshing required?	No	No	Yes
Volatile?	No	Yes	Yes

Figure 4.61 Some major characteristics of IC memories.

Two key factors in the design of a memory system are its hardware cost and its speed of operation. If an X- by Y-bit memory is to be built from N- by m-bit RAM ICs, then at least $n = XY/(Nm)$ of the latter are needed. Additional ICs may also be required for address decoding, signal driving, and similar peripheral activities. Generally speaking, hardware cost is minimized by using as few RAM ICs as possible, which implies employing ICs with the largest available storage capacity Nm. A basic measure of the operating speed of a memory is its *access time* t_A, which is the maximum time required to read a word from the memory. t_A is measured from the application of a new address to the memory's address terminals, to the appearance of all bits of the addressed word on the output data terminals of the memory. The process of reading (writing) a word, which requires various signals to be applied to the address, data, and control lines of the memory (see Fig. 4.55) is termed a read (write) *memory cycle*. Another important memory speed measure is the *memory cycle time* t_C, which is the minimum time that must elapse between the initiation of two successive memory cycles. Different cycle times may be defined for read and write operations; often they are identical, allowing a single memory cycle time t_C to be assigned to the memory. Typically $t_C = t_A$ for ROMs and static RAMs, while $t_C > t_A$ in the case of dynamic RAMs. In general, the t_A and t_C parameters of a memory system must be chosen to match the speed characteristics of the device that controls the memory, which, in the cases of interest here, is a microprocessor.

Proper operation of a RAM or ROM requires fairly precise timing of the signals applied to its IO lines to control read or write cycles. Consider, for instance, the Intel 2102 (also called the 8102), a popular 1K-bit RAM IC introduced in the mid-1970s, which uses static nMOS circuits. As indicated in Fig. 4.62 the 2102 is organized as a 1024- by 1-bit array, and so requires 10 address lines $A_9{:}A_0$. Separate input and output data lines are provided, as well as the standard control lines write enable, denoted $R/\overline{W}$, and chip select $\overline{CE}$ (for chip enable). $R/\overline{W} = 1$ specifies a read operation, and $R/\overline{W} = 0$ specifies a write operation. The 2102 is selected for a read or write operation by setting $\overline{CE} = 0$. When $\overline{CE} = 1$ the 2102 is disabled, and the output data line D_{out} is held in the high-impedance state Z; as will be seen later, this facilitates the interconnection of several 2102s to form larger RAMs. Two additional connections are needed for power ($+5$ V) and ground; hence the 2102 is packaged in a 16-pin DIP.

Figure 4.63 presents representative timing diagrams for the read and write cycles of the 2102 RAM; more detailed timing data can be found in the manufacturer's literature

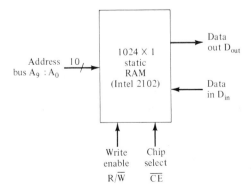

Figure 4.62 A 1K-bit nMOS static RAM IC, the Intel 2102.

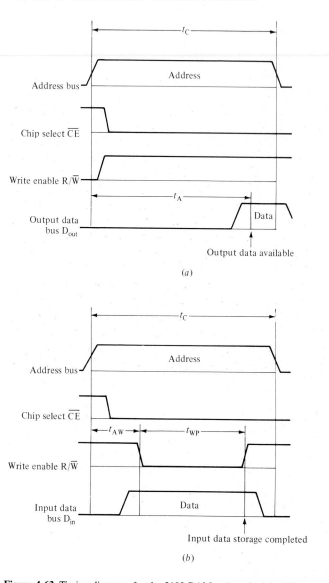

Figure 4.63 Timing diagrams for the 2102 RAM: (*a*) read cycle; (*b*) write cycle.

(Intel, 1975a). A read or write cycle begins with the application of a new address word to the address bus A. The chip-select line $\overline{CE}$ must be enabled ($\overline{CE} = 0$) at about the same time; it may be held at the 0 level for a sequence of memory cycles addressed to the same chip. In the case of a read operation, the write-enable signal R/$\overline{W}$ must be brought to the 1 level; it may be held at 1 for a sequence of read cycles. The data being read become available on the output data line D_{out} t_A seconds after the address application as indicated in Fig. 4.63a. The timing of a typical write cycle appears in Fig. 4.63b. The data to be written into the 2102 are applied to the input data line D_{in} at about the same time as the destination address is placed on the address bus A. The $R/\overline{W}$ line must be held at the 1 level for a minimum period called the *address setup time* t_{AW} to allow the individual address bits to stabilize at their final values. (Initiating the write operation before the address has stabilized could cause the input data to be written into one or more incorrect locations in the RAM.) After t_{AW} seconds $R/\overline{W}$ is changed from 1 to 0 to initiate the write process. It must be held at 0 for a minimum period t_{WP}, called the *write pulse width*, to ensure that the data have been stored in the RAM. During this period the input data D_{in} must not change. After t_{WP} seconds, $R/\overline{W}$ returns to 1, and the current address and data words can be removed, allowing a new memory cycle to begin. Note that a sequence of write cycles requires a sequence of 0 pulses on $R/\overline{W}$, not a continuous 0 signal. The permissible values of t_A, t_C, t_{AW}, t_{WP} and other timing parameters that we have ignored appear in the data sheets for the 2102.

As observed in the discussion of SSI/MSI circuits, component expansion. is a fundamental design issue. In memory design, component expansion has two aspects: increasing the word size m and increasing the word storage capacity N. Word-size expansion presents no difficulties. Suppose that a given $N \times m$ RAM IC is to be used to implement an $N \times km$ memory. It suffices to take k copies of the $N \times m$ RAM and interconnect them as indicated in Fig. 4.64. The external address and control lines are connected in common to all k ICs, while the k bidirectional data buses are merged to make a single km-bit data bus.

Increasing the word-storage capacity implies increasing the number of addresses used. As illustrated in Fig. 4.65, this may require the use of additional address decoding circuits. Suppose that it is desired to expand the capacity of a RAM from $N = 2^p$ to $2^k N = 2^{p+k}$ words, while retaining the word size at m bits. Obviously a total of 2^k copies of the basic RAM are required, and the number of address lines must be raised from p to $p + k$. As indicated in the figure, the p low-order address lines $A_{p-1}:A_0$ are connected in common to the address input terminals of all 2^k RAM ICs. The k new high-order address lines $A_{p+k-1}:A_p$ are connected to the inputs of a 1-out-of-2^k decoder circuit. The 2^k output lines of this decoder are connected to the chip-select (CS) inputs of the 2^k RAM ICs. Hence each $(p + k)$-bit address pattern applied to the memory system causes just one of the RAM ICs to be enabled. The RAM that is selected is determined by address bits

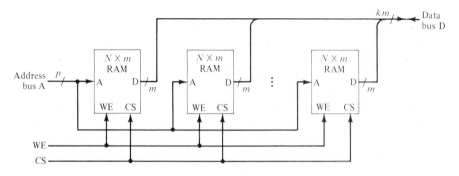

Figure 4.64 Design of an N- by km-bit RAM from k N- by m-bit RAMs.

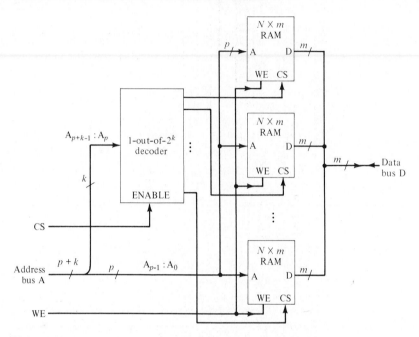

Figure 4.65 Design of a $2^k N$- by m-bit RAM from 2^k N- by m-bit RAMs.

$A_{p+k-1}:A_p$; the word location within this RAM chip is selected by address bits $A_{p-1}:A_0$. The external chip-select and write-enable lines are connected in the straightforward fashion shown in Fig. 4.65. As noted earlier, RAMs are generally designed so that when disabled (CS = 0), the output data bus goes to the high-impedance state Z. Thus corresponding data lines from the RAM ICs may be directly wired together, effectively forming a three-state data bus. (See Sec. 2.3.3. for a discussion of three-state logic.) In the memory system of Fig. 4.65 only the RAM IC that has 1 applied to its CS input line can transfer data to or from the bidirectional external data bus at any time.

The word-size and storage-capacity expansion techniques illustrated in Figs. 4.64 and 4.65 can easily be combined in the same circuit. Figure 4.66 shows a 4096- by 2-bit RAM constructed from eight copies of the 2102 static RAM IC discussed above; see Figs. 4.62 and 4.63. Note how this circuit forms a two-dimensional array of ICs whose structure is similar to that of the storage-cell array within each IC (Fig. 4.59). The right-hand column of RAM ICs stores bit 0 of each word in the memory, while the left-hand column stores bit 1. A 1-out-of-4 decoder with inverted outputs is used to decode the two extra address bits A_{10} and A_{11}. The corresponding (unidirectional) data lines of each column are wired together, forming a pair of 2-bit three-state input and output data buses.

Figure 4.67 shows another commercially available 1K-bit RAM, the Intel 2111 (also called the 8111), which has a 256- by 4-bit organization and employs static nMOS circuits. Unlike the 2102, the 2111 has a single bidirectional data bus and two chip-select inputs $\overline{CE}_1$ and $\overline{CE}_2$. The chip-select lines are ANDed inside the 2111, so that both must be enabled, that is, $\overline{CE}_1 = \overline{CE}_2 = 0$, to enable the 2111. When either $\overline{CE}_1$ or $\overline{CE}_2$ is 1, the

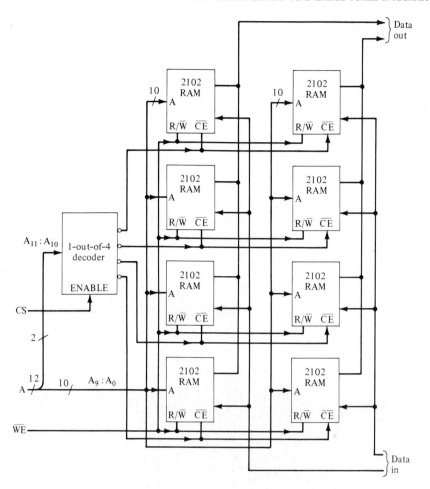

Figure 4.66 A 4096- by 2-bit RAM constructed from eight 2102 1K-bit RAMs.

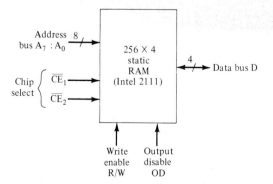

Figure 4.67 Another 1K-bit nMOS static RAM IC, the Intel 2111.

2111's data bus enters the high-impedance state. This RAM chip also has an extra input control line called OD (output disable), which disables the output circuits of the 2111, independent of the states of the write-enable and chip-select lines. The OD line is activated during write cycles to prevent spurious internal data from being read from the 2111 onto the common data bus, while the latter is being used as an input bus to transfer externally supplied data into the RAM. (This problem does not arise in RAMs such as the 2102 that have separate input and output data buses.)

The extra chip-select line of the 2111 RAM is intended to simplify expansion of the word storage capacity. Two examples will be given to illustrate this. Suppose that a 1024-by 8-bit RAM, that is, a 1K-byte RAM, is to be designed using 2111s. Clearly eight 2111s are necessary, and they can be configured in essentially the same 4×2 organization appearing in Fig. 4.66. However, the 1-out-of-4 decoder can be replaced by a pair of inverters as depicted in Fig. 4.68; even these can be dispensed with if the address

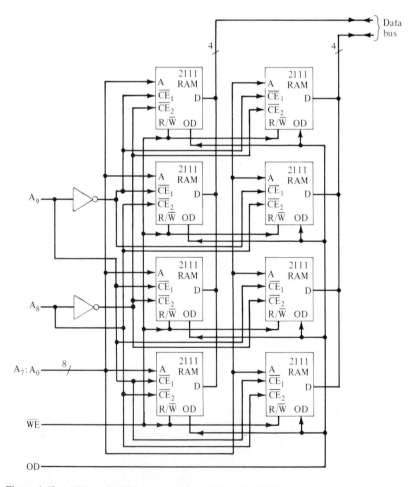

Figure 4.68 A 1K-byte RAM constructed from eight 2111 1K-bit RAMs.

bits are available in both true and complemented form. These inverters, in combination with the AND gates inside the 2111s that link the $\overline{CE}_1$ and $\overline{CE}_2$ signals, perform the required 1-out-of-4 address decoding function. The advantage of several chip-select lines is more apparent in the design of very large memories. Consider, for instance, the design of an 8K-byte RAM from 2111s. A total of 64 RAM ICs are required, which must arranged in 32 rows and two columns. To address the rows using the general scheme of Fig. 4.65, a 1-out-of-32 address decoder is necessary. A possible design for such a decoder requiring three ICs is shown in Fig. 4.18. Each output of this decoder is connected to all the chip-select inputs of the 2111s in a single row of the memory. A simpler addressing scheme using only two small decoder ICs is given in Fig. 4.69. The five extra address lines $A_{12}{:}A_8$ are divided into two groups of two and three lines, which are decoded separately via the two decoders. The outputs of the 1-out-of-4 decoder are connected to $\overline{CE}_1$ terminals of the RAM ICs, while the outputs of the 1-out-of-8 decoder are connected to the $\overline{CE}_2$ terminals. These connections are designed to give each row of 2111s a unique 5-bit address $A_{12}A_{11}A_{10}A_9A_8$. For example, consider the row appearing in Fig. 4.69 whose address is

$$A_{12}A_{11}A_{10}A_9A_8 \;=\; 10100$$

The $\overline{CE}_1$ inputs of the RAMs in this row are connected to the output of the 1-out-of-4 decoder that is enabled by $A_{12}A_{11} = 10$. The $\overline{CE}_2$ inputs in the same row are connected to the output of the 1-out-of-8 decoder that is enabled by $A_{10}A_9A_8 = 100$. This row therefore is selected by the coincidence of enabling signals from the decoders on the row's chip select lines. In effect, the row address is being split into X and Y coordinates, each of which has its own chip-select terminal and address decoder.

The practical design considerations discussed in Sec. 2.3 should receive careful attention when designing a memory system. In circuits such as that of Fig. 4.69, certain lines have large fan-out, and buffers may be necessary to meet loading constraints. To minimize noise problems, memory arrays should be carefully laid out on printed-circuit boards or other IC carriers, and decoupling capacitors should be used in accordance with the IC manufacturer's recommendations; see, for instance, Fig. 2.74.

4.3.4 ROM-Based Design

ROMs and PROMs constitute very useful LSI/VLSI building blocks for complex digital systems. As we show here, they are general-purpose logic elements in the sense that they can be programmed to realize essentially any desired function. ROMs and PROMs differ from each other in the way they are programmed. However, there is no significant difference in the way they are used in digital systems, or in their impact on system performance. Because they can be erased and reprogrammed using fairly simple equipment, PROMs are particularly convenient for use in one-of-a-kind designs. ROMs are better suited to mask programming and similar mass production techniques. For simplicity, only the term ROM will be used from now on, but all the discussion is directly applicable to PROMs as well as ROMs.

A ROM (or PROM) has the external connections shown in Fig. 4.70a, which include a p-bit address bus A, an m-bit output data bus D, and a chip-select control line CS.

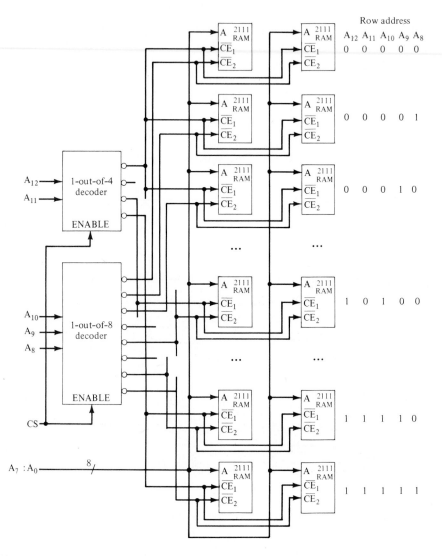

Figure 4.69 Addressing circuitry for an 8K-byte RAM constructed from 64 2111s.

When the ROM is enabled (CS = 1), and a p-bit address is applied to A, the m-bit word whose storage address is on A is read out onto D. The signal D_i appearing on each data line is determined by the address A, and therefore can be treated as a logic function $F_i(A)$ = $F_i(A_0, A_i, \ldots, A_{p-1})$ of the p address bits. If a set of p logic variables $X = (x_0, x_1, \ldots, x_{p-1})$ is applied to the ROM's address bus as depicted in Fig. 4.70b, then the logic function

$$F(X) = F_0(X), F_1(X), \cdots, F_{m-1}(X)$$

is produced on the data bus. Clearly a 2^p- by m-bit ROM can be used in this manner to

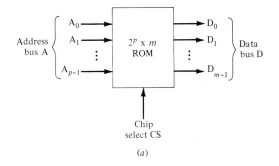

(a)

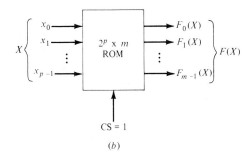

CS = 1

(b)

Figure 4.70 A 2^p- by m-bit ROM: (a) as a memory; (b) as a combinational function generator.

realize any combinational logic function F involving up to p input and m output lines. The ROM causes a propagation delay in the generation of F equal to the ROM's access time t_A. Therefore ROMs may be seen as universal logic elements that can replace SSI/MSI-based combinational circuits of the kind considered earlier in this chapter and in Chap. 2. They permit LSI technology to be applied efficiently to the production of many types of complex combinational circuits.

The 2^p- by m-bit ROM of Fig. 4.70 stores a complete description of the function F in a form that closely resembles a truth table for F. Let $b_{ij} \in \{0, 1\}$ be the bit appearing in the ith row and jth output column of a truth table defining F. Then b_{ij} is the value stored (programmed) in the jth bit position of the ROM word location whose address is i. Hence a truth table for F can be directly mapped into a ROM of appropriate size. This type of ROM-based design is sometimes called *table look-up*, because for each input combination X, the corresponding output value $F(X)$ is "looked up" in the (truth) table stored in the ROM. While it is a design method of great generality, it has the disadvantage that ROM size grows exponentially with the number of input variables needed. Each additional input variable requires the ROM's storage capacity to be doubled. Although LSI allows ROMs and PROMs of very high capacity to be manufactured, ROM function generators are limited to functions of about 12 variables.

Figure 4.71 shows the implementation of 3-bit binary addition using a ROM. There are seven input variables: the two 3-bit operands $X = x_2x_1x_0$ and $Y = y_2y_1y_0$, and the carry-in signal C_{in}. There are four output signals: the 3-bit sum $Z = z_2z_1z_0$ and the carry-out signal C_{out}. Hence a $2^7 \times 4 = 512$-bit ROM is required with the line assignment given in Fig. 4.71a. Figure 4.71b shows the data that must be stored in the ROM to implement binary addition; note that this figure is simply a truth table for addition.

The foregoing way of implementing a p-input m-output combinational function requires a ROM with a storage capacity of $m2^p$ bits, a number that increases very rapidly with p. Frequently a network of several small ROMs can be used instead of a single large ROM. Consider, for example, the design of a 6-bit version of the binary adder of Fig. 4.71. The number of input variables is now 13, and the number of output signals is seven. The ROM's storage capacity must be increased to $2^{13} \times 7 = 57,344$ bits, which is quite large by current LSI/VLSI standards, and is an excessive amount of logic to devote to this relatively simple function. Note that a rather similar problem was encountered in Sec. 3.3 when we considered the design of two-level adder circuits using standard gates; even with only 6 bits per operand, a huge number of gates is necessary. The solution developed there was to partition the addition process into several small addition steps, each of which could be implemented by a two-level circuit, with ripple-carry propaga-

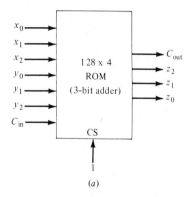

(a)

Address							Stored Data			
C_{in}	y_2	y_1	y_0	x_2	x_1	x_0	C_{out}	z_2	z_1	z_0
0	0	0	0	0	0	0	0	0	0	0
0	0	0	0	0	0	1	0	0	0	1
0	0	0	0	0	1	0	0	0	1	0
			$\cdots$						$\cdots$	
1	1	0	0	0	0	1	0	1	1	0
1	1	0	0	0	1	0	0	1	1	1
1	1	0	0	0	1	1	1	0	0	0
1	1	0	0	1	0	0	1	0	0	1
			$\cdots$						$\cdots$	
1	1	1	1	1	0	1	1	1	0	1
1	1	1	1	1	1	0	1	1	1	0
1	1	1	1	1	1	1	1	1	1	1

(b)

Figure 4.71 A 2^7- by 4-bit ROM implementing 3-bit binary addition: (a) symbol; (b) truth table representing stored data.

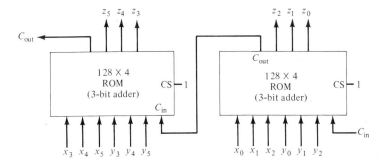

Figure 4.72 A 6-bit binary adder implemented from two 128- by 4-bit ROMs.

tion (or carry lookahead) between the small adders. We adopt the same approach here using ROMs. As illustrated in Fig. 4.72, the 6-bit adder is implemented by two 3-bit adder ROMs with ripple-carry propagation between them. Each 3-bit adder stage requires a small 2^7- by 4-bit ROM of the sort specified by Fig. 4.71. The total ROM storage requirements of this two-stage ripple-carry adder are 1024 bits, which is considerably less than the 57,344 bits necessary for a single-ROM design. While the adder circuit of Fig. 4.72 greatly reduces the effective ROM complexity, it also increases the maximum addition time from t_A to $2t_A$—a typical hardware-speed trade-off.

By combining ROMs used as combinational function generators with registers, sequential circuits can be designed. For example, the general sequential circuit structure of Fig. 3.58, which consists of a combinational part C and a memory part M, can be designed using a ROM for C and a register for M. Consequently, the design of any sequential circuit can be based on a ROM. Figure 4.73 shows a variant of the foregoing ROM-register design, which is very common. Since it is mainly used in the design of special- or general-purpose control circuits, we term it a ROM-based control unit. In a typical controller application the ROM's contents correspond directly to control signals, and hence the ROM is called a *control memory* (CM). In the ROM-based controller of Fig. 4.73, each input (address) X causes a specific word to be read from the CM into the register R. R may then be used to supply control signals to external devices that are controlled by this control unit. Some of the information in R may also be fed back to the address inputs of CM and used to determine the next word read from CM. In this fashion,

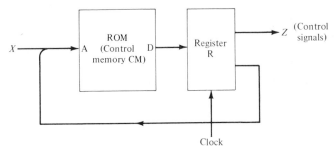

Figure 4.73 General structure of a ROM-based control unit.

CM can be used to generate via R binary sequences of arbitrary length and complexity. ROM-based control units are contrasted with hardwired control units, such as the multiplier controller of Fig. 4.49. In the latter, the control signals reside in "hard" form in the wiring of the combinational decoding circuit D, whereas in ROM-based designs this information is in "soft" or programmable form in the control memory CM.

A simple application of the ROM-based controller approach to the design of a binary up-down counter is illustrated in Fig. 4.74. (The design of up-down counters using SSI circuits was examined in detail in Sec. 3.3.6.) The present counter is required to count either up or down in the standard binary number sequence in response to 1-pulses appearing on the count-in line CI. The 4-bit count output Z is incremented if the DOWN control line is 0; Z is decremented if DOWN = 1. The counter is composed of a 32- by 4-bit ROM CM, and a 4-bit D-type register R. The ROM's contents or program appears in Fig. 4.74b. The DOWN control line is connected directly to the high-order address input A_5 of CM, implying that the count-down function is implemented by the half of the ROM

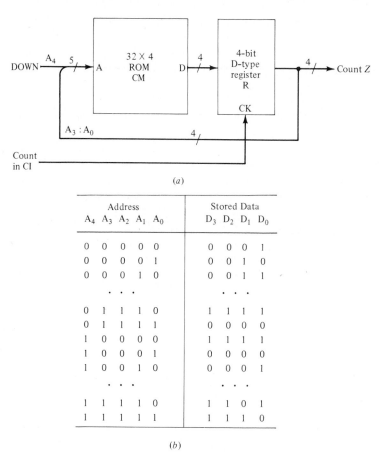

(a)

Address					Stored Data			
A_4	A_3	A_2	A_1	A_0	D_3	D_2	D_1	D_0
0	0	0	0	0	0	0	0	1
0	0	0	0	1	0	0	1	0
0	0	0	1	0	0	0	1	1
		$\cdots$				$\cdots$		
0	1	1	1	0	1	1	1	1
0	1	1	1	1	0	0	0	0
1	0	0	0	0	1	1	1	1
1	0	0	0	1	0	0	0	0
1	0	0	1	0	0	0	0	1
		$\cdots$				$\cdots$		
1	1	1	1	0	1	1	0	1
1	1	1	1	1	1	1	1	0

(b)

Figure 4.74 ROM-based modulo-16 up-down binary counter; (a) circuit diagram; (b) data stored in the ROM.

with addresses 10000 to 11111; the other half of the ROM with addresses 00000 to 01111 implements the count-up function. The output of R, that is, the current count $Z = z_3z_2z_1z_0$, is connected to the remaining address lines A_3: A_0. Consequently the data word stored in the ROM location with address $0z_3z_2z_1z_0$ is $Z + 1$, while $Z - 1$ is stored in the location with addresses $1z_3z_2z_1z_0$. The count line CI is connected to the clock input of the register R, so that whenever a 1-pulse appears on CI, one of the values $Z + 1$ or $Z - 1$ is read from CM into R, as determined by the state of the DOWN line.

Figure 4.75 lists some of the more important applications of ROMs (and PROMs) in the design of digital systems. ROMs are often employed as encoder/decoder circuits for converting data from one type of representation or code into another. Suppose, for instance, that it is desired to convert data from the widely used 7-bit ASCII (American Standards Committee for Information Interchange) code to the EBCDIC (Extended Binary-Coded Decimal Interchange Code) used in many IBM and IBM-compatible computers. Each of these codes allows a full range of alphabetic and numeric symbols to be represented by a 7-bit word. The code conversion process can be accomplished by a 2^7- by 7-bit ROM that stores a suitable code-conversion (truth) table. For each input ASCII character X applied to the ROM's address bus, the ROM outputs the corresponding EBCDIC codeword $F(X)$. The same $2^7 \times 7$ ROM type can, if suitably programmed, be used to convert from EBCDIC to ASCII, or, indeed, perform conversions between any two 7-bit alphanumeric codes.

An important related application of ROMs is as character generators for converting alphanumeric characters from word form, for example, ASCII code, into a two-dimensional pattern suitable for displaying on a CRT terminal, a dot-matrix printer, or similar output device. Figure 4.76 shows a representative commercial character generation IC, the Motorola MCM66720 (Motorola, 1978). It is an 8K-bit ROM that is programmed to store 128 common typographical symbols, each of which is formed by a 7×9 matrix of 1s and 0s. The actual contents of the MCM66720 are listed in Fig. 4.76b, where the small black and white squares denote stored 1s and 0s respectively. Each stored character has a unique 7-bit address A_6:A_0; for example, the character $ has the address A_6:$A_0 = 0100100$. The nine rows R0:R9 within each character can be addressed individually via the four row-select lines RS_3:RS_0. Thus the 11-bit pattern

$$A_6:A_0,RS_3:RS_0 = 0100100,0100$$

Function Type	Application
Combinational	Code conversion
	Character generation
	Arithmetic functions:
	Simple functions (addition, subtraction, etc.) using nonstandard
	number codes
	Complex functions (logarithms, trigonometric functions, etc.)
Sequential	General-purpose sequential circuits
	Microprogrammed control units

Figure 4.75 Some common applications of ROMs.

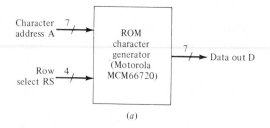

(a)

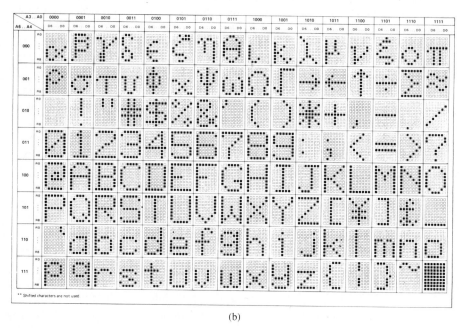

(b)

Figure 4.76 Commercial 8K-bit ROM for character generation, the Motorola MCM66720: *(a)* symbol; *(b)* stored data. *(Courtesy Motorola Inc.)*

addresses the middle row R4 of the $ character, and causes the data

$$D_6 : D_0 = 0111110$$

to be read out. A complete character is read out row by row using nine consecutive read operations. First the character's 7-bit address is placed on the A bus, then the sequence $0000, 0001, \ldots, 1001$ is applied to RS. The data bits defining the character are supplied to the output device in question, where they are used to construct a visual image of the character.

Although simple arithmetic functions such as standard binary addition can be realized by ROM-based circuits, as in the designs of Figs. 4.71 and 4.72, it is usually more efficient in terms of hardware cost to use standard logic-circuit implementations of the kind considered earlier. However, ROMs have significant advantages when non-standard number codes are used; such codes can complicate the implementation of otherwise simple arithmetic operations. Suppose, for instance, that it is desired to design an octal (base 8) adder that uses the nonstandard "binary-coded octal" code specified in Fig. 4.77. The 3-bit codewords of this code have been randomly assigned to the eight octal digits 0, 1, 2, ..., 7 so that the individual bits have no obvious weight or similar properties that might be exploited in designing the adder. This structural randomness is of no consequence in a ROM-based design; all that is required is a truth table for the desired addition function. Figure 4.78 shows such a truth table for one-digit octal addition employing the nonstandard code. A one-digit octal adder can then be realized by the 128-by 4-bit ROM of Fig. 4.71a with the data of Fig. 4.78 programmed into it. Two copies of this ROM can be connected in the ripple-carry configuration of Fig. 4.72 to produce a two-digit nonstandard octal adder.

ROMs are also useful in the design of circuits to implement relatively complex arithmetic functions, where it may be simpler to store the function values in a table rather than build processing circuits to compute them. ROM-implemented functions have the further advantage of high speed, since even the most complex function value is obtained via a single read operation. Consider the task of multiplying two 8-bit unsigned binary integers to produce a 16-bit result. Two possible techniques for implementing this operation were discussed already: the sequential shift-and-add design of Figs. 4.47–4.49, and combinational array approach of Fig. 4.53. A one-ROM implementation of 8-bit multiplication would require a ROM with a storage capacity of $2^{16} \times 16 = 1,048,578$ bits (1 megabit), which is presently difficult to fabricate on a single IC chip. It

Octal Digit	Standard Binary Code	Nonstandard Binary Code
0	000	010
1	001	101
2	010	110
3	011	000
4	100	111
5	101	100
6	110	001
7	111	011

Figure 4.77 Standard and nonstandard binary codes for representing octal numbers.

Address							Stored Data			
C_{in}	y_2	y_1	y_0	x_2	x_1	x_0	C_{out}	z_2	z_1	z_0
0	0	0	0	0	0	0	0	0	0	1
0	0	0	0	0	0	1	1	1	0	1
0	0	0	0	0	1	0	0	0	0	0
			...						...	
1	1	1	1	1	0	1	0	0	0	1
1	1	1	1	1	1	0	0	0	1	1
1	1	1	1	1	1	1	1	1	0	1

Figure 4.78 ROM program for implementing one-digit nonstandard octal addition.

is, however, possible to build the desired multiplier using a network of smaller ROMs and some additional circuits. As in the previous binary addition example, the basic approach is to break the required operation into several smaller operations of the same type. Let $X = X_7{:}X_0$ and $Y = Y_7{:}Y_0$ denote the input operands, the multiplier and multiplicand, and let $Z = Z_{15}{:}Z_0$ be the desired product $X \times Y$. We can bisect the input operands as follows:

$$X = 2^4(X_7{:}X_4) + X_3{:}X_0$$

$$Y = 2^4(Y_7{:}Y_4) + Y_3{:}Y_0$$

The product Z can now be expressed as

$$\begin{aligned} Z &= (2^4(X_7{:}X_4) + X_3{:}X_0) \times (2^4(Y_7{:}Y_4) + Y_3{:}Y_0) \\ &= 2^8 \, (X_7{:}X_4 \times Y_7{:}Y_4) + 2^4(X_7{:}X_4 \times Y_3{:}Y_0) \\ &\quad + 2^4(X_3{:}X_0 \times Y_7{:}Y_4) + (X_3{:}X_0 \times Y_3{:}Y_0) \end{aligned} \qquad (4.30)$$

Equation (4.30) defines Z as the sum of four shifted partial products. Each of the four partial products

$$P = X_7{:}X_4 \times Y_7{:}Y_4$$

$$Q = X_7{:}X_4 \times Y_3{:}Y_0$$

$$R = X_3{:}X_0 \times Y_7{:}Y_4$$

$$S = X_3{:}X_0 \times Y_3{:}Y_0$$

can be implemented by a 2^8- by 8-bit ROM programmed as a 4-bit multiplier; the 2K-bit capacity of this ROM presents no problems. Figure 4.79 shows how Eq. (4.30) can be realized using this approach. A network of 4-bit adders is used to compute the sum of the shifted partial products. The shifting, which is denoted by multiplication by 2^i in (4.30), is implicit in the interconnection pattern of the adders (cf. the combinational array multiplier of Fig. 4.53). If desired, each 4-bit adder can be a 2^9- by 5-bit ROM programmed in the manner indicated in Fig. 4.71. It is probably more economical to use a standard 4-bit adder IC such as the 74283.

ROM-based controllers (Fig. 4.73) are used extensively to design I-units for microprocessors and larger CPUs. In this application the control memory CM has its contents organized into formatted control words called *microinstructions*, each of which defines a set of control signals to be activated during some clock cycle. A sequence of one or more microinstructions designed to control a specific operation, such as addition or multiplication to be performed by the E-unit, is called a *microprogram*, and the control unit is said to be microprogrammed. (Note that the terms microprogram and microprocessor are independent; the prefix micro means small in each case.) The operation to be performed by the E-unit is specified by an *instruction* word I, part of which, the operation-specification part or *opcode*, is transmitted to the microprogrammed control unit. The opcode provides the starting address in CM of a microprogram MP(I) that implements I. The microinstructions forming MP(I) are read one by one from CM to produce the sequence of control signals required in the execution of the instruction I.

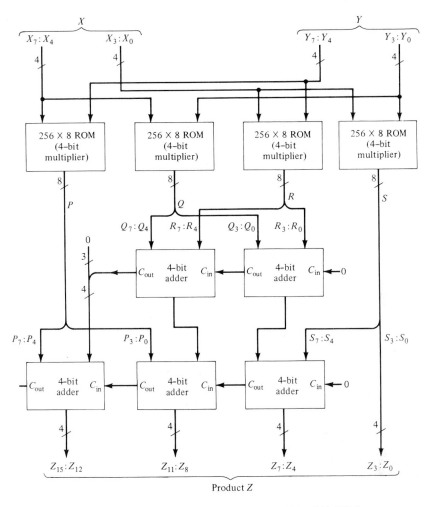

Figure 4.79 An 8-bit binary multiplier constructed using four 256- by 8-bit ROMs.

The main advantage of microprogrammed over hardwired control is the relative ease with which the contents of CM can be changed to rectify design errors, or accommodate changes in the specifications of the system being controlled. PROMs are especially flexible in this regard. Similar changes in a hardwired unit require redesigning the basic circuit structure. In the microprogrammed case it suffices to reprogram the control memory without altering the system structure. Another advantage of microprogramming is that the task of designing a control unit is made simpler and more systematic. The use of microprogramming in the microprocessor context is considered further in Chap. 8. In the next chapter we turn to the basic organization of the CPU itself.

4.4 SUMMARY

Digital components in the MSI range (100 to 1000 transistors per IC) are primarily word-processing devices, where the words of interest are numbers, alphanumeric characters, addresses, instructions, and the like. A typical MSI device has several input-output data buses, each one word wide, and several control lines. The control lines specify the operations to be performed on the data appearing on the input data buses. Control lines also play an important role in expanding a component to increase data word size. A large set of MSI ICs with standard functions and part numbers can be found in the 7400 series of TTL and related devices.

The main combinational MSI component types are multiplexers, decoders, priority encoders, and various types of arithmetic-logic circuits. A multiplexer is usually employed to route data words from one of several sources to a common destination. Multiplexers may also be used as general-purpose Boolean function generators. A decoder is designed to activate a specific output line when a corresponding word (address) is placed on its input data bus. Decoders are principally used in addressing logic, and similar data-selection circuitry. They are also employed as demultiplexers to route data from a common source to one of several possible destinations. An encoder produces a specific output pattern or address for each active input line; the priority attribute ensures that when several input lines are activated simultaneously, a unique output pattern, corresponding to the input line of highest priority, is produced. A wide variety of MSI arithmetic-logic circuits are available, ranging from binary adders to multifunction ALUs that perform fixed-point addition, subtraction, magnitude comparison, and various word-oriented logic operations. There are two major techniques for expanding arithmetic circuits to accommodate larger word sizes: ripple-carry propagation, which is simple but relatively slow, and carry lookahead, which is faster but requires extra support circuits.

The most basic sequential ICs at the MSI level are multibit latches and registers. These are word-storage elements that employ parallel (i.e., word-by-word) input-output data transfer. Shift registers, on the other hand, employ serial (i.e., bit-by-bit) data transfer, which may be combined with parallel input or output transfer in several combinations, such as serial-in parallel-out. Shift registers are used for converting data between serial and parallel form, and for various control functions. Another useful class of MSI devices are counters, which are distinguished by their timing behavior (synchronous or asynchronous) and modulus (the maximum number of different count values produced). The most common counter types are n-bit binary and decade counters, whose moduli are 2^n and 10 respectively.

Circuits constructed from MSI components often take the form of register-transfer systems, in which operations of the form

$$R_0 := F(R_1, R_2, \cdots, R_k); \qquad (4.31)$$

play a central role. Here R_0, R_1, $\cdots$, R_k are registers and F denotes a (combinational) logic or arithmetic operation. F acts on the contents of the registers R_1, R_2, $\cdots$, R_k yielding a result $F(R_1, R_2, \cdots, R_k)$, which is transferred to the results register R_0. Register-transfer circuits often decompose naturally into two parts: a data-processing unit that performs the main computation, data-transfer, and storage tasks; and a control unit that supplies the control signals necessary to select and sequence the operations carried out by the data-processing unit. Data-processing units are typically designed in an ad-hoc fashion based on data-flow considerations. Control unit designs fall into two major categories: hardwired units whose functions are permanently wired in, and (micro)programmed control units whose functions reside in a programmable control memory. The behavior of a register-transfer system may be specified using flowcharts and/or formal descriptions written in register-transfer languages (RTLs). RTLs employ statements such as (4.31), but their use in the design process has not been standardized.

At the LSI design level (over 1000 transistors per IC), the major component types are memories, general-purpose data-processing circuits such as microprocessors and microcomputers, and special-purpose circuits such as complex arithmetic function generators and IO controllers. Memory ICs are often the most numerous ICs in LSI/VLSI systems. They are of two main kinds: read-only memories (ROMs), which store data that can be read but not changed during normal system operation, and random-access memories (RAMs) that allow unrestricted reading and writing of data. ROMs and RAMs are composed of arrays of addressable word stores with a random-access addressing mechanism that permits any stored word to be read out in a fixed time called the access time t_A. A type of ROM called a programmable ROM or PROM has the useful property of being easy to erase and reprogram. RAMs are found in two varieties, static and dynamic. The latter have the simpler storage cells, but require periodic refreshing to prevent loss of the stored data. Most semiconductor RAMs are volatile, which means that the stored data are lost if the power supply is disconnected. ROMs and RAMs can be expanded systematically to increase both the word size and the word-storage capacity of the memory; the latter may require extra address decoding circuits.

ROMs and PROMs provide a straightforward way of applying LSI technology to the implementation of arbitrary combinational and sequential logic functions. A combinational function F can be realized by storing its truth table in a ROM of suitable size. The input combination X is applied as an address to the ROM causing the corresponding function value $F(X)$ to be read out as data. With the addition of one or more registers, a ROM can realize any sequential function. Great redesign flexibility results from the fact that the ROM can be reprogrammed or replaced to alter the function being realized. ROM-based circuits are useful for code conversion, character generation, and arithmetic operations involving complicated operations or nonstandard number codes. These applications are limited mainly by ROM size; a doubling of storage capacity accompanies each additional input variable. This drawback can be overcome by replacing a single large ROM by a network of smaller ROMs. Sequential circuits often can be efficiently realized in the form of ROM-based control units, in which the control signals of interest are stored in a ROM called a control memory.

4.5 FURTHER READING

Perhaps reflecting the lack of a comprehensive design theory at the MSI/LSI levels, there are few systematic treatments of MSI/LSI-based design. Manufacturers' data manuals remain among the best sources of information concerning IC characteristics and applications at all complexity levels. The Fairchild *TTL Applications Handbook* (Fairchild, 1973) contains a thorough discussion of digital system design using commercially available MSI components. A comprehensive digital design methodology is developed by Blaauw in his text *Digital System Implementation* (Blaauw, 1976) using the standard programming language APL as an RTL; the inherent compactness of APL often makes for difficult reading, however. Another RTL (DDL) and its uses are covered in depth in Dietmeyer and Duley (1975). A detailed treatment of semiconductor ROMs and RAMs and their applications appears in Hnatek (1977), while the design and use of arithmetic circuits are discussed in Cavanagh (1984).

4.6 PROBLEMS

4.1 Let B_n^m denote the set of all logic functions of up to n variables, where each variable is an m-bit word as in Eq. (4.1).

    (a) Define by means of equations the operations AND, OR, and NOT with respect to B_n^m.

    (b) Identify the unit and zero elements of B_n^m.

    (c) Prove that B_n^m is a Boolean algebra by showing that it satisfies all the axioms of Fig. 3.59.

4.2 Explain why so many MSI ICs in the 7400 series have input-output lines that are active or enabled in the 0 state, while they are inactive or disabled in the 1 state.

4.3 Besides those discussed in the text, a frequently mentioned application of multiplexers is parallel-to-serial data conversion. Explain how a multiplexer is used for this purpose.

4.4 Using only the four types of multiplexers defined in Fig. 4.9, design a 64-input 2-bit multiplexer containing as few ICs as possible.

4.5 Use the 74153 four-input 2-bit multiplexer of Fig. 4.9c to construct a 32-input 2-bit multiplexer, again employing as few ICs as possible.

4.6 Consider the problem of realizing an arbitrary n-variable Boolean function $z(x_0, x_1, \ldots, x_{n-1})$ using a 2^{n-1}-input multiplexer MUX. Let $D = D_0 : D_{2^{n-1}-1}$ and $S = S_{n-2} : S_0$ be the data and select input lines, respectively, of MUX. Assuming that z is defined by a truth table, give a concise set of rules for selecting the values to be applied to the input lines of MUX so that it realizes the function z.

4.7 Show how to use a single four-input 2-bit multiplexer such as the 74153 to realize the standard full adder function defined in Fig. 3.38.

4.8 *(a)* Construct a truth table for the 74154 1-out-of-16 decoder defined in Fig. 4.15b.

    (b) Carry out the gate-level logic design for a 74154 using only NAND gates in your design.

4.9 Design a 1-out-of-64 decoder using five copies of the 74154 1-out-of-16 decoder.

4.10 Using 7400-series MSI ICs defined in the text, design a circuit that can be used to transfer a 4-bit word via a shared 4-bit bus from any of 16 sources to any of 16 destinations.

4.11 A circuit C is required to monitor the state of a 10-bit bus $B = B_0 : B_9$. If any line of B assumes the 0 value, C should activate a "zero present" line P. It should also generate a 4-bit word Z indicating the bus line B_i that is 0. If 0s appear on several bus lines simultaneously, only the line B_i with the highest index i should be indicated. Carry out the logic design of C using any appropriate SSI/MSI circuits from the 7400 series.

4.12 *(a)* Construct a truth table for the 74148 eight-input priority encoder defined in Fig. 4.20b.

    (b) Carry out the gate-level logic design for a 74148 using only NOR gates in your design.

4.13 Discuss the advantages and disadvantages of ripple-carry propagation versus carry lookahead in the design of adder circuits for long words.

4.14 Consider the 4-bit carry-lookahead structure of Fig. 4.23b. Using the detailed logic circuit of Fig. 3.19 as a guide, obtain logic equations in sum-of-products form that define the behavior of the subcircuits S_i, CL_i, and GP_i, for $i = 0, 1, 2, 3$.

4.15 *(a)* Design a 16-bit comparator using four 7485 4-bit comparators connected in series as in Fig. 4.25.

(b) Faster comparator circuits can be designed by avoiding the series configuration of Fig. 4.25. Instead the outputs of several different comparators are compared directly by another comparator, producing a two-level tree-structured comparison circuit. Use this parallel comparison approach to design a 16-bit comparator composed of 7485s.

4.16 Design a 12-bit ALU using three copies of the 74181 4-bit ALU (Fig. 4.26). Carry lookahead is to be used, with any necessary carry-lookahead circuits implemented using only NAND ICs from the small catalog in Fig. 3.37.

4.17 A 64-bit ALU with carry lookahead is to be designed using the 74181 4-bit ALU, and the 74182 carry-lookahead generator.

(a) Determine the function of the four input-output signals of the 74182, which are shown unidentified in Fig. 4.27, and are intended to allow interconnection of several 74182s to form larger carry-lookahead generators. Give sum-of-product Boolean equations defining the two unidentified output lines of the 74182.

(b) Construct a clearly labeled logic diagram for the complete 64-bit ALU.

4.18 Figure 4.80 describes the 74350, a 4-bit combinational shifter with three-state output lines. Input data are

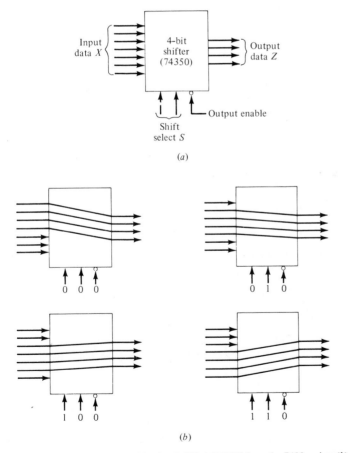

Figure 4.80 *(a)* A 4-bit combinational shifter (74350) from the 7400 series; *(b)* possible shift patterns of the 74350.

shifted zero, cne, two, or three bit positions, as determined by the shift select control lines S. Figure 4.80b illustrates the four possible shift patterns.

(a) Describe two applications of this type of shifter in digital system design.

(b) Design a circuit composed of 74350s that allows a 16-bit word to be shifted left zero, one, two, or three places.

4.19 Design a 16-bit positive edge-triggered register using the 74100 8-bit latch IC (Fig. 4.28), and any necessary additional logic.

4.20 Explain clearly why there are n-bit shift registers, but no n-bit "shift latches" in the MSI component repertoire.

4.21 Carry out the logic design of a 4-bit shift register with serial-in, parallel-in, serial-out, and clear capabilities. The shift register should be built from SR flip-flops that have preset and clear inputs. Both the parallel load and clear operations should be synchronous.

4.22 Using the 74194 4-bit universal shift register as the basic building block (see Fig. 4.30d), design the following types of shift registers:

(a) A 12-bit serial-in parallel-out left-shift register

(b) A 12-bit parallel-in serial-out right-shift register

(c) A 16-bit universal shift register

4.23 Modify the logic circuit for a synchronous modulo-16 binary counter given in Fig. 4.33b, to form a synchronous decade counter. Make as few changes to the original circuit as possible.

4.24 Again using as little extra logic as possible, modify the 74163 modulo-16 counter of Fig. 4.36a to obtain each of the following:

(a) A modulo-9 counter employing the count sequence 0111, 1000, 1001, ..., 1110, 1111, 0111.

(b) A modulo-9 counter with the count sequence 0000, 0001, 0010, ..., 1000, 1001, 0000.

4.25 The 74160 is a decade counter with the same pin assignments as the 74163 modulo-16 counter defined in Fig. 4.36a. Using four 74160s, design a BCD counter that counts from 0000 to 9999.

4.26 Figure 4.81 shows a high-speed multistage counting circuit formed by cascading 74163 4-bit counters. The three enable signals EIP, EIT, and EO of the 74163 play key roles in this design; their behavior is defined as follows. EO becomes 1 when the 74163 reaches its maximum count value and EIT = 1. The other enable in line EIP is internally ANDed with EIT to form a signal EIP $\wedge$ EIT that is used to enable the flip-flops forming the counter. The interconnection scheme of Fig. 4.81 is sometimes called carry lookahead, and is significantly faster than the ripple-carry expansion method illustrated by Fig. 4.34.

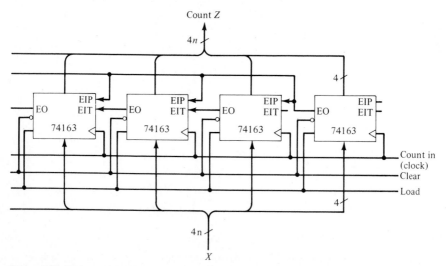

Figure 4.81 High-speed counter expansion technique (carry lookahead).

Show that the delay of an n-stage ($4n$-bit) carry-lookahead counter is the same as the delay of a single stage.

4.27 Assuming that the ALU performs the eight operations specified for the 74381 in Fig. 4.26c, indicate the settings of the control lines appearing in Fig. 4.37 to make the circuit perform the following register-transfer operations:

$$A := A - B;$$

$$BUS_1 := B \vee C;$$

$$A := BUS_0;$$

4.28 (a) Using the RTL of this book, which is defined in Fig. 4.44, describe concisely the 16-bit instruction register IR of Fig. 4.82, clearly identifying the subregisters OPCODE, MOD, and ADDRESS.

(b) Write an RTL description of the following operations involving IR and another 16-bit register DR[0:15]. If OPCODE contains 000, then DR should be cleared. If OPCODE contains some other value, and MOD contains 00, then ADDRESS should be transferred to the leftmost 11 bit positions of DR while the remaining bits of DR are set to 1; if MOD ≠00, then the contents of ADDRESS should be replaced by its logical complement.

4.29 Explain why the compound RTL statement (4.23) and the three-statement sequence (4.24) can yield different results, even though each is composed of the same set of simple RTL statements written in the same order.

4.30 In the unsigned binary multiplication of Fig. 4.48, the right half of the accumulator A is initially empty, and is filled in the course of multiplication. The multiplier register Q, on the other hand, is full initially, but is gradually emptied. This suggests that A and Q can be merged into a single ($2n + 1$)-bit register AQ, whose right half is used to store the multiplier X. Redesign the circuit of Fig. 4.47 and the RTL description of Fig. 4.48 to incorporate this change.

4.31 Redraw the unsigned binary multiplier of Fig. 4.47 incorporating all the changes necessary to implement the TC multiplication algorithm of Fig. 4.51. Provide a list of all the control signals required by the modified circuit.

4.32 The product of two numbers X and Y is sometimes computed by adding Y to itself X times. Although slow, this multiplication method is easy to implement, especially where nonstandard number codes are used. Carry out the design at the register-transfer level of a multiplier for 8-bit SM binary numbers where this approach is used. Give a block diagram and an RTL description of your design. Estimate the worst-case multiplication time, assuming your multiplier circuit operates with a clock rate of 2MHz.

4.33 A special type of multiplier called a *serial-parallel multiplier* is shown in Fig. 4.83. A fixed n-bit multiplicand Y is applied in parallel to the circuit. A multiplier X of arbitrary length is then applied to the circuit serially. The circuit computes the product XY and outputs it serially at the same rate the input X arrives. Carry

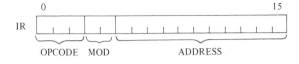

Figure 4.82 A 16-bit register IR containing three subregisters.

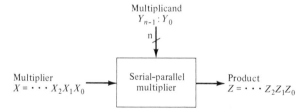

Figure 4.83 Symbol for a serial-parallel multiplier.

out the design at the register-transfer level of a serial-parallel multiplier for unsigned binary numbers, where the multiplicand size n is 8 bits. Provide both a block diagram and an RTL description of your design.

4.34 A division algorithm known as *restoring division* is described by the flowchart of Fig. 4.84a. This is a variant of the pencil-and-paper method used for decimal long division, which is intended for machine implementation using unsigned binary integers. It closely parallels the multiplication scheme of Fig. 4.48, and uses similar hardware. The input operands are an n-bit divisor and a $2n$-bit dividend; the output operands are an n-bit remainder and a $2n$-bit quotient. Three main registers are used: an n-bit divisor register M, a $2n$-bit

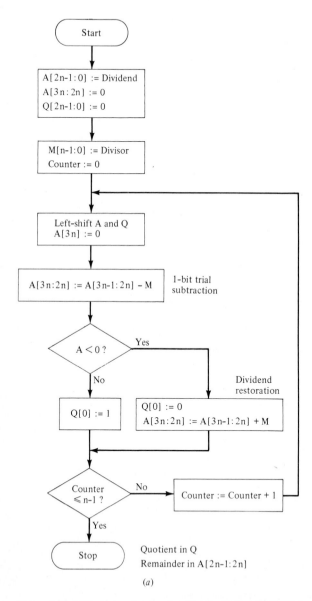

(a)

Figure 4.84 (a) Restoring division algorithm for unsigned n-bit binary integers; (b) illustration with $n = 2$.

Dividend $= 1101_2 = 13$
Divisor $= 11_2 = 3$

	Accumulator A	Quotient register Q
	0 00 1101	0000
Shift	0 01 1010	0000
Subtract	11	
	1 10 1010	0000
Add	11	
	0 01 1010	0000
Shift	0 11 0100	0000
Substract	11	
	0 00 0100	0001
Shift	0 00 1000	0010
Subtract	11	
	1 01 1000	0010
Add	11	
	0 00 1000	
Shift	0 01 0000	0100
Subtract	11	
	1 10 0000	0100
Add	11	
	0 01 0000	0100 = Quotient = 4
	Remainder = 1	

(b)

(Figure 4.84 continued)

quotient register Q, and a $(3n + 1)$-bit accumulator register A. Both A and Q are left-shift registers. The dividend is initially placed in $A[2n - 1:0]$, and the remainder eventually appears in $A[3n - 1:2n]$; the leftmost bit $A[3n]$ serves as a sign indicator following subtraction. M and $A[3n{-}1:2n]$ are connected to an n-bit adder-subtracter circuit. Division is accomplished by a sequence of $2n$ 1-bit shift-and-subtract steps. If the result of a subtraction is nonnegative, then the rightmost bit $Q[0]$ of the quotient register is set to 1. If the result is negative, which is indicated by $A[3n] = 1$, then $Q[0]$ is set to 0, and A is restored to its previous state by adding M to it. An application of this algorithm in the case where $n = 2$ appears in Fig. 4.84b.

(a) With the multiplier circuit of Fig. 4.47 serving as a model, design a circuit that implements the restoring division algorithm of Fig. 4.84a.

(b) Give an RTL description of your divider circuit along the lines of Fig. 4.48.

(c) Indicate how this restoring division algorithm might be modified to reduce the size of some of the operand registers used.

4.35 (a) Draw a logic diagram for a 3- by 3-bit combinational multiplier that uses the LSI array organization of Fig. 3.53.

(b) Estimate the number of transistors and logic gates necessary to design a 16- by 16-bit combinational array multiplier using typical nMOS circuits. Estimate the propagation delay (multiplication time) of this circuit, assuming an average gate delay of 1 ns.

4.36 Answer each of the following true or false questions, and explain your reasoning in each case.

(a) ROM circuits are significantly simpler than dynamic RAM circuits of the same storage capacity.

(b) The ROM circuit of Fig. 4.56 is volatile, since its switching transistors cannot operate with the power turned off.

(c) The access time of a static RAM can be expected to be much less than that of a dynamic RAM, assuming both employ comparable circuit technologies.

4.37 Using the theory described in Sec. 3.1.2, construct a CSA model for the static MOS RAM cell of Fig. 4.58a. Give a detailed state table describing its behavior in terms of the seven-member set of logic values V_7.

4.38 Treating the dynamic RAM cell of Fig. 4.60 as a primitive element or black box, use it to construct a 2- by 2-bit RAM Draw a complete logic diagram for your design, which should include all the logic needed to restore the RAM's state automatically at the end of each read cycle.

4.39 A certain memory has the parameters t_A = 300 ns and t_C = 470 ns. What is the maximum number of read operations that can be completed in 1 second?

4.40 Many RAM ICs permit a read and a write operation to be combined in a single memory cycle called a *read-modify-write cycle*. This allows a single memory location to be addressed, its old contents read, and new data entered in a time that is somewhat less than that required by separate read and write cycles addressed to the same location. Using the timing diagrams appearing in Fig. 4.63 as a guide, construct a similar timing diagram for a read-modify-write cycle for the 2102 RAM. Give an appropriate formula for its cycle time, using the parameters appearing in Fig. 4.63.

4.41 *(a)* Draw a logic diagram for an 8192- by 1-bit RAM that uses the 2102 RAM IC of Fig. 4.62.

(b) Draw a logic diagram for a 512-byte RAM that uses the 2111 RAM IC of Fig. 4.67.

4.42 A 16K- by 4-bit RAM is to be designed using the Intel 2111 RAM IC. Any necessary addressing circuitry is to be built exclusively around the Intel 8205, a high-speed 1-out-of-8 decoder, whose external connections are given in Fig. 4.85. The three enable lines E_1, E_2, and E_3 are internally ANDed, so that the 8205 is enabled if and only if $E_1 \wedge E_2 \wedge E_3 = 1$. Assuming that no line may have fanout greater than 20, design the addressing logic for the 16K × 4 RAM using as few 8205s as possible.

4.43 Repeat Prob. 4.42 using the Intel 2142, a 4K-bit RAM, in place of the 2111. Figure 4.86 presents a summary data sheet for the 2142 (Intel, 1979); note that it has the same word size as the 2111, but four times the storage capacity.

4.44 A ROM is shown in Fig. 4.70b and elsewhere as a combinational function generator. As a memory element, however, a ROM is also a sequential circuit, suggesting that it is both combinational and sequential at the same time. Explain this apparent contradiction.

4.45 Using the ripple-carry structure of Fig. 4.72, design a combined adder-subtracter for 6-bit TC numbers that employs two identical 1K-bit ROMs.

4.46 A ROM-based converter circuit C is to be designed that converts binary data obtained from a 24-hour clock into standard decimal format for display purposes. The clock is a free-running counter that supplies C periodically with a binary number denoting the number of minutes that have elapsed since midnight. C then

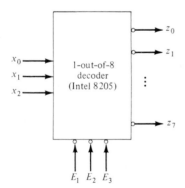

Figure 4.85 The Intel 8205 high-speed 1-out-of-8 decoder.

2142
1024 X 4 BIT STATIC RAM

	2142-2	2142-3	2142	2142L2	2142L3	2142L
Max. Access Time (ns)	200	300	450	200	300	450
Max. Power Dissipation (mw)	525	525	525	370	370	370

- High Density 20 Pin Package
- Access Time Selections From 200-450ns
- Identical Cycle and Access Times
- Low Operating Power Dissipation .1mW/Bit Typical
- Single +5V Supply

- No Clock or Timing Strobe Required
- Completely Static Memory
- Directly TTL Compatible: All Inputs and Outputs
- Common Data Input and Output Using Three-State Outputs

The Intel® 2142 is a 4096-bit static Random Access Memory organized as 1024 words by 4-bits using N-channel Silicon-Gate MOS technology. It uses fully DC stable (static) circuitry throughout — in both the array and the decoding — and therefore requires no clocks or refreshing to operate. Data access is particularly simple since address setup times are not required. The data is read out nondestructively and has the same polarity as the input data. Common input/output pins are provided.

The 2142 is designed for memory applications where high performance, low cost, large bit storage, and simple interfacing are important design objectives. It is directly TTL compatible in all respects: inputs, outputs, and a single +5V supply.

The 2142 is placed in a 20-pin package. Two Chip Selects ($\overline{CS}_1$ and CS_2) are provided for easy and flexible selection of individual packages when outputs are OR-tied. An Output Disable is included for direct control of the output buffers.

The 2142 is fabricated with Intel's N-channel Silicon-Gate technology — a technology providing excellent protection against contamination permitting the use of low cost plastic packaging.

PIN CONFIGURATION   LOGIC SYMBOL   BLOCK DIAGRAM

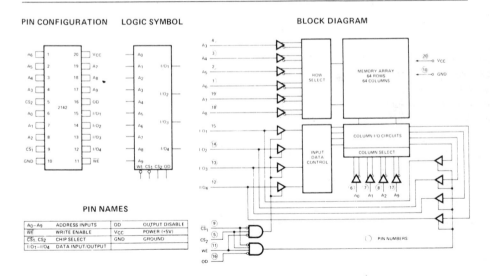

PIN NAMES

A_0–A_9	ADDRESS INPUTS	OD	OUTPUT DISABLE
$\overline{WE}$	WRITE ENABLE	Vcc	POWER (+5V)
$\overline{CS}_1$, CS_2	CHIP SELECT	GND	GROUND
I/O_1–I/O_4	DATA INPUT/OUTPUT		

Figure 4.86 Summary data sheet for a 4K-bit nMOS static RAM IC, the Intel 2142. *(Courtesy Intel Corp.)*

outputs the time in hours and minutes using four-digit BCD code. For instance, the input 1100011000_2, denoting 792 minutes after midnight, causes C to generate 0001001100010010_{BCD}, denoting 13:12 hours.

(a) What is the ROM size required for a single-ROM implementation of C?

(b) Design a multichip converter for this application that uses smaller ROMs and additional standard circuits. The total ROM capacity in this case should be less than half that of a single-ROM implementation of C.

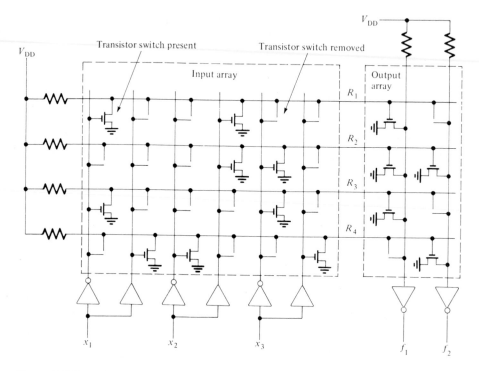

Figure 4.87 Example of a programmed logic array (PLA).

4.47 Using the ROM-based controller organization, design a two-digit modulo-100 BCD (up) counter. Show how two copies of this counter can be cascaded to yield a four-digit counter.

4.48 Three kinds of multiplication circuits were discussed in this chapter: a sequential shift-and-add design (Figs. 4.47–4.49), a combinational array design (Fig. 4.53), and a ROM-based design (Fig. 4.79). Compare and contrast these designs from the following viewpoints:

    (a) The number of logic gates or transistors used

    (b) The maximum multiplication time

    (c) Ease of expansion to handle larger operands

4.49 ROMs are only one of several LSI structures that are suitable as general-purpose function generators. Another such structure is the *programmable logic array* (PLA), one form of which is illustrated by Fig. 4.87. It consists of two regular arrays or grids of conductors, an input array and an output array. Transistor switches can be placed selectively at the grid points during manufacture by mask programming or similar means. The locations of the transistor switches in the input and output array determines the functions being realized. Each row in the input array realizes a Boolean NOR function. For example, the topmost row R_1 of the input array in Fig. 4.87 realizes the function

$$R_1 = \overline{x_1 \vee \bar{x}_2}$$

Each column of the output array computes another NOR function of the R_i's on the rows to which it is connected. Thus in the PLA of Fig. 4.87.

$$f_1 = \overline{\overline{R_1} \vee \overline{R_2} \vee \overline{R_3}}$$

$$= \bar{R}_1 \wedge \bar{R}_2 \wedge \bar{R}_3 \qquad by \ De \ Morgan's \ laws$$

$$= (x_1 \vee \bar{x}_2) \wedge (\bar{x}_2 \vee x_3) \wedge (x_1 \vee x_3)$$

(a) Determine in POS form the second function f_2 realized in Fig. 4.87.

(b) Show that the PLA structure of Fig. 4.87 with n input variables can be used to realize any n-input combinational function.

(c) Given a combinational function f in POS form, derive a set of rules for programming the PLA to realize f.

4.50 Consider the realization of Boolean functions using ROMs or PLAs; the latter are defined in the preceding problem. Assume that each ROM storage cell requires only a single transistor of the same type used at the PLA's grid points. Let the total area of the IC chip needed to manufacture a ROM or a PLA be proportional to the number of these transistors. (The other transistors used in IO drivers, address circuits, and so on, account for only a small fraction of the total number of transistors used in ROMs and PLAs.)

(a) Demonstrate that, in general, a given set of combinational functions can be generated with a smaller chip if a PLA rather than a ROM implementation is used.

(b) Explain why the design process is usually more difficult when PLAs are employed.

BASIC MICROPROCESSOR ORGANIZATION

"Dear reader, this notice will serve to inform you that I am submitting to the public a small machine of my own invention, by means of which you alone may, without any effort, perform all the operations of arithmetic, and may be relieved of the work which has oftentimes fatigued your spirit . . ."

[Blaise Pascal: *Notice to Those Interested in Seeing and Operating the Arithmetic Machine*, 1645]

This chapter presents a general introduction to the structure and behavior of microprocessors. The basic concepts of computer organization are briefly reviewed. A simple programmable controller, the Motorola 14500, is introduced. This device is intermediate in complexity between conventional microprocessors and the nonprogrammable processing elements discussed in the preceding chapters. The general principles of CPU design and operation are discussed, and the instruction, address, and data types commonly used in microprocessors are defined. Two important 8-bit microprocessor families based on the Motorola 6800 and the Intel 8080 microprocessors and their derivatives are described in detail.

5.1 INTRODUCTION

We begin by reviewing the basic structure of microprocessors and microcomputers. A commercial microprocessor, the Motorola 14500, which is intended for the design of simple control systems, is used as an example. Besides being easy to describe concisely and completely, the 14500 serves as a bridge between the special-purpose digital systems encountered earlier and conventional general-purpose microprocessors.

5.1.1 Computer Organization

As discussed in Chap. 1, a typical digital computer has three main components or subsystems: a CPU (central processing unit), a main memory, and an IO (input-output) system. The CPU has overall control of the computer, and is responsible for fetching, interpreting, and executing sequences of instructions, that is, computer programs. The tasks of fetching and decoding the instructions are carried out by a part of the CPU called the I-unit (instruction unit). The instructions are executed by the CPU's E-unit (execution unit), which contains an ALU (arithmetic-logic unit) and a set of working or scratchpad registers. The main memory M stores instructions and data for processing by the CPU. The IO subsystem connects the CPU and M to the outside world. It includes a set of IO or peripheral devices that communicate with the rest of the computer via special interface circuits. Among the more common IO devices are secondary memories such as magnetic disk and tape units, and user consoles such as CRT terminals and teletypewriters. Sensors and actuators are important IO devices in many microcomputer systems. Most computers employ a set of shared interconnection lines called the system bus as the principal communication link between the CPU, the main memory, and the IO system. Figure 5.1 shows the structure of a typical computer of this kind.

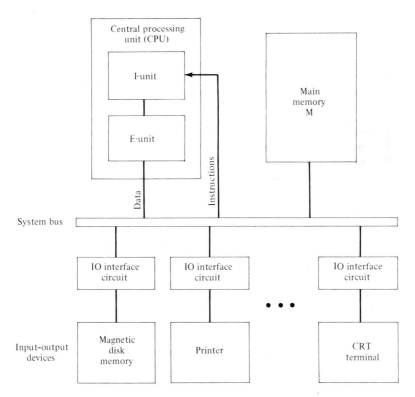

Figure 5.1 Organization of a typical computer.

The functions performed by the CPU are defined by its instruction set. A typical computer has from about 50 to 200 different instruction types. It is convenient to group instructions into three major classes: data-transfer, data-processing, and program-control instructions. Data-transfer instructions move information without altering its content from one part of the computer to another. This data movement may be within the CPU, between the CPU and M, or between the IO system and the CPU or M. Data-processing instructions transform information using the ALU circuits in the E-unit of the CPU. This instruction group includes arithmetic instructions such as add, multiply, and increment; and logical instructions such as and, exclusive-or, and complement. Program-control instructions determine the sequence in which instructions are executed. They allow control to be transferred from one part of a program to another, or between different subprograms. Jump (go to), call subroutine, and return from subroutine are typical examples of program-control instructions.

The I-unit is responsible for keeping track of the locations or addresses of the instructions in M that are currently needed by the CPU. Instructions are normally fetched and executed in the sequence in which they are stored in M. The I-unit maintains a special register (actually a counter) called the *program counter* PC, which stores the address of the next instruction, or portion of an instruction, that the CPU expects to require. After each instruction fetch operation, PC is automatically incremented to construct the memory address required for the next instruction fetch. Program-control instructions can alter the contents of PC, thereby influencing the instruction execution sequence. The CPU usually contains other registers that facilitate the accessing of instructions and data. For example, a region of main memory called a stack is often used when transferring control of the system between different subprograms. A *stack* is a set of contiguous storage locations that can be accessed on a last-in/first-out (LIFO) basis. An address register called the *stack pointer* is used by the CPU to keep track of the stack's entry/exit location (the top of the stack).

Information is transferred and stored within a computer system in the form of groups of bits called words. Different word sizes are employed by different parts of the computer. Main memory stores words of a fixed size w_M, the memory word size; a typical value for w_M is 8 bits (1 byte). Address words, on the other hand, are typically 16 bits long. A CPU designed to process data words of size n bits is called an n-bit (micro) processor. CPU word size ranges from 1 to 64 bits or more. The smaller word sizes, such as 8 bits, are typical of microprocessors. The Motorola 14500 and 6800 microprocessors, which are described later in this chapter, are examples of 1-bit and 8-bit microprocessors respectively.

The actions of a CPU are timed by a clock signal whose period t_{CPU}, called the *CPU cycle time*, is a fundamental measure of CPU operating speed. t_{CPU} is the minimum time required by the CPU to change its state; its duration is largely determined by the IC technology used to manufacture the CPU. The quantity $1/t_{CPU}$, which is called the CPU clock rate, is also used to define the CPU operating speed. For example, some versions of the Intel 8080 microprocessor have maximum clock rates of 2 MHz, corresponding to a clock period of 500 ns. Another simple measure of CPU performance is the time required to fetch and execute an instruction, that is, the instruction cycle time. Since instruction cycle times vary with the complexity of the instruction, the execution time of a common instruction such as add is often selected as representative.

Microcomputers are distinguished from other computers primarily by the fact that the CPU (called a microprocessor), main memory, and IO interface circuits are fabricated from a very small number of integrated circuits. In the extreme case only one IC is used, resulting in a one-chip microcomputer. This represents perhaps the ultimate step in minaturization, because it reduces an entire computer (except its IO devices, which, by their nature, cannot normally be minaturized) to one small inexpensive component. Frequently a microcomputer takes the form of a printed circuit (PC) board on which are mounted several dozen ICs (not to mention some discrete components), including a microprocessor, a memory consisting of RAMs and (P)ROMs, and various IO interface circuits. The precise number of ICs used and their configuration depend on the system application. Figure 5.2 shows an example of a general-purpose one-board microcomputer, the Intel SBC 80/10 (Garrow et al., 1976), which is based on the 8080 microprocessor.

Microprocessor and microcomputer components are supplied by manufacturers in related groups or families. Members of the same component family can be expected to exhibit a high degree of hardware and software compatibility, and offer various trade-offs between processing speed, system cost, and design flexibility. For example, the 8080 and 8085 microprocessors studied in Sec. 5.4 are members of the same microprocessor family. They have essentially the same instruction sets, and are designed to communicate with common memory and IO interface circuits via similar system buses. However, the 8085 is a complete one-chip CPU, whereas an 8080-based CPU requires three ICs: the 8080 microprocessor and a pair of auxilliary or support ICs. Different versions of both the 8080 and 8085 exist that are distinguished by their package types and clock rates.

Microprocessors often have simpler instruction sets than do large mainframe computers. Shorter processor and memory word sizes are used in microcomputers, with 8 bits (1 byte) being typical. Few microprocessors have instructions for multiplication, division, or any floating-point operations. When required for some application, these operations must be implemented either by software routines or by auxiliary hardware processors. Several reasons may be cited for these apparent limitations of microcomputers vis-à-vis larger minicomputers or mainframe computers.

1. The circuits required to implement more powerful instruction sets require more or larger microprocessor chips, and thereby increase manufacturing difficulty and cost.
2. Chip packaging considerations limit the number of external connections (pins) that a microprocessor may have; dual in-line packages (DIPs) are limited to about 64 pins. In general, the shorter the word sizes used by an IC, the fewer pins are needed.
3. Simple instruction and data types are adequate for many microprocessor applications. Often little or no numerical processing is needed.

It should be noted that some microcomputers are basically more compact versions of larger machines. The Digital Equipment Corp. LSI-11, for example, is a microcomputer version of DEC's PDP-11 minicomputer (Digital Equipment Corp., 1976). The distinctions between micro-, mini-, and large (mainframe) computers are now rather vague, and can be expected to diminish further as LSI and VLSI technology penetrates all levels of computer design.

(a)

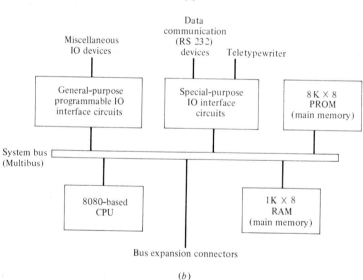

(b)

Figure 5.2 The Intel SBC 80/10 single-board microcomputer: (a) photograph *(Courtesy Intel Corp.)*; (b) black diagram.

5.1.2 The 14500 Microprocessor

The Motorola 14500 is a 1-bit programmable processor intended for building relatively simple control systems, where logical decisions rather than numerical calculations are required (Motorola, 1977). A typical application of the 14500 in industrial process control is to switch some machine on and off in response to changes in its environment. For example, if the main power switch S_1 is on, a motion limit switch S_2 is off, and a thermostatic switch S_3 is also off, then motor M should be turned on. Logical control operations of this type were often implemented in the past by electromechanical relay circuits and, more recently, by hardwired or nonprogrammable logic circuits employing SSI/MSI devices. The 14500 and its support circuits are intended to provide a low-cost alternative to hardwired logic circuits in industrial applications of the foregoing kind. For this reason the 14500 is referred to as an *industrial control unit* (ICU) in the manufacturer's literature.

The 14500 is basically the E-unit of a simple 1-bit microprocessor. Because of its short word size and its relatively small instruction set (only 16 instructions are used), the 14500 can be packaged efficiently in a 16-pin DIP. Figure 5.3 shows its internal structure. The principal data-processing part of the ICU is the logic unit LU, which corresponds to the arithmetic-logic unit of conventional processors. Reflecting its intended applications, the 14500 has logical instructions, but no explicit arithmetic instructions. The LU receives its input operands from a 1-bit accumulator AC (actually a D flip-flop) and a bidirectional data line called DATA. DATA acts as the main data bus of

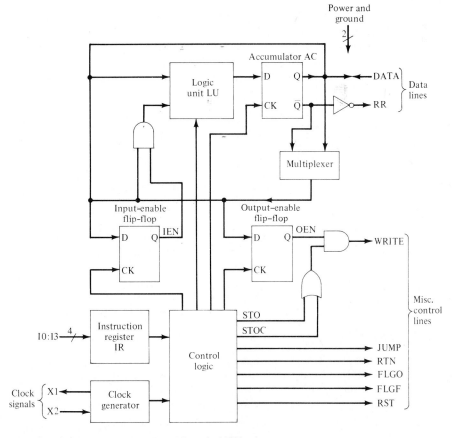

Figure 5.3 Internal organization of the Motorola 14500 microprocessor.

the ICU. Results computed by the LU are placed in AC, from which they can be transferred to external destinations via the DATA line. The contents of AC are also continuously available at the output pin called RR. (RR denotes result register, the name used for the accumulator by Motorola). Besides the LU and AC, the 14500 contains a clock generator, a 4-bit instruction register IR, and logic circuits that generate a variety of timing and control signals used to communicate with external devices, including an I-unit, main memory, and IO devices.

The 14500 has 16 input-output terminals or pins, whose functions are defined in Fig. 5.4. The operations to be performed by the ICU are specified by a 4-bit instruction that is applied to input pins I0:I3. A clock signal appearing on output pin X1 may be used as the system clock; alternatively the ICU may be controlled by an external clock signal connected to input pin X2. CMOS circuit technology is used by the 14500, which requires two pins for power ($+5$ V) and ground. A reset signal RST serves to initialize all registers. The WRITE output signal is used to enable external memory during the execution of store instructions. The four control signals JMP, RTN, FLGO, and FLGF are typically transmitted to the external I-unit during the execution of program control instructions. Instruction timing is quite simple. Once each clock cycle the signals on I0:I3 are transferred to IR; then they are decoded and executed.

The 14500 has a total of 16 instructions as listed in Fig. 5.5, with their behavior defined using the RTL notation introduced in Chap. 4. The nine data-transfer and data-processing (logical) instructions are quite straightforward. They all make use of the 1-bit accumulator AC and the bidirectional terminal DATA as data sources or destinations.

Type	Name	Function
Data	DATA	Bidirectional input-output data line
	RR	Output line from the accumulator (result register)
Instruction	I0:I3	Instruction input lines (4 bits)
Power supply	V_{DD}	Power ($+5$ V)
	V_{SS}	Ground (0 V)
Timing	X1	System clock signal generated by the 14500
	X2	An external clock source may be connected to X2. Alternatively a resistor connected between X1 and X2 may be used to set the frequency of the internal clock X1.
Misc. control	WRITE	Signal activated by store instructions. Used to enable external memory writes.
	JMP	Signal activated by the jump instruction. Used to load an external program counter with a branch address.
	RTN	Signal activated by the return from subroutine instruction. Used to enable a pop operation in an external instruction stack.
	RST	Reset signal used to clear all registers
	FLGO, FLGF	Flag signals activated by the "no operation" instructions **NOPO** and **NOPF** respectively. Miscellaneous user-defined uses.

Figure 5.4 Names and functions of the 16 IO pins of the 14500.

Type	Instruction	Mnemonic	Action on Registers and Pins (no input-output disabling)*
Data transfer	Load accumulator	**LD**	$AC := \overline{DATA}$;
	Load accumulator complemented	**LDC**	$AC := \overline{DATA}$;
	Store accumulator	**STO**	$DATA := AC$, $WRITE := 1$;
	Store accumulator complemented	**STOC**	$DATA := \overline{AC}$, $WRITE := 1$;
Logical	And	**AND**	$AC := AC \wedge DATA$;
	And complemented	**ANDC**	$AC := AC \wedge \overline{DATA}$;
	Or	**OR**	$AC := AC \vee DATA$;
	Or complemented	**ORC**	$AC := AC \vee \overline{DATA}$;
	Exclusive-nor	**XNOR**	$AC := \overline{AC \oplus DATA}$;
Program control	Jump	**JMP**	$JMP := 1$;
	Return	**RTN**	$RTN := 1$;
	Skip on zero	**SKZ**	**if** $AC = 0$ **then** skip next instruction;
	No operation/set flag	**NOPO**	$FLGO := 1$;
		NOPF	$FLGF := 1$;
	Input enable	**IEN**	$IEN := DATA$;
	Output enable	**OEN**	$OEN := DATA$;

* To account for input and output disabling by **IEN** and **OEN,** replace DATA by DATA ∧ IEN in **LD, LDC,** and all logical instructions. Replace WRITE := 1 by WRITE := OEN in **STO** and **STOC.**

Figure 5.5 The instruction set of the 14500.

DATA is typically connected via external circuitry to memories, switches, sensors, and other IO devices, which therefore can be directly controlled by 14500 instructions. The load instruction **LD**, for example, inputs a data bit from the DATA pin to AC, as defined by the RTL statement

$$AC := DATA;$$

The corresponding store instruction **STO** specified by

$$DATA := AC, \ WRITE := 1;$$

is intended for transferring data from the 14500 to an external ROM or RAM. It causes the contents of the accumulator AC to be transferred to the DATA terminal. It then activates the WRITE control line, signaling the presence of data at the DATA pin to be read by the external memory. **STO** may also be used to transfer data directly to IO devices.

The program-control instructions **JMP** (jump) and **RTN** (return from subroutine) are conventional unconditional branch instructions. Since the 14500 does not contain a program counter, these instructions merely cause the 14500 to generate control signals at the JMP and RTN pins, where they can be used to enable the appropriate actions in an external user-defined I-unit. **SKZ** (skip on zero) is a conditional branch instruction that tests the value of the accumulator AC. If $AC = 1$, then the instruction applied to pins I0:I3 during the next clock cycle is executed normally. If, on the other hand, $AC = 0$, the next instruction is skipped and the CPU idles for one clock cycle. The two "no operation" instructions **NOPO** and **NOPF** activate the flag output signals FLGO and FLGF respectively; they do not otherwise affect the state of the ICU. No specific functions are defined for these flag signals. They may, for example, be used to control IO devices. **NOPO** and **NOPF** are also useful as the last instructions of programs, where they can be used to generate completion signals, or to reset the program counter.

Perhaps the most unusual instructions in the 14500's repertoire are the input-enable and output-enable instructions **IEN** and **OEN**, which are used to control data transfers to and from the 14500. **IEN** causes the current signal on the DATA pin to be loaded into the input-enable flip-flop IEN. As can be seen from Fig. 5.3, the signal IEN is ANDed with the signal DATA so that all instructions using DATA as an input operand source obtain the effective value DATA $\wedge$ IEN. Thus if **IEN** sets IEN to 0, subsequent instructions obtain the value DATA $\wedge$ 0 = 0 from the DATA pin. It is necessary for another **IEN** instruction to be executed with DATA = 1 for the DATA input signal to be enabled. In a similar way, the output-enable instruction **OEN** controls the WRITE output signal. Executing **OEN** causes the current value of DATA to be loaded into the output-enable flip-flop OEN. The data output instructions **STO** and **STOC** place the value OEN on the WRITE line. If OEN = 0, then the WRITE signal is disabled; otherwise it is enabled. Since WRITE must be enabled to carry out a data transfer from the 14500, **OEN** can block output data transfer, just as **IEN** can block input data transfer.

Figure 5.6 is a timing diagram showing the events that occur during the execution of a representative sequence of four instructions

> **STO**
> **NOPF**
> **LD**
> **IEN**

which forms a short symbolic program for the 14500 ICU. Each instruction cycle (instruction fetching, decoding, and execution) takes place during one clock period t_{CPU}. An instruction is loaded into IR when the clock signal X1 goes from 1 to 0; it is then decoded and executed. The output control signals WRITE, JMP, RTN, FLGO, and FLGF, which are activated by various instructions, remain active for a fixed duration not exceeding t_{CPU}, and so appear as pulses. The internal control signals IEN and OEN remain active until reset by appropriate **IEN** or **OEN** instructions.

5.1.3 14500-Based Systems

To construct a complete control system around the 14500 ICU, it is necessary to provide the following components:

1. Interface circuits to the system IO signals associated with switches, actuators, sensors, and so forth
2. A program memory M to store the instructions required by the 14500 and, if necessary, a memory or register set for temporary data storage
3. An I-unit to generate instruction addresses

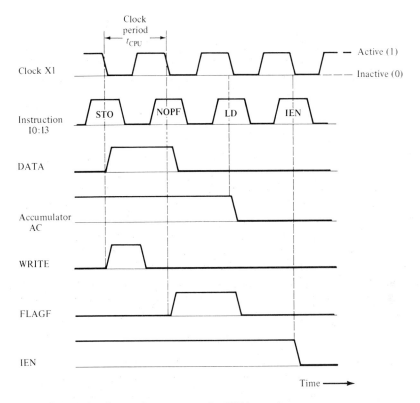

Figure 5.6 Timing diagram for a representative ICU instruction sequence.

The resulting control unit takes the form of a primitive multichip microcomputer.

Figure 5.7 shows a complete 14500-based controller. The memory M, which may be a ROM or PROM, stores a single program that is executed continuously. The I-unit consists of a program counter PC, which is a standard binary counter with count (CI), clear (CLR), and parallel load (LD) capabilities. PC is the source of the addresses used to access M. System input signals are connected to a multiplexer MUX, which places input data on the bidirectional DATA line of the 14500. System output signals are sent via the DATA line to an addressable multibit latch L. System operation begins when a pulse is applied to the external reset line, which clears the 14500 registers and sets the contents of PC to address zero, the start address of the system program. PC is subsequently incremented by the system clock signal X1. By using **NOPF** as the last instruction to be executed, the PC address automatically can be reset to zero by FLGF as indicated in Fig. 5.7. The system program in a typical application monitors the state of the q system inputs, and initiates control functions by altering the values of the r system output signals.

The instructions stored in M have the form

OP   ADR

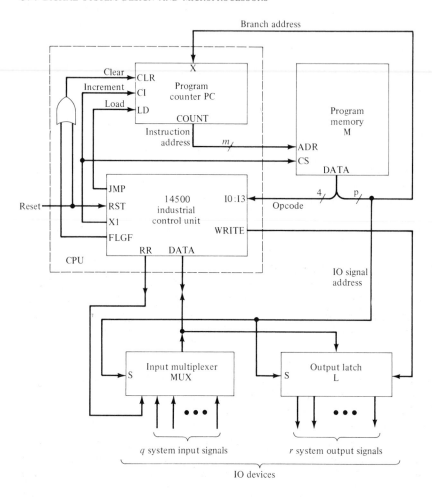

Figure 5.7 Simple control system based on the 14500.

where **OP** is a 4-bit opcode representing one of the 16 instructions listed in Fig. 5.5, and ADR is the address of some operand. ADR often specifies one of the system IO signals, but it can also be designed to address other quantities of interest. For example, the 14500 accumulator AC can be addressed directly by connecting the ICU's output data pin RR to the system input multiplexer MUX as shown in Fig. 5.7. In the case of jump instructions, ADR is a branch address that is loaded into PC. Note that the JMP output line of the 14500, which is activated by the **JMP** instruction, is used to load the branch address into PC in the circuit of Fig. 5.7. The 14500 itself imposes no restrictions on the various system parameters such as memory address size m, instruction length $4 + p$, the number of system input signals q, and the number of system output signals r.

We now consider how the system of Fig. 5.7 might be programmed to solve some elementary control problems. Suppose that an electric motor is controlled by an on–off switch represented by the logic signal F. The decision to turn F on or off is determined by three signals X, Y, Z which must be monitored continuously. The relationships between F, X, Y, and Z are specified by the truth table of Fig. 5.8a. Equating 0 with off and 1 with on, it is readily seen that this truth table is equivalent to the Boolean equation

$$F = X \lor (\overline{Y} \land Z) \tag{5.1}$$

Figure 5.8b shows a hardwired logic implementation of this control equation, while Fig. 5.8c shows a programmed implementation for the 14500-based controller. For the latter it is assumed that the input variables X, Y, Z are connected to the multiplexer MUX of Fig. 5.7, while F is connected to one of the output lines of the latch L. The program of Fig. 5.8c is in symbolic assembly-language format, in which F, X, Y, Z are symbolic addresses assigned to the corresponding IO signals. The logic-oriented instruction set of the 14500 allows implementation of Boolean equations in a very straightforward manner, as can be seen by comparing Eq. (5.1) for F with the program of Fig. 5.8c. The final

Input signals			Output signal
X	Y	Z	F
On	d	d	On
d	Off	On	On
Off	On	d	Off
Off	d	Off	Off

Note: d = don't care

(*a*)

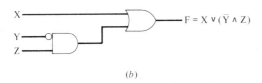

(*b*)

Address in M	Instruction	Comment
000	**LDC** Y	AC := $\overline{Y}$;
001	**AND** Z	AC := AC $\land$ Z making AC = $\overline{Y} \land Z$;
010	**OR** X	AC := AC $\lor$ X making AX = X $\lor$ ($\overline{Y} \land Z$);
011	**STO** F	F := AC making F = X $\lor$ ($\overline{Y} \land Z$);
100	**NOPF**	FLGF := 1 causing PC to be reset to zero;

(*c*)

Figure 5.8 Control problem: (*a*) truth-table specification; (*b*) hardwired implementation using standard gates; (*c*) programmed implementation using the 14500.

NOPF instruction is used to reset the program counter PC to zero, thereby returning to the first instruction of the program. Note that **NOPF** could be replaced in this program by **JMP** 0.

The **IEN** and **OEN** instructions are mainly intended for modifying the effects of other instructions. As an illustration of this, suppose that **IEN** W is added to the beginning of the program in Fig. 5.8c, where W is a new system input variable. The resulting program is

```
IEN   W
LDC   Y
AND   Z
OR    X
STO   F
NOPF
```

If W = 1 when **IEN** W is executed, then the new instruction has no effect on the program. If, however, **IEN** W is executed with W = 0, then the three instructions following **IEN** W effectively become

```
LDC   1
AND   0
OR    0
```

and always result in AC = 0, independently of the values of X, Y, and Z. Hence the next instruction **STO** F sets F to 0. Clearly F cannot be set to 1 as long as W remains at 0. Thus in this example, **IEN** W overrides all the signals X, Y, Z, making W act as a master switch. As observed by the manufacturer (Motorola, 1977), **IEN** and **OEN** must be used with caution, since their effects on subsequent instructions may be quite subtle.

Numerical computations are occasionally needed in control applications where the 14500 is used. For example, it may be necessary to transmit a specific number of pulses, or wait a specified length of time before initiating some action. An ICU-based system can be endowed with the ability to count, add, and so on, by supplying appropriate arithmetic routines. Since its instruction set implements a logically complete set of operations, any arithmetic function can be programmed, although the resulting programs may be extremely long.

Figure 5.9 contains a program to perform 1-bit addition. It may be viewed as a software implementation of the full adder equations

$$SUM = X \oplus Y \oplus CIN$$

$$COUT = (X \wedge Y) \vee (X \wedge CIN) \vee (Y \wedge CIN)$$

where X and Y are the input data bits and CIN and COUT are the input and output carry bits respectively. Note the nonstandard use of the IEN flip-flop as a temporary data register in this example. More complex programs will require the use of an external set of scratchpad registers for temporary data storage, since very little is provided by the 14500 itself. The writing of long programs for the 14500 is also facilitated by the use of subroutines. The **JMP** and **RTN** instructions provide primitive mechanisms for implementing subroutine call and return operations.

uction		Comment
LDC	CIN	$AC := CIN$;
XNOR	Y	$AC := \overline{AC \oplus Y}$ making $AC = \overline{Y} \oplus CIN$;
XNOR	X	$AC := \overline{AC \oplus X}$ making $AC = X \oplus Y \oplus CIN$;
STO	SUM	$SUM := AC$;
LD	Y	$AC := Y$;
OR	CIN	$AC := AC \vee CIN$ making $AC = Y \vee CIN$;
AND	X	$AC := AC \wedge X$ making $AC = (X \wedge Y) \vee (X \wedge CIN)$;
IEN	Y	$IEN := Y$; IEN is being used as a temporary data register
OR	CIN	$AC := AC \vee (CIN \wedge IEN)$ making $AC = (X \wedge Y) \vee (X \wedge CIN) \vee$ $(Y \wedge CIN)$;
STO	COUT	$COUT := AC$;
IEN	1	$IEN := 1$, which enables the DATA line for future instructions;

Figure 5.9 A 1-bit addition program for the 14500.

The 14500 affords a good illustration of one of the major uses of microprocessors, namely, to replace hardwired logic in fairly simple control applications. As can be seen from Fig. 5.8, a hardwired logic circuit can be mapped directly into a microprocessor program. Although the resulting microprocessor-based system may contain far more gates and flip-flops than the hardwired logic it replaces, the cost of the microprocessor system is very low, when measured by the number of ICs it contains. Furthermore, greater design flexibility is achieved by implementing control logic in software instead of hardware.

The 14500 ICU is basically a 1-bit microprocessor intended for rather simple decision-oriented control tasks. Its word size is too small, and its instruction set too limited, to make it suitable for applications that involve all but the simplest numerical computations. It can be regarded as a serial processor, since it must process words one bit at a time. Despite these limitations, the 14500 is a general-purpose processor that is, in principle, capable of performing any desired computation.

5.2 CPU ORGANIZATION

Having examined a specific, although simple, microprocessor in some detail, we are now in a position to discuss microprocessor design from a more general point of view. The purpose of this section is to introduce the key concepts of CPU organization, emphasizing those that are most relevant to the design and application of microcomputers.

5.2.1 CPU Functions

The primary function of a CPU such as a microprocessor is to execute programs. During their execution, programs are stored wholly or in part in a (main) memory M that lies outside the CPU proper. M contains a set of 2^N storage locations, each capable of storing a w_M-bit word. A given location in M may contain an instruction or data item, or a portion of one. The CPU accesses M for reading or writing by sending to it the N-bit address

ADR of the location M[ADR] it desires to read from or write into. During write or store operations, the CPU also sends M a w_M-bit word to be stored in M[ADR]. During read (also called load or fetch) operations, M transmits the w_M-bit contents of M[ADR] to the CPU. Information received from M is stored in registers in the CPU.

To carry out the operations specified by an instruction I stored in M, the CPU must perform the following actions:

1. Construct the address(es) of the location(s) in M that contain I.
2. Fetch I from M by executing one or more memory read operations.
3. Inspect or decode I to determine its data-processing requirements.
4. If necessary, fetch any operands required by I that are stored in M.
5. Execute the operations specified by I.
6. If required by I, store the results in M.

The six steps listed constitute an *instruction cycle*. During normal operation the CPU repeatedly goes through instruction cycles. The complexity and duration of an instruction cycle depend on the particular instruction I being processed.

The CPU is often divided logically, if not physically, into two subsystems, an instruction or I-unit concerned mainly with instruction fetching and interpretation (steps 1–3) and an execution or E-unit that is responsible for instruction execution (steps 4–6). Thus in the 14500-based microprocessor depicted in Fig. 5.7, the I-unit consists of the program counter PC, the instruction register IR, and the control logic in the 14500 microprocessor. The rest of the 14500, including the (arithmetic-) logic unit and the accumulator register AC, forms the E-unit. In more conventional microprocessors, both the I- and E-units are augmented by additional registers and processing circuits. The complexity of these circuits is roughly proportional to the complexity of the CPU's instruction set.

The CPU contains a variety of registers for the temporary storage of addresses, instructions, and data. Some of these, termed the *programmable registers*, can be accessed via instructions in the CPU's instruction set; the others are inaccessible to the programmer. The CPU registers can be accessed more quickly than M, and hence instructions whose operands are in CPU registers are faster than equivalent instructions whose operands are in M. Most CPUs contain a special register called an accumulator AC, which is used as an implicit operand source or destination by many instructions. In addition to the program counter PC employed to store instruction addresses, there may be other address registers present to support various memory-addressing modes. A special register, called here the *status register* SR, stores information on conditions occurring during instruction execution, such as overflow or carry generation in arithmetic operations or the appearance of an all-0 result. The status information can be tested and used to modify program behavior. Many CPUs have a set of general-purpose programmable registers, sometimes referred to as a scratchpad memory, which can be used by a programmer in any way desired. The number of general-purpose registers in the CPU is kept small deliberately, so that they can be identified by very short addresses, typically 2 to 4 bits. The various CPU registers can communicate internally with one another, the data-processing circuits, and the CPU buses to the outside world. Figure 5.10 shows the internal structure of a typical microprocessor.

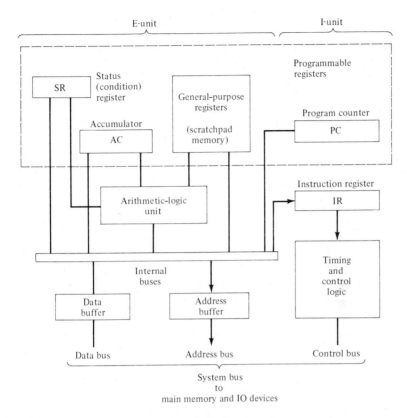

Figure 5.10 Internal organization of a typical microprocessor.

Besides fetching and executing instructions from M, the CPU also acts as the central controller for the entire computer. It therefore is equipped to communicate with IO devices. Communication between the CPU and IO devices normally utilizes the same set of lines, the system bus, used for communication with main memory. The ways in which the CPU, M, and the IO devices communicate form an important aspect of microprocessor architecture, which is considered in detail later.

An instruction I specifies an operation F to be performed and a set of operands or data items $X_1, X_2, \cdots, X_n$ to be processed. We use the term *operand* to include both the input quantities, or arguments of the instruction, and also the results that are produced by the instruction. Instructions may be represented in several different ways. Our RTL notation allows instruction I to be written as a register-transfer statement thus:

$$X_1 := F(X_2, X_3, \cdots, X_n);$$

The assembly language of the computer in question represents I by a symbolic expression of the form

$$F \quad X_1, X_2, \cdots X_n$$

Every microprocessor family has its own unique assembly language. Although standard formats and mnemonics for assembly languages have been proposed, they have not been generally accepted. I can also be described in the microprocessor's machine language format, which is the pattern of bits used to represent I within the computer itself. Representative examples of assembly-language and machine-language instruction formats appear in Fig. 5.11.

There is usually a close correspondence between a computer's assembly- and machine-language instruction formats. Each consists of an operation code or *opcode* that defines F, followed by a list of operand identifiers called *addresses*. Thus in the Z80 load instruction

LD   A,2FA1H

appearing in Fig. 5.11, the opcode is LD (load), and the addresses consist of a CPU register name A and a main memory address written as a hexadecimal number $2FA1_{16}$. The corresponding machine-language instruction contains the same information in a somewhat different form consisting of 3 bytes. (The memory word size of the three microprocessors mentioned in Fig. 5.11 is 1 byte.) The first byte 00111010 is called the opcode byte; it identifies the instruction as a load instruction using register A. The next 2 bytes contain the 16-bit binary number corresponding to $2FA1_{16}$. Note that every machine-language instruction in Fig. 5.11 is stored in M as a sequence of from 1 to 3 bytes.

As the examples in Fig. 5.11 indicate, corresponding 8080/8085 and Z80 instructions have different assembly-language formats but identical machine-language formats. Two processors whose instruction sets are related in this manner are said to be *software compatible* at the machine-language or object-code level, but incompatible at the assembly-language or source-code level. The instruction set of the 8080 is a proper subset of the Z80's; the Z80 is therefore said to be *downward compatible* with the 8080, while the 8080 is *upward compatible* with the Z80. The 6800 is not software compatible with the other microprocessors in Fig. 5.11, despite occasional similarities in their assembly languages.

5.2.2 Addressing Modes

Many instructions make use of CPU registers such as the accumulator to store operands. There may be no need to identify these registers explicitly in the instruction format, since they can be determined from the opcode. For example, all the 14500's data transfer and logical instructions (see Fig. 5.5) implicitly address the accumulator AC; only the storage device currently connected to the DATA line needs to be explicitly addressed. The add instruction ABA of the 6800 microprocessor appearing in Fig. 5.11 implicitly specifies two CPU registers A and B. This type of operand specification is called *implicit addressing*. The most obvious advantage of implicit addressing of this kind is that it results in shorter instruction formats. Shorter instructions take up less space in M. Equally important is the fact that shorter instructions can usually be processed more rapidly. Compare, for instance, the 6800 instructions ABA and LDA A 2FA1H, which appear in Fig. 5.11. The machine code for ABA is only 1 byte long, whereas that of the load instruction is 3 bytes long. Since the 6800 can fetch information from M only 1 byte

Instruction	RTL Description	Microprocessor	Assembly-Language Format	Machine-Language Format
Move (immediate) data to register	A := 64;	8080/8085	MVI A,64	00111110 01000000
		Z80	LD A,64	
		6800	LDA A #64	10000110 01000000
Load register from memory	A := M[2FA1$_{16}$];	8080/8085	LDA 2FA1H	00111010 10100001 00101111
		Z80	LD A, 2FA1H	
		6800	LDA A 2FA1H	10110110 00101111 10100001
Add register to register	A := A + B;	8080/8085	ADD B	10000000
		Z80	ADD B	
		6800	ABA	00011011
Unconditional branch	PC := 18;	8080/8085	JMP 18	11000011 00010010 00000000
		Z80	JMP 18	
		6800	JMP 18	01111110 00000000 00010010

Figure 5.11 Examples of microprocessor instruction formats.

at a time, it takes three times as long to fetch the 3-byte load instruction as it does to fetch ABA.

The purpose of an instruction address is to identify an operand value to be used in executing the instruction. Sometimes the operand value is contained in the instruction itself, a mode of operand specification called *immediate addressing*. For example, the 8080/8085 instruction

$$\text{MVI} \quad \text{A,64} \tag{5.2}$$

which is defined in Fig. 5.11 causes the (decimal) number 64 to be transferred to the A register; the mnemonic opcode MVI denotes move immediate. The quantity 64 appearing in (5.2) is called an immediate address.

Very frequently, an operand is identified by naming the device that stores its current value; this is called *direct addressing*. The operand identifier used, which is called a direct address, is usually a CPU register name or a main memory address. (A storage device's name is synonymous with its address.) In the following Z80 instruction

$$\text{LD} \quad \text{A,64} \tag{5.3}$$

for example, there are two direct addresses—namely, A, a CPU register name, and 64, a main memory address. Note that the same symbol 64 is an immediate address in (5.2) but a direct address in (5.3).

It is occasionally useful to have instructions that identify their operands in a less direct fashion than by immediate or direct addressing. An operand identifier is called an *indirect address* if it is the (direct) address of a storage device whose contents in turn form the direct address of the desired operand. As an illustration, the Z8000 microprocessor allows instructions of the form

$$\text{LD} \quad \text{R1} \quad @\text{R2} \tag{5.4}$$

in which R1 is a direct address and @R2 is an indirect address. R1 and R2 are the names (direct addresses) of two CPU registers. Instruction (5.4) specifies the operation R1: = M[R2], that is, move to register R1 the contents of the memory location whose direct address is stored in register R2. In the assembly language of the Z8000 and other processors, @R is used to denote an indirect address if R stores the direct address of the required operand. Indirect addressing can be extended, in principle, to many levels by allowing instruction addresses of the form @@ ... @R.

Indirect addressing is useful when it is desired to use specific storage locations as address registers. It is frequently used to implement multiway branches in a program. For example an instruction such as

$$\text{JMP} \quad 18$$

(examples of which appear in Fig. 5.11) causes an unconditional branch to the instruction at memory location 18. It is implemented by the operation PC : = 18. An instruction of the form

$$\text{JMP} \quad @18 \tag{5.5}$$

which reads jump to 18 indirectly, corresponds to PC : = M[18]. Thus if M[18] = 19, (5.5) is equivalent to JMP 19. If the contents of M[18] are determined by a branch condition, then (5.5) suffices to implement a conditional branch to a large number of different destinations.

Immediate, direct, and indirect addressing form a natural hierarchy of addressing modes, as illustrated in Fig. 5.12. They require, respectively, zero, one, and two read operations to obtain the operand value from the instruction address. While the extra read steps take time, they also increase the number of different operand values that a single address can specify at different times. For example, an immediate address always yields the same value, a direct address for a k-bit storage device can yield up to 2^k different values, while an indirect address can refer to up to 2^k direct addresses, each of which can yield many different values of the target operand. Most microprocessors have immediate and direct addressing; a smaller number have instructions with indirect addressing ability.

Another dimension is added to instruction addressing by the use of address modification. An address ADR1 can be modified by a second address ADR2 so that the *effective address* ADR used to locate the operand in question is determined by the relation

$$ADR = ADR1 + ADR2 \qquad (5.6)$$

ADR1 and ADR2 may be immediate, direct, or indirect addresses in any combination. Frequently one of these two addresses is treated as a relatively fixed *reference address* that is modified by the other; the modifier address may be called an *offset* or *displacement*. Several important address modification schemes are based on (5.7) that differ principally in the types of address registers used and the choice of reference address.

In *indexed addressing* the address ADR1 appearing in the instruction is usually the reference address, while the offset ADR2 is stored in a register called an index register. For example, the 6800 instruction

$$LDA \quad A \ ADR1,X \qquad (5.7)$$

is an indexed load instruction that specifies the operation $A := M[ADR1 + X]$. Here a symbolic direct memory address ADR1 is added to the contents of the 6800's index register, which is named X, to form the effective direct address ADR1 + X. The symbol ,X appearing in (5.7) is usually regarded as an address modifier that indicates indexing.

Addressing Mode	Number of Reads to Obtain Operand Value V	Typical Notation	Location of operand value V		
			Instruction	X	Y
Immediate	0	Constant name (with prefix #)	V		
Direct	1	Variable name	X⟶	V	
Indirect	2	@ Variable name	@X⟶	Y⟶	V

Figure 5.12 Three basic addressing modes.

When the instruction address is viewed as the offset address and the reference address is stored in a register R, the term *base addressing* is used, and R may be called a base register. An example of a microprocessor with separate indexed and base addressing is the Z8000.

Indexed addressing is useful for processing ordered arrays or lists of words of the form N[0], N[1], ... We can store these items in contiguous locations in M so that consecutive items have consecutive addresses thus:

Address	Contents
ADR1	N[0]
ADR1 + 1	N[1]
ADR1 + 2	N[2]
...	...

Any word N[i] in the array can be conveniently referenced by an indexed instruction address ADR1 whose index register stores the quantity i. The term indexed addressing comes from the fact that i is the index of N[i]. If the instruction (5.7) is used to access the above array, then setting X to some value, say seven, causes N[7] to be loaded into register A.

An address field ADR appearing in a branch instruction is typically the (direct) address of data used to replace the contents of the program counter PC. There is another addressing mode used for branch instructions called *relative addressing,* in which a new address to be loaded into PC is constructed by adding an (immediate) address ADR1 appearing in the branch instruction to the old PC contents as follows:

$$PC := PC + ADR1;$$

ADR1 is thus used as an offset with respect to PC. Relative addressing has the advantage of allowing short address fields to specify branch addresses, thereby decreasing branch instruction size. It also allows the branch addresses of a program to be made independent of the program's location in main memory M. Programs with this property are termed *relocatable,* because they can be repositioned in M without affecting their executability.

Figure 5.13 summarizes the three address modification schemes described here: indexed, base, and relative addressing. They all define ways to construct an effective address from two partial addresses. They are thus independent of the immediate, direct, and indirect addressing modes discussed earlier, which specify how to track down an operand value. The six addressing modes defined in Figs. 5.12 and 5.13 can be combined with one another in various ways to produce the seemingly large number of different addressing modes found in some microprocessors.

5.2.3. Data Types

Every operand of an instruction has a data type that assigns a meaning to the operand. The most common data types encountered in microprocessors are numbers, logical constants denoting the values **true** and **false**, and words representing alphanumeric

Addressing Mode	Usual Role of Instruction Address ADR1	Usual Role of Modifier Address	Modifier Register Name	Construction of the Effective Address ADR
Indexed	Reference	Offset	Index register X	
Base	Offset	Reference	Base register B	
Relative	Offset	Reference	Program counter PC	

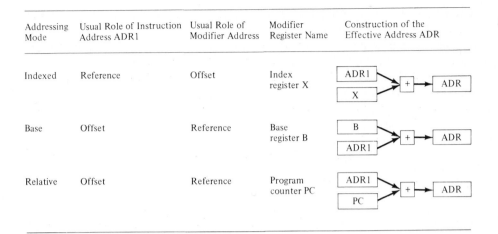

Figure 5.13 Three addressing modes that modify the instruction address.

characters. Numbers fall into two major groups, fixed point and floating point. They may be further subdivided by the number bases or radixes used, two in the case of binary numbers and 10 in the case of decimal numbers. Figure 5.14 shows the basic data types. More complex data types can be formed by concatenating words of one data type to form longer units that, depending on the context, are called blocks, strings, lists, or arrays. Because of the short word sizes of microcomputers, it is often necessary to represent a single item such as a long number by a block of words within the computer.

Fixed-point numbers, which were examined in detail in Sec. 3.1.4, are reviewed briefly here. Binary fixed-point numbers are most often represented in twos-complement (TC) code, mainly because it allows addition and subtraction to be implemented by means of very simple logic circuits. Decimal numbers generally use BCD (binary-coded decimal) code. Each decimal digit is then encoded in 4 bits, which allows two digits to fit exactly into the 1-byte memory word size found in many microcomputers. The instructions provided for processing decimal numbers are often rather limited, implying the

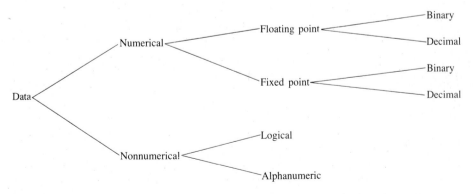

Figure 5.14 Some basic data types.

need for software routines to obtain a full range of decimal operations. BCD number words do not normally store a sign (plus or minus); a separate word or portion of a word must be reserved for this purpose. Figure 5.15 gives some examples of the fixed-point number formats found in such 8-bit machines as the 6800 and 8080.

Sometimes the CPU or memory word size of a microcomputer is too short to represent fixed-point numbers of the required range or precision. Longer numbers can be accommodated by breaking them into word-size pieces that can be processed sequentially. For example, the number $-4\ 227\ 075$ is equivalent to the TC number

$$101111110111111111111101_{TC}$$

To store this 24-bit number in a typical byte-organized memory, we can split it into 3 bytes that can be stored in consecutive memory locations thus:

$$10111111$$

$$01111111$$

$$11111101$$

This is a 3-byte block representing the original number. Three memory reads are required to fetch the number, and operations such as addition and subtraction must be applied to each byte in sequence. Recall that the TC code permits all bits of word, including the sign bit, to be processed in a uniform fashion, which is an advantage when dealing with blocks of the above type.

Much larger number ranges can be represented by floating-point numbers. They correspond to the scientific notation commonly used to represent very large or very small numbers. For example, one and a half trillion, which has the lengthy fixed-point form

$$1\ 500\ 000\ 000\ 000$$

can be written more concisely as

$$1.5 \times 10^{12} \tag{5.8}$$

Similarly, the very small number one and a half trillionth can be written as 1.5×10^{-12}. In this scientific notation a number has three components: a mantissa, an exponent, and a

Data Type	Data Word		Number Represented
	Binary	Hexadecimal	
Twos complement	01000000	40	$+64$
(signed)	01111111	7F	$+127$
	10000001	81	-127
	11111111	FF	-1
BCD decimal	01000000	40	40
(unsigned)	10000001	81	81
	11111111	FF	Invalid

Figure 5.15 Examples of 8-bit fixed-point number formats used in many microprocessors.

base, which, in the case of (5.8), are the quantities 1.5, 12, and 10 respectively. It is often convenient, in the display of a pocket calculator for instance, to omit the base (its value is understood) and rewrite (5.8) in the form

$$1.5 \qquad 12$$

This is the floating-point number format, which, with suitable binary encoding, is employed for machine computation. In general a floating-point number consists of a pair of fixed-point numbers, a mantissa M and an exponent E, which represent the number $M \times B^E$ using some implicit base B. When M and E are binary (decimal) numbers, it is most convenient to make B equal to two (10). Number precision is determined by the length of M, while the range of the numbers that can be represented is determined by the length of E.

Figure 5.16 depicts the format proposed as a standard for representing 32-bit floating-point numbers in microcomputers by the Institute of Electrical and Electronics Engineers (IEEE), and known as the IEEE 754 Standard (Stevenson, 1981). It consists of three components: a 23-bit mantissa or fraction field M; an 8-bit exponent field E, which implicitly contains the sign of the exponent; and a sign bit S, which is the sign of the mantissa, and therefore of the entire floating-point number. E and M are binary fixed-point numbers, so that the B is two. M denotes a binary fraction, which with S forms a sign-magnitude number. There is, however, an implicit 1 to the left of the binary point associated with M, so that the complete mantissa, also called the *significand*, can be expressed as 1.M. This means that mantissas of the form 101.011, 10.10111, 0.101011, 0.000101011, and so on, must all be replaced by 1.01011, a process called *normalization*. A floating-point number is normalized by shifting the mantissa to the left or right, and making a compensating adjustment to the exponent. Normalization ensures that every number has a unique floating-point representation. Since a floating-point number conforming to the IEEE Standard must have a 1 immediately before the binary point of the mantissa, that 1 need not be stored with the number; however, it must be restored by the arithmetic circuits that process the number. The E field in Fig. 5.16 represents a positive unsigned integer from which the exponent value is obtained by subtracting 127. Hence the actual exponent is $E - 127$, and it ranges in value from -127 to $+128$. E is called a *biased exponent,* and 127 is called the *bias*. Exponent biasing simplifies certain operations involving floating-point numbers.

It follows from the foregoing discussion that the number N defined by a 32-bit word conforming to the IEEE 754 Standard can be expressed by the formula

$$N = (-1)^S \, 2^{E-127} \, (1.M) \tag{5.9}$$

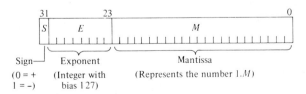

Figure 5.16 The IEEE 754 Standard for 32-bit floating-point numbers.

in all but a few special cases. Zero is one such case, and is represented by a sequence of thirty-two 0s. The number -1.5, for instance, is denoted by

$$1 \quad 01111111 \quad 10000000000000000000000$$

which, according to (5.9), has the value

$$N = (-1)^1 \, 2^{127-127} \, (1.1_2) = (-1) \, 2^0 \, (1.5) = -1.5$$

The IEEE 32-bit floating-point standard allows numbers up to about 3.4×10^{38} to be represented (see Prob. 5.8). Note that a 32-bit fixed-point integer format cannot represent numbers larger than $2^{31} - 1$, which is about 2.1×10^9. The IEEE 754 Standard also covers 64-bit or double-precision floating-point numbers, which have a 52-bit mantissa field and an 11-bit exponent field, allowing numbers up to about 1.7×10^{308} to be represented.

Arithmetic operations such as addition become quite complex when floating-point rather than fixed-point numbers are involved. Consequently very few microprocessors have the instructions or arithmetic circuits required for direct processing of floating-point numbers. The ability to do such processing can be added to any microprocessor in two ways:

1. By providing it with software routines that implement the desired floating-point operations
2. By attaching suitable floating-point arithmetic circuits to the microprocessor

As will be discussed in Sec. 8.3, a variety of one-chip arithmetic processors are commercially available that provide a simple and efficient way of endowing a system with floating-point hardware.

The two binary signal values 1 and 0 can be used in a very natural way to denote the logic values **true** and **false**. Logical variables can be associated with binary devices such as switches (**true** = on, **false** = off), with program branching conditions (**true** = condition is satisfied, **false** = condition is not satisfied) or, in general, with the presence or absence of any system state of interest. An n-bit word can represent n independent logical variables, which can be processed in parallel by logical instructions. All microprocessors contain a variety of logical instructions; see, for example, the 14500 instruction set in Fig. 5.5.

When communicating with IO devices, a microprocessor is sometimes required to handle alphanumeric data. Such data are most conveniently represented by a string or sequence of words, each of which denotes an alphanumeric character in some suitable binary code. One of the codes for this purpose that is very widely used is the ASCII (American Standards Committee on Information Interchange) code, which is defined by Fig. 5.17. It uses 7 bits for character specification, thus allowing 128 different combinations. This is sufficient to represent the English alphabet in both lowercase and uppercase form, the 10 decimal digits, and certain common symbols such as punctuation marks. Some 32 control or nonprinting ASCII characters in the leftmost two columns of Fig. 5.17 are used for communication with and control of IO devices. The 7 bits $c_6 c_5 c_4 c_3 c_2 c_1 c_0$ of an ASCII character usually have an eighth bit $p = c_7$ appended to them. p is a parity bit

Most Significant Bits $c_6c_5c_4$

$c_3c_2c_1c_0$	000		001		010	011	100	101	110	111
0000	NUL	Null	DLE	Data link escape	(Space)	0	@	P	`	p
0001	SOH	Start of heading	DC1	Device control 1	!	1	A	Q	a	q
0010	STX	Start of text	DC2	Device control 2	"	2	B	R	b	r
0011	ETX	End of text	DC3	Device control 3	#	3	C	S	c	s
0100	EOT	End of transmission	DC4	Device control 4	$	4	D	T	d	t
0101	ENQ	Enquiry	NAK	Negative acknowledge	%	5	E	U	e	u
0110	ACK	Acknowledge	SYN	Synchronous idle	&	6	F	V	f	v
0111	BEL	Bell	ETB	End of transmission block	'	7	G	W	g	w
1000	BS	Backspace	CAN	Cancel	(	8	H	X	h	x
1001	HT	Horizontal tab	EM	End of medium	)	9	I	Y	i	y
1010	LF	Line feed	SUB	Substitute	⋆	:	J	Z	j	z
1011	VT	Vertical tab	ESC	Escape	+	;	K	[	k	{
1100	FF	Form feed	FS	File separator	,	<	L	∖	l	|
1101	CR	Carriage return	GS	Group separator	-	=	M	]	m	}
1110	SO	Shift out	RS	Record separator	.	>	N	↑	n	~
1111	SI	Shift in	US	Unit separator	/	?	O	↓	o	(Delete)

Least Significant Bits $c_3c_2c_1c_0$

Figure 5.17 The 7-bit ASCII code.

used for error detection. In even (odd) parity ASCII codes, p is set to a value that makes the total number of 1s in the 8-bit character $C = c_7c_6c_5c_4c_3c_2c_1c_0$ even (odd). An error in data transmission or storage that alters any single bit of C can be detected by recomputing the parity of C and comparing it with the previously computed value c_7. If they differ, an error has occurred. Parity checking is implemented by special hardware or software routines. Even when parity checking is not performed, it is convenient to append an extra (unused) bit to form 8-bit ASCII characters that fit neatly into the byte-oriented st͏͏ ͏age devices found in most microcomputers.

5.2.4 Instruction Types

An instruction, as we have seen, specifies an operation and a set of operands. The operation is determined by an opcode, which is usually the first or leftmost field of the instruction's assembly and machine language formats. The number of basic operations that a computer can perform is fairly small. However, the number of possible instructions greatly increases when the operand addressing modes and data types that may be used with each opcode are taken into account.

In machine-language instructions the opcode field usually specifies all the addressing modes and data types to be used. Thus by decoding the opcode, the CPU can find out how to obtain the operands, and what actions to perform on the operands. At the assembly-language level, the mnemonic opcode defines the basic operation type. In some machines the opcode also defines addressing modes and data types. It is desirable from a programming viewpoint to include these operand characteristics in the instruction address fields rather than in the opcode field. Thus in the move immediate instructions depicted in Fig. 5.11, the prefix # is used in some cases to designate the immediate operand. In the 8080/8085 case, however, the assembly-language opcode MVI (move immediate) specifies the immediate addressing mode.

The differences between assembly- and machine-language opcodes are illustrated by Fig. 5.18, which shows the possible variants of the add instruction in the 6800 microprocessor. In all cases the operand data type is an 8-bit twos-complement fixed-point number, a fact that is implicit in all the opcodes. There are only three basic opcodes at the assembly-language level, namely, ABA, ADD, and ADC. When combined with the 6800's possible addressing modes, the result is 17 distinct machine-language opcodes, each of which can be represented by 8 bits or two hexadecimal digits; the latter notation is used in Fig. 5.18. In counting the instructions of a particular computer, usually only the distinct assembly language opcodes are counted. Thus Fig. 5.18 contributes three instructions (ABA, ADD, ADC) to the 72 instructions normally considered to constitute the 6800's instruction set in 6800 literature. The 6800 has 197 distinct machine language opcodes.

As noted in Sec. 5.1.1, we divide instructions into three broad classes:

1. Data-transfer instructions that move information (addresses, operand values, instructions, etc.) unchanged from one part of the computer to another
2. Data-processing instructions that transform data, thereby carrying out the main computational tasks required

Instruction Type	RTL Description	Assembly Language	Machine Language (hex)	Comment
Add accumulators	A := A + B;	ABA	1B	6800 has two accumulators A and B.
Add immediate	A := A + 64;	ADD A #64	8B 40	
	B := B + 64;	ADD B #64	CB 40	C is the 6800 carry bit.
Add immediate with carry	A := A + C + 64;	ADC A #64	89 40	
	B := B + C + 64;	ADC B #64	C9 40	
Add direct	A := A + M[64];	ADD A 64	9B 40	"Direct" addresses are 1 byte long.
	B := B + M[64];	ADD B 64	DB 40	
Add direct with carry	A := A + C + M[64];	ADC A 64	99 40	
	B := B + C + M[64];	ADC B 64	D9 40	
Add extended	A := A + M[256];	ADD A 256	BB 01 00	"Extended" (direct) addresses are 2 bytes long.
	B := B + M[256];	ADD B 256	FB 01 00	
Add extended with carry	A := A + C + M[256];	ADC A 256	B9 01 00	
	B := B + C + M[256];	ADC B 256	F9 01 00	
Add indexed	A := A + M[X + 64];	ADD A 64,X	AB 40	X is the 6800 index register.
	B := B + M[X + 64];	ADD B 64,X	EB 40	
Add indexed with carry	A := A + C + M[X + 64];	ADC A 64,X	A9 40	
	B := B + C + M[X + 64];	ADC B 64,X	E9 40	

Figure 5.18 The add instructions of the 6800 microprocessor.

3. Program-control instructions that are mainly used to determine the order in which instructions are executed

Data-transfer instructions are often further classified by the sources and destinations of the transfers, which include CPU registers, main memory, and IO devices. Thus there are register-to-register data transfer instructions, register-to-memory instructions, and so on. Instructions that use IO devices as sources or destinations are called input-output (IO) instructions. There are two special types of data-transfer instructions called push and pop (or pull), which are used to transfer data to and from a stack storage area. The stack is implemented by a set of registers or, more often, by a set of consecutive memory locations, which are accessed via a special address register, the stack pointer SP. A stack has the property that the last word written into the stack is the first word read out; this access method is called LIFO (last-in/first-out). After a push or pop operation has been performed, SP is adjusted automatically to point to the next consecutive location in the stack. The end at which data are appended to or removed from the stack is conventionally known as the "top" of the stack. Since SP automatically keeps track of the stack top, it is not necessary to include stack addresses in push or pop instructions.

Data-processing instructions fall into two main categories: arithmetic instructions, which operate on numbers, and logical instructions, which operate on logical data. The logical instructions should include a set of operations that is (logically) complete in the sense discussed in Sec. 3.3.2, for example, AND, OR, and NOT. Logical instructions acting on n-bit words treat each bit position independently, and therefore perform n independent 1-bit logical operations simultaneously. The fundamental nature of logical instructions is indicated by the fact that the 14500 microprocessor discussed in the preceding section has only logical data-processing instructions.

Arithmetic instructions are distinguished on the basis of the number types they process. Almost all microprocessors handle fixed-point binary numbers, and many include some fixed-point decimal instructions also. Most arithmetic instructions handle operands whose length is the microprocessor's nominal word size; these may be referred to as single-precision instructions. Some instructions for double-precision (double-word) operations may also be available, as well as instructions that facilitate the programming of multiple precision or block operations. The most widely implemented arithmetic instructions are add, subtract, increment (add one), decrement (subtract one), and negate (change the sign). Multiply and divide require more complicated logic circuits than add and subtract; hence they are found only in the more powerful micro-processors. Floating-point arithmetic is usually implemented by software routines or auxiliary hardware processors.

Another useful class of data-processing instructions are the shift instructions, which can be viewed as either arithmetic or logical. All shift instructions move a data word a specified number of places to the left or right. Logical shift (often simply called shift) instructions cause the vacated positions resulting from the shift to be filled with 0s; data shifted beyond the word boundary are lost. Arithmetic shift instructions differ from logical in that they cause all the vacated bit positions to be set to the value of the leftmost (in right shifts) or rightmost (in left shifts) bit of the original data word. Multiplication (division) by 2^i can be implemented by left (right) shifting an appropriately encoded number i places. Consider, for example, the following negative TC number

$$11011110_{TC}$$

which denotes -34. An arithmetic right shift of this number by one bit position results in

$$11101111$$

which is the proper TC representation of $-34/2 = -17$. Note how arithmetic, unlike logical, shifts preserve the leading or trailing 1s associated with negative TC numbers. Another instruction that involves shifting is rotate, which causes the data that are shifted out from one end of the data word to be shifted back in at the other end.

Program-control instructions change the flow of control during program execution by modifying the contents of the program counter PC. Normally instructions are executed in the sequence in which they are stored in main memory. PC is used by the CPU to store instruction addresses; it is incremented automatically during each instruction cycle to point to the next consecutive instruction. The simplest way to modify PC is by means of a branch or jump instruction that specifies an operand (the address of a new instruction) that is used to replace the current contents of PC. Branch instructions may be unconditional, or they may be made conditional on the presence of certain CPU states. Branch conditions are commonly specified by a status register SR (also called a flag or condition-code register), which is tested by the conditional branch instructions. If the indicated condition is present, PC is modified and a program branch takes place; otherwise the branch instruction does not change PC. Among the more common condition bits stored in SR are the following:

1. A carry bit C, which is set whenever a carry or borrow bit is generated from the leftmost bit of the result of an arithmetic operation
2. A zero bit Z, which is set whenever an all-0s result is produced
3. An overflow bit V, which is set whenever the result of a signed arithmetic operation is too long, causing the magnitude part to overflow into the leftmost (sign) position (see Prob. 5.13)
4. A sign bit S, which is set to the value in the sign position of the current result

Normally the contents of SR are updated after the execution of every data-processing instruction; the bits affected vary from instruction to instruction.

Two very important kinds of branch instructions named call and return are used to transfer control between two programs. A call instruction, sometimes called jump to subroutine, contains a branch address ADR, which is the starting address of the program or subroutine to which control is to be transferred. Before replacing the PC contents by ADR, a call instruction causes the old PC contents, known as the return address, to be saved in a predefined location, for example, at the top of a stack. A return instruction is used to transfer control from a previously called program back to the calling program. Return is implemented by transferring the previously saved return address back to PC. Like simple branch instructions, call and return can be made conditional on the CPU status.

Figure 5.19 lists some of the most common instruction types found in micro-processors. Also shown is a set of representative mnemonic names for use in assembly language programs (Fischer, 1979); most commercial microprocessors have similar opcode mnemonics.

5.2.5 External Communication

The major components of a microcomputer communicate with one another via a set of shared lines called the system bus B. At any one time only two devices may be logically connected to B—one to send or transmit data (the source device), and the other to receive the data (the destination device). Of particular importance is communication between the following pairs of units:

1. The CPU and main memory M
2. The CPU and IO interface circuits
3. IO interface circuits and M

Each storage location in M and each access point of the IO devices is assigned an address that is used to select it for participation in bus operations. No address is assigned to the CPU, since it is selected directly by specific control lines in B. In a simple microcomput-er all bus activities are initiated and controlled by the CPU. Most microprocessors are designed so that the CPU can yield control of B to certain IO devices, usually via special IO control circuits. One such circuit is a *DMA (direct-memory-access) controller,* whose main purpose is to control data transfers between IO devices and M, a mode of IO communication called *direct memory access (DMA).*

A typical data transfer via a microcomputer system bus B involves the following sequence of actions:

1. A "master" device DEV1 such as the CPU or a DMA controller associated with the IO system assumes control of B.
2. The bus master DEV1 places on the appropriate lines of B an address word, which is used to select a second or "slave" device DEV2 to participate in the data transfer.
3. Once DEV2 has been activated, data transfer begins; either device can act as the data source or destination.

Usually separate sets of lines in B, called the address and data buses, are employed for address and data transmission respectively. Sometimes address and data words are transmitted sequentially via common address-data lines, in which case the address-data lines are said to be multiplexed. Additional bus lines, collectively referred to as control lines, are used mainly to initiate and terminate data transfers over the bus.

Three-state lines are often used for buses, since the third high-impedance or Z state greatly facilitates the transfer of bus control. A device that is physically connected to a line L can be logically disconnected from the bus by driving it to the Z state. When all connections to L are in the Z state, L is said to be floating. A bus master relinquishes control of the bus by allowing the address, data, and certain control lines to float, thus enabling a different device to take control.

Type	Typical Mnemonic	Instruction
Data transfer	MOV	Move one word
	LD	Load register from memory
	ST	Store register in memory
	IN	Input a word from an input port to a register or memory
	OUT	Output a word from a register or memory to an output port
	PUSH	Move data from register(s) to the top of a stack
	POP	Move data from the top of a stack to register(s)
	MOVBK	Move a block of words
	SET	Move 1s into all operand bit positions
	CLR	Move 0s into all operand bit positions (clear)
	XCH	Exchange (swap) the specified operands
Data processing	ADD	Add
	ADDC	Add with carry
	SUB	Subtract
	SUBC	Subtract with borrow
	INC	Increment by one
	DEC	Decrement by one
	MUL	Multiply
	DIV	Divide
	NEG	Negate (replace operand by its arithmetic complement)
	CMP	Compare operands and set status bit(s) based on the outcome
	AND	And
	OR	Or
	XOR	Exclusive-or
	NOT	Not (replace operand by its logical complement)
	SHR/SHL	Logical right/left shift
	SHRA/SHLA	Arithmetic right/left shift
	ROR/ROL	Rotate right/left
Program control	BR	Branch unconditionally
	BRc	Branch if condition bit c is 1
	BRNc	Branch if condition bit c is 0
	SKIP	Increment PC to skip the next instruction
	SKc/SKNc	Skip next instruction if condition bit c is 1/0
	CALL	Call subroutine
	CALLc/CALLNc	Call subroutine if condition bit c is 1/0
	RET	Return from subroutine
	RETc/RETNc	Return from subroutine if condition bit c is 1/0
	HALT	Stop executing instructions
	WAIT	Stop executing instructions until a specified external event occurs
	NOP	"No operation." PC is incremented to continue program execution

Figure 5.19 Common microprocessor instruction types.

All communication via bus B must be properly timed, so that the communicating devices can be kept in step. This means that the destination device should not attempt to read data from the bus until all data lines have assumed their proper values. Similarly, the source device should not remove the data from the bus until the data have been read from the bus at the destination. Allowance must be made for fluctuations in signal-transmission times by proper sequencing of the bus signals involved in the data transfer. For example, a data word D should be placed on the bus some time δ before a control line S indicating the presence of D is activated. The delay δ should be sufficient to ensure that all bits of D reach the destination device before the signal on S; othewise the destination device may read the data lines prematurely and receive improper data values. The timing of the signals involved in a bus operation can be described by a timing diagram such as that of Fig. 5.6, which is designed to show the sequence in which signals change value, as well as the permissible delays between various events.

Once an active communication path has been established between two devices, data transfer is timed by one or more control signals. A simple approach that requires very little hardware is a free-running clock as the timing reference for all bus activities; this is called *synchronous communication*. A single clock signal such as the CPU clock may be sent to all devices connected to the system bus. Alternatively the communicating devices can have independent clock sources of the same frequency, provided the clocks can be kept in synchronism. A clock period provides a rising and a falling signal edge, each of which can serve as a reference point for determining signal rise and fall times on other lines. Synchronous data transmission has the merit of great simplicity, since one or two clock signals suffice to time all bus activities. The clock period is, in general, decided by the worst-case delays in the signal-transmission paths. The communicating devices should have comparable operating speeds; othewise the slower device will tend to drag the other down to an inefficient, and possibly unacceptable, level of operation.

Synchronous communication requires that the starting and finishing times of bus operations be predictable within reasonable tolerances. If only the starting times are predictable, then a mode of operation for which we coin the term *semisynchronous* may be used. In this mode, a special control signal is used to initiate the bus operation, a data transfer, for example. Once started, the bus operation must be completed within some prescribed period. When a semisynchronous data transfer is initiated by the destination device, the initiating control signal is normally named (data) request. The initiating control signal for a data transfer started by the source device has the generic name (data) ready. Figures 5.20a and 5.20b give timing diagrams for general semisynchronous data transfers. Note how the delays δ_1, δ_2, and δ_3 are deliberately inserted by the communicating devices to ensure that the data lines always have valid data when they are read by the destination device. A limited time is allowed for the destination to read the data bus; if it fails to do so within the allotted time, a data-transmission error may result. Note also that the source device has no way of knowing whether the data word has actually reached its destination.

Figure 5.21 shows a timing diagram for a representative semisynchronous data transfer of the kind found in some microcomputers. It is a destination-initiated transfer from main memory M to the CPU, that is, a memory read cycle. The chip-select line serves as the data request line to M. Thus M, which is unclocked, receives read requests

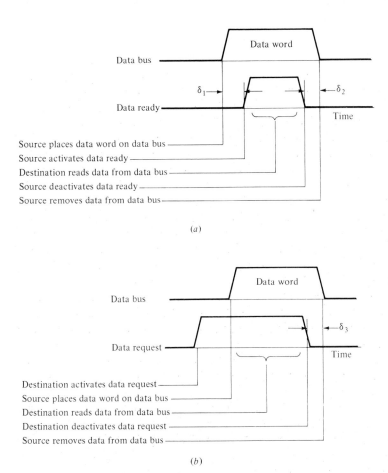

Figure 5.20 Semisynchronous data transfer: (*a*) source initiated; (*b*) destination initiated.

at times that are, for it, unpredictable. It must respond, however, to a read request within a certain maximum time. In the case of the CPU, it is often convenient to coordinate (synchronize) memory read cycles with the operation of its internal clock ϕ, because all internal CPU operations are synchronized by ϕ. Thus in the case shown in Fig. 5.21 a memory read cycle begins at time t_0 when ϕ goes from 0 to 1. The CPU first sets the write-enable line to 0 to indicate a read operation, and places the address of the memory location that is to be read on the address bus. Then after a delay of t_{AW} (the address setup time), at time t_1 it activates the memory-select line, causing M to perform a read operation. The CPU then waits t_{A} seconds (the access time) until t_2, at which time it reads the contents of the data bus into a CPU (buffer) register. The memory circuits must have an access time that does not exceed t_{A}; otherwise they are too slow for use with this particular CPU. It should be noted that t_1 and t_2 are fixed times relative to t_0, the starting time of the memory read cycle. A semisynchronous memory write cycle has a timing

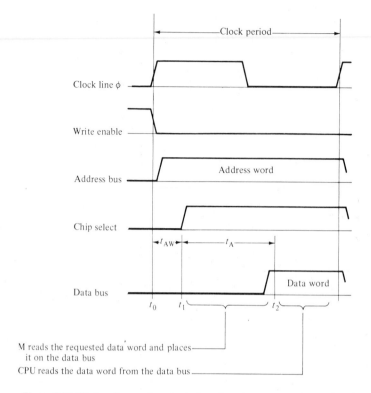

Figure 5.21 Timing diagram for a typical semisynchronous memory read cycle.

diagram similar to that of Fig. 5.21. The write-enable line is set to 1 to indicate write, and the CPU places a data word on the data bus before it selects the memory. Again a fixed maximum delay is allowed for the memory to complete its internal write operation.

When both the start and completion times of a bus operation are unpredictable, a second control signal with the generic name acknowledge can be introduced to indicate completion. Thus the operation is timed by a pair of control signals, ready/request and acknowledge. This mode of communication is termed (fully) *asynchronous*. A representative destination-initiated asynchronous data transfer is depicted in Fig. 5.22. Specific events are triggered by the rise or fall of the control signals. Unlike the semisynchronous case of Fig. 5.20b no constraint is placed on the maximum time taken to complete the data transfer. The interaction between the control signals illustrated in Fig. 5.22 is often referred to as *handshaking*.

Fully asynchronous communication of the foregoing type is encountered in various computer actions. It is used, for example, when the CPU yields control of the system bus B to a DMA control unit. The DMA controller requests access to B by activating a DMA request line. (This line is called the hold line in some microcomputers.) At a suitable breakpoint such as the end of the current CPU machine cycle, the CPU responds to DMA request by allowing the data, address, and certain control lines of B to float to the high-impedance state Z. It informs the requesting controller that the bus is available by

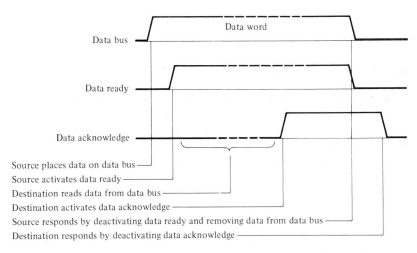

Figure 5.22 Source-initiated asynchronous data transfer.

activating a DMA acknowledge line as shown in Fig. 5.22. The DMA controller now takes control of the bus, and can execute one or more data transfers between M and the IO device(s) managed by that controller. On completion of the DMA operation, the DMA controller again allows the bus to float, and signals the CPU by deactivating DMA request. The CPU then regains control of B and deactivates DMA acknowledge.

Most data transfers over a microcomputer bus are memory read or write operations resulting from instruction fetching and execution by the CPU. As an illustration, consider the instruction cycle for the 8080/8085 store accumulator instruction

STA   2FA1H

which is equivalent to $M[2FA1_{16}] := A$. The machine-language instruction is 3 bytes long, since it comprises an opcode byte and 2 bytes forming the memory address $2FA1_{16}$

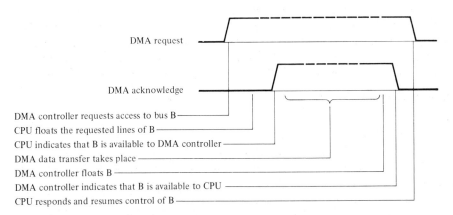

Figure 5.23 Timing diagram for a DMA operation.

(cf. Fig. 5.11). The instruction cycle for this instruction involves four 1-byte data transfers via the 8080/8085 system bus, three consecutive memory read cycles to fetch the instruction from M, and one memory write cycle to transfer the contents of the accumulator A to M.

The CPU-initiated IO operations, which generally involve data transfers between the CPU and IO devices, are implemented in a manner similar to memory read and write operations. The IO devices are typically connected to the system bus via addressable registers called *IO ports*. The IO instructions address IO ports in much the same way as memory-referencing instructions address locations in M. Some microcomputers, such as the 6800, have no IO instructions per se. IO devices are accessed by memory-referencing instructions; they, therefore, must be connected to the CPU via the same data, address, and control lines as M. This mode of IO operation, called *memory-mapped IO,* requires the IO devices and M to share a common address space. In microcomputers such as the 8080/8085, which have distinct IO instructions, separate control lines are used to select M and IO devices. This mode of operation, called *isolated IO,* allows IO and memory addresses to be kept logically separated.

As noted earlier, IO devices can communicate with the CPU via DMA control units to obtain temporary control of the system bus. Another important mechanism for communication between IO devices and the CPU is an interrupt. An *interrupt* allows an IO device, often via a special interrupt controller, to ask the CPU to suspend execution of its current program temporarily and branch to another program, an interrupt routine, that is designed to service the interrupting device in some way. A typical reason for an interrupt request is the need for an IO device to send data to or receive data from the CPU or M. A pair of asynchronous control lines, interrupt request and interrupt acknowledge, are frequently used for interrupt timing. An IO device activates the interrupt request line to inform the CPU of a pending interrupt. When it responds to the interrupt request, which it usually does between instruction cycles, the CPU saves the program counter as in a subroutine call, and loads PC with the interrupt address, which is the starting address of an interrupt routine. Normally a variety of different interrupt routines are needed to perform all the services required by IO devices. In microprocessors such as the 6800, interrupts cause program control to be transferred to a fixed interrupt address, thus requiring the CPU to execute additional instructions to determine which of the possible interrupt routines is to be used. Other microprocessors, such as the 8080/8085, allow the interrupting IO device to transmit interrupt addresses (also called interrupt vectors) directly to the CPU, thus permitting immediate transfer of control to the desired interrupt routine. This is known as *vectored interrupt* control.

5.3 THE 6800 FAMILY

We turn next to a representative 8-bit microprocessor family that derives from the Motorola 6800 microprocessor. The organization of the 6800, its instruction set, and its major support circuits are introduced. Two derivatives of the 6800, the 6801 one-chip microcomputer and the 6809 microprocessor, are also briefly discussed.

5.3.1 The 6800 Microprocessor

The 6800 microprocessor was introduced by Motorola in 1974 (Young et al., 1974). It is an 8-bit machine that is roughly comparable in complexity and performance to the Intel 8080 described in Sec. 5.4; indeed these two microprocessors have been major rivals in the marketplace. The 6800 and 8080 architectures differ in several important respects; for example, the 6800 has more addressing modes and the 8080 has more registers. Since the 6800 is somewhat easier to understand than the 8080 we consider it first here. The 6800 has been widely used and, like most successful microprocessors, it is the progenitor of a large family of microprocessors, microcomputers, and support circuits with various degrees of hardware and software compatibility. For example, the 6801 one-chip microcomputer, introduced by Motorola in 1979, is downward software compatible with the 6800 at the machine-language level, and has many of the 6800's hardware features. Another important microprocessor family whose design philosophy is derived from that of the 6800 is the 6500 series originated by MOS Technology Inc. (now a division of Commodore International Ltd.)

The internal organization of the 6800 is depicted in Fig. 5.24. This microprocessor is designed to process 8-bit data words and 16-bit addresses. It is housed in a standard 40-pin DIP to which are connected an 8-bit bidirectional data bus and a 16-bit address bus. The 6800 has an unusually small number of control lines. In fact, so sparing is the use of control lines in the 6800 that several of the 40 pins available are unused.

The 6800 contains six programmable registers: a pair of general-purpose 8-bit data registers A and B, an 8-bit status register CC, and three 16-bit address registers—a program counter PC, a stack pointer S (also called SP in 6800 literature), and an index register X (also called IX). The A and B registers are referred to as accumulators, because they are used as the main operand source or destination registers by many instructions. The CC register stores a condition code consisting of six flag bits whose functions are listed in Fig. 5.25. Bits 6 and 7 of CC are unused. Four of the CC flags—namely, C (carry), V (overflow), Z (zero), and N (negative or sign bit)—can be tested by conditional branch instructions. The H (half-carry) flag is used in certain decimal operations where each half of an 8-bit operand represents a BCD digit. The remaining I (interrupt) flag is an interrupt mask bit that allows a programmer to enable or disable one of the 6800's interrupt request lines.

The three CPU address storage registers PC, S, and X are of fairly conventional design. PC stores the next instruction address, and is incremented automatically during each instruction cycle. S is used to access a user-defined LIFO stack region of main memory. 6800 stacks grow "downward" in the sense that after a byte is added to the stack by a push operation, S is automatically decremented by one. In the case of a stack read or pop operation, S is automatically incremented by one prior to the data transfer from the stack. X is an index register whose contents are added to an instruction's address field to form an effective main memory address whenever the indexed addressing mode is specified.

Data processing within the 6800 is implemented by an 8-bit ALU capable of fixed-point addition and subtraction and some standard logical operations. Memory-mapped IO is used; therefore, the memory and IO devices connected to a 6800 must share the

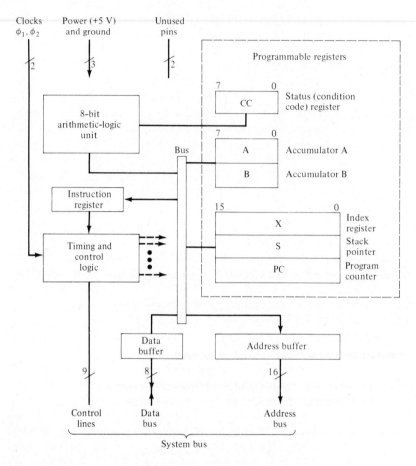

Figure 5.24 Internal organization of the Motorola 6800 microprocessor.

Bit	Name	Condition Specified When Bit Is 1 (0)
0	C (Carry)	Carry or borrow signal was (not) generated.
1	V (Overflow)	Arithmetic overflow occurred (did not occur) during twos-complement operation.
2	Z (Zero)	All 0s result was (not) generated.
3	N (Negative)	Leftmost or sign bit of result was 1 (0).
4	I (Interrupt mask)	CPU is not (is) responding to maskable interrupt requests.
5	H (Half carry)	Carry was (not) generated from right half of result.
6, 7		Unused bits, which are permanently set to 1.

Figure 5.25 The status (condition code) flag bits of the 6800.

402

available set of 2^{16} = 64K address combinations. As Fig. 5.24 indicates, nine external control lines are employed for controlling data transfers, DMA operations, and interrupts. There are three interrupt request lines which are not vectored; that is, they cause program control to be transferred to fixed interrupt addresses that are generated internally by the CPU.

The 6800 has a repertoire of 72 instructions; in other words, there are 72 distinct assembly-language opcodes. The 6800 instruction types are summarized in Fig. 5.26; all three major types—data processing, data transfer, and program control—are represented. A complete description of the 6800's instruction set and assembly language can be found in the manufacturer's literature (Motorola, 1975a). Some representative assembly-language and machine-language instructions for the 6800 appear in Figs. 5.11 and 5.18. Additional instructions used in this book will be defined when they are introduced.

Most 6800 instructions process 8-bit operands that may represent either numeric or nonnumeric data. Addresses are treated as 16-bit unsigned positive numbers. Two different number types are used for 8-bit numeric data, binary and decimal. Signed binary numbers use TC code, while BCD code is used for decimal numbers; see Fig. 5.15 for some examples. Almost all the 6800's arithmetic instructions are designed to process 8-bit binary numbers. As in some other microprocessors such as the 8080/8085 and Z8000, decimal arithmetic is implemented indirectly via a special instruction called decimal adjust accumulator (DAA).

Two-digit (8-bit) decimal addition is implemented in the 6800 by executing two instructions in sequence, a binary add instruction (ADD or ADC) followed by DAA. When binary addition is performed on decimal numbers, the result is not, of course, the decimal sum. The purpose of DAA is to transform this "incorrect" sum into the proper decimal sum required. It does so by executing an algorithm that is equivalent to the two-step process described in Fig. 5.27; the correctness of this algorithm can easily be verified. To illustrate it, suppose that it is desired to add the two decimal numbers 57 and 67, which in BCD code are

$$N1 = 0101\ 0111_{BCD}$$

and

$$N2 = 0110\ 0111_{BCD}$$

respectively. If N1 is stored in the 6800 accumulator A, we can execute the instruction

$$ADD \quad A\ N2$$

which computes the binary sum 1011 1110 of N1 and N2 and places it in the A accumulator. ADD also affects the carry flag C and the half-carry flag H, so that the results of this addition are

$$A = 1011\ 1110$$
$$C = 0$$
$$H = 0$$

Major Type	Subtype	Instruction	Comment
Data transfer	CPU only	Move accumulator to accumulator Move address register to address register Set/clear register/flag	
	CPU memory	Move register to memory (Store) Move memory to register (Load) Move register to stack (Push) Move stack to register (Pop)	Adjust stack pointer S.
Data processing	Arithmetic	Add with/without carry Subtract with/without borrow Negate Increment/decrement Decimal adjust accumulator A	Used with 8-bit twos complement numbers. Used for BCD addition.
	Logical	And Or Exclusive-or Complement (Not)	
	Shift	Rotate left/right Arithmetic shift left/right Logical shift left/right	All shift instructions include the carry flag C.
Program control	Branch	Jump unconditionally Jump conditionally Call subroutine Return from subroutine	Tests flag condition. Stack used as the save area.
	Other	No operation Compare and set flag Enable/disable interrupts Wait for interrupt	

Figure 5.26 Summary of the 6800 instruction set.

Step 1: If the right half (least significant 4 bits) of the accumulator contains a number greater than nine, or if the half-carry flag H is 1, add 00000110_2, i.e. six, to the accumulator using binary addition.

Step 2: If the left half (most significant 4 bits) of the accumulator contains a number greater than nine, or if the carry flag C is 1, add six to the left half of the accumulator.

Figure 5.27 Algorithm used by the decimal adjust accumulator (DAA) instruction.

Note that neither half of A contains a valid BCD number. Suppose that the instruction

$$DAA$$

is now executed. Step 1 of the DAA algorithm results in

$$A = 1100\ 0100$$

$$C = 0$$

while step 2 yields

$$A = 0010\ 0100$$

$$C = 1$$

The contents of A interpreted as a decimal number are 24, while the fact that $C = 1$ indicates the occurrence of a decimal carry digit 1; thus we have obtained the correct decimal sum 124.

As Fig. 5.26 shows, the 6800 has no multiplication or division instructions. It also has no explicit IO instructions because memory-mapped IO is used. Memory-referencing instructions must be used for all IO operations. The 6800's other data-transfer instructions and its logical and shift instructions are quite conventional. The program-control instructions include the usual conditional and unconditional branches and the subroutine call and return. There are also some variants of call and return intended mainly for interrupt handling. An unusual instruction of the latter kind is wait for interrupt WAI, which causes all CPU registers, except the stack pointer S, to be saved in the stack area, whereupon program execution is suspended until an interrupt request is received from an external device.

The 6800 machine-language instructions can be 1, 2, or 3 bytes long, depending on the operation to be performed and the addressing modes used; again see Figs. 5.11 and 5.18 for examples. The first, or opcode, byte of an instruction specifies the operation required and the addressing modes to be used. The opcode can also implicitly address a CPU register, for example, an accumulator. The remaining 1 or 2 bytes, if present, form an explicit address field. The various possible addressing modes are listed in Fig. 5.28. The immediate addressing mode is quite conventional. There are two kinds of direct memory addressing—the so-called "direct" addressing mode, which uses a short 8-bit address, and an "extended" mode, which uses a full 16-bit address. The 8-bit direct

Type	Variant	Name Used in 6800 Literature	Effective Address of Operand	Comment
Immediate		Immediate	Operand is instruction byte 2 (occasionally bytes 2 and 3)	Denoted by prefix # in assembly-language addresses
Direct	Register	Inherent	Contained in instruction byte 1 (opcode)	
	Memory, short	Direct	Instruction byte 2	
	Memory, long	Extended	Instruction bytes 2 and 3	
Indexed		Indexed	Index register X + (unsigned) instruction byte 2	Denoted by suffix ,X in assembly-language addresses
Relative		Relative	PC + 2 + (signed) instruction byte 2	Used only in certain branch instructions

Figure 5.28 Addressing modes of the 6800.

addressing mode allows only the 256 memory locations with the lowest addresses to be accessed. An instruction that specifies indexed addressing contains a 1-byte address, which is added to the 2-byte address stored in the index register X to form the effective address. (It is not unreasonable to view this as base addressing.) The relative addressing mode is used by branch instructions only. Relative addresses are 1 byte long and are added to the program counter PC to form the effective branch address. The 6800 relative addressing mode allows the effective address to range from PC $-$ 126 to PC $+$ 129, where PC is the start address of the branch instruction in question.

5.3.2 Programming Example

To illustrate 6800 assembly-language programming, consider the task of adding two 32-digit fixed-point decimal numbers called ALPHA and BETA. The short word size of the 6800 and similar microprocessors frequently calls for multiprecision operations of this kind. The CPU word size is only 8 bits, that is, 2 BCD digits; hence the required addition must be implemented by a sequence of 16 one-word addition steps. Since the main memory word size is also 8 bits, each number must be stored as a block or array of 16 words. Figure 5.29 shows how the two numbers ALPHA and BETA might be stored in M. We will assume that the desired sum ALPHA $+$ BETA is to be stored in the same locations as BETA; thus our program will implement the operation

$$BETA := ALPHA + BETA$$

It is natural to use an indexed expression such as ALPHA[I] to denote the Ith word of the 16-word array representing ALPHA. This suggests using the 6800's index register to store the index I. Specifically we will assign the word ALPHA[I] to the main memory

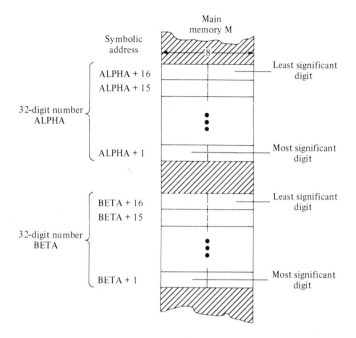

Figure 5.29 Location of the 32-digit addition operands in main memory.

address ALPHA + I, and permit I to range from 1 to 16. Note that I can be conveniently altered via the instructions INX and DEX, which increment and decrement, respectively, the 6800 index register. Clearly BETA can also be indexed easily in step with ALPHA. From these considerations we obtain the 32-digit addition algorithm described by the flowchart of Fig. 5.30. A 6800 assembly-language program implementing this algorithm appears in Fig. 5.31.

The addition program operates as follows: The index register X is initially set to 16, so that the three indexed instructions LDA (load accumulator), ADC (add with carry), and STA (store accumulator) all effectively address the least significant digit pairs of ALPHA and BETA. After the first one-word addition has been completed, X is decremented by one using the DEX instruction, which makes the LDA, ADC, and STA instructions effectively address the next most significant digit-pairs of the corresponding numbers. This process continues until X reaches zero, a condition that causes the Z flag to become 1. Note that DEX, like most arithmetic instructions, affects the flags in the CC register each time it is executed. The Z flag is continually tested by the branch if not equal (to zero) instruction BNE. Whenever DEX decrements X to a nonzero quantity, it also resets Z to 0, causing BNE to transfer control back to the instruction with the symbolic address or label LOOP. When X finally reaches zero and Z becomes 1, no branch takes place, and control goes to the next sequential instruction after BNE. The 6800 lacks a halt instruction; thus to cause program execution to halt, we use a dynamic program halt implemented by the last instruction appearing in Fig. 5.31. Here the unconditional branch instruction JMP (jump) causes a branch to itself. It therefore continually loads the

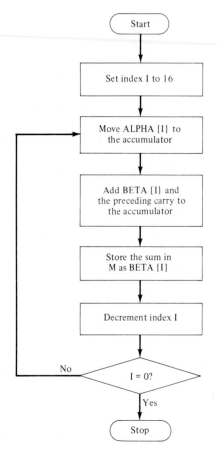

Figure 5.30 Flowchart of the 32-digit addition program.

Location	Instruction		Comment
START	CLC		Clear carry flag C.
	LDX	#16	Load index register X with byte count 16.
LOOP	LDA A	ALPHA,X	A := M[ALPHA + X].
	ADC A	BETA,X	A := A + C + M[BETA + X].
	DAA		Decimal adjust accumulator A.
	STA A	BETA,X	M[BETA + X] := A.
	DEX		Decrement index register X.
	BNE	LOOP	Branch to LOOP if zero flag Z is not 1.
STOP	JMP	STOP	Dynamic program halt.

Figure 5.31 6800 assembly-language program to add two 32-digit decimal numbers.

program counter with the same address STOP, thus effectively halting the micro-processor. Other features of this program worth noting are the use of DAA to obtain decimal addition and the important role played by the carry flag C in extending addition across the number arrays.

It is also useful to look at the machine-language version of this program, which is called the *object program,* and is generated by an assembler from the original assembly-language *source program* of Fig. 5.31. The source and object programs appear side by side in Fig. 5.32. Note how all symbolic addresses in the source code are replaced by numeric values in the object code. Thus, for example, the label LOOP corresponds to the (hexadecimal) memory address 0104_{16}. The source addresses ALPHA and BETA have been assigned to memory locations 0030_{16} 0010_{16} respectively. This means that the number BETA must occupy the 16 memory locations with addresses 0011_{16} through 0020_{16}. The branch instruction BNE, unlike JMP, uses relative addressing, a fact that is not apparent from the assembly-language code. On examining the machine-language version of the BNE instruction, we see that it consists of 2 bytes, an opcode byte 26_{16} stored in location $010C_{16}$, and a 1-byte relative address $F6_{16}$ stored in location $010D_{16}$. The effective branch address used by BNE ADR is computed as PC + 2 + ADR, where, as Fig. 5.28 indicates, ADR is treated as a signed binary number. In this case PC is initially $010C_{16}$, and ADR is $F6_{16}$, which is equivalent to 11110110, the twos-complement code for minus 10. Hence the effective address placed in PC is $010C_{16} - 8 = 0104_{16}$. As can be seen from Fig. 5.32, 0104_{16} is the location of the LDA instruction whose symbolic address in the assembly-language program is LOOP.

5.3.3 Control Signals and Interrupts

The nine external control lines of the 6800, excluding the two clock lines, are listed in Fig. 5.33. They have three main functions:

1. To control data transfers across the system bus
2. To allow external devices to gain control of the system bus, mainly for DMA operations
3. To allow external devices to interrupt the CPU by forcing it to transfer program control to certain predefined memory locations

The data-transfer control group consists of a read/write select line R/$\overline{\text{W}}$ and a line called VMA (valid memory address), which, in conjunction with the clock signal ϕ_2, is

Object Code (hex)		Source Code	
Location	Instruction	Location	Instruction
0100	OC	START	CLC
0101	CE 00 10		LDX #16
0104	A6 30	LOOP	LDA A ALPHA,X
0106	A9 10		ADC A BETA,X
0108	19		DAA
0109	A7 10		STA A BETA,X
010B	09		DEX
010C	26 F6		BNE LOOP
010E	7E 01 OE	STOP	JMP STOP

Figure 5.32 Machine- and assembly-language versions of the 32-digit decimal addition program.

Type	Name	Function
Data-transfer control	R/$\overline{\text{W}}$	Read/write enable. Specifies a read operation (R/$\overline{\text{W}}$ = 1), write operation (R/$\overline{\text{W}}$ = 0), or inactive condition (R/$\overline{\text{W}}$ = 1 or Z).
	VMA	Valid memory address. Indicates the presence of an address on the address bus.
Bus-access control	$\overline{\text{HALT}}$	DMA request. Causes the 6800 to float the data, address, R/$\overline{\text{W}}$, and VMA lines at the end of the current instruction cycle.
	BA	Bus available. DMA acknowledge line used to respond to $\overline{\text{HALT}}$.
	TSC	Three-state control. Causes the 6800 to float the address bus and R/$\overline{\text{W}}$.
	DBE	Data bus enable. Causes the 6800 to float the data bus.
Interrupt request	$\overline{\text{RESET}}$	Reset. Sets the interrupt mask flag I to 1 to block maskable interrupt requests, and loads the address M[FFFE$_{16}$].M[FFFF$_{16}$] into PC.
	$\overline{\text{NMI}}$	Nonmaskable interrupt request. Saves the CPU registers PC, X, A, B, and CC in the stack, sets I to 1, and loads M[FFFC$_{16}$].M[FFFD$_{16}$] into PC.
	$\overline{\text{IRQ}}$	Maskable interrupt request. Saves PC, X, A, B, and CC in the stack, sets I to 1, and loads M[FFF8$_{16}$].M[FFF9$_{16}$] into PC.

Figure 5.33 The nine control lines of the 6800.

used to enable external devices for data-transfer operations. Since memory-mapped IO is used by the 6800, a single line R/$\overline{\text{W}}$ suffices to indicate the direction of all data transfers on the system bus; R/$\overline{\text{W}}$ = 1 indicates a read operation, that is, a data transfer to the device that controls the system bus, while R/$\overline{\text{W}}$ = 0 indicates a write operation, that is, a data transfer from the bus controller. When no data transfer is taking place, R/$\overline{\text{W}}$ is set either to 1 or to the high-impedance state Z. VMA is set to 1 to indicate that an address has been placed on the address bus, marking the start of a data transfer. Thus VMA acts rather like a data-request line during read operations, and like a data-ready line during writes. The timing of a CPU-initiated read operation in a 6800-based system is shown in Fig. 5.21, where R/$\overline{\text{W}}$ acts as the read/write enable line and VMA acts as the chip-select line.

The four control lines $\overline{\text{HALT}}$, BA, TSC, and DBE are used in transferring control of the system bus between the CPU and external control units. $\overline{\text{HALT}}$ and BA are conventional DMA request and acknowledge lines, respectively, which are used in the manner depicted in Fig. 5.23. When $\overline{\text{HALT}}$ is activated by an external DMA controller ($\overline{\text{HALT}}$ = 0), the 6800 causes the data and address buses and the R/$\overline{\text{W}}$ and VMA control lines to float to the Z state. It then activates BA to indicate to the requesting device that it may assume control of the system bus. In this mode of operation the CPU always completes execution of its current instruction before relinquishing the bus. Thus several machine cycles may elapse before the device that activates $\overline{\text{HALT}}$ gains access to the system bus. The TSC control signal can be used in place of $\overline{\text{HALT}}$ to gain faster access to the system bus for very short periods of time. This rapid DMA technique, which is called "cycle stealing," involves temporarily stretching a clock period defined by the system clocks ϕ_1 and ϕ_2, to allow several data transfers to take place across the system bus during a single extended clock period; for details of this rather complicated design trick, see Motorola (1975b).

The remaining three control lines, $\overline{RESET}$, $\overline{NMI}$, and $\overline{IRQ}$, which are listed in Fig. 5.33, are referred to as interrupt request lines in 6800 literature. They all cause program control to be transferred to an interrupt address that is stored in some fixed pair of locations at the high-address end of main memory. With the exception of $\overline{RESET}$, whose inclusion among the interrupt lines is therefore questionable, the 6800 interrupt lines also automatically save the contents of the CPU registers PC, X, A, B, and CC in the stack region of main memory before control is transferred to the interrupt routine. The CPU responds to interrupt request signals at the end of its current instruction cycle; the highest priority is assigned to $\overline{RESET}$ and the lowest priority to $\overline{IRQ}$. RESET is normally used only when the system is first powered up; it is designed to transfer control to a routine that initializes the system. $\overline{NMI}$ is typically used to respond to emergency conditions such as a pending power failure. $\overline{IRQ}$ is the line used to channel routine interrupt requests from external devices to the CPU. It alone is maskable, that is, the CPU responds to $\overline{IRQ}$ requests only if the interrupt mask flag is disabled (I = 0). The interrupt mask flag I can be altered by two special 6800 instructions, SEI (set interrupt mask), which sets I to 1, and CLI (clear interrupt mask), which resets it to 0. When responding to an interrupt request, the CPU automatically sets I to 1; it subsequently must be cleared by executing CLI.

A 6800 interrupt sequence may be initiated by activating any of the three interrupt request control lines. During the interrupt sequence the 6800 automatically adjusts the value of the stack pointer S to account for the data added to, or removed from, the stack. An interrupt sequence can also be carried out by executing an instruction called software interrupt SWI. SWI saves the CPU registers (except S) in the stack, enables I, and causes PC to be loaded with an interrupt address obtained from a part of main memory reserved for SWI. SWI is usually executed in response to program errors such as arithmetic overflow, divide by zero, and the like. Such errors can be viewed as program-generated interrupts or *traps*. SWI is used to transfer control to an error recovery routine. 6800 interrupt-handling routines normally end with the instruction RTI (return from interrupt), which restores to the CPU the contents of the CC, B, A, X, and PC registers that were saved in the stack when the interrupt began.

SWI and the interrupt request control lines of the 6800 always cause interrupt addresses to be obtained from fixed memory locations; Fig. 5.34 shows the locations used. This is an example of a nonvectored interrupt scheme. If a choice must be made among many different interrupt service routines, then a software-implemented poll of the possible interrupt sources must be carried out to identify the interrupting device and the desired interrupt routine. Thus the response time of the 6800 to interrupt requests may be much slower that that of systems such as the 8080/8085 that support vectored interrupts. The transfer of control to and from interrupt service routines in the 6800 is implemented in essentially the same way as a transfer to and from a subroutine. Indeed the main difference between SWI and a subroutine call is the fact that SWI sets the

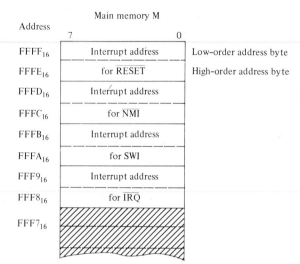

Address

Main memory M

Address		
FFFF$_{16}$	Interrupt address	Low-order address byte
FFFE$_{16}$	for $\overline{\text{RESET}}$	High-order address byte
FFFD$_{16}$	Interrupt address	
FFFC$_{16}$	for $\overline{\text{NMI}}$	
FFFB$_{16}$	Interrupt address	
FFFA$_{16}$	for SWI	
FFF9$_{16}$	Interrupt address	
FFF8$_{16}$	for $\overline{\text{IRQ}}$	
FFF7$_{16}$		

Figure 5.34 Location of the 6800 interrupt addresses.

interrupt mask. The use of the stack as the interrupt save area means that interrupt calls can be nested to a depth that is limited only by the stack size.

The internal timing and sequencing of operations within the 6800 are quite simple. As observed earlier, each machine cycle corresponds to one clock cycle. During a machine cycle, the 6800 can complete a register transfer operation of the form $X_1 := F(X_2, \ldots)$ involving 1-byte operands. One of the operands at most can be in main memory M; the rest must be in CPU registers. F is typically a function such as addition or a logical operation that requires only one pass through the main ALU. A 2-byte function, such as the 16-bit addition required to construct an effective address when indexed addressing is used, requires two passes through the ALU and therefore takes two machine cycles. If an instruction is k bytes long, then k machine cycles are required to fetch the instruction from M. In general, the number of machine cycles needed to fetch and execute a 6800 instruction varies from two to 12. Two examples will serve here to illustrate the actions occurring during a 6800 instruction cycle.

First consider the add immediate instruction

ADD   B #64

which, as shown in Fig. 5.18, specifies the register-transfer operation $B := B + 64$. The instruction is 2 bytes long, and its instruction cycle is composed of two machine cycles. During the first machine cycle, the 6800 performs a memory read operation to fetch the opcode byte. It decodes the opcode during this cycle and identifies it as an add immediate instruction that uses accumulator B. The CPU also increments the program counter PC so that it automatically points to the second byte of the instruction. In the second machine cycle, the CPU fetches the second half of the instruction, the immediate address, and adds it to the contents of the B register, placing the resulting sum in B. The CPU also recomputes the values of the H, N, Z, V, and C flags on the basis of the results of this addition. During the second machine cycle, the CPU again increments PC so that it now points to the next consecutive instruction. Note that each of the two machine cycles involves a memory read cycle of the kind depicted in Fig. 5.21.

We next examine another version of the add instruction, namely,

$$\text{ADD} \quad \text{B} \quad 64,\text{X}$$

which uses indexed addressing. As shown in Fig. 5.18, it specifies the operation $B := B + M[X + 64]$. Again the instruction is 2 bytes long, but this time it requires five machine cycles. In the first machine cycle, the CPU fetches and decodes the instruction opcode byte; it also increments PC. The opcode identifies the function to be performed, the CPU register to be used, and the addressing modes. The address part of the instruction is fetched in the second machine cycle, and PC is incremented again. The next two machine cycles are used to perform the 16-bit addition necessary to obtain the effective address $ADR = X + 64$. In the fifth and final cycle, the CPU reads memory location ADR and performs the addition $B := B + M[ADR]$. As always when executing arithmetic-logic instructions, the values of the relevant flags are recomputed.

The overall behavior of the 6800 is shown in simplified form in Fig. 5.35. Before entering a new instruction cycle, the 6800 checks the state of $\overline{\text{HALT}}$ and the interrupt request control lines. An active $\overline{\text{HALT}}$ line causes the CPU to relinquish control of the system bus and enter a wait state of indefinite duration. If $\overline{\text{HALT}}$ is inactive, the CPU checks the nonmaskable interrupt request line $\overline{\text{NMI}}$, and then the maskable line $\overline{\text{IRQ}}$. If there are no unmasked interrupt requests pending, the next instruction cycle is entered; otherwise the CPU first responds to an interrupt by saving the main CPU registers, enabling I, and loading PC with the appropriate interrupt address.

5.3.4 6800-Based Systems

The 6800 component family includes a variety of compatible memory ICs, IO interface circuits, and other support ICs. The simplest 6800-based microcomputer requires about six ICs. Figure 5.36 shows such a system, comprising a 6800 CPU, a clock generator, ROM and RAM memory circuits, and an IO interface circuit. The ROM is used for permanent storage of programs and data, while the RAM is used for temporary scratchpad storage; note that the 6800 itself contains very few scratchpad registers. An external RAM is also needed to implement the stack used by the 6800. The IO interface circuits are essentially addressable registers that can communicate with both the 6800 system bus and IO devices. Since memory-mapped IO is used, these IO ports are accessed in the same manner as ROM or RAM locations. The 64K different addresses that are available are shared among the memory and IO interface circuits. Each address that is assigned to an IO interface circuit defines an IO port of the system.

The interconnections among the ICs forming a microcomputer are largely determined by the characteristics of the system bus. The memory and IO interface circuits have data and address pins that must be connected to the corresponding lines of the system bus. The lines $R/\overline{W}$, VMA, and ϕ_2 supply the control signals needed to coordinate communication between the CPU, main memory, and IO circuits. $R/\overline{W}$ is used to specify the direction of a data transfer. The E (enable) signal derived from ϕ_2 and VMA serves as a system clock signal, and is sent to all support circuits to synchronize

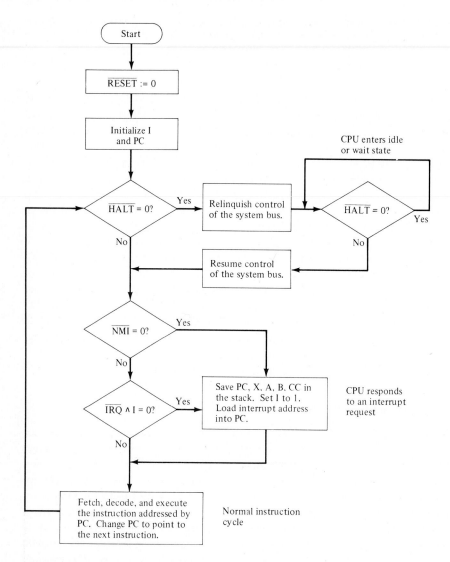

Figure 5.35 Overview of the internal operation of a 6800-based CPU.

them with the CPU. A memory location or IO port is selected to participate in a data transfer when its address appears on the address lines of the system bus; the data transfer is enabled when E is activated.

The number of signals that an IO device presents to a microcomputer and the timing characteristics of those signals, in other words, the IO device's interface, can vary over a very wide range. Serial IO devices transmit data 1 bit at a time, whereas parallel IO devices transmit data a word at a time; 8-bit words are typical. Serial devices are the least expensive when long communication distances are involved. In addition to its serial or

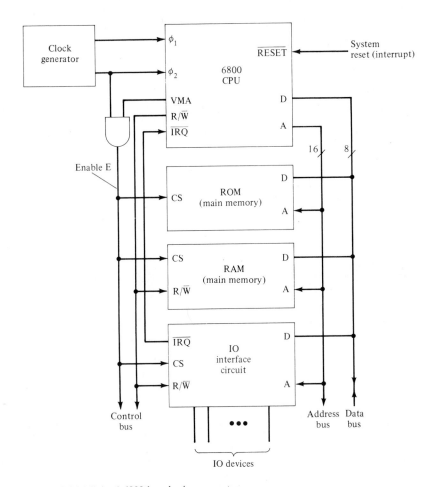

Figure 5.36 Minimal 6800-based microcomputer.

parallel data lines, an IO device normally has various control lines that also must be connected to the host computer. To simplify the task of interfacing with IO devices, there are several general-purpose 6800-compatible interface circuits that can be modified under program control to match the interface characteristics of many common IO devices. Two such circuits are shown in Fig. 5.37—the 6821 programmable interface adapter (PIA) intended for parallel IO devices, and the 6850 asynchronous communications interface adapter (ACIA) intended for use with serial IO devices.

As Fig. 5.37a shows, the 6821 PIA contains two independent IO ports called A and B. Each port can be connected to an IO device or devices via ten lines whose direction (input or output) can be programmed by means of a control word that is transmitted from the 6800 to the 6821, where it is stored in a control register. In a typical application eight of the ten lines connected to a 6821 port might be used as input or output data lines, while the remaining two lines are used as control lines (e.g. request/acknowledge handshak-

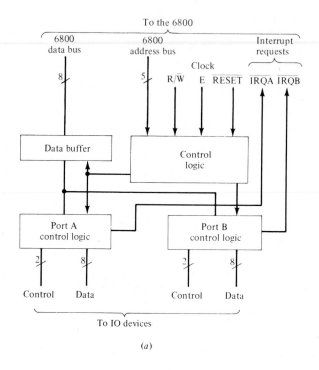

(a)

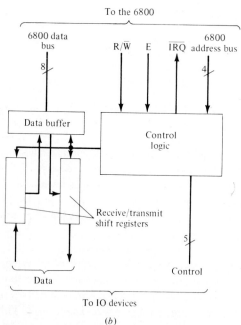

(b)

Figure 5.37 Two 6800-series IO interface circuits: (a) the 6821 PIA for parallel IO devices; (b) the 6850 ACIA for serial IO devices.

ing lines). The PIA contains buffer registers for storing temporarily the data passing through its IO ports. It also is capable of sending interrupt request signals to the CPU. It might be programmed to generate an interrupt when, for example, new data are required at one of its IO ports.

The 6850 ACIA shown in Fig. 5.37b is a type of IO interface circuit that is usually called a UART (universal asynchronous receiver/transmitter). The 6850 presents to an IO device a set of serial data lines and various control lines. Serial data received by the 6850 from an IO device are converted to parallel 8-bit words for transmission to the 6800 system bus. Conversely, when transmitting data from the system bus, the 6850 performs parallel-to-serial conversion. The 6850 can be programmed to adapt to certain characteristics of IO devices; for example, it may be programmed to use any one of a set of standard signal transmission rates (baud rates) when communicating with IO devices. Like the 6821 PIA, the 6850 ACIA is programmed during normal operation by means of control words sent from the 6800 and stored in control registers in the interface circuit.

In the late 1970s, as IC manufacturing techniques allowed chip gate densities greater than that of the 6800, Motorola introduced several microprocessors and one-chip microcomputers exhibiting a relatively high degree of hardware and software compatibility with the 6800 (Wiles et al., 1978). The 6802 microprocessor, for example, is a 6800 with a clock generator and a 128-byte portion of read/write main memory on the same IC chip. The 6801 one-chip microcomputer has most of the features of the 6802 and, in addition, contains a 2K-byte ROM, four IO ports, a programmable timer, and several new instructions. The 6809 microprocessor introduced in 1979 is an 8-bit microprocessor containing some significant additions to the 6800 architecture. We next look briefly at the 6801 and 6809, since they are good examples of architectural enhancement within a microprocessor family.

5.3.5 The 6801 Microprocessor

The 6801 is basically a one-chip version of the 6800 one-board microcomputer shown in Fig. 5.36. It contains within a single IC a CPU similar to the 6800, a clock generator, a substantial part of main memory distributed between a ROM and a RAM, and various IO interface circuits. The internal organization of the 6801 appears in Fig. 5.38. When it is acting as a self-contained microcomputer, most of the 6801's 40 IO pins can be directly connected to external IO devices via four IO ports. The 6801 was also designed to allow both its internal memory capacity and IO interfacing abilities to be expanded using 6800-series support circuits. To make this possible, the internal system bus of the 6801 can be extended to the outside world through ports 3 and 4. Thus the 6801 has several distinct modes of operation, depending on the way ports 3 and 4 are used; the particular mode to be used is specified by certain signals applied to port 2 during system initialization. The three major operating modes of the 6801 are

1. The single-chip mode
2. The expanded multiplexed mode
3. The expanded nonmultiplexed mode

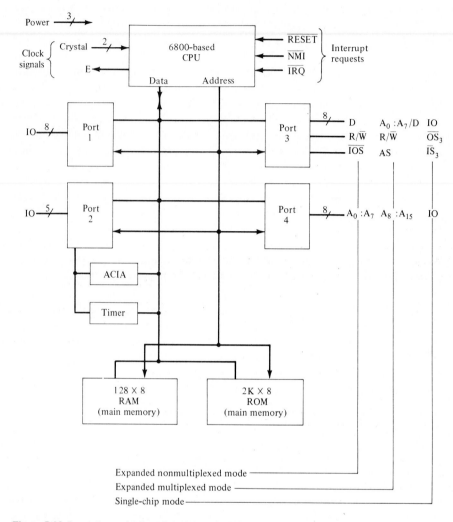

Figure 5.38 Internal organization of the Motorola 6801 one-chip microcomputer.

The functions assigned to the lines of ports 3 and 4 in these three modes are summarized in Fig. 5.38.

In the 6801's single-chip mode of operation, all its ports, including ports 3 and 4, are directly addressable IO ports. Each IO port is assigned an address within the 6801's 64K address space; as in the 6800 case, memory-mapped IO addressing is used. Ports 1 and 4 are 8-bit parallel IO ports. Port 3 may be used to transmit a data byte (denoted "IO" in Fig. 5.38) between the 6801 and an external device. It also has two control lines denoted $\overline{\text{IS}}$ (input strobe) and $\overline{\text{OS}}$ (output strobe), which can be used to control data transfers through port 3. The directions of the lines at the IO ports are user programmable. Thus in the single-chip mode port 3, and to a lesser extent ports 1 and 4, perform functions similar to the 6821 PIA; (cf. Fig. 5.37a). Port 2 is primarily a serial IO port, and is connected to circuits in the 6801 that resemble the 6850 ACIA of Fig. 5.37b. This port is also connected to a programmable timer circuit.

In the two expanded modes of operation, ports 3 and 4 become connections to the 6801's internal system bus, and present a 6800-compatible interface to external devices. In the expanded nonmultiplexed mode, port 3 extends the 8-bit bidrectional data bus D, while port 4 extends eight lines designated $A_0:A_7$ of the 6800 address bus. This allows up to 256 additional memory or IO addresses to be used. The read/write select line $R/\overline{W}$ is extended through one of the two control lines of port 3; the other is used as a control line for data transfers and is called $\overline{IOS}$ (input-output strobe). To achieve the full 64K addressing capability of the 6800 CPU, the expanded multiplexed mode must be used. Again port 4 is used to supply 8 address bits, this time the high-order bits $A_8:A_{15}$. The eight data lines of port 3 are used to extend the remaining address lines $A_0:A_7$ and the data bus D. Thus data and address bytes are multiplexed through port 3. During a data transfer, the 6801 first transmits a 16-bit address to ports 3 and 4. Bits $A_0:A_7$ must be stored in an external latch as depicted in Fig. 5.39. To simplify the connection of this latch to the 6801, the 6801 automatically generates a control signal AS (address strobe) via port 3 that can be used to load the address byte $A_0:A_7$ into the latch. After the entire address is set up, port 3 is used to transmit a data byte to or from the 6801.

To maintain compatibility with 6800-series components, many of the 6800's external control signals also appear in the 6801. As Fig. 5.38 shows, the three 6800 interrupt request lines are present. There are no DMA control lines since the 6801 has no DMA facilities. The VMA (valid memory address) and ϕ_2 clock signals used by the 6800 to enable external devices (see Fig. 5.36) are replaced in the 6801 by a single enable line E, which serves as the system clock signal. In the expanded modes of operation, the 6801 also supplies the 6800 read/write enable signal $R/\overline{W}$ via port 3.

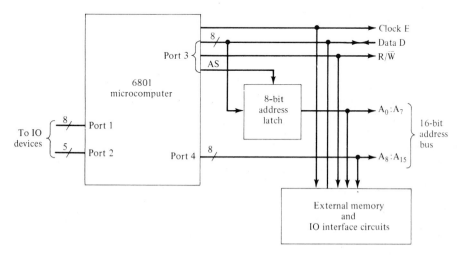

Figure 5.39 Multiplexed expansion of the 6801 microcomputer.

Port 2, like ports 3 and 4, can be used for different purposes at different times. It can serve as a programmable serial IO port that resembles the 6850 ACIA of Fig. 5.37b. Two lines are used to transfer serial data to and from the 6801, while a third line carries an internally or externally generated signal used to synchronize the serial data transmission. As in the 6850 ACIA, data are transferred to a pair of shift registers connected to port 2. When an input register is full or an output register is empty, an interrupt is automatically generated by port 2. Port 2 also allows external access to a programmable timer. This timer contains a 16-bit counter T, which is continuously incremented by the system clock. Several addressable registers are available that can copy ("capture") the contents of T, or compare their contents with those of T. An interrupt can be generated under various circumstances, for instance, when T and some other register have the same contents. An external signal applied to port 2 can be used to transfer the contents of T to a predefined capture register. This is a very convenient way of allowing the 6801 to time external events. Yet another function of port 2 is to select the operating mode that determines the roles of ports 3 and 4. Using some external circuitry, three lines of port 2 are connected to the $\overline{\text{RESET}}$ line, allowing the mode of operation to be defined during system reset.

In addition to the entire 6800 instruction set, the 6801 has 10 new instructions; the 6801 is therefore downward software compatible with the 6800. Most of the new instructions perform 16-bit or double-precision operations. For these operations the A and B accumulators are concatenated to form a 16-bit register $D = A.B$. For example, the 6801's double-precision add instruction ADDD adds a specified 16-bit operand to D and places the resulting sum in D. A new multiply instruction performs the operation D $:= A \times B$ treating the operands as unsigned binary numbers.

5.3.6 The 6809 Microprocessor

The 6809 is a one-chip microprocessor that is a major architectural extension of the 6800. It is approximately downward software compatible with the 6800 (and also with the 6801) at the assembly-language or source-code level; note that there are some discrepancies between the 6800 and 6809 that the manufacturer's literature often ignores. The 6800 and 6809 machine languages are entirely incompatible, however, because corresponding instructions have completely different opcodes. The 6809 has all the 6800's programmable registers and most of its external data, address, and control lines. It can be used with most 6800-series support chips; hence the 6809 can be said to be hardware compatible with the 6800.

The 6809 has more programmable registers, more instruction types, and more addressing modes than the 6800. A measure of its greater computational power is the fact that the 6809 has 1464 different machine language opcodes, whereas the 6800 has only 197. Figure 5.40 shows the programmable registers of the 6809; the registers not found in the 6800 are shaded. As in the 6801, the A and B registers can be combined to form a single 16-bit accumulator called D. There is a second index register Y and a second "user" stack pointer U. All the address registers X, Y, S, U can be used as index registers, if desired.

Much of the increased power of the 6809 comes from its new addressing features.

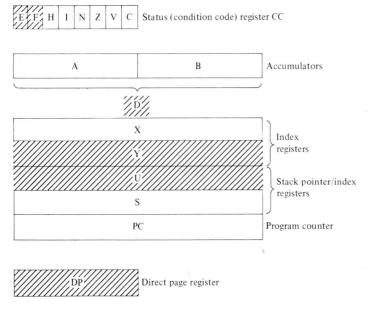

Figure 5.40 The programmable registers of the Motorola 6809 microprocessor (registers not in the 6800 are shaded).

The use of short (1-byte) and long (2-byte) addresses for direct addressing in the 6800 (see Fig. 5.28) is extended to indexed, immediate, and relative addressing in the 6809. The 6800's short direct addresses are restricted to the range 0000_{16} to $00FF_{16}$, that is, to a *page* of 256 words at the low-address end of M. In the 6809 a 1-byte "direct page" register DP is provided whose contents are appended to the high-order end of all short direct addresses. By altering the contents of DP, short direct addresses can be used to refer to any of 256 pages in main memory. Thus the advantages of short addresses are obtained without limiting the address range to a small region of memory. In the 6809 direct addressing using DP is an example of *paged addressing*.

All the 16-bit address registers X, Y, S, U can be used as address registers in a symmetric fashion. For example, we can write

LDA ,X

to specify the operation A := M[X]. Note that the opcode mnemonic LDA (load accumulator) replaces the 6800 mnemonic LDA A. This instruction can also be written with Y, S, or U replacing X. The addressing mode indicated by ,X in the above instruction is indexing using index register X with an instruction address or offset of zero; this is functionally equivalent to indirect addressing using register X as the direct address store.

Two new address modification schemes called predecrementing and postincrementing are also included in the 6809. They allow index register contents to be modified in the course of an instruction cycle that involves indexed addressing. For example, the instruction.

$$\text{LDA} \quad ,-\text{Y}$$

specifies predecrementing of the index register Y. When execution begins, the index register is first decremented by one thus:

$$Y := Y - 1;$$

Then the main operation A := M[Y] is carried out using the newly modified index register. Just as predecrementing is indicated by the prefix $-$, postincrementing is indicated by the suffix $+$. Thus the instruction

$$\text{LDA} \quad ,\text{S}+$$

results in the operations

$$A := M[S]; \quad S := S + 1;$$

Figure 5.41 shows a 6809 version of the 32-digit decimal addition program from Fig. 5.31 that illustrates some of the addressing modes discussed above. Index modification methods such as pre- and postincrementing and decrementing are sometimes called *autoindexing*.

Like the 6801, the 6809 has a multiplication but no division instruction. Many of the new instruction types perform 16-bit operations using D = A.B as a 16-bit accumulator. While the 6809 retains the 8-bit external data bus of the 6800, its internal data bus and associated circuits are 16 bits wide. Hence the 6809 can be regarded as a 16-bit microprocessor.

The 6809 has several external control signals not found in the 6800. The VMA and ϕ_2 signals used to enable external transfers in 6800-based systems are replaced by a single enable line E as in the 6801. An input signal called memory ready MRDY is present that allows the 6809 to communicate with certain slow memory and IO interface circuits. Data transfers over the 6809 system bus are normally conducted in the semi-synchronous fashion depicted in Fig. 5.21. In this mode of operation, which is the only

Location	Instruction		Comment
START	CLC		Clear carry flag C.
	LDX	ALPHA + 17	Initialize register X used to point to ALPHA.
	LDY	BETA + 17	Initialize register Y used to point to BETA.
LOOP	LDA	,−X	X := X − 1; A := M[X];
	ADC	A,−Y	Y := Y − 1; A := A + C + M[Y];
	DAA		Decimal adjust accumulator A.
	STA	,Y	M[Y] := A;
	CMPX	BETA + 1	Compare X with BETA + 1; if equal, set Z to 1.
	BNE	LOOP	Branch to LOOP if Z is not equal to 1.
	BRA	*	Dynamic program halt.

Figure 5.41 6809 version of the 32-digit decimal addition program of Fig. 5.31.

one used in the 6800, MRDY is permanently held at the active level (MRDY = 1). A device that cannot perform a data transfer within the normal clock period defined by the system clock E can be given control of MRDY. By holding MRDY in the inactive state, the slow device can stretch the clock period temporarily to accommodate its slow response time. When it is ready, it indicates that fact to the 6809 by activating MRDY. Thus MRDY allows a type of asynchronous data transfer to take place.

The 6809 has a new interrupt request line $\overline{\text{FIRQ}}$ (fast interrupt request). It is fast in the sense that it saves only the program counter PC and the status register CC. The other interrupt lines $\overline{\text{IRQ}}$ and $\overline{\text{NMI}}$, like their counterparts in the 6800, save all CPU registers except S in the stack region defined by S. Bits 6 and 7 of CC, which are unused in the 6800 (see Fig. 5.25), are associated with $\overline{\text{FIRQ}}$ in the 6809. Bit 6 of CC, which is denoted F, acts as a mask bit for interrupt requests received on $\overline{\text{FIRQ}}$. When F is set to 1, it disables $\overline{\text{FIRQ}}$. Bit 7 of CC is called E (entire), and is used to distinguish interrupts caused by $\overline{\text{FIRQ}}$ from interrupts generated by all other interrupt sources, including software interrupts. Whenever the entire CPU state is saved in the S stack in response to an interrupt call, the E flag is set to 1. The partial save caused by $\overline{\text{FIRQ}}$ resets E to 0. When a return from interrupt instruction RTI is executed, E is checked to determine which CPU registers should be restored from the stack save area.

5.4 THE 8080/8085 FAMILY

This section reviews in detail another important 8-bit microprocessor family based on the Intel 8080 and 8085 microprocessors. The organization and programming of these devices and their major support circuits are discussed. Zilog Inc.'s Z80 microprocessor is also introduced.

5.4.1 The 8080 and 8085 Microprocessors

The 8008 introduced by Intel Corp. in 1972 was the first commercial 8-bit microprocessor. It employed relatively slow pMOS technology and, as was often the case with early microprocessors, had some design features that were soon perceived as unduly primitive. The 8080 8-bit microprocessor, which was introduced by Intel in 1973, uses faster nMOS technology, and was intended to overcome some of the limitations of the 8008 (Shima & Faggin, 1974). The 8080 rapidly superseded the 8008, and came to be one of the most widely used microprocessors. Like the 6800, it gave rise to a large number of support circuits, as well as other microprocessors and microcomputers with various degrees of compatibility with the 8080. The Intel 8085 introduced in 1977 (Sohn & Volk, 1977) is another version of the 8080 architecture with minor modifications and improvements. Since it is almost identical to the 8080 from a programming point of view, we will consider the 8080 and 8085 as a single microprocessor denoted 8080/8085; differences between the two will be noted as they arise. The 8080 and 8085 families are sometimes called the MCS-80 and MCS-85 families, respectively, in the literature. (MCS stands for microcomputer set.) Another important 8080 derivative is the Zilog Z80, which appeared in 1976. Several more recent devices, for example, the Intel 8086

16-bit microprocessor (see Sec. 8.1.1) and NEC Corp.'s 7801 one-chip microcomputer are also based on the 8080 architecture. The National Semiconductor NSC800 microprocessor family, which was introduced in 1980, is downward compatible at the machine-language level with the Z80, the 8085, and the 8080.

Like the 6800, the 8080/8085 is designed to process 8-bit data words in both the CPU and main memory M. A 16-bit address is required to access M, resulting in a maximum memory capacity 64K bytes. The 8080/8085 uses many more control lines than the 6800. Largely because of this, there are insufficient pins in the standard 40-pin DIP used by the 8080/8085 to allow all the system bus lines to be connected directly to the 8080/8085. Both the 8080 and the 8085 multiplex—that is, time-share—certain pins to overcome this pin shortage. The 8080 multiplexes data and control signals, whereas the 8085 multiplexes data and address signals. Each microprocessor also has some control lines not found in the other. Despite these differences, the system buses of the 8080 and 8085 are quite similar, so that the 8080 and 8085 share many memory, IO interface and other support circuits.

A complete 8080-based CPU requires three ICs, an 8080 and two support circuits as shown in Fig. 5.42a. One of these support ICs supplies the system clock signals; like the 6800, the 8080 lacks an on-chip clock generator. The second support circuit, called the status latch, allows control information to be multiplexed over the 8080's 8-bit data bus D. At the beginning of each machine cycle, a status word is transmitted to this status latch via D, where it determines the setting of the control lines that emanate from the latch. In most 8080-based CPUs, an IC called the 8028 system controller is used to serve both as the external status latch and as a driver for the system data bus to increase the number of TTL-compatible loads that can be attached to it. Note that all 16 address lines $A_0:A_{15}$ of the system address bus connect directly to the 8080. Most system control lines are connected to either the 8080 or the status latch. Several control signals (e.g., reset) enter the CPU via the clock generator so that they can more easily be synchronized with the system clock.

An 8085-based CPU appears in Fig. 5.42b. Improvements in IC manufacture allow the 8085 to have an on-chip clock generator. All control lines of the system bus are connected directly to the 8085, as is the 8-bit bidirectional data bus. However, only the eight high-order address lines $A_8:A_{15}$ are attached directly to the 8085. The remaining eight address bits are multiplexed with data words over the 8-bit address/data bus AD. Thus, to obtain 16 parallel address lines, an external 8-bit address latch must be used as shown in Fig. 5.42b. A data transfer to the CPU is carried out in two steps. The 8085 first places a 16-bit address on lines A and AD. The eight address bits $A_0:A_7$ are present on AD only long enough to allow them to be loaded into the address latch. AD is then used to transfer a data byte to or from the 8085. Some 8085 memory and IO support circuits have built-in address latches and can demultiplex AD. Such circuits allow the 8085 to be used as a one-chip CPU. In applications where eight address bits suffice, the 8085 can also be used as a one-chip CPU simply by ignoring the temporary address signals on AD, and using $A_8:A_{15}$ as the system address bus.

The 8080 and 8085 have a very similar internal organization, which is depicted in Fig. 5.43. There is an 8-bit ALU, an 8-bit accumulator A, a 5-bit status or flag register SR (this is unrelated to the 8080's external status latch), and six general-purpose

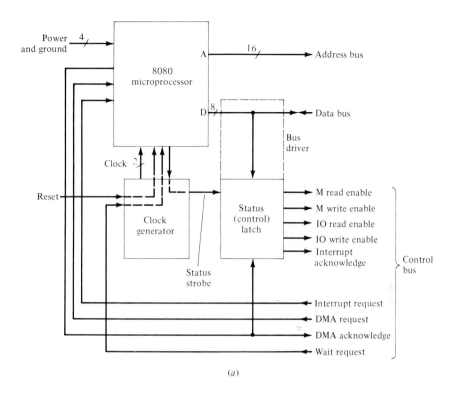

(a)

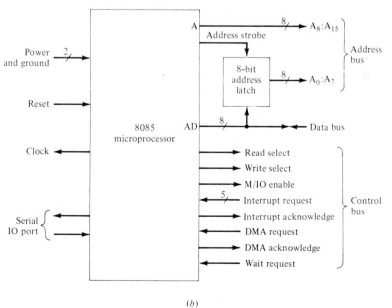

(b)

Figure 5.42 Basic CPU circuit using (a) the 8080 and (b) the 8085.

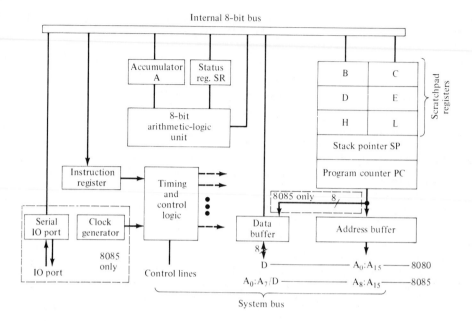

Figure 5.43 Internal organization of the Intel 8080/8085 microprocessor.

scratchpad registers B, C, D, E, H, and L. The functions of the five flag bits in SR are listed in Fig. 5.44. In comparing them with the 6800 flags described in Fig. 5.25, we see that the microprocessors have four flags in common—namely, carry, zero, negative or sign, and half or auxiliary carry. The 8080/8085 lacks the 6800's arithmetic overflow flag, while the 6800 has no parity flag. The 8080/8085 parity flag P is intended for error detection; an erroneous bit in a result (a 0 that should be a 1, or vice versa) is reflected in the value of P. All the 8080/8085 flags can be tested by program control instructions. The 8080/8085 interrupt mask bits are not considered part of SR and will be discussed later.

There are two dedicated 16-bit address registers in the 8080/8085, the program counter PC and the stack pointer register SP. PC stores the address of the next instruction word and SP stores the address of the topmost byte of a user-defined stack in main memory M. PC is automatically incremented by one whenever an instruction byte is fetched from M. Each time a byte is popped from (pushed into) the stack region, SP is

Name	Condition Specified When Bit Is 1 (0)	Equivalent 6800 Flag
CY (Carry)	Carry or borrow signal was (not) generated	C
Z (Zero)	All 0s result was (not) generated	Z
S (Sign)	Leftmost or sign bit of result was 1 (0)	N
AC (Auxiliary carry)	Carry was (not) generated from the right of half of the result	H
P (Parity)	The result contained an even (odd) number of 1s	None

Figure 5.44 The status flag bits of the 8080/8085.

automatically incremented (decremented) by one; the 8080/8085 program counter and stack pointer register behave in exactly the same way as their counterparts in the 6800. Unlike the 6800, the 8080/8085 has no index register. Additional address registers are obtained in the 8080/8085 by pairing the six scratchpad registers to form three 16-bit registers BC, DE, and HL. The register-pair HL has special significance because it is used as an implicit memory address register by many instructions such as ADD A,M, which specifies the operation $A := A + M[HL]$.

Isolated or non-memory-mapped IO is used in the 8080/8085. The IO address size is limited to 8 bits, so that up to $2^8 = 256$ addresses can be assigned to IO devices. These addresses are used by IO instructions only, and therefore are independent of the $2^{16} = 64K$ addresses that can be assigned to M. Facilities are provided for both DMA and vectored interrupt processing, with the 8085 having more interrupt features than the 8080. The 8085 also has a serial IO port not found in the 8080. By requiring only a single $+5$-V power supply, the 8085 overcomes a major disadvantage of the 8080, which requires three different power supply voltages: $+5$ V, -5 V and $+12$ V.

The 8080/8085 has over 70 instruction types, approximately the same number as the 6800. (Different assembly-language format conventions make exact comparison between the two families difficult.) A summary of the 8080/8085 instruction set appears in Fig. 5.45; a more detailed description can be found in Intel (1979). Some representative examples of 8080/8085 assembly- and machine-language formats are given in Fig. 5.11.

Most 8080/8085 instructions process 8-bit operands; a few, intended mainly for address manipulation, have 16-bit operands. Data words may be either numeric or nonnumeric (logical). There are two basic number types, binary and decimal, with BCD code used for the latter. Addresses are treated as 16-bit unsigned binary numbers. Most arithmetic instructions in the 8080/8085 process 8-bit twos-complement numbers. Decimal arithmetic is implemented indirectly via the decimal adjust accumulator DAA instruction. This instruction works just as DAA does in the 6800, using the algorithm given in Fig. 5.27. Thus to perform 1-byte or two-digit decimal addition in the 8080/8085, a 1-byte binary add instruction is followed by DAA. For example, the two-instruction sequence

ADI   17H

DAA

specifies the decimal addition $A := A + 17$. (ADI is the mnemonic opcode for the binary add immediate to accumulator instruction.)

As indicated in Fig. 5.45, the 8080/8085 has a variety of instructions in the three major groups: data transfer, data processing, and program control. The 8085 has two multipurpose instructions, called RIM (read interrupt masks) and SIM (set interrupt masks) that are not found in the 8080. Otherwise the 8080 and 8085 instruction sets are identical.

The 8080/8085 data-transfer instructions move data unchanged among storage locations in the CPU, main memory M, and the IO ports. M can be accessed by simple load and store instructions, and also by push and pop instructions that access the top of the stack defined by the stack pointer SP. There are two parallel IO instructions called IN

Major Type	Subtype	Instruction	Comment
Data transfer	CPU only	Move register(-pair) to register(-pair) Set/clear carry flag CY	
	CPU-memory	Move register(-pair) to memory (Store) Move memory to register(-pair) (Load) Move register(s) to stack (Push) Move stack to register(s) (Pop)	Adjust stack pointer SP.
	Input-output	Move accumulator to output port (OUT) Move input port to accumulator (IN) Move bit to/from serial IO port (SIM/RIM)	8085 only
Data processing	Arithmetic	Add with/without carry Substract with/without borrow Increment/decrement Add register-pair to HL Decimal adjust accumulator A	8-bit twos-complement operations Unsigned 16-bit addition Used for BCD addition
	Logical	And Or Exclusive-or Complement (Not)	
	Shift	Rotate CY. A left/right Rotate A left/right	
Program control	Branch	Jump (un)conditionally Call subroutine (un)conditionally Return from subroutine (un)conditionally	Stack used as the save area.
	Other	No operation Compare and set flags Enable/disable interrupts Halt	

Figure 5.45 Summary of the 8080/8085 instruction set.

and OUT in the 8080/8085 that transfer a byte of data between the CPU accumulator and an IO port specified by an 8-bit address. Note that this address is transmitted to the IO port via the 16-bit system address bus. IO ports and locations in M are distinguished by the use of different select and enable control lines; see Fig. 5.42. The input instruction

$$\text{IN} \quad 12\text{H}$$

transfers a byte from the IO port with address $12_{16} = 00010010_2$ to the accumulator; that is, it performs the data transfer $A := IO[12_{16}]$. Similarly the output instruction

$$\text{OUT} \quad 12\text{H}$$

specifies the operation $IO[12_{16}] := A$. The 8085's RIM instruction is used as a serial input instruction to transfer a bit from the serial input data SID line of the 8085 to accumulator bit A_7. SIM transfers the contents of A_7 to the serial output data line SOD.

The 8080/8085's arithmetic processing ability is limited to addition and subtraction; it has no multiply or divide instructions. As noted above, decimal arithmetic requires the use of the DAA instruction. The standard logical operations and, or, exclusive-or, and complement are included in the 8080/8085 instruction set. There are four rotate instructions: two rotate the accumulator contents to the left and right, and the other two include the carry flag CY in the rotation. For example, the instruction RAR called rotate right through carry performs the operation

$$A_0,CY,A_7,A_6,A_5,A_4,A_3,A_2,A_1 := CY,A_7,A_6,A_5,A_4,A_3,A_2,A_1,A_0;$$

Since the carry flag can be set, reset, and tested by various instructions, RAR and RAL (rotate left through carry) are useful for testing or modifying individual bits of the accumulator. There are no explicit arithmetic or logical shift instructions corresponding to those of the 6800, but shifting can be performed indirectly using the 8080/8085's rotate instructions. The values of some or all of the five flags CY, Z, S, AC, and P are recomputed after the execution of most data-processing instructions. It is important to consult the complete instruction set specification to determine which flags are affected by any particular instruction, since there are certain apparent inconsistencies. For example, the decrement register instructions denoted by the opcode DCR affect all flags except CY. However, the decrement register-pair instructions denoted by DCX affect none of the status flags.

The program control group of instructions includes jump, call, and return instructions, all of which can be made conditional on the states of the four flags CY, Z, S, and P. For example, RET is a conventional return from subroutine instruction that replaces the contents of the program counter PC with the two topmost words of the stack defined by SP. There are also eight conditional return instructions of the form Rc, where c denotes a flag state or condition code. Thus RZ (return if zero) causes a return to be performed if $Z = 1$; no return takes place if $Z = 0$. Similarly, RNZ (return if not zero) results in a return operation if and only if $Z = 0$. CALL instructions cause the PC contents to be saved in the stack, then PC is loaded with the (16-bit) address of the subroutine to which control is being transferred. Thus most 8080/8085 call instructions are 3 bytes long. A special 1-byte call instruction called restart RST is used during interrupt processing, and is discussed later.

As the examples of Fig. 5.11 show, 8080/8085 machine-language instructions are 1, 2, or 3 bytes long. The first byte is the opcode; the second and third bytes, if present, form an immediate address or else a direct memory address. Note that neither indexed nor relative addressing is allowed. In 8080/8085 assembly language the addressing mode is usually specified by the mnemonic opcode rather than by the address field as in the 6800. Thus the move immediate operation A := 64 is specified by the assembly-language instruction

MVI   64

where MVI denotes move immediate. The move direct operation A := B, on the other hand, requires the instruction

MOV   A,B

with MOV (move) replacing MVI. Direct addressing is used both for CPU registers and main memory M. All direct memory addresses are 2 bytes long. For instance, the load accumulator direct instruction

LDA   100FH

performs the operation A := $M[100F_{16}]$ using direct addressing. Indirect addressing may be achieved using any of the three register-pairs BC, DE or HL as address registers. For example, the load accumulator indirect instruction

LDAX   B

invokes the operation A := M[BC] in which BC acts as the memory address register. The HL register-pair is frequently used for indirect addressing of M, and is designated by the symbol M in an instruction address field; for example, the 8080/8085 instruction

MOV   A,M

is equivalent to A := M[HL].

5.4.2 Programming Examples

Consider again the 32-digit decimal addition program developed for the 6800 in Sec. 5.3.2. The problem is to implement the operation

BETA := ALPHA + BETA

where ALPHA and BETA are 32-digit unsigned BCD numbers. Assume that these numbers are stored as 16-byte arrays in M in the same manner as before; see Fig. 5.29. Since the 8080/8085 lacks the 6800's indexed addressing mode, a different method of processing the arrays is required. Figure 5.46 shows a suitable addition algorithm for the 8080/8085. Two register-pairs DE and HL are used as address registers to point to bytes ALPHA + I and BETA + I respectively. By decrementing DE and HL in step, all 16 pairs of bytes in ALPHA and BETA can be accessed in sequence and added. To determine when all bytes have been added, a third register C from the 8080/8085's scratchpad memory is used as a byte counter. An assembly-language program that

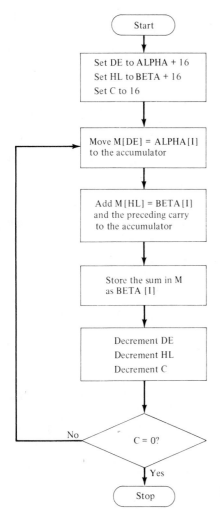

Figure 5.46 Flowchart of a 32-digit decimal addition algorithm for the 8080/8085.

implements this approach appears in Fig. 5.47. The advantages of indexed addressing are apparent when this program is compared with the corresponding 6800 program in Fig. 5.31. The 6800's index register plays the role of all three registers DE, HL, and C in the 8080/8085 program. Comments may be appended to any statement in 8080/8085 assembly language, but must be preceded by a semicolon.

As a second example, consider the task of searching a block of words in main memory for a specific byte. The block may be of arbitrary size, and the desired word may be stored anywhere within the block. This type of block searching is very useful in such nonnumeric tasks as text editing. Let BLOCK and SIZE denote the starting address and length in bytes, respectively, of the block to be searched. Figure 5.48 lists an 8080/8085 assembly-language program that carries out the desired block search. The memory bytes

Location	Instruction	Comment
START:	XRA A	; Clear carry flag CY by executing A := A ⊕ A.
	LXI D, ALPHA + 16	; Load immediate operand ALPHA + 16 into DE.
	LXI H, BETA + 16	; Load immediate operand BETA + 16 into HL.
	MVI C, 16	; Load 16 into register C, which is used as a ; byte counter.
LOOP:	LDAX D	; A := M[DE].
	ADC M	; A := A + CY + M[HL].
	DAA	; Decimal adjust accumulator.
	MOV M, A	; M[HL] := A.
	DCX D	; Decrement register pair DE.
	DCX H	; Decrement register-pair HL.
	DCR C	; Decrement register C. Z is set to 1 when C. ; becomes zero; Z is reset to 0 otherwise.
	JNZ LOOP	; Branch to LOOP if Z is not 1.
	HLT	; Halt.

Figure 5.47 8080/8085 assembly-language program to add two 32-digit decimal numbers.

with the addresses BLOCK, BLOCK + 1, ..., BLOCK + SIZE − 1 are fetched in sequence and compared with the desired byte, which we shall call BYTE and store in the accumulator A. The fetch-and-compare operation is performed by the compare memory instruction

$$CMP \quad M$$

which compares M[HL] to A, and sets certain flags based on the outcome of the comparison. By testing the Z flag after executing CMP M, it can be determined if M[HL] = BYTE. This byte-by-byte comparison continues until either a match is found or the entire block has been searched without finding the desired byte. When a match is found, the contents of HL are the address of the matching byte in M. The register-pair BC is used as a counter that is initially set to SIZE, and is decremented after each 1-byte comparison. If BC reaches zero, an exit is made to the instruction labeled NOMAT, which indicates an unsuccessful search. BC is decremented by means of the decrement register-pair instruction DCX, which does not affect any of the 8080/8085 flags. Thus to test for BC = 0, the program of Fig. 5.48 uses the pair of instructions

$$MOV \quad A,B$$

$$ORA \quad C$$

which are equivalent to

$$A := B;$$

$$A := A \vee C;$$

and together perform the operation A := B ∨ C. (ORA denotes the logical instruction called or accumulator.) If the result A = 0 is produced by the ORA instruction, then all bits of registers B and C must be 0. ORA then sets the Z flag to 1, a situation that can be detected by the conditional branch instruction JNZ (jump if not zero).

Location	Instruction		Comment
START:	LXI	B, SIZE	; Load block length SIZE into BC.
	LXI	H, BLOCK	; Load start address BLOCK of block into HL.
LOOP:	MVI	A, BYTE	; Load byte to be matched BYTE into A.
	CMP	M	; Compare A with M[HL]. Set Z to 1 if A =
			; M[HL]; set Z to 0 otherwise.
	JZ	MATCH	; Branch to MATCH if Z is 1.
	INX	H	; Increment register-pair HL.
	DCX	B	; Decrement register-pair BC. No flags are affected by
			; this instruction.
	MOV	A, B	; Check whether BC = 0 by computing B $\vee$ C and
	ORA	C	; setting Z to 1 if the result is zero.
	JNZ	LOOP	; Branch to LOOP if Z is not 1.
NOMAT:	. . .		; No match found
	. . .		
MATCH:	. . .		; Match found
	. . .		

Figure 5.48 8080/8085 program to search a block of arbitrary size for a specific byte.

5.4.3 Control Signals and Interrupts

The major external control lines found in CPUs based on the 8080 and the 8085 are listed together in Fig. 5.49. The directions of the control lines with respect to the CPU are indicated by in (into the CPU) and out (from the CPU). As Fig. 5.42a shows, some control signals in an 8080-based CPU are connected to the two support ICs rather than to the 8080 chip itself. The functions of the 8080/8085 control lines include timing of the CPU and system operations, control of memory and IO data transfers, and control of DMA and interrupt processing.

The 8080 requires a two-phase external clock source like that of the 6800. The 8085 can supply its own clock signals, in which case lines X_1 and X_2 can be connected to an external quartz crystal that helps to keep the internal clock frequency constant. Alternatively the 8085 can be driven by an external clock generator connected to X_1 and X_2. The 8085's clock signal is also made available on the CLK line for use as a system clock source.

The data-transfer control lines are used to direct data transfers over the system bus. Since isolated IO is used, memory and IO devices are distinguished by certain control signals. In the 8080, for example, a memory read cycle activates the $\overline{\text{MEMR}}$ (memory read) line, whereas an IO read operation, which can be initiated only by the input instruction IN, activates the $\overline{\text{I/OR}}$ (input-output read) line. Similarly, $\overline{\text{MEMW}}$ and $\overline{\text{I/OW}}$ enable memory and IO write operations respectively. These four read/write control signals are replaced by the three signals $\overline{\text{WR}}$, $\overline{\text{RD}}$, and IO/$\overline{\text{M}}$ in the 8085 as described in Fig. 5.49.

In a data transfer across the 8080/8085 system bus, the slave device to or from which data are being transferred normally is expected to respond within a specified time period; otherwise the data may be lost. This is the usual semisynchronous type of transfer illustrated in Fig. 5.21. The READY control line allows the 8080/8085 to communicate with arbitrarily slow memory and peripheral devices, thus permitting a kind of

Type	Name 8080	Name 8085	Function
Clocks	ϕ_1, ϕ_2 (in)	X_1, X_2 (in)	Input clock signals. X_1 and X_2 may be connected to an external clock that overrides the 8085's internal clock.
		CLK (out)	Output clock signal for use as a system clock
Data-transfer control		WR (out)	Write enable for M or IO
		$\overline{RD}$ (out)	Read enable for M or IO
		IO/$\overline{M}$ (out)	IO or M select. IO/$\overline{M}$ = 1 (0) selects IO (M).
	$\overline{MEMR}$ (out)		M read enable
	$\overline{MEMW}$ (out)		M write enable
	$\overline{I/OR}$ (out)		IO read enable
	$\overline{I/OW}$ (out)		IO write enable
	READY (in)	READY (in)	Wait request. Indicates that memory or IO device is ready to send or receive data.
DMA control	HOLD (in)	HOLD (in)	DMA request. Causes the CPU to float the data, address, and data-transfer control lines.
	HLDA (out)	HLDA (out)	DMA acknowledge line used to respond to HOLD
Reset	RESET (in)	$\overline{RESET\ IN}$ (in)	Resets the program counter PC to zero
		RESET OUT (out)	System reset line activated by $\overline{RESET\ IN}$
Interrupt	INT (in)	INTR (in)	Maskable interrupt request line
	$\overline{INTA}$ (out)	$\overline{INTA}$ (out)	Interrupt acknowledge line used with INT and INTR. The interrupting device responds to $\overline{INTA}$ with an interrupt vector in the form of a RESTART or CALL instruction.
		TRAP (in)	Nonmaskable interrupt request
		RST 5.5 (in) RST 6.5 (in) RST 7.5 (in)	Maskable interrupt request lines that generate a predefined RESTART instruction internally which is used as the interrupt vector
Miscellaneous	STSTB (out)		Strobe signal for the external status (control) latch
		ALE (out)	Strobe signal for the external address latch
	WAIT (out)		Indicates that the 8080 is in a wait state
	INTE (out)		Indicates the state of the interrupt enable flip-flop
	SYNC (out)		Indicates the start of a machine cycle

Figure 5.49 Major control lines of the 8080 and 8085.

asynchronous data transfer. Normally, with fast devices, READY is held active all the time to indicate that the unit U being addressed is ready to send or receive data. If, however, U controls the READY line and pulls it to the inactive (0) state, then the CPU enters a wait state, where it remains indefinitely until READY is reactivated. Thus READY serves as a data-ready or data-acknowledge line to indicate completion of the data transfer by the slave device. READY can also be regarded as a wait request line, a function that is useful during system testing (see Prob. 5.41).

Direct memory access is implemented in a standard manner in the 8080/8085 by using HOLD as a DMA request line and HLDA (hold acknowledge) as a DMA acknowledge line. HOLD and HLDA function in precisely the manner described in Fig. 5.23. The CPU responds to an active HOLD line by allowing the system data, address, and data-transfer control lines to float so that they can be taken over by the requesting DMA controller. The CPU signals that the bus is available by activating HLDA. The CPU completes any ongoing operations that do not require the system bus. It then enters a wait state, where it remains until HOLD is deactivated, at which point it regains control of the system bus.

The 8080/8085 uses a vectored interrupt scheme in which each interrupt request from an external device must be accompanied by a vector that specifies the interrupt address to be used, that is, the start address of an interrupt-servicing program stored in M. There is a general-purpose interrupt request line INT/INTR (called INT in the 8080 and INTR in the 8085) that is used by IO devices to signal the CPU that they require interrupt processing. At the end of each instruction cycle, the CPU checks the state of INT/INTR. If INT/INTR is active and is not disabled (masked), a special interrupt sequence is initiated. First the interrupt acknowledge $\overline{\text{INTA}}$ is activated by the CPU. The device requesting the interrupt responds by placing a call subroutine instruction on the system data bus. This instruction I, which serves as the interrupt vector, is read by the CPU and is executed as if it were an ordinary instruction obtained from M. I causes the contents of the program counter PC to be saved in the stack. PC is reloaded with an address obtained from I, which therefore is the interrupt address. Execution of the interrupt program then begins. If it is desired to save other CPU registers besides PC, then the first few instructions of the interrupt program should move the register contents to a save area in M. This saving is most conveniently done using the 8080/8085's push instructions to save the CPU registers in the stack. For example, the instruction PUSH PSW, called push processor status word, saves both the accumulator and the flag register in the stack.

There is a special 1-byte call instruction called restart RST that is designed for use as the vector I in 8080/8085 interrupt processing. RST contains a 3-bit address field ADR that specifies the interrupt address ADR $\times$ 8. Thus only eight memory addresses can be used as interrupt addresses by RST, namely, 0, 8, 16, 24, 32, 40, 48, and 56. The 8080 can only accept RST instructions from interrupting devices. The 8085, however, also accepts regular 3-byte subroutine call instructions of the form CALL ADR in which ADR is a full 16-bit memory address; this allows any address in M to be used as an interrupt address.

Figure 5.50 illustrates the effects of the instruction RST 2 when used as an interrupt vector. Immediately before the restart instruction is received by the CPU, the registers SP and PC contain the addresses 1000_{16} and $741F_{16}$ respectively. The top of the stack M[SP]

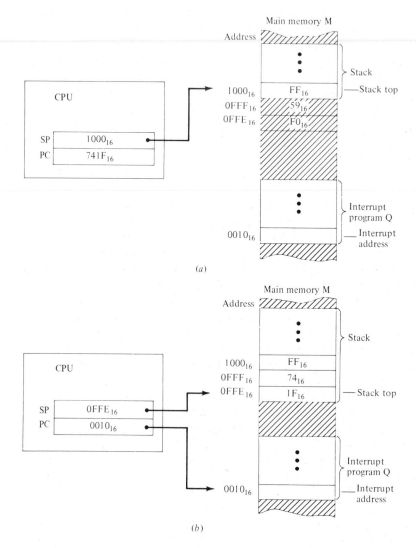

Figure 5.50 Microcomputer state (*a*) immediately before and (*b*) immediately after executing the RST 2 instruction.

contains the byte FF_{16}. When RST 2 is executed, the contents of PC are pushed into the stack 1 byte at a time. After each byte transfer to the stack, SP is automatically decremented by one. (Note that 8080/8085 stacks, like those of the 6800, grow downward with respect to the memory address space.) Thus after the return address has been saved, SP = $0FFE_{16}$ and the top of the stack M[SP] contains $1F_{16}$, which is the right (low-order) half of the return address. Then the address $2 \times 8 = 0010_{16}$ is loaded into PC. As Fig. 5.50 shows, this is the starting address of an interrupt program Q. Q is typically used to transfer information to or from the interrupting IO device. The last instruction executed in Q should be a return instruction that restores the return address to PC, so that execution of the interrupted program can resume at the point at which it was suspended.

The 8080/8085 responds to interrupt requests received on the INT/INTR line only if an interrupt enable flip-flop called INTE has been set to 1. INTE corresponds to the interrupt mask flag in the 6800 (Fig. 5.25). INTE can be set and reset via the 8080/8085 instructions EI (enable interrupt) and DI (disable interrupt) respectively.

The 8085 has four interrupt request lines, in addition to INTR, that cause a restart instruction to be generated internally by the 8085. These lines act as nonvectored interrupt request lines, and free the requesting device from the need to generate an RST or CALL instruction. The four extra interrupt request lines of the 8085 are called TRAP, RST 5.5, RST 6.5, and RST 7.5, and are associated with the interrupt addresses 36, 60, 52, and 44 respectively. TRAP is a nonmaskable interrupt request line and has the highest priority. Like the 6800's NMI line, TRAP is intended for use in emergency situations such as a pending power failure. The lines RST 7.5, RST 6.5, and RST 5.5 have successively lower priority, while interrupt requests received on INTR have the lowest priority of all. The RST X.5 interrupt request lines have individual enable (mask) flip-flops that can be inspected and altered using the 8085's special instructions RIM (read interrupt masks) and SIM (set interrupt masks).

An instruction cycle of the 8080/8085, which is the process of fetching an instruction from M and excuting it, is composed of from two to five machine cycles. There are some 10 different types of machine cycles, most of which involve a 1-byte data transfer over the system bus (i.e., a read or write operation) and some internal CPU operations. The number and types of machine cycles used in any instruction cycle depend on the instruction being processed. As an example, consider the store accumulator direct instruction STA 10FFH, which specifies the operation $M[10FF_{16}]:=A$. The machine-language version of this instruction consists of the 3 bytes (in hexadecimal) 32_{16}, FF_{16}, 10_{16}. The instruction cycle for STA 10FFH comprises the following four machine cycles $MC_1:MC_4$.

MC_1: an opcode fetch cycle to read from memory and decode the instruction opcode byte $32_{16}=$ STA

MC_2: a memory read cycle to fetch the second byte of the instruction, which is the low-order half of the instruction's address field

MC_3: a memory read cycle to fetch the third byte of the instruction, which is the high-order half of the address field

MC_4: a memory write cycle to transfer the contents of the accumulator to main memory

The machine cycles $MC_1:MC_3$ serve to fetch the instruction from M; the instruction is executed in MC_4. During each of the cycles $MC_1:MC_3$, PC is incremented by one, so that PC always contains the address required for the memory read operations in $MC_1:MC_3$. The instruction address field supplies the address used in the memory write operation of MC_4. In addition to the three types of machine cycles used by STA, there are IO read and write cycles and cycles to handle interrupt, DMA, and certain idle conditions.

All machine cycles in the 6800 are one CPU clock period in duration. In the 8080/8085, however, a machine cycle lasts three or more clock periods, each of which is associated with a distinct state T_i of the CPU. Most machine cycles consist of three states T_1, T_2, and T_3. For example, in an 8080/8085 memory read or write cycle the following actions occur.

T_1: During this period the address and control signals for the memory access are set up. In the 8080 the address is placed on the address bus $A_0:A_{15}$, and a status word specifying control signals is sent to the external status latch via the 8080's data bus D. In the 8085, half the address $A_8:A_{15}$ is placed on the 8085's eight address lines; the remaining half $A_0:A_7$ is sent to the external address latch via the address/data bus AD.

T_2: The CPU checks the READY and HOLD control lines. If READY $= 0$, indicating a slow memory device, the CPU enters a wait state until READY becomes 1. If HOLD $= 1$, indicating a DMA request, then the CPU floats the data-transfer lines and enters a wait state until HOLD $= 0$.

T_3: In a memory read cycle the CPU transfers a byte from the data bus to an internal register; in a memory write cycle the CPU transfers a byte from an internal register to the data bus.

Note that T_2 can be followed by an indefinite number of wait states to accommodate different memory response times, or to allow DMA transfers to take place. Unlike the 6800, the 8080/8085 can allow DMA transfers of any length to occur at the start of any CPU machine cycle.

Figure 5.51 shows a simple timing diagram for the STA instruction cycle discussed above. The memory read and write cycles $MC_2:MC_4$ each contain three states or CPU clock periods. The opcode fetch cycle MC_1 has four states: three to read the opcode from main memory and a forth to decode it and set up the subsequent machine cycles. Thus a

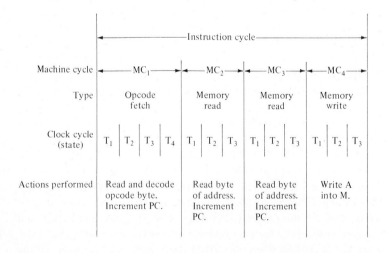

Figure 5.51 Instruction cycle timing for the store accumulator direct (STA) instruction

total of 13 clock cycles or states are used in processing STA. With a typical clock frequency of 2 MHz, this results in an instruction cycle time of 6.5 μs for STA.

As a second example of 8080/8085 instruction processing, consider the add immediate instruction ADI 64, which is equivalent to A := A + 64. Like its counterpart ADD A,#64 in the 6800, this instruction is 2 bytes long and has an instruction cycle containing two machine cycles. The first machine cycle is a four-state opcode fetch cycle in which the instruction's opcode is read into the CPU and decoded; PC is also incremented. The second machine cycle, a three-state memory read cycle, is used to read the immediate address byte into the CPU, where it is added to the accumulator A. PC is again incremented, and all five status flags are reevaluated on the basis of the result of the addition. (In some versions of the 8080/8085, only the transfer of the data byte to the CPU is completed during the second machine cycle; one or two more clock cycles are needed to complete the addition. However, these extra clock cycles are overlapped with the opcode fetch machine cycle of the next instruction, so that ADI effectively uses only two machine cycles with seven states.)

Figure 5.52 is a simplified flowchart of the overall behavior of the 8080/8085. The CPU continuously executes machine cycles that make up instruction cycles. A normal machine cycle can be altered by various external events. If the READY control line is found to be inactive in state T_2, the CPU enters a wait state. If HOLD is active, the CPU floats the system bus and again enters a wait state. Note that in the 8080/8085's various wait states the CPU clock signals continue to function normally. Since the 8080/8085, like many microprocessors, uses dynamic MOS circuit technology, its clocks cannot be stopped or slowed down significantly without losing information stored in the CPU. At the end of each instruction cycle the CPU responds to any pending interrupt requests that are not masked. In the case of the 8085, which has five separate interrupt request lines, the pending request with the highest hardwired priority is chosen for service. The CPU enters a special interrupt sequence of machine cycles in which it reads an instruction I, either RST or CALL, from the interrupting device. I is then executed by the CPU in the same manner as any other instruction.

5.4.4 8080/8085-Based Systems

The 8080/8085 series contains a relatively large number of ROMs, RAMs, IO interface ICs, and other support circuits. All 8080-compatible circuits can be used with the 8085. There are also some ICs designed specifically for the 8085. Figure 5.53 shows how two basic system components, a 2708 PROM and an 8212 IO port, are connected to the 8080/8085 system bus.

The 2708 (also called the 8708) is a 1K- by 8-bit PROM that is typically used for program storage in a microcomputer. It can be erased by exposure to ultraviolet light and then reprogrammed electrically. In the application illustrated in Fig. 5.53, the eight output data lines OD of the 2708 are wired directly to the system data bus. The 2708's 10 address lines are connected to 10 of the 16 system address lines; the particular lines used determine the position of the 2708's addresses within the system's 64K address space. Finally, a control signal that enables a read operation must be connected to the chip-select $\overline{\text{CS}}$ line of the 2708. If the 8080 is used, $\overline{\text{MEMR}}$ provides the required read-enable signal.

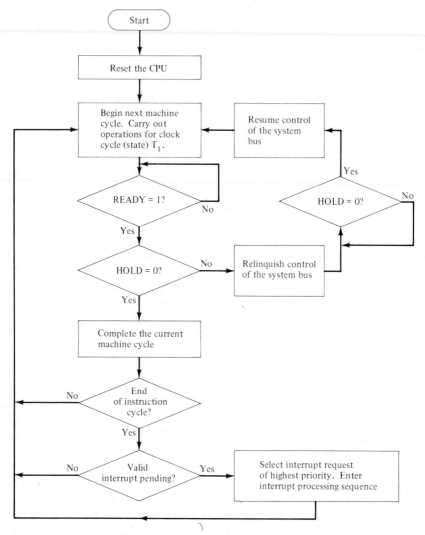

Figure 5.52 Overview of the internal operation of an 8080/8085-based CPU.

If the 8085 is used, $\overline{CS}$ can be connected to the composite 8085 control signal $\overline{RD} \vee$ $IO/\overline{M}$. A RAM is connected to the 8080/8085 bus in a similar fashion; an additional control signal is used to distinguish read and write operations.

The 8212, which is used as an input port in Fig. 5.53, is an addressable 8-bit latch that can also be used as an output port. It consists of eight clocked D latches whose outputs are connected to tristate buffer gates. Two device-select lines $\overline{DS1}$ and DS2 are available for addressing purposes; the 8212 is enabled for reading by the CPU when DS1 $\wedge$ DS2 $= 1$. Data can be written into the 8212 independently of the values of $\overline{DS1}$ and DS2 by activating the strobe line STB. Thus in the configuration of Fig. 5.53 the input

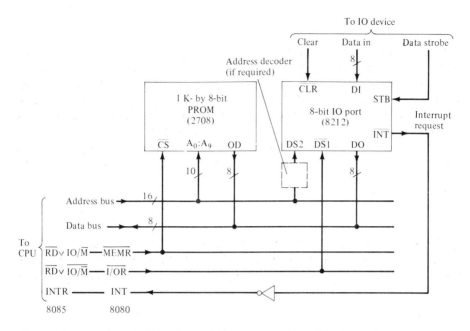

Figure 5.53 Interfacing a PROM and a parallel input port to an 8080/8085-based microcomputer.

device can load data asynchronously into the 8212 by means of STB. To read the data from the 8212, the 8080/8085 CPU must place an appropriate address on the system address bus and activate the IO read-enable line(s)—$\overline{I/OR}$ for the 8080 and $\overline{RD} \vee IO/\overline{M}$ for the 8085. Any 8-bit address can be assigned to the 8212. In small systems it is often possible to make this assignment so that no explicit address decoding is required; a single address line can be connected to DS2, which selects the 8212 whenever its address is applied to the system address bus. Note that isolated IO is used in the system of Fig. 5.53. It is easily converted to memory-mapped IO by replacing the IO read-enable line by memory read enable. The 8212 also is able to generate interrupt request signals to the CPU via its $\overline{INT}$ line. It contains a service request flip-flop that is changed along with $\overline{INT}$ to the active state by a signal on the strobe line STB. When the 8212 is subsequently selected by the CPU, the service request flip-flop and $\overline{INT}$ are deactivated. The 8212 can be used as an output port by connecting its data lines DI and DO to the 8080/8085 data bus and the IO device respectively.

The 8080/8085 family contains several programmable IO interface circuits. The 8255 programmable peripheral interface (PPI) chip provides a set of parallel IO ports, while the 8251 communications controller is a UART for serial IO devices; these devices closely resemble the 6821 PIA and 6850 ACIA of the 6800 family, which were discussed earlier (see Fig. 5.37). There are also some specialized ICs that interface the 8080/8085 system bus to specific IO devices such as keyboards, printers, and floppy disk units, as well as special-purpose interface circuits for standard communication buses such as the IEEE 488 bus for digital instruments, which is also known as the GPIB (general-purpose interface bus). Finally, it should be noted that there are various support ICs to control the sharing of the 8080/8085's interrupt and DMA facilities among sets of IO devices. Such specialized interface circuits are discussed in Chap. 7.

One of the most useful of the 8080/8085's IO interface circuits is the 8255 PPI. It serves to connect two or three parallel IO ports to the 8080/8085 system bus. A total of 24 IO pins are available on the 8255's 40-pin DIP for connection to IO devices. The direction (input, output, or bidirectional) and function (data or control) of these pins are determined during normal operation by an 8-bit control word that is transmitted to the 8255 from the CPU. Many different operating modes can be specified by this control word, three of which are shown in Fig. 5.54. In Fig. 5.54a the 8255's 24 IO pins are programmed to form three parallel ports A, C, and B, with A acting as an input port and B and C acting as output ports. In the configuration of Fig. 5.54b, all three ports A, C, and B are input ports. The port C lines are also designed for use as control lines for asynchronous data transfers that require handshaking signals. Half the C lines are associated with port A; the other half provide control lines for port B. Figure 5.54c shows a mode of operation in which ports A and B are used as asynchronous input and output ports respectively. Three C lines are used to control data transfers into port A. $\overline{STB}_A$ is a strobe signal used to load data from an IO device into the 8-bit data buffer register connected to port A. In response to $\overline{STB}_A$, the 8255 can supply an automatic acknowledge signal IBF_A (input buffer A full) to the IO device and, at the same time, send an interrupt request $INTR_A$ to the CPU. In a similar manner, three C lines are used to control data transfers through output port B in Fig. 5.54c. $\overline{OBF}_B$ (output buffer B full) is activated after the CPU loads a byte into port B's data buffer register; $\overline{OBF}_B$ serves as a data-ready signal to the output device connected to port B. This device responds by reading the data from port B and activating the acknowledge line ACK_B. The 8255 responds by generating an interrupt request signal $INTR_B$ to inform the CPU that the output device has received the data and is ready for more.

As shown in Fig. 5.42b, an external latch is necessary to read address bytes from the 8085's multiplexed address/data bus AD. Several support circuits were designed for the 8085 that have this address latch built into them. Figure 5.55 shows a three-chip 8085-based microcomputer that uses two such circuits, an 8355 ROM-IO chip and an 8155 RAM-IO-timer chip. This microcomputer is a minimum-chip system for the 8085; a comparable 8080-based microcomputer would contain at least eight ICs. Note, however, that the 6801 microcomputer appearing in Fig. 5.38 provides similar functions using just one IC.

The 8155 RAM-IO-timer contains a 256- by 8-bit RAM, which is assigned the memory addresses $0000_{16}{:}00FF_{16}$; it thus obtains all the eight address bits it needs via the address/data bus AD. Since the 8155 can demultiplex the AD bus internally, only eight pins of the 40-pin DIP housing the 8155 are needed for address and data transmission. This allows 22 pins to be used as IO interface lines. These 22 lines are organized into three programmable IO ports A, B, and C, which are roughly equivalent to the corresponding IO ports of the 8255 PPI. They can be used as three independent IO ports. Alternatively, the six C lines of the 8155 can be used as ready/acknowledge and interrupt request signals for data transfers through ports A and B in the manner shown in Fig. 5.54c. Finally, the 8155 contains a programmable timer, which is basically an addressable 14-bit counter that counts down in response to pulses received on the TIMER IN line.

It generates various types of signals on the TIMER OUT line when some user-defined value is reached by the counter. These signals can be used for IO device control; they can also be used to interrupt the CPU.

The second 8085 support chip appearing in Fig. 5.55 is the 8355 RAM-IO chip, which combines a 2K- by 8-bit mask-programmed ROM with a pair of 8-bit IO ports. Like the 8155, it contains an address latch to capture the address bits $A_0:A_7$; it is also connected to three other 8085 address lines so that it can obtain $2^{11} = 2K$ distinct

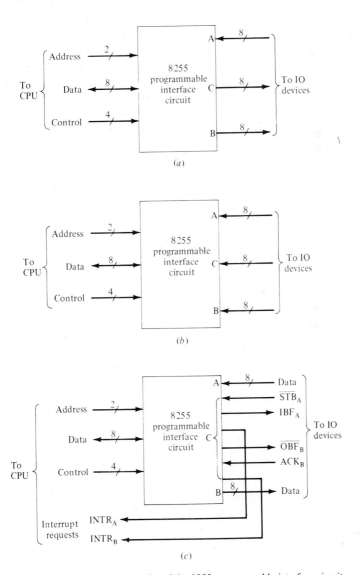

(a)

(b)

(c)

Figure 5.54 Three operating modes of the 8255 programmable interface circuit.

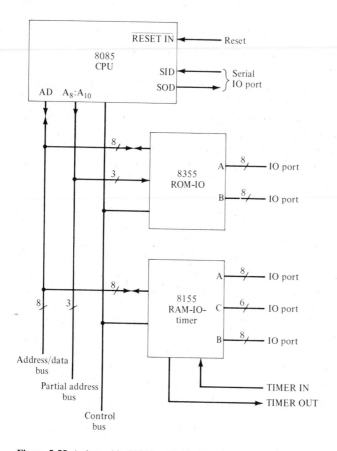

Figure 5.55 A three-chip 8085-based microcomputer.

addresses. The IO section of the 8355 contains two parallel IO ports A and B whose direction is programmable during normal operation. There is no provision for the automatic generation of handshaking or interrupt signals of the kind found in the 8155 and 8255.

5.4.5 The Z80 Microprocessor

The Z80, introduced by Zilog Inc. in 1976, was intended to supersede the 8080 (Shima et al., 1976). It is a one-chip microprocessor that includes essentially all the hardware and software features of the 8080 with many significant additions. It is worth noting that Zilog's founders included former Intel employees who had participated in the design of the 8080. The 8085, which appeared later, can be viewed as Intel's response to the Z80.

The Z80 is packaged in a standard 40-pin DIP. As in the 8080, 16 parallel address lines and eight bidirectional data lines are connected directly to the Z80. Several design changes reduce the number of control lines used. The Z80 contains its own clock generator, and a single clock signal is used in place of the 8080's two. Two pins are saved by the use of a single $+5$-V power supply instead of the three ($+5$ V, -5 V, and $+12$ V) used in the 8080. Note that these design improvements also appeared in the 8085. Unlike the 8085, however, the Z80 adds only one new interrupt request line, a nonmaskable interrupt request that is similar to the 6800's $\overline{\text{NMI}}$ and the 8085's TRAP lines. Static nMOS technology is used in the Z80, which means that it can function correctly at any clock frequency below the maximum, a convenience during system debugging.

Roughly speaking, the Z80 has twice as many registers and instructions as the 8080/8085. The programmable registers of the Z80 appear in Fig. 5.56; those that are not also in the 8080/8085 are shown shaded. The main general-purpose registers, the accumulator A, the status (flag) register F, and the scratchpad registers B, C, D, E, H, L are mirrored by an auxiliary set of registers designated by primes: A', F', B', C', D', E', H', and L'. Z80 instructions normally apply to the main (unprimed) registers. However, by using certain exchange instructions, the contents of the main and auxiliary registers can be quickly swapped. For example, the instruction EXX (exchange register pairs) swaps the contents of the six scratchpad registers in the main set for those of the auxiliary

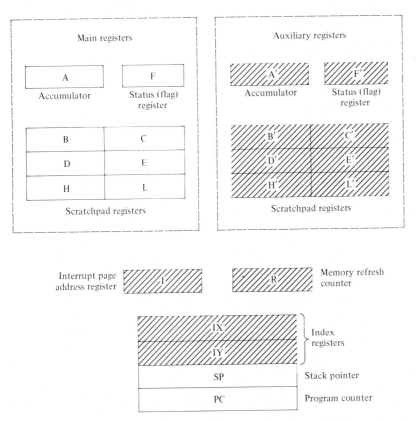

Figure 5.56 The programmable registers of the Zilog Z80 microprocessor (registers not in the 8080/8085 are shaded).

set. Such exchange instructions provide a rapid mechanism for state saving during subroutine and interrupt processing. The auxiliary registers also effectively double the temporary storage space in the CPU.

Borrowing from the 6800, the Z80 has a pair of 16-bit index registers IX and IY. These allow the Z80 to support all the addressing modes of both the 8080/8085 and the 6800, namely, immediate, direct, indirect, indexed, and relative. The Z80 also contains a new 8-bit register I called the interrupt page address register. I provides the high-order half of the interrupt address used in processing certain interrupt requests. Specifically, the interrupting device can send the CPU the opcode of the CALL instruction, followed by a byte that acts as the low-order half of the interrupt address. The Z80 appends this address byte to the contents of I to obtain a 16-bit address vector that can point to any location in main memory. Note that the same result is achieved in the 8085 by allowing the interrupting device to transmit a complete 3-byte CALL instruction to the CPU.

The Z80 contains an 8-bit register R called the memory refresh counter that is not found in any of the microprocessors discussed so far. Its purpose is to enable the Z80 to supply the signals required for periodic refreshing of external dynamic memory circuits. During each opcode fetch cycle, while it is decoding the opcode, and therefore not using the system bus, the Z80 places the contents of R on the system address bus and activates a special refresh control signal $\overline{\text{RFSH}}$. This information can be used by simple refresh circuits to control the refresh operations for a set of memory locations whose addresses correspond to R. R is automatically incremented after each instruction fetch, allowing it to sweep through a range of memory addresses. The memory refresh counter functions entirely automatically; it can be accessed by the programmer for testing purposes only. Note that the refreshing operation has no effect on the CPU's operating speed.

The Z80 is upwardly software compatible with the 8080 at the machine-language level. As the instruction format examples of Fig. 5.11 show, the Z80 and 8080 assembly languages are quite incompatible. The Z80 has about 158 assembly-language opcodes and 696 different machine-language opcodes; the corresponding figures for the 8080 are 78 and 244 respectively. Most of the new Z80 instructions use 2-byte opcodes at the machine-language level. The first byte of these opcodes contains one of the few patterns not used as an opcode by the 8080; the second byte defines the Z80 instruction. Thus whenever it decodes a non-8080 opcode byte, the Z80 goes through another opcode fetch cycle to obtain a second opcode byte. Because of the use of 2-byte opcodes, Z80 instructions range in length from 1 to 4 bytes.

The Z80 augments the 8080 instruction set mainly by introducing many new addressing modes and data types. As observed earlier, both indexed and relative addressing of the kind used by the 6800 are available. Besides the many 8080-type instructions for 8-bit data processing, the Z80 has instructions for 1-bit, 4-bit, and 16-bit data, both logical and numeric. It also has an important new class of instructions for moving and searching blocks of data of arbitrary length.

The 8080 has only a few simple instructions for 16-bit operands, which are intended mainly for address computation. The Z80, on the other hand, has 16-bit versions of essentially all the 8080's 8-bit data transfer and arithmetic instructions. For example, the Z80's 16-bit arithmetic instruction set includes the following instruction types.

1. Add register-pair to HL.
2. Add register-pair to HL with carry.
3. Add register-pair to index register.
4. Subtract register-pair from HL with borrow.

Only the first of these four instruction types is found in the 8080.

The Z80 has instructions for setting, resetting, and testing a specified bit in a word stored in a CPU register or main memory. For example, the bit test instruction

$$\text{BIT} \quad 7,(\text{HL})$$

causes the complement of $M[HL]_7$, which is the leftmost bit of the memory word addressed by the HL register-pair, to be transferred to the Z (zero) flag flip-flop, where it can be tested by a subsequent conditional branch instruction. The bit set and reset instructions SET 7,(HL) and RES 7,(HL) change the value of $M[HL]_7$ to 1 and 0 respectively. Note the use of parentheses to indicate indirect addressing in these instructions.

Perhaps the most powerful of the new Z80 instructions are those designed to manipulate blocks of data. Instructions exist that move a block of data from one part of memory to another, or between main memory and an IO port. These instructions use certain specific CPU registers as memory or IO address registers and byte counters. Addresses are incremented or decremented automatically, and the data are transferred byte by byte until the byte count reaches zero. For example, the block move instruction LDIR (load, increment, and repeat) moves a block of data within main memory. The register-pairs HL and DE are assumed to store the start addresses of the source and destination blocks, respectively, while BC stores the number of bytes to be moved. LDIR causes the sequence of operations

$$M[DE] := M[HL]; \quad DE := DE + 1; \quad HL := HL + 1; \quad BC := BC - 1;$$

to be executed repeatedly until BC = 0. A variant of LDIR called LDDR (load, decrement, and repeat) decrements the address registers DE and HL after each byte transfer. There are similar instructions to move blocks of data between main memory and IO ports. For instance, INIR (input, increment, and repeat) is a block input instruction causing the operations

$$M[HL] := IO[C]; \quad B := B - 1; \quad HL := HL + 1; \qquad (5.10)$$

to be executed repeatedly until B = 0. Here HL is the memory address register, C is the IO port address register, and B is the byte counter. The corresponding block output instruction is OTIR (output, increment, and repeat), which replaces $M[HL] := IO[C]$ in (5.10) by $IO[C] := M[HL]$.

The Z80 also has two block search instructions that scan a block of memory for an occurrence of a specific byte. The data are compared byte by byte with the contents of the accumulator A. When a match is found, a flag is set, and HL stores the address of the matching byte in M. The compare, increment, and repeat CPIR instruction compares A with M[HL] repeatedly. After each comparison, HL is incremented and BC, which is again used as a byte counter, is decremented. If a match between A and M[HL] is found, the Z flag is set to 1 and execution terminates. If no match exists, CPIR continues executing until BC reaches zero. Figure 5.57 shows a Z80 block search program that uses CPIR and is equivalent to the much longer 8080/8085 program of Fig. 5.48. The Z80's other block search instruction is CPDR (compare, decrement, and repeat), which decrements rather than increments HL after each 1-byte comparison, and thus scans M in the direction opposite to that of CPIR.

5.5 SUMMARY

The Motorola 14500 is one of the simplest devices that can be called a microprocessor. It is basically the E-unit or data-processing part of a small CPU. It has a repertoire of 16 instructions that process data 1 bit at a time. With a few additional ICs, a programmable digital control system can be constructed that is suitable for certain relatively simple industrial control applications, where logical rather than numeric computations are required.

A typical microprocessor contains both the E-unit and I-unit or instruction-processing part of a CPU. Certain functions such as clock signal generation may require one or two support chips to complete the CPU; this is true of early microprocessors such as the 6800 and 8080. A microprocessor contains the logic circuits necessary to execute up to several hundred different types of instructions. It also contains the logic circuits to fetch and decode instructions from an external memory M. Data processing is carried out in the microprocessor's arithmetic-logic unit, while a variety of CPU registers are used for the temporary storage of instructions, addresses, and data. The CPU communicates with and controls external devices such as M and IO interface circuits via a set of address, data, and control lines that constitute the system bus. A computer composed of a microprocessor, main memory, and IO interface circuits is called a microcomputer. A microcomputer often takes the form of a set of interconnected ICs mounted on a printed circuit board. In some cases, such as the Motorola 6801, an entire microcomputer is contained within a single IC chip.

Location	Instruction		Comment
START:	LD	BC, SIZE	; Load block length SIZE into BC.
	LD	HL, BLOCK	; Load start address BLOCK of block into HL.
	LD	A, BYTE	; Load byte to be matched BYTE into A.
	CPIR		; Compare A with M[HL], increment HL, decrement BC,
			; and repeat. If A = M[HL], set Z to 1 and exit;
			; otherwise continue until BC = 0 and set Z to 0.
	JR	Z, MATCH	; Jump (relative) to MATCH if Z = 1.
NOMAT:	. . .		; No match found
	. . .		
MATCH:	. . .		; Match found
	. . .		

Figure 5.57 Z80 program for searching a block of arbitrary size for a specific byte.

The primary function of a CPU is to fetch and execute instructions. The CPU actions associated with processing a single instruction define an instruction cycle. Instructions are normally divided into machine cycles, which may be further subdivided into clock cycles. The normal pattern of an instruction cycle may be broken by DMA (direct memory access) or interrupt requests. A DMA request causes the CPU to relinquish control of the system bus and enter a wait state. This allows a device with DMA control capabilities to transfer data directly to or from main memory. An interrupt request causes the CPU to suspend temporarily the execution of its current program and to begin executing another program stored at a specified interrupt address; this program is typically used to transfer data to or from the interrupting device. When vectored interrupts are used, the interrupt address is supplied by the interrupting device; otherwise it is supplied by the CPU.

The computational ability of a microprocessor is determined mainly by its instruction set. Instructions are characterized by the types of data they process, the data-addressing modes they use, and the operations they perform. In an n-bit microprocessor, most instructions are designed to process data n bits at a time; a typical value of n is eight. Many addressing modes are used, the more important of which are immediate, direct, indirect, indexed, and relative. The types of operations performed by microprocessor instructions fall into three main groups: data transfer, data processing, and program control. Data-transfer instructions copy information from one part of the computer to another. Data-processing instructions include arithmetic and logical instructions. Arithmetic operations are typically limited to addition and subtraction, but multiplication and division instructions are becoming common in newer microprocessors. The basic data types used for arithmetic operations are fixed-point binary and decimal numbers. More complex data types must be processed by software routines or special hardware processors. Many microprocessor applications involve very little numeric computation, and hence a simple instruction set is quite adequate. Often more important is the ability to respond rapidly to service requests, such as DMA and interrupt requests, from IO devices. In judging a microprocessor, account must also be taken of the other ICs in the microprocessor's family, as well as the availability of hardware and software design aids.

We have examined in detail two of the most widely used and influential 8-bit microprocessor families, those based on the Motorola 6800 and the Intel 8080. Figure 5.58 shows a family tree indicating the relationships among the 8080, the 6800, and their more important derivatives. The 8080 and 6800 have many similarities. Each has around 70 instructions (as measured by the number of distinct assembly-language opcodes), which perform similar operations on similar data types. They employ the same stack mechanism to facilitate the transfer of program control. Each family contains a similar range of support circuits, including RAMs, ROMs, PROMs, general-purpose programmable IO interface circuits, and various special-purpose IO interface circuits. The 6800 and 8080 differ in some important respects, however. The 8080 requires three CPU chips and three different power supply voltages. The 6800 requires only a single 5-V power supply, and two ICs suffice to form a 6800-based CPU. Each microprocessor has addressing modes not found in the other. The 6800 has more addressing modes, but the 8080 has more CPU scratchpad registers. The 8080 has isolated IO and vectored interrupts, neither of which is found in the 6800, and so on.

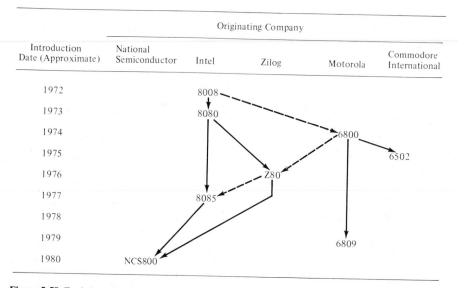

Figure 5.58 Evolution of some important 8-bit microprocessors; solid (broken) arrows show major (minor) influence directions.

As the 8080 and 6800 came into widespread use, and improvements in IC manufacture allowed higher chip densities and performance, new products began to appear that eliminated many of the shortcomings of the earlier microprocessors while preserving some degree of compatibility with them. Frequently the newer microprocessors are designed to execute the instructions of the microprocessors on which they are based, as well as some new instructions. This type of (upward) software compatibility can be achieved at the assembly-language level, as in the case of the 6800 and the 6809, or at the machine-language level, as in the 8080 and Z80. Hardware compatibility requires the use of similar, but by no means identical, data, address, and control signals, so that common memory, IO interface circuits, and other support circuits can be used by the compatible microprocessors. Not all the changes in the later microprocessors are desirable in all applications; often they involve subtle trade-offs between circuit design and performance. Thus while the 8085 reduces the number of ICs needed for an 8080-type CPU from three to one, it also introduces address and data multiplexing that is inherently slower than nonmultiplexed operation. It also requires the use of extra demultiplexing circuitry. The very large instruction set of the Z80 contributes greatly to its computing power, but also makes the Z80 assembly language more difficult to learn and, perhaps, to use.

5.6 FURTHER READING

Among the general texts available on computer organization and architecture, Hamacher et al. (1978) and Hill and Peterson (1978) provide good introductory treatments, and more advanced material can be found in Tanenbaum (1976), Hayes (1978), and Baer (1980). The Motorola 14500 ICU and its applications are described in the *MC14500B Industrial Control Unit Handbook* (Motorola, 1977), on which Sec. 5.1 is based; see also Tabachnik et al. (1981). Detailed specifications of the 6800 and 8080/8085 series and their derivatives can be found in the various manufacturers' manuals and data sheets (Motorola, 1981; Intel, 1979). Bishop's book *Basic Microprocessors and the 6800* (Bishop, 1979) is a readable elementary introduction to the 6800 series; and a very thorough treatment of 6800 applications can be found in Motorola (1975b). There are many introductory books concerning the 8080/8085 family (Rony et al., 1977; Cohn & Melsa, 1977). A valuable reference work that describes and evaluates the microprocessor families discussed in this chapter is that by Osborne and Kane (1981a).

5.7 PROBLEMS

5.1 Give two specific system control applications for which the Motorola 14500 ICU is well suited, and two for which it is not suited. List all the reasons for your answers.

5.2 Consider the following program segment for the 14500.

LD	X
ANDC	Y
AND	Z
OEN	RR
STO	F

X, Y, and Z are binary system input variables, Z is a binary system output variable, and RR is the signal appearing at the ICU pin called RR. Suppose that before the code is executed, the relevant system variables have the following values:

$$F,OEN,RR,X,Y,Z = 1,1,1,1,0,0$$

What are the values of these quantities after all five instructions have been executed?

5.3 Write a 1-bit subtraction program for the 14500 that is analogous to the addition program of Fig. 5.9.

5.4 The 14500-based system of Fig. 5.7 has no scratchpad storage space apart from the 14500's internal flip-flops. For many applications more scratchpad storage capacity is needed. Describe how a standard 256- by 1-bit RAM chip can be added to the circuit of Fig. 5.7 to act as a scratchpad memory. Draw a block diagram showing the RAM and all its connections to the rest of the circuit. Give a brief narrative description of the way in which the RAM is used.

5.5 Design a hardware stack memory that can be used to save subroutine return addresses in a 14500-based system. Assume that addresses are 8 bits long, and that at most eight return addresses need to be saved at any time. Design the stack around an 8- by 8-bit RAM IC, with suitable support circuits constructed from standard SSI/MSI ICs. Show clearly how the stack is connected to the 14500 CPU. Describe briefly how your circuit operates.

5.6 The 6800 and 8080/8085 are considered to have fewer than 80 different instruction types. All machine-language instructions for these microprocessors have 8-bit opcodes. Since 7 bits can represent $2^7 = 128 > 80$ different patterns, it might be thought that using an 8-bit opcode wastes 1 bit. Explain why this is not so.

5.7 Determine whether or not the following statements are true. Justify your answers.

(*a*) Let P, Q, and R be three related microprocessors. If P is upward software compatible with Q, and Q is upward software compatible with R, then R is downward software compatible with P.

(*b*) If P is (upward or downward) software compatible with Q at the assembly-language level, then P is also compatible with Q at the machine-language level.

5.8 Consider the IEEE 754 floating-point number format depicted in Fig. 5.16. The largest value 11111111_2 $= 255_{10}$ of the exponent field E is reserved for representing certain invalid numbers, such as the result of dividing a floating-point number by zero; $E = 255$ can be thought of as denoting infinity. Thus E is restricted to the range 0 to 254 for valid numbers.

(a) Give the binary floating-point representation of the numbers -1.2, 255.0, and 0.5×10^6.

(b) What are the largest valid positive and negative numbers that are representable in this format?

5.9 Explain why the IEEE 754 Standard, like other floating-point number formats, uses an all-0 representation of the number zero, in violation of Eq. (5.9).

5.10 A hypothetical 8-bit microprocessor called SIMP has the following specifications. It contains a program counter PC, two general-purpose 8-bit registers A and B, and two status flags—a carry flag C and a zero flag Z. Main memory is byte organized, and has a maximum capacity of 256 bytes. All SIMP's machine language instructions must be 1 or 2 bytes long. There are three possible addressing modes: immediate, direct, and indirect. SIMP uses memory-mapped IO.

You are to specify a general-purpose instruction set for SIMP, assuming that at most eight different instruction types are allowed. Assign a suitable mnemonic opcode to each instruction. For each instruction you choose, provide some justification for its inclusion in the instruction set.

5.11 Consider again the SIMP microprocessor defined in the preceding problem. Assume that its instruction set contains only one data transfer instruction, which is denoted MOV. MOV can transfer a single byte of data between the CPU and main memory, or between two CPU registers. Using MOV only, write programs in assembly-language format for each of the following tasks.

(a) Exchange the contents of the A and B registers.

(b) Exchange the contents of the memory locations $M[00_{16}]$ and $M[FF_{16}]$.

(c) Transfer the contents of PC to the memory location whose address is in register B.

5.12 What common addressing modes are not implemented in the following microprocessors: (a) the 6800? (b) the 8080?

5.13 Most microprocessors have an overflow flag OVF in their status registers that is set when the result of a signed arithmetic operation exceeds the normal word size. In signed binary addition, for example, OVF is set whenever a carry is generated from the bit position to the right of the sign bit. Note that in unsigned arithmetic operations the normal carry flag, which is set by a carry signal from the leftmost bit position, suffices to indicate overflow. The 8080/8085 has no overflow flag, a design deficiency that is remedied in the Z80.

Consider an 8-bit microprocessor that performs the following addition and subtraction operations on the twos-complement numbers X and Y.

$$Z_7Z_6Z_5Z_4Z_3Z_2Z_1Z_0 := X_7X_6X_5X_4X_3X_2X_1X_0 \pm Y_7Y_6Y_5Y_4Y_3Y_2Y_1Y_0$$

Let $Q = 0$ (1) indicate that the current operation is addition (subtraction). OVF is normally computed from X, Y, Z, and Q. Derive a sum-of-products Boolean expression for $OVF(X,Y,Z,Q)$.

5.14 (a) Explain clearly why the algorithm for the DAA algorithm given in Fig. 5.27 always corrects the result of a 1-byte binary addition instruction that has been applied to two decimal numbers.

(b) Show by means of a counterexample that this algorithm does not correct the results of a binary subtraction instruction.

5.15 The 8086 microprocessor has two decimal adjust instructions: decimal adjust for addition DAA, which uses the algorithm of Fig. 5.27, and decimal adjust for subtraction DAS. DAS converts the result of applying a binary subtraction instruction to 1-byte decimal operands to the proper decimal form. Determine the algorithm used by DAS. (Note that the Z80 has a single decimal adjust instruction that works for both addition and subtraction.)

5.16 The use of decimal adjust instructions as discussed in the two preceding problems is a nuisance from a programming point of view. Describe how a microprocessor could be designed to perform decimal and binary arithmetic without the use of decimal adjust instructions.

5.17 Not all microprocessors have a stack mechanism for saving return addresses when processing subroutines or interrupts. An example is the Intersil 6100, which is a microprocessor version of the PDP-8, a 12-bit minicomputer introduced by Digital Equipment Corp. in the mid-1960s. The subroutine call instruction JMS (jump to subroutine) of the 6100 and PDP-8 is implemented by the following operations

$$M[ADR] := PC + 1; \qquad PC := M[ADR + 1];$$

where ADR is the address field of the JMS instruction. Thus the return address $PC + 1$ is saved in the subroutine in memory location M[ADR], while the first instruction of the subroutine is stored in the next location M[ADR + 1].

(a) Describe how the return from subroutine instruction is implemented in this architecture.

(b) What are the disadvantages of JMS compared with the stack-implemented CALL instructions of the 6800 and 8080/8085?

5.18 The no-operation instruction NOP is found in the instruction sets of most microprocessors. List as many uses for this instruction as you can.

5.19 Draw a timing diagram similar to Fig. 5.22 for a general destination-initiated asynchronous data transfer.

5.20 A microprocessor has a single pair of DMA request and acknowledge lines. It is desired to allow eight different IO devices, each with a different hardwired priority, to have access to the microprocessor's system bus for DMA operations. Each IO device has its own DMA request and acknowledge lines, as well as all the logic needed to control DMA operations. Design a logic circuit C using standard SSI/MSI ICs to interface the eight pairs of DMA request/acknowledge lines from the IO devices to those of the microprocessor. (Most microprocessor families contain single-chip DMA controllers for performing this function.)

5.21 List the advantages and disadvantages of memory-mapped IO.

5.22 (a) A microcomputer employing memory-mapped IO uses k-bit addresses for all data transfers over the system bus. If the microcomputer contains n addressable IO ports, what is the length in words of the longest program that can be stored in main memory?

(b) Microprocessors such as the 8080/8085 are designed for isolated IO. Nevertheless memory-mapped IO can easily be used with these microprocessors, if desired. Explain why this is so.

5.23 The 6800's clock period can be stretched to allow a few DMA byte transfers to take place during one machine cycle. Explain why the clock period cannot be made arbitrarily long to allow DMA transfers of long blocks of data during one machine cycle.

5.24 Explain why the 6800, unlike the 8080/8085, cannot be used with main memory ICs whose access time is much longer than the CPU clock period.

5.25 Why does the 6800 lack an interrupt acknowledge line corresponding to the $\overline{INTA}$ line of the 8080/8085?

5.26 Write down the 6800 assembly-language instructions needed to carry out the following operations. Use as few instructions as you can; in most cases one or two suffice.

(a) Exchange the contents of registers A and B.

(b) Add 47 to the accumulator A, where all operands are binary numbers.

(c) Add 47 to A, where all operands are decimal numbers.

(d) Subtract 47 from A where all operands are decimal numbers.

(e) Or the contents of $M[10F6_{16}]$ to accumulator A.

(f) Negate the binary number stored in $M[10F6_{16}]$.

(g) Set all flag bits to 1.

(h) Shift the accumulator A one bit to the left thus

$$A_6A_5A_4A_3A_2A_1A_00 := A_7A_6A_5A_4A_3A_2A_1A_0;$$

without altering any flags.

(i) Call the subroutine SUB1 if and only if the Z flag is 1.

(j) Return from the subroutine SUB1.

5.27 List as many ways as you can of clearing the 6800's A register by using just one instruction.

5.28 In a 6800 program it is required to jump to one of eight memory locations JUMP0, JUMP1, ..., JUMP7 based on the contents of the A register. If the ith bit A_i of A is 1, and $A_j = 0$ for all $j > i$, then the jump should be made to JUMPi. No jump should be made if all bits of A are 0. Write as short an assembly-language program as you can to implement this multiway branch operation.

5.29 The following assembly-language routine PROG is to be executed by a 6800-based microcomputer:

```
LDA A   EFH
LDX     #17
ADC A   EFH,X
DAA
STA A   0100H
```

(*a*) How many bytes does the object program obtained by assembling PROG contain?

(*b*) Immediately before PROG is executed, let A = 76_{16}, X = 0000_{16}, PC = 1234_{16}, M[$00EF_{16}$] = 99_{16}, and M[0100_{16}] = 01_{16}. Determine the contents of all these registers and storage locations immediately after PROG has been executed.

5.30 Suppose that the order of the bytes forming the 32-digit decimal numbers ALPHA and BETA in Fig. 5.29 is reversed, so that ALPHA + 1 and BETA + 1 contain the least significant instead of the most significant digits. Rewrite the 6800 program of Fig. 5.31 to accommodate this change.

5.31 Explain why the 32-digit decimal addition program for the 6800 appearing in Fig. 5.32 is not relocatable; that is, if the object program is moved to a different part of main memory, errors may occur during its execution. Outline the changes that must be made to this program to make it relocatable.

5.32 Write a 6800 assembly-language program similar to that of Fig. 5.31 that performs the 32-digit decimal subtraction

$$BETA := ALPHA - BETA$$

5.33 Write a 6800 assembly-language program to do the 8- by 8-bit unsigned binary multiplication

$$A.B := A \times B$$

The unsigned product is placed in the A.B register pair. Give both a flowchart of your algorithm and a program listing with comments. (Note that this multiplication operation is performed by a single instruction MUL in both the 6801 and 6809.)

5.34 Write a 6800 block search program analogous to that of Fig. 5.48 that searches a memory block BLOCK of arbitrary length SIZE for a specific byte BYTE.

5.35 Suppose that the byte-storage order of the numbers ALPHA and BETA of Fig. 5.29 is reversed, as specified in Prob. 5.30. Rewrite the 6809 program of Fig. 5.41 to accommodate this change. Use postincrementing instead of predecrementing to scan the number arrays.

5.36 The following program is written in the assembly language of the 6502 microprocessor, an 8-bit machine whose architecture and instruction set are similar to, but not compatible with, the 6800. Using your knowledge of the 6800, decode each instruction and add a comment stating the actions performed by the instruction. What is the overall function of this program?

```
        LDX   #0
        CLC
START   LDA   OP1,X
        ADC   OP2,X
        STA   OP3,X
        INX
        CPX   #7
        BNE   START
```

5.37 (*a*) Why does every instruction cycle of the 6800 contain at least two machine cycles?

(*b*) The maximum number of machine cycles in any 6800 instruction cycle is 12. This maximum is reached by the software interrupt instruction SWI, which acts as a program-generated interrupt request. Using the information provided in Sec. 5.4, deduce the main actions occurring during each of SWI's 12 machine cycles.

(*b*) The 6800's return from interrupt instruction RTI basically reverses all the operations performed by SWI, but uses only 10 machine cycles. Explain this apparent discrepancy in instruction cycle length between SWI and RTI.

5.38 List all the reasons why the 8080/8085 uses far more external control lines than the 6800.

5.39 List all the major differences in hardware and software between the Intel 8080 and 8085 microprocessors.

5.40 How many pins does the 8085 save by multiplexing address and data bits? What is the impact of this multiplexing on the pin requirements of memory and IO circuits in an 8085-based microcomputer?

5.41 A useful design aid is a single-step circuit, which, when connected to a microprocessor-based system, allows a manual button to be used to make the system execute a single machine cycle and then halt until the single-step button is depressed again. Design a simple single-step circuit for the 8080 that uses the 8080's READ and SYNC control lines.

5.42 Repeat Prob. 5.26 using 8080/8085 assembly language in place of that of the 6800.

5.43 Using the 8080/8085's rotate instructions, write minimum-length programs that are equivalent to the 6800's left and right arithmetic and logical shift instructions. Be sure to set all status register bits to the proper values.

5.44 The following assembly-language program PR1 is to be executed by an 8080/8085-based computer.

```
LXI    H, 017FH
MOV    A, M
DCR    A
DCR    H
STA    007FH
RZ
```

(*a*) How many bytes does the object program obtained by assembling PR1 contain?

(*b*) Immediately before PR1 is executed, let $A = 21_{16}$, $PC = 0FFF_{16}$, $SP = ABCD_{16}$, $HL = 2358_{16}$, $M[017F_{16}] = 01_{16}$, and $M[007F_{16}] = 00_{16}$. Determine the contents of these registers and memory locations immediately after PR1 has been executed.

5.45 Write an 8080/8085 assembly-language program similar to that of Fig. 5.47 that performs the 32-digit decimal subtraction

$$BETA := ALPHA - BETA$$

5.46 Decimal numbers that stored two digits to the byte are said to be in *packed* format; numbers storing only one digit per byte are said to be *unpacked*. Unpacked number formats are used when storing a mixture of alphabetic characters and numbers, in which case the ASCII code defined in Fig. 5.17 is often used.

Write an 8080/8085 program that converts a 16-byte packed decimal number NPK into the equivalent unpacked ASCII-coded number NUNPK.

5.47 Design an algorithm suitable for the 8080/8085 that converts a packed, unsigned *N*-byte decimal number DNUM into its binary equivalent BNUM. The algorithm should be designed with ease of programming as the main objective; execution speed and storage efficiency are secondary considerations. Describe your algorithm by means of a flowchart, and write an 8080/8085 program that implements it.

5.48 An 8080 assembly-language program is to be written that transfers a block of 100 bytes from IO port 7 to a region of main memory with the starting address $00FF_{16}$. The data transfer can begin only if a status flag SF controlled by the IO device in question is set to 1. SF is continuously available as data bit 3 of IO port 6. The CPU should monitor SF continuously until it becomes 1, and then transfer the data block.

5.49 Why does the 8080/8085 employ different types of machine cycles for IO read operations and memory read operations, since each involves a similar 1-byte data transfer to the CPU? (IO and memory write machine cycles are also different.)

5.50 Identify two 8080/8085 instructions that employ the maximum and minimum number of machine cycles. For each instruction list all its machine cycles in sequence and describe the purpose of each one.

5.51 Analyze the advantages and disadvantages of the techniques used in the Z80 to maintain software compatibility with the 8080.

SIX

MICROCOMPUTER PROGRAMMING

"Without the aid of this language [the Mechanical Notation] I could not have invented the Analytical Engine; nor do I believe that any machinery of equal complexity can ever be constructed without the assistance of that or some other equivalent language."

[Charles Babbage: *Passages from the Life of a Philosopher,* 1864]

Writing programs for microcomputers is the focus of this chapter. The major features of high-level and assembly languages are described and compared, using examples drawn mainly from the high-level language Pascal and the assembly languages for the 6800 and 8080/8085 microprocessors. The criteria for measuring program quality are examined, and a systematic approach to program design is presented. Programming techniques for microcomputers are discussed in detail, first using assembly languages and then high-level languages.

6.1 PROGRAMMING LANGUAGES

This section presents an overview of the main features of computer programming languages. Two broad classes of languages are considered—high-level languages and assembly languages. The instruction and data types common to most programming languages are examined.

6.1.1 Language Types

A great number of languages have been devised for writing computer programs. Two types of languages are of interest here: a class of general-purpose problem-oriented languages called high-level languages, which are represented by FORTRAN, COBOL, BASIC, and Pascal; and a class of machine-oriented languages called assembly languages, which are represented by the 6800 and 8080/8085 assembly languages introduced in the preceding chapter. High-level languages are designed to resemble the languages, such as mathematical notation and narrative English text, most often used to specify problem solution techniques or algorithms. Ideally there is a one-to-one correspondence between statements, that is, instructions written in the high-level language, and the steps in the algorithm being programmed. For example, the algorithm step

"Compute the (positive) square roots of the numbers X and Y, add them, and call the result ALPHA."

corresponds directly to the FORTRAN statement

$$ALPHA = SQRT(X) + SQRT(Y) \tag{6.1}$$

An assembly-language statement, on the other hand, is typically a simple instruction for a specific computer. Thus the statement

$$ABA \tag{6.2}$$

which is an assembly-language instruction of the Motorola 6800 microprocessor, corresponds to the English statement

"Add the contents of register A to register B."

The key differences between the two kinds of languages can be seen by comparing statements (6.1) and (6.2). ABA is an opcode acronym or mnemonic name for add B to A, which is only meaningful in the few machines that have CPU registers named A and B. The 8080 is one such machine; however, the 8080/8085 assembly language employs the statement

$$ADD \quad B \tag{6.3}$$

instead of ABA. Thus, for all practical purposes, the use of ABA and the rest of the 6800 assembly language is restricted to 6800-based systems. In general, an assembly language reflects the structure of a particular computer family, and its use is restricted to that family. The high-level language statement (6.1) does not reflect the structure of any specific computer. The computation it specifies, two square-root extractions followed by an addition, cannot be performed by a single primitive instruction of any computer. In fact, most computers lack a single instruction for the square-root operation. Consequently, to execute (6.1), it must be broken down into a sequence of lower-level operations that correspond directly to primitive instructions in the computer's instruction set. This breaking down, or translation, can be done using any computer, thus making high-level language statements such as (6.1) machine independent. The machine independence of (6.1) can also be seen in the fact that the programmer has assigned arbitrary names ALPHA, X, and Y to variables, whereas in (6.2) and (6.3) the machine-dependent names A and B must be used.

Before a high-level-language or assembly-language source program prepared by a programmer can be executed by a computer, it must be translated into an executable object program. The language of the object program is machine language, which is the binary program format that can be directly executed by the computer. For example, the machine-language version of the 6800 assembly-language statement (6.2) is

$$00011011$$

or $1B_{16}$. Figure 6.1 illustrates the computer-language translation process, which normally is done automatically by special systems programs that are available in most computer installations. A high-level-language program is translated by a machine-specific systems program called a compiler into the machine language of the computer that is to execute it. The corresponding translator for assembly-language programs is called an assembler. Occasionally programs are written or modified by the programmer using machine language, thereby bypassing the translation step. A comparison of the machine- and assembly-language versions of a program (see Fig. 5.32 for an example) shows clearly that machine languages are much less intelligible to human beings. Machine-language programs are extremely difficult to write and debug, and therefore are unsuitable for most programming tasks.

A high-level programming language is usually designed for a broad range of computational tasks, and therefore may be called general purpose. FORTRAN and COBOL are two of the earliest such languages, and are still among the most widely used. FORTRAN is aimed principally at numerical programming applications in science and engineering. COBOL (COmmon Business Oriented Language) was designed for commercial data processing, where efficient manipulation of large alphanumeric files is more important than efficient numeric computation. Pascal (named in honor of the inventor of the first mechanical calculator, Blaise Pascal) is a more recent high-level language whose structure simplifies program design and debugging. Because of this, and the fact that Pascal is widely known, we employ Pascal for most of the high-level programming

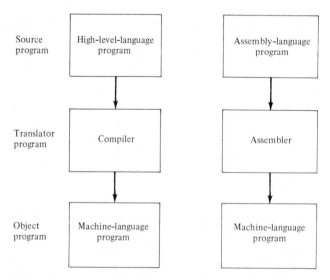

Figure 6.1 Translation of user-written programs into executable form.

examples in this book. Note that Pascal is also the basis for the RTL notation introduced in Chap. 4. Another class of high-level languages was introduced in the 1970s intended specifically for programming microprocessors (Crespi-Reghizzi et al., 1980). These languages, which include PL/M (Programming Language Microcomputer) designed by Intel, have many of the high-level features of languages such as Pascal, but also have machine-dependent features of interest to the designer of microprocessor-based systems. They thus can be viewed as intermediate between conventional high-level languages and assembly languages.

Despite the widespread use of high-level programming languages, assembly languages are still heavily used for programming all types of computers. An indication of this can be seen in the results of a 1977 survey of programming language usage for administrative data processing in the United States (Phillipakis, 1977). Not surprisingly, COBOL was found to be the most widely used language with a usage index of 63 percent. Assembly languages came second with a usage index of 16 percent, while the high-level language PL/1 (Programming Language One) was a distant third at 6 percent. In general scientific and technical programming, FORTRAN is the dominant language. Assembly languages are the types of programming languages most widely used in designing microprocessor-based systems, but the use of high-level languages—notably, Pascal, BASIC (Beginner's All Purpose Symbolic Instruction Code), and PL/M—for these applications is increasing steadily.

6.1.2 Comparative Example

To illustrate the nature of high-level and assembly languages, we next consider the use of two representative languages, Pascal and 8080/8085 assembly language, to implement a specific algorithm. The problem to be solved is that of finding the first location of a given character in a string or one-dimensional array of characters; this is a common task in word-processing applications of microcomputers. Figure 6.2 shows a flowchart of the algorithm to be used. The string to be searched is called BLOCK, and is viewed as an indexed array of the form BLOCK[0], BLOCK[1], ..., BLOCK[SIZE − 1]. BLOCK[I] is the *I*th character in the array, and SIZE is the total number of characters in the array. The character for which a matching character is to be found in the array, if one exists there, is called BYTE. The search is carried out in straightforward fashion by examining every character BLOCK[I] in turn, and comparing it with BYTE. The comparison proceeds character by character until a match is found, in which case the final value of the index I points to the matching character. If BLOCK does not contain BYTE, the search terminates unsuccessfully after every character in BLOCK has been examined.

Figure 6.3 lists a high-level language program written in Pascal that implements the foregoing search algorithm. It illustrates the basic features of a typical high-level language; a detailed description of Pascal will be given in Sec. 6.4. The boldface words **program, var, integer, char, array, begin, end, while, do, if, then** have special meanings in Pascal, and are called *keywords*. Roughly speaking, the keywords and the mathematical operator symbols : = , = , <, and so on constitute the "opcode" symbols of Pascal. The mnemonic names SEARCH, I, SIZE, BYTE, BLOCK, MATCH, NOMATCH, and READATA are defined by the programmer, and are called *identifiers*.

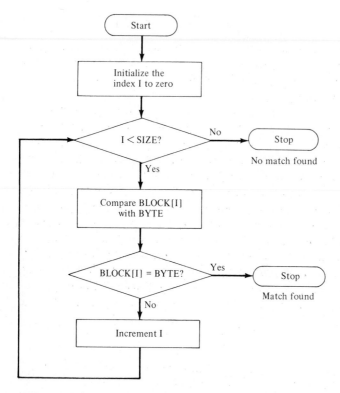

Figure 6.2 Algorithm to search an array BLOCK for the element BYTE.

SEARCH is the name assigned to the entire program. The identifiers I, SIZE, BYTE, and BLOCK are the names of variable operands used in the program. The identifiers READATA, MATCH, and NOMATCH are the names of subprograms, which are called *procedures* in Pascal, that are assumed to be defined elsewhere. READATA is an input procedure that obtains the values of the operands BLOCK, BYTE, and SIZE from main memory or an input device of the system. MATCH is a procedure that defines the actions taken after a match has been found, while the procedure NOMATCH is executed when the search program fails to find a matching character. It is assumed that the MATCH and NOMATCH procedures contain halt statements corresponding to the stop blocks in the flowchart. As in the RTL examples encountered previously, indentation and comments are used in Fig. 6.3 to improve program readability.

High-level languages allow a programmer to specify the meaning or (data) type to be assigned to each variable in a program. In the Pascal program of Fig. 6.3, the statement

var I, SIZE: **integer**;

specifies that I and SIZE are to be treated as integer variables. Similarly the variable BYTE is defined to be of type **char**, that is, an alphanumeric character. The statement

BLOCK: **array** [0..255] **of char**;

```
program SEARCH;
{Purpose: To search a character string BLOCK for the first occurrence of the character BYTE.}

var I,SIZE: integer;
    BYTE: char;
    BLOCK: array [0..255] of char;

begin
READATA(BLOCK,BYTE,SIZE);
I := 0;

while I < SIZE do
  begin
  if BLOCK[I] = BYTE then MATCH;
  I := I + 1
  end;

NOMATCH

end.
```

Figure 6.3 Array-search program written in the high-level language Pascal.

which is also included in the scope of the **var** statement, declares BLOCK to be an array of 256 characters that are indexed from 0 to 255. The precise formats or codes used to represent integers and characters depend on the computer used to execute the program. Different computers require different formats, which are produced by the corresponding compilers. The high-level language programmer is usually not interested in machine-specific details of this sort.

Several symbols and keywords are reserved in Pascal for use as delimiters or punctuation marks to separate various parts of the program. The curly brackets { and } are used here to delimit comment statements; in some implementations of Pascal, (* and *) replace { and } as comment delimiters. Comments are ignored by compilers during program translation; they are included in programs to enhance their readability for human beings. A simple statement such as the assignment statement

$$I := 0;$$

must terminate in a semicolon, which is the main delimiter for separating statements in Pascal. A sequence of simple statements can be grouped into a unit called a compound statement by enclosing the sequence between the pair of delimiters **begin** and **end**. A compound statement can be used in much the same way as a simple statement when constructing programs. Note that the main body of the program SEARCH, which follows the heading and declaration statements, has the form of a compound statement. The usual terminating semicolon may be omitted when a statement is immediately followed by an **end** delimiter. A period is placed after the last **end** delimiter to mark the end of the program.

The main steps of the array-searching process are implemented by the two Pascal *program-control statements* of the form **while** . . . **do** and **if** . . . **then** in Fig. 6.3. Each of these English-like statements contains a decision whose outcome is yes or no; the decision outcome determines which of two possible actions should be performed next. For example, the source-code segment

$$\textbf{while} \quad I < SIZE \quad \textbf{do}$$
$$\textbf{begin}$$
$$\ldots$$
$$\textbf{end};$$

which is called a **while** statement, makes the decision: Is I less than SIZE? by comparing these two integers. If I is found to be less than SIZE, then the compound statement following **do** is executed. If I equals or exceeds SIZE, indicating that the entire array has been searched unsuccessfully, then the statement immediately after the **while** statement, in this case the invocation of the procedure NOMATCH, is executed. In general, the statements between **begin** and **end** in the **while** statement are executed repeatedly as long as the condition after **while** is satisfied; when this condition is no longer satisfied, an exit is made from the **while** statement. In a similar manner, the **if** statement

$$\textbf{if} \quad BLOCK[I] = BYTE \quad \textbf{then} \ MATCH; \tag{6.4}$$

makes the decision: Do the characters BLOCK[I] and BYTE have the same value? If the answer is yes, then the procedure MATCH is executed; otherwise control is transferred to the statement immediately following the **if** statement, which in this case is the assignment statement

$$I := I + 1 \tag{6.5}$$

Note the difference between the symbol $=$ in (6.4), which means "is equal to" or "has the same value as," and the symbol $:=$ in (6.5), which means "is to be assigned the value of." The Pascal assignment symbol $:=$ is intended to resemble the arrow $\leftarrow$. The usual terminating semicolon is omitted from statements that, like (6.5), are immediately followed by **end**.

Figure 6.4 gives an assembly-language program for the 8080/8085 microprocessor that also implements the search algorithm of Fig. 6.2. (This program was examined in Sec. 5.4.3.) It is immediately apparent that the 8080/8085 program is much less English-like or readable than the equivalent Pascal program in Fig. 6.3. In fact, without detailed comments of the sort given in Fig. 5.48, to which the reader is again referred, the program of Fig. 6.4 is unintelligible to all but experienced 8080/8085 programmers. The machine-dependent features of this program include the use of opcodes that are unique to the 8080/8085 family, such as LXI (load register-pair immediate); the naming of specific CPU registers, such as the A, B, HL, and Z registers; and the use of the microprocessor-oriented data types byte (an 8-bit word) and "word" (a 16-bit word).

All the statements in Fig. 6.4 between START and NOMAT are described in detail in Fig. 5.48. The remaining statements illustrate some additional features of assembly languages. The program opens with a comment; in 8080/8085 assembly language, each comment or portion of a comment on every line must be preceded by a semicolon. Thus comments are delimited by ; and the end of a line. The statements from START to

```
;     Purpose: To search a character string BLOCK for the first occurrence
;     of the character BYTE.

              ORG      0100H
              READ     BLOCK, BYTE, SIZE
I             SET      0
START:        LXI      B, SIZE
              LXI      H, BLOCK
LOOP:         MVI      A, BYTE
              CMP      M
              JZ       MATCH
              INX      H
              DCX      B
              MOV      A, B
              ORA      C
              JNZ      LOOP


NOMAT:        . . .
              . . .


MATCH:        . . .
              . . .


              END
```

Figure 6.4 Array-search program written in 8080/8085 assembly language.

NOMAT are typical assembly-language instructions. The general format of such instructions is

label: opcode   operand-list   ;comment

Each such statement corresponds to a single machine-language instruction.
The three statements

ORG   0100H

. . .

I SET   0

. . .

END

are examples of assembler directives. A *directive* or *pseudoinstruction* is a command to the assembler concerning actions to be taken during the program translation or assembly process. The ORG (origin) directive in Fig. 6.4 tells the assembler that the first machine-language instruction that is generated during assembly should be assigned to main memory location 0100_{16}; the H in the source code denotes hexadecimal or base-16 format. The ORG location provides a reference point for the construction of all subsequent machine-language addresses during assembly. Thus the first LXI instruction appearing in Fig. 6.4 is 3 bytes long, and is therefore assigned to the three consecutive 8080/8085 memory addresses 0100_{16}, 0101_{16}, 0102_{16}; the second LXI instruction is assigned to the next three locations 0103_{16}, 0104_{16}, 0105_{16}, and so on. Note that the

Pascal program contains no references to physical memory addresses; symbolic addresses only are used. The 8080/8085 directive

$$\text{I} \quad \text{SET} \quad 0$$

in which SET plays the role of opcode, instructs the assembler to assign the initial value zero to the variable I during assembly. The final END directive informs the assembler that the end of the source program has been reached.

The statement

$$\text{READ} \quad \text{BLOCK, BYTE, SIZE}$$

invokes a user-defined macroinstruction called READ. A *macroinstruction*, or simply a *macro*, is a sequence of instructions that can be represented by a simple name, READ in this case, that can be used as a new opcode. A macro, like a procedure in Pascal, represents a subprogram that can be invoked by naming it in another program. A macro is one of two important mechanisms (the other is the subroutine) for adding structure to assembly-language programs. The macro READ of Fig. 6.4 performs the same function as the READATA procedure of Fig. 6.3; it obtains the values of the input operands BLOCK, BYTE, and SIZE.

In comparing Figs. 6.3 and 6.4 we see that the Pascal has several more powerful or higher-level statement types and data types than the 8080/8085 program. For example, the Pascal control statement

if BLOCK[I] = BYTE **then** MATCH;

corresponds to the three assembly-language statements

$$
\begin{array}{lll}
\text{LOOP:} & \text{MVI} & \text{A, BYTE} \\
& \text{CMP} & \text{M} \\
& \text{JZ} & \text{MATCH}
\end{array}
$$

A simple one-to-one correspondence exists between the statements

$$\text{I} := \text{I} + 1$$

and

$$\text{INX} \quad \text{H}$$

both of which specify the increment operation.

Much of the complexity of the 8080/8085 program arises because arrays are not treated as primitive data types as they are in Pascal. Thus the programmer must devise a complex mechanism for manipulating the BLOCK array using various general-purpose CPU registers. The 8080/8085 registers HL, BC, and A are used to store the index I, the size of the unsearched portion of the array, and the reference character BYTE respectively. The Z flag register is also used to store the outcome of the main decisions made in the program. No registers or other special features of the host computer are mentioned in the Pascal program.

It should be noted that the term "high level" is a relative one in the context of programing languages. The Pascal program of Fig. 6.3 is low level in comparison with the two-statement array search program shown in Fig. 6.5a. The latter uses a hypothetical language that is typical of those employed by commercial text-editing programs. (There are as yet no standard programming languages for text editors.) This example demonstrates that, in general, a shorter and more readable program can be written by using a language that is specialized for the application at hand, rather than a general-purpose language. Figure 6.5b shows yet another version of the search program, this time written in the assembly language of the Z80 microprocessor; see Fig. 5.57 for detailed comments on this program. The Z80's CPIR (compare, increment, and repeat) instruction is a "high-level" instruction that is equivalent to portions of several Pascal statements. The use of this instruction makes the overall length of the assembly-language program about the same as that of its Pascal equivalent.

6.1.3 Instruction Specification

A computer program is a list of instruction statements that describe an algorithm to be executed by a computer. The program must define the actions to be performed on the data being processed, as well as the sequence, or order of execution, of those actions.

Most computational tasks can be expressed in the following general form: Evaluate some function F of the operands X1, X2, ..., Xn and assign the resulting value to the variable Y. This action is specified in most programming languages (and RTLs) by means of an *assignment statement* of the form

$$Y := F(X1, X2, \ldots, Xn);$$

```
load      BLOCK [255]
find      $BYTE$
```

(*a*)

```
          ORG     0100H
          READ    BLOCK, BYTE, SIZE

I         SET     0

START:    LD      BC, SIZE
          LD      HL, BLOCK
          LD      A, BYTE
          CPIR
          JR      Z, MATCH

NOMAT:    . . .
          . . .

MATCH:    . . .
          . . .

          END
```

(*b*)

Figure 6.5 Two more array-search programs written in (*a*) a text-editor command language and (*b*) Z80 assembly language.

The simplest assignment statement is the data-transfer statement

$$Y := X;$$

which simply assigns the current value of X to Y. Data-transfer statements have many names, such as copy, move, load, store, and replace. Interestingly, they are the most frequently used statements in many programming languages (Knuth, 1971). All languages allow some basic arithmetic and logical operations to be expressed by a single assignment statement. For example, the 8080/8085 assembly-language instruction

$$SUB \quad B$$

specifies the subtraction operation, which is defined in Pascal thus:

$$A := A - B;$$

High-level languages allow very complex expressions to be included in assignment statements, for example,

$$A := B * LOG(C - 2.71825) + PI ** 2;$$

Instruction execution sequence can be controlled in various ways. In most cases instructions are required to be executed in the order in which they are written down by the programmer. The instruction order in the source program is generally preserved intact during translation to object program form. Thus, unless the programmer specifies otherwise, execution of each instruction is followed by execution of the instruction appearing immediately after it in the (source or object) program. For instance, the three-instruction program segment

$$
\begin{aligned}
C &:= A; \\
A &:= B; \\
B &:= C;
\end{aligned}
\qquad (6.6)
$$

implies the following sequence. First execute the instruction

$$C := A;$$

then execute the instruction

$$A := B;$$

and finally execute

$$B := C;$$

The program (6.6) is intended to exchange A and B, that is, it assigns to A and B the values possessed by the other variable before (6.6) is executed. It is easily seen that if the three statements are not executed in the order described, then (6.6) no longer exchanges the values of A and B.

The order in which instructions are executed can be varied by means of program-control or *branch statements*. The simplest such statement that is available in all high-level and assembly languages is the unconditional branch or **goto** instruction. These instructions are typically written in the format

JUMP   NEXT

or

goto   NEXT;

where NEXT is a label or symbolic address assigned to the next instruction to be executed after the branch instruction itself has been executed. The program

$$
\begin{array}{ll}
 & C := A; \\
 & \textbf{goto}\ \ 20; \\
10: & B := C; \\
 & \textbf{goto}\ \ 30; \\
20: & A := B; \\
 & \textbf{goto}\ \ 10; \\
30: & \ldots
\end{array}
\qquad (6.7)
$$

is functionally equivalent to (6.6). The **goto**'s in (6.7) serve to unscramble the assignment statements so that they are executed in the order specified in (6.6). While this use of **goto**'s is logically correct, it makes the flow of control among the various instructions difficult to follow and therefore error-prone. Branch instructions of this sort should be used cautiously in program design.

Conditional branch statements allow one of several possible execution sequences to be followed, depending on the outcome of a test performed on some specified condition. All programming languages allow two-way conditional branch statements. For example, the 8080/8085 jump-on-zero instruction

JZ   TEN   (6.8)

causes the CPU flag bit named Z to be tested. If $Z = 1$, implying that an all-0's result was produced by a preceding instruction, then a branch is made to the instruction labeled TEN. If, on the other hand, $Z = 0$, then the next sequential instruction, that is, the instruction immediately after (6.8), is executed. An equivalent conditional branch instruction in the FORTRAN language has the format.

IF (Z .EQ. 1) GO TO 10   (6.9)

while in Pascal it is expressed thus:

if $Z = 1$ **then goto** 10;   (6.10)

Note that both FORTRAN and Pascal require instruction labels to be integers, while 8080/8085 assembly language requires labels to begin with a letter of the alphabet. If the condition test in any of (6.8) – (6.10) fails, that is, if the condition specified in the instruction is not currently satisfied, then the next sequential instruction is executed. Pascal and other languages also allow two-way branch instructions of the form

if $Z = 1$ **then goto** 10 **else goto** 20;

that permit the two possible next instructions to be positioned anywhere in the program. Many high-level languages have other program control statements, such as multiway branches and the **while** statement encountered in Fig. 6.3; these are discussed in Sec. 6.4.

Figure 6.6 summarizes the programming language elements considered above. For comparison, the flowchart symbols corresponding to the main elements in programming languages are shown. This figure implies that there is an equivalence among flowcharts, high-level-language programs, and assembly-language programs, so that each can be used to describe any algorithm. Flowcharts allow the flow of control within a program to be displayed in a two-dimensional graphic form that is easily understood by humans, but not by machines.

A programming language provides a set of fixed symbolic names for standard operations. These are used in accordance with certain specified rules of syntax to construct instructions and programs. Many programming tasks can be simplified if the programmer can assign symbolic names to special operations that are often used in the programming task at hand, but are not available as predefined operations of the language being used. Each special operation of this sort is named and described by means of a (sub)program written using the standard facilities of the programming language in

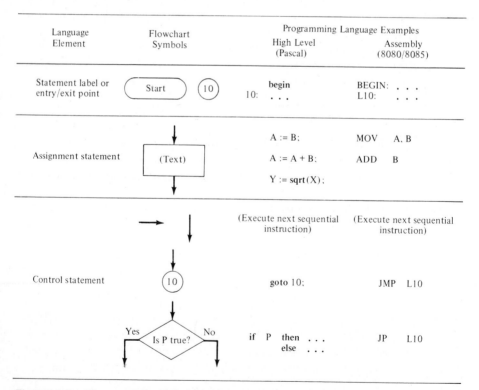

Figure 6.6 Possible representations of some basic elements of programming languages.

question. Execution of the new operation can then be specified by simply naming it or "calling" it in some standard fashion. Computer programming languages provide several facilities for introducing user-defined operations of this kind.

Almost all programming languages, both high level and assembly, allow subprograms to be defined as subroutines. The term "procedure" is used in place of subroutine in some programming languages, including Pascal; these two terms are used interchangeably here. A subroutine is invoked for execution by writing its name, often preceded by the word CALL. For example, in FORTRAN or 8080/8085 assembly language, a subroutine named GAMMA is invoked by the statement

CALL GAMMA

In Pascal it suffices to write the (procedure) name GAMMA by itself. Each language has its own conventions for writing the program that defines the actions to be performed by a subroutine. A typical definition has the following general format:

SUBROUTINE GAMMA

(Statements defining the subroutine)

END

During source-program translation, the subroutine definition is translated into a self-contained object program. When the subroutine is called for execution, program control is transferred to this subroutine program, and is subsequently returned by the subroutine to the calling program (which may itself be a subroutine). Because they are self-contained programs, subroutines can be written independently by different programmers. Subroutines of general interest are often placed in a *program library,* where they can easily be accessed by many programmers. The standard facilities of popular programming languages are often augmented by program libraries in this way. A typical object program has the form of a collection of subroutines, either user written or obtained from a program library, all linked to a main program. The necessary links among these routines are often provided automatically by the translator program used, or else by a special systems program called a *link editor,* which processes the object program before execution.

Another mechanism for augmenting a programming language by user-defined operations is the macro (macroinstruction), whose use is confined mainly to assembly languages. A macro is defined and invoked in a source program in much the same way as a subroutine. For example, in 8080/8085 assembly language a macro named GAMMA is defined by a subprogram with the format

GAMMA MACRO

(Statements defining the macro)

ENDM

This macro is invoked simply by writing the opcode

GAMMA

The central difference between macros and subroutines lies in the way in which they are handled during translation from source to object code. Each time a macro is invoked, a copy of the entire macro is inserted at that point in the object code. Thus is a macro is invoked n times in the source code, n distinct copies of that macro appear in the object code. A subroutine, on the other hand, appears just once in the object program, no matter how many time it is invoked. Figure 6.7 illustrates this basic difference between macros and subroutines. The relative merits of these important programming concepts are examined later.

    Programming languages contain various types of statements that are directed at the translator program, and are used to control some aspects of the translation of source to object code. We refer to such statements as (translator) directives. Unlike ordinary

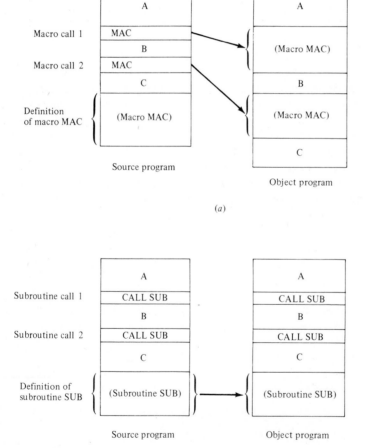

(a)

(b)

Figure 6.7 Generation of object code for (a) macros and (b) subroutines or procedures.

instructions, directives are not translated directly into object code. Directives are typically used to control storage allocation for the object program, delimit program structures such as subroutines and macros, identify data types, and perform similar bookkeeping tasks. Examples of compiler and assembler directives were encountered in the programs of Figs. 6.3 and 6.4 respectively.

6.1.4 Data Specification

High-level programming languages furnish a wider range of basic instruction types and formats than assembly languages. A somewhat similar disparity exists in the realm of data or operand types. Assembly languages provide only a few predefined data types, which are usually highly dependent on the computer being programmed. High-level languages, on the other hand, often have many predefined data types that are largely machine independent. The programmer can overcome the deficiencies of any given language in the data specification area by defining new data types, either directly by means of explicit data type declarations, or indirectly via subroutine or macro definitions.

In high-level languages every data variable has a *type* associated with it, which is the set of (constant) values that the variable can assume. The two most common types of numeric data are **integer** and **real**. Integer and real numbers in high-level languages correspond to fixed-point and floating-point numbers within the computer. Integer constants are typically written as decimal numbers without decimal points, for example, 1, $+17$, -10200. Real numbers may be written with decimal points as in $+17.0$ and -3.1415926. They may also be written in scientific notation with a scale factor denoting a power of 10, for example, $2.17E+3$, which is equivalent to 2.17×10^3. A variable's type is specified in a high-level language program by means of a *(type) declaration statement*. For example, the variables LAMDA and MU are defined to be real numbers in FORTRAN programs by the declaration statement

REAL   LAMDA, MU

The equivalent Pascal declaration statement is

var   LAMDA, MU: real;

Besides the types **integer** and **real**. Pascal has the type **char** whose values are the alphanumeric characters A, B, ..., Z, 0, 1, ..., 9, !, @, ... Another basic type in many high-level languages is **boolean**, whose values are **true** and **false**. Pascal is one of the few languages that allows the programmer to define new data types explicitly. For example, a special type named COLOR with the five values BLACK, BLOND, BROWN, RED, and WHITE may be specified by the following Pascal statement:

type: COLOR = (BLACK,BLOND,BROWN,RED,WHITE);

A variable, say NU, may then be declared to be of type COLOR thus:

var   NU: COLOR;

The foregoing data types apply only to variables that can assume one value at a time;

such variables are called simple variable or *scalars*. There are many useful composite data types where a single name or identifier represents a collection of data items. High-level languages generally include, as a predefined composite data type, the type **array**, denoting a set of objects that are ordered by one or more index parameters. In FOR-TRAN, for example, the declaration statement

REAL   LAMDA(50)

defines LAMDA as a 50-element array of variables whose members are the real numbers LAMDA(1), LAMDA(2), ..., LAMDA(50). The corresponding array declaration statement in Pascal is

var   LAMDA: **array** [1..50] **of real**;

Individual data items within an array are referred to by appending parenthetic index numbers to the array name. The Ith item in the array LAMDA defined above is specified by the name LAMDA(I) in FORTRAN and by LAMDA[I] in Pascal.

Another useful composite data type defined in Pascal is **record**. A record, like an array, is a named collection of related items. Unlike an array, however, the items in a record need not all be of the same type. Each item or *field* in the record has its own identifying name and data type. A field is referred to by appending its name to that of the record that contains it. For example, the identifier EMPLOYEE.NAME refers to the field NAME within the record EMPLOYEE. The structure of a Pascal record is specified by means of a record declaration statement such as the following simple EMPLOYEE record, which contains three fields called NAME, AGE, and SEX:

EMPLOYEE: **record**
           NAME: **array** [1..32] **of char**;
           AGE: 0..100;
           SEX: (MALE,FEMALE)
      end;

A rather different approach to data specification is taken in assembly languages. The name of a variable is treated as the address of some physical storage location in the underlying computer, for example, a CPU register, a main memory location, or an IO port. The value of the variable is the contents of the corresponding storage location. In most cases a storage location can store any type of data that fits in it, implying that its data type is not fixed. Consider the use of the name A in 8080/8085 assembly-language programs. A denotes a general-purpose register in the CPU to which the programmer can assign any type of 8-bit data, such as an 8-bit binary number, a 2-digit decimal number, an ASCII character, or half of a main memory address. Thus it is not meaningful to assign a data type of the kind discussed earlier to A or similar variable names in assembly-language programs. It appears that the main distinguishing feature of data types at the assembly-language level is their length. This is reflected in the 8080/8085 version of Intel's PL/M programming language, which allows only two simple data types to be declared: **byte**, denoting the set of 8-bit words, and **address**, denoting 16-bit words. In general, explicit data-type declaration facilities are not included in assembly languages.

Constants can be expressed in a variety of ways in assembly languages. While high-level languages restrict the programmer to decimal number types, various number bases that are powers of two can be used at the assembly-language level. In 8080/8085 assembly language the number 17 can be written in all the following ways:

Hexademical: 11H

Decimal: 17D or 17

Binary: 00010001B

In most languages, character constants are indicated by quotation marks, for example, '17'.

Assembly languages permit certain composite data types to be processed in a fairly direct manner by the use of special addressing modes. Consider, for example, the following add-with-carry-indexed instruction

$$\text{ADC} \quad \text{A BETA,X} \tag{6.11}$$

which appears in the 6800 assembly-language program of Fig. 5.31. This instruction is equivalent to the high-level-language statement

$$A := A + C + \text{BETA}[X];$$

Thus in (6.11) BETA denotes an array with index X; X also represents a specific CPU register called the index register. When programming in assembly languages that lack an indexed addressing mode, arrays must be handled in a less direct fashion than that of (6.11). For example, the programmer may substitute certain general-purpose CPU registers for index registers. The DE and HL registers serve this purpose in the 8080/8085 program of Fig. 5.47.

A composite data type commonly found in assembly languages but not in high-level languages is a stack. (A stack is an ordered set of data items that are accessed via one end of the stack, which is called the top of the stack.) The special instructions PUSH and POP are used to transfer data to and from the top of the stack. For example, PUSH A moves the contents of register or memory location A to the stack. The address of the top of the stack is computed automatically by the CPU and maintained in a special register (the stack pointer) for use by PUSH and POP instructions.

Although assembly and high-level languages differ significantly in the specification and processing of their basic data types, these differences can often be bridged by the judicious use of subroutines, macros, and other structuring facilities. Binary data types may be added to Pascal programs by using **type** statements to define them. Similarly a stack can be defined as a special Pascal data type, and procedures called PUSH and POP can be defined to transfer data to and from the stack. Array- or record-processing instructions similarly can be added to assembly-language programs. For instance, we could define a macro

$$\text{ADDM} \quad \text{XI,YJ,ZK}$$

in 8080/8085 assembly language to perform the matrix addition operation

$$X[I] := Y[J] + Z[K];$$

In general, such programmed operations and data types are less convenient to use and take more time to process than those that are built into the programming language being used.

6.2 PROGRAM DEVELOPMENT

The control programs of a microcomputer constitute a software system that is often of considerable complexity. As discussed in Sec. 1.4, an orderly design methodology is essential to the successful implementation of any complex system. This section examines the program design process, emphasizing the need for design methods that simplify program debugging and testing.

6.2.1 Quality and Cost

The success of a program design project depends on two main factors: the quality of the programs produced, and the total cost of producing them. Figure 6.8 lists some important criteria for judging the quality of a computer program. Foremost among these is the requirement that the program behave correctly, that is, that it meet its original specifications. This correctness criterion is more stringent in the case of programs than in most other systems because a minor design flaw such as an incorrect opcode or a displaced bit can result in total failure of the program. Program correctness is achieved by clear specification of the desired behavior of the program, careful and systematic implementation of the programming process, and thorough testing of the prototype design.

While all computer programs are required to produce correct results, the relative importance of the other quality measures listed in Fig. 6.8 depends on the type of program being designed and the way in which it is to be used. In general, it is desirable to maximize the program's execution speed, ease of use, and flexibility, while minimizing its utilization of memory space and other scarce resources in the host computer. These factors involve various trade-offs that must be evaluated in the context of the program being designed. To illustrate these trade-offs, we consider briefly the design of the control program for a hand-held electronic game.

The major design objectives for a typical hand-held game are small size and low production cost. To minimize size and cost, the controlling electronic circuits are usually

Correctness:	Does the program produce the desired results?
Execution speed:	Is the program fast enough?
User convenience:	Is the program easy to use?
Design flexibility:	Is the program easy to modify, extend, or transfer to a new computer?
Resource utilization:	Does the program make efficient use of the available memory, input-output facilities, and other system resources?

Figure 6.8 Criteria for measuring program quality.

implemented entirely in a one-chip microcomputer. Since the memory capacity of such a microcomputer is limited, say, to 4K words of program space, it is essential that the control program fit completely in the available memory space. The addition of an extra memory chip would add perhaps a few dollars to the cost of each unit. However, since production runs for electronic games may be in the hundreds of thousands or millions, an extra IC would add substantially to total production costs. Thus minimizing the control program size is an important design criterion in this case. Ease of use is also important, so considerable attention should be devoted to the design of the game's IO routines. A typical electronic game has a production life of only one or two years, and so there is probably no requirement for modifying or extending the original design, unless the manufacturer plans a "new and improved" version for future production. Whether or not program execution speed is a significant design goal depends on the complexity of the game. The microcomputer's reaction time is measured in microseconds, while that of the human interacting with it is measured in seconds. This million-to-one speed advantage of the computer means that relatively simple games can be implemented without encountering any speed problems. If a complex game such as chess is to be played, however, enormous numbers of computations must be made by the game for each of its moves, and fast program execution becomes very important.

The two main stages in the life of a program are the initial design phase and the production phase. Program production involves transfer of the program to a suitable storage medium, delivery to users, and installation. The cost of the program to its manufacturer is determined by several factors: the development cost c_D of the initial design; the cost c_P of packaging, distributing, and installing the program; and n, the number of copies of the program that are produced. To achieve a return on investment of r percent, the program must be sold at a price p given by the following equation:

$$p = \frac{\left(\dfrac{c_D}{n} + c_P\right)(100 + r)}{100} \tag{6.12}$$

Usually c_D is far greater than c_P. If n is very large, as in the case of the electronic game, then c_D has very little influence on p or r because the term c_D/n in (6.12) tends to zero as n increases. c_P is the dominant cost factor in such cases. On the other hand, when n is small (e.g., one), c_D becomes the dominant cost, making the minimization of program development cost a central design objective. Since computer programming is a labor-intensive activity, c_D is directly proportional to the number of person-months devoted to program development.

6.2.2 Design Process

Figure 6.9 lists the main steps in the development of a computer program. These steps constitute a particular instance of the general system design process described in Fig. 1.43. A rough indication of the relative cost of each design step was given in Fig. 1.44.

The first step in program development is to obtain or construct a clear set of design specifications for the desired program. These specifications should include a definition of

Design Step	Actions Required
Planning	Obtain specifications of the desired program behavior and quality. Estimate overall project costs and work schedule.
Preliminary design	Select the programming language(s) to be used. Identify the major program modules and the algorithms to implement them. Document by means of flowcharts or pseudocode.
Detailed design	Code the program module by module in top-down order using the chosen programming language(s).
Debugging	Identify and correct programming errors. Execute and evaluate the program using appropriate test data. Modify the program until satisfactory operation is achieved.
Final documentation	Complete the program documentation, including a user's manual and documents on program installation and maintenance.

Figure 6.9 Main steps in program development.

the computational tasks to be performed, the input-output formats to be used, and a description of the general environment in which the program is to be developed and used. The last includes the computer families that are to execute the program, the system software with which the program must interact, and the languages in which it may be written. In microprocessor programming projects it is important to know what design aids, such as microprocessor development systems, are available to the project. It is also important to identify, and to attempt to quantify, the program quality objectives, including execution speed, computer resource utilization, and design flexibility; see Fig. 6.8. Any requirements for compatibility with existing programs should also be determined. Finally, the budget and personnel available to the project should be identified, and a schedule for completing each of the steps in Fig. 6.9 should be worked out. The importance of careful initial planning should not be underestimated. It is not uncommon for a program to be designed that fully meets the initial specifications, but is found to be unsatisfactory because of omissions or inaccuracies in those specifications.

In the preliminary design phase, the major modules of the program and their relationships are determined. A program module should perform a clearly defined and self-contained task that can be implemented by a single subroutine, procedure, or macro. Typical tasks performed by a single module include:

1. Reading from an input device
2. Checking and updating status conditions
3. Computing a numerical function
4. Generating a pseudorandom number
5. Sorting a data set
6. Searching a data set
7. Reformatting or editing a data item
8. Writing to an output device

Unless a module is simple enough to be implemented by one or two instructions, it is necessary to identify an algorithm that implements it. For common programming tasks such as items 4 and 5, standard well-tested algorithms can be found in the computer literature (for example, Knuth, 1969). In more specialized applications, the programmer must devise his or her own algorithms, or consult a specialist in the relevant application area. Often the ultimate users of the program can provide the necessary advice on algorithm selection or design.

Flowcharts form a convenient tool for documenting the preliminary design of a computer program. The purpose of a flowchart is to present in easily readable form the sequence of operations to be performed by a yet-to-be-written program or program module. The basic symbols used to construct flowcharts have been encountered already in numerous examples. Some additional widely used flowchart symbols appear in Fig. 6.10. Generally speaking, the entries in flowchart blocks should be independent of the programming language being used, so that they may be understood by nonprogrammers. The entries should be written in ordinary English or mathematical notation, with careful abbreviation to make them fit within the narrow confines of the flowchart symbols. To prevent it from becoming unwieldly, the flowchart of a program module generally should be tailored to fit on a single page. And to simplify the interfaces between different modules, the number of entry and exit points of a flowchart should be kept small. A basic tenet of "structured" program design is that modules should have a single entry point and a single exit point wherever possible to enhance their intelligibility and simplify the debugging process.

An alternative to flowcharts favored by some programmers is *pseudocode,* which is a program-like description of an algorithm that makes use of English statements to describe operations that have yet to be programmed. The pseudocode typically has a framework of control statements written in the programming language to be used, so that a complete program can, in principle, be constructed by converting the English statements into real program code. Figure 6.11 shows both a flowchart (cf. Fig. 6.2) and a Pascal-based pseudocode description of the block search algorithm discussed earlier in this section. Note that the pseudocode description is a skeleton of the final Pascal program in Fig. 6.3. Flowcharts and pseudocode not only provide the basis for the detailed program design phase, but they also form a useful part of the final program documentation.

The detailed program design step is primarily one of mapping algorithms from flowcharts or pseudocode into complete source programs; this mapping process is called *coding.* It is best carried out in top-down fashion, by first coding the highest-level module, the main program P, then coding the modules $\{P_i\}$ called by P, then coding the modules called by the P_i's, and so on. Module code should be designed to be as readable as possible. Mnemonic names should be used for identifiers wherever appropriate. Statements should be indented and spaced in such a way as to clarify the internal structure of the module. The total length of the module should be restricted to about one page or 40 lines of code, again to simplify understanding and debugging. Liberal use should be made of comments in ordinary English to explain the program's behavior, particularly the actions taken when exceptional conditions occur. It is good practice to begin a program module with a block of comments that identify the module, state its purpose, explain its IO requirements, and define any constraints on its use.

Flowchart Symbols	Meaning

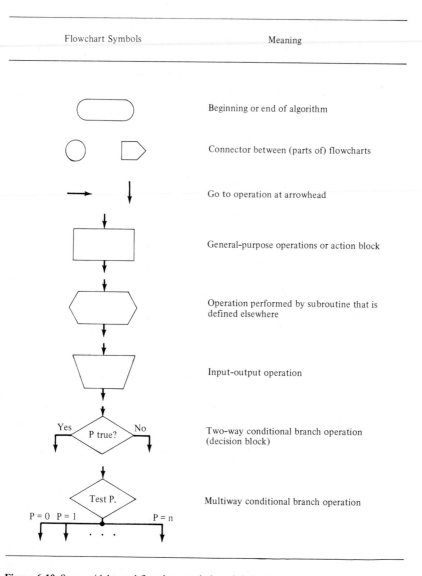

Beginning or end of algorithm

Connector between (parts of) flowcharts

Go to operation at arrowhead

General-purpose operations or action block

Operation performed by subroutine that is defined elsewhere

Input-output operation

Two-way conditional branch operation (decision block)

Multiway conditional branch operation

Figure 6.10 Some widely used flowchart symbols and their meanings.

Once a module has been coded, it must be tested and debugged. Since program modules are self-contained units, they can be subjected to considerable testing in isolation from the rest of the program. After careful manual checking, an attempt can be made to translate (assemble or compile) the module into object code. Many translator programs produce useful error message that can assist debugging. Successful translation indicates only that the program is free of syntactical errors. It remains to test the logic of the program. This is done by carrying out test executions of the (object) program using

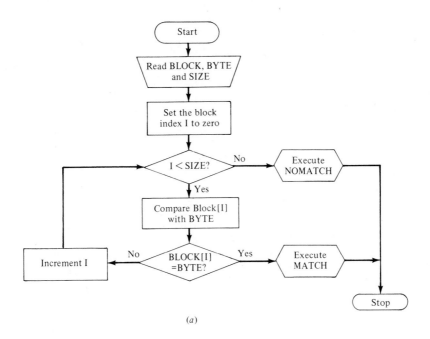

(a)

```
program SEARCH;
{Read BLOCK, BYTE and SIZE.}
{Set the block index I to zero.}
while I < SIZE do
    begin
    {Compare BLOCK[I] with BYTE. If equal, execute MATCH and halt.}
    {Increment I.}
    end;
{Execute NOMATCH and halt.}
end.                            (b)
```

Figure 6.11 Two preliminary design descriptions for the array-search programs: (a) flowchart; (b) pseudocode.

representative input data D_{in} for which the corresponding output data D_{out} is either known, or can be obtained independently of the program being tested. The actual results D'_{out} computed by the program are then compared with the expected results D_{out}, and any necessary corrections are made to the program when $D_{out} \neq D'_{out}$. It is generally not possible to test the program under all possible input conditions, so that the test data must be carefully chosen to ensure that all portions of the code are exercised and checked. In addition to checking computational correctness, it may be necessary to measure the program's size, speed, and resource utilization to ensure that it is within specifications. After a module has been adequately tested in isolation, it should be tested in conjunction with other modules to which it is linked. Finally, the entire program should be tested while running on a computer system of the type on which it will be normally used. Microprocessor development systems are particularly useful tools for debugging microcomputer software at all stages of its development.

The final step in the design process is to prepare the program documentation. The purpose of the documentation is to enable the designers and others to understand, use, and, if necessary later, modify the program in question. It should usually consist of the following items:

1. A narrative English description of the program describing its purpose and the computer environments in which it may be used
2. A user's manual with a complete description of system configurations, input-output formats, and other information needed to use the program
3. A set of annotated flowcharts describing the overall design of the program
4. A listing of the source program, which should be fully annotated by comment statements, describing the detailed design of the program
5. Information needed for program installation, modification, or other maintenance functions

6.2.3 Language Selection

Unless specified a priori, the programming language to be used must be selected during the preliminary design process. The choice is frequently limited by the availability of assemblers, compilers, MDSs, and other support facilities in the project design environment. In the design of a microprocessor-based system, programming language selection often reduces to a choice between a high-level language and assembly language. Figure 6.12 lists the main factors to be considered when comparing these two language types. In general, assembly languages are more difficult to use because of the low level of the instruction and data types available, and the necessity of understanding the internal structure of a particular target computer. Because they are easier to use and are machine

Factor	Assembly Language	High-level Language
Difficulty of coding and debugging	Higher	Lower
Program expandability and portability	Lower	Higher
Programmer availability	Lower	Higher
Program development time and cost	Higher	Lower
Source program length	Longer	Shorter
Object program length	Shorter	Longer
Program execution speed	Faster	Slower
Efficiency of input-output operations	Higher	Lower

Figure 6.12 Factors to be considered when comparing high-level and assembly languages.

independent, high-level languages are more widely known, and consequently experienced high-level-language programmers are often easier to hire. Assembly-language source programs tend to be longer and less readable than their high-level-language equivalents, and thus they are more difficult to debug or modify. They are also limited to use on a single family of computers. High-level-language programs are easier to debug and change. They are also portable in the sense that they can be used on any computer for which the necessary translation programs are available. Thus, when adequate support facilities are provided, a program development project can usually be completed more quickly and at less cost if a high-level language is used. However, in many microprocessor applications, the program quality criteria of high execution speed and efficient resource utilization cannot be met by using high-level languages.

While source programs written in high-level languages tend to be shorter than their assembly-language counterparts, the reverse is true of object programs. Because of unavoidable inefficiencies in the program compilation process, the object code generated from a high-level-language program is usually significantly longer; consequently it requires more program memory capacity in the target computer. Since assembly-language programs yield shorter object code, they are preferred for microcomputer applications where program storage capacity is restricted. Furthermore, the assembly-language programmer has much greater control over a computer's resources than a high-level-language programmer, and therefore can make more efficient use of them. This is particularly true of IO facilities, many of which are invisible to the high-level-language programmer. The combination of efficient resource utilization and shorter object code means that higher execution speeds can be achieved by using assembly languages. Figure 6.13 summarizes the application areas for which each language type is more suitable than the other. It should also be noted that it is possible to write some modules of a multimodule program in assembly language and other modules in a high-level language to exploit the advantages of each type of language.

6.2.4 Design Example

To illustrate the foregoing design issues, we now consider in detail a specific program design project. The problem is to produce a program that will convert an input temperature in degrees Celsius (centigrade) to the corresponding output temperature in degrees

Language	Characteristics of Suitable Applications
Assembly language	High-volume production with limited program memory space Maximum program execution speed required Simple bit-oriented operations only required Extensive use of complex or real-time IO operations
High-level language	Low-volume (e.g., one-of-a-kind), production without severe hardware cost constraints Software to be portable across several computer families Extensive use of complex numeric operations

Figure 6.13 Applications favoring assembly languages versus high-level languages.

Fahrenheit. This program is intended for an electronic thermometer that is controlled by a microprocessor in the 8080/8085 series. The use of two representative programming languages will be considered: the high-level language Pascal and the 8080/8085 assembly language.

The first step in the design process is to determine complete specifications for the behavior and quality of the desired program. The range of input temperatures expected and the accuracy with which the temperature is to be measured should be obtained. We will assume that the input temperature range is $-50°C$ to $+50°C$, and that only integer temperature values are to be used. Other design and program quality considerations such as design cost, execution speed, program size, and program flexibility will be considered later.

The next major step, preliminary design, includes selection of the computational algorithm and the programming language to be used. Perhaps the best-known temperature-conversion algorithm is embodied in the following equation:

$$°F = °C \times 9/5 + 32 \tag{6.13}$$

If Pascal is used to implement this equation, the result is the simple one-module program CONV1 appearing in Fig. 6.14. Equation (6.13) is implemented directly by the Pascal statement

$$DEGF := \textbf{round}(DEGC * 9/5 + 32);$$

where **round** is a function built into the Pascal compiler used that rounds off the possibly nonintegral expression DEGC * 9/5 + 32 to the nearest whole number. CONV1 also

Program CONV1 (**input, output**);

```
{ **************************************************************
*                                                            *
*   Programmer:    John P. Hayes, February 1981              *
*                                                            *
*   Purpose:       To convert an input temperature in degrees Celsius to the corresponding   *
*                  output temperature in degrees Fahrenheit.  *
*                                                            *
*   Method:        The standard temperature conversion formula is used:   *
*                     Fahrenheit = Celsius * 9/5 + 32        *
*                                                            *
*   Input:         Integer representing degrees Celsius       *
*                                                            *
*   Output:        Integer representing degrees Fahrenheit rounded off to the nearest integer   *
*                                                            *
************************************************************** }

var DEGC, DEGF: integer;
begin
  readln (DEGC);
  DEGF := round (DEGC*9/5 + 32);
  writeln (DEGC, ' deg. C = ', DEGF, ' deg. F')
end.
```

Figure 6.14 Pascal temperature-conversion program CONV1.

employs two other standard Pascal functions—**readln**, denoting read line, and **writeln**, denoting write line. **readln** and **writeln** are input-output commands used to transfer data between the Pascal program and designated IO files. The files to be used, in this case **input** and **output**, are specified as arguments in the first statement of the program. These file names may be assigned to various IO devices such as disk memories or interactive terminals. The statement

$$\textbf{readln} \text{ (DEGC);}$$

appearing in CONV1 reads a line from the input file **input**. This line should contain an integer value, say -25, which is to be assigned to the variable DEGC representing the input temperature. Similarly, the statement

$$\textbf{writeln} \text{ (DEGC, ' deg. C = ', DEGF, ' deg. F')}$$

transfers to the output file **output** a line of the form

$$-25 \text{ deg. C} = -13 \text{ deg. F}$$

in which the current values of the variables DEGC and DEGF are inserted at the specified points in the line; the items between apostrophes are transferred unchanged to the output file.

CONV1 is sufficiently simple that merely compiling and executing it with some test values of DEGC are adequate for testing and debugging. While this program is largely self-explanatory, it is desirable to include in it some in-source documentation that identifies the program and describes it in ordinary English. In CONV1 this documentation takes the form of a set of comments or preamble preceding the program proper, which specifies the programmer, the date programmed, the overall methods used, and the input-output data formats.

Very little development effort was required to produce CONV1, a direct result of using the high-level language Pascal. CONV1 is also relatively flexible. For example, it is not restricted to the given input temperature range $-50°C$ to $+50°C$. A typical Pascal compiler might use 32-bit words to represent integers, thereby allowing the direct use of numbers with magnitudes up to about two billion. Pascal also allows the programmer to treat multiplication and division as primitive operations; these operations are not available in 8080/8085 assembly language. However, the 8080/8085 machine-language object program obtained by compiling CONV1 is likely to be relatively long and inefficient. The compiler translates the multiplication and division operations into subroutines written in 8080/8085 machine code; these subroutines are typically obtained from a program library accompanying the compiler. Because they are general-purpose, the multiply and divide subroutines are likely to be unnecessarily long and complex for the very simple calculations required by Eq. (6.13). Furthermore, the compiler probably uses a number format such as a 32-bit integer for DEGC and DEGF. This means that the addition operation of Eq. (6.13) must be executed by a multibyte addition subroutine similar to that of Fig. 5.47. Consequently the compiled object program can be expected to contain general-purpose data types and arithmetic subroutines that make it much longer than the specific application requires. To minimize object program length and execution time, we must turn to assembly-language programming.

An assembly-language version of the temperature-conversion program can also be based on Eq. (6.13); this is left as an exercise (Prob. 6.35). Because of the fact that the 8080/8085, like most of the simpler microprocessors, lacks multiply and divide instructions, it seems desirable to avoid these operations entirely. We therefore consider a different approach based on the table-look-up technique employed in the ROM designs of Sec. 4.3.4. The key idea is to store the temperature-conversion data in the form of a table. The input temperature DEGC is used to construct the address of an entry in the table that represents the desired output temperature. This entry is then read, or looked up, to obtain the desired result. At first sight, it appears that we should construct a table that stores the output temperature DEGF for every input temperature DEGC in the desired range. Each entry is then computed in advance according to the equation

$$\text{DEGF} = 1.8 \times \text{DEGC} + 32$$

The table size can be halved by storing $1.8 \times \text{DEGC}$ for positive values of DEGC only. If DEGC is negative, then all that is necessary is to look up the table entry for $|\text{DEGC}|$, the absolute value of DEGC. This entry is then negated and added to 32 to obtain the value of DEGF. It will also be seen that it is simpler to use positive numbers as table pointers or addresses, since memory addresses in the 8080/8085 and other microcomputers are always treated as unsigned positive integers. We thus arrive at the temperature-conversion algorithm described by the flowchart of Fig. 6.15.

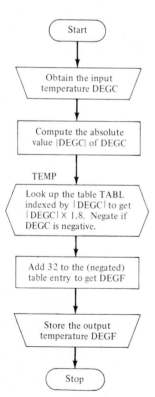

Figure 6.15 Flowchart for a temperature-conversion program based on table look-up.

We turn next to the detailed design of a program in 8080/8085 assembly language that implements the foregoing table-look-up algorithm. An examination of the flowchart in Fig. 6.15 suggests that the program should consist of the following three modules:

1. A main program
2. A subroutine called TEMP to perform table look-up
3. A table TABL containing temperature-conversion data

Figure 6.16 shows a complete source listing of an 8080/8085 program called CONV2 that implements Fig. 6.15. Note how the three program modules are clearly labeled and separated from one another. Each module consists of a sequence of assembly-language statements preceded by a block of comments that serve as the main documentation for the module. Comments are also sprinkled liberally throughout the program code to enhance its readability.

Before detailed coding begins, it is important to decide how the program modules are to be stored in the main memory of the eventual host computer. Figure 6.17 gives a memory map that provides this information. The main program is assigned the (low-order) starting address 0500_{16}, and is followed immediately by the code for the subroutine TEMP and the data table TABL. Since CONV2 includes subroutine call and return instructions that require a stack, the programmer must define a stack area in main memory. The stack can be regarded as a fourth program module. In the present example, the stack is assigned to a memory region immediately preceding the main program. Only the "bottom" of the stack (which actually has the highest address number) is defined explicitly in CONV2. Recall that 8080/8085 stacks grow downward in the direction of decreasing memory addresses. The maximum size of the stack is determined by the manner in which the stack is used during program execution. In CONV2 the stack is only used in a single subroutine call, and hence it need only store a single 2-byte return address.

When writing assembly-language programs for microprocessors, particular attention must be paid to the size and type of the basic data items to be processed. Often the standard data word size, 1 byte in the 8080/8085 case, is so short that a single item, such as a number, must be stored as a sequence of words. For the present problem, it is necessary to handle numbers in the range -50 to $+50$ to represent degrees Celsius; the corresponding range for degrees Fahrenheit is -58 to $+122$. A single byte in 8080/8085 binary code (twos complement) can accommodate numbers from -128 to $+127$. Thus all numbers can be represented by 1-byte binary words, and normal single-precision arithmetic can be used. A considerable increase in program complexity is required to perform multiprecision arithmetic, as the multibyte addition program of Fig. 5.47 suggests.

CONV2 contains several types of assembly-language instructions not previously encountered. The directive DB (define byte) is used to place byte-sized data values in main memory. The second statement of the main program, namely,

DEGC: DB -25

causes the number -25 to be placed, in 8-bit twos-complement form, in the main

```
;;;;;;;;;;;;;;;;;;;;;;;;;;;;;;;;;;;;;;;;;;;;;;;;;;;;;;;;;;;;;;;;;;;;;;;;;;;;;;;;;;
;                                                                              ;
;        Program CONV2                                                         ;
;                                                                              ;
;        Programmer:      John P. Hayes, February 1981                         ;
;                                                                              ;
;        Purpose:         To convert an input temperature DEGC in degrees Celsius to the ;
;                         corresponding output temperature DEGF in degrees Fahrenheit. ;
;                                                                              ;
;        Method:          The formula DEGF = DEGC * 9/5 + 32 is used. DEGC * 9/5 is stored in ;
;                         a data table called TABL which is read by a table look-up subroutine called ;
;                         TEMP. To reduce the size of TABL, only data for positive values of DEGC ;
;                         are stored.                                          ;
;                                                                              ;
;        IO data:         DEGC and DEGF are stored in main memory locations of the same name ;
;                         as twos-complement binary numbers.                   ;
;                                                                              ;
;        Constraints:     Input temperature range is −50 to +50 deg. C. An increase in this range ;
;                         requires TABL to be extended.                        ;
;                                                                              ;
;;;;;;;;;;;;;;;;;;;;;;;;;;;;;;;;;;;;;;;;;;;;;;;;;;;;;;;;;;;;;;;;;;;;;;;;;;;;;;;;;;


;        Main Program
;
              ORG        500H
;        (Additional input routines may be inserted here)
DEGC:         DB         − 25        ; Test value
DEGF:         DS         1
;
;        Read DEGC and check its sign
              LDA        DEGC        ; Read DEGC into the accumulator A
              CMA                    ; Negate A setting S to 0 (1) if DEGC
              INR        A           ;   is negative (nonnegative)
;
;        Compute DEGF
              LXI        SP, 500H    ; Initialize the stack pointer SP
              CALL       TEMP        ; Look up DEGC*9/5 in TABL and put in A
              ADI        32          ; Add 32 to A to form DEGF
              STA        DEGF        ; Store result in M
              HLT
;
;        End of main program
;;;;;;;;;;;;;;;;;;;;;;;;;;;;;;;;;;;;;;;;;;;;;;;;;;;;;;;;;;;;;;;;;;;;;;;;;;;;;;;;;;
```

(a)

Figure 6.16 Temperature conversion program CONV2 written in 8080/8085 assembly language; (a) main program; (b) subroutine TEMP; (c) data table TABL.

memory location whose symbolic address is DEGC. Since this statement occurs immediately after the origin statement

ORG   500H

```
; ;;;;;;;;;;;;;;;;;;;;;;;;;;;;;;;;;;;;;;;;;;;;;;;;;;;;;;;;;;;;;;;;;;;;;;;;;;;;;;;;;;;;
;                                                                                  ;
;      Subroutine TEMP                                                             ;
;                                                                                  ;
;      Purpose:        Table look-up. TEMP fetches an entry from the byte-organized table TABL   ;
;                      corresponding to the absolute value of DEGC and places it in reg. A. If   ;
;                      DEGC is negative, indicated by S = 0, then TEMP also negates A before      ;
;                      returning.                                                  ;
;                                                                                  ;
;      Method:         HL is used to store the base address of TABL. The absolute value of       ;
;                      DEGC is added to HL to obtain the absolute address of the desired entry    ;
;                      in the table.                                               ;
;                                                                                  ;
;      Inputs:         DEGC, TABL, A = −DEGC, S = 0 (1) if DEGC is negative         ;
;                      (nonnegative).                                              ;
;                                                                                  ;
;      Outputs:        The result is placed in the A register.                     ;
;                                                                                  ;
; ;;;;;;;;;;;;;;;;;;;;;;;;;;;;;;;;;;;;;;;;;;;;;;;;;;;;;;;;;;;;;;;;;;;;;;;;;;;;;;;;;;;;
;
;      Set DE to the absolute value of DEGC
TEMP:      LHLD      DEGC      ; Place (byte) DEGC in the L half of HL
           MOV       E,L       ; Move DEGC to E
           MVI       D,0
           JM        S1        ; Check sign of DEGC
           MOV       E,A       ; Negate DEGC in E
;
;      Construct absolute address of table entry and place in HL
S1:        LXI       H,TABL    ; Place TABL base address in HL
           DAD       D         ; Add DE to HL forming table pointer P
;
;      Read from the table into A. If DEGC is negative (S = 0) negate the result in A
           JP        S2
           MOV       A,M       ; DEGC is positive
           RET
S2:        MOV       A,0       ; DEGC is negative
           SUB       M
           RET
;
;      End of subroutine TEMP
; ;;;;;;;;;;;;;;;;;;;;;;;;;;;;;;;;;;;;;;;;;;;;;;;;;;;;;;;;;;;;;;;;;;;;;;;;;;;;;;;;;;;;
```

(b)

(Figure 6.16 Continued)

which specifies the start address of the object code, the assembler will make the symbolic address DEGC correspond to the physical memory address 0500_{16}. The data table TABL is completely specified by a simple sequence of DB directives, as indicated in Fig. 6.16c. The first entry 0 of TABL is placed in memory location TABL, the second entry 2 is placed in location TABL + 1, and so on. The 51st and last entry 90 is placed in location TABL + 50.

```
; ;;;;;;;;;;;;;;;;;;;;;;;;;;;;;;;;;;;;;;;;;;;;;;;;;;;;;;;;;;;;;;;;;;;;;;;;;;;;;;;;;;;;;
;
;    Data table TABL
;
;    Purpose:        Partial conversion of degrees C to degrees F. The I-th entry (byte) is the
;                    quantity I * 9/5 rounded off to the nearest integer. I runs from 0 to 50.
;
;
; ;;;;;;;;;;;;;;;;;;;;;;;;;;;;;;;;;;;;;;;;;;;;;;;;;;;;;;;;;;;;;;;;;;;;;;;;;;;;;;;;;;;;;
;
TABL:      DB           0, 2, 4, 5, 7, 9, 11, 13, 14, 16
           DB           18, 20, 22, 23, 25, 27, 29, 31, 32, 34
           DB           36, 38, 40, 41, 43, 45, 47, 49, 50, 52
           DB           54, 56, 58, 59, 61, 63, 65, 67, 68, 70
           DB           72, 74, 76, 77, 79, 81, 83, 85, 86, 88, 90
;
;      End of data table TABL
; ;;;;;;;;;;;;;;;;;;;;;;;;;;;;;;;;;;;;;;;;;;;;;;;;;;;;;;;;;;;;;;;;;;;;;;;;;;;;;;;;;;;;;
           END
```

(c)

(Figure 6.16 Continued)

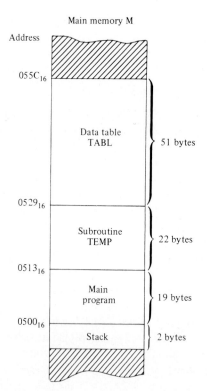

Figure 6.17 Memory map for the assembly-language program CONV2 of Fig. 6.16.

The third statement of the main program

DEGF: DS 1

is another example of a memory-allocation directive. DS (define storage) states that the number of bytes appearing in the operand field, in this case one, is to be reserved in a block with the starting address DEGF. The values to be stored in this block are not specified by DS; the block is merely reserved for future use. In the above DS statement, a single memory location is being reserved to store the result to be computed by CONV2.

The logic of CONV2 is fairly straightforward, and may be deduced by analyzing Fig. 6.16. The first step is to determine the sign of the input temperature. DEGC is loaded into the A register and negated via a logical complement (CMA) and increment (INR) operation. This places $-$DEGC in A, and sets the sign flag S to 0 if DEGC is negative; S is set to 1 otherwise. S $=$ 0 is used throughout CONV2 to indicate that DEGC is negative (see Prob. 6.22). Since S $=$ 1 normally indicates a negative number, this irregular use of S should be noted by appropriate comments. The table-look-up step executed by the subroutine TEMP is accomplished by constructing the address P of the desired table entry, and then transferring the entry to A via a move statement. P is obtained by adding |DEGC| to the base address TABL of the data table, and placing the result in the principal memory address register-pair HL. Note how the 8080/8085's only 16-bit add instruction DAD (add register-pair to HL) is used for this purpose.

The extensive amount of in-source documentation used in CONV2 should also be noted. As in CONV1, a long preamble identifies each program module, defines its purpose and method of operation, and specifies its input-output requirements. It is important that any special or hidden constraints imposed by the programmer or the program specifications be spelled out, whose violation could result in erroneous program execution. For example, the values of DEGC supplied to CONV2 must be confined to the range -50 to $+50$. If a value outside this range, say $+100$, is used, the program will run to completion without indicating an error. CONV2 will construct a pointer P $=$ TABL $+$ 100 that addresses a memory location in the unused region following the data table; (see Fig. 6.17), and hence produces a meaningless value for DEGF.

CONV2 can be tested by assembling it and executing it with representative test values for DEGC. Coding errors such as invalid opcodes or missing delimiters are usually detected by the assembler and reported to the programmer. Errors in the logical design of the program are detected by carrying out test runs after the program has been successfully assembled. This type of testing may be done using any 8080/8085-based computer. Alternatively, the test runs may be performed using a suitable simulation program. Figure 6.18 shows the output listing from a test run for CONV2 using the latter approach with a commercially available simulation program called Interp/80 (Intel, 1975b). This program simulates the operation of a typical 8080-based microcomputer. It was written in FORTRAN, and therefore can be executed by almost any type of computer. Interp/80 simulates the execution of 8080 machine code, and allows the user to monitor program execution in various ways. The actions taken by Interp/80 are controlled by user-supplied commands.

The commands given to Interp/80 in the CONV1 test run of Fig. 6.18 instruct it to load the object code for CONV2, initialize the simulated program counter PC to the

INTERP/80 VERS 1.6

$F = 1

LOAD 7 7.

91 LOAD OK

SET PC = 502H.

SET OK

TRACE 0 TO 1500.

TRACE OK

BASE HEX.

HEX BASE OK

GO.

```
CYZSP   A     B     C     D     E     H     L     HL      SP      PC
*0000  *00H  *00H  *00H  *00H  *00H  *00H  *00H  *0000H  *0000H  *0502H
LDA 500H
 0000  *E7H   00H   00H   00H   00H   00H   00H   0000H   0000H  *0505H
CMA
 0000  *18H   00H   00H   00H   00H   00H   00H   0000H   0000H  *0506H
INR A
 0000  *19H   00H   00H   00H   00H   00H   00H   0000H   0000H  *0507H
LXI SP 500H
 0000   19H   00H   00H   00H   00H   00H   00H   0000H  *0500H  *050AH
CALL 513H
 0000   19H   00H   00H   00H   00H   00H   00H   0000H  *04FEH  *0513H
LHLD 500H
 0000   19H   00H   00H   00H   00H  *E7H  *00H  *00E7H   04FEH  *0516H
MOV EL
 0000   19H   00H   00H   00H  *E7H   00H   E7H   00E7H   04FEH  *0517H
MVI D OH
 0000   19H   00H   00H   00H   E7H   00H   E7H   00E7H   04FEH  *0519H
JM 51DH
 0000   19H   00H   00H   00H   E7H   00H   E7H   00E7H   04FEH  *051CH
MOV EA
CYZSP   A     B     C     D     E     H     L     HL      SP      PC
 0000   19H   00H   00H   00H  *19H   00H   E7H   00E7H   04FEH  *051DH
LXI H 529H
 0000   19H   00H   00H   00H   19H  *05H  *29H  *0529H   04FEH  *0520H
DAD D
 0000   19H   00H   00H   00H   19H   05H  *42H  *0542H   04FEH  *0521H
JP 526H
 0000   19H   00H   00H   00H   19H   05H   42H   0542H   04FEH  *0526H
MOV AB
 0000  *00H   00H   00H   00H   19H   05H   42H   0542H   04FEH  *0527H
SUB M
*1010  *D3H   00H   00H   00H   19H   05H   42H   0542H   04FEH  *0528H
RET
 1010   D3H   00H   00H   00H   19H   05H   42H   0542H  *0500H  *050DH
ADI 20H
*0011  *F3H   00H   00H   00H   19H   05H   42H   0542H   0500H  *050FH
STA 501H
 0011   F3H   00H   00H   00H   19H   05H   42H   0542H   0500H  *0512H
HLT
HLT CYCLE 172
```

Figure 6.18 Test run for CONV2 using the Interp/80 simulation program.

490

address 0502_{16} of the first executable instruction of CONV2, and execute the program in trace mode, printing in hexadecimal form the contents of all flags and registers in the simulated CPU at the end of every instruction cycle. The final command GO initiates program execution, causing Interp/80 to generate one line of information on the CPU state after each instruction of CONV2 is executed. Other information, such as the contents of specified main memory locations, can also be provided by Interp/80 if requested. Thus from Fig. 6.18 we see that the simulated test run begins with PC = 0502_{16} and all other CPU registers set to zero. After execution of the first instruction

LDA   DEGC

we see from the Interp/80 run that A contains $E7_{16}$. This represents the test value of DEGC, namely, -25, because -25_{10} is equivalent to the twos-complement number $11100111 = E7_{16}$. Two instruction cycles later A has become $19_{16} = +25_{10}$ and S = 0, indicating that the negation of DEGC was carried out correctly. The remaining instructions of CONV2 are checked in a similar fashion from the Interp/80 output listing. After the ADI instruction has been executed, completing the computation of DEGF, we find A = $F3_{16}$, which represents -13_{10} and indicates that the correct result has been generated by CONV2. Additional test runs were carried out using other test values of DEGC, including zero and the boundary values -50 and $+50$. Since all gave correct results, a high degree of confidence can be placed in the correctness of CONV2.

In conclusion, we consider the pros and cons of the design approach implemented by CONV2. It is a relatively short program whose object code including the 51-byte table TABL is 92 bytes long. CONV2 is also fast; about 17 instructions must be executed to perform the desired temperature conversion. A program using multiplication or division instead of table look-up would probably be much slower. On the negative side, CONV2 was much harder to design than the Pascal program CONV1. CONV2 is also much less flexible. For instance, to expand the temperature range accommodated, the size of TABL must be increased. If the input temperature range exceeds -88 to $+55$, then 8-bit words are no longer sufficient for DEGC or DEGF. CONV2 would have to be rewritten completely to process multibyte number formats.

6.3 ASSEMBLY-LANGUAGE PROGRAMMING

We now examine in more detail the requirements and techniques for writing microprocessor programs at the assembly-language level. Examples are based mainly on the assembly languages of the 6800 and 8080/8085 microprocessor families introduced in Chap. 5.

6.3.1 General Features

The earliest digital computers were programmed directly in binary-coded machine languages. Assembly languages were soon developed to allow instructions to be coded using alphabetic symbols and decimal digits, which are far more convenient for human programmers. Assembly-language programs are, to a first approximation, symbolic and more readable versions of machine-language programs. As computer usage increased, programs grew larger and more complex, and the need was recognized for a way of constructing large programs from small independently written subprograms or modules. Thus features were introduced into assembly languages to permit program modules to be written as independent units that subsequently could be combined or assembled in various ways to form a single executable program. This assembly process is the origin of the term "assembly language" (Barron, 1969). At the present time almost every computer, large or small, is delivered with an assembly language and associated software. The assembly language is normally defined by the computer's primary manufacturer, and is unique to a particular computer family. Occasionally several different assembly languages may exist for the same machine. Although standards for assembly languages have been proposed (Fischer, 1979), there is little evidence that such standards are likely to be adopted by the computer industry.

A machine-language instruction generally consists of an opcode, which specifies the operations to be performed, followed by a list of operands thus:

$$\text{opcode} \quad \text{operand} \quad \text{operand} \quad \ldots \quad \text{operand}$$

To simplify hardware design, the lengths of the opcode and operand fields are usually multiples or submultiples of the main memory and word size, which in microcomputers is often 8 bits. The above format for machine instructions is mirrored directly in assembly-language instructions, which have the following general appearance:

$$\text{label} \quad \text{opcode} \quad \text{operand} \quad \text{operand} \quad \ldots \quad \text{comment}$$

The constraints imposed on the format and size of the various fields appearing in an assembly-language instruction vary from computer to computer. The fields must be written in a fixed order and be separated by various delimiters such as spaces, commas, or other punctuation marks. In some computers a more rigid format is used in which each field must begin in a fixed position or column within the instruction line. Only the symbolic name appearing in the opcode field is fixed for most instructions; the set of permissible opcode names are predefined keywords of the language being used. Fixed names are also assigned to the CPU registers; these names may be used in the operand fields. In many cases, however, the operands are defined by symbolic names introduced by the programmer. Similarly, a user-defined name may be used in the optional label field. The programmer may place any desired information in the comment field, which is an optional item in the instruction that is intended to enhance a program's readability by humans.

When an assembly-language source program is assembled into a machine-language object program, the opcode and operand fields of each instruction are translated more or less directly into suitable binary form. The binary forms to be used for opcodes are fixed; those used for programmer-defined symbolic names are determined by the assembler from its analysis of the program. The label field of an instruction is translated into the address of a memory location used to store the first word of the instruction during program execution. In most cases the assembler can compute the locations to be assigned to an instruction from the instruction's position in the program. Consequently the majority of assembly-language instructions do not require label fields. Comments in an assembly-language program have no effect on its object code. Figure 6.19 contains an

MOTOROLA M6800 CROSS ASSEMBLER, RELEASE 1.2

```
00001                          NAM    ADDD32
00002                      * M6800 PROGRAM TO ADD TWO 32-DIGIT DECIMAL NUMBERS
00003       0030       ALPHA  EQU    $30
00004       0010       BETA   EQU    $10
00005 0100                    ORG    $100
00006 0100  OC         START  CLC                    CLEAR CARRY FLAG (C := 0)
00007 0101  CE  0010          LDX    #16             LOAD INDEX REGISTER X WITH 16
00008 0104  A6  30      LOOP  LDA  A  ALPHA,X  A := M[ALPHA + X]
00009 0106  A9  10             ADC  A  BETA,X   A := A + C + M[BETA + X]
00010 0108  19                 DAA                    DECIMAL ADJUST ACCUMULATOR A
00011 0109  A7  10             STA  A  BETA,X   M[BETA + X]:= A
00012 010B  09                 DEX                    DECREMENT INDEX REGISTER X
00013 010C  26  F6             BNE    LOOP            BRANCH TO LOOP IF Z = 0
00014 010E  7E  010E    STOP  JMP    STOP            DYNAMIC PROGRAM HALT
00015                          END
```

SYMBOL TABLE

ALPHA 0030 BETA 0010 START 0100 LOOP 0104 STOP 010E

Figure 6.19 Assembly listing for a 32-digit decimal addition program written in 6800 assembly language.

assembly listing generated during the assembly of a 6800 program, which shows the correspondence between the assembly-language source code and the machine-language object code. (This program performs 32-digit decimal addition and is described in detail in Sec. 5.3.2.) The object code is listed in hexadecimal representation on the left of Fig. 6.19, and the source code, which has been slightly edited by the assembler, appears on the right; cf Fig. 5.32. The second column from the left lists the memory addresses to which the machine language instructions are assigned; the instructions themselves appear immediately to the right of this column. The assembler also creates a *symbol table*, which is shown in Fig. 6.19, that defines the correspondence between the symbolic names in the source program and the names used in the object program. Note that some object program names, such as 0030_{16} for ALPHA and 0100_{16} for START, are specified in the source program, while others, such as $010E_{16}$ for STOP, are computed by the assembler.

An assembly language contains various features that have no counterparts at the machine-language level. Certain commands called directives are provided for controlling the assembly process, and are not translated into machine code. Typical examples are the NAM (which merely serves to assign a name to the program for use by the assembler), ORG, EQU, and END directives appearing in Fig. 6.19. Assembly languages also allow the programmer to define new operations and opcodes. The main mechanisms for this are macros and subroutines, which are examined in detail later in this section. The macro feature makes it possible to define macro languages that are tailored to a specific application. By the skillful use of macro facilities, a programmer can make an assembly-language program take on the appearance of one written in a higher-level language. For example, the macro statement

IF_P   THEN_Q,   ELSE_R

has the opcode IF_P, and two operand fields THEN_Q and ELSE_R. It is designed to resemble, at least superficially, a two-way conditional branch statement of a type common in high-level programming languages.

Most assembly languages permit complex numerical or logical expressions to be used to identify operands. Consider, for instance, the 8080/8085 add immediate instruction

$$\text{ADI} \quad \text{KEY*2} - 16 \tag{6.14}$$

The arithmetic expression KEY*2 − 16 is evaluated by the assembler during the assembly process, and the resulting value is inserted in the operand field of the machine instruction into which (6.14) is translated. Thus if KEY has the value 20 when the translation of (6.14) begins, the output of the assembler is the machine language equivalent of

$$\text{ADI} \quad 24$$

As noted earlier, assembly languages were originally intended to aid program design by allowing programs to be composed from independently written program modules. An important aspect of module independence is relocability, which is the property of a program that allows it to be positioned anywhere in a computer's main memory space and still execute properly. Modules whose branch instructions use relative addressing only (see Sec. 5.2.2) are inherently relocatable, because all instruction addresses are computed relative to the program counter contents during execution. In other cases relocability can be achieved by modifying the address fields appearing in the object code immediately before it is loaded into memory for execution. This address modification can be carried out by a system program called a (relocating) *loader*.

6.3.2 Executable Instructions

The assembly language for any given computer includes a set of instruction types that correspond directly to the hardware-implemented instruction set of the computer's CPU. Instruction sets and their symbolic representation were discussed in detail in Chap. 5. Here we summarize their main features from a programming viewpoint.

It is convenient to group executable instructions into three broad classes: data-transfer, data-processing, and program-control instructions. The purpose of data-transfer instructions is to copy or move data unchanged from one storage location to another. The source and destination locations may be CPU registers, main memory locations, or IO ports. These instructions are identified by mnemonic opcodes such as MOVE, LOAD, STORE, READ, WRITE, IN, and OUT in assembly languages. Data-processing instructions perform arithmetic, logical, and other operations on various types of data. The instruction sets of most microprocessors can only process directly data that are in the form of fixed-point numbers or nonnumeric (logical) words. Some powerful microprocessors, such as the Intel iAPX 432, have instructions that operate on floating-point numbers and other types of data. Logical operations are performed bitwise, that is, the data in each bit position of the instruction's operands are processed independently. Data-processing instructions have opcodes such as ADD, SUB, MULT, DIV, AND, OR, XOR, and NOT. The execution of these instructions is monitored by CPU circuits that record, as status or flag bits, certain characteristics of the results produced. Status bits typically identify the numeric sign of a result, the occurrence of an all-0 result, arithmetic overflow, and the like.

The third group of instructions, program-control instructions, are used to control the sequence in which the instructions of a program are executed. A simple way to control the instruction sequence is to use unconditional branch instructions that load a specified branch address into the program counter; these instructions have mnemonic names such as JUMP and BRANCH. Conditional branch instructions test one or more designated status bits; a branch is made if and only if specified test conditions are satisfied. The special branch instructions CALL (or JUMP TO SUBROUTINE) and RETURN are used to transfer control between different programs or subroutines. These instructions are often designed to use stack memory for passing control information between programs.

A comprehensive listing of the instruction types encountered in microprocessors appears in Fig. 5.19. Figure 6.20 lists all the assembly-language instruction types (excluding assembler directives) and opcodes used in the Motorola 6800 microprocessor. Recall that the 6800 has a rather small set of CPU registers comprising two general-purpose data registers; the accumulators A and B; three address registers—the program counter PC, the stack pointer register S, and the index register X; and a set of six status bits. The 6800 employs memory-mapped IO, and therefore has no explicit IO instructions.

An assembly-language instruction generally contains an opcode field followed by a list of $k \geq 0$ operand fields or addresses. The main purpose of the opcode is to define the set of operations F to be performed during the instruction cycle. The address fields provide the CPU with information needed to locate some or all of the $n \geq k$ operands used by F. Often the opcode field also contains some implicit operand addresses, particularly those associated with CPU registers such as the accumulator, the program counter or the status register. Consider, for instance, the 8080/8085 instruction

ANA   B

which specifies the logical and operation $A := A \wedge B$. It contains one explicit address field B denoting the B register. The accumulator A, which stores one input operand as well as the final result, is considered to be addressed implicitly by the opcode ANA. While A and B are the major operands of this instruction, it also affects the 8080/8085 program counter and the flag bits CY, Z, S, AC, and P (see Fig. 5.44). Thus PC and the flags are also, in a sense, implicitly addressed by this instruction. A complete description of the effect of ANA B on the programmable registers of the 8080/8085 can be given as follows; this information is normally obtained from the microprocessor manufacturer's literature (Intel, 1979):

$$A_7, A_6, \ldots, A_0 := A_7 \wedge B_7, A_6 \wedge B_6, \ldots, A_0 \wedge B_0;$$
$$Z := \overline{A_7} \wedge \overline{A_6} \wedge \overline{A_5} \wedge \overline{A_4} \wedge \overline{A_3} \wedge \overline{A_2} \wedge \overline{A_1} \wedge \overline{A_0}$$
$$S := A_7,$$
$$CY := 0,$$
$$P := A_7 \oplus A_6 \oplus A_5 \oplus A_4 \oplus A_3 \oplus A_2 \oplus A_1 \oplus A_0,$$
$$AC := A_3 \vee B_3; \quad \text{(8080 case)}$$
$$AC := 1; \quad \text{(8085 case)}$$
$$PC := PC + 1;$$

Type	Opcode	Instruction
Data transfer	LDA x	Load accumulator x from memory, where x is A or B.
	LDy	Load address register y from memory, where y is S or X.
	STA x	Store accumulator x in memory, where x is A or B.
	STy	Store address register y in memory, where y is S or X.
	Tvw	Move (transfer) register v to register w, where vw is AB, BA, SX, XS, AP, or PA; P denotes the (processor) status register.
	PSH x	Push accumulator x into stack.
	PUL x	Pop (pull) data from stack into accumulator x.
	CLR	Clear accumulator or memory.
	CLf	Clear flag f, where f is C, I, or V.
	SEf	Set flag f, where f is C, I, or V.
Data processing	ADD x	Add (without carry) memory to accumulator x.
	ADC x	Add with carry memory to accumulator x.
	ABA	Add accumulator B to accumulator A.
	SUB x	Subtract (without borrow) memory from accumulator x.
	SBC x	Subtract with carry (borrow) memory from accumulator x.
	SBA	Subtract accumulator B from accumulator A.
	NEG	Negate (twos complement) accumulator or memory.
	INC	Increment accumulator or memory.
	INy	Increment address register y, where y is S or X.
	DEC	Decrement accumulator or memory.
	DEy	Decrement address register y, where y is S or X.
	DAA	Decimal adjust accumulator A.
	AND x	And memory to accumulator x.
	ORA x	Or memory to accumulator x.
	EOR x	Exclusive-or memory to accumulator x.
	COM	Form ones complement of accumulator or memory.
	ROL	Rotate left (through carry flag) accumulator or memory.
	ROR	Rotate right (through carry flag) accumulator or memory.
	ASL	Arithmetic shift left accumulator or memory (into carry flag).
	ASR	Arithmetic shift right accumulator or memory (into carry flag).
	LSR	Logical shift right accumulator or memory (into carry flag).
	CMP x	Compare accumulator x to memory and set flags based on the outcome.
	CPX	Compare index register to memory and set flags.
	CRA	Compare accumulators and set flags.
	BIT x	Compare accumulator x to memory and set flags.
	TST	Compare accumulator or memory to zero and set flags.
Program control	BRA	Branch unconditionally (uses relative addressing).
	JMP	Branch unconditionally (uses other addressing modes).
	Bcc	Branch if flag condition cc is true, where cc is CC, CS, EQ, GE, GT, HI, LE, LS, LT, MI, NE, PL, VC or VS.
	BSR	Call subroutine (uses relative addressing).
	JSR	Call subroutine (uses other addressing modes).
	RTS	Return from subroutine.
	SWI	(Software interrupt) Call subroutine and save registers in stack.
	WAI	(Wait for interrupt) Call subroutine, save registers in stack, and suspend execution until interrupted.
	RTI	(Return from interrupt) Return from subroutine and restore registers from stack.
	NOP	No operation.

Figure 6.20 Executable instruction types of the 6800 microprocessor.

The primary advantage of implicit addressing is that it allows shorter instruction formats in both the source and object programs. An instruction such as ANA B is referred to as a one-address instruction because it contains only one explicit address field, namely, B.

The addresses, both implicit and explicit, of an instruction specify operand values in various ways that are referred to as addressing modes. Each operand has its own addressing mode, so that several different modes may occur in the same instruction. Every addressing mode has two major characteristics: the number of levels of indirection used, and the manner in which the address information obtained from the instruction is modified to form a final or effective address.

An address ADR1 of an operand whose current value is V is said to be *n-level indirect* if it is necessary to perform a sequence of n read operations of the following kind to retrieve V.

$$ADR2 := M[ADR1];$$
$$ADR3 := M[ADR2];$$
$$\cdots$$
$$V := M[ADRn];$$

Alternatively, we could write:

$$V := M[M[\ldots M[ADR1] \ldots]]$$

The cases where $n = 0, 1,$ and 2 are the most widely used, and are called immediate, direct, and indirect addressing respectively. These three cases are illustrated in Fig. 5.12. The number of levels of indirection associated with a particular address may be indicated by a special (prefix) character in the address field as is done in the 6800. The 8080/8085, on the other hand, specifies indirection in the opcodes. Figure 6.21 illustrates these notational differences, and gives examples of all the addressing modes of the 6800 and 8080/8085.

Effective address construction takes several forms, but typically involves the addition of a second address field ADR2 to the address field ADR1 obtained from the instruction to form an effective address ADR thus:

$$ADR := ADR1 + ADR2; \tag{6.15}$$

Action of Instruction	Operand Addressing Modes	Instruction Formats	
		8080/8085	6800
A := B;	A,B both direct	MOV A,B	TAB[1]
A := 17;	A direct, 17 immediate	MVI A,17	LDA A #17
A := M[17];	A direct, M direct	LDA 17[2]	LDA A 17
A := M[HL];	A direct, M indirect	MOV A,M	
A := A + B;	A,B both direct	ADD B[2]	ABA[1]
B := M[17 + X];	B direct, M indexed		ADD B 17,X
PC := 17₁₆;	PC direct, 17₁₆ immediate	JMP 17H[3]	JMP $17[3]
PC := PC + 17 + 2;	PC direct, 17 relative		BRA 17[3]

Notes: (1) A and B addresses implicit. (2) A address implicit. (3) PC address implicit.

Figure 6.21 Comparison of addressing modes in the 8080 and 6800 microprocessors.

Various names are used to describe this process, depending on the source of ADR2, and the interpretation assigned to the address modification process. Often ADR2 is supplied by a CPU register R, thus making the effective address relative to R. The effective address can then be easily changed by changing the contents of R. In indexed addressing, a CPU address register called an index register stores ADR2, and an effective main memory address is constructed according to (6.15). In relative addressing, PC stores ADR2, and the effective address ADR is placed in PC. Figure 6.21 shows examples of indexed and relative addressing.

Another form of address modification found in some computers is the use of constants (usually one) to increment or decrement ADR automatically at some point during the instruction cycle. This is sometimes termed autoindexing. An example can be seen in the 6809 assembly-language program of Fig. 5.41 where the address $-X$ in the instruction

$$\text{LDA} \quad , -X$$

indicates that the contents of address register X should be (pre)decremented by one, and the result used as an effective memory address.

The motivation for addressing schemes such as indirect and indexed addressing is to allow a single address to refer to different data items at different times without having to alter the instruction that contains the address. The necessary address calculations are performed in the CPU during program execution. Indexed addressing is used in programs such as the addition program of Fig. 6.19 where ordered sets of words or arrays are being processed. Consider, for example, the following piece of 6800 code of the type found in this program:

$$\text{LDX} \quad \text{J}$$
$$\text{LDA} \quad \text{A ALPHA,X}$$

These instructions specify the following actions involving the index register X:

$$\text{X} := \text{J};$$
$$\text{A} := \text{M[ALPHA} + \text{X]};$$

Here indexing enables the LDA instruction to address the Jth item of the array ALPHA, where J is defined by the index register. Instructions such as INX (increment index register) and DEX (decrement index register) make it easy to step through and process all items in an array.

Indirect addressing may be used in much the same fashion to process arrays. Consider the following code for a hypothetical microprocessor with indirect addressing features:

$$\text{LD} \quad \text{R,ALPHA}$$
$$\text{ADD} \quad \text{R,J}$$
$$\text{LDA} \quad @\text{R}$$

The R register is used for indirectly addressing main memory, as the following equivalent instructions indicate:

$$R := ALPHA;$$
$$R := R + J;$$
$$A := M[R];$$

Thus the LDA instruction again has the effective address ALPHA + J; however, unlike the version with indexed addressing, an explicit add instruction is needed to construct this address. Figure 6.22 gives an assembly listing for an 8080/8085 32-digit addition program that is equivalent to the 6800 program of Fig. 6.19. (The design of the 8080/8085 program is covered in Sec. 5.4.3.) The 8080/8085 has no indexed addressing mode. However, unlike the 6800, it can address main memory indirectly using the DE and HL registers as memory address registers. These registers therefore are used to address ALPHA and BETA in lieu of the 6800's index register X. Note that this results in

```
8080 MACRO ASSEMBLER, VER 2.4        ERRORS = 0 PAGE 1
    ADDD32

            TITLE 'ADDD32'
         ;     8080/8085 PROGRAM TO ADD TWO 32-DIGIT NUMBERS
0030                ALPHA    EQU    30H
0010                BETA     EQU    10H
0100                         ORG    100H
0100    AF          START:   XRA    A              ; CLEAR CARRY (CY := 0)
0101    114000               LXI    D,ALPHA + 16   ; LOAD ALPHA + 16 INTO DE
0104    212000               LXI    H,BETA + 16    ; LOAD BETA + 16 INTO HL
0107    0E10                 MVI    C,16           ; C := 16
0109    1A          LOOP:    LDAX   D              ; A := M[DE]
010A    8E                   ADC    M              ; A := A + CY + M[HL]
010B    27                   DAA                   ; DECIMAL ADJUST A
010C    77                   MOV    M,A            ; M[HL] := A
010D    1B                   DCX    D              ; DECREMENT DE
010E    2B                   DCX    H              ; DECREMENT HL
010F    0D                   DCR    C              ; DECREMENT C
0110    C20901               JNZ    LOOP           ; BRANCH TO LOOP IF Z = 1
0113    76                   HLT
                             END
NO PROGRAM ERRORS


8080 MACRO ASSEMBLER, VER 2.4        ERRORS = 0 PAGE 2
    ADDD32

                             SYMBOL TABLE
*  01
A      0007    ALPHA   0030    B      0000    BETA    0010
C      0001    D       0002    E      0003    H       0004
L      0005    LOOP    0109    M      0006    PSW     0006
SP     0006    START   0100 *
```

Figure 6.22 Assembly listing for the 8080/8085 version of the 32-bit decimal addition program.

a slightly longer and slower program, since the DE and HL registers must be modified separately, whereas in the 6800 program, it suffices to modify the single index register. The 6800 also uses the X register as a byte counter, whereas a separate counter (register C) must be used in the 8080/8085 program.

The complexity of most assembly languages is a consequence of the large number of opcodes and addressing modes used. The number of different instruction types needed to construct a general-purpose computer is actually very small. The Motorola 14500 1-bit microprocessor examined in Sec. 5.1 has only 16 instructions. The Scientific Micro Systems MicroController (also known as the 8X300), an early 8-bit bipolar microprocessor, has only eight basic instruction types as listed in Fig. 6.23 (Liccardo, 1975). However, the effective number of instructions is increased somewhat by the inclusion of opcode modifiers, such as rotate operand *n* places, among the instruction's address fields. The 70 or so instruction types listed for the 6800 in Fig. 6.19 are more typical of microprocessor instruction sets. While a small instruction set is easier to learn, it requires multi-instruction programs to perform operations that can be carried out by a single instruction in machines with larger instruction repertoires.

6.3.3 Assembler Directives

Instructions such as those listed in Figs. 6.20 and 6.23 are called executable, because each assembly-language statement containing one of these instructions is translated into an executable machine-language instruction by the assembler. There is a second class of assembly-language instructions called directives or pseudoinstructions that do not directly produce executable object code. Instead they serve as commands to the assembler, and thereby direct the assembly process itself.

Directives are written according to the same format conventions as executable instructions; the following format is typical.

label   opcode   operand   operand   . . .   comment

Since a directive's opcode defines an operation that has no counterpart in machine language, it is sometimes called a pseudo-operation. The label field of a directive may be

Type	Opcode	Instruction
Data transfer	XMIT	Move (transmit) immediately addressed data.
	MOVE	Move data (uses other addressing modes).
Data processing	ADD	Add data from source to destination.
	AND	And data from source to destination.
	XOR	Exclusive-or data from source to destination.
Program control	JMP	Branch unconditionally.
	NZT	(Nonzero transfer) Branch if specified operand is nonzero.
	XEC	Execute instruction at specified address without altering the program counter.

Figure 6.23 Executable instruction types of the MicroController (8X300).

used as a symbolic address in the usual sense. However, it may also name one of the operands of the directive, such as the macro's name in a MACRO declaration directive. Like memory address labels, directive labels of this sort can be referred to from elsewhere in the program. As in the case of executable instructions, the operand field(s) of a directive may contain symbolic names or expressions that are evaluated by the assembler. Assembler directives may be classified into four major groups with the following functions:

1. Symbol definition
2. Memory assignment
3. Program structuring
4. Miscellaneous formating and bookkeeping

Figure 6.24 lists a typical set of directives which are found in the original version of the Intel 8080 assembly language (Intel, 1976a). An 8080/8085 program that employs most of these directives appears in Fig. 6.25.

A basic requirement of every assembly language is to permit the programmer to define arbitrary symbolic names for variables and their values. EQU (equivalent or equals) and SET are the main pseudo-operations provided for this purpose. The principal function of EQU is to equate two different names that are used for the same thing in different parts of a program (Barron, 1969). For instance, the directive

$$\text{ALPHA} \quad \text{EQU} \quad \text{BETA} \tag{6.16}$$

defines the new symbolic name ALPHA, and declares that it must always have the same

Type	Opcode	Directive
Symbol definition	EQU	Equate new and old symbolic names.
	SET	Assign new value to symbolic name.
Memory assignment	ORG	Origin. Assign starting address to program section.
	DB	Define byte. Define a sequence of data constants of type byte.
	DW	Define word. Define a sequence of data constants of type (16-bit) word.
	DS	Define storage. Reserve consecutive storage locations for a specified number of bytes.
Program structuring	MACRO	Begin macro definition.
	ENDM	End macro definition.
Miscellaneous	IF	Begin block to be assembled if and only if a specified condition is satisfied.
	ENDIF	End conditional assembly block.
	TITLE	Use specified title as a heading on each page of the assembly listing.

Figure 6.24 Assembler directives of the Intel 8080 assembly language.

```
                TITLE 'MACRO DEMONSTRATION PROGRAM'
;
;       8080/8085 MACRO 'ADDDN' TO ADD TWO N-BYTE DECIMAL
:       NUMBERS: OPND2 := OPND1 + OPND2
ADDDN    MACRO   OPND1, OPND2, N
         XRA     A                    ; CLEAR CARRY FLAG CY
         LXI     D,OPND1 + N          ; LOAD OPND1 ADDRESS
         LXI     H,OPND2 + N          ; LOAD OPND2 ADDRESS
         MVI     C,N                  ; LOAD BYTE COUNT N
LOOP:    LDAX    D                    ; A := M[DE]
         ADC     M                    ; A := A + CY + M[HL]
         DAA                          ; DECIMAL ADJUST A
         MOV     M,A                  ; M[HL] := A
         DCX     D                    ; DECREMENT DE
         DCX     H                    ; DECREMENT HL
         DCR     C                    ; DECREMENT C
         JNZ     LOOP                 ; BRANCH TO LOOP IF Z = 0
         ENDM
;
;       TEST PROGRAM
         ORG     100H
ALPHA    EQU     30H
BETA     EQU     10H
GAMMA    EQU     50H
N        SET     16
         ADDDN   ALPHA, BETA, N
N        SET     8
         IF      N - 4
         ADDDN   GAMMA, BETA, N
         ENDIF
         HLT
         END
```

Figure 6.25 8080/8085 assembly-language program illustrating the use of assembler directives and macros.

value as the previously defined quantity BETA. The SET opcode, on the other hand, is used to assign a temporary value to a variable. For example,

$$PI \quad SET \quad 3142 \qquad (6.17)$$

assigns the value 3142 to the new or old symbolic variable PI. This assignment subsequently may be changed by another SET directive such as

$$PI \quad SET \quad 1944 \qquad (6.18)$$

The assembler replaces all occurrences of the name PI in instructions falling between (6.17) and (6.18) by the value 3142. After processing the directive (6.18), the assembler begins to use 1944 as the value of PI until the next SET occurs. The difference between (6.16) and the following SET directive should be noted.

$$ALPHA \quad SET \quad BETA \qquad (6.19)$$

While directive (6.19) assigns the current value of BETA to ALPHA, later SET statements may change one but not the other, so that the names ALPHA and BETA are no longer synonymous. The foregoing distinction between EQU and SET is found in the assembly languages of such microprocessors as the 8080/8085; some languages follow different conventions.

Besides translating symbolic names into binary values, the assembler must also determine the absolute or relative locations in main memory to which instructions and data must be assigned for proper later execution of the program being assembled. The ORG (origin) directive specifies an absolute starting address to be used to store succeeding instructions or data. ORG effectively initializes a memory location counter LC maintained by the assembler during the assembly process. LC is continuously modified as the translation proceeds; it provides the memory-allocation data appearing in the leftmost column of the assembly listing in Fig. 6.22. After a k-word object instruction is created by the assembler and assigned to starting location LC, the assembler increments LC by k to obtain the location to which the next instruction should be assigned. ORG directives can be placed anywhere in a program, allowing the object program to be assigned to several disjoint regions of main memory, if desired. Special types of "relative origin" directives are employed by assemblers that support the generation of relocatable object code.

Two kinds of directives are used to allocate storage for constants. Directives with the typical opcode Dx (define data of type x) are used to command the assembler to assign a block of memory locations to store one or more specified constants of type x. The label of the Dx directive, either explicit or implicit, defines the starting address of the memory region to be used. Thus the 8080/8085 directive

DATA   DB   'AB&3'

where DB means define byte, causes the assembler to assign the character string AB&3, with each character encoded into an ASCII byte, to four successive 1-byte memory locations as follows:

Symbolic Address	Symbolic Contents	Hexadecimal Contents
DATA	A	41_{16}
DATA + 1	B	42_{16}
DATA + 2	&	26_{16}
DATA + 3	3	33_{16}

Figure 6.16 shows a lengthy table of numbers defined via the DB directive. The 8080/8085 directive DW (define word) is used to assign constants to memory in 16-bit units. For example, if ALPHA is a 16-bit address with the current value $01AB_{16}$, the directive

ADR1   DW   ALPHA

causes the assembler to assign AB_{16} to memory location ADR1 and 01_{16} to location ADR1

+ 1. To reserve a specific block of memory locations without defining their contents, the directive DS (define storage) is used. The 8080/8085 directive

DATA   DS   4

therefore reserves memory locations DATA through DATA + 3 for future use.

The third group of directives mentioned earlier is concerned with adding structure to assembly-language programs in the form of macros, procedures, and so on. Many assemblers have facilities for defining macros; they are sometimes distinguished by the term *macro assemblers*. Two special directives are required for a macro definition: a MACRO directive to mark the start of a block of instructions that compose the macro definition, and an ENDM (end macro) directive to mark the end of the definition. The MACRO directive also names the macro, and lists any parameters or operands that may be used when invoking the macro. In the 8080/8085 program of Fig. 6.25 a macro named ADDDN is defined that is a macro version of the multibyte decimal addition routine used as an example earlier (see Fig. 5.47 and 6.22). The definition of this macro begins with the directive

ADDDN   MACRO   OPND1, OPND2, N

The label field names the macro, while the operand list specifies three parameters. These are *dummy parameters* that are replaced by *actual parameters* each time the macro is invoked. Thus the macro call

ADDDN   ALPHA, BETA, N

causes the assembler to generate a copy of the body of the macro definition with ALPHA, BETA, and N replacing the dummy parameters OPND1, OPND2, and N respectively. Thus the basic macro may be modified via parameters each time it is used in the program.

Most assembly languages, such as those of the 6800 and 8080/8085, have no special directives for defining or delimiting subroutines. In these languages a subroutine or procedure is distinguished only by a symbolic name that is used as the start address of the defining code. The subroutine terminates with one or more return instructions. The programmer typically uses comments to convert a subroutine into a clearly defined module of the source program; see, for example, Fig. 6.16b. A few more powerful assembly languages, such as that of the 8086 microprocessor (Intel, 1978a), have directives for defining procedures with features resembling those found in high-level languages.

It is occasionally useful to make the assembly of a particular piece of source code conditional on certain specified conditions. This allows the code in question to be included in some assembly runs and ignored in others. Conditional assembly directives with an IF opcode are provided for this purpose. In the program of Fig. 6.25, the statement

IF   N − 4

causes the expression N − 4 to be evaluated by the assembler and compared with zero. If it is zero, the statements between the IF and ENDIF directives are skipped by the assembler; otherwise they are assembled in the usual fashion. Most assembly languages also include various directives for controlling the format of the output data produced during program assembly. The TITLE directive used in Fig. 6.25, for example, provides the assembler with a title that it uses as a page heading in assembly listings. 6800 assembly language has an OPT (option) directive that provides extensive control over the object code and assembly listing formats (Motorola, 1975a).

6.3.4 Macros and Subroutines

Macros and subroutines are the two basic mechanisms that allow an assembly-language programmer to treat a block of source-program instructions as a single higher-level instruction. Thus they enable the original instruction set supplied with the assembly language to be augmented by programmer-defined instructions, whose use can greatly simplify program coding and debugging. As discussed earlier, macros and subroutines differ primarily in the way they are translated into object code and subsequently executed. Each time the assembler encounters a macroinstruction in the source program, it inserts a copy of the block of instructions that define the macro into the object program. On the other hand, the assembler creates only a single object-code version of a subroutine. Links are established between the subroutine code and the points in the (main) program where it is to be executed by means of call and return instructions. The assembler translates subroutine call and return instructions into the corresponding machine-language instructions. There are no macro call or return instructions at the machine-language level. Once assembled, a macro becomes an integral part of the program that "calls" it. Figure 6.7 illustrates the differences in the object code resulting from the assembly of macros and subroutines.

A macro is defined by a listing of the instructions that compose it, enclosed in appropriate delimiter statements. These delimiter statements are directives that tell the assembler where the macro definition begins and ends. The 8080/8085 assembler directives MACRO (begin macro definition) and ENDM (end macro definition) appearing in Fig. 6.24 are typical. The begin macro directive is also used to name the macro itself and any parameters used by the macro.

Macros may be used to augment an assembly language by new opcodes for all types of operations, including data-transfer, data-processing, and program-control operations. Macros are particularly useful for introducing data-transfer instructions with addressing modes not available in the underlying machine language. The 8080/8085, for instance, has no indirect addressing mode that allows two memory locations rather than a CPU address register to be specified as the location of the address of an operand held in main memory. Suppose that we often specify a load operation that uses this type of addressing, which is represented symbolically thus:

$$A := M[M[ADR]];$$

A macro named LDA@ (load accumulator indirect) that implements this function can be defined as follows in 8080/8085 assembly language.

```
LDA@    MACRO    ADR    ; Begin macro definition
        LHLD     ADR    ; HL := M[ADR + 1].M[ADR]
        MOV      A, M   ; A := M[HL]
        ENDM            ; End macro definition
```

This macro is invoked by a statement of the form

LDA@   ALPHA   ; A := M[M[ALPHA]]

Here ALPHA is an actual parameter (a symbolic name for a 16-bit address) defined elsewhere in the program, which is used by the assembler to replace the dummy parameter ADR appearing in the macro definition. Note that LDA@ replaces only two executable instructions. Macros are typically used to replace short, frequently occurring pieces of code of this type.

As a second example, consider the design of an 8080/8085 macro that performs the memory-to-memory addition operation

M[OPND2] := M[OPND1] + M[OPND2];

where OPND1 and OPND2 are the addresses of two 1-byte decimal numbers stored in main memory M. A macro named ADDD that implements this add function can be defined as follows:

```
ADDD   MACRO   OPND1, OPND2   ; Begin macro definition
       LXI     D, OPND1       ; Load OPND1 into address register DE
       LXI     H, OPND2       ; Load OPND2 into address register HL
       LDAX    D              ; A := M[DE]
       ADD     M              ; A := A + M[HL]
       DAA                    ; Decimal adjust accumulator A
       MOV     M, A           ; M[HL] : = A
       ENDM                   ; End macro definition
```

To use this macro in a (source) program, we must write a statement of the form

ADDD   ALPHA, BETA

where the operands ALPHA and BETA are actual parameters that are substituted for the dummy parameters OPND1 and OPND2, respectively, by the assembler.

Figure 6.25 lists an 8080/8085 program containing an N-byte version named ADDDN of the above addition macro. ADDDN adds two N-byte decimal numbers by means of the multibyte addition algorithm used in various earlier examples. N, the number of bytes to be added, appears as the third member of the parameter list of ADDDN. Figure 6.25 also gives a test program that uses the macro ADDDN twice with various parameters. An assembly listing of this program is shown in Fig. 6.26 which

```
8080 MACRO ASSEMBLER, VER 2.4          ERRORS = 0 PAGE 1
   MACRO DEMONSTRATION PROGRAM

                         TITLE 'MACRO DEMONSTRATION PROGRAM'

            ;
            ;   8080/8085 MACRO 'ADDDN' TO ADD TWO N-BYTE DECIMAL
            ;   NUMBERS: OPND2 := OPND1 + OPND2
     1            ADDDN    MACRO    OPND1, OPND2, N
     1                     XRA      A             ; CLEAR CARRY FLAG CY
```

Figure 6.26 Assembly listing for the macro-demonstration program of Fig. 6.25.

```
        1                      LXI    D,OPND1 + N   ; LOAD OPND1 ADDRESS
        1                      LXI    H,OPND2 + N   ; LOAD OPND2 ADDRESS
        1                      MVI    C,N           ; LOAD BYTE COUNT N
        1              LOOP:    LDAX   D             ; A := M[DE]
        1                      ADC    M             ; A := A + CY + M[HL]
        1                      DAA                  ; DECIMAL ADJUST A
        1                      MOV    M,A           ; M[HL] := A
        1                      DCX    D             ; DECREMENT DE
        1                      DCX    H             ; DECREMENT HL
        1                      DCR    C             ; DECREMENT C
        1                      JNZ    LOOP          ; BRANCH TO LOOP IF Z = 0
                              ENDM
                       ;
                       ;   TEST PROGRAM
0100                          ORG    100H
0030           ALPHA   EQU    30H
0010           BETA    EQU    10H
0050           GAMMA   EQU    50H
0010           N       SET    16
        1              +       ADDDN  ALPHA, BETA, N
0100    1  AF          +       XRA    A             ; CLEAR CARRY FLAG CY
0101    1  114000      +       LXI    D,ALPHA + N   ; LOAD OPND1 ADDRESS
0104    1  212000      +       LXI    H,BETA + N    ; LOAD OPND2 ADDRESS
0107    1  0E10        +       MVI    C,N           ; LOAD BYTE COUNT N
0109    1  1A          + LOOP:  LDAX   D             ; A := M[DE]
010A    1  8E          +       ADC    M             ; A := A + CY + M[HL]
010B    1  27          +       DAA                  ; DECIMAL ADJUST A
010C    1  77          +       MOV    M,A           ; M[HL] := A
010D    1  1B          +       DCX    D             ; DECREMENT DE
010E    1  2B          +       DCX    H             ; DECREMENT HL
010F    1  0D          +       DCR    C             ; DECREMENT C
0110    1  C20901      +       JNZ    LOOP          ; BRANCH TO LOOP IF Z = 0
0008           N       SET    8
        1                      IF     N - 4
        2              +       ADDDN  GAMMA, BETA, N
0113    2  AF          +       XRA    A             ; CLEAR CARRY FLAG CY
0114    2  115800      +       LXI    D,GAMMA + N   ; LOAD OPND1 ADDRESS
0117    2  211800      +       LXI    H,BETA + N    ; LOAD OPND2 ADDRESS
011A    2  0E08        +       MVI    C,N           ; LOAD BYTE COUNT N
011C    2  1A          + LOOP:  LDAX   D             ; A := M[DE]
011D    2  8E          +       ADC    M             ; A := A + CY + M[HL]
011E    2  27          +       DAA                  ; DECIMAL ADJUST A
011F    2  77          +       MOV    M,A           ; M[HL] := A
0120    2  1B          +       DCX    D             ; DECREMENT DE
0121    2  2B          +       DCX    H             ; DECREMENT HL
0122    2  0D          +       DCR    C             ; DECREMENT C
0123    2  C21C01      +       JNZ    LOOP          ; BRANCH TO LOOP IF Z = 0
                              ENDIF
0126       76                  HLT
                              END
```

(Figure 6.26 Continued)

indicates how macros are handled by the assembler. Note that there is no object code corresponding to the macro definition statements. Each macro call statement in the source code gives rise to a complete copy of the macro object code with the appropriate actual parameters inserted. For debugging purposes, the assembly listing includes both the object code derived from the macro call and the equivalent source code with the actual parameters in symbolic form. Note also that although the symbolic address LOOP appears in the body of each copy of the macro, the assembler generates a different object-code value for LOOP in each case.

The foregoing examples illustrate the use of macros to specify data-processing operations. Macros may also be employed to enhance the program-control facilities of an assembly language, thereby making it more closely resemble a high-level language. For instance, the Pascal-type conditional branch statement

if P = Q **then go to** EXIT;

can be mimicked by the 8080/8085 macro statement

IFF   P, Q, EXIT

where the macro named IFF is defined as follows.

```
IFF    MACRO    OPND1, OPND2, ADR    ; Begin macro definition
       LXI      H, OPND1             ; HL = OPND1
       LXI      D, OPND2             ; DE := OPND2
       LDAX     D                    ; A := M[DE]
       CMP      M                    ; Compare M[HL] with A; if equal
                                     ;   (unequal), set Z = 1 (0)
       JZ       ADR                  ; Branch to ADR if Z = 1
       ENDM                          ; End macro definition
```

Since macro call statements are constrained to follow the format conventions of the assembly language for which they are defined, only a rough approximation to most high-level instruction formats can be achieved in this manner.

Like a macro, a subroutine is defined by listing the instructions that compose it. Unlike a macro definition, however, the definition of a subroutine is assembled directly into executable object code. To execute the subroutine, an instruction of the type CALL SUB1 is placed in the main program. Here CALL is the opcode of the host computer's built-in subroutine call instruction, and SUB1 is the name of the particular subroutine that is to be executed. SUB1 may also be equated with the address of the first executable instruction in the subroutine definition. CALL SUB1 is typically translated into a machine-language subroutine call instruction that performs the following actions:

1. CALL saves the contents RADR of the program counter PC in a predetermined storage location, usually the top of a stack area in main memory. RADR is the return address of the calling program.
2. CALL then transfers the subroutine start address SUB1 to PC, causing execution of the subroutine to begin in the next instruction cycle.

To return control to the (main) calling program, the subroutine must execute a return instruction that restores the previously saved return address RADR to the program counter PC.

Figure 6.27 shows an 8080/8085 subroutine named ADDDN designed to perform the same function, addition of two *N*-byte decimal numbers, as the ADDDN macro of

```
                TITLE 'SUBROUTINE DEMONSTRATION PROGRAM'
;
;       8080/8085 SUBROUTINE 'ADDDN' TO ADD TWO N-BYTE
;            DECIMAL NUMBERS: OPND2 := OPND1 + OPND2
;
;       SUBROUTINE DEFINITION
;            OPND1 START ADDRESS ASSUMED TO BE IN DE
;            OPND2 START ADDRESS ASSUMED TO BE IN HL
;            BYTE COUNT N ASSUMED TO BE IN C
                ORG       200H
ADDDN:          XRA       A              ; CLEAR CARRY FLAG CY
LOOP:           LDAX      D              ; A := M[DE]
                ADC       M              ; A := A + CY + M[HL]
                DAA                      ; DECIMAL ADJUST A
                MOV       M,A            ; M[HL] := A
                DCX       D              ; DECREMENT DE
                DCX       H              ; DECREMENT HL
                DCR       C              ; DECREMENT C
                JNZ       LOOP           ; BRANCH TO LOOP IF Z = 0
                RET                      ; RETURN
;
;       MAIN PROGRAM
                ORG       100H
ALPHA           EQU       30H
BETA            EQU       10H
GAMMA           EQU       50H
N               SET       16
                LXI       SP,500H        ; INITIALIZE STACK POINTER
;
;       FIRST CALL TO SUBROUTINE
                LXI       D,ALPHA+N      ; LOAD ADDRESS OF OPND1
                LXI       H,BETA+N       ; LOAD ADDRESS OF OPND2
                MVI       C,N            ; LOAD BYTE COUNT N = 16
                CALL      ADDDN
;
;       SECOND CALL TO SUBROUTINE
N               SET       8
                LXI       D,GAMMA+N      ; LOAD ADDRESS OF OPND1
                LXI       H,BETA+N       ; LOAD ADDRESS OF OPND2
                MVI       C,N            ; LOAD BYTE COUNT N = 8
                CALL      ADDDN
;
RADR:           NOP                      ; RESERVED FOR FUTURE USE
                HLT                      ; HALT
                END
```

Figure 6.27 8080/8085 program illustrating the use of subroutines.

Fig. 6.25. The main program of Fig. 6.27 contains two calls to the ADDDN subroutine using different sets of parameters. Since this assembly language does not allow parameters to be included in subroutine call instructions, explicit instructions must be written to transfer actual parameters to the subroutine. In the present example, several data-transfer instructions (LXI and MVI) are placed in the main program for this purpose immediately in front of the subroutine calls. Figure 6.28 is an assembly listing for this program. Observe the differences between the object code associated with the subroutine of Fig. 6.28 and the object code for the equivalent macro program appearing in Fig. 6.26.

Figure 6.29 illustrates the way call and return instructions are used to link a main program and a subroutine for the case of an 8080/8085-based microcomputer that is executing the program of Fig. 6.28. Like most microprocessors, the 8080/8085 supports a main-memory stack that is controlled by a stack pointer register SP in the CPU. The stack is intended for return address storage and is used automatically by all subroutine call and return instructions. A call pushes the return address from the program counter PC into the stack, while a return instruction pops the stack back into PC. After each 1-byte portion of an instruction has been fetched from M by the CPU, PC is automatically incremented by one. Thus after all 3 bytes (the opcode byte CALL and the 2-byte address ADDDN) of the second call instruction appearing in Fig. 6.28 have been fetched by the CPU, the computer is in the state depicted symbolically by Fig. 6.29a. PC stores the next sequential address RADR occurring in the main program and SP contains the current top-of-the-stack address 0500_{16}. Execution of CALL causes RADR to be pushed from PC into the stack, an operation that is implemented by two 1-byte memory write cycles. SP is decremented automatically during the push operation to provide the addresses needed for writing into the stack. Next the start address ADDDN of the subroutine is transferred from the CPU address buffer register to PC, resulting in the situation depicted in Fig. 6.29b. Execution of the subroutine then proceeds until the RET (return) instruction is reached. RET pops the stack into PC, thereby returning control to the instruction labeled RADR in the main program.

As the multibyte addition routines used in Figs. 6.25 and 6.27 suggest, it is generally possible to implement any function either as a macro or as a subroutine. It thus is natural to ask how one decides which of these program structures to use in a given situation. No simple answer can be given, since macros and subroutines affect several important program quality criteria in different ways. The affected criteria include:

1. Object program size
2. Program execution speed
3. Ease of programming
4. Program modularity

To illustrate the trade-offs involved, suppose that a block of code B in some program P is a candidate for definition as a macro M(B) or a subroutine S(B). Assume that B and M(B) contain n executable instructions, all of which are executed each time the macro is invoked. It is reasonable to assume that each time S(B) is used, $n + 2$ instructions must be executed, including a call and a return instruction not required by M(B). Let k be the number of times B must be executed when P is run. Finally, let us assume that the

```
                              TITLE 'SUBROUTINE DEMONSTRATION PROGRAM'

                  ;
                  ;   8080/8085 SUBROUTINE 'ADDDN' TO ADD TWO N-BYTE
                  ;      DECIMAL NUMBERS: OPND2 := OPND1 + OPND2
                  ;
                  ;   SUBROUTINE DEFINITION
                  ;      OPND1 START ADDRESS ASSUMED TO BE IN DE
                  ;      OPND2 START ADDRESS ASSUMED TO BE IN HL
                  ;      BYTE COUNT N ASSUMED TO BE IN C
0200                           ORG    200H
0200  AF          ADDDN:       XRA    A            ; CLEAR CARRY FLAG CY
0201  1A          LOOP:        LDAX   D            ; A := M[DE]
0202  8E                       ADC    M            ; A := A + CY + M[HL]
0203  27                       DAA                 ; DECIMAL ADJUST A
0204  77                       MOV    M,A          ; M[HL] := A
0205  1B                       DCX    D            ; DECREMENT DE
0206  2B                       DCX    H            ; DECREMENT HL
0207  0D                       DCR    C            ; DECREMENT C
0208  C20102                   JNZ    LOOP         ; BRANCH TO LOOP IF Z = 0
020B  C9                       RET                 ; RETURN

                  ;
                  ;      MAIN PROGRAM
0100                           ORG    100H
0030              ALPHA        EQU    30H
0010              BETA         EQU    10H
0050              GAMMA        EQU    50H
0010              N            SET    16
0100  310005                   LXI    SP,500H      ; INITIALIZE STACK POINTER

                  ;
                  ;      FIRST CALL TO SUBROUTINE
0103  114000                   LXI    D,ALPHA+N    ; LOAD ADDRESS OF OPND1
0106  212000                   LXI    H,BETA+N     ; LOAD ADDRESS OF OPND2
0109  0E10                     MVI    C,N          ; LOAD BYTE COUNT N = 16
010B  CD0002                   CALL   ADDDN

                  ;
                  ;      SECOND CALL TO SUBROUTINE
0008                           SET    8
010E  115800                   LXI    D,GAMMA+N    ; LOAD ADDRESS OF OPND1
0111  211800                   LXI    H,BETA+N     ; LOAD ADDRESS OF OPND2
0114  0E08                     MVI    C,N          ; LOAD BYTE COUNT N = 8
0116  CD0002                   CALL   ADDDN
                  ;
0119  00          RADR:        NOP                 ; RESERVED FOR FUTURE USE
011A  76                       HLT                 ; HALT
                               END
```

Figure 6.28 Assembly listing of the subroutine demonstration program of Fig. 6.27.

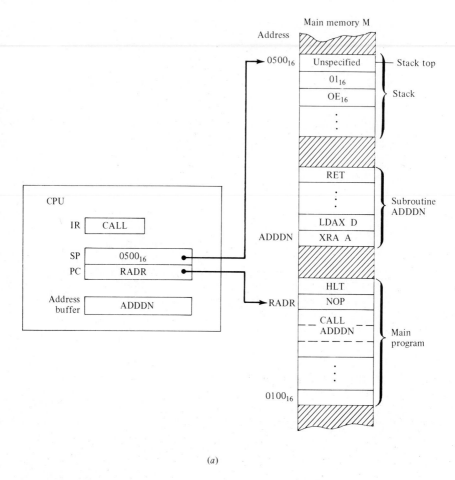

(a)

Figure 6.29 Microcomputer state during the execution of the program of Fig. 6.28: (a) immediately after fetching the second CALL instruction; (b) immediately after executing this instruction.

instructions appearing in P have an average length of p words and an average execution time of t seconds. Thus the impact of M(B) or S(B) on object program length and program execution time can be summarized as follows:

	Using Macro M(B)	Using Subroutine S(B)
Object code (words) due to B:	knp	$(n + 2k)p$
Execution time (seconds) due to B:	knt	$k(n + 2)t$

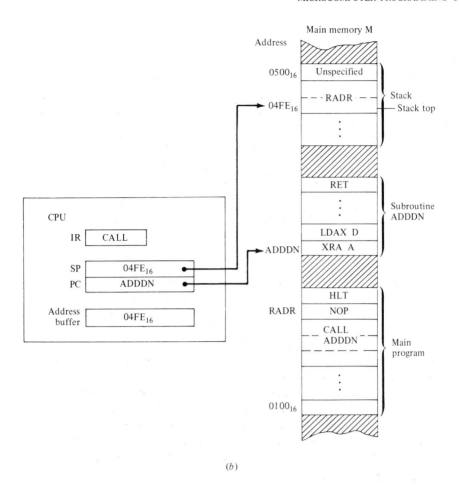

(b)

(Figure 6.29 Continued)

Clearly the version of P that uses the subroutine S(B) is slower by $2kt$ seconds, due to the overhead of executing subroutine call and return instructions. However, the length of the object code for the subroutine version of P is less than that of the macro version if the following inequality is satisfied.

$$kn > n + 2k \qquad (6.20)$$

Inequality (6.20) holds for all k only if $n \geq 3$. Thus for very short routines consisting of one or two instructions, macros always produce shorter object code than subroutines. The contribution of macros to the length of P increases very rapidly as k and n increase. Consequently, if k and n are both fairly large, shorter object code is obtained by using subroutines. For example, if $k = n = 8$, $knp = 64p$ words for the macro version of P, whereas $(n + 2k)p = 24p$ words for the subroutine version. However, it should be noted that the subroutine version requires additional storage space for return address storage.

Macros and subroutines should also be compared from the viewpoint of programming ease. Macros generally allow high-level instructions to be written in a fairly natural form with a list of parameters following an opcode in a macro call statement. The task of substituting actual for dummy parameters is done by the assembler. Assembly languages rarely permit parameters to be included in subroutine call statements; hence explicit instructions must be used for parameter passing. (This important issue is examined in the next subsection.) Macro statements, therefore, may be slightly more readable and less error-prone than the corresponding subroutine constructions (cf. Figs. 6.25 and 6.27). Macros and subroutines both contribute to the design of programs in small independent units or modules at the source program level. As discussed in Sec. 6.2, the use of such modules has an important bearing on program quality and development costs. However, only subroutines contribute to the modularity of the object program. After assembly, the identity of individual macros is essentially lost. A subroutine retains its identity at the machine-language level, and may be modified or relocated independently of the programs that call it.

6.3.5 Subroutine Design

Because they constitute self-contained executable program modules at both the assembly-language and machine-language levels, subroutines are probably the most important structuring device for computer programs. As the various examples encountered earlier indicate, a subroutine is entered via a call instruction executed by the calling (main) program, and it is exited via a return instruction executed by the subroutine itself. The call instruction saves the current contents of the program counter PC, which are used as a return address to the calling program. A LIFO stack implemented in the main memory M is the most convenient place for storing return addresses. Most microprocessors, including the 8080/8085 and the 6800, have stack-support facilities for this purpose.

Besides saving PC when a subroutine is called, it may be necessary to save other CPU registers whose contents are required by the calling program after the subroutine has been executed. Again a stack is the most convenient temporary storage mechanism for saving these registers. To save a register R in the stack, an instruction of the type

PUSH R

is placed at the beginning of the code defining the subroutine. R can be subsequently restored to its original state by executing

POP R

immediately before a return is made to the main program. Consider again the subroutine ADDDN appearing in the 8080/8085 program of Fig. 6.27. ADDDN affects almost all the CPU registers, including the status (flag) register. To save the complete CPU state in the stack on entering ADDDN, its first executable instruction should be replaced by the following code:

```
ADDDN:   PUSH   PSW   ; Push 2-byte "program status" word consisting
                      ;  of the accumulator A and the status (flag)
                      ;  register into the stack
```

```
PUSH   B      ; Push register-pair BC into the stack
PUSH   D      ; Push register-pair DE into the stack
PUSH   H      ; Push register-pair HL into the stack
XRA    A      ; Clear carry flag CY
```

To restore the state of these registers before returning to the calling program, the final return instruction should be preceded by

```
POP    H      ; Pop the stack into register-pair HL
POP    D      ; Pop the stack into register-pair DE
POP    B      ; Pop the stack into register-pair BC
POP    PSW    ; Pop the stack into A and the flag register
```

Note that the sequence of pop addresses is the reverse of the push sequence, reflecting the last-in first-out access method of the stack. Unlike the 8080/8085, the 6800 has a special call instruction named SWI (software interrupt), which automatically saves all CPU registers, including PC, in the stack. A corresponding return instruction RTI (return from interrupt) restores all the CPU registers from the stack.

Another key issue in subroutine design is parameter passing, which refers to the method used to transfer data representing arguments or parameters of the subroutine from the calling program to the subroutine. This can be done directly in the call statement in most high-level languages. For example, the FORTRAN call statement

CALL (PARAM)

includes the actual parameter PARAM, which is then used to replace the corresponding dummy parameter in the subroutine definition. Most assembly languages, on the other hand, do not permit a parameter list to be included in a call instruction. Hence the programmer must write instructions to implement the passing of parameters to the subroutine being called. For example, in the program of Fig. 6.28 the first subroutine call instruction is preceded by three data-transfer instructions

```
LXI    D,ALPHA + N
LXI    H,BETA + N
MVI    C,N
```

whose purpose is to transfer the 2-byte address parameters ALPHA + N and BETA + N and the 1-byte integer parameter N to the subroutine ADDDN.

The essence of parameter passing is for the calling program to place in a communication area C that is known to the subroutine either the values of the actual parameters to be passed, or address information from which the subroutine can determine their location. Figure 6.30 summarizes four of the most useful methods for passing parameters to subroutines. These methods differ principally in the choice of C, the communication area, which can be in the CPU, in a data area of M, in the stack, or in the calling program itself. Note that C can be used in a similar fashion to transfer results from the subroutine back to the calling program.

Perhaps the simplest and fastest way to pass parameters is to use CPU registers to hold the parameter values. This is done in the case of the byte count parameter N in the program of Fig. 6.27. An instruction in the main program simply places the current value

Communication Area C	Actions by Main Program	Actions by Subroutine
CPU registers	Place parameter values in CPU registers	Read CPU registers
Data area in M	Place parameter address in CPU register R	Read M using R as address register
Stack in M	Push parameter values into stack	Pop stack
Main program in M	None; parameter values are listed as data in the main program	Read data from the main program

Figure 6.30 Some techniques for passing parameters to a subroutine.

of N in the C register, which the subroutine ADDDN then uses as a byte count register. The main limitation on using CPU registers to store parameter values is the small number of CPU registers available in most microprocessors. If the operand set is too large to be stored in the CPU, then it can be stored in a data area of main memory M. In that case it is sufficient for the main program to pass the address and, if necessary, the size of the data area to the subroutine; this address information can then be passed via CPU registers. The subroutine ADDDN of Fig. 6.27 is designed to process two N-byte numeric operands. Since the 8080/8085's CPU storage capacity is too small to store these operands for most values of N, the operands in question are stored in M in two data areas whose start addresses are passed to the subroutine via the address registers DE and HL. As noted above, the size of these data areas is passed to the subroutine via the C register.

Passing parameters to subroutines written in 6800 assembly language presents some problems, because the CPU contains so few registers, either for holding parameter values or for holding the addresses of parameters whose values are in M. Furthermore the 6800 instruction types for transferring data between the CPU and M are quite restrictive (see Fig. 6.20). For example, there are no push or pop instructions that apply to 16-bit addresses. To illustrate these difficulties, consider the task of writing a 6800 version of the N-byte decimal addition subroutine ADDDN considered above. Figure 6.19 lists a 6800 decimal addition program that might be taken as a starting point for designing the subroutine ADDDN. The addresses ALPHA and BETA in this program correspond to the OPND1 and OPND2 parameters used in ADDDN. ALPHA and BETA are fixed address fields of instructions in the program of Fig. 6.19. They cannot be modified as required for parameter passing without modifying the instructions themselves during execution, an extremely undesirable procedure. As in the 8080/8085 version of ADDDN, it would be useful to have two CPU registers to store the addresses ALPHA and BETA; however, only one general-purpose address register, the index register X, is available in the 6800. Thus it appears to be necessary to use additional locations in M as address registers, and pass parameter addresses via M.

Figure 6.31 lists a 6800 version of the ADDDN subroutine based on the above considerations. Space is reserved at the start of the subroutine for storing the two main address parameters OPND1 and OPND2. The 6800's RMB (reserve memory bytes) directive is equivalent to the 8080/8085's DS (define storage) directive; see Fig. 6.24. The index register X is used as an ordinary address register to access the data bytes addressed by the contents of the reserved memory locations. Since the 6800 has no

```
              NAM        SUBROUTINE DEMONSTRATION PROGRAM NO. 2
*
*     6800 SUBROUTINE 'ADDDN' TO ADD TWO N-DIGIT DECIMAL NUMBERS:
*          OPND2 := OPND1 + OPND2
*
*     SUBROUTINE DEFINITION
*          OPND1 START ADDRESS ASSUMED TO BE IN MEMORY LOCATION OPND1
*          OPND2 START ADDRESS ASSUMED TO BE IN MEMORY LOCATION OPND2
*          BYTE COUNT N ASSUMED TO BE IN CPU REGISTER B
              ORG        $200
OPND1    RMB        2              RESERVE 2 BYTES FOR OPND1 ADDRESS
OPND2    RMB        2              RESERVE 2 BYTES FOR OPND2 ADDRESS
ADDDN    CLC                       CLEAR CARRY FLAG C
LOOP     LDX        OPND1          X := M[OPND1]
         LDA   A    #0,X           A := M[X]
         DEX                       DECREMENT OPND1
         STX        OPND1          SAVE NEW VALUE OF OPND1
         LDX        OPND2          X:= M[OPND2]
         ADC   A    #0,X           A := A + C + M[X]
         DAA                       DECIMAL ADJUST A
         STA   A    #0,X           M[X] := A
         DEX                       DECREMENT OPND2
         STX        OPND2          SAVE NEW VALUE OF OPND2
         DEC        B              DECREMENT B
         BNE        LOOP           BRANCH TO LOOP IF Z = 0
         RTS                       RETURN FROM SUBROUTINE
*
*     MAIN PROGRAM
              ORG        $100
ALPHA    EQU        $30
BETA     EQU        $10
GAMMA    EQU        $50
N        EQU        16
         LDS        $500           INITIALIZE STACK POINTER
*
*     FIRST CALL TO SUBROUTINE
         LDX        #ALPHA+N       )
         STX        OPND1           )
         LDX        #BETA+N          )  PASS PARAMETERS
         STX        OPND2           )
         LDA   B    #N             )
         JSR        ADDDN          CALL (JUMP TO SUBROUTINE)
*
*     SECOND CALL TO SUBROUTINE
NO       EQU        8
         LDX        #GAMMA+NO      )
         STX        OPND1           )
         LDX        #BETA+NO          )  PASS PARAMETERS
         STX        OPND2           )
         LDA   B    #NO            )
         JSR        ADDDN          CALL (JUMP TQ SUBROUTINE)
*
RADR     NOP                       RESERVED FOR FUTURE USE
STOP     JMP        STOP           DYNAMIC HALT
         END
```

Figure 6.31 6800 program containing a subroutine ADDDN.   517

indirect addressing modes, it is necessary to load X directly from OPND1 and OPND2, and then use a special case of indexed addressing to employ X as an address register. For example, the instruction

$$\text{STA} \quad \text{A} \quad \#0,\text{X}$$

computes the effective address $0 + X = X$ and thus performs the store accumulator operation $M[X] := A$. After each use of X for accessing an operand, it is decremented, and the new address value is saved in M. Because of these extra load and store operations, the 6800 ADDDN subroutine is significantly longer and slower than the comparable nonsubroutine 6800 program (Fig. 6.19) and the 8080/8085 version of ADDDN (Fig. 6.27).

The third technique for parameter passing listed in Fig. 6.30 uses the same stack that is used for storing return addresses and other saved data as a communication area for parameter values. The parameters to be passed are pushed by the main program before the subroutine is called; the subroutine then obtains the parameters by executing an appropriate sequence of pop instructions. Neither the 8080/8085 nor the 6800 provides very good support for this method of parameter passing. For example, neither microprocessor allows immediate addresses or direct memory addresses to be used with push or pop. Thus to push an immediate address ALPHA in an 8080/8085 program requires two instructions, such as

```
LXI     D, ALPHA      ; Load immediate data ALPHA into DE
PUSH    D             ; Push register-pair DE into stack
```

Even more instructions are necessary if 6800 assembly language is used, since there are no instructions for pushing addresses.

```
LDX     #ALPHA        Load immediate data ALPHA into X
STX     TEMP          Store ALPHA temporarily in M[TEMP]
LDA A   TEMP          Load high-order half of ALPHA into A
PSH A                 Push A into stack
LDA A   TEMP+1        Load low-order half of ALPHA into A
PSH A                 Push A into stack
```

None of the foregoing methods of passing parameters allows a subroutine to be called in the simple and natural fashion used by high-level languages, in which the actual parameters are listed in the call statement as arguments of the subroutine name, for example,

$$\text{CALL} \quad \text{SUB(PAR1, PAR2)}$$

A reasonably close approximation to this format can be achieved in assembly-language programs by listing the parameters as data constants following the subroutine call, as in the following 8080/8085 code:

```
        CALL    SUB
        DB      PAR1, PAR2
RADR:   . . . .
```

This means that the parameter values are stored in M as part of the main program itself. To obtain the actual parameters, therefore, the subroutine must read the data list following the subroutine call in the main program. Note that the execution of CALL SUB causes the address RADR $-$ 2, which points to the start of the parameter list, to be pushed into the stack. This address can be popped by the subroutine to access the parameter list. After the parameters have been obtained by the subroutine, it should ensure that the address RADR, which is the return address to the calling program, is at the top of the stack.

Figure 6.32 shows a useful technique for programming the parameter passing operation discussed above. It makes use of the 8080/8085 instruction XTHL that exchanges the contents of the two top-of-the-stack bytes for the contents of the HL address register. When CALL SUB is executed, RADR $-$ 2 is pushed into the stack. Then the first XTHL instruction transfers RADR $-$ 2 from the stack to HL, which now points to the parameter list. Next a sequence of move instructions is executed to transfer the actual parameters from the calling program to the dummy parameter locations used by the subroutine, in this example, the CPU registers A and B. Each 1-byte move operation is followed by an increment instruction addressed to HL, so that after all the parameter values have been passed, HL contains the return address RADR. A second XTHL instruction then transfers RADR to the top of the stack, where it can be used by a subsequent return instruction.

From the foregoing discussion it follows that an assembly-language subroutine has the general organization illustrated in Fig. 6.33. Immediately after entering the subroutine, any necessary save operations are carried out. The subroutine then executes the instructions, if any, required to obtain its input parameters. The main part of the subroutine is executed next. Finally, any output parameters (results) are made available to the calling program, the previously saved registers are restored to their original state, and a return instruction is executed. Output parameters are usually transferred to the CPU or a data area in main memory.

```
; Definition of the subroutine SUB

SUB:    XTHL                    ; Exchange HL and the top of the stack
        MOV     A,M             ; Move PAR1 to the A register
        INX     H               ; Increment HL
        MOV     B,M             ; Move PAR2 to the B register
        INX     H               ; Increment HL
        XTHL                    ; Exchange HL and the top of the stack, placing the return address RADR
                                ;     at the top of the stack

        . . . .

; Main program

        . . . .

        CALL    SUB             ; Call subroutine SUB
        DB      PAR1, PAR2      ; Actual parameter list
RADR:   . . . .
```

Figure 6.32 Parameter passing to an 8080/8085 subroutine where the parameters are stored in the calling program.

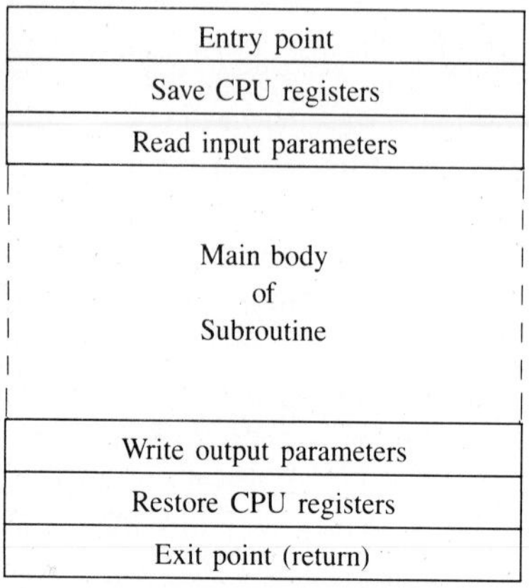

Entry point
Save CPU registers
Read input parameters
Main body of Subroutine
Write output parameters
Restore CPU registers
Exit point (return)

Figure 6.33 General structure of an assembly-language subroutine.

A stack that is maintained automatically by the CPU in main memory M is extremely useful for processing subroutines. It can be used as a save area, as a parameter-storage area, and as temporary storage for intermediate results. An important aspect of stack operation is the fact that space is assigned in the stack only as it is needed. Thus the stack space used as a save area on entry to a subroutine is effectively released for other uses on leaving the subroutine. This efficient use of RAM space is an asset in microcomputers, where RAM capacity is sometimes very limited. Unfortunately not all assembly languages have a good set of stack-accessing instructions of the push and pop type, which allow the assembly-language programmer to make maximum use of the stack.

The LIFO access method used by program-control stacks makes it easy to include subroutine calls within a subroutine definition. Such *nested* subroutine calls do not interfere with one another, provided that, on each return, the stack is restored to the state that existed before the corresponding subroutine was called. Note that a sequence of calls is always followed by a sequence of returns in the last-in/first-out order that a stack naturally supports. One can go further and define a subroutine that calls itself; such a subroutine is said to be *recursive*.

Figure 6.34 contains a short recursive subroutine written in 6800 assembly language. It computes the sum of the first N natural numbers according to the following recursive relationship.

$$SUM(0) = 0$$

$$SUM(N) = SUM(N - 1) + N$$

The subroutine SUM in Fig. 6.34 computes the result zero whenever it is called with N = 0. If N ≥ 1, then SUM calls itself with the input parameter N − 1. A total of N + 1 calls to SUM is made in this manner. The final call is with N = 0, and SUM returns the value SUM(0) = 0. A sequence of N returns ensues; after the ith return, SUM(i) = SUM(i − 1) + i is computed and placed in the accumulator A. After the final return to the main program, A contains the desired result SUM(N). Figure 6.35 shows a simulated execution of this program for N = 3. Note how the stack pointer S varies during program execution.

```
          NAM        SUMN
*    6800 PROGRAM TO COMPUTE THE SUM OF THE FIRST N NATURAL
*       NUMBERS USING A RECURSIVE SUBROUTINE THAT IMPLEMENTS
*       THE FORMULA:   SUM(0) := 0;
*                           SUM(N) := SUM(N - 1) + N;
*       WHERE N LIES BETWEEN 0 AND 23
*
*    MAIN  PROGRAM
          ORG        $100
N         EQU        3                   TEST VALUE
          LDS        #$100               INITIALIZE STACK POINTER S
          LDA   B    #N                  PLACE PARAMETER N IN ACCUMULATOR B
          JSR        SUM                 CALL SUBROUTINE 'SUM'
HALT      BRA        HALT                DYNAMIC HALT
*
*    SUBROUTINE 'SUM' DEFINITION
*       PARAMETER N ASSUMED TO BE IN REGISTER B
*       RESULT SUM(N) PLACED IN REGISTER A
*
*       CHECK IF N = 0
SUM       TBA                            TRANSFER B TO A
          TST   A                        TEST A. SET FLAG Z TO 1 IF A = 0.
          BNE        NZERO               BRANCH TO NZERO IF Z = 0
          RTS                            RETURN FROM SUBROUTINE
*    N IS NONZERO. COMPUTE   SUM (N - 1)
NZERO     DEC   B                        DECREMENT B
          JSR        SUM                 CALL SUBROUTINE 'SUM'
          INC   B                        RESTORE N TO B
*    COMPUTE SUM (N - 1) + N
          ABA                            ADD B TO A
          RTS                            RETURN FROM SUBROUTINE
          END
```

Figure 6.34 6800 program containing a recursive subroutine.

6.4 HIGH-LEVEL LANGUAGE PROGRAMMING

In this section the structure of high-level languages and their use in programming microprocessor-based systems are considered. Examples are presented mainly in the language Pascal, which is described in detail.

6.4.1 General Features

High-level languages were introduced to allow computer programs to be written in a format that reflects a program's application rather than the structure of a particular computer that executes the program. Thus FORTRAN, as its name implies, allows instructions to a computer to be written in the form of ordinary algebraic formulas. For example, the equation

$$y = 2.5(\tfrac{1}{2}x_1 + x_2^3 - \pi) \tag{6.21}$$

```
OC  =  OPCODE
P   =  PROGRAM COUNTER
A   =  ACCUMULATOR A
B   =  ACCUMULATOR B
C   =  CONDITION CODE (FLAGS)
S   =  STACK POINTER
```

```
OC     P     A  B     C      S
LDS   *0103  00 00 000000*0100
LDA   B*0105 00*03 000000 0100
JSR    *010A 00 03 000000*00FE
TBA    *010B *03 03 000000 00FE
TST   A*010C 03 03 000000 00FE
BNE    *010F 03 03 000000 00FE
DEC   B*0110 03*02 000000 00FE
JSR    *010A 03 02 000000*00FC
TBA    *010B *02 02 000000 00FC
TST   A*010C 02 02 000000 00FC
BNE    *010F 02 02 000000 00FC
DEC   B*0110 02*01 000000 00FC
JSR    *010A 02 01 000000*00FA
TBA    *010B *01 01 000000 00FA
TST   A*010C 01 01 000000 00FA
BNE    *010F 01 01 000000 00FA
DEC   B*0110 01*00 000Z00 00FA
JSR    *010A 01 00 000Z00*00F8
```

```
OC     P     A  B     C      S
TBA    *010B *00 00 000Z00 00F8
TST   A*010C 00 00 000Z00 00F8
BNE    *010E 00 00 000Z00 00F8
RTS    *0113 00 00 000Z00*00FA
INC   B*0114 00*01 000000 00FA
ABA    *0115 *01 01 000000 00FA
RTS    *0113 01 01 000000*00FC
INC   B*0114 01*02 000000 00FC
ABA    *0115 *03 02 000000 00FC
RTS    *0113 03 02 000000*00FE
INC   B*0114 03*03 000000 00FE
ABA    *0115 *06 03 000000 00FE
RTS    *0108 06 03 000000*0100
BRA    0108  06 03 000000 0100
```

END OF SIMULATION

Figure 6.35 Simulated execution in trace mode of the program in Fig. 6.34.

which is written in ordinary mathematic notation, can be translated into the following FORTRAN statement

$$Y = 2.5 * (X(1)/2.0 + X(2)**3 - PI) \qquad (6.22)$$

Note that the changes introduced by the translation are mainly typographical. Subscripts and superscripts are replaced by parenthetical expressions, while the special symbol π is replaced by PI; these changes are made to accommodate the limited printing capabilities of most IO terminals. Multiplication by 2.5, which is implicit in (6.21), is made explicit in (6.22) by means of the multiply symbol *. Thus as an instruction to compute Y according to the given formula, (6.22) is much closer to a problem specification than assembly or machine language. The symbolic names X, Y, and PI appearing in the FORTRAN statement are meaningful to the programming application, but not to the computer C being used. For instance, their data type (real numbers) may not correspond to a number representation used in C. Moreover, the exponentiation operation denoted by ** in (6.22) is not found in the instruction set of any computer. Thus high-level programming languages can be viewed as problem oriented rather than machine oriented. To be executed on a specific computer C, a source program written in a high-level language must be translated into the machine language of C, a task usually performed by a compiler program.

As discussed in Sec. 6.2.3, high-level languages have a number of advantages over assembly languages. They are easier to learn and use. They are much more readable than assembly languages, and so simplify program debugging and maintenance. The higher-level data types and operators used as building blocks in high-level languages permit more to be said with fewer statements—which tends to increase programmer productivity, and can significantly lower the cost and duration of system development. High-level languages are machine independent in the sense that they can be used on any computer for which the necessary compilers and other support software is available. It is therefore a relatively easy task to transfer programs written in these languages from one computer to another.

On the negative side, a high-level language, because of its inherent machine independence, cannot make the most efficient use of the resources of a particular computer. Programs can be expected to produce longer object code and to execute more slowly than assembly-language programs written to perform the same tasks. High-level languages are designed for efficient specification of high-level tasks involving real-number arithmetic or text processing; they are often inefficient for programming low-level tasks such as bit manipulation or timing control. Figure 6.12 summarizes the advantages and disadvantages of high-level languages. Figure 6.13 lists the main types of programming tasks for which high-level languages are best suited.

Since the 1950s a large number of high-level languages have been created for various programming applications. Figure 6.36 contains a representative set of high-level languages, most of which have been very widely used. International standards exist for the more popular languages such as FORTRAN and COBOL, but most high-level languages exist in many dialect forms with varying degrees of compatibility. Dialects usually result from modifications to the standard language introduced by a computer manufacturer or software company to accommodate some special features of a particular computer series. Despite such differences, however, high-level languages are much more standardized and portable than assembly languages.

From the beginning, high-level languages have been designed with certain types of programming tasks in mind. Languages such as FORTRAN, ALGOL, and BASIC are considered scientific languages, since they are most suited to numeric calculations of the kind encountered in science and engineering. Nonnumerical tasks such as text editing and file processing can be programmed in FORTRAN, for example, but relatively long

Intended Applications	Language	Approximate Date of Introduction	Originator
Scientific programming	FORTRAN (Formula Translation)	1955	IBM Corp.
	ALGOL (Algorithmic Language)	1960	International committee
	BASIC (Beginner's All Purpose Symbolic Instruction Code)	1965	Dartmouth College
Business programming	COBOL (Common Business-Oriented Language)	1960	U.S. industry/ government committee
Multipurpose	PL/I (Programming Language One)	1965	IBM Corp.
	Pascal (after Blaise Pascal)	1970	N. Wirth (ETH, Zurich)
	Ada (after Ada Lady Lovelace)	1980	CII-Honeywell-Bull (France)
Machine oriented	Forth (from Fourth-Generation Computer)	1970	C. H. Moore (U.S. National Radio Observatory)
	PL/M (Programming Language Microcomputer)	1975	Intel Corp.

Figure 6.36 Some important high-level programming languages.

and complex programs must be written for such tasks. COBOL is the main language used for business and commercial data processing tasks, which are characterized by complex nonnumeric operations such as the processing of large payroll files. These applications involve fairly simple numeric calculations; COBOL's features for supporting numeric operations thus are quite limited. Later languages, such as PL/I, Pascal, and Ada (named for Ada Augusta Byron (1816–1852), Countess of Lovelace, who collaborated with Charles Babbage on the first mechanical computers) attempt to cover both scientific and business applications, and therefore may be called multipurpose.

The languages mentioned were developed for large mainframe computers, and their design indicates little concern for machine-efficiency considerations. A number of high-level languages have been introduced whose primary concern is efficient use of such machine resources as memory space and CPU instruction execution speed. An example is the language Forth (Moore & Rather, 1974), which was designed to yield programs that would run very efficiently on small computer systems. Other languages were developed by adding features of high-level languages such as **while** control structures and **array** data types to assembly languages. Interest in such languages increased greatly with the appearance of microprocessors in the 1970s. Microprocessor applications have some special features that make high-level languages with machine-dependent features particularly attractive:

1. The memory space available for program or data storage is often severely restricted.
2. Efficient and direct control may be required over such machine features as IO ports.
3. Programs must interact with timing signals such as clock and interrupt signals.

A variety of microprocessor-oriented high-level languages have appeared that address these special problems (Crespi-Righizzi et al., 1980); one such language, PL/M, will be briefly considered.

PL/M was developed for programming Intel microprocessors, including the 8080/8085 and 8086 series. It has various high-level constructs such as **if** .. **then** .. **else** statements, and procedure calls of the form **call** PROCNAME (parameter list). At the same time, PL/M includes low-level operations such as **shl** (shift left) that are more typical of assembly languages. PL/M has the usual arithmetic operators $+$, $-$, $*$, and $/$, but they can only act on short integers corresponding exactly to the number formats implemented in the hardware of the underlying microprocessor. A PL/M procedure may be given the machine-dependent attribute **interrupt** n, which allows it to be interrupted whenever an interrupt request of priority n or less is received while executing the procedure. Because of their close correspondence to machine code, PL/M programs can readily be compiled into very efficient object code.

There are certain microprocessor applications—for example, hand-held calcula-tors—which are designed to be programmed directly in a high-level language, but have fairly small memories. A compiler is usually a large program and this may require more storage space than is available. In such cases the compiler may be dispensed with entirely, and replaced by a smaller and simpler translator program called an *interpreter*. As shown in Fig. 6.37, the interpreter P_I is stored in the target computer along with the original source programs P_S. P_I translates each statement of P_S into machine language immediately before it is executed. After execution the machine language instructions can be discarded, so that no complete object-code version of P_S is created. This mode of program execution is called interpretive. It is particularly suited to interactive program-ming with simple high-level languages such as BASIC. Since each statement in the source program must be translated into object code every time it is executed, interpretive program execution is much slower than the execution of compiled object code.

Compilers and interpreters exist that allow all major high-level languages to be used for programming microcomputers. The more complex languages such as FORTRAN or COBOL tend to require large main memories, both in the target microcomputer and in the microprocessor development systems used as design aids. While this has limited the use of high-level languages in microprocessor-based design, this problem is likely to diminish as higher-capacity RAM and ROM ICs become available. It is interesting to note that Ada, which is perhaps the most complex of current high-level languages (Katzan, 1982), is intended for use in "embedded" computer systems where, as in most microprocessor-based systems, the target computer is a component of some larger system.

6.4.2 Programming Example

Several small programs written in Pascal were presented earlier that illustrate the basic features of this particular programming language; see Figs. 6.3 and 6.14. We next describe a more complex Pascal program that introduces additional features of Pascal, and demonstrates the use of high-level languages for programming microprocessor-based systems.

The system to be programmed consists of an electric oven controlled by a micro-

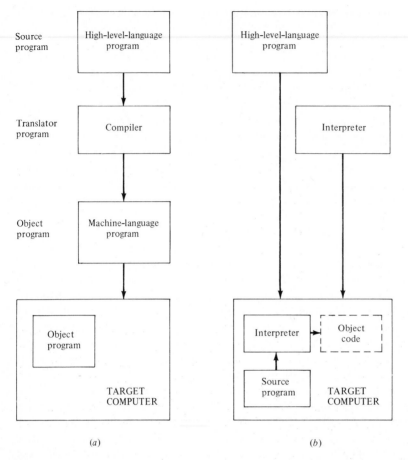

Figure 6.37 Program translation and execution: (*a*) using a compiler; (*b*) using an interpreter.

computer C that is based on a typical 8-bit microprocessor such as the 8080/8085 or the 6800. Figure 6.38 depicts the structure of this system. The main purpose of C is to keep the oven temperature within a narrow range around a reference temperature REF_TEMP indicated by thumbwheel switches on a control panel attached to the microcomputer. The temperature of the oven can be varied by increasing or decreasing the electric current supplied to the oven's heating element. The current level is specified by a data word CURRENT generated by C. A temperature-sensing device in the oven supplies a signal SENSOR to C from which it computes the actual temperature of the oven in degrees Celsius. This computed temperature OVEN_TEMP is then compared with REF_TEMP to determine what changes, if any, need to be made to CURRENT to maintain the oven at the desired temperature. To prevent excessive heat loss, and to protect human beings working nearby, the oven door should always be closed while the oven is in operation. A safety switch DOOR_SWITCH therefore is built into the oven and is turned on when the oven door is fully closed. The state of this switch is monitored continuously by C. If DOOR_SWITCH is found to be turned off while the oven is operating, C is required to

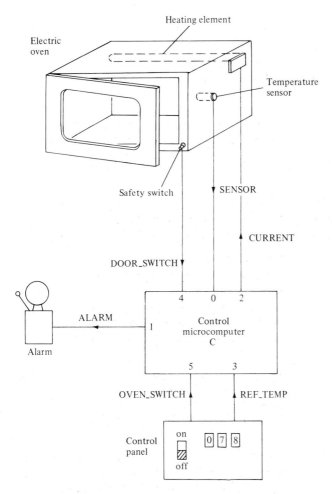

Figure 6.38 Microprocessor-controlled electric oven.

turn the oven off by reducing CURRENT to zero. C also activates an alarm signal under these conditions.

A flowchart describing an algorithm for controlling this microprocessor-based system appears in Fig. 6.39. Input signals provided by the various input devices attached to the oven and the control panel are read and checked periodically. It is assumed that these input signals are made available in digital form at IO ports of C. A subroutine named CONVERT is employed to convert the output of the temperature sensor into a temperature value OVEN_TEMP. For simplicity it is assumed that if the heater control signal CURRENT is set to the value REF_TEMP, then the temperature of the oven becomes approximately equal to REF_TEMP. If REF_TEMP and OVEN_TEMP are sufficiently close, say within 2°C of each other, then C holds CURRENT at the value REF_TEMP. If, however, OVEN_TEMP exceeds REF_TEMP by more than 2°C, then C decreases CURRENT by one unit to lower the oven temperature. Similarly, if

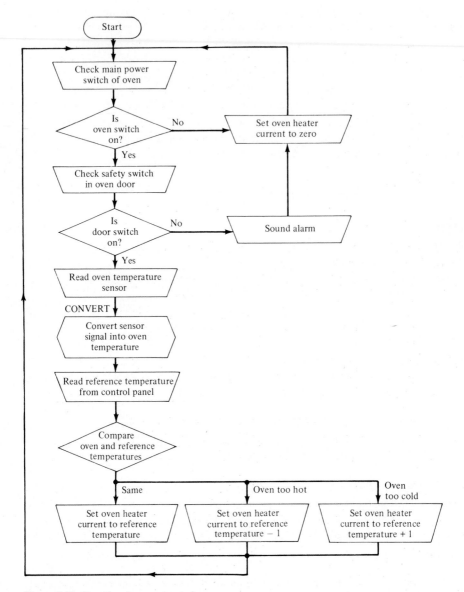

Figure 6.39 Algorithm for oven control.

OVEN_TEMP is found to be too low, CURRENT is increased by one unit. Consequently, if the oven temperature fluctuates, C repeatedly adjusts the heater current to maintain OVEN_TEMP within the range REF_TEMP ± 2.

It can be seen from Fig. 6.39 that the microcomputer C executes a fixed sequence of operations that are repeated indefinitely during normal operation of the system. The overall structure of the flowchart thus has the form of an endless loop. If the main power switch OVEN_SWITCH on the control panel is off, then C enters a waiting loop in which it continually sets CURRENT to zero and checks the state of OVEN_SWITCH. C also checks the safety interlock switch DOOR_SWITCH. If the condition OVEN_SWITCH = ON and DOOR_SWITCH = OFF ever occurs, then C activates an alarm before shutting off the heater current. Clearly most of the operations performed by C involve IO operations as indicated by the many trapezoidal boxes in the flowchart. C therefore must be equipped with a set of IO ports through which it can communicate with the system's IO devices. We will not be concerned here with the detailed structure of these IO ports, such as the number of bits used or their exact configuration. As will be evident later, these details are largely hidden from the high-level-language program that implements the algorithm of Fig. 6.39.

Translation of the flowchart into a high-level language program is a rather straightforward process. Figure 6.40 lists a Pascal implementation of Fig. 6.39. This program, which is named OVEN, contains three modules:

1. A numeric procedure or subroutine called CONVERT that converts the output signal from the temperature sensor into degrees Celsius. A very simple relationship is assumed to exist between these quantities in order to keep the procedure short. By making CONVERT a procedure, it can easily be replaced by another procedure that implements a more complex conversion algorithm.
2. A procedure called SET_OVEN that computes the heater control signal CURRENT and transmits it to the oven. Again, for brevity, a very simple relationship is assumed to exist between CURRENT and the reference temperature REF_TEMP.
3. A main program that reads the various input ports in sequence, calculates the status of the system, and transmits appropriate command signals to the output ports.

Pascal conventions require that the procedure definitions precede the main program; the latter therefore is at the end of the source code. At the beginning of the program is a preamble containing various directives to the Pascal compiler; these will be discussed later.

The program OVEN illustrates the principal advantage of a high-level language over assembly languages, namely, shorter and more readable source code. This results from the use of long mnemonic names for data and procedures, and the use of complex instruction formats that resemble ordinary English sentences. For instance, the statement

if abs(OVEN_TEMP − REF_TEMP) < = 2 **then** SET_OVEN(REF_TEMP)

appearing in Fig. 6.40 is a fair approximation of the following statement in ordinary English:

"If the absolute value of the difference between the oven temperature and the reference temperature is less than or equal to two, then set the oven temperature to the reference temperature."

The foregoing Pascal statement contains a call to a predefined procedure named **abs** that calculates the absolute value of a number. It also contains a call to the special procedure SET_OVEN, which is defined in the program under consideration. Note that the use of different typefaces for program identifiers has no significance as far as Pascal is

program OVEN:

```
{ ********************************************************************
*      This is a Pascal program named OVEN used to control the operation of a microprocessor-     *
*      based electric oven. It is required to keep the oven temperature within a specified range, and   *
*      prevent unsafe operation. OVEN communicates with the oven and the outside world via six    *
*      IO ports whose functions are defined as follows:                                           *
*      PORT_0:     Input signal SENSOR from oven temperature sensor                               *
*      PORT_1:     Output signal ALARM to warning device                                          *
*      PORT_2:     Output signal CURRENT to oven heater                                           *
*      PORT_3:     Input reference temperature signal REF_TEMP from control panel switches        *
*      PORT_4:     Input signal DOOR_SWITCH from safety interlock switch in oven door             *
*      PORT_5:     Input signal OVEN_SWITCH from main power switch                                 *
* ****************************************************************************** }
```

{Declarations}

```
const      OFF = '0';
           ON = '1';
           ALARM = '1';
           ZERO = 0;
type       TEMP = 0..255;
           SWITCH = '0'..'1';
var        OVEN_TEMP, REF_TEMP, SENSOR:   temp;
           OVEN_SWITCH, DOOR_SWITCH:   switch;
           PORT_0, PORT_1, PORT_2, PORT_3, PORT_4, PORT_5:   file of char;
```

{Procedure to set oven heater current to a specified value}

```
procedure SET_OVEN (TEMPERATURE: temp);
var        CURRENT:   integer;
begin
  CURRENT := TEMPERATURE;
  write (PORT_2, CURRENT)
end;
```

{ Procedure to convert sensor output signal to temperature in degrees C }

```
procedure CONVERT (var SENSOR_OUTPUT, TEMPERATURE: temp);
begin
  TEMPERATURE := round (SENSOR_OUTPUT/2) + 10
end;
```

{Main program}

```
begin
{Name and initialize physical files representing IO ports}
reset (PORT_0, 'IN.0');
rewrite (PORT_1, 'OUT.1');
rewrite (PORT_2, 'OUT.2');
reset (PORT_3, 'IN.3');
reset (PORT_4, 'IN.4');
reset (PORT_5, 'IN.5');
```

Figure 6.40 Pascal implementation of the oven control algorithm of Fig. 6.39.

```
{Begin oven control operations}
while true do
   begin          {Check main power switch}
   read (PORT_5, OVEN_SWITCH);
   if OVEN_SWITCH = OFF then SET_OVEN (ZERO) else
      begin          {Check oven door switch}
      read (PORT_4, DOOR_SWITCH);
      if DOOR_SWITCH = OFF then
         begin          {Sound alarm}
         write (PORT_1, ALARM);
         SET_OVEN (ZERO)
         end else
         begin          {Check and adjust oven temperature}
         read (PORT_0, SENSOR);
         CONVERT (SENSOR, OVEN_TEMP);
         read (PORT_3, REF_TEMP);
         if abs (OVEN_TEMP - REF_TEMP) < = 2 then SET_OVEN (REF_TEMP)
            else if OVEN_TEMP > REF_TEMP then SET_OVEN (REF_TEMP - 1)
            else SET_OVEN (REF_TEMP + 1)
         end
      end
   end
end.
```

(Figure 6.40 Continued)

concerned. Normally a Pascal compiler does not distinguish between typefaces or between upper- and lowercase characters.

Another feature that distinguishes Pascal from most assembly languages is its use of blocks. A block in this context is a related group of statements comprising the declaration and executable parts of a procedure or main program. Blocks serve to isolate parts of a program from one another, since a variable name has no meaning outside the block where it is defined. Thus no conflict results from the fact that the procedures CONVERT and SET_OVEN of Fig. 6.40 both use the name TEMPERATURE for an internal (local) variable.

In Pascal compound statements can be constructed systematically from simple statements. A compound statement is a sequence of simple statements enclosed by the keywords **begin** and **end**. Most of the main program of OVEN, for example, consists of a **while** statement with the following structure:

while true do begin   statements   end;

Here **begin** and **end** enclose a compound statement that is executed as long as the condition following the keyword **while** holds. In this case the condition is: Is **true** = **true**?, which always holds. Note that a statement can have other compound statements embedded or nested in it. In the above **while** statement, we find several compound and nested **if** statements. Indenting is used to make clear which statements are being grouped together. Different **begin-end** pairs are indented differently, with the amount of indentation increasing for each new compound statement encountered.

All the main types of statements used in Pascal programs are represented in the program OVEN, including compiler directives, assignment (data-processing) statements, program-control statements and procedure calls. The preamble contains various instructions to the Pascal compiler that correspond to directives in assembly languages. Their purpose is to assign symbolic names and data types to data items used in the program. Statements beginning with the keyword **const** are used to assign symbolic names to constants. For instance, the statement

const   OFF = '0';

assigns the name or identifier OFF to the character constant 0, while

ZERO = 0;

which is also governed by the preceding **const** keyword, assigns the name ZERO to the integer constant 0. Every data item occurring in a Pascal program must be assigned a (data) type. This may be done using the predefined Pascal types, which include **integer, real, character,** and **boolean**. Alternatively the programmer may create new data types via type declarations. A data type called TEMP is created in OVEN by the statement

type   TEMP = 0..255;

which states that variables of type TEMP may only assume integer values in the range 0 through 255. Pascal statements beginning with the keyword **var** (variable) are used to specify or declare the type of a variable. The variable OVEN_TEMP is declared to be of type TEMP by means of the statement

var   OVEN_TEMP: temp;

The type of every variable must be declared in Pascal programs. This has the advantage of allowing the compiler to detect certain design errors of the "adding apples to oranges" variety. If the statement

OVEN_TEMP := 256;

were in OVEN, an error would be signaled during program compilation, because OVEN_TEMP is a variable of type TEMP, and therefore may not assume the value 256.

Data-processing statements in Pascal take the form of assignments of the following general kind:

variable := expression to be evaluated;

Calls to procedures are made by simply writing the procedure name followed by a list of actual parameters thus:

CONVERT (SENSOR, OVEN_TEMP);

Pascal has a small number of predefined procedures, whose names therefore are keywords of the language. Examples of such procedures in OVEN are **round, abs, reset, read, rewrite,** and **write**.

Program-control statements play a particularly important role in the construction of Pascal programs. Pascal has a relatively large number of program-control constructs.

Two of the most useful are illustrated by OVEN: the **while** statement

> **while** condition **do** statements;

and the **if** statement

> **if** condition **then** statements A **else** statements B;

In each case a true-or-false condition is tested to decide which of several actions to perform. The **if** statement implements a two-way conditional branch operation and corresponds to a diamond-shaped decision box in a flowchart. The given condition is tested once; if true statements A are executed, if false statements B are executed. The condition specified in a **while** statement is tested repeatedly; each time it is found to be true, the statements after **do** are executed. When the **while** condition is found to be false, the statement immediately after the **while** statement is executed. Thus a **while** statement corresponds to a loop in a flowchart with a single conditional exit.

Like most high-level programming languages, Pascal has just a few simple predefined procedures, such as **read** and **write**, for specifying IO operations. These IO procedures were designed to communicate with IO devices such as CRT terminals, line printers, and secondary memory devices that process data in the form of alphanumeric strings or *files*. Although the IO devices of the oven-control microcomputer do not handle alphanumeric files, it is necessary to assume that they do in the control program OVEN; otherwise they cannot be accessed by **read** or **write** statements. Thus in OVEN all the IO ports are declared to be variables of the predefined type **file of char**, that is, files of alphanumeric characters. In most implementations of Pascal, characters are represented by 8-bit ASCII words, so there is a rough correspondence between a Pascal **read** or **write** operation with character data and the IN and OUT machine instructions found, say, in the 8080/8085 microprocessor. The **reset** and **rewrite** statements appearing in OVEN are needed to initialize Pascal IO files for reading and writing respectively. It is not possible in standard Pascal to address individual bits of an IO port, which would be very desirable in the case of the variables of type SWITCH used in OVEN. These binary variables can be represented by single bits in assembly-language programs; in OVEN they must be represented by (8-bit) characters. This inefficiency, which is a serious problem in microprocessor programming applications, can be overcome by the addition of nonstandard features to Pascal for IO operations and bit processing (Wakerly, 1981). Alternatively, these operations can be programmed in assembly language, and the resulting assembly-language routines can be coupled with the main Pascal source code.

By way of contrast, Fig. 6.41 outlines another version of the OVEN program written in the microprocessor-oriented language PL/M developed by Intel Corp. (McCracken, 1978). This language has assignment and control statement formats that are similar to those of Pascal. For example, the Pascal construction

> **while** condition **do**
>   **begin**
>   · · ·
>   **end**;

```
/* PL/M version of the oven control program (outline only) */
OVEN:
do;
/* Declarations */
declare (OVEN$TEMP, REF$TEMP, SENSOR, ALARM) byte;
declare (OVEN$SWITCH, DOOR$SWITCH) byte;
/* Procedures CONVERT and SET$OVEN are defined here */
/* Main program */
do while 1;
  OVEN$SWITCH = input(5);
  if OVEN$SWITCH = 0 then call SET$OVEN(0); else
    do
    DOOR$SWITCH = input(4);
    if DOOR$SWITCH = 0 then
      do;        /* Sound alarm */
      output(1) = ALARM;
      call SET$OVEN(0);
      end; else
      do;        /* Check and adjust oven temperature */
      SENSOR = input(0);
      call CONVERT (SENSOR, OVEN$TEMP);
      REF$TEMP = input(3);
      /* Compare OVEN$TEMP with REF$TEMP and set oven heater current */
      end;
    end;
  end;
end OVEN;
```

Figure 6.41 Outline of a PL/M version of the oven-control program.

becomes in PL/M

$$\textbf{do while } condition;$$
$$\cdots$$
$$\textbf{end};$$

PL/M has a much more restricted set of data types than Pascal. In the 8080/8085 version of PL/M only two types are allowed: **byte** representing 8-bit data words and **address** representing 16-bit words. Note that these are the inherent data types of the 8080/8085 microprocessor. The **declare** statements of Fig. 6.41 are used to specify the type, either **byte** or **address**, of each variable appearing in the program. The four basic arithmetic operations $+$, $-$, $*$, and $/$ can be used in PL/M programs; however, they are effectively restricted to 8-bit and 16-bit integer arithmetic by the PL/M constraints on data types.

An advantage of PL/M over Pascal in microprocessor applications is that bits within data items can be manipulated directly. For example, to make a decision based on the leftmost bit of the byte variable DOOR$SWITCH, we can use the PL/M **if** statement

$$\textbf{if } (DOOR\$SWITCH \textbf{ and } 80H) = 00H \textbf{ then } \ldots \textbf{ else } \ldots;$$

Here 80H denotes the hexadecimal byte $80_{16} = 10000000_2$, and **and** is the bitwise logical and operator. PL/M has the predefined identifiers **input** and **output**, which correspond directly to IO instructions in machine language. For example, the statement

$$DOOR\$SWITCH = \textbf{input}(4);$$

occurring in Fig. 6.41 causes the 1-byte quantity DOOR$SWITCH to assume the value at IO port 4. This PL/M statement is essentially equivalent to the following statements in 8080/8085 assembly language:

```
IN    4              ; Input byte from IO port 4 to accumulator
STA   DOOR$SWITCH    ; Store accumulator in memory location DOOR$SWITCH
```

Note that in PL/M, but not in standard Pascal, we can also represent the two-valued variables, OVEN$SWITCH and DOOR$SWITCH by single bits within a data word, thereby making more efficient use of the memory and IO space of the host computer.

6.4.3 Language Elements (Pascal)

We now examine the main data and instruction specification mechanisms provided by high-level programming languages, again using Pascal as the running example. A complete and more formal definition of Pascal can be found in Jensen and Wirth (1974) and Ravenel (1979).

A typical Pascal program has the overall structure shown in Fig. 6.42. The program starts with a *header statement* that names the program. The program name is followed by an optional list of program parameters in parentheses; these parameters are usually the names of files associated with IO devices of the system that will execute the program. For example, the header statement from the Pascal program of Fig. 6.14 is

program CONV1 (**input, output**);

which states that the program's name is CONV1 and that it makes use of the the standard or built-in IO files named **input** and **output**. All read and write statements in a Pascal program refer to the files **input** and **output**, respectively, unless other files are explicitly specified. The program header is followed by a list of declaration statements that assign meanings to the programmer-defined identifiers (symbolic names) appearing in the program, including statement labels, data constants, and data variables. Each variable must be assigned a data type. Any nonstandard types to be used must also be defined in this part of the program.

Included in the declaration part are the definitions of any special procedures and subroutines to be used by the program. The definition of a Pascal procedure has essentially the same structure as the program definition of Fig. 6.42, with the keyword

```
program PROGRAM_NAME (parameters);
Declarations
    labels
    constants
    types
    variables
    procedure definitions
begin
Executable statements
end.
```

Figure 6.42 General structure of a Pascal program.

procedure replacing **program** in the header statement. Note that procedures can be defined within other procedures with few restrictions. The procedure definitions are followed by the executable statements that form the main program. The main program takes the form of a compound or structured statement enclosed by **begin** and **end**. As observed earlier, statements can be nested within statements in a systematic manner. The microprocessor program OVEN of Fig. 6.40 is a particular instance of the general structure of Fig. 6.42 that contains two procedure definitions. To execute a procedure in Pascal, it is only necessary to write the procedure name followed by the appropriate parameters. Other high-level languages such as FORTRAN and PL/M (cf. Fig. 6.41) require the keyword **call** to precede the procedure name.

Like other high-level languages, Pascal recognizes a special class of procedures called functions that are designed to compute a single value (the function value) that is returned directly to any statement that calls the function. This allows functions to be treated as operands in arithmetic and logical expressions. Many generally useful procedures such as **read** and **write**, and functions such as **round** and **abs**, all of which are used in the program OVEN, are built into standard Pascal. This means that the corresponding procedure definitions are known to the Pascal compiler and need not be provided by the programmer. These built-in procedures and functions are considered part of the Pascal language.

Pascal is said to be a (strongly) typed language, which implies that the (data) type of every program variable must be explicitly declared. A variable's type determines the set of values it can take, and the set of operations that may be applied to it. Four simple or scalar types are built into Pascal that are identified by the keywords **integer**, **real**, **char**, and **boolean**. All **integer** quantities assume integer values from the set

$$-\text{MAXINT}, \ -\text{MAXINT} + 1, \ \ldots, \ -1, 0, 1, \ \ldots, \ \text{MAXINT} - 1, \text{MAXINT}$$

where the maximum value MAXINT is determined by the compiler and, indirectly, by the computer being programmed. **Real** data are assigned the values of floating-point numbers whose range and precision are also compiler dependent. Variables of type **char** (character) can assume values corresponding to a character set that contains the 10 decimal digits, the letters of the alphabet, and certain special symbols. The ASCII character set (see Fig. 5.17) is often used to define **char**. Finally, **boolean** variables can be assigned only the two values denoted by the keywords **true** and **false**.

The way in which a variable can be combined with other variables and operators depends on the variable's type. Pascal possesses the set of arithmetic-logic operators listed in Fig. 6.43. The arithmetic operators $+$, $-$, and $*$ apply to **integer** and **real** numbers in the normal fashion. Division among **real** numbers is specified by $/$. Two division operators are associated with integers; **div** yields an **integer** quotient corresponding to the truncated **real** quotient, while **mod** yields the **integer** remainder. The logical operators **and**, **or**, and **not** are the standard operators of Boolean algebra, and apply only to **boolean** data. The various relational operators are used for comparing data items of the same type, and yield **boolean** results. For example, if X is an integer, then the expression

$$X < > 273$$

Operator Type	Operator	Description	Input Operand Type	Output Operand Type
Arithmetic	+	Addition	**integer**	**integer**
			real	**real**
	−	Subtraction	**integer**	**integer**
			real	**real**
	*	Multiplication	**integer**	**integer**
			real	**real**
	/	Division	**real**	**real**
	div	Division yielding the quotient	**integer**	**integer**
	mod	Division yielding the remainder	**integer**	**integer**
Logical	**and**	Boolean and	**boolean**	**boolean**
	or	Boolean (inclusive) or	**boolean**	**boolean**
	not	Boolean complementation	**boolean**	**boolean**
Relational	=	Equal to	Any type	**boolean**
	< >	Not equal to ($\neq$)	Any type	**boolean**
	<	Less than	Any ordered type	**boolean**
	< =	Less than or equal to ($\leq$)	Any ordered type	**boolean**
	>	Greater than	Any ordered type	**boolean**
	> =	Greater than or equal to ($\geq$)	Any ordered type	**boolean**

Figure 6.43 Operators available in Pascal and the associated data types.

has the value **true** whenever $X \neq 273$, and the value **false** otherwise. Note that the composite operator symbols $\neq$, $\leq$, and $\geq$ are not included in character sets such as ASCII, and therefore are replaced by pairs of symbols from the set $=$, $<$, and $>$. The relational operators are used with **boolean** input operands under the assumption that **false** is less than or equal to **true**, that is,

$$\textbf{false} < = \textbf{true} \tag{6.23}$$

Various logical interpretations can be given to the relational operators in such all-**boolean** expressions; for instance, the operator $< =$ in (6.23) represents Boolean implication.

The foregoing symbolic operators can be used to construct complex expressions in Pascal programs according to the usual laws of arithmetic and Boolean algebra. These operators are augmented by a set of built-in functions, a representative subset of which appears in Fig. 6.44. Functional variables of the form $f(x)$ may be used as operands in arithmetic or logical expressions in a straightforward fashion, for example,

$$X := \textbf{round} \ ((X + 2.674 * Y)/\textbf{sqr} \ (\textbf{ln} \ (Y - 3.157E-2)));$$

As noted earlier, new functions may be defined by the programmer and added to the built-in-set.

The composite data types of Pascal include **file**, **array**, **record**, **set**, and **pointer**. A variable of type **file** usually consists of a stream of data items of the same simple type that are stored sequentially on an IO device. Files are accessed by the IO procedures **read**,

Function f(x)	Description	Type of x	Type of $f(x)$
abs(x)	Absolute value of x	**integer** **real**	**integer** **real**
atan(x)	Arc tangent in radians of x	**real**	**real**
cos(x)	Cosine of x radians	**real**	**real**
eof(F)	End-of-file function; **true** if the end-of-file symbol has been read from F; **false** otherwise.	**file**	**boolean**
exp(x)	Exponential function e^x	**real**	**real**
ln(x)	Logarithm of x to the base e	**integer** **real**	**real** **real**
log(x)	Logarithm of x to the base 10	**integer** **real**	**real** **real**
pred(x)	Predecessor function; returns value of immediate predecessor of x	Any ordered type	Same as x
round(x)	Nearest integer to x	**real**	**integer**
sin(x)	Sine of x radians	**real**	**real**
sqr(x)	Square of x	**integer** **real**	**integer** **real**
sqrt(x)	Square root of x	**real**	**real**
succ(x)	Successor function; returns value of immediate successor of x	Any ordered type	Same as x
trunc(x)	Truncation function; returns nearest integer y, where $y < x$ if $x > 0$, and $y > x$ if $x < 0$	**real**	**integer**

Figure 6.44 Some typical functions that are built into Pascal.

readln (read line), **write**, and **writeln** (write line), as illustrated by the programs of Figs. 6.3 and 6.40. A file is identified in a Pascal program by assigning it a type of the form **file of** TYPE where TYPE is the simple type of the file's component data items. Thus in Fig. 6.40 the character files PORT_0 to PORT_5 are declared to be **file of char**. A sequence of read operations addressed to a particular file causes data to be read in sequence from the file until the end of the file is reached, a condition causing the corresponding **eof** function (see Fig. 6.44) to change value from **false** to **true**. As shown in the program of Fig. 6.40, files are initialized for reading and writing by the built-in procedures **reset** and **rewrite**. A file name may appear as the first parameter in a file-processing procedure; if none is given, one of the standard files **input** or **output** is assumed to be the default file name.

One of the most useful composite data types provided by high-level languages is **array**. An array is an indexed set of data items that, like the components of a file, are all of the same type. Pascal allows multidimensional arrays to be defined, whose components can be of any simple or composite type. For example, a 50 × 100 two-dimensional array X of **real** numbers can be defined by the following statement:

var X: **array** [1..50,1..100] **of real**;

or equivalently by

var X: **array** [1..50] **of array** [1..100] **of real**;

The element in the ith row and jth column of X is automatically assigned the name X[i,j]. The notation a..b in the array definitions indicates a sequence of index values whose first and last members are a and b respectively. Recognizing that compilers often transform arrays into object-code forms that use the memory space of the target computer inefficiently, Pascal permits the keywords **packed array** to be used instead of **array**. The word packed tells the source-code translator that the object program should be constructed to economize storage space, even at the expense of increasing program execution time.

We will discuss one other Pascal data type, namely, the type **record**. While files and arrays must contain components of uniform types, a record can group together data items called fields, which may be of many different types. A record variable X may be specified by the following kind of declaration statement:

> **var** X: **record**
> > FIELD1:   type;
> > FIELD2:   type;
> > . . .
> > FIELDn: type
> > **end**;

Any field, say FIELDk of X, can be referenced by the identifier X.FIELDk obtained by appending a period and the field name to the record name.

The Pascal program of Fig. 6.45 illustrates many of the concepts introduced above. The purpose of this program, which is named ROLLBOOK, is to read data records from the standard file **input**, perform some simple processing, and write data onto the file **output**. The input files is assumed to be organized as a sequence of three-line records. To process these records, ROLLBOOK defines a variable STUDENT of type **record.** This particular record structure contains three fields, one of type **array of char** to accommodate alphanumeric character strings, and two of type **integer** to accommodate numeric data. ROLLBOOK illustrates the use of a new program-control statement

> **repeat**   statements   **until**   condition;

which causes the statements after **repeat** to be repeatedly executed until the condition following **until** is found to be true. In this example records on the file **input** are processed repetitively until an end-of-file symbol is detected, an event that changes the built-in **eof** function from **false** to **true**. This program also shows how a special function is defined in Pascal. The function in question is named AVERAGE and yields an **integer** result. Note how the term AVERAGE appears as a parameter in the final **writeln** procedure call.

New data types may be introduced into a Pascal program in two ways. Every type corresponds to a set of values that variables of that particular type may assume. A *subrange type* has a value set defined as a subrange of the values of an existing (ordered) type. For example, the subrange type called TEMP in Fig. 6.40 is defined as the set of 256 integers 0, 1, ..., 255, which is a subrange of the type **integer**. TEMP is defined by the type declaration

> **type**   TEMP = 0..255;

program ROLLBOOK (**input, output**);

```
{ *********************************************************
*     This is a Pascal demonstration program that extracts grades from a student record file and      *
*     computes an average grade. The records are stored sequentially on the file input using the       *
*     following format:                                                                                 *
*              Line 1:   Name (One to 20 alphanumeric characters)                                       *
*              Line 2:   Rank (1 = undergraduate; 2 = graduate student)                                 *
*              Line 3:   Grade (integer)                                                                 *
* ********************************************************* }
```

{Declarations}

```
var   COUNT, SUM:  integer;
      STUDENT:   record
                  NAME:   array[1..20] of char;
                  RANK:   integer;
                  GRADE:  integer
                 end;
```

{Function to compute average grade}
```
function AVERAGE: integer;
begin
AVERAGE := SUM div COUNT
end;
```

{Main program}

```
begin
COUNT := 0;
SUM := 0;
repeat
  readln (STUDENT.NAME);
  readln (STUDENT.RANK);
  readln (STUDENT.GRADE);
  writeln ('NAME = ', STUDENT.NAME);
  writeln ('GRADE = ', STUDENT.GRADE);
  COUNT := COUNT + 1;
  SUM := SUM + STUDENT.GRADE
until eof;
writeln ('AVERAGE GRADE = ', AVERAGE)
end.
```

Figure 6.45 Pascal program to process student grades.

Similarly, SWITCH is defined as a subrange of the type **char** consisting of the two values '0' and '1'. In general, operators that can be applied to a particular type can also be applied to the subrange types derived from it. An *enumerated type* is defined by listing all the possible values allowed by the type. For instance,

$$\textbf{type} \quad COLOR = (green, white, orange);$$

defines by enumeration the three-valued type COLOR. If a variable X is declared to be of type COLOR thus

var   X: COLOR;

X may assume any of the values GREEN, WHITE, and ORANGE, but no other values. Although Pascal allows a programmer to define new data types in the above ways, it does not allow the operators that are applicable to the new data types to be defined.

Figure 6.46 shows the general layout of the declaration part of a Pascal program or procedure. Note that the various declaration statements must be listed in the order given in this figure.

6.4.4 Statement Types

The building blocks of high-level languages are simple statements that correspond roughly to instructions at the assembly-language level. Complex expressions can be used as the operands of statements, so that statement length and internal complexity are not fixed. In Pascal and some other languages, the end of a statement is indicated by a semicolon; the semicolon may be omitted if the statement is followed by certain keywords such as **end** or **else**. A compound statement is formed by enclosing a sequence of simple or compound statements between the delimiters **begin** and **end**. This construction makes it possible to embed statements in other statements in an orderly fashion, and greatly adds to the expressiveness of the language.

The executable instructions of assembly languages were grouped into three broad classes: data-transfer, data-processing, and program-control instructions. A similar classification can be made of the simple statements of a high-level language, but the relative importance of the various groups differs considerably from assembly languages. While assembly languages have many different types of data-transfer instructions (MOVE, LOAD, STORE, etc.), high-level languages rely on an assignment statement with the following format:

destination operand(s) : = source operand(s);

Languages such as PL/M and FORTRAN use = in place of the assignment operator : = , which, however, does not indicate the direction of the data transfer, and may also be

```
label    N1, N2, ..., Nk;
const    CONST1 = value;
         CONST2 = value;
         . . .
type     TYPE1 = value set;
         TYPE2 = value set;
         . . .
var      VARA1, VARA2, ...: type;
         VARB1, VARB2, ...: type;
         . . .
Procedure and function definitions
```

Figure 6.46 General structure of the declaration part of a Pascal program or procedure.

confused with the relational operator "equal to." Input-output transfers are usually specified by special procedures of the **read** and **write** types.

Data-processing instructions are expressed in high-level languages by general assignment statements thus:

$$\text{variable} := \text{expression to be evaluated;}$$

The value of the expression on the right of the assignment operator is to be computed and then assigned to the variable on the left. As discussed earlier, these expressions are constructed from the available data types, operators, and functions according to the usual laws of arithmetic and Boolean algebra. Procedure calls to data-processing routines may also be viewed as data-processing instructions in high-level languages, whereas in assembly languages they are generally considered to be program-control instructions. High-level languages have more types of program-control statements than assembly languages, and these statements play a more important role in the design of high-level programs.

The program-control statements of high-level languages fall into two main groups: branch and loop control. Branch control statements such as **if** .. **then** .. **else** select a (compound) statement from one or more alternatives and cause it to be executed once. These instructions are similar to, but somewhat more general than, branch instructions found in assembly languages. High-level languages also have loop control statements such as **do** .. **while**, which cause a (compound) statement to be executed repeatedly under the control of a specified test condition. Loop control statements are characteristic of modern high-level programming languages, and are considered to be key constructs in the design of well-structured programs. They have only rudimentary counterparts in assembly languages, for example, the Z80's repetitive control instruction CPIR used in Fig. 5.57. Figure 6.47 lists the program-control statement types of Pascal, and also shows equivalent flowcharts.

Simple unconditional branches may be expressed as follows in Pascal

goto n;

...

n: statement S;

where n is an integer denoting a statement label. The use of **goto** statements in high-level language programs is frequently discouraged because, as discussed in Sec. 6.1, their presence can complicate program structure. Moreover, it is better in most applications to replace **goto's** by the other more powerful and more structured control statements of Pascal. The **goto** statement is sometimes useful as an "escape" statement to leave a procedure when some unexpected condition is encountered, for example, an error condition. The appearance of the statement **goto** n; in a Pascal program or procedure requires the insertion of a label declaration statement of the form

label   n;

at the beginning of the corresponding set of declaration statements; see Fig. 6.46.

Conditional branches are implemented by **if** statements of the form

if B **then** S1 **else** S2;

where B is an expression that yields a **boolean** value. If B = **true**, then statement S1 is executed; otherwise S2 is executed. Multiway branches can be constructed by nesting several **if** statements. For instance, the main program in Fig. 6.40 contains a three-way branch statement with the following structure:

if B1 **then** S1 **else if** B2 **then** S2 **else** S3;

Pascal Statement	Equivalent Flowchart Structure

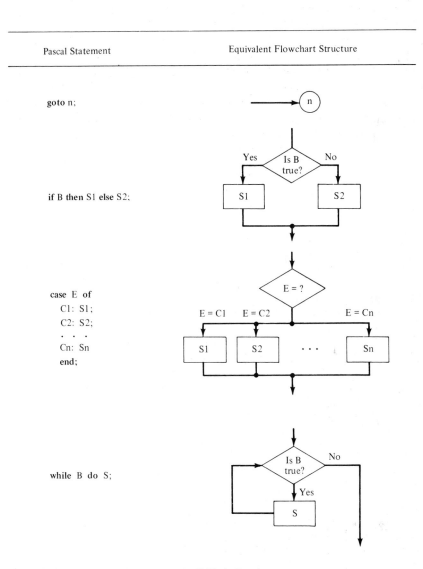

Figure 6.47 Program-control statements available in Pascal.

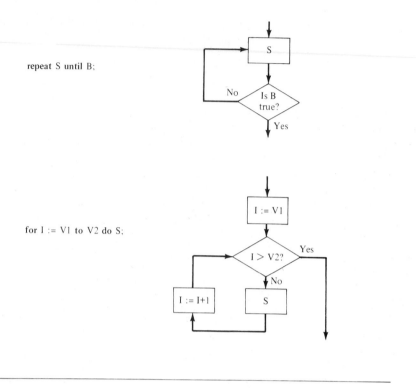

repeat S until B;

for I := V1 to V2 do S;

(Figure 6.47 Continued)

n-way branches formed from nested **if** statements become quite cumbersome when *n* is large. Suppose, for example, that an eight-way branch based on the value of a character variable named FLAG is to be implemented. If FLAG = 'i', then the statement Si is to be executed, where $0 \leq i \leq 7$. This requires the following kind of nested **if** construction:

$$
\begin{aligned}
&\textbf{if } \text{FLAG} = \text{`0' } \textbf{then } \text{S0 } \textbf{else} \\
&\textbf{if } \text{FLAG} = \text{`1' } \textbf{then } \text{S1 } \textbf{else} \\
&\textbf{if } \text{FLAG} = \text{`2' } \textbf{then } \text{S2 } \textbf{else} \\
&\textbf{if } \text{FLAG} = \text{`3' } \textbf{then } \text{S3 } \textbf{else} \\
&\textbf{if } \text{FLAG} = \text{`4' } \textbf{then } \text{S4 } \textbf{else} \\
&\textbf{if } \text{FLAG} = \text{`5' } \textbf{then } \text{S5 } \textbf{else} \\
&\textbf{if } \text{FLAG} = \text{`6' } \textbf{then } \text{S6 } \textbf{else } \text{S7;}
\end{aligned}
\tag{6.24}
$$

Not only is statement (6.24) very long, it is likely to be translated into object code that tests FLAG repeatedly, and therefore executes slowly.

Pascal provides another branch instruction, called the **case** statement, which implements multiway branches more efficiently than the nested **if** construction. The **case** statements have the general format

$$\text{\textbf{case} E \textbf{of}}$$
$$\text{C1: S1;}$$
$$\text{C2: S2;}$$
$$\cdots$$
$$\text{Cn: Sn}$$
$$\text{\textbf{end};}$$

where E is an expression of some simple type except **real** that yields values in the set C1, C2, ..., Cn. When the case statement is executed, E is evaluated once and found to have some value Ci. Then the statement Si with the label Ci in the **case** statement is executed directly. The multiway branch statement (6.24) is equivalent to the following simpler and more efficient **case** statement:

$$\text{\textbf{case} FLAG \textbf{of}}$$

| '0': S0; | '1': S1; | '2': S2; | '3': S3; |
| '4': S4; | '5': S5; | '6': S6; | '7': S7 |

$$\text{\textbf{end};}$$

Many computer programs contain loops consisting of sequences of statements that are executed repeatedly. A specified condition is tested periodically to determine when an exit should be made from the loop. Loops may be implemented with conditional branch statements thus:

$$
\left.
\begin{array}{l}
\text{1:} \quad \text{start of loop} \\
\qquad \cdots \\
\text{\textbf{if} B \textbf{then goto} 1;}
\end{array}
\right\} \quad \text{Loop statement(s) S} \qquad (6.25)
$$

This is the commonest loop construction used in assembly-language programming; it is used, for example, in the multibyte addition routines of Figs. 6.19 and 6.22. The loop control statements found in some high-level languages allow loop routines such as (6.25) to be written as a single control statement. The use of these loop control statements can improve program structure and intelligibility. Pascal provides three control constructs for defining program loops—the **while**, **repeat**, and **for** statements.

The formats used for **while** and **repeat** statements are

$$\text{\textbf{while} B \textbf{do} S;} \qquad (6.26)$$
$$\text{\textbf{repeat} S \textbf{until} B;}$$

where B is an expression with a **boolean** value and S is a (compound) statement forming the body of the loop. Note the equivalence between (6.25) and (6.26), and the fact that the

while and **repeat** statements eliminate the need for the statement label and **goto** appearing in (6.25). The loop control statements (6.26) allow S to be executed an indefinite number of times as determined by the test condition B. As Fig. 6.47 indicates, the key difference between **while** and **repeat** is in the position of the condition test performed on B. In a **while** statement B is tested before each execution of S. If B = **true**, then S is executed; otherwise an exit is made from the **while** statement. Hence if B is **false** initially, S is not executed at all. In a **repeat** statement, on the other hand, B is tested after each execution of S, so that S is always executed at least once. In this case the condition B = **true** causes an exit to be made from the **repeat** loop. Examples of the use of **while** and **repeat** statements in Pascal programs can be found in Figs. 6.40 and 6.45 respectively.

There are some programming situations—for example, when processing data of type **array**—where it is desired to repeat certain program statements a fixed number of times. The **while** and **repeat** statements can be used for this purpose by introducing an index or counting variable into the loop statement S, as in the following example.

$$\text{INDEX} := 1;$$

while INDEX $<=$ 100 **do**

    begin

    A[INDEX] := B[INDEX];   (6.27)

    INDEX := INDEX + 1

    end;

Pascal has a third loop control statement called a **for** statement that has built-in indexing to allow the loop statements to be executed a specified number of times. The general structure of this statement is

    for index := initial-value **to** final-value **do** S;

Thus (6.27) can be replaced by the following **for** statement:

    for INDEX := 1 **to** 100 **do** A[INDEX] := B[INDEX];   (6.28)

Note that the index variable of a **for** statement may be used as a parameter within the **for** loop S as is done in (6.28); however, statements in S that explicitly alter the index variable are forbidden since such statements interfere with the automatic changes made to the index during the execution of the **for** statement. The keyword **to** may be replaced by **downto**, causing the index values to be generated in descending rather than ascending order. Consequently (6.28) may be rewritten as

    for INDEX := 100 **downto** 1 **do** A[INDEX] := B[INDEX];

Figure 6.48 shows a second version of the program of Fig. 6.45, which illustrates the application of the **for** statement to array processing.

program ROLLBOOK2 (**input, output**);

```
{ ************************************************************
*      Second version of Pascal demonstration program to extract grades from a student record file   *
*      and compute an average grade. The records are stored on input using the following format:      *
*            Line 1: Name (One to 20 alphanumeric characters)                                          *
*            Line 2: Rank (1 = undergraduate; 2 = graduate student)                                    *
*            Line 3: Grade (integer)                                                                   *
* ************************************************************ }
```

{Declarations}

type   MATRIX1 = **array** [1 . . 100] **of array** [1 . . 20] **of char**;
       MATRIX2 = **array** [1 . . 100] **of integer**;
       INFILE = **file of char**;
var   NAME_LIST: matrix1;
       RANK_LIST: matrix2;
       GRADE_LIST: matrix2;
       I: **integer**;

{Procedure to transfer data from external file to internal arrays}

procedure READFILE (**var** CLASS_FILE: infile; CLASS_SIZE: **integer**; **var** NAME: matrix1; **var** RANK, GRADE: matrix2);

var   J: **integer**;
       STUDENT: **record**
                 NAME: **array** [1 . . 20] **of char**;
                 RANK: **integer**;
                 GRADE: **integer**
                 end;
begin
for J := 1 **to** CLASS_SIZE **do**
   begin
   readln (STUDENT.NAME);
   readln (STUDENT.RANK);
   readln (STUDENT.GRADE);
   NAME[J] := STUDENT.NAME:
   RANK[J] := STUDENT.RANK;
   GRADE[J] := STUDENT.GRADE
   end

end;

{ Function to compute average grade }

function AVERAGE (GRADE: matrix2; CLASS_SIZE: **integer**): **integer**;
var SUM: **integer**;
begin
SUM := 0;
for I := 1 **to** CLASS_SIZE **do** SUM := SUM + GRADE[I];
AVERAGE := SUM **div** CLASS_SIZE
end;

Figure 6.48 Another version of the grade-processing program of Fig. 6.45.

{ Main program }

begin
READFILE (**input**, 50, NAME_LIST, RANK_LIST, GRADE_LIST);
for I := 1 **to** 50 **do**
    writeln ('NAME = ', NAME_LIST[I], 'GRADE = ', GRADE_LIST[I]);
writeln ('AVERAGE GRADE = ', AVERAGE (GRADE_LIST, 50))
end.

(Figure 6.48 Continued)

6.4.5 Procedures and Functions

Procedures or subroutines provide the basic means for constructing computer programs in a modular or structured form. A procedure (we henceforth use only the Pascal term) is a self-contained program module that usually can be written, compiled, and debugged independently of other modules. By judiciously choosing procedure names, the readability of a program can be improved. For example, in the Pascal program of Fig. 6.40, the command to set the oven temperature to the reference temperature is expressed by a call to the procedure named SET_OVEN thus:

$$SET\_OVEN\ (REF\_TEMP);$$

Also, as will be discussed later, procedures of the kind found in Pascal programs can reduce a program's data storage requirements. A special type of procedure called a function is definable in most high-level languages. A main program is defined in essentially the same manner as a procedure, so it too can be regarded as a sort of procedure.

A function F is distinguished from other types of procedures by the fact that it computes or returns a single value denoted by F(X), where X is the set of parameters of the function. F(X) can be used like a variable operand in program statements and, like an ordinary variable, its type must be declared. Thus while a procedure P(X) that is not a function can only appear in procedure call statements of the form

$$P(X);$$

a function F(X) can appear as an operand in any expression that is appropriate to its particular type. For instance, the **real** function **sin**(x) can appear in any valid arithmetic expression involving **real** numbers, for example,

$$Y := \mathbf{sqrt}\ (1.7635 - \mathbf{sin}(x));$$

Pascal, like most high-level languages, has numerous built-in procedures and functions; see Fig. 6.44. A programmer can introduce new ones by employing the definition structures shown in Fig. 6.49. Definitions of a procedure named READFILE and a function named AVERAGE appear in Fig. 6.48. A definition consists of a header statement identified by the keyword **procedure** or **function**, followed by a sequence of statements called a block. Each header statement contains a list of formal parameters, and defines certain attributes of these parameters, including their types. For example, a

Procedure header { **procedure** PROCEDURE_NAME (formal parameters);

Declaration part

    labels

    constants

    types

Block   variables

    other procedure and function definitions

Statement part

    begin

    . . .

    end;

(*a*)

Function header { **function** FUNCTION_NAME (formal parameters): type;

Declaration part

    labels

    constants

    types

Block   variables

    other procedure and function definitions

Statement part

    begin

    . . .

    end;

(*b*)

Figure 6.49 General structure of (*a*) procedure and (*b*) function definitions in Pascal.

procedure named SUM that computes the sum S of the elements of an array X of integers might have the following header:

$$\textbf{procedure } \text{SUM } (X: \textbf{ array } [1..50] \textbf{ of integer}; \textbf{ var } S: \textbf{ integer}); \qquad (6.29)$$

Since SUM assigns a new value to the quantity S, the latter is declared to be a variable parameter indicated by the keyword **var** appearing in the header. The procedure definition should contain a statement of the form

$$S := \text{expression}; \qquad (6.30)$$

that yields the procedure's final result. A function named SUM that performs the same calculation could have the header statement

$$\textbf{function } \text{SUM } (X: \textbf{ array } [1..50] \textbf{ of integer}): \textbf{ integer};$$

In this case the desired result is referred to by the function name SUM, and a declaration that SUM(X) is of type **integer** is included in the function header. The function definition must contain the statement

$$\text{SUM} := \text{expression};$$

in place of (6.30).

The block part of a procedure or function definition, which follows the header statement, has two sections: a declaration part and a statement part. The *declaration part* is a sequence of nonexecutable statements that declare or define all the special identifiers used in the block. These statements serve as directives to the program translator. All nonstandard names used for labels, constants, variables, and types must be declared. The declaration part also includes the definitions of any other procedures or functions, excluding built-in ones, that are called in the statement part of the block. The internal layout of the declaration part of a Pascal block appears in Fig. 6.46. The *statement part* of the block is a compound statement enclosed by **begin** and **end** containing the executable statements that form the main body of the procedure or function.

A Pascal program can be viewed as a set of blocks, with the main program constituting the outermost block. Blocks may be nested within other blocks to an arbitrary number of levels. The declaration part of a block typically defines identifiers that are unique to that block. An important feature of Pascal is that each identifier has a well-defined *scope*, that is, a region of the program for which the identifier is valid or meaningful. An identifier's scope is determined by the program's block structure. Generally speaking, the scope of an identifier X is the block B where it is declared, and all blocks that are contained in B. (If the identifier X happens to be redefined in some block B' contained in B, then B' is excluded from the scope of the original X.) In the program of Fig. 6.47, for example, the scope of the variable NAME_LIST is the entire program, while that of the variable STUDENT is confined to the procedure READFILE. The identifiers declared in a block B are said to be *local* to B, whereas identifiers that are defined in a block that contains B are said to be *global* to B. The scope rules of Pascal mean that statements in B can only access variables that are either local or global to B.

Storage space is allocated to the local variables of a procedure only when the procedure is entered (called). This space can be deallocated, and thereby made available for other uses, on exiting from the procedure. Hence the scope concept can be used to improve memory space utilization while a program is executing. Furthermore, it allows the same identifiers to be used with different meanings in different procedures. This can facilitate the construction of a program from modules written by different groups of programmers.

The passing of parameters between procedures, a complex task in assembly-language programming, is quite simple in Pascal and most high-level languages. When a procedure is called, the actual parameters to be passed are listed in parentheses after the procedure name in the call statement. These parameters must correspond with the formal (dummy) parameters appearing in the header statement of the procedure definition, with respect to both position and data type. The formal parameters are a set of variables that are local to the procedure. Parameters of Pascal procedures are of two principal kinds, value and variable. (The use of procedure and function names as parameters will not be covered here.) A *value parameter* is basically an input operand to the procedure; the actual (dummy) parameter is an expression whose current value is assigned to the corresponding formal parameter in the procedure definition. A *variable parameter*, on the other hand, can act as an output operand of the procedure because, unlike a value parameter, it can be assigned new values during procedure execution. In effect, all changes made to a variable formal parameter are also made to the corresponding actual parameter.

To illustrate the above concepts, consider again the procedure SUM with the header statement appearing in (6.29). X is a value parameter, while S, as specified by the prefix **var**, is a variable parameter. SUM is called by a statement of the form

$$SUM \ (Y,T);$$

and the actual parameters Y and T are placed in correspondence with the formal parameters X and S respectively. Y must be declared to be of type **array** [1..50] **of integer** to match X, and T must be of type **integer** to match S. When the procedure call is executed, the value of Y is assigned to X, but Y is not altered by the execution of SUM. The variable parameter T effectively replaces S during procedure execution, so that all operations performed on S are performed on T. A procedure READFILE with five parameters of various kinds appears in Fig. 6.47. The actual mechanism used for parameter passing in high-level-language programs is determined by the compiler and is largely hidden from the programmer.

6.5 SUMMARY

Programming languages fall into two main groups—high level and assembly. High-level languages such as FORTRAN, COBOL, and Pascal were developed for describing numeric and text-processing algorithms in a way that approximates mathematical notation or a simplified version of English. They provide the programmer with a more powerful (higher-level) set of instructions and data types than can be found in assembly languages. High-level languages are also machine independent in the sense that they can be executed by any computer for which the necessary translation program, compilers or interpreters, are available. Because of this machine independence, however, they do not allow the programmer to have direct control over such computer resources as IO ports and main memory, an important issue in microprocessor-based systems. A few microprocessor oriented high-level languages such as PL/M provide the programmer with access to certain resources of the target microcomputer; these languages are less widely used, however.

Most assembly languages were designed for programming specific computer families. Unlike high-level languages, they give the programmer essentially complete control over a computer's resources. They provide instruction and data types that correspond directly to the low-level instruction and data types that are implemented in the hardware of the underlying machine. Consequently assembly-language programs tend to be longer, less readable, and more difficult to debug than equivalent programs written in high-level languages. Before it can be executed, a source program written in assembly language must also be translated into machine-language object code; translation in this case is done by an assembler program. Because of the close correspondence between assembly and machine language, shorter object programs can be obtained if the source program is written in an assembly language rather than a high-level language. At the present time, assembly languages are the more widely used group of languages for programming microprocessor-based systems.

Developing the software for a complex system is a costly and time-consuming task. The chief goal in all program design projects is ensuring the correctness of the resulting code. Secondary design goals, whose relative importance is application dependent, are fast execution, flexibility in making changes to the program, and efficient utilization of the CPU, memory, and IO resources of the host computer. Minimization of program memory space is an important design objective for some microprocessor-based systems that are to be produced in high volume at low cost per unit. Program development costs can be reduced by employing a systematic design methodology such as the following five-step process:

1. Planning: Define the desired program behavior and also the computing environment that is to be used.
2. Preliminary design: Specify the overall structure and identify the major components (program modules) of the program.
3. Detailed design: Code the program module by module following a top-down sequence.
4. Debugging: Identify and correct design errors.
5. Documentation: Prepare the documents required to understand, use, and maintain the program.

Flowcharts and pseudocode are useful for preliminary design, and also for documentation. Step 4 (debugging) has been found to be the most costly step in large projects, so minimizing design errors is an important general design objective.

Assembly languages have a fixed instruction format of the following kind:

label   opcode   operands   comment

The opcode defines an operation to be carried out using the specified operands and, possibly, other implicit operands. Operands are typically stored in CPU registers, main memory locations, IO ports, and other locations known to the programmer. Most assembly languages provide a variety of different addressing modes for indicating an operand's location, including direct, indirect, indexed, and relative addressing. Operand types are usually limited to a few simple machine-dependent word formats. Instruction formats and opcode mnemonics have not been standardized.

Assembly-language instructions may be classified as executable and nonexecutable. The nonexecutable instructions, which are called directives, are used by the assembler for symbol definition, memory space assignment, program structuring, and various bookkeeping tasks. The executable instructions, which can be translated directly into machine-language instructions, fall into three major groups: data transfer (including IO instructions), data processing, and program control. A typical assembly language has about 50 to 100 different opcodes. These built-in instructions may be augumented by programmer-defined macroinstructions or macros. A macro is an instruction with its own unique opcode that is defined to be equivalent to a sequence of regular instructions. During program translation, the assembler replaces each occurrence of the macro by the corresponding instruction sequence. Macros are mainly useful as a shorthand notation for short, frequently occurring instruction sequences.

A subroutine is a sequence of instructions whose execution, like that of a macro, is invoked by a programmer-defined name. Whereas a macro is reproduced in expanded form each time it is called, a subroutine appears only once in the object program. A subroutine thus constitutes a self-contained module of a program at the source- and object-code levels. Links are established between a calling program and a subroutine by means of call and return instructions. In many microprocessor systems an automatically maintained stack region of main memory is used for communication between call and return instructions. A call instruction places a return address to the calling program at the top of the stack before transferring control to the first instruction of the subroutine. A return instruction retrieves the return address from the stack, causing execution of the calling program to be resumed. Explicit instructions are usually required for passing parameters to or from an assembly-language subroutine.

A high-level-language program consists of a header statement followed by a list of nonexecutable declarations, followed in turn by executable statements. The declaration part defines the special identifiers, including constant, variable, and procedure (subroutine) names, used in the program. High-level languages allow program statements (instructions) to be constructed from a much wider range of primitive data types and operators than assembly languages. Most data-transfer and data-processing operations are expressed by assignment statements thus:

$$\text{variable} := \text{expression to be evaluated};$$

Program-control statements play an especially important role in program design using high-level languages. Modern languages such as Pascal have two kinds of control statements: branch statements such as **if** and **case** statements, and loop statements such as **while**, **repeat**, and **for** statements. Program construction is also aided by the ability to enclose a sequence of instructions between the delimiters **begin** and **end**, thereby forming a compound statement that can be treated as a single unit.

High-level programming languages have more powerful features for defining and calling procedures (subroutines) than assembly languages. They also provide a class of procedures called functions, which return a single value and can be used as operands in expressions. Many common operations are implemented by built-in procedures and functions. For example, IO operations are typically performed by built-in procedures named **read** and **write**. A procedure definition in Pascal consists of a header followed by a block of declarations and executable statements. Other procedure definitions may be included in the declaration section, thus allowing procedures to be systematically nested. The scope of each declared identifier is limited to the block B where it is defined, and to certain subblocks of B. Scoping rules allowing the same identifier to be used with different meanings in different procedures, and also permit efficient use of data storage space during program execution.

6.6 FURTHER READING

A broad overview of program design issues in the context of microprocessors appears in Ogdin (1978), and a more detailed treatment of microcomputer programming can be found in Wakerly (1981). A formal and rigorous discussion of programming concepts for both assembly and high-level languages is presented in Ullman (1976). Van Tassel examines program design issues, including program efficiency and debugging (Van Tassel, 1978). A series of books by Leventhal cover assembly-language programming for several important microprocessors, including the 8080/8085 (Leventhal, 1978a) and the 6800 (Leventhal, 1978b). There are several good textbooks on Pascal programming (e.g., Bowles, 1977; Findlay & Watt, 1978). The use of PL/M for programming microprocessors is treated in depth by McCracken (1978). Despite numerous standardization efforts, different implementations of a given programming language often differ in small but significant ways. Reference should be made to the appropriate user's manual for a complete description of any particular version of a programming language.

6.7 PROBLEMS

6.1 Explain why computer programs are rarely written directly in machine language. Under what circumstances is machine-language programming likely to be used today?

6.2 Give examples in both high-level and assembly languages of typical instructions or statements for implementing each of the following operations:
  (*a*) Two-way conditional branches
  (*b*) Subroutine calls
  (*c*) Input-output data transfers
  (*d*) One-bit shift operations

6.3 Describe three typical built-in data types found in most high-level programming languages. Describe two typical data types found in assembly languages. Explain why most programming languages require the type of programmer-defined identifier to be specified explicitly by means of directives or declaration statements.

6.4 Define what is meant by a macroinstruction. Explain why most assembly languages have macro-definition capabilities, whereas most high-level languages do not. Suggest a suitable statement format for adding a macro-definition capability to a high-level language such as Pascal.

6.5 Explain the differences between compilers and interpreters of high-level languages. Under what circumstances would an interpreter be preferred to a compiler for use with a microprocessor-based system?

6.6 Occasionally one encounters a system program called a *disassembler,* whose purpose is to convert a machine language (binary) object program back into assembly-language form. Suggest some possible practical uses for disassemblers. Explain why it is generally impossible to recover the entire original source program from the object program by means of a disassembler.

6.7 For each of the following microprocessor applications, list what you think are the two most important design goals or program quality criteria to be used in developing the system control software.
  (*a*) Microwave oven
  (*b*) Domestic sewing machine
  (*c*) Hand-held computer programmable in BASIC
  (*d*) Traffic-light controller at a major intersection
Give reasons for your answers in each case.

6.8 Describe in general terms the way a complex computer program should be developed so that new features (enhancements) can be added periodically to the program in a cost-effective manner.

6.9 List the program design rules that should be followed to minimize the amount of time that must be devoted to debugging.

6.10 Write a short essay comparing and contrasting high-level and assembly languages as the media for writing microprocessor software. Explain the relative advantages and disadvantages of each kind of language. List several design situations where you would prefer to use a high-level language, and explain why.

6.11 Analyze the relative merits of high-level and assembly languages with respect to the following steps in program development: design debugging, system documentation.

6.12 Indicate which kind of language, high level or assembly, is more suited to the following programming tasks, giving the reasons for your answers in each case.

(*a*) Computing the square root of a floating-point number

(*b*) Creating a time delay of 400 ms duration

(*c*) Reading serial data from a disk unit and formatting the data into 32-bit integers

(*d*) Justifying a page of text by inserting extra blanks between words to make each line of equal width

6.13 It is planned to build a microcomputer dedicated to text editing that is to be used in an intelligent CRT terminal. The necessary software will be written in assembly language, and one of the following microprocessors will be used: 8080, 8085, Z80, 6800. Which microprocessor do you think is most suitable for this application? Justify your answer.

6.14 Write an essay comparing and contrasting the 6800 and 8080/8085 assembly languages from the following viewpoints: addressing modes, assembler directive capabilities, parameter passing to subroutines.

6.15 Describe the main differences between macros and subroutines in assembly languages. Discuss the factors that determine whether a frequently used piece of source code should be made into a macro or a subroutine.

6.16 (*a*) Give two ways of clearing the A accumulator of the 6800 microprocessor by means of a single assembly-language instruction.

(*b*) Design a minimum-length 6800 program to transfer all programmable CPU registers except SP to the top of the stack.

(*c*) Define a 6800 subroutine called SUBD (subtract decimal) that subtracts the B register from the A register, assuming that all operands are decimal numbers.

6.17 (*a*) Give two ways of clearing the accumulator of the 8080/8085 microprocessor by means of a single assembly-language instruction.

(*b*) Define an 8080/8085 macro called ADDD (add decimal) that adds the B register to the A register, assuming that all operands are decimal numbers.

(*c*) Define an 8080/8085 subroutine called SUBD (subtract decimal) that subtracts the B register from the A register using decimal operands.

6.18 Consider the addition programs for the 6800 and 8080/8085 appearing in Figs. 6.19 and 6.22 respectively. Identify the addressing modes used for all explicit operands in each instruction.

6.19 (*a*) Explain how indirect addressing can be used in 8080/8085 assembly-language programs to carry out the tasks normally implemented by indexed addressing in 6800 programs. Discuss the trade-offs involved.

(*b*) Give an example of an array-processing task where an 8080/8085 program can be expected to be shorter and faster than an equivalent 6800 program. Explain your answer.

6.20 Macros are useful for introducing new addressing modes into assembly language programs. Write 8080/8085 macro definitions to implement the following macroinstructions, each of which involves a new type of addressing mode.

Macro Statement	Name	Action Performed
JMP@ ADR	Jump indirect	PC := M[ADR + 1].M[ADR]
STR@ R, ADR	Store register indirect	M[M[ADR + 1]. M[ADR]] := R
XLDA ADR	Indexed load accumulator	A := M[ADR + DE] where DE simulates an index register

6.21 The following short 8080/8085 program is proposed to replace the much longer temperature-conversion program CONV2 given in Fig. 6.16

```
           ORG    500H
DEGC:      DB     − 25
DEGF:      DS     1
           LDA    DEGC            ; Place input temperature in A
           MOV    B, A * 9/5 + 32 ; Compute output temperature and place in B
           MOV    A, B
           STA    DEGF            ; Store result
           HLT
```

Most assembly languages allow complex expressions of the type appearing in the first MOV statement to be used as instruction operands. Thus the above program is syntactically correct and will assemble without error. Nevertheless this program is useless for the required temperature-conversion task. Explain clearly why that is so.

6.22 The CONV2 program of Fig. 6.16 uses the S flag for communication between the main program and the subroutine TEMP. This may be viewed as poor programming practice, since it is often difficult to keep track of flag states in assembly-language programs. Rewrite CONV2 to eliminate the use of flags in this way.

6.23 Redesign the 8080/8085 program of Fig. 6.27 so that subroutine calls to ADDDN can be written as follows in the main program:

```
           CALL   ADDDN
           DW     OPND1, OPND2    ; Operand start addresses
           DB     N               ; Operand byte count
```

6.24 Redesign the 6800 program of Fig. 6.31 so that subroutine calls to ADDDN can be written as follows in the main program:

```
           JSR    ADDDN
           FDB    OPND1, OPND2    Operand start addresses
           FCB    N               Operand byte count
```

The 6800 directives FDB (form double constant byte) and FCB (form constant byte) correspond exactly to the 8080/8085 directives DW and DB respectively; see Fig. 6.24.

6.25 Draw a diagram similar to Fig. 6.29 that shows the states of the relevant CPU registers and main memory locations immediately before and immediately after the execution of the final RET (return from subroutine) instruction in the program of Fig. 6.27.

6.26 Analyze the instruction set of the MicroController listed in Fig. 6.23 from the viewpoints of programming ease and execution efficiency. All instructions are 16 bits long and contain one or two address fields of various lengths. Operand length can be specified, and can vary from 1 to 8 bits. Addition uses twos-complement numbers. The main address modes available are direct, indirect, and immediate.

6.27 Consider a hypothetical microprocessor called the 8079½, which has no stack support facilities, but is otherwise identical to the 8080. The 8079½ lacks the stack pointer register SP and all instructions that affect SP including PUSH, POP, CALL, and RET. However, these instructions can be added effectively to the 8079½'s instruction repertoire by writing suitable macros that use a software-implemented stack mechanism. Design two 8079½ assembly-language macros that simulate the 8080's CALL and RET instructions as closely as possible using the BC register-pair of the 8079½ as a stack pointer register. Provide a flowchart, source listing, and brief narrative description of each macro.

6.28 Repeat Prob. 6.27, replacing the 8080 by the 6800 and the 8079½ by the equally fictitious 6799½, which is identical to the 6800 without its stack hardware or instructions. Assuming that the 6799½ assembly language is similar to that of the 6800 without its stack instructions, but with the addition of the assembler directives listed in Fig. 6.24, write macros to simulate the 6800's JSR and RTS instructions. Any suitable CPU register or memory location may be used to store the stack pointer.

The following problems marked by asterisks are to be solved using the assembly language of the 6800, 8080/8085, or any similar 8-bit microprocessor. In all cases prepare the following documentation: a flowchart, a source program listing with suitable comments, and a clear narrative description of your program. If the necessary assembly and execution facilities are available, also provide an assembly listing, and one or two test runs demonstrating the correctness of your program.

6.29* In low-speed systems, multiplication is sometimes implemented by repeated addition. The key idea is to obtain the product PQ by adding P to itself Q times. This technique is computationally feasible as long as P and Q are relatively small. It can also easily accommodate unusual or nonstandard number types. Write an assembly-language program that computes the product PQ by repeated addition, where P and Q are unsigned two-digit decimal numbers, and PQ is a four-digit result.

6.30* Write an assembly-language subroutine called MOVE that transfers a contiguous block of bytes from one part of memory to another. The source data are stored in the memory locations with addresses BLK1, BLK1 + 1, ..., BLK1 + SIZE − 1, where SIZE is a variable denoting the number of bytes in the block. The destination addresses are BLK2, BLK2 + 1, ..., BLK2 + SIZE − 1. The input parameters of MOVE are the addresses BLK1 and BLK2, and the block size SIZE. SIZE can take any value between one and 2^{15}. Assume that the source and destination areas do not overlap.

6.31* Repeat Prob. 6.30 with the assumption that the source and destination blocks do not overlap removed.

6.32* Design an algorithm to convert a packed decimal number DNUM containing N bytes (i.e. $2N$ digits) into the equivalent binary number BNUM, where DNUM and BNUM are both unsigned positive integers. The algorithm should be designed with ease of programming as the main objective. Execution speed and storage efficiency are secondary goals, but should be taken into account. Write an assembly-language program called DTOB that implements your algorithm.

6.33* An assembly-language program is required to implement the formula

$$z_0 = \frac{x_1 + 2x_2 - x_3}{2}$$

where x_1, x_2, and x_3 are even positive integers between zero and 100; z_0 should also be a positive integer. Your program should test the parity of x_1, x_2, and x_3, and also the sign of z_0. If any x_i is odd, or if z_0 is negative, the CPU's zero flag should be set to 1. If no error conditions are detected, execution should terminate with the zero flag set to 0.

Write your program in the form of a subroutine named ZED with input parameters x_1, x_2, and x_3. The values of these parameters should be placed immediately after the subroutine call statement in the calling program. The final result z_0 should be placed in the accumulator.

6.34* The goal of this problem is to construct a macro called DAB that mimics the actions of the decimal adjust accumulator DAA found in the 6800, 8080/8085, and some other microprocessors. DAB may be written using any instructions except DAA or its equivalent. Like DAA, which it will replace, DAB should correct the result obtained by applying a 1-byte binary add instruction to decimal data. The CPU state after executing DAB should be as close as possible to the state existing after the execution of DAA.

Write an assembly-language macro defining DAB. List the differences, if any, between DAA and DAB. Calculate the "slow-down" factor for DAB by dividing the (average) number of machine cycles needed to execute DAB by the number of machine cycles used by DAA.

6.35* Consider again the Celsius-to-Fahrenheit temperature-conversion program CONV2 of Fig. 6.16. You are to write a program CONV3 that realizes the conversion equation

$$°F = 1.8 * °C + 32$$

directly, using multiplication instead of table look-up. Like CONV2, the new program CONV3 should handle temperatures in the range $\pm 50°C$. However, it is known that sometime in the future a new version CONV4 will be needed to handle the expanded temperature range $\pm 100°C$. The primary goal in designing CONV3 is to minimize the length of the object program. The secondary design goal is to minimize the extra development costs needed to convert CONV3 to CONV4. Describe the steps taken in the design of CONV3 to meet both these goals. Estimate, showing all your calculations, the percentage increase in object program length resulting from the conversion of CONV3 to CONV4.

6.36* A standard way to test a RAM memory for hardware faults is to execute a test algorithm called CHECKERBOARD, which works as follows (Breuer & Friedman, 1976): First write 0s and 1s into alternating bit positions in the entire RAM to produce the following checkerboard pattern of stored data:

Address	Contents
0000_{16}	0 1 0 1 0 1 0 1
0001_{16}	1 0 1 0 1 0 1 0
0002_{16}	0 1 0 1 0 1 0 1
0003_{16}	1 0 1 0 1 0 1 0
	...

Then read the entire RAM contents and verify that each bit location contains the expected value. The preceding actions are repeated with the 0 and 1 positions interchanged. Thus CHECKERBOARD verifies that a 0 and a 1 can be written into and read from every cell of the RAM. If on reading some cell a d is obtained where a $\bar{d}$ is expected, then a fault has been detected.

You are to write a CHECKERBOARD test program in assembly language that can be executed by a microprocessor to test its own main memory. Assume that this RAM contains 512 consecutive bytes with starting address 0000. Your program should be designed to execute in the shortest possible time so that testing interferes with normal CPU operation as little as possible. Compute the number of machine cycles required to execute your version of CHECKERBOARD.

6.37* Write a recursive assembly-language subroutine that computes the nth Fibonacci number FIB(n), which is defined as follows:

$$FIB(0) = 0$$

$$FIB(1) = 1$$

$$FIB(n) = FIB(n-1) + FIB(n-2) \quad \text{for } n \geq 2$$

Assume that n lies in the range of zero to 12. The Fibonacci numbers form a famous number series with many interesting applications (Knuth, 1969).

6.38 Pascal is in most respects a better designed and more powerful programming language than FORTRAN. Explain why FORTRAN is still much more widely used for programming all types of computers than Pascal.

6.39 List the main deficiencies of Pascal as a programming language for microprocessor-based real-time control systems. Describe how two of these deficiencies are avoided in the programming language PL/M.

6.40 Describe two features of the Pascal language that can be exploited to reduce the amount of temporary data storage needed for program execution.

6.41 Write down the shortest possible valid Pascal program named PROG. PROG may be a dummy program that serves no useful purpose other than to indicate the minimum elements of a Pascal program.

6.42 (*a*) Explain why the built-in Pascal procedures **read** and **write** are not also functions in the formal Pascal sense.

(*b*) Specify which of the following built-in procedures of Pascal that were not encountered earlier are functions.

Name	Description
length(x)	Compute the number of characters in the character string x.
page(F)	Eject a page before writing to the (printer) file F.
odd(x)	Return the value **true** if the integer x is odd; otherwise return the value **false**.

6.43 Rewrite the main program part of the Pascal program OVEN appearing in Fig. 6.40 to replace the **while** statement by an equivalent **repeat** statement.

6.44 Let A be a 20×30 and B a 30×50 array or matrix of **real** numbers. We wish to compute the matrix product $C = A \times B$, where the entry in the ith row and jth column of C is defined by the usual formula

$$C[i, j] = \sum_{k=1}^{30} A\,[i, k] \times B\,[k, j] \qquad (6.31)$$

Write Pascal loop routines to compute the 20×50 matrix C:

(a) Using a **while** statement for loop control
(b) Using a **repeat** statement for loop control
(c) Using a **for** statement for loop control

6.45 Write a complete Pascal procedure named MULT that performs **real** matrix multiplication according to (6.31). The matrices A, B, and C with the dimensions given in Prob. 6.44 are to be the parameters of this procedure. Note that standard Pascal does not support dynamic arrays whose dimensions can be treated as variable parameters.

6.46 Modify the ROLLBOOK program of Fig. 6.45 so that the list of student names is written out in alphabetical order. Assume that the records on the input file **input** are in random order and that the statement **reset** may be used to reset or rewind the file **input** so that reading starts at the beginning of the file. Write your program in such a way that the structure of the original ROLLBOOK program is changed as little as possible.

The remaining problems in this chapter can be tackled using any desired high-level programming language, although Pascal is preferred. In all cases provide a flowchart and a source program listing with a comprehensive set of comments. If the necessary support facilities are available, also provide annotated test run listings that demonstrate that your program is correct.

6.47 A program called ALARM is to be written that that will control a microprocessor-based burglar alarm system in a small plant. ALARM receives inputs from 50 door and window switches denoted SWITCH_1:SWITCH_50, any one of which can be activated by an intruder. The program is required to monitor these switches continuously. When SWITCH_i is activated by an intruder, the message

INTRUDER AT LOCATION i

should be displayed on a guard's CRT console. The guard should be able to enter the command RESET i to ALARM, causing it to ignore SWITCH_i until a subsequent SET i command is entered. The commands RESET ALL and SET ALL are to be used to disable and (re)enable the entire burglar alarm system. Design the source program of ALARM to be as short and readable as possible.

6.48 Write a high-level language program that reads a file of alphanumeric text and computes the frequency f with which the letter E or e occurs among the nonblank characters of the text. The program should print a result of the form

f PERCENT OF THE NONBLANK CHARACTERS ARE E'S

6.49 Sparse matrices, in which most of the elements are zero, are often encountered in numerical analysis. It is inefficient to store a large $n \times m$ sparse matrix in the form of a two-dimensional array of nm entries since most of those entries are known to be zero entries that can be ignored in many calculations. Memory space can be saved by storing only the nonzero entries explicitly, and storing the positions and dimensions of the all-zero subarrays of the sparse matrix.

Devise a suitable format (data type) for storing sparse matrices so that storage space is minimized. Assume that a typical **real** sparse matrix contains 100 rows and 100 columns, and that 95 percent of its entries are zero. Write a high-level-language procedure named ADDSM that adds two sparse matrices, and produces a sum sparse matrix in the compressed format.

6.50 Write a fast program that computes and prints out the first 50 Fibonacci numbers; see Prob. 6.37 for a definition of these numbers. Demonstrate that your program indeed has a relatively high execution speed.

6.51 Suppose that I, J, and K are positive integers less than 32. Write a high-level language program that computes all values of I, J, and K that satisfy the equation

$$I^2 + J^3 = K^4$$

Design your program to be both readable and easily extensible to handle larger operand values. Estimate the speed of your program by calculating the number of "basic operations" it performs using Fig. 6.43 to define the basic operations.

INTERFACING TECHNIQUES

"A system is no better than its sensory organs. . . . To those within a system, the outside reality tends to pale and disappear."

[John Gall: *Systemantics*, 1975]

This chapter addresses the important issue of communication between a microprocessor and the input-output devices that link it to the outside world. The process of attaching an IO device to a microprocessor-based system is termed interfacing, and involves a close interaction between hardware and software design. The interfacing characteristics of common analog and digital IO devices are examined here. The role of shared buses in the interfacing process is considered in detail. The general methods used for communicating with IO devices are also discussed, including programmed IO, interrupt-driven IO, and direct memory access (DMA).

7.1 DIGITAL INPUT-OUTPUT

The overall characteristics of microprocessor IO devices and their associated interface circuits are considered in this section. The interfacing requirements of some basic digital IO devices, including switches, keyboards, and LED-based display units, are examined in detail.

7.1.1 Basic Interface Concepts

The noun "interface" is a general term for the boundary or point of contact between two parts of a system. In digital systems it usually refers to the set of signal connection points that the system or any of its components presents to the outside. The verb "to interface" means to link two or more components or systems via their respective interface points, so that information can be transferred between them. In a microprocessor-based system there are two main types of interfaces: the microprocessor or microcomputer interface, which, as shown in Fig. 7.1, corresponds to the system bus; and the interfaces presented by the system's IO devices. The latter depend on the kinds of IO devices with which they are associated, and vary greatly in complexity. To link an IO device to a microprocessor, an IO interface circuit is typically interposed between the device and the system bus. This circuit serves to match the signal formats and timing characteristics of the microprocessor interface to those of the IO device interface. The overall task of linking microprocessors and IO devices in the manner illustrated in Fig. 7.1 is termed *interfacing*.

The microprocessor interfacing problem has two principal aspects—hardware and software. Among hardware interfacing issues are selecting the most appropriate interface circuits, connecting the right wires to one another, and ensuring that all interface signals have the proper electrical characteristics (voltage level, current drive capability, waveform, etc.). The software side of interfacing involves the writing of programs, called *IO programs*, that control the transfer of information to and from IO devices. This information flow may be between the IO devices and the CPU (microprocessor). In most cases, however, IO operations involve the transfer of data between IO devices and main memory. The individual steps of a typical IO operation—for example, input or output a word of data—are fairly simple, and can be readily specified using a typical micro-

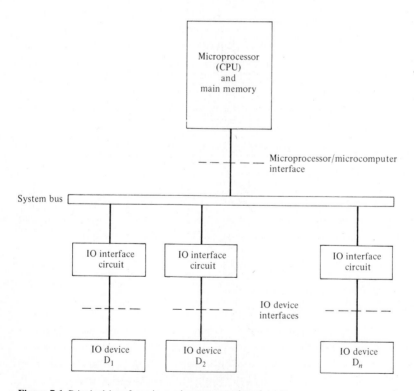

Figure 7.1 Principal interfaces in a microprocessor-based system.

processor's instruction repertoire. Some microprocessors, such as the 8080/8085, provide special instructions, collectively called *IO instructions*, that are intended to facilitate the construction of IO programs.

The interface characteristics of an IO device, such as the word size used for external data transfer and the maximum data-transfer rate, are often significantly different from those of the microprocessor to which it is attached. As discussed in Sec. 1.1.3, many of the physical variables with which a microprocessor must interact are nonelectrical in nature, and can assume analog (continuous) rather than digital (discrete) values. The maximum rate at which new data can be produced or accepted by an IO device often differs greatly from that of the microprocessor. In particular, IO devices that involve mechanical motion operate at much lower speeds. If several IO devices are attached to the same microprocessor, a means must be provided for selecting only one device at a time to participate in an IO operation, thereby preventing conflicting use of the system bus.

The foregoing considerations imply that IO interface circuits must perform the following functions:

1. Data conversion
2. Synchronization
3. Device selection

Data conversion refers to matching the physical and logical characteristics of the data signals employed by the IO device to those employed by the system bus. This includes conversion of signals between analog and digital form, and conversion between the serial (bit-by-bit) data-transmission format used by some IO devices and the parallel (word-by-word) formats used by almost all microprocessors. Synchronization is needed to accommodate the different operating speeds of the CPU, main memory, and IO devices. This usually requires the inclusion of one or more words of temporary or buffer storage in the interface circuits. The IO devices and the CPU operate independently in the sense that their internal clocks are not synchronized with one another. Hence handshaking control signals (ready, request, acknowledge, etc.) of the type discussed in Sec. 5.2.5 must be exchanged via the interface circuits to initiate or terminate IO operations. Device selection also involves the exchange of control signals. Selection of an IO device by the CPU may be implemented in much the same way as a memory read or write operation. The CPU places an address word associated with the device in question on the system address bus, and activates appropriate input- (read) or output- (write) enable control lines. Indeed some microprocessors, such as the 6800, employ the same control signals and instructions for accessing either main memory or IO devices. The IO operations may also be initiated by an IO device, for example, by transmitting an interrupt request signal to the CPU.

Figure 7.2 shows the structure of the interface circuitry needed to attach a specific input device, a typewriter-style keyboard, to an 8-bit microprocessor such as the 6800 or 8080/8085. The keyboard is assumed here to generate a unique 8-bit word (e.g., an ASCII codeword) for each key depressed. It also signals the availability of a new input word by activating a data-ready control line. Direct connection of the keyboard's

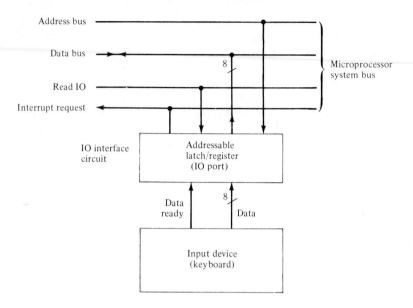

Figure 7.2 Interfacing a parallel input device (keyboard) to a microprocessor.

interface lines to the system bus is not possible because of the unpredictable times at which keys are depressed and new data produced. An interface circuit is therefore introduced to act as a buffer between the keyboard and the microprocessor bus. This is basically an 8-bit addressable latch or register with some additional control logic, and is termed an (input) IO port. It performs the following functions:

1. It receives and stores data words one at a time from the keyboard; each new data word replaces the preceding one.
2. It signals the presence of new data at the IO port by sending an interrupt request signal to the CPU via a control line in the system bus.
3. It responds to a read IO command from the CPU by transferring its stored data word to the system data bus, thus allowing the data to be read into the CPU.

Note that in this example the execution of a program by the CPU, specifically a read IO port instruction, controls the final stage in the data transfer across the microprocessor interface. This instruction specifies the IO port address to be used, as well as the type of data transfer required.

A more complicated IO interfacing problem is illustrated by Fig. 7.3. Here the microprocessor is connected to remote IO devices, with which it communicates via a (long-distance) telephone line; the latter therefore defines the local IO interface. Data transmission over telephone lines is serial, since only two wires are available, and uses analog signals to represent the data. Typically, a sinusoidal electric signal (see Fig. 2.15a) called a *carrier* is employed. The carrier is modulated to have two distinct frequencies that represent logical 0 and 1, as indicated in Fig. 7.3. When voice-grade

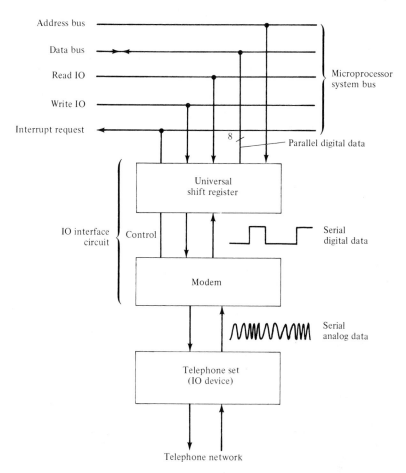

Figure 7.3 Interfacing a serial input-output device (telephone) to a microprocessor.

telephone lines are used, these signal frequencies can be heard as tones or beeps of different pitches. Data transmission, therefore, uses sequences of beeps. An electronic device called a *modem* (modulator–demodulator) serves to convert data from the beep format to the ordinary digital pulse format used within the microcomputer, and vice versa. Data transmission through the modem is serial, whereas data transmission over the system bus is parallel. Hence we also require a circuit to convert data from serial to parallel form during input operations and from parallel to serial form during output operations. A universal shift register of the sort described in Sec. 4.1.5 can easily be adapted to this task, and can also serve as the IO port for the modem.

Some of the more common IO devices encountered in microprocessor-based systems are listed in Fig. 7.4. Among the simplest input devices are on–off switches and *keyboards* consisting of sets of depressible switches called *keys*. Switches are inherently digital devices that generate binary electric signals that can be readily interfaced with a

Type	Device
Input	On–off switch
	Keyboard
	Transducer (sensor)
Output	LED display
	CRT display
	Electric motor/actuator
	Printer
Input-output	Interactive terminal
	Secondary memory
	Magnetic disk unit
	Cassette tape recorder
	Communication link
	Standard bus
	Telephone line

Figure 7.4 Widely used IO devices in microprocessor-based systems.

microprocessor. A microprocessor is frequently required to sense or measure nonelectrical variables such as temperature, position, velocity, pressure, and light intensity. For this purpose a *transducer* or *sensor* is necessary to detect the physical variable of concern, and generate a proportional electric signal; the conversion of physical to electrical parameters is termed *transduction*. A transducer typically produces an electric data signal that is analog rather than digital. This signal must be converted to digital form before it can be sent to a microprocessor. Analog-to-digital conversion is therefore associated with most transducers.

Output devices that display digital information in visual form are present in many microprocessor-based systems. Seven-segment LED displays (see Fig. 1.11, for instance) are often used to output small amounts of numerical information. Large amounts of alphanumeric data can be conveniently displayed on a television-style CRT unit. A CRT is also useful for displaying graphical ("graphics") images that are computer processed. When mechanical motion is to be controlled by a computer, electric motors often serve as output devices. The motors also may be incorporated in more complex output devices such as hard-copy printers and robot arms.

Input and output devices of the foregoing kinds can be combined in a single unit to form a device with both input and output capability. The combination of a keyboard and a CRT display yields a video terminal, a common IO device for human interaction with a computer. Another important class of IO devices are secondary memories, such as magnetic tape and disk memory devices. These memories use magnetic storage media and electromechanical read/write mechanisms. They provide very large storage capacity at relatively low cost, but are much slower than main memory devices that contain semiconductor RAMs and ROMs. When a computer is linked to a relatively remote device, the communication link is seen as the computer's local IO device for interfacing purposes. A number of standard buses have been defined to simplify interfacing in certain applications areas, for example, the IEEE 488 bus, sponsored by the IEEE and other organizations, and intended for interfacing digital instrumentation to (micro) computers.

Interface circuits range in complexity from simple addressable latches as used in Fig. 7.2, to sophisticated IO controllers that carry out all the data conversion, synchronization, and selection operations required by a particular class of IO devices. LSI/VLSI technology has made it feasible to put all the interfacing circuitry for complex IO devices such as a disk memory unit in a single IC. Clearly such special-purpose interface circuits can greatly simplify the interfacing problem. There are also general-purpose interface circuits whose characteristics can be altered by software to match the interface requirements of many different types of IO devices. Thus, like many aspects of digital system design, IO interfacing involves hardware–software trade-offs that can substantially affect the development and production costs of the overall system. Most microprocessor families contain a variety of special-purpose and general-purpose IO interface circuits. Selecting the most cost-effective interface circuits for a given application consequently is an important step in microprocessor-based design.

An example of a simple, but extremely useful, interface circuit is the Intel 8212 IO port, an IC intended primarily for interfacing to 8080/8085-based systems. The 8212 was introduced in Sec. 5.3 (see Fig. 5.53); a data sheet for this device appears in Fig. 7.5 (Intel, 1979). It contains eight clocked D-type latches intended for temporary data storage. The data in (DI) and data out (DO) buses of these latches are 8080/8085 compatible, which means they can be wired directly to the data lines of an 8080/8085 system bus, or to any similar 8-bit data bus in a microprocessor-based system. When used as an output port, the 8212's DI bus is connected to the microprocessor data bus, while the DO bus is connected to the IO (output) device. Conversely, when used as an input port, the DO lines, which form a three-state bus, are connected to the microprocessor data bus and the DI lines are attached to the IO (input) device.

The remaining logic circuits and control lines of the 8212 are used for synchronization and addressing (device-selection) purposes. For example, an input device can employ the STB (strobe) control line to clock the D latches, thereby loading a data word into the 8212. The microprocessor subsequently can execute an input instruction to read the data stored in the 8212. This requires activating the 8212's device-select lines $\overline{DS1}$ and DS2, which enables the DO bus and causes the data in the latches to be transferred to the system data bus and thence into the microprocessor itself. It is also possible to have the 8212 signal the presence of new input data, or request new output data in the case of an output port, by activating its interrupt-request line $\overline{INT}$ in response to an STB signal from the IO device. Thus the 8212 can act either as a passive IO port, completely under the control of the CPU, or as an interrupting IO port capable of relaying a service request from its IO device to the CPU.

7.1.2 Switches and Keyboards

Some basic IO devices, and their interfacing requirements, are considered next. Perhaps the simplest input device is a manual on–off switch or key. Figure 7.6a shows how a (two-terminal) switch may be used to produce a logic signal z that is suitable for interfacing with a microprocessor. When the switch is in the on or closed position, the input signal $x = 0$ (ground) is applied to the inverter, causing its output z to become 1 ($+5$ V). When the switch is in the off or open position, x is pulled up to the 1 level by the

8212
8-BIT INPUT/OUTPUT PORT

- Fully Parallel 8-Bit Data Register and Buffer
- Service Request Flip-Flop for Interrupt Generation
- Low Input Load Current — .25mA Max.
- Three State Outputs
- Outputs Sink 15mA

- 3.65V Output High Voltage for Direct Interface to 8008, 8080A, or 8085A CPU
- Asynchronous Register Clear
- Replaces Buffers, Latches and Multiplexers in Microcomputer Systems
- Reduces System Package Count

The 8212 input/output port consists of an 8-bit latch with 3-state output buffers along with control and device selection logic. Also included is a service request flip-flop for the generation and control of interrupts to the microprocessor.

The device is multimode in nature. It can be used to implement latches, gated buffers or multiplexers. Thus, all of the principal peripheral and input/output functions of a microcomputer system can be implemented with this device.

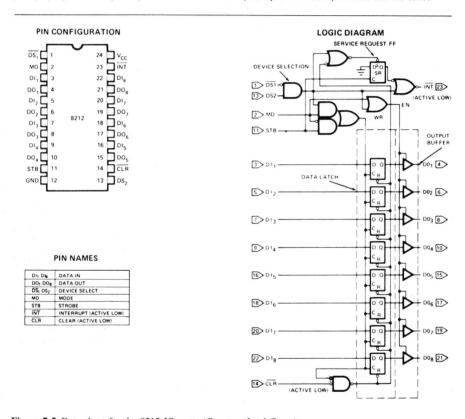

PIN NAMES

DI_1 DI_8	DATA IN
DO_1 DO_8	DATA OUT
$\overline{DS_1}$ DS_2	DEVICE SELECT
MD	MODE
STB	STROBE
$\overline{INT}$	INTERRUPT (ACTIVE LOW)
$\overline{CLR}$	CLEAR (ACTIVE LOW)

Figure 7.5 Data sheet for the 8212 IO port. *(Courtesy Intel Corp.)*

resistor R, causing the inverter's output to become 0. If, as is generally the case, a TTL inverter is used, R may be omitted, because a disconnected TTL input line automatically floats to the logical 1 value.

Ideally a switch should have the logical behavior depicted in Fig. 7.6b. In practice the physical contact points in an (electro) mechanical switch tend to bounce when they

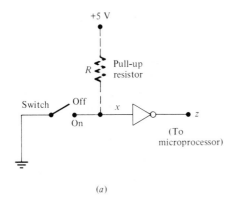

(a)

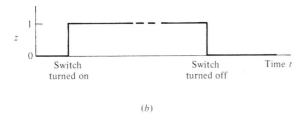

(b)

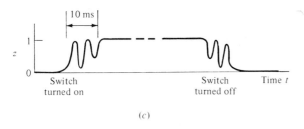

(c)

Figure 7.6 (a) Two-terminal on-off switch as a microprocessor input device; (b) ideal behavior; (c) actual behavior showing contact bounce.

are pressed together or pulled apart. This bouncing, although usually imperceptible to the person operating the switch, causes the signal x produced by the switch to oscillate between the 0 and 1 levels several times before settling at its final value. The duration of the bouncing period is in the region of 10 ms. This is very long compared with the propagation delay of a logic gate, which is typically a few nanoseconds. Consequently any signal bounce affecting x in the circuit of Fig. 7.6a is reflected in the inverter output z, resulting in the distorted waveform of Fig. 7.6c. If the values of z are supplied to a microprocessor when the switch contacts are bouncing, an incorrect decision may be made concerning the state of the switch. For example, the condition $z = 1$ immediately followed by $z = 0$ does not ncecessarily mean that the switch is being turned off; it could be caused by contact bounce when the switch is actually being turned on.

To eliminate the confusion caused by this phenomenon, which is called *switch bounce*, a hardware or software process called *debouncing* is employed. Figure 7.7 shows another type of on-off switch that is easy to debounce by means of a hardware-implemented debouncing circuit. The switch has three terminals instead of two, so that separate contact points are associated with the on and off positions.* The two NAND gates of Fig. 7.7 constitute an SR latch (cf. the NOR latch of Fig. 3.30). This latch has 11 as its quiescent input combination, and it is set or reset by the arrival of a 0 on one of its input lines x_1 or x_2. Application of 0 to, say, x_1 for a few nanoseconds suffices to set the latch to the state $z = 1$. Subsequent applications of 0 or 1 to x_1 have no effect on the latch's state, provided x_2 stays at 1. Hence contact bounce in the off position does not appear at the output of the latch. The same is true for bouncing that occurs when the switch is moved to the on position. The behavior of this circuit thus closely approximates the ideal behavior of Fig. 7.6b.

A keyboard is a collection of on–off switches, usually of the two-terminal variety, each of which is associated with a specific function such as entering a digit or a command into a microprocessor-based system. Figure 7.8 depicts a small keyboard of the type used in simple calculators. Each of its 16 keys is a two-terminal switch that is turned on when the key is depressed and off when the key is released. All the keys have one terminal in common, so that the keyboard presents an interface of 17 external electrical connections.

A straightforward way of interfacing this keyboard to a microprocessor is demonstrated in Fig. 7.9. Two 8212 8-bit IO ports, which are defined in Fig. 7.5, serve as the interface circuits. Each is configured as a passive (non-interrupting) input port with a unique address. The three-state DO output buses of the 8212s are attached directly to the

---

*This type of switch is also called a single-pole double-throw switch, to contrast it with the single-pole single-throw switch of Fig. 7.6a. The two-terminal and terminal switches can also be thought of as one-input and two-output demultiplexers respectively.

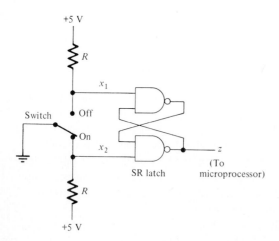

Figure 7.7 Three-terminal on-off switch with a debouncing circuit.

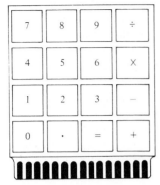

Figure 7.8 16-key calculator-type keyboard.

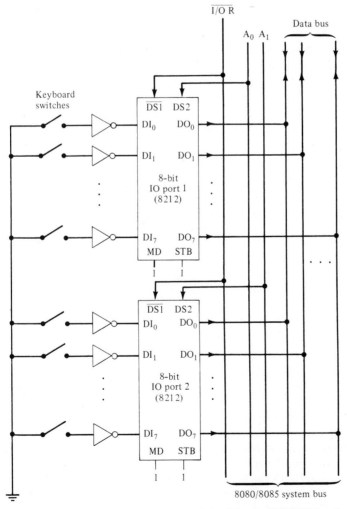

Figure 7.9 Interfacing the 16-key keyboard of Fig. 7.8 to an 8080/8085-based microprocessor.

571

microprocessor data bus. The keyboard switches are connected via inverters to the DI input lines of the 8212s; it is assumed that no pull-up resistors are necessary. The STB (strobe) and MD (mode) control lines are set so that the 8212's data latches are constantly enabled. This implies that the states of the keyboard switches are transferred continuously to the D latches. Note, however, that these latches do not serve as debouncing circuits in the manner of the SR latch of Fig. 7.7.

It remains to provide circuitry to select (address) each 8212 port, and enable its DO output lines. This requires simultaneously activating the 8212's two device-select lines $\overline{DS1}$ and DS2, that is, making $\overline{DS1} \wedge DS2 = 1$. Now execution of an 8080/8085 input instruction IN ADR has the following effect:

1. The specified IO port address ADR is placed on the system address bus.
2. One or two control lines are activated to enable the transfer of a data byte from the addressed IO port to the system data bus; in the 8080 case, a single line named $\overline{I/O\,R}$ (IO read) is employed for this purpose.

Thus we see that ADR and $\overline{I/O\,R}$ must be used to activate the $\overline{DS1}$ and DS2 inputs of the 8212 ports. Clearly we can connect $\overline{I/O\,R}$ directly to $\overline{DS1}$ in each 8212. Separate addresses must now be assigned to each port and used to activate its DS2 input. A simple way of doing this appears in Fig. 7.9. Two address lines A_0 and A_1 from the system bus are connected to the DS2 inputs of ports 1 and 2 respectively. This means that port 1 is selected by any address of the form dd . . . d1, where d is a don't care value. For example, execution of the instruction

$$\text{IN} \quad 1 \qquad ; \text{Input data byte from IO port no. 1}$$

causes the address

$$A_7{:}A_0 = 00000001$$

to be placed on the system address bus; note that only the eight low-order lines of the 8080/8085's 16 address lines are used to address IO ports. The CPU then activates the read IO control line ($\overline{I/O\,R} = 0$), which enables input port 1. The word currently in its data latches is transferred to the system data bus, from which it is loaded into the accumulator of the CPU. In a similar manner IO port 2 can be read by the instruction IN 2, which uses the address 00000010.

The keyboard interface circuit of Fig. 7.9 is designed to operate in conjunction with an IO program that acts as a keyboard service routine. Although only a few instructions, including the two input instructions IN 1 and IN 2, suffice to read the keyboard's current state, additional processing must be done if the keyboard is to function properly. Normally only one key is depressed at a time. The keyboard service routine must identify that key, and transfer control to another routine that performs some action specific to the key in question. Thus the two 8-bit words representing the keyboard state in this example must be scanned or decoded to identify the depressed key. For example, if the key marked " + " is depressed, that fact must be identified by the keyboard service routine so that an appropriate addition routine can be invoked. Since it is possible for two or more keys to be depressed simultaneously, either by accident or by design, provision must be made in the keyboard software to handle the situation in which several keys are on at once. Finally, as discussed above, the individual keys are subject to switch bounce, which is transmitted directly to the CPU via the 8212 ports. Debouncing must also be included in the keyboard service routine. This can be achieved by reading the keyboard several times, at intervals of, say, 10 ms. The successive keyboard states are then compared, and any temporary states that can be attributed to bouncing are detected and eliminated from consideration.

In summary, the interface software supporting the hardware interface of Fig. 7.9 must carry out the following actions:

1. It must transfer data from the two input ports used by the keyboard to the CPU.
2. It must decode the input data and transfer control to an action routine corresponding to a depressed key.
3. It must resolve any ambiguities caused by contact bounce or multiple depressed keys.

Thus the simplicity of the hardware interface for the calculator keyboard is offset by the need for relatively complex interface software.

Figure 7.10a lists an IO subroutine called RDKEY designed to read and decode the keyboard of Fig. 7.9. This program, which is written in 8080/8085 assembly language, reads the input ports 1 and 2 in turn using two IN instructions. It examines each bit of the input words in a fixed sequence to determine which bits, if any, are 1, indicating a depressed key. If no 1 is detected, RDKEY returns to the calling program with CY, the CPU's carry flag, set to 0. If a 1 bit is detected, indicating that key number i is on, a return is made with $CY = 1$, and the number i stored in the B register. The data words from the keyboard are scanned using the RLC (rotate accumulator left and set carry) instruction, which has the following effects:

$$A_6,A_5,A_4,A_3,A_2,A_1,A_0,A_7 := A_7,A_6,A_5,A_4,A_3,A_2,A_1,A_0, \quad CY := A_7;$$

RLC thus puts the leftmost bit of the accumulator in the carry flag where it can be tested by the RC (return if carry flag is 1) conditional branch instruction. By carrying out eight rotations of this type, every bit in the accumulator can be individually identified. After each rotation, RDKEY decrements the B register, whose contents therefore serve to label the accumulator bit that is currently being examined. When CY is found to be 1, the RC instruction is executed, terminating execution of RDKEY. If $CY = 0$, the scanning operation continues until all 16 bits of input data have been checked, at which point the final unconditional return instruction RET is executed. RDKEY is representative of IO routines used to detect specific signals at the IO interface.

To implement debouncing in software, a keyboard-reading routine such as RDKEY is executed several times in sequence, with an interval of about 10 ms between each execution. The results of the read operations are stored and compared. Only when a sequence of, say, three or more consistent values is read is the keyboard assumed to be in a stable nonbouncing condition, at which point the action necessary to service the decoded key is carried out. The 10-ms delay between the reads can be obtained by executing the software delay routine, such as the DELAY program of Fig. 7.10b. This

```
;    8080/8085 SUBROUTINE 'RDKEY' TO READ AND DECODE THE 16-KEY KEYBOARD
;    OF FIGS. 7.8 AND 7.9. RDKEY RETURNS WITH CY = 0 IF NO KEY IS
;    DEPRESSED; OTHERWISE IT RETURNS WITH CY = 1 AND A VALUE CORRE-
;    SPONDING TO THE FIRST DEPRESSED KEY IN REGISTER B.
;
RDKEY:  IN      1       ; INPUT BYTE FROM KEYBOARD IO PORT NO. 1
        MVI     B,16    ; INITIALIZE REGISTER B WITH HIGHEST KEY NO.
        MVI     C,9     ; INITIALIZE REGISTER C (USED AS COUNTER)
RDK1:   DCR     C       ; DECREMENT C
        JNZ     RDK2    ; BRANCH TO RDK2 IF ZERO FLAG Z = 0
        IN      2       ; INPUT BYTE FROM KEYBOARD IO PORT NO. 2
RDK2:   RLC             ; ROTATE ACCUMULATOR A TO LEFT, AND SET
                        ;   CARRY FLAG CY TO OLD VALUE OF A[7]
        DCR     B       ; DECREMENT B (CY IS NOT AFFECTED BY DCR)
        RC              ; RETURN TO CALLING PROGRAM IF CY = 1
        JNZ     RDK1    ; CONTINUE SCANNING CURRENT HALF OF KEYBOARD
        RET             ; RETURN (WITH CY = 0)
```

(a)

```
;    8080/8085 SUBROUTINE 'DELAY' TO CREATE A DELAY OF APPROXIMATELY 10
;    MS, ASSUMING A CPU CLOCK RATE OF 2 MHZ
;
DELAY:  PUSH    PSW     ; SAVE ACCUMULATOR AND FLAGS (PROGRAM STATUS WORD)
        PUSH    D       ; SAVE REGISTER PAIR DE
        LXI     D,800   ; LOAD INITIAL COUNT INTO DE
DEL1:   DCX     D       ; DECREMENT DE
        MOV     A,D     ; COPY D TO ACCUMULATOR A
        ORA     E       ; OR REGISTERS A AND E INTO A (TO TEST DE)
        JNZ     DEL1    ; BRANCH TO DEL1 IF DE IS NOT ZERO
        POP     D       ; RESTORE DE
        POP     PSW     ; RESTORE A AND FLAGS
        RET             ; RETURN
```

(b)

Figure 7.10 Subroutines of keyboard service program: (a) read and decode keyboard; (b) 10-ms delay.

subroutine simply loads a number N into a CPU register, the register-pair DE in this instance, and decrements it to zero. This is a "useless" activity that is intended merely to eat up CPU time. The execution time of this program constitutes the desired delay. Its value is determined by the number N and by the execution times of the instructions composing DELAY. The analysis required is quite straightforward. The main program loop of DELAY contains the four instructions DCX, MOV, ORA, and JNZ. From the microprocessor manufacturer's data manuals it can be determined that to execute these four instructions requires about 25 CPU clock cycles or machine states. (The 8080 and the 8085 microprocessors differ slightly in the number of clock cycles they employ for some instructions.) These instructions are executed N times, implying a total of about $25N$ clock cycles to execute DELAY. If the CPU clock rate is 2 MHz, then the clock period is 0.5 μs. Hence to achieve a delay of 10 ms = 10,000 μs, we require

$$25N \times 0.5 = 10,000$$

implying that N should be 800. This indeed is the initial value loaded into DE by the LXI (load register-pair immediate) instruction in Fig. 7.10b. Note that testing for DE = 0 is complicated by the fact that the DCX (decrement register-pair) instruction does not affect the CPU flags, a quirk of the 8080/8085 that was noted previously (see Fig. 5.48). If several keys are on simultaneously, then RDKEY only detects the one that it encounters first during its examination of the 16 input bits read from the keyboard. This examination is carried out according to a predetermined sequence, and can lead to improper keyboard operation if, for instance, an incorrect key K_1 is momentarily depressed in conjunction with the correct key K_2. RDKEY may then detect K_1 first and incorrectly assume it to be the desired active key. This problem can be solved in much the same way as debouncing by repeated readings of the keyboard with appropriate delays inserted.

If the interfacing technique of Fig. 7.9 is extended to large keyboards of the kind used in interactive terminals and the like, the number of interface lines and IO ports becomes excessive. A 64-key keyboard, for instance, would require 64 inverters and eight 8-bit IO ports. This interface hardware can be greatly reduced by adopting the *walking-1s* keyboard-scanning method illustrated in Fig. 7.11. Here the 64-key keyboard is organized as a two-dimensional 8 × 8 array of horizontal and vertical conductors, with a switch at the intersection of each row and column. Depressing a key causes the corresponding row and column to be electrically connected. Two 8-bit IO ports are attached to the keyboard array: an input port, which is attached to the eight conductor

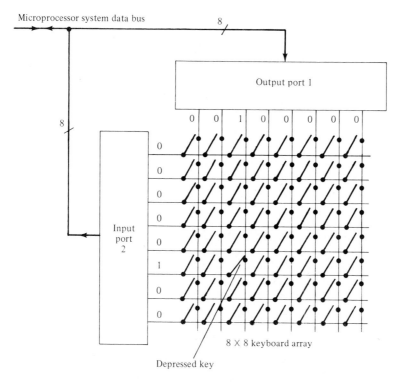

Figure 7.11 Microprocessor interface for a 64-key keyboard using the walking-1s scanning technique.

rows, and an output port, which is attached to the eight conductor columns. Again the Intel 8212 is a suitable IC for implementing these IO ports.

The state of the keyboard in Fig. 7.11 is determined by a sequence of eight write and eight read operations addressed to its IO ports. First the pattern 10000000 is written into output port 1. In an 8080/8085-based system this can be accomplished by executing the following two instructions:

    MVI   A,10000000B   ; Load 10000000_2 into accumulator A
    OUT   1   ; Output accumulator to IO port 1

The equivalent instructions in a 6800-based system would be:

    LDA   A   #10000000B   Load 10000000_2 into accumulator A
    STA   A   P1   Output accumulator A to IO port P1

Since the 6800 microprocessor uses memory-mapped IO, the symbolic "memory" address P1 must be assigned to output port 1. Once an output word is stored in port 1, it is applied directly to the eight columns of the keyboard matrix. The signals appearing on the eight rows are applied to input port 2, where they are stored for subsequent reading by the microprocessor. If any key is depressed, a 1 signal can pass from the corresponding column into the corresponding row; it can be arranged so that rows in which no key is depressed apply 0 to the corresponding input of port 2. Figure 7.11 demonstrates the situation when a 1 is applied to the third column, and the key in the third column and sixth row is depressed. If IO port 2 is now read (e.g., by means of the input instruction IN 2), the pattern 00000100 is returned to the microprocessor. By comparing this input word with the word 00100000 previously sent out to port 1, the depressed key can be identified; an IO routine similar to RDKEY (Fig 7.10a) may be used for this purpose. All the switches of the keyboard can be checked by sending out the eight-pattern sequence

$$
\begin{array}{l}
10000000 \\
01000000 \\
00100000 \\
00010000 \\
00001000 \\
00000100 \\
00000010 \\
00000001
\end{array}
\qquad (7.1)
$$

to port 1, and reading the corresponding eight patterns induced at port 2. Note that (7.1) can be seen as "walking" a 1 bit across a background of 0s—hence the name of this keyboard-scanning approach. As before, the keyboard service software must, in addition to identifying the keyboard state, deal with switch bounce, and resolve conflicts due to multiple depressed keys (see Prob. 7.3).

The walking-1s keyboard-scan method, and all the logic necessary for switch debouncing, key encoding, and multiple-key resolution, can be packaged in a single LSI chip termed a *keyboard encoder*. A representative example, the National Semiconductor MM57499 serial keyboard interface circuit (National Semiconductor, 1980), is shown in Fig. 7.12. This device is designed for interfacing large keyboards with up to 96 keys that

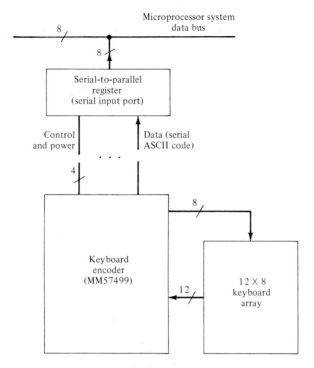

Figure 7.12 Application of a 96-key keyboard encoder circuit, the National Semiconductor MM57499.

are detached, that is, at a distance of 0.5 m or more, from the host microprocessor interface. The MM57499 generates an ASCII codeword representing a depressed key, which it transmits in serial form to the host system; this serial transmission minimizes the number of wires that must link the host to a detached keyboard and encoder circuit. A serial-to-parallel shift register can be used as the input port that transfers the ASCII codeword to the microprocessor data bus.

The main functions performed by the MM57499 keyboard encoder circuit are as follows:

1. It scans a keyboard arranged as a 12 × 8 array using the walking-1s approach discussed previously. The generation of the sequence of patterns to be applied to the keyboard's columns and the reading of the resulting row patterns are all handled by sequential logic circuits inside the MM57499. The scanning is repeated continuously at a predetermined rate.

2. Switch debouncing and multiple-key resolution are handled automatically in the MM57499 by detecting the relative times at which keys are depressed, and measuring the relative duration of the on periods. Thus if a key is depressed and held on for a minimum period, subsequent pressed keys are ignored until the first one has been released.

3. Once a valid depressed key has been identified, the corresponding ASCII codeword

is selected from a ROM in the MM57499, and is transmitted serially to the host microprocessor.

A number of other useful features are included in this interface circuit; for details see the manufacturer's data sheets (National Semiconductor, 1980). The use of sophisticated IO controllers such as the MM57499 reduces the interface software needed to service the keyboard to a simple routine that merely has to read the serial input port of Fig. 7.12 periodically.

7.1.3 LED-Based Devices

An output device that is the counterpart of a switch is a light source or lamp with two states, on (illuminated) and off (dark). Incandescent lamps are occasionally used as microprocessor output devices. Light-emitting diodes (LEDs), whose electrical charac-teristics were examined in Sec. 2.1.2, are more suitable for this purpose for the following reasons:

1. They consume less electric energy and produce less heat.
2. Displays for numeric and alphanumeric characters are easily constructed from sets of LEDs.

Although their electric power requirements are less than those of incandescent lamps, LEDs consume relatively high currents in the 15–30-mA range. Furthermore, the brightness of an LED increases with the magnitude of the current flowing through it.

Figure 7.13a shows how a single LED might be driven from the output port of a microcomputer. The resistor R serves as a current-limiting device to prevent the LED from drawing an excessive current and destroying itself. The LED is turned on when the gate input z is logical 0 corresponding to 0 V; it is turned off when $z = 1$ ($+5$ V). In the

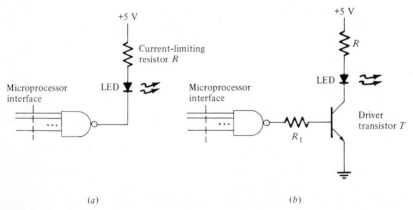

Figure 7.13 Interfacing an LED: (a) directly via a logic gate; (b) via a driver (power) transistor to increase brightness.

on state the current drawn by the LED should not exceed the minimum guaranteed output current I_{OL} of the NAND gate, which is 16 mA for standard TTL-compatible logic gates (see Fig. 2.63). This is sufficient to light up the LED, but at less than the most desirable brightness level. To make the LED brighter, the current flowing through it should be increased to 20 mA or more. This can be done by using a high-output buffer NAND gate or, as shown in Fig. 7.13b, by using a (discrete) transistor T as a current amplifier. The circuit of Fig. 7.13b is also suitable for driving a small (flashlight-size) incandescent light bulb in place of the LED.

A set of LEDs can be combined in a single DIP package in such a way that a variety of visual characters can be displayed by selectively switching LEDs on and off. Two important examples appear in Fig. 7.14: a seven-segment LED display designed to output the 10 decimal digits 0, 1, ..., 9, and a *matrix LED* display designed to output a full range of alphanumeric characters. The matrix display contains 35 separate LEDs forming an array of seven rows and five columns. Packages containing clusters of these LED display circuits are commercially available, and are very convenient output devices for calculators and other microprocessor-based systems; see Figs. 1.11 and 1.40 for examples.

From an interfacing viewpoint, the individual LED segments composing the displays of Fig. 7.14 must be controlled by circuits that are functionally equivalent to those of Fig. 7.13. Figure 7.15 illustrates a straightforward but inefficient way of controlling a single seven-segment LED display. To minimize pin count, the seven LED segments have one terminal (in this case, the positive (anode) terminal) connected to a single pin. The seven negative (cathode) terminals of the LEDs are connected to separate gates via current-limiting resistors in the manner of Fig. 7.13a. These gates in turn are connected to, or form part of, a microprocessor IO (output) port. The microprocessor must be supplied with the necessary IO program to generate the output signals needed to display a particular digit. A more efficient interfacing scheme is depicted in Fig. 7.16. Here the microprocessor must supply the output digit in BCD code, which is the usual internal representation of a decimal digit. The BCD digit is passed to the 7447 decoder/driver IC, which drives the seven-segment display via the usual current-limiting resistors. For each BCD digit, the 7447 selects and switches on the proper subset of the LED segments. For example, when presented with 0010_{BCD}, denoting the digit 2, the 7447 switches on the three horizontal segments and the upper right and lower left vertical segments to form the symbol "2," as illustrated in Fig. 7.16. All 10 decimal digits can be displayed in this

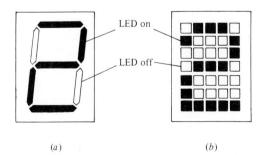

(a)   (b)

Figure 7.14 LED-based output devices displaying the digit 2: (*a*) seven-segment LED display; (*b*) 5 × 7 matrix LED display.

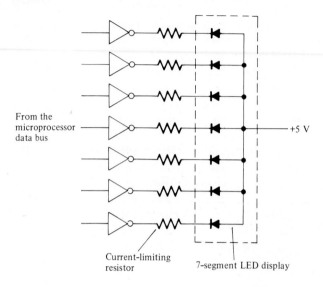

Figure 7.15 Simple circuit for driving a seven-segment LED display.

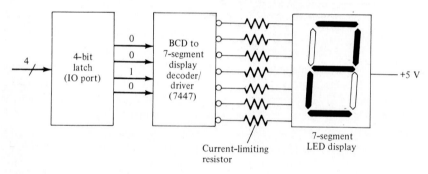

Figure 7.16 Interfacing a seven-segment LED display to a decimal (BCD) data source.

manner; for the inputs 1010:1110 the 7447 displays five special symbols, while 1111 leaves the display dark (blank symbol). As indicated by its "driver" appellation, the 7447 can produce the large currents (up to 40 mA) needed to achieve maximum brightness. It should be noted that other interface ICs are available that can reduce the number of components needed to drive an LED display. For instance, the Signetics 8T74 decoder/driver/latch IC can replace the entire interface circuit of Fig. 7.16, including the seven resistors.

To display a particular digit via the foregoing interface circuit, the host microprocessor typically must execute two instructions. The first instruction loads the digit to be displayed into the CPU's accumulator register. The second instruction is an output instruction addressed to the IO port attached to the LED; this causes the BCD character to be transferred from the accumulator to the system data bus, and from there to the latch in the IO port. The LED display continuously displays the digit in question until a new character is sent to the IO port.

More complex circuits must be employed to control a 5 × 7 matrix LED display. The 35 LEDs are arranged into seven rows and five columns, as indicated in Fig. 7.17, with each LED connected between a conductor in some row and a conductor in some column. The 12 row/column conductors are, in turn, connected to external pins. This organization reduces the number of pins, but allows only one row or one column of the matrix display to be activated at a time. Consequently circuitry is required that selects, say, one column of the display and selectively activates its LEDs for a brief period. Each column is selected in turn until a complete character has been displayed. If this process is repeated sufficiently often (at least 60 times a second), the persistence of human vision allows a steady image of the entire character to be perceived. The fact that each LED is illuminated for a period of, say, T_{on} seconds, and is off for a longer period of T_{off} seconds, means that the perceived brightness B is approximately

$$B = \frac{B_{on} \, T_{on}}{T_{off}}$$

where B_{on} is the brightness or light intensity during the on period. Thus B varies with the "duty factor" T_{on}/T_{off}, which typically will be around 15 percent.

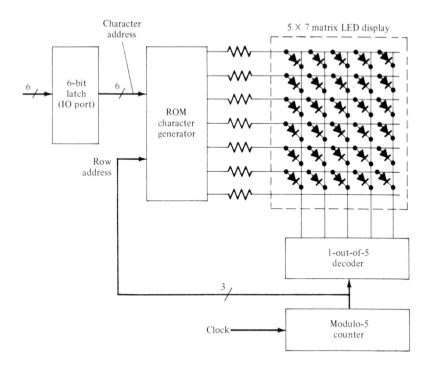

Figure 7.17 Interface circuit for a 5 × 7 matrix LED display.

Figure 7.17 shows a somewhat simplified scheme for using a matrix LED display as an output device for alphanumeric characters. A modulo-5 counter driven by a free-running clock signal is used in conjunction with a 1-out-of-5 decoder to produce the signals necessary continuously to select or strobe the five LED columns of the display. A ROM character generator of the type described in Sec. 4.3.5. (see Fig. 4.76) stores the repertoire of characters that can be displayed in the form of 5×7 bit patterns. The data outputs of the ROM are connected to the seven rows of the matrix display, via current-limiting resistors, if necessary. In this example, the ROM can store up to $2^6 = 64$ characters. A particular character to be displayed is identified by a 6-bit word that is transmitted from the host microprocessor and stored in a latch at the display's IO port. This 6-bit word is applied to the character address lines of the ROM, causing the corresponding character pattern stored in the ROM to be selected. The pattern is then read out column by column and applied to the matrix LED display. The character column to be read out is determined by the 3-bit column-select input of the ROM (which corresponds to the row-select input of Fig. 4.76). The column address is obtained from the modulo-5 counter, so that the LED display and the character generator operate in step: column i of the selected ROM character is applied to column i of the LED matrix. Hence, as long as the clock is operating, the desired character is continuously read out in five 7-bit slices, and is displayed slice by slice in the matrix LED display unit.

An output display unit for a microprocessor-based system generally consists of a set of single-character LED display circuits, which collectively allow a multidigit number or a short alphanumeric message to be displayed. Consider, for example, an output device composed of 10 seven-segment LED displays. The interfacing scheme of Fig. 7.16 could be replicated 10 times, resulting in an interface circuit containing ten 4-bit IO ports (or five 8-bit IO ports), and 10 decoder/driver ICs with up to 70 resistors. This rather large number of interface components can be greatly reduced by multiplexing the 10 seven-segment displays in somewhat the same way as the five LED columns are multiplexed in Fig. 7.17. The result is a multiplexed seven-segment LED display of the kind illustrated by Fig. 7.18. In this circuit, a single BCD to seven-segment display decoder/driver, the National Semiconductor 8857, is used to drive the seven LED segments for each of the 10 digits to be displayed. The 8857 is logically equivalent to the 7447 decoder/driver of Fig. 7.16, but can produce a higher output current without the need for external current-limiting resistors. (The 8857 is also designed for seven-segment displays that have a common cathode rather than a common anode connection for the seven-segment LEDs.) Each of the 10 digits in the display unit is enabled in sequence, so that at any time only one digit is actually being driven by the 8857 and illuminated. As in the matrix LED control circuit of Fig. 7.17, each digit must be activated repeatedly in a manner that produces a bright flickerfree image. Thus a control program is necessary that repeatedly outputs each digit to be displayed, as well as the signals required to select the proper seven-segment LED unit to display each digit. Digit selection is implemented by the 7445 1-out-of-10 decoder discussed in Sec. 4.1.3, which supplies an enable signal to the common (cathode) terminal of the various digits. The digit to be enabled is specified in a 4-bit number supplied by the host processor.

A flowchart defining the required behavior of a control program for the multiplexed

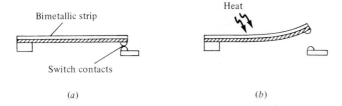

Figure 7.25 Bimetallic thermal transducer: (*a*) closed; (*b*) open.

the temperature rises above another specified level T_H. This type of thermostat can thus maintain the ambient temperature at an average value of about $(T_H + T_L)/2$.

Accurate temperature measurement and control over a wide range of temperatures can be obtained with a transducer called a *thermocouple*. This again is composed of two thin pieces (wires) of different metals joined at one end A as depicted in Fig. 7.26a. The other end B is attached to electrical conductors that serve as output lines of the thermocouple. When A and B are held at different temperatures, a small potential difference develops between them (the Seebeck effect). Thus if end B is held at a fixed reference temperature T_{ref}, the junction end A can be used to sense a temperature T_M that

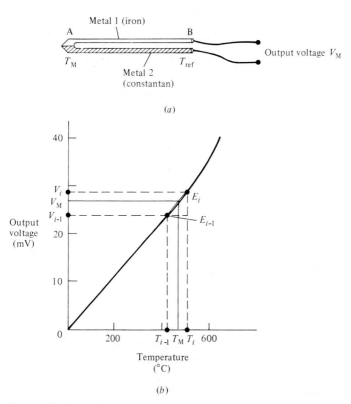

Figure 7.26 Type J (iron-constantan) thermocouple: (*a*) structure; (*b*) temperature–voltage characteristics.

is to be measured. The voltage V_M produced is approximately proportional to $T_M - T_{ref}$. Standard types of thermocouples are available commercially, and are designated by letters indicating the metals they contain. For example, a type J thermocouple is composed of iron and constantan (an alloy of copper and nickel), and is used for temperature measurements in the range -200 to $+800$ °C. Figure 7.26b plots the relation between T_M and V_M for this type of thermocouple when $T_{ref} = 0$ °C. Since this relation is slightly nonlinear, tables are used to determine T_M from V_M; such tables are published in the United States by the National Bureau of Standards (Powell et al., 1974).

The hardware structure of a microprocessor-based thermometer employing a thermocouple is shown in Fig. 7.23a. The voltage V_M generated by the thermocouple, after suitable conditioning and analog-to-digital conversion, is used to determine the measured temperature T_M, which is then displayed on a seven-segment LED display unit. We next turn to the software needed to operate this system. It consists of one or more IO routines P that perform the following sequence of operations.

1. P reads the digital word V_M from IO port 0, which is attached to the output of the ADC; V_M represents the thermocouple's output signal, possibly weighted by a scaling factor.
2. P then scans an internal temperature–voltage table to find the temperature value T_M corresponding to V_M. This table can hold only a small number of the potentially infinite range of voltage values produced by the thermocouple. Hence V_M is likely to fall between two adjacent entries V_{i-1} and V_i of the table, as suggested by Fig. 7.26b. An interpolation technique is normally used to compute T_M from the temperature values available in the table.
3. Once T_M has been determined, it is sent out to the LED display attached to IO port 1.

Suppose that the desired temperature–voltage pair (T_M, V_M) falls between the two table entries $E_{i-1} = (T_{i-1}, V_{i-1})$ and $E_i = (T_i, V_i)$. Since the relation between voltage and temperature for thermocouples is nearly linear, it is reasonable to assume that (T_M, V_M) lies on the straight line joining E_i and E_{i-1}; see Fig. 7.26b. The slope of this line is described by

$$\frac{V_i - V_{i-1}}{T_i - T_{i-1}} = \frac{V_M - V_{i-1}}{T_M - T_{i-1}}$$

from which it follows that

$$T_M = T_{i-1} + \frac{(T_i - T_{i-1})(V_M - V_{i-1})}{V_i - V_{i-1}} \tag{7.2}$$

Thus in response to an input reading V_M, the system software retrieves the table values V_i, V_{i-1}, T_i, and T_{i-1} and computes T_M by means of the interpolation equation (7.2).

A Pascal implementation of the foregoing software to control the microprocessor-based thermometer is listed in Fig. 7.27. As observed in Chap. 6, the IO facilities of standard Pascal are inadequate for systems of this type; hence a number of simplifying assumptions have been made. The input voltage V_M, representing the thermocouple output in millivolts, is assumed to be available in integer format at input port PORT_0,

Program THERMOMETER;
{ Pascal program to read a voltage from a J-type thermocouple via an ADC, transform it to temperature by table look-up with interpolation, and output the result to an LED display. }

{ Declarations }

```
const    TABLE_SIZE  =  15;
type     MILLIVOLTS  =  0..63;
         TEMPERATURE  =  0..1023;
         ARRAY1  =  array [0..table_size] of millivolts;
var      PORT_0, PORT_1: file of integer;
         V: array1;
         T: array[0..table_size] of temperature;
         VM:  millivolts;
         TM:  temperature;
         I:  integer;
```

{ Procedure to look up table to find position i of entry E[i] that is closest to but does not exceed a given value EM. }

```
procedure SCAN_TABLE (TABLE: array1; EM: millivolts; var i: integer);
begin
   i := 1;
   while EM > TABLE[i] do i := i + 1
end;
```

{ Main program }

```
begin
```
{ Define voltage-temperature table for thermocouple }

T[0] := 0;	V[0] := 0;	T[8] := 400;	V[8] := 16;
T[1] := 50;	V[1] := 2;	T[9] := 450;	V[9] := 19;
T[2] := 100;	V[2] := 4;	T[10] := 500;	V[10] := 21;
T[3] := 150;	V[3] := 6;	T[11] := 550;	V[11] := 23;
T[4] := 200;	V[4] := 8;	T[12] := 600;	V[12] := 25;
T[5] := 250;	V[5] := 10;	T[13] := 650;	V[13] := 27;
T[6] := 300;	V[6] := 12;	T[14] := 700;	V[14] := 29;
T[7] := 350;	V[7] := 14;	T[15] := 750;	V[15] := 31;

```
reset (PORT_0, 'UNIT = 2');
rewrite (PORT_1, 'UNIT = 1');

while true do
   begin
   read (PORT_0, VM);
   SCAN_TABLE (V,VM,I);
   TM := T[I-1] + (T[I] - T[I-1]) * (VM - V[I-1]) div (V[I] - V[I-1]);
   write (PORT_1, TM)
   end
end.
```

Figure 7.27 Pascal program to control the microprocessor-based thermometer of Fig. 7.23a.

while the output temperature T_M is transmitted as an integer to output port PORT _1. A small temperature–voltage table is defined in Fig. 7.27 by means of a set of Pascal assignment statements. This awkward table definition reflects the fact that Pascal does not permit constant declarations to specify array values. The PL/M language, on the other hand, does allow such declarations. A PL/M version of the table of Fig. 7.27 can be specified thus:

    declare T(16) **address data** (0, 50, 100, 150, 200, 250, 300, 350, 400, 450, 500, 550, 600, 650, 700, 750);

    declare V(16) **byte data** (0, 2, 4, 6, 8, 10, 12, 14, 16, 19, 21, 23, 25, 27, 29, 31);

A procedure called SCAN_TABLE is used to determine the index value i such that V_{i-1} is the largest entry in the voltage table satisfying the relation $V_{i-1} \leq V_M$. (V_M and V_{i-1} are represented by VM and V[I − 1], respectively, in the program listing.) The desired temperature is then computed by a Pascal statement that is a direct implementation of the interpolation equation (7.2). It is not difficult to construct an assembly-language version of this program. The table-look-up operation is readily implemented in assembly language; see, for instance, the temperature-conversion program of Fig. 6.16. Implementing the interpolation process is likely to be more difficult, especially if multiplication and division instructions or subroutines are not available.

7.2.3 Actuators

In many applications a microprocessor controls mechanical variables such as the position or orientation of an object. This requires an output device, generally called an *actuator,* that can translate electronic control signals into mechanical motion. A relay may be regarded as a simple type of actuator to control the position of a mechanical on–off switch. More complicated movement is controlled by more powerful electromechanical devices, of which solenoids and electric motors are the most important. The industrial process control system depicted in Fig. 1.36, for example, employs three electric motors: two to control the spatial position of the insulation extrusion unit, and a third to control the speed of the cable drive mechanism.

A *solenoid* is a fairly simple type of actuator, which, like a relay, is a form of electromagnet. It contains a cylindrical coil of insulated wire that is activated by passing an electric current through it. This creates a strong magnetic field in the hollow core of the solenoid, which exerts a strong attractive force on a sliding plunger made of soft iron. Thus, when activated, the solenoid draws the plunger towards its center; when deactivated by switching off the current flowing through the coil, a return spring withdraws the plunger to a noncentral rest position. Figure 7.28 shows a solenoid being used to operate a door-lock mechanism. The motion of the solenoid's plunger is transmitted to a sliding bolt via a lever. A solenoid can also be used to produce rotary motion via a ratchet. Rotary motion, as well as linear motion over longer distances, is generally the province of electric motors.

A more complicated output device employing solenoids as positional actuators— namely, a low-cost printer of the kind found in desk calculators, POS terminals, and the

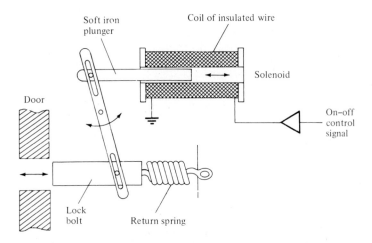

Figure 7.28 Solenoid actuator for a door-lock mechanism.

like—is illustrated in Fig. 7.29a. This device can print up to 42 different characters in a 16-column format on a roll of paper. The characters in question are found in mirror-image relief on the surface of a rotating drum. As shown in Fig. 7.29b, the print drum has 16 columns, each containing 42 characters spaced evenly around the circumference. For each of the 16 columns of the drum there is a solenoid-actuated hammer that presses an ink ribbon and the paper against the drum, thereby transferring the character under the hammer to the paper. A row of 16 characters is printed one character at a time. The drum rotates continuously; when the desired character for column i is positioned under the corresponding hammer, the hammer's solenoid is activated for a precise period to complete the printing operation. This process is repeated until an entire row of up to 16 characters has been printed. Then the paper is advanced to the next row to be printed, for example, by means of another solenoid. At the same time the ink ribbon may be advanced, and printing of the next row begins.

In this example the print drum is continually rotated by a synchronous electric motor that is designed to have a constant rotational speed. The speed may fluctuate slightly, however, due to the intermittent pressing of the paper against the print drum, and other factors. This necessitates some form of information feedback from the printer to its controller, that indicates the precise position of the print drum at all times. This positional information is provided by a set of magnetic transducers attached to the drum drive mechanism. (Optical transducers are also suitable for this application.) A permanent magnet M_1 is embedded in the surface of the print drum. A detecting device called a read head is placed so that M_1 rotates past it. The read head is like an electromagnet in reverse. It consists of a coil of insulated wire wound around a soft magnetic core; when M_1 moves past the read head, its magnetic field induces a voltage in the coil which is sent as the signal P_1 to the microprocessor that controls the printer. A pulse from P_1, therefore, indicates the drum's rotational position, and hence the character currently under the 16 hammers. P_1 is designed as a reset signal to mark the start of a character print cycle.

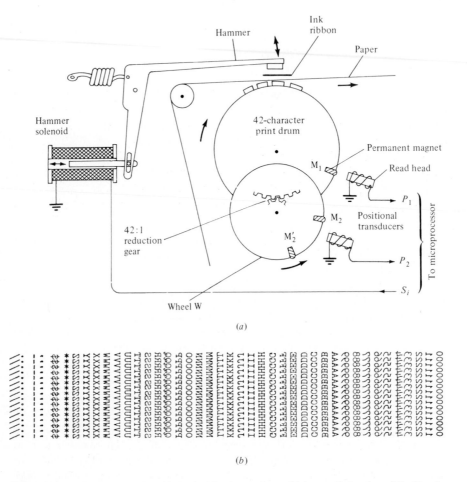

Figure 7.29 (a) Cross section (simplified) of a 16-column printer; (b) the unrolled surface of the 16-column 42-character print drum.

It is also desirable to have the printing mechanism indicate when the hammer solenoids should be activated and deactivated. For this purpose a second magnetic transducer is employed, as shown in Fig. 7.29a. Two additional permanent magnets M_2 and M_2' are embedded in a wheel W that is geared to the print drum. W is designed so that it rotates 42 times for every revolution of the print drum. Hence one rotation of W occurs in the time it takes one character of the print drum to pass under the heads of the hammers. M_2 and M_2' are placed so that they provide positional signals P_2 via a second magnetic read head, which indicate when the hammers should be activated and deactivated respectively. Thus a pulse on P_2 produced by M_2 is used by the microprocessor to activate the solenoid in some selected column i by setting S_i to 1. A subsequent pulse on P_2 generated by M_2' causes S_i to be reset to 0. Figure 7.30 depicts the waveforms appearing on P_1 and P_2 when the printer is in operation. It also indicates the sequence in

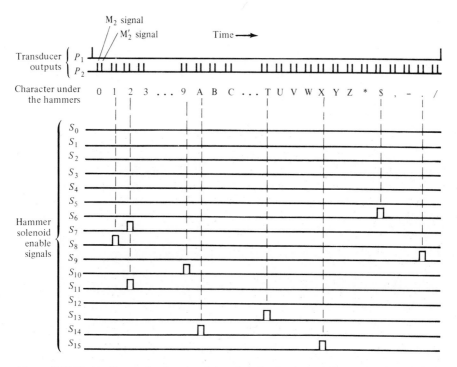

Figure 7.30 Timing diagram for the printer's interface signals when printing the row $21.92 TAX.

which the print hammers must be actuated to print the following right-justified row of characters

$21.92 TAX

Note that all copies of the same character, in this case the two 2s, are printed simultaneously, so that an entire row is printed during one rotation of the drum.

A total of 19 logic signals are used to interface the printer to a host microprocessor. Sixteen output signals $S_0:S_{15}$ control the solenoid-operated hammers. Drive (amplifier) circuits are required to meet the relatively large current requirements of the solenoids. One additional output S_{16} controls a solenoid that advances the paper and the ink ribbon. The two input signals P_1 and P_2 produced by the magnetic transducers are transmitted from the printer to the microprocessor. A convenient means of interfacing these 19 IO signals is a general-purpose IO controller IC such as the 6821 PIA in the Motorola 6800 series (see Fig. 5.37) or the 8255 IC in the Intel 8080/8085 series (see Fig. 5.54). These are both programmable devices whose IO interface lines are easily configured by a software command to match the 19 lines attached to the printer. Figure 7.31 shows how to use the 6821 to interface the printer to a 6800-compatible system bus (Motorola, 1975b). The 16 data lines constituting IO ports A and B of the 6821 are programmed to be output lines, and are connected via suitable drive circuits to the hammer-enable lines $S_0:S_{15}$. The 6821 has four additional programmable IO lines that are intended primarily as control

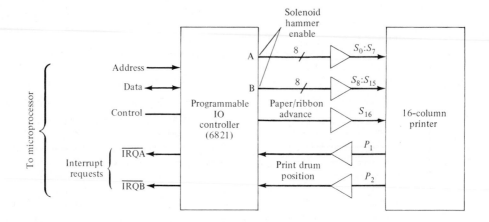

Figure 7.31 Printer interface circuit using a general-purpose IO controller IC (the 6821 PIA).

lines for the data ports. In this application one of these lines is used to enable the paper/ribbon advance solenoid via S_{16}. Two of the remaining lines are used to relay the transducer outputs P_1 and P_2 to the host microprocessor. Specifically, the 6821 is programmed so that a signal pulse on P_1 causes an interrupt request to be sent to the CPU via the 6821's interrupt request line $\overline{\text{IRQA}}$. In a similar fashion, P_2 produces a second interrupt request via $\overline{\text{IRQB}}$.

The software part of the printer interface consists of two interrupt-handling routines that are invoked by $\overline{\text{IRQA}}$ and $\overline{\text{IRQB}}$. $\overline{\text{IRQA}}$, which is activated once every revolution of the print drum, may be used to enable the solenoid actuator that advances the paper and ink ribbon. This requires the microprocessor to send a pulse of the proper duration to the solenoid by setting and resetting S_{16}. $\overline{\text{IRQA}}$ is also used to initialize an address variable or pointer identifying the character currently under the hammers. A second interrupt-handling routine responds to $\overline{\text{IRQB}}$, which, as demonstrated in Fig. 7.30, is activated 84 times as often as $\overline{\text{IRQA}}$, that is, twice for every character row on the print drum. $\overline{\text{IRQB}}$ signals are generated alternately by the magnet elements M_2 and M_2' as wheel W of the printer rotates. An interrupt request from M_2' causes the microprocessor to deactivate any previously active print hammers by resetting their S_i enable signals to 0. The interrupt routine also updates its pointer to the next character c due to appear under the hammers. It then scans the current row of characters to be printed, which is stored in a buffer area in main memory. If the character c appears in this row, flags are set to indicate that the c should be printed in certain columns, and a return is made to the interrupted program. A short time later $\overline{\text{IRQB}}$ is activated by M_2, indicating that the drum is now in position for printing the character c. If the previous execution of the $\overline{\text{IRQB}}$ routine has indicated that c is to be printed, the hammer-enable signals S_i in the appropriate columns are set to 1, and a return is made.

The 16-column printer is likely to be only one of a number of IO devices in the same microprocessor-based system. In a POS terminal, for example, the IO devices include a keyboard, an LED display, a modem, a UPC scanner, and so on; see Fig. 1.33. Thus an important question arises as to how much of the microprocessor's time must be devoted to controlling the printer. This can be estimated as follows: Suppose that the printer is designed to print an average of two lines/second. Assuming one rotation of the print drum per line, each rotation takes 500 ms, and hence each rotation of the wheel W containing the transducers M_2 and M_2' takes $500/42 = 12$ ms. During this 12-ms period the $\overline{IRQB}$ interrupt-request line is activated twice. The number of instructions executed by the microprocessor in response to the interrupt request is variable, but can reasonably be expected to lie in the range 5 to 50; note that in most cases no character will be printed, requiring no special actions by the microprocessor beyond updating its print drum position information. If an average of 25 instructions are executed by the microprocessor in response to each $\overline{IRQB}$ interrupt, at an average rate of one instruction every 5 μs, then 125 μs must be devoted to servicing a typical interrupt. Thus about 250 out of every 12,000 μs are spent by the microprocessor controlling the printer, which is approximately 2 percent of its available processing time.

Electric motors are used to control more complicated forms of mechanical motion. Figure 7.32 shows a motor that controls the movement of a tool back and forth along a linear path. The rotary motion of the motor's drive shaft is converted to linear motion by means of a screwed rod (a lead screw), which is threaded through the tool holder. The direction of motion of the tool is altered by reversing the direction of rotation of the electric motor; the latter is usually performed by reversing the direction of electric current flow through the motor. Limit switches are used to turn the motor off when the tool holder approaches the ends of the lead screw. Additional switches may be used to halt the tool in intermediate positions; optical or magnetic transducers are particularly useful for this application.

A large variety of different types of electric motors are available. All are based on the conversion of electric currents to magnetic fields that are arranged to create attractive or repulsive magnetic forces producing rotation. An electric motor has two major parts: a cylindrical rotor that rotates and a fixed stator that surrounds the rotor. The rotor and/or the stator are typically equipped with sets of coils or windings, which produce the magnetic fields necessary to operate the motor. Electric motors can be designed to operate from ac or dc power supplies. They can be further distinguished by their operating speeds, their power, and their torque or turning-force characteristics.

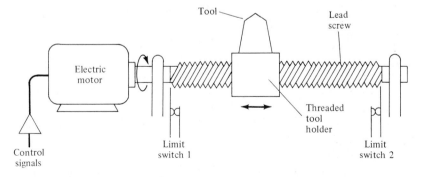

Figure 7.32 Use of an electric motor to control the motion of a tool along a linear path.

A special type of electric motor that is well suited to many position-control tasks is a *stepping motor* (also called a step or stepper motor). Unlike a conventional motor, whose only mode of operation is continuous rotation, a stepping motor can be rotated through a small precise angle or step, then halted. This step movement is controlled by a (digital) pulse of electric current supplied to the motor's windings. n such pulses in sequence cause the motor to rotate through n steps and halt in a known repeatable position; a continuous stream of pulses produces continuous rotation. The step size is determined by the motor's design, and can range from 1.8 degrees to 30 degrees, that is, from 200 to 12 steps per revolution.

The operating principle of a representative stepping motor is illustrated by Fig. 7.33. The rotor has the form of a cylindrical permanent magnet with gearlike teeth around the circumference. Each tooth is either a north (N) or south (S) magnetic pole, and N and S teeth occupy alternating positions. The stator also has a set of teeth, which, however, are

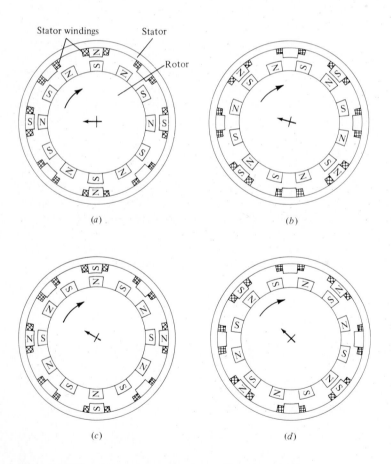

Figure 7.33 The behavior of a stepping motor (single-phase mode).

formed from soft (nonpermanent) magnetic material, and are surrounded by electric windings. A stator tooth can be converted into either an N or an S magnetic pole by passing an electric current through its winding; the magnetic polarity is determined by the direction of the current. Figure 7.33a shows the motor with half the stator teeth magnetized in an alternating N-S configuration. Each magnetized stator tooth is directly opposite a rotor tooth of different polarity, which it strongly attracts (unlike magnetic poles attract and like poles repel.) Thus the rotor is firmly fixed in the position shown in the figure. Suppose that the active stator teeth are switched off and the remaining stator teeth are switched on, yielding the stator pole configuration of Fig. 7.33b. The active stator teeth exert attractive and repulsive forces on the two nearest rotor teeth, which act in unison to produce rotation in the clockwise direction. This rotation continues until each active stator tooth is aligned with a rotor tooth of opposite polarity. The rotor then locks in the position shown in Fig. 7.33b. It is easily seen that the total angle of rotation or step size s is given by

$$s = \frac{360}{2n} \text{ degrees}$$

where n is the number of stator teeth. In the present case, $n = 12$ and $s = 15$ degrees. If the stator configuration is now changed to that of Fig. 7.33c, another rotation by s degrees occurs. The fourth configuration of Fig. 7.33d causes another step to take place. Additional steps are produced by repeating the four stator patterns of Fig. 7.33a–d in the same sequence. Thus to control a stepping motor, it is necessary to supply the stator windings with four distinct current patterns that produce stator pole configurations similar to those shown in the figure. It is easily seen that if the stator configurations of Fig. 7.33 are generated in the reverse order, stepwise rotation in the counterclockwise direction is obtained.

The magnetic-pole patterns of Fig. 7.33 can be produced in various ways. A popular approach is to supply each stator tooth with two separate windings, one to produce an N pole and the other to produce an S pole; the result is a *bifilar stepping motor*. The four patterns of Fig. 7.33 are produced by passing a current through four different sets of stator windings, with the windings in each set connected in series. For example, to produce the pole configuration of Fig. 7.33a, the N windings of the topmost and bottommost stator teeth are connected in series with each other and with the S windings of the two teeth midway between them; let the resulting circuit be denoted W_a. In a similar way, the remaining pole configurations of Figs. 7.33b, 7.33c, and 7.33d correspond to the three disjoint sets of windings W_b, W_c, and W_d respectively. To operate the stepping motor, the four composite windings W_a, W_b, W_c, and W_d are connected to a power supply and four switches x_a, x_b, x_c, and x_d, as shown in Fig. 7.34a. By activating these switches in the sequence shown in Fig. 7.34b, the stepping action of Fig. 7.33 is obtained. Stepping motors are normally operated using the slightly more complicated switching sequence given in Fig. 7.34c. In this mode of operation two of the four windings are activated simultaneously, so that all stator teeth are magnetized simultaneously and can contribute to the motor's torque. It is easily demonstrated that this normal or *dual-phase* control method of Fig. 7.34c produces a stepping motion of the same size and direction as the *single-phase* method of Fig. 7.34b (see Prob. 7.18). While

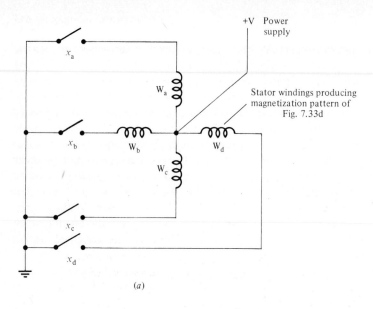

(a)

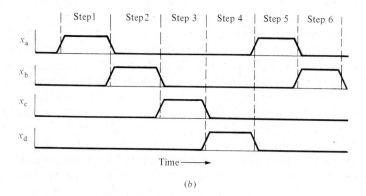

(b)

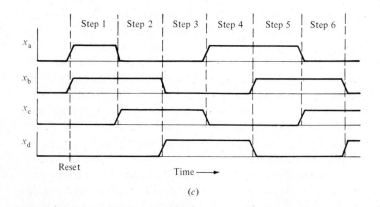

(c)

Figure 7.34 (a) Control circuit for a bifilar stepping motor; (b) single-phase (low-power) mode of operation; (c) dual-phase (normal) mode of operation.

the latter produces lower torque, it has the advantage of consuming less power than the dual-phase mode.

A stepping motor can be interfaced to a microprocessor by means of the circuit of Fig. 7.35, which is designed for normal dual-phase operation. The microprocessor outputs three signals to control the motor: a STEP signal containing a train of pulses, each of which is of sufficient duration to cause the motor to rotate through one step; a direction signal DIR, which determines the direction of rotation; and an initialization signal RESET. These signals are connected to a modulo-4 up-down counter as specified in Fig. 7.35. The 2-bit output of the counter is then decoded to obtain the sequence of drive signals appearing in Fig. 7.34c. The software to control the motor via this interface circuit is fairly simple. First the DIR signal, which is attached to the up-down control input of the counter, is set to indicate the desired direction of rotation. Then RESET is activated, and a sequence of n pulses is applied to STEP, producing a rotation of n steps. This position control scheme is an example of an *open-loop* control system, since no feedback is needed to attain the proper final position (cf. the closed-loop temperature control and printer control systems of Figs. 7.23b and 7.31 respectively).

7.2.4 Analog–Digital Conversion

Numerous techniques are known for converting IO data between analog and digital forms. They involve various trade-offs between speed and accuracy, and also between hardware and software complexity. While ADCs and DACs can be implemented largely in hardware using LSI circuits, it is also possible to use very simple interface circuits, and employ microprocessor software to carry out the conversion functions; this software can also be quite simple. We now examine some basic analog–digital conversion methods, illustrating the role that the microprocessor can play in the data-conversion process.

A simple interface between the analog and digital worlds can be created by an electronic circuit called a *comparator*, which is defined by Fig. 7.36a. Like the logic comparator discussed in Sec. 4.1.4 (see Fig. 4.24), this comparator compares two input signals and generates an output signal indicating their relative magnitudes. In the present case the inputs are two analog voltages v_1 and v_2, and the output z is a binary logic signal;

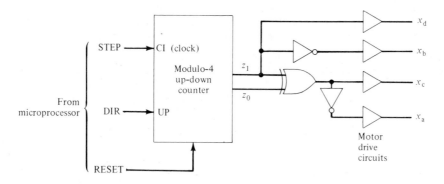

Figure 7.35 Interface circuit for a stepping motor (dual-phase operation).

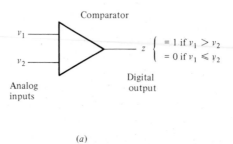

(a)

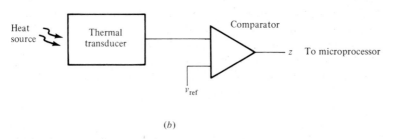

(b)

Figure 7.36 Analog comparator: (a) symbol; (b) simple application.

$z = 1$ if $v_1 > v_2$, while $z = 0$ if $v_1 \leq v_2$. By themselves, comparators are useful in alarm circuits, as illustrated by Fig. 7.36b. Here the analog output v of a (thermal) transducer is applied to a comparator whose digital output z is monitored by a microprocessor. When v exceeds a predetermined value specified by the reference voltage v_{ref}, z changes from 0 to 1, effectively sounding an alarm that, in this case, might indicate an excessive temperature. Comparators are also used in many other types of analog-to-digital conversion circuits, as will be seen shortly.

Digital-to-analog conversion is generally done exclusively in hardware by special-purpose ICs. To illustrate the principles involved, consider the switched resistor network of Fig. 7.37a in which the switches are controlled by the n variables $x_{n-1}x_{n-2} \cdots x_0$ of the digital input word that is to be converted to analog form. Suppose that $x_{n-1}x_{n-2} \cdots x_0$ represents an unsigned binary integer N, so that bit x_i has the numerical weight 2^i. Bit x_i is assigned to the switch controlling the resistor whose resistance is $2^{n-i-1}R$ ohms. The effective resistance R_e between the terminals a and b of the resistor network is determined by the switch states, and is given by the following equation (Eq. 2.11):

$$\frac{1}{R_e} = \frac{x_{n-1}}{R} + \frac{x_{n-2}}{2R} + \cdots + \frac{x_0}{2^{n-1}R}$$

$$= \frac{1}{2^{n-i}R}(x_{n-1}2^{n-1} + x_{n-2}2^{n-2} + \cdots + x_0)$$

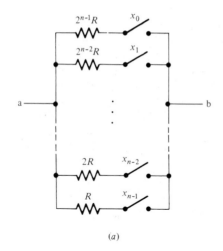

(a)

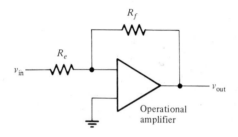

(b)

Figure 7.37 Components of a DAC: (a) weighted resistor network; (b) amplifier circuit.

Hence

$$R_e = 2^{n-1} R/N \qquad (7.3)$$

implying that R_e is inversely proportional to the magnitude N of the digital input word.

It remains to use R_e to produce an analog voltage signal that is proportional to N. This is done by connecting the resistor network to a voltage-amplifying circuit of the kind given in Fig. 7.37b. At the heart of this circuit is an *operational amplifier* ("op amp"), which is a very sensitive analog voltage amplifier capable of amplifying an input voltage by a factor of 100,000 or more. (A comparator is a modified form of operational amplifier, and hence the same circuit symbol is used for both.) The resistors of Fig. 7.37b, including the feedback resistor R_f, give the circuit the following IO behavior:

$$v_{\text{out}} = \frac{R_f}{R_e} v_{\text{in}} \qquad (7.4)$$

Combining Eqs. (7.3) and (7.4) yields

$$v_{out} = -\frac{R_f v_{in}}{2^{n-1} R} N$$

Hence if v_{in} is fixed, the analog output voltage v_{out} becomes proportional to the digital input as required. The values of R, R_f, and v_{in} are chosen to make v_{out} cover some desired voltage range, for example, 0 to $+5$ V. Figure 7.38 shows an 8-bit weighted-resistor DAC of the foregoing kind, with bipolar transistors serving as the input switches. When n is large, this type of DAC has the disadvantage of requiring precision resistors whose resistance values vary over a wide range; such resistors are difficult to manufacture using IC technology. Consequently a different type of resistor network is used in practice (see Prob. 7.20). DACs are commercially available that are suitable for interfacing with most

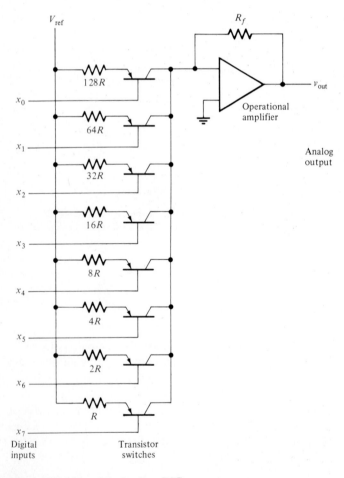

Figure 7.38 8-bit weighted-resistor DAC.

types of microprocessors. The typical input word size is 8 to 12 bits, with a propagation delay (digital-to-analog conversion time) of 100 ns or more.

A conceptually simple analog-to-digital conversion method called *direct conversion* is depicted in Fig. 7.39. Suppose that an analog input voltage v is to be converted to an n-bit unsigned binary integer. This means that the ADC must generate 2^n distinct output words $0 \ldots 00, 0 \ldots 01, \ldots, 1 \ldots 11$ corresponding to 2^n fixed analog input voltages V_0, $V_1, \cdots, V_{2^n-1}$, where $V_{i+1} > V_i$. In the direct conversion approach, v is compared simultaneously with each of the 2^n voltage values $V_0, V_1, \cdots, V_{2^n-1}$, which are generated

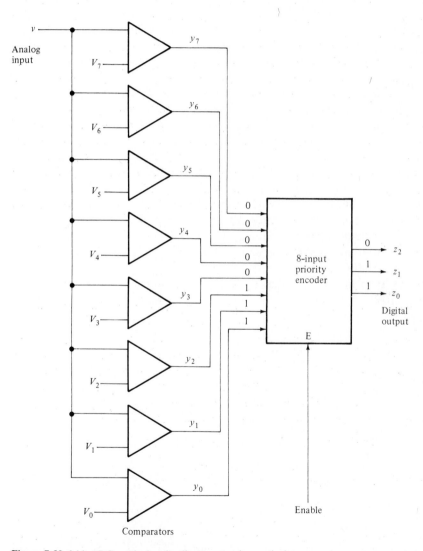

Figure 7.39 3-bit ADC employing the direct conversion method.

internally by the ADC. This comparison is performed by 2^n comparators of the kind defined in Fig. 7.36a. The output signals from the comparators take the form

$$Y = y_{2^n-1}\, y_{2^n-2} \cdot\cdot\, y_{i+1}y_iy_{i-1} \cdot\cdot\, y_1y_0 = 00 \cdot\cdot\, 011 \cdot\cdot\, 11 \qquad (7.5)$$

containing from zero to 2^n consecutive 1s. If the leftmost 1 in (7.5) corresponds to comparator output y_i, then the input voltage v lies between V_i and V_{i+1}, and is uniquely represented in digital form by Y. As indicated in Fig. 7.39, Y is transformed to an ordinary n-bit binary number by means of a priority encoder. The output Z of the encoder is the desired digital version of the analog input v. Direct conversion is a relatively fast analog-to-digital conversion technique, allowing conversion times of less than 100 ns. Because the number of comparators grows exponentially with n, the number of output bits, direct-conversion ADCs are limited to $n = 3$ or 4. Thus the precision with which v can be measured by a direct-conversion ADC is relatively low.

The foregoing conversion method is fast because it compares the unknown voltage v with all possible (digital) reference voltages simultaneously. Several analog-to-digital conversion methods employ an indirect conversion approach in which v is compared with one reference value v_{ref} at a time. v_{ref} is changed systematically until it is as close as possible to v. This implies a slower conversion process, but allows greater precision to be achieved. Furthermore, the hardware part of the ADC can be reduced to the very simple circuit in Fig. 7.40. Here, a digital word VREF is converted to the reference analog voltage v_{ref} by a DAC. A comparator is then used to compare v with v_{ref}, producing the digital outcome bit COMP. When COMP indicates that v and v_{ref} are approximately equal, VREF is then the desired digital representation of v. The circuit of Fig. 7.40 has an all-digital interface comprising the signals VREF and COMP, which is easy to connect to a special-purpose (hardwired) logic circuit or to a microprocessor. We next describe two popular analog-to-digital conversion methods that employ this hardware, and are easily implemented in software.

One way to obtain the trial values for VREF is simply to count from zero to 2^{n-1}. Each time VREF is incremented, it is compared with v via the DAC and comparator.

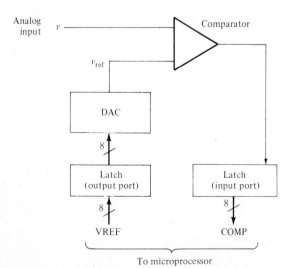

Figure 7.40 Hardware for indirect analog-to-digital conversion methods.

Counting continues until a change in the value of COMP from 1 to 0 indicates that v_{ref} just exceeds v, at which point the conversion is complete, and VREF is the result. This is sometimes called the *ramp* conversion method, since v_{ref} increases by constant increments and so has a waveform resembling a ramp. Figure 7.41 gives a 6800 assembly-language implementation of the ramp technique that contains only five instructions. VREF and COMP are assigned IO addresses within the 6800's memory address space. VREF is incremented from 0 to 255, until a test of COMP indicates that v_{ref} has reached the value of v, at which point the conversion process is complete. The obvious disadvantage of the ramp method is a long conversion time. The worst-case execution time for the ramp subroutine of Fig. 7.41 is approximately 2 ms, assuming a CPU clock rate of 2 MHz. For many applications, however, this is sufficiently fast. If v spans the range 0 to 5 V, then each increment step changes v_{ref} by 5/256 V = 19.5 mV. This is the smallest measurable change in v, and is referred to as the *resolution* of the ADC. Resolution is increased by increasing the number of bits n in VREF, which also requires a larger DAC. To obtain a resolution of, say, 1 mV using the foregoing example, n must satisfy the relation

$$\frac{5}{2^n} \leq 10^{-3}$$

which implies $n \geq 13$ bits.

A faster algorithm for analog-to-digital conversion called the *successive approximation* method is specified by Fig. 7.42. Again the simple indirect comparison interface circuit of Fig. 7.40 is assumed. This method determines the proper value of VREF bit by bit, beginning with the most significant bit VREF[n − 1]. The VREF latch is cleared, and VREF[n − 1] is set to 1, so that VREF = 100 . . . 0 is compared with the input v. If VREF is found to exceed v, then VREF[n − 1] must be 0, and therefore is changed back to 0; otherwise VREF is left unchanged. Then the next bit VREF[n − 2] is set to 1, VREF is compared with v, and VREF[n − 2] is either left at 1 or reset to 0. This process continues for n steps, so that the final value of VREF represents the best digital approximation of v. The successive approximation method is considerably faster than the ramp method, since the latter requires up to 2^n rather than n comparison steps. A straightforward 6800

```
*      6800 SUBROUTINE 'RAMP' TO PERFORM 8-BIT ANALOG-TO-DIGITAL CONVERSION
*          VIA THE INDIRECT RAMP METHOD USING THE CIRCUIT OF FIG. 7.32
*

RAMP    CLR    VREF       CLEAR OUTPUT LATCH ATTACHED TO THE DAC
LOOP    INC    VREF       INCREMENT THE REFERENCE VOLTAGE
        TST    COMP       TEST OUTPUT OF COMPARATOR; IF ZERO, SET CPU'S Z
*                         FLAG TO 1, OTHERWISE RESET Z TO 0
        BNE    LOOP       BRANCH TO LOOP IF Z ≠ 1
        RTS               RETURN FROM SUBROUTINE; RESULT IN VREF
```

Figure 7.41 Subroutine implementing the ramp analog-to-digital conversion method using the circuit of Fig. 7.40.

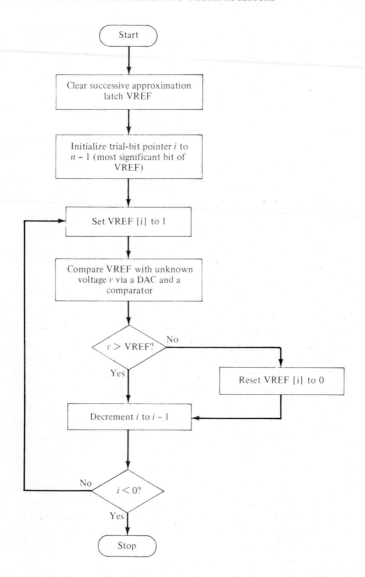

Figure 7.42 Successive approximation method for analog-to-digital conversion.

implementation of successive approximation for the circuit of Fig. 7.40 is listed in Fig. 7.43 (Frank, 1976). The desired digital equivalent of the analog input v is constructed bit by bit in accumulator A for transmission to output port VREF. Accumulator B is employed as a mask register to allow individual bits of register A to be set, reset, or tested. The initial mask pattern used is 10000000, and it is rotated to the right by one bit position after each comparison step, using the 6800's ROR (rotate right) instruction. Since ROR rotates the selected accumulator through the carry flag C, the conditional

```
*     6800 SUBROUTINE 'SUCROX' TO PERFORM 8-BIT ANALOG-TO-DIGITAL CONVERSION
*        VIA THE SUCCESSIVE APPROXIMATION METHOD USING THE CIRCUIT OF FIG. 7.40
*

SUCROX   CLR  A                   CLEAR ACCUMULATOR A
         LDA  B #%10000000        LOAD MASK PATTERN '10000000' INTO ACCUMULATOR B
LOOP     ABA                      ADD B TO A TO SET TRIAL BIT TO 1
         STA  A VREF              OUTPUT A TO LATCH ATTACHED TO THE DAC
         LDA  A COMP              INPUT COMPARATOR RESPONSE TO RIGHTMOST BIT OF A
         AND  A #%00000001        CHECK COMPARATOR RESPONSE; IF ZERO, SET CPU'S Z
*                                 FLAG TO 1, OTHERWISE RESET Z TO 0
         BNE    CONTIN            BRANCH TO CONTIN IF Z ≠ 1
         LDA  A VREF              INPUT VREF TO A
         SBA                      SUBTRACT B FROM A TO RESET TRIAL BIT TO 0
         BRA    SHIFT             GO TO SHIFT
CONTIN   LDA  A VREF              RETAIN THE TRIAL BIT AT 1
SHIFT    ROR  B                   ROTATE THE MASK THROUGH B AND THE CARRY FLAG C
         BCC    LOOP              IF C = 0, BRANCH TO LOOP
         RTS                      RETURN FROM SUBROUTINE; RESULT IN VREF AND A
```

Figure 7.43 Subroutine implementing the successive approximation analog-to-digital conversion method using the circuit of Fig. 7.40.

branch instruction BCC (branch if carry flag is clear) is used as a test for termination of the algorithm. Setting and resetting the trial bits of A is accomplished by addition or subtraction of the current mask pattern using the ABA (add B to A) and SBA (subtract B from A) instructions. At a 2-MHz CPU clock rate, execution of this program requires about 125 μs, making it 15 times faster than the corresponding 6800 ramp program (Fig. 7.41).

7.3 COMMUNICATION METHODS

Interaction between the major components of a microprocessor-based system requires information transfer over common communication lines or buses. This section examines the characteristics of the two basic types of buses, parallel and serial. The use of standard buses is discussed, as well as the techniques used for implementing interrupts and DMA.

7.3.1 Microprocessor Buses

As defined previously, a bus is a set of associated lines used to transfer digital data from one place to another. The simplest bus is a set of one or more data lines that transmit data words from one fixed device to another. If the communicating devices are complex or operate asynchronously, then it is also necessary to transmit synchronizing control information between the devices. These synchronizing signals may be sent over the data lines along with the data, or else may be sent in parallel with the data over special control lines. To minimize wiring complexity a bus is often time-shared (multiplexed) among many different devices, all of which are physically connected to the bus lines. At any time only two of these devices are logically connected to the bus in the sense of being able to use it for a data-transfer operation; one of these devices acts as the data source and the other as the data destination. (Occasionally more than one destination device may be logically connected to the bus.) To realize this type of bus sharing, a means of selecting or addressing individual devices for logical connection to the bus is needed. To this end, each data source and destination is assigned a unique address, and addresses are transmitted over the bus, either via the data lines or via separate address lines. Finally to ensure that no conflicting use of the bus is made—for example, two devices attempting to act as data sources simultaneously—requests for logical connection to the bus must be supervised, a process called bus-access control or bus arbitration. Bus-access control also requires the use of dedicated control lines. In general, therefore, a bus is a collection of data, address, and control lines designed for systematic data transfer among a set of system components. The bus lines may be either unidirectional or bidirectional, with the latter typically employing three-state logic (see Sec. 2.3.2).

The main communication path in a microcomputer is the system bus, to which are attached the CPU (microprocessor), the ROM or RAM circuits forming main memory, and the interface circuits for IO devices. It is termed a parallel bus because data are transmitted over the system bus n bits at a time, where n is usually either the data word size of main memory or the CPU. Microprocessors such as the 6800 and the 8080/8085 have a memory and CPU data word size of 8 bits; hence it is natural to transmit data 8 bits at a time over the corresponding system bus. Since each main memory location and IO port is a potential data source or destination, a large number of addresses must be handled by the system bus. A separate address bus that can transmit all bits of an address word in parallel is thus usually included in the system bus. Finally, a variety of control lines are provided for synchronization, bus-access control, and signaling special conditions such as interrupts.

Control of the system bus in a microcomputer is mainly the CPU's responsibility, and so the structure of the bus is largely dictated by the lines attached to the CPU itself. The IO devices can take control of the system bus from the CPU through the agency of a DMA (direct memory access) controller, which can transfer data directly between the IO devices and main memory without the assistance of the CPU. Bus-access control signals are used by the DMA controller to communicate with the CPU and obtain control of the system bus from it.

Figure 7.44 shows the major features of two typical system buses, those of the 6800 and 8085 8-bit microprocessors. (A more detailed description of the control signals of these buses can be found in Secs. 5.3 and 5.4.) The 6800 bus of Fig. 7.44a contains an 8-bit bidirectional data bus and a 16-bit address bus that permits up to $2^{16} = 64K$ distinct addresses to be used. Some 10 control lines are provided whose functions include indicating the data-transfer direction (read/write enable), data-transfer timing, bus-access control (for DMA operations), and requesting interrupts. The 8085 system bus of Fig. 7.44b is also designed to transmit 8-bit data and 16-bit address words. However, only 16 bus lines are provided for this purpose, and hence the low-order half (bits $A_0:A_7$) of each address word is multiplexed with the corresponding data word via a common address data bus AD. This reduces the number of pins required by the 8085 IC and other system components, as well as the size of the system bus itself. (A separate 16-bit address bus can be obtained, if desired, by demultiplexing the AD bus as shown in Fig. 5.42b.)

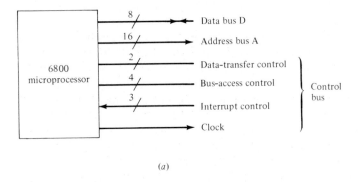

Data bus D

Address bus A

Data-transfer control

Bus-access control

Interrupt control

Clock

(a)

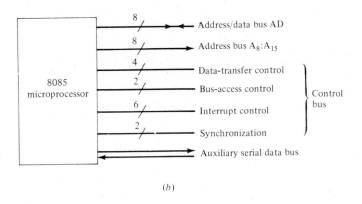

Address/data bus AD

Address bus $A_8:A_{15}$

Data-transfer control

Bus-access control

Interrupt control

Synchronization

Auxiliary serial data bus

(b)

Figure 7.44 Examples of microprocessor system buses: (a) the 6800 bus; (b) the 8085 bus.

The control signals of the 8085 bus perform functions similar to those of the 6800. Note that while the 6800 supplies a clock signal to synchronize all data transfers, the 8085 does not, but instead allows data transfers to be (partially) asynchronous. Another unusual feature of the 8085 is an auxiliary bus that allows an IO device to be directly connected to the CPU via two serial data lines. The timing and control information needed for serial data transmission is sent along with the data over these two lines.

Two key characteristics of buses can be deduced from the foregoing discussion: the degree of parallelism used in information transfer, and the methods used to synchronize the devices communicating over the bus. A bus is considered *parallel* if all bits of a data word of specified size are transmitted simultaneously or in parallel; it is *serial* if data are transmitted 1 bit at a time. Roughly speaking, a parallel bus for n-bit data words is n times faster than a corresponding serial bus, but uses n times more hardware (signal lines, line driver and receiver circuits, etc.). The parallel bus is therefore more costly, and its cost increases with the physical length of the bus. The parallel transmission of data over long distances (20 m or more) is also complicated by a phenomenon called signal *skew*. This refers to the fact that a set of signals leaving a data source simultaneously along separate wires do not always arrive simultaneously at the data destination; instead they arrive at slightly different times, or "skewed." Skew is caused by minor variations in electrical resistance and capacitance that determine a line's signal-propagation delay. It is corrected by deskewing, which involves delaying the signal-transmission process until the slowest signal arrives at the destination. This can significantly reduce the maximum operating speed of a parallel bus. For these reasons, serial buses, which are also referred to as communication lines, are used for data communication over longer distances.

In simpler microcomputers all interfacing is done directly with the main system bus. It is sometimes desirable to interface IO devices first to a special IO bus, which in turn is interfaced to the main system bus. These IO buses can be serial or parallel, and are tailored to the operating characteristics of the particular class of IO devices that they serve. Thus a microprocessor-based system may contain up to three different types of buses as depicted in Fig. 7.45: the microprocessor system bus, one or more parallel IO buses, and one or more serial IO buses. A parallel IO bus is quite similar to a microprocessor system bus, and is designed to accommodate IO devices with high data-transfer rates such as disk memories or complex measuring instruments. It is often under the direct control of an IO processor that can execute IO programs, thereby freeing the CPU for other tasks. The IO processor also serves as a communications link between the IO and system buses. Serial IO buses are used to attach relatively slow IO devices such as interactive terminals and printers to a microcomputer. A UART (universal asynchronous

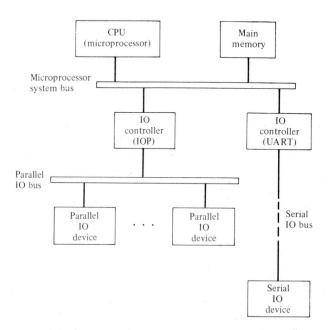

Figure 7.45 Bus types present in microprocessor-based systems.

receiver-transmitter) is commonly used to interface a serial bus to the system bus. A serial bus may also be used to connect a microcomputer to a modem and thence to a telephone network; see Fig. 7.3.

Every microprocessor tends to have its own distinctive system bus, which differs in the number of lines present, the types of control signals used, signal transmission timing, and so on, from the buses of other microprocessors. A similar disparity exists among the buses of minicomputers and large (main-frame) computers. For these reasons, various standard buses have been proposed over the years, which attempt to make the hardware aspect of interfacing independent of the particular (micro)processor being employed. A list of some standard buses that are widely used in microprocessor-based systems is given in Fig. 7.46. They are divided into three groups corresponding to the three bus types illustrated in Fig. 7.45. Most of these buses first appeared in commercial products and were subsequently adopted as standards by such standard-making bodies as the IEEE in the United States and the Comité Consultatif International de Téléphonie et Télégraphie (CCITT), an international organization that falls under the aegis of the United Nations. The specifications for each bus standard, which can be obtained from the sponsoring organization, include the following:

1. A standard set of bus signal (line) names
2. The functions assigned to individual signals and signal sequences
3. The electrical characteristics of the bus
4. The mechanical characteristics of the cables and connectors to be used when implementing the bus

Multibus is a microprocessor system bus for 8-bit and 16-bit microprocessors originally developed by Intel Corp. for its 8080-based Intellec microprocessor development system (MDS) in the mid-1970s. It has since been used as a bus standard by other microprocessor manufacturers, and is the basis for the IEEE 796 bus standard. The S-100 was the 100-line system bus used in the Altair computer, an 8080-based machine introduced in 1974 by the now defunct MITS Inc. The Altair may be regarded as the first low-cost personal computer, and its S-100 bus rapidly became a de facto standard for other personal computers. Again it is the basis for a formal standard, the IEEE 696 bus.

The second group of buses listed in Fig. 7.46 were designed mainly for parallel data transmission among complex digital instruments, which may themselves be microprocessor controlled. The CAMAC (Computer Automated Measurement and Control) standard was developed around 1970 by the nuclear engineering industry in Europe, and allows 24-bit data transfers. The GPIB (General-Purpose Interface Bus) is derived from an instrumentation bus designed by Hewlett-Packard Co., and allows 8-bit data transmission. The third group of serial IO buses have their origins in the telephone industry, and were intended to standardize the interfacing of data terminals and other communications equipment to telephone networks. The RS-232 and CCITT V.24 are broadly similar serial bus standards sponsored by the U.S. Electronic Industries Association (EIA) and the CCITT respectively.

Bus Type	Name	Origins	Equivalent IEEE Bus Standard
Microprocessor system bus	Multibus	System bus for Intel Corp.'s Intellec microprocessor development system (MDS) series (1975)	IEEE 796
	S–100	System bus of the MITS Inc. Altair personal computer introduced in 1974	IEEE 696
Parallel IO bus	CAMAC	Standard bus for nuclear instrumentation defined by the Committee for European Standards on Nuclear Equipment (1969)	IEEE 583
	GPIB	Interface bus for programmable digital instruments designed by Hewlett-Packard Co.	IEEE 488
Serial IO bus	RS–232	Standard serial bus defined by the EIA for interconnecting data terminal and data communication equipment	
	CCITT V.24	Standard serial bus defined by the CCITT	

Figure 7.46 Standard buses that are widely used in microprocessor-based systems.

7.3.2 The System Bus

The interface most frequently encountered by the system designer is the microprocessor system bus, which will be examined in detail. It is a parallel bus, since it transfers data in the form of n-bit words via an n-bit data (sub)bus, where n is typically the CPU or main memory word size. Of course, smaller words also may be transferred over the bus simply by not using all the available data lines. An address bus is provided to allow large numbers of uniquely addressable data sources and destinations to be connected to the system bus. The remaining bus lines are control lines that perform various control functions, including synchronization of data transfers, the control of access or logical connection to the system bus, and the transfer of interrupt signals.

During a data-transfer operation, only two units may be logically connected to the system bus. One of the units has overall control of the system bus, and is often referred to as the *bus master* or *bus controller*. A bus master can issue data-transfer commands via the bus's control lines, and can place addresses on the address bus. The other unit logically connected to the bus has a more passive role, and may be called the *bus slave*. The slave device can receive and decode addresses, and respond to commands from the bus master; it cannot, however, issue addresses or commands itself. Either the master or the slave can act as the data source. In many microprocessor-based systems only the CPU can be the bus master; the main memory and IO interface circuits serve as bus slaves. When present, DMA controllers and IOPs can also be bus masters. In *multiprocessors*, which are defined as computer systems containing more than one CPU, each CPU is a potential bus master.

The timing of bus data transfers was discussed in Sec. 5.2.5, and is summarized here. Three transfer methods were identified: synchronous, semisynchronous, and asynchronous, all of which are supported by standard microprocessor system buses. Synchronous timing employs a free-running clock signal that is generated by the bus master, or else by a central clock generator circuit, and is used as a timing reference for the main steps in the data transfer. These steps are the placement (writing) of data on the data bus by the source unit, the placement of an address on the address bus by the bus master, the placement of a command (read or write) on the control bus by the bus master, the decoding of the address by the destination unit, and the reading of the data from the data bus by the destination unit. The clock signal must be supplied to both the master and the slave. Typically each unit uses the rising and falling edges of clock pulses as reference times during a data-transfer operation, and the transfer of one data word is completed during one clock cycle. Because both source and destination must "see" the edges of the clock signal at approximately the same time, fully synchronous data transfer is practical only for short buses and for communication between units with very similar read and write times. If the operating speeds of the two devices differ appreciably, then the clock frequency must be set to a low worst-case value, thereby limiting the rate at which data transfers can take place. Figure 7.47 is a representative timing diagram for a fully synchronous data-transfer operation over a parallel bus. The rising edge of the clock signal causes the bus master to initiate the data transfer by issuing the address of the desired slave unit and a set of control signals or command indicating the type of data transfer to be carried out, either read (transfer to the bus master) or write (transfer from the bus master). After the slave unit has had time to respond to the address and data-

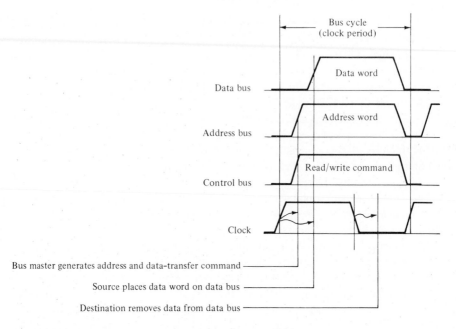

Figure 7.47 Synchronous data-transfer operation using a parallel bus.

transfer command, the source device places a data word on the data bus; again the timing of this action is determined by the rising edge of the clock. The clock's falling edge is used here to trigger the transfer of data from the bus by the destination unit, thus completing a bus cycle.

In synchronous bus transfers the times at which a data word is transferred to and from the bus are determined by the bus clock. In a semisynchronous data transfer, on the other hand, only one of these operations is explicitly timed. The clock signal is replaced by a data-ready or data-request control signal that is specially activated for each one-word data transfer. Examples of semisynchronous data transfers appear in Figs. 5.20 and 5.21.

Asynchronous data transfer is especially important in bus communication, since it allows devices with very different communication speeds to transfer data efficiently to one another. It is characterized by the use of pairs of handshaking control signals (request/ready and acknowledge), which are used by each communicating unit to signal the successful completion of a data-transfer step to the other unit. By delaying the activation or deactivation of a handshaking signal, each device can make the other wait indefinitely until it has completed some action affecting the data-transfer operation. Figure 7.48 shows two typical asynchronous read and write operations. A read or write command, corresponding to data request and data ready, respectively, is activated by the master to signal the slave that the indicated data transfer is to take place. The slave responds by transferring data to or from the data bus as commanded, and it signals completion of this operation by activating the data-acknowledge line. The master responds by deactivating the command signal, which in turn causes the data-acknowledge line to be deactivated. In the case of the read operation of Fig. 7.48a, deactivation of

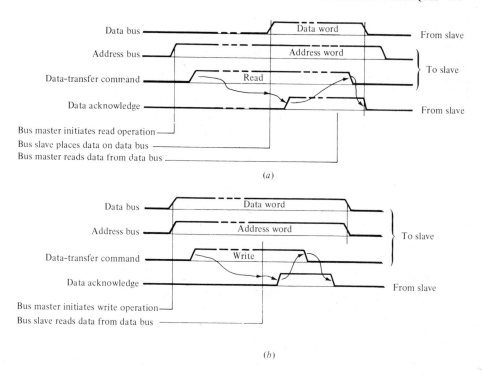

Figure 7.48 Asynchronous data-transfer operations: (*a*) read (to master); (*b*) write (from master).

the command line(s) tells the slave that the data it has transmitted were successfully received by the master. In all cases the data source is informed of the receipt of the transmitted data by the destination unit. The cause-and-effect relationship among the handshaking signals is suggested by arrows in Fig. 7.48. Another important aspect of bus timing is the fact that the master should not activate the read/write command lines until some time after it has placed a new address on the address bus. This is to ensure that all address bits seen by the slave have stabilized at their final values before it attempts to decode the address. Similarly, the master should not remove the current address from the address bus until after it has deactivated the command lines.

The data-transfer command or control lines specify the direction of the data transfer, and are generally called read/write enable lines. As observed in Sec. 5.2.5, microprocessors such as the 8080/8085 that employ isolated IO addressing have one set of read/write lines for IO devices and another set for main memory. This allows the same address patterns to be assigned to memory and IO ports without conflict. Microprocessors such as the 6800 have just one set of read/write enable lines, implying that all memory and IO addresses must be distinct. This is termed memory-mapped IO, and reduces the number of bus lines and data-transfer instructions at the expense of a smaller overall address space. The actual structure of the data-transfer control subbus varies greatly from microprocessor to microprocessor. Figure 7.49 compares the data-transfer command methods used by the 6800 and 8085; see Figs. 5.33 and 5.49 for definitions of all the relevant control signals. Data transfers via the 6800's system bus are semi-

	8085 Microprocessor		6800 Microprocessor	
Data-Transfer Operation	Command Signals	Acknowledge Signal	Command Signals	Acknowledge Signal
Read word from memory	$IO/\overline{M} = 0$ $\overline{RD} = 0$	READY $= 1$	$R/\overline{W} = 1$ VMA $= 1$	None used
Read word from IO device	$IO/\overline{M} = 1$ $\overline{RD} = 0$	READY $= 1$	$R/\overline{W} = 1$ VMA $= 1$	None used
Write word to memory	$IO/\overline{M} = 0$ $\overline{WR} = 0$	READY $= 1$	$R/\overline{W} = 0$ VMA $= 1$	None used
Write word to IO device	$IO/\overline{M} = 1$ $\overline{WR} = 0$	READY $= 1$	$R/\overline{W} = 0$ VMA $= 1$	None used

Figure 7.49 Control signals for bus transfer operations in the 6800 and 8085 microprocessors.

synchronous with the VMA (valid memory address) line acting as the CPU's data-ready/ request line for read and write operations. The 8085 system bus permits asynchronous data transfer. The data-transfer command is defined by three lines: $IO/\overline{M}$ (IO or memory select), $\overline{RD}$ (read enable), and $\overline{WR}$ (write enable). The READY line serves as a data-acknowledge line for asynchronous transfers. A slow memory or IO device can delay activation of READY, causing the CPU to enter a wait state of indefinite duration.

Systems containing several potential bus masters need a systematic procedure for transferring control of the bus from one master to another. Provision must be made for resolving conflicts that result from an attempt by several units to become the bus master simultaneously. This problem is solved by assigning different priorities to the potential masters, so that when several masters are requesting control of the system bus at the same time, only the device with the highest priority is allowed to assume control of the bus. If only two potential bus masters are physically attached to the bus, exchange of bus control can be accomplished by including among the bus's control lines a pair of asynchronous lines with the generic names bus request and bus acknowledge. In many microprocessor buses these lines are called DMA request and DMA acknowledge, or equivalent, since they are intended for sharing the bus between a DMA controller and the CPU. If one of the bus devices U_1 is the current bus master, the other device U_2 requests access to the bus by activating the bus request line. When U_1 is ready to relinquish control of the bus, it signals that fact by activating bus acknowledge, and logically disconnecting itself from the bus lines needed for data transfers. U_2 then responds by logically connecting itself to the released bus lines and deactivating bus request. The subsequent deactivation of bus acknowledge by U_1 completes the transfer of bus control to U_2, which is the new bus master. U_1 can again regain control of the bus by activating bus request, initiating another transfer of bus control. Note that the release of shared bus lines can be implemented simply by driving the corresponding physical connections of the bus to the high-impedance state Z.

The Intel Multibus (Intel, 1978b; Boberg, 1980) illustrates the foregoing bus design concepts. This bus has been widely used in commercial computer systems employing 8-bit and 16-bit microprocessors. It is found, for instance, in the 8080-based SBC 80/10 single-board microcomputer depicted in Fig. 5.2. The large edge connector on the bottom left of the SBC 80/10 is its Multibus interface. This edge connector contains 86 connection points or pins, with 43 on each side of the PC board. The size and spacing of these pins, as well as the overall dimensions of the PC board, form part of the mechanical specifications for the Multibus. The electrical specifications for the Multibus signals are based on those of the standard TTL logic family, which are considered in Sec. 2.4.1. In this section we briefly examine the functional specifications of the Multibus.

Of the 86 pins used in a standard Multibus connector, 61 represent data, address, and control lines; the remainder are used for power and ground connections or are reserved for future use. The 61 functional lines of the Multibus are summarized in Fig. 7.50. Sixteen bidirectional data lines named $\overline{\text{DAT0}}$, $\overline{\text{DAT1}}$, $\overline{\text{DAT2}}$, ..., $\overline{\text{DATF}}$ are provided for data-transfer purposes. An address bus containing 20 lines is provided for address transmission in conjunction with the transfer of 8-bit data words over the data bus. Thus a maximum of 2^{20} bytes or 1 megabyte of byte-organized memory can be addressed directly. Should a data word size of 16 bits (2 bytes) be used, the auxiliary address line $\overline{\text{BHEN}}$ (byte high enable) must be active ($\overline{\text{BHEN}} = 0$). $\overline{\text{BHEN}}$ therefore effectively selects the high-order byte of a 2-byte word that is addressed by the 20 address lines ADR0:ADR13; note that a hexadecimal rather than a decimal numbering convention is used for these lines. The two inhibit lines $\overline{\text{INH1}}$ and $\overline{\text{INH2}}$ are designed to allow ROM and RAM units to time-share a common set of addresses (see Prob. 7.31).

Data transfers via the Multibus may be timed in a number of different ways. By using the common system clock line $\overline{\text{CCLK}}$ to distribute a clock signal to all bus devices,

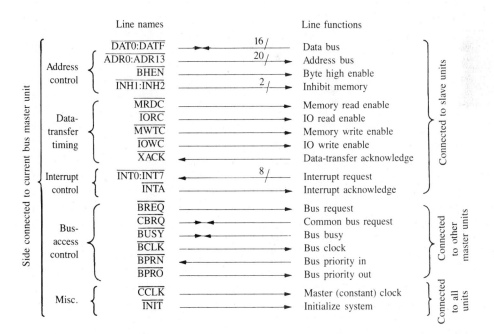

Figure 7.50 Structure of the Multibus standard system bus (excluding power and ground lines).

synchronous data transfer can be implemented along the lines of Fig. 7.47. The various read/write enable lines can be used by themselves to implement semisynchronous data transfers; in conjunction with the data-transfer acknowledge line $\overline{\text{XACK}}$ they permit fully asynchronous operation of the Multibus. Asynchronous data transfers via the Multibus are required to follow the signal-sequencing conventions depicted in Fig. 7.48. The Multibus standard specifies the minimum and maximum delays allowable between various signal changes. For example, all address bits must be at stable values for at least $t_{AS} = 50$ ns before the data-transfer command lines (read/write enable) are activated; t_{AS} is thus the address setup time. The command lines must be held in the active state for at least $t_{CMD} = 100$ ns, which is therefore the minimum command pulse width. Since separate memory and IO read/write enable lines are present, the Multibus supports both memory-mapped and isolated IO addressing.

The Multibus contains a set of eight interrupt-request lines that are used by bus units to interrupt the current activity of the CPU and cause it to execute an interrupt service routine. Each interrupt-request line is assigned a different priority, with $\overline{\text{INT0}}$ having the highest priority and $\overline{\text{INT7}}$ the lowest. By themselves, these lines can be used to invoke interrupt service routines whose locations (starting memory addresses) are known to the CPU, that is, nonvectored interrupt control. To implement vectored interrupt control, in which case the interrupting unit must supply an address vector via the data bus, the Multibus provides an interrupt-acknowledge line $\overline{\text{INTA}}$. This line is activated by the CPU in response to an interrupt request to tell the interrupting device to place an interrupt vector on the data bus; it thus acts as an asynchronous data-request line, where the data word is the interrupt vector. The 8085 microprocessor, for example, employs both vectored and nonvectored interrupts.

A set of six bus access-control lines allow control of the Multibus to be transferred from one bus master to another. The bus-busy line $\overline{\text{BUSY}}$ is activated by the current bus master to indicate that the Multibus is in use; no other bus unit can become the master while $\overline{\text{BUSY}}$ is active. This line must be deactivated by the current master after it has completed its current bus transactions. The bus clock line $\overline{\text{BCLK}}$ is used to synchronize the exchange of control signals that occurs when a new master gains control of the Multibus. The remaining bus-access lines are used in various ways to determine priority when several bus units request control of the bus at the same time. Each potential bus master has a priority-in line $\overline{\text{BPRN}}$ that must be enabled for the unit in question to become the bus master. Hence the priority of the Multibus master units can be determined by controlling their $\overline{\text{BPRN}}$ lines. Figure 7.51 depicts a priority resolution method

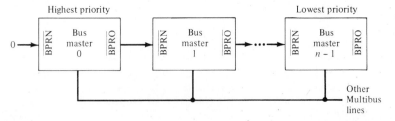

Figure 7.51 Serial technique (daisy chaining) for bus-access control in Multibus systems.

called *daisy chaining*, in which all the potential bus masters are connected in series by their priority-in and -out lines $\overline{\text{BPRN}}$ and $\overline{\text{BPRO}}$. Each master unit has a fixed priority determined by its position along the $\overline{\text{BPRN}}/\overline{\text{BPRO}}$ chain. The unit with the highest priority has its priority-in line permanently enabled as indicated in the figure. This device thus can always gain immediate access to the Multibus whenever the current bus master relinquishes control of the Multibus. If the highest-priority unit does not require the bus, it enables its priority-out line ($\overline{\text{BPRO}} = 0$), thereby enabling the priority-in line of the unit with the next highest priority. If this unit also does not require the Multibus, it enables its $\overline{\text{BPRO}}$ line, and so on. In effect, a bus-available signal is propagated serially through all the master units via the priority-in/out lines. Each unit can, if it wishes, block the propagation of this signal to lower-priority units and assume control of the Multibus. Daisy chaining is a relatively slow method of transferring control of the Multibus; a faster parallel method for determining bus-access priority is described in Prob. 7.32.

When interfacing to a standard bus such as the Multibus, care must be taken to ensure that electrical loading and signal-noise conditions imposed by the bus lines and the other units attached to the bus are met (see Sec. 2.4). Longer lines are normally terminated by line driver and receiver circuits, which provide high current output and minimize noise due to transmission-line effects. For bidirectional bus lines a combination driver–receiver circuit, or *transreceiver*, is used. The bus's data and control lines are normally connected directly to lines with corresponding names on the various bus units, a straightforward task. The address bus is connected, possibly via decoding logic, to the corresponding address- or (chip-) select input lines on the bus slave units. The interfacing of address lines is examined in detail in the context of memory system design in Sec. 4.3.3. In some simpler microprocessor applications only a small number of the 2^m possible addresses allowed by an m-bit address bus are actually needed. In such cases it is possible to dispense with address-decoding circuits by employing the so-called *linear addressing* scheme depicted in Fig. 7.52, in which individual address lines are used as chip-select lines. In this example, for instance, the address line A_6 serves as the chip-select line for the 32- by 8-bit ROM. Hence any address pattern with $A_6 = 1$ selects the ROM for logical connections to the system bus; the specific memory location within the ROM to be used for a data-transfer (read) operation is then determined by the address bits $A_5{:}A_0$. Resetting A_6 to 0 serves to disconnect the ROM from the system bus. This implies that none of the 512 address patterns with $A_6 = 0$ can be allocated to any addressable unit of this system. The price paid for the elimination of address-decoding circuits thus is a large reduction in the number of available addresses. In general, if k out of the m lines of the address bus are used as select lines in a linear addressing configuration, the number of usable addresses is reduced from 2^m to at most $k2^{m-k}$. Another example of an IO interface that uses linear addressing appears in Fig. 7.9.

7.3.3 IO Programming

From an interfacing viewpoint, most IO devices can be seen as relatively passive sources (in the case of input devices) or destinations (in the case of output devices) of data that are processed by the system's microprocessor or CPU. The CPU itself has little storage space internally, and hence data that are to be transmitted to an output device, or are to be

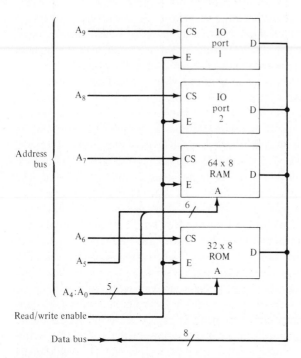

Figure 7.52 System bus interface employing linear addressing.

received from an input device, must be stored, at least temporarily, in a reserved region of main memory. This IO data storage region also serves as a buffer between the CPU and IO devices, which often differ greatly in their data-transmission rates. Most IO operations thus involve the transfer of data between main memory and external IO devices. IO operations are supervised by IO programs, which differ from other programs in that they address IO ports as well as main memory. They also often involve time-critical tasks, for which the IO programs must interact with external events in "real" time, that is, when they actually occur. We next turn to consideration of the hardware and software mechanisms needed for controlling IO operations.

Three general methods of controlling IO operations can be distinguished:

Programmed IO
Interrupt-driven IO
Direct memory access (DMA)

In *programmed IO* all steps of an IO operation require the execution of instructions by the CPU, implying that the steps in question are under continual software control. This is in many respects the simplest and slowest method of IO control, and can be used with all computer systems. Frequently the CPU cannot predict when an IO device will be ready to participate in an IO operation. Consequently the CPU must periodically execute instructions that check or "poll" the IO device to determine its status (ready or not ready); for this reason the terms *polled IO* and *status-driven IO* are also used for programmed IO. The execution of a status-polling routine by the CPU is time consuming, and reduces the maximum rate at which data can be transferred to or from the IO device involved. An IO device that is ready to send or receive data is forced to wait until the next polling period before it can make the CPU aware of its need for service. Thus programmed IO control may be unsuitable for systems containing IO devices that require very rapid access to the CPU.

The foregoing speed deficiencies of programmed IO can be alleviated by employing interrupts, which enable an IO device to send an immediate signal to the CPU whenever it is ready to send or receive data. This signaling is accomplished by activating an interrupt-request line that goes from the IO interface directly to the CPU, and forms part of the system bus. The CPU responds to an interrupt request by temporarily suspending the execution of its current program, while it executes a program P that has been previously placed in memory to handle the interrupt in question. P, which is referred to as an interrupt service routine, is typically an IO program that reads data from input devices into memory or writes data from memory to output devices. Since the execution of P is initiated by an interrupt request from an IO device, this type of IO control is termed *interrupt-driven IO*.

Although an interrupt mechanism relieves the CPU from the tedious task of checking the status of IO devices, it still requires the CPU to execute the IO programs that actually transfer data between main memory and the IO subsystem. By adding a fairly modest amount of control hardware to the IO interface circuits, they can be endowed with the ability to transfer data to and from main memory directly, thereby bypassing the CPU. This type of IO control is called direct memory access or DMA, and interface circuits that implement DMA are called DMA controllers. A DMA controller is capable of taking charge of the system bus and initiating read or write operations addressed to main memory; in other words, it can act as a bus master. It can also increment or decrement addresses automatically, and keep track of the number of data words being transferred through it. A block of words thus can be moved between an IO device and main memory under the supervision of the DMA controller without intervention by the CPU. This method of IO control reduces the CPU's role to that of initializing the DMA controller by supplying it with the starting address of the IO buffer region in main memory to be used, as well as the maximum number of words to be transferred. When the DMA controller determines that it has transferred the last data word, it can signal that fact to the CPU by generating an interrupt request. DMA control allows blocks of data to be transferred over the system bus at the maximum rate allowed by the bus. Consequently DMA is most suitable for interfacing IO devices that input or output blocks of data at very high speed, such as graphics devices that must display very large amounts of rapidly changing information on a CRT screen. Figure 7.53 summarizes the characteristics of the three IO control techniques.

Next we consider the implementation of the programmed IO method for controlling IO operations. It is characterized by the fact that there is no direct communication from the IO devices to the CPU that can inform the CPU of the IO device's status. In addition, all IO data pass through the CPU, implying that two or more instructions must be executed to effect the transfer of a word between the main memory and the IO device. To

| | IO Control Method | | |
Function or Parameter	Programmed IO	Interrupt-Driven IO	Direct Memory Access
Initiation of IO operation	CPU reads and tests status of IO device (polling).	IO device sends interrupt request to CPU. CPU transfers control to interrupt service routine P.	IO device sends interrupt request to CPU. CPU transfers control to interrupt service routine P'. P' initializes DMA controller.
Transfer of IO data	CPU executes data-transfer program PD.	CPU executes data-transfer program PD.	DMA controller transfers block of data over the system bus.
Termination of IO operation	End of execution of PD	End of execution of PD	DMA word count reaches zero. DMA controller sends interrupt request to CPU.
IO interface circuit complexity	Lowest	Low	Moderate
Speed of response to data-transfer request from IO device	Slow	Fast	Fastest
Maximum IO data-transfer rate	Moderate	Moderate	High

Figure 7.53 Comparison of three basic IO control methods.

output a word, for example, the CPU first must execute a load instruction that transfers the word to a CPU register such as the accumulator. Then the CPU can execute an output instruction to transfer the data from the CPU to the output port. Similarly, to transfer a word from an input device to memory, the CPU must execute an input instruction, followed by a store instruction. Additional bookkeeping instructions may be needed to update addresses, count the number of words being transferred, and so on. Thus a substantial overhead in processing time is incurred in programmed IO operations.

The proper execution of an input or output instruction requires that the IO device or port being addressed accept or transmit a data word within a prescribed IO instruction cycle. If the IO device is not ready in time then the instruction cycle may be completed without the proper data transfer taking place; for example, the CPU may simply read a meaningless word from the system data bus that represents the bus's inactive state. In some instances an IO device is always ready for data transfer, so that an IO instruction addressed to such a device will always be executed successfully. This situation exists, for example, in measurement instructions such as the microprocessor-based thermometer of Fig. 7.23a. The input port attached to the thermal transducer provides a digitized representation of the current temperature on a continuous basis; this port therefore can be read at any time by the system control software. Similarly, new data can be written to the output port connected to the LED display unit at any time.

A different situation arises when IO devices such as secondary memory units are present in the system. Consider the reading of data from a magnetic-tape memory device, which records digital data in magnetically encoded form on the surface of a plastic tape in essentially the same way as a domestic audio (video) tape recorder stores analog sound (visual images). When operating, the tape moves continuously past a read/write head that serves as an IO transducer; data are written a bit or a word at a time in closely spaced columns along the surface of the tape. The host microprocessor must read each column during the brief time it is positioned in front of the read/write head. To ensure that this happens, the control circuits of the IO device should provide a synchronization or status signal S to indicate that it is ready for reading or writing. S may then be polled by the system control program to decide when data should be transferred to or from the IO device under consideration. Figure 7.54 shows a general hardware interface for this type of programmed IO. The IO device is provided with two ports, one for data transfer and a second for status or timing control. One bit of the status IO port represents S and may, in general, be viewed as a data-ready/request signal from the IO device. The polling process then involves reading the status port and checking the value of bit S. If S = 1 (active or ready), then a data read or write operation can be addressed to the associated data port. If S = 0, then the CPU may switch to other tasks, returning periodically to recheck S. It may also check S continuously by repeatedly reading the status port; the CPU is then, in effect, waiting for S to change value. If desired, another bit A of the status IO port may be used to transfer a data-acknowledge signal to the IO device. By writing a 1 and then a 0 into A, the CPU can send an acknowledge pulse to the IO device indicating the receipt or transmission of a data word. In this manner, the exchange of handshaking signals required for asynchronous data transmission between the CPU and the IO device can be programmed.

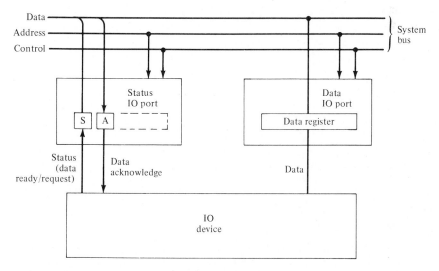

Figure 7.54 Interface circuit for programmed IO with status polling.

Figure 7.55 gives the general structure of a system control program that services a set of IO devices by polling their status periodically. Each device's status is polled in turn, and a data-transfer routine is executed if the status indicator is found to be active, implying that the IO device is ready to send or receive data. Each one-word data-transfer step typically has some bookkeeping actions associated with it, such as sending acknowledge signals, updating the memory address to be used for the next data transfer, and decrementing a data word count to determine if the IO buffer area of memory is full.

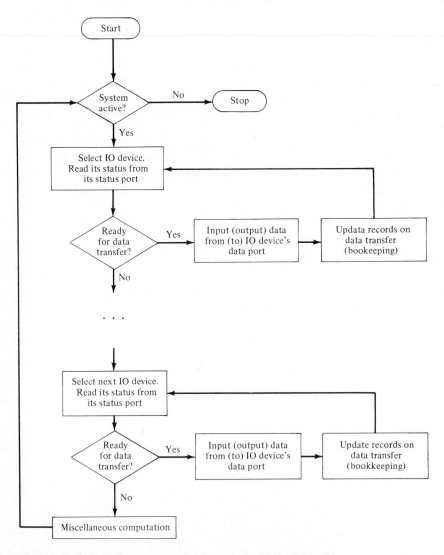

Figure 7.55 Typical software organization for programmed IO with polling.

These various IO operations may be interspersed with other non-IO operations that the CPU must carry out.

An IO program that polls an IO device and transfers a block of data to main memory is listed in Fig. 7.56. This program, which is written in 6800 assembly language, follows the general algorithm of Fig. 7.55, and uses an IO interface circuit like that of Fig. 7.54. The data and status ports are assigned the symbolic names DATA and STATUS, respectively, in the 6800's memory-mapped IO address space; the required status bit is in the leftmost (sign) position of the word stored at the status port. It is assumed that no acknowledgement signals are required by the IO device. The number of words in the block of data to be transmitted to memory is placed in the 6800's X (index) register. This number is decremented after each data-transfer step, so that $X = 0$ can be used as a termination condition. IO data words are transferred from the IO data port via a load accumulator (LDA) to the CPU's A accumulator. They are then transferred to the stack region of main memory, which serves as the IO buffer area, via a push instruction. The push instruction has the advantage over ordinary store instructions of not requiring an explicit memory address operand, which would require updating via an additional instruction after each word transfer. Note also that the 6800 CPU contains only three address registers: the program counter PC, which is not available for general use; the index register X, which is already being used as a counter; and the stack pointer register S. The S register is automatically used as an address register by push and pop instructions. The status bit, which is in the sign position of the STATUS word, is tested by means of the 6800's BPL (branch if plus) conditional branch instruction. The IO program of Fig. 7.56 continues to read data words from the IO device as long as they are available (indicated by the status bit) and the count in X is nonzero.

An important question relates to how fast data can be transferred using programmed IO. The answer clearly depends on the number of instructions needed to implement the transfer, and their execution time. Consider again the POLL routine of Fig. 7.56. It requires execution of six instructions, including several bookkeeping instructions, to transfer one data word from the input device to main memory. With the indicated addressing modes, these instructions consume a total of 24 CPU clock cycles per data word, which is 12 μs at a CPU clock rate of 2 MHz. The maximum IO data-transfer rate is achieved when POLL is executed repeatedly. Hence at 12 μs per word, the maximum achievable data rate is $10^6/12 = 8.33 \times 10^4$ words/s.

```
        LDS    IOBUF    INITIALIZE STACK POINTER TO IO BUFFER AREA
        LDX    COUNT    INITIALIZE X AS WORD COUNT REGISTER
        ...
POLL    LDA A  STATUS   INPUT STATUS WORD TO ACCUMULATOR A
        BPL    NEXT     TEST SIGN (N) BIT OF. A; IF N ≠ 1 THEN GO TO NEXT AND
                          POLL OTHER IO DEVICES
        LDA A  DATA     INPUT DATA WORD TO ACCUMULATOR A
        PSH A           TRANSFER (PUSH) DATA WORD TO STACK
        DEX             DECREMENT WORD COUNT IN X
        BNE    POLL     CONTINUE POLLING CURRENT DEVICE UNLESS X = 0
NEXT    ...             PROCEED TO NEXT (IO OR NON-IO) TASK
```

Figure 7.56 6800 routine for IO data transfer with polling.

The major microprocessor families contain some general-purpose IO interface circuits designed to simplify the implementation of programmed IO control. These circuits fall into two major groups determined by the data-transfer mode, serial or parallel, of the IO devices that they interface to the microprocessor system bus. The parallel IO interface circuits are represented by the 6821 PIA (Fig. 5.37a) of the 6800 series, and its 8080/8085-series counterpart, the 8255 PPI interface circuit (Fig. 5.54). The corresponding serial IO interface circuits, which are generally termed UARTs, are the 6850 ACIA (Fig. 5.37b) and the 8251 programmable communication interface circuit. The 8251 is also called a *USART (universal synchronous/asynchronous receiver/ transmitter)* because, unlike the 6850, it can control synchronous as well as asynchronous serial IO data transfers. A common characteristic of all these IO circuits is that they can be programmed on-line to match the interface requirements of a wide range of different types of IO devices. We next briefly consider the role played by these interface circuits in programmed IO systems, using the 8255 and 8251 ICs from the 8080/8085 series as examples (Intel, 1981a).

Figure 7.57 shows the internal organization of the 8255 PPI, which is intended to link the 8080 system bus, or any similar 8-bit microprocessor bus, to a set of 24 IO interface lines. The IO lines can be configured as IO ports in various ways under software control. Generally speaking, ports A and B are used as 8-bit data ports, and may be individually specified to be input, output, or bidirectional. Port C may also be programmed to be a data port; however, it is primarily designed to transmit and receive control signals associated with data transfers through ports A and B. Port C is therefore very suitable as a status port in programmed IO operations. The 8255 has two address lines that allow ports A, B, and C to be addressed directly for input (read) and output (write) operations. The fourth possible address on these lines refers to an 8-bit control or command register CR within the 8255. The 8255 is programmed or configured by

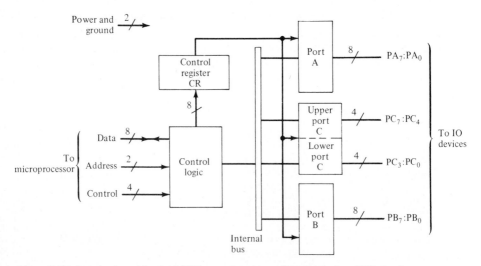

Figure 7.57 Organization of the Intel 8255 programmable peripheral interface (PPI) circuit.

transmitting commands to CR that specify the directions of the IO lines, and the use to be made of port C. Three of the many possible programmable configurations of the 8255 appear in Fig. 5.54; a complete listing can be found in the manufacturer's literature (Intel, 1981a).

Figure 7.58a shows a specific configuration of the 8255 for programmed IO control with polling, which implements the general interface of Fig. 7.54. This configuration is programmed by storing the command 10011000 in the 8255's CR register, which can be accomplished by executing the following 8080/8085 assembly-language instructions:

MVI A, 10011000B ; Load command for 8255 into accumulator A

OUT CRADR ; Output command to 8255's CR register

Here CRADR is the symbolic address within the system's IO address space that the system designer has assigned to register CR. After execution of these instructions, the 24 IO lines of the 8255 assume the directions shown in Fig. 7.58a. The upper and lower halves of port C become input and output subports, respectively, allowing the former to be used as data-ready/request or status lines and the latter as data-acknowledge lines. Status can be checked by the CPU simply by reading port C and testing the bits containing status information. Acknowledge signals are transmitted by writing to port C. Since this must be done without disturbing the other port C lines, the 8255 has special command words that are addressed to CR and set and reset port C lines individually. For

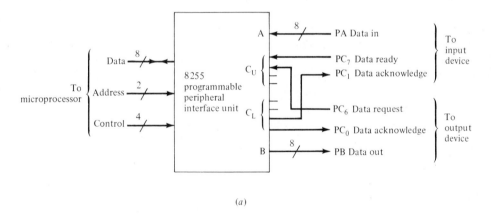

(a)

```
WAIT:   IN    PORTC   ; INPUT STATUS WORD FROM PORT C TO ACCUMULATOR A
        RAL           ; ROTATE A LEFT THROUGH CARRY FLAG CY. CY THEN
                      ;   CONTAINS A STATUS BIT
        JNC   WAIT    ; JUMP TO WAIT (CONTINUE POLLING) IF CY ≠ 1
INPUT:  IN    PORTA   ; INPUT DATA WORD FROM PORT A TO ACCUMULATOR A
        MOV   M, A    ; MOVE A TO MAIN MEMORY LOCATION M[HL]
```

(b)

Figure 7.58 (a) Possible configuration of the 8255 for programmed IO; (b) routine to poll and read a data word from the input device attached to port A.

example, the command 00000011 sets line PC_1 to 1, while the command 00000010 resets PC_1 to 0. Thus an acknowledge signal can be sent to the input device of Fig. 7.58a by executing the instructions

MVI   A, 00000011B   ; Load 8255 command to set line PC_1

OUT   CRADR   ; Output command to 8255

The acknowledge line subsequently can be deactivated by executing

MVI   A, 00000010B   ; Load 8255 command to reset line PC_1

OUT   CRADR   ; Output command to 8255

By including appropriate delay routines in the IO programs, the duration (pulse width) of the acknowledge signals can be precisely controlled.

Figure 7.58b shows a simple IO routine written in 8080/8085 assembly language that checks IO device status and transfers a data word when it becomes available. This program is designed for use with the 8255 IO interface of Fig. 7.58a. The first three instructions continuously check the status of the IO device, and constitute a "busy wait" loop. The data at port C, which contains the status bit of interest, are moved to the CPU's accumulator via an input instruction. The status bit is then shifted into the CPU's carry flag flip-flop, which can be tested by conditional branch instructions. If the test indicates that data are available, a word is transferred from port A to the accumulator and thence to main memory.

The structure of the 8251 USART is given in Fig. 7.59. It presents much the same interface to the microprocessor system bus as the 8255 (cf. Fig. 7.57). On the IO device side, however, it has a serial interface comprising an output data line TxD (transmitter data), an input data line RxD (receiver data), and a set of associated control lines. In a typical application binary encoded alphanumeric characters are transferred serially between the 8251 and an IO device via the TxD and RxD lines. The 8251 automatically performs serial-to-parallel character conversion during input operations and parallel-to-serial conversion during output operations. It can be programmed to handle the data-transmission conventions of many types of serial IO devices, and such standard serial IO buses as the RS-232 bus.

The 8251 has two major operating modes, termed synchronous and asynchronous. Asynchronous communication is most often used with lower-speed IO devices such as CRT terminals and teletypewriters. In this mode of operation the 8251 and the IO device to which it is connected operate at approximately the same speed, but are controlled by independent clock sources. The bits of a character are transmitted serially at a predetermined rate called the *baud rate*, for the nineteenth century French inventor J. M. E. Baudot. A rate of n bauds means that n distinct signals are transmitted per second; n bauds corresponds to n bits/second, provided each transmitted signal contains 1 bit of information. While character bits must be transmitted at a specified speed, individual characters can be separated by arbitrary intervals. This is achieved by preceding and following each character by synchronization bits termed the start and stop bits, a process named *framing*. For example, if the idle state of a serial input data line such as RxD is 0, the arrival of a 1 start bit indicates that transmission of a new character is about to begin. The

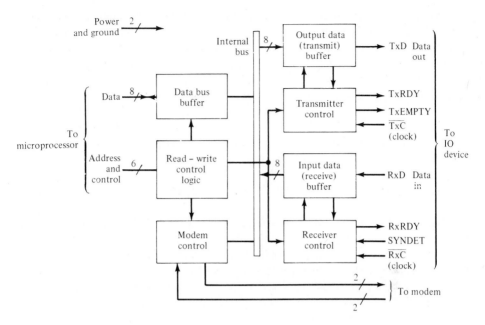

Figure 7.59 Organization of the Intel 8251 universal synchronous/asynchronous receiver/transmitter (USART) circuit.

start bit is then followed by a sequence of from 1 to 8 character bits transmitted at a known baud rate. Finally, the transmission of a 0 stop bit effectively allows the receiver to return to the idle state for an indefinite period. Thus the framing requirements of asynchronous data communication involve an overhead of at least 2 start/stop bits per character transmitted. Note that the 8251 can be programmed to insert and remove start/stop bits automatically during asynchronous IO operations. Figure 7.60 shows how the

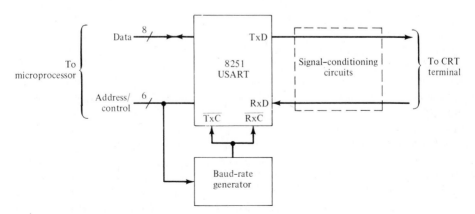

Figure 7.60 Using the 8251 in asynchronous mode to interface a CRT terminal.

8251 might be used as an asynchronous IO interface circuit to a CRT terminal. Data transmission is accomplished via the RxD and TxD lines; if necessary, signal-conditioning circuits must be added to match the electrical requirements of the serial bus linking the USART to the CRT terminal. A clock circuit called a *baud rate generator* serves as the 8251's local timing reference, and is connected to its transmit and receive clock input lines $\overline{\text{TxC}}$ and $\overline{\text{RxC}}$.

When used for synchronous data communication, the 8251 receives clock signals directly from the IO device via its $\overline{\text{TxC}}$ and $\overline{\text{RxC}}$ lines. This eliminates the need for character framing, thus allowing higher data-transmission rates to the achieved. Special synchronizing characters must be transmitted from time to time to enable the boundaries between characters to be identified. In its synchronous mode, the 8251 can be programmed to detect predefined "sync" characters in input streams, and insert them into output streams.

Programming the 8251 or other UART/USARTs is quite similar to programming the 8255 discussed earlier. The data bus buffer (Fig. 7.59) constitutes an addressable IO port to which or from which the host microprocessor can transfer IO data by executing IO instructions. The 8251 has another IO port corresponding to the 8255's control register CR to which 8-bit commands can be sent by the CPU. The CPU can also input a status byte from the 8251, which indicates the 8251's readiness to receive or transmit data, and any error conditions detected by the 8251 during data transmission. The operating mode of the 8251 is determined by a pair of commands issued by the CPU. A "mode" command word specifies the type of data transfer (synchronous or asynchronous), the baud rate, the character length, and the synchronization conventions to be followed. A second command word is used to reset the 8251, and to initialize IO transfers by activating control lines going to the IO device. Several special IO control lines are provided to facilitate interfacing the 8251 to a modem (cf. Fig. 7.3).

7.3.4 Interrupts

IO instructions, or, in the case of systems with memory-mapped IO addressing, memory-referencing instructions, enable a microprocessor to communicate directly with its IO devices. Interrupts provide a direct means of communication in the opposite direction. By activating an interrupt-request line, which is considered to be part of the system bus, an IO device can immediately attract the attention of the CPU. A device normally generates an interrupt request when it requires the execution of an interrupt service program P to transfer data between it and main memory or the CPU. To respond to an interrupt, the CPU must suspend execution of its current program P' and execute the interrupt routine P before resuming execution of P'. This temporary exchange of program control is precisely what occurs when a subroutine or procedure is called by another program. In the interrupt case, the source of the call to P is an external IO device, and the programs P and P' are generally unrelated. The structure of the interrupt service program P, however, can be expected to resemble closely that of an ordinary subroutine.

Interrupt mechanisms are divided into two broad classes based on the manner in which the CPU obtains the starting address of the interrupt service routine P; this address is commonly called the interrupt address or interrupt vector. In microprocessors such as the 6800, whose interrupt structure is discussed in detail in Sec. 5.3.3, each interrupt-request line I is associated with a fixed interrupt address ADR. When I is activated by an interrupting device, the CPU responds as follows.

1. It completes execution of its current instruction, and then saves the contents of the program counter PC in main memory, typically by pushing the contents of PC into a stack. Other CPU registers may also be saved.
2. The CPU next constructs and loads the interrupt address ADR into PC.
3. Normal instruction processing is then resumed, causing the interrupt routine P, whose starting address is ADR, to be executed.

Like an ordinary subroutine, P should include instructions to save, and subsequently restore, any programmable CPU registers that are modified during the execution of P. Moreover, the last instruction executed by P should be a return instruction that restarts execution of the previously interrupted program.

The foregoing scheme may be termed *nonvectored* interrupt control, since the interrupting IO device is not required to provide the CPU with an interrupt vector; the vector ADR in question is wired into the CPU's interrupt control circuits. Nonvectored interrupts have the advantage of a very simple hardware interface. All that is necessary is to connect a data-ready/request line from the IO device to an interrupt request line IR in the system bus. The system designer must also ensure that the fixed address ADR invoked by IR is used as the starting address or entry point of the corresponding interrupt-handling program P. Note that P can be positioned anywhere in main memory, provided the instruction stored at ADR is a branch instruction to P, for example, **goto** P. The main drawback of nonvectored interrupts is the lack of flexibility arising from the use of one fixed address per interrupt-request line. The 6800 microprocessor, for example, has only three interrupt-request lines, $\overline{\text{RESET}}$, $\overline{\text{NMI}}$, and $\overline{\text{IRQ}}$, of which only $\overline{\text{IRQ}}$ is a truly general interrupt request line. Problems occur, therefore, when the number of different interrupt service routines needed in a system exceeds the number of interrupt-request lines present. In such cases it is necessary to provide software that polls the interrupting devices to determine which interrupt routine to execute.

Figure 7.61 shows how a 6800-based system, or any similar microcomputer with nonvectored interrupts, might be configured to handle a large number of interrupts by software polling. All interrupt sources are connected to a common interrupt-request line, in this case, the 6800's $\overline{\text{IRQ}}$ line. The CPU always responds to an interrupt signal on $\overline{\text{IRQ}}$ by saving PC and the remaining CPU registers (except the stack pointer register S) in the stack region of main memory. It then loads into PC the address POLL stored in memory locations FFF8_{16} and FFF9_{16} (see Fig. 5.34), which transfers control to a polling routine named POLL. The POLL program proceeds to read and decode certain status information provided by each potential interrupt source to determine which interrupt routine to use or, equivalently, the source of the interrupt request signal on $\overline{\text{IRQ}}$. The IO devices are polled in turn according to some predetermined priority sequence; usually the faster IO

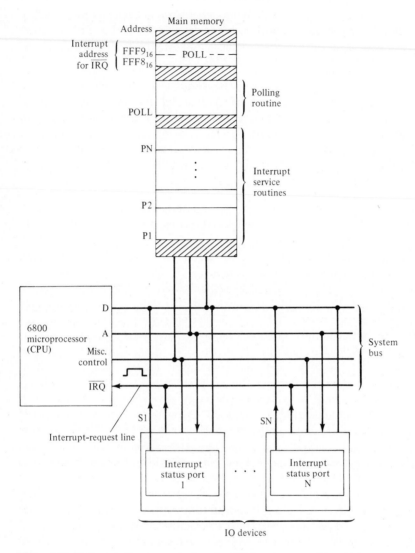

Figure 7.61 Hardware/software organization of a 6800-based system with multiple nonvectored interrupts.

devices have the more urgent service needs and are polled first. A suitable polling routine for the interrupt scheme of Fig. 7.61 might have the following structure:

```
POLL   LDA A   S1        Input status bit from source 1 (highest priority)
       BMI     P1        Test status bit. If set, execute program P1
       LDA A   S2        Input status bit from source 2
       BMI     P2        Test status bit. If set, execute program P2
       . . .
       LDA A   SN-1      Input status bit from source N-1
```

| BMI | PN-1 | Test status bit. If set, execute program PN-1 |
| BRA | PN | Execute program PN (lowest priority) |

Here the LDA (load accumulator) instruction transfers a status word from an IO port to the A register, and sets the 6800's sign flag N to the value of the sign bit A_7 of A, which represents the status Si. N is then tested via the BMI (branch if minus) instruction, which transfers CPU control to the interrupt-handling routine Pi whenever $N = Si = 1$. Note that although POLL uses the CPU's accumulator A and flags (condition code), it need not save them explicitly, since the 6800 always saves all CPU registers automatically when it responds to $\overline{IRQ}$. Other microprocessors will require the polling routine to contain save instructions. Each of the programs P1, P2, ..., PN should have RTI (return from interrupt) as its final instruction. Execution of this instruction restores the CPU to the state existing before it began its current interrupt sequence.

The second type of interrupt control, vectored interrupts, eliminates the need for software polling when dealing with many interrupt sources. Instead an interrupting device supplies the interrupt vector ADR it needs to the CPU via the system bus. Special control lines can be used to transmit ADR to the CPU; however, it is normally more convenient to use the system data bus for this purpose. To synchronize the transmission of ADR, the CPU issues a control signal called interrupt acknowledge, which causes the interrupt source to place the interrupt vector on the data bus, from which it is then read into the CPU. As in the nonvectored interrupt case, when the CPU responds to an interrupt-request signal, it must save the old contents of PC before loading the interrupt address ADR into PC. Thus the actions taken by the CPU (the interrupt cycle) are quite similar to those occurring during execution of the subroutine call instruction

$$\text{CALL ADR} \tag{7.6}$$

Note that in each case the new program address ADR is sent to the CPU via the system bus; the main difference is the source of ADR, which is main memory for a subroutine, and an IO device for an interrupt. This similarity between subroutine calls and interrupt cycles is exploited in 8080/8085-series microprocessors by having interrupting devices generate a complete call instruction such as (7.6) rather than just the address part ADR. As explained in Sec. 5.4.3, all 8080/8085 microprocessors have a special 1-byte call instruction RST (restart), which can be used by IO devices to specify any of eight interrupt addresses. The 8085 allows a complete 3-byte CALL instruction to be supplied by an interrupting device, thus permitting any of the 64K possible memory addresses to be used as the interrupt address.

Figure 7.62 depicts a representative interface circuit for an interrupting IO device in an 8080-based system. The CPU and the IO device are directly linked via the interrupt-request line INT and the interrupt-acknowledge line $\overline{INTA}$. Two 8212 general-purpose IO ports (see the 8212 data sheet in Fig. 7.5) compose the interface circuit, one serving as a data port and the other providing the RST instruction that incorporates the desired interrupt vector. A data-ready control signal accompanying the loading of data into the 8212 data port is used to activate the 8212's STB (strobe) control input, which in turn activates the $\overline{INT}$ output line. As its name suggests, $\overline{INT}$ is intended to be connected via an inverter to the system's interrupt request line INT. Thus the loading of new data into

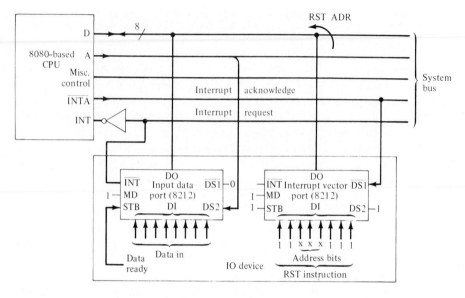

Figure 7.62 Interface circuit for vectored interrupts in an 8080-based system.

the data port automatically sends an interrupt-request signal to the CPU. When the CPU is ready to respond to this interrupt request, it activates the interrupt-acknowledge line $\overline{\text{INTA}}$, which is attached to the device- (chip-) select inputs of the second 8212. The control inputs of this IC are set to make it act as an input (data) port when selected. Its data-in lines are wired to constant signals that define the RST ADR instruction to be used. When $\overline{\text{INTA}}$ is activated, the second 8212 is selected ($\overline{\text{DS1}} \wedge \text{DS2} = 1$), causing the restart instruction RST ADR to be placed on the data bus. The CPU then reads this instruction from the data bus and processes it as any other 1-byte instruction. The execution of RST results in the following actions:

M[SP-1],M[SP-2] := PC;   {Save old PC}
SP := SP − 2;   {Update stack pointer SP}
PC := 0000000000xxx000$_2$;   {Load interrupt address ADR}

where xxx denotes the 3-bit address field obtained from the RST instruction itself. Use of CALL instead of RST permits all bits of the interrupt address to be specified by the IO device, but requires slightly more complicated interface circuitry.

If many vectored interrupt sources are present in a system, the possibility exists that several will generate interrupt requests simultaneously. A method therefore is needed to select one of the competing interrupt requests for service, and return the interrupt acknowledge only to the selected device. This problem is basically the same as that discussed earlier (Sec. 7.3.1) for the selection of a bus master from a set of simultaneous requests for control of the system bus. Observe that interrupting devices also need temporary control of the data bus to transmit an interrupt vector to the CPU. As in the previous problem, interrupts are selected on the basis of priorities assigned to the various

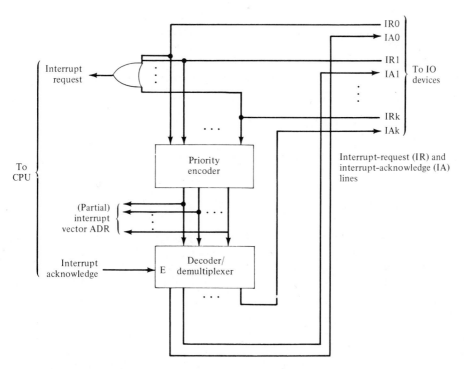

Figure 7.63 Parallel technique for interrupt priority control.

interrupt sources. This implies that the interrupt-acknowledge signal should be made available only to the interrupting device whose priority is highest. One way of accomplishing this is to transmit the interrupt-acknowledge signal serially in daisy-chain fashion from IO device to IO device in the manner of Fig. 7.51. Each device must be supplied with interface circuits to block transmission of the acknowledge signal if it has an interrupt request pending; otherwise it should relay the interrupt-acknowledge signal to the next lower-priority device.

Figure 7.63 demonstrates a faster parallel technique for selection among competing interrupt requests. Again each interrupt source is assigned a fixed priority, which is determined by the encoder input and decoder output lines to which it is connected. The interrupt-request lines from the IO devices are connected to the input of a priority decoder, whose output is therefore the address ADR of the active interrupt-request line with the highest priority. ADR is then fed to a standard decoder/demultiplexer circuit, which is designed to route the interrupt-acknowledge signal received from the CPU back to the interrupt source represented by ADR. Thus the effect of the circuit of Fig. 7.63 is to connect the interrupt-request/acknowledge line pair from the highest-priority active interrupt source to the corresponding lines of the system bus. Note also that the output ADR of the priority encoder can be used to construct a unique interrupt vector for each interrupting device, if desired.

The assignment of priorities to IO interrupt sources should reflect the urgency with which they must be serviced; faster IO devices normally need higher priority. It is generally desirable to allow execution of an interrupt service routine to be itself interruptable by interrupts of higher priority. Such nesting of interrupts is analogous to nesting subroutines, and is easily implemented if a call-return stack is available. By the same token, it may be desirable to prevent an interrupt service routine from being interrupted by an interrupt of lower priority. Selective blocking or masking of interrupt requests can be achieved by including interrupt-enable and -disable instructions in the CPU's instruction set. Execution of an interrupt-disable instruction causes the CPU to ignore a specified set of interrupt-request signals by setting interrupt mask flip-flops that block the request signals from the CPU's program control logic circuits. The interrupt-request lines remain disabled until they subsequently are enabled by an appropriate interrupt-enable instruction. The 8080/8085, for example, has the instruction DI (disable interrupts), which disables the main INT/INTR interrupt-request line by setting an interrupt mask flip-flop INTE (interrupt enable). The corresponding EI (interrupt-enable) instruction resets the INTE flip-flop, thereby enabling the interrupt system. The 8085 has three additional nonvectored interrupt-request lines (RST 5.5, RST 6.5, and RST 7.5) that can be enabled and disabled by the special SIM (set interrupt mask) instruction. The 8085 has a fourth nonvectored interrupt-request line, called TRAP, which is nonmaskable, that is, it cannot be enabled or disabled by the system software. The 6800 microprocessor has a single interrupt-enable instruction CLI (clear interrupt mask) and disable instruction SLI (set interrupt mask) to control its only maskable interrupt request line $\overline{\text{IRQ}}$.

The general structure of an interrupt service routine P is illustrated by Fig. 7. 64. The entry point of P is determined by the available set of interrupt addresses. If it is desired to make the routine uninterruptible, its first instructions should disable all or part of the interrupt system; in some cases disabling of other interrupts is done automatically by the CPU when it responds to an interrupt. Then any CPU registers that are modified by P should be saved; this can be done conveniently by pushing the registers in question into

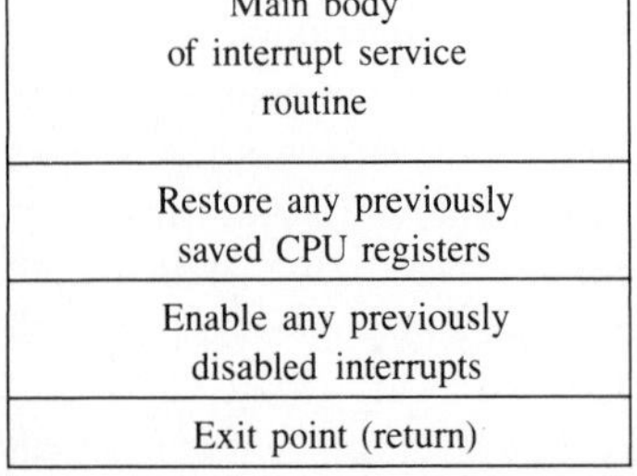

Entry point
Disable other interrupts, if required
Save any CPU registers to be modified
Main body of interrupt service routine
Restore any previously saved CPU registers
Enable any previously disabled interrupts
Exit point (return)

Figure 7.64 General structure of an interrupt service routine.

a stack region in main memory. The main body of the interrupt routine follows. It is typically concerned with the transfer of data to and from an IO device, and any associated bookkeeping operations. P terminates by restoring any previously saved CPU registers, enabling any previously disabled interrupt-request lines, and finally executing a return instruction to restart execution of the program that was originally interrupted by P.

Figure 7.65 lists a simple 8080 interrupt service routine named OUTWD that is intended to output a word from a fixed location (DATA) in main memory to IO port 9 in response to an interrupt request received on the INT line. All other interrupts are required to be disabled during the execution of OUTWD. The 8080 automatically disables INT blocking all further interrupts when it begins processing an interrupt request. Thus, on entering OUTWD, the interrupt system is already fully disabled. OUTWD uses the accumulator A as a temporary data register, and so this register must be saved. Since the 8080 has no instruction that pushes A by itself, the PUSH PSW (push program status word) instruction is used, which pushes both A and the status register SR into the stack. The main IO data-transfer operation is implemented via a load memory to accumulator (LDA) instruction followed by an output accumulator to IO port (OUT) instruction. The accumulator is then restored to its original state, and the interrupt system is enabled via an EI instruction. EI is then followed by the final return (RET) instruction. It should be noted that the interrupt system of the 8080 is not enabled by EI until immediately after execution of the instruction following EI, in this case the return instruction RET. This one-instruction delay ensures that a return from the interrupt routine can always be completed successfully before the CPU enters another interrupt cycle.

The major microprocessor families contain special interface circuits commonly called *(priority) interrupt controllers*, which simplify the various design tasks associated with interrupt-driven IO, and allow the number of available interrupt-request lines to be increased systematically. A powerful IC of this kind, the Intel 8259 programmable interrupt controller designed for use with the 8085 and 8086 series, is outlined in Fig. 7.66 (Intel, 1979). The 8259 handles eight vectored interrupt-request lines; several 8259s can be interconnected to control more interrupt lines, if necessary. Each interrupt-request line is associated with a priority level, a mask flip-flop, and an interrupt vector, all of whose values are programmable. The 8259 is programmed on-line via command words transmitted from the host microprocessor in a way similar to that used for the 8251 and 8255 programmable interface circuits examined in the preceding section. If the

```
;  8080 INTERRUPT SERVICE ROUTINE 'OUTWD' TO OUTPUT A WORD FROM A
;     FIXED LOCATION IN MEMORY TO AN OUTPUT DEVICE AT IO PORT NO. 9. OTHER
;     INTERRUPTS ARE TO BE DISABLED DURING THE EXECUTION OF 'OUTWD'
;
OUTWD:  PUSH  PSW       ; SAVE ACCUMULATOR A (AND FLAGS) IN STACK
        LDA   DATA      ; MOVE WORD FROM M[DATA] TO A
        OUT   9         ; OUTPUT WORD FROM A TO IO PORT NO. 9
        POP   PSW       ; RESTORE A (AND FLAGS) FROM STACK
        EI              ; ENABLE INTERRUPT SYSTEM
        RET             ; RETURN TO INTERRUPTED PROGRAM
```

Figure 7.65 8080 interrupt routine to perform a one-word output data transfer.

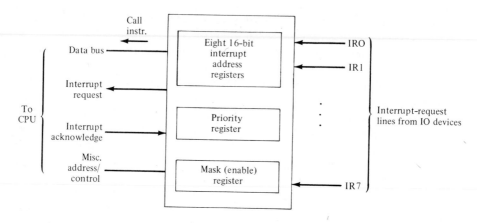

Figure 7.66 The Intel 8259 programmable interrupt controller.

8259 receives an interrupt request (unmasked) on one or more of its IR0:IR7 lines, it transmits an interrupt request to the CPU via its INT line. When the CPU responds with an interrupt-acknowledge signal on the INTA line, the 8259 selects the interrupt address corresponding to the active IR line of highest priority, and transmits it over the data bus to the CPU embedded in a call instruction. If the CPU is the 8085 microprocessor, the 8259 constructs a 3-byte call instruction consisting of a 1-byte CALL opcode followed by a 2-byte interrupt address. To control the transmission of this call instruction from the 8259, the 8085 executes a modified instruction fetch cycle during which it activates its INTA line three times to strobe each byte of the call instruction from the 8259. Although the 6800 microprocessor was not designed with vectored interrupts in mind, the 6800 support chip set nevertheless includes a priority interrupt controller intended to eliminate the need for polling a set of interrupt sources as in Fig. 7.61 (see Prob. 7.46).

7.3.5 Direct Memory Access

As observed earlier, the objective of most IO operations is the transfer of data, sometimes in long blocks of words, between IO devices and main memory. Both programmed and interrupt-driven IO require the active participation of the CPU, that is, the execution of data-transfer software by the CPU, in every step of an IO operation. DMA control of IO operations, to which we now turn, removes the CPU from the data-transfer process proper; instead the data are transferred directly between main memory and the IO interface under the supervision of a special interface circuit called a DMA controller. A DMA controller is capable of acting as the master of the system bus, and issuing read and write commands to main memory. It also has the control logic necessary to direct the transmission of a block of data words to or from a set of consecutive memory locations. DMA-controlled data transfer can thus take place at the maximum rate allowed by the system bus and main memory. This is many times faster than the maximum speed achievable with CPU-controlled IO operations. The typical data-transfer program POLL listed in Fig. 7.56 requires the fetching and executing of at least six instructions, or about

24 CPU clock cycles, to transfer one word of IO data to main memory. To transfer the same data word to main memory under DMA control requires just a single memory write cycle, which can be accomplished in from one to four CPU clock periods, depending on the system organization. Hence DMA provides significantly higher IO data-transmission rates than other IO control methods. It is primarily used with such relatively fast IO devices as disk memories, graphics display devices, and high-speed printers.

The key components of a DMA controller are depicted in Fig. 7.67. They include an address register AR that specifies the memory location to be used as the source or destination for the next data word to be transferred, and a word count register WC that specifies the number of data words that remain to be transferred in the current IO operation. AR and WC each is configured as an addressable output port so that it can be initialized by CPU-executed software. The DMA controller also contains buffer registers to accommodate data that are en route between the memory and IO subsystems. Since the

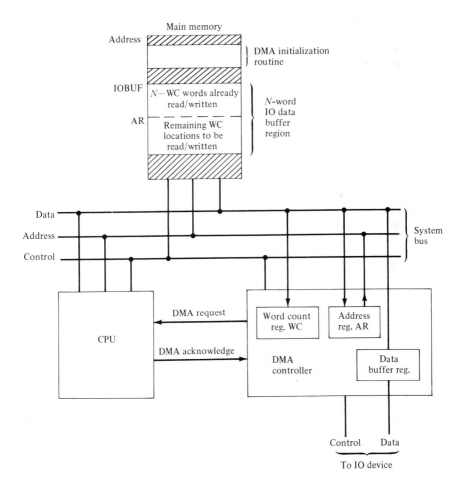

Figure 7.67 Hardware/software organization of a system with DMA-controlled IO.

DMA controller and the CPU must share the system bus, a bus-access control procedure is necessary. This is usually provided by a pair of control lines with the generic names DMA request and DMA acknowledge, which link the DMA controller directly to the CPU as indicated in Fig. 7.67. It can be viewed as a special case of a more general bus-access method such as that found in the Multibus (cf. Fig. 7.50). Whenever the DMA controller needs to gain control of the system bus, it activates the DMA request line. The CPU responds to this request at an appropriate breakpoint by allowing the parts of the system bus used for data transfer—namely, the data, address, and data-transfer command lines—to float to the high-impedance state. It then activates the DMA acknowledge line to indicate that the system bus has been released. The DMA controller responds by logically connecting itself to the system bus as the new bus master. It then proceeds to transfer IO data directly to or from memory. It eventually releases the bus by making its connections to the relevant bus lines float, and deactivating the DMA request line. The CPU thereupon resumes its normal role as the system bus master, and deactivates DMA acknowledge.

A DMA-controlled IO operation or, more simply a DMA operation, is set up by executing a short initialization routine. This consists of several output instructions that place initial values in the AR and WC registers. AR is loaded with the starting address IOBUF of the IO data buffer region in main memory to or from which data are to be transferred by the DMA controller. The number N of data words to be transferred, that is, the maximum size of the IOBUF region, is placed in WC. Thus initialized, the DMA controller proceeds to transfer data between IOBUF and its IO device without further intervention by the CPU. It does so by taking control of the system bus from time to time and, depending on its mode of operation, transferring one or more words of data. The times at which DMA requests are made depend on the characteristics of the IO device involved; typically a DMA transfer is needed whenever the IO device requests or produces data at the IO interface. After each one-word data-transfer step, the DMA controller automatically decrements WC by one, and increments or decrements AR to point to the next location of IOBUF to be used. The DMA operation terminates when WC reaches zero, at which point the DMA controller can signal completion of its current task by sending an interrupt request to the CPU. It takes no further action until it is reinitialized for a new DMA operation by the CPU. This can be expected to occur after the CPU has processed the input data in IOBUF, in the case of an input device, or placed new data there, in the case of an output device. Figure 7.68 summarizes the steps in a DMA-controlled input operation. A DMA output operation is similar with the direction of the data flow reversed.

The ways in which DMA can be implemented with a given microprocessor depend heavily on the timing of the CPU's operations, and the use it makes of the system bus. A key time unit in this regard is the CPU machine cycle, which is the time required to perform a basic step, roughly corresponding to a compound register-transfer operation, during instruction processing. Examples of machine cycles are opcode fetch cycles, memory read or write cycles, IO read (input) or write (output) cycles, and interrupt response cycles. An important feature of all these machine cycles is the fact that they include the transfer of at least one word of information over the system bus; this operation may be called a *bus cycle*. Clearly the CPU must complete its current bus transaction before it can relinquish the system bus to a DMA controller. A convenient breakpoint for

1. The IO (input) device transmits a new data word to the DMA controller's data buffer register. The DMA controller activates the DMA request line to the CPU.
2. At the next breakpoint—the end of the current machine cycle, for example—the CPU allows the data-transfer lines of the system bus to float and activates the DMA acknowledge line.
3. The DMA controller assumes control of the system bus, and executes a memory write cycle to transfer the contents of the data buffer register to the memory location M[AR] specified by the AR address register.
4. The word count register is decremented by one, and AR is updated to point to the next empty location in the IO buffer area of main memory.
5. If no new data are available, the DMA controller releases the system bus and deactivates the DMA request line. If additional IO data words are available, steps 3 and 4 may be repeated.
6. When WC reaches zero, indicating that the current IO operation has been completed, the DMA controller halts and sends an interrupt request to the CPU.

Figure 7.68 Main steps in a DMA-controlled input data-transfer operation.

this purpose, therefore, is the end of the machine cycle during which a DMA request signal is received. Figure 7.69 shows the timing of the CPU's actions during the transfer of control to and from a DMA controller, with the end of a machine cycle serving as the DMA breakpoint. This technique is used by many microprocessors, including the 8080/8085 and the Z80.

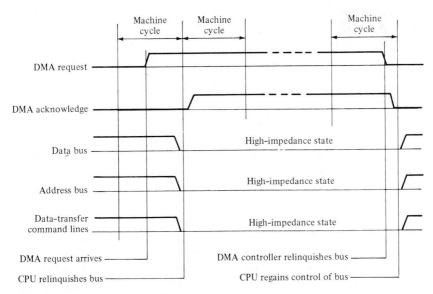

Figure 7.69 CPU actions associated with a DMA operation.

DMA control methods fall into broad classes, block transfer and cycle stealing. *Block DMA transfer* allows a block or sequence of data words of arbitrary length to be transferred via a DMA controller in one continuous burst while the controller is the system bus master. Although it provides the maximum IO data-transmission rate, block DMA transfer forces the CPU to wait in an idle state for relatively long periods, since it cannot obtain instructions from memory while a DMA operation is taking place. *Cycle stealing* refers to a class of DMA transfer methods in which the DMA controller periodically "steals" one, or perhaps several, bus cycles from the CPU for a DMA operation, after which it immediately returns control of the system bus to the CPU. Thus to transfer a block of N data words via cycle stealing requires up to N DMA steps, which are separated from one another by periods during which the CPU controls the system bus. A stolen bus cycle represents all or part of a machine cycle. It is possible to arrange DMA in a system, so that the DMA controller always relinquishes the system bus after transferring a single word over it. This word-at-a-time cycle stealing reduces the IO data-transfer rate, but also reduces the interference by the DMA controller in the CPU's activities. It may even be possible to eliminate this interference completely by confining DMA operations to periods when the CPU is not actively using the system bus, for example, while it is decoding an opcode or performing internal register-transfer operations. This DMA mode, which can be implemented in Z80-based systems, is termed *transparent DMA*. Yet another approach, found in the 6800 microprocessor, is to extend or stretch temporarily a CPU machine cycle to allow time for a DMA transfer to be squeezed in after the normal CPU bus transaction.

As discussed in Sec. 5.4.3, the 8080/8085 microprocessor implements block DMA transfer in the straightforward fashion illustrated by Figs. 7.67 through 7.69. The control lines HOLD and HLDA (hold acknowledge) correspond to DMA request and DMA acknowledge respectively. The CPU always responds to a HOLD signal by floating the relevant system bus lines at the end of the current machine cycle and entering a waiting or "hold" state until HOLD is deactivated. Cycle stealing can be implemented by designing the DMA controller to return the system bus to the CPU after a specific number of DMA bus cycles, normally one. The 6800 has a similar form of DMA control in which the $\overline{\text{HALT}}$ and BA (bus-available) lines serve as DMA request and acknowledge respectively (see Sec. 5.3.3). Unlike the 8080/8085, however, the 6800 does not relinquish the system bus in response to a $\overline{\text{HALT}}$ signal until the end of its current instruction cycle. Since 6800 instruction cycles contain two or more machine cycles, this results in a slower response to DMA requests. The 6800 also supports a cycle-stealing mode of operation with a shorter response time, although it requires extra support circuits. Using the TSC (three-state control) line in place of $\overline{\text{HALT}}$, the CPU machine cycle (which is the same as a clock cycle) is stretched to allow an IO data word to be transferred by a DMA controller.

The Z80 has the unusual ability to support transparent DMA. An opcode fetch machine cycle of the Z80 comprises four CPU clock cycles, during the first two of which a memory read bus cycle takes place using the CPU's program counter PC as the memory address source. This results in an opcode byte of an instruction being transferred to the instruction register. During the second two clock cycles of the machine cycle, the CPU decodes the opcode byte, increments PC, and performs other internal operations. At the same time it carries out a second memory read cycle using the memory refresh counter R as the address source. As explained in Sec. 5.4.5, this is designed for refreshing dynamic RAMs attached to the system bus; of course, it performs no useful function if only static RAM circuits are present. Transparent DMA is achieved in Z80-based systems by having a DMA controller "steal" the refresh bus cycles from opcode fetch machine cycles. The Z80 CPU issues a special control signal $\overline{M1}$ (machine cycle 1) that identifies an opcode fetch cycle. The DMA controller uses $\overline{M1}$ to determine when to override the refresh operation and seize control of the system bus. It then performs a one-word DMA operation, and returns the bus to the CPU at the normal end of the current opcode fetch machine cycle, thereby ensuring that the CPU is not delayed.

DMA controller ICs are included in all major microprocessor families. They are programmable devices containing all the logic necessary for supervising DMA operations involving one or more IO devices. Figure 7.70 shows the structure of a typical DMA controller with facilities for supporting four independent DMA operations that time-share the system bus. Commercially available controllers of this type include the Motorola 6844 and the Intel 8237 ICs, which are members of the 6800 and 8080/8085 series respectively. The control logic associated with each of the four DMA operations is termed a *DMA* or *IO channel*; thus Fig. 7.70 depicts a four-channel DMA controller. Each DMA channel contains its own memory address register AR_i, word count register WC_i, and data buffer register DR_i, and is separately addressable by the CPU. The mode

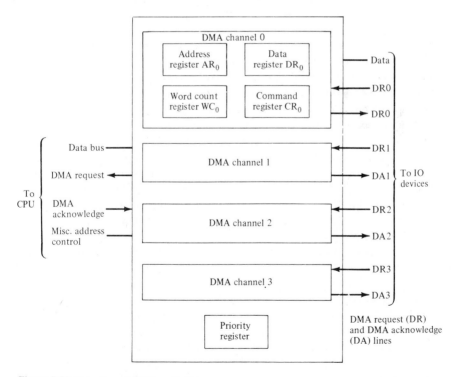

Figure 7.70 Four-channel DMA controller.

of DMA control to be used by the channel (block DMA, cycle stealing, etc.) is specified by the channel's command register CR_i. A priority register specifies each channel's priority of access to the system bus to conduct DMA operations. All of the foregoing registers are programmable during system operation, giving the CPU dynamic control of IO task selection and priority.

Each channel of a DMA controller can carry out an independent IO data transfer. It requires the services of the CPU to initialize its various control registers AR_i, WC_i, and CR_i. The power of a DMA controller could be further extended by enabling it to load these registers itself. This suggests extending the command register to form a general-purpose instruction unit (I-unit), analogous to that of the CPU, but oriented toward IO instructions. This would include an instruction address register corresponding to the CPU's program counter, capable of specifying IO instructions in main memory to be fetched and executed by the DMA controller. At this point we have a specialized processor capable of independently executing IO programs that control a set of DMA channels. Such devices are called *IO processors* (IOPs), and are considered further in Sec. 8.3.3.

7.4 SUMMARY

Interfacing is concerned with the connection of IO devices to microprocessors and the problems of communicating with and controlling the IO devices. It involves a close interaction between hardware in the form of IO interface circuits and software in the form of IO programs. The major tasks performed by the hardware and software are IO operations in which data are transferred between the IO devices and the main memory of the system. Various tasks supporting IO data transfers must also be carried out, including synchronization, data-format conversion or encoding, and selection on a priority basis of one of several IO devices that may be competing at any time for access to the system. Microprocessor families contain a variety of both special- and general-purpose interface circuits designed to match most IO devices to the interfacing characteristics of the microprocessors in question. These circuits range from simple addressable registers (IO ports) that require extensive software support, to sophisticated programmable controllers that can independently control complex IO operations with minimal CPU involvement. Since IO programming involves time-dependent and machine-dependent interactions among binary signals, assembly languages are generally more suitable than high-level programming languages for writing IO software.

An on–off mechanical switch, which is a 1-bit data source, is probably the simplest and most common input device. A keyboard is a collection of switches used to input numeric or alphanumeric data to a digital system. Despite their apparent simplicity, switches pose a nontrivial interfacing problem, namely, debouncing to remove ambiguities caused by contact bounce on opening or closing the switch. Like most interfacing problems, this one can be solved by hardware (a debouncing latch) or software (a debouncing routine). Keyboard interfacing introduces the additional problems of locating the depressed key or keys, selecting one key, if several are depressed simultaneously, and encoding the selected key into a suitable data format such as ASCII code. To reduce the number of physical lines at the keyboard's interface, a scanning technique such as the walking-1s method is often used with larger keyboards. LSI has made it possible to place all keyboard functions, including key scanning and encoding, debouncing, and the resolution of multiple depressed keys, in a single IC known as a keyboard encoder.

An LED is a simple 1-bit output device with the useful property that sets of LEDs can be grouped to represent numeric and alphanumeric data. For example, numeric data are commonly displayed by means of seven-segment LED display circuits. Interface circuits for LED-based output devices typically contain decoding, current-driving, and current-limiting components. Larger LED display units employ multiplexing, in which the display elements are switched on and off in sequence; this reduces the number of interface circuits and interconnections, as well as the total current needed to operate the display units. LED-based optocouplers are used to interface microprocessors to devices such as domestic appliances that require large currents or voltages.

Microprocessors, which can only process digital data directly, must frequently interact with devices that deal with analog or continuous quantities such as temperature, pressure, and spatial position. Analog interfaces are encountered in most measurement and process-control applications. A typical analog input interface employs a transducer or sensor to convert a nonelectrical analog variable into a proportional analog electric signal; the latter is then converted to digital form by an ADC. Conversely an analog output interface can be expected to contain a DAC that produces the analog electric signals needed to control an analog output device.

Transducers come in many forms, and are based on a variety of electrical phenomena. An important class of transducers depend on the ability of the analog variable of interest to alter their electrical resistance. Resistance-based transducers include thermistors, strain gauges, and position-sensing potentiometers. The relation between the transducer's output signal and the original analog input signal may be nonlinear and complex. However, the power of the microprocessor can readily be used to overcome this problem; for instance, by storing the transducer's characteristics in tabular form in the system's memory, from which they can be retrieved by appropriate table-look-up software. Electromechanical actuators, such as solenoids and stepping motors, permit microprocessors to control such mechanical output variables as the position or velocity of an object. These devices are key components in a wide range of IO devices, including printers, disk memory units, and industrial process-control equipment.

Analog-to-digital and digital-to-analog conversion involve a number of trade-offs between hardware and software control, and also between speed of operation and digital precision. DACs generally are hardware devices built around a weighted resistor network. Many techniques are used to implement ADCs, including all-hardware direct conversion, the ramp method, and the successive approximation method. The latter two can be realized by software ADC routines using relatively simple interface circuits.

Shared buses constitute the principal medium for intrasystem communication in microprocessor-based systems. The system bus is a parallel bus that links the CPU, main memory, and IO interface circuits, and determines the hardware characteristics of the microprocessor's IO interfaces. Additional buses, both serial and parallel, may be used to link IO devices to IO interface circuits or controllers. Several standard buses have been proposed for various classes of microprocessors and microprocessor applications, and are in widespread use in commercial systems. Typical of these is the Multibus or IEEE 796 bus, a standard system bus for use with 8- and 16-bit microprocessors. Such buses are designed to support data transfers between two devices at a time, a bus master device, such as a CPU or DMA controller, and a bus slave device, such as a memory unit or IO port. Various data-transmission methods may be used, depending on the timing characteristics of the communicating devices and their distance apart. These methods include synchronous or clocked communication, semisynchronous communication, and asynchronous communication, with the last providing the flexibility for data transfer between devices with very different timing characteristics. Most buses contain a set of bus-access control lines to allow control of the bus to be transferred systematically from one bus master to another. Additional bus lines support other aspects of data transfer, including addressing, data-transfer command specification, and interrupt control.

Three major approaches to the problem of establishing and supervising IO data-transfer operations have been identified: programmed IO, interrupt-driven IO, and DMA. Programmed IO requires the active participation of CPU-executed instructions in all phases of an IO operation, including initiation, data transfer, and termination. The initiation of a programmed IO operation may be implemented by a polling routine that periodically inputs and tests the status (ready or not ready for an IO operation) of a set of IO devices; this may be termed status-driven IO. When an IO device's status assumes the ready state, an appropriate IO data-transfer routine addressed to that device is executed by the CPU. Programmed IO control has the advantage of needing only the simplest interface hardware. It is suitable for relatively slow IO devices that do not require a rapid response from the CPU when they are ready to send or receive data. General-purpose programmable IO interface circuits are available that greatly ease the task of implementing programmed IO. These include interface circuits for both parallel and serial IO data transmission.

Faster response to IO service requests can be obtained by interrupt-driven IO. In this case the IO devices are linked directly to the CPU via interrupt-request lines, which they activate when they require the services of the CPU. In response to an interrupt-request signal, the CPU suspends execution of its current program and executes an interrupt-handling program that is typically designed to transfer data to or from the interrupting device. As in the programmed IO case, all data-transfer steps are under direct CPU software control. The address of the interrupt-handling routine corresponding to a particular interrupt request may be fixed or, in the case of vectored interrupt control, it may be supplied by the interrupt source. When many interrupt sources are present in a system, interrupt requests are routed through a programmable interrupt controller that can resolve conflicting interrupts on a priority basis.

The highest IO data-transmission rates are achieved by DMA. This IO control method requires the presence of a DMA controller that can act as a bus master and supervise data transfers directly between main memory and one or more IO devices. A pair of DMA request/acknowledge lines enable the DMA controller to obtain control of the system bus from the CPU when it is ready for data transmission. For each IO device or IO channel under its supervision, the DMA controller maintains a memory address register and a word count register, which it updates after each one-word data transfer. The implementation of DMA reduces the role of the CPU in IO operations to that of initializing the DMA controllers. DMA operations may be performed in block-transfer mode, in which a sequence of many words can be transferred in one step by the DMA controller. An alternative to block transfer is cycle stealing, which allows IO data to be transferred by the DMA controller one word at a time, possibly during periods when the system bus is not required by the CPU. An IO processor can be regarded as a DMA controller with the added ability to initiate new DMA operations by itself, thereby becoming able to execute IO programs independently of the CPU.

7.5 FURTHER READING

An excellent treatment of microprocessor interfacing from a more advanced standpoint appears in Stone's book *Microcomputer Interfacing* (Stone, 1982). Another useful text oriented toward systems employing the S-100 (IEEE 696) standard bus is that by Libes and Garetz (1981). Johnson's *Process Control Instrumentation Technology* covers transducers and actuators in the industrial control context (Johnson, 1977). The *M6800 Microprocessor Applications Manual* (Motorola, 1975b), although aimed at the design of systems employing the 6800 microprocessor, contains a great deal of general information on IO devices and their interfacing requirements, with many detailed hardware and software examples. The Intel *Peripheral Design Handbook* (Intel, 1981a) has data sheets and application notes covering the extensive range of interface circuits, including many advanced programmable IO controllers, that are available for systems based on the 8080/8085 and similar microprocessors. Interface circuits from many vendors, as well as standard microprocessor buses, are described and evaluated by Kane and Osborne (1978).

7.6 PROBLEMS

7.1 Figure 7.71a shows a common way of connecting a three-terminal (single-pole double-throw) switch S to a microprocessor-based system to produce a binary input signal z. Mechanical contact bounce occurs whenever S is moved to either the on or the off position. An oscilloscope attached to z yields the waveform shown in Fig. 7.71b. Explain why no bounce is observed in z when S is turned off.

7.2 The interface circuit for the 16-key keyboard in Fig. 7.9 is to be modified so that an interrupt is generated each time a key is depressed. The CPU should respond to a keyboard interrupt by executing a subroutine called SERV that reads the keyboard and places a binary number from zero to 15 in register B that uniquely identifies a depressed key. SERV should resolve any ambiguities caused by contact bounce, and by depressing several keys simultaneously.

(a) Draw a logic diagram for the complete interface circuit linking the keyboard to the 8080/8085 system bus. Use only commercially available SSI/MSI ICs in your design.

(b) Draw a flowchart for the keyboard service routine SERV.

(c) Write a program in 8080/8085 assembly language that realizes SERV.

7.3 A few problems arise in the walking-1's keyboard-scanning scheme illustrated in Fig. 7.11 if several keys are depressed simultaneously. Whenever two switches in the same row are depressed, the corresponding columns are connected together or short-circuited. This effectively connects two output signals from port 1, resulting in indeterminate signal values. Suppose that three switches with the row-column coordinates (i, j), (i, k), and (h, j) are depressed simultaneously. When output port 1 applies a 1 test signal to column k, a 1 can travel down column k to switch (i, k), across row i to switch (i, j), up column j to switch (h, j), and finally across

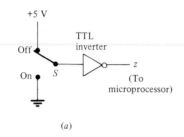

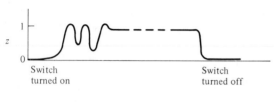

Figure 7.71 (a) Simple switch circuit; (b) its behavior.

row h to port 2. The 1 signal then detected on line h would normally be interpreted as indicating that switch (h, k) has been depressed; this is referred to as the "ghost key" phenomenon.

Describe hardware and/or software measures that can be taken in implementing walking-1s keyboard scanning to eliminate the foregoing short-circuited columns and ghost key problems.

7.4 Investigate the problem of interfacing an 8×8 keyboard to an 8-bit microprocessor via a two- or three-port programmable interface circuit such as the 6821 PIA or the 8255. Depressed keys are to be identified via the walking-1s scanning method. All necessary keyboard service functions (scanning, debouncing, key encoding, etc.) are to be implemented by software, using as little additional hardware as possible.

(a) Draw a logic diagram of the interface showing the keyboard, the system bus, and all ICs used.

(b) Carry out the system design of the keyboard service software. Provide a flowchart showing the overall structure of this software, and give a short narrative description of the function of each of its major (sub)routines.

7.5 Suppose that the direct-drive method of Fig. 7.16 is used to interface a 10-digit seven-segment LED display unit to an 8-bit microprocessor. Construct a logic diagram for the interface circuit required and a flowchart for the software necessary to control the display. Explain why the control software is not significantly less than that needed for the multiplexed 10-digit display circuit of Fig. 7.18, despite the fewer ICs used by the latter.

7.6 Implement the flowchart of Fig. 7.19 for controlling a multiplexed LED display unit using the following:

(a) An assembly language, for example, 6800 or 8080/8085 assembly language

(b) A high-level language such as Pascal

Analyze the suitability for each language type for this particular IO programming task.

7.7 Redesign the multiplexed LED display unit of Fig. 7.18 to allow for storage in a local RAM or register file of all the digits to be displayed at any time. The objective here is to eliminate the need for repeatedly executing an IO program that refreshes the display. New data to be displayed are loaded once into the RAM and subsequently are retrieved under automatic hardware control to refresh the display elements. Give a logic diagram for the modified display unit and a flowchart for the software needed to communicate with it.

7.8 Electromechanical relays are sometimes used to interface high-current or high-voltage electric circuits to microprocessors. Figure 7.72 shows a relay connection to a 12-V dc motor of the sort used in automobiles. The relay-controlled switch S turns on and off in step with digital logic pulses applied to the z input. The relay thus performs the same function as the LED optocoupler in Fig. 7.21. Write a brief note comparing and contrasting optocouplers and relays as interface devices for microprocessor-based systems.

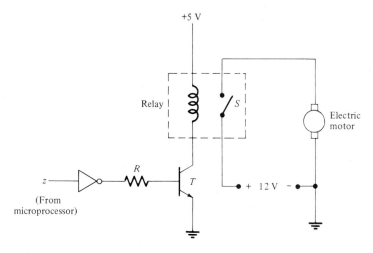

+5 V

Relay

S

Electric
motor

R

z

T

+ 12 V −

(From
microprocessor)

Figure 7.72 Using a relay to interface a 12-V dc electric motor.

7.9 Explain what is meant by open-loop and closed-loop control systems in the microprocessor context. Outline the advantages and disadvantages of each. Give a practical example of each type of system that is different from any mentioned in the text.

7.10 Explain briefly why many systems that process analog physical variables have analog input devices but digital output devices.

7.11 Suggest a suitable type of transducer for each of the following IO devices, and outline its hardware and software interfacing requirements.

(*a*) A weighing scales to be attached to a POS terminal

(*b*) A moisture sensor in a domestic clothes dryer, which is used to switch off the dryer automatically when the clothes are sufficiently dry

(*c*) A device to monitor the thickness of the brake linings in an automobile and alert the driver when they become excessively worn

(*d*) A device to monitor a gas-fired furnace and shut off the flow of gas automatically in the event of a failure of the mechanism used to ignite the gas burners

7.12 The transducer circuits of Figs. 7.24a and 7.24b, which are called voltage divider and bridge circuits, respectively, yield an output voltage v whose value is a function of the transducer's resistance R. Prove that the bridge configuration is inherently the more sensitive of the two, in that a given change in R can produce a larger change in v than is possible with the voltage divider circuit.

7.13 A problem with some resistance-based transducers is their sensitivity to temperature, which can disturb the resistance changes produced by other analog quantities being sensed. The following approach is taken to compensate for unwanted thermal effects when using strain gauges (see Fig. 7.24b). A second strain gauge G′ that is identical to the original strain gauge G is mounted close to G, but is oriented so that it is unaffected by the forces being measured by G. Typically G and G′ are mounted at right angles to each other. Because of their proximity, the resistances R and $R′$ of G and G′, respectively, are subject to the same temperature fluctuations. R and $R′$ are combined with two other resistors in a bridge circuit such as that of Fig. 7.24b. Determine the most suitable positions for R and $R′$ in the bridge configuration, and explain your reasoning.

7.14 Consider the potentiometer transducer for measuring the depth of a liquid in a reservoir, which appears in Fig. 7.24c. Assume the following parameters are known. When the float is in the highest position, the liquid depth D is D_{max} and the potentiometer resistance R being measured is R_{max}. When the float is in the lowest position, $D = D_{min}$ and $R = 0$. The length of the float arm measured from the wiper axis to the surface of the liquid is r. A change in the liquid depth from D_{min} to D_{max} causes the float arm to rotate through the angle a_{max}.

(a) Derive an equation relating the transducer output voltage $v(D)$ to the liquid depth D.

(b) Write a Pascal program that determines D from $v(D)$, assuming that the length of the object program should be as small as possible, while D must be computed with an accuracy of ± 5 percent.

7.15 Redesign the table-look-up procedure SCAN_TABLE of the Pascal temperature-conversion program THERMOMETER (Fig. 7.27) as an assembly-language subroutine for either the 6800 or 8080/8085 microprocessor.

7.16 Consider the interrupt-driven 16-column printer discussed in Sec. 7.2.3. Suppose that it is interfaced to a 6800 microprocessor via a 6821 PIA as indicated in Fig. 7.31. Construct a detailed set of flowcharts for a set of assembly-language interrupt routines to control all phases of printer operation.

7.17 Determine a possible configuration of rotor teeth for a stepping motor that has only four stator teeth and a step size of 36 degrees. Explain its operation (single-phase mode only) by means of a timing diagram such as Fig. 7.33.

7.18 (a) Redraw Fig. 7.33 to show the behavior of the stepping motor in the dual-phase mode of operation with the input signal pattern of Fig. 7.34c. Show clearly that the same step size s is obtained as in the single-phase mode, but the stable positions are displaced by $\frac{1}{2}s$ from the stable positions occurring in single-phase operation.

(b) On the basis of the foregoing analysis, devise a control method for stepping motors that cuts the normal step size from s to $\frac{1}{2}s$ Draw a timing diagram similar to Figs. 7.34b and 7.34c for this mode of operation.

7.19 The printer of Fig. 7.29 is to be redesigned as follows: The number of different characters on the print drum is to be increased from 42 to 48. The print drum is to be driven by a stepping motor in place of a continuous (servo)motor. The feedback signals P_1 and P_2 from the position transducers are to be eliminated, so that the printer changes from a closed-loop to an open-loop system.

Outline the hardware and software interface required by the modified printer. Explain clearly how the printer and the system microprocessor are kept in step.

7.20 The weighted-resistor DAC network of Fig. 7.37a is difficult to manufacture using IC technology, because it requires a wide range of different resistance values. Figure 7.73 shows an alternative weighted-

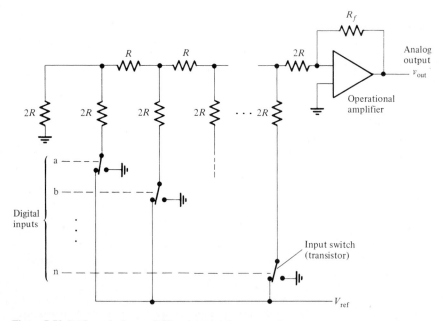

Figure 7.73 DAC employing an R-$2R$ weighted-resistor network.

resistor network for DAC design called an *R-2R* or *multiplying* DAC. It has the advantage of requiring only two different resistor values denoted R and $2R$. Consequently it is much easier to manufacture, and is widely used. Prove that the ith input switch, when closed, contributes a term proportional to 2^i to the effective resistance of the *R-2R* resistor network. From this determine which of the digital input bits a, b, ..., n is the most significant bit.

7.21 Suppose that the digital input to the 8-bit DAC of Fig. 7.38 is a two-digit BCD number rather than an 8-bit binary number. What values must the eight resistors have in this case?

7.22 Write a brief essay comparing and contrasting the three analog-to-digital conversion methods discussed in Sec. 7.2.3—direct conversion, the ramp method, and the successive approximation method—from the viewpoints of hardware complexity, conversion speed, and resolution.

7.23 Consider the 3-bit direct-conversion ADC circuit of Fig. 7.39. Suppose that the input analog voltage v varies from 0 to 8 V.

(*a*) What values should the reference voltages V_0:V_7 have?

(*b*) What is the output value $Z = z_2 z_1 z_0$ corresponding to each of the following values of the input v: 0 V, 0.8 V, 3.0 V, 7.9 V?

7.24 A thermal transducer TT has a sensitivity of 0.75 mV/°C over its working range. It is desired to use TT in a temperature-measuring instrument whose range is 0 to 250°C and whose sensitivity is 0.2 °C, that is, temperature can be measured to within a fifth of a degree. The output of TT is to be applied to an ADC that generates an n-bit digital representation of TT's millivolt reading. What should n be?

7.25 Rewrite the ramp analog-to-digital conversion routine of Fig. 7.41 using the 8080/8085 assembly language. Compare and contrast the relative efficiency of the 6800 and 8080/8085 instruction sets for this type of IO programming.

7.26 Write a Pascal program to implement the successive approximation algorithm of Fig. 7.42 using the interface circuit of Fig. 7.40. Discuss the advantages and disadvantages of using a high-level programming language for this application.

7.27 (*a*) Explain why most microprocessors have unidirectional address buses, but bidirectional data buses.

(*b*) In the 8085 system bus (Fig. 7.44b) the low-order address bits A_0:A_7 are multiplexed with data over the common AD bus. Suggest why this might be preferable to multiplexing data with the high-order address bits A_8:A_{15}.

7.28 Write a short essay on bus standardization, covering motivation, the impact of bus standards on system cost (including design development and hardware and software costs), and the limitations of such standardization efforts.

7.29 A 6800-based system is to be designed with the Multibus as its system bus. Draw a diagram showing the connections that must be made between the 6800's interface lines and those of the Multibus; label each connection with the corresponding 6800 and Multibus signal names. List two features supported by the Multibus that are not supported by the 6800.

7.30 An 8085 CPU is required to communicate with a RAM unit M via the Multibus. M is organized as a 32K-by 16-bit memory with address bus A_0:A_{14} and data bus D_0:D_{15}.

(*a*) Draw a logic diagram showing all connections of the 8085 and M to the Multibus. Label each connection with its proper Multibus name.

(*b*) Write two assembly-language macros that use the foregoing bus connections, and perform the following 16-bit load and store operations.

Macro Statement	Name	Actions Performed
LWD	Load word	A := M[HL]; B := M[HL + 1];
SWD	Store word	M[HL] := A; M[HL + 1] := B;

7.31 The Multibus inhibit lines $\overline{\text{INH1}}$ and $\overline{\text{INH2}}$ are intended for temporarily preventing certain memory or IO units from responding to read or write commands. This allows the units in question to be assigned the same physical addresses, provided all but one of the units is always inhibited. In a typical application a RAM M and a PROM M′ are assigned the same set of addresses. M is connected to $\overline{\text{INH1}}$ and is inhibited by activating $\overline{\text{INH1}}$ whenever it is desired to address M′. Similarly M′ is inhibited via $\overline{\text{INH2}}$ whenever M is being addressed.

Suggest two applications of this type of RAM/ROM address multiplexing in microcomputer design, and explain why it is preferable not to assign separate addresses to the memory units.

7.32 Figure 7.74 depicts a parallel method for resolving Multibus interrupt requests that is faster than the serial daisy-chain scheme of Fig. 7.51. Each potential master unit U_i is again assigned a fixed priority. When it desires to take control of the Multibus, U_i activates its bus request line $\overline{\text{BREQ}}$, which, along with the $\overline{\text{BREQ}}$ lines from other bus masters, is connected to a combinational priority-resolving circuit P. If there is no active interrupt request from a device of higher priority than U_i, P activates U_i's priority-in line $\overline{\text{BPRN}}$, permitting it to become the new bus master.

Carry out the logic design of P using standard MSI components for the case where there are at most eight potential bus masters.

7.33 Write an essay comparing the three IO control methods—programmed IO, interrupt-driven IO, and DMA—from the viewpoints of interface hardware complexity, control software complexity, and IO data-transmission speed.

7.34 Modify the interface system for the 16-column printer of Figs. 7.29–7.31 to use status-driven programmed IO in place of interrupt-driven IO. Give a logic design for the new interface circuit, employing standard ICs as much as possible. Estimate the loss of CPU efficiency, using some suitable efficiency measure of your choosing, resulting from the elimination of interrupts.

7.35 With the IO programs of Figs. 7.56 and 7.58b serving as examples, compare and contrast the 6800 and 8080/8085 instruction sets in terms of their suitability for implementing programmed IO with polling.

7.36 Convert the 8080/8085 input program listed in Fig. 7.58b into a subroutine named INSUB that transfers blocks of IO data via the 8255 programmable interface circuit. INSUB should read a specified number ION of data bytes from input port A, and transfer them to an IO buffer region in main memory that occupies addresses IOBUF, IOBUF + 1, ..., IOBUF + ION − 1. The input device supplies data bytes to port A asynchronously, each accompanied by a data-ready signal. The values of ION and IOBUF are to be stored in memory locations of the same names.

7.37 (a) Write an output program corresponding to the input program of Fig. 7.58b that transfers one word of data asynchronously to the output device attached to the 8255 circuit of Fig. 7.58a.

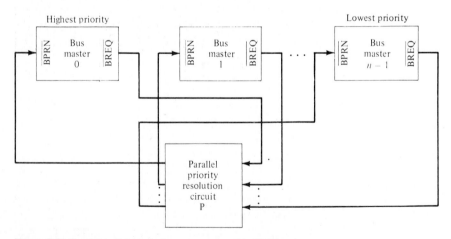

Figure 7.74 Parallel technique for bus-access control in Multibus systems.

(*b*) Expand your program from part (*a*) of this problem into an output subroutine OUTSUB that transfers blocks of ION data bytes from an IO buffer region named IOBUF in main memory. (See also Prob. 7.36.)

7.38 Redesign the POLL routine for the 6800 microprocessor given in Fig. 7.56 into a subroutine that transfers a block of ION bytes from the input device to the system stack. The subroutine should be invoked by the standard 6800 call instruction

JSR   POLL

Your modifications should keep the data-transfer operation as fast as possible. (*Caution*: POLL uses the system stack as a data buffer, while JSR uses it to store return addresses.)

7.39 The Z80 microprocessor augments the IN and OUT IO instructions of its 8080 predecessor with the set of instructions listed in Fig. 7.75. These enable both 1-byte and block IO transfers to be programmed via a single instruction. Main memory and IO ports are addressed indirectly using the HL and C registers as address registers. Register B also serves as a byte counter during block transfers.

(*a*) Write a set of 8080/8085 macros that are functionally equivalent to the Z80's input instruction set.

(*b*) Execution of any of the instructions INDR, INIR, OUTDR, or OUTIR by itself causes a block of IO data to be transferred to or from main memory; however, the data-transfer rate is slower by a factor of f than that achievable by an equivalent block DMA transfer. Explain why this is so, and estimate the value of f.

7.40 Let D be an input device connected to IP port 7 of an 8080/8085-based microcomputer. The CPU responds to an interrupt from D by executing an interrupt service routine named DREAD. The functions of DREAD are to input a data byte from port 7 and store it in a 64-byte IO buffer IOBUF in main memory. DREAD also maintains a byte count variable DCOUNT, which specifies the number of data bytes that have been transferred from D into IOBUF. DCOUNT is checked periodically by another program that empties IOBUF when it is full, and resets DCOUNT to zero. Code DREAD in 8080/8085 assembly language.

7.41 The 8255 programmable interface circuit is to be used to interface a single seven-segment LED display unit (i.e., one digit) and an 8-bit DIP switch to an 8085-based system. (A DIP switch is a set of two-terminal

Type	Instruction		Actions Performed
Input	IN	A, (port)	A := IO[port]; (Input byte from IO port no. 'port' to accumulator A)
	IN	reg, (C)	reg := IO[C]; (Input byte from IO port addressed by register C to register 'reg' = A, B, C, D, E, H, or L)
	IND		M[HL] := IO[C]; HL := HL − 1, B := B − 1;
	INDR		Repeat IND until B = 0;
	INI		M[HL] := IO[C]; HL := HL + 1, B := B − 1;
	INIR		Repeat INI until B = 0;
Output	OUT	(port), A	IO[port] := A;
	OUT	(C), reg	IO[C] := reg;
	OUTD		IO[C] := M[HL]; HL := HL − 1, B := B − 1;
	OUTDR		Repeat OUTD until B = 0;
	OUTI		IO[C] := M[HL]; HL := HL + 1, B := B − 1;
	OUTIR		Repeat OUTI until B = 0;

Figure 7.75 IO instruction set of the Z80 microprocessor.

manual on–off switches mounted in a standard dual in-line package.) The LED unit and the DIP switches are to be attached to separate 8-bit IO ports numbered 6 and 7 respectively.

(*a*) Draw a logic diagram showing all connections between the LED, the DIP switch, the 8255, and the system bus. Show also any additional components needed, such as driver circuits.

(*b*) Write an IO program that reads the DIP switch and, if bit *i* is switched on, causes the corresponding decimal digit *i* to be displayed by the LED display unit.

7.42 Consider the general nonvectored interrupt scheme for 6800-based systems, which appears in Fig. 7.61. The status ports merely indicate to the CPU whether or not the corresponding IO device has an active interrupt request. It is not difficult to extend this design so that each status port contains not only an interrupt status flag, but also a (partial) interrupt address vector. It thus not only indicates the presence of an interrupt, but also specifies the interrupt routine to service it.

(*a*) Sketch a 6800 assembly-language routine that polls the interrupt status ports and uses their contents as interrupt vectors.

(*b*) Is this modified interrupt polling scheme equivalent to vectored interrupt control? Explain your answer.

7.43 Write an essay analyzing the relative merits of vectored and nonvectored interrupt control, and considering interface circuit complexity, program design difficulty, and IO data-transfer speed.

7.44 Describe how the daisy-chaining method illustrated in Fig. 7.51 can be adapted for priority interrupt control in microprocessor-based systems employing vectored interrupts. Briefly compare this method with the parallel priority control method in Fig. 7.63.

7.45 Carry out the design at the register-transfer level of a priority interrupt controller for 8080-based microcomputers. The controller should handle up to eight separate interrupt requests, and resolve priorities by the parallel method of Fig. 7.63. A unique RST (restart) instruction should be generated by the controller for each interrupt request line.

7.46 The 6800 microprocessor has no built-in circuits to support vectored interrupts. Nevertheless, something similar can be obtained in a 6800-based microcomputer by introducing a special circuit C that allows the IO devices to modify the addresses transmitted over the system bus during normal interrupt processing. Specifically, when in response to an interrupt request on $\overline{IRQ}$ the CPU reads the memory locations with addresses $FFF8_{16}$ and $FFF9_{16}$ (see Fig. 5.34), C intercepts these addresses en route from the CPU to main memory and modifies them.

Design C using standard SSI/MSI circuits so that it produces eight different address-pairs corresponding to eight different interrupt sources by modifying the three high-order bits of the addresses $FFF8_{16}$ and $FFF9_{16}$ generated by $\overline{IRQ}$. When two or more interrupt requests are received simultaneously by C, it should select the one with the highest wired-in priority for service. Provide a logic circuit for C and a brief narrative description of its operation. Explain clearly how C is synchronized with the CPU.

7.47 A microprocessor-based system is often called on to time external events. This can be done by causing the microprocessor to execute a timing program such as the delay routine of Fig. 7.10b. Another approach is to attach a hardware-implemented IO device called a *programmable timer* to the system. This is basically a counter (or set of counters) that operates as follows:

(*1*) It is loaded with a number representing a time interval *T*.

(*2*) It is subsequently triggered to start counting down automatically at a fixed rate; the count input signal is derived from a clock generator, for example, the system clock.

(*3*) When the count reaches zero, the timer generates an interrupt request to the CPU.

Carry out the logic design of a programmable timer for use in a 6800- or 8080/8085-based system. The time interval *T* can range from 1 to 1000 ms. The clock signal available for the timer is a 2-MHz system clock. The timer may be assigned up to four IO port addresses in the range 0020_{16} to 0023_{16}. The service routine that responds to timer interrupts has the starting address 0010_{16}. Use standard 74LS00-series SSI/MSI ICs for your design, which should include all the logic needed to interface the programmable timer to the system bus of the host microprocessor.

7.48 (*a*) Explain why a CPU can halt at the end of its current machine cycle to allow a DMA operation to take place, but must continue to the end of its current instruction cycle before allowing an interrupt operation to begin.

(*b*) Almost all microprocessors have instructions for masking interrupt requests from IO devices. Explain why they do not have similar instructions for masking DMA requests.

7.49 Suppose that a microcomputer must accommodate a large number of DMA channels, say 32. A four-channel DMA controller such as that of Fig. 7.70 is available. Describe how to interface eight such DMA controllers to the system bus to ensure that

(*1*) No more than one DMA channel is logically connected to the system bus at any time.

(*2*) No DMA channel is permanently excluded from access to the system bus by the continual arrival of DMA requests in channels of higher priority.

7.50 It is desired to link two similar microprocessor-based systems to that they can exchange messages. A message is a fairly short sequence of data words that must be transferred from the main memory of one system to that of the other system. Message transfer is accomplished by each system treating the other as one of its IO devices. The message source performs an output operation addressed to the other system, while at the same time the other system performs an input operation. Using either the 6800 or the 8080/8085 to implement the host microprocessors, carry out the following:

(*a*) Describe a practical design situation where this type of intersystem message transfer is necessary.

(*b*) Design a suitable hardware interface for intersystem communication based on programmable interface circuits such as the 6821/8255 or 6850/8251.

(*c*) Outline the structure of the software needed for message transfer, explaining clearly how the activities of the two microprocessors are synchronized.

EIGHT

ADVANCED MICROPROCESSOR ORGANIZATION

"[In 1951] I went to see Professor Douglas Hartree, who had built the first differential analyzers in England and had more experience in using these very specialized computers than anyone else. He told me that, in his opinion, all the calculations that would ever be needed in this country could be done on the three digital computers that were then being built–one in Cambridge, one in Teddington, and one in Manchester. No one else, he said, would ever need machines of their own, or would be able to afford to buy them."

[Lord Bowden, *American Scientist*, 1970]

A variety of approaches to the construction of more powerful microprocessor-based systems are presented in this chapter. The characteristics of advanced one-chip microprocessors are reviewed, with the Intel 8086 and Motorola 68000 serving as examples. The use of bit-sliced circuits and microprogramming to custom-design microprocessors is considered. The AMD 2900 series of bit-sliced components is introduced and applied to the design of a high-speed CPU that emulates the 8080 microprocessor. Various ways of improving system performance by employing several processors are discussed, including the use of arithmetic processors, IO processors, and multiple CPUs (multiprocessors).

8.1 16-BIT MICROPROCESSORS

The motivations for and architecture of powerful microprocessors with CPU word sizes of 16 bits or more are examined in this section. Two representative 16-bit microprocessors, the Intel 8086 and the Motorola 68000, are considered in some detail.

8.1.1 General Characteristics

Since the introduction of the first commercial microprocessor family, the Intel MCS-4 series, in 1971, there has been a steady growth in the computational power of micro-processors and their support circuits. As discussed in Sec. 1.2, this progress has been spurred by continual improvements in IC manufacturing technology, which by the early 1980s allowed chips containing 100,000 or more transistors to be mass produced at very low cost per chip. The evolution of microprocessor architecture in the 1970s and 1980s to a considerable degree has paralleled that of (large) computers through the first three electronic generations. The features of more powerful computers are gradually being incorporated into new microprocessor and microcomputer chip designs as the necessary silicon "real estate" to accommodate them becomes available.

A very rough but convenient measure of a microprocessor's computing capability is its principal CPU word size. Commercial microprocessors have word sizes that range from 1 bit, such as the Motorola 14500 studied in Sec. 5.1, to 32 bits. Four-bit microprocessors appear to be used in the largest numbers for devices such as pocket calculators and toys, whose computational requirements are fairly modest. "Standard" microprocessor architecture is typified by 8-bit microprocessors such as the 6800 and 8080/8085 families covered in Chap. 5. These microprocessors find perhaps the widest range of applications, from simple appliance controllers to low-cost personal computers. Thirty-two-bit microprocessors such as the National Semiconductor 16032 and the Intel iAPX 432 approach the power and complexity of minicomputers, and are used for similar applications, such as general-purpose scientific computation (Gupta & Toong, 1983). In this section we consider the design and application of 16-bit microprocessors, which provide some insight into the more advanced aspects of microprocessor-based systems.

The first 16-bit microprocessor on a single IC chip was the National Semiconductor PACE (Processing And Control Element), which was introduced in 1976 and had only limited commercial success. It was followed by 16-bit microprocessor series from several manufacturers; three of the more popular 16-bit microprocessors are summarized in Fig. 8.1. The first of these, the Intel 8086, appeared in 1978 as part of the MCS-86 series, later renamed the iAPX-86 series. Like some other 16-bit microprocessors, it can be regarded as a 16-bit enhanced version of an earlier 8-bit machine, in this case the 8080. In addition to handling 16-bit and smaller data words, the 8086 has new hardware-implemented instruction types, including fixed-point multiplication and division instruc-tions, and several new addressing modes. It also has a larger memory address space (2^{20} bytes or 1M bytes, compared with the 8080's 2^{16} bytes) to accommodate larger amounts of software, especially programs written in high-level languages. It has some hardware and software features to support multiprocessor design, that is, the linking of several microprocessors in a single system. A fair degree of hardware compatibility has been maintained between the 8086 and the 8080. For example, many interface and support circuits designed for the 8080 can also be used directly in 8086-based systems. Although the 8086 has instructions that are functionally equivalent to almost all those of the 8080 (and 8085), there is no real compatibility between the assembly languages or machine languages of the two families. The 68000 and Z8000 microprocessors, which also appear in Fig. 8.1, have the same general capabilities as the 8086, with some additional features. They are only loosely related to their 8-bit predecessors, the 6800 and Z80, and are best regarded as new architectures. Their data types include 32-bit "long" words, so that they can, to a limited extent, be viewed as 32-bit machines.

The rapid proliferation of microprocessors in the mid-1970s saw the introduction of new and relatively sophisticated applications that favored the use of high-level programming languages such as Pascal and PL/M. Microprocessors in the 8-bit range are not well suited to support the use of such languages. For example, such basic features of high-level languages as integer multiplication, real (floating-point) arithmetic, and data types such as arrays and character strings have no counterparts in the machine language of simpler microprocessors. Consequently they must be represented indirectly via subroutines and the like, which tends to increase program size and reduce processor throughput. Compilation of a moderately large high-level language program can easily produce object code that is too big to fit in the 64K-byte main memory space provided by such microprocessors as the 6800 and 8080/8085. Complex microprocessor-based systems may contain a set of relatively independent "user" programs that may also have been written by different programmers (users). Coordination of the execution of the user programs is often assigned to a system control program or operating system. The operating system supervises all program activity to ensure that the available resources of the system, including processor execution time, main memory space, and shared software routines, are used fairly and efficiently. It must, for example, prevent one user program from accidentally or deliberately destroying information associated with another program. It must also prevent two programs from attempting to use the same shared resource simultaneously. Implementation of resource sharing, memory protection, and other operating system functions on 8-bit microprocessors is generally quite difficult.

To solve the foregoing problems, microprocessors such as those of Fig. 8.1 contain a number of features to facilitate the implementation of operating systems and programs written in high-level languages. These features, which are borrowed from second- and third-generation computers, are listed in Fig. 8.2. By providing larger address buses, a larger main memory is obtained that can accommodate more software. The address bus of the 68000, for instance, permits direct addressing of up to 2^{24} bytes $= 16M$ bytes of main memory. The addition of a support circuit called a *memory management unit*

Item	Microprocessor		
	8086	68000	Z8000
Introduction date (approximate)	1978	1980	1980
Originating company	Intel	Motorola	Zilog
Number of transistors	29,000	70,000	17,500
IC pin count	40	64	40
Typical CPU clock frequency (MHz)	8	10	4
Number of basic instruction types	95	61	110
Number of directly addressable main memory locations (bytes)	2^{20}	2^{24}	6×2^{20}

Figure 8.1 Specifications for some widely used 16-bit microprocessors.

(MMU) allows this large memory space to be supervised efficiently. Most 16-bit microprocessors have fixed-point multiply and divide instructions, as well as all the instruction types found in smaller machines. They also typically have instructions for processing words of various fixed lengths, character strings of arbitrary length, and arrays of words. Few one-chip microprocessors yet have hardware-implemented floating-point operations. However, these operations, and other useful numerical functions, can be placed on an auxiliary chip called an *arithmetic coprocessor,* which acts as an extension to the CPU's execution unit. Instructions for the coprocessor can be included in program instruction streams in the usual manner. They are fetched from main memory by the CPU, but are turned over to the coprocessor for execution.

Systems requiring very large amounts of on-line software use secondary memory devices, such as magnetic disk memory units, for bulk storage of information. Programs and data are transferred from secondary to main memory only when they are required for processing. After processing is complete, any new or modified information is returned to secondary storage, and the main memory space allocated to the process in question is released for use by new processes. The movement of information back and forth between main and secondary memory in this manner is normally controlled by IO routines that form part of the operating system. This data movement is invisible to user programs, making the system appear to have a single, very large addressable memory whose capacity equals that of main and secondary memory combined. A one-level logical memory composed of several levels of physical memory devices is termed a *virtual memory.* The management of virtual memory is a major function of a typical operating system, and is supported by some hardware features of the newer microprocessors. For example, information stored in the main memory of an 8086-based system is grouped into logically related modules called *segments.* Typical segments include procedures, arrays, and stacks. Segments are accessed via special address registers called segment registers. Segments are convenient units for transferring information between main and secondary memory; and are easily relocated anywhere in main memory by altering the contents of the associated segment registers. The MMUs found in 16-bit microprocessor series greatly simplify the implementation of virtual memory (see Prob. 8.4).

Another useful feature of some 16-bit microprocessors, notably the 68000, is the provision of two major CPU states or operating conditions: a *supervisor* or *system state* intended for the sole use of the operating system, and a *user state* intended for the execution of user or applications programs. Certain *privileged instructions* can only be executed by the CPU when it is in the supervisor state; these instructions are effectively reserved for the exclusive use of the operating system. This provides a simple but

---

1. Large main memory address space
2. Powerful instruction and data types
3. Coprocessors for instruction-set expansion
4. Management of virtual memory systems
5. Program- and data-protection mechanisms
6. Control methods for multiple (concurrent) processes

Figure 8.2 Design features of more powerful microprocessors.

powerful means of protecting programs and data, since user programs cannot execute the privileged instructions that alter the system's major resource-allocation mechanisms.

The coupling of two or more microprocessors to form a multiprocessor makes possible a substantial increase in system performance or throughput. Higher system reliability can also be achieved by multiprocessors, since if one microprocessor fails, its functions can be taken over by other microprocessors. Such *fault-tolerant systems* are becoming increasingly important as microprocessors find their way into such applications as the control of transportation or life-support systems, where a computer failure can threaten human life or property. Multiprocessor design involves the ability to share the hardware and software resources among interacting and concurrently executing processes. A representative microprocessor-based multiprocessing system, or *multimicroprocessor* system, is illustrated in Fig. 8.3. It is composed of a number of microprocessors, each with its own private or local resources. A common or global set of resources are shared by all microprocessors and accessed via a global bus. Interprocessor communication is accomplished by the transfer of messages to or from the global main memory. To prevent conflicting use of the shared resources by different microprocessors, a means must be provided for testing the status of each global resource and, if it is not busy, permitting only one microprocessor to gain access to it. The 8086, for example, allows instructions to contain a lock field that can be used to give a processor exclusive control of the global bus during the critical step of taking charge of a global resource that other processors also may wish to control at the same time.

8.1.2 The 8086 Microprocessor

The 8086 was introduced by Intel Corp. in 1978 to "extend the 8080 family into the 16-bit arena" (Katz et al., 1978). The extensions include 16-bit as well as 8-bit operations, more powerful instructions and addressing modes, a larger memory address space, support for virtual memory and multiprocessing, and auxiliary processors for numeric

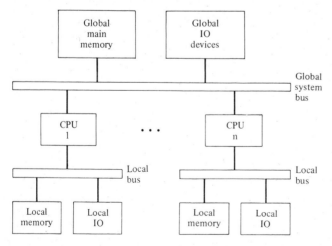

Figure 8.3 Multimicroprocessor system with both local and global resources.

computation and IO control. The 8086 is the principal CPU chip in a microprocessor family variously known as the MCS-86 and iAPX-86; we refer to it simply as the 8086 family. The 8086 chip is housed in a 40-pin DIP, and has 16 pins for connection to an external data bus. A variant of the 8086, called the 8088 microprocessor, has an eight-line rather than a 16-line external data bus, but is otherwise much the same as the 8086. Two other distinctive members of the 8086 family are the 8089 IO processor, intended for independent control of high-speed IO operations, and the 8087 numeric processor, both of which are studied later in this chapter. The 8087, which performs a large set of arithmetic operations, including high-precision fixed-point arithmetic, floating-point arithmetic, and trigonometric function calculation, is designed to be linked as a coprocessor to an 8086 or 8088 CPU. The 8086 architecture is also the basis of two subsequent more powerful 16-bit microprocessors, the 80186 and 80286, which define the iAPX-186 and iAPX-286 series respectively.

The internal organization of the 8086 appears in Fig. 8.4. Like any CPU, it is designed to fetch instructions and operands from an external memory, decode and execute the instructions, and store the results produced either in CPU registers or in main memory. At the heart of the 8086 is a 16-bit ALU that performs all data processing, and communicates with a set of fourteen 16-bit programmable registers that are used for data, address, and status flag storage. External data and address transfer employs a 16-bit bidirectional multiplexed bus AD, which is analogous to the 8-bit bus of the same name in the 8085. Four additional address lines allow 20-bit addresses to be produced by the 8086. An unusual feature of this microprocessor is the provision of an instruction buffer memory that is organized as a first-in/first-out (FIFO) queue. Instruction bytes may be prefetched (e.g., when the CPU is busy with some internal operation and the system bus is idle) and stored in the instruction buffer for subsequent execution. This reduces the time the CPU spends waiting for new instructions to be fetched from memory, thereby increasing the system's effective instruction-execution rate. To facilitate the separation of instruction fetching and execution, the 8086 contains a bus interface unit that supervises the system bus and prefetches up to six instruction bytes whenever the status of the system bus and the CPU permit.

The 14 programmable registers of the 8086 fall into several groups. The four registers designated AX, BX, CX, and DX are general-purpose data registers. The AX register, for instance, serves as the main operand register or accumulator. The high-order (H) and low-order (L) halves of these registers are also directly addressable with the names given in Fig. 8.4. The stack pointer register SP, the program counter PC, and the status or flag register are quite conventional. As indicated by shading in Fig. 8.4, all the foregoing registers, with the exception of the high-order half AH of the accumulator AX, can be mapped directly into the programmable registers of the 8080/8085 (cf. Fig. 5.43). (The value of this correspondence is questionable, however, since the 8080/8085 and 8086 families have incompatible machine and assembly languages.) The 8086 registers designated BP (base pointer), SI (source index), and DI (destination index) are used for several addressing modes, including base and indexed addressing, which are not found in the 8080/8085. The four remaining address registers are segment registers, which, as explained below, support the implementation of virtual memory management.

From a programmer's viewpoint, the main memory of an 8086-based system stores

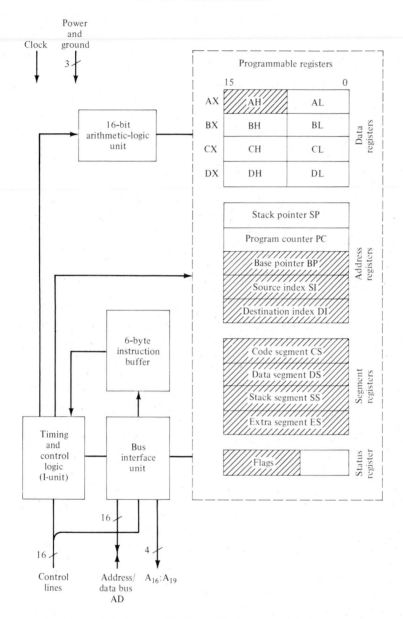

Figure 8.4 Internal organization of the Intel 8086 microprocessor (registers not in the 8080/8085 are shaded).

up to 2^{20} individually addressable 8-bit bytes. Sixteen-bit word transfers are accomplished by accessing two adjacent bytes simultaneously (see Prob. 8.6). The megabyte of memory is also seen as a set of segments, where a segment is a contiguous block of up to 2^{16} (64K) memory locations. Each segment represents an independently accessible and relocatable entity such as a program module or a data set. It is assigned a starting (base) address called the *segment address* ADR_s. A byte within a segment is identified by a 16-bit displacement or offset address ADR_d. The displacement ADR_d is typically specified by an address field within an instruction; the manner in which ADR_d is calculated depends on the addressing mode (direct, indirect, indexed, etc.). The segment address is obtained from one of the CPU's four segment registers. Figure 8.5a shows the general way in which a memory location (byte) is addressed via ADR_s and ADR_d. To obtain the 20-bit absolute or effective address ADR of a particular memory byte, ADR_s and ADR_d, which are both 16 bits long, are combined as follows: ADR_s is shifted four bit positions to the left and then added (via unsigned binary addition) to ADR_d thus:

$$ADR = 16 \times ADR_s + ADR_d \tag{8.1}$$

The final 20-bit address ADR may be termed the *physical address* of the memory location in question, while ADR_d is its *logical address*. By modifying ADR_s, which is a function usually assigned to an operating system, the relation between the physical and logical addresses can be altered without affecting program executability.

Whenever the 8086 constructs a physical address ADR, it obtains a segment address ADR_s from one of its segment registers. Hence up to four segments may be in use at any time. The segment register employed in a given addressing operation may be specified either by the assembly-language programmer using special ASSUME directives, or by the 8086 itself according to certain default rules. Figure 8.5b illustrates the typical use made of the 8086's segment registers. The code segment register CS, as its name implies, is designed to point to a segment storing an executable program module such as a subroutine or procedure. Suppose, for example, that the instruction pointed to by the current contents of PC is to be fetched. The 8086 places on the system address bus the address corresponding to $16 \times CS + PC$. In a similar way, the stack segment register SS is used to access a segment representing a LIFO stack in main memory. The other two segments have various possible uses; in Fig. 8.5b they point to data segments. Note that at any time an active segment can be replaced by simply reloading the corresponding segment register; there is no restriction on overlap among segments.

Machine-language instructions for the 8086 vary in length from 1 to 6 bytes; most have the general format defined in Fig. 8.6a. The first byte is the opcode specifying the instruction's general type. The second byte, if present, defines a source or destination register REG to be used, while its MOD (modifier) and R/M (register/memory) fields specify how addresses for main memory are to be constructed. Additional instruction bytes may be present to specify a memory address or an operand value (immediate address); the memory address field may contain a single byte D_L or 2 bytes $D_H.D_L$. The rules for obtaining the displacement address ADR_d are listed in Fig. 8.6b. ADR_d is then combined with a segment address to obtain a final physical address ADR according to (8.1). Despite the large number of possible addressing modes, address specification in assembly-language programs is fairly simple because many of the details of address construction can be left to the assembler. Consider, for instance, the statement

$$MOV \quad ALPHA, AL \tag{8.2}$$

which means move a byte from the lower half AL of the accumulator AX to the memory location ALPHA. Depending on the program context, this statement may be translated

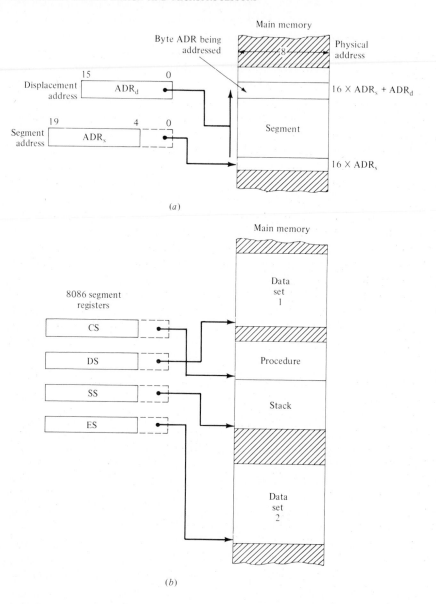

Figure 8.5 (a) Addressing a byte within a segment; (b) typical use made of the 8086's segment registers.

into the following 3-byte machine-language instruction:

$$\underbrace{1\,0\,0\,0\,1\,0\,0}_{\text{Opcode}}\quad \underbrace{0\,1}_{\text{MOD}}\ \underbrace{0\,0\,0}_{\text{REG}}\ \underbrace{1\,1\,1}_{\text{R/M}}\quad \underbrace{0\,1\,1\,0\,1\,0\,1\,1}_{D_L}$$

Here the opcode byte means "move byte from register"; REG = 000 indicates that AL is to serve as the data source register. The data-destination address in memory is obtained

Optional

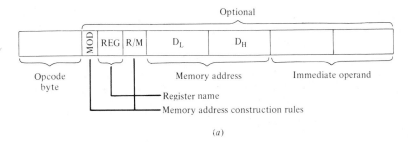

(a)

	Effective Address ADR_d		
R/M	MOD = 00	MOD = 01	MOD = 10
000	BX + SI	BX + SI + D_L	BX + SI + $D_H.D_L$
001	BX + DI	BX + DI + D_L	BX + DI + $D_H.D_L$
010	BP + SI	BP + SI + D_L	BP + SI + $D_H.D_L$
011	BP + DI	BP + DI + D_L	BP + DI + $D_H.D_L$
100	SI	SI + D_L	SI + $D_H.D_L$
101	DI	DI + D_L	DI + $D_H.D_L$
110	$D_H.D_L$	BP + D_L	BP + $D_H.D_L$
111	BX	BX + D_L	BX + $D_H.D_L$

(b)

Figure 8.6 (a) General 8086 instruction format; (b) memory address calculation methods.

from the 1-byte address component D_L in accordance with the address construction rules specified by REG = 111 and MOD = 01. From Fig. 8.6b it can be seen that the address ADR_d to be used relative to the current data segment is expressed by

$$ADR_d = BX + D_L \qquad (8.3)$$

BX may be interpreted as an implicit base register. If the data segment register DS defines the current segment address for this MOV instruction, then the logical address ALPHA in (8.2) is mapped into the physical address defined by (8.1) and (8.3) as follows:

$$ADR = 16 \times DS + BX + D_L$$

The 8086's instruction set includes all the types found in the 8080/8085, but with more addressing modes and more operand types. Thus we find all the 8080/8085 data-transfer instructions for moving data among CPU registers, between the CPU and memory (including stack push and pop instructions), and between the CPU and IO ports. The basic arithmetic-logic instructions include add and subtract with or without carry/borrow, increment and decrement, and various Boolean and rotation operations. As in the 8080/8085 case, decimal operations are implemented via binary (twos-complement) instructions followed by special decimal-adjust instructions. The 8086 also implements most of the 8080/8085's program-control instructions, including conditional and unconditional jumps and unconditional subroutine call and return instructions.

Figure 8.7 summarizes the 8086 instruction types that have no 8080/8085 counterparts. The exchange (XCHG) instructions swap the locations of two designated operands in a single step, and replace three move instructions. The translate instruction XLAT performs the operation

$$AL := M[16 \times ADR_s + BX + AL];$$

which is intended for 8-bit code conversion and similar table-look-up tasks. BX serves as a pointer to a 256-byte conversion table in main memory. The current contents of AL are used as an index to an entry in the table; the contents of that entry are fetched and become the new contents of AL. The 8086's multiply and divide instructions can apply to 8-bit or 16-bit signed or unsigned operands. Multiplication is realized by a hardware-implemented algorithm similar to those discussed in Sec. 4.2.4. Depending on the size and location of its operands, execution of an unsigned multiply (MUL) instruction takes from about 70 to 150 CPU clock cycles; signed multiplication and division are somewhat slower. Decimal addition is performed on packed decimal numbers (two BCD digits per byte) using a DAA instruction that is similar to the DAA instruction of the 6800 and

Type	Instruction	Comment
Data transfer	Exchange (swap) two registers Exchange register and memory location Translate byte via table look-up	
Data processing	Multiply signed/unsigned integers Divide signed/unsigned integers Decimal adjust for addition/subtraction ASCII adjust for add/subtract multiply/divide Arithmetic shift left/right Logical shift left/right	Used with packed decimal Used with unpacked decimal
Program control	Decrement counter and branch conditionally (loop instruction)	Uses relative addressing
String manipulation	Move byte and update source and/or destination index registers Compare source and destination bytes, set flags, and update index registers Compare destination word to accumulator, set flags, and update index registers (scan) Repeat the following instruction until counter CX is zero; decrement CX after each repetition	Prefix instruction for string manipulation instructions
External synchronization	Lock system bus during execution of following instruction Fetch instruction for coprocessor (escape) Wait for signal from external (co)processor	Prefix instruction used in multiprocessing

Figure 8.7 Summary of the 8086 instruction types not in the 8080/8085 instruction set.

8080/8085 microprocessors defined in Fig. 5.27. In the 8086 case, however, DAA means decimal adjust for addition, to distinguish it from a similar decimal adjust for subtraction (DAS) instruction. Decimal subtraction is implemented by following a binary subtraction instruction by DAS. The 8086 also provides a second set of decimal adjust instructions for arithmetic operations on ASCII-coded numbers, which represent unpacked decimal numbers containing only one BCD digit per byte (see Prob. 8.8). Another minor addition to the 8086's instruction repertoire is a set of arithmetic and logical shift instructions of the kind found in the 6800 microprocessor.

In the program-control instruction category, the 8086 has a class of loop instructions that combine the decrementing of a loop counter (the CX register) with a conditional branch based on the counter value. Like the 6800's branch instructions, the 8086's loop instructions employ relative addressing. For example, the loop statement

LOOP   NEXT

first decrements CX by one. If CX is then nonzero, the number of bytes from the end of the loop instruction to the instruction labeled NEXT is added to PC, thereby effecting a jump-relative operation to NEXT. If CX = 0, no branching occurs.

An unusual aspect of the 8086 is its character string manipulation instructions, which are useful in non-numerical applications such as word processing. A *string* is defined as a set of 8-bit or 16-bit words stored in consecutive locations in main memory; the contents of the string are arbitrary. There are five basic types of string instructions designed to move a word from a source string or to a destination string, compare words in two strings, or compare a string word with a fixed word. All the string instructions use the SI and DI registers as implicit pointers to the current words in the source and destination strings respectively. After the current data words have been moved or otherwise processed, SI and DI are automatically updated by either incrementing or decrementing them by one. Thus by repeatedly executing the same string instruction, entire strings or blocks of words can be processed. To facilitate this, the 8086 has several repeat instructions that can be prefixed to the basic string-manipulation instructions, causing them to be repeated the number of times specified by the CX register. CX is automatically decremented after each repetition, and the string operations continue until CX reaches zero. Suppose, for example, that it is desired to transfer an N-byte string from a memory region ALPHA to a memory region BETA. This can be implemented by the following 8086 assembly language code:

```
        MOV     DI, BETA      ; Load address of destination string into DI
        MOV     SI, ALPHA     ; Load address of source string into SI
        MOV     CX, N         ; Load string length (bytes) into CX
  REP   MOVSB                 ; Repeatedly move string bytes from source to
                              ; destination and update CX,DI,SI. Stop
                              ; when   CX = 0
```

Note how the REP (repeat) instruction is used as a prefix to the string-manipulation instruction MOVSB (move string of bytes). Since REP and MOVSB are each 1 byte long, the combination REP MOVSB amounts to a 2-byte memory-to-memory block-move instruction. The string instruction MOVSW is similar to MOVSB, except it moves

16-bit words rather than bytes. The remaining (synchronization) instructions listed in Fig. 8.7 are discussed in Sec. 8.3 in the context of systems with multiple processors.

The assembly language for the 8086 (Intel, 1978a) is similar to, but richer than, that of the 8080/8085, especially in the number of directives available for program structuring. A few representative aspects of the 8086 assembly language will be mentioned here. A part of a program representing a well-defined logical entity can be designated a segment by enclosing it between the directives SEGMENT and ENDS (end segment). Thus a segment named SEG1 is delimited as follows:

SEG1   SEGMENT

. . .

Body of segment

. . .

SEG1   ENDS

Similarly, subroutines or procedures are precisely delimited by the directives PROC (start procedure) and ENDP (end procedure). Note that neither the start nor the end of a subroutine is explicitly specifiable, except by comments, in 8080/8085 or 6800 assembly-language programs. Various additional 8086 directives exist for manipulating segment addresses and for linking program modules that may have been assembled independently.

Programming in 8086 assembly language is illustrated by Fig. 8.8. Two segments are specified: a program or code segment named DEC_ADD, which does the addition operation

BETA := ALPHA + BETA;

using 32-digit packed decimal operands; and a data segment named DEC_DATA, which defines the input values of ALPHA and BETA. (This particular example was developed in detail for the 6800 and 8080/8085 in Secs. 5.3.2 and 5.4.2 respectively.) The decimal addition algorithm is essentially the same as that used in Chap. 5. The numbers to be added are moved from the memory to the CPU one word at a time, and are added in the 8-bit accumulator AL via the ADC (binary add with carry) and DAA (decimal adjust for addition) instructions. Memory addressing is simplified, compared with the corresponding 8080/8085 routine in Fig. 5.47, by using indexed addressing with SI serving as the index register. In its use of indexed addressing DEC_ADD more closely resembles the 6800 addition program of Fig. 5.31. The loop instruction LOOP combines the steps of decrementing the byte counter CX, and making a branching decision based on the resulting value of CX. The ASSUME directive at the beginning of the DEC_ADD segment tells the assembler which segment registers will be used during the execution of DEC_ADD. ASSUME is mainly intended to enable the assembler to double-check that segment addressing is consistent throughout the program. Segment registers must be loaded by explicit move instructions, except where default values are used. The ASSUME statement at the start of DEC_ADD indicates that CS is to store the segment address for DEC_ADD itself, while DS is to store the segment address for DEC_DATA.

Location	Instruction		Comment
DEC_ADD	SEGMENT		; Define start of code segment DEC_ADD
	ASSUME	CS: DEC_ADD	; Define code segment usage
&		DS: DEC_DATA	; Define data segment usage
START:	MOV	AX, DEC_DATA	; Load data segment register DS
	MOV	DS, AX	
	MOV	CX, 16	; Load data byte count into CX
	MOV	SI, 0	; Initialize index register SI to zero
	CLC		; Clear carry flag CY
LOOP1:	MOV	AL, ALPHA[SI]	; Load byte SI of ALPHA into AL
	ADC	AL, BETA[SI]	; Add byte SI of BETA and carry flag CY to AL
	DAA		; Decimal adjust AL for addition
	MOV	BETA[SI], AL	; Store result in memory
	DEC	SI	; Decrement index register SI
	LOOP	LOOP1	; Decrement CX and jump to LOOP1 if CX $\neq$ 0
CONTINUE:	: : :		
DEC_ADD	ENDS		; Define end of code segment DEC_ADD
DEC_DATA	SEGMENT		; Define start of data segment DEC_DATA
ALPHA	DB	12H, 90H, 55H, 28H, 30H, 19H, 77H, 84H	
	DB	33H, 92H, 56H, 82H, 11H, 10H, 30H, 90H	
BETA	DB	79H, 20H, 38H, 88H, 61H, 40H, 90H, 99H	
	DB	11H, 10H, 33H, 33H, 78H, 29H, 10H, 43H	
DEC_DATA	ENDS		; Define end of data segment DEC_DATA

Figure 8.8 8086 assembly-language program and data segments for 32-digit (packed) decimal addition.

DS is loaded by move statements in DEC_ADD. The code segment register CS must be loaded with the value DEC_ADD before execution of the DEC_ADD segment begins. The DEC_DATA segment is nothing more than a table of DB (define byte) directives, with appropriate constant entries.

The 8086 communicates with the external world in much the same way as the 8-bit microprocessors encountered already. Figure 8.9 shows an 8086-based CPU suitable for controlling small single-processor systems, with the system bus set to a "minimum-mode" configuration; its external appearance differs little from that of an 8085-based CPU (cf. Fig. 5.42b). An address latch is used to separate addresses from data transmitted over the common AD bus. As in the 8085 case, memory and IO interface chips are available that can themselves demultiplex the AD bus to separate addresses from data. The control lines named $\overline{\text{WR}}$, $\overline{\text{RD}}$, M/$\overline{\text{IO}}$, and READY are used for data-transfer control, and have exact counterparts in the 8085 (see Fig. 5.49). Interrupts and DMA operations are supervised in much the same way as they are in the 8080/8085 via the vectored interrupt control lines INTR (interrupt request) and $\overline{\text{INTA}}$ (interrupt acknowledge), and the DMA control lines HOLD (DMA request) and HLDA (DMA acknowledge). In a typical 8086-based microcomputer, interrupts and DMA functions are directed by priority interrupt controllers and DMA controllers, respectively, of the sort presented in Sec. 7.3. For more complex system configurations, especially those containing IOPs or multiple CPUs, the 8086 has a Multibus-compatible "maximum mode" in which the functions of the control lines emanating from the 8086 are changed and additional bus control circuits are required. The bus mode to be used is determined by the setting of the

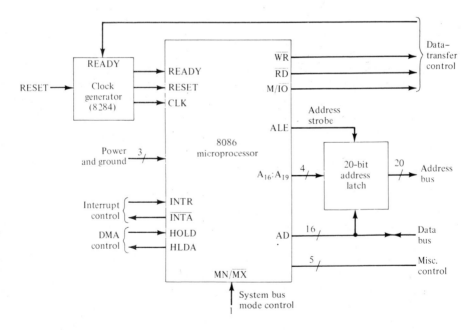

Figure 8.9 8086-based CPU in a minimum-mode system bus configuration.

8086's MN/$\overline{\text{MX}}$ (minimum/maximum) control pin. The use of the 8086's maximum bus mode will be illustrated later in this chapter.

8.1.3 The 68000 Microprocessor

The 68000 represents a substantial extension of the 6800 and 6809 architectures discussed in Sec. 5.3. Although usually classified as a 16-bit machine, it provides a full range of 8-bit and 16-bit operations, and a large number of 32-bit functions. The last, coupled with the fact that its main programmable registers are 32 bits wide, gives the 68000 the general appearance of a 32-bit microprocessor. The 68000's instruction repertoire is not compatible with that of the 6800 at any level. It includes new operations such as multiplication and division, as well as some data types and addressing modes not found in the 6800. The 68000 also has a much larger number of general-purpose data and address registers. It has, however, a slightly smaller number of basic instruction types than the 6800, a consequence of using a more systematic way of specifying opcodes and addresses in assembly-language statements. The 68000 has its own family of support circuits, but it is also designed to be directly compatible with 6800-series memory and IO interface circuits. Notable members of the 68000 family include the 68451 memory management unit (MMU), which supports segment addressing, memory protection, and other aspects of virtual memory systems, and the 68881 numerical processor for floating-point arithmetic.

The internal organization of the 68000 is depicted in Fig. 8.10. Remedying a major shortcoming of the 6800, there is a large number of general-purpose CPU registers. These include eight data registers D0:D7 and seven data registers A0:A6, all of which are 32 bits wide. An eighth address register position is occupied by a pair of stack pointer registers designated A7 (user stack pointer) and A7' (supervisor stack pointer). The data and address registers are quite general in the sense that, with the exception of A7 and A7', any data or address register can be used for any data or address storage purpose respectively. Any address register, for example, can be defined by the programmer to be an index or base register. There is no special accumulator register; any data register Di may be treated as an accumulator. Di can serve as the source or destination of either 8-, 16-, or 32-bit operands, in which case only its low-order 8, 16, or 32 flip-flop, respectively, are used. Operand size is specified by instruction opcodes; hence the one name "Di" serves to designate data register Di as an 8-, 16-, or 32-bit operand storage location. In a similar manner, the address registers can be used to accommodate either 16-bit partial addresses or 32-bit full addresses. A program counter PC and a status (flag) register SR complete the 68000's programmable register set.

The 68000 has a relatively large 64-pin DIP as its standard package (see Fig. 1.24). This makes it possible to connect separate address and data buses directly to the 68000. The data bus is 16 bits wide, which, as much as anything, contributes to the 68000's designation as a 16-bit microprocessor. Like most microprocessors, the 68000 treats the 8-bit byte as the smallest addressable unit of main memory. Its 32-bit internal address registers make it capable, in principle, of addressing up to 2^{32} bytes of memory. The original version of the 68000 can address only 2^{24} memory bytes, however. Since two adjacent bytes can be transferred simultaneously via the 16-bit system data bus, 23 address lines emerge from the 68000, as indicated in Fig. 8.10. This truncation of the external address bus by 8 bits is primarily due to an insufficient number of pins being available, even with the 64-pin package. Newer 68000-series microprocessors have non-DIP packages with more pins, and allow all 32 possible address bits to be fully used.

The 68000 machine-language instructions may include from one to four 16-bit words. The first word contains the opcode, and specifies the operand addressing modes to be used. Short addresses, such as CPU register names, may also be included in the opcode word. Additional words are used to specify immediate operands and memory addresses. The addressing modes of the 68000 are described by Fig. 8.11. Most of the

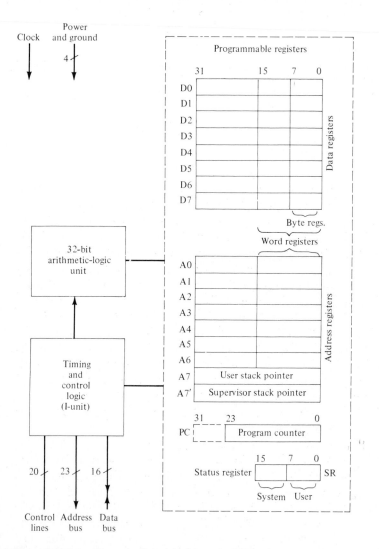

Figure 8.10 Internal organization of the Motorola 68000 microprocessor.

Major Type	Subtype	Address Fields in Instruction	Operand Location	Additional Operations
Immediate	Immediate	8-, 16-, or 32-bit data item	Instruction	
Direct	Register direct	Name R of data, address, or status register	Register R	
	Memory direct (absolute addressing)	16- or 32-bit main memory address ADR	M[ADR]	
Indirect	Indirect	Name Ai of address register	M[Ai]	
	Indirect with displacement	Name Ai of address register and 16-bit displacement DISP	M[Ai + DISP]	
	Indirect with predecrement	Name Ai of address register	M[Ai − N] where N is the operand size in bytes	Ai := Ai − N
	Indirect with postincrement	Name Ai of address register	M[Ai]	Ai := Ai + N
Indexed	Indexed indirect with displacement	Address register Ai, index (address or data) register Rj, and 16-bit displacement DISP	M[Ai + Rj + DISP]	
Relative	Relative	16-bit displacement DISP	M[PC + DISP]	
	Relative indexed	Index (address or data) register Rj and 8-bit displacement DISP	M[PC + Rj + DISP]	

Figure 8.11 Addressing modes of the 68000.

addressing techniques encountered already, including immediate, direct, indirect, indexed, and relative addressing, are implemented. The autoindexing methods of the 6809, namely, predecrementing and postincrementing of address registers, are also used by the 68000. Instructions may contain up to two explicit address fields defining operands in main memory or the CPU. The permissible combinations of addressing modes vary from instruction to instruction. The largest number of combinations are allowed with move instructions. Figure 8.12 gives a sampling of move statements in 68000 assembly language, which indicates the range of addressing possibilities. Note that, unlike any of the microprocessors studied so far, memory-to-memory data transfers can be specified by a single move instruction. There are no provisions for segment addressing like that of the 8086. Figure 8.11 also illustrates how different operand sizes are defined by appending a size parameter B (byte), W (16-bit word), or L (32-bit long word) to the basic opcode, in this case MOVE. W is the default size parameter, so that MOVE and MOVE.W are equivalent opcodes for "move word."

The 68000's instruction types are summarized in Fig. 8.13. The data-transfer instructions are noteworthy for the large number of source-destination combinations allowed, including register to register, register to or from memory, and memory to memory. There are no explicit instructions for IO data transfers since, like its predecessors, the 68000 employs memory-mapped IO. The usual push and pop stack instructions are also missing, as they are easily implemented via move instructions and the 68000's autoindexing addressing modes. For example, the instruction

$$\text{MOVE.L} \quad D1, \ -(A7) \tag{8.4}$$

is equivalent to the operation push D1. A7 serves as the stack pointer, and the predecre-

Instruction	Meaning
MOVE D0, D1	Move 16-bit word from data register D0 to data register D1
MOVE.B D1, D0	Move byte from data register D1 to data register D0
MOVE.L D2, A6	Move 32-bit long word from data register D2 to address register A6
MOVE.L #63490, D7	Move immediate 16-bit operand representing 63490_{10} to data register D7
MOVE.W $1000, A0	Move word at $M[1000_{16}]$ to A0
MOVE.B $170924, $213FFF	Move byte from $M[170924_{16}]$ to $M[213FFF_{16}]$
MOVE.L #$FFFFFFFF, 0	Move immediate long operand $FFFFFFFF_{16}$ to $M[0]:M[3]$
MOVE.B (A6), (A0)	Move byte from $M[A6]$ to $M[A0]$
MOVE ALPHA, $1000(A6)	Move word from $M[ALPHA]$ to $M[A6 + 1000_{16}]$
MOVE.L $-$(A1), (A2)$+$	Predecrement A1 by four, move long word from $M[A1]$ to $M[A2]$, and postincrement A2 by four
MOVE.W ALPHA(A5), BETA(A4,D0)	Move word from $M[A5 + ALPHA]$ to $M[A4 + D0 + BETA]$, where D0 serves as an index
MOVE.B $FFFF(A0,D6), $-$(A7)	Predecrement A7 by one, and move byte from $M[A0 + D6 + FFFF_{16}]$ to $M[A7]$

Figure 8.12 Examples of move instructions in 68000 assembly language.

ment operation causes it to be decremented by four, before the contents of D1 are transferred to M[A7]. The new value of A7 now points to the topmost location of the (downward-growing) stack area in main memory. The pop operation corresponding to (8.4) is

$$\text{MOVE.L} \quad (A7)+, \ D1$$

The data-processing instructions include a standard complement of arithmetic operations, Boolean functions, and shifts. To facilitate the programming of multiprecision arithmetic operations, the usual add/subtract with carry/borrow instructions are provided. For these operations the 68000 has an "extend" flag X that duplicates the normal carry flag in most respects. The 68000 also has signed and unsigned multiply and divide instructions similar to those of the 8086. For decimal arithmetic there are proper

Type	Instruction
Data transfer	Move byte/word/long word
	Move register set to/from memory
	Move effective address to register or stack
	Exchange two registers
	Exchange left and right halves of register
	Clear register or memory location
	Set register or memory location conditionally
Data processing	Binary add with/without carry
	Binary subtract with/without borrow
	Binary multiply with signed/unsigned operands
	Binary divide with signed/unsigned operands
	Binary negate
	Decimal add/subtract/negate with carry/borrow
	And
	Or
	Exclusive-or
	Complement (not)
	Rotate left/right with/without extend flag
	Arithmetic shift left/right
	Logical shift left/right
Program control	Jump conditionally/unconditionally
	Call subroutine
	Return from subroutine
	Decrement counter and branch conditionally (loop)
	Test bit and modify bit and/or flag
	Compare operands and set flags
	Allocate/deallocate working area in stack (link/unlink)
	Trap conditionally/unconditionally (supervisor call)
	Check register bounds
	Reset external devices
	Halt
	No operation

Figure 8.13 Summary of the 68000 instruction set.

decimal add and subtract instructions, which eliminate the cumbersome decimal-adjust instructions found in earlier microprocessors.

In the program control area we find standard conditional and unconditional branch instructions, as well as subroutine call and return instructions. Also present is a loop instruction that, as in the 8086, combines the functions of iteration counting and conditional branching. Several instructions allow individual bits within an operand to be tested and modified. A pair of instructions called link and unlink are intended for allocating and deallocating temporary storage areas in the main memory stack. This space may be used, for example, to pass parameters to a procedure. The link instruction

$$\text{LINK} \quad \text{Ai}, \ \#-\text{n} \tag{8.5}$$

has the following effect. The contents of the named address register Ai are pushed into the stack. The stack pointer A7 is automatically updated as part of the push operation, and the new value of A7 is loaded into Ai. Then the displacement $-$ n from (8.5) is added to the stack pointer value in A7. Figure 8.14 shows the relevant parts of a 68000-based system before and after execution of this link instruction. The contents of Ai are termed a *frame pointer* because, along with the stack pointer A7, they serve to frame or delimit an *n*-byte working storage area at the top of the stack. The stack space allocated by LINK can be subsequently deallocated or freed by executing the unlink instruction

$$\text{UNLK} \quad \text{Ai}$$

which reverses the process depicted in Fig. 8.14.

The 68000 has two major modes of operation or system states determined by the value of the S (supervisor) flag bit in its status register SR. When S $= 1$, the CPU is in the supervisor state, which is intended to be the state used during the execution of operating system routines or similar supervisory programs. Most programs are executed in the user state, which is indicated by S $= 0$. There is a small set of privileged instructions that can only be executed by the 68000 when it is in the supervisor state. An obvious example of a privileged instruction in the 68000 is the halt instruction STOP; one does not want ordinary programs to be able to halt the CPU in a multiuser environment. Instructions that affect the supervisor flag S are also privileged to prevent user programs from changing the system state from the user to the supervisor state, thereby becoming able to execute the privileged instructions. When stack instructions are executed in the supervisor state, A7' is used as the stack pointer in place of A7. This makes it possible to maintain a clear separation between the stacks used by the operating system and those of user programs.

Various errors occurring during program execution are automatically detected by the 68000. Examples of such errors are:

1. An attempt to divide by zero during the execution of a division instruction
2. An attempt to execute a privileged instruction while in the user state; this is called a *privilege violation*
3. An attempt to execute an *illegal instruction* whose first word does not contain a valid opcode field
4. Receipt of an error signal from an external device

The 68000 responds to any of these error conditions by saving SR, switching the supervisor flag S from 0 to 1, saving the program counter PC in the system stack area defined by A7′, and finally loading PC with a new address that it fetches from an address in main memory that is preassigned to the error in question. This address is normally the entry address of an operating-system routine designed to handle the error. A privilege violation, for instance, may be handled by aborting the responsible user program.

The detection and processing of errors in the foregoing manner by the CPU is called a *trap*. A trap may also be defined as a CPU-initiated interrupt, since the CPU's actions during a trap are similar to its response to an externally generated IO interrupt. Traps, interrupts, and related system conditions are lumped together under the heading of *exceptions*. The 68000 has been designed to deal with all forms of exceptions in a consistent way. Exception processing can also be initiated by user programs via special trap instructions. These correspond to *supervisor call* instructions in some large comput-

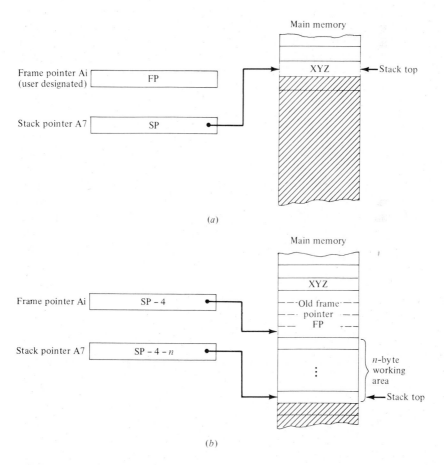

Figure 8.14 State of a 68000-based system (*a*) before, and (*b*) after execution of the link instruction LINK Ai, #n.

ers, and they enable user programs to communicate directly with an operating system. The basic trap instruction in the 68000 takes the form

$$\text{TRAP} \quad \#\text{ADR}$$

Execution of this instruction causes SR and PC to be saved in the system stack; S is set to 1 and the address ADR is loaded into PC. Another useful trap instruction is the register bounds check instruction CHK. For example,

$$\text{CHK} \quad \#\text{BOUND, Di}$$

compares the variable X stored in data register Di with the value BOUND. If $X >$ BOUND or $X < 0$, then a trap to a predefined address occurs. CHK is useful for determining if an index value for an array lies within its proper range.

Figure 8.15 illustrates the 68000 assembly language for the 32-digit decimal addition problem

$$\text{BETA} := \text{ALPHA} + \text{BETA}$$

which has served as a running example since Chap. 5. The language itself is quite conventional, and has none of the structuring features of the 8086 assembly language (cf. Fig. 8.8). The 68000 has one decimal add instruction ABCD called add decimal with extend, that is, add with carry. ABCD is restricted to 1-byte operands, and thus 32-digit addition requires 16 successive 1-byte additions as do all the previous versions of this program. Only two addressing modes are allowed with ABCD, namely, data-register-to-data-register direct and memory-to-memory indirect with predecrementing. The latter addressing method is used in Fig. 8.15. Termination is controlled in standard fashion by comparing the contents of one of the address registers with its final expected value.

The 64 external pins of the 68000 are assigned to the functions shown in Fig. 8.16. As discussed earlier, 39 pins are used for data (16) and address (23) transmission. Four pins act as power (+ 5 V) and ground connections, and one receives a clock signal CLK from an external clock generator. The remaining 20 pins are used for control purposes, including data transfer, interrupt, and system bus-access control. These lines allow the 68000 to be attached to a fairly powerful system bus with many of the features found in the Multibus (cf. Fig. 7.50).

Location	Instruction	Comment
	MOVE #0, CCR	Clear condition code part, including carry flags, of SR
	MOVE #ALPHA + 17, A0	Initialize pointer to operand ALPHA
	MOVE #BETA + 17, A1	Initialize pointer to operand BETA
LOOP	ABCD − (A0), − (A1)	A0 := A0 − 1, A1 := A1 − 1; M[A1] := M[A0] + M[A1] + X; (Add decimal with extend/carry flag X)
	CMPI #BETA + 1, A1	Compare immediate BETA + 1 to A1 and set Z flag to 1 if equal; reset Z to 0 otherwise
	BNE LOOP	Branch to LOOP if Z is nonzero

Figure 8.15 68000 assembly-language program to add two 32-digit decimal numbers.

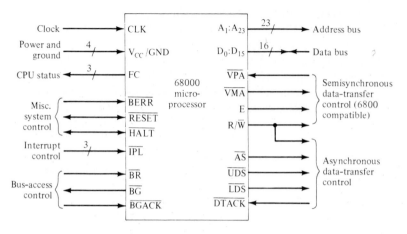

Figure 8.16 External connections of the 68000.

To simplify interfacing to 6800-series devices, the 68000 has three control lines E (enable), $\overline{\text{VMA}}$ (valid memory address), and R/$\overline{\text{W}}$, which are exact counterparts of data-transfer control signals in the 6800, and control 6800-style semisynchronous data transfers over the system bus. The $\overline{\text{VPA}}$ (valid peripheral address) signal forces the 68000 into a 6800-compatible mode of operation for handling data transfers and interrupt requests. There is an additional set of control lines, including data ready/request and data acknowlege lines, which control more general asynchronous data transfers in conventional fashion.

Three lines are used for system bus-access control when several bus masters are present, including multiple CPUs and DMA controllers. Consider the case in which a 68000 shares the system bus with a DMA controller. The latter requests access to the bus by activating the $\overline{\text{BR}}$ (bus request) line. The 68000 responds at the end of its current bus cycle by floating the data-transfer lines and activating $\overline{\text{BG}}$ (bus grant). The DMA controller now becomes the bus master, and indicates this fact by activating the bus-busy signal $\overline{\text{BGACK}}$ (bus grant acknowledge). If several potential bus masters can request bus access simultaneously, the $\overline{\text{BG}}$ signal must be processed by a priority resolution circuit that transmits $\overline{\text{BG}}$ only to the requesting device of highest priority.

A set of three control lines named $\overline{\text{IPL}}$ (interrupt priority level) are used in 68000-based systems both to signal the presence of an interrupt and to specify its priority level. The all-0 condition $\overline{\text{IPL}} = 000$ indicates that there are no pending interrupt requests. A nonzero value n on $\overline{\text{IPL}}$ signals an interrupt request of priority level n; thus interrupts may be assigned seven different priority levels. The 68000's status register SR stores a programmable 3-bit interrupt mask. The 68000 responds to an interrupt only if its priority level n exceeds the value currently stored in the interrupt mask in SR. Interrupts are processed by saving both SR and PC in the supervisor stack area, and loading an interrupt address or vector into PC, which points to an appropriate interrupt service program. The supervisor flag S is also set to 1 since interrupts, like all 68000 exceptions, are designed to be processed in the supervisor mode.

The 68000 can respond to nonmasked interrupt requests in two different ways. If the $\overline{\text{VPA}}$ line is active, then the CPU uses the value of n appearing on the $\overline{\text{IPL}}$ lines to construct one of seven predefined interrupt vectors ADR(n). This is termed automatic vectoring, and can be considered as a limited form of vectored interrupt control, where the interrupting device supplies a 3-bit partial interrupt address to the CPU; compare the use of 1-byte RST call instructions in 8080/8085-based systems. The 68000 also supports a more general form of vectored interrupt control in which the interrupt source supplies an 8-bit address via the system data bus. A somewhat complex exchange of control signals is used with this second type of interrupt. The 3-bit FC (function code) bus signals the interrupt-acknowledge condition, and the asynchronous data-transfer control lines are used to control the transfer of the interrupt vector over the data bus to the CPU.

Besides their role in interrupt processing, the FC lines have the general task of signaling the CPU's overall status, including the current value of the S flag and the type of the current bus cycle (instruction fetch or data transfer). The information provided by FC can be used for memory protection by separating supervisor and user storage regions, or separating program and data regions (see Prob. 8.13). The remaining control lines of the 68000 perform various system control functions. $\overline{\text{RESET}}$ may be used as an input signal to initialize the 68000 at the beginning of system operation. It also serves as an output signal that is activated by executing the RESET instruction, in which case the $\overline{\text{RESET}}$ signal is normally used to initialize other components of the system, for example, IO device controllers. $\overline{\text{HALT}}$ can be used to force the 68000 into a waiting state at the end of its current bus cycle, at which time it deactivates or floats all its connections to the system bus. It can also be used as an output line to indicate to external devices that the CPU has halted. $\overline{\text{BERR}}$ (bus error) is intended to inform the CPU of problems occurring in external devices, such as a device's inability to complete its part of a bus cycle. For example, if the device fails to respond to an asynchronous read request within a reasonable time, a suitable timing circuit monitoring the system control lines can be used to activate $\overline{\text{BERR}}$, thus bringing the problem to the CPU's attention. The CPU can respond either by retrying the unsuccessful bus cycle, or else by initiating a bus-error trap sequence.

8.2 BIT-SLICED MICROPROCESSORS

Bit slicing is the basis of a powerful class of integrated components that allow system designers to specify their own unique microprocessor architecture. This section examines bit slicing and the related control method of microprogramming, which are used in most bit-sliced systems. The 2900 bit-sliced microprocessor series is reviewed and applied to the design of a microprocessor that emulates the 8080.

8.2.1 Bit Slicing

All the microprocessors discussed so far have their structure and behavior fully defined during manufacture. The acceptable instruction and data types, for example, are wired into the data-processing E-unit and the program-controlling I-unit. If different operations and data types must be processed (e.g., multiplication of fixed-point numbers of nonstandard length), then the necessary instructions and operands must be simulated by software. This, of course, is much slower than direct hardware implementation. The speed of most microprocessors is also limited by their use of MOS circuit technologies that allow high component densities at the expense of lower operating speeds as measured, say, by the maximum permissible CPU clock rate. Thus the very high speeds achievable with various TTL and ECL bipolar technologies have not been widely available in standard microprocessors. Bit slicing solves these problems by providing flexible building blocks for microprocessor design that can take advantage of the fastest current IC technologies.

The fundamental bit-sliced device is a (micro) *processor slice,* which is the E-unit for a simple CPU with a small data word size, typically 4 bits. The key property of a k-bit processor slice is the fact that n copies of the slice can be interconnected in a simple and regular manner to form an nk-bit processor that performs the same functions as a single slice on nk-bit rather than k-bit operands. The processor slices are interconnected in the form of a cascade circuit or one-dimensional array, as depicted in Fig. 8.17. The term "bit slicing" arises from the similarity between the processor array and a large processor that has been sliced into n identical subprocessors, each operating on a k-bit portion or slice of the data being processed by the array. As indicated in the figure, the same control lines are connected to all slices, so that, in general, they all perform the same operations at the same time; these operations are independent of n, the number of slices in the processor array. The k-bit data buses that transmit operands to or from the slices are simply merged to form kn-bit data buses for the array. Additional data connections may link adjacent slices, for instance, to allow the transmission of carry/borrow signals from slice to slice during arithmetic operations.

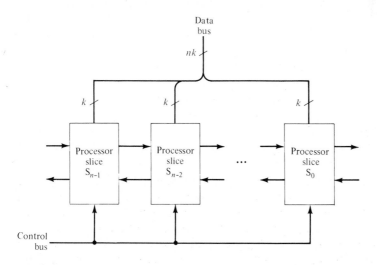

Figure 8.17 General structure of an nk-bit bit-sliced microprocessor composed of n k-bit slices.

Clearly bit slicing makes it easy to tailor a microprocessor's data word size to a particular application. By using six 4-bit slices, for example, a 24-bit processor can be constructed. Moreover, a bit-sliced processor can easily be partitioned dynamically into subarrays of various sizes, which simplifies the processing of operands of different sizes—16-bit data words and 24-bit addresses, for example. Since the individual slices correspond to simple microprocessors without the usual I-units, they are small enough for fabrication using TTL or ECL circuit designs. The small word size used for the processor slices also alleviates another common problem in microprocessors, namely, the limited number of pins available in standard DIP packages.

It is apparent that the operations carried out in a bit-sliced processor must be such that all interactions between slices can be reduced to a transfer of signals between adjacent slices. In the terms used in Chap. 4, the slices must be expandable via the array interconnection structure of Fig. 8.17. A review of the MSI and LSI circuits discussed there will show that all the functions found in simpler microprocessors can be realized by components that are expandable in bit-sliced fashion. Data-transfer instructions primarily involve data buses and parallel registers, which can easily be bit sliced, since no interaction occurs between adjacent data bits. The 7400-series latch and register of Figs. 4.28 and 4.29, respectively, clearly display the bit-sliced structure of Fig. 8.17. Boolean operations such as and, or, and exclusive-or similarly involve no interactions between adjacent data bits, and can be realized by bit-sliced gate arrays (word gates). Ripple-carry adders constitute bit-sliced implementations of binary add and subtract with carry/borrow signals propagated from slice to slice. Other examples of bit-sliceable devices encountered earlier are shift registers and counters. Combinational ALU circuits such as the 74181 4-bit ALU are simple processor slices capable of addition, subtraction, logical, and data-transfer operations. Figure 4.27a shows a bit-sliced 16-bit ALU composed of four 74181s. The processor slices considered in this chapter are basically ALU slices of this type, with the addition of small RAMs (register files) and the input-output buses and control functions needed to support a general microprocessor-type instruction set.

To construct a complete CPU, it is necessary to combine a bit-sliced E-unit with an I-unit that can fetch and decode the instructions to be executed by the E-unit. The I-unit of a bit-sliced CPU is usually microprogrammed, and has the general organization shown in Fig. 8.18. Microprogramming, which was briefly introduced in Sec. 4.3.5, gives the designer flexibility in designing the I-unit similar to that provided by bit slicing in the case of the E-unit. The control sequences to be activated during the execution of the instructions are stored as lists of microinstructions, that is, microprograms, in a special memory (usually a ROM or PROM) called the control memory CM. This is contrasted with hardwired control, in which the control sequences produced by the I-unit are generated by special-purpose sequential logic circuits. The circuits needed to fetch microinstructions from CM are collectively referred to as a *microprogram sequencer* or microprogram controller. As we will see shortly, the bit-slicing concept can also be applied to microprogram sequencers.

The first commercial bit-sliced component families appeared quite early in the evolution of microprocessors (Hayes, 1981). In 1973, National Semiconductor introduced a pMOS microprocessor series called GPC/P (General Purpose Controller/

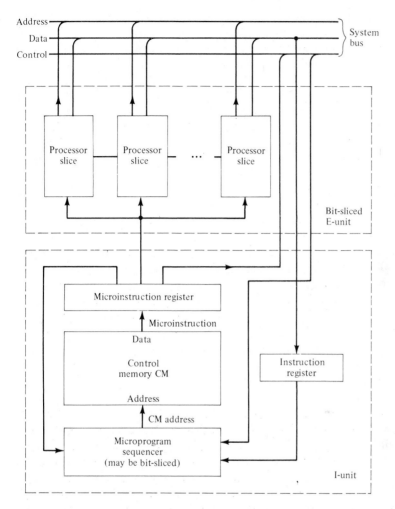

Figure 8.18 Outline of a bit-sliced microprocessor employing microprogrammed control.

Processor) based on a 4-bit processor slice named a RALU (register and arithmetic-logic unit). It was followed by the more widely used Intel 3000 series, which employed much faster Schottky TTL technology. The 3002 processor slice of this series was unusual in its use of a 2-bit data word size (see Prob. 8.30). One of the most popular bit-sliced families was the 2900 series introduced by Advanced Micro Devices (AMD) in 1976, which, like the 3000 series, employs Schottky TTL logic, but with 4-bit processor slices. This important family is discussed in detail in the remainder of this section. Several ECL bit-sliced microprocessor series also exist, including the Motorola 10800 and the Fairchild 100200 series; the latter is one of the first to include an 8-bit processor slice.

Figure 8.19 summarizes the advantages and disadvantages of using bit slicing in microprocessor design. The system designer can specify the processor word size(s), the

1. Data word size(s) of processor can be customized
2. Instruction set can be customized via microprogramming
3. Faster IC technologies such as TTL and ECL can be used
4. A large number of ICs are required to form a complete CPU
5. High development costs are incurred for hardware design and microprogramming

Figure 8.19 Main characteristics of bit-sliced microprocessors.

composition of the instruction set, and other key architectural features, and can optimize them for a particular application. In addition, faster IC technologies can be used, which might be unsuitable for fabricating larger non-bit-sliced microprocessors because of restrictions on IC component density, power dissipation, and pin count. The price paid for this increase in flexibility and speed is the large number of ICs needed to build a CPU, and the substantial increase in the total design effort required. A further disadvantage is the nonstandard instruction sets usually designed for bit-sliced computers, which prevent the use of widely available standard software.

Bit-sliced microprocessors have found their main applications in special-purpose systems requiring unusually high data-transfer or arithmetic-processing rates. Examples of such systems are graphics display terminals, navigation control systems, and large general-purpose computers. These applications exploit the inherent speed advantage of the faster IC logic families used, as well as the design flexibility resulting from bit slicing and microprogramming. The speed advantage deriving from the IC technology used can be expected to diminish as manufacturing improvements allow those technologies to be applied to conventional non-bit-sliced microprocessors.

8.2.2 Microprogramming

The I-unit, or program-control unit, of a CPU is responsible for fetching instructions from main memory, interpreting their opcodes, and activating the control signals that trigger the various steps required to execute the instructions. It must also respond to external control signals generated by the E-unit or IO devices that affect the instruction execution sequence. For example, status (flag) signals from the E-unit influence the behavior of conditional branch instructions. Instruction execution is also modified by interrupt and DMA requests from IO devices. Because it usually must deal with hundreds of different machine-language opcodes and a comparable number of different control signals, the I-unit is one of the most complex parts of a computer, and therefore one of the most difficult to design.

Two basic approaches to I-unit design have evolved—hardwiring and microprogramming. Hardwired I-units employ a fixed sequential logic circuit to produce the required control signals; see Fig. 8.20a. The design of the I-unit is thus tailored to a specific instruction set, and can be optimized with respect to operating speed and hardware cost. The control information associated with each instruction is effectively embedded in the I-unit's logic circuits. Hardwired I-units tend to have unstructured or "random" interconnections, especially when an attempt is made to minimize the number of gates or transistors used in their design. Changes in the instruction set (e.g.. to

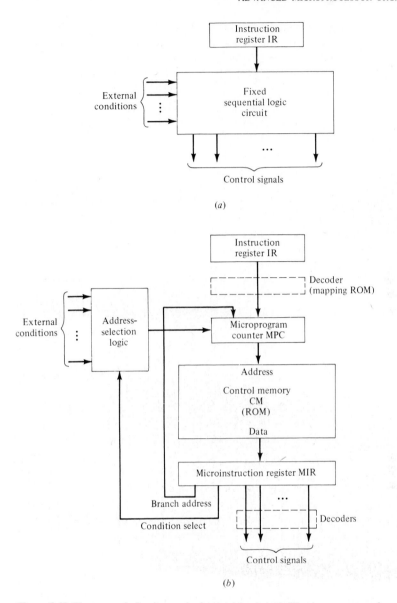

Figure 8.20 The two main I-unit organizations: (*a*) hardwired; (*b*) microprogrammed.

correct errors during design development) require some or all of the I-unit to be redesigned, and this is a costly and time-consuming process. Because of their complexity, hardwired I-units are particularly prone to design errors. They are also difficult to redesign to extend the instruction set, a common requirement in the evolution of microprocessor families.

Microprogramming was defined by Maurice V. Wilkes of Cambridge University, and others, in the 1950s as a technique for making I-unit design more systematic and flexible. Consequently, despite their common micro prefix, the concepts of microprogramming and microprocessor are unrelated. The typical organization of a microprogrammable I-unit is illustrated in Fig. 8.20b. Control information is stored in the form of microprograms—related sequences of microinstructions—in a control memory CM. There is usually one microprogram for each instruction type, with additional microinstructions for such functions as instruction fetching, operand address calculation, and interrupt processing. A microprogram is executed by fetching its constituent microinstructions one by one from CM. Each microinstruction is loaded into the microinstruction register MIR from which the corresponding control signal values are obtained, possibly after some additional decoding. The microprogram counter MPC serves as the address register for CM. MPC is incremented by one during the execution of each microinstruction, so that it points to the next consecutive microinstruction stored in CM. The address-selection logic connected to MPC allows it to be loaded with a nonconsecutive branch address in response to external conditions. The branch address is normally obtained from an address field within the current microinstruction in MIR; a condition-select field specifies which of the possible external signals is to be used as the branching condition.

A microprogrammed computer has two distinct levels of control: the instruction level and the microinstruction level. At the instruction level the CPU continually executes instruction cycles that involve the following steps.

1. The CPU fetches from main memory M an instruction I whose address is stored in the program counter PC.
2. The opcode part of I is placed in an instruction register IR; the operation specified by IR is then decoded and executed.
3. PC is altered to point to the next instruction to be fetched from M.

A similar sequence of operations takes place at the lower microinstruction level, where the I-unit continually executes *microinstruction cycles* as follows:

1. The addressing portion (microprogram sequencer) of the I-unit fetches from the control memory CM a microinstruction MI whose address is stored in the microprogram counter MPC.
2. MI is loaded into the microinstruction register MIR and is decoded, if necessary, to produce the required control signals.
3. MPC is altered to point to the next microinstruction to be fetched from CM.

A microinstruction cycle can be executed faster than an instruction cycle, since microinstructions are stored within the CPU, whereas instructions must be fetched from an external memory. Microinstructions also normally require less decoding than instructions.

The actions controlled by microinstructions take the form of *microoperations* that can be performed directly by the underlying hardware. These microoperations include loading registers, routing data via multiplexers, decoders, buses, and so on through a

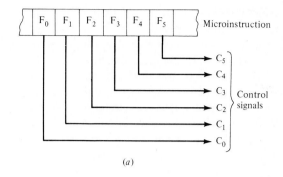

(a)

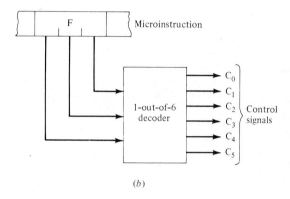

(b)

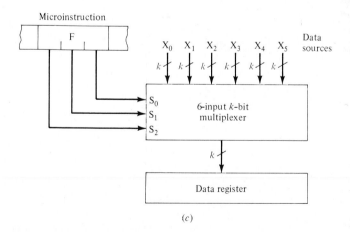

(c)

Figure 8.22 Partial microinstructions showing: (a) unencoded control fields; (b) encoded control field requiring decoding; (c) encoded control field not requiring decoding.

control functions of the form "load data from source X_i into register R." The data are routed to the register in the conventional manner via a multiplexer. Clearly, with an appropriate choice of bit patterns for F, the three lines from F can be connected directly to the select inputs S of the multiplexer as shown.

As an illustration of microprogrammed control design, consider the unsigned binary multiplication process discussed in Sec. 4.2.4, which uses the circuit of Fig. 4.47 and the shift-and-add algorithm of Fig. 4.48. The multiplier circuit resembles a simple CPU, since it is capable of implementing such instructions as add, shift, multiply, etc. (see Prob. 8.19). A hardwired control unit for this multiplier appears in Fig. 4.49. A microprogrammed control unit might have the structure shown in Fig. 8.23a; note that it contains essentially the same hardware as the microprogrammed I-unit of Fig. 8.20b. A straightforward horizontal microinstruction format is used in which a 1-bit control field is associated with every control signal identified in the original design; the mnemonic names of these control signals indicate their functions. A 4-bit branch address field BA permits a 16-word CM to be used, which is ample for the multiply microprogram, and a few additional microprograms. Conditional branching is controlled by a 3-bit condition-select field CS, which allows six branching conditions, unconditional branching, and no branching to be specified. The meaning of a microinstruction with this format may be defined symbolically as follows.

$$C_0 := F_0, C_1 := F_1, \ldots, C_7 := F_7, \textbf{if } CS = \textbf{true then } MPC := BA$$
$$\textbf{else } MPC := MPC + 1;$$

An analysis of the multiplication algorithm yields the conditions that must be tested, which are the value of the low-order multiplier bit $Q[0]$, the value of the START line, and the counter output EO, which is activated when the counter reaches its maximum value.

Figure 8.24 contains a microprogram implementing multiplication using the "E-unit" of Fig. 4.47 and the "I-unit" of Fig. 8.23. The following meanings have been attached to the condition select fields.

CS	Meaning
000	No branching
001	Unconditional branching
010	Branch if $Q[0] = 0$
011	Branch if START $= 0$
100	Branch if EO $= 0$

The microprogram consists of eight microinstructions, including those needed to load the input operands and output the results. The first microinstruction MI_0 is stored in CM location 0000. It has no active control fields and serves as a conditional branch microinstruction. Its condition-select field $CS = 011$ indicates that the branch condition is START $= 0$. The branch address is 0000, that is, the address of MI_0 itself. Hence MI_0 can be described as follows:

$$\textbf{if } START = 0 \textbf{ then } MPC := 0000 \textbf{ else } MPC := 0001;$$

MI_0 thus causes the control unit to wait until START becomes 1, at which point the

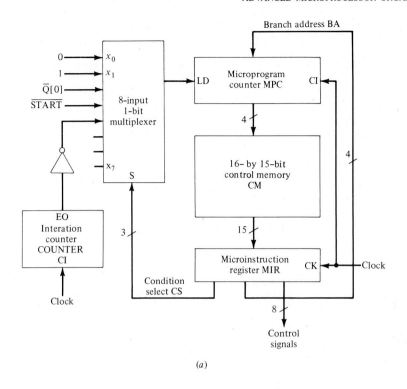

(a)

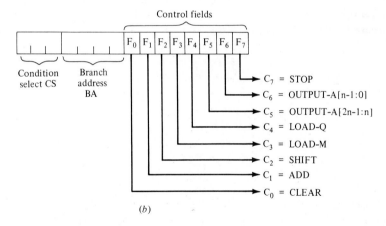

(b)

Figure 8.23 (a) Microprogrammed control unit for the multiplier of Fig. 4.47; (b) its microinstruction format.

second microinstruction MI_1 is fetched from location 0001. MI_1 activates the CLEAR control signal, which resets the accumulator A and the iteration counter COUNTER to zero; it also activates LOAD-Q, which transfers a word, the multiplier operand, from the

Microinstruction

Location in CM	Condition Select CS	Branch Address BA	Control Fields								Comment
			CLEAR	ADD	SHIFT	LOAD-M	LOAD-Q	OUTPUT-A[2n-1:n]	OUTPUT-A[n-1:0]	STOP	
0000	011	0000	0	0	0	0	0	0	0	0	Wait until START = 1.
0001	000	1111	1	0	0	0	1	0	0	0	Clear A and COUNTER; load multiplier.
0010	000	1111	0	0	0	1	0	0	0	0	Load multiplicand.
0011	010	0101	0	0	0	0	0	0	0	0	Test Q[0] and skip add step if Q[0]=0.
0100	000	1111	0	1	0	0	0	0	0	0	Add M to A.
0101	100	0011	0	0	1	0	0	0	0	0	Shift A and Q; go to 0011_2 if EO = 0.
0110	000	1111	0	0	0	0	0	1	0	1	Output high-order half of product.
0111	001	0000	0	0	0	0	0	0	1	0	Output low-order half of product and go to 0000_2.

Figure 8.24 Microprogram for unsigned binary multiplication.

input bus DATA-IN to the multiplier register Q. No branching is required after executing MI_1; hence its CS field is set to 000, and its branch address field is not used and so can contain arbitrary values. MI_1 thus performs the following microoperations:

$$Q := \text{DATA-IN}, \ A := 0, \ \text{COUNTER} := 0, \ \text{MPC} := 0002;$$

The remaining microinstructions are similarly interpreted; they have been derived directly from the algorithm listed in Fig. 4.47. As Fig. 8.23a demonstrates, the address-selection logic for the control unit consists of a simple multiplexer whose output line is attached to the parallel load line LD of the MPC. The various test condition signals are applied to the data inputs of the multiplexer, while the microinstruction CS field is applied to its select input S. Thus, during each microinstruction cycle, the condition signal selected by CS is applied directly to LD. When the condition signal is 1, the branch address BA is loaded into MPC; otherwise MPC is automatically incremented by one via the system clock signal.

Commercial microprogramed CPUs generally have much more complicated I-units and microinstructions than those of Fig. 8.23. This complexity results from attempts to reduce the number of components and interconnections used, an especially important consideration in one-chip microprocessors and microcomputers. Figure 8.25 shows a simplified version of the microprogrammed I-unit of the 8086 microprocessor (McKevitt & Bayliss, 1979). At its heart is a 504×21 control memory CM storing an emulator for the 8086 instruction set. To reduce the chip area occupied by CM, it is realized by a PLA rather than a ROM (see Probs. 4.49 and 4.50). A fairly short 21-bit microinstruction is used, which is of the vertical type. Instructions are passed to the I-unit from the 8086's 6-byte instruction buffer. A portion of the opcode of the current instruction is placed in the instruction register IR for use as the entry address of a microprogram that interprets the instruction. Certain control information is obtained directly from the instruction via a supplementary decoder ROM (e.g., the main function to be performed by the ALU in the case of arithmetic instructions). The operand fields of the instruction are loaded into two temporary registers designated M and N; these serve as working registers for the I-unit and are not programmable at the instruction level. Microinstructions are fetched from the control memory by the microprogram counter MPC in a more or less conventional way. A subroutine register SR is attached to MPC for use as a one-address stack for storing a return address during a subroutine call within a microprogram. It is convenient to make certain common microprograms, such as a microprogram that computes the effective address for a main memory access, into subroutines, so that their code does not have to be repeated throughout the emulator. Since most microprograms contain only a few micro-instructions, a simple subroutine scheme suffices.

Consider, for example, the 8086 instruction

$$\text{INC} \quad \text{AX}$$

which increments the 16-bit AX register by one. On being fetched from the instruction buffer, part of this 16-bit instruction word is loaded into MPC via IR to provide a starting address to the microprogram that performs the increment operation. An address field in the instruction that names the AX register is loaded into the M register. Finally, the part of the instruction's opcode that specifies the increment operation is applied via the supple-

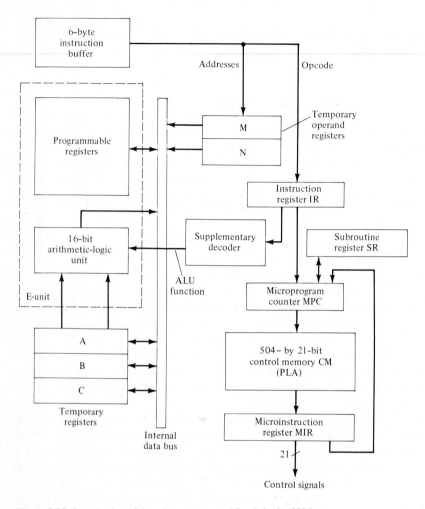

Figure 8.25 Organization of the microprogrammed I-unit in the 8086.

mentary decoder directly to the control inputs of the 8086's main ALU. This completes the instruction fetch operation, and execution of the increment microprogram proper begins. This microprogram consists of two microinstructions. The first of these moves the contents of the programmable register addressed by the M register, in this case AX, to a temporary data register named A, which is connected to one of the two data ports of the ALU; at the same time the ALU is initialized for the increment operation. The second microinstruction performs the operation

$$\text{REGISTER[M]} := A + 1;$$

which increments the contents of the A register and transfers the result to the register addressed by the M register (i.e., AX). Note that the use of the M register for indirectly addressing the main operand allows any increment-register instruction to be executed by the same microprogram. Moreover, the use of the opcode to determine the ALU function directly also allows this microprogram to be used unchanged to implement all the 8086's decrement-register instructions.

8.2.3 The 2900 Family

Since its introduction in 1976, the AMD 2900 series has become one of the most widely used bit-sliced microprocessor families (Advanced Micro Devices, 1978; Mick & Brick, 1980). It comprises a large set of compatible ICs, all with 2900 part numbers, for constructing bit-sliced microprogrammable microcomputers. The series employs low-power Schottky TTL technology, which combines high speed with moderate power consumption. The members of the 2900 family may be grouped as follows:

1. Processor slices
2. Microprogram sequencers, some of which are bit-sliced
3. Memories (RAMs and PROMs)
4. Miscellaneous SSI and MSI circuits (bus transceivers, decoders, registers, etc.)

Standard 74LS00-series ICs may also be used in 2900-based systems. Software design support facilities include the AMDASM microassembly language, and microprocessor development systems with special facilities for microprogram design and testing. A complete microprocessor or microcomputer constructed from 2900-series components can be expected to contain 50 or more ICs. This high component count is balanced by the fact that significantly higher performance can be achieved than is possible with single-chip MOS microprocessors or microcomputers.

The first processor slice in the 2900 series is the 2901 4-bit processor, whose internal organization is illustrated in Fig. 8.26. It is a fairly simple E-unit housed in a 40-pin package. It contains an eight-function combinational ALU and a 16- by 4-bit RAM, which constitutes a set of 16 general-purpose programmable registers; there is also an accumulator-like result register denoted Q. The ALU can perform addition and subtraction on 4-bit twos-complement numbers, as well as some conventional Boolean operations. A pair of shifter circuits allow the contents of the Q register and the ALU result F to be shifted one position either to the left or right. The ALU produces sign, zero, and overflow status flags, as well as the carry information needed for both ripple-carry propagation and carry lookahead. The 2901's RAM is of the dual-port variety, which means that two reads can be performed simultaneously. It is supplied with two addresses A and B, and has two corresponding A and B data output ports; a single input port to the RAM employs only the B address. The RAM's two 4-bit addresses are obtained from microinstruction control fields supplied by the controlling I-unit, as indeed are all the 2901's input control signals. Two 4-bit data buses D and Y allow external data to be transferred to or from the 2901 respectively.

The (micro)operations performed by the 2901, and hence by a bit-sliced array of 2901s, are determined by a 9-bit I (instruction) bus. I is subdivided into three major subfields, which we term I_S, I_F, and I_D. I_S specifies the sources of the ALU's R and S input operands. I_F specifies the function to be performed by the ALU. Finally, I_D indicates the

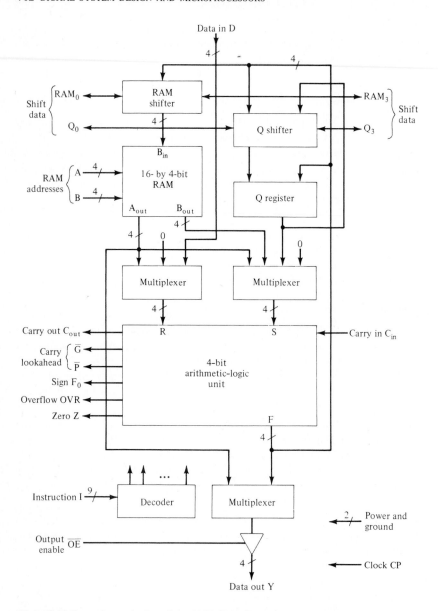

Figure 8.26 Internal organization of the AMD 2901 4-bit microprocessor slice.

destination of the ALU's result F; I_D is also used to specify shifting operations for both F and Q. Figure 8.27 defines all possible ways of specifying I. The ALU has five different input operand sources, including the RAM locations RAM[A] and RAM[B] addressed by the A and B address buses, the Q register, the data bus D, and the constant 0000 (zero). Figure 8.27 gives the eight allowable combinations of these ALU data sources. The

$I_S = I_0{:}I_2$	ALU Sources	
	R	S
000	RAM[A]	Q
001	RAM[A]	RAM[B]
010	0	Q
011	0	RAM[B]
100	0	RAM[A]
101	D	RAM[A]
110	D	Q
111	D	0

$I_F = I_3{:}I_5$	ALU Function
000	$R + S + C_{in}$ (add)
001	$S - R - \overline{C}_{in}$ (subtract)
010	$R - S - \overline{C}_{in}$ (subtract)
011	$R \vee S$ (or)
100	$R \wedge S$ (and)
101	$\overline{R} \wedge S$ (complement-and)
110	$R \oplus S$ (exclusive-or)
111	$\overline{R \oplus S}$ (exclusive-nor)

$I_D = I_6{:}I_8$	ALU Destinations and Shift Functions		
	Y	RAM[B]	Q
000	F	—	F
001	F	—	—
010	RAM[A]	F	—
011	F	F	—
100	F	F/2	Q/2
101	F	F/2	—
110	F	2F	2Q
111	F	2F	—

Figure 8.27 Microoperations specified by the main control bus I of the 2901.

ALU's add and subtract functions include C_{in} as a carry/borrow in signal to allow arithmetic operations to be easily extended across a bit-sliced array of 2901s. It is readily seen that the five Boolean functions of the ALU are logically complete. The 4-bit result F generated by the ALU can be transferred to the Y bus, the Q register, or the RAM location RAM[B], as specified by I_D. In some cases, F is left-shifted or right-shifted (denoted by multiplication and division by two, respectively, in Fig. 8.27) en route to RAM[B]; an auxiliary shift may also be performed on the contents of Q. Note that the 2901 has four bidirectional shift lines that allow shift operations to be extended across an array of 2901s.

Suppose, for example, that it is desired to perform the register-to-register add-and-shift operation

$$RAM[9] := (RAM[7] + RAM[9])/2;$$

This is specified by the following partial microinstruction consisting of six control fields:

$$A, B, I_S, I_F, I_D, C_{in} = 0111, 1001, 001, 000, 101, 0 \qquad (8.7)$$

Note that the intermediate result $F = RAM[A] + RAM[B]$ is placed on the Y bus during the execution of (8.7); the Q register is not affected. A negation operation such as

$$RAM[15] := -RAM[15];$$

can be microprogrammed via subtraction thus:

$$A, B, I_S, I_F, I_D, C_{in} = dddd, 1111, 011, 010, 011, 1$$

where d denotes a don't care value. A simple data transfer such as

$$Q := D;$$

is implemented by the following "dummy" OR operation

$$Q := D \vee 0;$$

which is specified by

$$A, B, I_S, I_F, I_D, C_{in} = dddd, dddd, 111, 011, 000, d$$

This demonstrates the usefulness of zero as an ALU operand.

A $4n$-bit processor is formed by interconnecting n 2901s in the array pattern of Fig. 8.17. Figure 8.28 shows a 16-bit processor composed of four 2901s. The 4-bit D and Y buses of the individual slices are merged to form 16-bit IO buses for the array. Adjacent slices are linked in straightforward fashion by connections between their shift data lines and their carry-in and carry-out lines C_{in} and C_{out}. The instruction bus I, the RAM address buses, and other input control lines are connected in common to all slices. With the indicated connections among the ALU status flags, which are discussed below, the result is a 16-bit processor that behaves as a 16-bit version of the 2901 with a 16- by 16-bit RAM, 16-bit data-processing circuits, and 16-bit buses. Note that the ALUs of the four slices are linked via ripple-carry propagation.

The 2901 generates a conventional set of three flag bits indicating the status of the current ALU result F. The flag information is typically sent to the microprogram sequencer where it can influence microinstruction sequencing. The sign flag F_3 is simply the leftmost bit of F. The zero flag Z (which is called $F = 0$ in AMD literature) is set to 1 whenever $F = 0000$, and is set to 0 otherwise. The remaining flag OVR indicates arithmetic overflow resulting from any of the 2901's three arithmetic operations. Figure 8.28 shows how the individual flag lines are connected in a bit-sliced processor array. The sign and overflow flags are taken directly from the most significant (leftmost) slice;

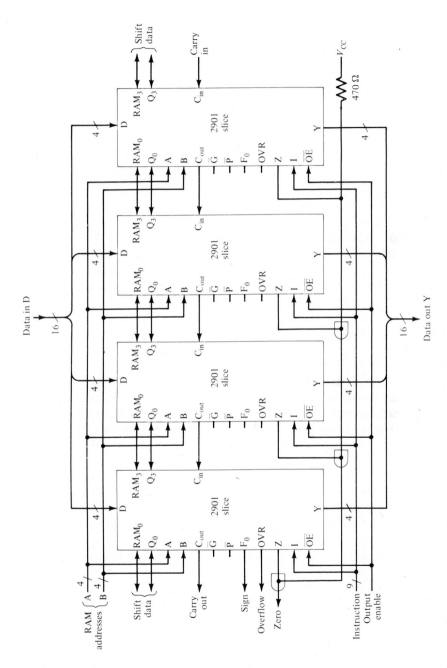

Figure 8.28 16-bit bit-sliced processor array employing ripple-carry propagation.

the corresponding outputs of the other slices are ignored. The zero flag for the array is obtained by tying together the Z outputs of all slices, which are open-collector output lines designed to form a wired AND gate, as indicated in the figure. This means that all Z signals must be 1 in order for a 1 to appear on the zero status line of the array, an event that occurs only when the effective 16-bit ALU of the array produces an all-0 result.

The organization of Fig. 8.28 depends on ripple-carry propagation to extend addition and subtraction across the bit-sliced array. This has the usual drawback that the add or subtract time for an n-slice array increases with n. To provide faster arithmetic operations, the 2901 and all other commercial processor slices support the carry-lookahead technique described in Sec. 4.1.4. This requires replacing the carry-out signal C_{out} by the generate $\overline{G}$ and propagate $\overline{P}$ signals, and using an auxiliary carry-lookahead generator to produce the carry-in C_{in} signals for all except the least significant (rightmost) slice. Figure 8.29 shows how the 16-bit processor of Fig. 8.28 is modified to implement carry lookahead; the signals not shown here are interconnected in the manner of Fig. 8.28. The 2902 carry-lookahead generator is functionally identical to the 74182 IC discussed earlier (cf. Fig. 4.27b).

Multiplication is not a bit-sliceable operation in the same sense as addition, subtraction, or shifting. However, it can be implemented in a bit-sliced processor via a short add-and-shift microprogram of the type discussed in the preceding section. Suppose, for example, that the 2901 array of Fig. 8.28 is to perform 16- by 16-bit multiplication of unsigned binary numbers. The 16-bit Q register formed from the four slices is used to store the multiplier operand, while the RAM register RAM[A] stores the multiplicand. RAM[B] is used an accumulator register for partial products. These 16-bit registers must have the logical configuration shown in Fig. 8.30, with RAM[B] and Q forming a single 32-bit right-shift register. This organization is the same as that of the dedicated multiplier circuit in Fig. 4.47, except for the merging of the accumulator and multiplier registers. The merging is based on the fact that the accumulated partial product P is initially $n = 16$ bits long, and increases in length by 1 bit during each add-and-shift iteration. The multiplier Q is also initially n bits in length, but is reduced by 1 bit during each iteration to shift the next multiplier bit into the control unit. In the merged scheme of Fig. 8.30a, P

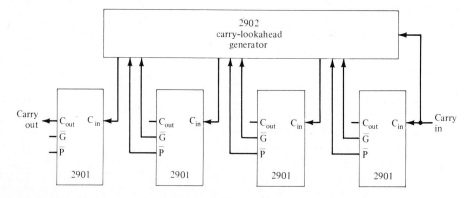

Figure 8.29 Modification to the 16-bit processor array to implement carry lookahead.

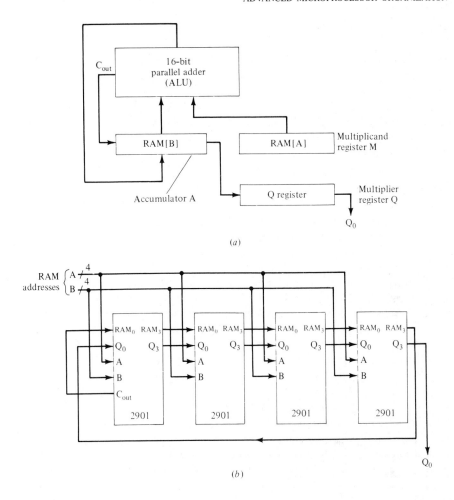

Figure 8.30 (*a*) Register organization of a 2901 processor array; (*b*) the corresponding interconnections for 16-bit unsigned binary multiplication.

simply expands into the Q register to take up the space vacated by the shifted multiplier. At the end of the multiplication process the multiplier operand has disappeared, and the 32-bit final product has its high-order half in RAM[B] and its low-order half in the Q register. To realize the structure of Fig. 8.30a in the 16-bit 2901 array of Fig. 8.28, the shift-data lines must be interconnected as in Fig. 8.30b. These connections link the RAM and Q shifters into a single 32-bit shifter, permitting an ALU result F being loaded into RAM[B] to be concatenated with the contents of the Q register and shifted in unison. Note that the Q shift defined by the I_D control field (see Fig. 8.27) is designed for just this type of operation. If faster multiplication is desired, the carry-lookahead circuit of Fig. 8.29 can be used with the scheme of Fig. 8.30.

Before multiplication proper begins, the input operands are loaded into RAM[A] and the Q register, and RAM[B] is cleared. The desired product is obtained by executing

16 conditional add-and-shift operations based on the value of the multiplier bit Q_0 (which corresponds to Q[0] in Fig. 4.47) produced by the least significant 2901 slice. The add-and-shift step can be expressed formally as follows:

if Q_0 = 1 **then** RAM[B] := RAM[A] + RAM[B]; **right-shift** RAM[B].Q;   (8.8)

The foregoing operations can easily be implemented by two or three microinstructions as in the multiplication microprogram of Fig. 8.24. If Q_0 is allowed to modify the data source part I_S of the 2901 command bus, then (8.8) can be implemented by a single microinstruction thus:

$$I_S, I_F, I_D = 0 \ \overline{Q}_0 1,000,100 \tag{8.9}$$

Here advantage is being taken of the fact that when I_F specifies addition, changing I_S from 001 to 011 changes the action of the ALU from

$$F := RAM[A] + RAM[B];$$

to

$$F := 0 + RAM[B];$$

which effectively skips addition. To complete the microinstruction cycle, F is right-shifted by the RAM shifter before being loaded into RAM[B], while Q simultaneously is right-shifted by the Q shifter, as specified by the I_D control field of (8.9). By making a small change in the circuit of Fig. 8.30, the foregoing multiplication technique can be used for twos-complement multiplication; see Prob. 8.24.

The 2903 4-bit processor slice is an enhanced version of the 2901 that has the following new features. The 4-bit input data bus D is replaced by a pair of 4-bit buses; an input bus DA and a bidirectional IO bus DB. Besides adding a useful new data path to the processor slice, DB makes it possible to attach external RAM ICs to the 2903 to increase the effective capacity of its internal RAM register file, which, as in the case of the 2901, can store 16 4-bit words (see Prob. 8.25). The 2903 also has a new set of "special" arithmetic-logic functions, mostly of the conditional add/subtract-and-shift variety, which facilitate the microprogramming of multiplication, division, and related operations.

Another important class of components in the 2900 series are microprogram sequencers, which generate the addresses of the microinstructions to be executed to control the overall behavior of a bit-sliced system; see Fig. 8.18. The 2909 microprogram sequencer IC is designed to generate 4-bit addresses, but is itself bit sliced, so that n copies of the 2909 can be cascaded to form a $4n$-bit microprogram sequencer. The internal structure of a 2909 slice is shown in Fig. 8.31. The function of the 2909 is to transfer an address from one of several internal or external sources to its output bus Y, which goes directly to the address port of the control memory CM. Four address sources are used by the 2909: an external data bus D; a register R, which is attached to a second external data bus; a microprogram counter MPC; and a small four-word stack ST. D and R are typically used to channel branch addresses from the microinstruction register to the microprogram sequencer, and thence to CM. MPC is composed of a 4-bit register and a combinational incrementer circuit, which is designed so that MPC receives the address Y

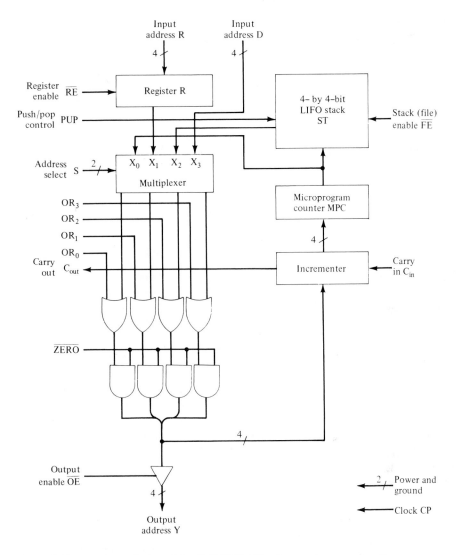

Figure 8.31 Internal organization of the AMD 2909 4-bit microprogram sequencer slice.

$+ C_{in}$ every clock cycle. The next address Y is taken from MPC when executing a sequence of microinstructions stored in consecutive locations of CM. The LIFO stack ST is intended to support subroutine calls and returns in microprograms; it plays the same role as the 8086's subroutine register (Fig. 8.25). During a call operation the current contents of MPC are pushed into the stack, and the address of the subroutine being called is obtained from R or D. To execute a return-from-subroutine operation, the return address is popped from ST and placed on the Y bus.

The 2909 contains a four-input 4-bit multiplexer that selects one of R, D, MPC, or ST as the next address source. Its two select lines S are therefore driven by condition-select information obtained from the current microinstruction in the microinstruction register MIR. The output of the multiplexer can be modified before it reaches the Y bus by signals applied to the OR and $\overline{ZERO}$ control lines. For example, if $\overline{ZERO}$ is activated, Y is forced to 0000; this is useful for implementing a reset operation in response to, say, an external reset switch. Individual bits of the output address from the multiplexer can be set to 1 via the four control lines $OR_0{:}OR_3$. If $OR_0{:}OR_3 = 1111$ and $\overline{ZERO}$ is inactive, Y is forced to 1111. If the low-order control bit OR_0 is connected to a condition variable, then a conditional skip can be implemented, since Y can be changed from ddd0 to ddd1 by the value of OR_0. In general, the control inputs of a 2909-based microprogram sequencer are grouped together to form one or more condition-select fields within the system's microinstruction format. Suppose, for instance, that a microinstruction is to include an unconditional branch to a CM address ADR that is applied to the D input bus of the microprogram sequencer. This **goto** ADR microoperation is defined by the following microinstruction fields

$$S,\overline{FE},PUP,OR,\overline{ZERO} = 11,1,d,0000,1 \qquad (8.10)$$

whose effect is to disable the stack and the OR-AND address-modification logic and route the external branch address ADR from D to Y. A microsubroutine call to the same address ADR is specified by

$$S,\overline{FE},PUP,OR,\overline{ZERO} = 11,0,1,0000,1$$

which pushes (defined by PUP = 1) the contents of MPC into the stack ST, and again routes ADR from D to Y. A return from the microsubroutine is defined as follows:

$$S,\overline{FE},PUP,OR,\overline{ZERO} = 10,0,0,0000,1$$

The interconnection of several 2909s to generate larger CM addresses is quite simple. Figure 8.32 shows a three-slice array that produces 12-bit addresses. The only data connection between adjacent slices is a ripple-carry link between their incrementers. The D, R and Y buses of the slices are merged to form three 12-bit address buses as indicated. This circuit can address a control memory storing up to $2^{12} = 4{,}096$ microinstructions, which should be sufficient to implement an emulator for a fairly powerful instruction set. The 2900 series also contains a single-chip 12-bit microprogram sequencer, the 2910, which is not bit sliced. The 2910 is quite similar to the 2909 array of Fig. 8.31, but has a number of improvements. The R register can be used as an iteration counter to simplify the microprogramming of such functions as multiplication and division. The condition-select input lines are organized into a set of 16 control words, which can be made conditional on external variables or the internal counter R. This provides, in a more direct fashion than the 2909, a set of conditional and unconditional microprogram control instructions, including jump, call, return, and loop.

8.2.4 An 8080 Emulator

Bit-sliced components have found extensive use in new processor and controller designs, but they also have been used to construct microprogrammed emulators for some existing CPUs. In particular, several bit-sliced versions of the 8080 microprocessor have been

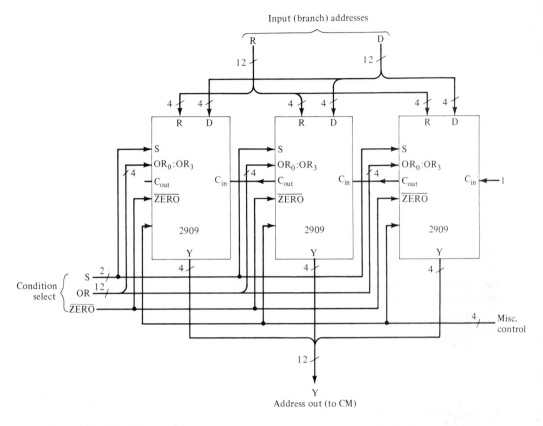

Figure 8.32 12-bit bit-sliced microprogram sequencer.

designed—a reflection of the 8080's great popularity. An 8080 emulator based on the Intel 3000 bit-sliced family was marketed in kit form by Signetics Corp. in the late 1970s (Signetics, 1977; Lau, 1978). Another emulator for the 8080 was designed by AMD using its 2900 series, which was covered in the preceding section (Shavit, 1978). We now study the AMD 8080 Emulator as an example of microprocessor design using commercial bit-sliced components.

A number of reasons may be cited for building a bit-sliced version of an existing microprocessor such as the 8080. The major one is to achieve faster program execution. There are several possible sources of this higher operating speed—including the use of a faster bipolar IC technology in place of the nMOS technology of the original 8080; the inclusion of architectural improvements such as instruction or microinstruction overlap; and the realization in firmware of operations such as multiplication and division that must be implemented by instruction-level software in the original machine. A bit-sliced implementation also can easily be designed to accept enhancements to the hardware or software of the original microprocessor, such as an extended instruction set or a different system bus.

The AMD Emulator is designed to replace the standard MOS CPU circuit of Fig. 5.42a, comprising the 8080 chip proper, a clock generator, and a status (control) latch. It therefore must have precisely the same set of external data, address, and control lines as the MOS version, and generate signals on those lines that are fully compatible with it. Moreover, the emulator must be able to emulate every instruction in the 8080's repertoire of about 70 instruction types. To do all this the AMD Emulator uses about 60 ICs, including four 2901 processor slices, three 2909 microprogram sequencer slices, 11 PROM chips, and a large number of SSI/MSI chips. The resulting microprocessor, operating at a clock rate of 5 MHz, can execute 8080 object code about four times faster than the 2-MHz MOS version of the 8080 that it replaces.

The AMD Emulator follows the general bit-sliced microprocessor organization depicted in Fig. 8.18. The 8080's programmable registers and ALU circuits are mapped into a bit-sliced processor array, while its instruction-decoding logic and associated timing and control circuits are mapped into a microprogrammable I-unit. The data and address parts of the system bus are connected mainly to the processor array, which contains the logic required for data and address manipulation. The control part of the system bus is connected primarily to the I-unit. The ease with which the target CPU's functions can be mapped into the emulator depends on the similarity between their underlying architectures. Extra logic and/or microcode is normally required to emulate any function of the target machine that is not found in the processor slices used to construct the E-unit of the emulator. For example, the 8080's parity flag (see Fig. 5.44) has no counterpart in the 2901 processor slice used in the AMD Emulator; special circuits thus are added to the emulator's E-unit to generate a parity flag signal. Other 8080 flags, however, can be obtained directly from the flag signals produced by the 2901.

The design of a bit-sliced emulator requires a thorough analysis of the instruction set to be emulated. Each machine instruction type must be dissected to determine a possible sequence of microoperations by the emulator that will implement all the steps of its instruction cycle. These steps typically include fetching the instruction, decoding its opcode, constructing addresses, transferring and processing data, and setting flag signals. Figure 8.33 contains a representative sampling of the 8080 instruction set, indicating some salient features. About half of the 8080's instruction types are of the data-processing variety, including twos-complement addition and subtraction, increment and decrement, and, or, exclusive-or, complement, and rotate. These operations are quite similar to the data-processing functions of the 2901, and therefore are easy to emulate. (A notable exception is the DAA instruction.) The remainder of the 8080 instruction set is about evenly divided between data-transfer and program-control instructions. Note that most instructions involve both 8-bit data operations and 16-bit address operations—e.g., to increment the 16-bit program counter PC. There are three main addressing modes: immediate, direct, and indirect. Instruction length varies from 1 to 3 bytes, depending on the addressing modes used. The first byte of every instruction is an opcode, which, as illustrated in Fig. 8.33, may contain one or two 3-bit address fields designating CPU registers as operand sources or destinations. Longer instructions contain either an additional immediate operand or a direct address pointing to a main memory location or an IO port. Note that the 8080's six general-purpose data registers B, C, D, E, H, and L can be coupled to form three 16-bit register-pairs BC, DE, and HL for

Type	Instruction	Description	No. of Bytes	Assembly-Language Format	Opcode Format
Data transfer	Move register to register	$R_1 := R_2;$	1	MOV R_1,R_2	0 1$d_2d_1d_0s_2s_1s_0$ [3]
	Move memory to register	$R := M[HL];$	1	MOV R,M	0 1$d_2d_1d_0$1 1 0
	Move immediate to memory	$M[HL] := X;$	2	MVI M,X	0 0 1 1 0 1 1 0
	Load accumulator direct	$A := M[ADR];$	3	LDA ADR	0 0 1 1 1 0 1 0
	Input from IO port P	$A := IO[P];$	2	IN P	1 1 0 1 1 0 1 1
	Push register-pair to stack	$M[SP-1] := B;$	1	PUSH B	1 1 0 0 0 1 0 1
		$M[SP-2] := C;$			
		$SP := SP - 2;$			
Data processing	Add register	$A := A + R;$ SF; [1]	1	ADD R	1 0 0 0 0$s_2s_1s_0$
	Add memory with carry	$A := A + M[HL] + CY;$ SF;	1	ADC M	1 0 0 0 1 1 1 0
	Add register-pair	$HL := HL + BC;$ SF;	1	DAD B	0 0 0 0 1 0 0 1
	Subtract immediate	$A := A - X;$ SF;	2	SUI X	1 1 0 1 0 1 1 0
	Increment register	$R := R + 1;$ SF;	1	INR R	0 0 $d_2d_1d_0$1 0 0
	Increment register-pair	$HL := HL + 1;$	1	INX H	0 0 1 0 0 0 1 1
	And memory	$A := A \wedge M[HL];$ SF;	1	ANA M	1 0 1 0 0 1 1 0
	Or immediate	$A := A \vee X;$ SF;	2	ORI X	1 1 1 1 0 1 1 0
	Exclusive-or register	$A := A \oplus R;$ SF;	1	XRA R	1 0 1 0 1$s_2s_1s_0$
Program control	Jump	$PC := ADR;$	3	JMP ADR	1 1 0 0 0 0 1 1
	Jump on zero	**if** $Z = 1$ **then** $PC := ADR;$	3	JZ ADR	1 1 0 0 1 0 1 0
	Call subroutine	$M[SP-1] := PC_{15}:PC_8;$	3	CALL ADR	1 1 0 0 1 1 0 1
		$M[SP-2] := PC_7:PC_0;$			
		$SP := SP - 2;$			
		$PC := ADR;$			
	Return from subroutine	$PC_7:PC_0 := M[SP];$	1	RET	1 1 0 0 1 0 0 1
		$PC_{15}:PC_8 := M[SP+1];$			
		$SP := SP + 2;$			
	Compare register	Set flags based on value of $A - R$	1	CMP R	1 0 1 1 1$s_2s_1s_0$
	No operation	None [2]	1	NOP	0 0 0 0 0 0 0 0

Notes: (1) SF denotes set flags; the specific flag settings are instruction dependent.
(2) All instructions increment PC by the number of bytes they contain.
(3) $s_2s_1s_0$ and $d_2d_1d_0$ denote the source and destination register addresses respectively.

Figure 8.33 Details of some representative 8080 instructions.

use as address registers in indirect addressing. The remaining programmable registers are an 8-bit accumulator A, a status register SR that stores 5 flag bits, and a pair of 16-bit address registers—the program counter PC and the stack pointer register SP.

The internal organization of the E-unit portion of the AMD Emulator is shown in Fig. 8.34. It roughly resembles the organization of the standard 8080 chip (Fig. 5.43), with the ALU and most of the programmable registers buried within the bit-sliced processor array. Four 2901 slices are used that can act either as a pair of separate 8-bit processors or as a single 16-bit processor. The logical coupling and uncoupling of the left and right 8-bit processors are under microprogram control, and are designed to allow the

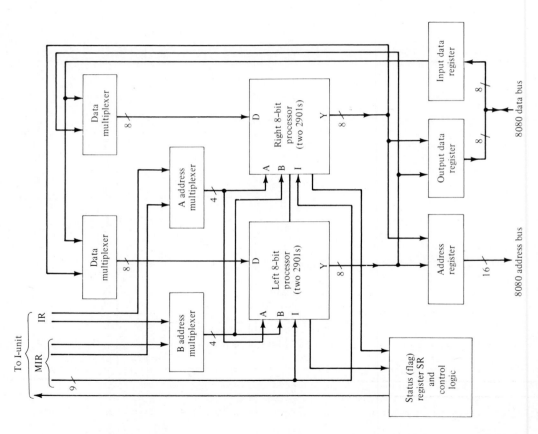

Figure 8.34 E-unit of the AMD Emulator.

8080's registers and register-pairs to be processed uniformly. The other circuits in the E-unit include multiplexers for routing data and control information through the E-unit, buffer registers for the system bus, and logic to process and store flag signals. As noted earlier, the 2901's flags do not exactly match those of the 8080.

The 16- by 16-bit RAM within the 2901 array of Fig. 8.34 provides more than enough space to accommodate the programmable registers of the 8080, and any additional temporary (scratchpad) registers needed. A natural way to assign the 8080 registers to 2901 RAM locations is to place the B, D, and H registers in the RAM of the left 8-bit processor and the C, E, and L registers in the corresponding locations of the RAM in the right 8-bit processor. The register-pairs BC, DE, and HL then automatically become single addressable registers within the overall 16-bit processor. This scheme is indeed used in the AMD Emulator but, as can be seen from Fig. 8.35, the 8080 registers are duplicated so that each 8-bit register appears in both the left and right 8-bit processors, and the register-pairs appear in the complementary forms R_1R_2 and R_2R_1. This redundant register-allocation scheme allows every register-to-register instruction of a particular type, such as move or add, to be implemented by a single microprogram, instead of requiring different microprograms for the left and right processors. Suppose, for example, that an 8-bit 8080 register with address $s_2s_1s_0$ is to be used as an operand source in some microoperation. This address is obtained from the current opcode (see Fig. 8.33), and is sent in the form of $0s_2s_1s_0$ to the left processor, and in the form $0s_2s_1\bar{s}_0$ to the right processor, where it is used to address their internal RAMs. The address assignment of Fig. 8.35 results in the same register being addressed within each 8-bit processor. Each processor receives the same command via its I bus, and so all 8-bit operations are executed in parallel in each 8-bit processor. Note, however, that when a 16-bit operation is performed on a register-pair, say BC, changing its contents, the comple-

RAM Address	Contents in Left 8-bit Processor	Contents in Right 8-bit Processor
0000	B	C
0001	C	B
0010	D	E
0011	E	D
0100	H	L
0101	L	H
0110	Not used	A
0111	A	Not used
1000	Not used	Not used
1001	SP_{15}:SP_8	SP_7:SP_0
1010	Scratchpad	Scratchpad
1011	Scratchpad	Scratchpad
1100	00000000	00111000
1101	00111000	00000000
1110	Not used	Not used
1111	PC_{15}:PC_8	PC_7:PC_0

Figure 8.35 Allocation of RAM locations in the 2901 processor array.

mentary pair CB must be updated via a separate operation. The overhead in execution time that this entails is considered to be small.

Figure 8.36 illustrates the organization of the I-unit of the AMD 8080 Emulator. It is intended to replace the instruction register IR and the hardwired timing and control unit of the 8080 chip (Fig. 5.43). At its heart is a 512- by 56-bit control memory CM that stores the 352 microinstructions used to emulate the 8080's instruction set. Twelve-bit addresses for CM are generated by a bit-sliced microprogram sequencer composed of three 2909s in the configuration of Fig. 8.32; the capacity of CM can easily be increased

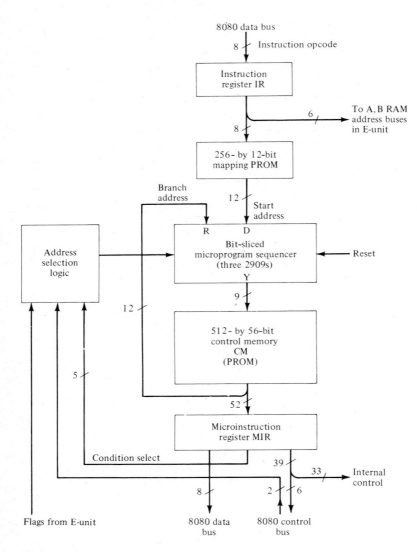

Figure 8.36 I-unit of the AMD Emulator.

to 4096 microinstructions, if desired. The 56-bit microinstruction format used is outlined in Fig. 8.37. It is of the horizontal type containing a 12-bit branch address field, a 5-bit condition select field, and some 22 control fields of various sizes. The rightmost five control fields, comprising bits 16:0, specify the RAM addresses and the main control bus I of the 2901 processor array. Bits 32:27 define the values of six control lines that form part of the 8080 system bus. The remaining control fields define the internal operations of the AMD Emulator, and are peculiar to its design.

Instruction processing in the 8080 is implemented by the AMD Emulator as follows. A microprogram named FETCH is used to fetch the next instruction to be executed from main memory as specified by the program counter PC. FETCH loads the opcode byte of the instruction into the instruction register IR, as shown in Fig. 8.36. The opcode is decoded via a small PROM called a mapping PROM, which produces a 12-bit address pointing to the first microinstruction in the microprogram designed to emulate the current instruction. If the opcode contains register address fields, they are sent directly from IR to the RAM address buses of the 2901 array. The starting address provided by the mapping PROM is sent to the D input of the microprogram sequencer, and thence to its microprogram counter MPC and the address port of CM. A read cycle by CM produces the required microinstruction, which is placed in the microinstruction register MIR, from which its control information is extracted. Subsequent microinstructions within the same microprogram may be addressed by incrementing MPC and using it as the address source. Branching is implemented by returning the 12-bit branch address field of the current microinstruction directly from the output port of CM to the microprogram sequencer via its R input bus. When no branching is needed, 8 bits of this address field can be used to transfer an 8-bit data word from the microinstruction to the 2901 processor array via the main data bus. The address-selection logic of the I-unit monitors the condition-select field in the MIR, the flag signals generated by the E-unit, the 8080 system bus lines INT (interrupt request) and HOLD (DMA request), and certain other signals that affect microinstruction sequencing. The access circuitry of the control memory CM is designed so that the execution of the current microinstruction can be overlapped with the fetching of the next consecutive microinstruction, a process called *pipelining*.

We now briefly consider the organization of the microcode stored in CM. A short initialization microprogram called RESET has the starting address 000_{16}. It is invoked by activating an external reset control line, corresponding to the 8080's $\overline{\text{RESET}}$ input, which is attached to the $\overline{\text{ZERO}}$ input of the 2909-based microprogram sequencer.

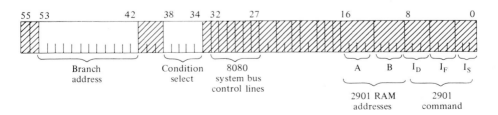

Figure 8.37 Microinstruction format of the AMD Emulator (control fields are shaded).

Execution of the RESET microprogram resets the 8080 program counter to zero by loading 0000_{16} into location 1111_2 of the 2901 processor's RAM. It also loads constants used by various microprograms into RAM locations 1100_2 and 1101_2. After certain other initialization actions, RESET transfers control to the microprogram FETCH, causing instruction processing to begin. FETCH requests a memory read operation via the system bus using PC as the main memory address source, and loads the incoming opcode byte into the instruction register IR. Decoding via the mapping PROM yields the address of a microprogram designed to emulate the instruction's execution cycle, including the fetching of any necessary addresses or operands from main memory, the processing of data and addresses by the E-unit, and the storing of results either in the emulator or elsewhere. Execution of this microprogram normally terminates with a return to FETCH, whose address is saved in the stack memory of the 2909 microprogram sequencer. The status of the DMA request line HOLD is checked routinely by most microinstructions; receipt of a DMA request results in an immediate transfer to a subroutine that causes the emulator to relinquish control of the system bus and enter a wait loop until HOLD is deactivated. The interrupt-request line INT is checked during each execution of the FETCH microprogram, which, when necessary, calls an interrupt-handling microprogram that carries out an 8080-style interrupt cycle.

To illustrate the task of microprogramming the AMD Emulator, consider the microprogram named MOVRR that emulates the execution of all 8080 register-to-register move instructions of the type MOV R_1,R_2. These instructions have the 1-byte format given in Fig. 8.33. The addresses of the source register R_2 and the destination register R_1 are obtained directly from the instruction register IR, and thus need not be specified in the microprogram. MOVRR must specify, however, that these addresses are to be routed from IR to the A and B address buses of the processor arrays. The required move operation is defined by the OR operation.

$$RAM[B] := 0 \lor RAM[A];$$

which requires the following 2901 control fields:

$$I_S,I_F,I_D = 100,011,011$$

MOVRR must also set various other control fields governing internal operations of the emulator, and test for a pending DMA request by specifying that a branch should occur to a routine named HLDF if the external HOLD control line is active. If HOLD is inactive, then a return is made to the FETCH microroutine, causing a new instruction cycle to begin.

All the foregoing operations required by MOVRR can be included in a single microinstruction. In the AMDASM microassembly language (Advanced Micro Devices, 1978) used to microprogram the AMD Emulator, this microinstruction/microprogram is written thus:

MOVRR: ALU,,,FTOB.F & ALUC & BASW SW,SW & OR & ZA & IOC &

       /IF R.F, INV,HOLD & NUM, HLDF & NOC   (8.11)

Forbidding as this appears at first sight, it is far more legible than the following binary object-code version of MOVRR, which shows how it is stored in CM.

11000000 00101111 10101011 11110000 01110101 01010100 11011100   (8.12)

The various symbolic names in (8.11) are microprogrammer-defined identifiers for fields within the microinstruction or (constant) values to be assigned to those fields. The name OR for example, specifies that the I_F control field of the ALU (bits 5:3 of the binary microinstruction) should be set to 011 to select the ALU's logical OR function. The AMDASM microassembler thus derives the three underlined bits of (8.12) from the presence of OR in (8.11). The second line of (8.11) defines the method to be used to obtain the address of the next microinstruction to be executed after MOVRR. This line can be loosely translated thus: Test the HOLD control line. If HOLD is not active, take the next CM address from the 2909 stack which is denoted by F (file) in (8.11); as indicated above, this returns control to the FETCH microprogram. If HOLD is active, a branch should be made to the microprogram called HLDF that handles DMA requests. Execution of instructions of the MOV R_1,R_2 type by the AMD Emulator requires a total of three microinstruction (clock) cycles: two to execute the two-microinstruction FETCH microprogram and one to execute MOVRR. The standard MOS version of the 8080 requires five of its slower CPU clock cycles to execute the same move instruction.

8.3 SYSTEMS WITH SEVERAL PROCESSORS

The performance of a microprocessor-based system can be improved significantly by employing auxiliary processors of various kinds. Two types of special-purpose auxiliary processors, arithmetic processors and IO processors, are discussed in this section. The design of multiprocessor systems containing several general-purpose (micro)processors or CPUs is also examined.

8.3.1 Rationale

The microprocessor-based systems encountered previously have the conventional archi-tecture depicted in Fig. 8.38, in which essentially all data-processing and control functions reside in a single central processor, the CPU. The memory M serves as a temporary or permanent store for programs and data that are to be processed by the CPU. The IO interface circuits link the CPU and M to the outside world via a set of IO devices. Intrasystem communication takes place over a set of shared signal lines, the system bus, which allow information to be transferred between the CPU and M, the CPU and the IO interface circuits, or M and the IO interface circuits. Some CPU functions can be transferred to the IO interface—for example, by the use of DMA controllers—but these functions are limited to the control of simple IO data-transfer operations. Although the computer organization of Fig. 8.38 is adequate for the vast majority of microprocessor applications, there are, nevertheless, important applications that require a different system structure.

A basic drawback of microprocessors, as compared with large central processors, is their low instruction execution rate or *throughput*. A typical mainframe computer, for instance, has a throughput in the range of 1 to 10 million instructions per second, or *MIPS*, whereas the throughput of a microprocessor such as the 6800 is about 0.1–0.01

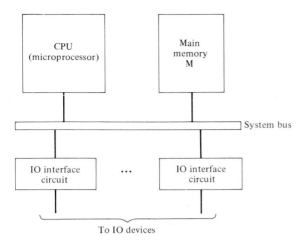

Figure 8.38 Basic microcomputer organization with all data-processing functions residing in a single CPU.

MIPS. A microprocessor's performance in numerical computations is further diminished by its short data word length and its lack of floating-point instructions. Larger computers may have a single hardware- or firmware-implemented instruction to, say, add two 32-bit floating-point numbers. A typical 8-bit microprocessor must carry out the same floating-point addition by executing a relatively long and slow software routine. The speed at which floating-point addition and other complex arithmetic operations are executed by a microprocessor can be greatly increased by providing an auxiliary arithmetic (co)processor as an extension to the microprocessor's E-unit. The microprocessor acting as the CPU provides the arithmetic processor with instructions and operands that are then processed in the arithmetic processor, and the results returned to the CPU. Figure 8.39a shows the position of an arithmetic processor within a standard microcomputer; it communicates with the CPU via the system bus and, possibly, via special control lines. A number of single-chip arithmetic processors are commercially available. A representative example to be studied later is AMD's 9511 chip, which performs addition, subtraction, multiplication, and division on 32-bit floating-point numbers, as well as both 16-bit and 32-bit fixed-point numbers. It also computes square roots, logarithms, and trigonometric functions. It is designed with an 8-bit external data interface that can easily be attached to the system bus of most 8-bit microprocessors.

Many microprocessors require the CPU to devote an appreciable amount of time to supervising IO operations, which primarily involve the transfer of data between the main memory and IO devices. If a few very fast IO devices are present, or else a large number of slower devices, the CPU may have insufficient time to carry out its principal data-processing tasks. Hence the number and types of IO devices that can be attached to a system may be restricted by the throughput of the CPU. A further constraint on IO transfer rates is the shared bus structure of Fig. 8.38, which requires all intrasystem data transfers to take place sequentially. The performance of microprocessor-based systems with heavy IO workloads can be improved by using another kind of special-purpose

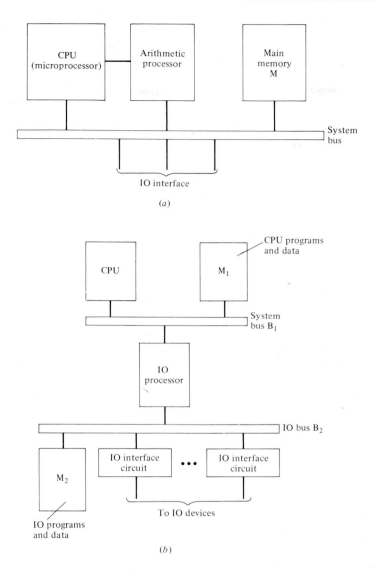

Figure 8.39 Microprocessor-based systems containing (a) an arithmetic (co)processor and (b) an IO processor.

auxiliary processor, in this case an IO processor or IOP, to relieve the CPU of the job of directly controlling routine IO operations. An IOP can be regarded as a DMA controller augmented by an I-unit that enables it to initiate, direct, and terminate a set of IO data-transfer operations without intervention of the CPU. The CPU, however, retains an overall supervisory role, and is the ultimate source of all tasks executed by the IOP.

An IOP can be attached to a microprocessor system in the same manner as the IO interface circuits of Fig. 8.39a. The IO programs executed by the IOP are stored in the main memory M, which also contains the data buffer areas used during IO operations. Each time the IOP needs to fetch an instruction or transfer a word to or from M, it must become the master of the system bus, thus preventing the CPU from using it. Contention between the CPU and the IOP for control of the system bus thus can be a limiting factor on overall system performance. Figure 8.39b shows a different system configuration that reduces the contention between the CPU and the IOP, and permits a higher degree of parallelism among CPU and IO operations. As before, there is a system bus B_1 linking the CPU, the IOP, and main memory M_1. The IOP is also connected to a second bus B_2, termed the IO bus, to which are attached the IO devices under the IOP's control. This bus, whose structure may be quite similar to that of the system bus, also links the IOP to a RAM M_2 used to store the IOP's programs and data buffer space. This configuration allows CPU and IO operations to proceed simultaneously and independently via B_1 and B_2 respectively. Of course, it will be necessary from time to time to transfer data between M_1 and M_2, which can be accomplished by a high-speed block DMA transfer under the control of the IOP. An example of an IOP for use in microcomputer systems is the Intel 8089, a single-chip IOP that is a member of the 8086 microprocessor family. The 8089 has a repertoire of about 50 instructions, which are oriented toward IO operations, and are quite distinct from those of the 8086. It can be used in system organizations such as that of Fig. 8.39b, and can support programmed IO, interrupt-driven IO, or DMA, using most types of IO devices; the 8089 IOP is studied in Sec. 8.3.3.

All the foregoing systems are called *uniprocessors*, since they contain only one CPU, which exercises overall control of the system's activity. At any time, a uni-processor can be engaged in just one programmed activity or task, although associated subtasks may be processed concurrently in special-purpose arithmetic or IO processors. The presence of several CPU's—several general-purpose instruction-set processors—in the same system constitutes a multiprocessor or, where the CPUs are microprocessors, a multimicroprocessor. Unlike a uniprocessor, a multiprocessor can execute several equal and independent tasks simultaneously, each task being assigned to a different CPU. Multiprocessors can therefore achieve higher throughput than uniprocessors. Moreover, it is possible to design a multiprocessor so that it can tolerate the failure of one of its CPUs; the tasks of a failed CPU are reassigned to a faultfree CPU. Thus multiprocessor architectures are frequently employed for systems that have fault tolerance as a major design goal. Multiprocessors are also well suited to distributed processing environments, where separate but related tasks must be peformed in locations that are physically far apart (more than a few meters). The physical separation makes it inefficient to centralize all data processing in a single CPU; for example, the CPU's response time to interrupt requests increases rapidly with its distance from the interrupt source. Examples of suitable environments for distributed processing are an office that contains a set of IO terminals or work stations that must share a common file system, and an assembly line in a factory where a set of computer-controlled machine tools is engaged in a manufacturing process. In such applications a separate CPU can be placed at each work site and assigned responsibility for local tasks; a central computer may be used to coordinate the activities of the distributed CPUs.

Figure 8.3 shows a common system organization used for centralized (non-distributed) multiprocessing systems. Here each CPU has its own local bus, memory, and IO devices. It communicates with other CPUs and certain shared resources (global memory and IO devices) via a common system bus. A similar system organization is used to link the CPU and IOP in Fig. 8.39b. In the case of a distributed multiprocessor, the global system bus is usually replaced by a network of serial communication links, such as high-speed coaxial cables, which are more suitable for data transmission over longer distances. This results in the kind of system illustrated in Fig. 8.40. Note that this system structure is also used for *computer networks,* which are defined as independent

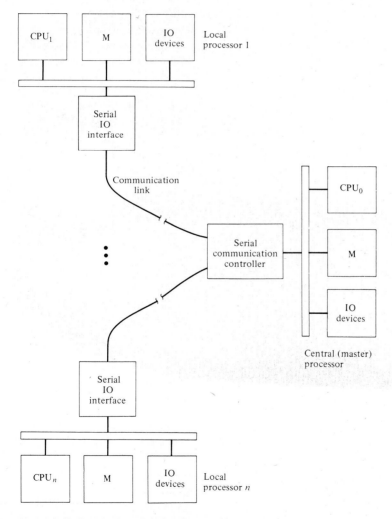

Figure 8.40 Organization of a distributed multiprocessor system.

computers linked by a communication network. A distributed multiprocessor is distinguished from a computer network by the fact that its processors cooperate in the execution of system tasks, and are usually under the control of a common operating system.

Another possible organization for a centralized multiprocessor is shown in Fig. 8.41. Here the shared global bus is replaced by a complex interconnection network called a crossbar switching network, or simply a *crossbar switch*. There is only one common main memory M, which is subdivided into a set of memory modules M_0, M_1, M_2, and M_3. Each memory module is assigned a distinct region of M's address space, and has its own independent read and write access circuitry. The crossbar switch contains a set of (vertical) buses that are connected to the memory modules, and another set of (horizontal) buses that are connected to the system's processors, including CPUs and IOPs. In response to a request from a processor, the crossbar switch can create a logical connection between any horizontal bus and any vertical bus, thus linking the processor directly to a memory module. Clearly only one processor can be connected to a given memory module at any time; however, different processors may be connected to different memory modules at the same time. For example, in the system of Fig. 8.41, CPU P_0 can be connected to memory module M_3 while CPU P_1 is connected to M_1 and IOP P_3 is

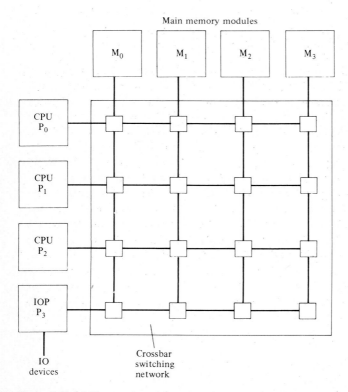

Main memory modules

Figure 8.41 Multiprocessor system employing a crossbar switch.

connected to M_0. A high degree of parallel processing thus is possible. The fact that all processors have equal access to main memory means that programs and data can be shared very easily. Crossbar switches tend to be costly and bulky, however, because of their very large number of external connections and their complex internal switching logic. The simpler and less expensive multiple-bus organization of Figs. 8.3 and 8.39 is usually preferred for multimicroprocessor systems.

Although a multiprocessor organization can increase a system's performance, reliability, and flexibility, it also increases design cost and complexity, especially in the area of software design. A basic problem with all multiprocessors is contention for the shared hardware and software resources of the system. Suppose, for instance, that all the processors in the system of Fig. 8.41 request access to the same memory module M_1 simultaneously. Only one processor can be connected to M_1, so the remaining processors must wait their turn. Under these conditions the performance of the multiprocessor is no better than that of a uniprocessor. Careful system design can reduce the performance loss resulting from contention among the processors. Since it is often a consequence of conditions that cannot be predicted precisely, for instance, the order in which memory addresses are generated during program execution or the arrival times of IO interrupt requests, contention cannot be eliminated completely. Contention is less of a problem in distributed or loosely coupled systems, where the various processors interact with one another infrequently.

8.3.2 Arithmetic Processors

The arithmetic processing capabilities of most microprocessors are limited by the lack of space on the microprocessor chip(s), since a considerable amount of space is devoted to hardware or firmware supporting nonarithmetic functions. If the latter is stripped away, it is possible to expand the remaining logic to implement an instruction set for arithmetic functions comparable to that of larger computers. The result is a one-chip arithmetic processor capable of performing a wide range of operations on long (16-bit, 32-bit, or longer) fixed-point and floating-point operands. Such a processor can provide direct hardware support for the **integer** and **real** operand types employed in most high-level programming languages, and eliminate the need for long, slow, software-implemented arithmetic routines. An arithmetic processor chip is functionally similar to the calculator chips found in pocket scientific calculators. Just as the calculator depends on a human operator to supply it via a keyboard with input data and instructions, an arithmetic processor relies on a host microprocessor or CPU for its data and instructions. In some cases the arithmetic processor is designed as a special-purpose IO device, and interacts with the host CPU via standard IO communication methods such as programmed IO and interrupts. In other cases the arithmetic processor is coupled to the host CPU so that it resembles an extension of the host's E-unit; the host fetches special arithmetic instructions and operands that it passes directly to the arithmetic processor for execution. Arithmetic processors of this type are sometimes termed coprocessors.

A representative and widely used arithmetic processor chip, the AMD 9511, is illustrated in Fig. 8.42 (Cheng, 1981; Croson et al., 1981). Internally it resembles a 16-bit microprogrammed CPU, but has a smaller and more specialized instruction set, and is not capable of fetching its own instructions. Data and instructions are transferred to, and results are removed from, the 9511 via an 8-bit bidirectional data bus, which, with its associated address and control lines, is easily connected to the system bus of standard microprocessors. To the host microprocessor the 9511 is a programmable IO interface circuit, and is typically used as follows:

1. The host CPU outputs the operands for an arithmetic operation to the 9511 in 8-bit segments via the system bus.
2. It then sends the 9511 an 8-bit instruction or command specifying the particular operation to be executed.
3. The 9511 executes the specified command, such as add two 32-bit floating-point numbers. Note that many of its operations require hundreds or thousands of CPU clock cycles to complete.

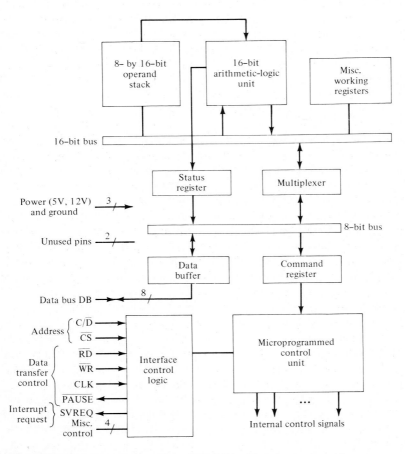

Figure 8.42 Internal organization of the AMD 9511 arithmetic processor chip.

4. Once the 9511 has computed the desired result, it signals that fact to the CPU by generating an interrupt.
5. The CPU then retrieves the result from the 9511 8 bits at a time by executing one or more input instructions.

Since the execution times of 9511 commands vary over a wide range, the 9511 must be able to inform the host CPU when execution is complete. Three distinct methods of doing this are provided. The command sent to the 9511 can tell it to activate an interrupt-request line SVREQ (service request) when the result is ready. The 9511 also maintains an 8-bit status word that indicates whether it is busy (still executing a command) or not busy (execution complete). This word can be read by the CPU at any time, thus allowing it to monitor the 9511's progress via programmed polling. Finally, the 9511 can use a third method of communication with microprocessors such as the 8080/8085 and 6809 that suppport asynchronous data transfers over the system bus. Any time after issuing a command to the 9511, the CPU can attempt to read the results from the 9511. If the 9511 is still busy executing the command, it simply withholds the data-acknowledge signal until it has the results ready, thus stretching the CPU-initiated read cycle by an arbitrary amount. The 9511's output signal $\overline{\text{PAUSE}}$ serves as the acknowledge line and must be connected (usually via additional logic) to the corresponding input line of the host CPU, for example, the READY line in the 8080/8085 case. This communication method forces the CPU to wait in an idle state while the 9511 is busy with its current command. The other methods, while requiring somewhat more complex hardware and software interfaces, allow the CPU to perform other tasks while the 9511 is busy.

All 9511 operations are invoked by an 8-bit command word that specifies the function to be performed and the type of operands to be used. The processing circuits of the 9511 employ the stack-oriented architecture found in some large computers, which eliminates the need to include address fields in data-processing instructions. An 8- by 16-bit LIFO stack within the 9511 serves as the source and destination of all operands used to execute arithmetic instructions. This stack is functionally similar to the stacks used by most microprocessors to implement such instructions as push, pop, call, and return. Data input and output instructions sent by the CPU to the 9511 are transformed internally into pop and push operations, respectively, that use the 9511's operand stack. For example, a 32-bit operand D is transferred to the 9511 via four 8-bit output (write) operations that result in the operand occupying the top-of-the-stack or TOS position. If a second operand D_2 is then transferred to the 9511, it is pushed into the TOS position, and D_1's location becomes the next-to-the-top position, referred to as NOS (next on stack) in 9511 literature. A command word f can now be sent to the 9511 to perform an arithmetic operation of the form

$$D_3 := f(D_1, D_2);$$

The command word is loaded into the 9511's command register where it invokes a microprogram to carry out the desired operation f, and put the final result D_3 at the top of the stack. The actions performed by this microprogram are equivalent to the following sequence of steps:

$$\text{POP } D_1;$$

$$POP\ D_2;$$

$$D_3 := f(D_1, D_2);$$

$$PUSH\ D_3;$$

Note that the input operands D_1 and D_2 are effectively destroyed. An arithmetic function with a single input operand such as square root calculation uses TOS as both the input and output operand location thus:

$$POP\ D_1;$$

$$D_2 := SQRT(D_1);$$

$$PUSH\ D_2;$$

The instruction set of the 9511 arithmetic processor is listed in Fig. 8.43. The basic operations add, subtract, multiply, divide and negate are provided for all three data types: 16-bit fixed-point numbers, 32-bit fixed-point numbers, and 32-bit floating-point numbers. Standard twos-complement code is used for fixed-point numbers. The format for floating-point numbers is shown in Fig. 8.44a; it represents the numerical value N given by the equation

$$N = (-1)^S (0.M)\ 2^E$$

except in the case where N is zero, which is represented by the all-0 word. This is a nonstandard format differing in several key respects from the more widely used IEEE 754 floating-point number format discussed earlier (see Fig. 5.16). The instruction format of the 9511 is quite simple, and is outlined in Fig. 8.44b. Five bits identify the arithmetic function to be performed, and 2 bits define the data type to be used. The remaining (leftmost) bit is set to 1 if an interrupt signal on the SVREQ line is desired at the end of execution. The 9511's status byte has the format shown in Fig. 8.44c. The leftmost bit is set to 1 while the 9511 is busy executing a command, in which case it will not accept a new command. The remaining status bits provide useful information about the results computed by the 9511, including any (potential) error conditions encountered.

The hardware aspect of interfacing the 9511 to a microprocessor is quite straightforward. Its bidirectional IO data bus is attached to the corresponding lines in the system bus of the microprocessor. The clock line CLK and the data-transfer control lines $\overline{RD}$ (read) and $\overline{WR}$ (write) are also attached directly to the corresponding lines of the system bus. The 9511 is enabled by activating its chip-select line $\overline{CS}$. Two addresses must be assigned to the 9511 in the host microprocessor's IO (or memory) address space: one for accessing the command and status registers and the other for accessing the 9511's data stack. The command/data-control line $C/\overline{D}$ is used by the 9511 to distinguish these two addresses. Figure 8.45 lists all the interface signal values used to transfer information to or from the 9511; these must be matched with address and control signals generated by the microprocessor during input (read) and output (write) operations.

A relatively large number of instructions is generally needed for data transfers involving the 9511. Sixteen- or 32-bit operands must be transmitted a byte at a time,

Operand Type	Operation
16-bit fixed-point	Add
	Subtract
	Multiply
	Divide
	Negate
32-bit fixed-point	Add
	Subtract
	Multiply
	Divide
	Negate
32-bit floating-point	Add
	Subtract
	Multiply
	Divide
	Negate
	Square root
	Sine
	Cosine
	Tangent
	Inverse sine
	Inverse cosine
	Inverse tangent
	Common logarithm (base 10)
	Natural logarithm (base e)
	Exponential e^x
	Power x^y
Miscellaneous	Convert from floating point to 16/32-bit fixed point
	Convert from 16/32-bit fixed point to floating point
	Push TOS into stack (duplicate TOS)
	Pop stack (delete TOS)
	Exchange TOS and NOS
	Push floating-point constant π into stack
	No operation

Figure 8.43 Instruction (command) set of the 9511.

usually to or from main memory. Figure 8.46a lists a subroutine named FLD written in 8080/8085 assembly language that moves a 32-bit operand from main memory to the 9511. Each byte of the operand is first transferred from M[HL] to the accumulator A via a move instruction, and thence to the 9511's operand stack via an output instruction. The memory address register HL is decremented after each move. Using FLD as a subroutine, the floating-point addition ALPHA + BETA can be implemented by the program of Fig. 8.46b. Two executions of FLD transfer the operands to the 9511 stack, with their bytes in the proper order. The symbolic address D9511 is used here to denote the stack; C9511 serves as the address of both the 9511's command and status registers.

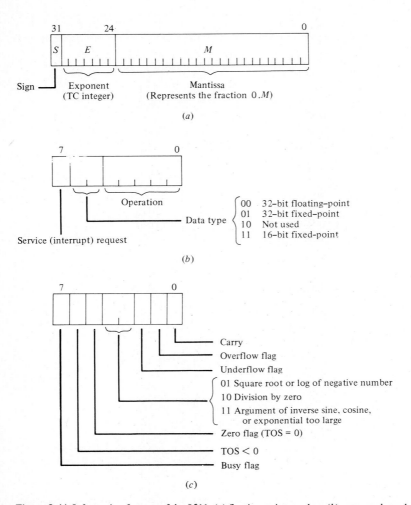

Figure 8.44 Information formats of the 9511: (*a*) floating-point number; (*b*) command word; (*c*) status word.

9511 Interface Signals				
$\overline{CS}$	C/$\overline{D}$	$\overline{RD}$	$\overline{WR}$	Operation Defined
0	0	1	0	Push operand byte from data bus to stack
0	0	0	1	Pop operand byte from stack to data bus
0	1	1	0	Transfer command byte from data bus to command register
0	1	0	1	Transfer status byte from status register to data bus
1	d	d	d	No operation

Figure 8.45 Interface signals required to transfer information to or from the 9511.

The command byte 10_{16} is loaded into the accumulator via a move immediate instruction, and transferred thence to the 9511's command register via another output instruction. If an end-of-execution interrupt request is desired, the command byte 90_{16} should be substituted.

The arithmetic processor now proceeds to execute a floating-point addition operation, taking its arguments from TOS and NOS and eventually placing the result in TOS. The CPU can check the 9511's busy-status byte periodically to determine when the results are ready. Figure 8.46c lists a suitable 8080/8085 polling routine for this purpose. It continually inputs the contents of the 9511's status register and tests the leftmost (busy)

```
;   8080/8085 SUBROUTINE 'FLD' TO TRANSFER A 32-BIT OPERAND FROM MAIN MEMORY TO
;       THE 9511 ARITHMETIC PROCESSOR

FLD:    MOV   A,M        ; LOAD LEAST SIGNIFICANT BYTE FROM M[HL] INTO A
        OUT   D9511      ; OUTPUT BYTE FROM A TO 9511'S OPERAND STACK
        DCX   H          ; DECREMENT MEMORY ADDRESS REGISTER HL
        MOV   A,M        ; TRANSFER SECOND BYTE
        OUT   D9511
        DCX   H
        MOV   A,M        ; TRANSFER THIRD BYTE
        OUT   D9511
        DCX   H
        MOV   A,M        ; TRANSFER FOURTH (EXPONENT) BYTE
        OUT   D9511
        RET              ; RETURN FROM SUBROUTINE
```

(*a*)

```
;   8080/8085 ROUTINE TO INITIATE A 32-BIT FLOATING-POINT ADDITION USING THE 9511
        LXI   H,ALPHA+3  ; LOAD ADDRESS OF LEAST SIGNIFICANT BYTE OF
                         ;    OPERAND ALPHA INTO HL
        CALL  FLD        ; TRANSFER ALPHA TO THE 9511'S OPERAND STACK
        LXI   H,BETA+3   ; LOAD ADDRESS OF OPERAND BETA INTO HL
        CALL  FLD        ; TRANSFER BETA TO THE 9511'S OPERAND STACK
        MVI   A,10H      ; LOAD FLOATING-POINT ADD COMMAND INTO A
        OUT   C9511      ; TRANSFER COMMAND TO 9511'S COMMAND REGISTER
```

(*b*)

```
;   8080/8085 SUBROUTINE TO POLL THE 9511'S BUSY STATUS FLAG

POLL:   IN    C9511      ; TRANSFER 9511'S STATUS BYTE TO A
        ANI   80H        ; SET Z = 1 (0) IF BUSY FLAG IS 0 (1) VIA AN AND-
                         ;    IMMEDIATE-TO-A INSTRUCTION
        JNZ   POLL       ; CONTINUE POLLING IF BUSY FLAG IS 1
        RET              ; RETURN FROM SUBROUTINE
```

(*c*)

Figure 8.46 8080/8085 assembly-language routines to communicate with the 9511: (*a*) load long operand; (*b*) issue command; (*c*) poll status.

bit, until that bit becomes 0, indicating that the result is ready. The CPU can now read out the result via a 4-byte 9511-to-memory transfer routine analogous to the memory-to-9511 transfer routine of Fig. 8.46a. Status polling can be eliminated if the 9511's interrupt facility is used; the end-of-execution interrupt signal SVREQ can transfer control directly to the routine that fetches the result from the 9511. Figure 8.47 shows the 9511 interfaced to the 8085 CPU with interrupt requests sent to the 8085's nonvectored RST 6.5 interrupt-request line. The predefined interrupt address vector 0034_{16} used by RST 6.5 should be the entry address of the routine that transfers results from the 9511.

The 8086 microprocessor family contains a one-chip arithmetic processor, designated the 8087 numeric data processor, which functions as a coprocessor with 8086-series CPUs (Intel, 1981b). It is a microprogrammed stack-oriented special-purpose processor with essentially the same set of instruction types as the 9511, but with a broader range of data types. (The 8087 is, in fact, a more complex chip than its host CPU, the 8086.) The 8087's data types include 16- and 32-bit number formats similar to those of the 9511. It can also operate on 64-bit fixed-point (twos-complement) and floating-point binary numbers, and 80-bit (10-digit) packed decimal numbers. Unlike the 9511, it employs the standard floating-point formats sponsored by IEEE.

The 8087 differs fundamentally from the 9511 in the way in which it is coupled to its host CPU. From a programmer's perspective, the 8086 CPU and 8087 coprocessor appear as a single processor executing a single instruction stream. As we now explain, instructions intended for the 8087 can be intermixed with 8086 instructions in a very natural fashion via the 8086's special class of ESC (escape) instructions. The ESC

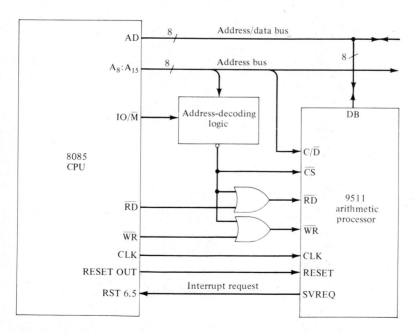

Figure 8.47 Interfacing the 9511 to the 8085 microprocessor.

instructions can take many programmer-defined forms, allowing them to convey a set of special commands to a coprocessor. The host CPU fetches ESC instructions from main memory in the normal manner but does not execute them. The 8087 arithmetic processor is connected to the system bus as shown in Fig. 8.48, in such a way that it can monitor instruction opcodes en route from memory to the host CPU. When the 8087 detects an ESC opcode, it reads it into its internal registers, and proceeds to execute it. Although the CPU does not execute the function defined by the ESC opcode, it performs the essential function of constructing a main memory address, if one is specified in the ESC instruction. Note that the construction of effective addresses employs various address registers—segment registers, for example—that are found only in the CPU. Having constructed the specified memory address, the CPU then executes a memory read or write cycle, but does not transfer any data to or from the system bus. The 8087, however, captures the address placed on the system bus by the CPU; it can also capture any data read from memory by this CPU-controlled bus transaction. The 8087 now has all the information it needs to communicate independently with main memory. Using the initial address provided by the CPU, it can fetch additional consecutive operand words from memory, or it can store a set of consecutive words in memory. Thus the CPU's dummy ESC instruction cycle can supply the 8087 coprocessor with a command and the source or destination address of an operand of any size in main memory. Since the 8087 is a bus master, it can load or store its memory operands without further CPU assistance. This ingenious technique completely eliminates the lengthy CPU-executed data- and command-transfer routines needed by the 9511.

As with all auxiliary processors, special measures must be taken to synchronize the activities of the 8086 and 8087. When executing an ESC command, the 8087 activates an external busy signal named BUSY, which corresponds to the 9511's $\overline{\text{PAUSE}}$ signal. BUSY is intended to be attached to the control input named $\overline{\text{TEST}}$ of the 8086, as shown in Fig. 8.48. The 8086 has an instruction called WAIT, which continually tests the $\overline{\text{TEST}}$

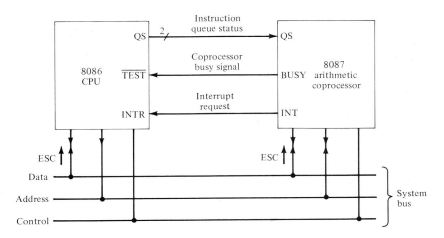

Figure 8.48 Interfacing the 8087 to the 8086 microprocessor.

line. If it is inactive ($\overline{\text{TEST}} = 1$) when first tested by WAIT, the 8086 enters an idle or waiting state and tests $\overline{\text{TEST}}$ every five clock cycles. When $\overline{\text{TEST}}$ is activated by the 8087, indicating that it has completed execution of an ESC instruction, the CPU emerges from the waiting state and executes the next instruction in its instruction stream. The 8086–8087 synchronization is normally achieved by preceding each ESC instruction by a WAIT instruction, thereby ensuring that the CPU does not perform its part of the ESC processing before the coprocessor is ready. Like the 9511, the 8087 also maintains a status word defining its overall state, and is capable of interrupting the CPU. Synchronization of the 8086 and 8087 is complicated by the fact that ESC instructions must pass through the 8086's instruction buffer, and hence may not be processed by the 8086 until some time after they have been fetched. To ensure that the 8086 and 8087 process ESC instructions simultaneously, the 8087 maintains an internal instruction buffer identical to that of the 8086. The 8086 also supplies the 8087 with 2 bits of instruction buffer status information that allow the 8087 to move its copy of the ESC opcode through its instruction queue in step with the CPU.

Figure 8.49 contains an example of an assembly-language program for execution by an 8086–8087 processor pair. It is designed to perform the addition operation

$$\text{GAMMA} := \text{ALPHA} + \text{BETA}$$

on 32-bit floating-point operands stored in main memory. Four ESC instructions are needed: two to transfer the input operands APLHA and BETA to the operand stack in the 8087, a third to specify the 32-bit floating-point add operation, and a fourth to transfer the result GAMMA from the 8087 to main memory. The symbolic command field following 'ESC' in each ESC statement is actually assembled as part of the machine-language ESC opcode. Its value is selected by the programmer to correspond to the desired 8087 operation. Thus the symbolic commands FLD (floating-point load to stack), FADD (floating-point add), and FST (floating-point store from stack to memory) are representations of the actual operations performed by the 8087 coprocessor. The WAIT instruction preceding each ESC statement allows the 8087 to complete all its actions on the current ESC instruction before execution of the next one begins. The 8086 can respond to external interrupts while executing WAIT, thus allowing it to perform other actions while the 8087 is busy. Note that on returning from an interrupt-servicing routine called while executing WAIT, the CPU resumes execution of the previously

```
;  8086/8087 ROUTINE TO PERFORM FLOATING-POINT ADDITION
   WAIT
   ESC    FLD, ALPHA     ; TRANSFER FIRST OPERAND ALPHA FROM MEMORY TO 8087
   WAIT
   ESC    FLD, BETA      ; TRANSFER SECOND OPERAND BETA FROM MEMORY TO 8087
   WAIT
   ESC    FADD           ; EXECUTE FLOATING-POINT ADD COMMAND
   WAIT
   ESC    FST, GAMMA     ; TRANSFER RESULT GAMMA FROM 8087 TO MEMORY
```

Figure 8.49 8086 assembly-language routine to perform floating-point addition using the 8087.

interrupted WAIT instruction; this deviates from the normal method of handling interrupts.

8.3.3 IO Processors

IO processors have been standard components of mainframe computers since the 1960s. They are useful in microcomputer systems that have unusually heavy processing loads or throughput requirements, making it desirable to off-load most IO processing from the CPU to a processor dedicated to IO operations. An IOP is a programmable device whose complexity falls between that of a general-purpose microprocessor and the specialized IO controllers encountered in Chap. 7. It has an instruction set that is designed for supporting IO operations, a task at which it can be expected to be more efficient than a standard microprocessor. An IOP is capable of fetching and executing its own IO programs from an external memory, and therefore can be programmed to control IO operations involving essentially any type of IO device. IOPs can support DMA data transfers of the type required by very fast IO devices such as disk memories. A typical IOP can supervise concurrent IO operations involving a few fast IO devices or a large number of slow IO devices. The data-transfer facilities provided by the IOP are time-shared or multiplexed by the active IO devices, each of which can be viewed as having its own DMA channel or data path through the IOP to main memory.

Figure 8.50 shows a basic way of including an IOP in a computer system. The IOP is attached to the system bus and the IO devices in the same way as a DMA controller (cf. Fig. 7.67). Unlike a DMA controller, however, the IOP can execute IO programs, which, in the case of Fig. 8.50, share the system's main memory with CPU programs. The CPU software has overall control of the system, and is responsible for selecting the IO tasks to be executed by the IOP; the CPU and IOP thus have a sort of master–slave relationship. IO operations are carried out by the system in the following manner:

1. The CPU writes a set of messages to the IOP in a predefined format in a fixed region of main memory that we will call IOMESS. These messages define an IO task—a sequence of data-transfer operations, for instance—to be carried out by the IOP. They include such information as the address of the IO program to be executed, the IO device to be used, the actions to be performed on termination of the IO program, and other relevant parameters.
2. The CPU executes an instruction that activates an "attention" line connected to the IOP. The IOP responds by reading the contents of IOMESS and beginning execution of the IO program pointed to by IOMESS.
3. The IOP and the CPU proceed independently with the execution of their respective programs, using normal DMA mechanisms to share the system bus. From time to time the IOP can place messages for the CPU in IOMESS where they can be read by the CPU to determine the current status of the IO task being executed by the IOP.
4. When the IOP completes its allotted task, it sends an interrupt signal to the CPU and enters a wait state, where it remains until a new IO task is assigned to it by the CPU.

As Fig. 8.50 indicates, the CPU and IOP communicate in two ways: directly via

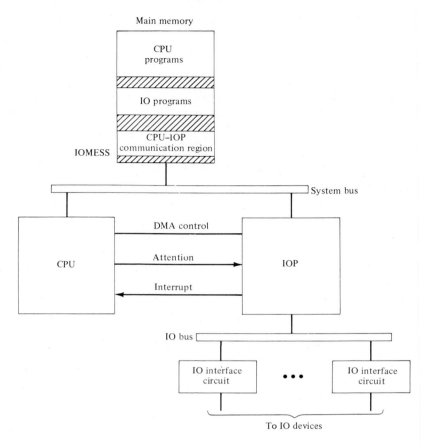

Figure 8.50 Organization of a computer containing an IOP.

special control lines and indirectly via messages in main memory. These control lines allow the processors to attract each other's attention very rapidly to request some service. The details of the service in question are stored, if necessary, in the message region IOMESS. The CPU uses the attention line to make the IOP execute some specified program; in much the same way, the IOP uses an interrupt-request line to make the CPU execute a predefined program. Standard DMA request lines are used by the IOP to force the CPU to relinquish control of the system bus. Note that the CPU cannot similarly force the IOP to relinquish the system bus to it; it must wait until the IOP has finished using the bus. The fact that the CPU and IOP must share the system bus for instruction and data transfer can limit overall performance in heavily loaded systems. Conflict between the CPU and IOP for access to the system bus can be reduced via the system organization of Fig. 8.39a, in which the IOP has a local memory for storing IO programs that it can access via a separate IO bus. CPU-IOP conflict can be reduced even further, but at much higher hardware cost, by using a crossbar switch as in Fig. 8.41.

The instruction set of a typical IOP contains a limited range of data-transfer, data-processing, and program-control instructions, all oriented toward IO operations. The only data-processing functions performed by the IOP are address construction, which requires unsigned binary addition or subtraction, word counting, data reformatting, and the like. Most instructions executed by the IOP take the form

$$\text{Transfer } N \text{ words to/from memory region IOBUF} \qquad (8.13)$$

using some previously selected IO device D that is attached to the IOP in question. Input operations require the IOP to transfer data from D to the IOP, and thence to main memory, while for output operations, the IOP reads data from main memory and then transfers the data to D. The IOP generally communicates with D via synchronous or asynchronous data transfer over an IO bus; it communicates with main memory via DMA. The number of DMA steps needed to execute an instruction such as (8.13) depends on the type of DMA control used (cycle stealing, block DMA transfer, etc.; see Sec. 7.3.5). Unlike a DMA controller, an IOP can carry out a sequence of unrelated DMA operations without CPU intervention.

Figure 8.51 presents an overview of the internal operation of a representative IOP. It remains in an inactive or wait state until it receives the appropriate attention signal from the CPU. In response to this, the IOP reads a set of task parameters from the CPU-IOP message area IOMESS in main memory. Note that the minimum information it requires is the starting address of an IO program, which it loads into an internal program counter to initiate program execution by the IOP. The IO program may be used to fetch additional control parameters not stored in IOMESS. Since the IOP typically controls several IO devices, an essential parameter is the address of the particular IO device D to be used. Once it has identified D, the IOP must activate D and prepare it for its role in the current IO operation. This requires a series of device-specific commands to be transmitted to D. These commands are treated as output data by the IOP, and are simply fetched under IO program control from main memory and passed to the IO device. Examples of such device-specific commands are:

Switch device on/off
Start/stop data transfer
Move read/write head of disk memory to specified position
Advance printer by a specified number of lines
Advance printer to next page
Advance magnetic tape to next record
Rewind magnetic tape

To control data transfer to or from D, the IOP must initialize a set of its internal registers to form a DMA channel for D; these registers include a memory address register, a word count register, and any necessary data buffer and channel status registers. Once the IOP's channel registers and the IO device have been initialized, the main IO task can proceed in normal DMA fashion. When the word count register for the current DMA operation reaches zero, a new DMA operation can be initiated by including the necessary DMA initialization instructions in the current IO program. When the IOP reaches the end of the

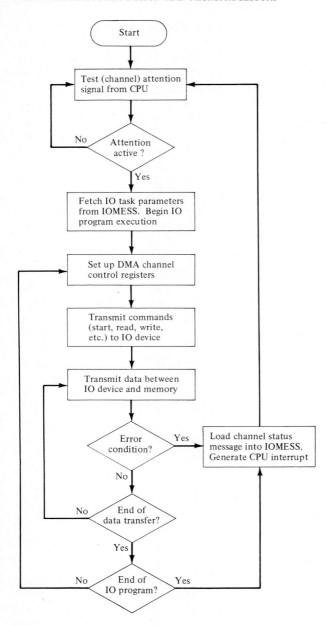

Figure 8.51 Operation of a typical IOP.

program, it writes a channel status message into the IOMESS region of main memory and sends an interrupt signal to the CPU. The IOP is normally programmed to abort an IO operation if it encounters an error condition such as an IO device that fails to respond to a data-transfer request signal. In that case it also places a status message in IOMESS to inform the CPU of the error condition.

The Intel 8086 series is one of the few microprocessor families containing a dedicated IOP, the 8089 (El-Ayat, 1979; Intel, 1981b). This one-chip IOP, packaged in a 40-pin DIP, has the internal structure depicted in Fig. 8.52. It comprises a pair of independent DMA channels, supported by specialized I- and E-units, and elaborate bus control circuits. Each channel contains its own program counter, termed a task pointer TP in 8089 literature, thus enabling two independent IO programs to be executed concurrently in time-shared fashion. Each channel also contains the usual DMA control registers, including address registers for the data source and destination, and a word count register indicating the number of bytes remaining to be transferred in the current

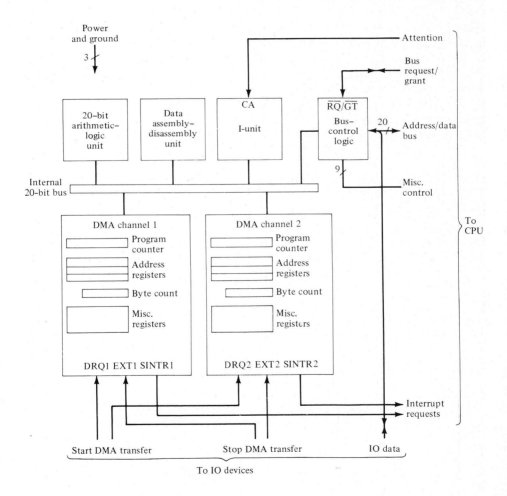

Figure 8.52 Internal organization of the Intel 8089 IOP.

IO operation. The DMA channels share a 20-bit ALU, whose large word size is designed to accommodate the 20-bit memory addresses used in 8086-based systems. Because of pin limitations, the 8089 uses a single bidirectional 20-bit bus for data and address communication with both main memory and IO devices. External latches and control circuits are necessary to separate data from address words and, if desired, to create separate system and IO buses. The 8089 is designed to handle both 8-bit and 16-bit data words. It automatically can assemble 8-bit words received from an input device into 16-bit words for transmission to memory; conversely, it automatically can disassemble 16-bit words obtained from memory for transmission to an output device.

The 8089 IOP has about 50 different instruction types, which are summarized in Fig. 8.53. These instructions form a general-purpose instruction set with rather primitive arithmetic and program-control capabilities, but with some specialized features for IO control. Most instructions handle 8-, 16-, and 20-bit data words, with the last, of course, being memory address words, which are treated as unsigned integers. Several bit-manipulation instructions are also provided. Four addressing modes may be used in 8089 instructions: immediate, base, indexed, and indexed with postincrementing. Operands may be stored in 8089 registers or in the system's memory or IO address space. It should be noted that the 8089's instruction set is not compatible with that of the 8086 at either the machine-language or assembly-language level. Software (IO programs) for the 8089 is generally written in an assembly language (ASM-89) that is unique to the 8089, although it has a family resemblance to that of the 8086; see Fig. 8.8.

Major Type	Subtype	Instruction	Comment
Data transfer		Move 8/16-bit data word	
		Move address (pointer)	
Data processing	Arithmetic	Add	Unsigned 20-bit
		Increment	operations, with shorter
		Decrement	operands sign-extended
			to 20 bits
	Logical	And	
		Or	
		Not	
	Bit manipulation	Set specified bit to 1	
		Clear specified bit to 0	
Program control	Branch	Jump unconditionally	
		Jump conditionally	
		Call subroutine	
	Other	Set logical bus width (WID)	
		Test and set while locked (TSL)	
		Begin DMA transfer (XFER)	
		Send interrupt to CPU	
		No operation	
		Halt	

Figure 8.53 Summary of the 8089 instruction set.

As Fig. 8.53 suggests, the 8089 has very limited data-processing capabilities. A few unsigned binary instructions are supplied, primarily for effective address calculation. The program-control instructions are also more restrictive than those of a typical microprocessor. For example, a subroutine call is expressed as

$$\text{CALL} \quad \text{SAVE, SUB} \tag{8.14}$$

where SAVE is a user-defined location in main memory used to save the old contents of the channel's program counter (task pointer), and SUB is the subroutine address to be loaded into the program counter. There is no stack mechanism of the kind usually employed with call instructions. There is also no return instruction per se. To effect a return from the subroutine called by (8.14), the return address SAVE must be moved back to the IOP channel in question via a MOVP (move pointer) instruction. The special instruction WID (set bus width) is used to define the data unit, or logical word size, for DMA transfers as either 8 or 16 bits, with the restriction that the logical width of a bus cannot exceed its physical width. The TSL (test and set while locked) instruction is intended to prevent conflicts for shared resources when the 8089 is used in a multi-processor configuration; its use is discussed in Sec. 8.3.4. Another noteworthy 8089 instruction XFER (transfer) causes the channel in question to begin a DMA-controlled data-transfer operation, after execution of the instruction immediately following XFER. This one-instruction delay gives the 8089 time to initialize its registers for the DMA operation before the actual data transfer begins. As noted earlier, IO devices receive their start commands as sequences of data words transmitted from the IOP. Fast IO devices such as disk memories may begin data transfer immediately after receiving their last command from the IOP. In such cases XFER should be placed immediately before the IOP instruction that transmits the last command to the IO device; reversal of the order of these two IO instructions could result in loss of data.

The 8089 is designed to connect to an 8086-based system in two ways, termed local and remote configurations. In local mode, which is illustrated in Fig. 8.54, the IOP and CPU share a single system bus, to which they are connected via various interface circuits, including address latches, bus transreceiver circuits, and a special bus controller chip, the 8288. The 8086 CPU is set to its maximum mode of operation, so that the system bus closely corresponds to the Multibus, but without the latter's bus-access control features which are not required here. A bidirectional bus-request/grant line $\overline{\text{RQ/}}$ $\overline{\text{GT}}$ links the 8086 and 8089, and allows the 8089 to obtain control of the system bus from the 8086 at any time; it combines in one line the functions of the standard DMA request and DMA acknowledge lines. Note that the 8086 cannot request control of the system bus from the 8089. The channel attention line CA is used by the CPU to initiate IOP activities. As shown in Fig. 8.54, CA is generally wired into the CPU's IO address space, so that it can be activated by executing an IO instruction such as OUT ADR, where ADR is the IO address assigned to CA. Because there is only one physical path for transferring data to or from the 8089, all IO devices are connected via appropriate interface circuits or IO controllers to the system bus. Each IO device is linked directly to one of the 8089's DMA channels via a pair of lines called DRQ (data request) and EXT (external terminate). A previously selected IO device activates DRQi to tell the IOP that it is ready to send or receive data via DMA channel i. Similarly, the device can activate EXTi to

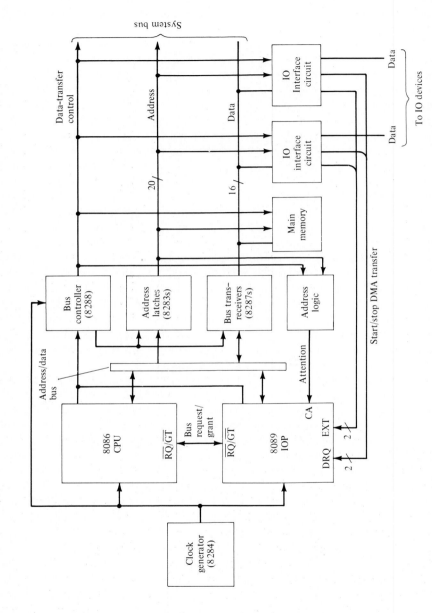

Figure 8.54 System configuration with the 8089 in local mode.

terminate a current DMA operation using channel *i*. It should be observed that, in the local mode of Fig. 8.54, every DMA word transfer requires at least two system bus cycles, one to send the word to the 8089 and another to retransmit the word from the 8089 to its final destination.

Using the 8089 in local mode requires relatively few system components, but leads to contention between the IOP and the CPU for use of the system bus. This contention is aggravated by the fact that the system bus forms the main data path between the IOP and the IO devices it controls. Using the 8089 in remote mode, as illustrated in Fig. 8.55, greatly reduces CPU-IOP contention for system bus cycles, at the cost of additional interface components and connections. In the remote mode, the 8089's interface lines are fanned out to two separate buses, a conventional system bus, and an IO bus, which is local or private to the 8089 and is not directly accessible by (i.e., is remote from) the CPU. As Fig. 8.55 shows, a second set of address latches and transreceivers are needed to drive the IO bus. Peripheral IO devices are now attached to the IO bus instead of the system bus, thus removing all data traffic between the IOP and the IO devices from the system bus. A local memory for the IOP is also attached to the IO bus and used to store the IO programs to be executed by the IOP. Consequently the IOP no longer needs to use the system bus to fetch instructions. It must, however, use the system bus to access the system's global memory, which stores information that must be equally accessible to both the CPU and the IOP. IOMESS, for instance, is located in the global memory. The 8089 distinguishes local from global memory by treating addresses assigned to local memory (and to IO devices) as part of its IO address space, while the addresses of devices attached to the system bus fall within the 8089's memory address space. In the remote configuration the 8086 and 8089 function as independent processors, and have equal access to the system bus using the Multibus bus-access conventions discussed in Sec. 7.3.2. Note that the 8089 no longer needs immediate access to the system bus to meet the data-transfer requirements of high-speed IO devices, since it can use its local memory as a temporary data buffer. The 8289 bus arbitration chip is used in the 8089 remote mode to control access to the system bus, which is now essentially the standard Multibus system bus. As will be seen in the following section, the interface structure of Fig. 8.55 is what is necessary to connect several 8086-series CPUs (and IOPs) to form a multiprocessor system.

8.3.4 Multiprocessors

A multiprocessor is a computer system containing two or more general-purpose (micro)processors or CPUs. As observed already, the three principal motivations for designing multiprocessing systems are:

1. High throughput
2. Efficient distributed computing
3. Fault tolerance

High throughput results from the fact that several instructions can be executed simultaneously or in parallel using the multiple CPUs. A multiprocessor organization is very

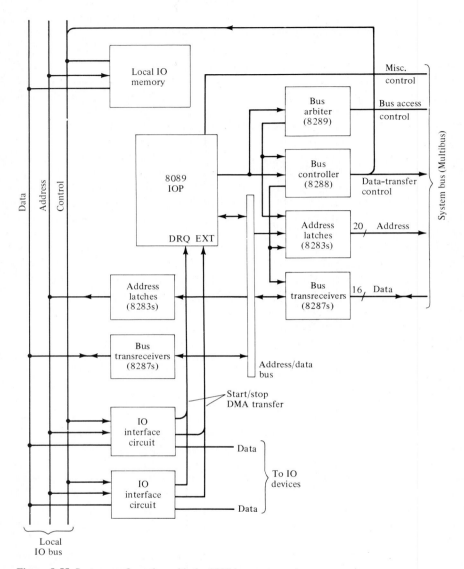

Figure 8.55 System configuration with the 8089 in remote mode.

suitable for a distributed system where related computational tasks must be performed at sites that are some distance from one another. Finally, fault tolerance and high reliability are possible because a multiprocessor, unlike a uniprocessor, can be made to continue operating in the presence of a failed CPU. Although these advantages have long been recognized, the use of multiprocessors in digital system design has been severely limited by their greater hardware costs, and by the difficulty of programming several CPUs to cooperate efficiently in the execution of common tasks. The advent of microprocessors has considerably reduced the hardware cost of such systems, but many of their software design problems remain poorly understood.

Multiprocessors are often divided into two basic groups, tightly coupled and loosely coupled, depending on the degree of cooperation among the system's CPUs. A *tightly coupled* multiprocessor allows its CPUs to interact frequently and rapidly to share programs and data. The CPUs typically share access to a common main memory and IO subsystem. Each system task must be partitioned into independent subtasks that can be executed in parallel by different CPUs. This type of task partitioning is by no means easy to achieve, except in special cases. Most algorithms implemented on computers are sequential in nature, that is, a new computation cannot be initiated until a current one is completed. Such algorithms can be executed no more efficiently by a multiprocessor than by a uniprocessor. Tightly coupled multiprocessors are generally restricted to applications where a high degree of easily exploitable parallelism is known to exist. Even for such applications it can be quite difficult to program a multiprocessor to achieve its maximum potential throughput. Contention among the CPUs for shared resources means that a CPU may have to wait for a resource it needs until it is relinquished by some other CPU; an idle CPU waiting for a busy resource to become available makes no contribution to the system's throughput. Consequently the n-fold increase in performance that might be expected to result from increasing the number of CPUs from one to n is rarely achieved in practice (see Prob. 8.50). The system of Fig. 8.41 employing a crossbar switch to link a set of CPUs to a common shared memory is an example of a tightly coupled multiprocessor.

A multiprocessor is said to be *loosely coupled* if there is relatively infrequent interaction among its constituent CPUs. Normally each CPU in such a system has its own local memory and IO devices, to which other CPUs do not have direct access. Most of the CPU's activities involve only its local or private resources, and thus do not bring it into conflict with the remaining CPUs. Communication between two CPUs of a loosely coupled system need not be especially fast. A global memory that is accessible to all CPUs may be used as a message store or "mailbox," as in the CPU-IOP communication discussed in the preceding section. Alternatively two CPUs may be linked via their IO systems, so that each sees the other as a sophisticated IO device. Since there is little CPU-CPU interaction in loosely coupled multiprocessors, high levels of parallel processing are readily achievable. Software design is usually simpler than in the tightly coupled case, since interprocessor communication can be implemented by asynchronous transfer of messages via the global resources. Loosely coupled systems also tend to be more fault tolerant; a failure of a CPU that is mainly devoted to local processing with private resources is likely to have little impact on the rest of the system. Most distributed multiprocessing systems, such as that of Fig. 8.40, fall into the loosely coupled category.

To illustrate the broad range of possible applications of microprocessors in multiprocessor design, we now examine three such systems containing the popular 8080 microprocessor studied in Sec. 5.4. The systems in question, all of which may be regarded as loosely coupled multimicroprocessors, are:

1. The Texas Instruments Model 763 portable communications terminal, which contains two microprocessors (Texas Instruments, 1978).

2. The Wang System 30, a distributed word-processing system containing up to 14 8080-based CRT terminals or work stations (Shackil, 1981).
3. The Siemens SMS (Structured Multiprocessor System) 201, an experimental multiprocessor containing 128 8080s and designed for high-speed numerical computations involving floating-point numbers (Kober & Kuznia, 1978).

The 763 is a general-purpose IO terminal with a typewriter-like keyboard and a dot-matrix printer, which is designed for communication with computer systems. It contains a magnetic bubble memory capable of storing several pages of alphanumeric text, which can be modified by means of text-editing software in the 763 before transmission to an external computer. The internal structure of the 763 is shown in Fig. 8.56. It employs an 8080 in conjunction with a 9980 16-bit microprocessor, a member of the Texas Instruments 9900 series (see Prob. 8.14). The two microprocessors share the tasks of control-

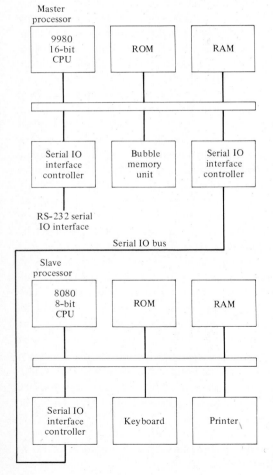

Figure 8.56 Organization of the Texas Instruments Model 763 portable terminal.

ling the 763's IO devices, which comprise the keyboard, the printer, the bubble memory system, and a serial interface controller that enables the 763 to be easily interfaced to a variety of external devices. The 9980 and the 8080 have a master–slave relationship similar to that between a CPU and an IOP. The more powerful 9980 is the master processor, and is responsible for controlling the bubble memory and the communications interface circuitry. It also executes the text-editing software, which is controlled by commands entered via the keyboard. The 8080 controls the remaining IO devices, namely, the keyboard and the printer. Each microprocessor has its own main memory, both ROM and RAM, permitting it to execute programs independently of, and in parallel with, the other microprocessor. The two microprocessors are linked by a 9600-baud serial IO bus, which allows them to exchange data with a minimum of interaction between their control software. Clearly the 9980 and the 8080 are very loosely coupled in this application.

The Wang System 30, a commercial word-processing system that was introduced in 1976, is a good example of a loosely coupled distributed multimicroprocessor. It is intended to provide comprehensive text-processing facilities for a number of secretaries in the same office. Each secretary is provided with an 8080-based work station containing a keyboard, a CRT display, and a 16K-byte RAM serving as a local memory. The 8080 microprocessor controls the keyboard and CRT and executes text-editing programs stored in its local memory. The work station is linked via a high-speed serial IO line (a coaxial cable) to a master processor that manages a large set of data and program files stored in a disk memory unit. The master processor, which is also 8080-based, has direct access to the RAMs of all the work stations, and can transfer programs or data to them from the central disk memory. The disk memory has a capacity of 10M bytes, enabling several thousand pages of alphanumeric text to be stored on-line. Data transfer between the work stations and the master processor is implemented as a DMA IO operation, thus giving each system user very fast access to the shared disk files. One or more hard-copy printers can be attached to the master processor and shared by the work stations. A typical configuration of the System 30 is shown in Fig. 8.57.

The Siemens 201 computer, which became operational in 1977, is an example of a more tightly coupled multiprocessor containing a very large number of microprocessors, 128 in all. It was designed for applications requiring fast floating-point computation of the type normally requiring a much more expensive mainframe computer. The overall structure of the SMS 201 is depicted in Fig. 8.58. It consists of an array of 128 microcomputers termed processing modules (PMs), each comprising an 8080-based CPU and 16K bytes of local memory. The PMs form an 8×16 array, with each row of 16 PMs attached to a common shared bus. The eight buses are, in turn, connected to a minicomputer that serves as the master processor (MP) of the system. The IO devices of the SMS 201 are also attached to the MP. As in the Wang System 30, the MP here has direct access to the local memories of all PMs. It can transfer programs or data directly to one PM, to a set of PMs, or to all PMs simultaneously. This broadcast mode of data transfer allows the MP to disseminate information to the PMs fairly rapidly, in spite of the use of relatively slow shared buses as communication links between the MP and the PMs. The PMs communicate with the MP via a conventional interrupt mechanism. In a typical application of this multiprocessor, the MP is responsible for assigning tasks to the PMs,

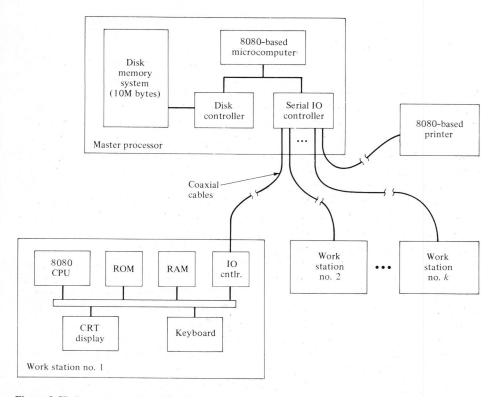

Figure 8.57 Organization of the Wang System 30 word-processing system.

which they then proceed to carry out independently by executing programs placed in their local memories. The MP can read the results generated by any PM from its local memory and transfer them to any other PM. This type of interprocessor communication is quite slow, and hence the SMS 201 is mainly suitable for applications that can be broken down into autonomous subtasks that interact infrequently. With such applications the SMS 201 can achieve throughputs of up to 32 MIPs, which exceeds the performance of many mainframe computers. Its designers note that by adding an arithmetic processor such as the AMD 9511 (see Sec. 8.3.2) to each PM, the system's throughput can be increased by a factor of about 20. Further performance improvements would result from replacing the 8080 by a more powerful microprocessor.

To illustrate the complex numerical tasks for which tightly coupled multiprocessors are suitable, we consider one of the applications of the SMS 201, namely, weather forecasting (Kober & Kuznia, 1978). In a typical mathematical model for this difficult problem, the geographic region of interest is marked with evenly spaced rectangular grid points $P_1, P_2, \ldots, P_n$, where n may be many thousands. Let $F_i(t)$ denote the values of some set of weather functions of interest (temperature, wind velocity, atmospheric pressure, etc.) that are present at grid point P_i at time t. The value $F_i(t + d)$ present after

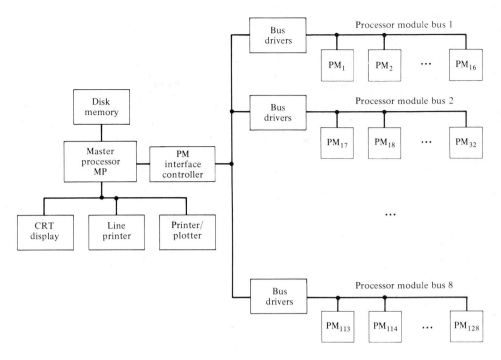

Figure 8.58 Organization of the experimental Siemens SMS 201 multiprocessor.

a short time interval d can be expressed in terms of $F_i(t)$ and the corresponding values $F_j(t)$ present at the four grid points P_{iN}, P_{iS}, P_{iE}, P_{iW} that are P_i's nearest neighbors in the north, south, east, and west directions respectively. This relation can be written as

$$F_i(t + d) = G[F_i(t), F_{iN}(t), F_{iS}(t), F_{iE}(t), F_{iW}(t)] \qquad (8.15)$$

For example, if T_i denotes the temperature at P_i, we can express T_i at time $t + d$ as the average of the surrounding temperatures at time t thus:

$$T_i(t + d) = \frac{T_{iN}(t) + T_{iS}(t) + T_{iE}(t) + T_{iW}(t)}{4}$$

In general, the function G of (8.15) is defined by sets of partial differential equations involving real (floating-point) variables. Thus, starting with a known set of $F_i(t)$ values, for example, the present measured weather conditions at all grid points, the desired weather parameters at some future time $t + kd$ can be estimated by executing (8.15) k times for every grid point—a total of kn times. For instance, if $n = 10,000$ and $d = 5$ minutes, a 24-hour weather forecast requires $12 \times 24 \times 10,000 = 2.88$ million evaluations of (8.15), with each evaluation requiring many floating-point calculations.

The advantage of a multiprocessor in solving the foregoing weather-forecasting problem is that all calculations required for each grid point P_i can be assigned to one processing module PM$_i$, and all PMs can evaluate (8.15) simultaneously for different grid points. After each evaluation step, the result $F_i(t + d)$ must be transferred from PM$_i$ to the four processing modules that perform the computations for the neighboring grid points P_{iN}, P_{iS}, P_{iE}, and P_{iW}. The time required for this interprocessor data exchange is very small compared with that required to compute $F_i(t + d)$. Consequently the weather-forecasting algorithm has the kind of inherent parallelism that can readily be exploited by a multiprocessor. The SMS 201, for example, can evaluate (8.15) for 128 different grid points at the same time. This evaluation has three major phases:

1. A control phase during which the master processor MP selects the programs to be executed by the PMs, and broadcasts a start-execution order to all PMs
2. A computation phase during which the PMs independently execute the indicated programs using only their local resources
3. A communication phase during which the MP transfers to each PM the results it needs from other PMs

Note that the main role of the MP is to coordinate the activities of the PMs. It also provides a communication link between the PMs and the system's IO devices, for instance, to print out the final results.

Unlike the 8080/8085 and other 8-bit microprocessors, most 16-bit microprocessors have hardware and software features specifically intended to support multiprocessing. The 8086, for example, is designed to allow moderate numbers of processors, both CPUs and IOPs, to be connected in a tightly coupled multiprocessor configuration, with the Multibus or IEEE 796 bus serving as the global system bus; see Fig. 8.59. Each CPU can

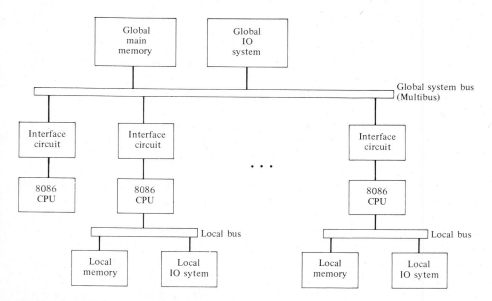

Figure 8.59 Multiprocessor system employing the 8086 microprocessor.

have a local or private bus with local memory and IO devices attached to it in the manner found in IOPs configured in the remote mode of Fig. 8.55. As illustrated in Fig. 8.60, a fairly complex multichip interface is necessary to connect an 8086 CPU to the over 60 lines forming the Multibus. This interface serves to isolate the 8086 from other processors connected to the Multibus. Since the Multibus supports the most general form of asynchronous communication, each processor can operate independently at its own distinct clock rate. Access to the Multibus is on a priority basis determined by the bus priority control lines $\overline{BPRN}$ and $\overline{BPRO}$, which, in the circuit of Fig. 8.60, are controlled by the 8289 bus arbiter chip. When the CPU is not using the Multibus, the data, address, and data-transfer control lines linking it to the Multibus are disabled, that is, placed in the high-impedance state. Suppose that the 8086 begins execution of an instruction that addresses global memory or IO, and hence requires access to the Multibus. The 8289 bus arbiter, which continuously monitors the Multibus $\overline{BUSY}$ line, determines whether the Multibus is available. If it is, the 8289 enables the 8288 bus controller, which is responsible for issuing read/write control signals. The 8289 also enables the 8283 address latches allowing an address from the 8086 to be transferred to the Multibus; a normal asynchronous data transfer then takes place over the Multibus. If the 8289 finds

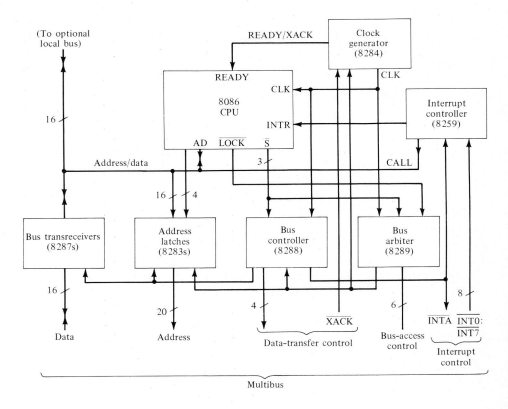

Figure 8.60 Interfacing the 8086 to the Multibus.

that the Multibus is unavailable ($\overline{\text{BUSY}} = 0$), it prevents, via the 8284 clock generator chip, the activation of the 8086's READY line. This causes the 8086 to enter a waiting state of indefinite duration. READY is eventually enabled by the 8289 after it gains control of the Multibus, and the requested bus cycle can be completed. By stretching Multibus access requests in this manner, the bus arbitration process is made transparent to the CPU software.

The sharing of global memory and IO resources in a multiprocessor can lead to possible conflict situations, which the system hardware or software must prevent. It is necessary, for example, to prevent a CPU from writing into a common data area of global memory while another CPU is reading from the same memory area. Similarly, a CPU should not be allowed to take control of a DMA channel or IO device that is actively being used by another CPU. A standard technique for avoiding such conflicts is to assign a special control variable S called a *semaphore* to each shared resource R. S indicates the status of R (busy or not busy), and is stored in a global memory location where it can be accessed, tested, and changed by any CPU. Before a CPU attempts to use the shared resource R, it must first read and check the corresponding semaphore S. If S is in the busy state (S = 1), then R is unavailable, and the CPU should not attempt to use it. If S = 0, indicating that R is available, the CPU in question should first set S to 1 to prevent other CPUs from using R, then it can take control of R. When it has finished using R, the controlling CPU should reset S to 0 to make R available to other processors.

Figure 8.61a lists a short program that might, at first sight, be thought suitable for testing and setting semaphores in the 8086-based multiprocessor of Fig. 8.59. However, as Fig. 8.61b shows, execution of this program by two or more CPUs at about the same time can result in a situation in which each CPU erroneously concludes that it alone has gained control of the shared resource R. This conflict arises from the fact that testing and setting the semaphore requires a sequence of Multibus cycles spread over a period during which several CPUs may control the bus. As indicated in Fig. 8.61b, two CPUs can fetch the semaphore S and determine that it is in the nonbusy state, before either has a chance to set S to the busy state. Each CPU independently sets S to the busy state and proceeds to use the shared resource R, with potentially disastrous consequences. This problem can be eliminated by using the semaphore control routine listed in Fig. 8.61c. A key component of this routine is the 8086's LOCK instruction, which causes the instruction that follows it, in this case XCHG (exchange), to have exclusive use of the system bus for the entire duration of its instruction execution cycle. Note that in 8086 assembly language, LOCK is written as a prefix of the instruction for which it locks the system bus. The execution of LOCK by the 8086 activates its $\overline{\text{LOCK}}$ control line (see Fig. 8.59), which causes the 8289 bus arbiter chip to activate the Multibus's $\overline{\text{BUSY}}$ line as soon as the Multibus becomes available. $\overline{\text{BUSY}}$ is held active for the duration of the several Multibus cycles needed to fetch and execute the XCHG instruction. (The 8086 normally deactivates $\overline{\text{BUSY}}$ at the end of every bus cycle so that a processor of higher priority can, if it requests, control the next Multibus cycle.) XCHG reads the current value of the semaphore S into the CPU register AL, and writes the busy value (S = 1) into the semaphore's storage location in global memory. Since the Multibus is locked for the duration of this instruction cycle, no other CPU can read S and find it in the nonbusy state. The first CPU now tests its copy of the previous value of S; if 0, the CPU assumes

```
;   INVALID 8086 ROUTINE FOR SEMAPHORE CONTROL (SHOULD NOT BE USED)
LOOP:  TEST   S, 0              ; FETCH SEMAPHORE S AND COMPARE TO 0. SET ZERO
                                ;   FLAG Z TO 1 IF S = 0
       JNE    LOOP             ; IF Z ≠ 1, JUMP TO 'LOOP'
       MOV    S, 1             ; SET S TO 1 (BUSY)
```

(*a*)

Multibus cycle	i	$i + 1$	$i + 2$	$i + 3$
Multibus transaction	CPU 1 fetches semaphore S	CPU 2 fetches semaphore S	CPU 1 sets S to 1	CPU 2 sets S to 1

(*b*)

```
;   VALID 8086 ROUTINE FOR SEMAPHORE CONTROL

LOOP:  MOV    AL, 1           ; MOVE 1 INTO CPU REGISTER AL
       LOCK   XCHG AL, S      ; SWAP THE CONTENTS OF AL AND THE MEMORY LOCATION
                              ;   STORING SEMAPHORE S WITH THE MULTIBUS LOCKED
       OR     AL, AL          ; SET ZERO FLAG Z TO 1 IF AL CONTAINS 0
       JNE    LOOP            ; IF Z ≠ 1, JUMP TO 'LOOP'
```

(*c*)

Figure 8.61 (*a*) Invalid 8086 semaphore control routine; (*b*) possible conflict situation arising from the use of this invalid code; (*c*) valid 8086 semaphore control routine.

control of R, otherwise it continues to execute the XCHG instruction until it finds S = 0. When a CPU has finished using the resource R, it should reset the semaphore S to 0 by executing the instruction

$$MOV \quad S, 0$$

The 8089 IOP has a semaphore control instruction TSL (test and set while locked), which permits the entire routine of Fig. 8.61c to be replaced by the following instruction:

$$LOOP: \quad TSL \ S, \ 1, \ LOOP$$

8.4 SUMMARY

Advances in IC manufacturing technology have resulted in continual improvements in the functional capabilities of one-chip microprocessors and microcomputers. Although 4-bit and 8-bit microprocessors account for the majority of applications, an increasingly important role is being played by 16-bit and 32-bit designs. Besides employing a larger CPU word size, these newer microprocessors have more powerful instruction sets, and a much larger main memory address space. They incorporate design features to support such advanced architectural concepts as virtual memory management, arithmetic coprocessors, and multiprocessing.

The Intel 8086 is representative of 16-bit microprocessors that have evolved from 8-bit predecessors, in this case, the 8080/8085. Its instruction set adds 16-bit operations, new functions such as multiplication and division, and more general addressing modes to the 8080/8085's instruction set. The capacity of main memory is increased from 64K bytes to 1 megabyte. The 8086 constructs a 20-bit physical address by combining a logical address with a segment address obtained from one of four segment registers. This segmented addressing mode facilitates the programming of certain memory management functions such as the relocation or the protection of stored information. A small instruction buffer in the 8086 allows instruction fetching and execution to be overlapped to a limited extent to increase the CPU's effective instruction execution rate or throughput. The 8086 is designed for use in multiprocessor systems employing the Multibus (IEEE 796 bus) as the global system bus. The 8086 family contains two useful special-purpose processors, the 8089 IO processor and the 8087 arithmetic coprocessor.

The Motorola 68000 is also generally viewed as a 16-bit microprocessor, but it has the internal architecture of a 32-bit CPU. Unlike its predecessors in the 6800 series, the 68000 has a relatively large number of general-purpose registers, which are designed to accommodate, in uniform fashion, 8-, 16-, and 32-bit operands. Physical addresses of up to 32 bits are used, allowing a maximum memory address space of 4096M bytes. Segmented addressing and other memory management functions can be implemented by adding a 68451 memory management unit to a 68000-based system. To support the design of operating systems, the 68000 has two system states: an unrestricted user state, and a supervisor state that is reserved for the operating system. The 68000's instruction set is noteworthy for its efficient exception handling via hardware- and software-implemented trap operations. Like the 8086, the 68000 has a large family of support circuits, including all those of the 6800 series.

Bit-sliced microprocessor families provide off-the-shelf ICs that enable system designers to define their own unique CPU architectures. Their key component is a (micro)processor slice, which constitutes the E-unit of a small, fast CPU. n copies of a k-bit processor slice can be connected to form an nk-bit CPU of the same kind as the basic slice. This allows the CPU word sizes to be tailored to a particular application; it also allows the use of high-speed low-density IC technologies such as TTL and ECL in microprocessor design. A bit-sliced microprocessor is controlled by an external I-unit, which typically is microprogrammed. Bit-sliced families also provide various building blocks for the design of microprogrammable control units and other system components. The disadvantages of bit-sliced systems are high development costs and parts counts as compared with systems based on conventional non-bit-sliced microprocessors.

Microprogramming refers to the storing of control signals in program-like form in a control memory. A particular operation or instruction I is executed by fetching and decoding a sequence of microinstructions that constitute a microprogram for I. Micro-programmed control has the advantage of being easier to design and modify than hardwired control. Consequently it is used to implement the I-units of more advanced microprocessors such as the 8086 and 68000, as well as in bit-sliced microprocessors.

The major parts of a microprogrammed control unit are the control memory CM and the microprogram sequencer, which generates the sequence of addresses used to fetch microinstructions from CM.

The AMD 2900 series is a comprehensive family of bipolar (Schottky TTL) components for designing bit-sliced systems. The 2901 chip is a representative 4-bit processor slice incorporating a 16-word register set, and an ALU capable of twos-complement addition and subtraction, Boolean operations, and shifting. A $4n$-bit processor can be constructed from n 2901s, using either ripple-carry propagation or carry lookahead to extend addition and subtraction from one slice to an n-slice array. More complex functions such as multiplication and division and floating-point operations are implemented by microprograms that control the 2901 array. To facilitate microprogramming, the 2900 series contains several microprogram sequencer chips. The 2909, for instance, is a 4-bit microprogram sequencer slice, n copies of which can be cascaded to form a microprogram sequencer that generates $4n$-bit addresses. The 2910 is a 12-bit microprogram sequencer that is not bit sliced.

Although they are mainly employed to realize new types of processors, bit-sliced families have also been used to construct emulators for existing microprocessors such as the 8080. The resulting bit-sliced microprocessors are generally significantly faster than the MOS microprocessors they replace. These speed improvements result from the use of a faster IC technology and the implementation of complex operations in microinstruction-level firmware rather than conventional instruction-level software.

In systems with heavy work loads, substantial performance increases can be achieved by offloading certain tasks from the CPU to more specialized auxiliary processors. Two such processors have come into widespread use: arithmetic processors for performing floating-point computations, and IO processors for controlling IO data transfers. An arithmetic processor can be designed to resemble an extension to its host CPU, deriving its instructions from the host's instruction stream, in which case it is said to be a coprocessor. The division of the work load of a system among several general-purpose microprocessors provides another method (multiprocessing) for improving overall performance.

The AMD 9511 is an early example of a one-chip arithmetic processor, which can be interfaced with any standard microprocessor. It executes a set of fixed-point and floating-point operations of the type found in scientific and engineering calculations. The 9511 is interfaced to a host microprocessor as if it were an IO device; data and commands are transferred between the 9511 and the CPU via IO operations. The 9511 can perform its computations independently and in parallel with the CPU. It can signal its status (busy or execution completed) via a busy signal, an interrupt request, or a status word that can be polled by the CPU. The 8086 family has a powerful arithmetic processor chip, the 8087 coprocessor. The 8087 can be programmed directly via CPU programs using the ESC (escape) instruction.

The IO processors are programmable devices capable of independently controlling a full range of IO operations involving a set of IO devices. They can be viewed as DMA controllers with the added ability to fetch and execute IO instructions without CPU intervention. Communication between a CPU and an IOP employs special control lines (attention and interrupt) and message areas in main memory. The 8089 IOP in the 8086 series is an example of a one-chip IOP designed for microprocessor-based systems. It comprises a pair of independent DMA channels and an instruction set oriented towards data-transfer control. The 8089 can be configured in local mode, in which case it communicates with the outside world via the main system bus. It also has a remote mode of operation that allows it to have connections both to the system bus and to a private IO bus. IO devices and an IO program memory may be attached to the IO bus, thereby reducing contention between the CPU and the IOP for access to the system bus.

Because of their low cost, microprocessors are attractive in the design of multi-processors, especially the loosely coupled variety where there is little interaction between the various microprocessors. Like all multiprocessors, multimicroprocessors present formidable software design problems due to the difficulty of programming several CPUs to operate in parallel while efficiently sharing common resources such as global memory and IO devices. The more advanced microprocessors have built-in features to support multiprocessor design. An example is the 8086's LOCK instruction, which enables a CPU to prevent other processors from gaining access to the global bus during such critical operations as testing and setting a semaphore. Another useful feature is a local bus system to allow a CPU to offload as much processing as possible from the global bus shared by all CPUs.

In conclusion, it should be noted that VLSI technology offers the possibility of building enormously complex multiprocessors at very low cost. It is presently possible to place a number of simple microprocessors on a single chip, thus making the one-chip multiprocessor feasible. Difficult problems in the design and application of such chips remain to be solved. Nevertheless, it is probable that, in the relatively few years since the introduction of the first microprocessors, we have barely scratched the surface of the powerful digital system design technology that is based on these devices.

8.5 FURTHER READING

The major 16-bit microprocessor families are described and compared, primarily from a software viewpoint, by Wakerly (1981). The Intel 8086 family and its applications are covered in the *iAPX 86,88 User's Manual* (Intel, 1981b), while a briefer treatment of the 68000 series appears in the *Motorola Microprocessors Data Manual* (Motorola 1981). Gupta and Toong (1983) present a useful collection of reprinted articles on 16- and 32-bit microprocessors. Section 8.2 on bit-sliced microprocessors is based, in part, on Hayes (1981), which surveys bit slicing from a broader perspective. Mick and Brick provide a comprehensive discussion of the AMD 2900 series and its applications in their book *Bit-Slice Microprocessor Design* (Mick & Brick, 1980). The AMD 9511 arithmetic processor and its interfacing requirements are examined by Cheng (1981) and Croson et al. (1981). The 8087 arithmetic processor, the 8089 IOP, and multiprocessing with the 8086 series are treated in Intel (1981b). Weitzman's text *Distributed Micro/Minicomputer Systems* discusses multimicroprocessor design in depth, with emphasis on loosely coupled systems (Weitzman, 1980).

8.6 PROBLEMS

8.1 Write a brief essay analyzing the influence, both good and bad, of its 8-bit predecessors on the design of either the 8086 or 68000 microprocessor. Indicate to what extent software compatibility has been maintained between the corresponding 8-bit and 16-bit families.

8.2 The architecture of a computer is said to be *orthogonal* if its instructions are designed in a uniform way from a small number of independent opcode types, data types, and addressing modes. Orthogonality implies little overlap in the functions of different instructions, and a high degree of regularity and consistency in instruction formats, all of which are desirable from a programming standpoint. Many 16-bit microprocessors have orthogonality as one of their design objectives.

    (*a*) What other microprocessor design objectives conflict with orthogonality, and why?

    (*b*) Compare and contrast the 8086 and 68000 from the point of view of the orthogonality of their instruction sets.

8.3 Describe the main differences in design and processing capabilities between general-purpose microprocessors, arithmetic processors, and IO processors.

8.4 Figure 8.62a shows how a memory management unit (MMU) might be added to a standard 8-bit microprocessor to increase its main memory address size from 16 to 24 bits, while also providing facilities for

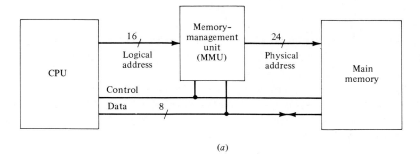

(*a*)

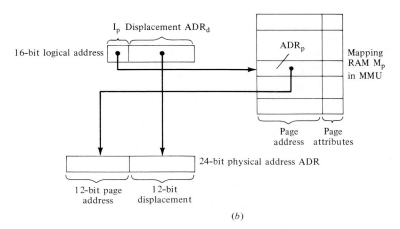

(*b*)

Figure 8.62 (*a*) Microcomputer containing an MMU; (*b*) address translation by the MMU.

relocation and protection of stored information. The main memory M is divided into 2^{12} nonoverlapping regions called *page frames,* each of which accommodates a 2^{12}-word block of information called a *page.* The 16-bit logical address generated by the CPU is divided into a 4-bit page index I_p and a 12-bit displacement ADR_d. A small RAM M_p in the MMU is used to translate I_p into a 12-bit page address ADR_p. The MMU constructs a 24-bit physical address ADR for transmission to M thus

$$ADR = 2^{12} \times ADR_p + ADR_d$$

as depicted in Fig. 8.62b. The contents of M_p are programmable, allowing the relationship between logical and physical addresses to be varied dynamically under software control. Each entry in the mapping memory M_p includes several bits defining the attributes of each page, such as read only (write protected). Page attributes are checked during address translation by the MMU. If it detects an invalid operation, such as an attempt to write into a page designated read only, it can abort the memory access and send an error interrupt (memory protection violation) to the CPU.

Carry out the logic design of this MMU at the register-transfer level, assuming that the system is to support virtual memory. Define an appropriate set of page attributes for inclusion in the entries of M_p.

8.5 (*a*) The 8086 and 68000 microprocessors have loop instructions that combine the functions of counter decrementing and conditional branching. Explain by means of examples how loop instructions can be used to implement **for** and **while** statements occurring in Pascal programs.

(*b*) Explain why the 8086 and 68000 have both signed and unsigned versions of their multiply and divide instructions, but not of their add and subtract instructions.

8.6 The 20-bit effective address $A_0:A_{19}$ generated by the 8086 references a particular 8-bit byte in main memory. It is often desirable to be able to access an entire 16-bit word during one memory cycle of an 8086-based system, implying the need to access two consecutively addressed bytes simultaneously. For this purpose the 8086 generates a memory control signal called $\overline{BHE}$ (byte high enable), which is equivalent to the $\overline{BHEN}$ signal used in the Multibus (see Fig. 7.50). Describe by means of a logic diagram how 1 megabyte of RAM may be interfaced to an 8086, so that the effective memory word size is 16 bits.

8.7 Explain how the 8086's XLAT (translate) instruction may be used to translate bytes denoting alphanumeric characters from ASCII to EBCDIC, an 8-bit code (including parity) that originated in IBM computers.

8.8 The 8086 has four "ASCII adjust" instructions AAA, AAS, AAM, and AAD, which apply to addition, subtraction, multiplication, and division respectively. In conjunction with the corresponding binary instructions, they allow arithmetic operations to be performed on 1-byte ASCII numbers (see Fig. 5.17 for the complete ASCII code), which constitute unpacked decimal numbers containing one decimal digit per byte. For example, the digit 5 has the 8-bit ASCII representation 00110101, where the right half is the usual binary of BCD representation of five and the left half has no numerical significance. To add two ASCII bytes requires the following steps:

1. Apply a binary add instruction (ADD or ADC) to the ASCII operands, placing the uncorrected result in the AL register.
2. Execute AAA, which produces the correct ASCII sum in AL, but with the 4 leftmost bytes set to 0000 instead of 0011; AAA also adjusts the carry flags.

The ASCII-like unpacked format with an all-0 left half may be used internally in place of standard ASCII code. In fact this form must be used for the input operands with the AAM and AAD instructions. When necessary, a standard ASCII codeword can be produced by executing the or-accumulator instruction

OR   AL, 00110000B

which replaces the all-0 left half of AL by 0011. AAS and AAM are used in much the same way as AAA; AAD, however, is applied to an ASCII dividend in the accumulator before a binary division is performed.

(*a*) Determine the algorithms used by AAA and AAM (cf. the DAA algorithm given in Fig. 5.27). AAM adjusts a 2-byte result stored in AX.

(*b*) Suggest why the 8086 has no decimal-adjust instruction for multiplication of packed decimal numbers.

8.9 Consider the decimal addition program for the 8086 listed in Fig. 8.8.

(*a*) Making as few changes as possible, modify the program segment to perform the 32-digit decimal subtraction

$$BETA := ALPHA - BETA;$$

(*b*) Again making as few changes as possible, redesign the program and data segments to perform 32-digit addition under the assumption that ALPHA and BETA are in ASCII code. Note that ASCII strings may be defined as follows using the 8086's DB (define byte) directive:

$$PI \ DB \quad '3.14159' \qquad ; Define \ PI \ as \ a \ 7\text{-byte ASCII-coded string}$$

8.10 In programming languages such as Pascal, the local variables of a procedure only need storage space allocated to them during the actual execution of the procedure; after execution the space can be deallocated and used for other purposes. Explain by means of a specific Pascal program how the 68000's LINK and UNLK instructions facilitate the temporary assignment of storage space to local variables. Give the 68000 code that implements the main features of the Pascal program, using an assembly-language format with comments.

8.11 (*a*) Describe the differences between the 68000's TRAP instruction and a conventional subroutine call instruction such as JSR (jump to subroutine).

(*b*) TRAP is useful in the implementation of diagnostic programs that are intended to exercise a microprocessor and detect faulty behavior. Explain why this is so.

8.12 Suppose that a set of four single-channel DMA controllers are to be attached to a 68000 system bus, with each controller assigned a fixed bus-access priority. Design the bus-access portion of the logic needed to interface the DMA controllers to the system bus.

8.13 The three FC (function code) output lines of the 68000 provide the CPU status information given in Fig. 8.63. This serves to identify the CPU state (user or supervisor) and the type of the current memory/bus cycle (data transfer or instruction fetch). Suppose that main memory is to be divided into two 2^{23}-byte regions, with the upper half intended for the sole use of the operating system, while the lower half may be used by applications programs. Using the FC lines, design a general interface between the 68000 and main memory that automatically blocks all attempts by applications programs to access the operating system's half of main memory.

8.14 One of the first 16-bit microprocessors is the Texas Instruments 9900 (Simpson et al., 1978) introduced in 1976, and derived from the earlier 900 series of minicomputers. It has the unusual design illustrated in Fig. 8.64 in which the CPU does not contain the usual set of general-purpose data and address registers. Instead a set of 16 word locations in main memory serve as CPU registers, and are termed the CPU's *workspace*. Like conventional CPU registers, the 9900's workspace registers are referenced by short 4-bit addresses in instructions. The base address of the workspace region of memory is stored in a CPU register WP called the workspace pointer. A workspace register R[i] is accessed by adding its 4-bit address i to WP and performing a conventional memory read or write cycle with the resulting 16-bit address. Thus a register-to-register operation

Function Code			CPU Status	
FC2	FC1	FC0	State	CPU Cycle Type
0	0	0	Not used	
0	0	1	User	Data transfer
0	1	0	User	Instruction fetch
0	1	1	Not used	
1	0	0	Not used	
1	0	1	Supervisor	Data transfer
1	1	0	Supervisor	Instruction fetch
1	1	1	Any	Interrupt acknowledge

Figure 8.63 Use made of the 68000's FC control lines.

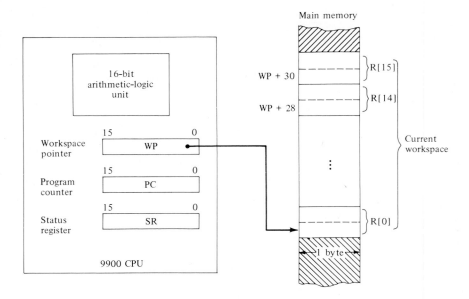

Figure 8.64 Memory-to-memory architecture of the Texas Instruments 9900 16-bit microprocessor.

is actually implemented by a memory-to-memory operation; for this reason, 990/9900-series computers are said to have *memory-to-memory architecture*. The current workspace can be changed at any time by executing an instruction that alters the contents of WP. The only other registers in the 9900 are a program counter PC and a status register SR, both of conventional design.

Write an essay analyzing the 9900's memory-to-memory architecture, and comparing it with the general-register architecture found in most CPUs.

8.15 Bit slicing is an attractive approach to the internal design of single-chip microprocessors. Explain why this is so.

8.16 An n-bit ripple-carry adder formed by cascading n full adder circuits forms a simple bit-sliced system (see Fig. 3.72). A full adder stage can be tested for faults—for example, internal short-circuit or open-circuit failures—by applying all eight possible signal patterns to its three input lines x_i, y_i, and C_{in}, and observing the eight response signals appearing on its two output lines z_i and C_{out}. Suppose that an n-bit ripple-carry adder must be tested for all faults affecting at most one of its full-adder stages. Test patterns may be applied to the $2n$ X and Y input lines and the external carry-in line C_{in}; responses may be observed at the n Z lines and the external carry-out line C_{out}. Internal carry lines may not be observed. Prove that all the faults of interest in the n-bit adder array can be detected by a set of eight test patterns, independent of the value of n. Describe how such a set of test patterns can be constructed.

8.17 What are the advantages of using microprogramming rather than hardwired logic to design the control part of a digital system? What are the disadvantages of microprogramming?

8.18 (*a*) Redesign the multiplier circuit of Fig. 4.47 to implement the twos-complement multiplication algorithm of Fig. 4.51. List all the new control signals needed and their functions.

(*b*) Modify the microprogrammed control unit and microinstruction format of Fig. 8.23 to control your twos-complement multiplier.

(*c*) Write a microprogram to implement the twos-complement multiplication algorithm. Present it in the tabular format of Fig. 8.24.

8.19 The circuit of Fig. 8.65a extends the multiplier of Fig. 4.47 to a simple, but complete, 16-bit CPU. A, M, and Q are now general-purpose programmable registers, and additional registers have been added to support

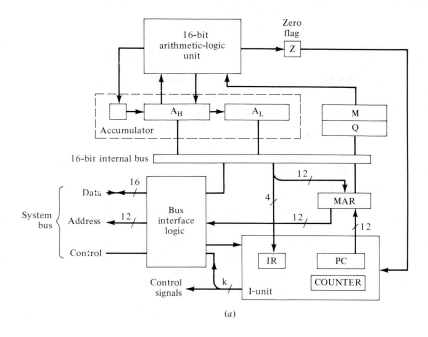

(a)

Instruction		Description
MOVE	ADR, R	Store contents of register R in memory location M[ADR]
MOVE	R, ADR	Load M[ADR] into R
ADD		Add register M to A_H
SUB		Subtract register M from A_H
MULT		Multiply M by Q using the algorithm of Fig. 4.48
SHIFT		Shift A and Q as in the algorithm of Fig. 4.48
JUMP	ADR	Branch unconditionally to ADR
JUMPZ	ADR	Branch to ADR if zero flag Z is 1

(b)

Figure 8.65 Simple CPU: (a) internal organization; (b) instruction set.

instruction processing and communication with an external bus connecting the CPU to memory and IO devices. MAR serves as a 12-bit memory address register for addressing instructions or data in main memory. Memory-mapped IO is used to access IO devices. A 16-bit instruction format is used that comprises a 4-bit opcode and an optional 12-bit memory/IO address ADR. Two bits of the opcode may be used as a register address R to specify the A_H, A_L, Q, or M register. An eight-member instruction set for this CPU is specified in Fig. 8.65b.

(a) Design a microprogrammable I-unit for this CPU using a horizontal microinstruction format like that of Fig. 8.23b. List all the control signals used and their functions.

(b) Following the format of Fig. 8.24, list a complete emulator for the instruction set of Fig. 8.65b. Include the microinstructions necessary to fetch instructions from the instruction register IR.

8.20 Consider again the microprogrammed CPU defined in the preceding problem. It is to be extended by adding a single nonvectored interrupt line that employs the fixed interrupt address vector FFF_{16}. Furthermore a one-level subroutine capability is to be added to the I-unit to allow a microprogram to call another microprogram, as in the 8086's I-unit. Repeat the I-unit design of Prob. 8.19, this time using a vertical microinstruction format that attempts to minimize microinstruction size. The emulator should be designed to respond to interrupts, and should take advantage of the I-unit's microsubroutine feature.

8.21 Using the data provided by Figs. 8.26 and 8.27, write short microprograms for a 2901 slice (or array of slices) that implement the following operations; only the values of the relevant control fields need be specified, as in (8.7).

    (*a*) Transfer the logical complement of the data on the D bus to the Q register.
    (*b*) Set all bits of register RAM[0] to 1.
    (*c*) Increment register RAM[10] by one.
    (*d*) Negate a twos-complement number stored in the Q register.

8.22 Design a 12-bit processor array from 2901 slices that can do unsigned 12-bit multiplication using carry lookahead. Show all interconnections among the slices as in Fig. 8.28. Instead of using an off-the-shelf carry generator IC such as the 2902, design your own carry-generation logic using NAND gates.

8.23 Consider the task of exchanging the low-order and high-order bytes of a 2-byte word stored in the internal RAM of a 16-bit 2901 processor array. Describe efficient ways of doing this under each of the following constraints:

    (*a*) The speed of the byte swap must be maximized
    (*b*) The amount of extra logic that is added to the processor array to support the byte swap must be minimized

In each case show the processor interconnections required, and list the microinstructions that implement the byte swap.

8.24 Figure 8.66 shows a simple modification of the 2901 array of Fig. 8.30 enabling it to perform multiplication of 16-bit twos-complement numbers. The line connecting C_{out} to RAM_0 in the most significant slice is replaced by an EXCLUSIVE-OR gate that applies the function $F_0 \oplus OVR$ to RAM_0. This change causes the sign bit F_0 of the partial product to be extended into RAM[B] when there is no overflow (OVR = 0); when overflow occurs (OVR = 1), $\overline{F}_0$ replaces F_0. Twos-complement multiplication is carried out by repeated execution of the conditional add-and-shift microinstruction (8.9), as in the unsigned case. In the last (16th) iteration, however, (8.9) is replaced by the corresponding conditional subtract-and-shift operation

$$I_S, I_F, I_D = 0\overline{Q}_0 1,001,100$$

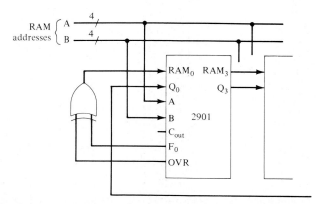

Figure 8.66 Modifying the 2901-based processor of Fig. 8.30 to handle twos-complement multiplication.

Prove that the foregoing scheme produces the correct twos-complement product for all combinations of positive and negative operands. *Hint:* Observe that the numerical value N of a positive or negative twos-complement integer $x_{n-1}x_{n-2} \ldots x_0$, where x_{n-1} is the sign bit, can be expressed as

$$N = -x_{n-1}2^{n-1} + \sum_{i=1}^{n-2} x^i 2^i$$

8.25 Figure 8.67a shows some important differences between the 2903 4-bit processor slice and its predecessor, the 2901 (cf. Fig. 8.26). The 2903's DA bus corresponds to the 2901's D bus, while DB is a new bidirectional 4-bit bus. Figure 8.67b shows another 2900-series IC, the 29704 16- by 4-bit dual-port RAM, which is basically similar to the internal RAMs of the 2901 and 2903 slices. Draw a logic diagram showing how two 29704s can be attached to a 2903 to expand its effective RAM capacity from 16 to 48 words.

8.26 Define, using a format as in (8.10), the control signals that must be applied to a 2909-based microprogram sequencer to realize each of the following microoperations:

(*a*) Go to the next consecutive microinstruction, that is, continue.

(*b*) Branch unconditionally to CM address zero.

(*c*) Perform an eight-way conditional branch based on the value of an external variable $X = x_2x_1x_0$. (This corresponds to a Pascal **case** statement).

8.27 One of the most frequent microoperations performed by the AMD 8080 Emulator is incrementing the program counter PC, which is assigned to RAM location 1111_2, and loading it into the memory address register AR. Define the control signals that must be applied to the 2901 processor array to complete this microoperation during one microinstruction cycle.

8.28 Using our symbolic RTL to specify microinstructions, outline microprograms suitable for use in the AMD Emulator to emulate each of the following 8080 instructions from the list in Fig.8.33. State any assumptions you make about unspecified details of the Emulator.

(*a*) Move memory to register.

(*b*) Add register pair.

(*c*) Call subroutine.

8.29 One of the more difficult 8080 instructions to implement using the AMD Emulator is DAA (decimal-adjust accumulator), an algorithm for which is defined in Fig. 5.27. Devise a symbolic microprogram to

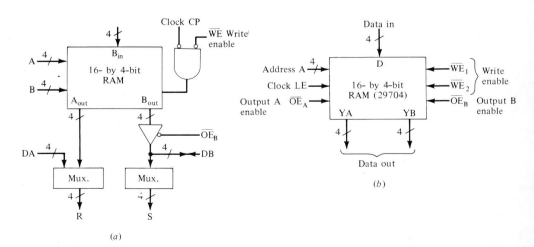

Figure 8.67 (*a*) Internal RAM and associated circuits of the AMD 2903 4-bit processor slice. (*b*) The 29704 16- by 4-bit dual-port RAM IC.

emulate DAA on the AMD Emulator, or any similar 2901-based processor, and point out the major implementation problems.

8.30 The structure of the Intel 3002 processor slice is shown in Fig. 8.68 (Intel, 1976b). It differs from the AMD 2901 primarily in its use of 2-bit rather than 4-bit data slices, and in having five rather than two external data bus connections.

(*a*) Write a brief note on the relative merits of the 2901 and 3002 for implementing a typical 16-bit microprocessor.

(*b*) The 3002 does not generate an overflow flag corresponding to OVR in the 2901. Describe in detail the extra logic that must be added to a 3002-based processor to generate an overflow signal.

8.31 (*a*) Explain the following statement: "In most computers, hardware floating point multiply and divide takes approximately the same amount of execution time as hardware fixed-point multiply and divide, but

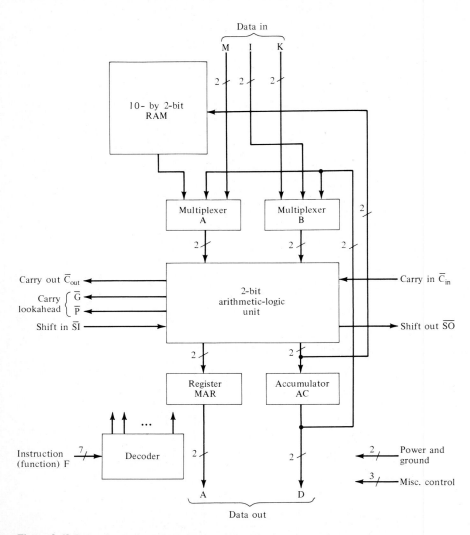

Figure 8.68 Internal organization of the Intel 3002 2-bit microprocessor slice.

hardware floating point add and subtract usually takes considerably more time than fixed point add and subtract'' (Cheng, 1981).

(*b*) Construct a flowchart for a floating-point addition algorithm that uses the 32-bit number format of the 9511 arithmetic processor (Fig. 8.44a). Assume that the algorithm is to be microprogrammed for a processor having a 32-bit ALU capable of fixed-point addition and subtraction, 1-bit shifting, numerical comparison, and other standard operations. A set of 32-bit working registers R0:R7 is also available.

8.32 Arithmetic processors such as the 9511 provide an efficient way of adding floating-point capabilities to a microprocessor. Another approach is to place a set of instruction-level floating-point subroutines in a ROM. For example, the Motorola 6839 floating-point ROM is an 8K-byte ROM chip that stores a complete set of floating-point subroutines employing the IEEE 754 standard format, and written in the machine language of the 6809 microprocessor. The 6839 is designed so that it can be positioned anywhere in the memory space of a 6809-based microcomputer, with its various subroutines accessed by conventional subroutine call instructions.

(*a*) Discuss the relative merits of the 6839 and an arithmetic processor such as the 9511 as "hardware" implementations of floating-point operations. Consider such factors as execution time, design requirements, and impact on overall system cost.

(*b*) Explain the type of operand addressing used by the 6839 in order for its subroutines to be executable independent of their location in the host system's address space.

8.33 Arithmetic processors can convey their execution status to their host CPU by three methods: interrupts, busy signals, and status words that the host can poll. Compare these three methods from the viewpoints of hardware and software design complexity, flexibility, and combined CPU–arithmetic processor throughput.

8.34 Consider the floating-point number format used in the 9511 arithmetic processor (Fig. 8.44a). The 24-bit mantissa M represents a fraction that, with the sign bit S, forms a sign-magnitude number. The 7-bit exponent E is a twos-complement integer. Floating-point results are always normalized by the 9511, meaning that there are no leading 0s in the mantissa M, that is, the 9511 always adjusts its results so that bit 23 is 1. (The only exception is zero, which is denoted by the all-0 word.)

(*a*) What are the largest positive and negative numbers that can be represented in this format?

(*b*) What are the disadvantages of this format compared with the IEEE 754 floating-point format used in the 8087 arithmetic processor?

8.35 Bits 0, 1, 2, 5, and 6 of the 9511's status word (Fig. 8.44c) are flag signals qualifying the results of the last command executed by the 9511. For each of these flags describe a realistic situation occurring during floating-point computation where the flag information should be used.

8.36 (*a*) List the advantages of the 8087 arithmetic processor over the 9511.

(*b*) Explain why the 8087, unlike the 9511, cannot be used with non-8086-series CPUs such as the 8080/8085 or the 68000.

8.37 Describe the role of the 8086's WAIT instruction in synchronizing CPU activities with those of the 8087 arithmetic processor.

8.38 The 8086's ESC (escape) instruction can be regarded as a call to a subroutine that is executed by an external coprocessor. This is suggested by the similarity between the instruction

ESC   SUB

and the conventional subroutine call instruction

CALL   SUB

Explore this analogy in detail, describing the various CPU steps (microoperations) necessary to implement ESC and CALL.

8.39 Write an 8086 assembly-language program that evaluates the Pascal assignment statement

$$Z := 32 * (X1 + X2)/X3 - 16.74523;$$

where X1, X2, X3 and Z are **real** variables represented by 32-bit floating-point numbers stored in main memory. Floating-point operations are to be executed by an 8087 coprocessor. Make up symbolic names for all 8087 commands that you need, and define them by comments. Assume that all arithmetic commands use a stack in the 8087 as the source and destination of their operands.

8.40 Repeat Prob. 8.39 for a microcomputer employing any standard 8-bit microprocessor and the 9511 arithmetic processor.

8.41 Briefly describe two different microprocessor applications where the use of an IOP can produce a significant improvement in system performance at an acceptable cost.

8.42 Write an essay comparing the 8089 IOP's local and remote modes in terms of hardware cost, software design complexity, and system throughput.

8.43 (*a*) Suppose that an 8089 is required to compute the difference ADR1 − ADR2 of two 20-bit memory addresses. Explain how this might be most efficiently programmed using the 8089's instruction set (Fig. 8.53), which lacks a subtract instruction.

(*b*) Consider the 8089's subroutine call instruction (8.13), which saves the return address in a random memory location. This has the disadvantage that subroutine calls cannot be easily nested. What advantages does it have?

8.44 A serious disadvantage of the 8089 IOP is its lack of software compatibility with its host CPU. It would be better from a software development standpoint to make an IOP's instruction set a compatible subset of the CPU's instruction set. Analyze the feasibility and cost of redesigning the 8089 to achieve this type of compatibility with the 8086 microprocessor.

8.45 List the advantages and disadvantages of multimicroprocessor systems compared with systems with a single microprocessor (unimicroprocessors).

8.46 Discuss the suitability of a large multimicroprocessor such as the SMS 201 for each of the following applications:

(*a*) General-purpose scientific computation in a university computer center

(*b*) Word processing, text editing, and related tasks in a newspaper's editorial office

(*c*) Monitoring and controlling the operation of a large number of robots working on an automobile assembly line.

8.47 (*a*) What is the purpose of the 8086's LOCK instruction?

(*b*) It is proposed to modify the semaphore test-and-set routine of Fig. 8.61a by preceding each of its three instructions by a LOCK instruction. Does this make the routine valid? Justify your answer.

8.48 Consider the problem of combining several copies of a standard 8-bit microprocessor such as the 6800 or 8080/8085 to construct a tightly coupled microprocessor. Describe in detail how you would implement a

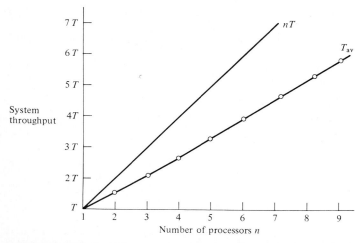

Figure 8.69 Maximum throughput nT and expected throughput T_{av} of a multiprocessor containing n processors of throughput T.

semaphore control mechanism to allow each microprocessor to obtain undivided control over shared system resources.

8.49 List all the features of the Multibus standard bus that facilitate the design of multiprocessors.

8.50 Some insight into interprocessor conflicts affecting the throughput of multiprocessors may be obtained by analyzing the crossbar-switch design of Fig. 8.41. Assume that there are n processors and n memory modules, and that the probability that processor P_i generates a read or write request addressed to memory module M_j at any time t is $1/n$. P_i is thus assumed continually to generate memory references that are uniformly distributed across the memory modules. Let p_i denote the probability that M_j is busy, that is, responding to an access request from some processor, at time t, thus forcing other processors that need access to M_j to wait. The throughput of waiting processors is assumed to be zero. If T is the maximum throughput of each processor in suitable units such as MIPS, prove that the average throughput T_{av} of the n-processor system is given by

$$T_{av} = \sum_{i=1}^{n} p_i T = n[1 - (1 - 1/n)^n]T \qquad (8.16)$$

T_{av} is plotted against n in Fig. 8.69 using Eq. (8.16). This graph shows that T_{av} tends to be significantly less than the maximum possible throughput nT.

REFERENCES

Advanced Micro Devices Inc.: "The Am2900 Family Data Book," Advanced Micro Devices, Inc., Sunnyvale, Calif., 1978.

Amdahl, G. M., G. A. Blaauw, and F. P. Brooks, Jr.: Architecture of the IBM System/360, *IBM J. Res. Dev.*, vol. 8, pp. 86-101, April 1964.

Andrews, M.: "Principles of Firmware Engineering in Microprogram Control," Computer Science Press, Potomac, Md., 1980.

Babbage, C.: "Passages From the Life of a Philosopher," Longman, Green and Company, London, 1864. [Extracts reprinted in "Charles Babbage and His Calculating Engines," P. Morrison and E. Morrison, (Eds.) Dover Publications, New York, 1961.]

Baer, J-L.: "Computer Systems Architecture," Computer Science Press, Potomac, Md., 1980.

Barron, D. W.: "Assemblers and Loaders," MacDonald, London, 1969.

Bell, C. G. and A. Newell: "Computer Structures: Readings and Examples," McGraw-Hill Book Company, New York, 1971.

Bishop, R.: "Basic Microprocessors and the 6800," Hayden Book Company, Inc., Rochelle Park, N.J., 1978.

Blaauw, G. A.: "Digital System Implementation," Prentice-Hall, Inc., Englewood Cliffs, N.J., 1976.

Blakeslee, T. R.: "Digital Design with Standard MSI and LSI," 2nd ed., Wiley-Interscience, New York, 1979.

Boberg, R. W.: Proposed Microcomputer System 796 Bus Standard, *IEEE Computer*, vol. 13, no. 10, pp. 89–105, October 1980.

Boole, G.: "The Laws of Thought," Macmillan and Company, Ltd., London, 1854. Reprinted by Dover Publications, Inc., New York, 1958.

Bowles, K. L.: "Microcomputer Problem Solving Using Pascal," Springer-Verlag, Inc., New York, 1977.

Braun, E., and S. MacDonald: "Revolution in Miniature: The History and Impact of Semiconductor Electronics," Cambridge University Press, Cambridge, England, 1978.

Breuer, M. A. (Ed.): "Design Automation of Digital Systems," Prentice-Hall, Inc., Englewood Cliffs, N.J., 1972.

Breuer, M. A., and A. D. Friedman: "Diagnosis and Reliable Design of Digital Systems," Computer Science Press, Woodland Hills, Calif., 1976.

Canepa, M., E. Weber, and H. Talley: VLSI in FOCUS: Designing a 32-Bit CPU Chip, *VLSI Design*, vol. IV, no. 1, pp. 20–24, January/February 1983.

Carr, W. N., and J. P. Mize: "MOS/LSI Design and Application," McGraw-Hill Book Company, Inc., New York, 1972.

Cavanagh, J. J. F.: "Digital Computer Arithmetic," McGraw-Hill Book Company, Inc., New York, 1984.

Cheng, S.: "Am9511A/Am9512 Floating Point Processor Manual," Advanced Micro Devices, Inc., Sunnyvale, Calif., 1981.

Chu, Y.: "Computer Organization and Microprogramming," Prentice-Hall Inc., Englewood Cliffs, N.J., 1972.

Cohn, D. L., and J. L. Melsa: "A Step by Step Introduction to 8080 Microprocessor Systems," Dilithium Press, Forest Grove, Oreg., 1977.

Colclaser, R. A.: "Microelectronics: Processing and Device Design," John Wiley & Sons, Inc., New York, 1980.

Crespi-Reghizzi, S., P. Corti, and A. Dapra: A Survey of Microprocessor Languages, *IEEE Computer*, vol. 13, no. 1, pp. 48–66, January 1980.

Croson, E. B., F. H. Carlin, and J. A. Howard: Integrated Arithmetic Processing Unit Enhances Microprocessor Execution Times, *Comput. Des.*, vol. 20, no. 4, pp. 163–171, April 1981.

Dietmeyer, D. L., and J. R. Duley: Register Transfer Languages and Their Translation. In "Digital Systems Design Automation: Languages, Simulation and Data Base," M. A. Breuer (Ed.)., Computer Science Press, Woodland Hills, Calif., 1975, pp. 117–218.

Digital Equipment Corporation: "Microcomputer Handbook," Digital Equipment Corporation, Maynard, Mass., 1976.

Duley, J. R., and D. L. Dietmeyer: A Digital System Design Language (DDL), *IEEE Trans. Computers*, vol. C-17, pp. 850–861, September 1968.

El-Ayat, K. A.: The Intel 8089: An Integrated I/O Processor, *IEEE Computer*, vol. 12, no. 6, pp. 67–78, June 1979.

Editors of *Electronics*: "An Age of Innovation: The World of Electronics 1930–2000," McGraw-Hill Book Company, Inc., New York, 1980.

Evans, C.: "The Micro Millenium," Viking Press, New York, 1980.

Fairchild Semiconductor: "The TTL Applications Handbook," Fairchild Semiconductor, Mountain View, Calif., 1973.

Fairchild Semiconductor: "Low Power Schottky and Macrologic TTL," Fairchild Semiconductor, Mountain View, Calif., 1975.

Falkoff, A. D., K. E. Iverson, and E. H. Sussenguth: A Formal Description of SYSTEM/360, *IBM Sys. J.,* vol. 3, pp. 198–263, 1964.

Findlay, W., and D. A. Watt: "Pascal, An Introduction to Methodical Programming," Computer Science Press, Potomac, Md., 1978.

Fischer W. P.: Microprocessor Assembly Language Draft Standard, *IEEE Computer*, vol. 12, no. 12, pp. 96–109, December 1979.

Fitzgerald, A. E., D. E. Higginbotham, and A Grabel: "Basic Electrical Engineering," 5th ed., McGraw-Hill Book Company, Inc., New York, 1981.

Fletcher, W. I.: "An Engineering Approach to Digital Design," Prentice-Hall, Inc., Englewood Cliffs, N.J., 1980.

Frank, R.: Microprocessor-Based Analog/Digital Conversion, *Byte*, vol. 1, no. 5, pp. 70–73, May 1976.

Gall, J.: "Systemantics," Quadrangle/New York Times, New York, 1975.

Garrow, B., J. Johnson, and M. Maerz: The Super Component: The One-Board Computer with Programmable I/O, *Electronics*, vol. 49, no. 3, pp. 77–84, February 5, 1976.

Gupta, A., and H. D. Toong (Eds.): "Advanced Microprocessors," IEEE Press, New York, 1983.

Hamacher, V. C., Z. A. Vranesic, and G. Zaky: "Computer Organization," McGraw-Hill Book Company, Inc., New York, 1978.

Hayes, J. P.: "Computer Architecture and Organization," McGraw-Hill Book Company, Inc., New York, 1978.

Hayes, J. P.: A Survey of Bit-Sliced Computer Design, *J. Dig. Sys.,* vol. 5, pp. 203–250, Fall 1981.

Hayes, J. P.: A Unified Switching Theory with Applications to VLSI Design, *Proc. IEEE*, vol 70, pp. 1140–1151, October 1982.

Hill, F. J., and G. R. Peterson: "Digital Systems: Hardware Organization and Design," 2nd ed., John Wiley & Sons., Inc., New York, 1978.

Hnatek, E. R.: "A User's Handbook of Semiconductor Memories," Wiley-Interscience, New York, 1977.

Intel Corporation: "MCS-4 Microcomputer Set User's Manual," Intel Corp., Santa Clara, Calif., 1974.

Intel Corporation: "Memory Design Handbook," Intel Corp., Santa Clara, Calif., 1975a.

Intel Corporation: "Interp/80 User's Manual," Intel Corp., Santa Clara, Calif., 1975b.

Intel Corporation: "Intel 8080 Assembly Language Programming Manual," Intel Corp., Santa Clara, Calif., 1976a.

Intel Corporation: "Series 3000 Reference Manual," Intel Corp., Santa Clara, Calif., 1976b.

Intel Corporation: "MCS-86 Assembly Language Reference Manual," Intel Corp., Santa Clara, Calif., 1978a.

Intel Corporation: "Intel Multibus Specification," Intel Corp., Santa Clara, Calif., 1978b.

Intel Corporation: "MCS-80/85 Family User's Manual," Intel Corp., Santa Clara, Calif., 1979.

Intel Corporation: "Peripheral Design Handbook," Intel Corp., Santa Clara, Calif., 1981a.

Intel Corporation: "iAPX 86, 88 User's Manual," Intel Corp., Santa Clara, Calif., 1981b.

Iverson, K. E.: "A Programming Language," John Wiley & Sons, Inc., New York, 1962.

Jenson, K., and N. Wirth: "Pascal User Manual and Report," Springer-Verlag, Inc., Berlin, 1974.

Johnson, C. D.: "Process Control Instrumentation Technology," John Wiley & Sons, Inc., New York, 1977.

Kabaservice, T. P.: "Applied Microelectronics," West Publishing Company, St. Paul, Minn., 1978.

Kane, J., and A. Osborne: "An Introduction to Microprocessors: Vol. 3. Some Real Support Devices," Osborne and Associates, Berkeley, Calif., 1978.

Katz, B. J., et al.: 8086 Microprocessor Bridges the Gap Between 8- and 16- Bit Designs, *Electronics*, vol. 51, no. 4, pp. 99–104, February 16, 1978.

Katzan, H., Jr.: "An Invitation to Ada and Ada Reference Manual," Petrocelli Books, New York, 1982.

Kneen, J.: "Logic Analyzers for Microprocessors," Hayden Book Company, Inc., Rochelle Park, N.J., 1980.

Knuth, D. E.: "The Art of Computer Programming: Vol. 2. Seminumerical Algorithms," Addison-Wesley Publishing Company, Inc., Reading, Mass., 1969.

Knuth, D. E.: An Empirical Study of FORTRAN Programs, *Software—Prac. Exp.*, vol. 1, pp. 105–133, 1971.

Kober, R., and C. Kuznia: SMS—A Multiprocessor for High Speed Numerical Calculations, *Proc. Int. Conf. on Parallel Processing*, Bellaire, Mich., pp. 18–24, 1978.

Larsen, D. G., and P. R. Rony: "Logic and Memory Experiments Using TTL IC's," Book 1, Howard W. Sams, and Company, Inc., Indianapolis, Ind., 1978.

Lau, S. Y.: Emulate Your MOS Microprocessor, *Elec. Des.*, vol. 26, no. 8, pp. 74–81, April 12, 1978.

Leventhal, L. A.: "8080A/8085 Assembly Language Programming," Osborne/McGraw-Hill, Berkeley, Calif., 1978a.

Leventhal, L. A.: "6800 Assembly Language Programming," Osborne and Associates, Berkeley, Calif., 1978b.

Libes, S., and M. Garetz: "Interfacing to S–100/IEEE 696 Microcomputers," Osborne/McGraw-Hill, Berkeley, Calif., 1981.

Liccardo, M.: Architecture of Microcontroller System, *AFIPS Conf. Proc.*, vol. 44, pp. 75–84, 1975.

McCluskey, E. J.: "Introduction to the Theory of Switching Circuits," McGraw-Hill Book Company, Inc., New York, 1965.

McCracken, D. D.: "A Guide to PL/M Programming for Microcomputer Applications," Addison-Wesley Publishing Company, Inc., Reading, Mass., 1978.

McKevitt, J., and J. Bayliss: New Options from Big Chips, *IEEE Spectrum*, vol. 6, no. 3, pp. 28–34, March 1979.

Mead, C., and L. Conway: "Introduction to VLSI Systems," Addison-Wesley Publishing Company, Inc., Reading, Mass., 1980.

Mick, J., and J. Brick: "Bit-Slice Microprocessor Design,"McGraw-Hill Book Company, Inc., New York, 1980.

Millman, J.: "Microelectronics," McGraw-Hill Book Company, Inc., New York, 1979.

Moore, G. E.: Cramming More Components onto Integrated Circuits, *Electronics*, vol. 38, no. 8, pp. 114–116, April 19, 1965.

Moore, C. H., and E. D. Rather: FORTH: A New Way to Program a Minicomputer, *Astron Astrophysics Suppl.*, vol. 15, pp. 497–511, 1974.

Motil, J. M.: "Digital Systems Fundamentals," McGraw-Hill Book Company, Inc., New York, 1972.

Motorola Inc.: "M6800 Microprocessor Programming Manual," 2nd ed., Motorola, Inc., Phoenix, Ariz., 1975a.

Motorola Inc.: "M6800 Microprocessor Applications Manual," Motorola, Inc., Phoenix, Ariz., 1975b.

Motorola Inc.: "MC14500B Industrial Control Unit Handbook," Motorola, Inc., Phoenix, Ariz., 1977.

Motorola Inc.: 8192-Bit Read Only Memories: Row Select Character Generators, Data sheet DS 9516, Motorola, Inc., Austin, Tex., 1978.

Motorola Inc.: "MC68000 16-Bit Microprocessor User's Manual," Motorola, Inc., Phoenix, Ariz., 1979.

Motorola Semiconductor Products: "Motorola Microprocessors Data Manual," 2nd ed., Motorola, Inc., Austin, Tex., 1981.

Muroga, S.: "Logic Design and Switching Theory," Wiley-Interscience, New York, 1979.

Myers, G. J.: "Advances in Computer Architecture," 2nd ed., John Wiley & Sons, Inc., New York, 1982.

National Semiconductor Corporation: "MOS Databook," National Semiconductor Corp., Santa Clara, Calif., 1980.

National Semiconductor Corporation: "CMOS Databook," National Semiconductor Corp., Santa Clara, Calif., 1981a.

National Semiconductor Corporation: "Logic Databook," National Semiconductor Corp., Santa Clara, Calif., 1981b.

Noyce, R. N., and M. E. Hoff, Jr.: A History of Microprocessor Development at Intel, *IEEE Micro*, vol. 1, no. 1, pp. 8–20, February 1981.

Ogdin, C. A.: "Software Design for Microcomputers," Prentice-Hall, Inc., Englewood Cliffs, N.J., 1978.

Osborne, A., and G. Kane: "Osborne 4 & 8-bit Microprocessor Handbook," Osborne/McGraw-Hill, Berkeley, Calif., 1981a.

Osborne, A., and G. Kane: "Osborne 16-bit Microprocessor Handbook," Osborne/McGraw-Hill, Berkeley, Calif., 1981b.

Philippakis, A. S.: A Popularity Contest for Languages, *Datamation*, vol. 23, no. 12, pp. 81–87, December 1977.

Phister, M.: Analyzing Computer Technology Costs—Part I: Development and Manufacturing, *Comput. Des.*, vol. 17, no. 9, pp. 91–98, September 1978; Part 2: Maintenance." *Ibid.*, no. 10, pp. 109–118, October 1978.

Powell, R. L., et al.: "Thermocouple Reference Tables based on the IPTS–68," NBS Monograph 125, U.S. Department of Commerce, National Bureau of Standards, Washington, D.C., March 1974.

Purchase, A.: The Impact of Electronics on the Point of Sale Market, Paper No. 22/2, *Proc. 1974 IEEE Intercon Tech. Program*, March 1974.

Randell, B., (Ed.): "The Origins of Digital Computers: Selected Papers," 3rd ed., Springer-Verlag, Inc., Berlin, 1982.

Ravenel, B. W.: Toward a Pascal Standard, *IEEE Computer*, vol. 12, no. 4, pp. 68–82, April 1979.

Reed, I. S.: Symbolic Design Techniques Applied to a Generalized Computer, Tech. Rept. TR-141, M.I.T. Lincoln Laboratory, January 1956. (Reprinted with revisions in *IEEE Computer*, vol. 5, no. 3, pp. 47–52, May/June 1972.)

Roddy, D.: "Introduction to Microelectronics," 2nd ed., Pergamon Press, Oxford, 1978.

Rony, P. R., and D. G. Larsen: "Logic and Memory Experiments Using TTL IC's," Book 2, Howard W. Sams and Company, Inc., Indianapolis, Ind., 1979.

Scientific American: "Microelectronics," W. H. Freeman, San Francisco, Calif., 1977.

Shackil, A. F.: Design Case History: Wang's Word Processor, *IEEE Spectrum*, vol. 18, no. 8, pp. 29–33, August 1981.

Shavit, M.: "An Emulation of the AM 9080A," Advanced Micro Devices, Inc., Sunnyvale, Calif., 1978.

Shima, M.: Demystifying Microprocessor Design, *IEEE Spectrum*, vol. 16, no. 7, pp. 22–30, July 1979.

Shima, M., and F. Faggin: In Switching to n-MOS Microprocessor Gets a 2-Microseconds Cycle Time, *Electronics*, vol. 47, no. 8, pp. 95–100, April 18, 1974.

Shima, M., F. Faggin, and R. Ungermann: Z80 Chip Set Heralds Third Microprocessor Generation, *Electronics*, vol. 49, no. 17, pp. 89–93, August 19, 1976.

Siewiorek, D., C. G. Bell, and A. Newell: "Computer Structures: Principles and Examples," McGraw-Hill Book Company, Inc., New York, 1982.

Signetics Inc.: "Signetics 8080 Emulator Manual," Signetics Inc., Sunnyvale, Calif., March 1977.

Simon, H. A.: "The Sciences of the Artificial," 2nd ed., M.I.T. Press, Cambridge, Mass., 1981.

Simpson, W. D., et al.: "9900 Family Systems Design and Data Book," Texas Instruments, Inc., Houston, Tex., 1978.

Smyth, R. K.: Microcomputer Applications to a Telephone Cable Plant Processor Controller, In *New Components and Subsystems for Digital Design: A Report*, Technology Services, Santa Monica, Calif., 1975, pp. 41–50.

Sohn, D. W., and A. Volk: Third Generation Microcomputer Set Packs It All into 3 Chips, *Electronics*, vol. 50, no. 10, pp. 109–113, May 12, 1977.

Stevenson, D.: A Proposed Standard for Binary Floating-Point Arithmetic, *IEEE Computer*, vol. 14, no. 3, pp. 51–62, March 1981.

Stone H. S.: "Microcomputer Interfacing," Addison-Wesley Publishing Company, Inc., Reading, Mass., 1982.

Tabachnick, R. L., et al.: Sequence Controllers with Standard Hardware and Custom Firmware, *IEEE Micro*, vol. 1, no. 2, pp. 9–25, May 1981.

Tanenbaum, A.: "Structured Computer Organization," Prentice-Hall, Inc., Englewood Cliffs, N.J., 1976.

Tektronix Inc.: "1983 Catalog," Tektronix Inc., Beaverton, Oreg., 1982.

Texas Instruments Inc.: "Model 763-765 Memory Terminals Systems Manual," Texas Instruments, Inc., Dallas, Tex., 1978.

Texas Instruments Inc.: "The TTL Data Book for Design Engineers," 2nd ed., Texas Instruments, Inc., Dallas, Tex., 1981.

Tseng, V. (Ed.): "Microprocessor Development and Development Systems," McGraw-Hill Book Company, Inc., New York, 1982.

Ullman, J. D.: "Fundamental Concepts of Programming Systems," Addison-Wesley Publishing Company, Inc., Reading, Mass., 1976.

Van Tassel, D.: "Program Style, Design, Efficiency, Debugging and Testing," 2nd ed., Prentice-Hall, Inc., Englewood Cliffs, N.J., 1978.

Wakerly, J. F.: "Microcomputer Architecture and Programming," John Wiley & Sons, Inc., New York, 1981.

Weitzman, C.: "Distributed Micro/Minicomputer Systems," Prentice-Hall, Inc., Englewood Cliffs, N.J., 1980.

Wiles, M., et. al.: Compatibility Cures Growing Pains of Microcomputer Family, *Electronics*, vol. 51, no. 3, pp. 95–103, February 2, 1978.

Wolff, M. F.: The Genesis of the Integrated Circuit, *IEEE Spectrum*, vol. 13, no. 8, pp. 45–53, August 1976.

Woolvet, G. A.: "Transducers in Digital Systems," Peter Peregrinus Ltd., Stevenage, England, 1977.

Young, L., T. Bennett, and J. Lavell: N-Channel MOS Technology Yields New Generation of Microprocessors," *Electronics*, vol. 47, no. 8, pp. 88–95, April 18, 1974.

INDEX